# THE
# BUSINESS
# JUDGMENT
# RULE

## Fiduciary Duties
## of Corporate Directors

Fifth Edition

Volume II

# THE
# BUSINESS
# JUDGMENT
# RULE

## Fiduciary Duties
## of Corporate Directors

DENNIS J. BLOCK
NANCY E. BARTON
STEPHEN A. RADIN

Fifth Edition
Volume II

ASPEN LAW & BUSINESS

# TABLE OF CONTENTS

## VOLUME I

**Acknowledgment** . . . . . . . . . . . . . . . . . . . . . . . . . . . xxiii

**About the Authors** . . . . . . . . . . . . . . . . . . . . . . . . . . . xxv

**Note to the Reader** . . . . . . . . . . . . . . . . . . . . . . . . . . xxvii

**Chapter I.  The Business Judgment Rule–An
             Introduction** . . . . . . . . . . . . . . . . . . . . . . .     1

A.  Historical Origins . . . . . . . . . . . . . . . . . . . . . . . . .     9

B.  Rationale . . . . . . . . . . . . . . . . . . . . . . . . . . . . .    12

C.  The Rule's Presumption and Its Effect . . . . . . . . . .    18

   1.  The Presumption . . . . . . . . . . . . . . . . . . . . . . .    19

   2.  The Shareholder Plaintiff's Burden . . . . . . . . . .    25

   3.  The Fairness Standard Where The
       Presumption Is Overcome . . . . . . . . . . . . . . . .    28

   4.  Business Judgment Versus Fairness . . . . . . . . . .    32

D.  Elements of the Rule . . . . . . . . . . . . . . . . . . . . . .    39

   1.  A Business Decision . . . . . . . . . . . . . . . . . . . .    40

   2.  Disinterestedness and Independence . . . . . . . . . .    41

      a.  Interestedness . . . . . . . . . . . . . . . . . . . . .    43

      b.  Independence . . . . . . . . . . . . . . . . . . . . .    45

      c.  Materiality . . . . . . . . . . . . . . . . . . . . . . .    47

d.  Examples of Findings of Interestedness
and Lack of Independence . . . . . . . . . . . . . .      53

e.  Receipt of Director's Fees  . . . . . . . . . . . .      61

f.  Ownership of Stock . . . . . . . . . . . . . . . .      63

g.  Ownership of Stock by Directors
Where Different Groups of Share-
holders Have Different Interests . . . . . . . . . .      67

h.  Codifications . . . . . . . . . . . . . . . . . . . .      70

3.  Due Care . . . . . . . . . . . . . . . . . . . . . . . .      74

4.  Good Faith . . . . . . . . . . . . . . . . . . . . . . .      80

5.  No Abuse of Discretion  . . . . . . . . . . . . . . .      84

E.  Fraud, Illegality and Ultra Vires Conduct . . . . . . . .      90

F.  Waste . . . . . . . . . . . . . . . . . . . . . . . . . . . .      93

G.  Application of the Business Judgment Rule to
Corporate Officers . . . . . . . . . . . . . . . . . . . . .      97

H.  Efforts to Codify the Business Judgment Rule  . . . . . .     100

1.  The Model Business Corporation Act . . . . . . . . .     101

2.  Principles of Corporate Governance:
Analysis and Recommendations  . . . . . . . . . . .     104

**Chapter II.  Fiduciary Duties of Corporate**
**Directors** . . . . . . . . . . . . . . . . . . . .     107

A.  The Duty of Care  . . . . . . . . . . . . . . . . . . . . .     109

1.  The Relationship Between the Business
Judgment Rule and the Duty of Care . . . . . . . .     110

2.  The Standard of Care . . . . . . . . . . . . . . . . .     117

3.  The Oversight Context  . . . . . . . . . . . . . . . .     126

4.  The Standard of Culpability for the
Imposition of Liability  . . . . . . . . . . . . . . . .     132

a.  The Gross Negligence Standard . . . . . . . . .     134

b.  The Oversight Context . . . . . . . . . . . . . .     140

      c. Van Gorkom . . . . . . . . . . . . . . . . . 146

      d. Technicolor . . . . . . . . . . . . . . . . . . 152

      e. Other Decisions Finding Liability for
         Money Damages Due to a Lack of Due
         Care . . . . . . . . . . . . . . . . . . . . . . . 167

      f. Decisions Granting Injunctive Relief
         Due to a Lack of Due Care . . . . . . . . . . 173

      g. Post-Van Gorkom Courts Finding Due
         Care and Upholding Board Conduct . . . . . . 179

   5. Reliance and Delegation . . . . . . . . . . . . . . . 198

      a. Reliance . . . . . . . . . . . . . . . . . . . . . 199

      b. Delegation . . . . . . . . . . . . . . . . . . . . 214

   6. Shareholder Ratification . . . . . . . . . . . . . . . 224

   7. Director Protection Statutes . . . . . . . . . . . . . 226

   8. Directors of Financial Institutions . . . . . . . . . . 242

   9. Financial Advisor Liability . . . . . . . . . . . . . 252

      a. Aiding and Abetting a Breach of
         Fiduciary Duty by Directors . . . . . . . . . . 252

      b. Breach of Duty to the Corporation . . . . . . . 254

      c. Breach of Duty to Shareholders . . . . . . . . . 256

B. The Duty of Loyalty . . . . . . . . . . . . . . . . . . . . 261

   1. The Relationship Between the Business
      Judgment Rule and the Duty of Loyalty . . . . . . . 264

   2. The Directors' Duty of Loyalty . . . . . . . . . . . 265

      a. Interested Director Transactions:
         Background . . . . . . . . . . . . . . . . . . . . 265

      b. Interested Director Transactions
         Approved by Disinterested Directors . . . . . . . 271

      c. Interested Director Transactions
         Approved by Disinterested Share-
         holders . . . . . . . . . . . . . . . . . . . . . . 274

d.  Interested Director Transactions
    Approved by the Court As Fair to
    Shareholders . . . . . . . . . . . . . . . . . . . . . .  282

e.  Interested Director Transactions:
    Variations from the Delaware Safe
    Harbor . . . . . . . . . . . . . . . . . . . . . . . . .  288

f.  The Corporate Opportunity Doctrine . . . . . . .  293

    (i)  Definition of a Corporate
         Opportunity . . . . . . . . . . . . . . . . . . .  294

    (ii) Judicial Review in Cases Where a
         Corporate Opportunity Has Been
         Taken . . . . . . . . . . . . . . . . . . . . . . .  300

g.  Director and Officer Compensation . . . . . . . .  308

h.  Stock Options . . . . . . . . . . . . . . . . . . . . .  321

    (i)  Stock Options Approved by
         Disinterested Directors . . . . . . . . . . . .  324

    (ii) Stock Options Approved by
         Interested Directors . . . . . . . . . . . . . .  328

3.  The Controlling Shareholders' Duty of
    Loyalty . . . . . . . . . . . . . . . . . . . . . . . . . .  342

a.  The Definition of Control . . . . . . . . . . . . . .  344

b.  The Interrelationship Between the
    Controlling Shareholder's Rights as a
    Shareholder and Fiduciary Duties as a
    Controlling Shareholder . . . . . . . . . . . . . .  349

c.  Sale of Control at a Premium . . . . . . . . . .  363

d.  The General Scope of the Controlling
    Shareholders' Duty to Demonstrate
    Fairness . . . . . . . . . . . . . . . . . . . . . . . .  368

e.  The Business Judgment Rule in Parent-
    Subsidiary Transactions . . . . . . . . . . . . . .  370

f.  Wholly-Owned Subsidiaries . . . . . . . . . . .  376

g. The Fairness Standard: Weinberger . . . . . . . 377

h. Majority of the Minority Shareholder
Approval . . . . . . . . . . . . . . . . . . . . . 400

i. Disinterested Director Approval and
Special Committees: Lynch and
. Tremont . . . . . . . . . . . . . . . . . . . . . 402

j. Additional Cases Where the Burden of
Proof with Respect to Fairness Has Not
Shifted Despite Existence of a Special
Committee . . . . . . . . . . . . . . . . . . . . 431

k. Special Committee Cases Where
Burden of Proof With Respect to
Fairness Has Shifted, And Unfairness
Has Not Been Proven . . . . . . . . . . . . . . 464

l. The Business Purpose Requirement In
Some Jurisdictions . . . . . . . . . . . . . . . 467

m. Principles of Corporate Governance
and the Committee on Corporate Laws
Guidelines . . . . . . . . . . . . . . . . . . . . 471

n. Appraisal: Principles Governing
Appraisal Proceedings . . . . . . . . . . . . . 476

o. Appraisal: When Appraisal Constitutes
an Exclusive Remedy . . . . . . . . . . . . . . 489

C. The Duty of Disclosure . . . . . . . . . . . . . . . . 499

1. The Reach of the Duty of Disclosure . . . . . . . . 500

2. The Role of the Business Judgment Rule . . . . . . 508

3. Materiality . . . . . . . . . . . . . . . . . . . . . . 510

a. The TSC Standard . . . . . . . . . . . . . . . 511

b. Cases Applying this Standard . . . . . . . . . 516

c. Opinions, Speculation, Inferences,
Characterizations, Legal Theories,
Pejoratives and Self-Flagellation . . . . . . . . 521

d.  Going-Private, Self-Tender Offer and
    Exchange Offer Transactions . . . . . . . . . . .  526

e.  Transactions Where A Vote Is
    Controlled by a Controlling
    Shareholder . . . . . . . . . . . . . . . . . . . . . .  527

4.  The Two Contexts in Which Shareholders
    May Vote  . . . . . . . . . . . . . . . . . . . . . . . .  528

    a.  Ratification of Interested Director or
        Controlling Shareholder Transactions  . . . . . .  528

    b.  Approval of Corporate Actions
        Required by Statute . . . . . . . . . . . . . . . . .  529

5.  Remedies . . . . . . . . . . . . . . . . . . . . . . . . .  530

    a.  Injunctive Relief . . . . . . . . . . . . . . . . . .  530

    b.  Money Damages:  The Need to Prove
        Economic Harm . . . . . . . . . . . . . . . . . . .  530

    c.  Money Damages:  Director Protection
        Statutes  . . . . . . . . . . . . . . . . . . . . . . .  535

D.  Wrongful Coercion  . . . . . . . . . . . . . . . . . . . . .  539

    1.  The Voting Context . . . . . . . . . . . . . . . . . .  540

    2.  Offers to Purchase Shares . . . . . . . . . . . . . .  547

E.  The Extent To Which Shareholders Must Be
    Treated Equally . . . . . . . . . . . . . . . . . . . . . . .  559

    1.  Common Shareholders  . . . . . . . . . . . . . . . .  559

        a.  The Majority Rule  . . . . . . . . . . . . . . .  560

        b.  The New York Rule  . . . . . . . . . . . . . . .  568

    2.  Preferred Shareholders . . . . . . . . . . . . . . . .  570

    3.  Zahn and Orban  . . . . . . . . . . . . . . . . . . .  582

F.  Fiduciary Duties of Directors of Financially
    Troubled Corporations  . . . . . . . . . . . . . . . . . . .  590

    1.  Fiduciary Duties Generally Not Owed to
        Creditors . . . . . . . . . . . . . . . . . . . . . . .  590

2. The Insolvent Corporation Context . . . . . . . . . . 596

    a. Cases Applying Trust Law Principles . . . . . . 599

    b. Cases Applying Business Judgment
       Rule Principles and Upholding Board
       Conduct . . . . . . . . . . . . . . . . . . . . . . . . 600

    c. Cases Applying Business Judgment
       Rule Principles and Not Upholding
       Board Conduct . . . . . . . . . . . . . . . . . . . . 604

    d. Healthco . . . . . . . . . . . . . . . . . . . . . . . . 605

3. Determining When a Corporation is
   Insolvent . . . . . . . . . . . . . . . . . . . . . . . . . . 619

**Chapter III.**    **The Business Judgment Rule
in Transactions Involving
Corporate Control** . . . . . . . . . . . . . . . 631

A. Introductory Issues . . . . . . . . . . . . . . . . . . . . . 632

1. Should the Rule Apply at All? . . . . . . . . . . . . 632

2. The Unocal Doctrine . . . . . . . . . . . . . . . . . . 638

    a. The Two-Prong Unocal Test . . . . . . . . . . . . 639

    b. The Defensive Conduct Requirement . . . . . . . 649

       (i) Cases Applying Unocal . . . . . . . . . . . . 649

       (ii) Cases Not Applying Unocal . . . . . . . . . . 655

       (iii) Cases Applying Unocal to Some
          But Not All Aspects of Board
          Conduct . . . . . . . . . . . . . . . . . . . . 659

    c. Reasonably Perceived Threat to
       Corporate Policy . . . . . . . . . . . . . . . . . . 662

       (i) Coercion . . . . . . . . . . . . . . . . . . . . . 663

       (ii) Price Inadequacy . . . . . . . . . . . . . . . . 666

       (iii) Insufficient Time or Information to
          Access Price Adequacy . . . . . . . . . . . . 672

(iv) Failure to Provide Shareholders an
Option to Remain Equity Holders . . . . . . 677

(v) Corporate Culture . . . . . . . . . . . . . . . 679

(vi) Antitrust and Other Regulatory
Issues . . . . . . . . . . . . . . . . . . . . . . . 680

d. Reasonable Response to Threat to
Corporate Policy . . . . . . . . . . . . . . . . . 681

e. The Law Outside of Delaware . . . . . . . . . . 686

3. The Revlon and QVC Doctrine: When It
Applies . . . . . . . . . . . . . . . . . . . . . . . . 694

a. From Revlon to QVC . . . . . . . . . . . . . . 698

b. QVC, Arnold and Santa Fe . . . . . . . . . . . 706

c. Other Delaware Cases . . . . . . . . . . . . . . 713

d. The Law Outside of Delaware . . . . . . . . . . 726

4. Evaluating Board Conduct Where the
Revlon and QVC Doctrine Applies . . . . . . . . . 730

a. The Revlon/QVC Standard . . . . . . . . . . . 733

b. Cases Enjoining Board Conduct . . . . . . . . . 736

c. Cases Upholding Board Conduct . . . . . . . . 754

d. Inducements . . . . . . . . . . . . . . . . . . . 771

e. Use of a Poison Pill Shareholder Rights
Plan as a Gavel . . . . . . . . . . . . . . . . . . 772

f. Confidentiality Agreements . . . . . . . . . . . 772

g. Board Responsibilities in Cases
Involving Competing Offers, Including
One By a Controlling Shareholder . . . . . . . 777

h. Equity-Linked Investors . . . . . . . . . . . . . 783

5. The Blasius Doctrine . . . . . . . . . . . . . . . . 790

a. Blasius . . . . . . . . . . . . . . . . . . . . . . . 791

b. Cases Construing Blasius . . . . . . . . . . . . . 792

      c.  Simultaneous Tender Offers and Proxy
Contests . . . . . . . . . . . . . . . . . . . . 799

      d.  The Law Outside of Delaware . . . . . . . . . . 805

  6.  Consideration of Non-Shareholder
Constituencies . . . . . . . . . . . . . . . . . . 808

      a.  Case Law . . . . . . . . . . . . . . . . . . . 808

      b.  State Statutes . . . . . . . . . . . . . . . . . 812

      c.  Charter Provisions . . . . . . . . . . . . . . 822

  7.  The Role of Outside Directors and Special
Committees . . . . . . . . . . . . . . . . . . . 823

  8.  Standing Considerations . . . . . . . . . . . . . 832

B.  White Squire Stock Transactions . . . . . . . . . . . . 834

  1.  Friendly Third Party Stock Acquisitions . . . . . . 834

      a.  Cases Upholding Friendly Third Party
Stock Acquisitions . . . . . . . . . . . . . . 835

      b.  Cases Not Upholding Friendly Third
Party Stock Acquisitions . . . . . . . . . . . . 846

  2.  Employee Stock Ownership Plans
("ESOPs") . . . . . . . . . . . . . . . . . . . . 853

      a.  Cases Invalidating ESOPs . . . . . . . . . . . . 855

      b.  Cases Upholding ESOPs Pursuant to
the Business Judgment Rule . . . . . . . . . . . 870

      c.  The Polaroid Fairness Standard . . . . . . . . . 872

      d.  Delaware Section 203 . . . . . . . . . . . . . 876

      e.  ERISA Considerations . . . . . . . . . . . . . 878

  3.  Bridge Financing . . . . . . . . . . . . . . . . . 901

C.  Crown Jewel Asset Sales . . . . . . . . . . . . . . . . 904

D.  White Knight Transactions and Mergers of
Equals . . . . . . . . . . . . . . . . . . . . . . . . 908

  1.  Leg-Up and Lock-Up Stock Options . . . . . . . . 909

      a.  Decision Upholding Stock Option
          Grants . . . . . . . . . . . . . . . . . . . . . . . . . . . . 909

      b.  Decisions Criticizing Stock Option
          Grants . . . . . . . . . . . . . . . . . . . . . . . . . . . . 914

  2.  Lock-Up Asset Options . . . . . . . . . . . . . . . . . . 918

      a.  Pre-1985 Decisions . . . . . . . . . . . . . . . . . . 918

      b.  Revlon, Macmillan and Hanson . . . . . . . . . . 921

      c.  Storer . . . . . . . . . . . . . . . . . . . . . . . . . . . . 928

      d.  Inadequate Consideration and Waste . . . . . . . 931

  3.  No Shop, Window Shop and Market Test
     Provisions . . . . . . . . . . . . . . . . . . . . . . . . . . . 935

      a.  No Shop Provisions . . . . . . . . . . . . . . . . . . 935

      b.  Window Shop Provisions . . . . . . . . . . . . . . 942

      c.  Market Test Provisions . . . . . . . . . . . . . . . 945

  4.  Termination Fees and Expense Reim-
     bursement Provisions . . . . . . . . . . . . . . . . . . . 957

      a.  Cases Upholding Termination Fees and
          Expense Reimbursement Provisions . . . . . . . 958

      b.  Cases Criticizing Termination Fees and
          Expense Reimbursement Provisions . . . . . . . 974

  5.  Topping Fees . . . . . . . . . . . . . . . . . . . . . . . . 979

  6.  Later, Better Offers . . . . . . . . . . . . . . . . . . . . 982

      a.  Cases Holding That Directors Cannot
          Contract Away Fiduciary Duties . . . . . . . . . 984

      b.  Cases Enforcing Merger Agreements
          Despite Changed Circumstances . . . . . . . . . . 994

      c.  Claims By Early Bidders Against Later
          Bidders . . . . . . . . . . . . . . . . . . . . . . . . . . . 1000

E.  Self-Tender Offers, Exchange Offers and
   Extraordinary Dividends . . . . . . . . . . . . . . . . . . . . 1003

  1.  Self-Tender Offers and Exchange Offers . . . . . . . 1003

a.  Pre-Unocal Repurchase, Self-Tender
    and Exchange Offer Cases . . . . . . . . . . . . 1004

b.  Unocal . . . . . . . . . . . . . . . . . . . . . . 1008

c.  Post-Unocal Repurchase, Self-Tender
    and Exchange Offer Cases . . . . . . . . . . . . 1011

d.  Unitrin . . . . . . . . . . . . . . . . . . . . . . 1024

e.  ITT . . . . . . . . . . . . . . . . . . . . . . . 1033

f.  Post-Unocal Exchange Offer Cases
    Involving Restrictive Covenants in
    Debt Securities . . . . . . . . . . . . . . . . . 1035

2.  Extraordinary Dividends . . . . . . . . . . . . . 1039

a.  Cases Upholding Extraordinary
    Dividends . . . . . . . . . . . . . . . . . . . . 1040

b.  Cases Enjoining Extraordinary Divi-
    dends . . . . . . . . . . . . . . . . . . . . . . 1045

F.  Super-Voting Common Stock . . . . . . . . . . . . . 1052

1.  Statutory Authority for Super-Voting Stock. . . . . 1054

2.  SEC Rule 19c-4 and Its Aftermath . . . . . . . . . 1055

3.  Cases Upholding the Adoption of
    Super-Voting Stock Plans . . . . . . . . . . . . . 1068

4.  Cases Enjoining the Adoption of
    Super-Voting Stock Plans . . . . . . . . . . . . . 1079

5.  Claims Involving Previously Adopted
    Super-Voting Stock Plans . . . . . . . . . . . . . 1083

G.  Poison Pill Shareholder Rights Plans . . . . . . . . . 1085

1.  Adoption of Poison Pill Rights Plans . . . . . . . . 1091

a.  Flip Over Provisions—Household . . . . . . . . 1091

b.  Flip In Provisions—Discrimination
    Among Shareholders . . . . . . . . . . . . . . . 1096

c.  Flip In Provisions—Business Judgment
    Rule Considerations . . . . . . . . . . . . . . . 1103

(i) Cases Upholding Flip In
Provisions . . . . . . . . . . . . . . . . . . . . 1104

(ii) Cases Not Upholding Flip In
Provisions . . . . . . . . . . . . . . . . . . . . 1107

(iii) Motion to Dismiss Decisions . . . . . . . . 1115

d. Back End or Debt Provisions . . . . . . . . . . 1121

e. Disproportionate Voting Provisions . . . . . . 1135

f. Exploding or Springing Warrants . . . . . . . . 1144

2. Use of Poison Pill Rights Plans During a
Contest for Control . . . . . . . . . . . . . . . . . 1146

a. The Auction Context . . . . . . . . . . . . . . . 1150

b. The Alternative Restructuring Context . . . . . . 1161

c. The "Just Say No" Defense . . . . . . . . . . . 1171

d. "Continuing Director" and "Dead
Hand" Restrictions Upon the the
Authority of Future Boards to Redeem
Rights . . . . . . . . . . . . . . . . . . . . . . 1184

e. Statutory Provisions . . . . . . . . . . . . . . . 1190

3. Shareholder Resolutions . . . . . . . . . . . . . . . 1194

## VOLUME II

H. Non-Structural Resistance to Contests for
Control . . . . . . . . . . . . . . . . . . . . . . . . 1203

1. Shareholder Meeting Dates . . . . . . . . . . . . . 1203

a. Cases Invalidating Board Decisions
Advancing or Delaying Meeting Dates . . . . . . 1204

b. Cases Upholding Board Decisions
Advancing or Delaying Meeting Dates . . . . . . 1217

c. Decisions Refusing to Enjoin
Shareholder Meetings . . . . . . . . . . . . . . 1240

d. Record Dates . . . . . . . . . . . . . . . . . . . 1241

2. Shark Repellent Charter and Bylaw
   Provisions . . . . . . . . . . . . . . . . . . . . . . . . . . 1245

   a. Shareholder Approved Shark Repellent
      Provisions . . . . . . . . . . . . . . . . . . . . . . . 1250

   b. Board Adopted Shark Repellent
      Provisions . . . . . . . . . . . . . . . . . . . . . . . 1253

   c. Bylaws Regulating Board Size . . . . . . . . . . 1253

   d. Bylaws Regulating Board Nominations,
      Shareholder Resolutions and Voting at
      Shareholder Meetings . . . . . . . . . . . . . . . 1257

   e. Bylaws Regulating Consent
      Solicitations . . . . . . . . . . . . . . . . . . . . . . 1274

   f. ITT's Staggered Board Bylaw . . . . . . . . . . 1278

   g. Other Shark Repellent Bylaw Decisions . . . . . 1283

   h. Statutory Restrictions . . . . . . . . . . . . . . . 1289

   i. Hollywood Park: Must a Valid Bylaw
      be Waived Where Enforcement Would
      be Inequitable? . . . . . . . . . . . . . . . . . . . 1292

3. Golden Parachute Severance Agreements . . . . . . 1296

   a. Barriers to Judicial Review . . . . . . . . . . . . 1299

   b. The Standard of Review . . . . . . . . . . . . . . 1301

   c. Cases Upholding Golden Parachutes . . . . . . . 1304

   d. Cases Enjoining or Questioning Golden
      Parachutes . . . . . . . . . . . . . . . . . . . . . . . 1312

   e. Legislation . . . . . . . . . . . . . . . . . . . . . . . 1319

   f. Employee Tin Parachutes . . . . . . . . . . . . . 1322

   g. Funding Trusts . . . . . . . . . . . . . . . . . . . . 1328

4. Antitrust and Other Regulatory Defenses . . . . . . 1332

5. The Pac-Man Defense . . . . . . . . . . . . . . . . . . 1339

6. Litigation . . . . . . . . . . . . . . . . . . . . . . . . . 1343

I. Settlements . . . . . . . . . . . . . . . . . . . . . . . . . . . 1349

    1.   Greenmail ........................... 1349

        a.  Cases Upholding Greenmail Trans-
             actions ............................ 1351

        b.  Cases Questioning Greenmail
             Transactions ...................... 1356

        c.  Anti-Greenmail Measures ............. 1364

    2.   Standstill Agreements .................. 1368

**Chapter IV.     The Business Judgment Rule in
                   Shareholder Derivative Litigation** ...... 1379

A.   The Nature of Shareholder Derivative Litigation
     and the Special Rules Governing Shareholder
     Derivative Litigation ...................... 1379

    1.   The Contemporaneous Ownership
        Requirement:  At the Time of the Alleged
        Wrongdoing ......................... 1385

    2.   The Contemporaneous Ownership Require-
        ment:  Throughout the Litigation .......... 1389

    3.   The Fair and Adequate Representation
        Requirement ......................... 1398

    4.   Security for Expenses ................... 1403

    5.   The Demand Requirement ............... 1407

    6.   Termination by Special Litigation Com-
        mittee .............................. 1407

    7.   Settlement ........................... 1408

    8.   Distinguishing Derivative from Non-
        Derivative Actions .................... 1411

    9.   Double Derivative Actions .............. 1415

   10.  Diversity Jurisdiction Issues ............. 1416

B.   The Demand Requirement .................... 1425

    1.   Definition ........................... 1425

2. Rationale . . . . . . . . . . . . . . . . . . . . . . 1440
3. The Two Means Of Complying with the
   Demand Requirement . . . . . . . . . . . . . . . . 1454
4. Choice of Law Considerations . . . . . . . . . . . . 1455
   a. State Law Governs . . . . . . . . . . . . . . . 1457
   b. The Federal Policy Exception . . . . . . . . . . 1460
5. Demand Futility . . . . . . . . . . . . . . . . . . 1467
   a. The Meaning of Futility, Generally . . . . . . . 1467
   b. The Delaware Approach: Aronson and
      Rales, Generally . . . . . . . . . . . . . . . . 1471
   c. Cases Explaining and Applying the
      Aronson Standard . . . . . . . . . . . . . . . . 1479
      (i) Cases Requiring Demand Under
          Aronson . . . . . . . . . . . . . . . . . . 1482
      (ii) Cases Excusing Demand Under
           Aronson . . . . . . . . . . . . . . . . . . 1504
   d. Cases Explaining and Applying the
      Rales Standard . . . . . . . . . . . . . . . . . 1529
   e. The New York Approach . . . . . . . . . . . . . 1543
   f. The California Approach . . . . . . . . . . . . 1560
   g. The Universal Demand Requirement
      Approach . . . . . . . . . . . . . . . . . . . . 1562
   h. The Effect of Changes in Board
      Composition Following Commence-
      ment of Litigation . . . . . . . . . . . . . . . 1572
   i. Waiver Considerations . . . . . . . . . . . . . 1578
      (i) Shareholder Demands . . . . . . . . . . . . 1578
      (ii) Board Delegation of Decision-
           Making Authority . . . . . . . . . . . . . 1586
   j. The Effect of Dismissal for Failure to
      Make a Demand . . . . . . . . . . . . . . . . . 1592

6.  The Response to a Demand . . . . . . . . . . . . . . 1593

    a.  The Board's Options . . . . . . . . . . . . . . . 1593

    b.  The Board's Entitlement to Adequate
        Time . . . . . . . . . . . . . . . . . . . . . . . . . . . . 1596

    c.  The Wrongful Refusal Doctrine . . . . . . . . . . 1605

    d.  Motions to Dismiss:  The Delaware
        Standard . . . . . . . . . . . . . . . . . . . . . . . . . 1613

    e.  Motion to Dismiss Decisions by Dela-
        ware Courts . . . . . . . . . . . . . . . . . . . . . . . 1618

    f.  Motion to Dismiss Decisions by Courts
        Construing Delaware Law Outside of
        Delaware . . . . . . . . . . . . . . . . . . . . . . . . . 1632

    g.  Decisions Construing New York, Illi-
        nois and Michigan Law . . . . . . . . . . . . . . 1636

    h.  Cases Involving Unlawful Conduct . . . . . . . . 1649

    i.  The Model Business Corporation Act
        and Statutory Provisions Similar to the
        Model Act . . . . . . . . . . . . . . . . . . . . . . . . 1655

    j.  Principles of Corporate Governance . . . . . . . 1665

        (i)  Section 7.04 Motions . . . . . . . . . . . . . . 1666

        (ii) Section 7.07 Through 7.13
             Motions . . . . . . . . . . . . . . . . . . . . . . 1668

7.  Discovery on the Demand Issue . . . . . . . . . . . 1673

8.  Standing to Raise Demand as a Defense . . . . . . 1681

9.  Section 16(b) Cases . . . . . . . . . . . . . . . . . . . 1684

10. Demand on Shareholders . . . . . . . . . . . . . . . 1686

C.  Termination by Special Litigation Committees . . . . . . 1689

    1.  The Power to Terminate . . . . . . . . . . . . . . . 1690

        a.  Gall, Auerbach and Zapata . . . . . . . . . . . 1690

        b.  Model and Statutory Provisions . . . . . . . . 1696

        c.  Miller and Alford . . . . . . . . . . . . . . . . . 1699

2. The Scope of Judicial Review—Auerbach Versus Zapata . . . . . . . . . . . . . . . . . . . . 1702

   a. The Auerbach Approach . . . . . . . . . . . . . . 1703

   b. The Zapata Approach . . . . . . . . . . . . . . 1711

   c. Applications of Zapata . . . . . . . . . . . . . . . 1722

   d. Variations of the Zapata Standard of Review by Courts Construing Connecticut, Massachusetts and North Carolina Law . . . . . . . . . . . . . . . . . . . 1738

   e. Director Disinterestedness and Independence . . . . . . . . . . . . . . . . . . . 1744

   f. The Structural Bias Theory . . . . . . . . . . . . 1765

   g. Effect of Procedural Context on the Level of Interest Required to Disqualify Directors . . . . . . . . . . . . . . . . . . 1773

   h. Considerations Involving Counsel . . . . . . . . 1775

   i. Model and Statutory Provisions . . . . . . . . . 1781

3. Discovery on the Termination Issue . . . . . . . . 1783

   a. After the Committee is Formed, But Before Its Recommendation . . . . . . . . . . . 1783

   b. After the Committee's Recommendation . . . . . . . . . . . . . . . . . 1786

      (i) The Delaware Approach . . . . . . . . . . . 1786

      (ii) The New York Approach . . . . . . . . . . 1795

      (iii) Model and Statutory Provisions . . . . . . 1798

4. The Special Litigation Committee—Some Practical Considerations . . . . . . . . . . . . . . 1800

D. The Limited Partnership Context . . . . . . . . . . . . 1804

1. The Demand Requirement . . . . . . . . . . . . . 1805

2. The Wrongful Refusal of Demand Doctrine . . . . . . . . . . . . . . . . . . . . . . . 1806

3. Special Litigation Committees . . . . . . . . . . . . 1808

E. Privilege and Work Product Considerations . . . . . . . 1819

    1. The Garner Doctrine . . . . . . . . . . . . . . . . . . 1820

    2. Public Access to Court Filings . . . . . . . . . . . . 1826

    3. Perrigo . . . . . . . . . . . . . . . . . . . . . . . . 1828

        a. The District Court Decisions . . . . . . . . . . . 1829

        b. The Sixth Circuit Decision . . . . . . . . . . . 1841

        c. The Sixth Circuit Dissent . . . . . . . . . . . . 1846

**Chapter V. Indemnification and Insurance** . . . . . . . . . 1851

A. Indemnification . . . . . . . . . . . . . . . . . . . . . . . 1852

    1. Underlying Policy Considerations . . . . . . . . . . . 1852

    2. Directors, Officers, Employees and Agents . . . . . . 1855

    3. Mandatory Indemnification . . . . . . . . . . . . . . 1857

        a. Statutory Provisions . . . . . . . . . . . . . . . 1857

        b. Charter, Bylaw and Contract Provisions . . . . . . . . . . . . . . . . . . . . . . . 1867

    4. Permissive Indemnification . . . . . . . . . . . . . . 1872

        a. Third Party Actions . . . . . . . . . . . . . . . . 1876

        b. Actions by or in the Right of the Corporation . . . . . . . . . . . . . . . . . . . . 1880

        c. Authorization . . . . . . . . . . . . . . . . . . . 1887

    5. Advancement . . . . . . . . . . . . . . . . . . . . . . 1894

        a. Permissive Advancement . . . . . . . . . . . . . 1895

        b. Mandatory Advancement . . . . . . . . . . . . . 1909

        c. Does "Indemnification" Include "Advancement"? . . . . . . . . . . . . . . . . . . 1928

    6. Court-Ordered Indemnification and Advancement . . . . . . . . . . . . . . . . . . . . . . 1932

a. Enforcement of Mandatory Indemni-
fication or Advancement Obligations . . . . . . . 1933

b. Court-Ordered Indemnification Where
Indemnification Is Not Otherwise
Required . . . . . . . . . . . . . . . . . . . . . . . 1938

c. Court-Ordered Advancement Where
Advancement Is Not Otherwise
Required . . . . . . . . . . . . . . . . . . . . . . . 1940

7. Types of Proceedings Covered . . . . . . . . . . . . 1946

8. Expenses Incurred Other Than as a
Defendant . . . . . . . . . . . . . . . . . . . . . . . . 1947

9. Types of Conduct Covered . . . . . . . . . . . . . . 1952

10. Exclusivity and Non-Exclusivity
Provisions . . . . . . . . . . . . . . . . . . . . . . . . 1959

11. Public Policy Limitations . . . . . . . . . . . . . . 1969

12. Funding Mechanisms . . . . . . . . . . . . . . . . . 1976

13. Notice to Shareholders . . . . . . . . . . . . . . . . 1979

B. Insurance . . . . . . . . . . . . . . . . . . . . . . . . . . . 1980

1. Statutory Provisions Authorizing Insurance . . . . . . 1980

2. The Need for Insurance . . . . . . . . . . . . . . . . 1983

3. Public Policy Limitations . . . . . . . . . . . . . . 1985

4. Typical Policy Structure and Terms . . . . . . . . . 1987

5. The Claim Made Requirement . . . . . . . . . . . . 1997

6. The Notice Requirement . . . . . . . . . . . . . . . 2008

7. The Wrongful Act Requirement . . . . . . . . . . . 2021

8. Losses Covered . . . . . . . . . . . . . . . . . . . . . 2025

9. Exclusions . . . . . . . . . . . . . . . . . . . . . . . . 2030

a. Common Exclusions . . . . . . . . . . . . . . . 2030

b. The Contest for Control Exclusion . . . . . . . 2040

c. The Insured Versus Insured Exclusion . . . . . 2044

d. The Insured Versus Insured Exclusion
in the Regulatory Context . . . . . . . . . . . . . 2054

e. The Insured Versus Insured Exclusion
in the Bankruptcy Context . . . . . . . . . . . . 2068

f. The Regulatory Exclusion: Ambiguity
Considerations . . . . . . . . . . . . . . . . . . . . 2074

g. The Regulatory Exclusion: Public
Policy Considerations . . . . . . . . . . . . . . . 2084

10. Advancement . . . . . . . . . . . . . . . . . . . . . . . 2092

11. Allocation . . . . . . . . . . . . . . . . . . . . . . . . . 2109

a. Allocation Between Defendants: The
Larger Settlement and Proportional
Fault/Relative Exposure Approaches . . . . . . 2109

b. Allocation Between Defendants: The
Case Law . . . . . . . . . . . . . . . . . . . . . . . 2113

c. Allocation Between Defendants: The
Burden of Proof . . . . . . . . . . . . . . . . . . . 2132

d. Allocation Between Defendants: New
Policy Approaches . . . . . . . . . . . . . . . . . 2135

e. Allocation Between Claims . . . . . . . . . . . . 2136

f. Allocation Where Some But Not All
Claims are Covered and Advancement
is Required . . . . . . . . . . . . . . . . . . . . . . 2137

12. Misrepresentations in Policy Applications . . . . . . 2139

a. General Principles . . . . . . . . . . . . . . . . . . 2140

b. Innocent Director Cases . . . . . . . . . . . . . . 2148

C. Self-Insurance and Insurance Pooling
Arrangements . . . . . . . . . . . . . . . . . . . . . . . . . 2153

D. The D & O Crisis of the Mid-1980s: The
Crisis, the Responses and the Current Market . . . . . . 2163

1. The Crisis . . . . . . . . . . . . . . . . . . . . . . . . . 2163

    2.   Responses . . . . . . . . . . . . . . . . . . . . . . . . 2167

        a.  Statutes Limiting Director Liability . . . . . . . 2168

        b.  Statutes Increasing the Availability of
           Indemnification and Insurance . . . . . . . . . . . 2169

        c.  Charter, Bylaw and Contract Provi-
           sions Maximizing Indemnification
           Rights . . . . . . . . . . . . . . . . . . . . . . . . . . 2169

        d.  Funding Mechanisms . . . . . . . . . . . . . . . . 2171

        e.  Self-Insurance and Insurance Pooling
           Arrangements . . . . . . . . . . . . . . . . . . . . . 2171

    3.   The Current Market . . . . . . . . . . . . . . . . . . 2172

**Table of Authorities** . . . . . . . . . . . . . . . . . . . . . . . 2177

**Index** . . . . . . . . . . . . . . . . . . . . . . . . . . . . . . . . 2445

# CHAPTER III

# The Business Judgment Rule in Transactions Involving Corporate Control

## [Sections A through G Appear in Volume I]

## H. Non-Structural Resistance to Contests for Control

There are additional defenses a corporation can utilize to deter a change in control of the corporation. As a general rule, these defenses are unlikely to win the control battle in and of themselves. Their principal advantage is that they may delay the completion of an unwanted bid for control long enough to provide a corporation the time it needs to secure a more favorable white knight offer or to implement a restructuring, recapitalization or other alternative defensive strategy.

### 1. Shareholder Meeting Dates

"Delaware Courts support the enfranchisement of Delaware's corporations' shareholders" and view "[t]he importance of allowing shareholders to vote at an annual meeting" as "critical to effective corporate governance."[3474] Indeed, so "central" and "long recognized" is the "role of annual meetings in the scheme of corporate

---

3474. *Mainiero v. Microbyx Corp.*, 1996 Del. Ch. LEXIS 107, at *7, 1996 WL 487939, at *3 (Del. Ch. Aug. 15, 1996).

governance" that "[e]ven the shareholders' power to approve amendments to the charter does not extend so far as to permit a Delaware corporation legitimately to dispense with the annual meeting."[3475] Likewise, even though any action that may be taken at a shareholders' meeting may be taken by written consent, the use of consents cannot satisfy the requirement that an annual meeting be held absent the unanimous consent of all shareholders.[3476]

A substantial body of case law addresses board efforts to advance or postpone the dates of shareholder meetings, both in Delaware and elsewhere. Most of these decisions enjoin inequitable efforts by directors to advance or postpone meeting dates. Several decisions, however, illustrate instances where meeting dates have been changed by directors acting in accordance with their fiduciary duties.

All things being equal, directors of corporations having certificates of incorporation and bylaws that do not specify particular dates for shareholder meetings have more flexibility in setting meeting dates than do directors of corporations required to schedule meetings on particular dates. All things being equal, certificate or bylaw provisions explicitly authorizing postponements or adjournments of meetings also provide directors more flexibility than they otherwise might have.

*a. Cases Invalidating Board Decisions Advancing or Delaying Meeting Dates.* The leading decision rejecting efforts by directors to advance or postpone scheduled shareholder meeting dates in order to accomplish an unjust or inequitable result is the Delaware Supreme Court's decision in *Schnell v. Chris-Craft Industries, Inc.*[3477] *Schnell* involved a board of directors that responded to a mid-October notice of a proxy contest by advancing the date of a shareholder meeting from January 11 to December 8.[3478] The mid-October to early-December period gave the dissident share-

---

3475. *Hoschett v. TSI Int'l Software, Ltd.*, 683 A.2d 43, 44 (Del. Ch. 1996).
3476. *Id.* at 43-46.
3477. 285 A.2d 437 (Del. 1971).
3478. *Id.* at 438-39.

holders "little chance, because of the exigencies of time, including that required to clear material at the S.E.C., to wage a successful proxy fight."[3479]

The Delaware Supreme Court stated that "[w]hen the by-laws of a corporation designate the date of the annual meeting of stockholders, it is to be expected that those who intend to contest the reelection of incumbent management will gear their campaign to the by-law date," and that "[i]t is not to be expected that management will attempt to advance that date in order to obtain an inequitable advantage in the contest."[3480] Here, however, the court concluded,

> management has attempted to utilize the corporate machinery and the Delaware Law for the purpose of perpetuating itself in office; and, to that end, for the purpose of obstructing the legitimate efforts of dissident stockholders in the exercise of their rights to undertake a proxy contest against management. These are inequitable purposes, contrary to established principles of corporate democracy. The advancement by directors of the by-law date of a stockholders' meeting, for such purposes, may not be permitted to stand.[3481]

The court rejected the director's contention that the board "complied strictly" with the Delaware General Corporation Law in changing the meeting date.[3482] To the contrary, the court replied, "inequitable action does not become permissible simply because it is legally possible."[3483] The court accordingly ordered that the January 11 meeting date be reinstated.[3484]

The Delaware Supreme Court repeatedly has cited and quoted *Schnell*, including, most recently, in *Farahpour v. DCX, Inc.*,[3485] *Paramount Communications Inc. v. QVC Network Inc.*,[3486] *Uni-*

---

3479. *Id.* at 439.
3480. *Id.*
3481. *Id.*
3482. *Id.*
3483. *Id.*
3484. *Id.* at 440.
3485. 635 A.2d 894, 901 (Del. 1994).
3486. 637 A.2d 34, 42 n.11 (Del. 1994).

*trin, Inc. v. American General Corp.*,[3487] *Williams v. Geier*[3488] and *Brody v. Zaucha*.[3489] These decisions all stand for the proposition that "inequitable action does not become permissible simply because it is legally possible,"[3490] and that "a fiduciary may not exercise legal rights if the action is inequitable either in its purpose or effect."[3491]

The Delaware Court of Chancery in *Aprahamian v. HBO & Co.*[3492] reached the same result that was reached in *Schnell*, except in the context of a board effort to postpone rather than advance a shareholder meeting. *HBO* involved a contest between an incumbent board and a dissident slate of director candidates proposing a program that the dissident slate contended would maximize the value of the corporation over a short-term period. The incumbent directors issued proxy materials opposing the dissident slate, but reversed course three business days before the scheduled meeting date and undertook to convince the corporation's shareholders that they would pursue the dissidents' plan, and that they were better qualified than the dissidents to complete that plan. Late in the afternoon on the day before the election, the incumbent directors received a report from their proxy solicitor, who advised the directors that the election was too close to call. The directors responded by postponing the meeting for five months, thus necessitating the setting of a new record date and invalidating the proxies that had been solicited by the dissident slate.[3493]

The court stated that an annual meeting may be postponed if the postponement is in the best interests of the corporation's shareholders, but that the burden of persuasion on this issue is upon the party seeking the postponement.[3494] The business judgment rule

---

3487. 651 A.2d 1361, 1378 (Del. 1995).
3488. 671 A.2d 1368, 1384 & n.35 (Del. 1996).
3489. 697 A.2d 749, 755 (Del. 1997).
3490. *Williams*, 671 A.2d at 1384.
3491. *Brody*, 697 A.2d at 755.
3492. 531 A.2d 1204 (Del. Ch. 1987).
3493. *Id.* at 1205-06.
3494. *Id.* at 1207.

has no applicability to a board decision to postpone a shareholder meeting even if made by outside directors, the court explained, because outside as well as inside directors are "obviously interested" in the outcome of the election.[3495] In the court's words:

> A candidate for office, whether as an elected official or as a director of a corporation, is likely to prefer to be elected rather than defeated. He therefore has a personal interest in the outcome of the election even if the interest is not financial and he seeks to serve from the best of motives.[3496]

The court noted the incumbents' assertion that shareholders needed time to examine the incumbents' decision three days before the scheduled meeting date to pursue the course previously advocated by the dissident slate, but concluded that if the directors had been sincere in their desire to ensure that shareholders were fully informed they would have postponed the meeting at the time they announced their new position rather than waiting until they heard their proxy solicitor's report the day before the scheduled meeting date.[3497] The court accordingly ordered that the meeting be convened the following day, the last day upon which it could be convened prior to the expiration of the proxies solicited by the dissident director slate.[3498] In order to protect the interests of shareholders "bewildered" by the sudden postponement of the original meeting and the ensuing litigation, however, the court also ordered that the meeting then be adjourned immediately, to be reconvened within a three week period.[3499]

The Delaware Court of Chancery's decision in *Gintel v. XTRA Corp.*[3500] involved a similar board decision, made two days before an annual meeting at which shareholders were scheduled to vote in a contested election, to delay the meeting for 30 days in order to provide the board an opportunity to arrange a sale

---

3495. *Id.* at 1206.
3496. *Id.*
3497. *Id.* at 1205, 1207.
3498. *Id.* at 1207, 1209.
3499. *Id.* at 1209.
3500. No. 11422 (Del. Ch. Feb. 27, 1990).

of the company. Balancing the interests underlying the two perspec-
tives from which a proxy contest can be viewed—(1) "fairness or
unfairness as between the two contending groups of candidates for
office" and (2) "the interests of the shareholders and the effective
exercise of the franchise"—the court ordered that the meeting be
held within 15 days, "in order to make known to all the shareholders that a significant development had occurred": the board's
"decision to seek to pursue an extraordinary transaction of some
kind."[3501] The court refused to allow the incumbent board time
to effectuate their plan because the plan had been developed "on
almost the virtual eve of a meeting at which there is every reason
to understand that there is a substantial question as to the stockholders' designation of the members of this board to continue" in
office.[3502]

In *Phillips v. Insituform of North America*,[3503] the Delaware
Court of Chancery held that a board's postponement of an annual
meeting required a showing by the directors that their action was
"necessary to protect an important corporate, as opposed to a personal, interest."[3504] Applying this standard, the court held that a
delay intended to ascertain how shares that recently had been placed
in the hands of court-appointed receivers would be voted at a meeting in which the only issue likely to be voted upon was the election
of directors was impermissible.[3505] The court stated that "it is
impossible to conclude that the court-appointed receivers of the
commanding block of . . . shares represented a threat to existing
policies, programs or interests" of the corporation "as to justify, if
ever it could be justified, ignoring the command of Section 211 [of
the Delaware General Corporation Law] to hold an annual meeting
within 13 months of the last such meeting."[3506]

---

3501. *Id.*, Tr. op. at 2-3, 5, 8.
3502. *Id.* at 7-8.
3503. 13 Del. J. Corp. L. 774 (Del. Ch. Aug. 27, 1987).
3504. *Id.* at 789.
3505. *Id.*
3506. *Id.*

A federal court construing Pennsylvania law in *Norfolk Southern Corp. v. Conrail Inc.*[3507] granted a motion for a preliminary injunction requiring that a Conrail Inc. shareholder meeting scheduled to vote upon a proposal pursuant to which Conrail would opt out of certain provisions of the Pennsylvania Business Corporation Law be convened and not be adjourned. Conrail stated in proxy materials that the meeting would not be convened "if Conrail has not received sufficient proxies to assure approval of the proposal."[3508] The court recognized that an order requiring Conrail to proceed with the vote without sufficient proxies to assure approval of the resolution would "not make very much difference" because the same proposal could be resubmitted to shareholders at another meeting.[3509] The court concluded, however, that not convening the meeting if the proposal was not assured of approval was not "a proper way to hold an election or a vote," and that "the way this vote is to be held is fundamentally unfair to those who may be opposed to the transaction."[3510] The court accordingly issued a preliminary injunction enjoining Conrail and its directors from "failing to convene, and/or from postponing, and/or from adjourning" the scheduled meeting "by reason of Conrail or its nominees not having received sufficient proxies to assure approval of the proposal."[3511]

*Shoen v. AMERCO*,[3512] a federal decision court construing Nevada law, reached the same result, first in the context of a motion for a temporary restraining order, and then on a motion for a preliminary injunction. The case involved AMERCO, a corporation split into two factions: the "Sam Shoen faction" and the "Joe Shoen faction." Each faction controlled approximately 47 percent of

---

3507. No. 96-7167 (E.D. Pa. Dec. 17, 1996).

3508. *Id.*, Tr. op. at 66.

3509. *Id.* at 68.

3510. *Id.* at 69.

3511. Order at 1.

3512. No. CV-N-94-0475-ECR (D. Nev. July 20, 1994), *subsequent proceedings*, 885 F. Supp. 1332 (D. Nev. 1994), *modified*, 1994 WL 904199 (D. Nev. Oct. 24, 1994), *vacated pursuant to settlement*, No. CV-N-94-0475-ECR (D. Nev. Feb. 9, 1995) (WL Insta-cite service).

AMERCO's common stock. AMERCO's remaining shares were
held by individual shareholders and an employee stock ownership
plan, with the ESOP's shares voted by ESOP trustees pursuant to
the instructions of individual ESOP participants or, to the extent no
instructions were given by individual participants to the trustees,
pursuant to the trustees' own determination. The Joe Shoen faction
controlled the company, and was held together by a shareholder
agreement providing that whoever controlled a majority of the
shares subject to the agreement had the power to vote all shares
subject to the agreement.[3513] AMERCO's bylaws provided for
the corporation's annual shareholder meeting to be held "on the last
Saturday of September of each year . . . , or on such other date as
may be determined by the Board of Directors."[3514] In the past,
AMERCO's annual meeting "almost always" had been held on the
last Saturday in September.[3515]

On April 8, 1994, Paul and Sophia Shoen, holders of approximately one-third of the Joe Shoen faction's 47 percent of
AMERCO's stock, notified AMERCO that they had commenced an
arbitration proceeding seeking termination of the shareholder agreement.[3516] If they were successful, the Joe Shoen faction would
control only about 32.6 percent of AMERCO's stock.[3517] The
arbitration decision, the court stated, "would likely come before the
traditional late September meeting date," and "[i]f so Joe would
probably lose control of AMERCO."[3518] On May 3, shortly after
failing to obtain a temporary restraining order enjoining the arbitration, AMERCO's board determined to advance AMERCO's annual
meeting date from September 24 to July 21.[3519]

At about the same time, Paul Shoen and others advised
AMERCO that they were seeking seats on AMERCO's board, and

---

3513. 885 F. Supp. at 1336-37.
3514. *Id*. at 1341-42.
3515. *Id*. at 1342.
3516. *Id*. at 1336, 1338.
3517. *Id*. at 1336.
3518. *Id*. at 1338.
3519. *Id*. at 1338, 1342.

submitted shareholder proposals intended to diminish the Joe Shoen faction's control of AMERCO.[3520] On July 8, AMERCO's ESOP trustees mailed AMERCO's proxy materials to ESOP participants.[3521] On July 12, Paul Shoen's proxy materials were cleared by the SEC, and on July 13 these proxy materials were delivered to the ESOP trustees for mailing to plan participants.[3522] On July 14, the trustees voted non-allocated shares in favor of incumbent management and against Paul Shoen's shareholder proposals.[3523] On July 15, the trustees determined "that Paul Shoen's proxy materials should not be forwarded to ESOP participants as there was insufficient time for participants to review the information and make an informed decision as to the positions contained therein."[3524]

On July 20, the court granted a motion for a temporary restraining order postponing the "suddenly moved up" annual meeting.[3525] The court stated that "[r]egardless of the reasons, whether innocent or otherwise, for moving up the annual meeting date from the traditional end of September date to July 21, the board had an obligation to inform its shareholders in advance when the annual meeting would be."[3526] The court held that the notice in this case, which was given on June 30—just three weeks before the meeting—was not "adequate to allow reasonable time for the preparation of proposals, proxy materials etc. such as plaintiff is trying to disseminate to the ESOP participants and others."[3527]

Furthermore, according to the court, "[w]hen considered together with the fact that Defendants' voting power may be diminished" by an arbitration decision that was scheduled to be released in the very near future concerning the validity of the Joe Shoen fac-

---

3520. *Id.* at 1337-38.
3521. *Id.* at 1339.
3522. *Id.*
3523. *Id.* at 1339-40.
3524. *Id.* at 1340.
3525. *Shoen v. AMERCO*, No. CV-N-94-475-ECR, slip op. at 2 (D. Nev. July 20, 1994).
3526. *Id.*
3527. *Id.*

tion's voting agreement, "it appears at first blush that there may have been some ulterior motives behind the AMERCO Board's decision to reschedule the meeting at a time before the arbitrator's decision was released and at a time that would prevent Plaintiff from being able to effectively mount his own campaign. . . . It appears from the record that Defendants may have been motivated for the purpose of perpetuating themselves in office and obstructing Plaintiff's legitimate efforts to exercise his rights."[3528] The court rejected AMERCO's claim that it might be harmed by the grant of the temporary restraining order because a court order of this type "would indicate strife and uncertainty within the corporation" and thus harm AMERCO's competitive position in its industry and make lenders less willing to loan money to the corporation.[3529] "[F]rustration of the right to vote," the court concluded, "substantially outweighs this speculative harm."[3530]

The court elaborated upon its reasoning in a decision granting a preliminary injunction.[3531] The court acknowledged that "Nevada law and the company's bylaws permit the board to set the time, place and date of the annual meeting," but explained—quoting *Schnell*—that this "literally true" statement "misses the point" because "'inequitable action does not become permissible simply because it is legally possible.'"[3532] The court—again quoting *Schnell*—stated that "it is to be expected that those who intend to contest the re-election of incumbent management will gear their campaign to the by-law date" of the meeting and that "[i]t is not to be expected that management will attempt to advance the date in order to obtain an inequitable advantage in the contest."[3533]

---

3528. *Id*. at 3.

3529. *Id*. at 2.

3530. *Id*.

3531. *Shoen v. AMERCO*, 885 F. Supp. 1332 (D. Nev. 1994), *modified*, 1994 WL 904199 (D. Nev. Oct. 24, 1994), *vacated pursuant to settlement*, No. CV-N-94-0475-ECR (D. Nev. Feb. 9, 1995) (WL Instacite service).

3532. *Id*. at 1342 (quoting 285 A.2d at 439).

3533. *Id*.

The court then concluded on the basis of the record before it that "incumbent managers afraid that they would lose an election held in late September" advanced AMERCO's meeting "for the purpose of interfering with free and fair voting by the shareholders."[3534] The court noted the AMERCO board's contention that at the time the meeting date was changed the board was not aware of Paul Shoen's candidacy for the board and his shareholder proposals, but rejected this contention because the board "certainly was aware of his attempt to terminate the shareholder agreement; indeed, it had sought only a week earlier to enjoin the arbitration. That attempt was unsuccessful. The board, controlled by Joe's faction, thus had ample reason to advance the date of the meeting, so that Joe would be able to vote all the shares subject to the agreement before its potential termination by the arbitrator's decision."[3535]

The court also rejected various "business justifications" such as "logistics and planning" pointed to by AMERCO's board in support of its decision to advance the date of the corporation's annual meeting to July, noting that the meeting "is held in the remote desert town of Tonopah, Nevada, at a hall that costs $25 to rent," and typically is attended by no more than 20 shareholders.[3536] The court also pointed to other conduct by AMERCO's directors as evidence of inequitable action by the directors, including violations of rules promulgated under Section 14(a) of the Securities Exchange Act of 1934, including Rules 14a-3 (proxy solicitations in employee newspapers and fliers before proxy materials were approved by the SEC), 14a-6 (proxy materials not filed with the SEC ten days before being sent to shareholders) and 14a-9 (false or misleading statements or omissions of material information in proxy solicitations).[3537] As further evidence of inequitable action, the court relied upon breaches of fiduciary duties by the trustees of AMERCO's ESOP plan, who also were members

---

3534. *Id.* at 1344.

3535. *Id.* at 1343-44.

3536. *Id.* at 1343.

3537. *Id.* at 1344-48 (citing 15 U.S.C. § 78n(a) and 17 C.F.R. §§ 240.14a-3, 14a-6 and 14a-9).

of incumbent management. These "flagrant" breaches of fiduciary duty included soliciting votes on behalf of management, preventing management's opponent from communicating with ESOP participants and voting against the opponent's proposals even though those proposals would benefit ESOP participants.[3538]

Because the board's decision to advance the shareholder meeting was "for the purpose of interfering with free and fair voting by the shareholders," the court stated, the board bore "the heavy burden of demonstrating a compelling justification" for its action.[3539] AMERCO's board, the court held, "offered no justification that is convincing, let alone compelling," for its decision to advance the meeting.[3540] Thus, the court concluded, AMERCO's board "at least at this preliminary stage of the case, appears very clearly to have violated its fiduciary duties."[3541] The court accordingly enjoined AMERCO's annual meeting for a period of 45 days from the date that new, neutral ESOP trustees were appointed, "to allow sufficient time for resolicitation."[3542] On a motion seeking modification of this order, the court rejected a contention that its order "improper[ly] . . . force[d] the company to hold its annual meeting while neutral trustees are in control of the ESOP and this litigation is pending."[3543] The court stated that its order "prevents a meeting from being held any earlier than 45 days from the time neutral trustees are chosen" but "does not affirmatively require that the meeting be held at any particular time."[3544]

---

3538. *Id.* at 1348-52; *see also* Chapter III, Section B 2 e (discussing this aspect of *AMERCO* case).

3539. *Id.* at 1341, 1344 (quoting *Blasius Indus. v. Atlas Corp.*, 564 A.2d 651, 660-61 (Del. Ch. 1988)).

3540. *Id.* at 1344.

3541. *Id.*

3542. *Id.* at 1355.

3543. *Shoen v. AMERCO*, 1994 WL 904199, at *2 (D. Nev. Oct. 24, 1994), *vacated pursuant to settlement*, No. CV-N-94-0475-ECR (D. Nev. Feb. 9, 1995) (WL Insta-cite service).

3544. *Id.*

*ER Holdings, Inc. v. Norton Co.*,[3545] a federal court decision construing Massachusetts law, involved a determination by the board of directors of Norton Company 28 days before the corporation's scheduled annual meeting in April 1990 to cancel the meeting and instead schedule a special meeting for two months later, in June 1990. This decision was made after ER Holdings, Inc. had made what the board considered an inadequate $75 per share cash offer for all Norton shares and announced its intent to mount a proxy contest at Norton's annual meeting.[3546]

The board based its determination to hold a special meeting in June rather than a regular meeting in April upon its belief that up to 60 days would be needed to explore alternatives to ER's offer, and a bylaw providing that (1) "[t]he Annual meeting of stockholders shall be held on the fourth Thursday of April in each year," and (2) "[i]f no annual meeting has been held on the date fixed above, a special meeting may be held in lieu thereof with all the force and effect of an annual meeting."[3547] ER challenged the board's decision on the basis of another bylaw provision, this one permitting bylaw amendments by the company's board so long as "[n]o change in the date of the annual meeting may be made within sixty days before the date fixed in these by-laws."[3548]

Norton's board contended that the 60 day rule relied upon by ER did not apply because the board's determination to cancel the corporation's annual meeting and instead schedule a special meeting did not "change . . . the date of the annual meeting."[3549] That interpretation of the bylaws, the court held, would allow the board to read the 60 day rule out of the company's bylaws completely, by changing an "annual meeting" to a "special meeting" simply by not holding an annual meeting on the date set by the bylaws—the fourth

---

3545. 735 F. Supp. 1094 (D. Mass. 1990), *aff'd*, No. 90-1314 (1st Cir. Apr. 18, 1990).

3546. *Id*. at 1096.

3547. *Id*. at 1096-97.

3548. *Id*.

3549. *Id*. at 1098.

Thursday of April.[3550] A more reasonable interpretation of the bylaws, the court concluded, would be (1) to construe the 60 day provision relied upon by ER prospectively to impose "a time limitation on affirmative action that would change the date of the [annual] meeting in the future," and (2) to construe the "special meeting may be held in lieu . . . of an annual meeting" provision relied upon by the board retrospectively, to provide "a vehicle for corporate reaction to a circumstance that has already occurred—the fact that, for some reason, 'no annual meeting has been held. . . .'"[3551] The court stated its view that "one of the most sacred rights of any shareholder is to participate in corporate democracy," and that it therefore was "unlikely that the Norton shareholders intended that the company's by-laws would permit the easy postponement of their voting rights that the Board's interpretation would allow."[3552]

The district court accordingly ordered Norton's board "to restore the annual meeting to its original date."[3553] The First Circuit affirmed the district court's opinion "substantially for the reasons set forth by the district court."[3554]

Another federal district court, this one construing New York law in *Ocilla Industries, Inc. v. Katz*,[3555] granted a preliminary injunction requiring that an annual meeting be held after the corporation's directors had scheduled the meeting for a date over five weeks "beyond the period contemplated by the . . . corporate by-laws and the applicable laws of the State of New York."[3556] The court held that the directors' delay was not justified by the directors' contention that the extra time was needed in order for the directors to "prepare for the impending proxy fight" and "present

---

3550. *Id.*

3551. *Id.*

3552. *Id.* at 1100-01.

3553. *Id.* at 1103.

3554. *ER Holdings, Inc. v. Norton Co.*, No. 90-1314, slip op. at 3 (1st Cir. Apr. 18, 1990).

3555. 677 F. Supp. 1291 (E.D.N.Y. 1987).

3556. *Id.* at 1301.

their views of what is best for the company."[3557] The court allowed the meeting to be held on the date chosen by the directors, however, for three reasons: (1) the plaintiffs had failed to demonstrate irreparable harm by the five week delay, (2) "confusion . . . could ensue if another date were arbitrarily selected by the court," and (3) "[a]t this point in the proceedings it is important that 'all concerned can be confident that . . . [a] shareholders' meeting will indeed take place . . . .'"[3558] The court stated that its order would "add 'certainty to the situation' and assure no further postponements."[3559]

As a federal court construing New Jersey law in *Danaher Corp. v. Chicago Pneumatic Tool Co.*[3560] summarized the law in a decision ordering Chicago Pneumatic Tool Company not to cancel a scheduled meeting:

> It has long been established that a board of directors may not manipulate the timing of the shareholders' annual meeting to perpetuate its reign of control. "Special scrutiny" is to be given where directors, bent on entrenchment, allegedly use their powers to restrict the ability of shareholders to replace them. The law is clear that when a board of directors has improperly postponed or manipulated the timing of the shareholders annual meeting, courts have the authority to compel the board to promptly hold such a meeting.[3561]

*b. Cases Upholding Board Decisions Advancing or Delaying Meeting Dates.* Not all board decisions advancing or postponing the dates of shareholder meetings are improper, of course.

---

3557. *Id.*

3558. *Id.* at 1302 (quoting *Silver v. Farrell*, 113 Misc. 2d 443, 448, 450 N.Y.S.2d 938, 942 (N.Y. Sup. Ct. Monroe Co. 1982)).

3559. *Id.* at 1302 (quoting *Silver*, 113 Misc. 2d at 448, 450 N.Y.S.2d at 942).

3560. 1986 U.S. Dist. LEXIS 24022, 1986 WL 7001 (S.D.N.Y. June 18, 1986).

3561. 1986 U.S. Dist. LEXIS 24022, at *36-37, 1986 WL 7001, at *15 (citations omitted).

The Delaware Court of Chancery in *Huffington v. Enstar Corp.*,[3562] for example, refused to grant a preliminary injunction enjoining a determination by directors to postpone a shareholders meeting for 28 days in order to allow the corporation's directors an opportunity to sell the corporation—something that a dissident shareholder group wanted done but believed it was better qualified to do than the corporation's incumbent directors. The dissident shareholders contended that an expeditious sale by the incumbent directors "would be tantamount to a scorched earth policy."[3563]

The court distinguished the *Schnell v. Chris-Craft Industries, Inc.*[3564] decision discussed in the preceding section of this Chapter,[3565] stating that "if the action of the Board in this case is to be condemned, it must be based on attendant circumstances that make it reasonably probable to assume that management intended to frustrate the vote of dissident stockholders."[3566] Here, the court stated, the dissident shareholders were "not being forced to prepare their proxy contest so hastily that they are denied sufficient time to effectively prepare for the contest" and were "not being denied the opportunity to vote or to participate in the annual meeting."[3567] The court rejected the plaintiffs' "hyperbole" that "'lame ducks' should not conduct a sale of the corporation" as a "fallacy" because "the 'worst scenario' suppositions of the Plaintiffs are based on speculation."[3568] The court explained:

> For instance, they want the Court to assume that there will be a sale and yet there is no guarantee that a sale will occur. They want the Court to assume that the Board will breach its fiduciary duties and conclude a sale that is not in the best interests of the stockholders or which is not fair. Should we speculate that this would occur? Even if it did occur, would not the stockholders have an opportunity to either seek an

---

3562. 9 Del. J. Corp. L. 185 (Del. Ch. Apr. 25, 1984).
3563. *Id.* at 187-88, 190.
3564. 285 A.2d 437 (Del. 1971).
3565. *See* Chapter III, Section H 1 b.
3566. 9 Del. J. Corp. L. at 189.
3567. *Id.* at 190.
3568. *Id.*

injunction to prevent the sale or to vote it down? And finally, why must this Court assume that if there is to be a sale, the Plaintiffs would conduct a more beneficial sale than the Defendants, the elected management of this corporation?[3569]

In sum, the court concluded, "[t]his Court is loath to intervene in the internal management of a corporation unless and until a plaintiff can make a case that the exercise of corporate governance, otherwise proper, is used as a tool to frustrate the legitimate rights of its stockholders."[3570] Here, the court concluded, it was "not convinced that the Plaintiffs have carried that burden."[3571]

The Delaware Court of Chancery also upheld a delay of an annual meeting for three weeks in *Hubbard v. Hollywood Park Realty Enterprises, Inc.*[3572] The meeting was delayed in this case by the incumbent board "in order to enable the shareholders to have sufficient time to be informed of the results" of court proceedings.[3573] The court stated that there was "no showing that this was done for the purpose of impairing or thwarting" a group soliciting proxies or would "have the effect of impairing or impeding the effective exercise of the corporate franchise."[3574] The Delaware Court of Chancery in *MAI Basic Four, Inc. v. Prime Computer, Inc.*[3575] similarly upheld a delay of an annual meeting "for a reasonable time in order to permit the stockholders to evaluate the new and much less attractive offer of Basic and in order to give the directors . . . reasonable time to find alternatives to Basic's new offer."[3576]

The Delaware Court of Chancery's decision in *Stahl v. Apple Bancorp, Inc.*[3577] involved a tender offer and proxy contest

---

3569. *Id.*

3570. *Id.* at 191.

3571. *Id.*

3572. No. 11902 (Del. Ch. Jan. 15, 1991).

3573. *Id.*, Tr. op. at 4.

3574. *Id.* at 7.

3575. 15 Del. J. Corp. L. 690 (Del. Ch. June 13, 1989).

3576. *Id.* at 693.

3577. 579 A.2d 1115 (Del. Ch. 1990).

announced by Stanley Stahl, a 30 percent shareholder of Apple
Bancorp, Inc., and a determination by Apple Bancorp's board to
respond by withdrawing an already established record date and
postponing an annual meeting that previously had been planned for
May 1990 until after the corporation could explore the advisability
of an alternative transaction.[3578] At the time of the board's decision to postpone the annual meeting, no specific date yet had been
set for the meeting and no proxy materials had been sent by the
corporation to shareholders. The board, however, had been advised
by the company's proxy solicitor that Stahl likely would prevail in
a proxy fight if the board did not present shareholders with an economic alternative to Stahl's bid.[3579] Stahl filed suit, seeking to
require the board to hold the corporation's annual meeting by mid-
June.[3580]

The court began its analysis by defining the fundamental
question to be determined in evaluating director conduct involving
the shareholder franchise as being "whether the directors' purpose
is 'inequitable'"[3581]—an inquiry requiring the court "to ask, in
the context of this case, whether they have taken action for the purpose of impairing or impeding the effective exercise of the corporate franchise and, if they have, whether . . . special circumstances
are present . . . warranting such an unusual step."[3582] The court
stated that such "special circumstances" must provide a "compelling justification" for board interference with the "high value"
traditionally placed upon the exercise of voting rights.[3583]

The court found no need to "inquire into the question of justification" in this case, however, because the court could not conclude that the board's determination to change its plan to hold the
corporation's annual meeting in May was made "for the primary
purpose of impairing or impeding the effective exercise of the cor-

---

3578. *Id.* at 1117-19.
3579. *Id.* at 1119.
3580. *Id.* at 1117.
3581. *Id.* at 1121.
3582. *Id.* at 1122.
3583. *Id.*

porate franchise."[3584] The court based its ruling "on the narrow ground that the action of deferring this company's annual meeting where no meeting date has yet been set and no proxies even solicited does not impair or impede the effective exercise of the franchise to any extent."[3585] Rather, the court stated, the election process will go forward at a time consistent with the company's bylaws and Section 211 of the Delaware General Corporation Law, which grants the Court of Chancery authority to order a shareholder meeting if no meeting has been held either within 30 days of the date designated by the corporation's board for a meeting or for a period of 13 months following the corporation's last annual meeting.[3586] The court acknowledged that "postponement of a noticed meeting will in some circumstances constitute an inequitable manipulation" of the corporate franchise, but concluded that the franchise process cannot "be said to be sufficiently engaged before the fixing of th[e] meeting date to give rise to that possibility."[3587]

The court then held that the *Blasius Industries, Inc. v. Atlas Corp.*[3588] standard of review[3589] was inapplicable because the board had postponed the corporation's annual meeting before a date for the meeting had been set.[3590] As a result, the court concluded, the postponement of the meeting date did not "impair or impede the effective exercise of the franchise to any extent."[3591] The court accordingly tested the board's conduct pursuant to the *Unocal Corp. v. Mesa Petroleum Co.*[3592] standard.[3593] With respect to the first prong of the *Unocal* test—"reasonable grounds for believing that a danger to corporate policy and effectiveness

---

3584. *Id.*

3585. *Id.* at 1123.

3586. *Id.* (citing Del. Gen. Corp. Law § 211).

3587. *Id.*

3588. 564 A.2d 651 (Del. Ch. 1988).

3589. *See* Chapter III, Section A 5.

3590. 579 A.2d at 1123.

3591. *Id.; see also* Chapter III, Section A 5 c (discussing this aspect of *Apple Bancorp* decision).

3592. 493 A.2d 946 (Del. 1985).

3593. *See* Chapter III, Section A 2.

existed"[3594]—the court held, as discussed earlier in this Chapter,[3595] that where a proxy contest is tied to a tender offer and shareholders are "in effect . . . asked to vote on the question whether the company should be sold," the absence of relevant information that "disaggregated shareholders are incapable of obtaining" without board involvement "may reasonably be seen as posing a threat" to the vote.[3596] With respect to the second prong of the *Unocal* test—a defensive measure "reasonable in relation to the threat posed"[3597]—the court upheld the board's "extremely mild" response to this threat—delay of a not yet scheduled annual meeting to a later date, consistent with the company's bylaws and Delaware's General Corporation Law.[3598] The court stated that "[t]o delay a meeting once called would constitute a more substantial question of disproportionality."[3599] "As one moves closer to a meeting date," the court added, "attempts to postpone a meeting would likely require a greater and greater showing of threat in order to justify interfering with the conclusion of an election contest."[3600]

The Court of Chancery's decision in *H.F. Ahmanson & Co. v. Great Western Financial Corp.*[3601] provides another example of a court that has upheld the postponement of an annual meeting, in this case for 50 days following the emergence of a unwanted bidder and a proxy contest by that bidder.

On January 28, 1997, before any contest for control began, Great Western Financial Corporation's board scheduled Great Western's annual meeting for April 22, 1997. At that meeting, four of eleven members of Great Western's board would stand for elec-

---

3594. 493 A.2d at 955.
3595. *See* Chapter III, Section A 2 c.
3596. 579 A.2d at 1124.
3597. 493 A.2d at 955.
3598. 579 A.2d at 1124.
3599. *Id.*
3600. *Id.*
3601. 1997 Del. Ch. LEXIS 84, 1997 WL 305824 (Del. Ch. June 3, 1997).

tion.[3602] On February 17, H.F. Ahmanson & Co. made an unsolicited offer to Great Western's board to acquire all of Great Western's shares in exchange for Ahmanson shares in a stock-for-stock merger. Ahmanson also announced that it would solicit proxies to elect three directors to Great Western's board at the corporation's April 22 meeting.[3603] Two potential white knights, one of which was Washington Mutual, Inc., contacted Great Western to express interest in a possible combination.[3604] On February 24, Great Western's board cancelled the April 22 meeting without setting a new date.[3605] On March 3, Ahmanson began soliciting consents to amend Great Western's bylaws to require that Great Western's annual meeting be held no later than May 6, 1997.[3606]

On March 5, Great Western entered into a merger agreement with Washington Mutual, subject to shareholder approval.[3607] Ahmanson responded by increasing its bid.[3608] Great Western's board "remained fully committed to the Western Mutual transaction and adamantly opposed to the Ahmanson proposal," and "announced that it would engage in no further negotiations with Ahmanson."[3609]

On April 9, Ahmanson delivered written consents to Great Western's registered agent, purporting to vote the number of shares needed to enact the bylaw Ahmanson had proposed in order to require that Great Western's annual meeting be held by May 6.[3610] On April 10, before the results of Ahmanson's consent obligations were certified (which, due to various delays, did not occur

---

3602. 1997 Del. Ch. LEXIS 84, at *5, 1997 WL 305824, at *2.

3603. 1997 Del. Ch. LEXIS 84, at *5-6, 1997 WL 305824, at *2.

3604. 1997 Del. Ch. LEXIS 84, at *6, 1997 WL 305824, at *2.

3605. 1997 Del. Ch. LEXIS 84, at *6-8, 1997 WL 305824, at *2-3.

3606. 1997 Del. Ch. LEXIS 84, at *9, 1997 WL 305824, at *3.

3607. 1997 Del. Ch. LEXIS 84, at *9-10, 1997 WL 305824, at *3.

3608. 1997 Del. Ch. LEXIS 84, at *10, 1997 WL 305824, at *4.

3609. 1997 Del. Ch. LEXIS 84, at *11-12, 1997 WL 305824, at *4.

3610. 1997 Del. Ch. LEXIS 84, at *12, 1997 WL 305824, at *4.

until May 5, 1997), Great Western's board scheduled the annual meeting for 2:00 p.m. on June 13.[3611] This date was chosen by Great Western's directors with the advice of counsel as "the earliest practicable date" that would (1) permit compliance with a federal rule requiring that broker search cards be mailed 20 business days before a record date (broker search cards are sent to brokers holding shares as record holders to notify them of an upcoming proxy solicitation in order "to afford the brokers sufficient time to identify the beneficial owners . . . to assure that they will receive the relevant proxy materials in timely fashion"), and (2) "afford the shareholders sufficient time to make an informed decision."[3612] Under the 20 day rule, May 9 was the earliest possible record date. Delaware law permits a meeting to be held ten days after the record date, but Great Western's counsel advised the board that "the 'normal' solicitation period between the record date and the annual meeting is 35 days."[3613]

No date was set for a special meeting to vote upon the Washington Mutual merger because Great Western did not yet know when it would receive comments from the Securities and Exchange Commission to draft proxy materials Great Western had submitted to the SEC in connection with Great Western's proposed merger with Washington Mutual.[3614] Great Western nevertheless began distributing broker search cards for both the June 13 annual meeting and the still unscheduled special meeting to vote on the merger.[3615] On April 28, Great Western fixed May 9 as the record date for the special meeting to vote on the merger, even though the date for the special meeting still had not been set.[3616]

---

3611. 1997 Del. Ch. LEXIS 84, at *3, 12, 1997 WL 305824, at *1, 4.

3612. 1997 Del. Ch. LEXIS 84, at *12-13, 14 n.7, 1997 WL 305824, at *4 & n.7.

3613. 1997 Del. Ch. LEXIS 84, at *13, 1997 WL 305824, at *4.

3614. 1997 Del. Ch. LEXIS 84, at *14-15, 1997 WL 305824, at *5.

3615. 1997 Del. Ch. LEXIS 84, at *15, 1997 WL 305824, at *5.

3616. *Id.*

On May 12, Great Western's board received the SEC's comments to Great Western's proxy materials concerning Great Western's proposed merger with Washington Mutual. The board met that same day and scheduled the special meeting to vote on the merger for June 13 at 10:00 AM—four hours before the previously scheduled annual meeting.[3617] The board set both meetings for the same date after being advised by Great Western's proxy solicitor that there was a "need to avoid confusion of stockholders as to what is being voted on at what time," and that having both meetings on the same day would result in the "least confusion potential."[3618] The board also was advised by counsel that the merger agreement with Washington Mutual required that the merger vote be held "as soon as practicable," and that a June 13 meeting date would provide shareholders sufficient time to review the proxy materials and make an informed decision.[3619] Ahmanson responded with an announcement that it would commence an exchange offer for all of Great Western's outstanding shares at the same price Ahmanson had offered Great Western's board in Ahmanson's proposed stock-for-stock merger, conditioned upon the redemption of Great Western's poison pill shareholder rights plan.[3620]

Beginning in early April, Ahmanson sought expedited proceedings and injunctive relief requiring Great Western to reschedule its annual meeting and elect directors "promptly and well in advance of the Washington Mutual merger meeting."[3621] The court denied a motion for expedited proceedings on the ground that Ahmanson's basis for claiming irreparable harm was speculative because as of that time no shareholder meeting to consider the Washington Mutual merger had been scheduled, and only "if and when that occurred" would there exist "a concrete, non-speculative

3617. 1997 Del. Ch. LEXIS 84, at *3, 15, 1997 WL 305824, at *1, 5.

3618. 1997 Del. Ch. LEXIS 84, at *15-16, 1997 WL 305824, at *5.

3619. 1997 Del. Ch. LEXIS 84, at *16, 1997 WL 305824, at *5.

3620. 1997 Del. Ch. LEXIS 84, at *17, 1997 WL 305824, at *5.

3621. 1997 Del. Ch. LEXIS 84, at *19, 1997 WL 305824, at *6.

basis to consider any application for injunctive relief and expedited discovery."[3622]

The court considered another application for injunctive relief after Great Western scheduled its annual meeting for June 13. This time, Ahmanson contended that Great Western's directors had breached their fiduciary duties and violated the following bylaw:

> The annual meeting of the stockholders of the Corporation shall be held on the fourth Tuesday in April in each year . . . or on such earlier or later date as the Board of Directors . . . may designate . . . . If any annual meeting shall not be held on the day designated or the directors shall not have been elected thereat or at any adjournment thereof, *thereafter the Board shall cause a special meeting of the stockholders to be held as soon as practicable for the election of directors.*[3623]

According to Ahmanson, Great Western's directors violated this bylaw "in two respects: by not calling a special (as distinguished from a rescheduled annual) meeting, and by not scheduling that meeting 'as soon as practicable,' which would be May 6, 1997 or shortly thereafter."[3624] The court determined that "it would consider scheduling an injunction proceeding" only if Ahmanson first demonstrated that it had stated legally cognizable claims for pre-meeting injunctive relief.[3625] Following briefing and argument, the court concluded that Ahmanson had not stated a claim for breach of fiduciary duty, but had stated a claim for a breach by Great Western's directors of Great Western's bylaw.[3626]

With respect to Ahmanson's breach of fiduciary duty claim, the court explained that Ahmanson did not allege any harm other than delay, and that to state a claim for cognizable irreparable harm

---

3622. *H.F. Ahmanson & Co. v. Great W. Fin. Corp.*, 1997 Del. Ch. LEXIS 55, at *3-4, 1997 WL 225696, at *1 (Del. Ch. Apr. 25, 1997).

3623. 1997 Del. Ch. LEXIS 84, at *42-43, 1997 WL 305824, at *13 (emphasis added by court).

3624. 1997 Del. Ch. LEXIS 55, at *4, 1997 WL 225696, at *2.

3625. 1997 Del. Ch. LEXIS 55, at *6-7, 1997 WL 225696, at *3.

3626. 1997 Del. Ch. LEXIS 55, at *7-11, 1997 WL 225696, at *3-4.

"delay must adversely threaten the exercise of the shareholders' right to vote in some tangible way."[3627] A claim for pre-meeting relief alleging "only a delay, without more," the court concluded, "is legally deficient."[3628]

With respect to Ahmanson's "as soon as practicable" bylaw claim, however, the court held that a violation of this bylaw, without more, was sufficient to support a claim seeking to enforce the bylaw's requirement. The court explained that "[t]he irreparable harm claimed . . . is not solely to the corporation's electoral process" but "encompasses harm to the corporation's governance process as well."[3629] The court stated that "[w]here the shareholders or the directors, by adopting a by-law, command the performance of a certain act, to hold that coercive relief cannot be had to enforce that command would violate basic concepts of corporate governance."[3630]

The court accordingly denied a motion to dismiss the claim for injunctive relief based upon this bylaw but stated that the fact that a claim had been stated did not by itself require that the court schedule expedited injunction proceedings.[3631] The court acknowledged that "[f]or this Court not to act" in the face of allegations that Great Western's directors allegedly "disregarded their own by-law, and (if the allegations of the complaint are correct) the right of Great Western's shareholders to have the corporation's bylaws observed . . . might be misread as judicial indifference to such conduct."[3632] This circumstance, the court stated, "should, at the least, obligate the Great Western board to account for its acts."[3633]

---

3627. 1997 Del. Ch. LEXIS 55, at *8, 1997 WL 225696, at *3.

3628. *Id.*

3629. 1997 Del. Ch. LEXIS 55, at *9, 1997 WL 225696, at *3.

3630. *Id.*

3631. 1997 Del. Ch. LEXIS 55, at *10, 1997 WL 225696, at *4.

3632. 1997 Del. Ch. LEXIS 55, at *11-12, 1997 WL 225696, at *4.

3633. 1997 Del. Ch. LEXIS 55, at *12, 1997 WL 225696, at *4.

Nevertheless, the court continued, Ahmanson was "seeking to move the June 13 meeting date backward primarily to serve its individual interests as a bidder," and "[n]o one representing the interests of unaffiliated shareholders has come forward to claim a need for a Court-ordered meeting before June 13, 1997."[3634] To the contrary, the sole concern addressed in class actions that had been commenced by Great Western shareholders was that a meeting on the Washington Mutual merger might be scheduled "before the shareholders could exercise an uninfluenced vote to elect directors."[3635] That scenario, the court stated, "would justify scheduling an expedited injunctive proceeding" but was "not yet (but soon may be) before the Court."[3636] Additionally, the court continued, "it would make little sense to schedule a proceeding of the kind Ahmanson desires if the objective facts show that it would be impracticable to hold a special shareholders meeting to elect directors at any point significantly in advance of June 13."[3637] The court stated that "prudence suggests" that the answer to this question should be known "before the defendants are subjected to a full-blown injunctive proceeding."[3638]

The court accordingly limited discovery and briefing to two issues: (1) the reasons why Great Western's board had postponed the corporation's annual meeting, and (2) the earliest practicable date upon which the meeting could be held. Once those issues were decided, the court stated, it would determine whether to schedule an injunction proceeding.[3639]

By this point in time, Ahmanson's goal of forcing an annual meeting by May 6 had been foreclosed by the passage of time. Ahmanson thus submitted a new request for injunctive relief. This time, Ahmanson sought a remedy that would allow the annual meeting to be held on June 13, which was quickly approaching, but that

---

3634. 1997 Del. Ch. LEXIS 55, at *11, 1997 WL 225696, at *4.
3635. *Id.*
3636. *Id.*
3637. 1997 Del. Ch. LEXIS 55, at *12, 1997 WL 225696, at *4.
3638. *Id.*
3639. 1997 Del. Ch. LEXIS 55, at *12-13, 1997 WL 225696, at *5.

then would require "a six week hiatus between the certification of the results of the election of directors and the special merger meeting."[3640] The court concluded that this proposed remedy was "highly unusual" and "inappropriate."[3641]

With respect to the board's decision to delay until June 13 the annual meeting originally noticed for April 22, the court explained that even if there had been a breach of a fiduciary duty or a breach of a duty arising under the contested bylaw, "the requested relief would still be inappropriate because it is entirely unrelated to the claimed wrong."[3642] "If, as plaintiffs contend," the court stated, "the directors wrongfully delayed the scheduling (or rescheduling) of the meeting to elect directors, the appropriate remedy would be an order mandating a prompt annual meeting"—relief that previously had been denied and the time for which had passed.[3643] The court rejected Ahmanson's reliance upon "the maxim that equity will not suffer a wrong without a remedy" as support for a contention that "a substitute remedy must be constructed" that would "replicate[ ] artificially the sequence and distance between the two meetings that would have occurred naturally had no wrongdoing occurred."[3644] To the contrary, the court reasoned, "[i]nherent in the very notion of a remedy is that it fits—remedies—the wrongful act."[3645]

With respect to the board's decision to schedule the Washington Mutual merger meeting for four hours before the rescheduled annual meeting, the court stated that this board determination did not threaten Great Western's shareholders with irreparable harm. The threatened harm, rather, was that shareholders would be deprived of deliberation concerning the Washington Mutual merger

---

3640. 1997 Del. Ch. LEXIS 84, at *20, 1997 WL 305824, at *6.

3641. 1997 Del. Ch. LEXIS 84, at *33, 1997 WL 305824, at *10.

3642. *Id.*

3643. *Id.*

3644. 1997 Del. Ch. LEXIS 84, at *34-35, 1997 WL 305824, at *10.

3645. 1997 Del. Ch. LEXIS 84, at *34, 1997 WL 305824, at *10.

by an eleven member board that included three Ahmanson nominees.[3646]

This threatened harm, according to the court, was "speculative and contingent" because it "would not occur unless the Ahmanson nominees were elected to the board, an event that might or might not occur."[3647] Any such harm, the court also concluded, "would be de minimis" and "immaterial" for two reasons.[3648]

First, the court explained, "as a real world, practical matter, Ahmanson's nominees would have no influence upon the decision of the remaining director majority to recommend the Washington Mutual transaction."[3649] In support of this conclusion, the court pointed to a letter Ahmanson had written to the Office of Thrift Supervision stating the following:

> [T]he Great Western board has demonstrated that it is implacably opposed to the Ahmanson offer and fully committed to its merger with [Washington Mutual]. The election of three directors nominated by Ahmanson . . . , who will represent only three of 11 directors, will not change that situation.[3650]

"The fact that the Great Western board is classified and that only a minority of directors will be elected," the court stated, "bears importantly on the conclusion that no irreparable harm is threatened by the delay in rescheduling the annual meeting."[3651] The court noted that "[i]f this case involved a 50 day delay in scheduling a meeting at which a majority of the directors would be elected (i.e., where control might pass), that would have far different implications from any irreparable harm analysis."[3652]

---

3646. 1997 Del. Ch. LEXIS 84, at *36, 1997 WL 305824, at *11.
3647. 1997 Del. Ch. LEXIS 84, at *37, 1997 WL 305824, at *11.
3648. *Id.*
3649. *Id.*
3650. *Id.*
3651. 1997 Del. Ch. LEXIS 84, at *38 n.27, 1997 WL 305824, at *11 n.27.
3652. *Id.*

Second, the court continued, "what is important to share-holders deciding how to vote are the substantive (and primarily economic) arguments for and against the Washington Mutual mer-ger."[3653] The court stated that "[t]hose arguments are and will be fully aired in the opposing sets of proxy materials that the Great Western board and Ahmanson each will disseminate to the share-holders."[3654] The court added that "[t]here is no suggestion that the Ahmanson nominees, if elected, would have anything substan-tive to add to the mix of information that would already be avail-able."[3655]

The court also stated that the premise underlying Ahmanson's irreparable harm argument—that Great Western's board had deprived shareholders of their right to vote for Ahmanson's nom-inees—was incorrect. The court explained that "[i]f Great West-ern's shareholders wish to elect Ahmanson's nominees to the board, they need only vote down the Washington Mutual merger proposal at the merger meeting, and then vote for Ahmanson's nominees at the rescheduled annual meeting."[3656] Indeed, the court noted, a letter from Ahmanson to Great Western's shareholders "acknowl-edged as much" by urging Great Western's shareholders to take "three simple steps": vote for Ahmanson's nominees, vote against the Washington Mutual merger, and tender Great Western shares into Ahmanson's exchange offer once it commences.[3657]

The court also held that the balance of equities did not favor an injunction postponing the vote by Great Western's shareholders on Great Western's merger with Washington Mutual. The court reasoned that an injunction would "delay the ability of Washington Mutual, Great Western, and their shareholders to begin realizing the economic benefits expected to result from the merger," and "significantly increase the risk that the value of Great Western

---

3653. 1997 Del. Ch. LEXIS 84, at *38, 1997 WL 305824, at *11.
3654. 1997 Del. Ch. LEXIS 84, at *38-39, 1997 WL 305824, at *11.
3655. *Id.*
3656. 1997 Del. Ch. LEXIS 84, at *39, 1997 WL 305824, at *12.
3657. 1997 Del. Ch. LEXIS 84, at *39-40, 1997 WL 305824, at *12.

would diminish, through losses of customers and key employees as a result of continued uncertainty surrounding the outcome of the bidding contest for control."[3658] The court held that these "costs of granting the requested injunctive relief would greatly outweigh the speculative, minimal benefits that the requested injunction would confer."[3659] The court added that "the only party likely to benefit" from an injunction delaying Great Western's merger with Washington Mutual would be Ahmanson because "Ahmanson's agenda, qua bidder, is to delay the vote on a competing transaction that, if approved, would foreclose Ahmanson's competing bid."[3660] The court stated that "Ahmanson is entitled to further that agenda, but the proper forum in which to do so is the economic and proxy information marketplace, not this Court."[3661]

The court then addressed the merits of Ahmanson's claims, beginning with Ahmanson's claim that Great Western's special meeting bylaw—quoted above—imposed a duty upon Great Western's board to schedule a special meeting "as soon as practicable" after February 24, 1997, the date the board postponed Great Western's annual meeting.[3662] Ahmanson contended that "the term 'thereafter'" in the bylaw "refers to the time of the decision not to hold the annual meeting, i.e., the date of the postponement."[3663] Great Western, by contrast, contended that "'thereafter' must be construed to refer to the time period following the 'day designated' for the 'annual meeting.'"[3664] The construction issue before the court therefore was "whether the word 'thereafter,' as it appears in the disputed sentence . . . , refers to the date the decision to cancel the annual meeting is made (here, February 24, 1997), as plaintiffs contend; or whether it refers to the designated date for the annual meeting (here, April 22, 1997), as defendants argue."[3665]

---

3658. 1997 Del. Ch. LEXIS 84, at *41, 1997 WL 305824, at *12.
3659. *Id.*
3660. *Id.*
3661. *Id.*
3662. 1997 Del. Ch. LEXIS 84, at *42, 1997 WL 305824, at *13.
3663. 1997 Del. Ch. LEXIS 84, at *43, 1997 WL 305824, at *13.
3664. *Id.*
3665. 1997 Del. Ch. LEXIS 84, at *46, 1997 WL 305824, at *14.

The court resolved this question in favor of Great Western, reasoning as follows:

> A corporation's by-laws are regarded as a contract between the corporation and its stockholders. Accordingly, issues of by-law interpretation are normally governed by principles of contract interpretation. A bedrock principle, which applies here, is that a contract must be construed as a whole, giving effect to all of its provisions and avoiding a construction that would render any of those provisions illusory or meaningless.
>
> That principle, when applied to the disputed portion of Section 2, results in the following analysis. The special meeting by-law describes three circumstances where the board is required to set a special meeting to elect directors as soon as practicable: "If [1] any annual meeting shall not be held on the day designated or [2] the directors shall not have been elected *thereat or* [3] at any adjournment *thereof, thereafter* the Board shall cause a special meeting of the stockholders . . . ." [emphasis and bracketed numbers added by court] The term "thereafter" refers to or relates to all three circumstances. Thus, if Ahmanson is correct that the first clause refers to the date the meeting is postponed rather than to the scheduled date for the meeting, then by parity of reasoning the terms "thereat" and "thereof" in the second and third clauses also must refer to the date of postponement and not to the date of the meeting.
>
> But the results that flow from that interpretation make no sense. It does not make sense for the second clause to mean that directors were not elected at a postponement, or for the third clause to mean that there was an adjournment at the postponement. The only interpretation that sensibly harmonizes and reconciles the second and third clauses with the first clause is for each to refer to the "meeting" and not (as Ahmanson suggests) to the postponement of the meeting. Under that interpretation the second and third clauses mean, respectively that a special meeting must be scheduled after an annual meeting is held at which either the directors were not elected or the meeting was adjourned.
>
> Ahmanson's construction of the disputed by-law is also flawed because it would lead to an absurd result and would be inconsistent with other provisions of the company's by-laws. The defendants argue that federal proxy rules require a

20 day period to conduct the broker search card process
before the record date, and that that 20 day period is ordinarily followed by a 35 day proxy solicitation period. Assuming without deciding that the defendants are correct, and that
a meeting must be scheduled 55 days in advance to satisfy
the "as soon as practicable" by-law requirement [plaintiffs, of
course, contend that an even shorter period was required],
then the board would have been mandated on February 24,
1997 to schedule a meeting to elect directors by April 21—
one day before the original meeting date that was canceled!
That reading would effectively nullify the board's express
power under Section 5 to cancel or postpone any previously
scheduled stockholders meeting, and its power under Section
2 to hold the annual meeting "on such earlier or later date"
than the fourth Tuesday in April.[3666]

Thus, the court concluded, "the Great Western board was not subject to a by-law-imposed duty to call a special meeting 'as soon as
practicable' on February 24, 1997."[3667]

The court then turned to Ahmanson's claim that fiduciary
duties separate and apart from the disputed bylaw required Great
Western's directors to schedule a meeting to elect directors for a
date earlier than June 13, 1997.[3668] The court applied the *Unocal*
standard of review after concluding that *Blasius* was inapplicable
because only a minority of Great Western's directors were being
voted upon.[3669] The court held that Great Western's board
"reasonably perceived" that Ahmanson's actions posed "a threat to
corporate policy or effectiveness."[3670] The court also held that
Great Western's response was "proportionate, i.e., is neither pre-

---

3666. 1997 Del. Ch. LEXIS 84, at *47-50, 1997 WL 305824, at
*14 (footnotes omitted or summarized in brackets).
3667. 1997 Del. Ch. LEXIS 84, at *52, 1997 WL 305824, at *15.
3668. 1997 Del. Ch. LEXIS 84, at *52-53, 1997 WL 305824, at
*15.
3669. 1997 Del. Ch. LEXIS 84, at *54-56, 1997 WL 305824, at
*16; *see also* Chapter III, Section A 5 c (discussing this aspect of *Great
Western* decision).
3670. 1997 Del. Ch. LEXIS 84, at *56-57, 1997 WL 305824, at
*16.

clusive nor coercive and falls within a range of reasonableness."[3671]

The court reasoned that Ahmanson's contention that "the only threat posed was the election of its slate of three directors" "ignores reality."[3672] The court explained that "Great Western's board was confronted with a multi-level attack," including "Ahmanson's hostile bid, its proxy contest, its consent solicitation, and this litigation."[3673] This "multi-level attack," the court continued, called for "an integrated response" and required Great Western's board "to fulfill its duty to provide adequate information to its shareholders concerning those events and the decisions they would be asked to make, including but not limited to the election of Ahmanson's three director nominees."[3674] The board's response, a 50 day delay of an annual meeting, "fell within a range of reasonable responses," the court held, because Great Western's shareholders "will have an effective opportunity to exercise their franchise rights in an informed manner."[3675]

The Delaware Court of Chancery refused to enjoin the scheduling of a shareholder meeting on short notice in *Dolgoff v. Projectavision, Inc.*[3676] This litigation involved an acrimonious relationship that had developed between Eugene Dolgoff, a co-founder and director of Projectavision, Inc., and other members of Projectavision's board. In February 1995, the board terminated Dolgoff's employment at Projectavision.[3677] Dolgoff refused a request by the board that he resign as a director, and Dolgoff sued the corporation for wrongful termination and misappropriation of intellectual property.[3678]

---

3671. 1997 Del. Ch. LEXIS 84, at *57, 1997 WL 305824, at *16.
3672. *Id.*
3673. *Id.*
3674. *Id.*
3675. 1997 Del. Ch. LEXIS 84, at *57-58, 1997 WL 305824, at *16.
3676. 21 Del. J. Corp. L. 1128 (Del. Ch. Feb. 29, 1996).
3677. *Id.* at 1129-30.
3678. *Id.* at 1132-33.

On January 24, 1996, the board, at a meeting called on one day's notice, approved a proxy statement proposing that the corporation's 1996 annual meeting be held early in calendar year 1996, on February 29, 1996 (the corporation had not yet held its 1995 meeting and previously had submitted a preliminary proxy statement to the Securities and Exchange Commission proposing that the 1995 meeting be held in early 1996).[3679] The proxy statement stated that the three year terms of both Dolgoff and Marvin Maslow, Projectavision's other co-founder, were expiring in 1996, proposed the re-election of Maslow, and stated that no one was being nominated to fill Dolgoff's term.[3680] Dolgoff filed suit, seeking to enjoin dissemination of the proxy statement and the holding of the 1996 meeting, and to compel the holding of the 1995 meeting, at which directors whose terms expired in 1995 would be required to stand for re-election.[3681] Projectavision's board responded with a revised proxy statement telling shareholders that three directors were up for re-election—Dolgoff, Maslow and one director whose term ended in 1995. Unlike Projectavision's prior proxy statement, the revised proxy statement proposed a nominee to fill Dolgoff's seat.[3682]

Dolgoff sought an order preliminarily enjoining Projectavision from holding its 1996 annual meeting on February 29, 1996. Dolgoff acknowledged that Projectavision's board had "the legal authority, under Projectavision's By-Laws, to set the date for the 1996 annual meeting in February," but contended that "[b]ased upon Projectavision's custom of holding annual meetings in November and the short amount of notice given to him, . . . the defendants' scheduling of the 1996 annual meeting was calculated in order to disadvantage him in his ability to mount a proxy contest; catching him by surprise and giving him inadequate time to propose an alternative slate of directors."[3683] According to Dolgoff, this conduct "impermissibly manipulated the electoral process," and

---

3679. *Id.*
3680. *Id.*
3681. *Id.* at 1133.
3682. *Id.*
3683. *Id.* at 1130, 1139.

constituted "inequitable interference with the shareholder franchise." [3684]

The court rejected this claim, explaining that "legal action can be the subject of equitable remedies if taken for the primary purpose of interfering with the effective exercise of the shareholder franchise," but that "such equitable power obviously must be invoked sparingly and only when circumstances make relatively clear that inequitable behavior or manipulation is present." [3685]

Here, the court found, "the Projectavision board was motivated to see Dolgoff's term expire and have him not reelected to the board, as soon as permissible." [3686] The court stated that in "the particular circumstances" of this case "this was certainly a permissible objective because, regardless of what originally led to the animosity that had developed between Dolgoff and the other board members, Dolgoff was now involved in litigation against the company over his termination and certain intellectual property rights." [3687] The court stated that the board "fixed a time for the annual meeting within the relevant provisions" of the Delaware General Corporation Law and the corporation's certificate and bylaws, "was not faced with a proxy contest or an expected contest when it did so," and "did not advance or delay the meeting after it had already been called." [3688] Thus, the court concluded, "while the board had strategic aims in calling a meeting for February, those were not inappropriate or inequitable . . . . The board did not seek to thwart the exercise of the shareholder franchise but sought, in a context where there was no reason to believe a proxy contest was at hand, to conclude Dolgoff's service on the board." [3689] "The fact that the scheduling of the meeting may have caught Mr. Dolgoff by surprise, arguably handicapping his ability to mount a counter-proxy campaign," the court stated, did not provide any

---

3684. *Id.*
3685. *Id.* at 1140.
3686. *Id.*
3687. *Id.*
3688. *Id.*
3689. *Id.* at 1141.

basis for enjoining "an otherwise properly and legally noticed shareholders' meeting."[3690]

A federal court construing Nevada law in *Hilton Hotels Corp. v. ITT Corp.*[3691] denied a motion for a preliminary injunction requiring ITT Corporation to conduct its annual meeting in May 1997, twelve months after its prior annual meeting.[3692] The ruling came in the context of a tender offer by Hilton Hotels Corporation for ITT Corporation's stock and a proxy contest seeking to replace ITT's board.[3693]

The court stated that if the intent of the Nevada Legislature or ITT was to require an annual meeting every twelve months, "they could have easily and clearly said so in the governing statutes and bylaws."[3694] Instead, the court continued, Section 78.330 of the Nevada General Corporation Law and ITT's bylaws provide that ITT's annual meeting "shall be held at such date, time and place as determined by the Board of Directors," and Section 78.345(1) of the Nevada statute provides that "[i]f any corporation fails to elect directors within 18 months after the last election of directors . . . , the district court has jurisdiction in equity, upon application of any one or more stockholders holding stock entitling them to exercise at least 15 percent of the voting power, to order the election of directors."[3695] The court observed that it could "divine no reason why the Nevada Legislature would postpone for six months a shareholder's remedy for a corporation's failure to hold an annual meeting which the Legislature intended to be held within twelve months of the prior annual meeting."[3696] The court thus held that "subject to the right of a board of directors to specify a shorter period,

---

3690. *Id.*

3691. 962 F. Supp. 1309 (D. Nev.), *aff'd mem.*, 116 F.3d 1485 (9th Cir. 1997).

3692. *Id.* at 1309-1310.

3693. *Id.* at 1311.

3694. *Id.* at 1310.

3695. *Id.*

3696. *Id.*

annual meetings for Nevada corporations are contemplated to occur no later than eighteen months after the last such meeting."[3697]

The court also rejected a contention that "even if consistent with Nevada law and ITT's bylaws, failure to conduct an annual meeting in May 1997 would constitute a breach of the fiduciary duty owed by ITT's incumbent Board of Directors to its shareholders."[3698] The court acknowledged that "[c]ourts have consistently prevented actions by an incumbent board of directors which were primarily designed to impair or impede the shareholder franchise," but concluded that ITT's board had not yet scheduled the corporation's annual meeting and was not required to schedule its annual meeting in May 1997.[3699] Citing *Apple Bancorp*, the court stated that "[t]he failure to hold an annual meeting in May, which has not even been set and is not yet required to be set, cannot be viewed as an inequitable manipulation by the incumbent Board primarily designed to impede the exercise of the shareholder franchise."[3700] The court added that a board has "reasonable discretion in setting an annual meeting to resist hostile takeover offers."[3701]

The court also rejected a contention by ITT shareholders that "a delay of the annual meeting beyond May 1997 may cause Hilton to withdraw its tender offer" as "simply not determinative."[3702] "Hilton, ITT and ITT's shareholders," the court stated, "are, within the limits of the law, permitted to do as they deem advisable in the marketplace with respect to their investment and business decisions."[3703]

In sum, the court concluded, "deciding when ITT's 1997 annual meeting should be held . . . is a matter for determination by the Board of ITT within the parameters set by Nevada law and

3697. *Id.*
3698. *Id.*
3699. *Id.* at 1310, 1311.
3700. *Id.* at 1311.
3701. *Id.*
3702. *Id.*
3703. *Id.* at 1311-12.

ITT's bylaws."[3704] "[T]here is no impairment of the shareholder franchise in this case," the court held, "because no annual meeting of shareholders has yet been set and the time for conducting the annual meeting has not yet expired."[3705]

The Ninth Circuit affirmed, stating that "[t]he record before us shows that the district court did not rely upon an erroneous legal premise or abuse its discretion in concluding that appellants' showing of probable success on the merits was insufficient to warrant preliminary injunctive relief."[3706]

*c. Decisions Refusing to Enjoin Shareholder Meetings.* Several courts have rejected requests by shareholders that shareholder meetings be postponed. In *Stroud v. Grace*,[3707] the Delaware Court of Chancery concluded that there was "no need for the extraordinary step" of enjoining an annual meeting at which shareholders were to vote on certificate of incorporation amendments limiting who could be elected as a director of the corporation.[3708] The court reasoned that the amendments would not be voted upon until after the election of directors at the meeting, that the amendments therefore could not have any "reasonably foreseeable practical effect" until the corporation's next annual meeting, and that there would be sufficient time after the amendments were voted upon for the court to consider plaintiffs' claims challenging the validity of the amendments.[3709]

The Delaware Court of Chancery in *Highland Capital, Inc. v. Longview Fibre Co.*[3710] denied a motion for a preliminary injunction that would have enjoined the holding of an annual meeting at which shareholders would be asked to vote upon a merger of the

---

3704. *Id.* at 1311.

3705. *Id.*

3706. *Hilton Hotels Corp. v. ITT Corp.*, 116 F.3d 1485 (unpublished opinion, text available at 1997 U.S. App. LEXIS 14893 and 1997 WL 345963) (9th Cir. June 19, 1997).

3707. 15 Del. J. Corp. L. 256 (Del. Ch. Apr. 21, 1989).

3708. *Id.* at 261.

3709. *Id.*

3710. 16 Del. J. Corp. L. 325 (Del. Ch. Jan. 22, 1990).

corporation into a wholly-owned subsidiary incorporated under the law of Washington. The plaintiff in the case alleged that "the real purpose of the merger and the change in domicile . . . is to entrench the existing board in office."[3711] The court explained that on September 5, 1989 the corporation's board considered the advisability of recommending that shareholders approve a certificate of incorporation amendment creating a board with directors having staggered terms and precluding the removal of directors except for cause. A proxy solicitation firm advised the board that this proposal was "likely to be approved by the shareholders but perhaps only by a narrow margin."[3712] The board then determined to accomplish its goal—i.e., creating a board with directors having staggered terms and precluding the removal of directors except for cause—by recommending that the corporation merge with a Washington subsidiary that already had a staggered board and a removal only for cause provision in its charter.[3713] The court rejected plaintiff's claim that the purpose and effect of the merger was not appropriately disclosed in the proxy statement sent by the corporation to shareholders.[3714]

*d. Record Dates.* Corporation law statutes require boards to set record dates for shareholder meetings. Section 213 of the Delaware General Corporation Law, for example, provides that the record date "shall not precede the date upon which the resolution fixing the record date is adopted by the board of directors, and . . . shall not be more than sixty or less than ten days before the date of such meeting."[3715]

Two decisions—*Wyser-Pratte v. Smith*[3716] and *WLR Foods, Inc. v. Tyson Foods, Inc.*[3717]—have addressed board decisions setting record dates for shareholder meetings.

---

3711. *Id.* at 327.

3712. *Id.* at 327-28.

3713. *Id.* at 328.

3714. *Id.* at 328-32.

3715. Del. Gen. Corp. Law § 213(a).

3716. 23 Del. J. Corp. L. 369 (Del. Ch. Mar. 18, 1997).

3717. 857 F. Supp. 496 (W.D. Va. 1994), *aff'd*, 65 F.3d 1172 (4th Cir. 1995), *cert. denied*, 516 U.S. 1117 (1996).

*Wyser-Pratte v. Smith*[3718] involved a board that set a record date that was 12 days before the meeting date. The court described this date as "within the statutory parameters" of Section 213 of the Delaware's statute but "disadvantages" to shareholders mounting a proxy contest.[3719] Plaintiffs alleged that the setting of the record date so close in time to the meeting date constituted a breach of fiduciary duty because the directors' intent was "to disenfranchise those who do not have record ownership, and even record holders, by discouraging them or their fiduciaries from being able to take timely steps to exercise their franchise."[3720] The Delaware Court of Chancery dismissed this claim, stating that plaintiffs' complaint "presents the classic allegations of suspicion of inequitable or unfair conduct accompanied by nefarious underlying motive, but fails to articulate specific facts supporting the underlying conclusory allegations."[3721]

The court stated its "commitment to the important principle" established in *Schnell v. Chris-Craft Industries, Inc.*[3722]: that "fraud or inequitable conduct, where well pleaded with allegations supported by specific facts, will result in careful judicial scrutiny and, where appropriate, the invocation of equitable principles to override otherwise permissible legal conduct."[3723] Here, however, the court concluded, "no cause of action has been adequately pleaded that supports a claim of inequitable conduct on the part of the incumbent Board."[3724]

The court also stated that courts "reserve intervention 'for those instances that threaten the fabric of the law, or which by an improper manipulation of the law, would deprive a person of a clear right.'"[3725] Here, the court held, "plaintiffs have not been

---

3718. 23 Del. J. Corp. L. 369 (Del. Ch. Mar. 18, 1997).

3719. *Id.* at 373.

3720. *Id.*

3721. *Id.* at 372.

3722. 285 A.2d 437 (Del. 1971); *see also* Chapter III, Section H 1 a (discussing *Schnell*).

3723. 23 Del. J. Corp. L. at 372.

3724. *Id.*

3725. *Id.* at 373.

deprived of a 'clear right' to a record date suiting their purposes."[3726] The court explained:

> The Board acquiesced, albeit reluctantly, in a shareholder demand for a special meeting, and noticed the meeting for the date, time and place requested. The Board then followed the statute and set a record date within permissible statutory limits. They did not move the date forward or backward to defeat any legitimate shareholder expectation or right. Plaintiffs knew or should have known that the record date could be set at any time within the statutory parameters. The complaint alleges no facts that would establish a skewed playing field unfairly manipulated to disadvantage parties to a proxy contest. The fact plaintiffs allege the Board or its chairman encouraged allies to buy shares before the record date, which presumably would then be voted to support the board at the meeting, has no legal bearing in these circumstances. Plaintiffs have equal time to do likewise.[3727]

Nor, the court stated, "can I fairly conclude that a board which follows the guideline of a Delaware Statute 'threatens the fabric of the law.'"[3728] To the contrary, the court observed, "[t]he impact of the selection of the record date on the logistics of a proxy contest were certainly known to the General Assembly when § 213 was enacted," and "[e]quity will not intervene now to frustrate legislative policy-making based on the conclusory allegations found in this complaint."[3729]

In sum, the court concluded, "the Board's selection of the record date twelve days before the meeting" was "authorized by statute."[3730] "[A]ll other contentions suggesting inequitable conduct by the Board" were "mere conclusory allegations unsupported by specific facts."[3731]

---

3726. *Id.*
3727. *Id.*
3728. *Id.*
3729. *Id.*
3730. *Id.* at 374.
3731. *Id.*

*WLR Foods, Inc. v. Tyson Foods, Inc.*[3732] involved a dispute concerning the record date for a vote by WLR Foods, Inc. shareholders requested by Tyson Foods, Inc., an entity seeking to acquire WLR, pursuant to Virginia's Control Share Act.[3733] The WLR Foods board set the record date to be the date on which Tyson had submitted its statutorily required control share acquisition statement, reasoning that this record date prevented Tyson from placing shares into friendly hands (under the Virginia Control Share Act shares held by Tyson could not be voted) between the submission of the control share acquisition statement and the record date.[3734] Tyson contended that the record date had been set in order to deprive shareholders who purchased shares after receiving Tyson's control share acquisition statement of the right to vote, and to increase the number of shares not voted because under the Virginia Control Share Act Tyson needed to obtain a majority of shares eligible to vote, not merely a majority of shares voted (Tyson assumed that shareholders who sold their shares after the record date would not be concerned enough to vote).[3735]

A federal court construing Virginia law held that "WLR plainly is permitted to set the record date as it has done in this case."[3736] The court explained that the only statutory limitations under the applicable Virginia law upon the board's authority in setting a record date required (1) that the record date may not be more than 70 days before the shareholder meeting and (2) that the decision selecting the record date—like any other board decision—must reflect "good faith business judgment" by the directors making the decision, with good faith "measured by the directors' resort to an informed decisionmaking process, not by the rationality of the decision ultimately taken."[3737]

---

3732. 857 F. Supp. 496 (W.D. Va.), *aff'd*, 65 F.3d 1172 (4th Cir. 1995), *cert. denied*, 516 U.S. 1117 (1996).

3733. *Id.* at 497.

3734. *Id.* at 498.

3735. *Id.*

3736. *Id.* at 499.

3737. *Id.* (citing Va. Stock Corp. Act §§ 13.1-660(A), 13.1-690).

Both of these requirements were satisfied, the court concluded, because the record date was within 70 days of the shareholder meeting and "WLR's directors undertook an informed decisionmaking process with regards to the selection of a record date."[3738] The court added that even if it were to review "the substantive rationality of the directors' decision to set the record date as they did, clearly that decision should stand" because "WLR's asserted desire to prevent any party from manipulating the Control Share Act" by placing shares in friendly hands prior to a record date "certainly qualifies as a rational decision."[3739]

Affirming this decision, the Fourth Circuit stated that "[t]he district court found, based on an examination of the record, that the WLR Board had acted in good faith, and we are not inclined to reverse its finding."[3740]

## 2. Shark Repellent Charter and Bylaw Provisions

Provisions in a corporation's charter or bylaws (bylaw provisions must be consistent with charter provisions; if they are not, the charter provision controls)[3741] "intended to deter a bidder's interest in that company as a target for a takeover" are called "shark repellents."[3742]

---

3738. *Id.*

3739. *Id.* at 499 n.5; *see also WLR Foods, Inc. v. Tyson Foods, Inc.*, 869 F. Supp. 419, 420, 424 (W.D. Va. 1994) (adopting factual findings and legal conclusions in prior decision), *aff'd*, 65 F.3d 1172 (4th Cir. 1995), *cert. denied*, 516 U.S. 1117 (1996).

3740. *WLR Foods, Inc. v. Tyson Foods, Inc.*, 65 F.3d 1172, 1187 (4th Cir. 1995), *cert. denied*, 516 U.S. 1117 (1996).

3741. *See Scotts African Union Methodist Protestant Church v. Conference of African Union First Colored Methodist Protestant Church*, 98 F.3d 78, 95 (3d Cir. 1996), *cert. denied*, 117 S. Ct. 688 (1997); *Oberly v. Kirby*, 592 A.2d 445, 457-61 (Del. 1991); *Centaur Partners, IV v. National Intergroup, Inc.*, 582 A.2d 923, 929 (Del. 1990); *Phillips v. Insituform of N. Am., Inc.*, 13 Del. J. Corp. L. 774, 790 (Del. Ch. Aug. 27, 1987); Del. Gen. Corp. Law § 109(b); 1 Model Bus. Corp. Act Annotated § 2.06(b) (3d ed. 1996).

3742. *Unitrin, Inc. v. American Gen. Corp.*, 651 A.2d 1361, 1377

(continued...)

Staggered director terms, pursuant to which (for example) one-third of a corporation's directors are elected each year, provide an important example of shark repellent provisions. Provisions of this type make it impossible for an unwanted bidder to replace a majority of a board at one annual meeting.[3743] Another important example are provisions eliminating or restricting the right of a majority of shareholders (1) to act by written consent, as is permitted in states such as Delaware, or (2) to call a special meeting, as is permitted in states such as Delaware if authorized by the corporation's certificate of incorporation or bylaws.[3744] Commentators have observed that the unsolicited tender offers by International Business Machines Corporation for Lotus Development Corporation in 1995 and by Johnson & Johnson for Cordus Corporation in 1996 were successful in large measure because Lotus and Cordus did not have staggered director terms and did not restrict the use of consents.[3745] The absence of these defenses permitted "a suitor that also owned the target's stock to solicit 'written consents' from

---

3742. (...continued)
n.19 (Del. 1995).

3743. 1 Robert H. Winter, Mark H. Stumpf & Gerard L. Hawkins, *Shark Repellents and Golden Parachutes: A Handbook for the Practitioner* § 4.1.1, at 115-17 & 131-160.22-46 (1992) (including examples); *see also Not All That Ends Well Is Good*, Corporate Control Alert, Dec. 1997, at 2 ("ITT couldn't hold off Hilton forever, because it hadn't installed one of the most common takeover defenses: a staggered board. Without a staggered board, all its directors would be up for reelection, and Hilton's slate could take control."). Massachusetts has enacted a statute mandating staggered terms for directors, with corporations permitted to opt out of the requirement by a majority vote of directors or a two-thirds vote of shareholders. *See* Mass. Bus. Corp. Law §§ 50A(a), (b); *Norton is Rescued From British BTR by the Massachusetts Legislature and Saint-Gobain*, Corporate Control Alert, May 1990, at 1 (discussing background of this statute); *see also The Siege of Atlanta*, Corporate Control Alert, Apr. 1997, at 2 (describing unsuccessful effort to adopt similar statutory provision in Georgia).

3744. *See* Del. Gen. Corp. Law §§ 211(d), 228; *see also* R. Winter, M. Stumpf & G. Hawkins § 8, at 243–260.4-18.

3745. Lipin, *Union Pacific Resources' Pennzoil Bid May Prompt the 'Just Say No' Defense*, Wall St. J., June 30, 1997, at A3.

investors," which allowed the suitor "to seek shareholder votes to replace the board immediately—a mechanism . . . that brought the targets to the negotiating table."[3746]

Another common shark repellent is an advance notice bylaw provision, which typically requires that a shareholder provide a specified number of days notice (often 45, 60 or 90 days) of the shareholder's intent to nominate a candidate for a board seat or to make a shareholder proposal or raise an issue in some other way at a meeting of shareholders.[3747] This type of provision "serve[s] the proper purpose of eliminating the element of surprise employed by many minority shareholders in voting themselves on the board of directors by requiring such shareholders to give management advance notice and other information."[3748]

Another example of shark repellent provisions are supermajority provisions, which "take various forms and are generally intended to offer protection to minority stockholders from a majority stockholder who would, but for the supermajority provision, be able to force a merger onto the corporation."[3749] "By requiring a greater percentage of stockholders to approve a proposed corporate action, stockholders are given more power to defeat actions adverse to their interests."[3750] Supermajority provisions, however, do not just "protect a minority shareholder against squeeze-out techniques employed by insurgents able to command a bare majority of votes"; they also "give minority shareholders the power to veto the will of the majority, effectively disenfranchising the majority."[3751]

---

3746. *Id.*

3747. *See, e.g., Unitrin, Inc. v. American Gen. Corp.*, 651 A.2d 1361, 1368-69 (Del. 1995); R. Winter, M. Stumpf & G. Hawkins § 8.2, at 244-244.1, 260.1–260.4-3, 260.4-260.15-18 (including examples).

3748. *American Gen. Corp. v. Torchmark Corp.*, 1990 WL 595282, at *4 (S.D.N.Y. Apr. 11, 1990), *preliminary injunction stayed pending an expedited appeal*, No. 90-2328 (5th Cir. Apr. 12, 1990), *appeal dismissed as moot*, 903 F.2d 825 (5th Cir. 1990).

3749. *Berlin v. Emerald Partners*, 552 A.2d 482, 488-89 (Del. 1989).

3750. *Id.* at 489 n.8.

3751. *National Intergroup*, 582 A.2d at 927; *see also Glazer v.*
(continued...)

Other examples of shark repellent provisions include fair
price and stock redemption provisions (typically requiring that any
transaction proposed by a shareholder who has acquired a specified
percentage of the corporation's stock must offer other shareholders
either the same average price—or in some cases the highest price—
paid by the acquiring shareholder to obtain its previously acquired
shares).[3752] Other shark repellent provisions eliminate or limit the
ability of shareholders (or, once an unwanted acquiror gains representation upon the corporation's board, less than a majority—or
supermajority—of directors) to remove directors without
cause,[3753] to increase the size of the board (a means by which
some unwanted acquirors have sought to nullify staggered board
provisions),[3754] to fill board vacancies,[3755] and/or to appoint
board members to board committees (including executive commit-

---

3751. (...continued)
*Pasternak*, 693 A.2d 319 (Del. 1997) (vacating on mootness grounds a
Court of Chancery ruling construing a certificate of incorporation provision requiring an 80 percent supermajority shareholder vote in favor of
certain mergers into the corporation; the Court of Chancery had decided
that the 80 percent shareholder approval requirement applied to mergers
not just into the corporation, but also into a corporate subsidiary); *Cede &
Co. v. Technicolor, Inc.*, 634 A.2d 345, 365-66, 373 n.40 (Del. 1993)
(noting supermajority provision requiring director unanimity with respect
to any sale of the corporation not approved by 95 percent of the corporation's outstanding shares); *National Intergroup*, 582 A.2d at 927-29
(holding that charter and bylaw provisions providing for a classified board
that could be modified only by an 80 percent supermajority vote were
clear and unambiguous and therefore enforceable); R. Winter, M. Stumpf
& G. Hawkins § 5, at 161-91.

3752. *See* R. Winter, M. Stumpf & G. Hawkins §§ 3.1-3.4, at 43-
56.1 & 7.1-7.4, at 213-242.10; Finkelstein, *Antitakeover Protection
Against Two-Tier and Partial Tender Offers: The Validity of Fair Price,
Mandatory Bid, and Flip-Over Provisions under Delaware Law*, 11 Sec.
Reg. L.J. 291, 296-98 (1984).

3753. 1 R. Winter, M. Stumpf & G. Hawkins § 4.1.2, at 117-122
(including examples).

3754. *Id.* § 4.1.3, at 122.1-124 (including examples).

3755. *Id.* § 4.1.4, at 124-126 (including examples).

tees).[3756] Additional examples include provisions allowing boards to consider the interests of non-shareholder constituencies as well as shareholders,[3757] provisions eliminating or limiting cumulative voting rights,[3758] voting rights ceilings and super-voting or dual class common stock plans,[3759] anti-greenmail provisions,[3760] reincorporation from one jurisdiction to another jurisdiction (typically enabling the corporation to take advantage of what directors believe to be a more favorable body of corporate law)[3761] and provisions limiting the means by which shark repellent provisions may be amended.[3762]

A 1995 study by the Investor Responsibility Research Center concluded that 895 or approximately 60 percent of 1500 major corporations have staggered terms for directors.[3763] The study also concluded that 657 or approximately 44 percent of these 1500 corporations have adopted advance notice provisions specifying deadlines for shareholders to nominate directors, 487 or approximately 32 percent have adopted fair price provisions, 466 or approximately 31 percent have adopted provisions limiting the circumstances under which special meetings may be called, 467 or approximately 31 percent have adopted provisions limiting action by written con-

---

3756. *Id.* § 4.1.5, at 126.1-128 (including examples).

3757. *Id.* § 6, at 193-212.8 (including examples).

3758. 2 R. Winter, M. Stumpf & G. Hawkins § 9.7, at 265 & 356–360-360.1 (including examples).

3759. *Id.* §§ 9.5, at 263 & 309-310, § 9.11, at 374.16–374.50-123 (including examples); *see also* Chapter III, Section F (discussing super-voting common stock).

3760. *Id.* § 9.10, at 270-270.1 & 374-374.16-10 (including examples); *see also* Chapter III, Section I 1 c (discussing anti-greenmail provisions).

3761. R. Winter, M. Stumpf & G. Hawkins § 9.2, at 261-62 & 270.9-302.40.

3762. *Id.* § 10, at 375-393 (including examples).

3763. *See Study Finds 1980s Corporate Defenses Remain Popular, But 'Hot Growth' Seen in Shareholder Action Constraints*, 10 Corporate Counsel Weekly (BNA) No. 40, Oct. 18, 1995, at 8.

sent, and 267 or approximately 18 percent have adopted provisions requiring a supermajority vote to approve mergers.[3764]

The following discussion begins by considering shareholder approved shark repellent provisions and then turns to decisions involving shark repellent provisions that directors have adopted without shareholder approval.

*a. Shareholder Approved Shark Repellent Provisions.* Judicial scrutiny is particularly deferential where shareholder approval of shark repellent provisions has been secured.

The Delaware Court of Chancery in *Henley Group, Inc. v. Santa Fe Southern Pacific Corp.*[3765] accordingly upheld a shareholder approved charter provision permitting the board to determine and alter its size by a majority vote so long as the board consisted of at least three but no more than 36 directors at any particular time.[3766] The court acknowledged that this provision "could result in some degree of stockholder disenfranchisement" but declined to grant a preliminary injunction enjoining enforcement of the provision because the corporation's shareholders had voted for this arrangement and "should the directors abuse their power, the shareholders are not without appropriate judicial remedies."[3767] The Delaware Court of Chancery in *Siegman v. Tri-Star Pictures, Inc.*[3768] likewise upheld a shareholder approved charter amendment granting directors authority to fill board vacancies and newly created directorships.[3769]

The Delaware Court of Chancery in *Seibert v. Gulton Industries, Inc.*[3770] similarly upheld the adoption by shareholders of a

---

3764. *Id.*

3765. 13 Del. J. Corp. L. 1152 (Del. Ch. Mar. 11, 1988).

3766. *Id.* at 1180.

3767. *Id.* at 1184.

3768. 15 Del. J. Corp. L. 218 (Del. Ch. May 5, 1989), *aff'd in part and rev'd in part on other grounds sub nom. In re Tri-Star Pictures, Inc., Litig.*, 634 A.2d 319 (Del. 1993).

3769. *Id.* at 232-34.

3770. 5 Del. J. Corp. L. 514 (Del. Ch. June 21, 1979), *aff'd mem.*, 414 A.2d 822 (Del. 1980).

supermajority charter provision requiring the approval of 80 percent of all shareholders before the corporation could enter into a business combination with a five percent shareholder unless the corporation's board of directors approved the business combination prior to the five percent shareholder's acquisition of its five percent interest.[3771] The court relied upon the failure by the shareholder challenging this provision "to cite any statute or case precedent which is done violence by the provision" or "to point convincingly to any public policy against the so-called 'shifting numbers' where corporate voting rights are concerned."[3772] A Massachusetts court reached the same result in *Seibert v. Milton Bradley Co.*[3773] The Delaware Court of Chancery in *Young v. Valhi, Inc.*[3774] enjoined an attempt by a shareholder to circumvent a charter provision adopted by Valhi, Inc. that was similar to the provisions upheld in *Gulton* and *Milton Bradley* by forming a wholly-owned subsidiary, and then merging the corporation into this subsidiary by means of a simple majority vote. The court labeled this maneuver "technically correct but devious."[3775] The court forbid this type of manipulation of corporate machinery "to accomplish an inequitable result, namely the unilateral elimination of any interest in Valhi on the part of its minority stockholders . . . by a vote of less than 80% of such corporation's voting stock."[3776]

A federal court construing Missouri law in *Torchmark Corp. v. Bixby*[3777] similarly refused to find a breach of fiduciary duty in a case involving charter and bylaw amendments proposed by a committee of independent directors and adopted by shareholders following disclosure of the fact that the amendments "might have the effect of deterring an unsolicited proposal" to acquire the cor-

---

3771. 5 Del. J. Corp. L. at 515.

3772. *Id.* at 518.

3773. 405 N.E.2d 131, 132-35 (Mass. 1980).

3774. 382 A.2d 1372 (Del Ch. 1978).

3775. *Id.* at 1378.

3776. *Id.* at 1378-79.

3777. 708 F. Supp. 1070 (W.D. Mo. 1988).

poration that was opposed by a family that held 48 percent of the corporation's stock.[3778]

A shark repellent provision generally requiring shareholder approval (because a change to the corporation's certificate of incorporation is required) is reincorporation from one jurisdiction to another jurisdiction in order to enable the corporation to take advantage of what the corporation's directors believe to be a more favorable body of corporate law. A federal court in California in *Plaza Securities Co. v. Lucky Stores, Inc.*[3779] refused to enjoin a shareholder vote on one such proposal. The proposal in *Lucky Stores* was presented as part of a restructuring program providing that Lucky Stores would repurchase 28 percent of its outstanding stock at $40 per share—a price approximately $10 per share above Lucky's then-market value and $3 per share above an unwanted offer from Asher Edelman.[3780] The court stated that "this is a transaction where the shareholders will vote and is not being done by the board alone," that a special committee of outside directors had studied and approved the proposal, and that both the board and the special committee had acted with the advice of independent financial and legal advisors.[3781] The court added that a single shareholder vote on the combined issue of the corporation's reincorporation from California to Delaware and the corporation's repurchase of shares was neither "illegal" nor "coercive" because shareholders may be offered "matters of incentives and disincentives in the same proxy material."[3782]

The court in *Lewis v. General Employment Enterprises, Inc.*,[3783] by contrast, granted a temporary restraining order

---

3778. *Id.* at 1080.

3779. No. C-86-7016 (N.D. Cal. Dec. 22, 1986).

3780. *See* Groves, *Lucky Holders, Wary of Restructuring Plan, OK Reincorporation*, L.A. Times, Dec. 23, 1986, at IV 1; *Lucky Stores Get Holders' Approval*, N.Y. Times, Dec. 23, 1986, at D4.

3781. *Plaza Sec.*, Tr. at 61, 68.

3782. *Id.* at 65-67.

3783. 1991 U.S. Dist. LEXIS 950, 1991 WL 11383 (N.D. Ill. Jan. 21, 1991), *reconsideration denied*, 1991 U.S. Dist. LEXIS 1140, 1991 WL 10826 (N.D. Ill. Jan. 31, 1991).

enjoining a special meeting at which shareholders were to vote upon a proposal to reincorporate an Illinois corporation as a Delaware corporation. The court based its conclusion upon a belief that the corporation's proxy material contained false and misleading statements.[3784]

*b. Board Adopted Shark Repellent Provisions.* Courts typically uphold shark repellent provisions adopted without shareholder approval where these provisions do not unjustifiably and inequitably interfere with shareholder voting or the consent solicitation process provided for in statutes such as Section 228 of the Delaware General Corporation Law, pursuant to which shareholders may take any action by written consent that could be taken at a shareholder meeting.[3785]

The following sections discuss decisions upholding and invalidating board adopted shark repellent provisions regulating (1) board size, (2) board nominations, shareholder resolutions and voting at shareholder meetings, (3) consent solicitations, (4) the adoption of a classified board and (5) various other subjects.[3786] The discussion below then turns to statutory restrictions upon board adopted shark repellent provisions and the question whether a board must waive enforcement of a bylaw where enforcement of the bylaw would be inequitable.[3787]

*c. Bylaws Regulating Board Size.* The leading decision addressing bylaws increasing or decreasing board size in order to effect an upcoming election is the *Blasius Industries, Inc. v. Atlas Corp.*[3788] decision announcing the *Blasius* standard discussed earlier in this Chapter.[3789]

*Blasius* involved a consent solicitation by Blasius Industries, a 9 percent shareholder of Atlas Corporation. This consent solicita-

---

3784. 1991 U.S. Dist. LEXIS 950, at *6-9, 1991 WL 11383, at *2-3.

3785. Del. Gen. Corp. Law § 228.

3786. *See* Chapter III, Sections H 2 c-g.

3787. *See* Chapter III, Sections H 2 h-i.

3788. 564 A.2d 651 (Del. Ch. 1988).

3789. *See* Chapter III, Section A 5.

tion sought to expand the size of the Atlas board from seven to fifteen members (the maximum number authorized in the corporation's charter) and to elect eight directors to fill the newly created
vacancies. The Blasius candidates for the board were committed to
a recapitalization that would include sales of certain of the corporation's businesses, borrowing, and substantial cash and debenture
dividends.[3790] The Atlas board responded by adopting a bylaw
amendment enlarging the board's size to nine and appointing two
new directors. This ensured that Blasius would not gain control of
the board even if Blasius gained the support of the holders of a
majority of the corporation's shares and filled the six board vacancies that then would exist.[3791] The court found that the board
"was not selfishly motivated simply to retain power" and that it
acted "in a good faith effort to protect its incumbency, not selfishly, but in order to thwart implementation of the recapitalization
that it feared, reasonably, would cause great injury to the Company."[3792]

As discussed in more detail earlier in this Chapter,[3793] the
court held that a board that acts "for the sole or primary purpose of
thwarting a shareholder vote" must overcome "the heavy burden of
demonstrating a compelling justification for such action."[3794] In
this case, the court held, the board failed to overcome this burden.
The court explained that there was no coercive action being taken
by "a powerful shareholder against the interests of a distinct shareholder constituency," and the board "had time . . . to inform the
shareholders of its views on the merits of the proposal subject to
stockholder vote."[3795] Under these circumstances, the court continued, "[t]he only justification that can . . . be offered for the
action taken is that the board knows better than do the shareholders
what is in the corporation's best interest."[3796] The court stated

---

3790. *Id*. at 654.
3791. *Id*. at 654-55.
3792. *Id*. at 656, 658.
3793. *See* Chapter III, Section A 5 a.
3794. 564 A.2d at 661-62.
3795. *Id*. at 662-63.
3796. *Id*. at 663.

that this premise "is irrelevant (except insofar as the shareholders wish to be guided by the board's recommendation) when the question is who should comprise the board of directors."[3797]

A federal court construing New Jersey law in *IBS Financial Corp. v. Seidman & Associates*[3798] invalidated a determination by the board of IBS Financial Corp. ("IBSF") to reduce its size from seven to six directors following an unsuccessful attempt by a group calling itself the IBSF Committee to Maximize Shareholder Value to elect two directors (only two board positions were voted upon) at IBSF's 1995 annual meeting. The committee was unsuccessful, and IBSF's board expected the committee to attempt again to obtain two board seats at IBSF's 1996 annual meeting, which was expected to be held in December 1996.[3799] On July 19, 1996, one of the two IBSF directors whose terms would expire at IBSF's 1996 annual meeting informed the board that he did not intend to seek re-election. The same day, the board voted to amend the corporation's bylaws to reduce the board's size from seven to six directors. As a result, one rather than two directors would be elected at the 1996 annual meeting.[3800]

The court found that the "primary motivation behind the IBSF board's decision" to eliminate a board seat was "to hinder the Committee's efforts in establishing a presence on IBSF's board."[3801] The court acknowledged that two other rationales suggested by the board—(1) that a smaller board was needed because the board performed many day-to-day tasks and (2) that the reduction was part of a long-range plan "to maintain flexibility in case future acquisitions necessitated adding directors" to the board —"[v]iewed in the abstract . . . amply justify the elimination of a board seat" but "[v]iewed against the backdrop of the impending proxy context . . . seem suspiciously pretextual."[3802] "Given

---

3797. *Id.*
3798. 954 F. Supp. 980 (D.N.J. 1997).
3799. *Id.* at 984, 993 n.6.
3800. *Id.* at 984.
3801. *Id.* at 985.
3802. *Id.* at 984-85.

these circumstances," the court stated, it "can only conclude that the IBSF board eliminated Lockhart's directorship primarily to hinder the Committee's proxy solicitation efforts."[3803]

The court, construing New Jersey law, looked to *Blasius* and cases construing *Blasius* in Delaware for guidance.[3804] The court held that "IBSF's elimination of a board seat constitutes the type of inequitable interference with the corporate franchise which *Blasius*, its predecessors and progeny, were designed to rectify" and that "IBSF has not and cannot establish a compelling justification of such action."[3805] The court reasoned as follows:

> The IBSF board, like the *Atlas* board [in *Blasius*], acted for the primary purpose of impeding the effectiveness of the shareholder vote. By reducing its membership by one, thereby reducing the seats up for election to one, the IBSF board effectively minimized the potential success of the Committee's impending proxy solicitation. After the reduction, if successful, the Committee could gain only one voice on the IBSF board—one sixth of the seats—as opposed to two—two-sevenths of the seats. Assuming another successful election the following year, the seat elimination could make the difference between a three-three deadlock and the Committee's outright control of IBSF—five-sevenths of the seats.
>
> Ochman's testimony conveys that the IBSF board, like the Atlas board, acted in subjective good faith to serve the corporation's best interests. Putting IBSF up for sale through an auction, as the board fears the Committee plans to do, may well be bad for the company and bad for the shareholders. *See* Ochman Dep. at 15 (expressing the board's firm belief that it, rather than the Committee, can best "build the franchise, develop the company further and maximize the shareholder value"). But as *Blasius* makes clear, this decision, when manifested as who should comprise the IBSF board, is one for the shareholders, not to be usurped by a board of directors, however good-intentioned.[3806]

---

3803. *Id*. at 985.
3804. *Id*. at 992.
3805. *Id*. at 994.
3806. *Id*. at 993-94.

The court accordingly determined to "invalidate the seat elimination as an unintended violation of the duty of loyalty owed to IBSF shareholders" and ordered IBSF to "restore its board membership to its prereduction size of seven, two seats of which to come up for election at the upcoming annual meeting."[3807]

  d. *Bylaws Regulating Board Nominations, Shareholder Resolutions and Voting at Shareholder Meetings.* The leading case addressing bylaws regulating board nominations is the Delaware Court of Chancery's decision in *Lerman v. Diagnostic Data, Inc.*[3808] *Lerman* involved a Diagnostic Data, Inc. ("DDI") bylaw requiring that board nominations be submitted to the corporation "not less than seventy days prior to any meeting of stockholders called for the election of directors."[3809] Against the backdrop of this bylaw, the board scheduled an annual meeting for a date 63 days in the future, with knowledge that a group of shareholders led by Henry Lerman had stated an intent to wage a proxy contest at the corporation's next annual meeting, made a demand for the corporation's shareholder list pursuant to Section 220 of the Delaware General Corporation Law, and filed a lawsuit seeking the list after the demand for the list had been refused.[3810]

  The court preliminarily enjoined the board's action, relying principally upon the Delaware Supreme Court's decision in *Schnell v. Chris-Craft Industries, Inc.*[3811]—a case discussed earlier in this Chapter that invalidated an inequitable board decision to accelerate the date of the corporation's annual meeting in order to shorten the time available to dissident shareholders to wage a proxy battle.[3812] The Court of Chancery in *Lerman* explained that "the action taken by DDI's board, whether designedly inequitable or not, has had a terminal effect on the aspirations of Lerman and his group" and "any other DDI shareholder who secretly might have

---

3807. *Id.* at 994.
3808. 421 A.2d 906 (Del. Ch. 1980).
3809. *Id.* at 909.
3810. *Id.* at 909-13.
3811. 285 A.2d 437 (Del. 1971).
3812. *See* Chapter III, Section H 1 a.

been harboring similar intentions."[3813] The court emphasized that "there was no way in which a DDI shareholder could possibly comply with the . . . 70-day requirement" in just 63 days, and that this fact "must clearly determine the issue."[3814]

The court rejected DDI's contention that "Lerman had plenty of time to have acted" before the meeting date was set and should have acted sooner.[3815] Even if true, the court stated, this circumstance "cannot serve to excuse the conduct of management if that conduct was both inequitable (in the sense of being unnecessary under the circumstances) and had the accompanying dual effect of thwarting shareholder opposition and perpetuating management in office."[3816] The court added that the combination of an advance submission requirement with an indefinite meeting date to be fixed at the discretion of management "has the effect of requiring those who would seek to wage a proxy challenge to remain in a constant state of readiness so as to have their materials and nominees available to go whenever management decides to drop the flag."[3817] According to the court, "[s]helf-readiness . . .—i.e., having all papers and filings prepared in advance and on the shelf so as to be able to pull them down and make the deadline once the meeting date is set"—is not required.[3818]

The court emphasized that "I do not address the question whether the 70-day requirement is unreasonable, and thus invalid, on its face."[3819] Rather, "I hold only that under the facts of this case the act of DDI's board, in fixing the date for the annual meeting at a time 63 days in the future, in the face of a by-law which required the plaintiff Lerman and his group to submit the names of their nominees, together with information concerning them, to the corporation at least 70 days in advance of the date of the annual

---

3813. 421 A.2d at 912.
3814. *Id.*
3815. *Id.* at 913.
3816. *Id.* at 914.
3817. *Id.*
3818. *Id.*
3819. *Id.* at 914.

meeting of shareholders, is invalid and cannot be permitted to stand so as to prevent the plaintiff and his group from placing the names of their candidates in nomination."[3820]

*Linton v. Everett*[3821] involved an advance notice bylaw provision in the context of a corporation's first election of directors in three years. The corporation, Security Investments Groups, Inc., had a single asset, Security Savings Bank—a bank over which the federal government had assumed control in 1992, following which Security Investments' primary activity had been the pursuit of litigation against the federal government for allegedly breaching promises made by the Federal Home Loan Bank Board (the "FHLBB") and the Federal Savings and Loan Insurance Corporation (the "FSLIC") to induce Security Bank to purchase two failing thrift institutions during the early 1980s.[3822] During this time period, Security Investments had no assets of value, forfeited its corporate charter and preserved the corporate entity solely as a vehicle to pursue litigation.[3823]

Following a favorable ruling in a case brought by similarly affected financial institutions, Security Investments' board noticed a shareholders meeting for September 17, 1996.[3824] Because there had been no election of directors for more than three years, the corporation's entire classified board would be voted upon at this meeting for terms of one, two or three years.[3825] The corporation's bylaws required that shareholders be provided 30 days notice of the meeting and that "a shareholder desiring to nominate an opposing slate must submit to the corporation specified biographical information about each opposition candidate within ten days of the mailing of the notice."[3826] The notice was mailed on August 19,

---

3820. *Id.*

3821. 1997 Del. Ch. LEXIS 117, 1997 WL 441189 (Del. Ch. July 31, 1997).

3822. 1997 Del. Ch. LEXIS 117, at *1-3, 1997 WL 441189, at *1.

3823. 1997 Del. Ch. LEXIS 117, at *6, 1997 WL 441189, at *2.

3824. 1997 Del. Ch. LEXIS 117, at *9-10, 14-15, 1997 WL 441189, at *3, 5.

3825. 1997 Del. Ch. LEXIS 117, at *16, 1997 WL 441189, at *5.

3826. 1997 Del. Ch. LEXIS 117, at *30, 1997 WL 441189, at *9.

1996, no opposing slate was nominated, the meeting was held on September 17, 1996, and all of the corporation's directors were re-elected.[3827]

Two shareholders sought to invalidate the election as inequitable because the thirty day notice period was "so short that as a practical matter the shareholders were deprived of any opportunity to nominate an opposing slate of directors."[3828] One of the two shareholders who sought to invalidate the election received notice of the meeting three days before he was required by the advance notice bylaw to send biographical information concerning potential candidates to the corporation. The other shareholder challenging the election received notice of the meting after the deadline for submitting biographical data had passed.[3829]

The court stated that the advance notice provision was not inequitable per se because "[i]n quite different circumstances, a case could arise where such a short notice period would be sufficient."[3830] "[I]n the unusual circumstances presented here," the court found, however, the notice period was not reasonable because no shareholder meeting had been held for three years and "[e]qually important, the directors did not follow their earlier practice of informing stockholders—well in advance—of the date by which shareholder proposals had to be submitted to the corporation in order to be included in the management proxy soliciting materials."[3831] Indeed, the court noted, "[i]n prior years that information was communicated to shareholders by a notice contained in the previous year's annual meeting proxy statement."[3832]

Thus, the court concluded, "in sharp contrast to the information the board furnished to shareholders between 1988 and 1992

---

3827. 1997 Del. Ch. LEXIS 117, at *15-16, 1997 WL 441189, at *5.

3828. 1997 Del. Ch. LEXIS 117, at *28, 1997 WL 441189, at *8.

3829. 1997 Del. Ch. LEXIS 117, at *30-31, 1997 WL 441189, at *9.

3830. 1997 Del. Ch. LEXIS 117, at *33, 1997 WL 441189, at *10.

3831. *Id.*

3832. 1997 Del. Ch. LEXIS 117, at *33-34, 1997 WL 441189, at *10.

when Security Investments shareholders meetings were held on a regular basis, in 1996 the stockholders were given no forewarning when a stockholders meeting would be called and had no reason to anticipate that one would be called imminently."[3833] The court stated that "[t]he defendants have offered no reason why such a tight notice period was necessary," and concluded that "[t]he only inference to be drawn is that the directors chose to proceed in this way in the hope of avoiding the risk of a proxy contest."[3834] "Even if that was not the board's intent," the court held, "the effect . . . was to deprive the shareholders of a fair opportunity to contest the election of management's nominees."[3835]

The court rejected a claim that "plaintiffs' lack of diligence, not the scheduling of the meeting, prevented them from complying with the advance notice provision."[3836] The court acknowledged that one of the plaintiffs in the case had asked to inspect the corporation's shareholder list months before the meeting was scheduled but was—in his own words—"too busy to review and copy the list" until it was too late.[3837] Quoting *Lerman*, the court stated that this contention was "unpersuasive" because "[e]ven if in theory the plaintiffs could have avoided the adverse effects of the advance notice provision by remaining in a constant state of preparedness to engage in a proxy contest, that 'cannot serve to excuse the conduct of management . . . that . . . was both inequitable (in the sense of being unnecessary under the circumstances) and [that] had the accompanying dual effect of thwarting shareholder opposition and perpetuating management in office.'"[3838] Quoting *Lerman* again, the court stated that shareholders "are not required to be 'shelf-

---

3833. 1997 Del. Ch. LEXIS 117, at *34-35, 1997 WL 441189, at *10.

3834. 1997 Del. Ch. LEXIS 117, at *35, 1997 WL 441189, at *10.

3835. 1997 Del. Ch. LEXIS 117, at *35 n.57, 1997 WL 441189, at *10 n.57.

3836. 1997 Del. Ch. LEXIS 117, at *31-32, 1997 WL 441189, at *9.

3837. 1997 Del. Ch. LEXIS 117, at *31, 1997 WL 441189, at *9.

3838. 1997 Del. Ch. LEXIS 117, at *32, 1997 WL 441189, at *9 (quoting 421 A.2d at 914).

ready,' i.e., in a constant state of alert that a shareholder meeting may be called and that certain information will be required to be filed without delay."[3839]

The court accordingly held that "the directors' decision to provide only thirty days' notice, which would inevitably trigger the advance notice provision in a manner foreseeably adverse to any shareholders desiring to nominate an opposing slate, constituted an inequitable manipulation of the election process."[3840] The election therefore was set aside, and a new election was ordered.[3841]

*Mesa Petroleum Co. v. Unocal Corp.*[3842] provides another example of a Delaware Court of Chancery decision enjoining enforcement of a bylaw provision on equitable grounds. The bylaw provision challenged in this case was adopted by Unocal's board in response to Mesa Petroleum's expression of interest in seeking control of Unocal. The bylaw prohibited shareholder consideration of matters raised by shareholders at the corporation's annual meeting unless specified information was submitted at least 30 days prior to the meeting. In accordance with this bylaw, Mesa announced 32 days prior to a scheduled meeting that it intended to present two proposals at the meeting. The first of these proposals would adjourn the meeting, and the second of these proposals would rescind any action taken at the meeting prior to the adjournment. Ten days later (i.e., 22 days before the meeting), Unocal's board announced that the bylaw precluded the presentation of proposals less than 30 days prior to the original date—not the adjourned date—of the meeting. Accordingly, Unocal contended, even if Mesa were successful in obtaining an adjournment of the meeting, Mesa would be precluded from presenting any proposals at the meeting when the meeting was reconvened.[3843] The court found the Unocal board's after-the-fact interpretation of the bylaw was inequitable and granted a prelim-

---

3839. *Id.*

3840. 1997 Del. Ch. LEXIS 117, at *35-36, 1997 WL 441189, at *10.

3841. 1997 Del. Ch. LEXIS 117, at *36, 1996 WL 441189, at *10.

3842. 1985 Del. Ch. LEXIS 461, 1985 WL 44692 (Del. Ch. Apr. 22, 1985).

3843. 1985 Del. Ch. LEXIS 461, at *5, 1985 WL 44692, at *1-2.

inary injunction enjoining enforcement of the bylaw.[3844] The court did not rule upon the validity of the bylaw in and of itself.[3845]

The Delaware Court of Chancery in *Kidsco Inc. v. Dins-more*[3846] upheld a determination by the board of The Learning Company ("TLC") to amend a bylaw that, prior to the amendment, allowed 10 percent of the corporation's shareholders to demand a special meeting of shareholders on a date to be set by the board between 35 days and 60 days following receipt of the request. The bylaw amendment substituted 60 days and 90 days for 35 days and 60 days, respectively.[3847]

The bylaw amendment was adopted on November 6, 1995, seven days after SoftKey International, Inc. announced (1) a cash tender offer for 50.1 percent of the TLC's shares, to be followed by a second step merger in which TLC's remaining shareholders would receive SoftKey stock, and (2) SoftKey's intent to solicit the holders of 10 percent of shareholders to call a special meeting in order to remove TLC's directors and replace them with TLC nominees who would exempt a merger of TLC and SoftKey from TLC's poison pill shareholder rights plan.[3848] "Thus, the sole purpose of the SoftKey-initiated special meeting was to facilitate SoftKey's hostile offer by removing the major obstacle to it."[3849] SoftKey's announcement came ten days before a scheduled November 9, 1995 TLC shareholder meeting at which shareholders were to vote on a merger agreement between TLC and Broderbund Software, Inc. that had been publicly announced on July 31, 1995.[3850]

---

3844. 1985 Del. Ch. LEXIS 461, at *7, 1985 WL 44692, at *5-6.

3845. 1985 Del. Ch. LEXIS 461, at *11, 1985 WL 44692, at *10-11.

3846. 674 A.2d 483 (Del. Ch. 1995), *aff'd*, 670 A.2d 1338 (unpublished opinion, text available at 1995 Del. LEXIS 426 and 1995 WL 715886) (Del. Nov. 29, 1995).

3847. *Id.* at 485, 487 & n.4.

3848. *Id.* at 487, 488-89.

3849. *Id.* at 487.

3850. *Id.* at 486-87.

According to the TLC board, the bylaw amendment was adopted in order to ensure that if shareholders disagreed with the board's belief that a merger of TLC and Broderbund best would serve shareholder interests, the board still would have time to seek alternatives to SoftKey's two-tier offer, including an auction of TLC to the highest bidder.[3851] As stated in a November 8, 1995 Schedule 14D-9 filing, the board adopted the bylaw amendment to assure that any special meeting called for the purpose of removing board members and replacing them with SoftKey nominees would be "conducted in an orderly time frame and to assure that the timing of the SoftKey Offer does not prevent the Company from protecting stockholder value under all possible circumstances."[3852] TLC's board also postponed the meeting at which shareholders would vote upon the proposed merger with Broderbund from November 9 until December 11.[3853]

On November 8, SoftKey delivered letters from the required 10 percent of TLC's shareholders demanding a special shareholders meeting in 35 days, on December 13, 1995.[3854] Pursuant to TLC's amended bylaw, TLC's board scheduled that meeting for the 60th day following receipt of the demand, on January 8, 1996.[3855]

The court denied a motion for a preliminary injunction enjoining enforcement of the bylaw, rejecting claims (1) that the bylaw amendment constituted a breach of a contract right held by Softkey and the other TLC shareholders who had demanded a special meeting to proceed under the pre-amendment bylaw, and (2) that the amendment constituted a breach of fiduciary duty.

With respect to SoftKey's breach of contract argument, the court explained that the corporation's certificate of incorporation expressly authorized the directors to amend or repeal bylaws with-

---

3851. *Id.* at 488-89.
3852. *Id.* at 489.
3853. *Id.* at 488.
3854. *Id.* at 489.
3855. *Id.*

out obtaining shareholder approval.[3856] Accordingly, "although the by-laws are a contract between the corporation and its stockholders, the contract was subject to the board's power to amend the by-laws unilaterally."[3857] "[W]here a corporation's by-laws put all on notice that the by-laws may be amended at any time, no vested rights can arise that would contractually prohibit an amendment."[3858]

With respect to SoftKey's breach of fiduciary duty claim, the court first rejected a claim that the amendment was invalid because it was intended to entrench TLC's board in office. The court explained that the bylaw was adopted for two purposes. First, the bylaw was adopted "to enable the board to present the Broderbund transaction to TLC's shareholders without having simultaneously to engage in a distracting proxy fight to retain their incumbency."[3859] Second, the bylaw was adopted "to give the board a reasonable time" if shareholders rejected the Broderbund transaction "to explore whether a superior alternative transaction could be developed, either in an auction or negotiated with SoftKey, Broderbund, or some other party."[3860]

In neither case, the court stated, would the amendment perpetuate the current board in office: "If the Broderbund transaction is approved, the TLC board will disappear, and only two of TLC's five directors will become directors of Broderbund. If the Broderbund deal is rejected and no alternative transaction is developed (and approved by shareholders), then the shareholders will be free, at the January 8 special meeting, to remove the current board if they do desire."[3861] Thus, the court concluded, "all that the plaintiffs have shown is a possibility that the directors tenure may be

---

3856. *Id*. at 492.
3857. *Id*. (citation omitted).
3858. *Id*.
3859. *Id*. at 493.
3860. *Id*.
3861. *Id*.

enlarged for an additional 25 days. That possibility does not an entrenched board make."[3862]

The court then held that the bylaw amendment satisfied the *Unocal Corp. v. Mesa Petroleum Co.*[3863] standard.[3864] The court stated that TLC's directors "reasonably perceived that the SoftKey offer and impending proxy contest posed a threat to corporate policy and effectiveness" because the timing of any SoftKey-initiated shareholders meeting threatened (1) "the shareholders' interest in making an informed choice about the Broderbund offer, free from the distraction of a concurrent proxy contest to replace the board," and (2) "TLC's (and the shareholders') interest in having in place a process that would yield the best possible value if the Broderbund transaction were turned down."[3865] The court emphasized the risk that if the Broderbund transaction were rejected at the December 11 meeting at which shareholders were to vote on that transaction and then a second meeting was held on December 13, as demanded by SoftKey, to consider removing TLC's directors in favor of SoftKey nominees, then TLC's directors "would have no time to explore whether a transaction superior to the SoftKey offer could be developed."[3866] Shareholders thus would be "limited to a choice between retaining the existing board, and accepting a SoftKey two-tiered proposal that had not yet been subject to negotiation or to any auction process."[3867]

The court stated that the directors' response to this threat was proportionate to this threat because the bylaw amendment "only delayed, but did not preclude, a shareholder vote," and "the 25 day

---

3862. *Id.*

3863. 493 A.2d 946 (Del. 1985).

3864. 674 A.2d at 496; *see also* Chapter III, Section A 2 (discussing *Unocal* standard); Chapter III, Section A 5 c (discussing *Kidsco* court's determination to utilize the *Unocal* standard rather than the standard provided for in *Blasius Industries, Inc. v. Atlas Corp.*, 564 A.2d 651 (Del. Ch. 1988)).

3865. 674 A.2d at 496.

3866. *Id.* at 497.

3867. *Id.*

delay clearly fell within a range of reasonable alternatives."[3868] The court stated that "[t]he board acted appropriately in responding to the last minute SoftKey offer by seeking to protect the ability of the stockholders to vote, up or down, on the pre-existing Broderbund merger, in a timeframe that would briefly delay SoftKey's special meeting so that the board would know the stockholders' wishes regarding the Broderbund merger, and then be in a position to exercise its fiduciary duties with knowledge of the stockholders' views."[3869] The court described this as an "'extremely mild'" response that "did not preclude SoftKey's ability to call a special meeting, nor could it alter or influence the vote in any respect."[3870] "The by-law amendment simply preserved an opportunity for TLC's board, if the Broderbund merger were rejected by the stockholders, to fulfill its duties to the shareholders to seek out the best value reasonably available."[3871]

This case, the court added, was "functionally indistinguishable from *Stahl v. Apple Bancorp, Inc.*,[3872] a case discussed earlier in this Chapter.[3873] The court in *Kidsco* explained:

> In *Stahl* . . . , Chancellor Allen denied a preliminary injunction sought by a hostile tender offeror that simultaneously was pursuing a proxy contest to oust the board. The target company's board responded by delaying the company's annual meeting (for which a record date had already been set) to a later date still in conformity with the company's by-laws and 8 Del. C. § 211. The board's justification for the delay was that the stockholders' best interests would be served by delaying the vote until the company had a fair opportunity to explore and pursue alternatives to the hostile offer. The Court held that the act of deferring the annual meeting, where no meeting date had been set and no proxies had been solicited, did not impair or impede the effective exercise of the franchise to any extent.

---

3868. *Id.*
3869. *Id.*
3870. *Id.* (quoting *Stahl*, 579 A.2d at 1125).
3871. *Id.* at 497.
3872. 579 A.2d 1115 (Del. Ch. 1990).
3873. *See* Chapter III, Section H 1 b.

> This case is functionally indistinguishable from *Stahl*. Here,
> the by-law amendment resulted in a brief deferral of a meet-
> ing that had not yet been demanded or called; and it was
> adopted for reasons similar to those validated in that
> case.[3874]

Under these circumstances, the court stated, "the franchise process"
could not be said in either the *Apple Bancorp* case or the *Kidsco*
case to be "sufficiently engaged" before the fixing of a meeting
date to give rise to the possibility of inequitable manipulation.[3875]

The Delaware Supreme Court affirmed, "on the basis of and
for the reasons stated by the Court of Chancery in its well-reasoned" decision.[3876]

Decisions outside of Delaware (construing the law of Delaware and other states, in some cases on the basis of Delaware law)
have reached conclusions similar to the holdings in the Delaware
decisions discussed above.

*Katz v. Chevron Corp.*[3877] involved the amendment of a corporation's bylaws in order to eliminate the right of shareholders to
call special meetings. A California court construing Delaware law
upheld this bylaw amendment. The court explained that the corporation's bylaws prior to the amendment had allowed any shareholder to call a special meeting for the purpose of removing the
corporation's existing board or using the threat of a special meeting
to pressure the board, and that the board had been advised that
under Delaware law shareholders had no "inherent right to call special meetings and that elimination of the right afforded by the
bylaws would not inhibit a proxy contest in connection with the
election of directors at annual shareholders' meetings."[3878]

---

3874. 674 A.2d at 496.

3875. *Id.* (quoting *Stahl*, 579 A.2d at 1123).

3876. *Kidsco Inc. v. Dinsmore*, 670 A.2d 1338 (unpublished opinion, text available at 1995 Del. LEXIS 426 and 1995 WL 715886) (Del.
Nov. 29, 1995).

3877. 22 Cal. App. 4th 1352, 27 Cal. Rptr. 2d 681 (Cal. Ct. App.
1994).

3878. *Id.* at 1374, 27 Cal. Rptr. at 694.

The Seventh Circuit in *Manbourne, Inc. v. Conrad*,[3879] construing Wisconsin law, enjoined enforcement of bylaw amendments that eliminated "the shareholders' power to require a special shareholders' meeting," stated that "the shareholders could remove a director only for cause and upon an affirmative vote of 80% of the outstanding shares," and required "a minimum of 50-days notice for a special shareholders' meeting."[3880] The court pointed to "the facts of this case," which included the arranging by the corporation's directors, shortly after an unwanted acquiror obtained control of 50.23 percent of the corporation's stock, for option holders to exercise their options "for the purposes of placing majority control in friendly hands," and maintaining the directors in office.[3881] Under these circumstances, the court held, the adoption of bylaw amendments "to entrench . . . directors in power" was a breach of the directors' fiduciary duty.[3882]

A federal court construing New York law in *International Banknote Co. v. Muller*[3883] enjoined enforcement of a bylaw requiring that director nominations be filed with the board of directors of International Banknote Company, Inc. ("IBC") no later than 45 days prior to an annual meeting. The bylaw amendment was adopted by the board 58 days prior to a previously scheduled annual meeting and one day after the announcement by a group of shareholders that the group intended to seek the removal of the corporation's directors.[3884] The court held that "the directors cannot seek refuge in the business judgment doctrine," because "[t]he record now before the Court suggests that the corporate board members breached their fiduciary duty of care by adopting without careful consideration a provision which drastically shortened the amount of time defendants had to prepare for the proxy contest."[3885] The court explained:

---

3879. 796 F.2d 884 (7th Cir. 1986).
3880. *Id.* at 886 & n.2.
3881. *Id.* at 886, 889-90.
3882. *Id.* at 889.
3883. 713 F. Supp. 612 (S.D.N.Y. 1989).
3884. *Id.* at 622.
3885. *Id.* at 625.

> [T]he IBC directors enacted by By-law less than 24 hours after receiving the Committee's Schedule 13D, and only 58 days before the previously scheduled annual meeting. Eugene Jonas, the Executive Vice President of IBC and a member of the Board, testified that it was his idea to adopt the By-law, but he also stated that before he received the Schedule 13D the day before the board meeting, he had never even considered amending the by-laws with an advance notice provision. Furthermore, Jonas testified that the purpose of the By-law was to disseminate nominee information to the shareholders, but he acknowledged that the By-law did not even require the Board to distribute the information supplied by the Committee.
>
> Neither Edward H. Weitzen, the President of IBC, Jonas, nor four of the directors who attended the March 28, 1989 Board meeting could recollect any specific discussion or questions about the By-law following the presentation by Jonas. In fact, the directors testified that the actual language of the By-law language had not even been prepared when the vote was taken.[3886]

The court thus found "a substantial likelihood that the IBC Board breached its fiduciary duty of care to the shareholders and that as a result, the business judgment rule does not apply."[3887] The court also found "a substantial likelihood that . . . the Board's primary motivation for adopting the By-law was entrenchment" and "a desire to maintain management's control rather than to act in the best interests of the shareholders."[3888] The court added that "[c]ourts have consistently found that corporate management subjects shareholders to irreparable harm by denying them the right to vote their shares or unnecessarily frustrating them in their attempt to obtain representation on the board of directors."[3889]

Another federal court construing New York law, *Holly Sugar Corp. v. Buchsbaum*,[3890] also enjoined enforcement of a bylaw.

---

3886. *Id.* (citations omitted).
3887. *Id.*
3888. *Id.* at 626.
3889. *Id.* at 623.
3890. [1981 Transfer Binder] Fed. Sec. L. Rep. (CCH) ¶ 98,366
(continued...)

The bylaw challenged in this case was adopted shortly after a group formed to mount a proxy context (1) commenced litigation contending that a quorum had not been present at a shareholder meeting at which there had been a vote to elect directors and (2) announced its intention to solicit proxies to call a special shareholders meeting to elect directors.[3891] The bylaw barred any shareholder "from calling a special meeting 'to vote on any matters voted on at a prior meeting the result of which is or may be dependent upon the outcome of court proceedings.'"[3892]

The court held that the "obvious and intended effect" of this "expedient amendment of by-laws" was "to deprive . . . shareholders of their valid right to vote in an election of directors . . . and, further, to preclude the defendants from soliciting shareholder support for their candidates."[3893] This conduct, the court stated, "is *per se* wrongful."[3894]

A federal court construing Missouri law in *AHI Metnall, L.P. v. J.C. Nichols Co.*[3895] granted a preliminary injunction enjoining enforcement of bylaw amendments adopted by J.C. Nichols Co. ("JCN"), a corporation whose chief executive office and board president, Lynn McCarthy, controlled over 50 percent of the corporation's stock. The bylaws were adopted in response to actions by Allen & Company Incorporated, a shareholder that owned approximately 6 percent of the corporation's stock. Allen's actions included (1) Allen's submission of a plan to McCarthy pursuant to which Allen would buy a controlling interest in JCN at a price JCN's board considered grossly inadequate, (2) a threat by Allen to commence a shareholder derivative action challenging alleged insider transactions by McCarthy, and (3) statements by an Allen representative at a JCN board meeting that litigation would follow

---

3890. (...continued)
(D. Colo. Oct. 28, 1981).
    3891. *Id.* at 92,234-35.
    3892. *Id.* at 92,235.
    3893. *Id.* at 92,238.
    3894. *Id.*
    3895. 891 F. Supp. 1352 (W.D. Mo. 1995).

if Allen's proposal to acquire a controlling interest in JCN was rejected.[3896] The bylaws adopted against this backdrop precluded nominations of directors or the making of business proposals at shareholder meetings by any shareholder who did not hold 20 percent or more of the corporation's stock.[3897] Because only one shareholder owned 20 percent or more of the corporation's stock, the court stated, "these bylaw amendments effectively preclude Plaintiff or any other shareholder from nominating a director or proposing any business at shareholder meetings."[3898]

With respect to the merits, the court held that Allen had shown "a very strong likelihood of success on the merits."[3899] The court rejected the directors' contention that their conduct was protected by the business judgment rule. The court explained that "these bylaw changes were adopted in response to a hostile takeover threat," and therefore the directors "will be afforded the protections of the business judgment rule only if their actions complied with the standards set forth in *Unocal*."[3900]

Under *Unocal*, the court continued, a board must show that "it had reasonable grounds for believing that a threat to corporate policy and effectiveness existed" and that the board's response to the perceived threat was "proportional to the threat posed."[3901] The court held that the directors' conduct failed both prongs of the *Unocal* test. First, "the Board's perception of a threat . . . based upon the above actions was not reasonable" in light of McCarthy's control of over 50 percent of JCN's stock and the fact that "the threatened derivative suit . . . was directed only at alleged insider transactions" by McCarthy—something "bothersome" to McCarthy but not "a legitimate threat to the corporation."[3902] Second, "[t]he total disenfranchisement of the right of every shareholder,

---

3896. *Id*. at 1355, 1356.
3897. *Id*. at 1355-56.
3898. *Id*. at 1356.
3899. *Id*. at 1358.
3900. *Id*. at 1356.
3901. *Id*.
3902. *Id*.

except Defendant McCarthy, to nominate directors or propose business was not a reasonable reaction to the perceived threats. . . . The Board's defensive measures clearly go too far and cannot be considered proportional to any perceived takeover threat."[3903]

Under *Blasius*, the court added, "[a] board's unilateral decision to adopt a defensive measure . . . that purposefully disenfranchises its shareholders is strongly suspect under *Unocal*, and cannot be sustained without a 'compelling justification.'"[3904] Here, the court concluded, there was "no such justification."[3905]

The court also relied upon Section 351.245(1) of Missouri's General Business and Corporation Law, a statute stating that "each outstanding share . . . should be entitled to one vote on each matter submitted to a vote at a meeting of shareholders."[3906] The court described "the rights to nominate director candidates and propose business" as "integral components of a shareholder's right to vote."[3907] "By effectively disenfranchising every shareholder of JCN except Defendant McCarthy," the court held, "the Board's 20% stock ownership requirements unreasonably impinge this right."[3908]

With respect to irreparable harm, finally, the court quoted the statement in *International Banknote* that "[c]ourts have consistently found that corporate management subjects shareholders to irreparable harm by denying them the right to vote their shares or unnecessarily frustrating them in their attempt to obtain representation on the board of directors."[3909]

---

3903. *Id.* at 1357.

3904. *Id.* (quoting *Stroud v. Grace*, 606 A.2d 75, 92 n.3 (Del. 1992)).

3905. *Id.* at 1357.

3906. *Id.* at 1357-58 (quoting Mo. Gen. Bus. & Corp. Law § 351.245(1)).

3907. *Id.* at 1358.

3908. *Id.*

3909. *Id.* at 1359 (quoting *International Banknote*, 713 F. Supp. at 623).

*e. Bylaws Regulating Consent Solicitations.* Two Delaware Supreme Court decisions—*Datapoint Corp. v. Plaza Securities Co.*[3910] and *Allen v. Prime-Computer, Inc.*[3911]—have granted preliminary injunctions enjoining enforcement of bylaws regulating consent solicitation procedures. In both cases, the bylaws were adopted by boards shortly after learning that shareholders intended to solicit consents to replace those boards pursuant to the consent solicitation process provided for by Section 228 of the Delaware General Corporation Law.[3912]

*Datapoint Corp. v. Plaza Securities Co.*[3913] involved a bylaw that delayed the effective date of shareholder consents until 60 days after the corporation's receipt of a shareholder's notice of an intent to solicit consents. The bylaw also stayed the effective date of any shareholder consent action until the termination of any lawsuit challenging the action.[3914] The court found that the purpose of the bylaw was not merely to facilitate a ministerial review of the sufficiency of consents by objective inspectors, but "to provide the incumbent board with *time* to seek to defeat the shareholder action by management's solicitation of its own proxies, or revocations of outstanding shareholder consents."[3915] Moreover, the court continued, the bylaw provision "staying the effective date of any shareholder consent action until termination of any lawsuits challenging such action effectively places within the incumbent board the power to stultify, if not nullify, the shareholders' statutory right" to solicit consents.[3916] The court concluded that this result "can only be found to be 'repugnant to the statute' which the bylaw is intended to serve, not master."[3917]

---

3910. 496 A.2d 1031 (Del. 1985).

3911. 540 A.2d 417 (Del. 1988).

3912. Del. Gen. Corp. Law § 228.

3913. 496 A.2d 1031 (Del. 1985).

3914. *Id*. at 1033-34.

3915. *Id*. at 1036.

3916. *Id*.

3917. *Id*. (quoting *Kerbs v. California E. Airways, Inc.*, 90 A.2d 652, 659 (Del.), *reargument denied*, 91 A.2d 62 (Del. 1952)).

The court cautioned, however, that its ruling did not bar a bylaw imposing "minimal essential provisions for ministerial review of the validity of the action taken by shareholder consent," "designed simply to defer consummation of shareholder action by consent in lieu of meeting until a ministerial-type review of the sufficiency of the consents has been performed by duly qualified and objective inspectors."[3918]

*Allen v. Prime Computer, Inc.*[3919] involved bylaw provisions that authorized the corporation to hire an inspector within three business days following the commencement of a consent solicitation. The bylaw also required the inspector to issue a preliminary report no sooner than 20 days following the commencement of the solicitation. The preliminary report then could be challenged within 48 hours.[3920]

The court pointed to three factors to be utilized "[i]n evaluating the reasonableness of a bylaw, which purports to establish ministerial review of the validity of consents."[3921] These three factors were the following:

> First, a court must determine the purpose sought to be served. A bylaw whose real purpose is delay of shareholder action is per se unreasonable. Second, the court should consider the impact of the bylaw upon the effective exercise of the power conferred under § 228. Finally, the bylaw should contain only the minimal requisites for a reliable and prompt ministerial review to ensure the orderly function of corporate democracy. Such ministerial review must not be unduly elaborate, should contain reasonable time periods only necessary to the circumstances, and should be one which, when administered in good faith, is reasonable and balanced.[3922]

The bylaws challenged in *Prime Computer*, the court stated, "clearly fail" to meet these standards. The court described the reasonableness of the 20 day provision as "not explained," and stated

---

3918. *Id.*
3919. 540 A.2d 417 (Del. 1988).
3920. *Id.* at 418-19.
3921. *Id.* at 420.
3922. *Id.*

that the 20 day provision "did more than 'defer consummation of shareholder action until a ministerial review of the validity of the consents' had occurred."[3923] The court added, however, that the purely ministerial review provisions in the bylaws, were they not coupled with the 20-day provision, "would probably be reasonable."[3924]

The Delaware Court of Chancery's decision in *Edelman v. Authorized Distribution Network, Inc.*[3925] refused to enjoin a bylaw governing consent solicitations. The bylaw challenged in this case required that (1) shareholders desiring to solicit written consents must request that the board fix a record date, and (2) a board receiving such a request must meet within 10 days, and, at that meeting, set a record date no later than 10 days after the board meeting (and thus no more than 20 days later than the shareholder request).[3926]

A shareholder who delivered a written consent to the corporation on September 7, 1989 contended that the bylaw requiring a shareholder request for a record date for a consent solicitation was invalid and that the delivery of his written consent therefore fixed September 7 as the record date. The board, by contrast, treated the consent as a request that the board fix a record date pursuant to the bylaw. The board accordingly met on September 17, and fixed September 27 as the record date. Between September 7 and September 27, affiliates of the corporation's chairman purchased approximately 30 percent of the corporation's outstanding stock. As a result, the corporation's chairman on the record date selected by the board had control of approximately 40 percent of the corporation's stock.[3927]

---

3923. *Id.* (quoting *Datapoint*, 496 A.2d at 1036).

3924. *Id.* at 421.

3925. 1989 Del. Ch. LEXIS 156, 1989 WL 133625 (Del. Ch. Nov. 3, 1989).

3926. 1989 Del. Ch. LEXIS 156, at *4-5, 1989 WL 133625, at *1-2.

3927. 1989 Del. Ch. LEXIS 156, at *6-7, 1989 WL 133625, at *2-3.

The court held that the challenged bylaw "on its face, does not appear to offend the letter or the spirit of the Delaware General Corporation Law" because the bylaw did nothing more than provide "for the orderly and efficient administration of the consent solicitation process."[3928] The challenged bylaw, according to the court, therefore could be distinguished from the bylaws invalidated by the Delaware Supreme Court in *Datapoint* and *Prime Computer* because the bylaws in those cases had "the effect of preventing the consummation of shareholder action by consent for an arbitrary period of time not reasonably related to the orderly functioning of corporate democracy."[3929] Nothing in the bylaw challenged in *Authorized Distribution*, the court stated, "impedes a stockholder's right to initiate a consent solicitation. Nor does it thwart the consummation or implementation of a stockholder consent solicitation action."[3930]

Due to "hotly disputed" factual issues surrounding the "intentions and motivations" of the directors in *Authorized Distributions*, however, the court concluded that it could not predict the outcome of litigation concerning the challenged bylaw with the confidence necessary to decide the pending motions for a preliminary injunction and/or summary judgment.[3931] The shareholder soliciting consents, the court also held, was not likely to suffer irreparable harm by the denial of injunctive relief because the record date fixed in accordance with the challenged bylaw provision was one day before the date on which the shareholder was permitted by Securities and Exchange Commission regulations to begin disseminating his consent solicitation materials to other shareholders.[3932]

The Delaware Court of Chancery in *In re Damon Corp. Stockholders Litigation*[3933] similarly refused to preliminarily

---

3928. 1989 Del. Ch. LEXIS 156, at *8-9, 13, 1989 WL 133625 at *3-4.

3929. 1989 Del. Ch. LEXIS 156, at *14, 1989 WL 133625, at *4.

3930. 1989 Del. Ch. LEXIS 156, at *11, 1989 WL 133625, at *4.

3931. 1989 Del. Ch. LEXIS 156, at *22-25, 1989 WL 133625, at *6-7.

3932. 1989 Del. Ch. LEXIS 156, at *25, 1989 WL 133625, at *7.

3933. [1988-1989 Transfer Binder] Fed. Sec. L. Rep. (CCH) (continued...)

enjoin bylaw amendments—adopted after the appearance of an
unwanted bidder—providing what the court described as "a reasonable mechanism for the setting of a record date to determine who is
a shareholder entitled to give effective written consent" and requiring 60 days notice prior to submitting a board nomination.[3934]
The court concluded that the shareholders challenging these bylaw
amendments had failed to show a reasonable probability of success
on the merits of their claim and had failed to articulate any irreparable harm.[3935] The court's opinion does not refer to any scheduled shareholders meeting that would be affected by the challenged
bylaw amendments.[3936]

   *f. ITT's Staggered Board Bylaw. Hilton Hotels Corp. v. ITT
Corp.*[3937] involved a classified board adopted as part of a restructuring plan announced by ITT Corporation in July 1997 in response
to a $55 per share tender offer by Hilton Hotels Corporation for all
shares of ITT stock and a proxy contest by Hilton seeking to
replace ITT's board. ITT's plan called for a self-tender offer by
ITT for approximately 26 percent of its shares at a price of $70 per
share and the splitting of ITT into three new entities: (1) ITT
Destinations, consisting of ITT's hotel and gaming business, which
represented approximately 93 percent of ITT's assets, (2) ITT
Education Services, consisting of ITT's technical schools, and (3)
ITT World Directories, consisting of ITT's European Yellow Pages
Division.[3938] The board of directors of ITT Destinations would

---

3933. (...continued)
¶ 94,040 (Del. Ch. Sept. 16, 1988).
      3934. *Id.* at 90,873.
      3935. *Id.*
      3936. *See International Banknote Co. v. Muller*, 713 F. Supp. 612,
624 (S.D.N.Y. 1989) (*Damon* "does not suggest that the provision was
aimed at a specific annual meeting or even that plaintiff had indicated an
intention to submit an alternative slate of directors at the next annual
meeting").
      3937. 978 F. Supp. 1342 (D. Nev. 1997).
      3938. *Id.* at 1344; Brinkley & Lipin, *ITT Plans to Split into Three
Companies: Firm to Take on New Debt, Buy Back Stock in Move to
Thwart Hilton Offer*, Wall St. J., July 17, 1997, at A3.

consist of the same members as ITT's current board. The new ITT Destinations board, unlike the current ITT board, however, would be a classified board divided into three classes, with each class of directors serving for a term of three years and one class being elected each year.[3939] An 80 percent shareholder vote would be required to repeal the classified board, to remove directors without cause, or to repeal the 80 percent requirement to remove directors without cause.[3940] Shortly after ITT's announcement of its restructuring plan, Hilton increased its tender offer price for all shares to $70 per share—the same amount ITT was offering for 26 percent of its stock.[3941]

"[C]ritical to the Court's analysis," ITT sought to implement the July restructuring plan without obtaining shareholder approval and prior to its upcoming annual meeting, which ITT's board had postponed from May until November after Hilton had announced its tender offer and proxy contest.[3942] The "dispositive issue presented in this case," the court stated, was whether an incumbent board "in the face of a hostile takeover attempt" may "entrench itself by effectively removing the right of the corporation's shareholders to vote on who may serve on the board of the corporation."[3943]

Nevada law governed, and the court looked to Delaware case law for guidance.[3944] The court "fully endorse[d]" Delaware precedents, including the *Unocal Corp. v. Mesa Petroleum Co.*[3945] and *Blasius Industries, Inc. v. Atlas Corp.*[3946] doctrines.[3947] Under *Unocal*, the court stated, two questions must be considered:

---

3939. 978 F. Supp. at 1344.

3940. *Id.*

3941. *Id.* at 1345.

3942. *Id.* at 1344; *Hilton Hotels Corp. v. ITT Corp.*, 962 F. Supp. 1309 (D. Nev.), *aff'd mem.*, 116 F.3d 1485 (9th Cir. 1997) (discussed in Chapter III, Section H 1 b).

3943. 978 F. Supp. at 1346.

3944. *Id.* at 1345-46.

3945. 493 A.2d 946 (Del. 1985).

3946. 564 A.2d 651 (Del. Ch. 1988).

3947. *See* Chapter III, Sections A 2 & 5.

"1) Does ITT have reasonable grounds for believing a danger to corporate policy and effectiveness exists? 2) Is the response reasonable in relation to the threat?"[3948] Under *Blasius*, the court continued, a third question must be considered: "If it is a defensive measure touching on issues of control, the court must examine whether the board purposefully disenfranchised its shareholders, an action that cannot be sustained without a compelling justification."[3949]

With respect to the first prong of *Unocal*, the court held that ITT had failed to demonstrate any threat to corporate policy or effectiveness. This aspect of the court's decision is discussed earlier in this Chapter.[3950] With respect to *Blasius*, the court held that the "primary purpose" of ITT's restructuring plan was to disenfranchise ITT's shareholders.[3951] The court reached this determination on the basis of the following six factors, none of which were dispositive but that "collectively . . . eliminate all questions of material fact"[3952]:

- *Timing*. The court described the timing of the plan as "transparent."[3953] The court explained that "all aspects" of ITT's plan "were formulated against the backdrop of Hilton's tender offer and proxy contest," the plan "was not announced until well after Hilton's initial tender offer," and "this major restructuring of ITT was announced and to be implemented in a little over two months" and was "designed to take effect less than two months before the annual meeting was to be held at which shareholders would have the opportunity to vote on an annually elected rather than a classified board."[3954]

---

3948. 978 F. Supp. at 1347.
3949. *Id.*
3950. *See* Chapter III, Section A 2 c (ii).
3951. 978 F. Supp. at 1348-49.
3952. *Id.* at 1349.
3953. *Id.*
3954. *Id.*

- *Entrenchment*. The court stated that "ITT and its advisors recognized from the outset that they were vulnerable because they did not have a staggered board of directors," and ITT's directors "appoint[ed] themselves to new, more insulated positions," with at least seven of ITT's eleven directors "avoiding the shareholder vote that would otherwise occur" at ITT's next annual meeting.[3955] This new staggered board comprised of incumbent directors, the court stated, "supports the conclusion" that ITT's plan was "primarily designed to entrench the incumbent board."[3956]

- *Stated Purpose*. The court stated that ITT's claim that it wanted "to avoid market risks and other business problems" was not a "credible justification" for not seeking shareholder approval of its restructuring plan.[3957] According to the court, "such vague generalizations do not approach the required showing of a reasonable justification other than entrenchment for the board's action."[3958]

- *Benefits*. The court acknowledged that it "may be true" that "there are economic benefits" to ITT's restructuring plan and the adoption of a classified board for ITT Destinations.[3959] The court held, however, that the "benefits of a plan infringing on shareholder voting rights do not remedy the fundamental flaw of board entrenchment."[3960]

- *Effect of Classified Board*. The court stated that the classified board provision in ITT's restructuring plan "absolutely precluded" ITT's shareholders from electing a majority of the directors nominated by Hilton for

---

3955. *Id.*
3956. *Id.*
3957. *Id.*
3958. *Id.*
3959. *Id.*
3960. *Id.*

election at ITT's 1997 annual meeting.[3961] This
effect, the court stated, was inconsistent with ITT's
earlier argument that a delay of the corporation's annual
meeting from May to November "would afford shareholders additional time to inform themselves and more
fully consider the implications of their vote for directors."[3962] ITT's position was "particularly anomalous," the court added, because "when ITT previously
split the company in 1995, it sought shareholder
approval."[3963] The court observed that although
"shareholder approval may not be absolutely required
to split ITT now anymore than it was in 1995, the fact
that the ITT board decided to subject the 1995 split of
the company to a shareholder vote" provided "strong
evidence" that the "primary purpose" of ITT's attempt
to implement its 1997 restructuring plan prior to ITT's
1997 annual meeting was to entrench the incumbent
ITT board.[3964]

- *Failure to Obtain an IRS Opinion.* The court also relied
  upon ITT's determination not to seek an Internal Revenue Service opinion concerning the tax consequences of
  ITT's restructuring plan. The court explained that it
  was "doubtful" ITT could obtain such an opinion
  before ITT's annual meeting, and that "ITT's counsel
  conceded that there is no binding precedent on point
  and that the issue was not free from doubt."[3965] The
  court stated that "obtaining a tax opinion from the
  Internal Revenue Service may not be mandatory," but
  "ITT's failure to seriously consider obtaining such an
  opinion provides additional evidence that ITT's primary

3961. *Id.*
3962. *Id.*
3963. *Id.*
3964. *Id.* at 1350.
3965. *Id.*

intention" in implementing its restructuring plan "was to impede the shareholder franchise."[3966]

In sum, the court concluded that "the structure and timing" of ITT's restructuring plan and its classified board provision for ITT Destinations was preclusive and "leaves no doubt that the primary purpose" for implementing the plan before ITT's annual meeting was "to impermissibly impede the exercise of the shareholder franchise by depriving shareholders of the opportunity to vote to re-elect or to oust all or as many of the incumbent ITT directors as they may choose at the upcoming annual meeting. It has as its primary purpose the entrenchment of the incumbent ITT board."[3967] The court held that there was no "compelling justification" for the infringement of the shareholder franchise that would occur if ITT's restructuring plan were implemented without a shareholder vote before ITT's upcoming annual meeting, and enjoined ITT from implementing the plan before ITT's annual meeting.[3968] The court added that "[i]f a majority of the incumbent ITT board is re-elected after a fully-informed and fair shareholder vote, the board will be free to implement any business plan it chooses so long as that plan is consistent with ITT's charter and by-laws, and governing law."[3969]

*g. Other Shark Repellent Bylaw Decisions.* Several additional decisions involving other types of shark repellent bylaw provisions are worth noting.

In *Treco, Inc. v. Land of Lincoln Savings & Loan,*[3970] a federal court construing Illinois law upheld a board's amendment of the corporation's bylaws in response to a threat of a contest for control (1) to add a provision stating that directors could be removed only for cause and by a 75 percent shareholder vote, and (2) to change the vote required in order for shareholders to amend

---

3966. *Id.*
3967. *Id.* at 1351.
3968. *Id.*
3969. *Id.*
3970. 749 F.2d 374 (7th Cir. 1984).

the corporation's bylaws from 50 percent to 67 percent.[3971] The court explained that

> (1) the directors reasonably believed the West Coast threat was serious, (2) the threat's implementation would be detrimental to Lincoln and its shareholders, (3) the defendants' amendments were adopted primarily to defend against the threat and on advice of counsel after consideration of alternatives, and (4) the directors' action was a reasonable exercise of business judgment.[3972]

The Delaware Court of Chancery denied a motion for a preliminary injunction in *American International Rent A Car, Inc. v. Cross*,[3973] a case involving a bylaw amendment eliminating a prior bylaw restriction upon any one shareholder owning more than 12,500 shares of the corporation's stock.[3974] The purpose of the bylaw amendment was to facilitate a sale of 273,500 shares to the corporation's existing shareholders in order to address financial difficulties faced by the corporation.[3975] The board had a "good faith belief that immediate action was necessary" and that "the stock sale was of paramount importance" to the corporation due to the corporation's financial difficulties.[3976] A special shareholders meeting was called to vote on this bylaw amendment, but at the meeting questions were raised concerning the need for the bylaw amendment and stock sales.[3977] One of the corporation's directors described the meeting as "rowdy" and "out of control."[3978] When the shareholders meeting recessed for lunch a special meeting of the board was convened and at that board meeting the board voted to adopt the bylaw on its own.[3979] The court stated that "[t]he record at this point does not establish whether, in light of the

---

3971. *Id*. at 375.
3972. *Id*. at 378 (citations omitted).
3973. 9 Del. J. Corp. L. 144 (Del. Ch. May 9, 1984).
3974. *Id*. at 145.
3975. *Id*. at 146.
3976. *Id*. at 146, 148.
3977. *Id*. at 146.
3978. *Id*.
3979. *Id*.

events of the morning, the Board members believed the stockholders would have voted down the proposed amendment," but that it was "reasonable to infer that the Board was, at least, concerned about the opposition expressed by some of the stockholders during the morning session."[3980]

The court held that the plaintiff in the case had "not met its burden of rebutting the presumption of the business judgment rule," and that it is not "a per se breach of fiduciary duty" for a board "to act in a manner which it may believe is contrary to the wishes of a majority of the company's stockholders."[3981] The court stated that "it would be expected that the stockholders' opposing views be given due consideration by the Board," but "I do not believe that stockholder opposition automatically overrides the other factors that the Board considers in exercising its business judgment."[3982] The court emphasized that if a majority of shareholders disapproved of the board's action "several recourses were, and continue to be, available to them," including "vot[ing] the incumbent directors out of office," "caus[ing] a special meeting of the stockholders to be held for the purpose of amending the bylaws and, as part of the amendment, they could remove from the Board the power to further amend the provision in question."[3983]

The Delaware Court of Chancery in *American Pacific Corp. v. Super Food Services, Inc.*[3984] granted a preliminary injunction enjoining a shareholders meeting at which shark repellent charter amendments were to be voted upon. The amendments, which were adopted following a repurchase of shares that increased an unwanted shareholder's holdings above 5 percent, included a supermajority voting provision and excluded all 5 percent or more shareholders from voting on any proposed alteration of this supermajority voting provision.[3985] The court rejected the corpora-

---

3980. *Id*. at 147.
3981. *Id*.
3982. *Id*.
3983. *Id*. at 148-49.
3984. 8 Del. J. Corp. L. 320 (Del. Ch. Dec. 6, 1982).
3985. *Id*. at 322-23, 324.

tion's contention that it sought nothing more than a supermajority voting provision and to "mak[e] it more difficult for holders of large stock blocks to amend the supermajority provision out of existence."[3986] Even if this were true, the court reasoned, it still was "troubling" that this was accomplished "by excluding, indeed disregarding, the vote of people who own 5% or more of the corporate stock."[3987] "At the least, in this particular context," the court stated, "such a proposition appears unjust."[3988] The court also found that the proxy statement advising shareholders of the vote on these amendments contained false statements concerning the proposed amendment, and that a supplemental proxy statement, "for whatever it is worth," had been mailed too late to be received by a large percentage of the corporation's shareholders.[3989]

In *Stroud v. Grace*,[3990] the Delaware Supreme Court reversed a preliminary injunction granted by the Court of Chancery enjoining enforcement of a bylaw governing the process by which board nominations could be made by shareholders. The bylaw required that a nomination of a candidate for the corporation's board be submitted 14 days prior to the shareholder meeting at which the vote would be taken and contain "information establishing such nominee's fulfillment of any qualification requirements set forth in the Corporation's Certificate of Incorporation, and such additional information with respect to such person as the Board of Directors may reasonably request."[3991] The bylaw also required a determination by the incumbent board at the shareholders' meeting (or the presiding officer at the meeting) with respect to "whether such person has met the qualification requirements."[3992] The Court of Chancery stated that these bylaw provisions "precluded the shareholders from knowing exactly what information to include

---

3986. *Id.* at 324.
3987. *Id.*
3988. *Id.*
3989. *Id.* at 323-24.
3990. 606 A.2d 75 (Del. 1992).
3991. *Id.* at 94.
3992. *Id.*

in their notice of nomination."[3993] Because of the requirement
that nominations and supporting information be submitted 14 days
before a shareholder meeting, the court continued, these bylaw provisions "gave the directors unfettered discretion to disqualify the
shareholders' candidates without recourse."[3994]

The Supreme Court described these possibilities as "hypothetical abuse," and held that the Court of Chancery had erred by
invalidating the bylaw upon this basis. The Supreme Court relied
upon the fact that the names of plaintiffs' nominees to the board
had been presented to the corporation's shareholders for a vote, and
had been "overwhelmingly rejected" by the shareholders.[3995] The
court stated that "every valid by-law is always susceptible to potential abuse," and that "[t]here was no basis to invoke some hypothetical risk of harm rather than an examination of the board's proven,
and entirely proper, conduct."[3996]

The Delaware Court of Chancery in *USACafes v. Office*[3997]
denied a motion for a preliminary injunction seeking to enjoin a
bylaw amendment requiring a 75 percent shareholder vote in order
to increase the size of the corporation's board and was adopted
after a potential acquiror had announced an intent to increase the
board's size from 7 directors to 16 directors and to elect new directors by means of a consent solicitation.[3998] The court stated that
the harm threatened by the bylaw was speculative and that "if consents are obtained from more than 50% but less than 75% of the
stockholders," "a prompt determination from the Court on the
validity of the contested bylaw amendments" could be
obtained.[3999]

---

3993. *Id*. at 95.
3994. *Id*.
3995. *Id*. at 95-96.
3996. *Id*. at 96.
3997. 11 Del. J. Corp. L. 1034 (Del. Ch. Oct. 28, 1985).
3998. *Id*. at 1036.
3999. *Id*. at 1039-40.

The Delaware Court of Chancery in *Highland Capital, Inc. v. Longview Fibre Co.*[4000] similarly denied a motion for a preliminary injunction without reaching the merits of a challenge to a bylaw amendment. The challenged bylaw amendment in this case required 90 days notice of any shareholder resolution to be presented at an annual meeting.[4001] This bylaw was challenged in connection with a meeting at which shareholders were to vote upon a merger of the corporation into a wholly-owned subsidiary incorporated under the law of Washington. The merger, according to the shareholder who brought this case, was intended to entrench the corporation's directors because the subsidiary's certificate of incorporation, unlike the parent's certificate of incorporation, provided for directors having staggered terms and who could not be removed except for cause.[4002] The court declined to "express a view concerning the validity" of the bylaw.[4003] The court reasoned as follows:

> [I]f one were to assume that that bylaw had not been adopted, plaintiff would as a practical matter be in an identical situation now. It received notice of the proposed merger in a timely way in December.
>
> An attempt to oust the incumbent board might (absent the 90 day bylaw) be a response that one might consider. Assuming, however, that one could marshal enough votes to oust the board, such a campaign to oust the board would be unnecessary, because plaintiff could instead launch a contest to defeat the proposal. That contest would be unaffected by the 90 day bylaw. Indeed, the principal path for stockholders who oppose a plan such as that proposed by defendants is to vote against it. Nevertheless, plaintiff has not been able to move quickly enough to conduct a proxy contest to defeat the proposal. How then can the existence of the 90 day notice provision which affects matters such as proxy contests to replace a board be thought material to the vote on the proposed merger? In my opinion, it cannot. Such matters as might be

---

4000. 16 Del. J. Corp. L. 325 (Del. Ch. Jan. 22, 1990).
4001. *Id.* at 327.
4002. *Id.* at 327-28.
4003. *Id.* at 332-33.

affected by the 90 day bylaw provision appear at this time to be entirely speculative and unable to support the relief requested.[4004]

Another Delaware Court of Chancery decision worthy of note is *Steinkraus v. GIH Corp.*[4005] The *GIH* court denied a motion to dismiss an action challenging a bylaw amendment requiring a majority vote of all outstanding shares of the corporation's stock in order to elect directors. The court explained that the amendment had been adopted after an action to compel a shareholder meeting had been filed and at a time when one shareholder could prevent trusts holding two-thirds of the corporation's stock from voting but could not control the votes of these trusts if the trusts voted, and that the complaint alleged "director action designed entirely to have the effect of precluding an effective vote"—a fact alleged to require "justification."[4006] Because the case arose in the context of a motion to dismiss, the court did not reach the corporation's contention that the bylaw amendment could be justified because if, as the plaintiff contended, the bylaw prevented the election of directors and thus perpetuated the incumbent board in office indefinitely, then "Delaware law provides a remedy in the power of the Court of Chancery under Section 226 of the General Corporation Law to appoint a custodian."[4007]

*h. Statutory Restrictions.* Charter and bylaw shark repellent provisions also have been struck down by the courts where they conflict with statutory provisions. In *Georgia-Pacific Corp. v. Great Northern Nekoosa Corp.,*[4008] for example, a federal court construing Maine law preliminarily enjoined enforcement of supermajority charter and bylaw provisions requiring the vote of 75 percent of the corporation's shareholders in order to remove directors. The court explained that Maine's corporation law statute specifically permitted removal of directors by the vote of only 67

---

4004. *Id.* at 333.

4005. 1991 Del. Ch. LEXIS 8, 1991 WL 3922 (Del. Ch. Jan. 16, 1991).

4006. 1991 Del. Ch. LEXIS 8, at *14, 1991 WL 3922, at *5.

4007. 1991 Del. Ch. LEXIS 8, at *13-14, 1991 WL 3922, at *5.

4008. 731 F. Supp. 38 (D. Me. 1990).

percent of a corporation's shareholders, or by a lesser vote if provided for in the corporation's charter.[4009] The court rejected the corporation's contention that the 67 percent statutory provision did not preclude a requirement of a greater majority than 67 percent, and held that another statutory provision generally authorizing charter or bylaw provisions that require a vote greater than a majority (including a unanimous vote) "cannot be read as providing license for corporations to bypass the Act's specific provisions."[4010]

The *Georgia Pacific* court also enjoined enforcement of charter and bylaw provisions establishing a 90 day notice requirement for nominating candidates for election as directors following the removal of directors at a shareholders meeting. This 90 day requirement, the court explained, conflicted with a statutory provision stating that new directors could be elected at the same meeting that directors were removed from the board.[4011]

The Court of Chancery in *Phillips v. Insituform of North America, Inc.*[4012] similarly granted a preliminary injunction enjoining enforcement of bylaw amendments in the context of a corporation having Class A and Class B common stock that was "identical except that the holders of Class B are entitled to elect 2/3 of the board of directors of the Company."[4013] Prior to the events underlying this litigation, two directors were designated by Class A shareholders and five directors were designated by Class B shareholders, but five of the seven directors (all but two of the five directors designated by Class B shareholders) owned A rather than B stock.[4014] The challenged bylaw amendments were adopted shortly after the board learned that Class B shares had been placed in the hands of court-appointed receivers and at the same time that the board resolved to recommend shareholder approval of "a

---

4009. *Id.* at 39-40.
4010. *Id.* at 40-41.
4011. *Id.* at 41-42.
4012. 13 Del. J. Corp. L. 774 (Del. Ch. Aug. 27, 1987).
4013. *Id.* at 778.
4014. *Id.* at 779, 791 n.9.

merger that would have the effect of eliminating the B stock."[4015]
The bylaw amendments "did several significant things":

> First, they determine that a quorum of the board is present
> only when a majority of the two A directors are present.
> Second, they dictate that the board may act only with the
> concurrence of a majority of the two A directors. They
> constitute the A directors and the Chairman of the Board as
> an executive committee. This committee is given power to
> call meetings, jurisdiction over certain matters relating to
> officers and power to call shareholder meetings.[4016]

The court concluded that these bylaws likely would be found
invalid following a trial because they resulted in "a fundamental
shift in the allocation of power between the A shareholders and the
B shareholders" that was inconsistent with the corporation's charter, which granted a "special right to the B shareholders to designate the persons to fill a majority of board positions."[4017] The
court also concluded that these bylaws were invalid because they
were adopted as a defense against the exercise of power by the B
shareholders to vote their shares and "were designed to equip the A
class of stock with an effective veto over future board
action."[4018]

The court described the corporation's directors as "intense
partisans waging war against the Class B stockholders."[4019]
"Whether regarded as individual owners of Class A stock, as
office-holders acting pursuant to a plan to remove the supervising
power of control shares (with a concomitant entrenchment effect) or
simply as directors choosing to favor the A shares over the B
shares," the court stated, the board's "exercise of the legal power
to enact by-laws, in this setting, requires a specific justification."[4020] Here, the court stated, "no reasonable apprehension of
injury to legitimate corporate interests has been put forward that

---

4015. *Id.* at 781-83.
4016. *Id.* at 783.
4017. *Id.* at 791.
4018. *Id.*
4019. *Id.*
4020. *Id.* (footnote omitted).

would justify, in these circumstances, this exercise by the board of the power conferred on it by the charter to amend by-laws."[4021] Nor, the court added, "does it appear that any palpable corporate benefit was actually a motivating force for these amendments."[4022]

   *i. Hollywood Park: Must a Valid Bylaw be Waived Where Enforcement Would be Inequitable? Hubbard v. Hollywood Park Realty Enterprises, Inc.*[4023] addresses the propriety of injunctive relief requiring a board to waive an otherwise valid and equitable bylaw because subsequent events render enforcement of the bylaw inequitable. This case involved a bylaw requiring shareholders of Hollywood Park Realty Enterprises ("Realty") who intended to nominate candidates for election to Realty's board at an annual meeting to furnish specified information to the corporation "not less than 90 days in advance of that meeting" or, if less than 90 days notice is given of the meeting, on "the seventh day following the first public announcement" of the meeting date.[4024]

   Prior to the 90 day deadline, a 9.9 percent shareholder announced a proxy contest and provided the information required by the advance notice bylaw.[4025] Three weeks later, and after the 90 day deadline had passed, Realty's board and the 9.9 percent shareholder agreed (1) that the 9.9 percent shareholder would be included on the "management" slate of candidates to be voted upon at Realty's upcoming annual meeting, and (2) that the 90 day advance notice requirement would not be amended or waived in order to permit any other shareholder to make any nominations or proposals at the meeting.[4026] Five directors of Hollywood Park Operating Company ("Operating"), an affiliated "sister" corporation (the stockholders of the two corporations were essentially

---

4021. *Id.* at 791-92.
4022. *Id.* at 792.
4023. 17 Del. J. Corp. L. 238 (Del. Ch. Jan. 14, 1991).
4024. *Id.* at 245.
4025. *Id.* at 245-46.
4026. *Id.* at 246-47.

identical and the common shares of the two companies traded together as a unit, but the corporation's respective boards were different) responded by commencing a solicitation of proxies to elect their own slate of nominees to the Realty board. The Operating directors also filed an action seeking to enjoin enforcement of the 90 day advance notice bylaw.[4027]

The court acknowledged that previous cases decided by the courts had involved "'affirmative' board action that change[d] the rules of the game in the midst of an election contest" and not "conduct amounting simply to a board refusal or failure to change the rules at a stockholder's behest," but concluded that "the case-by-case development of the law governing fiduciary obligations . . . cannot be constrained by so facile a distinction."[4028] From a semantic and even legal viewpoint," the court explained, "'inaction' and 'action' may be substantive equivalents, different only in form."[4029] According to the court, "occasions do arise where board inaction, even where not inequitable in purpose or design, may nonetheless operate inequitably."[4030]

Against this backdrop, the court defined the issue before it to be whether the settlement agreement entered into by Realty's board and the 9.9 percent shareholder equitably obligated Realty's board to waive the advance notice bylaw, and thus rendered the Realty board's refusal to waive the bylaw requirement inequitable even though the bylaw was "facially valid and . . . equitable at the time it originally became applicable."[4031] Answering this question "yes", the court pointed to "the fundamental nature of the shareholders' right to exercise their franchise, which includes the right to nominate candidates for the board of directors," and stated that "board-created procedural rules" restricting this fundamental right may not unreasonably infringe upon the exercise of this right.[4032]

---

4027. *Id.* at 247-48.
4028. *Id.* at 256-57.
4029. *Id.* at 257.
4030. *Id.*
4031. *Id.* at 256.
4032. *Id.* at 258.

Thus, the court continued, "an advance notice by-law will be validated where it operates as a reasonable limitation upon the shareholders' right to nominate candidates for director," but "must, on its face and in the particular circumstances, afford the shareholders a fair opportunity to nominate candidates."[4033]

Here, the court concluded, the agreement reached by the Realty board with the 9.9 percent shareholder following the 90 day advance notice deadline represented a "material change of circumstances" that distinguished this case from cases in which "shareholders, unprovoked by any board action, unilaterally and belatedly changed their minds and decided to nominate a slate of candidates for director."[4034] The court continued:

> [T]his is a case where the Realty board itself took certain action, after the by-law nomination deadline had passed, that involved an unanticipated change of allegiance of a majority of its members. It was foreseeable that that shift in allegiance would result in potentially significant changes in the corporation's management personnel and operational changes in its business policy and direction. Such material, post-deadline changes would also foreseeably generate controversy and shareholder opposition. Under those circumstances, considerations of fairness and the fundamental importance of the shareholder franchise dictated that the shareholders be afforded a fair opportunity to nominate an opposing slate, thus imposing upon the board the duty to waive the advance notice requirement of the by-law. And that duty exists, even though concededly the Realty board has acted in good faith and took no steps overtly to change the electoral rules themselves.[4035]

The court added that "policy, as well as purely equitable, considerations also require this result."[4036] The court explained that the bylaw was intended to assure that "stockholders and directors will have a reasonable opportunity to thoughtfully consider nominations and to allow for full information to be distributed to

---

4033. *Id.*
4034. *Id.* at 260.
4035. *Id.*
4036. *Id.*

stockholders, along with the arguments on both sides."[4037] The court stated that "[u]nless the advance notice requirement is waived here, . . . there will be no 'arguments on both sides' for shareholders to consider," and that "adequate time for information and reflection . . . can be achieved by a modest adjustment in the date of the annual meeting, if needed."[4038] "For these reasons," the court concluded, "the policy underlying the shareholders' fundamental right to exercise their franchise significantly outweighs the policies favoring the continued enforcement of the by-law," and "[t]he harm caused to shareholders from enforcing the by-law will greatly outweigh its benefits."[4039]

The court accordingly granted a preliminary injunction directing the Realty board "to waive the advance notice by-law requirement so as to afford any shareholder who so desires a reasonable opportunity to nominate a dissident slate of candidates for election to the Realty board."[4040] The *Hollywood Parks* litigation was settled before an appeal could be heard, but two months later, in a different context, the Delaware Supreme Court stated in a footnote in *Alabama By-Products Corp. v. Neal*[4041] that "[t]he invocation of equitable principles to override established precepts of Delaware corporate law must be exercised with caution and restraint. Otherwise, the stability of Delaware law is imperiled."[4042] The court acknowledged that equitable concepts are "an important part of our jurisprudence," but cautioned that such concepts "should be reserved for those instances that threaten the fabric of the law, or which by an improper manipulation of the law, would deprive a person of a clear right."[4043] The Supreme Court repeated this admonition in another footnote one month later in *Staar Surgical Co. v. Waggoner*,[4044] stating that "we emphasize that our courts

---

4037. *Id.*
4038. *Id.* at 260-61.
4039. *Id.* at 261.
4040. *Id.*
4041. 588 A.2d 255 (Del. 1991).
4042. *Id.* at 258 n.1.
4043. *Id.*
4044. 588 A.2d 1130 (Del. 1991).

must act with caution and restraint when granting equitable relief in derogation of established principles of corporate law."[4045] Observers suggested that these footnotes in *Alabama By-Products* and *Staar Surgical* were a response by the Delaware Supreme Court to the Court of Chancery's decision in *Hollywood Park*.[4046] The Supreme Court repeated the point made in its *Alabama By-Products* and *Staar Surgical* footnotes a year later in *Stroud v. Grace*,[4047] stating that "[i]t is important that there be certainty in the corporation law. We emphasize that the Court of Chancery must act with caution and restraint when ignoring the clear language of the General Corporation Law in favor of other legal or equitable principles."[4048]

## 3.  Golden Parachute Severance Agreements

"Golden parachute" employment contracts guarantee a corporation's top officers "continued employment, payment of a lump sum, or other benefits in the event of a change of corporate ownership."[4049] These benefits typically are triggered by (1) a change in control—a term defined, for example, to include a tender offer for a specified percentage of the corporation's shares, a proxy solicitation opposed by management, or a change in the majority of the members of the board of directors during a specified period of time unless the new directors are nominated or approved by the persons serving as the corporation's directors at the beginning of the specified period—and/or (2) a termination of an executive's employment or some other substantial change in the executive's responsibilities or compensation following a change in control. Some corporations have adopted provisions triggered by a "potential change of control" and that require executives to remain with the corporation for

---

4045. *Id.* at 1137 n.2.

4046. *See Is Delaware Supreme Court's Provocative Footnote a Critique of Hollywood Park?*, Corporate Control Alert, Apr. 1991, at 2-3.

4047. 606 A.2d 75 (Del. 1992).

4048. *Id.* at 87.

4049. *Schreiber v. Burlington N., Inc.*, 472 U.S. 1, 3 n.2 (1985); *In re Forum Group, Inc.*, 82 F.3d 159, 162 (7th Cir. 1996).

a specified period of time following the period surrounding a potential change of control.[4050] Agreements of the type described in this paragraph are labeled "golden" because the compensation often is very lucrative for the executive.[4051]

Golden parachutes are intended to enable corporate managers to perform their duties without worrying about the effect of a change in control upon their livelihood. Golden parachutes, according to their proponents, compensate employees who face a high risk that their employment will be terminated arbitrarily following a change in control. This enables corporations to attract and retain executives who might otherwise be attracted by employment opportunities offering greater job security. Golden parachutes also are said to encourage objective evaluations of takeover bids by executives subject to possible dismissal or reduction of responsibility following a change in control. Golden parachutes also discourage successful acquirors from arbitrarily eliminating good existing management.[4052] Golden parachutes triggered by a potential change of control and that require that the recipient remain with the corporation for a specified period of time following the period sur-

---

4050. *See* Stern & Lublin, *Chrysler Has Bold New Idea–In Parachutes*, Wall St. J., July 12, 1995, at B1.

4051. *Koenings v. Joseph Schlitz Brewing Co.*, 377 N.W.2d 593, 598 (Wis. 1985).

4052. *See, e.g., International Ins. Co. v. Johns*, 874 F.2d 1447, 1462-66 (11th Cir. 1989); *Nault v. XTRA Corp.*, [1992 Transfer Binder] Fed. Sec. L. Rep. (CCH) ¶ 97,022, at 94,501 (D. Mass. July 9, 1992); *Gaillard v. Natomas Co.*, 208 Cal. App. 3d 1250, 1266-67, 256 Cal. Rptr. 702, 711-12 (Cal. Ct. App. 1989); *Royal Crown Cos. v. McMahon*, 359 S.E.2d 379, 381 (Ga. Ct. App. 1987), *cert. denied* (Ga. Sept. 8, 1987); *Worth v. Huntington Bancshares, Inc.*, 540 N.E.2d 249, 254 (Ohio 1989); *Koenings v. Joseph Schlitz Brewing Co.*, 368 N.W.2d 690, 696 (Wis. Ct. App.), *rev'd*, 377 N.W.2d 593 (Wis. 1985); 2 Robert H. Winter, Mark H. Stumpf & Gerard L. Hawkins, *Shark Repellents and Golden Parachutes: A Handbook for the Practitioner* § 1.2, at 430-30.1, 436 n.3 (1992); American Bar Association Section of Corporation, Banking and Business Law, Subcommittee on Executive Compensation, *Executive Compensation: A Road Map for the Corporate Advisor*, 40 Bus. Law. 219, 349, 354 (1987).

rounding a potential change of control provide incentive for executives to remain with the corporation during a potentially protracted contest for control and (no matter who wins) the difficult period immediately following the contest.[4053]

Critics of golden parachutes dispute these benefits and question the appropriateness of granting executives special benefits to encourage action already mandated by their fiduciary obligations to the corporation and its shareholders. Critics also suggest that rather than inducing executives to remain with the corporation during a contest for control, golden parachutes encourage executives to resign at the conclusion of the contest, perhaps without real cause, in order to collect the parachute's rewards. Golden parachute payments also have been criticized as a reward for corporate officers who through poor performance fail to maximize shareholder values and thus provoke an offer for the company by someone interested in installing a new management team.[4054]

Golden parachutes often are thought of as a defensive measure but in fact rarely are useful as a takeover defense. This is because the dollar amount of the benefits promised to executives typically is *de minimus* in comparison to the hundreds of millions or billions of dollars required to acquire many corporations.[4055]

---

4053. *See* Stern & Lublin, Wall St. J., July 12, 1995, at B1.

4054. *See, e.g.*, *International Ins.*, 874 F.2d at 1466-67; R. Winter, M. Stumpf & G. Hawkins § 1.4, at 436 n.3.

4055. *See International Ins.*, 874 F.2d at 1459 ("[c]ommentators cannot agree on whether golden parachutes are truly takeover defenses"); *Brown v. Ferro Corp.*, 763 F.2d 798, 802 n.3 (6th Cir.) ("[i]n her briefs and in oral argument on appeal appellant did not seriously contend that the 'golden parachute' agreements would have a deterrent effect on future take-over attempts"), *cert. denied*, 474 U.S. 947 (1985); *Moore Corp. v. Wallace Computer Servs., Inc.*, 907 F. Supp. 1545, 1556 (D. Del. 1995) (concluding that "the golden parachute component of Cronin's employment agreement was not adopted as a defensive measure" because the board "fully intended to adopt an employment agreement for Cronin, identical in all pertinent respects to that of Dimitriou, Cronin's predecessor, but for some reason failed to get around to it" until after an unwanted tender offer had been made, and because "such agreements are commonplace among

(continued...)

*a. Barriers to Judicial Review.* Procedural barriers often fore-close judicial consideration of the merits of golden parachute sever-ance agreements. Challenges to golden parachute agreements as breaches of fiduciary duty or waste usually must be brought in the form of a shareholder derivative action on behalf of the corporation because the alleged injury is to the corporation as a whole. As explained in Chapter IV, a plaintiff who ceases to be a shareholder generally looses his standing to maintain a derivative action.[4056] Accordingly, where a corporation enters into golden parachute sev-erance agreements and then, following an acquisition of the corpo-ration by another corporation, is merged out of existence, a share-holder who had commenced an action challenging the adoption of the golden parachute agreements prior to the merger loses standing to continue the action.[4057] The result may be different in "direct

---

4055. (...continued)
chief executives of major companies"); *Kramer v. Western Pac. Indus., Inc.*, 546 A.2d 348, 352 n.3 (Del. 1988) (stating that "the issues raised in this case do not involve the area of defensive tactics": "Although some may view 'golden parachutes' as a defensive measure, others view this method of compensation as more a form of insurance for managers. More-over, some commentators have argued that golden parachutes actually benefit shareholders because they reduce the personal incentive of target managers to systematically reject takeover bids.") (citations omitted); *Heineman v. Datapoint Corp.*, [1990-1991 Transfer Binder] Fed. Sec. L. Rep. (CCH) ¶ 95,664, at 98,115 (Del. Ch. Oct. 9, 1990) (dismissing alleged entrenchment cause of action based upon payments of $15 million to directors and officers in a $400 million corporation because "[p]roof of these facts could not support a final judgment" that the payments "would act as a material deterrent to either a proxy or consent contest (the form of contest the complaint alleges was to occur) or even to a cash tender offer"); Robert C. Clark, *Corporate Law* § 13.6.1, at 577 (1986); R. Winter, M. Stumpf & G. Hawkins § 1.4, at 436 n.3, 436.7-.8.

    4056. *See* Chapter IV, Sections A 1-2.

    4057. *See Kramer v. Western Pac. Indus., Inc.*, 546 A.2d 348, 354-55 (Del. 1988); *Lewis v. Anderson*, 477 A.2d 1040 (Del. 1984); *Penn Mart Realty Co. v. Perelman*, 13 Del. J. Corp. L. 369, 374-75 (Del. Ch. Apr. 15, 1987), *appeal dismissed*, 529 A.2d 772 (Del. 1987); *Bershad v. Hartz*, 13 Del. J. Corp. L. 210, 214-16 (Del. Ch. Jan. 29, 1987). *Contra*
(continued...)

attacks against a given corporate transaction (attacks involving fair dealing or fair price)" but it is not enough to allege only that excessive compensation payments by the corporation directly affected the price paid in the transaction.[4058]

Where the corporation has not been merged out of existence and remains a publicly held company, shareholder plaintiffs face another hurdle—the requirement in shareholder derivative actions that plaintiffs must make a pre-litigation demand upon the corporation's board of directors that allows the board to determine whether litigation would serve the best interests of the corporation.[4059] In some jurisdictions, the plaintiff also must make a demand upon the corporation's shareholders.[4060] The rules governing this pre-litigation demand requirement are discussed in Chapter IV.[4061]

Finally, even if a shareholder plaintiff is able to satisfy the standing and demand requirements, the court may determine that the claims are not ripe for judicial consideration because a change

---

4057. (...continued)
*Gaillard v. Natomas Co.*, 173 Cal. App. 3d 410, 219 Cal. Rptr. 74 (Cal. Ct. App. 1985).

4058. *Kramer*, 546 A.2d at 354, *quoted in Rand v. Western Airlines, Inc.*, [1989-1990 Transfer Binder] Fed. Sec. L. Rep. (CCH) ¶ 94,751, at 94,052 (Del. Ch. Sept. 11, 1989). *Compare, e.g., Kramer*, 546 A.2d at 352-54 (finding no direct attack on merger terms and thus holding that former shareholder had no standing to litigate challenged payments) *with Rand*, [1989-1990 Transfer Binder] Fed. Sec. L. Rep. (CCH) at 94,052 (finding direct attack on merger terms and thus holding that former shareholders had standing to litigate challenged payments).

4059. *See, e.g., Smachlo v. Birkelo*, 576 F. Supp. 1439, 1443-45 (D. Del. 1983); *Colonial Sec. Corp. v. Allen*, 1983 Del. Ch. LEXIS 393, at *13, 1983 WL 19788, at *4 (Del. Ch. Apr. 18, 1983); *Fisher v. Weitzen*, No. 28159/82, slip op. at 3 (N.Y. Sup. Ct. N.Y. Co. May 26, 1983).

4060. *Compare Wolgin v. Simon*, 722 F.2d 389, 391-94 (8th Cir. 1983) (demand upon shareholders required) *with Zimmerman v. Bell*, 585 F. Supp. 512, 514-16 (D. Md. 1984) (demand upon shareholders not required).

4061. *See* Chapter IV, Sections B 1-9 (demand on directors) and B 10 (demand on shareholders).

of control has not yet taken place and the challenged golden parachute has not yet been triggered. As stated by the Delaware Supreme Court in *Grimes v. Donald*,[4062] a case dismissing a challenge to a contract requiring a $20 million payment in the event of a corporate officer's termination under "possible future circumstances," "[s]uch a set of facts has not been pleaded, is not before this Court, is based on speculation, and is not ripe for adjudication."[4063] The dissenting judge in a Sixth Circuit decision reaching the same conclusion, *Brown v. Ferro Corp.*,[4064] noted that the combination of the ripeness and standing requirements "has the plain consequence of eliminating any opportunity" to challenge golden parachutes because shareholders are "barred by the ripeness doctrine from challenging the parachutes before an acquisition or merger, and barred by the statutory passage of corporate property rights from challenging the parachutes after the acquisition or merger."[4065]

*b. The Standard of Review.* As discussed in Chapter II, executive compensation agreements generally are tested by a "reasonableness" standard, and most courts evaluating reasonableness have utilized a business judgment rule or a waste standard.[4066] Courts reviewing golden parachute compensation agreements similarly examine various indicia of reasonableness, including the amount of compensation provided for in the agreement[4067] and whether the

---

4062. 673 A.2d 1207 (Del. 1996).

4063. *Id.* at 1214; *see also Brown v. Ferro Corp.*, 763 F.2d 798, 801-03 (6th Cir.), *cert. denied*, 474 U.S. 947 (1985); *Mills v. Esmark, Inc.*, 544 F. Supp. 1275, 1290-91 (N.D. Ill. 1982); *Fisher,* slip op. at 2; *cf. Zimmerman*, 585 F. Supp. at 514 ("although the plaintiffs are seeking, as part of their relief, that the Court declare the contracts invalid (a dispute which may not yet be justiciable), the plaintiffs are also seeking damages from the defendants for breach of fiduciary duty in approving the contracts, a claim separate and distinct from relief with regard to the validity of the contracts").

4064. 763 F.2d 798 (6th Cir.), *cert. denied*, 474 U.S. 947 (1985).

4065. *Id.* at 803-04 (Merritt, J., dissenting).

4066. *See* Chapter II, Section B 2 g.

4067. *See International Ins. Co. v. Johns*, 874 F.2d 1447, 1467-68
(continued...)

parachute is triggered by a change in control itself or whether either termination of the executive or a substantial diminution in his job responsibilities or compensation also is required.[4068] As in

---

4067. (...continued)
(11th Cir. 1989); *Nault v. XTRA Corp.*, [1992 Transfer Binder] Fed. Sec. L. Rep. (CCH) ¶ 97,022, at 94,500 (D. Mass. July 9, 1992); *WLR Foods, Inc. v. Tyson Foods, Inc.*, 869 F. Supp. 419, 421, 422-23, 426 (W.D. Va. 1994), *aff'd*, 65 F.3d 1172 (4th Cir. 1995), *cert. denied*, 516 U.S. 1117 (1996); *Buckhorn, Inc. v. Ropak Corp.*, 656 F. Supp. 209, 232-35 (S.D. Ohio), *aff'd mem.*, 815 F.2d 76 (6th Cir. 1987); *Gaillard v. Natomas Co.*, 208 Cal. App. 3d 1250, 1269, 256 Cal. Rptr. 702, 714 (Cal. Ct. App. 1989); *Hedberg v. Pantepec Int'l, Inc.*, 645 A.2d 543, 547-49 (Conn. App. Ct.), *cert. granted*, 648 A.2d 879 (Conn. 1994) (cert. petition later withdrawn); *Kramer v. Western Pac. Indus., Inc.*, 12 Del. J. Corp. L. 1087, 1090-91 (Del. Ch. Nov. 7, 1986); *Worth v. Huntington Bancshares, Inc.*, 540 N.E.2d 249, 255 (Ohio 1989); *Koenings v. Joseph Schlitz Brewing Co.*, 377 N.W.2d 593, 599-604 (Wis. 1985). *But see Tate & Lyle PLC v. Staley Continental, Inc.*, [1987-1988 Transfer Binder] Fed. Sec. L. Rep. (CCH) ¶ 93,764, at 98,585 (Del. Ch. May 9, 1988) (upholding agreement notwithstanding "particularly troublesome . . . totality of the parachute benefits"); *Royal Crown Cos. v. McMahon*, 359 S.E.2d 379, 381 (Ga. Ct. App. 1987) (refusing to apply reasonableness standard to the amount of the compensation provided for by the agreement because to do so would interfere with the parties' freedom to contract), *cert. denied* (Ga. Sept. 8, 1987).

4068. *See Buckhorn*, 656 F. Supp. at 232 (upholding severance benefits that required that executives be fired or constructively discharged); *id.* at 233, 234 (refusing to uphold severance benefits requiring only a change of control); *Natomas*, 208 Cal. App. 3d at 1259-60, 1269-72, 256 Cal. Rptr. at 707, 714-16 (reversing grant of summary judgment dismissing challenge to golden parachute agreements providing that executives could terminate their employment for any reason following a six month transition period); *Hedberg*, 645 A.2d at 547-49 (reversing a trial court's invalidation of golden parachute employment agreement, where the trial court erred in concluding that the agreement permitted a corporate official to terminate his employment and receive severance pay benefits simply upon a change of control; rather, the appellate court held, the agreement required "an affirmative action by the company, after the change in control, that adversely impacts . . . compensation or responsibilities"); *In re Damon Corp. Stockholders Litig.*, [1988-1989 Transfer

(continued...)

other business judgment rule cases, the courts have focused upon the presence or absence of disinterested director approval of the severance agreement[4069] and the care or lack of care exercised by the corporation's board in approving the agreement.[4070] Several courts have expressed a preference for severance agreements adopted before the corporation is threatened with a change of control,[4071] although some courts have noted the importance of a

---

4068. (...continued)
Binder] Fed. Sec. L. Rep. (CCH) ¶ 94,040, at 90,872 (Del. Ch. Sept. 16, 1988) (upholding agreement requiring recipient of severance payments to remain with the company for six months following a change of control). *But see International Ins.*, 874 F.2d at 1468-69 (upholding severance agreement providing for payment upon a change of control); *Royal Crown*, 359 S.E.2d at 381 (upholding severance agreement triggered by voluntary resignation following a change in control).

4069. *See International Ins.*, 874 F.2d at 1451 & n.6, 1468, 1469; *Ocilla Indus., Inc. v. Katz*, 677 F. Supp. 1291, 1298-99 (E.D.N.Y. 1987); *Damon*, [1988-1989 Transfer Binder] Fed. Sec. L. Rep. (CCH) at 90,872; *Staley*, [1987-1988 Transfer Binder] Fed. Sec. L. Rep. (CCH) at 98,585; *cf. XTRA*, [1992 Transfer Binder] Fed. Sec. L. Rep. (CCH) at 94,501 (denying motion for summary judgment on claims seeking enforcement of a golden parachute agreement on the ground that "[t]he numerous defensive measures undertaken by the former Board" permit an inference that the golden parachute "was part of an attempt by the old Board to entrench itself"). *But see Natomas*, 208 Cal. App. 3d at 1259-60, 1268-72, 256 Cal. Rptr. at 707, 713-16 (reversing grant of summary judgment dismissing challenge to golden parachute agreements notwithstanding approval of compensation committee consisting of five outside directors).

4070. *See WLR*, 869 F. Supp. at 422-23; *Ocilla*, 677 F. Supp. at 1298-99; *Natomas*, 208 Cal. App. 3d at 1271-72, 256 Cal. Rptr. at 715; *Staley*, [1987-1988 Transfer Binder] Fed. Sec. L. Rep. (CCH) at 98,585.

4071. *See Buckhorn*, 656 F. Supp. at 232-35 (evaluating severance agreement provisions discussed before appearance of potential acquiror pursuant to business judgment rule criteria, but evaluating provisions not considered until after appearance of potential acquiror pursuant to the standard established in *Unocal Corp. v. Mesa Petroleum Co.*, 493 A.2d 946 (Del. 1985) (discussed in Chapter III, Section A 2), with all of the former but only some of the latter surviving the court's scrutiny); *Bender v. Highway Truck Drivers & Helpers*, 598 F. Supp. 178, 189 n.16 (E.D.
(continued...)

prompt response by a corporation to concerns by executives about job security that arise after a contest for control has been started or threatened.[4072] No single factor or combination of factors is dispositive.

*c. Cases Upholding Golden Parachutes.* Courts construing the laws of Delaware, Florida, Georgia, New York, Ohio and Wisconsin have upheld golden parachute payments.

The Delaware decisions include *Tate & Lyle PLC v. Staley Continental, Inc.*[4073] and *In re Damon Corp. Stockholders Litigation.*[4074]

In *Tate & Lyle PLC v. Staley Continental, Inc.*,[4075] the court refused to grant a preliminary injunction enjoining golden parachute agreements. The court stated that "[c]ompensation decisions are generally the sole prerogative of the directors," and that "[e]ven when a compensation decision directly benefits directors, if the decision is approved by a committee of disinterested directors,

---

4071. (...continued)

Pa. 1984) ("'golden parachute' clauses . . . may be unenforceable if enacted with notice of an impending tender offer or during a hostile takeover battle"), *aff'd mem.*, 770 F.2d 1066 (3d Cir. 1985); *Natomas*, 208 Cal. App. 3d at 1266, 256 Cal. Rptr. at 712 ("parachutes enacted in the midst of takeover negotiations should be discouraged"); *Staley*, [1987-1988 Transfer Binder] Fed. Sec. L. Rep. (CCH) at 98,585 (upholding pursuant to *Unocal* test severance agreements adopted "in a good faith response to possible future hostile tender offer advances"); *cf. International Ins.*, 874 F.2d at 1459-60 (court applies business judgment rule standard of review rather than *Unocal* standard based upon a finding that the challenged compensation agreements were intended to retain a talented management group rather than as a takeover defense).

4072. *See Buckhorn*, 656 F. Supp. at 232; *Koenings*, 377 N.W.2d at 603-04.

4073. [1987-1988 Transfer Binder] Fed. Sec. L. Rep. (CCH) ¶ 93,764 (Del. Ch. May 9, 1988).

4074. [1988-1989 Transfer Binder] Fed. Sec. L. Rep. (CCH) ¶ 94,040 (Del. Ch. Sept. 16, 1988).

4075. [1987-1988 Transfer Binder] Fed. Sec. L. Rep. (CCH) ¶ 93,764 (Del. Ch. May 9, 1988).

it is afforded the protection of the business judgment rule."[4076]
The outside directors who approved the parachutes, according to
the court, "seem to have shown that the plans were adopted in a
good faith response to possible future hostile tender offer
advances."[4077] This fact, the court found, created a "reasonable
probability that the directors' action in adopting the plans is
immune from further judicial scrutiny pursuant to the business judgment rule."[4078] The court reached this decision notwithstanding
its conclusion that both "the totality of the parachute benefits"—a
sum the court described as at least $20.3 million—and provisions in
the agreements reimbursing the beneficiaries for a 20 percent federal excise tax were "particularly troublesome."[4079]

The court in *In re Damon Corp. Stockholders Litigation*[4080]
also refused to grant a preliminary injunction enjoining golden
parachute agreements. The agreements that were challenged in this
case were approved by a compensation committee consisting of four
independent directors.[4081] The court stated that the actions of a
compensation committee consisting of independent directors are
"*prima facie* subject to the protections of the business judgment
rule" and may not be second-guessed by a court unless the plaintiffs can "show that the independent directors were primarily motivated by entrenchment motives or otherwise breached their duty of
loyalty or care."[4082]

A subsequent Delaware Court of Chancery decision, *Hills
Stores Co. v. Bozic*,[4083] states that *Staley* and *Damon* stand for
the proposition that "[w]hen a board provides severance benefits for
a defensive purpose, its action is subject to enhanced scrutiny"

---

4076. *Id.* at 98,585.

4077. *Id.*

4078. *Id.*

4079. *Id.* at 98,582-83, 98,585; *see also* Chapter III, Section G 3 e
(discussing federal excise tax referred to by the court).

4080. [1988-1989 Transfer Binder] Fed. Sec. L. Rep. (CCH)
¶ 94,040 (Del. Ch. Sept. 16, 1988).

4081. *Id.* at 90,872.

4082. *Id.*

4083. 23 Del. J. Corp. L. 230 (Del. Ch. Mar. 25, 1997).

under the *Unocal Corp. v. Mesa Petroleum Co.*[4084] standard.[4085] According to the *Hills Store* decision, *Staley* and *Damon* do not stand for the proposition that the business judgment rule governs determinations of this type.[4086]

The Eleventh Circuit, construing Florida law in *International Insurance Co. v. Johns*[4087] upheld severance agreements providing for the payment of bonuses to key executives if the executives remained with the corporation during a five year period or if there was a change of control during that five year period.[4088] The court, in the context of a dispute between a corporation and its insurer regarding the insurer's liability for $600,000 of $4,000,000 in payments pursuant to these parachutes that were returned by the recipients to the corporation in order to settle a shareholder derivative action, rejected the insurer's contention that the golden parachutes constituted illegal personal profits that were not covered by the corporation's insurance policy.[4089]

The court explained that the agreements had been adopted by a board committee that included a majority of disinterested directors, that the directors on the committee had sought to insure the retention of key members of management who had enjoyed "monumental success" in past years, and that the intended services had been performed with the corporation receiving the intended benefits.[4090] The court acknowledged that the agreements' provisions did not require that the covered executives be terminated in order to collect benefits and did not include a set-off clause that would take into account the possibility of continued work or immediate re-employment after the change in control, but concluded that it could not "in our hindsight" "second guess" the committee's predictions

4084. 493 A.2d 946 (Del. 1985).
4085. *See* Chapter III, Section A 2.
4086. 23 Del. J. Corp. L. at 238 n.4.
4087. 874 F.2d 1447 (11th Cir. 1989).
4088. *Id.* at 1451.
4089. *Id.* at 1452, 1455-56.
4090. *Id.* at 1451 & n.6, 1462-63, 1468, 1469.

regarding the displacement costs that would be suffered by the executives in the event of a change of control.[4091]

The Georgia Court of Appeals in *Royal Crown Cos. v. McMahon*[4092] reached the same result in a case involving a severance agreement providing that an executive would receive one year's salary as severance pay in the event of termination or resignation following a change of control.[4093] Following a change of control, the executive resigned but the corporation refused to pay the amount due under the agreement.[4094] The court stated that it was "unpersuaded" by the corporation's "attempt, largely without legal support, to defeat this otherwise enforceable severance agreement simply because it is contingent upon a change in corporate control."[4095] The court rejected the argument that golden parachute agreements are tainted by a conflict of interest favoring management beneficiaries to the detriment of shareholders. To the contrary, the court reasoned, golden parachutes protect shareholders "by inducing the continued employment" of an executive "during a time of uncertainty when he might otherwise have been distracted by concerns for his own financial security to seek employment elsewhere."[4096] The court declined to apply a reasonableness test to the amount of the compensation provided for by the severance agreement on the ground that to do so would interfere with the parties' freedom to contract.[4097]

A trial court in New York in *Silverman v. Schwartz*[4098] granted a motion to dismiss a complaint challenging an $18 million golden parachute payment by Loral Corporation to Loral's former chairman and chief executive officer, Bernard L. Schwartz. The payment followed a merger of Loral and Lockheed Martin Corpora-

---

4091. *Id.* at 1468-69.

4092. 359 S.E.2d 379 (Ga. Ct. App. 1987), *cert. denied* (Ga. Sept. 8, 1987).

4093. *Id.* at 380.

4094. *Id.* at 381.

4095. *Id.*

4096. *Id.*

4097. *Id.*

4098. N.Y.L.J., Mar. 17, 1997, at 27 (N.Y. Sup. Ct. N.Y. Co.).

tion, pursuant to which certain of Loral's assets were merged into Lockheed and other Loral assets were transferred to Loral Space, which then was spun off to Loral's common stockholders.[4099]

The court held that the shareholder who had commenced the action improperly challenged the transaction in the form of a shareholder derivative action of behalf of Loral Space. The claim asserted by the plaintiff, the court explained, did not involve any of the assets that had been spun off to Loral Space, and the plaintiff accordingly did not have standing to assert the claim.[4100] Even if the plaintiff did have standing, the court continued, "dismissal of the complaint would still be warranted, because the $9.1 billion tender offer resulted in a change of control within the contemplation of Mr. Schwartz' employment agreement with Loral. Mr. Schwartz, upon the happening of that event, was entitled as of right under his employment contract to the remaining monetary value of that contract. Plaintiff points to nothing that would have entitled or permitted the directors of Loral to force Mr. Schwartz to disgorge that right."[4101]

The Ohio Supreme Court in *Worth v. Huntington Bancshares, Inc.*[4102] held that a decision to enter into a golden parachute agreement guaranteeing a corporate officer continued employment or economic benefits following a change in control "is, like all other matters dealing with compensation of corporate executives, within the sound discretion of the corporation's board of directors."[4103] A decision of this type, the court stated, "most certainly" is "not void as against public policy."[4104] The court, however, affirmed a trial court finding that the employee in the case "did not resign because he in good faith determined that his status and responsibilities had diminished" following a takeover.[4105] As

---

4099. *Id.*
4100. *Id.*
4101. *Id.*
4102. 540 N.E.2d 249 (Ohio 1989).
4103. *Id.* at 255.
4104. *Id.*
4105. *Id.* at 254.

a result, the court concluded, benefits could not be collected under the terms of the agreement.[4106]

The trial court's opinion, *Orin v. Huntington Bancshares, Inc.*,[4107] had examined claims by two Huntington Bancshares employees that they had resigned from their positions on the basis of good faith determinations that their status and responsibilities had diminished following a change in control. The first of these employees had been an executive vice president who served on the board of directors and had been regarded as the number three executive in the company's hierarchy. The second of these employees— and the only one of the employees whose case reached the Supreme Court—had been a petroleum engineer. The trial court upheld the executive vice president's claim[4108] and rejected the petroleum engineer's claim.[4109]

The Wisconsin Supreme Court used a different line of reasoning in *Koenings v. Joseph Schlitz Brewing Co.*[4110] to uphold a termination provision in a Joseph Schlitz Brewing Company employment contract negotiated during the course of friendly merger negotiations in order to allow key employees "to feel secure in their jobs over the course of the takeover negotiations."[4111] The termination provision provided that an attorney and assistant corporate secretary earning $41,000 per year could, in the event of a substantial reduction in his responsibilities, treat the reduction as a termination but continue receiving full salary for the duration of the two year agreement. One year into the contract the employee invoked this provision and accepted another position paying more money.[4112]

---

4106. *Id.*

4107. Nos. 61129 & 61394 (Ohio Ct. Common Pleas Sept. 30, 1986), *aff'd sub nom. Worth v. Huntington Bancshares, Inc.*, 1987 Ohio App. LEXIS 9827, 1987 WL 25694 (Ohio Ct. App. Nov. 25, 1987), *aff'd in part and rev'd in part*, 540 N.E.2d 249 (Ohio 1989).

4108. *Id.*, slip op. at 4-14, 18-22.

4109. *Id.* at 14-18, 22-24.

4110. 377 N.W.2d 593 (Wis. 1985).

4111. *Id.* at 595-96.

4112. *Id.* at 596.

The court upheld the employment contract on the ground that the stipulated damages clause was reasonable under "the totality of the circumstances."[4113] The court reasoned as follows:

> [O]ffering the term contract with the stipulated damages clause was a method of purchasing employee loyalty during a time of employee uncertainty. Schlitz brewery operations conceivably could have been interrupted during the negotiation period if key employees had left Schlitz's employ. Rather than taking such a risk, Schlitz satisfied its need for greater corporate loyalty and lower employee attrition through the vehicle of a stipulated damages clause. The key employees' risk of salary and status loss was theoretically diminished, loyalty increased, and attrition decreased through the stipulated damages component of the contract.[4114]

The court added:

> It is conceivable that Schlitz could have purchased corporate loyalty by increasing the salaries of key employees, thereby increasing the employees' opportunity costs for leaving Schlitz. However, Schlitz may have felt that the least expensive method to purchase such loyalty was through the stipulated damages mechanism. The former method would require perhaps significant salary increases to seventy employees; the latter would require payment of the stipulated amount only upon a breach of a given contract.[4115]

The court explicitly rejected a lower court's holding that golden parachute employment contracts must include mitigation of damages provisions that take into account salary and benefits gained in subsequent employment.[4116] The court stated that the business judgment rule was "unnecessary to support our determination that the stipulated damages clause is reasonable under the totality of the circumstances."[4117] The court rejected the lower court's holding that

---

4113. *Id.* at 604.

4114. *Id.*

4115. *Id.* at 604 n.12.

4116. *Id.* at 599; *Koenings v. Joseph Schlitz Brewing Co.*, 368 N.W.2d 690, 698 (Wis. Ct. App.), *rev'd*, 377 N.W.2d 593 (Wis. 1985).

4117. 377 N.W.2d at 599.

the business judgment rule does not apply "to tactics such as golden parachutes" as "premature and wholly unwarranted."[4118]

An intermediate appellate court in Connecticut in *Hedberg v. Pantepec International, Inc.*[4119] reversed a trial court finding that an employment agreement entered into during a proxy contest was not reasonable in relation to the threat posed by a change of control. The appellate court noted the trial court's reasoning that

> according to the terms of the agreement, "if the pending proxy contest resulted in the election of Levinson's board, Hedberg was not obligated to provide services other than for a one month period after giving notice, and the corporation was obligated to pay severance pay for up to twenty-three months. Since the terms of the agreement entitled Hedberg to the same compensation and benefits for twenty-three months whether or not he chose to continue to work for Pantepec, the agreement was not reasonably calculated to achieve the continuity that director Hansen testified was the reason for its creation. Instead, the agreement protected Hedberg, an officer and director, at the expense of the corporation without even attempting to secure the stated advantage of continuity and expertise for the company."[4120]

The appellate court held that this ruling by the trial court was erroneous because the corporate official who was the beneficiary of the agreement could not terminate his employment and receive severance pay benefits upon a change of control.[4121] Rather, the appellate court held, the agreement required "an affirmative action by the company, after the change in control, that adversely impacts . . . compensation or responsibilities."[4122] The case was remanded for a new trial.[4123]

---

4118. *Id.;* 368 N.W.2d at 698.

4119. 645 A.2d 543 (Conn. App. Ct.), *cert. granted,* 648 A.2d 879 (Conn. 1994) (cert. petition later withdrawn).

4120. *Id.* at 547-48.

4121. *Id.* at 548-49.

4122. *Id.* at 549.

4123. *Id.*

*d. Cases Enjoining or Questioning Golden Parachutes.* The leading decision enjoining or questioning golden parachute agreements is *Gaillard v. Natomas.*[4124] In *Gaillard,* an intermediate appellate court in California reversed a grant of summary judgment dismissing a shareholder challenge to a series of golden parachute termination agreements on the ground that the directors' adoption of the agreements raised triable issues of fact. The termination agreements were approved by the corporation's compensation committee, which consisted of five outside directors, after the terms of a friendly merger between the corporation and a bidder that previously had made an unwanted tender offer had been concluded.[4125] The agreements provided that certain executives, some of whom already were entitled to golden parachute benefits, could terminate their employment within six months of the merger for "good reason" or after six months for any reason. Each agreement provided for a lump-sum payment equal in some cases to five times annual compensation, but the payment would be reduced in proportion to the length of time the recipient remained with the corporation following the six month period within which he could leave only for good reason.[4126] The key executives who were the beneficiaries of the agreements terminated their employment with the corporation shortly after the consummation of the merger and were paid a total of approximately $10 million. The court stated that "[t]he record supports the inference that the executives themselves created, at least in part, the 'good reason' for leaving."[4127]

The court held that the appropriateness of the reliance by the directors sitting on the compensation committee upon what the court found to be an attorney's conclusory representation during a two hour meeting that "continuity in management should be a concern of the . . . board and that the golden parachutes would serve that purpose" raised a question of fact that could not be decided in

---

4124. 208 Cal. App. 3d 1250, 256 Cal. Rptr. 702 (Cal. Ct. App. 1989).

4125. *Id.* at 1259-60, 256 Cal. Rptr. at 707-08.

4126. *Id.* at 1259, 256 Cal. Rptr. at 707.

4127. *Id.* at 1262, 256 Cal. Rptr. at 709.

the context of a summary judgment motion.[4128] The court stated its view that the agreements would not attract top-level management or secure objectivity in the face of a contest for control because (1) the agreements were entered into with executives who already worked for the company and who already had agreed to a friendly merger, (2) the terms of the agreements encouraged the executives to leave after six months by reducing their benefits in proportion to the length of time they remained with the company beyond six months, and (3) the agreements called for unreasonably high benefits.[4129] The court also noted that the drafting of the severance agreements by an attorney acting in accordance with the instructions of one of the recipients of the agreements supported an "inference of self-dealing which should have been investigated further."[4130]

The court acknowledged testimony that the purpose of the golden parachutes was to ensure a smooth six month transition period, and the court acknowledged that "a trier of fact might conclude that the compensation committee's reliance" upon counsel with respect to the sufficiency of this stated purpose "with no further inquiry" was "reasonable."[4131] The court also stated, however, that a trier of fact could "find that the evidence would reasonably support an inference to the contrary."[4132] The court reached the same conclusion with respect to the outside directors who were not on the compensation committee. The court stated that there was a triable issue of fact regarding the appropriateness of the directors' "total reliance" upon their colleagues on the compensation committee because "[t]he proposal of the golden parachutes here under somewhat suspicious circumstances, i.e., after the tender offer and in the midst of merger discussions, raise the question of whether these directors should have examined the golden parachutes more attentively."[4133]

---

4128. *Id.* at 1269, 256 Cal. Rptr. at 714.
4129. *Id.* at 1269-71, 256 Cal. Rptr. at 714-15.
4130. *Id.* at 1271, 256 Cal. Rptr. at 715.
4131. *Id.*
4132. *Id.*
4133. *Id.* at 1272, 256 Cal. Rptr. at 715-16.

Another California court issued a temporary restraining order blocking an initial payment of approximately $8 million of a reported $42 million golden parachute package for former Signal executives following a friendly merger with Allied in 1985. The case was settled prior to a ruling on plaintiff's motion for a preliminary injunction, with the former Signal executives reportedly agreeing to reduce the sum payable to them to $25 million.[4134] Litigation in Delaware challenging golden parachute agreements granted to Beatrice Foods executives also was settled. In that instance, a compensation package alleged to have been worth up to $63 million was reduced by approximately $25 million.[4135]

*Kramer v. Western Pacific Industries, Inc.*[4136] provides an example of a Delaware Court of Chancery decision that found "troublesome" the granting of two golden parachutes worth a total of $7 million the same day the board determined that the corporation was "in play."[4137] These termination agreements would be triggered if the corporation were acquired, and these agreements were granted notwithstanding the fact that the recipients both owned substantial amounts of the corporation's stock, had options to purchase additional shares at prices much lower than any likely tender offer price, and did not think that the payments were necessary to "induce them to obtain and consider proposals."[4138] Additionally, one of the recipients had no intention of remaining with the corporation after any acquisition, and the other was willing to remain with the corporation only if he was part of the acquisition group.[4139]

---

4134. Moore, *Business Grows Bolder In Giving Lucrative Golden Parachutes*, Legal Times, Mar. 24, 1986, at 1; Tracy, *Parachutes-A-Popping*, Fortune, Mar. 31, 1986, at 66; Work, *Are Golden Parachutes Turning Platinum?*, U.S. News & World Rep., Feb. 3, 1986, at 49.

4135. *In re Beatrice Co. Litig.*, 12 Del. J. Corp. L. 199, 207 (Del. Ch. Apr. 16, 1986), *aff'd*, 522 A.2d 865 (unpublished opinion, text available at 1987 Del. LEXIS 1036 and 1987 WL 36708) (Del. Feb. 20, 1987), *cert. denied*, 484 U.S. 898 (1987).

4136. 12 Del. J. Corp. L. 1087 (Del. Ch. Nov. 7, 1986).

4137. *Id.* at 1090.

4138. *Id.* at 1090-91.

4139. *Id.* at 1091.

On the basis of these facts, the court concluded that the plaintiff-shareholder had sustained his burden of showing a reasonable probability of success.[4140] A motion for a preliminary injunction was denied, however, due to the absence of irreparable injury.[4141] In *Bacine v. Scharffenberger*,[4142] another Delaware Court of Chancery decision denying a motion for a preliminary injunction, the court noted that its decision "in no way passed indirectly upon the propriety" of the "'golden parachute' benefits that will apparently be triggered in favor of City's board and management by shareholder approval of the very liquidation plan that has been proposed by City's board and management."[4143]

*Buckhorn, Inc. v. Ropak Corp.*,[4144] a federal court decision construing Delaware law, illustrates application of differing levels of judicial scrutiny by one court to a series of golden parachute agreements, with the presence or absence of a contest for control at the time of the board's consideration of each agreement determining the appropriate level of scrutiny.

The *Buckhorn* court began by upholding six "key employee" golden parachute agreements put into place by the board of Buckhorn, Inc. in response to an unwanted tender offer.[4145] Applying *Unocal Corp. v. Mesa Petroleum Co.*[4146] standard,[4147] the court held that the directors had a "good faith belief based upon reasonable grounds" that (1) the tender offer "posed a threat" to the corporation's key employees, and (2) the severance agreements were "reasonable in relation to the threat posed."[4148] The court explained that five of the six individuals who had received these severance agreements had relocated to facilitate long-range com-

---

4140. *Id.*

4141. *Id.*

4142. 10 Del. J. Corp. L. 603 (Del. Ch. Dec. 11, 1984).

4143. *Id.* at 610.

4144. 656 F. Supp. 209 (S.D. Ohio), *aff'd mem.*, 815 F.2d 76 (6th Cir. 1987).

4145. *Id.* at 217, 232.

4146. 493 A.2d 946 (Del. 1985).

4147. *See* Chapter III, Section A 2.

4148. 656 F. Supp. at 226-27, 232.

pany plans, and that these employees were concerned about the threat to their job security posed by a possible change of control.[4149] The court also pointed to the fact that these managers would be entitled to payments pursuant to the severance agreements only if they were fired or constructively discharged within twelve months after a change in control. Thus, the court reasoned, there was "no cost to the shareholders as long as the managers are allowed to retain their present position for one year after a change in control."[4150]

Also applying the *Unocal* standard, the court refused to uphold the adoption of new stock option plans (or the amendment of existing plans) for these employees that would vest upon a change of control. The court stated that the severance agreements discussed above had guaranteed these employees "employment or significant severance pay for up to one year following a change of control," and that issuing new stock options which would vest upon a change of control therefore did "little to add to the job security of these employees."[4151]

The court also considered a series of amendments to the employment contract of the company's chief executive officer, Richard P. Johnston.[4152] The court applied a business judgment rule analysis and upheld provisions granting stock options and a supplemental pension that had been discussed by the board prior to the announcement of an unwanted tender offer but that was not adopted until shortly after the tender offer was announced.[4153] The court concluded that consideration of these provisions was a response to events unrelated to the tender offer, including the board's previous decision to eliminate a pension plan for salaried employees and Johnston's previous determination, for tax reasons, to sell 230,000 shares of his shares of the corporation's stock to the corporation in exchange for the corporation's cancellation of an

---

4149. *Id.* at 232.
4150. *Id.*
4151. *Id.* at 233.
4152. *Id.* at 216-17.
4153. *Id.* at 233.

interest free loan that the corporation had made to him.[4154] The court held that the plaintiff had failed to satisfy its burden of showing that the directors who approved these benefits had been grossly negligent in concluding that a supplemental pension for Johnston, who was approaching retirement, was necessary.[4155]

By contrast, the court applied a *Unocal* analysis to the amendments to Johnston's employment agreement considered for the first time after the emergence of the bid for control.[4156] These amendments accelerated the vesting of Johnston's stock options and pension rights upon a change of control, added a severance pay provision entitling Johnston to receive the present value of future salary due to him in the event of a change in control, and extended Johnston's employment contract for six years.[4157] The court upheld the decision to accelerate the vesting of Johnston's stock options because the purpose of accelerating the options was to assure Johnston the right he would have if there were no change in control to exercise his options over time. The court stated that the tender offer "threatened to block Johnston from exercising his options," and there was "little else" the corporation's directors could do "to effectuate their initial purpose in granting Johnston the stock options" other than accelerate the options to vest upon a change of control.[4158]

The court, however, refused to uphold provisions allowing Johnston to accelerate his salary and pension benefits upon a change in control. The court explained that these amendments granted Johnston the right to benefits "at-will" following a change in control and thus increased the cost of an acquisition of the corporation without benefiting shareholders.[4159] The court stated that "[h]ad these amendments not been 'at-will,' but drafted more like the severance agreements for Buckhorn's six key employees, the Court

---

4154. *Id.* at 233-34.
4155. *Id.* at 234.
4156. *Id.*
4157. *Id.*
4158. *Id.*
4159. *Id.* at 235.

might take a different view."[4160] The court also stated that the corporation's directors had failed to demonstrate why the four years remaining on Johnston's existing contract did not provide adequate job security to encourage Johnston—who, as noted above, was approaching retirement—to stay with the corporation during troubled times.[4161]

*Nault v. XTRA Corp.*,[4162] another federal court decision construing Delaware law, denied a motion for summary judgment on claims seeking enforcement of a golden parachute severance agreement on the ground that "[t]he numerous defensive measures undertaken by the former Board" permit an inference that the golden parachute agreement "was part of an attempt by the old Board to entrench itself."[4163]

*Ocilla Industries, Inc. v. Katz*,[4164] a federal court decision construing New York law, found that "[s]erious questions" had been raised by the manner in which two golden parachute agreements had been adopted.[4165] The court noted that the only two individuals to speak to the attorney who drafted the agreements were the two beneficiaries of the agreements, and that these two individuals attended the board meeting at which the agreements were discussed and never left the meeting to allow the corporation's other directors to discuss the agreements outside of the presence of beneficiaries of the agreements.[4166] The court found that the totality of the circumstances surrounding the votes of the two directors who had approved the contracts and who were not beneficiaries of the contracts suggested that the review of the agreements by these two directors "was so 'shallow', and their approval so '*pro forma*', so lacking in even the "'reasonable diligence' [owed] in gathering and considering material information" as to be an inade-

---

4160. *Id.*

4161. *Id.*

4162. [1992 Transfer Binder] Fed. Sec. L. Rep. (CCH) ¶ 97,022 (D. Mass. July 9, 1992).

4163. *Id.* at 94,501.

4164. 677 F. Supp. 1291 (E.D.N.Y. 1987).

4165. *Id.* at 1298.

4166. *Id.*

quate performance of their fiduciary duty to . . . shareholders, even if reviewed under the 'business judgment' rule."[4167] A preliminary injunction was denied, however, due to the absence of irreparable injury.[4168]

Several additional courts not ruling upon the merits of golden parachute claims have expressed reservations similar to those stated in the cases discussed above. In *Schreiber v. Burlington Northern, Inc.*,[4169] the Third Circuit held that a corporation's failure to disclose the adoption of golden parachute agreements did not constitute a violation of Section 14(e) of the Securities Exchange Act of 1934.[4170] The court added, however, that its decision "by no means constitutes an endorsement of the conduct which the complaint attributes to the defendants."[4171] In *Brown v. Ferro Corp.*,[4172] one Sixth Circuit judge stated that he concurred with the court's finding that the case was not ripe for adjudication, but added his belief that it was "difficult to discern any advantage to shareholders in the broad benefits bestowed on certain corporate officials under the severance agreements in dispute."[4173]

*e. Legislation.* The Deficit Reduction Act of 1984 provides that payments made following a change of control that exceed three times the average compensation paid to the recipient over the preceding five year period are subject to a 20 percent non-deductible excise tax upon the recipient.[4174] The statute also provides that payments that exceed three times the average compensation paid over the five year period are not deductible by the corporation to the extent they exceed this limitation.[4175] This legislation was

---

4167. *Id.* at 1299 (quoting *Hanson Trust PLC v. ML SCM Acquisition Inc.*, 781 F.2d 264, 274 (2d Cir. 1986)).

4168. *Id.* at 1299-1300.

4169. 731 F.2d 163 (3d Cir. 1984), *aff'd on other grounds*, 472 U.S. 1 (1985).

4170. *Id.* at 165-66.

4171. *Id.* at 167.

4172. 763 F.2d 798 (6th Cir.), *cert. denied*, 474 U.S. 947 (1985).

4173. *Id.* at 803 (Wellford, J. concurring) (emphasis omitted).

4174. 26 U.S.C. § 280G.

4175. *Id.; see also* Department of the Treasury, Internal Revenue
(continued...)

intended to deter the granting of golden parachute severance agreements, but several of the cases discussed in the preceding sections of this Chapter[4176] suggest that the effect of the statute may have been to remove the stigma from parachute payments that fall within the limits established by the statute.[4177] The courts in *Buckhorn, Inc. v. Ropak Corp.*[4178] and *Worth v. Huntington Bancshares*[4179] expressly relied upon the fact that challenged severance payments were within the Deficit Reduction Act's limits as a factor demonstrating that the payments were reasonable in size.[4180] The court in *Gaillard v. Natomas Co.*[4181] similarly cited the Act's three year annual salary limit in support of its criticism of golden parachute agreements that promised benefits in excess of these limits.[4182] The Eleventh Circuit in *International Insurance Co. v. Johns*,[4183] a case construing Florida law, stated that "the 'three times' federal tax requirement should be a guiding factor . . . rather than an absolute rule" because "[c]onceivable corporate reasons could legitimize a golden parachute in excess of 'three times' annual salary."[4184]

---

4175. (...continued)
Service, *Golden Parachute Payments*, 26 C.F.R. Part 1; *Cline v. Commissioner*, 34 F.3d 480 (7th Cir. 1994) (holding that payments were excess golden parachute payments rather than simply compensation and/or bonus payments).

4176. *See* Chapter III, Sections G 2 b-d.

4177. *See* Tracy, *Parachutes A-Popping*, Fortune, Mar. 31, 1986, at 66.

4178. 656 F. Supp. 209 (S.D. Ohio), *aff'd mem.*, 815 F.2d 76 (6th Cir. 1987).

4179. 1987 Ohio App. LEXIS 9827, 1987 WL 25694 (Ohio Ct. App. Nov. 25, 1987), *aff'd in part and rev'd in part on other grounds*, 540 N.E.2d 249 (Ohio 1989).

4180. *Buckhorn*, 656 F. Supp. at 233; *Huntington Bancshares*, 1987 Ohio App. LEXIS 9827, at *81 n.11, 1987 WL 25694, at *30 n.11.

4181. 208 Cal. App. 3d 1250, 256 Cal. Rptr. 702 (Cal. Ct. App. 1989).

4182. *Id.* at 1270-71, 256 Cal. Rptr. at 715.

4183. 874 F.2d 1447 (11th Cir. 1989).

4184. *Id.* at 1462 n.30.

Adding to this unintended effect is the negotiation by some executives and corporations of golden parachutes exceeding the statutory restrictions, with the corporation committing itself to reimburse the executives for the excise tax imposed by the federal government.[4185] The court in *Tate & Lyle PLC v. Staley Continental, Inc.*[4186] described a provision of this type as "particularly troublesome."[4187] The court refused to grant a preliminary injunction enjoining the provision, however, because the outside directors who approved the parachutes "seem to have shown that the plans were adopted in . . . good faith."[4188]

Arizona and Minnesota have enacted statutes providing that a corporation may not "enter into or amend, directly or indirectly, agreements containing provisions, whether or not dependent on the occurrence of any event or contingency, that increase, directly or indirectly, the current or future compensation of any officer or director" during the course of any tender offer for the corporation's stock.[4189] The statutes do "not prohibit routine increases in compensation or other routine compensation agreements undertaken in the ordinary course of . . . business."[4190]

Securities and Exchange Commission Division of Corporation Finance no-action letters have required the inclusion in proxy materials of shareholder proposals prohibiting compensation payments that are contingent upon a merger or acquisition. These no-action letters distinguish compensation payments contingent upon a merger or acquisition from ordinary compensation issues concerning which shareholder proposals may be excluded for two reasons: (1) Internal

---

4185. *See* Wander & LeCoque, *Boardroom Jitters: Corporate Control Transactions and Today's Business Judgment Rule*, 42 Bus. Law. 29, 59 (1986); Moore, *Business Grows Bolder in Giving Lucrative Golden Parachutes*, Legal Times, Mar. 24, 1986, at 1.

4186. [1987-1988 Transfer Binder] Fed. Sec. L. Rep. (CCH) ¶ 93,764 (Del. Ch. May 9, 1988).

4187. *Id.* at 98,585.

4188. *Id.*

4189. Ariz. Gen. Corp. Law § 10-2705; Minn. Bus. Corp. Act § 302A.255(3).

4190. *Id.*

Revenue Code interpretations concerning "when payments are considered 'contingent' upon a change in ownership or control have assisted in differentiating 'golden parachute' payments from ordinary compensation arrangements," and (2) "public debate concerning potential anti-takeover, tax and legal implications of golden parachute arrangements reflect that such contingent arrangements increasingly are seen as raising significant policy issues."[4191]

*f. Employee Tin Parachutes.* Employee "tin parachutes," a variation of golden parachutes, cover a large number of a corporation's employees rather than a small number of the corporation's executives. Tin parachutes may serve valid corporate purposes such as employee compensation and promotion of employee morale and productivity. If the total compensation payable under the tin parachutes is substantial, then the parachutes may also deter hostile takeovers. Three decisions—*Tate & Lyle PLC v. Staley Continental, Inc.,*[4192] *GAF Corp. v. Union Carbide Corp.*[4193] and *WLR Foods, Inc. v. Tyson Foods, Inc.*[4194]—have refused to grant preliminarily injunctions enjoining tin parachute compensation plans. Two other decisions—*Minstar Acquiring Corp. v. AMF Inc.*[4195] and *Black & Decker Corp. v. American Standard, Inc.*[4196]—have granted preliminary injunctions enjoining tin parachute plans.

---

4191. TPI Enters., Inc., SEC No-Action Letter, 1990 SEC No-Act LEXIS 480, 1990 WL 286197 (S.E.C.) (Mar. 13, 1990); Crane Co., SEC No-Action Letter, 1990 SEC No-Act LEXIS 3, 1990 WL 286158 (S.E.C.) (Jan. 8, 1990); Transamerica Corp., SEC No-Action Letter, 1990 SEC No-Act LEXIS 46, 1990 WL 285806 (S.E.C.) (Jan. 10, 1990); *see also* Pittston Co., SEC No-Action Letter, 1990 SEC No-Act LEXIS 328, 1990 WL 286484 (S.E.C.) (Feb. 15, 1990) (similar language).

4192. [1987-1988 Transfer Binder] Fed. Sec. L. Rep. (CCH) ¶ 93,764 (Del. Ch. May 9, 1988).

4193. 624 F. Supp. 1016 (S.D.N.Y. 1985).

4194. 869 F. Supp. 419 (W.D. Va. 1994), *aff'd*, 65 F.3d 1172 (4th Cir. 1995), *cert. denied*, 516 U.S. 1117 (1996).

4195. 621 F. Supp. 1252 (S.D.N.Y. 1985).

4196. 682 F. Supp. 772 (D. Del. 1988).

In *Tate & Lyle PLC v. Staley Continental, Inc.*,[4197] the Delaware Court of Chancery denied a motion for a preliminary injunction seeking to enjoin tin parachutes providing that an employee terminated following a change in control, even for good cause, would be entitled to the greater of (1) one month's pay for each year of employment or (2) one month's pay for each $10,000 of annual salary.[4198] The potential cost of these benefits in the event of a change of control was estimated to be $3.5 million.[4199] The court stated that compensation payments generally are the sole prerogative of directors, and that the challenged compensation had been approved unanimously by a committee consisting of all of the corporation's outside directors.[4200] The court found that the directors "seem to have shown that the plans were adopted in a good faith response to possible future hostile tender offer advances and that the directors were not misinformed or uninformed and were not grossly negligent in adopting the plan."[4201] The court thus concluded that there was a "reasonable probability" that the directors' adoption of the plan was "immune from further judicial scrutiny pursuant to the business judgment rule."[4202]

In *GAF Corp. v. Union Carbide Corp.*,[4203] a federal court construing New York law denied a motion for a preliminary injunction seeking to enjoin an amendment to the corporation's retirement plan that would allow the corporation's board to allocate certain pension funds that had not yet vested to participating and retired employees in the event of an "unfriendly change of control."[4204] The court explained:

> The amendment does nothing more than allow the Board to treat the pensioners equitably and fairly in the manner and in

---

4197. [1987-1988 Transfer Binder] Fed. Sec. L. Rep. (CCH) ¶ 93,764 (Del. Ch. May 9, 1988).

4198. *Id.* at 98,582.

4199. *Id.*

4200. *Id.* at 98,585.

4201. *Id.*

4202. *Id.*

4203. 624 F. Supp. 1016 (S.D.N.Y. 1985).

4204. *Id.* at 1022.

the measure in which past negotiated transactions enabled the Board to do. Under friendly terms, the interests of employees can be ironed out on the bargaining table with equity to all sides. It was the Board's judgment, which appears entirely reasonable, that it was prudent to reserve to itself this power in the event of an unfriendly assault on control to prevent a takeover bidder from jeopardizing future appropriate and necessary increases of pension benefits by his use of the funds to finance a takeover. Labor, at whatever level, should not be victimized or go unrequited by control contests. It is entirely reasonable for a Board to take such steps as will assure workers against such a possibility arising from the necessity for financing the obligations incurred in a control contest.[4205]

The court in *WLR Foods, Inc. v. Tyson Foods, Inc.*[4206] reached the same conclusion with respect to severance agreements for corporate employees adopted at the same time that more lucrative golden parachutes for corporate officers were adopted.[4207] The court based its decision upon Virginia statutes providing that "[a] director shall discharge his duties . . . in accordance with his good faith business judgment of the best interests of the corporation,"[4208] and providing that this standard of conduct applies to "any action taken or not taken by directors" "with respect to any potential changes in control."[4209] In reaching this conclusion, the court stated that the directors "sought out and relied in good faith upon competent legal and financial advisors."[4210] The Fourth Circuit affirmed, without specifically discussing the board's decision to adopt severance agreements for corporate employees.[4211]

---

4205. *Id.*

4206. 869 F. Supp. 419 (W.D. Va. 1994), *aff'd*, 65 F.3d 1172 (4th Cir. 1995), *cert. denied*, 516 U.S. 1117 (1996).

4207. *Id.* at 421, 426.

4208. Va. Stock Corp. Act § 13.1-690; *see also* Chapter II, Section A 2 (discussing this statute).

4209. Va. Stock Corp. Act § 13.1-728.9; *see also* Chapter III, Section A 2 e (discussing this statute).

4210. 869 F. Supp. at 422.

4211. *See WLR Foods, Inc. v. Tyson Foods, Inc.*, 65 F.3d 1172

(continued...)

By contrast, in *Minstar Acquiring Corp. v. AMF Inc.*,[4212] a federal court applying New Jersey law granted a preliminary injunction enjoining employee pension parachute benefits adopted by AMF days after an unwanted tender offer had been commenced by Minstar. These benefits, which were conditioned upon a change in control within a six-month period, included a 20 percent increase in benefits accrued under a previously terminated retirement plan, and a doubling of the severance allowance for certain salaried employees.[4213]

The court concluded that the unwanted acquiror had raised a strong inference that the board's conduct was intended "not to benefit the employees but rather to solidify management's control."[4214] The court explained that AMF already had announced substantial staff reductions and that employees who already were scheduled to be terminated would receive twice as much in severance benefits if Minstar acquired control of the corporation than if Minstar did not acquire control.[4215] The court rejected AMF's contention that its increased severance benefits were needed to bring AMF in line with other companies. "If this was in fact the true justification," the court stated, "then conditioning the program on a change in control would be unnecessary."[4216]

A federal court construing Delaware law in *Black & Decker Corp. v. American Standard, Inc.*[4217] granted a preliminary injunction enjoining the amendment of a series of retirement plans and the creation of a new severance plan that together provided for the payment of $130 million in employee benefits following a change in corporate control.[4218] The court did not address the merits of the adoption of these benefits in and of themselves, but

---

4211. (...continued)
(4th Cir. 1995), *cert. denied*, 516 U.S. 1117 (1996).
    4212. 621 F. Supp. 1252 (S.D.N.Y. 1985).
    4213. *Id.* at 1255-56.
    4214. *Id.* at 1261.
    4215. *Id.*
    4216. *Id.*
    4217. 682 F. Supp. 772 (D. Del. 1988).
    4218. *Id.* at 776, 785-86.

focused instead upon the fact that the plans' definition of a change in control exempted a management and employee-backed recapitalization plan but not a competing tender offer.[4219] As discussed earlier in this Chapter, the court held that the directors' conduct triggered a duty under *Revlon, Inc. v. MacAndrews & Forbes Holdings, Inc.*[4220] to sell the company to the highest bidder, and that the $130 million advantage provided to the management and employee-backed recapitalization plan over the competing tender offer improperly placed the two bidders on unequal footing and thus constituted a breach of fiduciary duty.[4221]

Another decision, *Joy Manufacturing Corp. v. Pullman-Peabody Co.*,[4222] arose in the context of a decision on a shareholder's entitlement to an attorneys' fee award in an action challenging a pension parachute plan that was mooted by management's decision to sell the corporation. In this context, the court stated that "[c]ertainly a judicial challenge to the validity of such a scheme . . . would survive a . . . motion to dismiss."[4223] The court reasoned as follows:

> [T]he pension parachute could be found by a trier of fact to be a scorched earth plan which *when triggered* could not work to the benefit of the shareholders under any circumstance. Once the pension plan was activated by a so-called "Control Event," which under the plan included a hostile takeover *threat*, . . . the board could create the "Termination Event" which would thereafter result in "excess" pension fund monies being distributed to the pensioners so as thus to be unavailable to the unfavored acquiring entity. But, of course, these pension fund monies were assets of the corporation and its shareholders, and when the pension plan was triggered, those funds not only became unavailable to the hostile takeover entity, but also for all time to their rightful

---

4219. *Id.* at 776, 786.
4220. 506 A.2d 173 (Del. 1986).
4221. *See* Chapter III, Section A 3 c.
4222. 729 F. Supp. 449 (W.D. Pa. 1989).
4223. *Id.* at 457.

owners, the Joy shareholders, who incidentally, never were given the opportunity to vote on the plan.[4224]

A final decision, this one by the Delaware Court of Chancery in *Sutton Holding Corp. v. DeSoto, Inc.*,[4225] assumed but did not hold that provisions barring any amendment to the corporation's existing pension plans for a period of five years following a change in control constituted a breach of the duty of loyalty. The court stated that "[w]hen the . . . board injected this provision in the Company's pension plans, its dominant motivation was doubtlessly not to create a valuable economic right in plan beneficiaries," but rather to deter a change in control.[4226]

Massachusetts, Pennsylvania and Rhode Island have enacted legislation requiring "tin parachute" payments to employees terminated before or after a change of control. The Massachusetts statute provides for a payment equal to two weeks' pay for each completed year of service for any employee whose employment is terminated (1) during the period of time between an acquiror's acquisition of 5 percent of the corporation's stock and its acquisition of control or one year prior to the acquiror's acquisition of control, whichever is shorter, or (2) within two years after a transfer of control.[4227] The Pennsylvania statute provides for a payment equal to one week's pay for each completed year of service, up to a maximum of 26 weeks' pay, less any other severance payments made to the employee, for any employee terminated other than for willful misconduct within 90 days before (if the termination is pursuant to "an agreement, arrangement or understanding with the acquiror") or two years following a change of control.[4228] The Rhode Island statute is similar to the Massachusetts statute but only covers employees employed by the corporation for three or more years.[4229] A federal court has held that the Massachusetts statute

---

4224. *Id.*

4225. [1991 Transfer Binder] Fed. Sec. L. Rep. (CCH) ¶ 96,012 (Del. Ch. May 14, 1991).

4226. *Id.* at 90,064.

4227. Mass. Gen. Laws ch. 149, §§ 183(b), (c).

4228. Pa. Bus. Corp. Law §§ 2581, 2582(a).

4229. R.I. Gen. Laws §§ 28-7-19.2(b), (c), (d)(2).

impermissibly encroaches upon the federally controlled field of employee benefit plans implemented by the Employee Retirement Income Security Act ("ERISA") and therefore is preempted by ERISA.[4230]

g. *Funding Trusts*. Some corporations have established funding trusts, sometimes referred to as "rabbi trusts", that automatically and irrevocably fund compensation plans upon any change in control. In *Tate & Lyle PLC v. Staley Continental, Inc.*,[4231] the Delaware Court of Chancery preliminarily enjoined the funding of a trust that was intended to fund employee compensation plans within 10 days of a change in control, a term defined by the trust—in the court's words—as "(1) the hostile acquisition of more than 20% of Staley's stock; (2) the election of 20% or more of the members of Staley's Board without Board recommendation; or (3) stockholder approval of a plan of liquidation."[4232] The trust was financed by a $60 million letter of credit that cost the corporation $600,000 per year to maintain.[4233]

The court held that the directors who approved the trust's creation each had "a direct personal interest in one or another of the compensation plans to be funded."[4234] Accordingly, the court concluded, the creation of the trust was not protected by the business judgment rule.[4235]

The "most troublesome" of the plans, according to the court, was an "Outside Directors Retirement Plan" granting non-management directors an annual retainer upon retirement equal to $22,000 multiplied by the number of years the director had served on the corporation's board.[4236] This annual retirement retainer immedi-

---

4230. *See Simas v. Quaker Fabric Corp.*, 6 F.3d 849, 851-56 (1st Cir. 1993).

4231. [1987-1988 Transfer Binder] Fed. Sec. L. Rep. (CCH) ¶ 93,764 (Del. Ch. May 9, 1988).

4232. *Id.* at 98,582.

4233. *Id.*

4234. *Id.* at 98,586.

4235. *Id.*

4236. *Id.* at 98,585, 98,583.

ately and irrevocably would vest—costing the corporation at least $1.8 million—upon a change in control, a term defined for purposes of the Outside Directors Retirement Plan as "a tender offer for 10% or more of Staley's stock or 20% control of the voting stock or the nomination and election of hostile interests to 20% or more of Board membership."[4237] The court stated that the trust's protection of this plan "seriously taints the entire propriety" of the trust.[4238] The court explained that this plan "specifically benefits non-management directors upon a change of control" and was proposed to the full board by the corporation's compensation committee, which consisted of non-management directors.[4239] The court stated that "[t]his indicates a reasonable likelihood that the plan is not protected by the business judgment rule as it will, upon a change in control, immediately benefit the same directors who proposed its adoption."[4240] The court added its view that "[t]he use of the Funding Trust to fund the largesse to the non-management directors also on its face seems to serve no valid business purpose" because "[d]irectors have no right to expect to continue to be paid after the term of office for which they are elected by the stockholders expires."[4241]

The Delaware Court of Chancery in *Hills Stores Co. v. Bozic*[4242] denied a motion to dismiss a claim that the directors of Hills Stores Company breached their fiduciary duties by establishing and funding trusts to provide for the immediate payment of more than $30 million in severance benefits for six key executives and a consultant pursuant to employment agreements providing for these payments in the event of a change of control not approved by the corporation's board.[4243]

---

4237. *Id.* at 98,583.
4238. *Id.* at 98,585.
4239. *Id.*
4240. *Id.*
4241. *Id.*
4242. 23 Del. J. Corp. L. 230 (Del. Ch. Mar. 25, 1997).
4243. *Id.* at 236-37.

The employment agreements providing for these severance benefits had been adopted three days after Dickstein Partners, Inc. had commenced a consent solicitation and would be triggered by any change in control of Hills Department Stores Company, a regional retailer owned by Hill Stores that operated 156 stores. Claims that the adoption of those agreements constituted a breach of fiduciary duty previously had been the subject of settlement agreements and thus were not before the court.[4244] According to plaintiffs' complaint, the trust was created after the directors concluded that Dickstein Partners would succeed in electing a new slate of directors, who then would approve an offer by Dickstein Partners to purchase all shares of Hills Stores.[4245] At the same time that the funding trusts were established, the directors refused to approve Dickstein Partners' proposed change in control, and amended the employment agreements to provide for severance payments upon a change of control not just of Hills Department Stores but also Hill Stores itself. This change was made, the directors contended, "simply to correct a clerical error in the agreements."[4246] The creation and funding of the trusts caused Hills Department Stores to breach certain loan covenants and impair the relationships Hills Stores and Hills Department Stores Company had with these lenders.[4247]

The last business day before the results of the proxy contest were to be certified, the trustee was provided with a schedule of payments greater in several respects than provided for in the employment agreements, and on the day the results were certified the key executives who were the beneficiaries of the employment agreements resigned from their positions and received their severance benefits.[4248] Two weeks later, Dickstein Partners announced that it would not acquire (or seek to sell) Hills Stores stock due to the costs of the change of control.[4249]

---

4244. *Id.* at 236-37, 241.
4245. *Id.* at 237.
4246. *Id.* at 235-38.
4247. *Id.* at 236-37.
4248. *Id.* at 237.
4249. *Id.*

The directors contended that the terms of the employment agreements required that they not approve any proposed change in control that was the result of a proxy contest, and that as a result the decision not to approve the change of control was a proper exercise of business judgment.[4250] The court, however, held that this contract interpretation issue could not be decided in the context of a motion to dismiss.[4251]

The court continued, however, by holding that "[e]ven if the former directors' interpretation of the agreements is correct, or they had a good faith belief that it was, it is questionable how amending the agreements to apply to a change in control of Hill Stores or establishing trusts for the purpose of immediately paying the severance benefits were in the interest of the corporation."[4252] The court rejected the directors' contention that the amendment to the agreement simply corrected a clerical error as "a matter of proof that cannot be decided on the face of the complaint."[4253] The court also rejected the directors' contention that "it was surely proper to provide for the performance of the agreements" because "that does not answer the plaintiffs' allegation that establishing the trusts harmed the interest of the corporation by causing it to breach covenants and depriving the new board of an opportunity to persuade the key executives to remain with the corporation."[4254]

The court added that the challenged acts were defensive in nature, and thus "it is likely that some or all of the defendants' conduct at issue in this case will be subject to enhanced scrutiny" pursuant to the *Unocal Corp. v. Mesa Petroleum Co.*[4255] doctrine.[4256] This enhanced scrutiny, the court stated, "cannot be given on a motion to dismiss for failure to state a claim upon which

---

4250. *Id.*
4251. *Id.* at 238.
4252. *Id.*
4253. *Id.*
4254. *Id.*
4255. 493 A.2d 946 (Del. 1985).
4256. 23 Del. J. Corp. L. at 238; *see also* Chapter III, Section A 2 (discussing *Unocal* doctrine).

relief can be granted."[4257] Additionally, the court stated, "[e]ven
if the business judgment presumption applies," the plaintiffs' allegation that the directors acted for an improper purpose would be sufficient to survive the motion to dismiss.[4258] The court reasoned
as follows with respect to this conclusion:

> Directors must always act in what they believe in good faith
> to be in the best interest of the corporation. The plaintiffs
> allege that the defendants acted in bad faith. It may turn out
> that the plaintiffs' proof does not overcome the presumption
> that the former directors acted in good faith. But on a motion
> to dismiss, the court assesses the legal sufficiency of the
> complaint, not the probability of success. The plaintiffs have
> pled sufficient factually specific allegations to create a fair
> inference that in reacting to their defeat by the Dickstein
> Partners' nominees the former directors might have been
> motivated by concerns other than the best interest of the cor-
> poration and its stockholders.[4259]

## 4.   Antitrust and Other Regulatory Defenses

A board also may seek to thwart an unwanted contest for control by acquiring assets that create antitrust or other regulatory
problems for the potential acquiror. Such acquisitions have been
upheld pursuant to the business judgment rule when they serve
valid business purposes and are not motivated predominantly by
efforts to entrench incumbent management.

Thus, for example, in *Panter v. Marshall Field & Co.*,[4260]
the Seventh Circuit held that the business judgment rule protected a
board decision to acquire stores in an area where an unwanted
offeror already owned and operated a store. The court explained
that the business judgment rule imposes the "fairly stringent
burden" on plaintiffs of demonstrating that defeating an unwanted

---

4257. 1997 Del. Ch. LEXIS 47, at *9, 1997 WL 153823, at *3; *see
also* 1997 Del. Ch. LEXIS 47, at *3, 1997 WL 153823, at *1 (same);
Chapter III, Section A 2 a (discussing this aspect of *Unocal* doctrine).

4258. 1997 Del. Ch. LEXIS 47, at *10, 1997 WL 153823, at *3.

4259. 1997 Del. Ch. LEXIS 47, at *10-11, 1997 WL 153823, at *3
(footnote omitted).

4260. 646 F.2d 271 (7th Cir.), *cert. denied*, 454 U.S. 1092 (1981).

offer was "the sole or primary purpose" rather than just "among the motives of the board in entering the transactions."[4261] This burden was not met here, the court concluded, because uncontroverted evidence demonstrated that the acquisitions were "reasonable and natural" and in accordance with the board's long-range plans.[4262] The same result was reached in *Frank B. Hall & Co. v. Ryder System, Inc.*,[4263] another case involving an acquisition having "a recognized economic purpose" apart from defeating a contest for control.[4264]

By contrast, in *Royal Industries, Inc. v. Monogram Industries, Inc.*,[4265] the court concluded that "[s]ince the attempted acquisition of Sar by Royal was made solely to thwart Monogram's proposed tender offer, it serves no proper corporate purpose, is a waste of Royal's corporate assets, is calculated to serve the interest of Royal's Management to the exclusion or detriment of Royal shareholders, and should, therefore, be enjoined."[4266]

Antitrust litigation against an unwanted bidder also is a potential weapon in a corporation's defensive arsenal, although the potency of this weapon varies substantially in different jurisdictions. This is because the courts are divided regarding the standing of a corporation to seek injunctive relief against an unwanted bidder under Section 7 of the Clayton Act, which bars acquisitions where the effect "may be substantially to lessen competition, or tend to create a monopoly."[4267] Corporations also have lobbied regulatory agencies such as the Federal Trade Commission "in an effort to use the antitrust laws as a shield against a possible hostile takeover."[4268]

---

4261. *Id.* at 297.

4262. *Id.; see also id.* at 291.

4263. No. 82 C 0092 (N.D. Ill. July 12, 1982) (available on LEXIS without file number).

4264. *Id.*, slip op. at 8.

4265. [1976-1977 Transfer Binder] Fed. Sec. L. Rep. (CCH) ¶ 95,863 (C.D. Cal. Nov. 29, 1976).

4266. *Id.* at 91,138.

4267. 15 U.S.C. § 18.

4268. *In re Unitrin, Inc. Shareholders Litig.*, 1994 Del. Ch. LEXIS

(continued...)

The Second Circuit has upheld the standing of corporations to challenge unwanted acquisition attempts as violations of the Clayton Act in *Consolidated Gold Fields PLC v. Minorco, S.A.*[4269] and *Grumman Corp. v. LTV Corp.*[4270] The court explained in *Consolidated Gold Fields* that standing turns on whether what the corporation "is about to lose is an injury of the type the antitrust laws were intended to prevent, not on why [the corporation] has decided to complain of this injury."[4271] It therefore is irrelevant, the Second Circuit reasoned in *Consolidated Gold Fields*, whether a corporation's motivation for the litigation is to protect competition or to protect the job security of its management.[4272] The court added that to deny standing under these circumstances "would substantially impair enforcement of the antitrust laws to protect against anticompetitive takeovers."[4273] District courts in the Fifth and Seventh Circuits have reached the same result.[4274] The Sixth Cir-

---

4268. (...continued)
187, at *24, 1994 WL 698483, at *8 (Del. Ch. Oct. 13, 1994), *rev'd on other grounds sub nom. Unitrin, Inc. v. American Gen. Corp.*, 651 A.2d 1361 (Del. 1995).
    4269. 871 F.2d 252 (2d Cir.), *cert. denied*, 492 U.S. 939 (1989).
    4270. 665 F.2d 10 (2d Cir. 1981).
    4271. 871 F.2d at 259.
    4272. *Id.*
    4273. *Id.* at 260; *see also Square D Co. v. Schneider S.A.*, 760 F. Supp. 362, 364-65 (S.D.N.Y. 1991) (following *Consolidated Gold Fields*); *Square D Co. v. Schneider S.A.*, No. 91 Civ. 2928 (LBS), Tr. op. at 24-25 (S.D.N.Y. May 9, 1991) (noting that the ability of a corporation that is the target of an unwanted offer to raise antitrust claims "is meaningful only if the target is given a chance to have its claims judicially resolved," and refusing to enjoin the corporation's postponement of its annual meeting until after an antitrust action the corporation had commenced was resolved).
    4274. *See A. Copeland Enters., Inc. v. Guste*, 1989-2 Trade Cas. (CCH) ¶ 68,712, at 61,744-45 (E.D. La. Nov. 28, 1988); *Laidlaw Acquisition Corp. v. Mayflower Group, Inc.*, 636 F. Supp. 1513, 1516-17 (S.D. Ind. 1986); *Gearhart Indus., Inc. v. Smith Int'l, Inc.*, 592 F. Supp. 203, 211 n.1 (N.D. Tex.), *aff'd in part, rev'd in part and modified in part on other grounds*, 741 F.2d 707 (5th Cir. 1984); *Whittaker Corp. v. Edgar*,
(continued...)

cuit addressed the merits of a Clayton Act claim by a corporation facing an unwanted offer in *Marathon Oil Co. v. Mobil Corp.*[4275] without specifically discussing the question of standing. Several (but not all) of these decisions, it should be noted, pre-date the United States Supreme Court's 1986 decision in *Cargill, Inc. v. Montfort of Colorado, Inc.*,[4276] which deals with the standing of a competitor of a corporation facing an unwanted offer to assert Clayton Act claims. The *Cargill* case is discussed below.

Standing has been denied by the First, Fourth, Fifth and Tenth Circuits in *A.D.M. Corp. v. Sigma Instruments, Inc.*,[4277] *Burlington Industries, Inc. v. Edelman*,[4278] *Anago, Inc. v. Tecnol Medical Products, Inc.*[4279] and *Central National Bank v. Rainbolt*,[4280] and by district courts in the Third, Sixth, Ninth and Eleventh Circuits.[4281]

---

4274. (...continued)
535 F. Supp. 933, 950 (N.D. Ill. 1982), *aff'd mem.*, Nos. 82-1305 & 82-1307 (7th Cir. Mar. 5, 1982); *Frank B. Hall & Co. v. Ryder Sys., Inc.*, No. 82 C 0092, slip op. at 4 (N.D. Ill. July 12, 1982) (available on LEXIS without file number); *Chemetron Corp. v. Crane Co.*, 1977-2 Trade Cas. (CCH) ¶ 61,717, at 72,931-32 (N.D. Ill. Sept. 8, 1977).

4275. 669 F.2d 378 (6th Cir. 1981), *cert. denied*, 455 U.S. 982 (1982).

4276. 479 U.S. 104 (1986).

4277. 628 F.2d 753, 754 (1st Cir. 1980).

4278. [1987 Transfer Binder] Fed. Sec. L. Rep. (CCH) ¶ 93,339 (4th Cir. June 22, 1987) (affirming district court decision reported at 666 F. Supp. 799, 804-06 (M.D.N.C. 1987), "for the reasons sufficiently set forth in the district court's memorandum opinion").

4279. 976 F.2d 248, 250-51 (5th Cir. 1992), *cert. dismissed*, 510 U.S. 985 (1993).

4280. 720 F.2d 1183, 1187 (10th Cir. 1983).

4281. *See Moore Corp. v. Wallace Computer Servs., Inc.*, 907 F. Supp. 1545, 1565-67 (D. Del. 1995); *Hayden v. Bardes Corp.*, 1989-1 Trade Cas. (CCH) ¶ 68,477, at 60,620 (W.D. Ky. Feb. 27, 1989); *Burnup & Sims, Inc. v. Posner*, 688 F. Supp. 1532, 1534-35 (S.D. Fla. 1988); *Carter Hawley Hale Stores, Inc. v. The Limited, Inc.*, 587 F. Supp. 246, 248-50 (C.D. Cal. 1984).

These courts have explained that the injury allegedly suffered by a corporation that is merged into another corporation in violation of the Clayton Act includes harm such as the loss of independent decision making authority, loss of customers, loss of employees and loss of trade secrets. According to these courts, this injury is the result of the change in corporate control caused by the merger and not the result of a potential lessening of competition or some other anti-competitive effect of the merger.[4282] "In other words, these sequelae can occur with the consequence of any merger, even those that are not violative of the Clayton Act, and are divorced from any considerations that less competition may exist in the open market."[4283]

These courts also have reasoned that a corporation that is merged into another corporation in violation of the Clayton Act cannot show injury caused by a lessening of competition because after the merger the corporation becomes part of the very entity that it alleges will have the competitive advantage.[4284] The corporation and its shareholders thus "ultimately benefit from any increased prices or decreased competition stemming from the merger."[4285]

These courts also have pointed to "the evils of permitting target companies to make use of the antitrust laws as defensive weapons" because "disingenuous antitrust suits may be brought by targets to thwart the loss of control to be suffered by management, as opposed to any motives relating to antitrust."[4286] This litigation thus may constitute an "attempt by incumbent management to defend their own positions" rather than an "attempt to vindicate any public interest."[4287] As Judge Friendly put it in *Missouri Port-*

---

4282. *Moore*, 907 F. Supp. at 1566, 1567; *Burnup*, 688 F. Supp. at 1534; *Burlington*, 666 F. Supp. at 805.

4283. *Moore*, 907 F. Supp. at 1567.

4284. *Anago*, 976 F.2d at 251; *Hayden*, 1989-1 Trade Cas. (CCH) at 60,620; *Burnup*, 688 F. Supp. at 1534; *Burlington*, 666 F. Supp. at 805; *Carter Hawley Hale*, 587 F. Supp. at 250.

4285. *Moore*, 907 F. Supp. at 1566.

4286. *Id.*

4287. *Id.; Hayden*, 1989-1 Trade Cas. (CCH) at 60,620; *Burnup*,
(continued...)

*land Cement Co. v. Cargill, Inc.*,[4288] a decision that (without addressing the standing issue) reversed a preliminary injunction that had enjoined a tender offer until antitrust issues could be resolved: "[C]ompanies that have become the target of tender offers" often "seek shelter under § 7 of the Clayton Act," "[d]rawing Excalibur from a scabbard where it would doubtless remain sheathed in the face of a friendly offer," and hoping "to obtain a temporary injunction which may frustrate the acquisition since the offering company may well decline the expensive gambit of a trial or, if it persists, the long lapse of time could so change conditions that the offer will fail even if, after a full trial and appeal, it should be determined that no antitrust violation has been shown."[4289]

The courts also are divided concerning the standing of a competitor of a corporation faced with an unwanted acquisition attempt to challenge the acquisition as a violation of the Clayton Act. The United States Supreme Court in *Cargill, Inc. v. Montfort of Colorado, Inc.*[4290] held that a showing of loss or damage due merely to increased competition is not by itself sufficient to grant standing to the competitor.[4291] Rather, the competitor must demonstrate "threatened loss or damage 'of the type the antitrust laws were designed to prevent and that flows from that which makes defendants' acts unlawful.'"[4292] Circuit and district courts have expressed differing views concerning the *Cargill* decision. The Second Circuit in *R.C. Bigelow, Inc. v. Unilever N.V.*[4293] held that under the circumstances present in that case a competitor had standing.[4294] The Third, Fifth and Sixth Circuits in *Ansell Inc. v.*

---

4287. (...continued)
688 F. Supp. at 1534.
    4288. 498 F.2d 851 (2d Cir.), *cert. denied*, 419 U.S. 883 (1974).
    4289. *Id*. at 854.
    4290. 479 U.S. 104 (1986).
    4291. *Id*. at 122.
    4292. *Id*. at 113 (quoting *Brunswick Corp. v. Pueblo Bowl-O-Mat, Inc.*, 429 U.S. 477, 489 (1977)).
    4293. 867 F.2d 102 (2d Cir.), *cert denied*, 493 U.S. 815 (1989).
    4294. *Id*. at 107-11.

*Schmid Laboratories, Inc.*,[4295] *Phototron Corp. v. Eastman Kodak Co.*[4296] and *Axis, S.p.A. v. Micafil, Inc.*[4297] reached the opposite conclusion.[4298]

The Ninth Circuit's decision in *United States v. BNS Inc.*[4299] illustrates another means by which preliminary injunctive relief on an antitrust ground sometimes may be secured. In *BNS*, the United States and a bidder entered into a consent decree to remedy anticompetitive effects the government alleged would result from the bidder's acquisition of a corporation.[4300] Over the objections of both the United States and the bidder, the target corporation—which had been granted leave to "participate" in the proceedings pursuant to the Antitrust Procedures and Penalties Act[4301]—obtained a preliminary injunction from a district court barring the bidder's acquisition of a controlling interest in the corporation pending a ruling by the court approving or disapproving the consent decree.[4302] The Ninth Circuit upheld the district court's authority to issue the preliminary injunction on the ground that control by the bidder of the corporation during the pendency of the court's proceedings "could conceivably result in irreparable anticompetitive harm."[4303] The court modified the injunction in a later ruling to allow assumption of control of the relevant portion of the corporation's business by an independent trustee until the district court approved or disapproved the consent decree.[4304]

---

4295. 757 F. Supp. 467 (D.N.J.), *aff'd mem.*, 941 F.2d 1200 (3d Cir. 1991).

4296. 842 F.2d 95 (5th Cir.), *cert. denied*, 486 U.S. 1023 (1988).

4297. 870 F.2d 1105 (6th Cir.), *cert. denied*, 493 U.S. 823 (1989).

4298. *Ansell*, 757 F. Supp. at 478-85; *Phototron*, 842 F.2d at 98-102; *Axis* 870 F. Supp. at 1111-18; *see also Remington Prods. Inc. v. North Am. Philips, Corp.*, 755 F. Supp. 52 (D. Conn. 1991) (no standing).

4299. 848 F.2d 945 (9th Cir. 1988).

4300. *Id.* at 946.

4301. 15 U.S.C. §§ 16(b)-(h).

4302. 848 F.2d at 947.

4303. *Id.*

4304. *United States v. BNS Inc.*, 858 F.2d 456, 466 (9th Cir.
(continued...)

Finally, just as a corporation's board may seek to thwart an unwanted takeover by acquiring assets posing antitrust problems for a prospective acquiror or commencing litigation raising antitrust issues, so too can a board acquire assets posing other regulatory problems or commence litigation raising other regulatory issues for the acquiror. Examples of businesses subject to varying levels of government regulation include television and radio stations, public utilities, financial institutions, insurance companies, air carriers, and defense contractors.[4305] A related issue involves takeover bids by foreign entities, which may be subject to statutory restrictions on foreign investments[4306] or presidential review pursuant to the Exon-Florio provision of the Omnibus Trade and Competitiveness Act of 1988.[4307]

## 5. The Pac-Man Defense

Corporations also have countered unwanted tender offers by making their own tender offers for the stock of their would-be acquirors—a defense known as the "Pac-Man" ("I'll eat you before you eat me") defense. Pac-Man defenses were used in the Bendix-Martin Marietta, NLT-American General, Cities Services-Mesa Petroleum, Olympia Brewing-Pabst, Heublein-General Cinema and Houston Natural-Coastal takeover contests in 1982 through 1984.[4308] The defense reemerged in 1988 when American Brands

---

4304. (...continued)
1988).

4305. 1 Arthur Fleischer, Jr. & Alexander R. Sussman, *Takeover Defense* § 2.02[C], at 2-10 (5th ed. 1995).

4306. *Id.*

4307. *See* Pub. L. No. 100-418, 102 Stat. 1107 § 5021 (1988) (amending the Defense Production Act of 1950, 50 U.S.C. App. §§ 2061-2170); Pub. L. No. 102-99, 105 Stat. 487 (1991) (amending the Defense Production Act to permanently reauthorize the Exon-Florio provision of the Act, 50 U.S.C. App. § 2170).

4308. *See* Lipton & Brownstein, *Takeover Responses and Directors' Responsibilities–An Update*, 40 Bus. Law. 1403, 1419-20 (1985); Uchitelle, *The Origins of the 'Pac-Man' Defense*, N.Y. Times, Jan. 23, 1988, at 35.

successfully responded to E-II's offer to purchase American Brands stock by making a counter-tender offer for E-II's stock.[4309]

Martin Marietta's "Pac-Man" tender offer for Bendix following Bendix's tender offer for Martin Marietta is the only instance where a court addressed the adoption of a Pac-Man defense under state law fiduciary duty principles or the business judgment rule. There, in an effort to defeat Bendix's tender offer for Martin Marietta, Martin Marietta countered with a tender offer for Bendix.

In *Martin Marietta Corp. v. Bendix Corp.*,[4310] a federal court proceeding in Maryland, where Martin Marietta was incorporated, Bendix alleged that Martin Marietta's counter-offer violated the Martin Marietta board's fiduciary duty to Martin Marietta's shareholders because as a result of Bendix's tender offer Bendix held more than 58 percent of Martin Marietta's stock and thus was Martin Marietta's new majority shareholder.[4311] The court stated its view that it was "doubtful" that the Martin Marietta board was obligated "to accede to the wishes of a majority shareholder."[4312] Whatever fiduciary duties were owed by the Martin Marietta board to Bendix, the court stated, were owed to Bendix shareholders rather than Bendix management because "it is Bendix' shareholders, not Bendix' management, who beneficially own a majority of Marietta."[4313] According to the court, "[i]n exercising its equitable judgment this Court can—and, indeed, must—look beyond the corporate entity of Bendix to Bendix' shareholders in determining who, if anyone, Marietta's board owes fiduciary duties."[4314]

The court then held that Martin Marietta's board had acted in a manner it reasonably believed to be in the best interests of the

---

4309. *See* Feit, *Pac-Man Defense Upsets Majority Holder Rule*, Nat'l L.J., May 23, 1988, at 33; Labaton, *American Brands Set to Buy E-II*, N.Y. Times, Feb. 1, 1988, at D1.

4310. 549 F. Supp. 623 (D. Md. 1982).

4311. *Id.* at 625, 633.

4312. *Id.* at 633.

4313. *Id.*

4314. *Id.*

Bendix shareholders. The court explained:

> The record shows that Marietta's board reasonably believes
> that a combination of the two corporations would be best
> achieved pursuant to the terms of Marietta's offer rather than
> Bendix' offer. There is substantial evidence that it is the con-
> sidered view of Marietta's board that Bendix' current man-
> agement has little managerial competence or experience in
> Marietta's business and, as a result, Marietta's management
> would be more competent to manage the combined Bendix-
> Marietta entity than Bendix' management. While the record
> also shows that Marietta's management has little experience
> in Bendix non-aerospace businesses, this Court cannot, in
> keeping with the Maryland business judgment rule, say that it
> is unreasonable for Marietta's board to adhere to its
> view.[4315]

The court added that Bendix, as the majority shareholder of Martin
Marietta, owed a fiduciary duty to Martin Marietta's other shareholders not to force Martin Marietta to abandon a desirable business opportunity.[4316]

In *Martin Marietta Corp. v. Bendix Corp.*,[4317] a state court
proceeding in Delaware, where Bendix was incorporated, the Court
of Chancery held that Bendix could call a special shareholders
meeting on short notice before the date Martin Marietta could
acquire Bendix shares pursuant to its tender offer, and ask shareholders at that meeting to adopt charter amendments intended to
make an acquisition of control of Bendix by Martin Marietta more
difficult to complete even if Martin Marietta's tender offer succeeded and Martin Marietta became the holder of a majority of
Bendix shares.[4318] One of the amendments provided that any
merger with a 20 percent or more shareholder required—as the
court described the amendment—the "prior approval of Bendix
management" or (1) an 80 percent vote of all shareholders and (2)

---

4315. *Id.* at 633-34.

4316. *Id.* at 634.

4317. *See Martin Marietta Corp. v. Bendix Corp.*, No. 6942 (Del.
Ch. Sept. 19, 1982) (available on LEXIS without file number), *aff'd*, No.
298, 1982 (Del. Sept. 21, 1982).

4318. *Id.*, slip op. at 3-4.

a 67 percent vote of all shares not controlled by the 20 percent or more shareholder.[4319] A second amendment provided that no action requiring shareholder approval could be taken without a shareholder meeting unless written consents had been executed by all (rather than 50 percent, as required by Section 228 of the Delaware General Corporation Law, unless the corporation's certificate of incorporation states otherwise) of the corporation's shareholders.[4320]

The court stated that the standard to be applied in evaluating the proposed shark repellent provisions is whether the board adopting them "engaged in inequitable conduct under the facts of the present case."[4321] Applying this standard, the court stated that the circumstances and time constraints under which Bendix sought to adopt charter amendments designed to block Marietta's attempt to take control of Bendix "were imposed by Martin Marietta by virtue of the terms of its defensive tender offer."[4322] Accordingly, the court concluded, "I fail to see how . . . I can find a likelihood of unfair and inequitable conduct on the part of the Bendix board for calling a meeting to put a matter to the vote of its shareholders within the only time span afforded to it by the defensive tender offer of Martin Marietta."[4323]

On appeal, the Delaware Supreme Court expressed no opinion concerning the legality of the proposed amendments, but held that the Court of Chancery had not abused its discretion in denying Martin Marietta's application for preliminary injunctive relief.[4324] The Supreme Court stated that any attempt by Marietta—whose "position here is not as a representative of Bendix shareholders but that of a personal combatant"—to gain control of the Bendix board would be "a violation of a duty to its own majority stockholder,

---

4319. *Id*. at 4.
4320. *Id*.
4321. *Id*. at 15.
4322. *Id*. at 15-16.
4323. *Id*. at 16.
4324. *Martin Marietta Corp. v. Bendix Corp.*, No. 298, 1982, slip op. at 3 (Del. Sept. 21, 1982).

Bendix," and that Martin Marietta was "in effect asking the Court of Chancery to assist it in a violation" of this duty.[4325] Other Delaware cases arising in different contexts have held that the fact that many or even most "shareholders would prefer the board to do otherwise than it has done does not . . . afford a basis to interfere with the effectuation of the board's business judgment."[4326]

In *American General Corp. v. NLT Corp.*,[4327] the court rejected challenges to a Pac-Man defense on federal securities and state insurance law grounds. The plaintiffs in *NLT* did not allege any state law fiduciary duty violations, and the court stated that the counter-tender offer was "decided upon as the best alternative available to NLT and its shareholders and is a bona fide tender offer."[4328]

## 6.  Litigation

A corporation also may respond to an unwanted contest for control by commencing litigation against the unwanted bidder and alleging violations of securities laws or any other laws. In the words of the Delaware Supreme Court in *Unocal Corp. v. Mesa*

---

4325. *Id.*

4326. *Paramount Communications Inc. v. Time Inc.*, [1989 Transfer Binder] Fed. Sec. L. Rep. (CCH) ¶ 94,514, at 93,284 (Del. Ch. July 14, 1989), *aff'd*, 571 A.2d 1140 (Del. 1990); *see also* 1 R. Franklin Balotti & Jesse A. Finkelstein, *The Delaware Law of Corporations and Business Organizations* § 6.52, at 6-120 (3d ed. 1998) (describing the Delaware Supreme Court's statement in *Bendix* as "inconsistent with the cases that recognize and uphold the duty of directors to exercise their own business judgment in a manner they believe most appropriate for the welfare of the corporation and its stockholders as a whole") (citing *Unocal Corp. v. Mesa Petroleum Co.*, 493 A.2d 946 (Del. 1985) (discussed in Chapter III, Sections A 2 and E 1 b), *GM Sub Corp. v. Liggett Group, Inc.*, 1980 Del. Ch. LEXIS 581, at *4, 1980 WL 6430, at *2 (Del. Ch. Apr. 25, 1980), and *American Int'l Rent A Car, Inc. v. Cross*, 9 Del. J. Corp. L. 144, 148 (Del. Ch. May 9, 1984)).

4327. [1982 Transfer Binder] Fed. Sec. L. Rep. (CCH) ¶ 98,808 (S.D. Tex. July 1, 1982).

4328. *Id.* at 94,142.

*Petroleum Co.*,[4329] "[l]itigation, supported by corporate funds, aimed at the raider has long been a popular device."[4330] The business judgment rule protects board decisions to commence non-frivolous litigation in the same manner that the rule protects other board decisions made in response to an unwanted contest for control.[4331] Frivolous claims, of course, are barred by the rules of most courts.[4332]

---

4329. 493 A.2d 946 (Del. 1985).

4330. *Id.* at 957; *see also Katz v. Chevron Corp.*, 22 Cal. App. 4th 1352, 1374-75, 27 Cal. Rptr. 681, 694-95 (Cal. Ct. App. 1994) (upholding board decision to commence litigation); *Grand Metro. PLC v. Pillsbury Co.*, No. 10319, Tr. at 3-6 (Del. Ch. Oct. 4, 1988), 14 Del. J. Corp. L. 1042, 1043-44 (Del. Ch. Nov. 7, 1988) and 558 A.2d 1049, 1053 (Del. Ch. 1988) (refusing to enjoin board decision to institute tied house statute proceedings in multiple states due to the lack of a colorable claim that directors had violated their fiduciary duties by invoking these statutes).

4331. *See, e.g., Panter v. Marshall Field & Co.*, 646 F.2d 271, 297 (7th Cir.), *cert. denied*, 454 U.S. 1092 (1981); *Berman v. Gerber Prods. Co.*, 454 F. Supp. 1310, 1318-19 (W.D. Mich. 1978).

4332. *See, e.g.,* Fed. R. Civ. P. 11(b):

By presenting to the court (whether by signing, filing, submitting, or later advocating) a pleading, written motion, or other paper, an attorney or unrepresented party is certifying that to the best of the person's knowledge, information, and belief, formed after an inquiry reasonable under the circumstances,–

(1) it is not being presented for any improper purpose, such as to harass or to cause unnecessary delay or needless increase in the cost of litigation;

(2) the claims, defenses, and other legal contentions therein are warranted by existing law or by a nonfrivolous argument for the extension, modification, or reversal of existing law or the establishment of new law;

(3) the allegations and other factual contentions have evidentiary support or, if specifically so identified, are likely to have evidentiary support after a reasonable opportunity for further investigation or discovery; and

(4) the denials of factual contentions are warranted on the

(continued...)

Litigation as a defensive measure may provide a corporation several advantages.

First, and most obvious, litigation provides a corporation an opportunity to raise substantive legal issues.

Second, litigation may provide a means by which delay may be imposed upon an unwanted offeror. This delay, in turn, provides the corporation with more time than it otherwise would have to find a white knight or implement another defensive strategy. As the Delaware Court of Chancery observed in one case, even if litigation efforts by the corporation in that case over a two week period "may be viewed as simply buying time, it cannot be said that such conduct was not a proper exercise of managerial judgment as part of an overall effort to resist a potentially destructive tender offer."[4333]

Third, litigation may provide a means by which a corporation may obtain otherwise unavailable information from and concerning an unwanted bidder through discovery, including information concerning the bidder's finances and plans for the corporation. The discovery process also may distract the opposition's key personnel.[4334]

Fourth, litigation may provide a means by which a corporation may score public relations points. The grant of a temporary restraining order or a preliminary injunction often may be interpreted by shareholders (with the successful litigant's active encouragement) as evidence of wrongdoing, thus possibly advancing the

---

4332. (...continued)
   evidence or, if specifically so identified, are reasonably based
   on a lack of information or belief.
   4333. *Edelman v. Phillips Petroleum Co.*, 10 Del. J. Corp. L. 835, 843 (Del. Ch. Feb. 12, 1985).
   4334. *See generally* 1 Arthur Fleischer, Jr. & Alexander R. Sussman, *Takeover Defense* § 11.01[A] (5th ed. 1995); 1 Martin Lipton & Erica H. Steinberger, *Takeovers & Freezeouts* § 6.06[1], at 6–121-22 (1997); *Union Pacific Strikes a Dry Well with Pennzoil*, Corporate Control Alert, Dec. 1997, at 7, 9-10; Cherno & Sussman, *Tender-Offer Litigation*, Litigation, Winter 1984, at 41; Wachtell, *Special Tender Offer Litigation Tactics*, 32 Bus. Law. 1433 (1977).

successful litigant's position in the overall battle. Among the decisions noting this fact in considering whether to grant such relief are the following:

- *D-Z Investment Co. v. Holloway*[4335] and *Jewelcor Inc. v. Pearlman*[4336] (if preliminary injunctive relief is granted, "no matter how such [relief] was explained to the shareholders by the present management, a substantial number of shareholders would regard its issuance as a determination of the alleged Securities Act violations on the merits and a finding that the incumbent management had acted improperly");[4337]

- *Warnaco Inc. v. Galef*[4338] ("to delay either the vote or any implementation until a further hearing can be concluded would effectually grant the . . . motion and perhaps cloud the shareholders' vote on the plan");[4339]

- *Ocilla Industries, Inc. v. Katz*[4340] ("it is possible" that the granting of a preliminary injunction "will have a misleading effect on some shareholders");[4341]

- *Dolgoff v. Projectavision, Inc.*[4342] and *Columbia Pictures Industries, Inc. v. Kerkorian*[4343] ("The issuance of a preliminary injunction now would undoubtedly come to the attention of the stockholders. No matter how clearly it was indicated that the issuance was in no

---

4335. [1973-1974 Transfer Binder] Fed. Sec. L. Rep. (CCH) ¶ 94,588 (S.D.N.Y. June 11, 1974).

4336. 397 F. Supp. 221 (S.D.N.Y. 1975).

4337. *D-Z*, [1973-1974 Transfer Binder] Fed. Sec. L. Rep. (CCH) at 96,061-62 (quoting *Jewelcor*, 397 F. Supp. at 252).

4338. No. B-86-146 (PCD) (D. Conn. Apr. 25, 1986), *aff'd mem.*, 800 F.2d 1129 (2d Cir. 1986).

4339. *Id.*, slip op. at 19.

4340. 677 F. Supp. 1291 (E.D.N.Y. 1987).

4341. *Id.* at 1300.

4342. 21 Del. J. Corp. L. 1128, 1143 (Del. Ch. Feb. 26, 1996).

4343. No. 6334 (Del. Ch. Dec. 16, 1980).

way adjudication on the merits, it would be inevitable that at least a substantial number of stockholders would reach the conclusion that such a holding was tantamount to a determination of wrongdoing by the management.");[4344]

- *Davis Acquisition Inc. v. NWA Inc.*[4345] (the "spectre" that an "expression of opinion by a court may have an impact upon the outcome of the election . . . requires that a court in such a setting exercise particular care and imagination to minimize the risks of such danger);[4346] and

- *Abbey v. Montedison S.p.A.*[4347] ("an injunction might well be interpreted by shareholders as a finding of wrongdoing on defendants' part, which could in turn substantially diminish the possibility of the offer's success, even if it is ultimately upheld in all respects").[4348]

As the Second Circuit noted in *Kennecott Copper Corp. v. Curtiss-Wright Corp.*,[4349] a case where preliminary injunctive relief had been granted by a district court, "[t]here is a strong likelihood . . . that the election results were influenced by the criticism of Curtiss-Wright contained in the district court's election-eve decision."[4350]

Fifth, finally, the initiation of litigation by the corporation before a bidder initiates litigation affords the corporation the ability

---

4344. *Dolgoff*, 21 Del. J. Corp. L. at 1143 (quoting *Columbia Pictures*, slip op. at 1).

4345. [1990 Transfer Binder] Fed. Sec. L. Rep. (CCH) ¶ 95,434 (Del. Ch. Apr. 25, 1989).

4346. *Id*. at 97,213.

4347. 143 Misc. 2d 72, 539 N.Y.S.2d 862 (N.Y. Sup. Ct. N.Y. Co. 1989).

4348. *Id*. at 82, 539 N.Y.S.2d at 868.

4349. 584 F.2d 1195 (2d Cir. 1978).

4350. *Id*. at 1200. *But see Norfolk S. Corp. v. Conrail Inc.*, No. 96-7167, Tr. op. at 69 (E.D. Pa. Dec. 17, 1996) (rejecting claim that preliminary injunction should not be granted because "it may present some sort of bad publicity").

to choose the forum that the corporation believes best will suit its needs. Once the corporation or the unwanted bidder commences litigation, later filed claims often will be forced into the forum chosen by the first litigant as compulsory counterclaims.[4351] The selection of forum may be a particularly important advantage because "[t]argets have obtained instantaneous temporary restraining orders in home districts" and "[p]reliminary injunctions seem to be more frequently granted against a tender offer in the target's home court."[4352]

In short, as one court aptly has stated, takeover litigation is "often but one of a host of tactics employed in a larger strategy designed to accomplish ulterior objectives, either to acquire control of the target company or to prevent a takeover. All of this occurs in an environment often involving ongoing media publicity, where each development and court ruling may impact upon financial markets in ways only dimly perceptible by courts."[4353]

---

4351. *Compare Crouse-Hinds Co. v. InterNorth, Inc.*, 634 F.2d 690, 699-701 (2d Cir. 1980), *and Cyprus Corp. v. Whitman*, 93 F.R.D. 598, 603-06 (S.D.N.Y. 1982) (both holding that claim in second litigation constituted compulsory counterclaim) *with Koppers Co. v. American Express Co.*, 121 F.R.D. 46, 48-51 (W.D. Pa. 1988) (holding that claim in second litigation did not constitute a compulsory counterclaim); *see also Tullos v. Parks*, 915 F.2d 1192, 1194-96 (8th Cir. 1990) (rejecting a contention that district court lacked jurisdiction to adjudicate an unwanted tender offeror's state law claims; the court held that the state law claims were compulsory counterclaims to federal claims brought by the corporation against the unwanted offeror and that ancillary jurisdiction was conferred on this basis).

4352. Fleischer § 11.01[B], at 11-7.

4353. *Plaza Sec. Co. v. Office*, 12 Del. J. Corp. L. 1145, 1154 (Del. Ch. Dec. 15, 1986); *see also CRTF Corp. v. Federated Dep't Stores, Inc.*, 683 F. Supp. 422, 424 (S.D.N.Y. 1988) ("either the offeror or the target is likely to seek immediate judicial relief, seeking to enlist the court as its ally in the battle being waged in the marketplace"); *Tate & Lyle PLC v. Staley Continental, Inc.*, [1987-1988 Transfer Binder] Fed. Sec. L. Rep. (CCH) ¶ 93,764, at 98,584 (Del. Ch. May 9, 1988) ("this Court may be merely a pawn in a take-over battle which is just emerging").

# I.   Settlements

The final option available to a corporation seeking to resist an unwanted contest for control is reaching an accommodation or settlement with the unwanted bidder. This most often is accomplished by repurchasing stock held by the unwanted bidder (or finding a third party willing to repurchase the stock and/or entering into a standstill agreement. Both of these defensive mechanisms end hostilities, at least for the time being.

## 1.   Greenmail

The repurchase by a corporation of its shares—often at a substantial premium over market value—from a potential acquiror who has accumulated a block of the corporation's stock has become known as "greenmail." Greenmail repurchases were a common defensive strategy during the early-to-mid 1980s. According to one survey, $4 billion was paid by corporations to repurchase blocks of their own stock from individual shareholders between April 1983 and April 1984.[4354] According to another survey, eight investors earned between $32 million and $400 million each by selling their stock back to corporations between November 1983 and December 1984.[4355] The practice came under intense criticism, with the "payment of 'greenmail' to 'raiders'" being called "everything from 'extortion' and 'a disgrace' to '[u]nfair, unjust, [and] wrong.'"[4356] As one commentator put it: "one element of virtual consensus has emerged: greenmail . . . is bad."[4357] Some green-

---

4354. *See* Macey & McChesney, *A Theoretical Analysis of Corporate Greenmail*, 95 Yale L.J. 13, 13-14 (1985).

4355. *See* Note, *Greenmail: Targeted Stock Repurchases and the Management Entrenchment Hypothesis*, 98 Harv. L. Rev. 1045, 1046 & n.8 (1985); *see also Greenmail is Back—Just Ask Skadden Arps's Clients*, Corporate Control Alert, Jan. 1987, at 1; Nash, *Wall Street Bemoans a New 'Greenmail' Season*, N.Y. Times, Dec. 28, 1986, at E4; *A Flurry of Greenmail Has Stockholders Cursing*, Bus. Wk., Dec. 8, 1986, at 32.

4356. Macey & McChesney, 95 Yale L.J. at 14 (footnotes omitted).

4357. Gilson, *Drafting an Effective Greenmail Prohibition*, 80 Colum. L. Rev. 329, 329-30 (1988).

mail-type transactions accordingly have been "disguised"—a practice called "pale green greenmail" or "camoumail" (a play on the word camouflage)[4358]—or not disclosed to the public at all.[4359]

The term greenmail typically is used to describe a stock repurchase at a price above the stock's market value at the time of the sale. Some observers, however, have contended that greenmail includes stock repurchases from a potential acquiror at any price above what the stock's market value would have been absent the effect of stock purchases by the potential acquiror. Thus, for example, Ashland Oil's 1986 repurchase of a 9.2 percent block of Ashland stock held by the Belzberg family at $0.50 below the market value at the moment of the purchase—but $2.34 to $12.50 per share above the prices paid by the Belzbergs to acquire the stock and $1.25 above the market value at the close of trading on the day of the repurchase—was labeled greenmail by many Wall Street observers, but not Ashland.[4360] One arbitrager put it this way: "Greenmail is when you buy back the stock of a potential raider to get them off your back. . . . Ashland's stock was artificially high because of their presence, and now it's down."[4361]

---

4358. *See* Sandler, *'Pale Green Greenmail' is Spreading as Firms Buy Out Raiders as Part of Broader Purchases*, Wall St. J., Nov. 25, 1986, at 59; Bleakley, *Talking Deals; Buying Back, and Buying Off*, N.Y. Times, Nov. 13, 1986, at D2.

4359. *See* Nussbaum, *The Greenmailers Learn to Play in the Shadows*, Bus. Wk., May 5, 1986, at 105 ("Below the 5% mark is where most of the greenmail action is now taking place. Keeping away from the . . . automatic-disclosure trigger [under § 13(d) of the Securities Exchange Act of 1934, 15 U.S.C. § 78m(d)] allows the greenmailer and corporate manager to do business in the shadows, away from the prying eyes of shareholders and the SEC."); *In re BF Goodrich Co.*, Exchange Act Release No. 34-22792, [1985-1986 Transfer Binder] Fed. Sec. L. Rep. (CCH) ¶ 83,958 (Jan. 15, 1986) (finding that corporation's Form 10-K and proxy materials violated Sections 13(a) and 14(a) of the Exchange Act, 15 U.S.C. §§ 78m(a), 78n(a), by failing to disclose a repurchase of 4.9 percent of the corporation's outstanding stock at a 25 percent premium over market price).

4360. *See* Hicks, *Ashland to Buy Out Belzbergs*, N.Y. Times, Apr. 2, 1986, at D1.

4361. Hertzberg & Lubove, *Wall Street Winces as Belzbergs Agree*
(continued...)

*a. Cases Upholding Greenmail Transactions.* Greenmail trans-actions repeatedly have been upheld by the Delaware courts. The first of these decisions was the Delaware Supreme Court's decision in 1952 in *Martin v. American Potash & Chemical Corp.*[4362] The court in that case held that there is "no sound reason why . . . the method of reducing capital by purchasing shares at private sale for retirement may not be invoked simply because the purpose or motive of the reduction is to eliminate a substantial number of shares held by a stockholder at odds with management policy."[4363]

The Delaware Supreme Court reached the same result in 1964 in *Cheff v. Mathes.*[4364] This time, the court quoted *Bennett v. Propp*[4365]—an open market stock repurchase case discussed earlier in this Chapter[4366]—for the proposition that directors bear the burden of justifying the purchase of shares in the face of a contest for control of the corporation as being "primarily in the corporate interest."[4367] The court explained that "[w]e must bear in mind the inherent danger in the purchase of shares with corporate funds to remove a threat to corporate policy when a threat to control is involved" because under these circumstances "directors are of necessity confronted with a conflict of interest, and an objective decision is difficult."[4368] The court added, however, that "[t]o say that the burden of proof is upon the defendants is not to indicate . . . that the directors have the same 'self-dealing interest' as is present, for example, when a director sells property to the corporation."[4369] Rather, while the usual presumption provided by the

---

4361. (...continued)
*to Sell Stock, Run,* Wall St. J., Apr. 2, 1986, at 2.
    4362. 92 A.2d 295 (Del. 1952).
    4363. *Id.* at 302; *see also Kors v. Carey,* 158 A.2d 136, 140-42 (Del. Ch. 1960) (same result).
    4364. 199 A.2d 548 (Del. 1964).
    4365. 187 A.2d 405 (Del. 1962).
    4366. *See* Chapter III, Section E 1 a.
    4367. 199 A.2d at 554 (quoting 187 A.2d at 409).
    4368. *Id.*
    4369. *Id.* at 554.

business judgment rule may not apply, "the directors satisfy their burden by showing good faith and reasonable investigation" and "will not be penalized for an honest mistake of judgment, if the judgment appeared reasonable at the time the decision was made."[4370]

American Potash and Cheff v. Mathes were followed in a series of cases decided during the period beginning in the mid-1970s and concluding in the mid-1980s in the Delaware Court of Chancery[4371] and in federal court.[4372] The Delaware Supreme Court's 1985 decision in Unocal Corp. v. Mesa Petroleum Co.[4373]—another case discussed earlier in this Chapter[4374]— accordingly described "the principle of selective stock repurchases" as "neither unknown nor unauthorized" under Delaware law.[4375] The court in Unocal took this principal one step further by upholding a selective exchange offer open to all shareholders except a shareholder making a hostile tender offer, Mesa Petroleum. The court stated that "[t]he only difference is that heretofore the approved transaction was the payment of 'greenmail' to a raider or dissident posing a threat to the corporate enterprise. All other stockholders were denied such favored treatment, and given Mesa's past history of greenmail, its claims here are rather ironic."[4376]

The Delaware Supreme Court reached the same result in 1986 in Polk v. Good,[4377] a case involving a proposed settlement of an

---

4370. *Id.* at 555.

4371. *See Edelman v. Phillips Petroleum Co.*, 10 Del. J. Corp. L. 835, 844-45 (Del. Ch. Feb. 12, 1985); *Citron v. Burns*, 10 Del. J. Corp. L. 830, 834 (Del. Ch. Feb. 4, 1985); *Lewis v. Daum*, 9 Del. J. Corp. L. 481, 485-86 (Del. Ch. May 24, 1984); *Amsellem v. Shopwell, Inc.*, 5 Del. J. Corp. L. 367, 375-76 (Del. Ch. Sept. 6, 1979); *Kaplan v. Goldsamt*, 380 A.2d 556, 568-69 (Del. Ch. 1977).

4372. *See Heine v. Signal Cos.*, [1976-1977 Transfer Binder] Fed. Sec. L. Rep. (CCH) ¶ 95,898, at 91,322-23 (S.D.N.Y. Mar 4, 1977).

4373. 493 A.2d 946 (Del. 1985).

4374. *See* Chapter III, Sections A 2 and E 1 b.

4375. 493 A.2d at 957.

4376. *Id.*

4377. 507 A.2d 531 (Del. 1986).

action challenging a repurchase by Texaco, Inc. of a block of its shares at a 3 percent premium above market price.[4378] The court summarized the applicable law as follows:

> A Delaware corporation has the power to deal in its own stock, and may acquire a dissident's shares provided the transaction is free from fraud or unfairness. Unless the primary or sole purpose was to perpetuate the directors in office, such an acquisition will be sustained if, after reasonable investigation, a board has a justifiable belief that there was a reasonable threat to the corporate enterprise. When properly accomplished, such matters are protected by the business judgment rule.[4379]

The court found that the directors whose conduct was challenged in *Polk* had demonstrated that "reasonable grounds for believing that a danger to corporate policy existed," and that the board's action was "reasonable in relation to the threat posed."[4380] The court explained as follows:

> The events occurring from the outset of the Bass group's acquisition of Texaco stock, up to the repurchase, created reasonable grounds for a justifiable belief by the directors that there was a threat to Texaco. The payment of a premium of approximately 3% over market seems reasonable in relation to the immediate disruptive effect and the potential long-term threat which the Bass group posed. Clearly, that was a benefit to the company and most of its shareholders.[4381]

The court rejected a contention that shares could be repurchased at a premium over market price from dissident shareholders who "threaten to interfere with the day-to-day business operations of a company," but not from those who threaten what the plaintiffs characterized as "such activities as proxy fights and tender offers—the exercise of legitimate corporate 'democratic processes'."[4382]

---

4378. *Id.* at 533-34, 537.
4379. *Id.* at 536-37 (citations omitted).
4380. *Id.* at 537.
4381. *Id.*
4382. *Id.*

In 1988, in *Grobow v. Perot*,[4383] the Delaware Supreme Court again held that "[t]he law of Delaware is well established that, in the absence of evidence of fraud or unfairness, a corporation's repurchase of its capital stock at a premium over market from a dissident shareholder is entitled to the protection of the business judgment rule."[4384] Thus, the court stated, repurchases "by a corporation, at a premium over market, of its own stock held by a single dissident shareholder or shareholder group at odds with management . . . have repeatedly been upheld as valid exercises of business judgment."[4385]

The court accordingly dismissed an action challenging a $750 million repurchase by General Motors of stock and notes held by H. Ross Perot, a GM director and officer and the corporation's largest shareholder (holding approximately 0.8 percent of GM's stock).[4386] The court described the transaction as one intended to "resolve an internal rift in management of serious proportions and at the highest executive level," and concluded that "the repurchase of dissident Perot's interests can only be viewed legally as representing an exercise of business judgment by the General Motors Board with which a court may not interfere."[4387] The court reached this conclusion notwithstanding Perot's agreement in connection with the repurchase of his shares to stop criticizing GM and to pay GM damages if Perot violated this agreement in a liquidated sum of up to $7.5 million—a provision described as "hushmail," a play upon "greenmail" and "hush money."[4388] The court adhered to its determination to dismiss the *Grobow* action in *Levine v. Smith*,[4389] a 1991 ruling in the same litigation.[4390] The *Grobow* and *Levine* decisions arose in the context of motions to dismiss a

---

4383. 539 A.2d 180 (Del. 1988).
4384. *Id*. at 189.
4385. *Id*. (quoting *Grobow v. Perot*, 526 A.2d 914, 927 (Del. Ch. 1987), *aff'd*, 539 A.2d 180 (Del. 1988)).
4386. *Id*. at 184-85.
4387. *Id*. at 191.
4388. *Id*. at 184 & n.3, 190.
4389. 591 A.2d 194 (Del. 1991).
4390. *Id*. at 201-08.

shareholder derivative action due to plaintiffs' failure to make a pre-litigation demand, a subject discussed in Chapter IV.[4391]

The Delaware Supreme Court reaffirmed this principle again in 1991 in *Oberly v. Kirby*.[4392] The court stated that "[i]f . . . a corporation's directors believe that a large stockholder poses a threat to the corporation, the corporation may pay a premium to eliminate that threat."[4393]

The Supreme Court stated again in *Kahn v. Roberts*[4394] in 1996 that "[w]e have repeatedly ruled that a board may repurchase the stock of a dissatisfied shareholder."[4395] The Supreme Court accordingly affirmed a Court of Chancery decision upholding a board determination to repurchase shares based upon the board's "sincere belief" that "removing dissident shareholders and directors would maintain business practices considered to be in the best interest of the corporation" and "promote a more harmonious corporate policy structure."[4396] In an earlier decision in the case, the Court of Chancery held that a pre-litigation demand was not excused by the board's determination to repurchase shares at a premium over market value shares held by a director having "diametrically opposed views as to the future direction" of the corporation from the board, and who had been asked to (and did) resign as an officer of the corporation."[4397] Under these circumstances, the court held, the corporation's board "could have properly determined that it was in the best interests of the company" to purchase the shares held by this director.[4398] The court, however, held that demand was excused by an allegation that the corporation's directors did not

---

4391. *See* Chapter IV, Section B.

4392. 592 A.2d 445 (Del. 1991).

4393. *Id.* at 470-71.

4394. 679 A.2d 460 (Del. 1996).

4395. *Id.* at 466 n.6.

4396. *Kahn v. Roberts*, 21 Del. J. Corp. L. 674, 688 (Del. Ch. Dec. 6, 1995), *aff'd*, 679 A.2d 460 (Del. 1996).

4397. *Kahn v. Roberts*, [1993-1994 Transfer Binder] Fed. Sec. L. Rep. (CCH) ¶ 98,201, at 99,413 (Del. Ch. Feb. 28, 1994).

4398. *Id.*

act with due care.[4399] That allegation later was rejected in a ruling by the Court of Chancery on a motion for summary judgment,
which the Supreme Court affirmed.[4400]

Courts applying New York law have upheld greenmail transactions in *Karfunkel v. USLIFE Corp.*,[4401] *Lewis v. Kurshan*[4402] and
*Traub v. Barber.*[4403]

Federal courts have held that greenmail transactions are not
voidable and cannot be rescinded on grounds of duress or coercion,[4404] and do not constitute extortion under the Hobbs
Act[4405] and thus are not a predicate act upon which a claim under
the Racketeer Influenced and Corrupt Organizations Act
("RICO")[4406] may be premised.[4407]

*b. Cases Questioning Greenmail Transactions.* Standing in
sharp contrast to the Delaware and New York cases discussed
above[4408] is *Heckmann v. Ahmanson*,[4409] a litigation in which

4399. *Id.*

4400. 21 Del. J. Corp. L. at 685-88; 679 A.2d at 466; *see also
Drage v. Ameritrust Corp.*, 1988 Ohio App. LEXIS 3972, 1988 WL
113631 (Ohio Ct. App. Sept. 29, 1988) (construing Delaware law and upholding repurchase of shares from one shareholder), *appeal dismissed*, 550
N.E.2d 948 (Ohio 1990); *Lacos Land Co. v. Arden Group, Inc.*, 1986
Del. Ch. LEXIS 495, at *6-7, 1986 WL 14525, at *3-5 (Del. Ch. Dec.
24, 1986) (approving settlement of litigation including a corporation's
repurchase of plaintiff's stock at a price $5 per share higher than the price
to be offered to other shareholders in a self-tender offer).

4401. 116 Misc. 2d 841, 844-46, 455 N.Y.S.2d 937, 939-41 (N.Y.
Sup. Ct. N.Y. Co. 1982), *aff'd mem.*, 98 A.D.2d 628, 469 N.Y.S.2d
1020 (N.Y. App. Div. 1st Dep't 1983).

4402. N.Y.L.J., Dec. 1, 1983, at 6 (N.Y. Sup. Ct. N.Y. Co.).

4403. N.Y.L.J., July 9, 1987, at 7 (N.Y. Sup. Ct. N.Y. Co.)

4404. *Kamerman v. Steinberg*, 891 F.2d 424, 431-32 (2d Cir.
1989).

4405. 18 U.S.C. § 1951.

4406. 18 U.S.C. §§ 1961–1968.

4407. *Viacom Int'l Inc. v. Icahn*, 747 F. Supp. 205, 210-14
(S.D.N.Y. 1990), *aff'd on other grounds*, 946 F.2d 998 (2d Cir. 1991),
*cert. denied*, 502 U.S. 1122 (1992).

4408. *See* Chapter III, Section I 1 a.

an intermediate appellate court in California granted a preliminary injunction in 1985 and the trial court denied a motion for summary judgment seeking dismissal of the action in 1989. Also standing in contrast to the Delaware and New York cases discussed above are two federal court decisions—*Feinberg v. Carter*[4410] and *Fry v. Trump*[4411]—denying motions to dismiss.

*Heckmann v. Ahmanson*,[4412] an intermediate California appellate court decision, upheld a preliminary injunction imposing a constructive trust on a $60 million profit earned by Saul Steinberg and his associates (the "Steinberg Group") upon their 1984 resale of Walt Disney Productions stock back to Disney. The court concluded that although it could find no cases in which "a greenmailer was ordered to return his ill-gotten gains,"[4413] it believed that the Disney shareholder plaintiffs had established "a reasonable probability of proving a breach of fiduciary duties by the Steinberg Group."[4414]

The court first found a breach of fiduciary duty by Disney's directors. The court explained that the "acts of the Disney directors —and particularly their timing—are difficult to understand except as defensive strategies against a hostile takeover."[4415] These acts, the court stated, included the following:

> The Steinberg Group began acquiring Disney stock in March 1984. In May 1984 the Disney directors announced Disney would acquire Arvida and its $190 million debt. Trying to make the target company appear less attractive is a well-recognized defensive tactic by a board seeking to retain control. . . . Furthermore, the Steinberg Group announced its

---

4409. (...continued)

4409. 168 Cal. App. 3d 119, 214 Cal. Rptr. 177 (Cal. Ct. App. 1985), *subsequent proceedings*, [1989 Transfer Binder] Fed. Sec. L. Rep. (CCH) ¶ 94,447 (Cal. Super. Ct. Apr. 12, 1989).

4410. 652 F. Supp. 1066 (S.D.N.Y. 1987).

4411. 681 F. Supp. 252 (D.N.J. 1988).

4412. 168 Cal. App. 3d 119, 214 Cal. Rptr. 177 (Cal. Ct. App. 1985).

4413. *Id.* at 126, 214 Cal. Rptr. at 182.

4414. *Id.* at 123, 214 Cal. Rptr. at 180.

4415. *Id.* at 128, 214 Cal. Rptr. at 183.

tender offer for 49 percent of the outstanding Disney shares on June 8, 1984. Immediately following this announcement, the Disney directors began negotiations to repurchase the Steinberg Group's stock and reached an agreement on the repurchase two days later.[4416]

Under California law, the court continued, "[o]nce it is shown a director received a personal benefit from the transaction, which appears to be the case here, the burden shifts to the director to demonstrate" that "the transaction was entered in good faith" and "to show its inherent fairness from the viewpoint of the corporation and those interested therein."[4417] The court found that the only evidence concerning good faith and fairness presented by Disney's directors was a "vague" and "conclusory" assertion that their objective was to "avoid the damage to Disney and its shareholders which would have been the result of [the] announced tender offer."[4418] The court held that this evidence was insufficient to overcome the directors' burden of showing of good faith and fairness.[4419]

The court next concluded that the Steinberg Group could be held liable as an aider and abettor to the breach of fiduciary duty by Disney's directors: The court explained:

> The Steinberg Group knew it was reselling its stock at a price considerably above market value to enable the Disney directors to retain control of the corporation. It knew or should have known Disney was borrowing the $325 million purchase price. From its previous dealing with Disney, including the Arvida transaction, it knew that increased debt load would adversely affect Disney's credit rating and the price of its stock. If it were an active participant in the breach of duty and reaped the benefit, it cannot disclaim the burden.[4420]

As an alternative ground for its decision, the court found that the Steinberg Group's filing of a shareholder derivative action on

---

4416. *Id.*
4417. *Id.*
4418. *Id.*
4419. *Id.*
4420. *Id.* at 127, 214 Cal. Rptr. at 182-83.

behalf of Disney prior to the repurchase transaction in order to block defensive actions taken by Disney such as Disney's acquisition of Arvida constituted an assumption by the Steinberg Group of a fiduciary duty to represent all shareholders fairly and adequately.[4421] The court found that a trier of fact could reasonably find that the Steinberg Group had "used its position as class representative for its own financial advantage" by agreeing to abandon its claim when it sold its stock back to the corporation.[4422] The court reasoned:

> In filing its derivative suit, the Steinberg Group volunteered to prevent Disney from acquiring the large debt associated with Arvida "which" it alleged, "could materially diminish Disney earnings and . . . threaten its long-term profitability." Instead of preventing the Arvida acquisition, the Steinberg Group bailed out of the lawsuit, and out of Disney, with $325 million of Disney's money. According to plaintiffs, Disney borrowed the entire amount used to buy off the Steinberg Group. This loan together with the $190 million Arvida debt increased Disney's total indebtedness to about $830 million compared to about $585 million before the Steinberg Group came on the scene. This increased debt load resulted in a lowering of Disney's credit rating and a plunge of 16 points in the price of Disney stock from 65-1/8, the trading day before the repurchase agreement, to 49-1/2 a week later.

> Thus, it can be argued, with a reasonable probability of success, the Disney shareholders are worse off after the intervention of their "volunteer champion" than they were before. They are like the citizens of a town whose volunteer fire department quits fighting the fire and sells its equipment to the arsonist who set it (who obtains the purchase price by setting fire to the building next door).[4423]

Accordingly, and while acknowledging that "the final decision must await trial and a trial might well produce a different result," the court found that the Disney shareholder plaintiffs had demonstrated

---

4421. *Id.* at 128-29, 214 Cal. Rptr. at 183-84.
4422. *Id.* at 129, 214 Cal. Rptr. at 184.
4423. *Id.* at 132-33, 214 Cal. Rptr. at 186-87.

a reasonable probability of success on the merits and upheld the trial court's grant of a preliminary injunction.[4424]

Four years later, in 1989, the trial court in *Heckmann* denied a motion for summary judgment by the defendants in the case.[4425] Relying heavily upon *Gaillard v. Natomas Co.*[4426] (a case reversing a grant of summary judgment in favor of directors in an action challenging the adoption of golden parachute severance provisions),[4427] the court explained that the Disney repurchase transaction had been approved by a special committee of outside directors during a meeting that lasted less than an hour and by the corporation's board during a three hour meeting, and that the special committee had been advised by the same counsel that had represented the corporation with respect to anti-takeover strategies and that had formulated the repurchase transaction.[4428] The court stated that "[i]t may well be that a trier of fact might find" that the conduct of Disney's directors and their reliance upon the advice of counsel who had put together the proposed agreement complied with the directors' fiduciary obligations under California law, but the "evidence of the briefness of the consideration of the issue by the special committee would reasonably support an inference to the contrary."[4429] This was particularly true, the court stated, in light of "the suspect nature of paying a premium to a shareholder to head off a takeover bid."[4430] The court also stated that the "motive and intent of the director defendants in dealing with the threat to their control represented by a takeover effort . . . are

---

4424. *Id*. at 138, 214 Cal. Rptr. at 190.

4425. *Heckmann v. Ahmanson*, [1989 Transfer Binder] Fed. Sec. L. Rep. (CCH) ¶ 94,447 (Cal. Super. Ct. Apr. 12, 1989).

4426. 208 Cal. App. 3d 1250, 256 Cal. Rptr. 702 (Cal. Ct. App. 1989).

4427. *See* Chapter III, Section H 3 d (discussing *Natomas* decision).

4428. [1989 Transfer Binder] Fed. Sec. L. Rep. (CCH) at 92,871-72.

4429. *Id*. at 92,872.

4430. *Id*.

factual issues that do not lend themselves to determination as a matter of law."[4431]

Motions for summary judgment by the Steinberg Group, Drexel Burnham Lambert (the Steinberg Group's financial advisor, which had agreed not to "arrange financing for others for the purchase of shares in furtherance of a proposed change of control" of Disney for two years) and Morgan Stanley (Disney's financial advisor)—each of whom were alleged to have aided and abetted the directors' breach of fiduciary duty—also were denied.[4432]

*Feinberg v. Carter*,[4433] a federal court decision construing New York law, involved a challenge to B.F. Goodrich Company's 1984 repurchase of 4.9 percent of its common stock from Carl C. Icahn. According to plaintiffs' complaint, Icahn informed Goodrich's board of directors that he intended to acquire as much as 30 percent of the corporation's stock, and that he then would consider purchasing a controlling interest in the corporation or using his voting power to obtain a seat on Goodrich's board. Icahn, according to plaintiffs, also offered to sell his stock back to the corporation at $35 per share—approximately $7 or 25 percent above the stock's market price at the time. Goodrich's board accepted the offer, and Icahn agreed not to acquire any Goodrich stock for five years and not to disclose the transaction unless required by law.[4434]

The court denied a motion to dismiss the action. The court explained that the challenged transaction was "not supported by a showing of any underlying justification."[4435] To the contrary, the court stated:

> The Defendant Directors posit no proper business justification for their purchase of Icahn's stock at $35 per share, when this stock possessed a market value of $28 per share. This repurchase cost Goodrich a total of $41 million, or about $8

---

4431. *Id.*
4432. *Id.* at 92,873-78.
4433. 652 F. Supp. 1066 (S.D.N.Y. 1987).
4434. *Id.* at 1069-70.
4435. *Id.* at 1073.

million . . . more than a purchase of the same volume of stock in the open market. In return for this $8 million premium, Goodrich received nothing more than the 4.9 percent shareholder interest in Icahn's hands, his promise that he would not acquire shares of Goodrich stock for five years, and his promise of silence about the transaction.

Defendants have nowhere suggested how the elimination of a potentially major purchaser of Goodrich stock would improve the position of others holding Goodrich stock or otherwise serve the interests of the corporation. Specifically, they have pointed to no evidence indicating that elimination of Icahn as a shareholder would so improve the company's financial position to justify an $8 million premium.[4436]

In short, according to the court, "[t]he only beneficiaries under repurchase, other than Icahn, were the Goodrich directors, who insured their continued control of the company."[4437]

The *Feinberg* court distinguished two New York state court decisions upholding stock repurchases noted in the preceding section of this Chapter[4438]—*Karfunkel v. USLIFE Corp.*[4439] and *Lewis v. Kurshan.*[4440] *USLIFE*, the *Feinberg* court stated, involved a repurchase from a shareholder who had not threatened to seek control and that was justified by a need to increase the small number of shares held in the corporate treasury.[4441] *Kurshan*, according to the *Feinberg* court, involved a repurchase from "a corporate raider whose goals would be detrimental to those of the corporation," a showing the Goodrich directors had not made with respect to Icahn because the "possibility of a change in management personnel, of itself, does not rise to the level of such a showing."[4442] The *Feinberg* court also stated its view that *Kurshan*

---

4436. *Id.*

4437. *Id.* at 1081.

4438. *See* Chapter III, Section I 1 a.

4439. 116 Misc. 2d 841, 455 N.Y.S.2d 937 (N.Y. Sup. Ct. N.Y. Co. 1982), *aff'd mem.*, 98 A.D.2d 628, 469 N.Y.S.2d 1020 (N.Y. App. Div. 1st Dep't 1983).

4440. N.Y.L.J., Dec. 1, 1983, at 6 (N.Y. Sup. Ct. N.Y. Co.).

4441. 652 F. Supp. at 1081-82.

4442. *Id.* at 1082.

was "inconsistent with the weight of New York authority."[4443] A federal court construing Kentucky law and federal law distinguished *Feinberg* in *Lou v. Belzberg*.[4444] The court in *Belzberg* explained that in *Feinberg* "the directors secretly had repurchased stock for $7 *above* the market price, had extracted a promise of silence from the seller, and had thereafter 'followed a continued policy of refusing to discuss or misrepresenting the transaction,'" while in *Belzberg* the directors had "repurchased the stock at *below* the market price level and immediately and publicly announced the acquisition."[4445]

*Fry v. Trump*,[4446] a federal court decision construing Delaware law, involved the repurchase at a premium by Bally Manufacturing Co. of approximately 10 percent of its stock from Donald Trump.[4447] The court held that plaintiffs adequately pleaded a breach of fiduciary duty by Bally's directors and accordingly denied a motion to dismiss the claim. The court acknowledged that a Delaware corporation has "the power to deal in its own stock" and "acquire a dissident's shares provided that the transaction is free from fraud or unfairness" but added that directors may not act "solely or primarily out of a desire to perpetuate themselves in office."[4448] The court concluded that plaintiffs "certainly alleged such a motive" and had pleaded facts supporting that claim, including an agreement by Trump to drop a lawsuit against Bally's directors and not to purchase Bally stock for ten years.[4449] These alleged facts, the court held, constituted enough to state a claim that the directors' motive in entering into the repurchase transaction was entrenchment.[4450]

---

4443. *Id.*

4444. 728 F. Supp. 1010 (S.D.N.Y. 1990).

4445. *Id.* at 1016 n.1, 1018-19.

4446. 681 F. Supp. 252 (D.N.J. 1988).

4447. *Id.* at 254-55.

4448. *Id.* at 257 (citing *Polk v. Good*, 507 A.2d 531, 536 (Del. 1986), and *Unocal Corp. v. Mesa Petroleum Co.*, 493 A.2d 946, 955 (Del. 1985) (both discussed in Chapter III, Section I 1 a)).

4449. *Id.* at 257.

4450. *Id.*

*c. Anti-Greenmail Measures.* A 1995 study by the Investor Responsibility Research Center Inc. concluded that 90 or approximately 6 percent of 1500 major corporations have adopted anti-greenmail charter provisions.[4451] These anti-greenmail provisions reflect the criticism greenmail payments have received and the experiences in the mid-1980s of companies like Avco Corporation, Phillips Petroleum Company, St. Regis Corporation and Walt Disney Productions, where a greenmail payment to one unwanted shareholder led directly or indirectly to the appearance of a second unwanted shareholder.[4452] These provisions typically prohibit the repurchase by the company of stock from a 5 percent or more shareholder at a premium over the stock's market price unless the repurchase is approved by a vote of a specified percentage of the corporation's shareholders.[4453] These provisions deter greenmail but also may deprive the board of the power to repurchase shares under circumstances where a repurchase would benefit the corporation and its shareholders.[4454]

---

4451. *Study Finds 1980s Corporate Defenses Remain Popular, But 'Hot Growth' Seen in Shareholder Action Constraints*, 10 Corporate Counsel Weekly (BNA) No. 40, Oct. 18, 1995, at 8.

4452. *See* Chapter III, Section I 1 Introduction; Note, *The Evolution of Greenmail: A Lawyer's Dilemma in Corporate Representation*, 2 Georgetown J. of Legal Ethics 533, 539 (1988); *Wall Street Bemoans a New 'Greenmail' Season*, N.Y. Times, Dec. 28, 1986, at E4; *The Dubious Value of Paying Greenmail*, Bus. Wk., Mar. 4, 1985, at 83; Cole, *Icahn Ends Offer for Phillips; All Shareholders to Get More*, N.Y. Times, Mar. 5, 1985, at A1; Taylor, *Project Fantasy: A Behind the Scenes Account of Disney's Desperate Battle Against the Raiders*, Manhattan, Inc., Nov. 1984, at 60; *Irv Jacobs is at It Again–At Avco*, Bus. Wk., Nov. 19, 1984, at 50; Barmash, *$757 Million Murdoch Offer to St. Regis; Concern May Find the Bid Hard to Fight*, N.Y. Times, July 19, 1984, at D1; *Another Run at St. Regis?*, Bus. Wk., July 16, 1984, at 38.

4453. *See* 2 Robert H. Winter, Mark H. Stumpf & Gerald L. Hawkins, *Shark Repellents and Golden Parachutes: A Handbook for the Practitioner* § 9.10, at 270-70.1 (1992); *see also id.* Exhs. 9.10A & 9.10D, at 374-74.3, 374.16-74.16-3 (providing examples of such provisions).

4454. *See* Macey & McChesney, *A Theoretical Analysis of Corporate Greenmail*, 95 Yale L.J. 13, 16 (1985) ("restrict[ing] greenmail
(continued...)

New York enacted an "anti-greenmail" statute in 1985. This statute prohibits the purchase by a corporation of more than 10 percent of its stock from a shareholder for a purchase price greater than the stock's market value unless (1) the transaction is approved by the corporation's board of directors and by an affirmative vote of a majority of the corporation's outstanding shares (unless the corporation's certificate requires a greater percentage), (2) the offer to purchase is made to all shareholders, or (3) the selling shareholder has held the shares being sold for more than two years.[4455] The statute defines "market value" as follows:

(A) in the case of stock, the highest closing sale price during the thirty-day period immediately preceding the date in question of a share of such stock on the composite tape for New York stock exchange-listed stocks, or, if such stock is not quoted on such composite tape or if such stock is not listed on such exchange, on the principal United States securities exchange registered under the Exchange Act on which such stock is listed, or, if such stock is not listed on any such exchange, the highest closing bid quotation with respect to a share of such stock during the thirty-day period preceding the date in question on the National Association of Securities Dealers, Inc. Automated Quotations System or any system then in use, or if no such quotations are available, the fair market value on the date in question of a share of such stock as determined by the board of directors of such corporation in good faith; and

(B) in the case of property other than cash or stock, the fair market value of such property on the date in question as determined by the board of directors of such corporation in good faith.[4456]

---

4454. (...continued)
across the board deprive[s] shareholders in at least some firms of a legitimate means of protecting or advancing their interests in certain situations") (footnotes omitted).
    4455. N.Y. Bus. Corp. Law § 513(c).
    4456. *Id.* § 912(a)(11).

The effectiveness of statutes (and charter provisions) of this type is limited because they permit repurchases at a premium (in New York) of up to 10 percent of the corporation's stock and repurchases of any amount of stock at (or below) market value even if that value has risen substantially as a result of the selling shareholder's activities. As one commentator has concluded, "rather than prohibiting greenmail, existing and proposed prohibitions in fact serve to legalize greenmail by creating a safe harbor within which it safely can be paid."[4457]

Ohio and Pennsylvania have adopted a different form of anti-greenmail statute. These statutes require the payment to the corporation by certain shareholders of all profits realized in stock sales, whether the sale is to the corporation or to any other person or entity. Ohio's statute provides that "any profit realized, directly or indirectly, from the disposition of any equity securities of a corporation by a person who, within eighteen months before disposition directly or indirectly, alone or in concert with others, made a proposal, or publicly disclosed the intention or possibility of making a proposal, to acquire control of the corporation, inures to and is recoverable by the corporation."[4458] Exceptions are created if the securities were acquired more than 18 months before the date of the proposal or public disclosure, the aggregate amount of the profit realized does not exceed $250,000, or the person disposing of the securities proves either of the following:

> (a)   At the time the proposals or public disclosures were made, the person's sole purpose in making the proposals or public disclosures was to succeed in acquiring control of the corporation and under the circumstances, including, without limitation, the person's proposed price, financing and other acquisition plans, the person's financial resources and capabilities, and all other alternatives reasonably anticipated to become available to the corporation's shareholders, there were reasonable grounds to believe that the person would acquire control of the corporation;

---

4457. Gilson, *Drafting an Effective Greenmail Prohibition*, 88 Colum. L. Rev. 329, 331 (1988).
4458. Ohio Sec. Law § 1707.043(A).

(b)   The person's public disclosure concerning the intention or possibility of making a proposal to acquire control of the corporation and all other potentially manipulative conduct and practices by or on his behalf were not effected with a purpose of affecting market trading and thereby increasing any profit or decreasing any loss which the person might realize, directly or indirectly, from the disposition of the equity securities and did not have a material effect upon the price or volume of market trading in the equity securities. Evidence with respect to the past practices of such person is admissible and relevant in respect to the person's intent or purpose.[4459]

Pennsylvania's statute covers any profit realized by a "controlling person or group," a term defined by the statute to include any person who has acquired or offered to acquire 20 percent of a corporation's voting shares, or who "has otherwise, directly or indirectly, publicly disclosed or caused to be disclosed . . . that it may seek to acquire control of a corporation through any means.[4460] The statute provides that any profit realized by a controlling person or group from any sale or other disposition of securities issued by the corporation belongs to and is recoverable by the corporation if (1) the securities were acquired within the 24 months before or the 18 months after the date the person or group became a controlling person or group, and (2) the securities were sold within the 18 months after the acquiring person or group became a controlling person or group.[4461]

Since 1987, the Internal Revenue Code has imposed a nondeductible 50 percent excise tax on any "gain or other income" realized as a result of the receipt of greenmail. The term greenmail is defined for the purpose of this provision as "any consideration" (presumably even at a below market price) "transferred by a corporation (or any person acting in concert with such corporation) to directly or indirectly acquire stock of such corporation" from any shareholder if (1) the selling shareholder has held the stock for less

---

4459. *Id.* § 1707.043(B)(2).
4460. Pa. Bus. Corp. Law §§ 2573(1)(i)-(ii).
4461. *Id.* § 2575.

than two years, (2) during this two year period the selling shareholder (or persons acting in concert with this shareholder) "made or
threatened to make a public tender offer," and (3) the corporation
acquired the stock "pursuant to an offer which was not made on the
same terms to all shareholders."[4462] The statute's reference to
payments by the corporation or any person acting in concert with
the corporation suggests that the statute may cover the purchase of
an unwanted bidder's shares by a competing bidder or by a white
knight or a white squire acting in accordance with the wishes of the
corporation. The statute does not include a definition of what constitutes a "threat" to make a public tender offer or specify who
makes this determination.

## 2.  Standstill Agreements

A standstill agreement is a "corporate peace treaty, designed
to inject a degree of stability, certainty, and cooperation into the
relationship between an issuer and a major investor."[4463] As
described by one court in the mid-1980s:

> The typical standstill agreement serves to relieve the antago-
> nism, suspicion, and hostility which, in this era of corporate
> takeover bids, often exists between a corporation and a sub-
> stantial shareholder. The essential provision of a standstill
> agreement is a limitation, usually expressed as a percentage
> figure, on the shareholder's holding of the corporation's
> stock, and generally prohibits the shareholder from making
> any tender offers for the corporation's stock during the
> term of the agreement. Such agreements may also restrict the
> shareholder's ability to transfer the corporation's shares by
> affording the corporation a right of first refusal. By entering
> into such agreements, the directors ensure that the relation-

----

4462. 26 U.S.C. § 5881; *see also* Department of the Treasury,
Internal Revenue Service, *Excise Tax Relating to Gain or Other Income
Realized By Any Person on Receipt of Greenmail*, 56 Fed. Reg. 65685
(1991) (codified at 26 C.F.R. § 156.5881-1).

4463. *Enterra Corp. v. SGS Assocs.*, 600 F. Supp. 678, 687 (E.D.
Pa. 1985) (quoting Bartlett & Andrews, *The Standstill Agreement: Legal
and Business Considerations Underlying a Corporate Peace Treaty*, 62
B.U. L. Rev. 143 (1982)).

ship between the corporation and an investor who has been purchasing significant blocks of stock will be clearly governed and defined. Such agreements also serve to avoid the unsettling impact on the corporation's business and workforce which could result from anticipation on the part of customers, shareholders, and employees that a takeover bid may be imminent. The corporation may seek to avert a costly control fight with the contracting shareholder by arriving at a negotiated understanding in advance of an anticipated bid for control. The corporation may also seek to "lock up" a significant block of stock with a "friendly" shareholder in the event that a third party attempts a takeover that the board believes is not in the corporation's best interest to accept.

The contracting shareholder, in return, receives assurance that the corporation will not oppose its acquisitions up to the specified limit. Often an investor's substantial purchases of the corporation's stock initially will cause the market price of the stock to rise, and it becomes more costly for the investor to acquire additional stock. The investor may therefore seek to clearly set forth its "investment-only" intentions in order to dispel any anticipation of a tender offer and reduce the market price for the corporation's stock. In entering into a standstill agreement, the investor may seek input into management decisions, and may also obtain certain valuable securities registration rights from the corporation.[4464]

Standstill provisions also frequently are utilized in confidentiality agreements providing potential bidders for a corporation non-public information in exchange for limitations upon the types of bids these bidders may make for the corporation—a subject discussed earlier in this Chapter.[4465]

The observations stated above, of course, are generalizations. The precise scope of any specific standstill agreement, like any other contract, depends upon the intent of the parties, as manifested by the language of the parties' agreement and any parole evidence not barred by the parole evidence rule. Examples of cases construing standstill agreements include the following:

---

4464. *Id*. at 687-88.
4465. *See* Chapter III, Section A 4 f.

- *General Portland, Inc. v. LaFarge Coppee S.A.*[4466] (holding that an agreement pursuant to which entities referred to by the court as the Lafarge group would not purchase shares of General Portland, Inc. stock while in possession of confidential information provided to it by General Portland without the approval of General Portland's board precluded a tender offer by the Lafarge group for General Portland stock because a tender offer "would require disclosure of information that the Lafarge group is obligated to hold in confidence").[4467]

- *West Point-Pepperell, Inc. v. Farley Inc.*[4468] (holding that a standstill agreement entered into by Odyssey Partners and J.P. Stevens & Co., Inc. pursuant to which Drexel Burnham Lambert Inc., as an advisor to Odyssey, received "evaluation materials" relating to J.P. Stevens, did not bind Drexel, which had become an advisor to a bidder for West Point-Pepperell, Inc., an entity that had acquired control of J.P. Stevens);[4469]

- *Mesa Partners v. Phillips Petroleum Co.*[4470] (holding that a standstill agreement entered into by Mesa Petroleum Company and General American Oil Company ("GAO") resolving competing efforts by Mesa and Phillips Petroleum Co. to acquire GAO and providing that Phillips would acquire GAO and that Mesa would receive compensation for its unsuccessful effort did not bar a subsequent effort by Mesa to acquire Phillips);[4471] and

---

4466. [1982-1983 Transfer Binder] Fed. Sec. L. Rep. (CCH) ¶ 99,148 (N.D. Tex. Aug. 28, 1981).

4467. *Id*. at 95,542-43.

4468. 711 F. Supp. 1088 (N.D. Ga. 1988).

4469. *Id*. at 1092-93.

4470. 488 A.2d 107 (Del. Ch. 1984).

4471. *Id*. at 108, 113-16.

- *Crescott Investment Associates v. Davis*[4472] (holding that a standstill agreement precluding DPC Acquisition Partners from obtaining control of Dataproducts Corporation (the "Company") but giving DPC "the right to commence a tender offer (and a related proxy or consent solicitation) for all stock of the Company" under certain specified conditions did not preclude the particular tender offer and consent solicitation that DPC had commenced).[4473]

Claims that board determinations to enter into standstill agreements constituted breaches of fiduciary duty have been considered in three litigations: one in Pennsylvania—*Enterra Corp. v. SGS Associates*[4474]—and two in Delaware—*Ivanhoe Partners v. Newmont Mining Corp.*[4475] and *Lewis v. Straetz*.[4476]

In *Enterra Corp. v. SGS Associates*,[4477] a federal court construing Pennsylvania law concluded that a standstill agreement did not constitute a breach of fiduciary duty. Pursuant to the business judgment rule, the court stated, if "a valid corporate purpose" exists for entering into a standstill agreement and "if management has consulted appropriate legal and business advisors before concluding the agreement," then "courts should not second-guess management's judgment that the corporation would benefit from an extended period of corporate peace.'"[4478] Applying this test, the court found that Enterra Corporation's board had "numerous valid corporate purposes" for entering into a standstill agreement with its largest shareholder, SGS Associates:

> [T]he Board, acting in part upon the advice of counsel and Enterra's financial advisors, determined that it was in the

---

4472. 16 Del. J. Corp. L. 274 (Del. Ch. Dec. 26, 1989).

4473. *Id*. at 289-97.

4474. 600 F. Supp. 678 (E.D. Pa. 1985).

4475. 535 A.2d 1334 (Del. 1987).

4476. 1986 Del. Ch. LEXIS 365, 1986 WL 2252 (Del. Ch. Feb. 12, 1986).

4477. 600 F. Supp. 678 (E.D. Pa. 1985).

4478. *Id*. at 688 (quoting Bartlett & Andrews, 62 B.U. L. Rev. at 150).

best interests of the corporation to execute the Agreement
because the stability created by the Agreement would provide
numerous benefits to the corporation, including the retention
(and recruitment) of key employees; allaying the 'takeover'
concerns of (and stabilizing relations with) various suppliers,
customers, and lenders; settling the trading market for
Enterra stock; and preserving the Board's ability to sell the
corporation (if at all) at a time and in a manner which is in
the best interests of the corporation and all shareholders.[4479]

The court accordingly denied a motion for a preliminary injunction
because the parties challenging the standstill agreement had not
demonstrated a reasonable likelihood of success on their claim that
the agreement constituted a breach of the board's fiduciary duty to
the corporation.[4480] The court did note, however, that it "would
be inclined to challenge" the validity of a standstill agreement
"requiring the shareholder to vote with management on any
material matter."[4481]

The Delaware Supreme Court in *Ivanhoe Partners v. Newmont Mining Corp.*[4482] upheld a standstill agreement pursuant to
which Consolidated Gold Fields increased its position in Newmont
Mining from 26 to 49.7 percent as part of Newmont's defense
against a 1987 tender offer by Ivanhoe Partners, an entity controlled by T. Boone Pickens.[4483] Gold Fields had agreed in 1983
to a 10-year standstill agreement restricting its ownership of
Newmont's stock and its representation on Newmont's board to 33-
1/3 percent. The 1983 standstill agreement also provided that Gold
Fields could terminate the agreement if any entity other than Gold
Fields acquired 9.9 percent or more of Newmont's stock.[4484] In
August 1987, Ivanhoe announced that it had purchased 9.95 percent

---

4479. *Id.* at 689.

4480. *Id.* at 692.

4481. *Id.* at 688; *cf. Good v. Texaco, Inc.*, 9 Del. J. Corp. L. 461,
469 (Del. Ch. May 14, 1984) (pre-litigation demand requirement held
excused in such a case; discussed in Chapter IV, Section B 5 c (ii)).

4482. 535 A.2d 1334 (Del. 1987).

4483. *Id.* at 1336-37 & n.1.

4484. *Id.* at 1338.

of Newmont's stock, and a short time later Ivanhoe announced a tender offer for an additional 42 percent of Newmont's stock at a price that Newmont's board determined was inadequate.[4485]

Gold Fields considered terminating its 1983 agreement with Newmont (as it was permitted to do because Ivanhoe had acquired more than 9.9 percent of Newmont's stock) and then utilizing open market purchases to acquire control of Newmont. Following negotiations between Gold Fields and Newmont, however, Gold Fields and Newmont agreed to enter into a revised standstill agreement. The new agreement provided that Newmont, one of the largest gold producers in North America, would declare a $33 per share dividend to be financed by the sale of the corporation's non-gold assets. The dividend was intended to reduce Newmont's liquidity and thus make Newmont a less attractive target to Ivanhoe, distribute value to all shareholders, and facilitate a "street sweep" by Gold Fields of up to 49.9 percent of Newmont's outstanding stock.[4486] The new standstill agreement provided that Gold Fields then would have 40 percent of the seats on Newmont's board, would support the board's slate of nominees for the remaining board seats, and would not transfer its interest to any entity that would not agree to be bound by the standstill agreement.[4487]

The parties signed this standstill agreement on September 20, 1987, Newmont declared the dividend, and Gold Fields "swept the street" until it had acquired 49.7 percent of Newmont's stock. On September 23, the Delaware Court of Chancery granted a temporary restraining order barring further purchases of Newmont stock by Gold Fields and requiring that shares acquired pursuant to the street sweep purchases be segregated and held separately from other shares.[4488] The court stated its preliminary belief that Gold

---

4485. *Id.* at 1338-39.

4486. *Id.* at 1336-37, 1339-40; *see also* Chapter III, Section E 2 a (discussing this dividend).

4487. *Id.* at 1340.

4488. *Id.; see also Ivanhoe Partners v. Newmont Mining Corp.*, 533 A.2d 585, 590 (Del. Ch.), *aff'd*, 535 A.2d 1334 (Del. 1987); *Ivanhoe Partners v. Newmont Mining Corp.*, 13 Del. J. Corp. L. 673 (Del. Ch. Sept. 28, 1987).

Fields' open market purchases would render Newmont's board "takeover proof" because Gold Fields would be a 49.7 percent shareholder required to vote for Newmont's director nominees and whose ability to transfer its shares would be severely restricted.[4489]

In response to these concerns, Newmont and Gold Fields amended their standstill agreement on September 27 (1) to allow Gold Fields to tender into any tender offer for all Newmont shares by an offeror having firm commitments for financing, and (2) to provide that Newmont and Gold Fields would use their best efforts to establish cumulative voting.[4490] On a motion for a preliminary injunction, the Court of Chancery reiterated its view that the September 20 standstill agreement "went too far" by "locking up" Gold Fields' 49.9 percent stock interest and thus "as a practical matter, assured the defeat of any hostile takeover attempt for possibly ten years."[4491] The court concluded, however, that the September 27 amendments to the agreement "appear to go far towards reducing, if not eliminating altogether, the violations preliminarily found to inhere in the September 20 standstill agreement."[4492] Preliminary injunctive relief therefore was unwarranted, the court stated, at least so long as no changes were made to the composition of Newmont's board prior to a determination whether Newmont's certificate of incorporation would be amended to permit cumulative voting.[4493] The court accordingly vacated its earlier temporary restraining order.[4494]

On appeal, the Delaware Supreme Court upheld Newmont's defensive strategy, including the standstill agreement entered into on September 20. The Supreme Court first noted the threat to Newmont created by "the stark possibility that Gold Fields would cancel the 1983 standstill agreement and acquire control of the

4489. 535 A.2d at 1340.
4490. Id.
4491. 533 A.2d at 608-09.
4492. Id. at 609.
4493. Id. at 610.
4494. Id.

company, thus leaving the remaining shareholders without protection on the 'back end'."[4495] The court reasoned as follows:

> A clear danger was posed by Ivanhoe's deliberate acquisition of 9.95% of Newmont shares, designed to free Gold Fields from the agreement, thereby permitting Ivanhoe and Gold Fields to ally themselves against Newmont. But even without Ivanhoe, Gold Fields now could wrest control away from the public shareholders. In addition, as the Newmont board was aware, Gold Fields had the necessary financial backing to unilaterally "sweep the street" and obtain control of Newmont. Finally, the threat which Gold Fields posed was real. The Gold Fields board had in fact paused to weigh its options. Throughout these maneuvers it had considered in earnest the possibility of either independently purchasing control of Newmont or selling its interest to Ivanhoe.[4496]

On this basis, the Supreme Court concluded that the September 20 standstill agreement was "a reasonable response to the Gold Fields threat."[4497] Quoting the court again:

> To forestall Gold Fields' entry into the open market to purchase a controlling interest to the detriment of Newmont's public shareholders, Newmont obtained the new standstill agreement which restricted Gold Fields' ability to purchase and exercise control of the corporation. Thus, Newmont exchanged the $33 dividend for a revised standstill agreement, which not only limited Gold Fields' ownership to 49.9%, but, significantly, restricted its board membership to 40%. This guaranteed Newmont's continued independence under a board consisting of 40% Gold Fields directors, 40% independent directors and 20% management nominated directors. Further, the 49.9% limit on Gold Fields' stock ownership protected Newmont's public shareholders from being squeezed out by an unbridled majority shareholder.[4498]

---

4495. 535 A.2d at 1342.
4496. *Id.* (citation omitted).
4497. *Id.* at 1343.
4498. *Id.*

The Supreme Court emphasized that the September 20 agreement "ensured an independent board."[4499] The transfer restriction "perpetuated the independent nature of the board" and the voting restriction "only required Gold Fields to cast its votes for the nominees of the entire independent board."[4500]

A subsequent decision by the Court of Chancery stated that although the Supreme Court's ruling provided "a highly persuasive (if not conclusive) ground for relieving" Newmont and Gold Fields "of their undertaking and obligation to institute cumulative voting . . . other factors must also be considered, namely possible 'intervening equities' that could make it inequitable for Newmont to be relieved of its undertaking to implement cumulative voting."[4501] The Court of Chancery, however, concluded that no such showing had been made and modified its preliminary injunction order to remove the condition requiring Newmont to implement cumulative voting.[4502]

The Delaware Court of Chancery in *Lewis v. Straetz*[4503] rejected an allegation that the board of directors of Textron, Inc. had breached its fiduciary duties by entering into a two-year standstill agreement with Chicago Pacific Corporation, a bidder that had made an all cash offer at a price representing a 27 percent premium over the then market price of Textron stock.[4504] The standstill agreement, plaintiffs alleged, deprived the corporation's shareholders of the ability to consider or decide upon any offer from Chicago Pacific for two years.[4505] Plaintiffs also alleged that

---

4499. *Id.* at 1345-46.

4500. *Id.* at 1346.

4501. *Ivanhoe Partners v. Newmont Mining Corp.*, 1988 Del. Ch. LEXIS 48, at *22, 1988 WL 34526, at *7 (Del. Ch. Apr. 7, 1988).

4502. *In re Newmont Mining Corp. Shareholders Litig.*, 1988 Del. Ch. LEXIS 95, at *3-4, 1988 WL 73750, at *1-2 (Del. Ch. July 15, 1988).

4503. 1986 Del. Ch. LEXIS 365, 1986 WL 2252 (Del. Ch. Feb. 12, 1986).

4504. 1986 Del. Ch. LEXIS 365, at *3, 1986 WL 2252, at *1.

4505. 1986 Del. Ch. LEXIS 365, at *4, 14, 1986 WL 2252, at *1, 4.

Textron had breached the standstill agreement by not providing Chicago Pacific with confidential information, as required by the standstill agreement.[4506]

Granting a motion to dismiss, the court stated that the facts alleged by plaintiffs, if true, would demonstrate nothing more than that the chairman of Chicago Pacific had written to the chairman of Textron to express his desire to meet and explore a possible combination of the two companies. The letter proposed, according to the court, that if a meeting took place Chicago Pacific would not purchase any shares for two years without the consent of Textron's board and would hold all information it obtained from Textron in strict confidence.[4507] The court concluded that these facts could not support a finding that the defendants had, as plaintiffs alleged, "in some way improperly induced or forced" Chicago Pacific to enter into the standstill agreement or that Textron had violated any part of the agreement by not providing Chicago Pacific with any non-public information.[4508]

---

4506. *Id.*
4507. 1986 Del. Ch. LEXIS 365, at *15-16, 1986 WL 2252, at *5.
4508. 1986 Del. Ch. LEXIS 365, at *4, 16, 1986 WL 2252, at *1, 5.

# CHAPTER IV

## The Business Judgment Rule in Shareholder Derivative Litigation

The business judgment rule plays three important roles in shareholder derivative litigation. First, as discussed in Chapters I, II and III, the business judgment rule protects directors by providing a defense on the merits to claims that directors have breached their fiduciary duties. Second, in many jurisdictions the business judgment rule plays a role in determining the necessity for a pre-litigation demand prior to the commencement of derivative litigation, and provides the standard of review pursuant to which courts evaluate a board decision to refuse a demand in cases where demand is made. Third, in cases where a pre-litigation demand is excused, the business judgment rule plays a role in motions to terminate derivative litigation by special litigation committees consisting of disinterested and independent directors.

This Chapter focuses first upon the nature of shareholder derivative litigation and the special rules governing this type of litigation, and then upon the demand requirement and the termination of derivative litigation by special litigation committees.

## A. The Nature of Shareholder Derivative Litigation and the Special Rules Governing Shareholder Derivative Litigation

A shareholder derivative action is a lawsuit brought by one or more minority shareholders in order "to enforce a *corporate* cause of action against officers, directors, and third parties."[1] This form of lawsuit evolved during the nineteenth century as an equitable device allowing courts to protect corporations and minority shareholders "against the frauds of the governing body of directors or trustees"[2] and "to place in the hands of the individual shareholder a means to protect the interests of the corporation from the misfeasance and malfeasance of 'faithless directors and managers.'"[3]

Unlike a claim a plaintiff brings on his or her own behalf to enforce a claim he or she personally possesses, a shareholder derivative claim is "a claim belonging not to the shareholder" bringing the action, "but to the corporation."[4] "The rights sought to be vindicated" are those of the corporation and "not those of the plaintiff suing derivatively on the corporation's behalf."[5] The claim is brought derivatively because "those in control of the company refuse or fail to assert" the claim belonging to the corporation."[6] A derivative action accordingly is "founded on a right of action existing in the corporation itself, and in which the corporation itself is the appropriate plaintiff," but that allows a shareholder "to step into

---

1. *Kamen v. Kemper Fin. Servs., Inc.*, 500 U.S. 90, 95 (1991) (quoting *Ross v. Bernhard*, 396 U.S. 531, 534 (1970)); *see also Lee v. Engle*, 1995 Del. Ch. LEXIS 149, at *9, 1995 WL 761222, at *3 (Del. Ch. Dec. 15, 1995) (citing earlier edition of this text for this proposition).

2. *Hawes v. City of Oakland*, 104 U.S. 450, 453 (1881).

3. *Kemper*, 500 U.S. at 95 (quoting *Cohen v. Beneficial Indus. Loan Corp.*, 337 U.S. 541, 548 (1949)).

4. *Levine v. Smith*, 591 A.2d 194, 200 (Del. 1991); *see also Klotz v. Consolidated Edison Co.*, 386 F. Supp. 577, 580-81 (S.D.N.Y. 1974); *Alabama By-Products Corp. v. Cede & Co.*, 657 A.2d 254, 265 (Del. 1995); *Rales v. Blasband*, 634 A.2d 927, 932 (Del. 1993); *In re MAXXAM, Inc./Federated Development Shareholders Litig.*, 698 A.2d 949, 956 (Del. Ch. 1996); *Marx v. Akers*, 88 N.Y.2d 189, 193, 666 N.E.2d 1034, 1036, 644 N.Y.S.2d 121, 123 (1996); *Auerbach v. Bennett*, 47 N.Y.2d 619, 631, 393 N.E.2d 994, 1000, 419 N.Y.S.2d 920, 927 (1979).

5. *Gall v. Exxon Corp.*, 418 F. Supp. 508, 514 (S.D.N.Y. 1976).

6. *Alabama By-Products*, 657 A.2d at 264.

the corporation's shoes and to seek in its right the restitution he could not demand in his own."[7]

The action thus is "two-fold" in nature: "First, it is the equivalent of a suit by the shareholders to compel the corporation to sue. Second, it is a suit by the corporation, asserted by the shareholders on its behalf, against those liable to it."[8] The claim belongs to the corporation,[9] the injury is to the corporation[10] and any damages recovered are paid to the corporation.[11] Accordingly,

---

7. *Daily Income Fund, Inc. v. Fox*, 464 U.S. 523, 528 (1984) (quoting *Hawes*, 104 U.S. at 460, and *Beneficial Indus. Loan*, 337 U.S. at 548).

8. *Aronson v. Lewis*, 473 A.2d 805, 811 (Del. 1984), *quoted in Kaplan v. Peat, Marwick, Mitchell & Co.*, 540 A.2d 726, 730 (Del. 1988) *and Spiegel v. Buntrock*, 571 A.2d 767, 773 (Del. 1990); *see also Alabama By-Products*, 657 A.2d at 264 65 ("[c]onceptually, there are two aspects to a derivative action: (1) an effort by the shareholders against the corporation to compel it to sue; and (2) the underlying claim by the corporation, asserted by shareholders on its behalf, against those who caused the corporation legal injury"); *Daily Income Fund*, 464 U.S. at 529 n.4 ("the derivative suit may be viewed as the consolidation in equity of, on the one hand, a suit by the shareholder against the directors in their official capacity, seeking an affirmative order that they sue the alleged wrongdoers, and, on the other, a suit by the corporation against these wrongdoers").

9. *Alabama By-Products*, 657 A.2d at 265; *Levine*, 591 A.2d at 200; *Marx v. Akers*, 88 N.Y.2d at 193, 666 N.E.2d at 1036, 644 N.Y.S.2d at 123; *Auerbach*, 47 N.Y.2d at 631, 393 N.E.2d at 1000, 419 N.Y.S.2d at 927.

10. *See, e.g., Crocker v. Federal Deposit Ins. Corp.*, 826 F.2d 347, 349 (5th Cir. 1987), *cert. denied*, 485 U.S. 905 (1988); *Gaff v. Federal Deposit Ins. Corp.*, 814 F.2d 311, 315 (6th Cir.), *vacated in part on other grounds*, 828 F.2d 1145 (6th Cir. 1987); *Langner v. Brown*, 913 F. Supp. 260, 264 (S.D.N.Y. 1996); *Jones v. H.F. Ahmanson & Co.*, 1 Cal. 3d 93, 107, 460 P.2d 464, 470, 81 Cal. Rptr. 592, 598 (1969); *In re Fuqua Indus., Inc. Shareholder Litig.*, 1997 Del. Ch. LEXIS 72, at *47, 1997 WL 257460, at *12 (Del. Ch. May 17, 1997); *Strasenburgh v. Straubmuller*, 683 A.2d 818, 829 (N.J. 1996).

11. *See, e.g., Ross*, 396 U.S. at 538; *Bagdon v. Bridgestone/Firestone, Inc.*, 916 F.2d 379, 383 (7th Cir. 1990), *cert. denied*, 500 U.S.

(continued...)

the action "is not an action against the corporation, but in the corporation's favor."[12] "The corporation is a necessary party to the action; without it the case cannot proceed. Although named a defendant, it is the real party in interest, the stockholder being at best the nominal plaintiff."[13] "[W]ithout the presence of the corporation complete relief cannot be achieved, and the corporation's interests cannot be protected."[14] "[A] corporation may defend a stockholder's derivative action (although theoretically any recovery rebounds to the benefit of the corporation) if the corporate interests are threatened by the suit."[15] Majority shareholders who have the

---

11. (...continued)
952 (1991); *Zimmerman v. Bell*, 800 F.2d 386, 390 & n.* (4th Cir. 1986); *Guzewicz v. Eberle*, 953 F. Supp. 108, 110 (E.D. Pa. 1997); *In re Salomon Inc. Shareholders' Derivative Litig.*, [1994-1995 Transfer Binder] Fed. Sec. L. Rep. (CCH) ¶ 98,454, at 91,118 (S.D.N.Y. Sept. 25, 1994); *Jones*, 1 Cal. 3d at 107, 460 P.2d at 470, 81 Cal. Rptr. at 598; *Alabama By-Products*, 657 A.2d at 265; *Phoenix Airline Servs., Inc. v. Metro Airlines, Inc.*, 397 S.E.2d 699, 702 (Ga. 1990); *Finci v. American Casualty Co.*, 593 A.2d 1069, 1082 (Md. 1991); *Marx*, 88 N.Y.2d at 193, 666 N.E.2d at 1036, 644 N.Y.S.2d at 123; *Outen v. Mical*, 454 S.E.2d 883, 886 (N.C. Ct. App. 1995).

12. *Grand Council v. Owens*, 620 N.E.2d 234, 238 (Ohio Ct. App. 1993).

13. *Ross*, 396 U.S. at 538; *see also Liddy v. Urbanek*, 707 F.2d 1222, 1224 (11th Cir. 1983); *Salomon*, [1994-1995 Transfer Binder] Fed. Sec. L. Rep (CCH) at 91,118; *Nejmanowski v. Nejmanowski*, 841 F. Supp. 864, 865 (C.D. Ill. 1994); *Jones*, 1 Cal. 3d at 107, 460 P.2d at 470, 81 Cal. Rptr. at 598; *Sternberg v. O'Neil*, 550 A.2d 1105, 1124 (Del. 1988); *Weinberger v. Lorenzo*, 16 Del. J. Corp. L. 1647, 1653 (Del. Ch. Oct. 11, 1990); *Dean v. Kellogg*, 292 N.W. 704, 707-08 (Mich. 1940).

14. *ZB Holdings, Inc. v. White*, 144 F.R.D. 42, 45 (S.D.N.Y. 1992).

15. *Blish v. Thompson Automatic Arms Corp.*, 64 A.2d 581, 607 (Del. 1948); *see also Alleghany Corp. v. Kirby*, 218 F. Supp. 164, 186 (S.D.N.Y. 1963) ("New York law allows a corporation to expend funds in defense of a derivative action presumptively brought in its behalf when some interest of the corporation is threatened"); *Fuller v. American Mach. & Foundry Co.*, 91 F. Supp. 710, 711 (S.D.N.Y. 1950); *Ireland v.*

(continued...)

ability to direct and control the corporation's activities and commence litigation in the corporation's name may not proceed derivatively,[16] but derivative actions have been permitted in instances where there are two 50 percent shareholders.[17]

"Because shareholder derivative actions are brought 'to enforce a *corporate* cause of action against officers, directors and third parties,' the shareholders, 'standing in the shoes of the corporation' have no rights greater than those of the corporation, nor can those they choose to sue be deprived of defenses they could assert against the corporation's claims."[18] One court has held that this includes any contractual right to arbitration, pursuant, for example, to the Constitution and rules of the New York Stock Exchange.[19] After the New York Stock Exchange declined to arbitrate the dispute in that case, as the Exchange is permitted by its rules to do, the court held that litigation was permitted.[20] The court rejected a claim that an alternative arbitrator had to be selected. The court explained that "we cannot compel a party to arbitrate a dispute before someone other than the NYSE when that

---

15. (...continued)
*Wynkoop*, 539 P.2d 1349, 1360 (Colo. Ct. App. 1975); *Godley v. Crandall & Godley Co.*, 181 A.D. 75, 78, 168 N.Y.S. 251, 254 (N.Y. App. Div. 1st Dep't 1917), *aff'd mem.*, 227 N.Y. 656, 126 N.E. 907 (1920); *Hornsby v. Lohmeyer*, 72 A.2d 294, 299 (Pa. 1950); *National Bankers Life Ins. Co. v. Adler*, 324 S.W.2d 35, 37 (Tex. Civ. App. 1959).

16. *See Hubner v. Schoonmaker*, 1991 U.S. Dist. LEXIS 4866, at *8, 1991 WL 60594, at *3 (E.D. Pa. Apr. 9, 1991); *Platt v. Richardson*, [1989-1990 Transfer Binder] Fed. Sec. L. Rep. (CCH) ¶ 94,786, at 94,235-36 (M.D. Pa. June 6, 1989).

17. *See Ono v. Itoyama*, 884 F. Supp. 892, 895-99 (D.N.J. 1995); *aff'd mem.*, 79 F.3d 1138 (3d Cir. 1996); *Executive Leasing Co. v. Leder*, 191 A.2d 199, 200, 594 N.Y.S.2d 217, 218-19 (N.Y. App. Div. 1st Dep't 1993).

18. *Salomon*, [1994-1995 Transfer Binder] Fed. Sec. L. Rep. (CCH) at 91,118 (citations omitted).

19. *In re Salomon Inc. Shareholders' Derivative Litig.*, 68 F.3d 554, 557-59 (2d Cir. 1995).

20. *Id.* at 555-61.

party had agreed to arbitrate disputes only before the NYSE and the NYSE, in turn, exercising its discretion under its Constitution, has refused the use of its facilities to arbitrate the dispute in question."[21]

The courts have recognized that "derivative actions brought by minority stockholders could, if unconstrained, undermine the basic principle of corporate governance that the decisions of a corporation—including the decision to initiate litigation—should be made by the board of directors or the majority of shareholders."[22] Likewise, "it has long been recognized," the derivative action is susceptible to abuse in cases where derivative claims are filed "more with a view to obtaining a settlement resulting in fees to the plaintiff's attorney than to righting a wrong to the corporation (the so-called 'strike suit')."[23] As the Delaware Court of Chancery observed in 1996 in *Gagliardi v. TriFoods International, Inc.*[24]:

> Asserting a derivative claim allows an attorney in the role of agent for shareholders to exert substantially magnified settlement pressure on a defendant . . . . Strike suits are a greater threat in this context than in civil litigation between two principles. Thus, in such cases the consequences of surviving a motion to dismiss are, as a practical matter, substantially more significant than in garden variety civil litigation.[25]

Prerequisites to the commencement of derivative litigation and other special rules governing derivative litigation therefore have developed in order "to filter such cases at an early stage more

---

21. *Id.* at 558.

22. *Daily Income Fund*, 464 U.S. at 530; *see also Kemper*, 500 U.S. at 101 ("the demand requirement implements 'the basic principle of corporate governance that the decisions of a corporation—including the decision to initiate litigation—should be made by the board of directors or the majority of shareholders'") (quoting *Daily Income Fund*, 464 U.S. at 530).

23. 2 Model Bus. Corp. Act Annotated §§ 7.40–7.47 Introductory Comment at 7-257 (3d ed. 1996).

24. 683 A.2d 1049 (Del. Ch. 1996) (published in part, complete text available at 1996 Del. Ch. LEXIS 87 and 1996 WL 422330).

25. *Id.* at 1054.

finely" than is the case in other types of litigation[26] and "prevent abuse of this remedy."[27] Most prominent among these prerequisites and special rules are the following requirements.

## 1. The Contemporaneous Ownership Requirement: At the Time of the Alleged Wrongdoing

To have standing to commence a derivative action, a shareholder-plaintiff must have owned stock in the corporation at the time of the alleged wrong to the corporation. Section 327 of the Delaware General Corporation Law is typical of this contemporaneous ownership requirement, providing as follows:

> In any derivative suit instituted by a stockholder of a corporation, it shall be averred in the complaint that the plaintiff was a stockholder of the corporation at the time of the transaction of which he complains or that his stock thereafter devolved upon him by operation of law.[28]

Delaware Court of Chancery Rule 23.1 likewise provides the following:

> In a derivative action . . . the complaint shall allege that the plaintiff was a shareholder . . . at the time of the transaction of which the plaintiff complains or that plaintiff's share . . . thereafter devolved upon him by operation of law.[29]

Similar provisions appear in the Federal Rules of Civil Procedure and statutes and rules adopted in other states.[30] Under these statutes and rules, where alleged wrongdoing occurs before a plaintiff was a shareholder, the plaintiff has no standing to assert a derivative claim arising out of the alleged wrongdoing.[31]

---

26. *Id.*
27. *Kemper*, 500 U.S. at 95-96.
28. Del. Gen. Corp. Law § 327.
29. Del. Ch. R. 23.1.
30. *See, e.g.*, Fed. R. Civ. P. 23.1; N.Y. Bus. Corp § 626(b).
31. *See, e.g.*, *Scattergood v. Perelman*, 945 F.2d 618, 62

(cr

The "long-recognized policy" underlying this rule "is to prevent strike suits whereby an individual purchases stock in a corporation with purely litigious motives, i.e., for the sole purpose of prosecuting a derivative action to attack transactions which occurred prior to the purchase of stock."[32] The fact that a shareholder-plaintiff does not know of alleged wrongs at the time he acquires stock is irrelevant because statutes such as the Delaware statute do "not include any provision exempting 'good faith' purchasers" from their terms.[33]

The Model Business Corporation Act states the contemporaneous ownership requirement in similar terms. The Model Act provides that a shareholder "may not commence or maintain a derivative proceeding unless the shareholder . . . was a shareholder of the corporation at the time of the act or omission complained of."[34] The Official Comment explains that relaxing the requirement that a plaintiff must have been a shareholder at the time of the alleged wrongdoing "might encourage the acquisition of shares in

---

31. (...continued)
1991); *7457 Partners v. Beck*, 682 A.2d 160, 162-63 (Del. 1996); *Lewis v. Anderson*, 477 A.2d 1040, 1045-47 (Del. 1984); *International Equity Capital Growth Fund, L.P. v. Clegg*, 23 Del. J. Corp. L. 259, 269 (Del. Ch. Apr. 21, 1997); *Levien v. Sinclair Oil Corp.*, 261 A.2d 911, 921-23 (Del. Ch. 1969), *aff'd in part and rev'd in part on other grounds*, 280 A.2d 717 (Del. 1971); *Schreiber v. Bryan*, 396 A.2d 512, 517 (Del. Ch. 1978); *Newkirk v. W.J. Rainey, Inc.*, 76 A.2d 121, 123-24 (Del. Ch. 1950); *Pogostin v. Leighton*, 523 A.2d 1078, 1083-85 (N.J. Super. Ct. App. Div.), *cert. denied*, 484 U.S. 964 (1987); *Brambles USA, Inc. v. Blocker*, 731 F. Supp. 643, 649-52 (D. Del.), *motion for reargument denied*, 735 F. Supp. 1239, 1241-42 (D. Del. 1990); *cf. Salomon Bros., Inc. v. Interstate Bakeries Corp.*, 576 A.2d 650, 652, 653-54 (Del. Ch. 1989) (fact that shareholder acquired stock after learning of merger transaction that would trigger right to commence an appraisal proceeding does not preclude an appraisal proceeding), *appeal refused*, 571 A.2d 787 (unpublished opinion, text available at 1990 Del. LEXIS 32 and 1990 WL 18152) (Del. Feb. 6, 1990).

32. *Alabama By-Products Corp. v. Cede & Co.*, 657 A.2d 254, 264 n.12 (Del. 1995).

33. *7547 Partners*, 682 A.2d at 163.

34. 2 Model Bus. Corp. Act Annotated § 7.41(1) (3d ed. 1996).

order to bring a lawsuit, resulting in litigation on peripheral issues such as the extent of the plaintiff's knowledge of the transaction in question when the plaintiff acquired the shares."[35] The Official Comment notes that "there has been no persuasive showing that the contemporaneous ownership rule has prevented the litigation of substantial suits, at least with respect to publicly held corporations where there are many persons who might qualify as plaintiffs to bring suit even if subsequent purchasers are disqualified."[36]

A California statute stands in contrast to the majority rule. This statute grants courts discretion "to maintain the action on a preliminary showing to and determination by the court" that (1) there is a "strong prima facie case in favor of the claim asserted," (2) "no other similar action has been or is likely to be instituted," (3) the plaintiff acquired his shares before learning of the wrongdoing or disclosure of the wrongdoing to the public, (4) "unless the action can be maintained the defendant may retain a gain derived" from a "willful breach of a fiduciary duty," and (5) "the requested relief will not result in unjust enrichment of the corporation or any shareholder of the corporation."[37] A Pennsylvania statute grants courts discretion to allow shareholders who purchase shares after an alleged wrong has occurred to commence a derivative action where "there is a strong prima facie case in favor of the claim asserted on behalf of the corporation and . . . without the action serious injustice will result."[38]

Principles of Corporate Governance: Analysis and Recommendations has adopted a variation of the California and Pennsylvania approach. Principles of Corporate Governance permits a shareholder to commence a derivative action if the shareholder acquired his shares "before the material facts relating to the alleged wrong were publicly disclosed or were known by, or specifically communicated to, the holder."[39] The drafters of Principles of

---

35. *Id.* § 7.41 Official Comment at 7-340.

36. *Id.*

37. Cal. Gen. Corp. Law § 800(b)(1).

38. Pa. Bus. Corp. Law § 1782(b).

39. 2 Principles of Corporate Governance: Analysis and Recom-
(continued...)

Corporate Governance reason that the majority rule requiring that a shareholder hold shares at the time of a challenged transaction is intended "to prevent unjust enrichment by those who acquired their shares with knowledge of the alleged wrong and to discourage the litigation of purchased grievances" but "sweeps overbroadly and goes well beyond these legitimate policy objections."[40] According to the drafters, "[u]nquestionably, some shareholders who purchased after the time of the alleged wrong may still have been injured by it" because "[i]f the alleged wrong has not yet been publicly disclosed, it is unlikely that the purchasing shareholder paid a properly discounted price."[41] The drafters thus adopt "public disclosure of the wrong as the better cut off point, in the belief that on disclosure the marketplace will adjust the security's price to reflect the injury."[42]

Some courts have adopted a "continuing wrong" modification to the requirement that a shareholder plaintiff must have been a shareholder at the time of the wrong alleged in a derivative action. This "continuing wrong" requirement permits a shareholder "to challenge a corporate action that occurred before the plaintiff became a shareholder if that action was part of a continuing fraud or impropriety that was begun but not completed at the time the plaintiff became a shareholder."[43] The continuing wrong rule is "less an exception to the contemporaneous ownership rule than an expansive definition of what constitutes a 'transaction.'"[44] "[F]ederal courts generally have rejected the . . . 'continuing wrong' notion."[45]

---

39. (...continued)
mendations § 7.02(a)(1) (1994).

40. *Id.* § 7.02 Comment at 37.

41. *Id.*

42. *Id.*

43. *Ensign Corp. v. Interlogic Trace, Inc.,* [1990-1991 Transfer Binder] Fed. Sec. L. Rep. (CCH) ¶ 95,766, at 98,677 (S.D.N.Y. Dec. 19, 1990).

44. *Id.*

45. 7C Charles Alan Wright, Arthur R. Miller & Mary Kay Kane, *Federal Practice and Procedure* § 1828, at 65 (1986 & Supp. 1998).

The Delaware Court of Chancery has held that a purchaser of stock is not a shareholder for purposes of the contemporaneous ownership requirement until settlement of the trade.[46] The Court of Chancery has permitted intervention by a new plaintiff after it was discovered, midway through trial, that the plaintiff in the case was not a shareholder at the time of the transaction challenged in the case.[47]

## 2. The Contemporaneous Ownership Requirement: Throughout the Litigation

To have standing, a shareholder-plaintiff must own stock in the corporation not just at the time of the alleged wrong to the corporation.[48] The shareholder-plaintiff also must continue to hold stock in the corporation from the commencement of the litigation until the termination of the litigation.[49] The rationale for this rule is as follows:

[A] shareholder is permitted to intrude upon the authority of the board by means of a derivative suit only because his status as a shareholder provides an interest and incentive to

---

46. *Avacus Partners, L.P. v. Brian*, [1991 Transfer Binder] Fed. Sec. L. Rep. (CCH) ¶ 96,232, at 91,213-14 (Del. Ch. Oct. 24, 1990).

47. *In re MAXXAM, Inc./Federated Dev. Shareholders Litig.*, 698 A.2d 949, 953-58 (Del. Ch. 1996).

48. *See* Chapter IV, Section A 1.

49. *See, e.g., Scattergood v. Perelman*, 945 F.2d 618, 626 (3d Cir. 1991); *Alabama By-Products Corp. v. Cede & Co.*, 657 A.2d 254, 264 (Del. 1995); *Kramer v. Western Pac. Indus., Inc.*, 546 A.2d 348, 354-55 (Del. 1988); *Lewis v. Anderson*, 477 A.2d 1040, 1045-47 (Del. 1984); *International Equity Capital Growth Fund, L.P. v. Clegg*, 23 Del. J. Corp. L. 259, 269 (Del. Ch. Apr. 21, 1997); *Balin v. Amerimar Realty Co.*, 22 Del. J. Corp. L. 1115, 1126-27 (Del. Ch. Nov. 15, 1996); *Grace Bros., Ltd. v. Farley Indus., Inc.*, 450 S.E.2d 814, 816 (Ga. 1994); *Tenney v. Rosenthal*, 6 N.Y.2d 204, 210-11, 160 N.E.2d 463, 466-67, 189 N.Y.S.2d 158, 162-63 (1959); *Rubinstein v. Catacosinos*, 91 A.D.2d 445, 446, 459 N.Y.S.2d 286, 287 (N.Y. App. Div. 1st Dep't), *aff'd*, 60 N.Y.2d 890, 458 N.E.2d 1247, 470 N.Y.S.2d 570 (1983); *Bronzaft v. Caporali*, 162 Misc. 2d 281, 283-86, 616 N.Y.S.2d 863, 865-67 (N.Y. Sup. Ct. N.Y. Co. 1994).

> obtain legal redress for the benefit of the corporation. Once
> the derivative plaintiff ceases to be a stockholder in the cor-
> poration on whose behalf the suit was brought, he no longer
> has a financial interest in any recovery pursued for the bene-
> fit of the corporation. . . . [B]ecause a plaintiff may lose his
> incentive to prosecute a suit by being divested of the property
> interest (shares of stock) in the corporation for whose behalf
> he acts, the derivative suit requires "continued as well as
> original standing."[50]

In other words, "[s]tanding is justified only by this proprietary
interest created by the stockholder relationship and the possible
indirect benefits the nominal plaintiff may acquire *qua* stockholder
of the corporation which is the real party in interest."[51] The Delaware Court of Chancery has permitted intervention by a new plaintiff after the original plaintiff sells his stock and loses standing,
even where two years had passed from the sale of stock by the original plaintiff to the discovery by plaintiff's counsel and the court
of the sale and the new plaintiff's motion to intervene.[52]

The Delaware courts have created exceptions to this rule in
cases where a merger or other corporate reorganization (1) "is the
subject of a claim of fraud, being perpetrated merely to deprive
shareholders of the standing to bring a derivative action," or (2) "is
in reality merely a reorganization which does not affect plaintiff's
ownership in the business enterprise."[53]

---

50. *Alabama By-Products*, 657 A.2d at 265-66 (quoting *Anderson*, 477 A.2d at 1047).

51. *Kauffman v. Dreyfus Fund, Inc.*, 434 F.2d 727, 735-36 (3d Cir. 1970), *cert denied*, 401 U.S. 974 (1971), *quoted in Schilling v. Belcher*, 582 F.2d 995, 1002 (5th Cir. 1978), *Lewis v. Knutson*, 699 F.2d 230, 238 (5th Cir. 1983), *Ashburn v. Wicker*, 381 S.E.2d 876, 879 (N.C. Ct. App. 1989), *White v. Banes Co.*, 866 P.2d 339, 342 (N.M. 1993) and *Christopher v. Liberty Oil & Gas Corp.*, 665 So. 2d 410, 411 (La. Ct. App. 1995).

52. *Steiner v. Meyerson*, 1997 Del. Ch. LEXIS 88, at *9-12, 1997 WL 349169, at *4-5 (Del. Ch. June 13, 1997).

53. *Kramer v. Western Pac. Indus., Inc.*, 546 A.2d 348, 354 (Del. 1988); *Bonime v. Biaggini*, 10 Del. J. Corp. L. 610, 614-15 (Del. Ch.
(continued...)

These exceptions are construed narrowly. The Delaware Supreme Court's decision in *Lewis v. Anderson*,[54] for example, involved a derivative action commenced by a shareholder of Conoco, Inc. ("Old Conoco") against Old Conoco directors and officers, challenging "golden parachute" employment agreements entered into by Old Conoco with nine officers, two of whom also were directors.[55] Old Conoco subsequently was merged into a subsidiary of E.I. Du Pont de Nemours and Company, which was re-named Conoco, Inc. ("New Conoco").[56] The merger was a stock-for-stock merger, with Old Conoco shareholders receiving shares of Du Pont stock in return for their Old Conoco shares.[57]

The court held that the requirement that the plaintiff be a shareholder at the time a litigation is commenced and maintain shareholder status throughout the litigation was "fully applicable to a question of post-merger standing."[58] The court held that the two exceptions to the contemporaneous ownership rule stated above— i.e., "(1) where the merger itself is the subject of a claim of fraud; and (2) where the merger is in reality a reorganization which does not affect plaintiff's ownership of the business enterprise"—were "not applicable to this case" because "[p]laintiff has not asserted that the merger was perpetrated to deprive Old Conoco of its claim against the individual defendants; and the merger was clearly not a reorganization resulting in a holding company."[59] The court then

---

53. (...continued)
Dec. 7, 1984), *aff'd mem.*, 505 A.2d 451 (Del. 1985); *Anderson*, 477 A.2d at 1046 n.10; *Bokat v. Getty Oil Co.*, 262 A.2d 246, 249 (Del. 1970); *Merritt v. Colonial Foods, Inc.*, 505 A.2d 757, 763-66 (Del. Ch. 1986); *Schreiber v. Carney*, 447 A.2d 17, 21-22 (Del. Ch. 1982); *Helfand v. Gambee*, 136 A.2d 558, 561-62 (Del. Ch. 1957).

54. 477 A.2d 1040 (Del. 1984).

55. *Id.* at 1042.

56. *Id.*

57. *Id.*

58. *Id.* at 1046.

59. *Id.* at 1046 n.10.

rejected plaintiff's effort "to carve out a further exception for pre-merger derivative claims."[60]

The Delaware Supreme Court in *Kramer v. Western Pacific Industries, Inc.*[61] reached the same result in a case where a shareholder of Western Pacific Industries, Inc. who had commenced a derivative action became a former shareholder following a cash-out merger.[62] The court re-affirmed the rule requiring that "[t]o have standing to maintain a shareholder derivative suit, a plaintiff must be a shareholder at the time of the filing of the suit and must remain a shareholder throughout the litigation."[63] The court then held that the two exceptions to this rule were "clearly inapplicable": "Kramer does not contend that the merger was fraudulent, perpetuated merely to deprive Western Pacific of its claim against the defendants; nor does plaintiff assert that Western Pacific has simply been through a reorganization not affecting plaintiff's ownership."[64] The Delaware Supreme Court in *In re Tri-Star Pictures, Inc., Litigation*[65] similarly stated that Tri-Star Pictures, Inc. shareholders lost their standing to pursue derivative claims on behalf of Tri-Star following a cash-out merger of Tri-Star into Sony U.S.A., Inc. The court added, however, that if Tri-Star merged with Sony "in order to deprive Tri-Star minority stockholders of their claims, then such an action would constitute fraud sufficient to sustain even derivative claims."[66]

The Third Circuit in *Scattergood v. Perelman*,[67] construing Delaware law, held that shareholders lost standing to pursue derivative claims upon the completion of a cash-out merger, and rejected the plaintiffs' contention in that case that the merger was "the subject of a claim of fraud, being perpetrated merely to

---

60. *Id.*
61. 546 A.2d 348 (Del. 1988).
62. *Id.* at 349.
63. *Id.* at 354.
64. *Id.* at 354-55.
65. 634 A.2d 319 (Del. 1993).
66. *Id.* at 331 & n.14.
67. 945 F.2d 618 (3d Cir. 1991).

deprive shareholders of the standing to bring a derivative action."[68] "[F]or this exception to apply," the court stated, "the sole or at least dominant motive of the merger must be to deprive the shareholders of standing to bring the derivative suit."[69] Here, the court concluded, "the complaint does not allege that the merger was so motivated; to the contrary, it alleges that the merger was a long planned move to freeze the minority shareholders out at an unreasonably low price."[70] Sufficient allegations that a merger was itself the product of fraud were found in *Richardson v. Gray*,[71] a New York decision construing Delaware law in a case where plaintiffs stated "a valid claim for rescission . . . and established the need for preliminary injunctive relief" and where there were "important factual issues about the timing of the merger, coming one month after commencement of stockholder derivative actions . . . and days after at least one of the defendants was served" with an order to show cause.[72]

A different approach was taken by the United States Supreme Court in *Gollust v. Mendell*,[73] a case holding in the context of an action brought under Section 16(b) of the Securities Exchange Act of 1934[74] that a shareholder plaintiff who owns stock at the time the shareholder institutes a derivative action does not lose standing to maintain the claim following the acquisition of the corporation in a transaction pursuant to which the shareholder receives cash and stock in the acquiror.[75] The Supreme Court based this conclusion upon its view that the shareholder in the case "retains a continuing financial interest in the outcome of the litigation derived from his stock" in the new owner of the corporation.[76]

---

68. *Id.* at 626.
69. *Id.*
70. *Id.*
71. N.Y.L.J., Nov. 14, 1996, at 28 (N.Y. Sup. Ct. N.Y. Co.).
72. *Id.*
73. 501 U.S. 115 (1991).
74. 15 U.S.C. § 78p(b).
75. 501 U.S. at 126-28.
76. *Id.* at 127-28.

The Third Circuit in *Blasband v. Rales*[77] found *Gollust* "instructive" and held under Delaware law that a shareholder who has standing to assert a derivative claim prior to a merger continues to have standing following the merger where as a result of the merger the shareholder receives a financial interest in the acquiring corporation and asserts a double derivative claim as a shareholder of the acquiring corporation.[78]

In subsequent proceedings, the district court issued an order certifying to the Delaware Supreme Court the standing question that the Third Circuit had decided. According to the district court, the Third Circuit's decision "ignored the mandate" of Delaware law, and "[i]f the decision of the Court of Appeals is found to be contrary to Delaware law, the Delaware Supreme Court should make that determination promptly in order to avoid future confusion from a non-binding source and to neutralize a contaminating opinion relating to Delaware corporate law."[79] The Third Circuit issued a writ of mandamus directing the district court to vacate that order on the ground that "[w]hether the Delaware Supreme Court might have reached a different result if the derivative suit had been brought in the state courts, or if the standing question had been certified to it before the district court dismissed the action, our opinion nevertheless was conclusive on the standing point in the derivative suit."[80]

In further subsequent proceedings, the Delaware Supreme Court stated in a decision determining a different certified question that "[t]he question of Blasband's standing to pursue the derivative claims in the amended complaint has already been decided by the Third Circuit," and that ruling "cannot be reconsidered by this Court in the present proceeding."[81] The court noted that "[o]ur recognition of the limited scope of the present proceeding should not be interpreted as either an acceptance or a rejection of the Third

---

77. 971 F.2d 1034 (3d Cir. 1992).
78. *Id.* at 1040-46 & n.7.
79. *Blasband v. Rales*, 979 F.2d 324, 326 (3d Cir. 1992).
80. *Id.* at 328.
81. *Rales v. Blasband*, 634 A.2d 927, 931 (Del. 1993).

Circuit's conclusions on matters of the substantive Delaware corporation law relating to the standing issue."[82]

The Superior Court of Pennsylvania in *Drain v. Convenant
Life Insurance Co.*,[83] relying largely upon two federal court
decisions construing Pennsylvania law, *Miller v. Steinbach*[84] and
*Keyser v. Commonwealth National Financial Corp.*,[85] rejected the
"more stringent standing requirements of Delaware law," and held
that shareholders do not lose standing to maintain a derivative
action where the loss of their shares is involuntary and "the result
of the defendants' wrongdoing in the challenged merger."[86] In
such cases, Pennsylvania courts balance on a case by case basis
"the interests of allegedly aggrieved shareholders and the corporate
interest in efficient execution of control transactions."[87]

Alabama, California, Indiana and North Carolina courts also
have rejected the majority rule. The Alabama Supreme Court in
*Shelton v. Thompson*[88] held that shareholders who exchange their
shares for shares of another corporation's stock in a merger do not
lose their standing to maintain derivative claims commenced prior
to the merger on behalf of the corporation whose shares they then
held. The court recognized that "[o]f course, where a stockholder
sells his stock, either to the corporation or to a third party, that

---

82. *Id* at 931 n.5; *see also Kessler v. Sinclair*, 641 N.E.2d 135,
137-38 (Mass. App. Ct. 1994) (following *Blasband* and holding under
Delaware law that a shareholder of a corporation that is merged into
another corporation in a stock-for-stock merger has standing to continue a
derivative suit initially brought on behalf of the first corporation prior to
the merger due to the shareholder's "clear continuity of interest" in the
two corporations, but that the suit must be amended to allege that it is on
behalf of the successor corporation), *review denied*, 646 N.E.2d 135
(Mass. 1995).

83. 685 A.2d 119 (Pa. Super. 1996), *appeal granted*, 698 A.2d 67
(Pa. 1997).

84. 268 F. Supp. 255 (S.D.N.Y. 1967).

85. 120 F.R.D. 489 (M.D. Pa. 1988).

86. *Drain*, 685 A.2d at 125-27.

87. *Id*. at 126.

88. 544 So. 2d 845 (Ala. 1989).

stockholder, generally speaking, cannot claim standing to maintain a derivative action on behalf of the corporation in which he no longer owns an interest."[89] The court, however, declined to extend this rule to shareholders who lose their shares as a result of a merger because, the court stated, to do so "would allow an otherwise valid and actionable derivative suit against an officer of the corporation to be abated simply by effecting a merger with another corporation, as if the mere act of merger wipes out the alleged culpable conduct."[90] The court noted "state and federal precedents to the contrary" but concluded that "[b]y their blind adherence to the absolution of the 'stockholder status' prerequisite, these cases use 'lack of standing' to abolish the remedy. We refuse to adopt such a rule."[91]

The California Court of Appeal in *Gaillard v. Natomas Co.*[92] also held that "there is no requirement" following a merger "for continuing stock ownership in order for an individual, who is a shareholder at the time of the transaction complained of and at the time the action is filed, to proceed with a derivative action."[93] To rule otherwise, the court reasoned, "would create an anomalous result": "a situation where a shareholder files a derivative action, navigates laboriously through the pleading stage, undertakes extensive discovery, incurs sizable monetary obligations, and then, after an elapse of several years, is precluded from proceeding further because his or her corporation has just merged with another."[94] The court acknowledged that Delaware law is to the contrary but stated that "[i]n contrast to Delaware, California follows the judicial and legislative trend of a liberal and expansive construction of derivative suit standing requirements."[95] The North Carolina Supreme Court in *Alford v. Shaw*[96] used similar

---

89. *Id.* at 848.
90. *Id.*
91. *Id.* at 849.
92. 173 Cal. App. 3d 410, 219 Cal. Rptr. 74 (Cal. Ct. App. 1985).
93. *Id.* at 414, 219 Cal. Rptr. at 76.
94. *Id.*
95. *Id.* at 420-21, 219 Cal. Rptr. at 80-81.
96. 398 S.E.2d 445 (N.C. 1990).

reasoning (and quoted the passage in *Galliard* quoted above) to reach the same result.[97]

The Indiana Supreme Court in *Gabhart v. Gabhart*[98] likewise held that if "the shareholders of the merged corporation are made shareholders of the surviving corporation by reason of the merger agreement, they may assert the cause of action in a suit derivative of their stockholder status in the surviving corporation."[99] Additionally, the court held, "since no wrong should be without a remedy, a Court of Equity may grant relief, pro-rata, to a former shareholder of a merged corporation, whose equity was adversely affected by the fraudulent act of an officer or director and whose means of redress otherwise would be cut off by the merger, if there is no shareholder of the surviving corporation eligible to maintain a derivative action for such wrong and said shareholder had no prior opportunity for redress by derivative action against either the merged or the surviving corporation."[100]

The Model Business Corporation Act follows the majority Delaware rule by requiring that "the proceeding should be dismissed if, after commencement, the plaintiff ceases to be a shareholder."[101] Principles of Corporate Governance: Analysis and Recommendations adopts a variation of the minority rule by requiring a shareholder to continue to be a shareholder until the time of judgment

> unless the failure to do so is the result of corporate action in which the holder did not acquiesce, and either (A) the derivative action was commenced prior to the corporate action terminating the holder's status, or (B) the court finds that the holder is better able to represent the interests of the shareholders than any other holder who has brought suit.[102]

---

97. *Id.* at 449-50.

98. 370 N.E.2d 345 (Ind. 1977).

99. *Id.* at 357.

100. *Id.* at 358.

101. 2 Model Bus. Corp. Act Annotated § 7.41(1) Official Comment at 7-341 (3d ed. 1996).

102. 2 Principles of Corporate Governance: Analysis and Recommendations § 7.02(a)(2) (1994).

According to the drafters of Principles of Corporate Governance, "an otherwise eligible shareholder who has been involuntarily eliminated should be permitted to continue or bring a corporate cause of action if unjust enrichment otherwise seems likely to result."[103]

## 3.  The Fair and Adequate Representation Requirement

The shareholder plaintiff in a derivative action also must "fairly and adequately" represent the interests of the corporation. Federal Rule of Civil Procedure 23.1, for example provides as follows:

> The derivative action may not be maintained if it appears that the plaintiff does not fairly and adequately represent the interests of the shareholders or members similarly situated in enforcing the right of the corporation or association.[104]

The United States Supreme Court in *Cohen v. Beneficial Industrial Loan Corp.*[105] explained the rationale underlying this rule as follows:

> [A] stockholder who brings suit on a cause of action derived from the corporation assumes a position, not technically as a trustee perhaps, but one of a fiduciary character. He sues, not for himself alone, but as representative of a class comprising all who are similarly situated. The interests of all in the redress of the wrongs are taken into his hands, dependent upon his diligence, wisdom and integrity. And while the stockholders have chosen the corporate director or manager, they have no such election as to a plaintiff who steps forward to represent them. He is a self-chosen representative and a volunteer champion. The Federal Constitution does not oblige the state to place its litigating and adjudicating processes at the disposal of such a representative, at least without imposing standards of responsibility, liability and accountability which it considers will protect the interests he elects himself to represent.[106]

---

103. *Id.* § 7.02 Comment at 39.
104. Fed. R. Civ. P. 23.1.
105. 337 U.S. 541 (1949).
106. *Id.* at 549-50.

These considerations are important because "a shareholder may bring a derivative action to gain leverage by which to settle an unrelated dispute, to advance the shareholder's primary interests as an employee, creditor, or hostile bidder in a tender offer, or for other reasons not shared by the holders as a class. Where courts have discerned such conflicts between the real interests of the plaintiff and the interests of the class the shareholder purports to represent, they have been ready to deny standing."[107]

Examples of federal decisions discussing and applying the fair and adequate representation requirement include the First Circuit's decision in *GA Enterprises, Inc. v. Leisure Living Communities, Inc.*,[108] the Fifth Circuit's decision in *Smith v. Ayres*,[109] the Sixth Circuit's decision in *Davis v. Comed, Inc.*,[110] the Eighth Circuit's decisions in *Quirke v. St. Louis-San Francisco Railway Co.*[111] and *Allright Missouri, Inc. v. Billeter*,[112] the Ninth Circuit's decisions in *Zarowitz v. BankAmerica Corp.*[113] and *Larson v. Dumke*[114] and district court decisions in cases such as *Hall v. Aliber*,[115] *Torchmark Corp. v. Bixby*,[116] *Jordon v. Bowman Apple Products Co.*,[117] *Banks v. Whyte*[118] and *Meimaris v. Hudner*.[119]

---

107. 2 Principles of Corporate Governance: Analysis and Recommendations § 7.02 Comment at 40 (1994).

108. 517 F.2d 24, 25-27 (1st Cir. 1975).

109. 977 F.2d 946, 948-49 (5th Cir. 1992), *cert. denied*, 508 U.S. 910 (1993).

110. 619 F.2d 588, 592-98 (6th Cir. 1980).

111. 277 F.2d 705, 708 (8th Cir.), *cert. denied*, 363 U.S. 845 (1960).

112. 829 F.2d 631, 639-40 (8th Cir. 1987).

113. 866 F.2d 1164, 1165-66 (9th Cir. 1989).

114. 900 F.2d 1363, 1366-69 (9th Cir.), *cert. denied*, 498 U.S. 1012 (1990).

115. 614 F. Supp. 473, 475-77 (E.D. Mich. 1985).

116. 708 F. Supp. 1070, 1076-77 (W.D. Mo. 1988).

117. 728 F. Supp. 409, 412-13 (W.D. Va. 1990).

118. 1994 U.S. Dist. LEXIS 11063, at *7-18, 1994 WL 418997, at *2-6 (E.D. Pa. Aug. 9, 1994).

119. 1995 U.S. Dist. LEXIS 9676, at *1-3, 1995 WL 413164, at
(continued...)

No language comparable to Federal Rule of Civil Procedure 23.1 is included in Delaware Chancery Court Rule 23.1.[120] The Delaware courts, however, have held that Delaware's rule was not "drafted so as to deliberately omit the requirement that a plaintiff in a derivative action must be qualified to represent the interests of similarly situated shareholders in a fair and adequate manner."[121] Rather, the sentence in Federal Rule of Civil Procedure 23.1 that is not included in Delaware Court of Chancery Rule 23.1 "merely spells out what was implicit" under federal law and Delaware law before Federal Rule 23.1 was adopted, "namely that a plaintiff shareholder in a derivative action must be qualified to serve in a fiduciary capacity as a representative of a class of persons similarly situated, whose interests are in plaintiff's hands and the redress of whose injuries is dependent upon his diligence, wisdom and integrity."[122]

Examples of Delaware decisions discussing the requirement that a derivative plaintiff must fairly and adequately represent the interests of the corporation include *Katz v. Plant Industries, Inc.*,[123] *Youngman v. Tahmoush*,[124] *Scopas Technology Co. v. Lord*,[125] *MacAndrews & Forbes Holdings, Inc. v. Revlon, Inc.*,[126] *Emerald Partners v. Berlin*,[127] *Scattered Corp. v. Chicago Stock Exchange, Inc.*,[128] *Balin v. Amerimar Realty Co.*[129]

---

119. (...continued)
*1 (S.D.N.Y. July 12, 1995).
    120. Del. Ch. Ct. R. 23.1.
    121. *Katz v. Plant Indus., Inc.*, 1981 Del. Ch. LEXIS 549, at *3, 1981 WL 15148, at *1 (Del. Ch. Oct. 27, 1981).
    122. *Id.; see also Emerald Partners v. Berlin*, 564 A.2d 671, 673 (Del. Ch. 1989); *Youngman v. Tahmoush*, 457 A.2d 376, 379 (Del. Ch. 1983).
    123. 1981 Del. Ch. LEXIS 549, at *3-4, 1981 WL 15148, at *1-2 (Del. Ch. Oct. 27, 1981).
    124. 457 A.2d 376, 379-82 (Del. Ch. 1983).
    125. 10 Del. J. Corp. L. 306, 309-11 (Del. Ch. Nov. 20, 1984).
    126. 1985 Del. Ch. LEXIS 545, at *8-11, 1985 WL 21129, at *3-5 (Del. Ch. Oct. 9, 1985).
    127. 564 A.2d 670, 673-74 (Del. Ch. 1989).
    128. 1996 Del. Ch. LEXIS 79, at *8 n.3, 1996 WL 417507, at *3
(continued...)

and *Steiner v. Meyerson.*[130] Cases discussing this requirement in state courts outside of Delaware include *Brandon v. Brandon Construction Co.,*[131] *Heckmann v. Ahmanson,*[132] *Moore v. 1600 Downing Street, Ltd.,*[133] *Barrett v. Southern Connecticut Gas Co.,*[134] *Fink v. Golenbock*[135] and *Palmer v. United States Savings Bank of America.*[136] The Delaware Court of Chancery's decision in *In re Dairy Mart Convenience Stores, Inc. Derivative Litigation*[137] discusses the type of discovery available to defendants with respect to the fairness and adequacy of a plaintiff in a derivative action.[138]

The decisions cited above have identified the following factors as relevant to the determination whether a particular derivative plaintiff can provide fair and adequate representation:

economic antagonisms between representative and class; the remedy sought by plaintiff in the derivative action; indications that the named plaintiff was not the driving force behind the litigation; plaintiff's unfamiliarity with the litigation; other litigation pending between the plaintiff and defendants; the relative magnitude of plaintiff's personal interests as compared to his interest in the derivative action itself; plaintiff's vindictiveness toward the defendants; and, finally, the degree

---

128. (...continued)
n.3 (Del. Ch. July 12, 1996), *aff'd on other grounds*, 701 A.2d 70 (Del. 1997).

129. 22 Del. J. Corp. L. 1115, 1124-26 (Del. Ch. Nov. 15, 1996).

130. 1997 Del. Ch. LEXIS 88, at *7-9, 1997 WL 349169, at *3-4 (Del. Ch. June 13, 1997).

131. 776 S.W.2d 349, 353-54 (Ark. 1989).

132. 168 Cal. App. 3d 119, 128-29, 214 Cal. Rptr. 177, 183-84 (Cal. Ct. App. 1985).

133. 668 P.2d 16, 20-21 (Colo. Ct. App. 1983).

134. 374 A.2d 1051, 1055-57 (Conn. 1977).

135. 680 A.2d 1243, 1255-57 (Conn. 1996).

136. 553 A.2d 781, 784-87 (N.H. 1989).

137. 1997 Del. Ch. LEXIS 173, 1997 WL 732467 (Del. Ch. Nov. 13, 1997).

138. 1997 Del. Ch. LEXIS 173, at *10-19, 1997 WL 732467, at *4-5.

of support plaintiff was receiving from the shareholders he purported to represent.[139]

\*          \*          \*

whether the named plaintiff is the real party in interest; the plaintiff's familiarity with the litigation and willingness to learn about the suit; the degree of control exercised by attorneys over the litigation; the degree of support given to the plaintiff by the other shareholders; the plaintiff's personal commitment to the action; the remedies sought by the plaintiff; the relative magnitude of the plaintiff's personal interests as compared to the plaintiff's interest in the derivative action itself; and the plaintiff's vindictiveness toward the other shareholders.[140]

These elements typically are "intertwined or interrelated" and are "non-exclusive" and "it is frequently a combination of factors which leads a court to conclude" that a plaintiff is not a fair and adequate representative of the corporation.[141] "Not all factors will come into play in all cases, and in some cases there may be additional factors for the court to consider."[142] "[A] strong showing of one way in which the plaintiff's interests are actually inimical to those he is supposed to represent fairly and adequately . . . will

---

139. *Comed*, 619 F.2d at 593-94, *quoted in, e.g., Moore*, 668 P.2d at 20-21, *Katz*, 1981 Del. Ch. LEXIS 549, at \*4, 1981 WL 15148, at \*2, *Youngman*, 457 A.2d at 379-90, *Scopas*, 10 Del. J. Corp. L. at 310, *Emerald Partners*, 564 A.2d at 673, *Balin*, 22 Del. J. Corp. L. at 1124, *and Dairy Mart*, 1997 Del. Ch. LEXIS 173, at \*10, 1997 WL 732467, at \*3.

140. *Larson*, 900 F.2d at 1367 (numbering and citation omitted), *quoted or paraphrased in Rothenberg v. Security Management Co.*, 667 F.2d 958, 961 (11th Cir. 1982), *In re Dayco Corp. Derivative Sec. Litig.*, 102 F.R.D. 624, 632 (S.D. Ohio 1984), *Newell Co. v. Vermont Am. Corp.*, 725 F. Supp. 351, 368-69 (N.D. Ill. 1989), *Elgin v. Alfa Corp.*, 598 So. 2d 807, 819 (Ala. 1992), *and Fink*, 680 A.2d at 1256.

141. *Larson*, 900 F.2d at 1367, *Comed*, 619 F.2d at 593; *Fink*, 680 A.2d at 1256; *Emerald Partners*, 564 A.2d at 673; *Scopas*, 10 Del. J. Corp. L. at 310; *Youngman*, 457 A.2d at 379; *Katz*, 1981 Del. Ch. LEXIS 549, at \*4, 1981 WL 1518, at \*2.

142. *Fink*, 680 A.2d at 1256.

suffice in reaching such a conclusion."[143] Thus, "[o]ne or any combination of these factors may be sufficient to warrant disqualification of the derivative plaintiff."[144] "[T]he fundamental inquiry which the Court makes is whether the plaintiff has a true interest in the case and is likely to pursue it with vigor on behalf of the corporation and the other shareholders."[145]

The Model Business Corporation Act provides that a shareholder may not commence or maintain a derivative proceeding unless the shareholder "fairly and adequately represents the interests of the corporation in enforcing the right of the corporation."[146] The drafters explain that the reference to the interests of "the corporation" in the Model Act rather than the interests of "the shareholders"—the formulation used in Federal Rule of Civil Procedure 23.1—"more properly reflects the nature of the derivative suit."[147] Principles of Corporate Governance: Analysis and Recommendations requires that a shareholder be "able to represent fairly and adequately the interests of the shareholders."[148]

## 4. Security for Expenses

A substantial minority of states, including California and New York, have enacted statutes that under certain circumstances permit the corporation, and in some cases the defendants, to require the posting of security by the plaintiff or plaintiffs in a shareholder derivative action to cover the expenses, including attorneys' fees, that may be incurred by the corporation in the action. These statutes generally apply where the plaintiff or plaintiffs own less than a specified percentage or dollar value of the corporation's stock. The expenses for which security may be sought generally

---

143. *Comed*, 619 F.2d at 593; *Emerald Partners*, 564 A.2d at 673; *Scopas*, 10 Del. J. Corp. L. at 310; *Youngman*, 457 A.2d at 379; *Katz*, 1981 Del. Ch. LEXIS 549, at *4, 1981 WL 15148, at *2.

144. *Scopas*, 10 Del. J. Corp. L. at 310.

145. *Steiner*, 1997 Del. Ch. LEXIS 88, at *7, 1997 WL 349169, at *3.

146. 2 Model Bus. Corp. Act Annotated § 7.41(2) (3d ed. 1996).

147. *Id.* § 7.41 Official Comment at 7–340-41.

148. Principles of Corporate Governance § 7.02(a)(4).

include expenses that may be incurred by persons entitled to indemnification from the corporation. The rationale underlying these statutes is to "to make a plaintiff having so small an interest liable for all expenses and attorney's fees of the defense if he fails to make good his complaint."[149]

Section 627 of the New York Business Corporation Law is typical. This statute provides that "unless the plaintiff or plaintiffs hold five percent or more of any class of the outstanding shares" of the corporation's stock or shares having "a fair value in excess of fifty thousand dollars," "the corporation in whose right such action is brought shall be entitled at any stage of the proceedings before final judgment to require the plaintiff or plaintiffs to give security for the reasonable expenses, including attorney's fees, which may be incurred by it in connection with such action and by the other parties defendant in connection therewith for which the corporation may become liable" by statute or contract.[150] "The amount of such security may thereafter from time to time be increased or decreased in the discretion of the court having jurisdiction of such action upon showing that the security has or may become inadequate or excessive."[151] Under New York's statute, "the corporation shall have recourse" to the security "in such amount as the court having jurisdiction of such action shall determine upon the termination of such action."[152] Pennsylvania's statute is similar, but it exempts plaintiffs who own five percent or more of any class of the corporation's stock or stock having a market value of more than $200,000.[153] Under statutes such as the New York and Pennsylvania statutes, a corporation is "statutorily entitled to require security for reasonable expenses" where the plaintiff or plaintiffs do not own the specified percentage or value of stock.[154]

---

149. *Cohen v. Beneficial Indus. Loan Corp.*, 337 U.S. 541, 544-45 (1949).

150. N.Y. Bus. Corp. Law § 627.

151. *Id.*

152. *Id.*

153. Pa. Bus. Corp. Law § 1782(c).

154. *In re Westinghouse Sec. Litig.*, 832 F. Supp. 989, 1002 (W.D.
(continued...)

California's statute takes a different form. The California statute provides that "within 30 days after service of summons upon the corporation or upon any defendant who is an officer or director of the corporation, or held such office at the time of the acts complained of, the corporation or the defendant may move the court for an order, upon notice and hearing, requiring the plaintiff to furnish a bond as hereinafter provided," upon one or both of the following grounds:

> (1) That there is no reasonable possibility that the prosecution of the cause of action alleged in the complaint against the moving party will benefit the corporation or its shareholders.
>
> (2) That the moving party, if other than the corporation, did not participate in the transaction complained of in any capacity.[155]

The 30 day period may be extended by the court for an additional period or periods not exceeding a total of 60 days.[156] A plaintiff voluntarily may furnish a $50,000 bond before or after a motion for security is made. At that point, "the plaintiff has complied with the requirements of this section and with any order for a bond theretofore made, and any such motion then pending shall be dismissed and no further additional bond shall be required."[157]

---

154. (...continued)
Pa. 1993), *aff'd mem.*, 92 F.3d 1175 (3d Cir. 1996); *see also In re Westinghouse Sec. Litig.*, No. 95-3079 (3d Cir. May 24, 1995) (requiring plaintiffs to post a $25,000.00 bond to secure payment of all expenses, including attorneys' fees, reasonably incurred by corporation during the course of appeal, and authorizing corporation to "apply for an increase in the amount of the bond, if and when the costs and expenses for which it claims to be entitled as a result of this appeal come to exceed $25,000.00"); *Rosengarten v. Buckley*, 565 F. Supp. 193, 200 (D. Md. 1982) (Maryland law); *Haberman v. Tobin*, 466 F. Supp. 447, 451 & nn. 11-12 (S.D.N.Y. 1979) (New York law); *Nemo v. Allen*, 466 F. Supp. 192, 196 (S.D.N.Y. 1979) (New York law); *Levine v. Bradlee*, 248 F. Supp. 395, 398 (E.D. Pa. 1965) (Pennsylvania law).

155. Cal. Gen. Corp. Law § 800(c).

156. *Id.*

157. *Id.* § 800(e).

The Model Business Corporation Act "eliminates the security-for-expenses requirement for small shareholders, but encourages the court to assess the costs of litigation against the plaintiff"[158] if the court "finds that the proceeding was commenced or maintained without reasonable cause or for an improper purpose."[159] Principles of Corporate Governance: Analysis and Recommendations similarly provides that a court "may award applicable costs, including reasonable attorney's fees and expenses, against a party, or a party's counsel" under two circumstances:

> (1) At any time, if the court finds that any specific claim for relief or defense was asserted or any pleading, motion, request for discovery, or other action was made or taken in bad faith or without reasonable cause; or
>
> (2) Upon final judgment, if the court finds, in light of all the evidence, and considering both the state and trend of the substantive law, that the action taken as a whole was brought, prosecuted, or defended in bad faith or in an unreasonable manner.[160]

State law security for costs requirements apply to derivative claims asserted both in state court and in federal court.[161] This includes claims asserting federal causes of action, "unless the particular state law in question is inconsistent with the policies underlying the federal statute."[162] As discussed more fully later in this Chapter,[163] the United States Supreme Court's decisions in *Kamen v. Kemper Financial Services, Inc.*[164] and *Burks v. Lasker*[165] hold that it is not inconsistent with federal policy for

---

158. Goldstein & Hamilton, *The Revised Model Business Corporation Act*, 38 Bus. Law. 1019, 1022 (1983).

159. 2 Model Bus. Corp. Act Annotated § 7.46 (3d ed. 1996).

160. 2 Principles of Corporate Governance: Analysis and Recommendations § 7.04(d) (1994).

161. *See, e.g., Cohen v. Beneficial Indus. Loan Corp.*, 337 U.S. 541 (1949); *Phelps v. Burnham*, 327 F.2d 812, 813-14 (2d Cir. 1964); *Weisfeld v. Spartans Indus., Inc.*, 58 F.R.D. 570, 578 (S.D.N.Y. 1972).

162. *Kamen v. Kemper Fin. Servs., Inc.*, 500 U.S. 90, 108 (1991).

163. *See* Chapter IV, Section B 3 a.

164. 500 U.S. 90 (1991).

165. 441 U.S. 471 (1979).

courts in actions involving federal statutory claims (*Kemper* and *Burks* both involved the Investment Company Act of 1940)[166] to enforce case-dispositive state law rules requiring a pre-litigation demand and permitting disinterested directors to terminate derivative actions.[167] *A fortiori*, it is not inconsistent with federal policy for federal courts to enforce state security for costs statutes, which are not case-dispositive.[168]

## 5. The Demand Requirement

In order to have standing to commence a derivative action, a shareholder must allege with particularity that a pre-litigation demand that the corporation's board of directors commence the litigation either is excused as futile or has been made and wrongfully refused. This demand requirement "was designed to limit" shareholder derivative litigation "to situations in which, due to an unjustified failure of the corporation to act for itself, it was appropriate to permit a shareholder 'to institute and conduct a litigation which usually belongs to the corporation.'"[169] The demand requirement is discussed in detail later in this Chapter.[170]

Some jurisdictions also require a demand on shareholders, as also discussed later in this Chapter.[171]

## 6. Termination by Special Litigation Committee

A derivative action, unlike other actions, is subject to a motion to terminate by the corporation or a special litigation com-

---

166. 15 U.S.C. §§ 80a-1–80a-64.

167. *Kemper*, 500 U.S. at 108; *Burks*, 441 U.S. at 480-86.

168. *But see McClure v. Borne Chem. Co.*, 292 F.2d 824 (3d Cir.), *cert. denied*, 368 U.S. 939 (1961); *Levine v. Bradlee*, 248 F. Supp. 395 (E.D. Pa. 1965) (pre-*Kemper* decisions holding that state security statutes do not apply to federal claims).

169. *Daily Income Funds, Inc. v. Fox*, 464 U.S. 523, 530 (1984) (quoting *Hawes v. City of Oakland*, 104 U.S. 450, 460 (1881)).

170. *See* Chapter IV, Sections B 1-9.

171. *See* Chapter IV, Section B 10.

mittee acting on behalf of the corporation. Like the demand requirement, termination by special litigation committees is discussed in detail later in this Chapter.[172]

## 7. Settlement

A derivative action cannot be discontinued or settled without court approval.[173] In determining whether to approve the settlement of a derivative action, courts "assess the strengths and weaknesses of the claims asserted in light of the discovery record" and "evaluate the fairness and adequacy of the consideration offered to the corporation in exchange for the release of all claims made or arising from the facts alleged."[174] The court's function "is to consider the nature of the [plaintiff's] claim, the possible defenses thereto, the legal and factual circumstances of the case, and then to apply its own business judgment in deciding whether the settlement is reasonable in light of these factors."[175] "The ultimate issue . . . is whether the proposed settlement appears to be fair to the corporation and its absent shareholders."[176] "As a general rule, in evaluating a proposed settlement, th[e] court does not attempt to make substantive determinations concerning disputed facts or the merits of the claims alleged."[177] Of course, compromises of dis-

---

172. *See* Chapter IV, Sections C 1-4.

173. *See, e.g.*, Fed. R. Civ. P. 23.1; Del. Ch. Ct. R. 23.1; N.Y. Bus. Corp. Law § 626(d); 2 Model Bus. Corp. Act Annotated § 7.45 (3d ed. 1996); 2 Principles of Corporate Governance: Analysis and Recommendations § 7.14 (1994).

174. *In re Caremark Int'l Inc. Derivative Litig.*, 698 A.2d 959, 961 (Del. Ch. 1996).

175. *Kahn v. Sullivan*, 594 A.2d 48, 59 (Del. 1991) (quoting *Polk v. Good*, 507 A.2d 531, 535 (Del. (1986)).

176. *Caremark*, 698 A.2d at 961; *see also Zimmerman v. Bell*, 800 F.2d 386, 391 (4th Cir. 1986); *Republic Nat'l Life Ins. Co. v. Beasley*, 73 F.R.D. 658, 667 (S.D.N.Y. 1977); *Polk*, 507 A.2d at 536; *Lewis v. Hirsch*, [1994-1995 Transfer Binder] Fed. Sec. L. Rep. (CCH) ¶ 98,382, at 90,616 (Del. Ch. June 1, 1994).

177. *Carlton Invs. v. TLC Beatrice Int'l Holdings, Inc.*, 1997 Del. Ch. LEXIS 86, at *5, 1997 WL 305829, at *1 (Del. Ch. May 30, 1997);

(continued...)

puted claims are favored by all courts, and derivative claims are no exception.[178] Indeed, settlements of shareholder derivative actions are "particularly favored because such litigation is 'notoriously difficult and unpredictable.'"[179] Courts "do not lightly reject such settlements."[180]

Examples of decisions approving settlements of derivative litigation include federal court decisions in *Shlensky v. Dorsey*,[181] *Maher v. Zapata Corp.*,[182] *Zimmerman v. Bell*,[183] *Bell Atlantic Corp. v. Bolger*[184] and *In re Metropolitan Life Derivative Litigation*,[185] Delaware decisions in *Polk v. Good*,[186] *Kahn v. Sullivan*,[187] *In re Caremark International Inc. Derivative Litigation*,[188] *Carlton Investments v. TLC Beatrice International Holdings, Inc.*[189] and *In re Bally's Grand Derivative Litigation*,[190]

---

177. (...continued)
*see also Bell Atl. Corp. v. Bolger*, 2 F.3d 1304, 1311 (3d Cir. 1993) ("The principal factor . . . is the extent of the benefit to be derived from the proposed settlement by the corporation, the real party in interest. . . . The adequacy of the recovery must be considered in the light of the best possible recovery, of the risks of establishing liability and proving damages in the event the case is not settled, and of the cost of prolonging the litigation.") (quoting *Shlensky v. Dorsey*, 574 F.2d 131, 147 (3d Cir. 1978)).

178. *See, e.g.*, *Williams v. First Nat'l Bank*, 216 U.S. 582, 595 (1910); *In re Metropolitan Life Derivative Litig.*, 935 F. Supp. 286, 291 (S.D.N.Y. 1996); *Polk*, 507 A.2d at 535; *Hirsch*, [1994-1995 Transfer Binder] Fed. Sec. L. Rep. (CCH) at 60,615.

179. *Maher v. Zapata Corp.*, 714 F.2d 436, 455 (5th Cir. 1983).

180. *Id.*

181. 574 F.2d 131, 142-49 (3d Cir. 1978).

182. 714 F.2d 436, 453-67 (5th Cir. 1983).

183. 800 F.2d 386, 391-92 (4th Cir. 1986).

184. 2 F.3d 1304, 1310-18 (3d Cir. 1993).

185. 935 F. Supp. 286, 291-94 (S.D.N.Y. 1996).

186. 507 A.2d 531, 536-39 (Del. 1986).

187. 594 A.2d 48, 58-63 (Del. 1991).

188. 698 A.2d 959, 967, 970-72 (Del. Ch. 1996).

189. 1997 Del. Ch. LEXIS 86, at *5-8, 42-72, 1997 WL 305829, at *1-2, 10-20 (Del. Ch. May 30, 1997).

190. No. 14644 (Del. Ch. Oct. 9, 1997).

and New York decisions in *Seinfeld v. Robinson*[191] and *Braddock v. Citicorp.*[192] Examples of decisions rejecting settlements of derivative actions include federal court decisions in *In re Pittsburgh & Lake Erie Railroad Co. Securities & Antitrust Litigation*[193] and *Goldsholl v. Shapiro*[194] and the Delaware Court of Chancery's decision in *In re MAXXAM, Inc./Federated Development Shareholders Litigation.*[195]

When a shareholder objecting to a settlement seeks discovery concerning the settlement, "the usual liberal discovery rules do not apply."[196] Rather, "targeted, well-defined discovery" is permitted where the objector "shows sufficient reasons that the specific information sought would be relevant to the court's duty in evaluating the settlement."[197]

Because a shareholder derivative action is brought to enforce a corporate cause of action, the only claims that can be adjudicated and/or released in a settlement of a derivative action are claims belonging to the corporation (or to defendants against whom claims have been asserted and who are subject to jurisdiction).[198] "[T]he corporation does not share rights in the property of its shareholders and may not release or assign that property as part of a settlement

---

191. 172 Misc. 2d 159, 162, 656 N.Y.S.2d 707, 709 (N.Y. Sup. Ct. N.Y. Co. 1997).

192. N.Y.L.J., Aug. 14, 1997, at 22 (N.Y. Sup. Ct. N.Y. Co.).

193. 543 F.2d 1058, 1069-70 (3d Cir. 1976).

194. 417 F. Supp. 1291, 1295-1300 (S.D.N.Y. 1976).

195. 659 A.2d 760, 775-77 (Del. Ch. 1995).

196. *Carlton Invs. v. TLC Beatrice Int'l Holdings, Inc.*, 22 Del. J. Corp. L. 1165, 1169 (Del. Ch. Jan. 28, 1997).

197. *Sullivan v. Hammer*, 1990 Del. Ch. LEXIS 20, at *1-2, 1990 WL 28020, at *1 (Del. Ch. Mar. 6, 1990), *aff'd sub nom. Kahn v. Sullivan*, 594 A.2d 48 (Del. 1991); *see also Lewis v. Hirsch*, 1995 Del. LEXIS 62, at *1-5, 1995 WL 54419, at *1-2 (Del. Ch. Jan. 31, 1995); *In re Amsted Indus., Inc. Litig.*, 521 A.2d 1104 (Del. Ch. 1986) (both discussing availability and scope of discovery permitted to a shareholder objecting to a proposed settlement of a derivative action).

198. *In re Louisiana-Pacific Corp. Derivative Litig.*, 705 A.2d 238, 239-41 (Del. Ch. 1997); *Carlton Invs. v. TLC Beatrice Int'l Holdings, Inc.*, 23 Del. J. Corp. L. 190, 194-97 (Del. Ch. Apr. 21, 1997).

of claims that it owns."[199] It therefore "is inappropriate . . . to attempt in any judgment . . . to purport to affect the non-representative rights" of the shareholder who has commenced the derivative action or other shareholders (except to the extent that other, non-derivative claims have been asserted against one or more shareholders), or to release claims belonging to shareholders that arise out of the same facts underlying claims belonging to the corporation for which a release is obtained.[200] Thus, "the broad generality that all claims belonging 'to the corporation and its stockholders' arising from the facts surrounding the complaint may validly be released by the corporation in the settlement of a derivative claim" is not true.[201]

## 8. Distinguishing Derivative from Non-Derivative Actions

Shareholder plaintiffs often characterize an action as non-derivative in an effort to evade the often case-dispositive restrictions upon derivative litigation discussed above.[202] Whether a complaint states a derivative claim or a non-derivative claim, however, is determined "from the body of the complaint rather than from the label employed" by plaintiff's counsel.[203] The law of the

---

199. *Carlton*, 23 Del. J. Corp. L. at 195.

200. *Id.* at 196.

201. *Id.*

202. *See* Chapter IV, Sections A 1-7.

203. *In re Sunrise Sec. Litig.*, 916 F.2d 874, 882 (3d Cir. 1990); *Miller v. Loucks*, 1992 U.S. Dist. LEXIS 16966, at *4, 1992 WL 329313, at *1 (N.D. Ill. Nov. 5, 1992) (quoting *Sunrise*); *see also Kramer v. Western Pac. Indus., Inc.*, 546 A.2d 348, 352 (Del. 1988) ("[i]n determining the nature of the wrong alleged, a court must look to 'the body of the complaint, not to plaintiff's designation or stated intention'") (quoting *Lipton v. News Int'l, Plc*, 514 A.2d 1075, 1078 (Del. 1986)); *In re Rexene Corp. Shareholders Litig.*, [1991 Transfer Binder] Fed. Sec. L. Rep. (CCH) ¶ 96,010, at 90,057 (Del. Ch. May 8, 1991) ("[t]he determination is based upon the allegations in the complaint, not plaintiffs' characterization of their claims"), *aff'd sub nom. Eichorn v. Rexene Corp.*, 604 A.2d 416 (unpublished opinion, text available at 1991 Del. LEXIS 333 and

(continued...)

state of incorporation governs this issue unless the state law is inconsistent with federal policy.[204]

The standards used by courts to distinguish between derivative claims brought by shareholders on behalf of a corporation and direct, non-derivative claims brought by shareholders on their own behalf and/or as class action claims "have been articulated many times," but still it is "often difficult to distinguish between a derivative and an individual action."[205] The line separating derivative and individual actions can become "particularly vague" in the context of defensive actions, contests for control of the corporation and proxy contests.[206]

---

203. (...continued)
1991 WL 210962) (Del. Oct. 10, 1991); *Harris v. Carter*, 582 A.2d 222, 229 (Del. Ch. 1990) ("the nature of the pleading itself and not the pleader's characterization of the claims determines whether a claim stated is derivative or not"); *Spillyards v. Abboud*, 662 N.E.2d 1358, 1363 (Ill. App. Ct. 1996) (quoting *Lipton*); *Grand Council v. Owens*, 620 N.E.2d 234, 237 (Ohio Ct. App. 1993) ("[i]n analyzing whether a complaint states a derivative claim or a direct claim, the court is required to look to the nature of the alleged wrong rather than the designation used by plaintiffs").

204. *Sunrise*, 916 F.2d at 879; *Krouner v. American Heritage Fund*, 1997 U.S. Dist. LEXIS 11445, at *5-6, 1997 WL 452021, at *2 (S.D.N.Y. Aug. 6, 1997); *Strougo v. Scudder, Stevens & Clark, Inc.*, 964 F. Supp. 783, 790 (S.D.N.Y. 1997); *King v. Douglass*, 973 F. Supp. 707, 723 (S.D. Tex. 1996); *Thompson v. Glenmede Trust Co.*, 1993 U.S. Dist. LEXIS 7677, at *15 n.4, 1993 WL 197031, at *5 n.4 (E.D. Pa. June 8, 1993); *Burghart v. Landau*, 821 F. Supp. 173, 176 (S.D.N.Y.), *aff'd mem.*, 9 F.3d 1538 (2d Cir. 1993), *cert. denied*, 510 U.S. 1196 (1994); *Seinfeld v. Bays*, 595 N.E.2d 69, 75-77 (Ill. App. Ct. 1992); *see also* Chapter IV, Sections B 3 a-b (discussing choice of law principles in the context of the pre-litigation demand requirement).

205. *Grimes v. Donald*, 673 A.2d 1207, 1213 (Del. 1996) (quoting *Rexene*, [1991 Transfer Binder] Fed. Sec. L. Rep. (CCH) at 90,057); *see also Alabama By-Products Corp. v. Cede & Co.*, 657 A.2d 254, 266 (Del. 1995) ("the line of separation between derivative and corporate class actions is sometimes obscure").

206. *Kramer*, 546 A.2d at 352 n.3 (Del. 1988); *see also Tandy-*
(continued...)

Generally speaking, a wrong to the incorporated group as a whole that depletes or destroys corporate assets and reduces the value of the corporation's stock gives rise to a derivative action; a breach of an individual shareholder's "membership" contract or some other interference with the rights that traditionally are viewed as part of an individual's ownership of stock such as the right to vote or an allegation that a particular transaction will unfairly affect minority shareholders gives rise to a direct, non-derivative action by the injured shareholder or shareholders.[207] Thus, as the Delaware Supreme Court stated in *Grimes v. Donald*,[208] "[t]o pursue a direct action, the stockholder-plaintiff 'must allege more than an injury resulting from a wrong to the corporation.'"[209] Rather, "[t]he plaintiff must state a claim for 'an injury which is separate and distinct from that suffered by other shareholders,' . . . or a wrong involving a contractual right of a shareholder . . . which exists independently of any right of the corporation.'"[210] As stated by the same court in *Lewis v. Spencer*,[211] "[f]or a plaintiff

---

206. (...continued)
*crafts, Inc. v. Initio Partners*, 562 A.2d 1162, 1166 (Del. 1989) ("where the shareholder's individual interests are directly and equally implicated, as in proxy contests, the distinction between individual and representative claims may become blurred").

207. *See* William L. Cary & Melvin A. Eisenberg, *Cases and Materials on Corporations* 1014 (7th ed. 1995 & Supp. 1997); Harry G. Henn & John R. Alexander, *Law of Corporations and Other Business Enterprises* § 360, at 1048 (3d ed. 1983 & Supp. 1986); *see also Moelis v. Schwab Safe Co.*, 706 F. Supp. 284, 286 (S.D.N.Y. 1989); *Cede & Co. v. Technicolor, Inc.*, 542 A.2d 1182, 1188 n.10 (Del. 1988) (both citing earlier edition of this text for this proposition).

208. 673 A.2d 1207 (Del. 1996).

209. *Id.* at 1213 (quoting *Kramer*, 546 A.2d at 351).

210. *Id.* (quoting *Moran v. Household Int'l Inc.*, 490 A.2d 1059, 1070 (Del. Ch.), *aff'd on other grounds*, 500 A.2d 1346 (Del. 1985)); *see also Lewis v. Spencer*, 577 A.2d 753 (unpublished opinion, text available at 1990 Del. LEXIS 154 and 1990 WL 72615) (Del. May 11, 1990) (similar quote, and offering "the right to vote, or to assert majority control" as examples of "a wrong involving a contractual right of a shareholder").

211. 577 A.2d 753 (unpublished opinion, text available at 1990 Del. LEXIS 154 and 1990 WL 72615) (Del. May 11, 1990).

to have standing to bring an individual action, he must be injured *directly* or *independently* of the corporation."[212] In the words of the New York Court of Appeals in *Abrams v. Donati*[213]: "For a wrong against a corporation a shareholder has no individual cause of action, though he loses the value of his investment or incurs personal liability in an effort to maintain the solvency of the corporation."[214]

---

212. 1990 Del. LEXIS 154, at *4, 1990 WL 72615, at *2 (citations omitted); *see also In re Tri-Star Pictures, Inc., Litig.*, 634 A.2d 319, 330 (Del. 1993) ("[a] special injury is established where there is a wrong suffered by plaintiff that was not suffered by all stockholders generally or where the wrong involves a contractual right of the stockholders, such as the right to vote."); *Lipton*, 514 A.2d at 1078 ("[t]o set out an individual action, the plaintiff must allege either 'an injury which is separate and distinct from that suffered by other shareholders,' . . . or a wrong involving a contractual right of a shareholder, such as the right to vote, or to assert majority control, which exists independently of any right of the corporation") (quoting *Household*, 490 A.2d at 1070); *Elster v. American Airlines, Inc.*, 100 A.2d 219, 222 (Del. Ch. 1953) (stockholder can maintain individual action only if he has sustained "special injury", defined as "a wrong inflicted upon him alone or a wrong affecting any particular right which he is asserting,—such as his preemptive rights as a stockholder, rights involving the control of the corporation, or a wrong affecting the stockholders and not the corporation").

213. 66 N.Y.2d 951, 489 N.E.2d 751, 498 N.Y.S.2d 782 (1985).

214. *Id.* at 953, 489 N.E.2d at 751, 498 N.Y.S.2d at 782; *see also Jones v. H.F. Ahmanson & Co.*, 1 Cal. 3d 93, 107, 460 P.2d 464, 470, 81 Cal. Rptr. 592, 598 (1969) (holding that claim was individual rather than derivative in nature where although plaintiff "does allege that the value of her stock has been diminished by defendants' actions, she does not contend that the diminished value reflects an injury to the corporation and resultant depreciation in the value of the stock"); *Grace Bros., Ltd. v. Farley Indus., Inc.*, 450 S.E.2d 814, 816 (Ga. 1994) ("a shareholder must be injured in a way which is different from the other shareholders or independently of the corporation to have standing to assert a direct action"); *Kamen v. Kemper Fin. Servs., Inc.*, 500 U.S. 90, 97 n.4 (1991) (declining to decide whether actions brought by investment company shareholders under § 20(a) of the Investment Company Act of 1940, 15 U.S.C. § 80a-20(a), are derivative in nature); *Daily Income Fund, Inc. v. Fox*, 464 U.S.

(continued...)

"The same claim sometimes may be characterized as direct where only injunctive or prospective relief is sought but as derivative where other legal theories are utilized and other relief, such as monetary recovery, is sought.[215]

## 9. Double Derivative Actions

A double derivative action is a derivative action in which a shareholder of a parent corporation seeks to enforce the parent corporation's derivative right to sue on behalf of a subsidiary corporation and seek recovery for a cause of action belonging to the subsidiary.[216] A triple derivative action is a double derivative action in which the parent corporation's control of the subsidiary possessing a claim is through an intermediate subsidiary.[217]

---

214. (...continued)
523 (1984) (actions brought by investment company shareholders under § 36(b) of the Investment Company Act, 15 U.S.C. § 80a-35(b), are not derivative in nature).

215. *Grimes v. Donald*, 673 A.2d 1207, 1210, 1213 (Del. 1996).

216. *See, e.g., Blasband v. Rales*, 971 F.2d 1034, 1042-43 (3d Cir. 1992); *Goldstein v. Groesbeck*, 142 F.2d 422, 425 (2d Cir.), *cert. denied*, 323 U.S. 737 (1944); *Murray v. Miner*, 876 F. Supp. 512, 516 & n.6 (S.D.N.Y. 1995); *West v. West*, 825 F. Supp. 1033, 1054 (N.D. Ga. 1992); *Rales v. Blasband*, 634 A.2d 927, 932 (Del. 1993); *Sternberg v. O'Neil*, 550 A.2d 1105, 1107 n.1 (Del. 1988); *Schreiber v. Carney*, 447 A.2d 17, 22 (Del. Ch. 1982); *Levine v. Milton*, 219 A.2d 145, 146 (Del. Ch. 1966); *Brown v. Tenney*, 532 N.E.2d 230, 231-36 (Ill. 1988); *Powell v. Gant*, 556 N.E.2d 1241, 1245 (Ill. App. Ct.), *appeal denied*, 564 N.E.2d 847 (Ill. 1990); *Pessin v. Chris-Craft Indus., Inc.*, 181 A.D.2d 66, 72, 586 N.Y.S.2d 584, 588 (N.Y. App. Div. 1st Dep't 1992).

217. *See, e.g., Marcus v. Otis*, 168 F.2d 649, 651 (2d Cir. 1948); *Saltzman v. Birrell*, 78 F. Supp. 778, 783 (S.D.N.Y. 1948); *see also Sternberg*, 550 A.2d at 1124-26 (holding that a non-Delaware corporation's ownership of a Delaware subsidiary may—and in this case did—constitute a sufficient basis upon which the non-Delaware corporation was subject to jurisdiction in Delaware in a double derivative action); *cf. Untermeyer v. Valhi, Inc.*, 665 F. Supp. 297, 299 (S.D.N.Y. 1987) (not permitting multiple derivative action in context of Section 16(b) of the Securities Exchange Act, 15 U.S.C. § 78p(b), because that statute "expli-
(continued...)

In a double or triple derivative action, pre-litigation demands must be made upon the boards of both the parent corporation and the subsidiary corporation(s).[218]

At least one court has permitted a shareholder to bring a double derivative action where the corporation in which the shareholder held stock was a minority shareholder of the corporation whose rights the plaintiff sought to enforce.[219] The drafters of Principles of Corporate Governance: Analysis and Recommendations have observed that "[t]he more frequent and better practice has been to limit the doctrine to situations in which the shareholder's corporation holds at least a de facto controlling interest in the injured corporation."[220]

## 10. Diversity Jurisdiction Issues

Diversity jurisdiction in federal court requires that an action must be between citizens of different states, and that the amount in controversy must equal or exceed $75,000.[221] Diversity jurisdiction thus is defeated when any plaintiff is a citizen of the same state

---

217. (...continued)
citly confers standing to sue, in behalf of the issuer, only on the issuer itself or on the owner of any security of the issuer"; accordingly, the court concluded, a shareholder of a corporation that owns all of the stock of a subsidiary lacks standing to sue under Section 16(b) on behalf of the subsidiary).

218. *Blasband*, 971 F.2d at 1050; *Rales*, 634 A.2d at 933-35; *Brown*, 532 N.E.2d at 235-36; *Powell*, 556 N.E.2d at 1245; 13 William M. Fletcher, *Cyclopedia of the Law of Private Corporations* § 5977, at 194 (1995 & Supp. 1997); *cf. Carlton Invs. v. TLC Beatrice Int'l Holdings, Inc.*, 21 Del. J. Corp. L. 1084, 1100 (Del. Ch. Apr. 16, 1996) (demand not required upon subsidiaries before instituting a quadruple derivative action where the subsidiaries were French corporations and the court could not "assume that these French enterprises are legal entities governed by the same rules as those that govern Delaware corporations").

219. *West*, 825 F. Supp. at 1054-55.

220. 2 Principles of Corporate Governance: Analysis and Recommendations § 7.02 Comment at 40-41 (1994).

221. 28 U.S.C. § 1332.

as any defendant.[222] The corporation's state of incorporation and principal place of business both are domiciles of the corporation, and a corporation often has directors who are citizens of the corporation's state of incorporation or principal place of business.[223] In such a case, the question arises whether the corporation upon whose behalf the action is brought should be aligned as a plaintiff or a defendant for the purpose of determining the existence or non-existence of diversity jurisdiction.

The answer to this question depends upon whether there is an "actual," "substantial" "collision of interests" between the shareholder who has brought the action and the management of the corporation.[224] As the United States Supreme Court explained in *Doctor v. Harrington*,[225] "[t]he ultimate interest of the corporation made defendant may be the same as that of the stockholder made plaintiff, but the corporation may be under a control antagonistic to him, and made to act in a way detrimental to his rights. In other words, his interests, and the interests of the corporation, may be made subservient to some illegal purpose. If a controversy hence arise, and the other conditions of jurisdiction exist, it can be litigated in a Federal court."[226] As the Supreme Court stated in *Koster v. Lumbermens Casualty Mutual Co.*,[227] "jurisdiction is saved in this class of cases by a special dispensation because the corporation is in antagonistic hands."[228]

The leading and most recent Supreme Court decisions addressing the presence or absence of "antagonism" between a shareholder plaintiff and the management of a corporation for the

---

222. *See, e.g., Strawbridge v. Curtiss*, 3 Cranch (7 U.S.) 267 (1806); 13B Charles Alan Wright, Arthur R. Miller & Edward H. Cooper, *Federal Practice and Procedure* § 3605 (1984 & Supp. 1998).

223. 28 U.S.C. § 1332(c); *Krueger v. Cartwright*, 996 F.2d 928, 931 (7th Cir. 1993).

224. *City of Indianapolis v. Chase Nat'l Bank*, 314 U.S. 63, 69 (1941).

225. 196 U.S. 579 (1905).

226. *Id.* at 587.

227. 330 U.S. 518 (1947).

228. *Id.* at 523.

purpose of alignment are *Smith v. Sperling*[229] and *Swanson v. Traer*,[230] companion cases decided in 1957 by five to four votes. *Sperling* involved an allegation that a pre-litigation demand was not made because it was futile.[231] *Swanson* involved an allegation that a pre-litigation demand had been made but was wrongfully refused.[232]

The Supreme Court in *Sperling* held that "[t]here will, of course, be antagonism between the stockholder and the management where the dominant officers and directors are guilty of fraud or misdeeds" but that "wrongdoing in that sense is not the sole measure of antagonism."[233] Rather, the court concluded, "[t]here is antagonism whenever the management is aligned against the stockholder and defends a course of conduct which he attacks."[234] The court stated that this issue is decided on the basis of the plaintiff's complaint. The court therefore held that it was irrelevant that the conduct challenged in the litigation constituted an exercise of independent business judgment, as the district court in *Sperling* had found following a 15 day hearing.

Applying this standard in *Sperling*, where the plaintiff alleged that demand was excused, the court held as follows:

> Here it is plain that the stockholder and those who manage the corporation are completely and irrevocably opposed on a matter of corporate practice and policy. A trial may demonstrate that the stockholder is wrong and the management right. It may show a dispute that lies in the penumbra of business judgment, unaffected by fraud. But that issue goes to the merits, not to jurisdiction. There is jurisdiction if there is real collision between the stockholder and his corporation. That there is such a collision is evident here.[235]

---

229. 354 U.S. 91 (1957).
230. 354 U.S. 114 (1957).
231. 354 U.S. at 92-93.
232. 354 U.S. at 115.
233. 354 U.S. at 95.
234. *Id.*
235. *Id.* at 97-98.

Applying this standard in *Swanson*, where a demand had been made and refused, the court held similarly:

> [T]his case is an instance where the management—for good reasons or for bad—is definitely and distinctly opposed to the institution of this litigation. The management is, therefore, antagonistic to the stockholders as that conception has been used in the cases.[236]

Put another way, the court observed in *Sperling*, "[t]he cause of action, to be sure, is that of the corporation. But the corporation has become through its managers hostile and antagonistic to the enforcement of the claim."[237]

Dissenting, Justice Felix Frankfurter (joined by three other justices) rejected the majority's "mechanical determination" of jurisdiction. Justice Frankfurter stated that "[i]f anything had been regarded as settled until today about federal jurisdiction, it was that 'It is our duty, as it is that of the lower federal courts, to 'look beyond the pleadings and arrange the parties according to their sides in the dispute.'"[238] Justice Frankfurter therefore would have accepted the district court's findings in *Sperling* and realigned the corporation as a plaintiff and dismissed the action, and remanded the *Swanson* case for a similar hearing.[239] Justice Frankfurter cautioned, however, that "[o]f course the charges of wrongdoing need not be determined to ascertain the jurisdiction of the federal courts. What must be determined when directors or other persons alleged to control the corporation are joined as defendants is the relation of these people to the corporation."[240]

As in *Sperling* and *Swanson*, antagonism was found in *Walden v. Elrod*[241] and *Van Gelder v. Taylor*.[242] In both of these cases, management was found to have "defend[ed] a course of

---

236. 354 U.S. at 116.
237. 354 U.S. at 97.
238. *Id.* at 111 (Frankfurter, J., dissenting) (citations omitted).
239. *Id.* at 111-13.
240. *Id.* at 110-11.
241. 72 F.R.D. 5 (W.D. Okla. 1976).
242. 621 F. Supp. 613 (N.D. Ill. 1985).

conduct" challenged by the shareholder plaintiff.[243] Likewise, in *Rogers v. Valentine*,[244] the Second Circuit stated that "[o]n the basis of the allegations of the complaint, which stated that the management of Virginia Iron had refused to institute suit on behalf of the corporation and that further demand would be futile, the [district] court found that the corporation was antagonistic to the institution of suit and consequently could not be aligned as a party plaintiff."[245] This ruling, the Second Circuit held, was "clearly correct."[246]

The same result was reached in *Reilly Mortgage Group, Inc. v. Mount Vernon Savings & Loan Ass'n*,[247] where shareholders alleged that the corporation's controllers "failed to remedy improper activities, failed to permit stockholders' efforts to compel remedies, and uniformly approved activities to both the corporation's and the stockholders' detriment."[248] The court held that a cross-claim by the corporation against a former director and officer did not establish a lack of antagonism to the litigation because "a cynical eye" could view the claim as "suspect . . . finger-pointing between warring defense camps."[249] The cross-claim also was insufficient to establish jurisdiction, the court stated, because jurisdiction must be determined on the basis of the facts at the commencement of the litigation and "once established, cannot be ousted by later events" within the control of litigants.[250] The court also rejected a contention that the plaintiffs' claim that the corporation was antagonistic to the cause of action asserted by plaintiffs was premature due to the plaintiffs' failure to make a prelitigation demand. The court explained that "[t]he mere failure to have made demand, standing alone, is not sufficient to support realignment," but here there were "numerous 'points of substantial

---

243. *Walden*, 72 F.R.D. at 15; *Van Gelder*, 621 F. Supp. at 624.
244. 426 F.2d 1361 (2d Cir. 1970).
245. *Id*. at 1363.
246. *Id*.
247. 568 F. Supp. 1067 (E.D. Va. 1983).
248. *Id*. at 1073.
249. *Id*. at 1074.
250. *Id*.

antagonism' between plaintiff and the corporation."[251] Additionally, the court held, a demand was excused as futile.[252]

Antagonism also has been found in cases alleging wrongdoing by controlling shareholders, including *Bennett v. Worden*,[253] *Raese v. Kelly*,[254] *ZB Holdings, Inc. v. White*[255] and *Crouch v. French Riviera Health Spa.*[256]

Where the plaintiff is a majority shareholder or for some other reason can be said to control the corporation, antagonism generally is not found. Thus in *Liddy v. Urbanek*,[257] for example, a court under these circumstances held that "the pleadings provide no basis on which to find" that the corporation was "actively opposed to this litigation through its management."[258] The court pointed to the fact that the plaintiff was a majority shareholder and president of the corporation, and previously had caused the corporation to file another litigation in another court.[259]

Antagonism also typically is not found in cases involving corporations having two fifty percent shareholder blocks or that are deadlocked in some other way. As stated in *Duffey v. Wheeler*,[260] "[m]ere inaction, or inability to act on the part of the corporation, because of a deadlock between those who control the corporation has not been found to be the equivalent of active antagonism."[261] As stated in *Gibson v. BoPar Dock Corp.*,[262] "[b]ecause the corporation is unable to act on its own behalf and the shareholders are deadlocked, the corporation cannot be considered antagonistic to the

---

251. *Id.* at 1075.
252. *Id.*
253. 225 F. Supp. 42, 43-44 (E.D. Ark. 1964).
254. 59 F.R.D. 612, 614, 615 (N.D. W. Va. 1973).
255. 144 F.R.D. 42 (S.D.N.Y. 1992).
256. 1995 U.S. Dist. LEXIS 9869, at *2, 1995 WL 405700, at *1 (E.D. La. July 7, 1995).
257. 707 F.2d 1222 (11th Cir. 1983).
258. *Id.* at 1225.
259. *Id.*
260. 820 F.2d 1161 (11th Cir. 1987).
261. *Id.* at 1163.
262. 780 F. Supp. 371 (W.D. Va. 1991).

plaintiff for purposes of realignment of the parties."[263] Another decision illustrating this principle is *Cohen v. Heussinger*.[264] The court in *Ono v. Itoyama*,[265] however, aligned the corporation in that case as a defendant, where the plaintiff and a defendant each held 50 percent of the corporation's shares but the defendant was the corporation's dominant officer and had imposed transactions upon the corporation that the plaintiff was unable to oppose because of her financial dependence upon the defendant.[266]

Additional examples of decisions finding a lack of antagonism and requiring the alignment of the corporation as a plaintiff for the purpose of determining the existence or non-existence of diversity jurisdiction include the following:

- *Lewis v. Odell*[267] (holding that corporation named as a defendant should be realigned as a plaintiff because the corporation was bankrupt and "[t]he nature of the dispute is such that none of the trustees will be harmed by a judgment for plaintiff or has any reason to oppose the suit," the corporation "has not only retained neutrality in its responses to appellant's complaints but has even reserved the right to take control of the action," and the corporation "has not even 'refuse[d] to take action,' for [plaintiff] has never made any demand on it");[268]

- *Tessari v. Herald*[269] (holding that corporation named as defendant should be aligned as a plaintiff, where "the individual defendants did not comprise the Board of Directors at the time the original complaint was filed

---

263. *Id.* at 375.

264. 1994 U.S. Dist. LEXIS 7119, 1994 WL 240378 (S.D.N.Y. May 26, 1994).

265. 884 F. Supp. 892 (D.N.J. 1995), *aff'd mem.*, 79 F.3d 1138 (3d Cir. 1996).

266. *Id.* at 900-01.

267. 503 F.2d 445 (2d Cir. 1974).

268. *Id.* at 447.

269. 207 F. Supp. 432 (N.D. Ind. 1962).

and for three and one-half months prior to that time to the present, nor were they in any way associated with the management" during that time");[270]

- *In re Penn Central Securities Litigation*[271] (holding that corporation named as a defendant should be realigned as a plaintiff, where "[a]lthough at the time of the filing of the plaintiffs' complaints Holding Co.'s management may have been antagonistic to the prosecution of the claims, the present directors have no ties with the old management and the actions of the directors to date indicate their desire and ability to prosecute Holding Co.'s claims in good faith"; the court noted that jurisdiction was founded on the federal securities laws and not on diversity and thus motion for realignment by Holding Co. had no effect on the court's jurisdiction, but stated "we should still be concerned with the proper alignment of parties according to their interests when this issue is raised by the parties");[272]

- *Taylor v. Swirnow*[273] (holding that corporations named as defendants should be realigned as plaintiffs, where "[p]laintiffs control a majority of the corporation's stock," "[t]he corporations, being bankrupt, no longer operate or function in any meaningful sense," and "[n]one of the individual defendants were in control of the corporation at the time suit was instituted, or are currently in control");[274]

- *Nejmanowski v. Nejmanowski*[275] (holding that corporation named as defendant should be realigned as a plaintiff despite the fact that the corporation's majority shareholder and controlling officer was a defendant in

---

270. *Id*. at 434-37.
271. 335 F. Supp. 1026 (E.D. Pa. 1971).
272. *Id*. at 1042.
273. 80 F.R.D. 79 (D. Md. 1978).
274. *Id*. at 83-84.
275. 841 F. Supp. 864 (C.D. Ill. 1994).

the suit and opposed the suit, because two of the corporation's three directors were plaintiffs in the suit and favored the suit, and thus the corporation's management was not aligned against the plaintiffs; the court rejected a contention that the management of the corporation in fact was aligned against the action because the board could be replaced by the corporation's majority shareholder if the board acted to replace him as controlling officer or sue him on behalf of the corporation: "This action has not happened yet, . . . and it is pure speculation that it will. The Court simply cannot speculate on what might happen in the future to determine if it currently has subject matter jurisdiction. This Court must determine its subject matter jurisdiction based on the facts as they are presented to it at the time it rules.");[276] and

- *First National Bancshares of Beloit, Inc. v. Geisel*[277] (holding that corporation was properly named as a plaintiff where the corporation's board was not alleged to be under the control of the defendants in the action at the time the action was commenced; the court stated that "the facts supporting realignment of the parties must be in existence at the time the action is commenced," and that here the defendants in the case, who represented a controlling shareholder, were elected directors of the corporation after the action was commenced).[278]

Of course, an absence of diversity jurisdiction matters only in cases where there is no other basis upon which jurisdiction may be exercised by a federal court. The court in *First National*, for example, aligned the corporation as a plaintiff and thus found that there was no diversity jurisdiction. Subject matter jurisdiction with respect to the derivative count in the complaint still existed, how-

---

276. *Id*. at 865-68.
277. 853 F. Supp. 1333 (D. Kan. 1994).
278. *Id*. at 1335.

ever, because the court had subject matter jurisdiction over other claims in the case and exercised supplemental or ancillary jurisdiction over the derivative claim."[279]

In *ZB Holdings, Inc. v. White*,[280] by contrast, the court found a lack of diversity jurisdiction and denied a request that the court exercise supplemental or ancillary jurisdiction. The court explained as follows:

> Because the derivative action was subject to dismissal for failure to name IGH as a party, no viable lawsuit was ever before this Court in the first instance. Therefore, this Court lacked 'original jurisdiction' over this action and cannot now invoke supplemental jurisdiction as a basis for making IGH a party to this lawsuit.

> Supplemental jurisdiction was not intended to be a crutch for lawsuits that cannot stand on their own feet; rather, it was intended only to supplement—i.e., to allow the addition of parties or claims to an existing lawsuit so that complete relief could be fashioned and scarce judicial resources could be conserved.[281]

The court held that the fact that this derivative action had been consolidated with a related non-derivative action in which jurisdiction was based upon the federal securities laws did not provide a basis for the exercise of supplemental jurisdiction, because consolidated actions require "an independent jurisdictional basis for each complaint."[282]

## B. The Demand Requirement

### 1. Definition

Prior to filing a derivative action on behalf of a corporation, a shareholder generally must demand that the corporation's board of directors cause the corporation to pursue the alleged claim on behalf of itself. The United States Supreme Court stated in 1991 in

---

279. *Id*. at 1335-36.
280. 144 F.R.D. 42 (S.D.N.Y. 1992).
281. *Id*. at 47-48.
282. *Id*. at 43 n.1, 48 n.10.

*Kamen v. Kemper Financial Services, Inc.*[283] that the demand requirement "clearly is a matter of 'substance,' not 'procedure.'"[284] The Delaware Supreme Court stated in that same year in *Levine v. Smith*[285] that the requirement "is not a 'mere formalit[y] of litigation,' but rather an important 'stricture[ ] of substantive law.'"[286] The Delaware Supreme Court re-affirmed this principle in 1995 in *Alabama By-Products Corp. v. Cede & Co.*,[287] stating that the demand requirement represents "a procedural restatement of the[ ] bedrock principles of Delaware corporate governance in the context of *standing* to maintain a derivative shareholder's suit."[288] The Delaware Supreme Court re-affirmed this principle again in 1996 in *Grimes v. Donald*,[289] stating that the demand requirement "is a 'basic principle of corporate governance' and is a matter of substantive law."[290] This principle has been stated in numerous additional decisions both in Delaware[291] and outside of Delaware.[292]

---

283. 500 U.S. 90 (1991).

284. *Id.* at 96-97.

285. 591 A.2d 194 (Del. 1991).

286. *Id.* at 207, 210 (quoting *Tandycrafts, Inc. v. Initio Partners*, 562 A.2d 1162, 1166 (Del. 1989)).

287. 657 A.2d 254 (Del. 1995).

288. *Id.* at 265 (quoting *Levine*, 591 A.2d at 200).

289. 673 A.2d 1207 (Del. 1996).

290. *Id.* at 1216 (quoting *Kemper*, 500 U.S. at 101).

291. *See Rales v. Blasband*, 634 A.2d 927, 932 (Del. 1993); *Rales v. Blasband*, 626 A.2d 1364, 1366 (Del. 1993); *Draper v. Paul N. Gardner Defined Plan Trust*, 625 A.2d 859, 865 & n.9 (Del. 1993); *In re Fuqua Indus., Inc. Shareholder Litig.*, 1997 Del. Ch. LEXIS 72, at *49, 1997 WL 257460, at *13 (Del. Ch. May 17, 1997).

292. *See Blasband v. Rales*, 971 F.2d 1034, 1048 (3d Cir. 1992); *Starrels v. First Nat'l Bank*, 870 F.2d 1168, 1171 (7th Cir. 1989); *In re Kauffman Mut. Fund Actions*, 479 F.2d 257, 263 (1st Cir.), *cert. denied*, 414 U.S. 857 (1973); *Olesh v. Dreyfus Corp.*, [1995-1996 Transfer Binder] Fed. Sec. L. Rep. (CCH) ¶ 98,907, at 93,368 (E.D.N.Y. Aug. 8, 1995); *Coyer v. Hemmer*, 901 F. Supp. 872, 887 (D.N.J. 1995); *In re Westinghouse Sec. Litig.*, 832 F. Supp. 989, 994 (W.D. Pa. 1993), *aff'd mem.*, 92 F.3d 1175 (3d Cir. 1996); *Miller v. Loucks*, 1992 U.S. Dist.

(continued...)

Compliance with the demand requirement must be pleaded with particularity[293]—a rule widely recognized as "a deliberate departure from the relaxed policy of 'notice' pleading."[294] "[C]onclusionary allegations of fact or law not supported by allegations of specific fact may not be taken as true."[295] A plaintiff's pleading burden is "more onerous than that required to withstand" an ordinary motion to dismiss.[296]

The letter in which a shareholder makes a demand must "demand that the directors take action to remedy the alleged corporate injury for which derivative relief is . . . sought."[297] The

---

292. (...continued)
LEXIS 16966, at *20-21, 1992 WL 329313, at *5 (N.D. Ill. Nov. 5, 1992); *Grill v. Hoblitzell*, 771 F. Supp. 709, 712 n.3 (D. Md. 1991); *Johnson v. Hui*, 752 F. Supp. 909, 911 (N.D. Cal. 1990); *Cottle v. Hilton Hotels Corp.*, 635 F. Supp. 1094, 1097 (N.D. Ill. 1986); *Stallworth v. AmSouth Bank*, 1997 Ala. LEXIS 483, at *11, 1997 WL 778838, at *3 (Ala. Dec. 19, 1997); *Grand Council v. Owens*, 620 N.E.2d 234, 238 (Ohio Ct. App. 1993); *Drage v. Procter & Gamble*, No. A-9401998, slip op. at 3 (Ohio Ct. Comm. Pleas Jan. 19, 1996), *aff'd* 694 N.E.2d 479 (Ohio Ct. App. 1997).

293. *See, e.g.*, Fed. R. Civ. P. 23.1; *Kamen v. Kemper Fin. Servs., Inc.*, 500 U.S. 90, 108 n.10 (1991); Cal. Gen. Corp. Law § 800(b)(2); Del. Ch. Ct. R. 23.1; N.Y. Bus. Corp. Law § 626(c).

294. *Heit v. Baird*, 567 F.2d 1157, 1160 (1st Cir. 1977); *see also Kauffman Mut. Fund*, 479 F.2d at 263; *Loucks*, 1992 U.S. Dist. LEXIS 16966, at *15, 1992 WL 329313, at *4; *Allison v. General Motors Corp.*, 604 F. Supp. 1106, 1112 (D. Del.), *aff'd mem.*, 782 F.2d 1026 (3d Cir. 1985); *Tabas v. Mullane*, 608 F. Supp. 759, 766 (D.N.J. 1985).

295. *Grobow v. Perot*, 539 A.2d 180, 187 (Del. 1988).

296. *Levine*, 591 A.2d at 207; *Grobow*, 539 A.2d at 187 n.6; *see also Levner v. Prince Alwaleed Bin Talal Bin Abdulaziz Al Saud*, 903 F. Supp. 452, 456 (S.D.N.Y. 1994), *aff'd*, 61 F.3d 8, 8-9 (2d Cir. 1995) (affirming "on the carefully reasoned opinion" of the district court); *Abrams v. Koether*, [1992 Transfer Binder] Fed. Sec. L. Rep. (CCH) ¶ 96,995 (D.N.J. Aug. 7, 1992); *Gagliardi v. TriFoods Int'l, Inc.*, 683 A.2d 1049, 1054 (Del. Ch. 1996) (published in part, complete text available at 1996 Del. Ch. LEXIS 87 and 1996 WL 422330).

297. *Blasband v. Rales*, 772 F. Supp. 850, 854 (D. Del. 1991),
(continued...)

demand "need not assume a particular form" or "be made in any specific language," but "it must inform the board 'with particularity' of the complained of acts and the potential defendants" and thus "must fairly and adequately apprise the directors of the potential cause of action."[298] The demand must, at a minimum, "identify the alleged wrongdoers, describe the factual basis of the wrongful acts and the harm caused to the corporation, and request remedial relief."[299] "In most instances, the shareholder need not specify his legal theory, every fact in support of that theory, or the precise quantum of damages."[300] The burden of showing that a demand has been made rests upon the party asserting that there was a demand.[301] According to Principles of Corporate Governance, "[t]he demand should give notice to the board, with reasonable

---

297. (...continued)
*aff'd and rev'd on other grounds*, 971 F.2d 1034 (3d Cir. 1992) (quoting *Herd v. Major Realty Corp.*, [1990-1991 Transfer Binder] Fed. Sec. L. Rep. (CCH) ¶ 95,772, at 98,717 (Del. Ch. Dec. 21, 1990)).

298. *Stoner v. Walsh*, 772 F. Supp. 790, 796 (S.D.N.Y. 1991) (citations omitted).

299. *Allison*, 604 F.Supp. at 1117, *quoted in Allright Mo., Inc. v. Billeter*, 829 F.2d 631, 638 (8th Cir. 1987) and *Stallworth v. AmSouth Bank*, 1997 Ala. LEXIS 483, at *13, 1997 WL 778838, at *4 (Ala. Dec. 19, 1997); *see also Rales v. Blasband*, 634 A.2d 927, 935 (Del. 1993) (a shareholder demand must, "at a minimum, notify the directors of the nature of the alleged wrongdoing and the identities of the alleged wrongdoers"); *Yaw v. Talley*, 1994 Del. Ch. LEXIS 35, at *22-23, 1994 WL 89019, at *7 (Del. Ch. Mar. 2, 1994) ("[t]o constitute a demand, a communication must specifically state: (i) the identity of the alleged wrongdoers, (ii) the wrongdoing they allegedly perpetrated and the resultant injury to the corporation, and (iii) the legal action the shareholder wants the board to take on the corporation's behalf").

300. *Allison*, 604 F. Supp. at 1117; *see also Kemper*, 500 U.S. at 106 n.9 (noting the statement in *Allison* that "'[i]n most instances, the shareholder need not specify his legal theory' in his demand" (quoting 604 F. Supp. at 1117), and concluding as a result that "directors frequently will not be able to tell whether the underlying claim is founded on state law or on federal law").

301. *Yaw*, 1994 Del. Ch. LEXIS 35, at *23-24, 1994 WL 89019, at *7-8.

specificity, of the essential facts relied upon to support each of the claims made therein."[302]

Applying these principles, a federal court construing Delaware and federal law in *Allison v. General Motors Corp.*[303] held that a three-page, single-spaced demand letter was adequate even though the letter "was couched in terms of breach of fiduciary duty and requested suit be instituted seeking compensatory damages" while the complaint that later was filed also asserted a claim under the Racketeer Influenced and Corrupt Organizations Act ("RICO")[304] and on that basis sought treble damages, costs and attorneys' fees.[305] The court explained that the demand "identified the alleged wrongdoers," "spelled out the perceived wrongful conduct," "specified the losses suffered by the corporation," and "requested relief for the corporation."[306] A federal court construing federal law in *Rubin v. Posner*[307] similarly held that a letter demanding that a corporation sue certain identified parties constituted a demand that the corporation sue two other parties because the letter described the role of the other parties in the alleged wrongdoing.[308] A federal court construing Pennsylvania law in *B.T.Z., Inc. v. Grove*[309] held that letters written by a shareholder, B.T.Z., Inc., to the board of JLG Industries, Inc., demanding that the board consider a potential acquiror's offer satisfied the demand requirement with respect to a claim that the corporation's directors breached their fiduciary duties by failing to consider the offer. The court stated that "BTZ gave the JLG board an opportunity to address BTZ's concerns about the proposed takeover bid,"

---

302. 2 Principles of Corporate Governance: Analysis and Recommendations § 7.03(a) (1994).

303. 604 F. Supp. 1106 (D. Del.), *aff'd mem.*, 782 F.2d 1026 (3d Cir. 1985).

304. 18 U.S.C. §§ 1961-68.

305. 604 F. Supp. at 1116-17.

306. *Id.* at 1117.

307. 701 F. Supp. 1041 (D. Del. 1988).

308. *Id.* at 1045.

309. 803 F. Supp. 1019 (M.D. Pa. 1992).

and "[t]he BTZ letters fulfilled the purposes of the demand requirement in the context of the takeover."[310]

The Delaware Court of Chancery in *Leslie v. Telephonics
Office Technologies, Inc.*[311] and *Yaw v. Talley*,[312] by contrast,
held that a letter enclosing a draft complaint does not constitute a
demand unless the letter "specifically request[s]" that the board
"embark upon a particular course of remedial corporate
action."[313] The court explained that "I do not accept that the mere
sending of a copy of a complaint constitutes a demand that the
board take the legal action therein embodied"; rather, "[f]or an
action to constitute a valid demand, it must embody a specific
request for the board to take legal action on behalf of the
corporation."[314] The court reasoned that under Delaware law—as
discussed more fully later in this Chapter[315]—the making of a
demand "is said to concede (and waive any challenge to) the
board's ability to exercise a binding business judgment" with
respect to the subject matter of the demand and that this waiver
should not be extended to ambiguous communications.[316] The
court explained:

> To interpret an ambiguous communication as a demand
> would discourage a shareholder from bringing potential
> wrongdoing to the corporation's attention in a forum other
> than the courtroom, for fear that his position, should he later
> decide to sue derivatively, would procedurally be more diffi-
> cult to support. Furthermore, to require a board to investigate
> claims asserted ambiguously in an equivocal communication
> would not be an efficient use of corporate resources, because

---

310. *Id.* at 1021.
311. 19 Del. J. Corp. L. 1237 (Del. Ch. Dec. 30, 1993).
312. 1994 Del. Ch. LEXIS 35, 1994 WL 89019 (Del. Ch. Mar. 2,
1994).
313. *Yaw*, 1994 Del. Ch. LEXIS 35, at *25-26, 1994 WL 89019, at
*8.
314. *Leslie*, 19 Del. J. Corp. L. at 1255.
315. *See* Chapter IV, Section B 5 i (i).
316. *Leslie*, 19 Del. J. Corp. L. at 1255, *quoted in Yaw*, 1994 Del.
Ch. LEXIS 35, at *24-25, 1994 WL 89019, at *8 (citations omitted).

the board would lack the information necessary to make a good faith inquiry.[317]

Accordingly, the court held, a communication that "does not clearly and specifically" state "(i) the identity of the alleged wrong-doers, (ii) the wrongdoing they allegedly perpetrated and the resultant injury to the corporation, and (iii) the legal action the shareholder wants the board to take on the corporation's behalf" "ought not to be considered a demand."[318] The court acknowledged that the plaintiff's letters to the board in *Yaw* did "allege wrongdoing by identified persons" and did describe the alleged harm to the corporation," but these letters did not "specifically request" that the board "embark upon a particular course of remedial corporate action."[319] Instead, the letters asked shareholder-directors to agree to sell their shares to a bidder seeking to acquire the corporation but stopped "just short of expressly demanding" that the board take action to stop alleged wrongdoing.[320]

An alleged demand also was held to be insufficient in *Levner v. Prince Alwaleed Bin Talal Bin Abdulaziz Al Saud*,[321] a case involving 1991 and 1992 transactions between Price Alwaleed and Citicorp: (1) a February 21, 1991 purchase agreement entered into by Alwaleed and Citicorp, pursuant to which Alwaleed purchased 11.8 million Citicorp depository shares for $590 million, each representing one/two-thousandth of a share of convertible preferred Citicorp stock, and the equivalent of 5,900 shares of preferred stock, and (2) a February 19, 1992 sale by Alwaleed of one million shares of Citicorp common stock on the open market at a price of $17 per share, and a March 5, 1992 repurchase by Alwaleed of one million shares of Citicorp common stock on the open market at an

---

317. 1994 Del. Ch. LEXIS 35, at *25, 1994 WL 89019, at *8.

318. 1994 Del. Ch. LEXIS 35, at *22-23, 25, 1994 WL 89019, at *7, 8.

319. 1994 Del. Ch. LEXIS 35, at *25-26, 1994 WL 89019, at *8.

320. 1994 Del. Ch. LEXIS 35, at *26 n.11, 1994 WL 89019, at *12 n.11.

321. 903 F. Supp. 452 (S.D.N.Y. 1994), *aff'd*, 61 F.3d 8 (2d Cir. 1995).

average price of $16.68.[322] A shareholder filed a derivative action on behalf of Citicorp, alleging a violation of Section 13(d) of the Securities Exchange Act of 1934 in connection with Alwaleed's 1991 purchase of preferred stock, claiming that Alwaleed falsely stated in a Schedule 13D filing that he was the beneficial owner of the convertible preferred stock, and that the source of the funds paid for this stock had been his personal funds.[323] The shareholder alleged short-swing trading in violation of Section 16(b) of the Exchange Act in connection with the 1992 purchase and sale of stock.[324]

The shareholder alleged compliance with the demand requirement as follows:

> [O]n August 3, 1992, plaintiff demanded that Citicorp directly bring the claims alleged [in the amended complaint] with respect to his sale and repurchase of Citicorp stock in violation of § 16(b), and with respect to Alwaleed's failure timely to file documents required by the SEC, concerning, *inter alia*, the transfer by Alwaleed, in the spring or early summer 1992, of his Citicorp stock to a Cayman Islands Corporation he purported to own. . . . *In light of [this transfer], plaintiff also requested that Citicorp take action with respect to the possibility that Alwaleed was acting on behalf of others in connection with his purported purchase of the Citicorp convertible shares. . . .*[325]

A federal district court, construing Delaware law, held that plaintiff "clearly alleges that a demand was made for the § 16(b) claim involving the 1992 transaction," but that the language italicized above did not allege "with sufficient particularity that a demand was made upon the Citicorp board for the claims arising out of Alwaleed's 1991 transaction involving the preferred stock."[326] The court explained that with respect to the 1991 transaction the letter identified Alwaleed as the alleged wrongdoer but

---

322. *Id.* at 454-55.
323. *Id.* at 455.
324. *Id.* at 454-55.
325. *Id.* at 455-56 (emphasis added by court).
326. *Id.* at 456.

lacked a factual basis for the alleged wrongful acts. The letter also requested that Citicorp "take action" but without suggesting any remedial relief.[327] The court stated that "'the possibility that Alwaleed was acting on behalf of others,' simply was not adequately particular to alert the Citicorp board as to the corporate injury, or the specific relief sought."[328] The Second Circuit affirmed on the basis of "the carefully reasoned opinion" of the district court.[329]

The Third Circuit, construing federal law, similarly held that a series of four letters were insufficient to constitute a demand in *Shlensky v. Dorsey*.[330] The first letter requested information concerning "the amounts and circumstances" of illegal political contributions by Gulf Oil Corporation."[331] The second letter requested information concerning "the payment by Gulf of any fines in connection with the illegal contributions and the corporation's intentions regarding reimbursement from the officers and directors responsible for making the contributions."[332] The third letter made what it called "a 'formal demand' that the board of directors seek reimbursement from the 'responsible individuals' 'for all damages' sustained by the corporation in connection with the payment of fines and injury to the corporation's reputation resulting from the illegal contributions."[333] The fourth letter "renew[ed] and expand[ed]" the prior "demand" by referring to recent newspaper disclosures and stating that "the Directors should seek reimbursement for the contributions, all fines imposed, litigation and counsel expenses, lost interest, taxes and increased public relations costs expended to repair Gulf's damaged reputation and for the damage to Gulf's reputation."[334] The court stated that the "expan-

---

327. *Id*.

328. *Id*.

329. *Levner v. Prince Alwaleed Bin Talal Bin Abdulaziz Al Saud*, 61 F.3d 8, 8-9 (2d Cir. 1995).

330. 574 F.2d 131 (3d Cir. 1978).

331. *Id*. at 140.

332. *Id*.

333. *Id*. at 140-41.

334. *Id*. at 141.

sion" of the demand in the fourth letter "referred, perhaps, to the increased dollar amounts of reimbursement which the corporation should seek in view of . . . the enlarged scope of related damages to Gulf."[335] Like the third letter, the fourth letter "referred . . . only to reimbursement from 'responsible individuals.'"[336]

The court upheld a dismissal of Price Waterhouse, Gulf's independent certified public accountant and auditor, as a defendant in a derivative action filed by the shareholders upon whose behalf these four letters had been written. The court stated that the first two letters were addressed to Gulf's president and not Gulf's board and "called for nothing more than a responsive communication" from Gulf's president.[337] The third letter, the court stated, was a demand for legal action, but "Price Waterhouse was not mentioned in it and there was nothing in the letter suggesting that Price Waterhouse . . . was intended to be included among the individuals referred to in the letter as responsible for damages incurred by the corporation."[338] The court stated that "obviously, there can be no claim for damages against an unknown and unspecified party," and thus "plaintiffs cannot mean that any of the first three letters or combination of them literally communicated to Gulf's directors the existence of a claim against Price Waterhouse which should be enforced by Gulf."[339] "[T]he request for action against the 'responsible individuals' 'for all damages' to Gulf" the court continued, "does not, considered in the context of all three letters, suggest any liability on the part of Price Waterhouse to Gulf" because "[i]t is completely lacking in the specificity which would give the directors a fair opportunity to initiate the action, which the shareholders subsequently undertook, which it is the purpose of the demand requirement to provide."[340] The fourth letter, the court concluded, also was insufficient with respect to Price Waterhouse:

---

335. *Id.*
336. *Id.*
337. *Id.* at 140.
338. *Id.* at 141.
339. *Id.*
340. *Id.*

"No mention of Price Waterhouse was made in the letter."[341] Accordingly, "this letter, like the others, did not encompass a demand to bring suit against Price Waterhouse."[342]

Shareholder communications also have been held not to constitute demands in the following decisions:

- *Blosvern v. Fisher*[343] (holding under Delaware law that a broker's "discussion with management" does not constitute a demand);[344]

- *Cottle v. Standard Brands Paint Co.*[345] (holding under Delaware law that a letter instructing the board of Standard Brands Paint Co. (1) to offer bidders for Standard, including Entregrowth International Ltd., which had made a proposal to acquire Standard, "access to confidential information, (2) to refrain from enacting defensive mechanisms that would deter the acquisition of Standard by a third party, and (3) to '[s]ue those responsible if the corporation takes actions contrary to those discussed in this letter'" did not constitute a demand; the court stated that the letter "does not identify any act or omission by the Standard directors that is allegedly wrongful"; instead, the letter "gives instructions to the directors on how to perform their duties and demands that suit be brought against any unnamed persons who fail to do so"—a directive that "is simply too vague and conclusory to satisfy the purposes of the demand requirement");[346]

---

341. *Id.*

342. *Id.*

343. 504 A.2d 571 (unpublished opinion, text available at 1986 Del. LEXIS 1030 and 1986 WL 16162) (Del. Jan. 30, 1986).

344. 1986 Del. LEXIS 1030, at *3, 1986 WL 16162, at *1.

345. [1990 Transfer Binder] Fed. Sec. L. Rep. (CCH) ¶ 95,306 (Del. Ch. Mar. 22, 1990).

346. *Id.* at 96,431-32.

- *Brook v. Acme Steel Co.*[347] (holding under Delaware law that a letter containing "a generalized admonition . . . to seek out the highest bidder for the company and to refrain from paying greenmail to any stockholder" and offering "prospective advice" that "essentially instructs the directors to auction the company to the highest bidder" but that did not "identify a wrong to the corporation which the directors are expected to correct" or "demand suit to be instituted against anyone" did not constitute a demand; the court stated that the letter "fail[ed] to provide the directors with information necessary for them to assess whether an alleged wrong to the corporation has actually occurred and to determine whether to take steps to rectify it");[348]

- *Herd v. Major Realty Corp.*[349] (holding under Delaware law that shareholder letters demanding termination of a merger agreement and postponement of a shareholders' meeting did not constitute a sufficient demand for claims relating to the sale of real estate at less than fair market value, the payment of excessive fees, and the bypassing of corporate opportunities);[350]

- *Seibert v. Harper & Row, Publishers, Inc.*[351] (holding under Delaware law that a letter written by counsel as a shareholder and as a representative of other shareholders (1) stating a belief that an "announced agreement in principle" pursuant to which the corporation would purchase one-third of the corporation's outstanding shares from a single shareholder was "not in the best interest of the shareholders or the employees" of the corporation, (2) identifying four "areas of concern,"

---

347. 15 Del. J. Corp. L. 149 (Del. Ch. May 11, 1989).
348. *Id.* at 154.
349. [1990-1991 Transfer Binder] Fed. Sec. L. Rep. (CCH) ¶ 95,772 (Del. Ch. Dec. 21, 1990).
350. *Id.* at 98,716-17.
351. 10 Del. J. Corp. L. 645 (Del. Ch. Dec. 5, 1984).

and (3) requesting "the opportunity to meet with the board of directors to discuss the matter" did not constitute a demand; the court stated that the letter's "stated purpose was not to demand that specific corrective action be taken" but rather that "counsel be given the opportunity to discuss the matter in person with the entire board of directors.");[352]

- *Blasband v. Rales*[353] (holding under Delaware law that a letter questioning why the proceeds of a note offering had been used to purchase securities other than the securities that had been described in the offering materials and requesting details concerning all securities purchased by the corporation with the proceeds of the offering did not constitute a demand; the court stated that the letter did not "demand that the directors take action to remedy the alleged corporate injury for which derivative relief is now sought");[354]

- *Abrams v. Koether*[355] (holding under Delaware law that (1) a letter complaining concerning fees paid to a director's law firm and a stock purchase and "requesting answers to a list of ten questions" concerning the stock purchase did not constitute a demand, and (2) a later letter demanding litigation against directors who profited from the stock purchase constituted a demand only with respect to that transaction, and not with respect to "unrelated transactions and alleged fraud . . . in various proxy statements)";[356]

---

352. *Id.* at 651.

353. 772 F. Supp. 850 (D. Del. 1991), *aff'd and rev'd on other grounds*, 971 F.2d 1034 (3d Cir. 1992).

354. *Id.* at 853-54; *see also* 971 F.2d at 1039 n.3 (conceding this point on appeal).

355. 766 F. Supp. 237 (D.N.J. 1991).

356. *Id.* at 244-46, 252-54.

- *Allright Missouri, Inc. v. Billeter*[357] (holding under federal law that the following allegations satisfied the demand requirement: "Between March 29, 1984, and July 5, 1984," plaintiff "demanded that the general partners of Downtown take whatever action was necessary to recover Downtown's property or to recover reasonable compensation therefor from defendants Burkhardt, Senturia and/or Riverside," "reiterated its demands at a meeting for all the general partners and all of the limited partners on May 17, 1984," and "[n]o action was taken by the general partners"; the court explained that "[t]he demand identified the alleged wrongdoers (i.e., Burkhardt and Senturia); described the wrongful act at issue (i.e., the conveyance to Riverside); implicitly denoted the harm caused to the partnership (i.e., implicit in the demand was the fact that there was an improper loss of a valuable partnership asset); and made a request for remedial relief (i.e., a return of the property, or in lieu thereof, reasonable compensation from Burkhardt, Senturia, and/or Riverside");[358]

- *Stallworth v. AmSouth Bank*[359] (holding under Alabama law that general references to "demands" "in the past" that directors "act in the best interests of the corporation" but that fail "to state what the subject" of the shareholder's prior demands "were, when they were made, what specific relief he requested, or how those demands related to the actions he desires in this case . . . are far too vague in themselves . . . to satisfy the particularity-of-pleading requirement");[360]

---

357. 829 F.2d 631 (8th Cir. 1987).

358. *Id.* at 638-39.

359. 1997 Ala. LEXIS 483, 1997 WL 778838 (Ala. Dec. 19, 1997).

360. 1997 Ala. LEXIS 483, at *15-16, 1997 WL 778838, at *5.

- *B.T.Z., Inc. v. Grove*[361] (holding under Pennsylvania law that a letter demanding action with respect to a potential acquiror's offer constituted a demand with respect to a claim that the corporation's directors breached their fiduciary duties by failing to consider the offer, but did not constitute a demand with respect to the exercise by directors of "golden parachute" stock options upon a change of control);[362]

- *Poland v. Caldwell* [363] (holding under federal law that a letter containing "vague allegations" of "reckless expansion" by Atlantic Financial Federal "that caused a 'negative impact . . . on the 'bottom line,'" with "[t]he most specific allegations" being a claim that "the 'reckless expansion of the Company has carried, in its wake, sloppy management, imprudent lending and, undoubtedly, understatement of loan loss reserves," did not constitute a demand; the court stated that "Plaintiffs have the responsibility to make specific charges against the management so that the management may redress these problems," that plaintiffs did "not point to one specific example of how this expansion harmed Atlantic Financial," that "[t]he directors do not have to play a guessing game about which policies Plaintiffs were complaining," and that the letter in this case was "completely lacking in specificity");[364]

- *Stoner v. Walsh*[365] (observing in a case governed by New York law that "it is doubtful" whether a letter that "merely restated well-publicized business setbacks and problems . . . without indicating with any specificity the causes of action available to the corporation or

---

361. 803 F. Supp. 1019 (M.D. Pa. 1992).

362. *Id.* at 1021.

363. 1990 U.S. Dist. LEXIS 13634, 1990 WL 158479 (E.D. Pa. Oct. 12, 1990).

364. 1990 U.S. Dist. LEXIS 13634, at *7-8, 1990 WL 158479, at *3.

365. 772 F. Supp. 790 (S.D.N.Y. 1991).

those persons potentially liable" constituted "a demand with the level of adequacy required by New York law," but declining to dismiss plaintiff's claims on this ground because defendants had not challenged the adequacy of the demand);[366] and

- *Diduck v. Kaszycki & Sons Contractors, Inc.*[367] (holding under federal law that "mere notification of the Fund's attorneys of the possibility of delinquent contributions in the context of a completely separate suit does not . . . constitute an adequate demand").[368]

The demand must be directed to the board as a whole, and not merely to the board's chairman and/or general counsel.[369] The demand also must identify the shareholder making the demand, and thus cannot be an attorney's letter that does not identify the shareholder upon whose behalf the attorney is acting.[370]

## 2. Rationale

A pre-litigation demand is required for at least three reasons.

The first and most important reason that a pre-litigation demand is required was stated by the United States Supreme Court in 1984 in *Daily Income Fund, Inc. v. Fox*[371] and in 1991 in *Kamen v. Kemper Financial Services, Inc.*[372] These decisions state that the demand requirement implements "the basic principle of corporate governance that the decisions of a corporation—including the decision to initiate litigation—should be made by the board of

---

366. *Id.* at 797.

367. 737 F. Supp. 792 (S.D.N.Y. 1990), *aff'd in part and rev'd in part on other grounds*, 974 F.2d 270 (2d Cir. 1992).

368. *Id.* at 802.

369. *See Greenspun v. Del E. Webb Corp.*, 634 F.2d 1204, 1209 (9th Cir. 1980); *Shlensky v. Dorsey*, 574 F.2d 131, 140-41 (3d Cir. 1978).

370. *See Smachlo v. Birkelo*, 576 F. Supp. 1439, 1444-45 (D. Del. 1983).

371. 464 U.S. 523 (1984).

372. 500 U.S. 90 (1991).

directors or the majority of shareholders."[373] The demand requirement thus affords directors "an opportunity to exercise their reasonable business judgment and 'waive a legal right vested in the corporation in the belief that its best interests will be promoted by not insisting on such right.'"[374] The demand requirement thus "may be thought of as the corollary of the business judgment rule."[375]

The Second Circuit in *Elfenbein v. Gulf & Western Industries, Inc.*,[376] *Lewis v. Graves*[377] and *RCM Securities Fund, Inc. v. Stanton*[378] explained that the "purpose of the demand requirement is to 'allow the directors the chance to occupy their normal status as conductors of the corporation's affairs,'" and that "[w]hether a corporation should bring a lawsuit is a business decision, and the directors are, under the laws of every state, responsible for the conduct of the corporation's business, including the decision to litigate."[379] The Third Circuit in *Blasband v. Rales*[380] and *Garber v. Lego*[381] stated that "[t]he decision to bring a lawsuit or to refrain from litigating a claim on behalf of the corporation is a decision concerning the management of the corporation and consequently is the responsibility of the directors."[382]

---

373. *Kemper*, 500 U.S. at 101 (quoting *Daily Income Fund*, 464 U.S. at 530).

374. *Kemper*, 500 U.S. at 96 (quoting *Daily Income Fund*, 464 U.S. at 533, and *Corbus v. Alaska Treadwell Gold Mining Co.*, 187 U.S. 455, 463 (1903)).

375. *Gall v. Exxon Corp.*, 418 F. Supp. 508, 515 n.16 (S.D.N.Y. 1976).

376. 590 F.2d 445 (2d Cir. 1978).

377. 701 F.2d 245 (2d Cir. 1983).

378. 928 F.2d 1318 (2d Cir. 1991).

379. *Id*. at 1326 (quoting *Graves*, 701 F.2d at 247 and *Elfenbein*, 590 F.2d at 450, and omitting other citations).

380. 971 F.2d 1034 (3d Cir. 1992).

381. 11 F.3d 1197 (3d Cir. 1993).

382. *Blasband*, 971 F.2d at 1048; *Garber*, 11 F.3d at 1201.

The Seventh Circuit in *Kamen v. Kemper Financial Services, Inc.*[383] and *Boland v. Engle*[384] likewise observed that the demand requirement

> allows directors to make a business decision about a business question: whether to invest the time and resources of the corporation in litigation. . . . Choosing between litigation and some other response may be difficult, depending on information unavailable to courts and a sense of the situation in which business executives are trained. . . . If principles such as the "business judgment rule" preserve room for managers to err in making an operational decision, so too they preserve room to err in deciding what remedies to pursue.[385]
>
> \*          \*          \*
>
> [W]hether a corporation should pursue a right of action is a complicated business question on which courts need assistance. Legal expertise is relevant to such business decisions, but hard-nosed business acumen will be a better judge of whether corporate norms have been violated and whether litigation would be worth the costs to the corporation. Litigation against corporate managers, for example, may benefit corporations in a number of ways, including both the recovery of damages and the deterrence of future misconduct. But even where litigation would be beneficial, "acts short of litigation could have net benefits exceeding those of litigation." Requiring demand thus serves as a valuable screen of potential lawsuits, both by giving corporations a crack at resolving shareholder complaints before litigation and by giving courts more information on which to decide the merits of those suits that remain after demand.[386]

As stated in a concurring opinion in another Seventh Circuit decision, *Starrels v. First National Bank*,[387] the demand requirement "allows directors to make a business decision about a business question: whether to invest the time and resources of the corpora-

---

383. 908 F.2d 1338 (7th Cir. 1990), *rev'd on other grounds*, 500 U.S. 90 (1991).

384. 113 F.3d 706 (7th Cir. 1997).

385. *Kemper,* 908 F.2d at 1342-43.

386. *Boland*, 113 F.3d at 712 (citations omitted).

387. 870 F.2d 1168 (7th Cir. 1989).

tion in litigation."[388] The Eighth Circuit in *Allright Missouri, Inc. v. Billeter*[389] put it this way: "The demand requirement . . . serves the purpose of notifying management so that it can make the initial decision as to the type of action that should be taken, be it a lawsuit or some other form of corrective action, to resolve the problem at hand."[390]

The Delaware Supreme Court in *Levine v. Smith*[391] similarly stated that "[t]he directors of a corporation and not its shareholders manage the business and affairs of the corporation, and accordingly, the directors are responsible for deciding whether to engage in derivative litigation."[392] Thus, according to the Delaware Supreme Court in *Grimes v. Donald*,[393] "[i]f a claim belongs to the corporation, it is the corporation, acting through its board of directors, which must make the decision whether or not to assert the claim."[394] Numerous additional Delaware Supreme Court decisions emphasize this same principle, including the following:

- *Aronson v. Lewis*[395] ("the demand requirement is a recognition of the fundamental precept that directors manage the business and affairs of the corporation");[396]

- *Spiegel v. Buntrock*[397] ("A basic principle of the General Corporation Law of the State of Delaware is that directors, rather than shareholders, manage the business and affairs of the corporation. . . . The decision to bring a law suit or to refrain from litigating a claim on

---

388. *Id.* at 1173 (Easterbrook, J., concurring).
389. 829 F.2d 631 (8th Cir. 1987).
390. *Id.* at 638.
391. 591 A.2d 194 (Del. 1991).
392. *Id.* at 200.
393. 673 A.2d 1207 (Del. 1996).
394. *Id.* at 1215.
395. 473 A.2d 805 (Del. 1984).
396. *Id.* at 812, *quoted in Grimes*, 673 A.2d at 1215.
397. 571 A.2d 767 (Del. 1990).

behalf of a corporation is a decision concerning the
management of the corporation. . . . Consequently,
such decisions are part of the responsibility of the board
of directors.");[398]

- *Rales v. Blasband*[399] (the demand requirement limits
the right of a stockholder to prosecute a derivative
action "[b]ecause directors are empowered to manage,
or direct the management of, the business and affairs of
the corporation");[400] and

- *Alabama By-Products Corp. v. Cede & Co.*[401] ("It is
a fundamental principle of the Delaware General Corporation Law that directors, rather than shareholders,
manage the business and affairs of the corporation.
Consequently, the decision to pursue or refrain from
undertaking a claim on behalf of the corporation is
entrusted to the board of directors as within the ambit
of its management responsibility.").[402]

The New York Court of Appeals used similar language in
*Auerbach v. Bennett*[403] and *Marx v. Akers.*[404] These decisions
state that "[a]s with other questions of corporate policy and management, the decision whether and to what extent to explore and
prosecute such [derivative] claims lies within the judgment and control of the corporation's board of directors."[405] As that court
explained further in *Auerbach*: "Necessarily such decision must be
predicated on the weighing and balancing of a variety of disparate
considerations to reach a considered conclusion as to what course

---

398. *Id.* at 772-73.
399. 634 A.2d 927 (Del. 1993).
400. *Id.* at 932.
401. 657 A.2d 254 (Del. 1995).
402. *Id.* at 265 (citations omitted).
403. 47 N.Y.2d 619, 393 N.E.2d 994, 419 N.Y.S.2d 920 (1979).
404. 88 N.Y.2d 189, 666 N.E.2d 1034, 644 N.Y.S.2d 121 (1996).
405. *Marx*, 88 N.Y.2d at 194, 666 N.E.2d at 1037, 644 N.Y.S.2d
at 124; *Auerbach*, 47 N.Y.2d at 631, 393 N.E.2d at 1000, 419 N.Y.S.2d
at 927.

of action or inaction is best calculated to protect and advance the interests of the corporation. This is the essence of the responsibility and role of the board of directors, and courts may not intrude to interfere."[406] The New York Court of Appeals similarly stated in *Barr v. Wackman*[407] that the demand requirement "derives from one of the basic principles of corporate control—that the management of the corporation is entrusted to its board of directors . . . , who have primary responsibility for acting in the name of the corporation."[408]

The Alabama Supreme Court in *Elgin v. Alfa Corp.*[409] and *Stallworth v. AmSouth Bank*[410] similarly stated that "[o]ne of the reasons for the director-demand requirement is that it allows the derivative corporation, on whose behalf the action is brought in the first place, to take over the litigation, thus permitting the directors the opportunity to act in their normal status as conductors of the corporation's affairs."[411] The Massachusetts Supreme Judicial Court in *Houle v. Low* likewise stated the following:[412]

> Our cases have long recognized that the question whether a corporation should pursue a given lawsuit involves factors other than the merits of the claim. It is often a question of business policy. "Intelligent and honest men differ upon questions of business policy. It is not always best to insist on one's rights. . . ." Indeed, the requirement that a stockholder wishing to bring suit make a demand on the directors and the other stockholders evolved within the equitable jurisprudence of the derivative action in large measure as a recognition of

---

406. 47 N.Y.2d at 631, 393 N.E.2d at 1000-01, 419 N.Y.S.2d at 927.

407. 36 N.Y.2d 371, 329 N.E.2d 180, 368 N.Y.S.2d 497 (1975).

408. *Id.* at 378, 329 N.E.2d at 185-86, 368 N.Y.S.2d at 505.

409. 598 So. 2d 807 (Ala. 1992).

410. 1997 Ala. LEXIS 483, 1997 WL 778838 (Ala. Dec. 19, 1997).

411. *Stallworth*, 1997 Ala. LEXIS 483, at *12, 1997 WL 778838 at *4; *Elgin*, 598 So. 2d at 814.

412. 556 N.E.2d 51 (Mass. 1990).

the fact that the decision whether to sue is properly left to the corporate authorities.[413]

An intermediate appellate court in Ohio in *Drage v. Procter & Gamble*[414] stated that "[t]he directors of a corporation are charged with the responsibility of making decisions on behalf of the corporation and are the proper parties to bring a suit on behalf of the corporation or, in their business judgment, to forego a lawsuit," and that "the directors have the right to govern the corporation, including making decisions about when the corporation should instigate litigation against its own directors."[415] In the words of the Pennsylvania Supreme Court in *Cuker v. Mikalauskas*,[416] "[d]ecisions regarding litigation by or on behalf of a corporation, including shareholder derivative actions, are business decisions as much as any other financial decisions. As such, they are within the province of the board of directors."[417] As Dean Robert C. Clark of Harvard has put it: "Whether to sue or not to sue is ordinarily a matter for the business judgment of directors, just as is a decision that the corporation will make bricks instead of bottles."[418]

---

413. *Id.* at 57 (citations omitted).

414. 694 N.E.2d 479 (Ohio Ct. App. 1997).

415. 694 N.E.2d at 482, 487; *see also Drage v. Procter & Gamble*, No. A-9401998, slip op. at 3 (Ohio Ct. Comm. Pleas Jan. 19, 1996) ("the responsibility for determining whether or not a corporation shall enforce in the courts a cause of action for damages is, like other business questions, ordinarily a matter of internal management left to the discretion of the directors") (quoting *Grand Council v. Owens*, 620 N.E.2d 234, 238-39 (Ohio Ct. App. 1993) & slip op. at 4 (quoting *Kemper*, 500 U.S. at 101, quoted in second paragraph of this section of text), *aff'd*, 694 N.E.2d 479 (Ohio Ct. App. 1997).

416. 692 A.2d 1042 (Pa. 1997).

417. *Id.* at 1048; *see also In re Prudential Ins. Co. Derivative Litig.*, 659 A.2d 961, 970 (N.J. Super. Ct. Ch. Div. 1995) ("[t]he decision to bring a lawsuit or to refrain from litigating a claim on behalf of the corporation is a decision concerning the management of the corporation and is thus normally the responsibility of the directors").

418. Robert C. Clark, *Corporate Law* § 15.2, at 641 (1986), *quoted in In re Consumers Power Co. Derivative Litig.*, 132 F.R.D. 455, 465 (E.D. Mich. 1990).

The second reason that a pre-litigation demand is required is because a demand "enables corporate management to pursue alternative remedies, thus often ending unnecessary litigation."[419] The demand requirement in this way "serves the interests of judicial economy since a demand may often result in corrective action short of suit and, thereby, not only relieve the courts from entanglement in the management of internal corporate affairs, but also protect them from vain rulings on challenged acts which are later ratified by the board."[420] In other words, the demand requirement "relieve[s] courts from deciding matters of internal corporate governance by providing corporate directors with opportunities to correct alleged abuses."[421] The demand requirement thus requires that a shareholder "exhausts his intracorporate remedies" and promotes "alternate dispute resolution, rather than immediate recourse to litigation."[422] Put another way, "[b]y requiring exhaustion of intracorporate remedies, the demand requirement invokes a species of alternative dispute resolution procedure which might avoid litigation altogether."[423]

---

419. *Cramer v. General Tel. & Elecs. Corp.*, 582 F.2d 259, 275 (3d Cir. 1978), *cert. denied*, 439 U.S. 1129 (1979); *see also Graves*, 701 F.2d at 247 ("[c]orporate managers may be in a better position to pursue alternative remedies, resolving grievances without burdensome and expensive litigation"); *Barr*, 36 N.Y.2d at 378, 329 N.E.2d at 186, 368 N.Y.S.2d at 505 (directors "are often in a position to correct alleged abuses without resort to the courts").

420. *Barr*, 36 N.Y.2d at 378, 329 N.E.2d at 186, 368 N.Y.S.2d at 504-05.

421. *Marx*, 88 N.Y.2d at 194, 666 N.E.2d at 1037, 644 N.Y.S.2d at 124.

422. *Aronson*, 473 A.2d at 811-12.

423. *Grimes*, 673 A.2d at 1216; *see also Hawes v. City of Oakland*, 104 U.S. 450, 460-61 (1881) (shareholder plaintiff must demonstrate that he has "exhausted all the means within his reach to obtain, within the corporation itself, the redress of his grievances"); *Starrels*, 870 F.2d at 1173-74 (Easterbrook, J., concurring) (demand "initiates a form of alternate dispute resolution, much like mediation"); *Graves*, 701 F.2d at 248 ("strong policy and practical advantages favor[ ] exhaustion of intracorporate remedies"); *Stallworth*, 1997 Ala. LEXIS 483, at *12-13, 1997 WL
(continued...)

The third reason that demand is required is to "provide corporate boards with reasonable protection from harassment by litigation on matters clearly within the discretion of directors."[424] The goal is to "deter costly, baseless suits by creating a screening mechanism to eliminate claims where there is only a suspicion expressed solely in conclusory terms."[425] The demand requirement thus discourages "strike suits" brought "not to remedy wrongs to the corporation, but to induce settlements beneficial to the named plaintiff or his counsel."[426]

---

423. (...continued)
778838, at *4 ("Practically speaking, the demand requirement promotes a form of 'alternative dispute resolution'—that is, the corporate management may be in a better position to pursue alternative remedies, resolving grievances without burdensome and expensive litigation") (quoting *Shelton v. Thompson*, 544 So. 2d 845, 850 (Ala. 1989)); *Rales*, 634 A.2d at 935 (describing the demand requirement "as a 'form of alternate dispute resolution' that requires the stockholder to exhaust 'his intracorporate remedies'") (quoting *Aronson*, 473 A.2d 811-12); *Pogostin v. Rice*, 480 A.2d 619, 624 (Del. 1984) (the demand requirement "exists at the threshold to prevent abuse and to promote intracorporate dispute resolution"); *Grand Council*, 620 N.E.2d at 238 ("[t]he demand requirement is essentially a requirement that a shareholder exhaust his intracorporate remedies before going to court with a derivative suit"); *Procter & Gamble*, 694 N.E.2d at 487 ("[t]he demand rule is designed to promote the resolution of disputes within the corporation without interference from the courts or a minority of dissatisfied shareholders").
424. *Marx*, 88 N.Y.2d at 194, 666 N.E.2d at 1037, 644 N.Y.S.2d at 124; *see also Barr*, 36 N.Y.2d at 378, 329 N.E.2d at 186, 368 N.Y.S.2d at 505 (the demand requirement "affords corporate directors reasonable protection from the harassment of litigious dissident shareholders who might otherwise contest decisions on matters clearly within the directors' discretion").
425. *Grimes*, 673 A.2d at 1216, *quoted in Scattered Corp. v. Chicago Stock Exch., Inc.*, 701 A.2d 70, 75 (Del. 1997).
426. *Cramer*, 582 F.2d at 275; *see also Graves*, 701 F.2d at 248 ("[d]eference to directors' judgment may also result in the termination of meritless actions brought solely for their settlement or harassment value"); *Aronson*, 473 A.2d at 812 (the demand requirement "provide[s] a safeguard against strike suits"); *Gagliardi v. TriFoods Int'l, Inc.*, 683 A.2d
(continued...)

In short, the demand requirement "weed[s] out unnecessary or illegitimate shareholder derivative suits."[427]

The rationale underlying the demand requirement in no way is diminished by the fact that causes of action having merit may exist that the corporation's directors have not pursued or may not be inclined to pursue. A board of directors may decide against bringing an action even if the suit has "some merit" where "the litigation costs and the adverse effect on the business relationship between the corporation and the potential defendant might outweigh any potential recovery in the lawsuit."[428] Even where "something must be done," acts short of litigation can have net benefits exceeding those of litigation, and, indeed, even where a lawsuit "seems to have good prospects and a positive value" the lawsuit "still may be an unwise business decision because of the value of managerial time that would have to be invested, time unavailable to pursue the principal business of the corporation."[429] The law thus gives directors an opportunity to determine "whether the chances for a successful

---

426. (...continued)
1049, 1054 (Del. Ch. 1996) (published in part, complete text available at 1996 Del. Ch. LEXIS 87 and 1996 WL 422330) (explaining that "[a]sserting a derivative claim allows an attorney in the role of agent for shareholders to exert substantially magnified settlement pressure on a defendant," making "[s]trike suits . . . a greater threat in this context than in civil litigation between two principles," and stating that the demand requirement is intended "to filter such cases at an early stage more finely" than is done in other types of litigation); *Marx*, 88 N.Y.2d at 194, 666 N.E.2d at 1037, 644 N.Y.S.2d at 124 (the demand requirement "discourage[s] 'strike suits' commenced by shareholders for personal gain rather than for the benefit of the corporation"); *Barr*, 36 N.Y.2d at 378, 329 N.E.2d at 186, 368 N.Y.S.2d at 505 (the demand requirement is "designed to discourage 'strike suits' by shareholders making reckless charges for personal gain rather than corporate benefit"); *Kaufman Malchman & Kirby, P.C. v. Hasbro, Inc.*, 897 F. Supp. 719, 723-24 (S.D.N.Y. 1995) (collecting additional cases).

427. *Marx*, 88 N.Y.2d at 194, 666 N.E.2d at 1037, 644 N.Y.S.2d at 124 (quoting *Barr*, 36 N.Y.2d at 378, 329 N.E.2d at 186, 368 N.Y.S.2d at 505).

428. *Cramer*, 582 F.2d at 275.

429. *Starrels*, 870 F.2d at 1173-74 (Easterbrook, J., concurring).

suit, the costs of maintaining a suit, and other factors" militate in favor of or against instituting litigation.[430]

As stated by the United States Supreme Court in *Burks v. Lasker*,[431] "[t]here may well be situations in which the independent directors could reasonably believe that the best interests of the shareholders call for a decision not to sue—as, for examples, where the costs of litigation to the corporation outweigh any potential recovery."[432] As stated by the Delaware Supreme Court in *Zapata Corp. v. Maldonado*,[433] "[t]he final substantive judgment whether a particular lawsuit should be maintained requires a balance of many factors—ethical, commercial, promotional, public relations, employee relations, fiscal as well as legal."[434] As stated by the New York Court of Appeals in *Auerbach v. Bennett*[435] (in a passage quoted more fully above), "the decision whether and to what extent to explore and prosecute . . . claims . . . [n]ecessarily . . . must be predicated on the weighing and balancing of a variety of disparate considerations to reach a considered conclusion as to what course of action or inaction is best calculated to protect and advance the interests of the corporation."[436] As a California court concluded in *Findley v. Garrett*[437]:

> The mere fact that a recovery for the corporation would probably result from litigation does not require that an action be commenced to enforce the claim. Even if it appeared to the directors . . . that at the end of protracted litigation substantial sums could be recovered from some or all of the defendants, that fact alone would not have made it the duty

---

430. *Zauber v. Murray Sav. Ass'n*, 591 S.W.2d 932, 936 (Tex. Civ. App. 1979), *error refused*, 601 S.W.2d 940 (Tex. 1980).

431. 441 U.S. 471 (1979).

432. *Id.* at 485.

433. 430 A.2d 779 (Del. 1981).

434. *Id.* at 788 (quoting *Maldonado v. Flynn*, 485 F. Supp. 274, 285 (S.D.N.Y. 1980) (Weinfeld, J.), *aff'd in part and rev'd in part on other grounds*, 671 F.2d 729 (2d Cir. 1982)).

435. 47 N.Y.2d 619, 393 N.E.2d 994, 419 N.Y.S.2d 920 (1979).

436. *Id.* at 631, 393 N.E.2d at 1000-01, 419 N.Y.S.2d at 927.

437. 109 Cal. App. 2d 166, 240 P.2d 421 (Cal. Ct. App. 1952).

of the directors to authorize the commencement of an action. It would have made it their duty to weigh the advantages of probable recovery against the cost in money, time and disruption of the business of the company which litigation would entail.[438]

In the words of two other courts:

"[T]wo areas of consideration" are relevant to a determination whether to assert an independent action against directors and officers: "(1) Are the merits of the case strong enough to make it likely that the corporation could maintain a successful action against its officers and directors for wrongdoing?," and "(2) Even if there is a meritorious suit against the directors of a corporation, should such an action be maintained in light of other factors? In other words, once other factors are evaluated, might bringing the derivative action work a potentially greater harm to the corporation than any possible gain from that action?"[439]

\*          \*          \*

The whole point of recognizing the board's authority and responsibility in this context is to allow the board's judgment concerning what is in the long-run best interest of the corporation to be acted upon. That may not be the same as maximizing the return from the law suit. The [corporation] can legitimately sacrifice present compensation . . . if its good faith, informed judgment indicates to it that that course is best for the corporation.[440]

Tying all of this together, the court in *In re E.F. Hutton Banking Practices Litigation*,[441] construing Delaware and federal law, concluded that demand was required in derivative actions filed on behalf of E.F. Hutton following revelation of criminal conduct consisting of excessive overdrafting from banks at which E.F. Hut-

---

438. *Id.* at 177-78, 240 P.2d at 428.

439. *In re Consumers Power Co. Derivative Litig.*, 132 F.R.D. 455, 485 (E.D. Mich. 1990).

440. *Carlton Invs. v. TLC Beatrice Int'l Holdings, Inc.*, 1997 Del. Ch. LEXIS 86, at \*45, 1997 WL 305829, at \*11 (Del. Ch. May 30, 1997).

441. 634 F. Supp. 265 (S.D.N.Y. 1986).

ton maintained accounts, a practice that allowed E.F. Hutton to gain interest-free use of large amounts of money.[442] The court stated that this case "aptly illustrates" the need for the demand requirement.[443] The court explained:

> The facts alleged in the complaint—supplemented by the public information surrounding Hutton's plea of guilty—suggest that, if the Corporation wished to pursue them, valid causes of action exist against many—if not all—of the defendants named in the complaint. However, it does not follow that a disinterested Board of Directors (even if we were to assume that it was a wholly new Board, having no involvement in the facts at issue) would conclude that the present was an appropriate time to institute litigation against the alleged miscreants . . . . [T]here are presently pending in this Court some 14 suits against the Corporation itself based upon, among other things, the conduct claimed to have been approved of by the directors that plaintiffs now seek to have the Corporation sue, while the complaint alleges that the Securities and Exchange Commission is contemplating litigation which might threaten the ability of the Corporation to conduct its business. It seems obvious that the directors that plaintiffs wish to sue would be important witnesses for the Corporation in all of this existing and threatened litigation, and that a disinterested board might well—upon the advice of counsel retained to defend the Corporation in this litigation—conclude it to be unwise to subject them to further litigation clearly calculated to undercut their veracity and general effectiveness as witnesses.[444]

As the Delaware Court of Chancery put it in *Richardson v. Graves*,[445] another derivative action arising out of alleged criminal conduct within a corporation:

> Yes, the facts in this case prompt an impulse to enter the fray and resolve the problems that have arisen from the admitted criminal acts. Our conscience and dedication to justice sug-

---

442. *Id*. at 267-68.

443. *Id*. at 269.

444. *Id*. at 269-70.

445. 1983 Del. Ch. LEXIS 466, 1983 WL 21109 (Del. Ch. June 17, 1983).

gest this is the kind of case that should remain on the docket and be subject to some judicial scrutiny. Upon reflection, however, one must conclude that the criminality has already been investigated and what remains, the issue to be decided here, is whether the uninterested members of the board are in a better position to decide the fate of this lawsuit or should [this question] be left to the single-mindedness of a stockholder or a few of them. Obviously, the fate of this litigation could have a dramatic influence on the remaining sixty-eight lawsuits. In the end, an unleashing of the present litigants could effectively destroy the corporation and jeopardize the investment of the general public. Under the circumstances, it appears best that the fate of this litigation, yes, even the fate of this corporation, should be left to the consensus of its duly elected uninterested members of the board.[446]

The Delaware Court of Chancery in *In re Baxter International, Inc. Shareholders Litigation*[447] similarly concluded that the fact that a board decision to pursue litigation on behalf of the corporation would adversely affect the corporation's ability to defend pending litigation against the corporation and would influence a Securities and Exchange Commission investigation of the corporation did not excuse demand.[448] A New York court construing Delaware law in *Katz v. Emmett*[449] similarly refused to excuse demand in a case where a corporation faced exposure in a federal litigation involving the same alleged wrongdoing underlying the derivative action and the corporation's board already had opposed those claims in the federal litigation.[450] The court stated that "[i]f there is a potential inconsistency in the legal position in the federal action and that espoused by plaintiffs in this action, that

---

446. 1983 Del. Ch. LEXIS 466, at *12-13, 1983 WL 21109, at *5.
447. 654 A.2d 1268 (Del. Ch. 1995).
448. *Id.* at 1354.
449. N.Y.L.J., Sept. 27, 1994, at 26 (N.Y. Sup. Ct. Westchester Co.), *aff'd*, 226 A.D.2d 588, 641 N.Y.S.2d 131 (N.Y. App. Div. 2d Dep't 1996).
450. *Id.*

is merely an issue for the board's consideration, not a basis to avoid such consideration" by excusing demand.[451]

For all of these reasons, "[i]n the usual case, a shareholder's remedy for a perceived wrong against the corporation is limited to a demand upon the board that the corporation pursue redress. The board, in the exercise of its statutorily conferred managerial powers then makes the ultimate decision of whether or not to prosecute the claim."[452] Shareholder derivative litigation thus constitutes an exception "to the usual rule that the proper party to bring a claim on behalf of a corporation is the corporation itself, acting through its directors or the majority of its shareholders."[453] In sum, a shareholder derivative claim is an "extraordinary remedy"[454] and an "extraordinary procedural device."[455]

## 3.   The Two Means of Complying with the Demand Requirement

There are two means by which shareholder plaintiffs may plead compliance with the demand requirement and have standing to commence derivative litigation: (1) shareholders may allege particularized facts that, if true, would demonstrate that demand is excused because a demand would be futile,[456] or (2) shareholders may allege particularized facts that, if true, would demonstrate that

---

451. *Id.*

452. *Heineman v. Datapoint Corp.*, 611 A.2d 950, 952 (Del. 1992).

453. *Daily Income Fund, Inc. v. Fox*, 464 U.S. 523, 531-32 (1984); *see also Good v. Getty Oil Co.*, 514 A.2d 1104, 1106 (Del. Ch. 1986) (the derivative action "is an encroachment upon the prerogative of the board of directors to manage the affairs of the corporation," and is available only in "exceptional situations where a matter of corporate concern . . . has not been or cannot be resolved by the board of directors through the exercise of business judgment which is untainted by personal interest or otherwise disqualified").

454. *Lewis v. Graves*, 701 F.2d 245, 247 (2d Cir. 1983).

455. *Stepak v. Addison*, 20 F.3d 398, 402 (11th Cir. 1994).

456. *See* Chapter IV, Section B 4.

a demand has been made and wrongfully refused.[457] "[T]he right of a stockholder to prosecute a derivative suit is limited to situations where the stockholder has demanded that the directors pursue the corporate claim and they have wrongfully refused to do so or where demand is excused."[458] Where a demand is made and wrongfully refused, the shareholder who made the demand "*ex post* . . . has the right to bring the underlying action with the same standing which the stockholder would have had, *ex ante*, if demand had been excused as futile."[459]

## 4. Choice of Law Considerations

Prior to the United States Supreme Court's decision in *Kamen v. Kemper Financial Services, Inc.*[460] in 1991, federal courts

457. *See* Chapter IV, Section B 5.

458. *Rales v. Blasband*, 634 A.2d 927, 932 (Del. 1993); *see also Alabama By-Products Corp. v. Cede & Co.*, 657 A.2d 254, 265 (Del. 1995) ("the right of a shareholder to prosecute a derivative suit" is limited "to those situations where the stockholder has demanded that the board pursue a corporate claim and is met with a wrongful refusal, or where demand is excused because the directors are incapable of reaching an impartial decision to pursue such litigation"); *Baron v. Siff*, 1997 Del. Ch. LEXIS 152, at *4, 1997 WL 666973, at *2 (Del. Ch. Oct. 17, 1997) (a derivative plaintiff must allege "that (1) he has made a demand on the corporation's board of directors that has been wrongfully refused or (2) that making such a demand would be futile"); *Charal Inv. Co. v. Rockefeller*, [1995-1996 Transfer Binder] Fed. Sec. L. Rep. (CCH) ¶ 98,979, at 93,761 (Del. Ch. Nov. 7, 1995) ("Delaware courts require shareholders to refrain from filing derivative suits until the shareholder either (1) makes a demand on directors of a corporation requesting them to pursue the desired action or (2) pleads 'with particularity why demand is excused' prior to filing a derivative action"); *Yaw v. Talley*, 1994 Del. Ch. LEXIS 35, at *19, 1994 WL 89019, at *6 (Del. Ch. Mar. 2, 1994) ("the plaintiff must demonstrate either that no pre-suit demand was made because it would have been futile, or that a demand was made but was wrongfully refused").

459. *Scattered Corp. v. Chicago Stock Exch., Inc.* 701 A.2d 70, 74 (Del. 1997) (quoting *Grimes v. Donald*, 673 A.2d 1207, 1219 (Del. 1996)).

460. 500 U.S. 90 (1991).

asked to consider claims concerning compliance with the demand requirement were divided on the choice of law question underlying the demand requirement. Some courts applied federal law,[461] some courts applied the law of the state of incorporation,[462] and some courts found that the results obtained by applying federal and state law were the same and therefore that there was no need to resolve the choice of law issue.[463] Under *Kemper*, as explained

---

461. *See, e.g., Sax v. World Wide Press, Inc.*, 809 F.2d 610, 613 (9th Cir. 1987); *Kaster v. Modification Sys., Inc.*, 731 F.2d 1014, 1017-20 (2d Cir. 1984); *Lewis v. Graves*, 701 F.2d 245, 248-49 (2d Cir. 1983); *Greenspun v. Del E. Webb Corp.*, 634 F.2d 1204, 1209-10 (9th Cir. 1980); *Johnson v. Hui*, 752 F. Supp. 909, 912 (N.D. Cal. 1990).

462. *See, e.g., RCM Sec. Fund, Inc. v. Stanton*, 928 F.2d 1318, 1325-30 (2d Cir. 1991); *Starrels v. First Nat'l Bank*, 870 F.2d 1168, 1170 & n.4 (7th Cir. 1989); *Grafman v. Century Broadcasting Corp.*, 743 F. Supp. 544, 547 (N.D. Ill. 1990); *Burt v. Danforth*, 742 F. Supp. 1043, 1046-49 (E.D. Mo. 1990); *Weiland v. Illinois Power Co.*, [1990-1991 Transfer Binder] Fed. Sec. L. Rep. (CCH) ¶ 95,747, at 98,587 (C.D. Ill. Sept. 17, 1990); *First Am. Bank & Trust v. Frogel*, 726 F. Supp. 1292, 1298 (S.D. Fla. 1989); *Washington Bancorp. v. Washington*, [1989-1990 Transfer Binder] Fed. Sec. L. Rep. (CCH) ¶ 94,893, at 94,885-86 (D.D.C. Sept. 26, 1989); *Shields v. Murphy*, 116 F.R.D. 600, 604 (D.N.J. 1987); *Cottle v. Hilton Hotels Corp.*, 635 F. Supp. 1094, 1097 (N.D. Ill. 1986); *In re BankAmerica Sec. Litig.*, 636 F. Supp. 419, 421 (C.D. Cal. 1986); *In re Consumers Power Co. Derivative Litig.*, 111 F.R.D. 419, 422-24 (E.D. Mich. 1986).

463. *See, e.g., Gaubert v. Federal Home Loan Bank Bd.*, 863 F.2d 59, 64 (D.C. Cir. 1988) (federal law same as Texas law); *Meltzer v. Atlantic Research Corp.*, 330 F.2d 946, 948-49 (4th Cir.) (federal law same as Virginia law), *cert. denied*, 379 U.S. 841 (1964); *Jordon v. Bowman Apple Prods. Co.*, 728 F. Supp. 409, 413 (W.D. Va. 1990) (federal law same as Virginia law); *Lou v. Belzberg*, 728 F. Supp. 1010, 1016 n.1 (S.D.N.Y. 1990) (federal law same as Kentucky law); *Brickman v. Tyco Toys, Inc.*, 722 F. Supp. 1054, 1063 (S.D.N.Y. 1989) (federal law same as Delaware law); *Shields v. Erickson*, 710 F. Supp. 686, 691 (N.D. Ill. 1989) (federal law same as Delaware law); *In re CPC Int'l Stock Repurchase Sec. Litig.*, No. 87-40, slip op. at 4-8 (D. Del. Feb. 3, 1989) (federal law same as Delaware law); *Smith v. Gordon*, 668 F. Supp. 520, 522-23 (E.D. Va. 1987) (federal law same as Virginia law); *In re E.F.*

(continued...)

below, the need for demand is governed by the law of the state of incorporation unless the law of that state is inconsistent with federal law.

    *a. State Law Governs.* The Supreme Court's decision in *Kamen v. Kemper Financial Services, Inc.*[464] holds that a shareholder's compliance with the demand requirement is governed by the law of the state of incorporation. The Supreme Court explained that Federal Rule of Civil Procedure 23.1 "clearly *contemplates* both the demand requirement and the possibility that demand may be excused" but "does not *create* a demand requirement of any particular dimension."[465] Rather, Rule 23.1 "[o]n its face . . . speaks only to the adequacy of the shareholder representative's pleadings."[466] The court explained that "the function of the demand doctrine in delimiting the respective powers of the individual shareholder and of the directors to control corporate litigation clearly is a matter of 'substance,' not 'procedure.'"[467] "[A]s a rule of procedure issued pursuant to the Rules Enabling Act," the court stated, "Rule 23.1 cannot be understood to 'abridge, enlarge or modify any substantive right.'"[468]

    Following *Kemper*, it is clear that the demand requirement "is governed by both federal procedural requirements and state substantive law."[469] The requirement that a plaintiff make a demand or

---

463. (...continued)
*Hutton Banking Practices Litig.*, 634 F. Supp. 265, 270-72 (S.D.N.Y. 1986) (federal law same as Delaware law); *Recchion v. Kirby*, 637 F. Supp. 1309, 1320-22 (W.D. Pa. 1986) (federal law same as Pennsylvania law); *Hall v. Aliber*, 614 F. Supp. 473, 477 (E.D. Mich. 1985) (federal law same as Michigan law); *Allison v. General Motors Corp.*, 604 F. Supp. 1106, 1116 (D. Del.) (federal law same as Delaware law), *aff'd mem.*, 782 F.2d 1026 (3d Cir. 1985); *Zimmerman v. Bell*, 585 F. Supp. 512, 514 (D. Md. 1984) (federal law same as Maryland law).

    464. 500 U.S. 90 (1991).

    465. *Id.* at 96.

    466. *Id.*

    467. *Id.* at 96-97.

    468. *Id.* at 96 (quoting 28 U.S.C. § 2072(b)).

    469. *Boland v. Engle*, 113 F.3d 706, 711 (7th Cir. 1997).

the excuses that are acceptable for failing to make a demand "are governed by state substantive law," but Federal Rule 23.1 requires plaintiffs "to give federal courts enough information in the pleadings for the courts to apply state law."[470] "The procedural and substantive concerns thus dovetail to a large degree because a federal court cannot decide whether a plaintiff's reasons for not making demand satisfy state law unless the plaintiff's pleadings tell the court what those reasons are."[471] Following *Kemper*, federal courts have applied substantive state law in decisions addressing the need for demand.[472] The Model Business Corporation Act likewise provides that state law governs the demand requirement.[473]

A similar choice of law issue arises where a state court is asked to consider the futility of a demand upon the board of a

---

470. *Id.*

471. *Id.* at 710.

472. *See, e.g., id.; Garber v. Lego*, 11 F.3d 1197, 1201 (3d Cir. 1993); *Blasband v. Rales*, 971 F.2d 1034, 1047 (3d Cir. 1992); *Gonzalez Turul v. Rogatol Distribs., Inc.*, 951 F.2d 1, 2-3 (1st Cir. 1991); *Strougo v. Scudder, Stevens & Clark, Inc.*, 964 F. Supp. 783, 793 (S.D.N.Y. 1997), *reargument denied*, [1997 Transfer Binder] Fed. Sec. L. Rep. (CCH) ¶ 99,533 (S.D.N.Y. Aug. 18, 1997); *In re Silicon Graphics, Inc. Sec. Litig.*, [1996-1997 Transfer Binder] Fed. Sec. L. Rep. (CCH) ¶ 99,325, at 95,968 (N.D. Cal. Sept. 25, 1996); *Coyer v. Hemmer*, 901 F. Supp. 872, 882 (D.N.J. 1995); *Levner v. Prince Alwaleed Bin Talal Bin Abdulaziz Al Saud*, 903 F. Supp. 452, 456 (S.D.N.Y. 1994), *aff'd*, 61 F.3d 8 (2d Cir. 1995); *Levine v. Prudential-Bache Properties, Inc.*, 855 F. Supp. 924, 940 (E.D. Ill. 1994); *Burghart v. Landau*, 821 F. Supp. 173, 177-78 (S.D.N.Y.), *aff'd mem.*, 9 F.3d 1538 (2d Cir. 1993), *cert. denied*, 510 U.S. 1196 (1994); *In re General Motors Class E Stock Buyout Sec. Litig.*, 790 F. Supp. 77, 80-81 (D. Del. 1992); *Citron v. Daniell*, 796 F. Supp. 649, 651 (D. Conn. 1992); *Batra v. Investors Research Corp.*, [1992 Transfer Binder] Fed. Sec. L. Rep. (CCH) ¶ 96,983, at 94,261 n.4 (W.D. Mo. Apr. 2, 1992); *Grill v. Hoblitzell*, 771 F. Supp. 709, 711 (D. Md. 1991); *In re Mortgage & Realty Trust Sec. Litig.*, 787 F. Supp. 84, 86 (E.D. Pa. 1991); *Katz v. Pels*, 774 F. Supp. 121, 128 (S.D.N.Y. 1991); *Abrams v. Koether*, 766 F. Supp. 237, 249 (D.N.J. 1991); *Ryan v. Aetna Life Ins. Co.*, 765 F. Supp. 133, 137 (S.D.N.Y. 1991).

473. 2 Model Bus. Corp. Act Annotated § 7.47 (3d ed. 1996).

corporation chartered in a state other than the forum state. "The demand requirements for a derivative suit are determined by the law of the state of incorporation," and where the state of incorporation is Delaware "the substantive corporation law of Delaware determines whether or not the demand requirements . . . have been satisfied."[474] State courts in Delaware and New York in one instance applied different laws and reached opposite results regarding the demand issue in separate lawsuits against the same defendants challenging the same transaction, on behalf of the same Delaware corporation.[475] The New York court's decision was reversed on appeal pursuant to the *forum non conveniens* doctrine.[476] In the appellate court's words, "[o]ne of the abiding principles of the law of corporations is that the issue of corporate governance, including the threshold demand issue, is governed by the law of the state in which the corporation is chartered, in this case Delaware."[477]

---

474. *Rales v. Blasband*, 634 A.2d 927, 932-33 n.7 (Del. 1993); *see also Blumenthal v. Teets*, 745 P.2d 181, 185 (Ariz. Ct. App. 1987); *Draper v. Paul N. Gardner Defined Plan Trust*, 625 A.2d 859, 864-68 (Del. 1993); *In re Walt Disney Co. Derivative Litig.*, 1997 Del. Ch. LEXIS 25, at *7, 1997 WL 118402, at *3 (Del. Ch. Mar. 13, 1997); *Kessler v. Sinclair*, 641 N.E.2d 135, 137, 139 (Mass. App. Ct. 1994) *review denied*, 646 N.E.2d 135 (Mass. 1995); *In re Prudential Ins. Co. Derivative Litig.*, 659 A.2d 961, 969 (N.J. Super. Ct. Ch. Div. 1995); *Teachers' Retirement Sys. v. Welch*, --- A.D.2d ---, ---, 664 N.Y.S.2d 38, 40 (N.Y. App. Div. 1st Dep't 1997); *Katz v. Emmett*, 226 A.D.2d 588, 589, 641 N.Y.S.2d 131, 132 (N.Y. App. Div. 2d Dep't 1996); *Hart v. General Motors Corp.*, 129 A.D.2d 179, 182-86, 517 N.Y.S.2d 490, 492-94 (N.Y. App. Div. 1st Dep't), *leave to appeal denied*, 70 N.Y.2d 608, 515 N.E.2d 910, 521 N.Y.S.2d 225 (1987).

475. *Compare Grobow v. Perot*, 526 A.2d 914 (Del. Ch. 1987), *aff'd*, 539 A.2d 180 (Del. 1988) (applying Delaware law and granting motion to dismiss for failure to make demand) *with Hart v. General Motors Corp.*, N.Y.L.J., Mar. 6, 1987, at 7 (N.Y. Sup. Ct. N.Y. Co.) (applying New York law and denying motion to dismiss for failure to make demand), *rev'd*, 129 A.D.2d 179, 517 N.Y.S.2d 490 (N.Y. App. Div. 1st Dep't), *leave to appeal denied*, 70 N.Y.2d 608, 515 N.E.2d 910, 521 N.Y.S.2d 225 (1987).

476. *Hart*, 129 A.D.2d at 182-86, 517 N.Y.S.2d at 492-94.

477. *Id.* at 182, 517 N.Y.S.2d at 492.

Were different results reached by applying different laws, plaintiffs would be encouraged to forum shop in order to find the court most willing to excuse demand. As a federal court in Delaware correctly noted in *Allison v. General Motors Corp.*,[478] "[i]t would be disquieting if a derivative plaintiff suing a Delaware corporation could achieve a different answer as to whether demand is excused as futile simply by filing, quite literally, 'across the street' in Chancery Court."[479]

The demand requirement in a derivative action brought in federal court on behalf of a federally chartered bank, according to the one court to address the question, is governed by the law of the bank's principal place of business.[480]

    *b. The Federal Policy Exception.* The Supreme Court's decision in *Kamen v. Kemper Financial Services, Inc.*[481] holds that the rule requiring federal courts to apply the law of the state of incorporation to determine the need for a demand does not govern cases based upon a federal statute where application of state law "would be inconsistent with the federal policy underlying the cause of action."[482] The Supreme Court's decision in *Burks v. Las-*

---

478. 604 F. Supp. 1106 (D. Del.), *aff'd mem.*, 782 F.2d 1026 (3d Cir. 1985).

479. *Id.* at 1116 n.11; *see also Hart*, 129 A.D.2d at 186 & n.6, 517 N.Y.S.2d at 495 & n.6 (noting assertion by plaintiff's counsel that "the outcome in New York may well differ from that in Delaware" on the demand issue).

480. *Country Nat'l Bank v. Mayer*, 788 F. Supp. 1136, 1139-42 (E.D. Cal. 1992).

481. 500 U.S. 90 (1991).

482. *Id.* at 99; *see also id.* ("gaps in [federal] statutes bearing on the allocation of governing power within the corporation should be filled with state law 'unless the state la[w] permit[s] action prohibited by [federal law], or unless '[its] application would be inconsistent with the federal policy underlying the cause of action . . . .'") (citations omitted); *id.* at 108 ("where a gap in the federal securities laws must be bridged by a rule that bears on the allocation of governing powers within the corporation, federal courts should incorporate *state* law into federal common law unless the particular state law in question is inconsistent with the policies underlying the federal statute").

*ker*[483] similarly holds that state law governs determinations by special litigation committees consisting of disinterested and independent directors to terminate derivative litigation on the basis of a determination by the committee that pursuit of the litigation will not serve the best interests of the corporation—a subject addressed later in this Chapter[484]—subject to the same "inconsistent with federal policy" exception.[485]

The Supreme Court considered the scope of the "inconsistent with federal policy" exception to the rule that state law governs these issues in both *Kemper* and *Burks*. The court held that requiring demand unless demand is excused by state law (in *Kemper*) and permitting disinterested directors to move to terminate an action under state law (in *Burks*) are not inconsistent with the policies underlying the Investment Company Act of 1940 (the "ICA").[486] The court in *Burks* explained its reasoning as follows:

> Congress' purpose in structuring the Act as it did is clear. It "was designed to place the unaffiliated directors in the role of 'independent watchdogs,'" who would "furnish an independent check upon the management" of investment companies.
> . . . Without question, "[t]he function of these provisions with respect to unaffiliated directors [was] to supply an independent check on management and to provide a means for the representation of shareholder interests in investment company affairs." . . .
>
> Congress entrusted to the independent directors of investment companies, exercising the authority granted to them by state law, the primary responsibility for looking after the interests of the funds' shareholders. There may well be situations in which the independent directors could reasonably believe that the best interests of the shareholders call for a decision not to sue—as, for example, where the costs of litigation to the corporation outweigh any potential recovery. In such cases, it would certainly be consistent with the Act to allow the independent directors to terminate a suit, even though not frivo-

---

483. 441 U.S. 471 (1979).
484. *See* Chapter IV, Section C.
485. 441 U.S. at 477-80, 486.
486. 15 U.S.C. §§ 80a-1–80a-64.

lous. Indeed, it would have been paradoxical for Congress to have been willing to rely largely upon "watchdogs" to protect shareholder interests and yet, where the "watchdogs" have done precisely that, require that they be totally muzzled.[487]

The court reiterated this point in *Kemper*, stating that "[a]s we emphasized in *Burks*, the ICA embodies a congressional expectation that the independent directors would 'loo[k] after the interests of the [investment company]' by 'exercising the authority granted to them *by state law.*'"[488]

A substantial number of Court of Appeals and district court decisions have reached varying results with respect to whether federal policy permits dismissal of claims under Section 14(a) of the Securities Exchange of 1934, which prohibits the making of false or misleading statements in proxy statements,[489] due to a plaintiff's failure to make a pre-litigation demand or a special litigation committee determination that the action should be terminated.

The leading decision finding that federal policy would be frustrated by termination of a derivative action pursuant to state law where the action asserts claims under Section 14(a) is *Galef v. Alexander*.[490] The plaintiff in *Galef* alleged that the board in that case improperly granted stock options to six corporate officers and violated Section 14(a) by failing to disclose material information concerning the options in proxy statements sent to shareholders in order to obtain shareholder approval of the options.[491] A special litigation committee consisting of directors who had been named as defendants (all directors had been sued) but who had not received

---

487. *Burks*, 441 U.S. at 484-85 (citations and footnotes omitted).

488. *Kemper*, 500 U.S. at 107 (quoting *Burks*, 441 U.S. at 485; emphasis added in *Kemper); see also Strougo v. Scudder, Stevens & Clark, Inc.*, [1997 Transfer Binder] Fed. Sec. L. Rep. (CCH) ¶ 99,533, at 97,623 (S.D.N.Y. Aug. 18, 1997) (noting this holding).

489. 15 U.S.C. §§ 78n(a).

490. 615 F.2d 51 (2d Cir. 1980).

491. *Id.* at 53-55.

any of the stock options concluded that the best interests of the corporation called for dismissal of the action.[492]

The Second Circuit held that "to the extent that a complaint states claims against directors under § 14(a) upon which relief may be granted, federal policy prevents the summary dismissal of those claims pursuant to the business judgment of those defendant directors."[493] The court explained that the "vital" purpose of Section 14(a) is "to prevent management or others from obtaining authorization for corporate action by means of deceptive or inadequate disclosure in proxy solicitation."[494] Achievement of this goal, the court stated, would "quite clearly be frustrated if a director who was made a defendant in a derivative action for providing inadequate information in connection with a proxy solicitation were permitted to cause the dismissal of that action simply on the basis of his judgment that its pursuit was not in the best interests of the corporation."[495]

A district court in Illinois in *Mills v. Esmark, Inc.*[496] followed *Galef* in another case involving a Section 14(a) claim. The court stated that the members of a special litigation committee were disinterested and independent "for purposes of Delaware law" because "disinterested independence" of directors "is not impaired" merely because directors are named as defendants, but that the committee nevertheless "should not be permitted to cause the dismissal of a federal securities law claim which alleges wrongdoing by committee members."[497] A district court in New York in *In re Par Pharmaceutical, Inc. Derivative Litigation*[498] followed *Galef* in a case asserting claims under Section 14(a) and under the Racketeer Influenced and Corrupt Organizations Act ("RICO").[499] The

---

492. *Id.* at 54-56.
493. *Id.* at 64.
494. *Id.* at 63 (quoting *J.I. Case Co. v. Borak*, 377 U.S. 426, 431-32 (1964)).
495. *Id.* at 63.
496. 544 F. Supp. 1275 (N.D. Ill. 1982).
497. *Id.* at 1283, 1284 n.6.
498. 750 F. Supp. 641 (S.D.N.Y. 1990).
499. 18 U.S.C. §§ 1961-1968.

court held that *Galef* "precludes dismissal of plaintiffs' federal securities and RICO claims pursuant to the business judgment of a five-director voting Board which includes four defendant directors."[500]

A district court in Pennsylvania in *In re Westinghouse Securities Litigation*[501] similarly excused demand in connection with a Section 14(a) claim on the ground that "the decision whether or not to violate securities laws, unlike the decision whether to pursue litigation on behalf of the corporation, is not one reserved exclusively to the directors."[502] "Misapplying the business judgment rule to a pure allegation of securities fraud under Section 14(a)," the court stated, "would emasculate the federal policy of 'prevent[ing] management or others from obtaining authorization for corporate action by means of deceptive or inadequate disclosure in proxy solicitation,' and render the statute a nullity."[503]

Other courts have rejected challenges based upon the "federal policy" exception to the general rule that state law governs director determinations concerning the question whether litigation will serve the best interests of the corporation.

The Ninth Circuit in *Lewis v. Anderson*[504] held that termination of an action challenging stock option grants to key employees and statements made in connection with securing shareholder approval of these stock options would not frustrate the policy underlying Section 14(a).[505] The case involved a special litigation committee consisting of one director who was named as a defendant but who did not benefit from the alleged wrongdoing and two outside directors appointed to the board after the alleged wrongdoing

---

500. 750 F. Supp. at 646.

501. 832 F. Supp. 989 (W.D. Pa. 1993), *aff'd mem.*, 92 F.3d 1175 (3d Cir. 1996).

502. *Id.* at 998.

503. *Id.* (quoting *J.I. Case*, 377 U.S. at 431).

504. 615 F.2d 778 (9th Cir. 1979), *cert. denied*, 449 U.S. 869 (1980).

505. *Id.* at 783-84.

had occurred.[506] The Ninth Circuit stated that "[a]llowing disinterested directors to exercise their business judgment to dismiss what they see as groundless causes of action would in no way weaken the regulatory provisions of the federal securities laws. So long as those accused of manipulating the proxy vote are excluded from deciding whether or not to pursue the claim there is no conflict between the business judgment rule and § 14(a)."[507] The court did not focus upon the fact that one of the three directors on the special litigation committee was a defendant in the case. The Ninth Circuit stated in a later case upholding the refusal of a demand, *Litton Industries, Inc. v. Hoch*,[508] that "[m]erely being named as a defendant does not disqualify a director from deciding whether the company should pursue a claim" asserted under Section 14(a).[509]

Subsequent decisions, including two in the Second Circuit, which decided *Galef—Abramowitz v. Posner*[510] and *Maldonado v. Flynn*[511]—have not followed *Galef* in Section 14(a) cases where no allegations were made against any special litigation committee directors.[512] The Second Circuit did not attempt in either *Abramowitz* or *Maldonado* to distinguish *Galef*. The district court in *Abramowitz* noted that *Galef*, "relied on by plaintiff in support of her position that the business judgment rule is inconsistent with the Act, is not to the contrary. Rather, the *Galef* Court held that Section 14(a) would be frustrated if the Court were to defer to a business judgment determination that the derivative action should not

---

506. *Id.* at 780.

507. *Id.* at 784.

508. 996 F.2d 1225 (unpublished opinion, text available at 1993 U.S. App. LEXIS 16992 and 1993 WL 241549) (9th Cir. July 2, 1993).

509. 1993 U.S. App. LEXIS 16992, at *4, 1993 WL 241549, at *2.

510. 672 F.2d 1025 (2d Cir. 1982).

511. 671 F.2d 779 (2d Cir. 1982).

512. *Abramowitz*, 672 F.2d at 1031-32; *Maldonado*, 671 F.2d at 731-32.

proceed made by, or under the influence of, the *defendant-directors*."[513]

The Sixth, Eighth and Ninth Circuits in *In re General Tire & Rubber Co. Securities Litigation*,[514] *Abbey v. Control Data Corp.*[515] and *Gaines v. Haughton*[516] distinguished *Galef* by finding no causal link between alleged failures to disclose illegal foreign payments in proxy statements pursuant to which directors were elected and damages suffered by corporations as a result of the illegal foreign payments. In order to state a claim under Section 14(a) for damages, in the *Control Data* court's words, "the harm to plaintiff-shareholders must have resulted from the corporate transactions which were authorized as a result of the false or misleading proxy solicitations."[517] *Galef*, these courts explained, involved a proxy statement used to obtain shareholder approval for challenged stock options. Without causation of this type, these courts concluded, there is no frustration of federal policy by dismissal of derivative litigation.[518]

The Ninth Circuit in *Litton Industries, Inc. v. Hoch*[519] and district courts in *Diduck v. Kaszycki & Sons Contractors, Inc.*[520] and *Allison v. General Motors Corp.*[521] have held without discussion of the federal policy underlying RICO that there is nothing in

---

513. *Abramowitz v. Posner*, 513 F. Supp. 120, 130 n.11 (S.D.N.Y. 1981), *aff'd*, 672 F.2d 1025 (2d Cir. 1982).

514. 726 F.2d 1075 (6th Cir.), *cert. denied*, 469 U.S. 858 (1984).

515. 603 F.2d 724 (8th Cir. 1979), *cert. denied*, 444 U.S. 1017 (1980).

516. 645 F.2d 761 (9th Cir. 1981); *cert. denied*, 454 U.S. 1145 (1982).

517. *Id.* at 732.

518. *General Tire*, 726 F.2d at 1082; *Gaines*, 645 F.2d at 774-76; *Control Data*, 603 F.2d at 731-32.

519. 996 F.2d 1225 (unpublished opinion, text available at 1993 U.S. App. LEXIS 16992 and 1993 WL 241549) (9th Cir. July 2, 1993).

520. 737 F. Supp. 792 (S.D.N.Y. 1990), *aff'd in part and rev'd in part on other grounds*, 974 F.2d 270 (2d Cir. 1992).

521. 604 F. Supp. 1106 (D. Del.), *aff'd mem.*, 782 F.2d 1026 (3d Cir. 1985).

the RICO statute that is inconsistent with director refusal of a demand or termination of derivative litigation.[522] A federal district court in Illinois in *Shields v. Erickson*,[523] a derivative action involving claims under Section 14(a), RICO and the Foreign Corrupt Practices Act of 1977,[524] also required demand without discussion of the federal policies underlying these statutes.[525] A federal district court in Connecticut in *Citron v. Daniell*[526] similarly required demand in a derivative action involving Section 14(a) claims.[527]

## 5. Demand Futility

The demand requirement will be excused and a shareholder will be permitted to proceed with litigation on behalf of the corporation where the role of a majority of the corporation's directors in the conduct or transaction underlying the litigation (or the alleged domination or control of the directors by the alleged wrongdoers) is such that demand would be "futile."

*a. The Meaning of Futility, Generally.* "In this context, futility does not mean that there is no likelihood that a board will agree to the demand.[528] Rather, demand is futile where "the directors are incapable of making an impartial decision regarding such litigation."[529] The phrase "demand futility" therefore may be "misleading" because it refers to cases in which "the board is personally interested in the matter" and not to cases where "it is apparent" that disinterested and independent directors "will not institute suit

---

522. *Litton*, 1993 U.S. App. LEXIS 16992, at *4-5, 1993 WL 241549, at *2; *Diduck*, 737 F. Supp. at 800; *Allison*, 604 F. Supp. at 1120.

523. 710 F. Supp. 686 (N.D. Ill. 1989).

524. 15 U.S.C. §§ 78a note, 78m, 78dd-1, 78dd-2, 78ff.

525. 710 F. Supp. at 688-93.

526. 796 F. Supp. 649 (D. Conn. 1992).

527. *Id.* at 650-53.

528. *Heineman v. Datapoint Corp.*, 611 A.2d 950, 952 (Del. 1992).

529. *Rales v. Blasband*, 634 A.2d 927, 932 (Del. 1993).

for sound reasons."[530] "Futility means that the directors' minds are closed to argument and that they cannot properly exercise their business judgment in determining whether the suit should be filed. It is not enough to show that the directors simply disagree with a shareholder about filing a suit."[531] "That the directors disagree with the merits of an argument does not mean that demand is futile. A demand is futile only if the directors' minds are closed to argument. Opposition should not be confused with futility."[532]

Thus, for example, the Seventh Circuit, construing Maryland law in *Kamen v. Kemper Financial Services, Inc.*,[533] rejected a shareholder's contention that a corporation's response to her suit—the filing of a motion to dismiss and deposition testimony expressing a "dim view" of the suit's substantive allegations—demonstrated the futility of a demand.[534] The court explained:

> This argument confuses futility with failure. A demand is "futile" only if the directors' minds are closed to argument. That the directors disagreed with an argument could show their unwillingness to listen, but also could show that the argument was feeble. Demand enables the directors to take the leading role in managing the corporation. Conscientious managers may conclude that legal action is unjustified because not meritorious, or because it would subject the firm to injury. This is why courts assess futility *ex ante* rather than *ex post*. To say that a demand would have been futile because directors proved unsympathetic to the lawsuit is like saying that sending Mickey Mantle to the plate with the bases loaded was futile because he struck out.
>
> [N]o state treats the directors' failure to capitulate in the lawsuit as forfeiting the firm's entitlement to demand before the suit commences. Directors will (and should) oppose weak claims. If that opposition eliminated the need for demand, we

---

530. *Harris v. Carter*, 582 A.2d 222, 228 n.12 (Del. Ch. 1990).

531. *Drage v. Procter & Gamble*, 694 N.E.2d 479, 482-83 (Ohio Ct. App. 1997).

532. *Stallworth v. AmSouth Bank*, 1997 Ala. LEXIS 483, at *17-18, 1997 WL 778838, at *5 (Ala. Dec. 19, 1997).

533. 939 F.2d 458 (7th Cir.), *cert. denied*, 502 U.S. 974 (1991).

534. *Id.* at 462.

would reach the curious pass that claims so weak that they should not be pursued at all could go straight to court, while claims strong enough to litigate about should be presented to the directors.[535]

"[D]emand is the norm," the court stated, and therefore "[i]t must follow that the directors' substantive opposition does not obviate demand."[536]

An appellate court in Ohio in *Drage v. Procter & Gamble*[537] similarly held that post-complaint events are not "relevant to the issue of futility" because "the futility of demand must be determined by looking at the positions of the parties when the derivative suit is initially filed."[538] The court noted that "[a]fter a suit is filed, the directors may take action in their defense that could be construed as contrary to the claims of the shareholders, but that might not have been taken if a suit had not been filed."[539] As the trial court stated in *Procter & Gamble*: "Post-complaint events not existing at the time Drage's original complaint was filed . . . cannot support an evaluation that needed to be made at the time the derivative action was originally filed. . . . The Court cannot allow the plaintiff to bottom her claim of demand futility upon Board action taken after the plaintiff had already attempted to take control of certain litigation."[540]

---

535. *Id.* (citations omitted).

536. *Id.* at 463; *see also In re Mortgage & Realty Trust Sec. Litig.*, 787 F. Supp. 84, 88 (E.D. Pa. 1991) (construing Maryland law, and stating that "to equate opposition with futility would lead to the illogical result that plaintiffs could avoid the demand requirement simply by virtue of the weakness of their claims");

537. 694 N.E.2d 479 (Ohio Ct. App. 1997).

538. *Id.* at 483-84.

539. *Id.* at 483.

540. *Drage v. Procter & Gamble*, No. A-9401998, slip op. at 5 (Ohio Ct. Common Pleas Jan. 19, 1996), *aff'd*, 694 N.E.2d 479 (Ohio Ct. App. 1997); *see also In re Prudential Ins. Co. Derivative Litig.*, 659 A.2d 961, 973 (N.J. Super. Ct. Ch. Div. 1995) (demand not excused by fact that directors have moved to dismiss the litigation that is the subject of the demand); *cf. Boland v. Engle*, 113 F.3d 706, 713 n.7 (7th Cir. 1997) (continued...)

In light of the rationale underlying the demand requirement, a shareholder's claim that demand is excused because it is futile generally is litigated in the context of a threshold motion to dismiss, and thus the motion "is typically directed to the face of the complaint."[541] The overwhelming majority of the cases deciding whether demand is required or excused accordingly arise in the context of motions to dismiss. Where the factual allegations in a complaint (which must be assumed true) are sufficient to overcome a motion to dismiss but are factually incorrect, or if defendants wish for some other reason to rely upon more than just what a shareholder has pleaded, the issue can be raised in the context of a motion for judgment on the pleadings, summary judgment or even at trial or on appeal.[542] The longer a shareholder proceeds with

---

540. (...continued)

(stating, in case governed by Indiana law, that the filing of a motion to dismiss a derivative complaint for failure to make a demand does not waive the corporation's right to establish a disinterested committee to consider a demand if it is made because any such rule "would make demand the exception rather than the rule . . . . If boards of directors are faced with the choice of either moving to dismiss a shareholder lawsuit for failure to make demand or setting up a disinterested committee, few boards would move to dismiss for fear of losing the right to appoint a committee. . . . Knowing that boards are unlikely to move for dismissal, few shareholders would bother to make demand."). *But see Olesh v. Dreyfus Corp.*, [1995-1996 Transfer Binder] Fed. Sec. L. Rep. (CCH) ¶ 98,907, at 93,369 (E.D.N.Y. Aug. 8, 1995) (excusing demand under Maryland law where directors had "actively opposed plaintiffs' administration efforts" to win the remedy they now sought by way of a derivative action "well before this litigation was commenced").

541. *Kahn v. Tremont Corp.*, 1994 Del. Ch. LEXIS 41, at *11, 1994 WL 162613, at *3 (Del. Ch. Apr. 21, 1994), *subsequent proceedings*, 1996 Del. Ch. LEXIS 40, 1996 WL 145452 (Del. Ch. Mar. 21, 1996), *rev'd on other grounds*, 694 A.2d 422 (Del. 1997).

542. *See, e.g., Gonzales Turul v. Rogayol Distribs.*, 951 F.2d 1, 1-3 (1st Cir. 1991); *Abrams v. Koether*, 766 F. Supp. 237, 240, 244 (D.N.J. 1991); *Cooke v. Oolie*, 1997 Del. Ch. LEXIS 92, at *26-31, 1997 WL 367034, at *7-8 (Del. Ch. June 23, 1997); *Tremont*, 1994 Del. Ch. LEXIS 41, at *11-12, 1994 WL 162613, at *3; *Kahn v. Roberts*, [1993-1994 Transfer Binder] Fed. Sec. L. Rep. (CCH) ¶ 98,201, at

(continued...)

derivative litigation that is subject to dismissal for failure to comply with the demand requirement, however, the greater the undermining of the three rationales supporting the demand requirement: (1) directors, not minority shareholders, should determine whether litigation of a claim belonging to the corporation should be pursued on behalf of the corporation, (2) directors should be permitted an opportunity to pursue remedies other than litigation and thus avoid unnecessary litigation, and (3) directors should be protected from the harassment of costly, baseless "strike suit" litigation.[543]

*b. The Delaware Approach: Aronson and Rales, Generally.* Prior to 1984, the Delaware courts considered claims that demand was excused only on an infrequent basis. The Delaware courts focused in the few cases that raised this issue primarily upon whether a corporation's directors were sufficiently disinterested to render an objective business judgment concerning the demand. The Delaware courts did not focus in these decisions upon the business judgment challenged in the demand.

The Delaware Supreme Court in 1927 in *Sohland v. Baker*,[544] for example, held that demand is not required if a corporation's directors, "whether by reason of hostile interest, or guilty participation in the wrongs complained of, cannot be expected to institute a corporate suit, or where even if they did institute such a suit, it is apparent that they would not be the proper persons to conduct the litigation incident thereto."[545] The Delaware Court of

---

542. (...continued)
99,411-13 (Del. Ch. Feb. 28, 1994); *Avacus Partners, L.P. v. Brian*, [1991 Transfer Binder] Fed. Sec. L. Rep. (CCH) ¶ 96,232, at 91,215 n.12 (Del. Ch. Oct. 24, 1990); *Siegman v. Tri-Star Pictures, Inc.*, 15 Del. J. Corp. L. 218, 241 & n.16 (Del. Ch. May 5, 1989), *aff'd in part and rev'd in part on other grounds sub nom. In re Tri-Star Pictures, Inc., Litig.*, 634 A.2d 319 (Del. 1993); *Bennett v. Instrument Sys. Corp.*, 66 A.D.2d 708, 708-09, 411 N.Y.S.2d 287, 288-89 (N.Y. App. Div. 1st Dep't 1978).

543. *See* Chapter IV, Section B 2 (discussing rationale for demand requirement).

544. 141 A. 277 (Del. 1927).

545. *Id.* at 281-82.

Chancery similarly stated in 1931 in *McKee v. Rogers*[546] that a shareholder "may sue in equity in his derivative right to assert a cause of action in behalf of the corporation, without prior demand upon the directors to sue, when it is apparent that a demand would be futile, that the officers are under an influence that sterilizes discretion and could not be proper persons to conduct the litigation."[547] The Court of Chancery likewise stated in 1961 in *Dann v. Chrysler Corp.*[548] that demand is excused where a complaint charges "all the board with being active or passive parties to the various alleged fraudulent schemes."[549]

Commentators have observed the following concerning this line of decisions:

> Historically, . . . in suits against directors of the corporation on behalf of which suit was brought, the requirement was honored more in the breach than in the observance. Stockholders almost never made demand upon their corporation before bringing suit, but merely commenced their actions, alleging in boilerplate fashion that demand was futile because directors could not be expected to sue themselves. The older court decisions generally accepted this excuse as legally valid. Over time, the demand requirement languished because few defendants found it worthwhile to challenge complaints for failure to make a demand where, as in virtually every derivative action, the action named some or all of the directors.[550]

Delaware's approach to claims that demand is excused has changed since the mid-1980s, in a series of Delaware Supreme

---

546. 156 A. 191 (Del. Ch. 1931).

547. *Id.* at 193.

548. 174 A.2d 696 (Del. Ch. 1961).

549. *Id.* at 700; *see also Bergstein v. Texas Int'l Co.*, 453 A.2d 467, 471 (Del. Ch. 1982), *appeal denied*, 461 A.2d 695 (Del. 1983); *Ainscow v. Sanitary Co.*, 180 A. 614, 615 (Del. Ch. 1935); *Miller v. Loft*, 153 A. 861, 862 (Del. Ch. 1931); *Fleer v. Frank H. Fleer Corp.*, 125 A. 411, 414 (Del. Ch. 1924).

550. 2 David A. Drexler, Lewis S. Black, Jr. & A. Gilchrist Sparks, III, *Delaware Corporation Law and Practice* § 42.03[2], at 42-11 (1998).

Court decisions beginning with *Aronson v. Lewis*[551] and *Pogostin v. Rice*[552] in 1984 and continuing since then with *Grobow v. Perot*[553] in 1988, *Levine v. Smith*[554] in 1991, *Heineman v. Datapoint Corp.*[555] in 1992, *Rales v. Blasband*[556] in 1993 and *Grimes v. Donald*[557] in 1996. These cases establish two tests, often called the *Aronson* test and the *Rales* test.

The *Aronson* test governs in the "common-occurring pattern"[558] in derivative litigation: "a *decision* of the board of directors is being challenged in the derivative suit."[559] In these cases, a plaintiff alleging that demand is excused has the burden of pleading particularized facts that, if true, would "raise a reasonable doubt as to (i) director disinterest or independence or (ii) whether the directors exercised proper business judgment in approving the challenged transaction."[560] As discussed in more detail in Chapter I,[561] director interest may be established by "particularized facts demonstrating either a financial interest or entrenchment,"[562] and to plead entrenchment a plaintiff "must allege facts sufficient to show that the 'sole or primary purpose' of the challenged board action was to perpetuate the directors in control of the corporation."[563] As also discussed in more detail in Chapter I,[564] a lack

---

551. 473 A.2d 805 (Del. 1984).

552. 480 A.2d 619 (Del. 1984).

553. 539 A.2d 180 (Del. 1988).

554. 591 A.2d 194 (Del. 1991).

555. 611 A.2d 950 (Del. 1992).

556. 634 A.2d 927 (Del. 1993).

557. 673 A.2d 1207 (Del. 1996).

558. *Harris v. Carter*, 582 A.2d 222, 230 (Del. 1990).

559. *Rales*, 634 A.2d at 933.

560. *Grobow*, 539 A.2d at 186; *see also Grimes*, 673 A.2d at 1216; *Rales*, 634 A.2d at 933; *Datapoint*, 611 A.2d at 952; *Levine*, 591 A.2d at 205; *Pogostin*, 480 A.2d at 624; *Aronson*, 473 A.2d at 814.

561. *See* Chapter I, Section D 2 a.

562. *Grobow*, 539 A.2d at 188.

563. *Green v. Phillips*, 22 Del. J. Corp. L. 360, 369 (Del. Ch. June 19, 1996); *Kahn v. Roberts*, [1993-1994 Transfer Binder] Fed. Sec. L. Rep. (CCH) ¶ 98,201, at 99,412-13 (Del. Ch. Feb. 28, 1994).

564. *See* Chapter I, Section D 2 b.

of independence may be established by alleging with particularity that directors are "dominated or otherwise controlled by an individual or entity interested in the transaction."[565]

The *Rales* test governs where "the board that would be considering the demand did not make a business decision which is being challenged in the derivative suit"—a situation that arises "in three principal scenarios: (1) where a business decision was made . . . but a majority of the directors making the decision have been replaced; (2) where the subject of the derivative suit is not a business decision of the board; and (3) where . . . the decision being challenged was made by the board of a different corporation."[566] The second scenario includes cases "where directors are sued derivatively because they have failed to do something (such as a failure to oversee subordinates).[567]

In these cases, under *Rales*, "a court must determine whether or not the particularized factual allegations of a derivative stockholder complaint create a reasonable doubt that, as of the time the complaint is filed, the board of directors could have properly exercised its independent and disinterested business judgment in responding to a demand. If the derivative plaintiff satisfies this burden, then demand will be excused as futile."[568] Thus, "in those three circumstances described in *Rales*, the Court will apply only the first ('disinterest' and 'independence') prong of *Aronson*."[569]

In determining whether the *Aronson* or *Rales* test governs, "many cases . . . hold that the proper time to measure demand futility is at the filing of the complaint."[570] Under both the *Aron-*

---

565. *Grobow*, 539 A.2d at 189; *see also Rales*, 634 A.2d 936; *Aronson*, 473 A.2d at 815.

566. *Rales*, 634 A.2d at 933-34 (footnotes omitted).

567. *Id.* at 934 n.9.

568. *Id.* at 934.

569. *In re Bally's Grand Derivative Litig.*, 1997 Del. Ch. LEXIS 77, at *9, 1997 WL 305803, at *3 (Del. Ch. June 4, 1997).

570. *Harris v. Carter*, 582 A.2d 222, 228 (Del. Ch. 1990); *see also Rales*, 634 A.2d at 934; *Pogostin*, 480 A.2d at 624; *Aronson*, 473 A.2d at

(continued...)

*son* test and the *Rales* test, the disqualifying interest or lack of independence must afflict a majority of the corporation's directors in order for demand to be excused.[571]

As noted above, both the *Aronson* test and the *Rales* test utilize the term "reasonable doubt." Whether reasonable doubt does or does not exist, the Delaware Supreme Court stated in *Grobow v. Perot*,[572] "must be decided by the trial court on a case-by-case basis" and not by any "rote and inelastic" criteria.[573] The Court of Chancery observed in *Harris v. Carter*[574] that "[t]erms like reasonable doubt . . . help guide judgment but are not scientific. In making the required judgment no single factor . . . may itself be dispositive in any particular case. Rather the question is whether the accumulation of all factors creates the reasonable doubt to which *Aronson* refers."[575]

This "reasonable doubt" standard has been criticized—most notably in the New York Court of Appeals in *Marx v. Akers*[576] and Judge Frank H. Easterbrook's concurring opinion in a Seventh Circuit decision construing Delaware law, *Starrels v. First National Bank*.[577] *Marx* described the "reasonable doubt" standard as "confusing" because it is "a standard of proof which is the heart of a jury's determination in a criminal case."[578] As stated by Judge

---

570. (...continued)
809-10; *Bally's Grand*, 1997 Del. Ch. LEXIS, at *8, 1997 WL 305803, at *3; *Katz v. Halperin*, 21 Del. J. Corp. L. 690, 703 (Del. Ch. Feb. 5, 1996).

571. *Grimes*, 673 A.2d at 1216; *Rales*, 634 A.2d at 930, 936-37; *Levine*, 591 A.2d at 205; *Bodkin v. Mercantile Stores Co.*, 22 Del. J. Corp. L. 1156, 1161 (Del. Ch. Nov. 1, 1996); *Green*, 22 Del. J. Corp. L. at 369; *Halperin*, 21 Del. J. Corp. L. at 703.

572. 539 A.2d 180 (Del. 1988).

573. *Id.* at 186.

574. 582 A.2d 222 (Del. Ch. 1990).

575. *Id.* at 229.

576. 88 N.Y.2d 189, 666 N.E.2d 1034, 644 N.Y.S.2d 121 (1996).

577. 870 F.2d 1168, 1172-76 (7th Cir. 1989) (Easterbrook, J., concurring).

578. 88 N.Y.2d at 196, 666 N.E.2d at 1038, 644 N.Y.S.2d at 125.

Easterbrook, the phrase "'reasonable doubt' summons up the standard applied in criminal law"—"a demanding standard, meaning at least a 90% likelihood that the defendant is guilty."[579] Judge Easterbrook continued:

> If "reasonable doubt" in the *Aronson* formula means the same thing as "reasonable doubt" in criminal law, then demand is excused whenever there is a 10% chance that the original transaction is not protected by the business judgment rule. Why should demand be excused on such a slight showing? Surely not because courts want shareholders to file suit whenever there is an 11% likelihood that the business judgment rule will not protect a transaction. *Aronson* did not say, and later cases have not supplied the deficit. If "reasonable doubt" in corporate law means something different from "reasonable doubt" in criminal law, however, what is the difference?, and why use the same term for two different things?[580]

The "reasonable doubt" standard also was criticized as "overly subjective, thereby permitting a wide variance in the application of Delaware law to similar facts."[581]

The Delaware Supreme Court's decision in *Grimes v. Donald*[582] recognized that "[s]ome courts and commentators" have questioned the use in derivative litigation of the term "reasonable doubt," "a concept normally present in criminal prosecution."[583] The court responded by describing the term "reasonable doubt" as an "apt" term that "achieves the proper balance."[584] The court explained that "[r]easonable doubt can be said to mean that there is a reason to doubt."[585] "Stated obversely," the court continued, "the concept of reasonable doubt is akin to the concept

---

579. 870 F.2d at 1175.

580. *Id.*

581. *Marx*, 88 N.Y.2d at 196, 666 N.E.2d at 1038, 644 N.Y.S.2d at 125 (citing 2 Principles of Corporate Governance: Analysis and Recommendations § 7.03 comment d at 57 (1994)).

582. 673 A.2d 1207 (Del. 1996).

583. *Id.* at 1217.

584. *Id.*

585. *Id.*

that the stockholder has a 'reasonable belief' that the board lacks independence or that the transaction was not protected by the business judgment rule"—"an objective test . . . found in various corporate contexts."[586] This concept, according to the Delaware Supreme Court, "is sufficiently flexible and workable to provide the stockholder with 'the keys to the courthouse' in an appropriate case where the claim is not based on mere suspicions or stated solely in conclusory terms."[587]

An issue not yet considered by the Delaware Supreme Court is the need for a demand in the context of a board that is evenly divided between interested directors and disinterested directors. The Court of Chancery in *Kaufman v. Beal*[588] and *Katell v. Morgan Stanley Group, Inc.*[589] held that demand is excused where a board is evenly divided because "the plaintiffs would face a Board of Directors deadlocked on the response to the demand"[590] and the disinterested directors would be unable to act on claims without the agreement of the interested directors.[591] A federal district court construing Delaware law in *Bilunka v. Sanders*[592] has reached the same conclusion. The court in *Bilunka* stated that "[w]hen fifty percent of the Board members are interested or implicated in wrongdoing, the remaining Board members are incapable of action as they fail to contain the majority necessary to enforce the decisions of the disinterested members."[593] Another federal district court, this one construing New York law, has reached the same result.[594]

---

586. *Id.* at 1217 n.17.

587. *Id.* at 1217.

588. 1983 Del. Ch. LEXIS 391, 1983 WL 20295 (Del. Ch. Feb. 25, 1983).

589. [1992-1993 Transfer Binder] Fed. Sec. L. Rep. (CCH) ¶ 97,437 (Del. Ch. Jan. 14, 1993).

590. *Kaufman*, 1983 Del. Ch. LEXIS 391, at *25, 1983 WL 20295, at *8.

591. *Katell*, [1992-1993 Transfer Binder] Fed. Sec. L. Rep. (CCH) at 96,441.

592. [1994-1995 Transfer Binder] Fed. Sec. L. Rep. (CCH) ¶ 98,454 (N.D. Cal. Mar. 1, 1994).

593. *Id.* at 90,192.

594. *Ono v. Itoyama*, 884 F. Supp. 892, 899 (D.N.J. 1995), *aff'd*

(continued...)

The Seventh Circuit in *Boland v. Engle*,[595] a case construing Indiana law, reached a different conclusion. The court in
*Boland* held that where a board is equally divided, "it may well be
useful to require a shareholder to take a complaint to the board
before taking it to the courts."[596] The court added, however, that
in the case before the court the alleged financial benefit to one
director on a two director board "was only indirect—the transactions had some arguable business merit" and the director "benefitted only by way of the interconnections of the companies in his
corporate pyramid."[597] The court stated that "[a] direct pilfering
of corporate assets, for example, might present a different
case."[598]

The "atypical, if not unique, situation" in *Katz v. Halperin*[599] also is worthy of note. This case involved challenged transactions entered into by a corporation having a board consisting of
five directors, two of whom constituted a special committee of
independent directors who approved a series of challenged transactions. The transactions resulted in the replacement of the three
board members who had not approved the transactions by two new
board members. A derivative action challenging the transactions
then was commenced. The court held that the relevant board for the
purpose of determining whether demand was excused was the board
as of the date the complaint was filed.[600] Because two members of
the four person board as of the date the complaint was filed had
approved the challenged transactions and two had not approved the
transactions, the court stated that the case "neither fits neatly into
the scenario contemplated by *Aronson* nor *Rales*."[601] Under these

---

594. (...continued)
*mem.*, 79 F.3d 1138 (3d Cir. 1996).
    595. 113 F.3d 706 (7th Cir. 1997).
    596. *Id*. at 711.
    597. *Id*. at 713.
    598. *Id*.
    599. 21 Del. J. Corp. L. 690 (Del. Ch. Feb. 5, 1996).
    600. *Id*. at 702.
    601. *Id*. at 703.

circumstances, the court concluded that the *Aronson* test governed.[602]

   *c. Cases Explaining and Applying the Aronson Standard.* As stated above, the Delaware Supreme Court's decision in *Aronson v. Lewis*[603]—reaffirmed in *Pogostin v. Rice*,[604] *Grobow v. Perot*,[605] *Levine v. Smith*,[606] *Heineman v. Datapoint Corp.*,[607] *Rales v. Blasband*[608] and *Grimes v. Donald*[609]—holds that where a board decision is challenged in a derivative action, the shareholder alleging that demand is excused has the burden of pleading particularized facts that, if true, would "raise a reasonable doubt as to (i) director disinterest or independence or (ii) whether the directors exercised proper business judgment in approving the challenged transaction."[610] The court in *Grimes* stated the test slightly differently, as a three-pronged standard that separates the interestedness and independence components of the first prong of the *Aronson* standard into two prongs, and makes the second, business judgment prong of the *Aronson* standard the third prong of the standard as stated in *Grimes*:

> The basis for claiming excusal would normally be that: (1) a majority of the board has a material financial or familial interest; (2) a majority of the board is incapable of acting independently for some other reason such as domination or control; or (3) the underlying transaction is not the product of a valid exercise of business judgment.[611]

---

602. *Id.* at 703-04.
603. 473 A.2d 805 (Del. 1984).
604. 480 A.2d 619 (Del. 1984).
605. 539 A.2d 180 (Del. 1988).
606. 591 A.2d 194 (Del. 1991).
607. 611 A.2d 950 (Del. 1992).
608. 634 A.2d 927 (Del. 1993).
609. 673 A.2d 1207 (Del. 1996).
   610. *Grobow,* 539 A.2d at 186; *see also Grimes,* 673 A.2d at 1216; *Rales,* 634 A.2d at 933; *Datapoint,* 611 A.2d at 952; *Levine,* 591 A.2d at 205; *Pogostin,* 480 A.2d at 624; *Aronson,* 473 A.2d at 814.
   611. 673 A.2d at 1216 (footnotes omitted).

The Supreme Court articulated and explained the *Aronson* standard in *Levine* as follows:

> In determining the sufficiency of . . . a claim of demand futility, . . . [t]he trial court is confronted with two related but distinct questions: (1) whether threshold presumptions of director disinterest or independence are rebutted by well-pleaded facts; and, if not, (2) whether the complaint pleads particularized facts sufficient to create a reasonable doubt that the challenged transaction was the product of a valid exercise of business judgment.
>
> The premise of a shareholder claim of futility of demand is that a majority of the board of directors either has a financial interest in the challenged transaction or lacks independence or otherwise failed to exercise due care. On either showing, it may be inferred that the Board is *incapable* of exercising its power and authority to pursue the derivative claims directly. When lack of independence is charged, a plaintiff must show that the Board is either dominated by an officer or director who is the proponent of the challenged transaction or that the Board is so under his influence that its discretion is "sterilize[d]."
>
> Assuming a plaintiff cannot prove that directors are interested or otherwise not capable of exercising independent business judgment, a plaintiff in a demand futility case must plead particularized facts creating a reasonable doubt as to the "soundness" of the challenged transaction sufficient to rebut the presumption that the business judgment rule attaches to the transaction. The point is that in a claim of demand futility, there are two alternative hurdles, either of which a derivative shareholder complainant must overcome to successfully withstand a Rule 23.1 motion [to dismiss].[612]

As the Supreme Court explained in *Pogostin*:

> As to the first *Aronson* inquiry, the court reviews the factual allegations of the complaint to determine whether they create a reasonable doubt as to the disinterestedness and independence of the directors at the time the complaint was filed. Those questions are measured in relation to certain basic or fundamental principles. Directorial interest exists whenever

---

612. *Levine*, 591 A.2d at 205-06 (citations omitted).

divided loyalties are present, or a director either has received, or is entitled to receive, a personal financial benefit from the challenged transaction which is not equally shared by the stockholders. The question of independence flows from an analysis of the factual allegations pertaining to the influences upon the directors' performance of their duties generally, and more specifically in respect to the challenged transaction. . . .

The second, or business judgment inquiry of *Aronson*, focuses on the substantive nature of the challenged transaction and the board's approval thereof. A court does not assume that the transaction was a wrong to the corporation requiring corrective measures by the board. Rather, the transaction is reviewed against the factual background of the complaint to determine whether a reasonable doubt exists at the threshold that the challenged action was a valid exercise of business judgment. If the Court of Chancery in the exercise of its sound discretion is satisfied that a plaintiff has alleged facts with particularity which, taken as true, support a reasonable doubt as to either aspect of the *Aronson* analysis, the futility of demand is established and the court's inquiry ends.[613]

The Supreme Court stated in *Grobow* and *Levine* that "conclusionary allegations of fact or law not supported by allegations of specific fact may not be taken as true" in determining whether facts excusing demand have been pleaded,[614] that "the general notice pleading standard" governing ordinary motions to dismiss for failure to state a claim does not govern motions to dismiss for failure to make a demand or plead facts that, if true, would demonstrate that demand is excused,[615] and that a plaintiff's pleading burden in a case alleging that demand is excused therefore is "more onerous than that required to withstand" other motions to dismiss.[616] As explained by the Court of Chancery in its decision in *Levine*, a motion to dismiss for failure to make a demand "is not intended to

---

613. 480 A.2d at 624-25 (citations omitted).

614. *Grobow*, 539 A.2d at 187.

615. *Levine*, 591 A.2d at 210; *see also Grobow*, 539 A.2d at 187 n.6 (noting Rule 12(b)(6)'s "less stringent standard").

616. *Levine*, 591 A.2d at 207.

test the legal sufficiency of the plaintiff's substantive claim. Rather its purpose is to determine who is entitled, as between the corporation and its shareholders, to assert the plaintiff's underlying substantive claim on the corporation's behalf."[617] As stated by the Court of Chancery in *Richardson v. Graves*[618]: "[N]otice pleading is not enough. Generalities, artistically ambiguous, all-encompassing conclusory allegations are not enough. What is required are pleadings that are specific and, if conclusory, supported by sufficient factual allegations that corroborate the conclusion and support the proposition that demand is futile."[619] The Court of Chancery explained in another case, *International Equity Capital Growth Fund, L.P. v. Clegg*,[620] that although a "plaintiff should be accorded the benefit of a pleading doubt," he "must however not rely on 'conclusions' but must plead specific 'facts' showing a reasonable doubt as to the applicability of the business judgment presumption."[621]

Finally, the Supreme Court in *Grimes* stated that the *Aronson* test "involves 'essentially a discretionary ruling on a predominantly factual issue.'"[622] The court in *Grimes* described the "exercise of discretion by experienced and capable judges" as "a satisfactory screening mechanism, in our view."[623]

*(i) Cases Requiring Demand Under Aronson.* The facts underlying the *Aronson v. Lewis*[624] and *Pogostin v. Rice*[625] decisions

---

617. *Levine v. Smith*, 16 Del. J. Corp. L. 333, 345 (Del. Ch. Nov. 27, 1989), *aff'd*, 591 A.2d 194 (Del. 1991), *quoted in Langner v. Brown*, 913 F. Supp. 260, 265 (S.D.N.Y. 1996).

618. 1983 Del. Ch. LEXIS 466, 1983 WL 21109 (Del. Ch. June 17, 1983).

619. 1983 Del. Ch. LEXIS 466, at *5, 1983 WL 21109, at *2, *quoted in In re Prudential Ins. Co. Derivative Litig.*, 659 A.2d 961, 971 (N.J. Super. Ct. Ch. Div. 1995) and *Coyer v. Hemmer*, 901 F. Supp. 872, 887 (D.N.J. 1995).

620. 23 Del. J. Corp. L. 259 (Del. Ch. Apr. 21, 1997).

621. *Id.* at 267.

622. 673 A.2d at 1217 n.15 (quoting *Grobow*, 539 A.2d at 186).

623. *Id.* at 1217 n.15.

624. 473 A.2d 805 (Del. 1984).

(as well as the *Grobow v. Perot*[626] and *Levine v. Smith*[627] decisions, which are discussed in Chapter III)[628] illustrate applications of the *Aronson* test requiring demand.

*Aronson v. Lewis*[629] involved allegations that the directors of Meyers Parking Systems, Inc. breached their fiduciary duties and wasted corporate assets by approving a consulting agreement with Leo Fink, a director and a 47 percent shareholder of Meyers.[630] Meyers had been a wholly owned subsidiary of Prudential Building Corporation until Meyers was spun off to Prudential's shareholders in 1979. Plaintiff alleged that prior to January 1, 1981, Fink, who at the time was 75 years old, had an employment agreement with Prudential providing that upon retirement Fink would become a consultant to Prudential for ten years. Fink retired in April 1980, following which Prudential and Meyers agreed to share Fink's consulting services, with Meyers reimbursing Prudential for 25 percent of the fees paid by Prudential to Fink.[631]

On January 1, 1981, Meyers and Fink entered into a new employment agreement. This agreement required Meyers to pay Fink $150,000 per year plus a bonus based upon Meyer's pre-tax profits. The contract had a five year term and provided for automatic annual renewals once the five year term ended. Fink could terminate the contract at any time, and Meyers could terminate the contract upon six months notice. Following a termination, the contract provided, Fink would become a consultant to Meyers and be paid $150,000 per year for three years, $125,000 per year for the next three years, and then $100,000 per year for life. Fink agreed "to devote his best efforts and substantially his entire busi-

---

625. (...continued)
    625. 480 A.2d 619 (Del. 1984).
    626. 539 A.2d 180 (Del. 1988).
    627. 591 A.2d 194 (Del. 1991).
    628. *See* Chapter III, Section I 1 a.
    629. 473 A.2d 805 (Del. 1984).
    630. *Id.* at 808-09.
    631. *Id.* at 808.

ness time to advancing Meyers' interests."[632] Meyers also agreed to make interest-free loans to Fink.[633]

Applying the test for determining whether demand is excused that it had established, the Supreme Court in *Aronson* concluded that director disinterestedness and independence was present even though it was alleged that the corporation's directors were nominated or elected at the behest of Fink, a 47 percent shareholder, because the "shorthand shibboleth of 'dominated and controlled directors' is insufficient" to establish demand futility.[634] Rather, the court held, particularized factual allegations "manifesting 'a direction of corporate conduct in such a way as to comport with the wishes or interests of the corporation (or persons) doing the controlling'" beyond mere stock ownership are required in order to negate the presumption of independence provided for by the business judgment rule.[635] Indeed, the court added, in the demand context "even proof of majority ownership of a company does not strip the directors" of the protection of the business judgment rule.[636] To excuse demand, according to the court, "[t]here must be coupled with the allegation of control such facts as would demonstrate that through personal or other relationships the directors are beholden to the controlling person."[637]

With regard to the plaintiff's argument that the board's approval of the consulting agreement constituted a waste of corporate assets and thus was not the product of a valid exercise of business judgment under the second prong of the *Aronson* test, the Supreme Court held that the complaint did not allege particularized facts indicating that the consulting agreement constituted waste. The court pointed to "the directors' broad corporate power to fix the compensation of officers," and stated that the plaintiff's bare asser-

---

632. *Id.*

633. *Id.* at 809.

634. *Id.* at 816.

635. *Id.* (quoting *Kaplan v. Centex Corp.*, 284 A.2d 119, 123 (Del. Ch. 1971)).

636. *Id.* at 815.

637. *Id.*

tion that Fink performed "little or no services" was a conclusory allegation based solely on Fink's age and the existence of the consulting agreement that Fink previously had entered into with Prudential.[638]

The Supreme Court in *Aronson* also held that the mere approval of the challenged agreement by a majority of the corporation's directors is insufficient to excuse demand under either prong of the *Aronson* test notwithstanding the threat of personal liability for such approval, although the court added that "in rare cases a transaction may be so egregious on its face that board approval cannot meet the test of business judgment."[639] The court also rejected a contention that demand should be excused because requiring a demand would place directors in the position of deciding whether to sue themselves.[640]

On remand following the filing of an amended complaint including new factual allegations, the Court of Chancery concluded that "although it is a close call, plaintiff has borne his burden" with regard to the first, director interest or lack of independence, prong of the *Aronson* test.[641]

The Court of Chancery began by noting that plaintiff's amended complaint alleged that Fink owned or controlled through his family more than 50 percent of Meyers' common stock, and that Fink had entered into an agreement with ISS-International Service Systems A/S, which at the time the challenged agreements were entered into held approximately 30 percent of both Meyer's stock and Prudential's stock.[642] Pursuant to this agreement, Fink designated one group of Meyers' directors, ISS designated a second

638. *Id.* at 817 & n.12 (citing Del. Gen. Corp. Law § 122(5)).

639. *Id.* at 815 (citing *Gimbel v. Signal Cos.*, 316 A.2d 599 (Del. Ch.), *aff'd*, 316 A.2d 619 (Del. 1974), and *Cottrell v. Pawcatuck Co.*, 128 A.2d 225 (Del. 1956), *appeal dismissed and cert. denied*, 355 U.S. 12 (1957)).

640. *Id.* at 818.

641. *Lewis v. Aronson*, 11 Del. J. Corp. L. 243 (Del. Ch. May 1, 1985).

642. *Id.* at 248.

group of Meyers' directors, and Fink and ISS together designated the remainder of Meyers' directors.[643] The Court of Chancery pointed to the Supreme Court's statements that "even proof of majority ownership would not, in the demand context, strip the directors of the presumption of independence," "[i]t is not enough to charge that a director was nominated or elected at the behest of those controlling the outcome of a corporate election," and "[t]here must be coupled with the allegation of control such facts as would demonstrate that through personal or other relationships the directors are beholden to the controlling person."[644] The court concluded that "[p]laintiff's allegations as to Mr. Fink's stock ownership and designation of the directors are therefore still insufficient to create a reasonable doubt as to the directors' disinterestedness."[645]

Other allegations, the Court of Chancery concluded, however, were sufficient to satisfy the first prong of the *Aronson* standard. These allegations included assertions that ISS and Prudential received benefits from Fink's employment contract with Meyers because Fink, after being assured of the employment contract with Meyers, withdrew demands for compensation from ISS and Prudential for (1) the sale of Fink's Prudential stock at a price different from a previously agreed upon price and (2) Fink's retirement from Prudential and relinquishment of his position as Prudential's chairman.[646] The court stated that seven of Meyers' ten directors were directors or officers of either ISS or Prudential and thus stood on both sides of the transaction.[647] On this basis, the court found a "reasonable doubt as to the disinterestedness" of a majority of the Meyers board.[648]

The Court of Chancery also found that plaintiff had satisfied the second prong of the *Aronson* test. The court explained that the

---

643. *Id.*
644. *Id.* at 249 (quoting 473 A.2d at 815-16).
645. *Id.* at 249.
646. *Id.* at 250.
647. *Id.*
648. *Id.* at 250, 251.

plaintiff's amended complaint, in addition to alleging everything
that was alleged in plaintiff's prior complaint, also alleged (1) that
the payment by Meyers required by the agreement between Prudential and Meyers to share Fink's consulting services constituted full
payment for Fink's services to Meyers, (2) that Fink lived in
Florida, while Meyers' principal offices were in New York and its
business was conducted in states other than Florida, and (3) that the
challenged contract called for payments even if Fink became unable
to perform any services (although, the court noted, plaintiff did not
allege that Fink was "in anything but good health").[649]

The court stated that "[w]hen coupled with the facts that Mr.
Fink may terminate the agreement at any time while Meyers must
give six months notice and upon termination of employment a consulting agreement to continue for life goes into effect, the allegations that Mr. Fink resides in Florida, far from the locations of the
conduct of Meyers' business and is already receiving compensation
from Meyers through the services sharing agreement with Prudential, suggest that the services Mr. Fink might render to Meyers,
pursuant to the challenged contract, are so grossly inadequate that
no ordinary person of sound business judgment would deem it
worth that which the corporation paid."[650] Based upon these additional allegations, the court concluded that the "plaintiff has, if only
barely, alleged facts sufficient to create a reasonable doubt that the
challenged transaction was the product of a valid exercise of business judgment and therefore should bear the further scrutiny of the
Court."[651] The court added that "[t]he allegations that the contract
was actually entered into to compensate Mr. Fink for benefits he
gave to Prudential and to ISS strengthen the allegations of waste
and further raises a reasonable doubt that the directors could have
validly exercised their business judgment as to the contract."[652]

---

649. *Id*. at 252.
650. *Id*. at 252-53.
651. *Id*. at 253.
652. *Id*.

*Pogostin v. Rice*[653] involved a challenge to allegedly excessive executive compensation payments and an allegedly improper rejection of a tender offer. The compensation payments were not a basis for demand futility, the court held, because they were made pursuant to an executive compensation arrangement adopted by a majority of disinterested directors (only four directors on the corporation's 14 member board had "any financial or other interest whatsoever"), ratified by shareholders, and administered by four outside directors.[654] The board's rejection of the tender offer, the court also held, could not be the basis for demand futility because no facts were pleaded that, if true, would support the plaintiffs' claim that the board (or any group of board members) had acted solely or primarily to retain control.[655] The court added that "[v]aluation studies, carefully prepared by outsiders, were presented to the board prior to its decision," and "[a] special committee of independent, outside directors was charged with gathering and analyzing this information."[656]

Following *Aronson* and its progeny, it is settled under Delaware law (and the law of most other jurisdictions that have addressed the issue) that demand is not excused merely because a majority of directors have participated in, approved or acquiesced in the conduct or transaction underlying a shareholder derivative action.[657] To the contrary, "[e]xcusing demand on the mere basis

---

653. 480 A.2d 619 (Del. 1984).

654. *Id.* at 626.

655. *Id.* at 627.

656. *Id.*

657. *Cases Construing Delaware Law: See Grimes v. Donald,* 673 A.2d 1207, 1216 n.8 (Del. 1996); *Aronson,* 473 A.2d at 815, 817; *Pogostin,* 480 A.2d at 627; *Katz v. Halperin,* 21 Del. J. Corp. L. 690, 706 (Del. Ch. Feb. 5, 1996); *Emerald Partners v. Berlin,* 19 Del. J. Corp. L. 1182, 1190, 1192 (Del. Ch. Dec. 23, 1993); *Lewis v. Fites,* 18 Del. J. Corp. L. 1046, 1051-52 (Del. Ch. Feb. 18, 1993); *Decker v. Clausen,* 15 Del. J. Corp. L. 1022, 1027 (Del. Ch. Nov. 6, 1989); *Grobow v. Perot,* 526 A.2d 914, 924 (Del. Ch. 1987), *aff'd,* 539 A.2d 180 (Del. 1988); *Kaufman v. Belmont,* 479 A.2d 282, 288 (Del. Ch. 1984); *Lewis v. Daum,* 9 Del. J. Corp. L. 481, 485 (Del. Ch. May 24, 1984);

(continued...)

657. (...continued)
*Haber v. Bell*, 465 A.2d 353, 359 (Del. Ch. 1983); *Langner v. Brown*, 913 F. Supp. 260, 265 (S.D.N.Y. 1996); *Mendelovitz v. Vosicky*, 1993 U.S. Dist. LEXIS 12936, at *5-6, 1993 WL 367091, at *2 (N.D. Ill. Sept. 16, 1993), *aff'd on other grounds*, 40 F.3d 182 (7th Cir. 1994); *Citron v. Daniell*, 796 F. Supp. 649, 652 (D. Conn. 1992); *Cottle v. Hilton Hotels Corp.*, 635 F. Supp. 1094, 1098 (N.D. Ill. 1986); *Stein v. Bailey*, 531 F. Supp. 684, 691 n.16 (S.D.N.Y. 1982).

*Cases Construing the Law of Jurisdictions Other Than Delaware:* *Boland v. Engle*, 113 F.3d 706, 711 n.5 (7th Cir. 1997) (Indiana law); *Kamen v. Kemper Fin. Servs., Inc.*, 939 F.2d 458, 461 (7th Cir.), *cert. denied*, 502 U.S. 974 (1991) (Maryland law); *Bach v. National W. Life Ins. Co.*, 810 F.2d 509, 514 (5th Cir. 1987) (Colorado law); *Lewis v. Graves*, 701 F.2d 245, 248 (2d Cir. 1983) (federal law); *Greenspun v. Del E. Webb Corp.*, 634 F.2d 1204, 1210 (9th Cir. 1980) (federal law); *Olesh v. Dreyfus Corp.*, [1995-1996 Transfer Binder] Fed. Sec. L. Rep. (CCH) ¶ 98,907, at 93,368 (E.D.N.Y. Aug. 8, 1995) (Maryland law); *In re Abbott Lab. Derivative Litig.*, 1994 U.S. Dist. LEXIS 938, at *5, 1994 WL 31034, at *2 (N.D. Ill. Feb. 2, 1994) (Illinois law); *In re Westinghouse Sec. Litig.*, 832 F. Supp. 989, 996 (W.D. Pa. 1993), *aff'd mem.*, 92 F.3d 1175 (3d Cir. 1996) (Pennsylvania law); *Faktor v. American Bromaterials Corp.*, 1991 U.S. Dist. LEXIS 11927, at *30, 1991 WL 336922, at *11 (D.N.J. May 28, 1991) (federal law); *Lou v. Belzberg*, 728 F. Supp. 1010, 1017 (S.D.N.Y. 1990) (Kentucky and federal law); *Pullman-Peabody Co. v. Joy Mfg. Co.*, 662 F. Supp. 32, 35 (D.N.J. 1986) (federal law); *In re Consumers Power Co. Derivative Litig.*, 111 F.R.D. 419, 426 (E.D. Mich. 1986) (federal law); *Mozes v. Welch*, 638 F. Supp. 215, 219 (D. Conn. 1986) (federal law); *Kaufman v. Kansas Gas & Elec. Co.*, 634 F. Supp. 1573, 1581 (D. Kan. 1986) (federal law); *Kolin v. American Plan Corp.*, [1984-1985 Transfer Binder] Fed. Sec. L. Rep. ¶ 92,051, at 91,242 (E.D.N.Y. Apr. 30, 1985) (federal law); *Recchion v. Kirby*, 637 F. Supp. 1309, 1320 (W.D. Pa. 1986) (federal law); *Hall v. Aliber*, 614 F. Supp. 473, 479 (E.D. Mich. 1985) (Michigan law); *Jerozal v. Cash Reserve Management Inc.*, [1982-1983 Transfer Binder] Fed. Sec. L. Rep. ¶ 99,019, at 94,823-24 (S.D.N.Y. Aug. 10, 1982) (federal law); *Weiss v. Temporary Inv. Fund, Inc.*, 516 F. Supp. 665, 672 (D. Del.), *reargument denied*, 520 F. Supp. 1098 (D. Del. 1981), *aff'd*, 692 F.2d 928 (3d Cir. 1982), *vacated and remanded on other grounds*, 465 U.S. 1001 (1984) (federal law); *Brooks v. American Export Indus.*, 68 F.R.D. 506, 511 (S.D.N.Y. 1975) (federal law); *Stallworth v. AmSouth*

(continued...)

of prior board acquiescence . . . would obviate the need for demand in practically every case" because "[d]erivative suits are almost invariably directed at major, allegedly illegal, corporate transactions," and "[b]y virtue of their offices, directors ordinarily participate in the decision making involved in such transactions."[658] As one federal court construing Delaware law thus has noted, "if mere director approval were enough to excuse demand, demand would be futile in almost every case" and "[t]he futility exception to the demand requirement would devour the rule."[659] As another federal court, construing Maryland law, has reasoned:

> The prevailing contemporary view is that demand is necessary if the directors are disinterested—and because of the business judgment rule directors may be financially disinterested even if they took part in the acts of which the plaintiff complains. Careless acts by directors are regrettable but not a source of personal liability. So a plaintiff who believes that directors violated their duty of care may ask them to take remedial action without putting their fortunes at risk.[660]

It also is settled under Delaware law (and the law of most other jurisdictions that have addressed the issue) that demand is not excused merely because a majority of directors:

- Are named as defendants in the litigation,[661]

---

657. (...continued)
*Bank*, 1997 Ala. LEXIS 483, at *14, 1997 WL 778838, at *4 (Ala. Dec. 19, 1997) (Alabama law); *Shields v. Singleton*, 15 Cal. App. 4th 1611, 1622 & n.5, 19 Cal. Rptr.2d 459, 466 & n.5 (Cal. Ct. App. 1993) (California law); *In re Prudential Ins. Co. Derivative Litig.*, 659 A.2d 961, 970-71, 974 (N.J. Super. Ct. Ch. Div. 1995) (New Jersey law); *Drage v. Procter & Gamble*, 694 N.E.2d 479, 484-86 (Ohio Ct. App. 1997) (Ohio law).

658. *Graves*, 701 F.2d at 248.

659. *Langner*, 913 F. Supp. at 265.

660. *Kemper*, 939 F.2d at 461.

661. *Cases Construing Delaware Law: See Grimes*, 673 A.2d at 1216 n.8; *Aronson*, 473 A.2d at 817; *Pogostin*, 480 A.2d at 625; *Gagliardi v. Trifoods Int'l, Inc.*, 683 A.2d 1049, 1055 (Del. Ch. 1996) (published in part, complete text available at 1996 Del. Ch. LEXIS 87 and

(continued...)

661. (...continued)
1996 WL 422330); *Caruana v. Saligman*, [1990-1991 Transfer Binder]
Fed. Sec. L. Rep. (CCH) ¶ 95,889, at 99,379 (Del. Ch. Dec. 21, 1990);
*Blasband v. Rales*, 971 F.2d 1034, 1052 n.18 (3d Cir. 1992); *Shields v.
Murphy*, 116 F.R.D. 600, 604 (D.N.J. 1987); *In re E.F. Hutton Banking
Practices Litig.*, 634 F. Supp. 265, 270 (S.D.N.Y. 1986) (Delaware and
federal law); *Richardson v. Graves*, 1983 Del. Ch. LEXIS 466, at *8,
1983 WL 21109, at *3 (Del. Ch. June 17, 1983); *Stein*, 531 F. Supp. at
691 n.16.
   *Cases Construing the Law of Jurisdictions Other Than Delaware:*
See *Bach*, 810 F.2d at 514; *Graves*, 701 F.2d at 249; *Lewis v. Curtis*, 671
F.2d 779, 785 (3d Cir.), *cert. denied*, 459 U.S. 880 (1982) (federal law);
*Heit v. Baird*, 567 F.2d 1157, 1162 (1st Cir. 1977) (federal law); *Abbott
Lab.*, 1994 U.S. Dist. LEXIS 938, at *5, 1994 WL 31034, at *2; *West-
inghouse*, 832 F. Supp. at 996; *Garber v. Lego*, 1992 WL 554239, at *3
(W.D. Pa. Oct. 2, 1992) (federal law), *aff'd*, 11 F.3d 1197 (3d Cir. 1993)
(Pennsylvania law); *In re Mortgage & Realty Trust Sec. Litig.*, 787
F. Supp. 84, 87-88 (E.D. Pa. 1991) (Maryland law); *In re UJB Fin.
Corp. Shareholder Litig.*, 1991 U.S. Dist. LEXIS 20710, at *19, 1991
WL 321909, at *7 (D.N.J. Jan. 22, 1991) (federal law), *aff'd and rev'd
on other grounds sub nom. Shapiro v. UJB Fin. Corp.*, 964 F.2d 272 (3d
Cir.), *cert. denied*, 506 U.S. 934 (1992); *Weiland v. Illinois Power Co.*,
[1990-1991 Transfer Binder] Fed. Sec. L. Rep. (CCH) ¶ 95,747, at
98,589 (C.D. Ill. Sept. 17, 1990) (Illinois law); *Kamen v. Kemper Fin.
Servs., Inc.*, 659 F. Supp. 1153, 1162 n.15 (N.D. Ill. 1987) (federal law),
*aff'd on other grounds*, 908 F.2d 1338 (7th Cir. 1990) (federal law), *rev'd
on other grounds*, 500 U.S. 90 (1991) (holding that Maryland law
governs); *Mozes*, 638 F. Supp. at 219; *Syphers v. Scardino*, 1985 U.S.
Dist. LEXIS 13161, at *8, 1985 WL 4283, at *4 (E.D. Pa. Dec. 5, 1985)
(federal law); *Lewis v. Sporck*, 612 F. Supp. 1316, 1323 (N.D. Cal.
1985) (federal law); *Hall*, 614 F. Supp. at 479; *Kolin*, [1984-1985
Transfer Binder] Fed. Sec. L. Rep. at 91,242; *Reilly Mortgage Group,
Inc. v. Mount Vernon Sav. & Loan Ass'n*, 568 F. Supp. 1067, 1076 (E.D.
Va. 1983) (Virginia law); *Weiss*, 516 F. Supp. at 673; *Markowitz v.
Brody*, 90 F.R.D. 542, 556 (S.D.N.Y. 1981) (federal law); *Brooks*, 68
F.R.D. at 511; *Lewis v. Akers*, 227 A.D.2d 595, 596, 644 N.Y.S.2d 279,
281 (N.Y. App. Div. 2d Dep't), *leave to appeal denied*, 88 N.Y.2d 813,
672 N.E.2d 606, 649 N.Y.S.2d 380 (1996); *Bildstein v. Atwater*, 222
A.D.2d 545, 546, 635 N.Y.S.2d 88, 89 (N.Y. App. Div. 2d Dep't 1995)
(New York law); *Lewis v. Welch*, 126 A.D.2d 519, 521, 510 N.Y.S.2d
(continued...)

    •    Would have to sue themselves,[662]

---

661. (...continued)
640, 642 (N.Y. App. Div. 2d Dep't 1987) (New York law); *General Elec. Co. v. Welch*, N.Y.L.J., Dec. 30, 1992, at 27 (N.Y. Sup. Ct. N.Y. Co.) (New York law).

    662. *Cases Construing Delaware Law: See Blosvern v. Fisher*, 504 A.2d 571 (unpublished opinion, text available at 1986 Del. Ch. LEXIS 1030 and 1986 WL 16162) (Del. Jan. 30, 1986); *Aronson*, 473 A.2d at 818; *Pogostin*, 480 A.2d at 625; *Seminaris v. Landa*, 662 A.2d 1350, 1355 (Del. Ch. 1995); *Litman v. Prudential-Bache Properties, Inc.*, [1992-1993 Transfer Binder] Fed. Sec. L. Rep. (CCH) ¶ 97,313, at 95,585 (Del. Ch. Jan. 4, 1993); *Silverzweig v. Unocal Corp.*, 1989 Del. Ch. LEXIS 4, at *7, 1989 WL 3231, at *2 (Del. Ch. Jan. 19, 1989), *aff'd*, 561 A.2d 993 (unpublished opinion, text available at 1989 Del. LEXIS 151 and 1989 WL 68307) (Del. May 19, 1989); *Grobow*, 526 A.2d at 924; *Fites*, 18 Del. J. Corp. L. at 1051-52; *Daum*, 9 Del. J. Corp. L. at 486; *Stotland v. GAF Corp.*, 1983 Del. Ch. LEXIS 477, at *15, 1983 WL 21371, at *6 (Del. Ch. Sept. 1, 1983), *appeal dismissed*, 469 A.2d 421 (Del. 1983); *In re Silicon Graphics, Inc. Sec. Litig.*, [1996-1997 Transfer Binder] Fed. Sec. L. Rep. ¶ 99,325, at 95,968 (N.D. Cal. Sept. 25, 1996); *Levine v. Prudential-Bache Properties, Inc.*, 855 F. Supp. 924, 941 (E.D. Ill. 1994); *Mendelovitz*, 1993 U.S. Dist LEXIS 12936, at *5-6, 1993 WL 367091, at *2; *Hilton*, 635 F. Supp. at 1098-99; *Allison v. General Motors Corp.*, 604 F. Supp. 1106, 1114-15 (D. Del.), *aff'd mem.*, 782 F.2d 1026 (3d Cir. 1985) (Delaware and federal law); *Katz v. Emmett*, N.Y.L.J., Sept. 27, 1994, at 26 (N.Y. Sup. Ct. Westchester Co.), *aff'd*, 226 A.D.2d 588, 641 N.Y.S.2d 131 (N.Y. App. Div. 2d Dep't 1996); *Weinstock v. Bromery*, N.Y.L.J., Mar. 28, 1996, at 29 (N.Y. Sup. Ct. N.Y. Co.), *aff'd sub nom. Teachers' Retirement Sys. v. Welch*, --- A.D.2d ---, 664 N.Y.S.2d 38 (N.Y. App. Div. 1st Dep't 1997).

    *Cases Construing the Law of Jurisdictions Other Than Delaware: See Curtis*, 671 F.2d at 787; *Greenspun*, 634 F.2d at 1210; *Heit*, 567 F.2d at 1162; *Abbott Lab.*, 1994 U.S. Dist. LEXIS 938, at *5-6, 1994 WL 31034, at *2; *Westinghouse*, 832 F. Supp. at 996; *Weisbein v. Metrobank*, 1992 U.S. Dist. LEXIS 20196, at *6, 1992 WL 398361, at *2 (E.D. Pa. Dec. 31, 1992) (federal law); *Garber*, 1992 WL 554239, at *2; *UJB*, 1991 U.S. Dist. LEXIS 20710, at *19-20, 1991 WL 321909, at *7; *Lou*, 728 F. Supp. at 1017; *Atkins v. Tony Lama Co.*, 624 F. Supp. 250, 256 (S.D. Ind. 1985) (federal law); *Consumers Power*, 111 F.R.D. at

(continued...)

- Would have to sue friends, business associates and board colleagues,[663]

- Sit on other boards of directors together or have other business or social relationships with each other[664] (two courts, however, have held in actions brought on behalf of investment funds that service on the boards of multiple investment funds managed by the same investment advisor is sufficient to excuse demand),[665]

- Failed to take corrective action prior to the filing of the lawsuit and in the absence of a demand,[666]

---

662. (...continued)
427; *Cooper v. USCO Power Equip. Corp.*, 655 So. 2d 972, 975 (Ala. 1995) (Alabama law); *Noble v. Baum*, 1991 Conn. Super. LEXIS 1231, at *15, 1991 WL 101360, at *8 (Conn. Super. Ct. May 17, 1991) (Connecticut law); *Powell v. Gant*, 556 N.E.2d 1241, 1245 (Ill. App. Ct.), *appeal denied*, 564 N.E.2d 847 (1990) (Illinois law); *Prudential*, 659 A.2d at 972; *Procter & Gamble*, 694 N.E.2d at 483; *Drain v. Covenant Life Ins. Co.*, 685 A.2d 119, 128 (Pa. Super. Ct. 1996) (Pennsylvania law), *appeal granted*, 698 A.2d 67 (Pa. 1997).

663. *Cases Construing Delaware Law: See Abrams v. Koether*, 766 F. Supp. 237, 256 (D.N.J. 1991); *Weinstock*, N.Y.L.J., Mar. 28, 1996, at 29.

*Cases Construing the Law of Jurisdictions Other Than Delaware: See Grill v. Hoblitzell*, 771 F. Supp. 709, 712 (D. Md. 1991) (Maryland law); *Prudential*, 659 A.2d at 972.

664. *Cases Construing Delaware Law: See Langner*, 913 F. Supp. at 266; *Miller v. Loucks*, 1992 U.S. Dist. LEXIS 16966, at *24-26, 1992 WL 329313, at *7 (N.D. Ill. Nov. 5, 1992); *Daniell*, 796 F. Supp. at 652; *Weinstock*, N.Y.L.J., Mar. 28, 1996, at 29.

*Cases Construing the Law of Jurisdictions Other Than Delaware: See Grill*, 771 F. Supp. at 712; *Prudential*, 659 A.2d at 972.

665. *Cases Construing the Law of Jurisdictions Other Than Delaware: See Strougo v. Scudder, Stevens & Clark, Inc.*, 964 F. Supp. 783, 794-95 (S.D.N.Y. 1997), *reargument denied*, [1997 Transfer Binder] Fed. Sec. L. Rep. (CCH) ¶ 99,533, at 97,622 (S.D.N.Y. Aug. 18, 1997) (Maryland law); *Olesh*, [1995-1996 Transfer Binder] Fed. Sec. L. Rep. (CCH) at 93,368-69.

666. *Cases Construing Delaware Law: See Litman*, [1992-1993 (continued...)

- Refused to reconsider the challenged conduct or transaction or rejected an earlier demand by another shareholder,[667]

- Have defended or face a threat of liability in related litigation,[668]

- Have sought to defend the derivative action on either substantive or procedural grounds,[669]

- Have been selected to serve as directors by corporate officers alleged to have benefitted from challenged conduct,[670]

---

666. (...continued)
Transfer Binder] Fed. Sec. L. Rep. (CCH) at 95,585; *Blasband v. Rales*, 971 F.2d 1034, 1052 (3d Cir. 1992); *Levine*, 855 F. Supp. at 941; *Mendelovitz*, 1993 U.S. Dist. LEXIS 12936, at *5-6, 1993 WL 367091, at *2; *Allison*, 604 F. Supp. at 1113, 1116.

 *Cases Construing the Law of Jurisdictions Other Than Delaware:* See *Graves*, 701 F.2d at 249; *Mozes*, 638 F. Supp. at 219; *Prudential*, 659 A.2d at 975; *Roney v. Joyner*, 356 S.E.2d 401, 403 (N.C. Ct. App. 1987) (North Carolina law); *Procter & Gamble*, 694 N.E.2d at 483.

 667. *Cases Construing Delaware Law:* See *Kaplan v. Peat, Marwick, Mitchell & Co.*, 540 A.2d 726, 731 n.2 (Del. 1988), *aff'g on this ground* 529 A.2d 254, 257 (Del. Ch. 1987); *Decker*, 15 Del. J. Corp. L. at 1028; *Maurer v. Johnson*, No. 9725, slip op. at 2 (Del. Ch. May 10, 1989); *Grobow*, 526 A.2d at 924-25; *Blasband*, 971 F.2d at 1052 n.18.

 *Cases Construing the Law of Jurisdictions Other Than Delaware:* See *Kaufman v. Safeguard Scientifics, Inc.*, 587 F. Supp. 486, 488-89 (E.D. Pa. 1984) (federal law); *Procter & Gamble*, 694 N.E.2d at 486-87.

 668. *Cases Construing Delaware Law:* See *Seminaris*, 662 A.2d at 1355; *Decker*, 15 Del. J. Corp. L. at 1028.

 669. *Cases Construing the Law of Jurisdictions Other Than Delaware:* See *Kemper*, 939 F.2d at 460, 462-63; *Mortgage & Realty Trust*, 787 F. Supp. at 88; *Sporck*, 612 F. Supp. at 1323; *Prudential*, 659 A.2d at 973; *Procter & Gamble*; 694 N.E.2d at 483-84; *see also* Chapter IV, Section B 5 a (discussing these cases).

 670. *Cases Construing the Law of Jurisdictions Other Than Delaware: See Kemper*, 939 F.2d at 460 (all "independent directors come to a board after being slated by corporate insiders").

- Are alleged in conclusory language to be dominated and controlled by persons or entities who have benefited from the challenged conduct[671] (this is the case even where the allegedly dominating and controlling party controls all of the corporation's voting stock and chooses all members of the corporation's board because "the relevant inquiry is not how the director got his position, but rather how he comports himself in that position"),[672]

- Are "self-perpetuating, appoint themselves and those upon whom they can rely" ("even assuming that the directors are 'self-perpetuating,' plaintiffs must further show that, at the time suit was brought, the directors

---

671. *Cases Construing Delaware Law: See Heineman v. Datapoint Corp.*, 611 A.2d 950, 955 (Del. 1992); *Aronson*, 473 A.2d at 816-17; *Green v. Phillips*, 22 Del. J. Corp. L. 360, 370 (Del. Ch. June 19, 1996); *Halperin*, 21 Del. J. Corp. L. at 704; *Kahn v. Roberts*, [1993-1994 Transfer Binder] Fed. Sec. L. Rep. (CCH) ¶ 98,201, at 99,412 (Del. Ch. Feb. 28, 1994); *Emerald Partners*, 19 Del. J. Corp. L. at 1189, 1192; *Canal Capital Corp. v. French*, 18 Del. J. Corp. L. 611, 618-19 (Del. Ch. July 2, 1992); *Andreae v. Andreae*, [1991-1992 Transfer Binder] Fed. Sec. L. Rep. (CCH) ¶ 96,571, at 92,650 (Del. Ch. Mar. 3, 1992); *Grobow*, 526 A.2d at 924; *Stein v. Orloff*, 11 Del. J. Corp. L. 312, 317 (Del. Ch. May 30, 1985), *appeal refused*, 504 A.2d 572 (unpublished opinion, text available at 1986 Del. LEXIS 1024 and 1986 WL 16298) (Del. Jan. 28, 1986); *Sundin v. Fisher*, 10 Del. J. Corp. L. 917, 919-20 (Del. Ch. Feb. 15, 1985), *aff'd sub nom. Blosvern v. Fisher*, 504 A.2d 571 (unpublished opinion, text available at 1986 Del. LEXIS 1030 and 1986 WL 16162) (Del. Jan. 30, 1986); *Blasband*, 971 F.2d at 1049, 1053-54; *Coyer v. Hemmer*, 901 F. Supp. 872, 886-87, 887-88, 889 (D.N.J. 1995); *Mendelovitz*, 1993 U.S. Dist. LEXIS 12936, at *5-6, 1993 WL 367091, at *2; *Shields v. Erickson*, 710 F. Supp. 686, 692 (N.D. Ill. 1989) (Delaware and federal law); *Seltzer v. Krieger*, N.Y.L.J., Aug. 1, 1996, at 24 (N.Y. Sup. Ct. N.Y. Co.).

*Cases Construing the Law of Jurisdictions Other Than Delaware: See Kemper*, 939 F.2d at 460-61; *General Elec.*, N.Y.L.J., Dec. 30, 1992, at 27; *Atkins*, 624 F. Supp. at 256.

672. *Cases Construing Delaware Law: See Andreae*, [1991-1992 Transfer Binder] Fed. Sec. L. Rep. (CCH) at 92,650.

would not have accepted demand"; "[a] lack of corporate democracy does not, in itself, show the directors to be self-interested and necessarily hostile to accepting demand"),[673]

- Receive compensation for service as directors,[674]

- Have financial ties to the corporation that are comparable to the financial ties that all shareholders have to the corporation, such as stock ownership[675] or

---

673. *Cases Construing the Law of Jurisdictions Other Than Delaware*: *Prudential*, 659 A.2d at 972.

674. *Cases Construing Delaware Law: See Grobow*, 539 A.2d at 188; *Litman*, [1992-1993 Transfer Binder] Fed. Sec. L. Rep. (CCH) at 95,583; *Unocal*, 1989 Del. Ch. LEXIS 4, at *7, 1989 WL 3231, at *2; *In re NVF Co. Litig.*, 16 Del. J. Corp. L. 361, 373-74 (Del. Ch. Nov. 21, 1989); *Decker*, 15 Del. J. Corp. L. at 1028; *Lewis v. Straetz*, 1986 Del. Ch. LEXIS 365, at *15, 1986 WL 2252, at *5 (Del. Ch. Feb. 12, 1986); *Moran v. Household Int'l, Inc.*, 490 A.2d 1059, 1074 (Del. Ch.), *aff'd on other grounds*, 500 A.2d 1346 (Del. 1985); *Langner*, 913 F. Supp. at 266; *Daniell*, 796 F. Supp. at 652, 653; *E.F. Hutton*, 634 F. Supp. at 271; *Spillyards v. Abboud*, 662 N.E.2d 1358, 1367 (Ill. App. Ct. 1996); *Weinstock*, N.Y.L.J., Mar. 28, 1996, at 29.

*Cases Construing the Law of Jurisdictions Other Than Delaware: See Kemper*, 939 F.2d at 460; *Strougo*, 964 F. Supp. at 794; *Olesh*, [1995-1996 Transfer Binder] Fed. Sec. L. Rep. (CCH) at 93,368; *Westinghouse*, 832 F. Supp. at 997; *Batra v. Investors Research Corp.*, [1992 Transfer Binder] Fed. Sec. L. Rep. ¶ 96,983, at 94,262 (W.D. Mo. Apr. 2, 1992) (Maryland law); *Stoner v. Walsh*, 772 F. Supp. 790, 805 (S.D.N.Y. 1991) (New York law); *In re Woolworth Corp. Shareholder Derivative Litig.*, No. 109465/94, slip op. at 4-5 (N.Y. Sup. Ct. N.Y. Co. May 3, 1995), *aff'd*, --- A.D.2d ---, 658 N.Y.S.2d 869 (N.Y. App. Div. 1st Dep't 1997) (New York law); *Ferber v. Armstrong*, No. 27878/91, slip op. at 2 (N.Y. Sup. Ct. May 6, 1992) (New York law).

675. *Cases Construing Delaware Law: See In re Rexene Corp. Shareholders Litig.*, [1991 Transfer Binder] Fed. Sec. L. Rep. (CCH) ¶ 96,010, at 90,058 (Del. Ch. May 8, 1991), *aff'd sub nom. Eichorn v. Rexene Corp.*, 604 A.2d 416 (unpublished opinion, text available at 1991 Del. LEXIS 333 and 1991 WL 210962) (Del. Oct. 10, 1991); *Shields v. Erickson*, [1989-1990 Transfer Binder] Fed. Sec. L. Rep. ¶ 94,723, at

(continued...)

bonuses tied to corporate profitability,[676]

- Wish to retain their positions as directors and the benefits and prestige of being directors,[677]

- Would not "jeopardize" their "position as directors and employees" of the corporation by agreeing to the demand,[678]

- Allegedly fear public scrutiny, criticism or embarrassment, or that they will not be re-elected to new terms as directors, where no facts are alleged demonstrating an actual threat to the directors' positions,[679]

- Are alleged to have acted pursuant to "an entrenchment theory based on supposition rather than alleged fact,"[680] with "no factual allegations to support this conclusion" other than opposition to an unsolicited tender offer[681] or where the challenged conduct "could, at

---

675. (...continued)
93,903 (N.D. Ill. Aug. 24, 1989).
*Cases Construing the Law of Jurisdictions Other Than Delaware: Batra*, [1992 Transfer Binder] Fed. Sec. L. Rep. at 94,262.

676. *Cases Construing Delaware Law: See E.F. Hutton*, 634 F. Supp. at 271.
*Cases Construing the Law of Jurisdictions Other Than Delaware: See Procter & Gamble*, 694 N.E.2d at 485.

677. *Cases Construing Delaware Law: See Daniell*, 796 F. Supp. at 652, 653; *Tabas v. Mullane*, 608 F. Supp. 759, 766 (D.N.J. 1985); *Spillyards*, 662 N.E.2d at 1367.

678. *Cases Construing Delaware Law: Kahn*, [1993-1994 Transfer Binder] Fed. Sec. L. Rep. (CCH) at 99,412.

679. *Cases Construing Delaware Law: See Grobow*, 539 A.2d at 188; *Green*, 22 Del. J. Corp. L. at 369; *Fites*, 18 Del. J. Corp. L. at 1052; *Loucks*, 1992 U.S. Dist. LEXIS 16966, at *8, 1992 WL 329313, at *28.

680. *Cases Construing Delaware Law: Kahn*, [1993-1994 Transfer Binder] Fed. Sec. L. Rep. (CCH) at 99,412.

681. *Cases Construing Delaware Law: Unocal*, 1989 Del. Ch. LEXIS 4, at *7, 1989 WL 3231, at *2; *see also Hilton*, 635 F. Supp. at 1100; *Spillyards*, 662 N.E.2d at 1367-68.

least as easily, serve a valid corporate purpose as an improper purpose, such as entrenchment,"[682]

- Refuse to provide shareholders a report prepared by counsel in anticipation of litigation in order to evaluate potential liability for alleged wrongful conduct,[683]

- Granted indemnification as part of a challenged transaction,[684]

- Are alleged in a generalized manner to have acted without due care or in a grossly negligent manner,[685] or

- Allegedly received misinformation that was not material.[686]

---

682. *Cases Construing Delaware Law: See Cottle v. Standard Brands Paint Co.*, [1990 Transfer Binder] Fed. Sec. L. Rep. (CCH) ¶ 95,306, at 96,432 (Del. Ch. Mar. 22, 1990).
*Cases Construing the Law of Jurisdictions Other Than Delaware*: *Pullman-Peabody*, 662 F. Supp. at 35.

683. *Cases Construing Delaware Law: See Loucks*, 1992 U.S. Dist. LEXIS 16966, at *27-28, 1992 WL 329313, at *7.

684. *Cases Construing Delaware Law: See Grobow*, 526 A.2d at 924 n.14; *Good v. Getty Oil Co.*, 514 A.2d 1104, 1109 (Del. Ch. 1986); *see also Tabas*, 608 F. Supp. at 768 ("The Delaware Corporation Law specifically authorizes corporations to indemnify present and former directors and officers. 8 Del. C. § 145. Board members have no personal interest arising from these obligations").

685. *Cases Construing Delaware Law: See Litman*, [1992-1993 Transfer Binder] Fed. Sec. L. Rep. (CCH) at 95,585; *Andreae* [1991-1992 Transfer Binder] Fed. Sec. L. Rep. (CCH) at 92,651-52; *Seltzer*, N.Y.L.J., Aug. 1, 1996, at 24.
*Cases Construing the Law of Jurisdictions Other Than Delaware:* *See Daniell*, 796 F. Supp. at 653; *Procter & Gamble*, 694 N.E.2d at 486; *General Elec.*, N.Y.L.J., Dec. 30, 1992, at 27.

686. *Cases Construing Delaware Law: See Grobow v. Perot*, [1989-1990 Transfer Binder] Fed. Sec. L. Rep. (CCH) ¶ 94,869, at 94,717 (Del. Ch. Jan. 2, 1990), *aff'd sub nom. Levine v. Smith*, 591 A.2d 194 (Del. 1991).

Demand also is not excused

- By allegations that the challenged conduct or transaction involved a violation of law or fraud by the corporation or for some other reason cannot be ratified[687] (the courts have explained that an allegation that demand is excused because challenged conduct is unlawful and cannot be ratified "misses the point" because "[r]atification is not the only option; the board must be given a fair opportunity to decide whether the corporation itself should bring the suit," "the fact that a claim may be founded on fraud does not differentiate it from other claims," and "[r]efusal to sue is not . . . a ratification of fraud"),[688]

- By allegations that the corporation is subject to a regulatory or criminal investigation,[689] or have agreed on behalf of the corporation to the entry of a Consent Order with the Securities and Exchange Commission that establishes a violation of law by the corporation but

---

687. *Cases Construing Delaware Law: See Spiegel v. Buntrock*, 1988 Del. Ch. LEXIS 149, at *11-12, 1988 WL 124324, at *4 (Del. Ch. Nov. 17, 1988), *aff'd on other grounds*, 571 A.2d 767 (Del. 1990); *Richardson v. Graves*, 1983 Del. Ch. LEXIS 466, at *7-8, 1983 WL 21109, at *3-4; *Erickson*, 710 F. Supp. at 691-92; *E.F. Hutton*, 634 F. Supp. at 289-72.

*Cases Construing the Law of Jurisdictions Other Than Delaware: See Elfenbein v. Gulf & Western Indus., Inc.*, 590 F.2d 445, 450-51 (2d Cir. 1978), *aff'g* 454 F. Supp. 6, 8 n.4 (S.D.N.Y.) (federal law); *In re Nuveen Fund Litig.*, 1996 U.S. Dist. LEXIS 8062, at *16, 1996 WL 328001, at *5 (N.D. Ill. June 11, 1996) (Minnesota law); *Sporck*, 612 F. Supp. at 1322-23.

688. *Sporck*, 612 F. Supp. at 1322-23; *Findley v. Garrett*, 109 Cal. App. 2d 166, 177, 240 P.2d 421, 428 (Cal. Ct. App. 1952); *see also* Chapter IV, Section B 6 h (discussing board refusals of demands alleging unlawful conduct).

689. *Cases Construing Delaware Law: See Levine*, 855 F. Supp. at 941.

does not contain any admission of wrongdoing or findings concerning the directors themselves,[690]

- By allegations that the corporation's directors' and officers' liability insurance policy includes an "insured versus insured" exclusion barring coverage for claims by one insured party against another insured party, and thus that the policy does not cover an action brought by the corporation against the corporation's directors but does cover an action brought by shareholders acting on behalf of the corporation in a derivative action against the corporation's directors,[691]

- By allegations that directors recommended for shareholder approval a certificate of incorporation provision eliminating or limiting the directors' liability pursuant to a statute authorizing such a certificate provision,[692]

---

690. *Cases Construing Delaware Law: See Fites*, 18 Del. J. Corp. L. at 1052-53.

691. *Cases Construing Delaware Law: See Caruana*, [1990-1991 Transfer Binder] Fed. Sec. L. Rep. (CCH) at 99,379; *Decker*, 15 Del. J. Corp. L. at 1028; *Mendelovitz*, 1993 U.S. Dist. LEXIS 12936, at *5-6, 1993 WL 367091, at *2; *Katz*, N.Y.L.J., Sept. 27, 1994, at 26; *see also Stepak v. Addison*, 20 F.3d 398, 411 (11th Cir. 1994) (rejecting allegation that demand was wrongfully refused because "counsel informed the outside directors that a rejection of the demand would leave intact a $140 million insurance umbrella whereas acceptance of the demand would expose the directors to personal liability").

*Cases Construing the Law of Jurisdictions Other Than Delaware: See Westinghouse*, 832 F. Supp. at 997; *Stoner v. Walsh*, 772 F. Supp. at 805; *Prudential*, 659 A.2d at 972-73; *Woolworth*, slip op. at 7; *General Elec.*, N.Y.L.J., Dec. 30, 1992, at 27. *But cf. Grill*, 771 F. Supp. at 713-14 (stating that this allegation "may" be sufficient to excuse demand under Maryland law but not deciding the issue); *Procter & Gamble*, 694 N.E.2d at 484 (stating that "a provision prohibiting directors from bringing suits against each other" would excuse demand but "[a]n allegation that coverage may be adversely affected falls far short"); *see also* Chapter V, Section B 9 c (discussing insured versus insured provisions).

692. *Cases Construing Delaware Law: See Caruana*, [1990-1991 Transfer Binder] Fed. Sec. L. Rep. (CCH) at 99,379; *Decker*, 15 Del. J. (continued...)

- By allegations that directors caused false proxy statements or other documents to be sent to shareholders in order to retain their positions, to obtain shareholder approval of a certificate of incorporation provision eliminating or limiting director liability pursuant to a statute authorizing such a certificate provision or for some other reason,[693]

- By allegations that a statute of limitations is about to expire,[694] or

- By allegations that directors have made public statements critical of management or past corporate actions (rather than excuse demand, one court has stated, such statements "evidence a degree of open-mindedness which belie any allegation that the present board would necessarily reject a legitimate demand").[695]

Demand also is not excused by allegations that directors "consistently made poor decisions" or that the corporation "suffered losses" because of those poor decisions,[696] "there are costs, even great costs, associated with a business decision"[697] or "a

---

692. (...continued)
Corp. L. at 1028; *see also* Chapter II, Section A 7 (discussing Del. Gen. Corp. Law § 102(b)(7) and other similar statutes).
*Cases Construing the Law of Jurisdictions Other Than Delaware:* See *Woolworth*, slip op. at 7; *Ferber*, slip op. at 2; *General Elec.*, N.Y.L.J., Dec. 30, 1992, at 27.

693. *Cases Construing Delaware Law:* See *Halperin*, 21 Del. J. Corp. L. at 706-07; *Daniell*, 796 F. Supp. at 652; *Seltzer*, N.Y.L.J., Aug. 1, 1996, at 24.
*Cases Construing the Law of Jurisdictions Other Than Delaware:* See *Kemper*, 939 F.2d at 460, 462; *Procter & Gamble*, 694 N.E.2d at 486-87.

694. *Cases Construing Delaware Law: See Sundin*, 10 Del. J. Corp. L. at 920.

695. *Cases Construing the Law of Jurisdictions Other Than Delaware: See Grill*, 771 F. Supp. at 712.

696. *Andreae*, [1991-1992 Transfer Binder] Fed. Sec. L. Rep. (CCH) at 92,652.

697. *Unocal*, 1989 Del. Ch. LEXIS 4, at *9, 1989 WL 3231, at *3.

corporation loses a large amount of money."[698] As the Delaware Court of Chancery observed in a case challenging an unsuccessful investment of corporate funds in the stock market:

> The Complaint . . . does not allege any particularized facts which, if true, would show that the directors failed to exercise due care in approving the unsuccessful investments in the stock market. Corporate investments in the stock market are natural and acceptable, but not all of them prove profitable. The mere decline of investments is not a sufficient fact to overcome the presumption of propriety of the business judgment rule. Many other investors lost significant amounts of money in the sudden stock market decline of 1987. Absent particularized allegations which, if true, would show that the directors of May Petroleum acted in an uninformed and grossly negligent manner, their decision to invest corporate funds in the stock market is protected from judicial scrutiny by the business judgment rule.[699]

Demand also is not excused by allegations that "paint a troubling picture" of misconduct by the corporation's president and chief executive officer, where no allegations "challenge any activity of the board of directors or otherwise impugn the integrity of the otherwise nameless directors."[700] Demand upon the directors of a parent corporation is not excused by allegations challenging the conduct exercised by the directors of a subsidiary corporation because "[u]nder normal circumstances, a board of directors ought to be able to rely on its subsidiary's directors to oversee that subsidiary's management and attend to any problems that may arise."[701]

The law is not as settled concerning whether an alleged need to obtain prompt judicial relief is an excuse for not making a demand. In *Stroud v. Milliken Enterprises, Inc.*,[702] the Delaware

---

698. *Weiland v. Illinois Power Co.*, [1990-1991 Transfer Binder] Fed. Sec. L. Rep. (CCH) ¶ 95,747, at 98,589 (C.D. Ill. Sept. 17, 1990).

699. *Emerald Partners*, 19 Del. J. Corp. L. at 1190-91; *see also Coyer*, 901 F. Supp. at 889.

700. *Coyer*, 901 F. Supp. at 889.

701. *Decker*, 15 Del. J. Corp. L. at 1029-30.

702. 1988 Del. Ch. LEXIS 38 (Del. Ch. Mar. 18, 1988) (published

(continued...)

Court of Chancery held that a need to obtain prompt judicial relief "does not automatically preclude the corporation's right to receive a pre-suit demand."[703] The court stated that "[m]any stockholder derivative suits in which a demand was made have sought some form of preliminary relief, premised on an asserted need for immediate relief."[704] In *Edelman v. Phillips Petroleum Co.*,[705] by contrast, the Court of Chancery held that "given . . . the time constraints involved, requiring demand as a preamble to enjoining a shareholder's meeting at which ratification is sought would be a meaningless deferral to the demand rule."[706]

Dictum in the Delaware Supreme Court's decision in *Tandycrafts, Inc. v. Initio Partners*[707] also addresses this issue. This dictum arose in the context of a holding that a shareholder may be entitled to an attorneys' fee award where the shareholder's litigation effort "confers a benefit upon the corporation, or its shareholders, notwithstanding the absence of a class or derivative component."[708] The court acknowledged as "legitimate" the concern that "permitting an individual plaintiff to seek the allowance of counsel fees creates the potential for abuse since such an individual will have initiated litigation without compliance with the demand requirements . . . or without the usual class obligations assumed in a representative capacity."[709] The court responded, however, that "[w]hile compliance is the norm, situations may arise, particularly in rapidly evolving contests for corporate control, including, as here, proxy contests, in which challenged transactions may become moot or superseded before appropriate demand can be made with any realistic hope of corrective action being taken by incumbent

---

702. (...continued)
in part at 585 A.2d 1306), *vacated on other grounds*, 552 A.2d 476 (Del. 1989).
    703. 1988 Del. Ch. LEXIS 38, at *13.
    704. *Id.*
    705. 10 Del. J. Corp. L. 835 (Del. Ch. Feb. 12, 1985).
    706. *Id.* at 842.
    707. 562 A.2d 1162 (Del. 1989).
    708. *Id.* at 1163.
    709. *Id.* at 1166.

management."[710] The court stated that a shareholder under these circumstances "is not foreclosed from commencement of an individual action to implement his right to informed participation in the corporate election process."[711]

*(ii) Cases Excusing Demand Under Aronson.* Post-*Aronson v. Lewis*[712] decisions (including the Court of Chancery's decision on remand in *Aronson* itself in *Lewis v. Aronson*,[713] which is summarized following the discussion of *Aronson* above[714]) illustrate that there are important instances where demand is excused under Delaware law. Demand thus "has been excused in many cases in Delaware under the *Aronson* test."[715]

The Delaware Supreme Court's decision in *Heineman v. Datapoint Corp.*,[716] for example, excused demand in a case challenging four transactions approved by the board of directors of Datapoint Corporation following the acquisition of control of Datapoint in a proxy contest by a group of shareholders led by Asher B. Edelman. Following this proxy contest, Edelman became the Chairman of Datapoint's board, and, with 15 percent of Datapoint's stock, the corporation's largest shareholder.[717] The court held that the plaintiff pleaded "in sufficient particularized detail claims of interlocking directorships, domination by Edelman and shared investments between Edelman and a majority of the Datapoint board to raise a reasonable doubt concerning the disinterest and independence of the Datapoint board."[718]

---

710. *Id.*

711. *Id.*

712. 473 A.2d 805 (Del. 1984).

713. 11 Del. J. Corp. L. 243 (Del. Ch. May 1, 1985).

714. *See* Chapter IV, Section B 5 c (i).

715. *Grimes v. Donald*, 673 A.2d 1207, 1217 (Del. 1996); *see also id.* at 1217 n.19 (citing over 30 examples of "[s]ome of the relatively recent cases" excusing demand in Delaware).

716. 611 A.2d 950 (Del. 1992).

717. *Id.* at 951 & n.2.

718. *Id.* at 956.

The first challenged transaction (the "Reimbursement Transaction") involved payments by Datapoint to a majority of Datapoint's directors, including Edelman, as reimbursement of expenses related to the proxy contest waged by Edelman and these directors to acquire control of the corporation. The court held that this claim was sufficient to excuse demand. The court reasoned as follows:

> The complaint alleges a successful contest for corporate control, with the victors in that contest using their newly acquired positions to cause the corporation to reimburse the costs of waging that contest. Proof of these facts at trial would represent a *prima facia* case of director self-dealing. . . . The plaintiff need only raise a reasonable doubt that the business judgment rule applies. And though he is not required to plead a *prima facia* case of breach of fiduciary duty in order to avoid the demand requirement, once he does make such allegations he has carried his burden and demand is excused.[719]

The second challenged transaction (the "Arbitrage Transaction") involved "an 'arrangement' by a majority of Datapoint's board to divert a substantial amount of the corporation's assets to an arbitrage pool whose participants include entities in which a majority of the directors hold an interest."[720] These allegations, the court stated, "paint a picture of directors funneling corporate assets to their private use, a practice at clear variance with the directors' fiduciary obligation" and constitute claims of "director self-dealing supported by particularized facts" that "raise a reasonable doubt as to director disinterest."[721]

The third challenged transaction (the "United Stockyards Transaction") involved an allegation that Datapoint entered into an agreement with United Stockyards pursuant to which United Stockyards would provide consulting services to Datapoint for an annual fee of $300,000.[722] According to plaintiff, United Stockyards was engaged primarily in the business of operating public shipyards,

---

719. *Id*. at 953.
720. *Id*. at 954.
721. *Id*.
722. *Id*.

and had no expertise in Datapoint's line of business—the design and manufacture of computer, computer software and related office communications equipment.[723] Plaintiff alleged that this transaction was entered into for the benefit of Edelman, who was the controlling shareholder of United Stockyards, and was approved by directors having substantial business dealings with Edelman through investments in numerous Edelman-controlled concerns and who occupy board positions in various Edelman-controlled entities "at the pleasure of Edelman."[724] In short, the court stated, "[t]he nub of this claim is that a majority of Datapoint's board were dominated by Edelman through his control of their positions as Datapoint directors coupled with his control of business organizations in which they were investors."[725]

The court held that "an allegation that directors are dominated and controlled, standing alone, does not meet the demand futility standard."[726] Rather, "a party attacking a corporate transaction must advance particularized factual allegations from which the Court of Chancery can reasonably infer that the board members who approved the transaction are acting at the direction of the allegedly dominating individual or entity."[727] The court stated that plaintiff's allegations "present a close question" because it is "at least arguable" that the plaintiff "has failed to allege that Edelman *directed* a majority of Datapoint's board to support the transaction and to that extent the factual allegations of the amended complaint may be deemed inadequate."[728] The court concluded, however, that in view of the fact that plaintiff had alleged sufficient facts to excuse demand with regard to the Reimbursement and Arbitrage transactions, "further proceedings will be required at the trial court level," and "[w]e therefore deem the better course to be a remand of this claim with direction to permit . . . a second amended com-

---

723. *Id.* at 951, 954-55.
724. *Id.* at 955.
725. *Id.*
726. *Id.*
727. *Id.*
728. *Id.*

plaint to further articulate the assertion of self-interest and lack of independence regarding the United Stockyards transaction."[729]

The fourth and final challenged transaction (the "Jetstar Transaction") involved an agreement between Datapoint and AAA Jetstar, a corporation whose sole shareholder was Edelman. Pursuant to this agreement, Datapoint paid Jetstar $245,000 in exchange for "transportation services."[730] According to plaintiff, "this transaction is simply another device whereby Edelman siphons cash from Datapoint for his personal benefit."[731] The court stated that this claim, like plaintiff's United Stockyards claim, relied upon plaintiff's claim that Datapoint's board was dominated and controlled by Edelman. The court thus again concluded that "the claim of lack of independence is arguably insufficient but since it is part of a larger dispute which must receive further judicial attention at the trial level . . . [t]his claim also will be remanded for the opportunity to enlarge upon the allegation of domination through the filing of a second amended complaint."[732]

Additional cases in which demand has been excused pursuant to the first prong of the *Aronson* standard include

- *Sealy Mattress Co. v. Sealy, Inc.*[733] (excusing demand where corporation's directors all were employees of, and were appointed to their board positions by, a parent corporation with whom the challenged transaction had been entered);[734]

- *Siegman v. Tri-Star Pictures, Inc.*[735] (excusing

---

729. *Id.*
730. *Id.* at 956.
731. *Id.*
732. *Id.*
733. 1987 Del. Ch. LEXIS 511, 1987 WL 15254 (Del. Ch. July 20, 1987).
734. 702. 1987 Del. Ch. LEXIS 511, at *15, 1987 WL 15254, at *5.
735. 15 Del. J. Corp. L. 218 (Del. Ch. May 5, 1989), *aff'd in part and rev'd in part on other grounds sub nom. In re Tri-Star Pictures, Inc., Litig.*, 634 A.2d 319 (Del. 1993).

demand in a case challenging Tri-Star's acquisition of Coca-Cola's entertainment business in return for Tri-Star stock that would be paid to Coca-Cola shareholders as a special dividend, where six of the ten directors on the Tri-Star board were Coca-Cola shareholders);[736]

- *Manchester v. Narragansett Capital, Inc.*[737] (excusing demand where the four directors who approved an alleged change in the corporation's compensation policy each derived a personal financial benefit from the policy change);[738]

- *In re NVF Co. Litigation*[739] (excusing demand where the corporation's chairman, president, chief executive officer and 38 percent shareholder, Victor Posner, was interested in the challenged transaction, and five of the corporation's six other directors had business and/or family relationships with Posner);[740]

- *Heineman v. Datapoint Corp.*[741] (excusing demand where all members of the corporation's board received challenged severance agreements);[742]

- *Strougo v. Carroll*[743] (excusing demand where eleven of fourteen directors were alleged to have obtained personal financial benefits from insider trading);[744]

---

736. *Id.* at 237-41.

737. 1989 Del. Ch. LEXIS 141, 1989 WL 125190 (Del. Ch. Oct. 18, 1989).

738. 1989 Del. Ch. LEXIS 141, at *19-20, 1989 WL 125190, at *6.

739. 16 Del. J. Corp. L. 361 (Del. Ch. Nov. 21, 1989).

740. *Id.* at 373-74.

741. [1990-1991 Transfer Binder] Fed. Sec. L. Rep. (CCH) ¶ 95,664 (Del. Ch. Oct. 9, 1990).

742. *Id.* at 98,115.

743. [1990-1991 Transfer Binder] Fed. Sec. L. Rep. (CCH) ¶ 95,815 (Del. Ch. Jan. 29, 1991).

744. *Id.* at 98,916-17.

- *Kells-Murphy v. McNiff*[745] (excusing demand where corporation, Applied Data, Inc. ("ADI"), sold substantially all of its operating assets and business and approximately 38 percent of the sale amount was paid to ADI's controlling shareholder, Robert J. McNiff, rather than to ADI, (1) in exchange for an agreement by McNiff not to compete with ADI and to provide consulting services, and (2) as an incentive payment based upon the achievement of certain income levels in the future; plaintiff alleged that each of these agreements "was a pretext or sham"; the court held that a reasonable doubt was pleaded with respect to the independence of ADI's directors other than McNiff because shortly before the challenged transaction the directors (1) voted to award McNiff a stock bonus for no consideration, and (2) permitted McNiff to allow ADI's option to renew a favorable building lease to lapse, purchase the building himself, lease less space to ADI that ADI previously rented in the building for the same rent ADI previously paid, and rent the remaining space to a third party, thus depriving ADI of the opportunity to rent that space for its own benefit).[746]

- *Leslie v. Telephonics Office Technologies, Inc.*[747] (excusing demand where plaintiffs "alleged that *all . . .* directors benefitted financially from the non-competition agreements allegedly negotiated as part of the asset sale");[748]

- *Yaw v. Talley*[749] (excusing demand where plaintiff alleged "overcompensation, expense account abuse and usurpation of corporate opportunity" that benefitted a

---

745. 17 Del. J. Corp. L. 632 (Del. Ch. July 12, 1991).
746. *Id.* at 634-37.
747. 19 Del. J. Corp. L. 1237 (Del. Ch. Dec. 30, 1993).
748. *Id.* at 1255.
749. 1994 Del. Ch. LEXIS 35, 1994 WL 89019 (Del. Ch. Mar. 2, 1994).

majority of the corporation's directors; demand was not
excused with respect to a claim for conversion of corporate funds by one director "with the complicity of the
board of directors" because no supporting facts were
pleaded in support of that claim);[750]

- *Kahn v. Tremont Corp.*[751] (excusing demand with
  respect to a transaction where all of the entities
  involved in the transaction were controlled by the same
  controlling shareholder, five of the corporation's eight
  directors were directors or officers of other entities
  involved in the transaction, and the remaining three
  directors each had "a history of personally beneficial
  affiliation" with entities and efforts controlled by the
  controlling shareholder);[752]

- *Steiner v. Meyerson*[753] (excusing demand with respect
  to a transaction between the corporation and the corporation's chairman and chief executive officer where a
  five member board included this individual, the corporation's chief financial officer, and an outside director
  who was "a partner at a small law firm bringing in
  close to $1 million in revenues" annually from the cor-
  poration; and excusing demand with respect to claims
  challenging outside director compensation where the
  five member board that approved this compensation
  included the three outside directors who would receive
  the compensation);[754]

---

750. 1994 Del. Ch. LEXIS 35, at *27-32, 1994 WL 89019, at *9-
10.

751. 1994 Del. Ch. LEXIS 41, 1994 WL 162613 (Del. Ch. Apr.
21, 1994), *subsequent proceedings*, 1996 Del. Ch. LEXIS 40, 1996 WL
145452 (Del. Ch. Mar. 21, 1996), *rev'd*, 694 A.2d 422 (Del. 1997).

752. 1994 Del. Ch. LEXIS 41, at *9-10, 12-19, 1994 WL 162613,
at *2, 3-5.

753. [1995 Transfer Binder] Fed. Sec. L. Rep. (CCH) ¶ 98,857
(Del. Ch. July 18, 1995).

754. *Id.* at 93,152.

- *Friedman v. Beningson*[755] (excusing demand with respect to a transaction between the corporation and a 36 percent shareholder who served as the corporation's chairman, chief executive officer and president and a 25% owner of the corporation's principal customer, where a three member board included this individual and a director who received $48,000 a year in consulting fees from the corporation);[756]

- *In re Fuqua Industries, Inc. Shareholder Litigation*[757] (excusing demand where five members of a six person board allegedly entered into corporate transactions "motivated solely" by a "desire to secure their positions in office");[758]

- *Noerr v. Greenwood*[759] (excusing demand where four of a corporation's nine directors were beneficiaries of one stock option plan for non-employee directors and at least one of the corporation's remaining directors was a beneficiary of a "nearly identical" stock option plan for employees, and the two plans were presented to the board at the same meeting and to shareholders in the same proxy solicitation, and the complaint could "fairly be read to allege that both Plans were part of a unified scheme to provide all board members with incentive options");[760] and

---

755. 21 Del. J. Corp. L. 659 (Del. Ch. Dec. 4, 1995), *appeal refused*, 676 A.2d 900 (unreported opinion, text available at 1996 Del. LEXIS 11 and 1996 WL 33704) (Del. Jan. 10, 1996).

756. *Id.* at 666-67.

757. 1997 Del. Ch. LEXIS 72, 1997 WL 257460 (Del. Ch. May 17, 1997).

758. 1997 Del. Ch. LEXIS 72, at *56-57, 1997 WL 257460, at *15.

759. 1997 Del. Ch. LEXIS 121, 1997 WL 419633 (Del. Ch. July 16, 1997).

760. 1997 Del. Ch. LEXIS 121, at *32-36, 1997 WL 419633 at *9-10.

- *International Equity Capital Growth Fund, L.P. v. Clegg*[761] (excusing demand in case involving transactions between the corporation and C. Stephen Clegg, a 56 percent shareholder and the corporation's chairman and chief executive officer, and who on three specified occasions had used his "power to designate and to remove" board members "for the purposes of removing directors who had exercised independent judgment," and where a majority of the board included (1) Clegg, (2) John Klikus, a corporate employee named to the board to replace a "long-standing independent board member" Clegg had removed, and (3) Jacob Pollack, who had benefited from other transactions entered into by the corporation and that were challenged in the litigation—"a clear pattern of mutual advantage" between Clegg and Pollack, the court stated—and who was the chief executive officer of another corporation, whose compensation committee included Clegg;[762] excusing demand with respect to transaction entered into by the corporation and Pollack, based upon similar reasoning;[763] and also excusing demand with respect to transactions between an 80 percent owned subsidiary of the corporation and Clegg, where a majority of the subsidiary's board included (1) Clegg, (2) Pollack, and (3) James M. Gillespie, an employee of the subsidiary;[764] demand was not excused with respect to a claim arising out of the sale of the subsidiary's stock to the public because "plaintiffs have not alleged any facts suggesting this transaction was an interested one or that the board was in any way unable to review this particular action independently").[765]

---

761. 23 Del. J. Corp. L. 259 (Del. Ch. Apr. 21, 1997).
762. *Id.* at 267-68, 270.
763. *Id.* at 272.
764. *Id.*
765. *Id.* at 277.

Decisions involving defensive conduct by directors and transactions involving corporate control provide another example of cases where demand may be excused. As discussed in Chapter III,[766] Delaware courts apply enhanced judicial scrutiny to defensive conduct by directors pursuant to the doctrine first announced in *Unocal Corp. v. Mesa Petroleum Co.*[767] In this context, directors are accorded the presumption of the business judgment rule only after they carry an initial two part burden requiring that the directors demonstrate (1) that they had "reasonable grounds for believing that a danger to corporate policy and effectiveness existed," and (2) that the defensive measure decided upon was "reasonable in relation to the threat posed."[768] The Delaware Supreme Court's decision in *In re Santa Fe Pacific Corp. Shareholder Litigation*[769] states that the enhanced judicial scrutiny provided for by the *Unocal* doctrine "will usually not be satisfied by resting on a defense motion merely attacking the pleadings."[770] Thus, the court concluded, cases such as *Santa Fe* illustrate the difficulty of expeditiously dispensing with claims seeking judicial scrutiny at the pleading stage where the complaint is not completely conclusory."[771]

The Court of Chancery in *Wells Fargo & Co. v. First Interstate Bancorp*[772] applied this principle to excuse demand. The court stated that "factual allegations which, if true, are sufficient to shift the burden to defendants to meet the 'enhanced business judgment' test of *Unocal* are similarly sufficient to raise a reasonable doubt concerning the board's ability to make a binding business judgment."[773] There is no difference, the court explained, between a business judgment by the board in a case such as *Wells Fargo* to resist an acquisition proposal and "the hypothetical judgment that this board would make if asked to institute this law

---

766. *See* Chapter III, Section A 2 a.

767. 493 A.2d 946 (Del. 1985).

768. *Id.* at 955.

769. 669 A.2d 59 (Del. 1995).

770. *Id.* at 72.

771. *Id.*

772. 21 Del. J. Corp. L. 818 (Del. Ch. Jan. 18, 1996).

773. *Id.* at 832.

suit."[774] The Court of Chancery followed *Wells Fargo* in *In re Gaylord Container Corp. Shareholders Litigation*,[775] a case holding that demand was excused because a board's adoption of a shareholder rights plan was "subject to enhanced scrutiny and the circumstances alleged in the complaint create an inference of improper purpose."[776] The Court of Chancery distinguished *Wells Fargo* in *Gagliardi v. TriFoods International, Inc.*[777] According to the court in *TriFoods*, "the reasoning employed in *Wells Fargo* in order to excuse pre-suit demand" does not apply where a shareholder alleges in a "general conclusory" manner that a board "has exercised otherwise permissible business discretion in bad faith in order to entrench itself" and "there are no allegations concerning a specific transaction that would threaten board incumbency."[778]

Pre-*Santa Fe*, *Wells Fargo*, and *Gaylord* Court of Chancery decisions also illustrate examples of cases where demand has been excused by non-conclusory allegations that directors have acted to entrench themselves in office.

In *Moran v. Household International, Inc.*,[779] for example, demand was excused on the ground that the plaintiffs in the case pleaded particularized facts alleging that a poison pill shareholder rights plan "deters *all* hostile takeover attempts through its limitation on alienability of shares and the exercise of proxy rights" and "sufficiently pleads a primary purpose to retain control, and thus casts a reasonable doubt as to the disinterestedness and independence of the board."[780] Demand also was excused in *Edelman v. Phillips Petroleum Co.*,[781] where the court found that particular-

---

774. *Id.*

775. 22 Del. J. Corp. L. 1207 (Del. Ch. Dec. 19, 1996).

776. *Id.* at 1214.

777. 683 A.2d 1049 (Del. Ch. 1996) (published in part, complete text available at 1996 Del. Ch. LEXIS 87 and 1996 WL 422330).

778. *Id.* at 1055.

779. 490 A.2d 1059 (Del. Ch.), *aff'd on other grounds*, 500 A.2d 1346 (Del. 1985).

780. *Id.* at 1071; *see also* Chapter III, Section G 1 a (discussing *Household* decision).

781. 10 Del. J. Corp. L. 835 (Del. Ch. Feb. 12, 1985).

ized allegations had been pleaded regarding the board's adoption of an employee stock ownership plan as a means of ensuring control.[782] The court added that "given the commitment of Phillips management to use its best efforts to secure approval" of a recapitalization plan that included the challenged employee stock ownership plan "and the time constraints involved, requiring demand as a preamble to enjoining a shareholder's meeting at which ratification is sought would be a meaningless deferral to the demand rule."[783]

Likewise, in *L A Partners, L.P. v. Allegis Corp.*,[784] demand was excused due to allegations stating a primary purpose by the directors of Allegis Corporation to retain control, including (1) the adoption by Allegis of a poison pill rights plan that the board believed "rendered the company invulnerable to any takeover," (2) following an employee proposal to acquire Allegis, quick approval and implementation by Allegis of a note agreement placing notes convertible into 15 percent of the corporation's stock in the hands of a third party, Boeing Company, in exchange for cash Allegis did not need, (3) a decision by Allegis to alter product acquisition plans in order to obtain Boeing's consent to the note agreement, (4) obtaining an agreement by Boeing not to execute a written consent on behalf of anyone seeking control of Allegis, (5) a request by Allegis to Boeing, following the announcement of the start of a consent solicitation seeking to replace a majority of the Allegis board, to exercise its conversion rights in order to oppose the solicitation, and (6) upon Boeing's refusal, a proposal by Allegis of a recapitalization plan pursuant to which Allegis would incur $3 billion in debt in violation of restrictive covenants contained in the notes.[785]

The same result was reached in *In re Chrysler Corp. Shareholders Litigation*.[786] This case involved an allegation that

---

782. *Id.* at 842.
783. *Id.*
784. [1987-1988 Transfer Binder] Fed. Sec. L. Rep. (CCH) ¶ 93,505 (Del. Ch. Oct. 23, 1987).
785. *Id.* at 97,246-48, 97,250.
786. [1992 Transfer Binder] Fed. Sec. L. Rep. (CCH) ¶ 96,996 (Del. Ch. July 27, 1992).

Chrysler's board reduced the trigger threshold in a poison pill rights plan from 20 percent to 10 percent in response to the purchase of Chrysler shares by "a 'passive investor'" who, according to plaintiffs, "constituted no threat to Chrysler or its shareholders."[787] The plaintiffs in the case also alleged that the rights plan would be triggered "even if a group or combination of shareholders (as distinguished from a single shareholder) collectively crossed the 10% threshold."[788] These pleaded facts, the court held, "create, in my view, a reasonable doubt that the board took this action solely or primarily for entrenchment purposes."[789] These pleaded facts, the court also held, "rebut the defendants' assertion that the directors' defensive response is as easily explained by a valid corporate purpose (to protect shareholders from the perceived deleterious threat of a takeover . . . ) as by an improper motive (entrenchment)."[790]

Another decision excusing demand on this basis is *Chrysogelos v. London*.[791] The *Abajian* case involved a poison pill rights plan, golden parachute severance agreements, certificate amendments restricting shareholder votes, and the use of corporate funds to place shares in friendly hands at a cost exceeding the corporation's net earnings for an entire year, all allegedly to entrench directors.[792] The court in *Abajian v. Kennedy*[793] also excused demand. This case involved an issuance of stock carrying 15 percent of the corporation's voting power, which would increase to 19 percent following a self-tender offer.[794] The recipient of this stock had agreed not to sell the stock without the corporation's consent and not "to act, alone or in concert with others, to seek to affect or influence the control of management or the Board of Directors of

---

787. *Id*. at 94,350.

788. *Id*.

789. *Id*.

790. *Id*. at 94,350-51.

791. 18 Del. J. Corp. L. 237 (Del. Ch. Mar. 25, 1992).

792. *Id*. at 251-54.

793. 18 Del. J. Corp. L. 179 (Del. Ch. Jan. 17, 1992).

794. *Id*. at 182-84.

the Company."[795] The court concluded that "at this stage of the proceeding it cannot be said that there is no reasonable likelihood that plaintiffs could prove a case entitling them to relief. Put differently, these circumstances are sufficient, in context, to require me to conclude at this pleading stage that a reasonable doubt exists that the directors of Alaska Air will qualify for the protection of the business judgment rule."[796] Demand therefore was not required.[797]

Demand also has been excused in cases where directors have accumulated substantial voting rights as a result of the transactions challenged in those cases. An example is *Good v. Texaco, Inc.*[798] *Texaco* involved a board faced with an unwanted shareholder holding 25 million shares, or 9.7 percent, of the corporation's outstanding common stock. The board determined to approve a repurchase by the corporation of 13 million of the shareholder's 25 million common shares at a price of $50 per share, approximately 12 percent above the stock's market price at the time (and a more substantial premium over the stock's market price prior to disclosure of the shareholder's position in the company). The board also determined to approve an issuance of preferred stock to the shareholder in exchange for the shareholder's remaining 12 million shares of the corporation's common stock. Each share of the preferred stock had a value of $50 per share and was to be voted in accordance with the board's direction. As a result of the transaction, the directors would have the right to control the vote of approximately 5 percent of the corporation's outstanding shares.[799] Shareholders were scheduled to vote at the corporation's next annual meeting upon certificate of incorporation amendments designed to discourage future accumulations of substantial stock positions in the corporation. Pursuant to these amendments, an 80 percent supermajority shareholder vote would be required to approve business combinations not approved by the corporation's board, to remove direc-

---

795. *Id.* at 183-84.
796. *Id.* at 190-91.
797. *Id.* at 191.
798. 9 Del. J. Corp. L. 461 (Del. Ch. May 14, 1984).
799. *Id.* at 467.

tors, or to repeal or alter these certificate amendments.[800] Excusing demand, the court explained that "[t]he interestedness charged to the directors is that they have benefited personally from the transaction complained of by acquiring at corporate expense the right to control the vote of corporate shares which they do not own."[801]

*Seibert v. Harper & Row, Publishers, Inc.*[802] involved a repurchase of over 30 percent of the corporation's shares and transfer of the repurchased shares to two employee benefit plans, which would vote the shares at the direction of the board except for the approximately 3 percent of the shares that were attributable to employees whose benefits were vested.[803] Citing *Texaco*, the court held that demand was excused because the board had gained voting control over more than 30 percent of the corporation's shares.[804] The court reached this result notwithstanding the absence of any allegation that non-management directors, who constituted a majority of the board, obtained any monetary benefit from their positions as directors or from the transaction and notwithstanding the fact that the board was required to vote its newly acquired shares as fiduciaries.[805]

*Texaco* and *Harper & Row* were distinguished in *L A Partners, L.P. v. Allegis Corp.*,[806] a case holding that allegations that a transaction placed notes convertible into 15 percent of Allegis Company's voting stock in the hands of The Boeing Company, which had agreed not to execute a written consent on behalf of anyone seeking control of Allegis, were insufficient to establish interestedness. The court explained that Boeing had no obligation to convert the notes, and even if Boeing did convert the notes Boeing

---

800. *Id.* at 468.
801. *Id.* at 469.
802. 10 Del. J. Corp. L. 645 (Del. Ch. Dec. 5, 1984).
803. *Id.* at 649-50, 652-54.
804. *Id.* at 652-53.
805. *Id.* at 654.
806. [1987-1988 Transfer Binder] Fed. Sec. L. Rep. (CCH) ¶ 93,505 (Del. Ch. Oct. 23, 1987).

could vote to remove directors at a shareholder meeting.[807] As discussed earlier in this section, however, demand was excused on other grounds in *L A Partners*.[808] *Texaco* and *Harper & Row* also were distinguished in *Spillyards v. Abboud*,[809] an Illinois decision construing Delaware law. In *Spillyards*, an 18.3 percent block of a corporation's stock was sold to a third party required by contract to vote the shares in favor of the nominees of the corporation's incumbent directors.[810] The court pointed to "the absence of any allegations of takeover threats as a motivating force for the directors' actions" and stated that "plaintiffs' own factual allegations show motives other than entrenchment" as reasons for defendants' approval of the challenged transaction.[811] These motives included "the need to 'counteract the huge losses in net worth and the resulting precarious position'" of the corporation.[812] The court also pointed to the fact that the transaction had been approved by a special committee of the board consisting of three outside directors acting with the advice of financial advisors and outside legal counsel.[813]

Demand also may be excused pursuant to *Aronson*'s second prong in "extreme cases in which despite the appearance of independence and disinterest a decision is so extreme or curious as to itself raise a legitimate ground to justify further inquiry and judicial review."[814] The test "is necessarily high, similar to the legal test for waste"[815]—i.e., that the corporation has entered into a transaction in which "what the corporation has received is so inadequate

---

807. *Id*. at 97,247, 97,248-49.

808. *Id*. at 97,249-50.

809. 662 N.E.2d 1358 (Ill. App. Ct. 1996).

810. *Id*. at 1362.

811. *Id*. at 1369.

812. *Id*.

813. *Id*. at 1367-69.

814. *Kahn v. Tremont Corp.*, 1994 Del. Ch. LEXIS 41, at *21, 1994 WL 162613, at *6 (Del. Ch. Apr. 21, 1994), *subsequent proceedings*, 1996 Del. Ch. LEXIS 40, 1996 WL 145452 (Del. Ch. Mar. 21, 1996), *rev'd on other grounds*, 694 A.2d 422 (Del. 1997).

815. *Id*.

in value that no person of ordinary, sound business judgment would deem it worth that which the corporation has paid."[816]

In *Kahn v. Tremont*,[817] for example, the Delaware Court of Chancery held that sufficient questions were raised by the plaintiff's pleading in that case to warrant denying a motion to dismiss an action challenging a transaction involving two corporations, Tremont Corporation and NL Industries, Inc., under the control of a common controlling shareholder. Tremont, which was in business only as an operating company, purchased a 15 percent block of stock in NL Industries as an investment at a "relatively high price," despite the "limited liquidity of the shares" and despite a recent announcement of discouraging news by NL: "that worldwide supply of the company's principal product, titanium dioxide, exceeded demand; and that the sale of titanium dioxide pigments, the staple of one of NL Industries' subsidiaries, were expected to drop."[818] These alleged facts, the court held, were sufficient to excuse demand.[819]

The same result was reached in *Friedman v. Beningson*,[820] a case involving a transaction between a corporation and a 36 percent shareholder who served as the corporation's chairman, chief executive officer and president, a 25% owner of the corporation's principal customer.[821] The corporation's three member board

---

816. *Grobow v. Perot*, 539 A.2d 180, 189 (Del. 1988) (quoting *Saxe v. Brady*, 184 A.2d 602, 610 (Del. Ch. 1962)); *see also* Chapter I, Section F (discussing waste).

817. 1994 Del. Ch. LEXIS 41, 1994 WL 162613 (Del. Ch. Apr. 21, 1994), *subsequent proceedings*, 1996 Del. Ch. LEXIS 40, 1996 WL 145452 (Del. Ch. Mar. 21, 1996), *rev'd on other grounds*, 694 A.2d 422 (Del. 1997).

818. 1994 Del. Ch. LEXIS 41, at *20-22, 1994 WL 162613, at *5-6.

819. 1994 Del. Ch. LEXIS 41, at *6, 21, 1994 WL 162613, at *2, 6; *see also* Chapter II, Section B 3 i (discussing *Tremont* litigation).

820. 21 Del. J. Corp. L. 659 (Del. Ch. Dec. 4, 1995), *appeal refused*, 676 A.2d 900 (unreported opinion, text available at 1996 Del. LEXIS 11 and 1996 WL 33704) (Del. Jan. 10, 1996).

821. *Id*. at 662-64.

included the chairman and a director who received $48,000 a year in consulting fees from the corporation.[822] The court pointed to the nature of the alleged wrongdoing: (1) the board's approval of interest-free loans to the chairman in an amount equal to approximately 50% of the corporation's total revenues, 100% of pre-tax income and more than 100% of net income, which the board chairman used to buy the corporation's stock, the value of which he then allegedly inflated by making unduly optimistic public statements, after which he sold the stock, which later dropped by more than 50% in value following an announcement that earnings would significantly vary from previously announced estimates, and (2) the board's agreement to settle a class action suit arising out of these events solely with a payment of corporate assets.[823] These allegations, the court stated, supported the conclusion that the complaint "states facts that raise a reasonable doubt that the board . . . is in a position to exercise a valid business judgment on the question whether the claims asserted should be litigated."[824]

Such a showing also has been made in cases where plaintiffs plead facts that, if proven, would constitute gross negligence and thus preclude business judgment rule protection of the challenged conduct or transaction.[825] *Tomczak v. Morton Thiokol, Inc.*,[826] for example, involved Morton Thiokol's sale of one of its divisions to Dow Chemical Company in exchange for cash, 1.4 million Morton Thiokol shares that Dow had accumulated, and a promise by Dow not to purchase any Morton Thiokol stock for 10 years.[827] The plaintiffs alleged that (1) only two of Morton Thiokol's twelve directors had "any real notice" of the proposed transaction prior to the board meeting at which the transaction was discussed, (2) Morton Thiokol's remaining ten directors, all of whom were outside directors, "had only two short oral presentations to guide them,"

---

822. *Id.* at 666-67.

823. *Id.* at 662-64, 667.

824. *Id.* at 667.

825. *See* Chapter I, Section D 3 and Chapter II, Section A 4 a (both discussing gross negligence standard).

826. 12 Del. J. Corp. L. 381 (Del. Ch. May 7, 1986).

827. *Id.* at 383.

(3) "no one on the Board questioned, nor were they apprised of," the basis of an investment banker's valuation of the assets being sold, (4) "the directors ignored obvious opportunities to obtain a higher price," and (5) there was no "emergency" requiring an immediate decision.[828] The court stated that plaintiffs "paint a picture very similar"[829] to the gross negligence found in *Smith v. Van Gorkom*[830]—a decision discussed in Chapter II[831]—and held that these allegations, "if true, preclude the protection from judicial scrutiny afforded by the business judgment rule."[832]

A later decision in the case, however, granted summary judgment in favor of the directors. The court noted that its prior decision refused to dismiss plaintiffs' complaint "because the '[p]laintiffs' allegations paint[ed] a picture very similar to that found in *Smith v. Van Gorkom*; and supported 'a claim of violation of fiduciary duty.'"[833] The court stated that "[a]t that stage of the proceedings, . . . this Court was bound to accept the allegations of the plaintiffs' Amended Complaint as being true. At the present stage, however, after over three years of discovery, it is clear that the plaintiffs have failed to adduce any facts to support their allegations of gross negligence."[834]

The same result was reached in *Kahn v. Roberts*,[835] where a plaintiff alleged that (1) the only action taken by a special committee appointed to negotiate a repurchase of shares from a corporate director was "a single telephonic meeting" with "no documents . . . distributed before or during this meeting," and (2) the corporation's board approved the transaction two days later "without the benefit of a recommendation from the special committee, without materials

---

828. *Id.* at 386.

829. *Id.*

830. 488 A.2d 858 (Del. 1985).

831. *See* Chapter II, Section A 4 c.

832. 12 Del. J. Corp. L. at 386.

833. *Tomczak v. Morton Thiokol, Inc.*, [1990 Transfer Binder] Fed. Sec. L. Rep. (CCH) ¶ 95,327, at 96,585 (Del. Ch. Apr. 5, 1990).

834. *Id.*

835. [1993-1994 Transfer Binder] Fed. Sec. L. Rep. (CCH) ¶ 98,201 (Del. Ch. Feb. 28, 1994).

having been distributed prior to or during the meeting, and without discussing alternatives to the repurchase."[836] As in *Morton Thiokol*, the court later granted summary judgment in favor of the directors.[837] The court concluded that "the Board made its decision in the best interest of the corporation, satisfying its responsibility to exercise due care."[838] The court found "no evidence from which any reasonable person could infer Defendants were grossly negligent in approving the repurchase."[839]

Demand also was excused in *In re NVF Co. Litigation*,[840] where plaintiffs' complaint contained "no evidence" that directors "did anything but vote for the challenged transaction" in a 10 minute telephone meeting, during which the directors received no materials or outside evaluation concerning the transaction.[841] In *Yaw v. Talley*,[842] similarly, demand was excused based upon allegations that (1) a board's failure to pay the corporation's debts in a timely manner gave rise to a potential claim (and lawsuit) against the corporation, and (2) the board's failure to file audited statements with the corporation's bank was a breach of the corporation's credit agreement with that bank.[843] "Those facts, as pleaded in this complaint," the court stated, "create a reasonable doubt that those board decisions were the products of a valid exercise of business judgment."[844]

A plaintiff pleading demand futility due to an alleged lack of due care must allege particularized facts demonstrating a reasonable doubt regarding the care exercised by a *majority*—not just some—of

---

836. *Id.* at 99,413.

837. *See Kahn v. Roberts*, 21 Del. J. Corp. L. 674 (Del. Ch. Dec. 6, 1995), *aff'd*, 679 A.2d 460, 466 (Del. 1996).

838. *Id.* at 687.

839. *Id.* at 688.

840. 16 Del. J. Corp. L. 361 (Del. Ch. Nov. 21, 1989).

841. *Id.* at 371, 374-75.

842. 1994 Del. Ch. LEXIS 35, 1994 WL 89019 (Del. Ch. Mar. 2, 1994).

843. 1994 Del. Ch. LEXIS 35, at *29, 1994 WL 89019, at *9.

844. *Id.*

the corporation's directors. Thus in *Levine v. Smith*,[845] the Delaware Supreme Court held that demand was required where plaintiffs' lack of due care allegations "implicated, at most, only two of GM's fourteen outside directors, thereby leaving at least twelve of the twenty-one directors . . . independent and 'capable of impartially considering a demand.'"[846] "[G]eneralized allegations" that do not mention any specific instances of how or in what manner directors failed to inform themselves "fail to rise to instances of gross negligence" or "to rebut the presumption that the business judgment rule attaches to the challenged transaction."[847] Conclusory allegations that "amount at best to simple negligence" are insufficient to excuse demand.[848]

Demand also is excused where particularized facts are alleged that, if proven, would constitute waste—i.e., as noted above, that the corporation has entered into a transaction in which "what the corporation has received is so inadequate in value that no person of ordinary, sound business judgment would deem it worth that which the corporation has paid."[849]

For example, in *Lewis v. Hett*,[850] demand was excused where the plaintiff alleged an absence of consideration for severance payments equal to $180,000 per year for five years and then $35,000 per year for life to a 49 year old officer who had earned approximately $285,000 per year and who "had no employment contract with the company and held his office at the pleasure of the

---

845. 591 A.2d 194 (Del. 1991).

846. *Id.* at 206.

847. *Litman v. Prudential-Bache Properties, Inc.*, [1992-1993 Transfer Binder] Fed. Sec. L. Rep. (CCH) ¶ 97,313, at 95,585 (Del. Ch. Jan. 4, 1993).

848. *In re Chrysler Corp. Shareholders Litig.*, [1992 Transfer Binder] Fed. Sec. L. Rep. (CCH) ¶ 96,996, at 94,351 (Del. Ch. July 27, 1992).

849. *Grobow v. Perot*, 539 A.2d 180, 189 (Del. 1988) (quoting *Saxe v. Brady*, 184 A.2d 602, 610 (Del. Ch. 1962)); *see* Chapter I, Section F (discussing waste).

850. 10 Del. J. Corp. L. 240 (Del. Ch. Sept. 4, 1984).

Board."[851] The court held that these facts created "a reasonable doubt that the severance payments constitute a gift or waste of corporate assets" and thus that the "challenged transaction was . . . the product of a valid exercise of business judgment."[852] Similarly, demand was excused in *Stein v. Orloff*,[853] a case involving an allegation that a board reduced the exercise price of stock options, 75 percent of which were held by members of the board, without any consideration.[854] The court held that this constituted "a sufficient allegation of facts to state a claim for waste and therefore to create a reasonable doubt that the transaction was the result of a valid exercise of business judgment."[855]

*Avacus Partners, L.P. v. Brian*[856] is another case where demand was excused based upon a complaint that "alleged a litigable case of waste."[857] The alleged facts in this case included "specific facts that quantify the alleged inadequacy of the consideration" paid by a corporation in two transactions in which the corporation allegedly paid over 10 times the fair market value for securities of one company, and over 100 times the price paid a year earlier for control of a second company[858]—payments a later court labeled "incredibly disproportionate."[859] Particularized allegations of waste also were held sufficient to excuse demand in *Emerald Partners v. Berlin*,[860] a case where a shareholder alleged that corporate assets were pledged in return for no consideration in

---

851. *Id.* at 242.
852. *Id.* at 246 (quoting *Aronson*, 473 A.2d at 814).
853. 11 Del. J. Corp. L. 312 (Del. Ch. May 30, 1985), *appeal refused*, 504 A.2d 572 (unpublished opinion, text available at 1986 Del. LEXIS 1024 and 1986 WL 16298) (Del. Jan. 28, 1986).
854. *Id.* at 319.
855. *Id.*
856. [1991 Transfer Binder] Fed. Sec. L. Rep. (CCH) ¶ 96,232 (Del. Ch. Oct. 24, 1990).
857. *Id.* at 91,215.
858. *Id.*
859. *Benerofe v. Cha*, 1996 Del. Ch. LEXIS 115, at *25, 1996 WL 535405, at *9 (Del. Ch. Sept. 12, 1996).
860. 19 Del. J. Corp. L. 1182 (Del. Ch. Dec. 23, 1993).

order to secure personal loans owed by the corporation's chief executive officer and 52.4 percent shareholder.[861]

In *Rothenberg v. Santa Fe Pacific Corp.*,[862] a shareholder alleged that directors "offered enhanced terms" under a revised exchange offer to shareholders "who previously had agreed to tender their debentures in accordance with the terms of a less generous offer."[863] The shareholder alleged that "there was no rational business reason for the directors to do that, because the directors could (and should) have determined to close the original offer and, thereafter, to commence a new offer on the revised terms."[864] "[B]y not doing that," the shareholder alleged, "the directors wasted the corporation's equity by distributing approximately 1.15 million shares of Santa Fe common stock for no consideration."[865] The court noted that the directors' motion to dismiss pointed to two business purposes that, according to the directors, justified the challenged transaction: (1) to avoid litigation, and (2) "to ensure that Santa Fe's larger plan to divest . . . two subsidiaries would proceed promptly, and to promote that goal, by lowering the exchange value to induce the debenture holders to tender the requisite number of debentures."[866] The court refused to consider these "explanations of director business judgment" because they were not pleaded in plaintiff's complaint.[867] The court acknowledged that it "seems far-fetched to suppose that the board of a public company such as Santa Fe would make a decision of this kind in a transaction of this magnitude without any rational business purpose."[868] The court concluded, however, that "at this early procedural stage" the court was required to accept plaintiff's

---

861. *Id.* at 1192-93.
862. 21 Del. J. Corp. L. 309 (Del. Ch. Sept. 5, 1995).
863. *Id.* at 318
864. *Id.*
865. *Id.*
866. *Id.* at 318-19.
867. *Id.* at 319.
868. *Id.*

allegations.[869] The court stated that "[t]he facts that would serve to rebut" plaintiffs' allegations will have to be placed in the record in a proper way, after which they may then properly be considered."[870]

Additional examples of cases excusing demand where facts were alleged that, if true, would demonstrate waste include *Lewis v. Aronson*,[871] *In re NVF Co. Litigation*,[872] *Rosan v. Chicago Milwaukee Corp.*,[873] *Harris v. Carter*[874] and *Andreae v. Andreae*.[875]

Allegations of waste that are not accompanied by particularized facts supporting the claim of waste are insufficient to excuse demand. *Caruana v. Saligman*[876] illustrates this principle. This case involved a board that accepted a $178 million offer for one of its businesses rather than a $190 million offer.[877] The court explained that "[t]he $12 million difference (which amounts to less than 7% on the pre-tax basis) cannot be said to constitute waste."[878] To the contrary, the court held, this monetary difference "is insignificant, alone, and especially in light of factors not addressed by the complaint, i.e., timing, structure and certainty of financing, that could account for the board's acceptance of the lower offer."[879] The court stated that "the highest bid is not necessarily the best bid" and that the complaint left the court "ill-

---

869. *Id.*

870. *Id.*

871. 11 Del. J. Corp. L. 243, 252 (Del. Ch. May 1, 1985); *see also* Chapter IV, Section B 5 c (i) (discussing this decision).

872. 16 Del. J. Corp. L. 361, 375-76 (Del. Ch. Nov. 21, 1989).

873. 16 Del. J. Corp. L. 378, 392 (Del. Ch. Feb. 6, 1990).

874. 582 A.2d 222, 229 (Del. Ch. 1990).

875. [1991-1992 Transfer Binder] Fed. Sec. L. Rep. (CCH) ¶ 96,571, at 92,651 (Del. Ch. Mar. 3, 1992).

876. [1990-1991 Transfer Binder] Fed. Sec. L. Rep. (CCH) ¶ 95,889 (Del. Ch. Dec. 21, 1990).

877. *Id.* at 99,379.

878. *Id.*

879. *Id.* at 99,379-80.

equipped" to determine which of the two bids was the better bid.[880] For these reasons, the court concluded, "plaintiffs have not alleged facts sufficient to create a reasonable doubt" that the board "did not properly exercise its business judgment."[881]

The court in *Kahn v. Roberts*[882] likewise held that "the fact that the board bought the stock at a $4 premium"—at $40 per share instead of at the stock's $36 per share market price—"does not constitute a claim for corporate waste."[883] This $4 per share premium, the court stated, is not "so outrageous that no person of ordinary, sound business judgment would deem it worth what the corporation paid."[884]

The court in *Benerofe v. Cha*[885] similarly refused to excuse demand in a case alleging that the directors of Inorganic Coatings, Inc. ("ICI") committed waste by agreeing to sell zinc silicate coatings to Kun Sul Painting Industries Co., Ltd. ("KSP"), which owned over 59 percent of ICI's stock, for $7 per gallon.[886] This $7 per gallon price, the plaintiff alleged, was $10 per gallon less than ICI previously had sold this product to other purchasers and $16 to $21 less per gallon than the price at which KSP was reselling those products in Korea.[887]

"Weighing the facts alleged . . . against the strong presumption of the business judgment rule," the court reasoned, "those facts do not create a reasonable doubt that the Defendants wasted ICI's assets."[888] The court recognized that "the facts alleged do allow me to infer that KSP probably is making a substantial profit

---

880. *Id.* 99,380.

881. *Id.*

882. [1993-1994 Transfer Binder] Fed. Sec. L. Rep. (CCH) ¶ 98,201 (Del. Ch. Feb. 28, 1994).

883. *Id.* at 99,413.

884. *Id.*

885. 1996 Del. Ch. LEXIS 115, 1996 WL 535405 (Del. Ch. Sept. 12, 1996).

886. 1996 Del. Ch. LEXIS 115, at *4, 24, 1996 WL 535405, at *1, 8.

887. 1996 Del. Ch. LEXIS 115, at *24, 1996 WL 535405, at *8.

888. 1996 Del. Ch. LEXIS 115, at *25, 1996 WL 535405, at *9.

on the distribution arrangement," but "this inference does not necessarily lead me to conclude that the price KSP pays to ICI is so inadequate" that it constitutes waste.[889] The court stated that "one can certainly imagine several legitimate reasons that the Defendants might allow the transaction to go forward."[890] For example, the court observed, "perhaps KSP sells ICI's products in such a great quantity that ICI grants KSP a discount on its prices," and "perhaps ICI cannot distribute to the Korean market absent KSP's contacts so that comparing the price KSP pays to the price other third parties pay is unhelpful."[891] The court concluded: "Clearly, one cannot conclude based on the alleged facts that the exchange 'is so one-sided that no person of sound judgment could conclude that' the consideration is adequate. Since reasonable minds might disagree as to whether the exchange is wasteful, this Court cannot conclude that Plaintiffs have satisfied their burden . . . to raise a reasonable doubt that the Defendants exercised business judgment in allowing the exchange to proceed."[892]

Additional examples of cases rejecting waste allegations and refusing to excuse demand on this ground include *Grobow v. Perot*,[893] *Strougo v. Carroll*[894] and *In re Rexene Corp. Shareholders Litigation*.[895]

*d. Cases Explaining and Applying the Rales Standard.* As noted earlier in this Chapter,[896] the two-pronged test for deter-

---

889. 1996 Del. Ch. LEXIS 115, at *25-26, 1996 WL 535405, at *9.

890. 1996 Del. Ch. LEXIS 115, at *26, 1996 WL 535405, at *9.

891. *Id.*

892. 1996 Del. Ch. LEXIS 115, at *26-27, 1996 WL 535405, at *9 (citations omitted).

893. 539 A.2d 180, 189-91 (Del. 1988).

894. [1990-1991 Transfer Binder] Fed. Sec. L. Rep. (CCH) ¶ 95,815, at 98,917 (Del. Ch. Jan. 29, 1991).

895. [1991 Transfer Binder] Fed. Sec. L. Rep. (CCH) ¶ 96,010, at 90,058 (Del. Ch. May 8, 1991), *aff'd sub nom. Eichorn v. Rexene Corp.*, 604 A.2d 416 (unpublished opinion, text available at 1991 Del. LEXIS 333 and 1991 WL 210962) (Del. Oct. 10, 1991).

896. *See* Chapter IV, Section B 5 b.

mining demand futility established by the Delaware Supreme Court in *Aronson v. Lewis*[897] and its progeny—pursuant to which a shareholder plaintiff alleging that demand is excused must plead particularized facts that, if true, would "raise a reasonable doubt as to (i) director disinterest or independence or (ii) whether the directors exercised proper business judgment in approving the challenged transaction"[898]—focuses upon "a paradigm" including an "essential predicate": "the fact that a decision of the board of directors is being challenged in the derivative suit."[899]

Accordingly, the Delaware Supreme Court held in *Rales v. Blasband*,[900] "a court should not apply the *Aronson* test for demand futility where the board that would be considering the demand did not make a business decision which is being challenged in the derivative suit."[901] "Because this test requires an application of the business judgment rule to the conduct of the board, the test should not be applied when the transaction at issue was not the result of a conscious business decision made by the board that would be considering demand ( . . . the board in existence when the complaint is filed)."[902]

The court in *Rales* observed that "[t]his situation would arise in three principal scenarios."[903]

First, the court stated, this situation arises "where a business decision was made by the board of a company, but a majority of the directors making the decision have been replaced" between the time of the decision and the time of litigation.[904]

---

897. 473 A.2d 805 (Del. 1984).
898. *Grobow v. Perot*, 539 A.2d 180, 186 (Del. 1988).
899. *Rales v. Blasband*, 634 A.2d 927, 933 (Del. 1993).
900. 634 A.2d 927 (Del. 1993).
901. *Id.* at 933-34.
902. *In re Fuqua Indus., Inc. Shareholder Litig.*, 1997 Del. Ch. LEXIS 72, at *49, 1997 WL 257460, at *13 (Del. Ch. May 13, 1997).
903. 634 A.2d at 934.
904. *Id.*

Second, the court stated, this situation arises "where the subject of the derivative suit is not a business decision of the board."[905] For example, the court explained, where a shareholder "brings a derivative suit alleging that a third party breached a contract with the corporation, demand should not be excused simply because the subject matter of the suit—the third party's breach of contract—does not implicate the business judgment rule."[906] Similarly, the court continued, "where directors are sued derivatively because they have failed to do something (such as a failure to oversee subordinates), demand should not be excused automatically in the absence of allegations demonstrating why the board is incapable of considering a demand."[907] Indeed, the court stated, "requiring demand in such circumstances is consistent with the board's managerial prerogatives because it permits the board to have the opportunity to take action where it has not previously considered doing so."[908]

Third, the court concluded, this situation arises "where . . . the decision being challenged was made by the board of a different corporation," such as a parent or a subsidiary corporation.[909]

Under any of these circumstances, the court in *Rales* held, "it is appropriate . . . to examine whether the board that would be addressing the demand can impartially consider its merits without being influenced by improper considerations."[910] Thus, the court continued, a court deciding whether demand is futile under these circumstances "must determine whether or not the particularized factual allegations of a derivative stockholder complaint create a reasonable doubt that, as of the time the complaint is filed, the board of directors could have properly exercised its independent and disinterested business judgment in responding to a demand. If the derivative plaintiff satisfies this burden, then demand will be

---

905. *Id.*
906. *Id.* at 934 n.9.
907. *Id.*
908. *Id.*
909. *Id.* at 934.
910. *Id.*

excused as futile."[911] The "appropriate inquiry" is whether a complaint "raises a reasonable doubt regarding the ability of a majority of the Board to exercise properly its business judgment in a decision on a demand had one been made at the time th[e] action was filed."[912]

As the Delaware Court of Chancery explained in *In re Fuqua Industries, Inc. Shareholder Litigation*[913]:

> The appropriate test in any of these cases, therefore, is not an examination of whether the board has already demonstrated an inability to exercise business judgment with respect to the challenged transaction or an examination of whether the board approving the transaction is unable to exercise disinterested and independent judgment with respect to demand because, in any of these cases, there will have been no exercise of business judgment with respect to the transaction or the majority of the board approving the transaction will not be represented on the current board that would be considering demand. The appropriate test, therefore, is whether the board in existence at the time the complaint is filed is able to properly carry out its fiduciary duty to evaluate demand in a disinterested and independent fashion. In such unique circumstance, only this test recognizes that it is the fundamental right of the board to manage the corporation's affairs and that this right should not be trampled unless plaintiffs are able to show that the board has already failed in this regard or is otherwise so tainted as to lead to the conclusion that it is unable to act in the best interests of the corporation.[914]

---

911. *Id.*

912. *Id.* at 937.

913. 1997 Del. Ch. LEXIS 72, 1997 WL 257460 (Del. Ch. May 13, 1997).

914. 1997 Del. Ch. LEXIS 72, at *50-51, 1997 WL 257460, at *13; *see also Harris v. Carter*, 582 A.2d 222, 230 (Del. Ch. 1990) (the *Aronson* test involves the "commonly-occurring pattern" where "the board that approves 'the challenged transaction' and the board upon whom a demand could be made is one and the same"; where there is "a change in board control between the date of the challenged transaction and the date of suit," the appropriate inquiry is "not whether the board that approved

(continued...)

When a certificate of incorporation provision adopted with shareholder approval pursuant to a statute such as Section 102(b)(7) of the Delaware General Corporation Law exempts directors from liability,[915] "the risk of liability does not disable them from considering a demand fairly unless particularized pleading permits the court to conclude that there is a substantial likelihood that their conduct falls outside the exemption" from liability provided by the statute.[916] Demand accordingly may be excused on this ground alone.[917]

The decisions by the Third Circuit in *Blasband v. Rales*[918] and the Delaware Supreme Court in *Rales v. Blasband*[919] illustrate the principles underlying the *Rales* approach in the context of a double derivative action, where the demand requirement must be satisfied with respect both to the parent corporation's board and to the subsidiary corporation's board.[920] Both decisions came in a case alleging wrongdoing by Easco Hand Tools, Inc. Between the time of the alleged wrongdoing and the time the litigation was commenced, Easco was acquired by and became a subsidiary of Dana-

---

914. (...continued)
the challenged transaction was or was not interested in that transaction but whether the present board is or is not disabled from exercising its right and duty to control corporate litigation"); *Abajian v. Kennedy*, 18 Del. J. Corp. L. 179, 186 n.3 (Del. Ch. Jan. 17, 1992) (noting that the *Aronson* test focuses upon "the board *that approved the transaction* sought to be reviewed" rather than "the board in office *at the time the suit is initiated*," and that the *Aronson* test therefore is relevant only in the usual case where the board that approved the transaction sought to be reviewed is the same board that is in office at the time the suit is initiated).

915. *See* Chapter II, Section A 7 (discussing director protection statutes).

916. *In re Baxter Int'l, Inc. Shareholders Litig.*, 654 A.2d 1268, 1270 (Del. Ch. 1995).

917. *Id.*

918. 971 F.2d 1034 (3d Cir. 1992).

919. 634 A.2d 927 (Del. 1993).

920. 971 F.2d at 1050; 634 A.2d at 933-35; *see also* Chapter IV, Section A 9 (including additional citations).

her Corporation, and the litigation was commenced in the form of a double derivative action by a Danaher shareholder.[921]

The Third Circuit, ruling first, held that in a shareholder challenge to a transaction approved by a subsidiary's board before the subsidiary was acquired by the parent, demand futility "can be demonstrated, if at all," with respect to the subsidiary's board "under either prong" of *Aronson* but with respect to the parent's board "only under the first prong" of *Aronson*.[922] The court explained that the second prong of *Aronson* "is designed to assess whether the board that was responsible for the challenged transaction is entitled to the protections of the business judgment rule" and "clearly has no applicability" to any board that was not responsible for the transaction.[923]

Applying this rule, the Third Circuit concluded that the plaintiff in the case had not pleaded facts demonstrating that either the parent or the subsidiary board lacked disinterestedness and independence pursuant to the first prong of *Aronson*, and that the plaintiff had pleaded facts demonstrating that the subsidiary's board was incapable of responding to a demand pursuant to the second prong of *Aronson* as of the time of the challenged transaction but not as of the time that the litigation was commenced.[924] The court remanded the case in order to give the plaintiff an opportunity to plead, if he could, (1) interestedness or a lack of independence with respect to the parent board and (2) either (a) interestedness or a lack of independence with respect to the subsidiary board or (b) that the subsidiary board was incapable of responding to a demand under the second prong of *Aronson* because "a controlling group of Easco board members that sat on that board at the time of the challenged transactions continued to control the board at the time [plaintiff] filed his complaint."[925]

---

921. 971 F.2d at 1037-38; 634 A.2d at 930-31.
922. 971 F.2d at 1052.
923. *Id.*
924. *Id.* at 1052-55.
925. *Id.* at 1055.

Plaintiff amended his complaint, and the district court certified to the Delaware Supreme Court the question whether plaintiff had alleged facts sufficient to establish that demand upon the parent corporation was excused.[926] The Delaware Supreme Court, like the Third Circuit, held that in a double derivative litigation challenging action by the subsidiary before the subsidiary was acquired by the parent (1) the need for a demand upon the subsidiary board is determined pursuant to the *Aronson* test, and (2) the need for demand upon the parent board, which has not made a business judgment that is challenged in the derivative suit, is determined pursuant to the *Rales* test: i.e., whether plaintiff has pleaded particularized factual allegations that "create a reasonable doubt that, as of the time the complaint is filed, the board of directors could have properly exercised its independent and disinterested business judgment in responding to a demand."[927]

Applying this rule, the Delaware Supreme Court held that demand upon the parent board was excused (as stated above, the question whether demand upon the subsidiary board was excused had not been certified). The court reasoned that a majority (five of eight) of the directors on the parent board either were interested or lacked independence.

The court explained that three of the directors—(1) Steven M. Rales, the chairman of the parent corporation's board, (2) Mitchell P. Rales, the chairman of the parent corporation's executive committee (together, the "Rales brothers") and (3) Mortimer Caplin— were directors on the subsidiary corporation's board, and that the Third Circuit already had held that facts had been pleaded raising the reasonable doubt required by the second prong of the *Aronson* test concerning the conduct of these individuals as directors of the subsidiary corporation.[928] This determination, the Delaware Supreme Court stated, was binding upon the Supreme Court in the context of the certified question before the Supreme Court.[929]

---

926. 634 A.2d at 929-30.
927. *Id.* at 934.
928. *Id.* at 936.
929. *Id.*

Therefore, the court stated, "the potential for liability is not 'a mere threat' but instead may rise to 'a substantial likelihood.'"[930] Accordingly, the court continued, a decision by the parent board to bring suit against the subsidiary's directors "could have potentially significant financial consequences" for these directors.[931] "Common sense," the court thus concluded, "dictates that, in light of these consequences," these three directors "have a disqualifying financial interest that disables them from impartially considering a response to a demand."[932]

The court then explained that two additional directors lacked independence: (1) George Sherman, the president and chief executive officer of the parent corporation, which, as noted above, was controlled by the Rales brothers, and who earned $1 million per year in that position, and (2) Donald E. Ehrlich, the president of a bank that also was controlled by the Rales brothers, and who earned $300,000 per year in this position and who had two brothers who were vice presidents of the bank.[933] The court concluded that "[b]ecause of their alleged substantial financial interest in maintaining their employment positions" with corporations controlled by the Rales brothers, "there is a reasonable doubt that these two directors are able to consider impartially an action that is contrary to the interests of the Rales brothers."[934]

Thus, the court held:

[T]he appropriate inquiry is whether Blasband's amended complaint raises a reasonable doubt regarding the ability of a majority of the Board to exercise properly its business judgment in a decision on a demand had one been made at the time this action was filed. Based on the existence of a reasonable doubt that the Rales brothers and Caplin would be free of a financial interest in such a decision, and that Sherman and Ehrlich could act independently in light of their employment with entities affiliated with the Rales brothers, we con-

---

930. *Id.*
931. *Id.*
932. *Id.*
933. *Id.* at 936-37.
934. *Id.* at 937.

clude that the allegations of Blasband's amended complaint establish that DEMAND IS EXCUSED on the Board.[935]

Delaware Court of Chancery decisions applying the *Rales* standard to allegations that boards have failed to exercise appropriate oversight and prevent wrongdoing within the corporation include *In re Baxter International, Inc. Shareholder Litigation*[936] and *Seminaris v. Landa.*[937]

*In re Baxter International, Inc. Shareholders Litigation*[938] involved an alleged scheme by employees of Baxter International, Inc., a seller of medical supplies, pursuant to which Baxter systematically overcharged the Veterans Administration for products that Baxter had agreed to provide to the Veterans Administration at preferred prices. The practice continued after the Veterans Administration began an investigation and informed Baxter of the investigation and after Baxter had sent the Veterans Administration a letter stating that corrective measures had been taken.[939] Plaintiffs alleged that Baxter's directors breached their fiduciary duty to exercise reasonable care in the oversight and supervision of Baxter's business by "failing to prevent" Baxter employees from engaging in this wrongful conduct.[940] Plaintiff also alleged that Baxter's directors "thereby caused or permitted violations of federal rules and regulations."[941]

The court held that demand was not excused because the claim of director culpability was conclusory and did not include any pleading of "anything specific about the alleged scheme suggesting that the directors must have known of it."[942] The court relied upon the Delaware Supreme Court's decision in *Graham v. Allis-Chalmers Manufacturing Co.,*[943] a case where "the directors of a

---

935. *Id.*
936. 654 A.2d 1268 (Del. Ch. 1995).
937. 662 A.2d 1350 (Del. Ch. 1995).
938. 654 A.2d 1268 (Del. Ch. 1995).
939. *Id.* at 1268-69.
940. *Id.* at 1269.
941. *Id.*
942. *Id.* at 1271.
943. 188 A.2d 125 (Del. 1963).

large corporation were charged with failing to prevent employees from violating antitrust laws."[944] The court in *Allis-Chalmers* held that "directors are entitled to rely on the honesty and integrity of their subordinates until something occurs to put them on suspicion that something is wrong."[945] The court in *Allis-Chalmers* also held that "a director may not be liable for failure to prevent employee wrongdoing unless the director ignores 'obvious danger signs of employee wrongdoing.'"[946]

Applying this standard, the court stated that the plaintiffs in *Baxter* had "not pled with particularity that the directors ignored obvious danger signs of employee wrongdoing. Rather, plaintiffs' claim is premised on a presumption that employee wrongdoing would not occur if directors performed their duty properly. Plaintiffs' position is inconsistent with *Graham*. . . . [T]he complaint does not plead with particularity what obvious danger signs were ignored or what additional measures the directors should have taken."[947] Thus, the court concluded, this was not "a rare case where the circumstances are so egregious that there is a substantial likelihood of liability."[948] Demand therefore was not excused.[949]

*Seminaris v. Landa*[950] involved allegations that the directors of Fidelity Medical, Inc. breached their fiduciary duties by failing to prevent misrepresentations of the corporation's financial condition by its former chief executive officer, Efraim E. Landa.[951]

Applying the *Rales* standard because the plaintiff in the case did "not challenge any specific board action that approved or ratified these alleged wrongdoings," the court held that no particularized facts were alleged creating a reasonable doubt concerning the

---

944. 654 A.2d at 1270.

945. *Id.* at 1270 (quoting *Allis-Chalmers*, 188 A.2d at 130).

946. *Id.; see also* Chapter II, Section A 3 (discussing the *Allis-Chalmers* decision).

947. 654 A.2d at 1270-71.

948. *Id.* at 1271.

949. *Id.*

950. 662 A.2d 1350 (Del. Ch. 1995).

951. *Id.* at 1352, 1354-55.

disinterestedness or independence of any of the corporation's directors. The court rejected plaintiffs' reliance upon allegations that these directors wished to avoid liability and therefore would not impartially review the merits of the claims.[952] The court also rejected plaintiff's reliance upon allegations that a decision by the board to pursue litigation would adversely affect the corporation's ability to defend pending federal lawsuits and would have influenced a pending Securities and Exchange Commission investigation of the corporation.[953] The court explained that the directors' potential personal liability and potential exposure to criminal sanctions for their alleged involvement in the corporation's misrepresentations was not a disabling interest excusing demand because this case, like the *Baxter* case, was "not the rare case . . . where defendants' actions were so egregious that a substantial likelihood of director liability exists."[954] The court stated that plaintiff attributed Landa's wrongdoing to the directors through "an alleged conspiracy to inflate the value of Fidelity Medical's stock," but the "only particular allegations that support plaintiff's conspiracy theory" are that three of the corporation's directors signed a misleading 10-K and a misleading registration statement.[955] These allegations, the court held, were insufficient.[956] The court thus concluded that plaintiff's allegations demonstrated "a substantial likelihood of personal liability for Landa" but did not demonstrate that any other director "faced a substantial likelihood of liability for conspiring with Landa."[957]

The court also rejected plaintiff's reliance upon an allegation that the directors could be held liable for failing to supervise Landa and other corporate employees involved in the alleged wrongdoing. The court explained that in order to hold the directors liable on this ground, "plaintiff will have to demonstrate that they were grossly

---

952. *Id.* at 1354.
953. *Id.*
954. *Id.*
955. *Id.*
956. *Id.*
957. *Id.*

negligent in failing to supervise these subordinates."[958] The court stated that the complaint contained "long descriptions of Landa's wrongdoing" but alleged only in a conclusory manner that the other directors "looked the other way."[959] Thus, the court concluded, plaintiff failed to allege particularized facts describing "such egregious conduct by the directors that they face a substantial likelihood of liability due to their failure to prevent Landa's misrepresentations."[960]

A New Jersey court, in a case of first impression under New Jersey law, followed Delaware law in *In re Prudential Insurance Co. Derivative Litigation.*[961] This litigation involved allegations that a subsidiary of Prudential Insurance Company, Prudential Securities Incorporated ("PSI"), improperly sold limited partnership interests by misrepresenting illiquid and speculative partnerships as safe, income-producing investments. An SEC investigation concluded that PSI had committed securities fraud in connection with its marketing and sale of these limited partnership interests, and that PSI had failed to comply with a 1986 SEC Order requiring PSI to implement and maintain improvements in supervisory and compliance oversight procedures. PSI paid fines totaling $41 million, Prudential and PSI established a $330 million disgorgement fund to be used to pay damages to limited partnership investors, and Prudential established an $800 million reserve for future losses.[962]

Prudential shareholders filed a derivative action. The shareholders alleged inaction by Prudential's directors, including the directors' failure to insure compliance by Prudential's PSI subsidiary with the 1986 SEC Order, and the directors' failure to stop the alleged illegal sales practices by PSI executives.[963] The court concluded that the failure of Prudential's directors to insure its subsidiary's compliance with the SEC Order and to stop alleged illegal

---

958. *Id.* at 1355.
959. *Id.*
960. *Id.*
961. 659 A.2d 961 (N.J. Super. Ct. Ch. Div. 1995).
962. *Id.* at 964-66.
963. *Id.* at 974.

activity was a "failure to oversee both subordinates and a subsidiary corporation."[964] Because a "failure to oversee subordinates is 'not a business decision of the board,'" the court concluded, the demand issue was governed by the *Rales* test.[965]

Applying this standard, the court held that demand was not excused. The court explained that the complaint alleged nothing more than conclusory assertions that Prudential's directors were not disinterested or independent and were controlled by "defendants at the heart of the wrongdoing."[966] The court stated that plaintiffs' complaint did not "single out . . . which directors participated in the alleged wrongdoing, which directors 'control' the board and which are, in turn, 'controlled.' No individual directors or group of directors are set apart; in fact, many allegations do not differentiate among the directors and the other defendants" in the case, who were alleged to have committed the wrongdoing that the directors failed to detect and stop.[967]

A New York court construing Delaware law reached the same result in *Weinstock v. Bromery*.[968] This case involved unauthorized Mexican peso foreign exchange transactions by a former vice president of Chemical Banking Corporation ("CBC"). According to plaintiffs, this unauthorized trading caused Chemical Bank to suffer a $70 million pre-tax trading loss. Plaintiffs alleged that the directors of Chemical Bank had breached their fiduciary duties by failing to detect and stop this conduct.[969]

The court held that plaintiffs failed "to plead specific facts showing that the directors had prior knowledge of the wrongdoing so as to excuse demand."[970] The court explained that 80 percent

---

964. *Id.* at 975.
965. *Id.* (quoting *Rales*, 634 A.2d at 934 n.9).
966. *Id.* at 971.
967. *Id.*
968. N.Y.L.J., Mar. 28, 1996, at 29 (N.Y. Sup. Ct. N.Y. Co.), and No. 100151/95 (N.Y. Sup. Ct. N.Y. Co. Oct. 30, 1996), *aff'd sub nom. Teachers' Retirement Sys. v. Welch*, --- A.D.2d ---, 664 N.Y.S.2d 38 (N.Y. App. Div. 1st Dep't 1997).
969. N.Y.L.J., Mar. 28, 1996, at 29.
970. *Id.*

of Chemical's directors at the relevant time were outside directors who were not involved in daily corporate activities and stated that where, as here, "there are no facts alleged supporting assertions of actual participation by outside directors in unauthorized trading activity, it becomes imperative that plaintiff allege a factual basis for its charge of ignoring obvious danger signs.'"[971] Here, however, the court continued, plaintiffs alleged no facts supporting their contention that the unauthorized trading was "'obvious,' especially given the fact that a majority of the directors were 'outside,' non-management directors."[972] The court rejected plaintiffs' contention that the size of the trading loss itself established—in plaintiffs' words—"that the improper and purportedly unauthorized trades were so 'extensive' and obvious that defendant directors, at a minimum, recklessly abdicated their fiduciary obligations of due care in overseeing the Bank's operations."[973] In sum, the court concluded, "conclusory allegations . . . that . . . directors 'knew or should have known' about the unauthorized conduct of others or could have prevented the misconduct if they had performed their duty properly are insufficient as a matter of law to excuse demand."[974]

A motion to dismiss an amended complaint also was granted. The court reasoned that "[t]he amended pleading, stating only that the defendant directors failed to inform themselves about the transaction, makes no sense in this case because the directors did not have a responsibility to inform themselves about the transactions at issue."[975]

An appellate court affirmed, stating that "[t]he essence of the complaint against the CBC directors is that they failed to inform themselves about the unauthorized and concealed transactions of an employee of the corporation's subsidiary. It is precisely in such

---

971. *Id.*
972. *Id.*
973. *Id.*
974. *Id.*
975. No. 100151/95, Mar. 28, 1996 Order.

facially meritless cases that directors' actions are particularly protected by the business judgment rule."[976]

Another New York court construing Delaware law reached
the same result in *Pittleman v. Tully*.[977] This case involved
"improper financial transactions by employees which resulted in
sanctions and unfavorable publicity" for Merrill Lynch & Co.,
Inc.[978] The court stated that "plaintiff has introduced no facts at
all in his effort to show futility of demand."[979] Instead, the court
stated, plaintiff "argues in essence that since the Merrill Lynch
board of directors was at the helm when the improper transactions
occurred, the board is automatically interested and incapable of
impartiality."[980] This argument, the court held, "is clearly insufficient."[981]

    *e. The New York Approach.* The leading cases defining the
circumstances where demand is excused as futile under New York
law are the New York Court of Appeals' 1975 decision in *Barr v.
Wackman*[982] and 1996 decision in *Marx v. Akers*.[983] Following
these two cases, the rule in New York is that demand is excused
"when a complaint alleges with particularity" one of the following
three circumstances: [1] "a majority of the board of directors is
interested in the challenged transaction," with interestedness defined
to include either "self-interest in the transaction at issue . . . or a
loss of independence because a director with no direct interest in a
transaction is 'controlled' by a self-interested director," [2] "the
board of directors did not fully inform themselves about the challenged transaction to the extent reasonably appropriate under the
circumstances," or [3] "the challenged transaction was so egregious

---

976. *Teachers' Retirement Sys. v. Welch*, --- A.D.2d ---, --- 664
N.Y.S.2d 38, 40 (N.Y. App. Div. 1st Dep't 1997).
977. N.Y.L.J., July 18, 1996, at 22 (N.Y. Sup. Ct. N.Y. Co.).
978. *Id.*
979. *Id.*
980. *Id.*
981. *Id.*
982. 36 N.Y.2d 371, 329 N.E.2d 180, 368 N.Y.S.2d 497 (1975).
983. 88 N.Y.2d 189, 666 N.E.2d 1034, 644 N.Y.S.2d 121 (1996).

on its face that it could not have been the product of sound business judgment of the directors."[984]

*Barr v. Wackman*[985] involved a decision by the board of Talcott National Corporation, which consisted of thirteen outside directors (called the "unaffiliated" directors by the court) and five inside directors (called the "affiliated" directors by the court) to reject a $24 per share merger proposal from Gulf & Western Industries, pursuant to which shareholders would receive $17 in cash and a warrant. Instead, the board accepted a $20 per share proposal (all cash) from Associated First Capital Corporation, a Gulf & Western subsidiary.[986] A shareholder alleged that Talcott's board made this determination because Talcott's five inside directors received new and favorable employment contracts from Associated. In addition, a company whose executive vice president was the son of Talcott's board chairman and chief executive officer received a $340,000 "finder's fee" for the transaction, which was paid by Gulf & Western and Associated First Capital.[987] Plaintiff also alleged that Talcott's board agreed to sell a Talcott subsidiary at a net loss of $6.1 million "solely to accommodate" Gulf & Western, which was not interested in acquiring that subsidiary.[988]

The court in *Barr* held that demand can, in the trial court's "sound discretion," be excused where a shareholder pleads "[p]articular allegations of formal board participation in and approval of active wrongdoing," whether or not a majority of the members of the board are "individually charged with fraud or self-dealing."[989]

---

984. *Id.* at 200, 666 N.E.2d at 1040-41, 644 N.Y.S.2d at 127-28.

985. 36 N.Y.2d 371, 329 N.E.2d 180, 368 N.Y.S.2d 497 (1975).

986. *Marx*, 88 N.Y.2d at 198, 666 N.E.2d at 1039, 644 N.Y.S.2d at 126; *Barr*, 36 N.Y.2d at 374-75, 329 N.E.2d at 183-84, 368 N.Y.S.2d at 501-04.

987. *Marx*, 88 N.Y.2d at 199, 666 N.E.2d at 1040, 644 N.Y.S.2d at 127; *Barr*, 36 N.Y.2d at 375-76, 329 N.E.2d at 184, 368 N.Y.S.2d at 503.

988. *Marx*, 88 N.Y.2d at 199, 666 N.E.2d at 1040, 644 N.Y.S.2d at 127; *Barr*, 36 N.Y.2d at 376, 329 N.E.2d at 184-85, 368 N.Y.S.2d at 503.

989. *Barr*, 36 N.Y.2d at 381, 329 N.E.2d at 188, 368 N.Y.S.2d at

(continued...)

The court stated that "it is not sufficient . . . merely to name a majority of the directors as parties defendant with conclusory allegations of wrongdoing or control by wrongdoers."[990] "This pleading tactic," according to the court, "would only beg the question of actual futility and ignore the particularity requirement."[991]

Upholding a trial court's determination that demand was excused pursuant to this standard, the court in *Barr* explained that the complaint did "much more than simply name the individual board members as defendants":

> It sets out, with particularity, a series of transactions allegedly for the benefit of Gulf & Western and the affiliated directors. Though there are no allegations that the unaffiliated directors personally benefited from the transactions, they are claimed to have disregarded Talcott's interests for the sole purpose of accommodating Gulf & Western, which, in turn, would allegedly reciprocate by promoting the self-interest of the affiliated directors. Acting officially, the board, qua board, is claimed to have participated or acquiesced in assertedly wrongful transactions.

> Considered most favorably to the plaintiff the board's acts, as a necessary part of a series of intertwined events and agreements which benefited the affiliated directors rather than Talcott, cannot be regarded as immune from question in a shareholder's derivative action as a matter of law. If true, the allegations of the complaint . . . state a cause of action against the defendants, including the unaffiliated directors, for breach of their duties of due care and diligence to the corporation. Plaintiff may prove that the exercise of reasonable diligence and independent judgment under all the circumstances by the unaffiliated directors, at least to meaningfully check the decisions of the active corporate managers, would have put them on notice of the claimed self-dealing of the affiliated directors and avoided the alleged damage to Talcott. If the unaffiliated directors abdicated their responsibility, they may be liable for their omissions. Taking their

---

989. (...continued)
507-08.
     990. *Id.* at 379, 329 N.E.2d at 186, 368 N.Y.S.2d at 506.
     991. *Id.*

potential liability from the face of the complaint, plaintiff's failure to make a demand on the board was warranted.[992]

As summarized in *Marx*, the *Barr* court held that demand was excused with respect to Talcott's inside directors "because of the self-dealing, or self-interest of those directors in the challenged transaction"; "the controlling directors 'breached their fiduciary obligations to Talcott in return for personal benefits.'"[993] Demand was excused with respect to Talcott's outside directors "even in the absence of their receiving any financial benefit from the transaction," the *Marx* court continued, due to allegations that (1) the acceptance by these directors of the lesser of two offers constituted a "breach of their duties of due care and diligence to the corporation," (2) performance of their duty of care would have "put them on notice of the claimed self-dealing," and (3) they had acted to the corporation's detriment by failing "to do more than passively rubber stamp the decisions of the active managers."[994]

*Marx v. Akers*[995] involved allegations that the directors of International Business Machines Corporation (IBM) breached their fiduciary duties and engaged in self-dealing by awarding excessive compensation to three inside directors and other IBM executives and to the corporation's fifteen outside directors.[996] After summarizing *Barr*, the court in *Marx* stated that during the 20 years that *Barr* had been the law, "various courts" had "overlooked" *Barr*'s "explicit warning" that demand is not excused simply because shareholder-plaintiffs "name a majority of the directors as parties defendant with conclusory allegations of wrongdoing."[997] The court pointed specifically to several decisions, including *Miller*

---

992. *Id.* at 379-80, 329 N.E.2d at 186-87, 368 N.Y.S.2d at 506.

993. *Marx*, 88 N.Y.2d at 199, 666 N.E.2d at 1040, 644 N.Y.S.2d at 127 (quoting *Barr*, 36 N.Y.2d at 376, 329 N.E.2d at 185, 368 N.Y.S.2d at 503).

994. *Id.* (quoting *Barr*, 36 N.Y.2d at 380, 381, 329 N.E.2d at 187, 188, 368 N.Y.S.2d at 506, 507).

995. 88 N.Y.2d 189, 666 N.E.2d 1034, 644 N.Y.S.2d 121 (1996).

996. *Id.* at 192, 666 N.E.2d at 1036, 644 N.Y.S.2d at 123.

997. *Id.* at 199-200, 666 N.E.2d at 1040, 644 N.Y.S.2d at 127 (quoting *Barr*, 36 N.Y.2d at 379, 368 N.Y.S.2d at 506).

*v. Schreyer*[998]—a case discussed in more detail below. Briefly, the court in *Miller* stated that demand is excused where acts are alleged ". . . 'for which a majority of the directors may be liable and plaintiff reasonably concluded that the board would not be responsive to a demand.'"[999] Applying that standard, the court in *Miller* excused demand where the alleged wrongdoing was an illegal parking scheme entered into by corporate employees with a Florida insurer and that continued for four years, and that plaintiffs alleged the corporation's directors should have discovered and stopped.[1000] "The problem with such an approach," the *Marx* court explained, "is that it permits plaintiffs to frame their complaint in such a way as to automatically excuse demand, thereby allowing the exception to swallow the rule."[1001]

In order to resolve the "problem" created by decisions such as *Miller*, the *Marx* court elaborated upon *Barr*'s demand futility standard by stating the three-pronged test quoted in the first paragraph of this section.[1002] Applying this test to the facts in *Marx*, the court required demand with respect to the plaintiff's challenge to compensation approved by IBM's board for the corporation's inside directors and executives. The court, however, excused demand with respect to compensation approved by IBM's board for the corporation's outside directors.

With respect to the compensation for IBM's inside directors and executives, the court explained that IBM's 18 member board included 15 outside directors who did not receive this compensation. Accordingly, the court held, plaintiffs had "failed to allege that a majority of the board was interested in setting executive compensation," as required in order to excuse demand under the

---

998. 200 A.D.2d 492, 606 N.Y.S.2d 642 (N.Y. App. Div. 1st Dep't 1994).
999. *Id.* at 494, 606 N.Y.S.2d at 644 (quoting *Barr*, 36 N.Y.2d at 377, 329 N.E.2d at 185, 368 N.Y.S.2d at 503).
1000. *Id.* at 492-94, 495, 606 N.Y.S.2d at 643-44.
1001. *Marx*, 88 N.Y.2d at 200, 666 N.E.2d at 1040, 644 N.Y.S.2d at 127.
1002. *Id.* at 200, 666 N.E.2d at 1040-41, 644 N.Y.S.2d at 127-28.

first prong of the *Marx* test.[1003] The court also held that plaintiff
had failed to satisfy either the second or the third prongs of the
*Marx* test because plaintiff's "allegations that the board used faulty
accounting procedures to calculate executive compensation levels"
did not "move beyond 'conclusory allegations of wrongdoing,'"
and "[t]he complaint does not allege particular facts in contending
that the board failed to deliberate or exercise its business judgment
in setting those levels."[1004]

With respect to the compensation for outside directors, the
court explained that a majority of IBM's board consisted of outside
directors who received this compensation, and thus the majority
was self-interested and demand was excused.[1005] The court stated:

> Directors are self-interested in a challenged transaction where
> they will receive a direct financial benefit from the transac-
> tion which is different from the benefit to shareholders gener-
> ally. A director who votes for a raise in directors' compensa-
> tion is always "interested" because that person will receive a
> personal financial benefit from the transaction not shared in
> by stockholders. Consequently, a demand was excused as to
> plaintiff's allegations that the compensation set for outside
> directors was excessive.[1006]

Plaintiff's claim challenging the outside directors' compensation
nevertheless was dismissed on a separate ground: the absence of

---

1003. *Id*. at 202, 666 N.E.2d at 1041, 644 N.Y.S.2d at 128.

1004. *Id*.; *see also In re Woolworth Corp. Shareholder Derivative
Litig.*, --- A.D.2d ---, ---, 658 N.Y.S.2d 869, 870 (N.Y. App. Div. 1st
Dep't 1997) ("[w]ith respect to the challenged severance package for one
of the corporation's directors, the only person with a direct financial
interest in that package was the compensated director, such that the rest of
the Board was not interested therein" and thus demand was not excused).

1005. 88 N.Y.2d at 202, 666 N.E.2d at 1042, 644 N.Y.S.2d at
129.

1006. *Id*. (citing 1 Principles of Corporate Governance: Analysis
and Recommendations § 5.03 comment g, at 250 (1994) and *Steiner v.
Meyerson*, [1995 Transfer Binder] Fed. Sec. L. Rep. (CCH) ¶ 98,857
(Del. Ch. July 18, 1995)).

non-conclusory "factually-based allegations of wrongdoing or waste which would, if true, sustain a verdict in plaintiff's favor."[1007]

The *Marx* standard is similar to the *Aronson v. Lewis*[1008] standard utilized in Delaware in cases challenging business decisions by the directors to whom a demand would be made.[1009] The *Marx* standard, however, does not include the term "reasonable doubt," which the *Marx* court described as "confusing" and "overly subjective"[1010] for the reasons discussed in the section of this Chapter discussing Delaware's "reasonable doubt" language.[1011] The first prong of both the *Aronson* and the *Marx* standard requires disinterestedness and independence and defines those terms with almost identical words. The second, business judgment rule prong of *Aronson* incorporates both the requirement that directors "inform themselves, prior to making a business decision, of all material information reasonably available to them"[1012]—the second prong of *Marx*—and the "abuse of discretion" exception to the business judgment rule in Delaware pursuant to which "in rare cases a transaction may be so egregious on its face that board approval cannot meet the test of business judgment"[1013]—the third prong of *Marx*. The closeness of the *Aronson* and *Marx* language could not be coincidental, and the "so egregious on its face" prong of the demand futility standard in *Marx* likely will be construed in the same manner that the term has been construed in Delaware.[1014]

---

1007. 88 N.Y.2d at 204, 666 N.E.2d at 1043, 644 N.Y.S.2d at 130; *see also* Chapter II, Section B 2 g (discussing this aspect of *Marx* decision).

1008. 473 A.2d 805 (Del. 1984).

1009. *See* Chapter IV, Section B 5 b.

1010. *Marx*, 88 N.Y.2d at 196, 198, 200-01, 666 N.E.2d at 1038, 1038, 1040-41, 644 N.Y.S.2d at 125, 126, 127-28.

1011. *See* Chapter IV, Section B 5 b.

1012. 473 A.2d at 812.

1013. *Id.* at 815; *see also* Chapter I, Section D 5 (discussing abuse of discretion exception to the business judgment rule).

1014. *See, e.g.*, Chapter IV, Section B 5 c; *Kahn v. Tremont Corp.*, 1994 Del. Ch. LEXIS 41, at *21, 1994 WL 162613, at * 6 (Del. Ch. Apr. 21, 1994) (the second prong of *Aronson* is directed to "extreme
(continued...)

The second and third prongs of the *Marx* standard raise a question previously raised by the second prong of *Aronson*: How is demand futility measured if no "business judgment" has been made by the board concerning the conduct alleged to be wrongful. This question arises most frequently in the context of an alleged failure by a board to do something, such as oversee subordinates or maintain adequate internal controls, and as a result (according to shareholder plaintiffs) wrongdoing within the corporation has not been detected and stopped by the board. The Delaware courts answered this question in 1993 in *Rales v. Blasband*,[1015] a case holding that where no business judgment has been made the second prong of the *Aronson* test is inapplicable, and the only issue to be decided is whether the directors to whom a demand would be made are disinterested and independent.[1016]

A series of New York cases—*Lewis v. Welch*,[1017] *Bildstein v. Atwater*,[1018] *Teachers' Retirement System v. Welch*[1019] and

---

1014. (...continued)
cases in which despite the appearance of independence and disinterest a decision is so extreme or curious as to itself raise a legitimate ground to justify inquiry and judicial review," such as allegations of waste, where the issue is "whether what the corporation has received is so inadequate in value that no person of ordinary, sound business judgment would deem it worth what the corporation has paid"), *subsequent proceedings on other grounds*, 1996 Del. Ch. LEXIS 40, 1996 WL 145452 (Del. Ch. Mar. 21, 1996), *rev'd*, 694 A.2d 422 (Del. 1997); *AC Acquisitions Corp. v. Anderson, Clayton & Co.*, 519 A.2d 103, 111 n.9 (Del. Ch. 1986) (noting the "possibility—perhaps more theoretical than real—that a decision by disinterested directors following a deliberative process may still be the basis for liability if such decision cannot be 'attributed to any rational business purpose,' . . . or is 'egregious.'").
 1015. 634 A.2d 927 (Del. 1993).
 1016. *See* Chapter IV, Section B 5 d.
 1017. 126 A.D.2d 519, 510 N.Y.S.2d 640 (N.Y. App. Div. 2d Dep't 1987).
 1018. 222 A.D.2d 545, 635 N.Y.S.2d 88 (N.Y. App. Div. 2d Dep't 1995).
 1019. No. 113271/94 (N.Y. Sup. Ct. Apr. 16, 1996), *aff'd*, --- A.D.2d ---, 664 N.Y.S.2d 38 (N.Y. App. Div. 1st Dep't 1997).

*In re Woolworth Corp. Shareholder Derivative Litigation*[1020]— illustrate cases alleging oversight failures where demand has been required. *Marx* touches upon this question: the intermediate appellate court in *Marx* rejected a claim that demand was excused due to the corporation's use of improper accounting practices because "[t]he complaint fails to establish that these accounting practices are improper, or that the directors had or should have had knowledge of or that they participated in these alleged improper accounting practices."[1021] The Court of Appeals dealt with this allegation merely by stating that "the allegations that the board used faulty accounting procedures to calculate executive compensation levels" did not "move beyond 'conclusory allegations or wrongdoing' which are insufficient to excuse demand."[1022]

In *Lewis v. Welch*,[1023] an intermediate appellate court decision, demand was required in a case where plaintiffs named a majority of the corporation's directors as defendants and alleged that these directors "caused or are chargeable with causing the Company to defraud the government by making wrongful charges with respect to the work it performed," and that "[as] a result of the defendants' mischarges, the Company was indicted on charges that if falsified claims for its services and misstated its work performed."[1024] The court stated that "the allegation that 'the individual defendants caused or are chargeable with causing the Company to defraud the government', etc., is unsupported by facts alleged in the complaint or even by allegations in the indictment referred to in

---

1020. No. 109465/94 (Sup. Ct. N.Y. Co. May 3, 1995) and N.Y.L.J., Apr. 22, 1996, at 28 (Sup. Ct. N.Y. Co), *aff'd*, 240 A.D.2d 189, 658 N.Y.S.2d 869 (N.Y. App. Div. 1st Dep't 1997).

1021. *Marx v. Akers*, 215 A.D.2d 540, 541, 626 N.Y.S.2d 276, 277 (N.Y. App. Div. 2d Dep't 1995), *aff'd in part and rev'd in part on other grounds*, 88 N.Y.2d 189, 666 N.E.2d 1034, 644 N.Y.S.2d 121 (1996).

1022. 88 N.Y.2d at 202, 666 N.E.2d at 1041, 644 N.Y.S.2d at 128 (quoting *Barr*).

1023. 126 A.D.2d 519, 510 N.Y.S.2d 640 (N.Y. App. Div. 2d Dep't 1987).

1024. *Id.* at 520, 510 N.Y.S.2d at 642.

the complaint which does not mention the name of any director."[1025] Thus, the court continued, "[t]his allegation, upon which the plaintiff's derivative action rests, is conclusory and legally ineffective."[1026] The court cited *Barr* for the proposition that "it is not sufficient merely to name a majority of the directors as parties defendant with conclusory allegations of wrongdoing" and stated that "the complaint herein spells out no details from which it may be inferred that the making of a demand would indeed be futile."[1027] In sum, the court concluded, it "was not reasonable for the plaintiff to conclude that the 17-member . . . board of directors, 14 of whom are independent 'outside' directors, would not be responsive to a demand."[1028]

*Bildstein v. Atwater*,[1029] another intermediate appellate court decision, involved allegations that directors failed to uncover and stop the wrongful payments by corporate employees in connection with the sale of aerospace equipment to Egypt. The court rejected these claims, concluding that that demand is not excused where a plaintiff "merely name[s] a majority of the directors as defendants and assert[s] conclusory allegations of wrongdoing."[1030]

*Teachers' Retirement System v. Welch*,[1031] a trial court decision, involved allegations that the directors of General Electric Company ("GE") breached their fiduciary duties by failing to detect improper trading practices at Kidder Peabody, a GE subsidiary, by Joseph Jett, a Kidder bond trader.[1032] The court explained that there were no allegations that GE's directors "knew of Jett's

---

1025. *Id.* at 521, 510 N.Y.S.2d at 642.

1026. *Id.*

1027. *Id.*

1028. *Id.*

1029. 222 A.D.2d 545, 635 N.Y.S.2d 88 (N.Y. App. Div. 2d Dep't 1995).

1030. *Id.* at 546, 635 N.Y.S.2d at 89.

1031. No. 113271/94 (N.Y. Sup. Ct. Apr. 16, 1996), *aff'd*, --- A.D.2d ---, 664 N.Y.S.2d 38 (N.Y. App. Div. 1st Dep't 1997).

1032. *Id.*, Tr. at 4-5.

scheme or profited from it."[1033] To the contrary, the court stated, "[t]he actions complained of involved failure to detect flaws in accounting procedures of a subsidiary and failing to detect fraud of a single individual."[1034] The court also pointed to the fact that the overwhelming majority of GE's directors were outside directors who did not stand to gain anything from the alleged wrongdoing.[1035] For all of these reasons, the court held that plaintiff's "allegations of inattentiveness" were "insufficiently particularized" and thus did not support plaintiffs' claim that demand was excused as futile.[1036] An intermediate appellate court affirmed.[1037]

*In re Woolworth Corp. Shareholder Derivative Litigation*,[1038] a case in which there have been two trial court decisions (before *Marx*), and one appellate court decision (after *Marx*), involved allegations that directors failed to uncover accounting irregularities. In the trial court's first decision, the court, as in *Teachers' Retirement*, stated that "[m]ost of the directors here are outside directors, who obviously were not involved in daily corporate operations," and that there were "no facts alleged supporting allegations of actual participation by outside directors in a scheme of accounting errors."[1039] Rather, the court continued, there were only "a series of sweeping statements that the individual defendants 'knew or should have known' or 'knew or were reckless in failing to know' that certain Woolworth subsidiaries were engaged in accounting improprieties."[1040] The court concluded it was "entirely possible" that the alleged accounting irregularities "may not have come to the attention of diligent outside members of the Board of

---

1033. *Id.* at 9.

1034. *Id.* at 11.

1035. *Id.*

1036. *Id.*

1037. *Teachers' Retirement Sys. v. Welch*, --- A.D.2d ---, 664 N.Y.S.2d 38 (N.Y. App. Div. 1st Dep't 1997).

1038. No. 109465/94 (N.Y. Sup. Ct. N.Y. Co. May 3, 1995) and N.Y.L.J., Apr. 22, 1996, at 28 (N.Y. Sup. Ct. N.Y. Co), *aff'd*, --- A.D.2d ---, 658 N.Y.S.2d 869 (N.Y. App. Div. 1st Dep't 1997).

1039. No. 109465/94, slip op. at 3.

1040. *Id.* at 4.

Directors and plaintiffs do not allege a single fact to indicate why that was not so."[1041]

In the trial court's second decision in the case, the court addressed an amended complaint in which plaintiffs sought "to correct the deficiency of their initial complaint" by alleging that Woolworth's directors' "created a 'corporate culture' which promoted the use of inflated accounting figures."[1042] The amended complaint also "more particularly described the availability of accurate accounting information by which Board members could have ascertained that there were in fact accounting irregularities."[1043] The court again dismissed the case. The court described plaintiffs' new allegations as "merely amplifications of the prior 'knew or should have known' allegations" and held that these allegations still were an "insufficient . . . basis upon which to claim demand futility."[1044]

An intermediate appellate court affirmed. The appellate court stated that plaintiffs' allegations with respect to the alleged accounting irregularities were "insufficient to establish with particularity that the subject corporation's Board would not have been responsive" to a demand to take action.[1045] Most of these allegations, the court stated, tracked a publicly disseminated report issued by a special board committee that investigated the irregularities and "in response to which the Board took remedial action."[1046] The court also rejected a claim that demand was excused by allegations that one of the corporation's directors was awarded a severance package "to buy the director's silence."[1047] The court stated that "the only person with a direct financial interest in that package was the compensated director, such that the rest of the Board was not interested therein," and that the allegation that "the reason for this sev-

---

1041. *Id.* at 6.
1042. N.Y.L.J., Apr. 22, 1996, at 28.
1043. *Id.*
1044. *Id.*
1045. --- A.D.2d at ---, 658 N.Y.S.2d at 869.
1046. *Id.*
1047. *Id.* at 1-2.

erance package was to buy the director's silence is conclusory."[1048]

Trial court decisions construing New York law in a federal court in California in *Benedict v. Brennan*[1049] and a state court in Illinois in *Lewis v. Brennan*[1050] reached similar conclusions in cases involving allegations that the directors of Sears, Roebuck & Co. failed to uncover a fraudulent car repair scheme.

The court in *Benedict v. Brennan*[1051] rejected a contention that the Sears board, consisting of a "clear majority" of outside directors, had knowledge of "a scheme to victimize customers of Sears, Roebuck's automotive-repair shops," which became public knowledge following an investigation by California's Department of Consumer Affairs/Bureau of Automotive Repair (the "DCA/BAR").[1052] Plaintiff alleged that Sears' outside directors knew about the scheme before it became public knowledge based upon "(a) a 6 December 1991 letter in which California Senior Assistant Attorney General Herschel Elkins and Contra Costa County Deputy District Attorney Curtis Hoffman outlined the scheme; (b) a 16 December 1991 meeting where the scheme was discussed; (c) thousands of consumer complaints relating to the conduct involved in the scheme; and (d) a quota/commission system."[1053]

The court rejected this claim. The court explained that "the 6 December 1991 letter: (a) was addressed only to Brennan; (b) identified him as president and chief executive officer, but not as chairman of the board of directors; and (c) did not indicate specifically that outside directors, as distinct from 'the highest echelon of [Sears, Roebuck] management,' should be made aware of the scheme."[1054] The December 16, 1991 meeting, the court stated, "was between DCA/BAR representatives and a group of Sears,

---

1048. *Id.*
1049. No. C-92-2236 (N.D. Cal. Sept. 3, 1993).
1050. No. 92 CH 5820 (Ill. Cir. Ct. Feb. 15, 1995).
1051. No. C-92-2236 (N.D. Cal. Sept. 3, 1993).
1052. *Id.*, slip op. at 1, 3.
1053. *Id.* at 3-4.
1054. *Id.* at 4.

Roebuck representatives who do not seem to include outside directors."[1055] The "thousands of consumer complaints," the court continued, were not alleged to have been "directed to anyone at Sears, Roebuck—as distinct from, for example, DCA/BAR—much less to outside directors."[1056] The quota/commission system, the court also reasoned, "was used—apparently without causing a substantial problem—in other parts of Sears, Roebuck's operations. Thus, even if the scheme involving the automotive-repair shops resulted from the quota/commission system, knowing about and supporting the quota/commission system is not the same as knowing about and supporting the scheme involving the automotive-repair shops."[1057]

In sum, the court concluded, plaintiff "has not pointed to any specific facts indicating: (a) that before the scheme became public knowledge, outside directors saw the letter, were made aware of the meeting, knew of the scheme, or were negligent in failing to learn of the scheme; or (b) that outside directors ever participated in, authorized, or approved the scheme."[1058]

The court in *Lewis v. Brennan*[1059] dismissed a similar complaint. The court in *Brennan* stated that the complaint failed "to allege any particularized facts showing wrongdoing by the Board which would excuse the requirement under New York law that a presuit demand must be made prior to filing a stockholders' derivative action."[1060] Instead, the court found, plaintiffs' complaint was "laced with conclusionary allegations that the Board members failed in their duty and supervision, without specifying how they should have known a fraudulent scheme has occurred."[1061]

The court stated that while plaintiffs contended that "many consumers complained about the repairs done to their vehicles" and

---

1055. *Id*. at 4-5.
1056. *Id*. at 4.
1057. *Id*.
1058. *Id*. at 5.
1059. No. 92 CH 5820 (Ill. Cir. Ct. Feb. 15, 1995).
1060. *Id*., Tr. at 6.
1061. *Id*.

that this "should have put the Board on notice," there was no "allegation that any complaints were made to any Board members."[1062] The court similarly stated that while plaintiffs alleged that the California Department of Consumer Affairs informed Sears of the investigation and that the fraudulent car repair scheme had not stopped, plaintiffs did not allege "that the Sears Board itself was notified, nor when the notification took place."[1063] The court also adopted the reasoning in the decision in *Benedict*.[1064]

The opposite conclusion is illustrated by *Miller v. Schreyer*,[1065] a decision that, as discussed above, the Court of Appeals in *Marx* rejected as wrongly decided.[1066] The court in *Miller* excused demand on the ground that *Miller* involved a "failure to monitor and oversee the Company's operations and establish procedures to protect against employee misconduct"—conduct that constituted "inaction, not action protected by the presumptions of the business judgment rule."[1067]

*Miller* involved allegations that the "abdication of . . . responsibilities" by the directors of Merrill Lynch & Co., Inc. "facilitated the perpetration of a $900-million illegal securities 'parking scheme.'"[1068] The plaintiffs alleged that for four consecutive years, a Florida insurer, Guaranty Security Life Insurance Co. ("GSLIC"), exchanged its "junk bond" holdings with Merrill Lynch for United States Treasury securities and similar high quality securities shortly before the end of the calendar and fiscal year. This was done, plaintiffs alleged, so that GSLIC could avoid insolvency by reflecting ownership of high quality securities rather than depreciated junk bonds on its year end financial statements. Soon after year-end reports were issued, the transactions allegedly

---

1062. *Id.*

1063. *Id.* at 7.

1064. *Id.* at 9.

1065. 200 A.D.2d 492, 606 N.Y.S.2d 642 (N.Y. App. Div. 1st Dep't 1994).

1066. *Marx*, 88 N.Y.2d at 200, 666 N.E.2d at 1040, 644 N.Y.S.2d at 127.

1067. 200 A.D.2d at 493-94, 606 N.Y.S.2d at 643-44.

1068. *Id.* at 492, 606 N.Y.S.2d at 643.

were unwound at previously agreed upon prices that assured that Merrill Lynch would suffer no loss. The transactions were alleged to be "a complete sham" in which "confirmation slips were altered to falsify trade dates."[1069] According to plaintiffs, "had proper supervisory controls been in place, the timing of the securities swaps at year-end, the four-year duration of the practice, the non-market prices at which the securities were exchanged and the alteration of confirmation slips are circumstances which should have come to the attention of senior managerial supervisors and aroused suspicion at the highest levels of the corporation."[1070]

The court held that under New York law (the case was governed by Delaware law, but the court stated that the law governing the need for demand in Delaware was not "materially different" from the law in New York) "no demand is necessary 'if the complaint alleges acts for which a majority of the directors may be liable and plaintiff reasonably concluded that the board would not be responsive to a demand.'"[1071] Here, the court held, "the alleged malfeasance of the majority of the board of directors, pleaded with particularity in the complaint, renders service of a demand a futile gesture.[1072]

As stated above, *Miller* was rejected by the Court of Appeals as wrongly decided in *Marx*. The problem with the *Miller* approach, the court in *Marx* stated, "is that it permits plaintiffs to frame their complaint in such a way as to automatically excuse demand, thereby allowing the exception to swallow the rule."[1073] *Miller* accordingly was dismissed in subsequent proceedings, on the ground that "the Court of Appeals has specifically referred to the decision in this matter as being in error."[1074]

---

1069. *Id.* at 493, 606 N.Y.S.2d at 643.

1070. *Id.*

1071. *Id.* at 494, 606 N.Y.S.2d at 644 (quoting *Barr*, 36 N.Y.2d at 377, 329 N.E.2d at 185, 368 N.Y.S.2d at 503).

1072. *Id.* at 495, 606 N.Y.S.2d at 644.

1073. *Marx*, 88 N.Y.2d at 200, 666 N.E.2d at 1040, 644 N.Y.S.2d at 127.

1074. *Miller v. Schreyer*, No. 29885/91, slip op. at 2 (Sup. Ct. N.Y. Co. May 6, 1997).

Additional decisions construing New York law and requiring demand include appellate decisions in *Bennett v. Instrument Systems Corp.*[1075] and *Lewis v. Akers*[1076] and trial court decisions in *Hagelberg v. Brunschwig,*[1077] *Auerbach v. Aldrich,*[1078] *Velez v. Feinstein,*[1079] *First New York Bank for Business v. Selzer,*[1080] *Ferber v. Armstrong,*[1081] *General Electric Co. v. Welch*[1082] and *Mills v. Andreasen*[1083] and a federal court decision in *Stoner v. Walsh.*[1084]

Additional decisions construing New York law and excusing demand include appellate court decisions in *Joseph v. Amrep Corp.,*[1085] *Miller v. Kastner,*[1086] *Schmidt v. Magnetic Head Corp.,*[1087] *Lauer v. Schoenholtz,*[1088] *Curreri v. Verni*[1089] and

---

1075. 66 A.D.2d 708, 709, 411 N.Y.S.2d 287, 288-89 (N.Y. App. Div. 1st Dep't 1978).

1076. 227 A.D.2d 595, 595-96, 644 N.Y.S.2d 279, 281 (N.Y. App. Div. 2d Dep't), *leave to appeal denied*, 88 N.Y.2d 813, 672 N.E.2d 606, 649 N.Y.S.2d 380 (1996).

1077. N.Y.L.J., June 29, 1977, at 15 (N.Y. Sup. Ct. Queens Co.).

1078. N.Y.L.J., Dec. 23, 1977, at 13 (N.Y. Sup. Ct. Westchester Co. 1977).

1079. N.Y.L.J., Oct. 28, 1981, at 7 (N.Y. Sup. Ct. N.Y. Co.).

1080. N.Y.L.J., July 11, 1990, at 21 (N.Y. Sup. Ct. N.Y. Co.).

1081. No. 27878/91, slip op. at 2 (N.Y. Sup. Ct. May 6, 1992).

1082. N.Y.L.J. Dec. 30, 1992, at 27 (N.Y. Sup. Ct. N.Y. Co.).

1083. No. 128824/93, slip op. at 3-4 (N.Y. Sup. Ct. Oct. 31, 1994).

1084. 772 F. Supp. 790, 798 (S.D.N.Y. 1991).

1085. 59 A.D.2d 841, 841, 399 N.Y.S.2d 3, 3 (N.Y. App. Div. 1st Dep't 1977).

1086. 100 A.D.2d 728, 728, 473 N.Y.S.2d 656, 657 (N.Y. App. Div. 4th Dep't 1984).

1087. 101 A.D.2d 268, 283, 476 N.Y.S.2d 151, 160 (N.Y. App. Div. 2d Dep't 1984).

1088. 106 A.D.2d 551, 552, 483 N.Y.S.2d 70, 71 (N.Y. App. Div. 2d Dep't 1984), *appeal dismissed*, 64 N.Y.2d 610, 479 N.E.2d 826, 490 N.Y.S.2d 1023 (1985).

1089. 156 A.D.2d 420, 421, 548 N.Y.S.2d 540, 541 (N.Y. App. Div. 2d Dep't 1989).

*Tong v. Hang Seng Bank, Ltd.,*[1090] trial court decisions in *Fair v. Fuchs,*[1091] *Tobias v. Tobias,*[1092] *Campanelli v. Solomon*[1093] and *Bouhayer v. Georgalis*[1094] and federal court decisions in *Norlin Corp. v. Rooney, Pace Inc.*[1095] and *Benfield v. Steindler.*[1096] Except for the *Bouhayer* decision, these decisions all pre-date *Marx.*

*f. The California Approach.* The leading case explaining when demand is excused as futile under California law—and, indeed, the only reported case on the subject during the last 35 years in California—is the Court of Appeal's 1993 decision in *Shields v. Singleton.*[1097] The court in *Singleton* held that the standard governing demand futility allegations in California is as follows: "[I]n order to evaluate the demand futility claim, the court must be apprised of facts specific to each director from which it can conclude that that particular director could or could not be expected to fairly evaluate the claims of the shareholder plaintiff."[1098]

Applying this standard, the court held that demand was not excused by breach of fiduciary duty claims arising out of an alleged failure by directors to prevent unlawful conduct by employees of a corporate subsidiary, including fraud and corruption in the procurement of military defense contracts. This conduct, the plaintiff alleged, resulted in damages to the corporation, including criminal and civil penalties, settlement payments and legal fees, and loss of future business.[1099] The court explained that "the complaint does

---

1090. 210 A.D.2d 99, 100, 620 N.Y.S.2d 42, 43-44 (N.Y. App. Div. 1st Dep't 1994).

1091. N.Y.L.J., Dec. 19, 1991, at 25 (N.Y. Sup. Ct. N.Y. Co.).

1092. N.Y.L.J., Aug. 13, 1992, at 22 (N.Y. Sup. Ct. N.Y. Co.).

1093. N.Y.L.J., Sept. 11, 1992, at 26 (N.Y. Sup. Ct. Nassau Co.).

1094. 169 Misc. 2d 779, 780-84, 645 N.Y.S.2d 1008, 1009-11 (N.Y. Sup. Ct. Queens Co. 1996).

1095. 744 F.2d 255, 261-62 (2d Cir. 1984).

1096. No. C-1-92-729, slip op. at 2-4 (S.D. Ohio May 3, 1993), *appeal dismissed,* No. 93-3652 (6th Cir. Aug. 13, 1993).

1097. 15 Cal. App. 4th 1611, 19 Cal. Rptr. 2d 459 (Cal. Ct. App. 1993).

1098. *Id.* at 1622, 19 Cal. Rptr. at 466.

1099. *Id.* at 1614, 19 Cal. Rptr. 2d at 460-61.

not allege a single fact which would indicate that the directors had any knowledge of, much less participated in, any criminal or fraudulent activities, nor does it allege that they benefitted directly from the wrongdoing or were otherwise disabled from exercising independent business judgment."[1100] "Broad, conclusory allegations against all directors of a corporation," the court held, are "insufficient to establish demand futility."[1101] In sum, the court concluded, "the general allegations which plaintiff here indiscriminately levels against all the directors of the Company are insufficient to establish that demand on the board would have been futile."[1102]

The court in *Findley v. Garrett*[1103]—a case discussed approvingly by the court in *Shields*[1104]—reached the same result. The *Findley* complaint alleged that directors had "full knowledge" of an alleged conspiracy and "'participated' in the acts committed pursuant to the conspiracy, 'became active participants' in the acts of conspiracy, and 'knowingly shielded' and 'actively concealed' said acts of conspiracy by 'affirmative representations' which were 'fraudulent concealments' of material facts."[1105] The court held that these were all "general statements" that were "not supported by allegations of specific facts" and that therefore were insufficient to overcome the demand requirement.[1106]

The *Findley* court stated that directors are entitled to determine whether or not to pursue alleged causes of action, even where the alleged wrongdoing consists of fraud or illegal conduct:

> Directors have the same discretion with respect to the prosecution of claims on behalf of the corporation as they have in other business matters. In this respect the fact that a claim may be founded in fraud does not differentiate it from other claims. Refusal to sue on a fraud claim is not, as plaintiffs

---

1100. *Id.* at 1621, 19 Cal. Rptr. 2d at 465.
1101. *Id.*
1102. *Id.* at 1622, 19 Cal. Rptr. 2d at 466.
1103. 109 Cal. App. 2d 166, 240 P.2d 421 (Cal. Ct. App. 1952).
1104. 15 Cal. App. 4th at 1621-22, 19 Cal. Rptr. at 465-66.
1105. 109 Cal. App. 2d at 176, 240 P.2d at 427.
1106. *Id.*

contend, a ratification of fraud. The mere fact that a recovery for the corporation would probably result from litigation does not require that an action be commenced to enforce the claim. Even if it appeared to the directors . . . that at the end of protracted litigation substantial sums could be recovered from some or all of the defendants, that fact alone would not have made it the duty of the directors to authorize the commencement of an action. It would have made it their duty to weigh the advantages of probable recovery against the cost in money, time and disruption of the business of the company which litigation would entail.[1107]

Demand was excused in *Reed v. Norman*,[1108] a case where particularized factual allegations described the appropriation of specified amounts of corporate funds over specified periods of time for the personal use of a director who dominated all corporate actions and in circumvention of an injunction barring such use of corporate funds.[1109] Demand also was excused in *Gottesfeld v. Richmaid Ice Cream Co.*,[1110] a case where particularized factual allegations described numerous specific instances of self-dealing, including the issuance of promissory notes in specified amounts to specified directors to whom no money was owed and the transfer of a specific property to a director after the corporation had spent a specified amount of money to improve the property.[1111]

*g. The Universal Demand Requirement Approach.* The drafters of the American Bar Association Section of Business Law's Model Business Corporation Act and the American Law Institute's corporate governance project—Principles of Corporate Governance: Analysis and Recommendations—have proposed a "universal" demand requirement mandating demand in all cases. There is one exception: cases where a requirement that a shareholder make a demand and then wait for a board response prior to filing litigation would result in irreparable injury to the corporation.[1112]

---

1107. *Id.* at 177-78, 240 P.2d at 428.
1108. 152 Cal. App. 2d 892, 314 P.2d 204 (Cal. Ct. App. 1957).
1109. *Id.* at 895, 314 P.2d at 205-06.
1110. 115 Cal. App. 2d 854, 252 P.2d 973 (Cal. Ct. App. 1953).
1111. *Id.* at 857-59, 252 P.2d at 976-77.
1112. *See* 2 Model Bus. Corp. Act Annotated § 7.42 (3d ed. 1996);
(continued...)

The Official Comment to the Model Business Corporation Act explains that the rationale underlying this universal demand rule is two-fold: First, "even though no director may be independent, the demand will give the board of directors the opportunity to re-examine the act complained of in the light of a potential lawsuit and take corrective action."[1113] Second, "the provision eliminates the time and expense of the litigants and the court involved in litigating the question whether demand is required."[1114] The drafters add that "requiring a demand in all cases does not impose an onerous burden" upon shareholders.[1115]

The drafters of Principles of Corporate Governance likewise conclude that "a universal demand rule eliminates much of the threshold litigation, collateral to the merits of the action, that today slows the pace and increases the cost of derivative actions."[1116] The drafters also state that "making demand on the board is a rela-tively costless step" that "places little burden on the plaintiff" and that "may sometimes induce the board to consider issues or take corrective action that either moots or permits the early resolution of the action."[1117]

While the Model Act and Principles of Corporate Governance "both are premised upon the concept of universal demand—that is, a requirement that demand must be made in every case," Principles of Corporate Governance and the Model Act "then go in directions which are different from Delaware law and different from each other in determining the manner in which derivative litigation is to be conducted or terminated after demand has been made."[1118] The differing standards of judicial review recommended by the

---

1112. (...continued)
2 Principles of Corporate Governance: Analysis and Recommendations §§ 7.03(a), (b) (1994).
    1113. Model Bus. Corp. Act Annotated § 7.42 Official Comment at 199.
    1114. *Id.*
    1115. *Id.*
    1116. Principles of Corporate Governance § 7.03 Comment at 57.
    1117. *Id.* at 57-58.
    1118. *Grimes v. Donald*, 673 A.2d 1207, 1218 n.21 (Del. 1996).

Model Act and Principles of Corporate Governance are discussed later in this Chapter.[1119]

To date, fourteen states—Arizona, Connecticut, Florida, Georgia, Maine, Michigan, Mississippi, Montana, Nebraska, New Hampshire, North Carolina, Texas, Virginia and Wisconsin—have adopted statutes enacting universal demand requirements.[1120] A fifteenth state, Pennsylvania, has adopted a universal demand requirement by judicial decision.[1121]

The universal demand requirement also was adopted by the Seventh Circuit in *Kamen v. Kemper Financial Services, Inc.*,[1122] a case construing federal common law—an error that, as noted below, was reversed by the Supreme Court. The Seventh Circuit described the futility exception to the demand requirement as "ambiguous in scope" and "a prodigious generator of litigation."[1123] The court concluded that "[i]f demand is useful, then let the investor make one; if indeed futile, the board's response will establish that soon enough."[1124] The court explained the "virtue of simplification" in the context of "three of the common battles about the meaning of 'futility.'"[1125] In the court's words:

> 1. The plaintiff may say that some or all of the members of the board approved or are interested in the transaction and

---

1119. *See* Chapter IV, Sections B 6 i-j.

1120. *See* Ariz. Bus. Corp. Act § 10-742; Conn. Bus. Corp. Act § 33-722; Fla. Bus. Corp. Act § 607.07401(2); Ga. Bus. Corp. Code § 14-2-742; Me. Bus. Corp. Act § 630; Mich. Bus. Corp. Act § 450.1493a(a); Miss. Bus. Corp. Act § 79-4-7.42; Mont. Bus. Corp. Act § 35-1-543; Neb. Bus. Corp. Act § 21-2072; N.H. Bus. Corp. Act § 293-A:7.42; N.C. Bus. Corp. Act § 55-7-42; Tex. Bus. Corp. Act § 5.14(C); Va. Stock Corp. Act § 13.1-672.1B(1); Wis. Bus. Corp. Law § 180.0742.

1121. *See Cuker v. Mikalauskas*, 692 A.2d 1042, 1048-49 (Pa. 1997) (adopting Section 7.03 of Principles of Corporate Governance).

1122. 908 F.2d 1338 (7th Cir. 1990), *rev'd*, 500 U.S. 90 (1991).

1123. *Id.* at 1344 (quoting Principles of Corporate Governance: Analysis and Recommendations § 7.03 comment at 64 (Tentative Draft No. 8 Apr. 15, 1988)).

1124. *Id.* at 1344.

1125. *Id.*

that demand is futile because they will not sue themselves or contest their own acts. Although directors are unlikely to sue themselves, they may well take some action to palliate the consequences of poorly conceived acts, including their own. Directors want the venture to succeed, and if shown how they can improve its prospects, are likely to act. One mistake at the time of the initial decision does not imply that the member of the board opposes remedial action. Even when the "action" involves suit against some of their number, this does not disable the board. . . . [T]he board may appoint a minority of disinterested members to evaluate the demand and act for the corporation. In the extreme case in which all members are implicated, the board may expand its size and authorize the new members to act for the firm. Of course it may choose to do none of these things, but if so it will just decline the demand. Making a demand is cheap, *especially* so when the board is disabled from acting. Why prefer extended, costly litigation to the cheap and quick expedient of a demand?

2. The board may be determined not to sue. Perhaps by the time the judge comes to consider whether plaintiff should have made a demand, the defendant will have moved to dismiss the case on the merits. Any demand in such a case would be doomed to failure, and even at an earlier stage it may be transparent that the directors want nothing to do with litigation. This application of the "futility" exception has both a practical and a conceptual difficulty. The practical one is that it is difficult to tell in advance just what position the firm would take if asked; disputes about the demand requirement usually are resolved before the defendants plead to the merits. It is easy for the plaintiffs to *say* (and for the defendants to deny) that the board has a closed mind; it is much harder to tell who is right.

The conceptual difficulty is that even an adamant unwillingness to sue may reflect the merits. Boards ought not pursue silly or frivolous claims. So certain knowledge that the board is unwilling to authorize litigation may reflect only confidence that the case is feeble or injurious to the firm and other investors. Why should the plaintiffs be authorized to sue, and without so much as a request to the board, just because the complaint is all heat and no light? . . . [A] formulation of the futility rule that inquires whether a demand would prompt the board to correct a wrong "assumes that there is a wrong to be corrected. The director's antagonism to an action may well be justified and flow from a sound judgment that the action is either not meritorious or would otherwise subject the corporation to serious injury." . . . A decision not to file a weak lawsuit would be protected by the business judgment rule, so it makes perfect sense to ask for the board's perspective.

3. A plaintiff may insist that even the independent directors are toadies, so that their judgment could not be respected. Perhaps they are friends of the putative defendants; perhaps they draw hefty directors' fees and fear loss of their offices if they authorize suit; perhaps they believe that the courts have no business supervising corporate affairs and would not authorize litigation no matter how meritorious (and no matter how little their regard for holding onto their offices). If demand is futile in fact for any of these reasons, then the board will say no with dispatch and the case may proceed. . . . [T]he plaintiff may employ this arsenal of arguments to argue that the decision not to sue ought not be respected; the board will stand on the business judgment rule. The court will resolve the question on the merits rather than trying to treat it as a procedural hurdle. Framing questions about the independence of the directors as exceptions to the demand requirement diverts attention from the real issues.[1126]

In short, the court concluded, courts should focus upon whether a board's decision to refuse a demand should be respected rather than upon hypothetical inquiries about what would happen if a demand were made.[1127]

The Supreme Court reversed the Seventh Circuit in *Kamen v. Kemper Financial Services, Inc.*[1128] The Supreme Court held that the demand requirement is governed by state rather than federal law unless a federal policy would be frustrated by the application of state law—an aspect of the court's decision discussed earlier in this

---

1126. *Id.* at 1344-46.
1127. *Id.* at 1347.
1128. 500 U.S. 90 (1991).

Chapter.[1129] The court added that "[w]hatever its merits as a matter of legal reform" as a matter of state law, a universal demand requirement would be inappropriate as a matter of federal law because a federal universal demand rule would require federal courts "to fashion an entire body of federal corporate law" to govern cases in which demands made pursuant to a federal universal demand requirement are refused.[1130] This process, the court stated, "would necessarily infuse corporate decisionmaking with uncertainty" and provide the "type of disruption to the internal affairs of the corporation" that has in the past led federal courts to avoid "establishing competing federal- and state-law principles on the allocation of managerial prerogatives within the corporation."[1131]

As an example, the court pointed to the fact that under Delaware law a shareholder who makes a demand cannot assert that demand was excused as futile.[1132] This rule, the court stated, "makes it crystal clear to the directors of a Delaware corporation" that if a demand is made, then "the decision whether to commit the corporation to litigation lies solely in their discretion."[1133] A federal law universal demand requirement, however, would require demand in all cases where a shareholder sought to commence a derivative action in federal court. Contrary to Delaware law, a shareholder who made such a demand could not be said to have conceded the board's entitlement to make a decision concerning the demand.[1134] Under these circumstances, the court stated, the directors of a Delaware corporation that received a demand would not at that point in time know whether the decision to commit or not commit the corporation to litigation would lie solely in the

---

1129. *See* Chapter IV, Sections B 4 a-b.
1130. 500 U.S. at 104-05.
1131. *Id*. at 105-06.
1132. *Id*. at 105.
1133. *Id*. (citing *Spiegel v. Buntrock*, 571 A.2d 767, 775 (Del. 1990); *see also* Chapter IV, Section B 5 i (i) (discussing this principle); Chapter IV, Section B 6 c-f (discussing the standard or review under Delaware law in cases where a demand is refused).
1134. *Id*. at 105.

board's discretion. To the contrary, "the directors could do no more than speculate as to whether they should access the merits of the demand themselves or instead incur the time and expense associated with forming a special litigation committee," a procedure required in Delaware only where demand is excused.[1135]

The court added that the directors' dilemma upon receiving a demand "would be especially acute if the shareholder were proposing to join state-law and federal claims."[1136] In such a case, the court explained, different standards might govern the state law and federal law aspects of the demand.[1137]

The Supreme Court acknowledged that "[r]equiring demand in all cases . . . might marginally enhance the prospect that corporate disputes would be resolved without resort to litigation."[1138] According to the Supreme Court, however, "nothing disables the directors from seeking an accommodation with a representative shareholder even after the shareholder files his complaint in an action in which demand is excused as futile."[1139] The court added its view that adoption of a universal demand requirement "is unlikely to avoid the high collateral litigation costs associated with the demand futility doctrine" because a universal demand requirement would "merely shift the focus of threshold litigation from the question whether demand is excused to the question whether the directors' decision to terminate the suit is entitled to deference under federal standards."[1140]

For all of these reasons, the Supreme Court concluded, "we do not view the advantages" associated with the proposed universal demand rule to be "sufficiently apparent to justify replacing 'the

---

1135. *Id.; see also* Chapter IV C (discussing special litigation committees).
1136. *Id.* at 105.
1137. *Id.* (citations omitted).
1138. *Id.* at 106.
1139. *Id.*
1140. *Id.*

entire corpus of state corporation law' relating to demand futility."[1141]

On remand, the Seventh Circuit held that demand was required under Maryland law. The court reasoned that "[l]ike most states, Maryland both requires demand as a norm and excuses demand when the request would be futile" but "Maryland has done little to develop the scope of its futility exception."[1142] The court stated that "[i]n resolving doubt about the scope of its demand requirement, Maryland could well be influenced by the recommendations of the American Law Institute and the American Bar Association, both of which believe that the futility exception to the demand requirement should be eliminated."[1143] The court, however, did not decide whether Maryland would or would not adopt a universal demand requirement. Instead, the court concluded that "[w]e think it likely . . . that if Maryland does not abolish the futility exception it will cast its lot with the states that require demand on directors who face no substantial risk of personal liability."[1144] Thus, even if Maryland did not adopt a universal demand requirement, demand still would be required.[1145]

A subsequent decision in the Seventh Circuit construing Indiana law, *Boland v. Engle*,[1146] stated that "we suspect" Indiana would adopt a universal demand requirement but determined not to

---

1141. *Id.* at 106-07; *see also RCM Sec. Fund, Inc. v. Stanton*, 928 F.2d 1318, 1328 (2d Cir. 1991) (pre-Supreme Court *Kemper* decision stating that "[w]ere we a state court fashioning a demand requirement, we would not quarrel" with the Seventh Circuit's reasoning in *Kemper*, but concluding that federal courts have no authority to fashion a federal demand requirement and that a federal universal demand requirement would create "daunting complexities"); *Starrels v. First Nat'l Bank*, 870 F.2d 1168, 1174 n.2, 1176 (7th Cir. 1989) (Easterbrook, J., concurring) (noting benefits of universal demand rule).

1142. *Kamen v. Kemper Fin. Servs., Inc.*, 939 F.2d 458, 460 (7th Cir.), *cert. denied*, 502 U.S. 974 (1991).

1143. *Id.* at 461.

1144. *Id.* at 462.

1145. *Id.* at 462-63.

1146. 113 F.3d 706 (7th Cir. 1997).

decide "whether Indiana's highest court would go all the way to a universal demand requirement."[1147] The court held that even if Indiana would not adopt a universal demand requirement, Indiana courts still would be "persuaded by the general trend in the law towards narrowing, if not eliminating, the exceptions from the demand requirement" and thus would require demand based upon the facts pleaded by plaintiff in the case before the court.[1148]

The Model Act specifies that no derivative action may be commenced until "90 days have expired from the date the demand was made unless the shareholder has earlier been notified that the demand has been rejected by the corporation."[1149] The Official Comment explains that "[n]inety days has been chosen as a reasonable minimum time within which the board of directors can meet, direct the necessary inquiry into the charges, receive the results of the inquiry and make its decision."[1150] The drafters recognize that "[i]n many instances a longer period may be required" but conclude that a fixed 90 day time period "eliminates further litigation" with respect to whether a period of 90 or fewer days "is or is not a reasonable time."[1151] If a suit is commenced after 90 days in a case where more than 90 days is needed to complete the appropriate inquiry, the Model Act provides that "the court may stay" the action "for such period as the court deems appropriate."[1152]

Most states that have adopted the Model Act's universal demand requirement follow the Model Act's 90 day rule and the Model Act's provision that "the court may stay" a derivative action that is commenced before a response to a demand is made "for such period of time as the court deems appropriate." The Texas statute, however, provides for a stay until the review of a demand is completed if the corporation provides the court "with a written

---

1147. *Id.* at 713.
1148. *Id.* at 711.
1149. Model Bus. Corp. Act § 7.42(2).
1150. *Id.* Official Comment at 7-343.
1151. *Id.* at 7–343-44.
1152. *Id.* § 7.43.

statement containing an undertaking to advise the court and the shareholder making the demand of the determination promptly on the completion of the review of the matter."[1153] The stay must be "reviewed as to its continued necessity every 60 days thereafter," and "the stay may be renewed for one or more additional 60-day periods" if the corporation provides the court and the shareholder making the demand "a written statement of the status of the review and the reasons a continued extension of the stay is necessary."[1154]

Principles of Corporate Governance provides that "the court should dismiss a derivative action that is commenced prior to the response . . . to the demand" unless the demand is not responded to "within a reasonable time."[1155] The commentary in Principles of Corporate Governance states the following with respect to what constitutes a "reasonable time":

> When . . . the board promptly indicates that it will undertake a further study and respond with its determinations within a reasonable period (such as 60 days), the plaintiff should not normally be able to commence the action in this interim (absent irreparable injury). In general, a lengthy interim between the making of the demand and the board's response should seldom be necessary. If the corporation fails to undertake and complete its inquiry within a reasonable period following demand (which period should never exceed several months even when a study is undertaken and seldom should be that long), the plaintiff may file the action, and it should not be deemed premature.[1156]

The Delaware Supreme Court declined to adopt a universal demand requirement in *Rales v. Blasband*.[1157] The court in *Rales* rejected a contention that this "stringent" test is required "to discourage 'strike suits.'"[1158] The New York Court of Appeals

---

1153. Tex. Bus. Corp. Act § 5.14(D).

1154. *Id.*

1155. Principles of Corporate Governance § 7.03(d).

1156. *Id.* Comment at 60-61.

1157. 634 A.2d 927 (Del. 1993).

1158. *Id.* at 934.

declined to adopt a universal demand requirement in *Marx v. Akers*.[1159] The court in *Marx* explained that "[s]ince New York's demand requirement is codified in Business Corporation Law § 626(c)"—a requirement similar to Federal Rule of Civil Procedure 23.1, Delaware Court of Chancery Rule 23.1 and comparable requirements that most states have adopted[1160]—"a universal demand can only be adopted by the Legislature."[1161]

  *h. The Effect of Changes in Board Composition Following Commencement of Litigation.* "[M]any cases . . . hold that the proper time to measure demand futility is at the filing of the complaint."[1162] The Delaware Court of Chancery has held in several cases that if demand is excused at the start of a litigation, then demand remains excused throughout the litigation even if a board upon which demand was excused is replaced with a board upon which demand would not have been excused if the litigation been commenced at a later date. The rule established in these cases does not apply where the change in board composition occurs after a

---

  1159. 88 N.Y.2d 189, 666 N.E.2d 1034, 644 N.Y.S.2d 121 (1996).

  1160. *See* N.Y. Bus. Corp. Law § 626(c) (in any derivative action, the plaintiff's complaint must "set forth with particularity the efforts of the plaintiff to secure the initiation of such action by the board or the reasons for not making such effort"); *see also, e.g.,* Fed. R. Civ. P. 23.1; Cal. Corp. Code § 800(b)(2); Del. Ch. R. 23.1.

  1161. *Marx,* 88 N.Y.2d at 198, 666 N.E.2d at 1039, 644 N.Y.S.2d at 126; *see also id.* at 197-98 & n.4, 666 N.E.2d at 1039 & n.4, 644 N.Y.S.2d at 126 & n.4 (noting that New York's Legislature "has . . . considered and continues to consider implementing a universal demand requirement").

  1162. *Harris v. Carter,* 582 A.2d 222, 228 (Del. Ch. 1990); *see also Rales v. Blasband,* 634 A.2d 927, 934 (Del. 1993); *Pogostin v. Rice,* 480 A.2d 619, 624 (Del. 1984); *Aronson v. Lewis,* 473 A.2d 805, 809-10 (1984); *In re Bally's Grand Derivative Litig.,* 1997 Del. Ch. LEXIS 77, at *8, 1997 WL 305803, at *3 (Del. Ch. June 4, 1997); *Katz v. Halperin,* 21 Del. J. Corp. L. 690, 703 (Del. Ch. Feb. 5, 1996); *Seminaris v. Landa,* 662 A.2d 1350, 1354 (Del. Ch. 1995).

challenged transaction or challenged conduct but before litigation is initiated.[1163]

The leading case is *Harris v. Carter*.[1164] In *Harris*, the plaintiff's first complaint was labeled a class action—not a derivative action. Later, after a new board was in place, the plaintiff filed an amended complaint that was labeled a derivative action on behalf of the corporation, Atlas Energy Corporation.[1165] The court concluded that the plaintiff was not required to make a demand before the time the amended complaint was filed "even if it were assumed that the Atlas board at the time of the filing of the amended complaint was capable of exercising a valid business judgment with respect to the question whether the corporation itself should assert these claims."[1166] The court explained that the original complaint raised the same claims later brought as derivative claims, and it is the nature of a pleading rather than the pleader's characterization of a claim that determines whether the claim is derivative or not derivative.[1167] The court noted that the term "'claim' for these purposes does not refer simply to legal theories of liability but refers broadly to the acts and transactions alleged in the original complaint."[1168]

The court stated that although "some tribute must be paid to the fact that the lawsuit was properly initiated,"[1169] a board composed of "new directors who are under no personal conflict with respect to prosecution of a pending derivative claim" has three options: (1) "move the court to take control of the litigation by being re-aligned as a party plaintiff," (2) "move to dismiss the case as not, in the board's business judgment, in the corporation's best interest," or (3) "through a formal understanding or by simply fail-

---

1163. *Blasband v. Rales*, 971 F.2d 1034, 1054-55 (3d Cir. 1992); *see also* Chapter IV, Section B 5 d (discussing this decision).

1164. 582 A.2d 222 (Del. Ch. 1990).

1165. *Id.* at 224-25, 228.

1166. *Id.* at 228.

1167. *Id.* at 229.

1168. *Id.* at 231.

1169. *Id.* (quoting *Zapata Corp. v. Maldonado*, 430 A.2d 779, 787 (Del. 1981)).

ing to act, allow the representative plaintiff and his counsel to carry the litigation forward."[1170] These options, the court stated, "fully protect the legitimate rights of the board . . . to manage the corporation's business and affairs."[1171] Thus, in the *Harris* court's view, the demand requirement does not provide a basis "to stall the derivative suit mechanism where it has been properly initiated."[1172] "When claims have been properly laid before the court and are in litigation," the court stated, neither the demand requirement nor the policy it implements "requires that a court decline to permit further litigation of those claims upon the replacement of the interested board with a disinterested one."[1173] Instead, the new board is required "to take one of the steps outlined above, should it decide to act at all with respect to the matter."[1174]

The Court of Chancery re-affirmed this analysis in *In re Fuqua Industries, Inc. Shareholder Litigation.*[1175] The court stated that the filing of an amended complaint affects the demand requirement only "to the extent that the amended complaint raises claims not already 'validly in litigation.'"[1176] "[O]nly with respect to those claims," the court stated, "will adherence to the policy of making demand upon the first board deprive a board of its right to control the business and affairs of the corporation."[1177] Accordingly, "claims alleged in an amended complaint, which were not already validly in litigation, should be presented to the board in existence at the time of filing of the amended complaint or the plaintiff should state with particularity why demand upon that board would be futile and, thus, should be excused."[1178]

---

1170. *Id.* at 230-31.

1171. *Id.* at 231.

1172. *Id.*

1173. *Id.*

1174. *Id.*

1175. 1997 Del. Ch. LEXIS 72, 1997 WL 257460 (Del. Ch. May 13, 1997).

1176. 1997 Del. Ch. LEXIS 72, at *52, 1997 WL 257460, at *13 (quoting *Harris*, 582 A.2d at 230).

1177. 1997 Del. Ch. LEXIS 72, at *52, 1997 WL 257460, at *13.

1178. *Id.*

The Court of Chancery also relied upon *Harris* in *Needham v. Cruver*,[1179] a case holding that demand was excused where directors were alleged to be financially interested in challenged conduct at the time a complaint was filed but not at the time that the demand issue was litigated.[1180] The Court of Chancery also followed *Harris* in *Uni-Marts, Inc. v. Stein*.[1181] The court in *Uni-Marts* stated that where the transaction challenged in an amended complaint "grows out of and represents a modified version" of a transaction challenged in an earlier complaint, the plaintiff "need not establish that the board that existed at the time of the filing of the Amended Complaint was sufficiently implicated in the acts complained of to deprive it of the ability to make a valid business judgment concerning this suit."[1182]

A pre-*Harris* decision reaching the same conclusion is *Kaufman v. Beal*.[1183] The court in *Kaufman* stated that it "offends notions of fairness to require a plaintiff in a stockholder's derivative suit to make a new demand every time the Board of Directors of the corporation is changed."[1184] The court reasoned that courts considering motions to dismiss "have consistently held that a plaintiff must show that a demand was excusable by relying on facts gauged at the time the derivative action was commenced—not afterwards."[1185] According to the court, it would "be unfair to impose a different standard on a plaintiff where the composition of the Board of Directors is changed after suit."[1186] The court noted that the *Kaufman* case did not involve "the question of whether a demand on a Board is required before the filing of an amendment

1179. [1993 Transfer Binder] Fed. Sec. L. Rep. (CCH) ¶ 97,673 (Del. Ch. May 12, 1993).

1180. *Id.* at 97,118.

1181. 1996 Del. Ch. LEXIS 95, 1996 WL 466961 (Del. Ch. Aug. 9, 1996).

1182. 1996 Del. Ch. LEXIS 95, at *41, 1996 WL 466961, at *12.

1183. 1983 Del. Ch. LEXIS 391, 1983 WL 20295 (Del. Ch. Feb. 25, 1983).

1184. 1983 Del. Ch. LEXIS 391, at *26, 1983 WL 20295, at *9.

1185. *Id.*

1186. *Id.*

which states an entirely new claim."[1187] "Because it is not before me," the court stated, "I do not rule on the question."[1188]

The same result was reached by the Colorado Court of Appeals in *New Crawford Valley, Ltd. v. Benedict*[1189] and a federal court in California in *Nelson v. Pacific Southwest Airlines.*[1190] Both courts held that to require a demand and an amended complaint "every time that a change in the composition of the board of directors occurred" would be "overly burdensome to plaintiffs in derivative suits" because "[e]lection of directors may occur annually, and more frequent changes may result from death, resignation, or removal."[1191] The result, both courts stated, "would be to further delay already protracted litigation, while the plaintiff repeatedly awaited board action and filed amended complaints."[1192] Thus, the *New Crawford* and *Nelson* courts concluded, "[a] proper demand upon the board of directors is a necessary condition precedent to the commencement of the litigation, unless such demand would be futile," but there is no requirement that a plaintiff "after suit is properly instituted" must "make a further demand upon the board, even if its composition has been changed in the interim."[1193] The same result also was reached by a federal court in New York in *Rothenberg v. United Brands Co.*[1194] The court in that case accordingly assessed the need for a demand on the date that a complaint was filed rather than on the next day, when a new board of directors assumed control of the corporation.[1195]

---

1187. 1983 Del. Ch. LEXIS 391, at *27, 1983 WL 20295, at *9.

1188. *Id.*

1189. 847 P.2d 642 (Colo. Ct. App. 1993).

1190. 399 F. Supp. 1025 (S.D. Cal. 1975).

1191. *New Crawford*, 847 P.2d at 645; *Nelson*, 399 F. Supp. at 1031.

1192. *Id.*

1193. *Id.*

1194. [1977-1978 Transfer Binder] Fed. Sec. L. Rep. (CCH) ¶ 96,045 (S.D.N.Y. May 11, 1977), *aff'd mem.*, 573 F.2d 1295 (2d Cir. 1977).

1195. *Id.* at 91,691.

The Second Circuit reached a different conclusion in a 1975 decision in *Brody v. Chemical Bank*,[1196] a case construing federal law. *Brody* holds that when an amended complaint is filed, the court must determine whether demand is required or excused on the basis of the composition of the board of directors as it existed on the date that the amended complaint was filed rather than on the date that the action was commenced.[1197] This result is required, according to the *Brody* court, because the "very purpose of the 'demand' rule is to give the derivative corporation itself the opportunity to take over a suit which was brought on its behalf in the first place."[1198] The court stated that "[i]t is manifest that this purpose could not be served by making (or excusing) a demand on the 1971 directors who were out of office in 1974 when the second complaint was filed."[1199]

The Second Circuit's decision in *Brody* has been followed by a federal district court in New York in *Lou v. Belzberg*[1200] and an Illinois decision construing New York law in *Lewis v. Brennan*.[1201] As stated by the court in *Belzberg*, "[t]o deprive the newly constituted Board the opportunity to decide whether Ashland would best be served by instituting its own suit . . . is to ignore the policy considerations" underlying the demand requirement.[1202] Another federal district court decision in New York, *Fischer v. CF&I Steel Corp.*,[1203] similarly concluded that a shareholder plaintiff who loses standing to maintain his derivative claim following the acquisition of the corporation in a stock for stock merger—a subject discussed earlier in this Chapter[1204]—may demand that

---

1196. 517 F.2d 932 (2d Cir. 1975).

1197. *Id.* at 934.

1198. *Id.*

1199. *Id.*

1200. 728 F. Supp. 1010, 1017-18 (S.D.N.Y. 1990).

1201. No. 92 CH 5820, slip op. at 8-9 (Ill. Cir. Ct. Feb. 15, 1995).

1202. 728 F. Supp. at 1018.

1203. 599 F. Supp. 340 (S.D.N.Y. 1984).

1204. *See* Chapter IV, Section A 2.

the board of new owner of the corporation take appropriate action.[1205] The court stated that the rationale supporting the demand requirement "strongly favors the proposition that the newly-constituted SFSP board should be given the opportunity to take a fresh look at the issues raised by plaintiffs and to decide whether or not it wishes to pursue the claims."[1206]

   *i. Waiver Considerations.* Two important lines of Delaware cases address (1) the extent to which a shareholder who makes a pre-litigation demand waives any right the shareholder otherwise would have to argue that demand is excused as futile or that the corporation's directors lack the disinterestedness and independence required to act upon a demand that is made, and (2) the extent to which a board delegation of decision-making authority in connection with a shareholder demand to a committee of disinterested and independent directors waives any right the board otherwise would have to argue that demand was required and that the board as a whole is sufficiently disinterested and independent to act upon the demand.

   *(i) Shareholder Demands.* Several Delaware Supreme Court decisions beginning with *Stotland v. GAF Corp.*[1207] hold that a shareholder demand waives a claim that demand is excused. *Stotland* involved a shareholder plaintiff who initially refused to make a demand, but then made a demand following dismissal of his case by the Court of Chancery for "failure to make a demand or to properly demonstrate its futility."[1208] The Supreme Court held that by making a demand the plaintiff had mooted the appeal of his claim that demand was excused.[1209]

   The Delaware Supreme Court in *Spiegel v. Buntrock*[1210] similarly held that a shareholder who commences derivative litigation "cannot stand neutral . . . with respect to the board of direc-

---

1205. 599 F. Supp. at 347.
1206. *Id.*
1207. 469 A.2d 421 (Del. 1983).
1208. *Id.* at 422.
1209. *Id.* at 423.
1210. 571 A.2d 767 (Del. 1990).

tors' ability to respond to a request to take legal action, by simultaneously making a demand for such action *and* continuing to argue that demand is excused."[1211] Rather, "[b]y making a demand, a stockholder tacitly acknowledges the absence of facts to support a finding of futility."[1212] As a result, "the question of whether demand was excused is moot."[1213] By making a demand, the *Spiegel* court also held, a shareholder also concedes that a majority of the corporation's board is disinterested and independent with respect to the subject matter of the demand.[1214]

The Delaware Supreme Court in *Levine v. Smith*[1215] and *Rales v. Blasband*[1216] similarly stated that a shareholder who makes a demand "concedes the independence and disinterestedness of a majority of the board to respond."[1217] As stated by the Supreme Court in *Scattered Corp. v. Chicago Stock Exchange, Inc.*,[1218] "[i]f the stockholders make a demand, . . . they are deemed to have waived any claim they might otherwise have had that the board cannot independently act on the demand."[1219] As stated in *Grimes v. Donald*[1220] and *Chicago Stock Exchange*, "[i]f a demand is made, the stockholder has spent one . . . 'arrow' in the 'quiver'"—"the right to claim that demand is excused."[1221] This waiver extends to all claims and remedies related to the subject matter of the demand.[1222]

---

1211. *Id.* at 775.
1212. *Id.*
1213. *Id.*
1214. *Id.* at 777.
1215. 591 A.2d 194 (Del. 1991).
1216. 634 A.2d 927 (Del. 1993).
1217. *Rales*, 634 A.2d at 935 n.12; *see also Levine*, 591 A.2d at 212-13 (similar language).
1218. 701 A.2d 70 (Del. 1997).
1219. *Id.* at 74; *see also id.* at 71.
1220. 673 A.2d 1207 (Del. 1996).
1221. *Grimes*, 673 A.2d at 1218-19, *quoted in Chicago Stock Exch.*, 701 A.2d at 74.
1222. *Grimes*, 673 A.2d at 1219-20.

Thus, even where demand otherwise would be excused, once a shareholder makes a demand, according to the Court of Chancery in *Thorpe v. CERBCO, Inc.*[1223]:

> [T]he shareholder is deemed to have made an important concession: that the board *is* able to function on the question. . . . This tacit concession appears to be not simply a factual presumption that might be rebutted by an allegation of fact but a conclusive presumption. . . . Thus, the current rule may be thought to exact a heavy price from shareholders who elect to try (in a context when they will not have much information) to employ internal corporate mechanisms before filing a claim on behalf of the corporation.[1224]

The court noted that this rule would apply even in cases involving "an allegation of later uncovered facts showing a self-interest of the board."[1225]

Other Court of Chancery decisions following the Supreme Court's decisions in *Stotland*, *Spiegel*, *Levine*, *Rales*, *Grimes* and *Chicago Stock Exchange* include the following:

- *Mount Moriah Cemetery v. Moritz*[1226] ("[b]y making demand, a plaintiff tacitly admits that demand was not futile and, therefore, concedes that a majority of the board is independent");[1227]

- *BTZ, Inc. v. National Intergroup, Inc.*[1228] ("[o]nce a plaintiff makes a demand . . . he can no longer argue that demand is excused");[1229]

---

1223. 611 A.2d 5 (Del. Ch. 1991).

1224. *Id.* at 10-11 (footnote omitted).

1225. *Id.* at 10 n.5.

1226. [1990-1991 Transfer Binder] Fed. Sec. L. Rep. (CCH) ¶ 95,900 (Del. Ch. Apr. 4, 1991), *aff'd*, 599 A.2d 413 (unpublished opinion, text available at 1991 Del. LEXIS 244 and 1991 WL 165558) (Del. Aug. 12, 1991).

1227. *Id.* at 99,442.

1228. 1993 Del. Ch. LEXIS 58, 1993 WL 133211 (Del. Ch. Apr. 7, 1993)

1229. 1993 Del. Ch. LEXIS 58, at *9, 1993 WL 133211, at *3.

- *Szeto v. Schiffer*[1230] ("[i]f a pre-suit demand is made upon the directors, the stockholder is deemed to have conceded that a failure to have made a pre-suit demand would not be excused");[1231]

- *Leslie v. Telephonics Office Technologies, Inc.*[1232] and *Yaw v. Talley*[1233] ("a demand on the board to take action is said to concede (and waive any challenge to) the board's ability to exercise a binding business judgment");[1234]

- *Boeing Co. v. Shrontz*[1235] ("by making a demand, a stockholder tacitly acknowledges the absence of facts to support a finding of futility," and "[t]hus, when a demand is made, the question of whether demand was excused is moot"; "[b]y making demand, plaintiffs concede the independence and disinterestedness of a majority of the Boeing board");[1236]

- *Charal Investment Co. v. Rockefeller*[1237] ("[i]f a shareholder makes a demand on the board, rather than pleading that demand is excused, the law presumes that the shareholder concedes the board's ability to make an independent decision on the matter");[1238] and

---

1230. 19 Del. J. Corp. L. 1310 (Del. Ch. Nov. 24, 1993).

1231. *Id.* at 1319.

1232. 19 Del. J. Corp. L. 1237 (Del. Ch. Dec. 30, 1993).

1233. 1994 Del. Ch. LEXIS 35, 1994 WL 89019 (Del. Ch. Mar. 2, 1994).

1234. *Leslie*, 19 Del. J. Corp. L. at 1255, *quoted in Yaw*, 1994 Del. Ch. LEXIS 35, at *24-25, 1994 WL 89019, at *8.

1235. 18 Del. J. Corp. L. 225 (Del. Ch. Apr. 20, 1992), *subsequent proceedings*, 1994 Del. Ch. LEXIS 14, 1994 WL 30542 (Del. Ch. Jan. 19, 1994).

1236. 18 Del. J. Corp. L. at 236; 1994 Del. Ch. LEXIS 14, at *6, 1994 WL 30542, at *2.

1237. [1995-1996 Transfer Binder] Fed. Sec. L. Rep. (CCH) ¶ 98,979 (Del. Ch. Nov. 7, 1995).

1238. *Id.* at 93,761.

- *Baron v. Siff*[1239] ("[b]y making a pre-suit demand, a plaintiff concedes the independence and disinterestedness of the board").[1240]

A shareholder plaintiff cannot evade the rule established in these cases by making a demand but stating in his demand letter that he is making the demand notwithstanding his belief that demand is futile.[1241] Nor can a shareholder evade this rule by making a demand but filing a complaint in the name of a second shareholder who has not made a demand and who contends that demand is excused.[1242] A shareholder also cannot evade this rule by contending that a demand was compelled by court order after the shareholder unsuccessfully had contended that demand was excused as futile.[1243]

A shareholder who makes a demand "does not, by making the demand, waive the right to claim that demand has been wrongfully refused."[1244] To the contrary, "[s]imply because the composition of the board provides no basis *ex ante* for the stockholder to claim with particularity . . . that it is reasonable to doubt that a majority of the board is either interested or not independent, it does not necessarily follow *ex post* that the board in fact acted independently, disinterestedly or with due care in response to the demand."[1245] In other words, "the making of a demand waives

---

1239. 1997 Del. Ch. LEXIS 152, 1997 WL 666973 (Del. Ch. Oct. 17, 1997).

1240. 1997 Del. Ch. LEXIS 152, at *5, 1997 WL 666973, at *2.

1241. *Boeing Co. v. Shrontz*, 18 Del. J. Corp. L. 225, 236 (Del. Ch. Apr. 20, 1992).

1242. *Id*.

1243. *Litton Indus., Inc. v. Hoch*, 996 F.2d 1225 (unpublished opinion, text available at 1993 U.S. App. LEXIS 16992, at *4 and 1993 WL 241549, at *1) (9th Cir. July 2, 1993), *aff'g* No. 89-1967 RG, slip op. at 5-6 (C.D. Cal. Oct. 31, 1991); *Varian Assocs., Inc. v. Superior Court*, No. H011025, slip op. at 11 (Cal. Ct. App. Aug. 31, 1993).

1244. *Scattered Corp. v. Chicago Stock Exch., Inc.*, 701 A.2d 70, 74 (Del. 1997) (quoting *Grimes v. Donald*, 673 A.2d 1207, 1219 (Del. 1996)).

1245. *Id*.

only any contention that the board was incapable of acting on the demand."[1246] It does not preclude a plaintiff from alleging that the board or a committee investigating and/or acting on the demand did not act "independently and in good faith" or did not conduct "a reasonable investigation."[1247] A shareholder who makes a request for information in a form that is not a demand does not concede that a demand is required or that the corporation's board lacks disinterestedness and independence.[1248]

The Delaware rule discussed above has been followed by a federal court construing Illinois law in *Weiland v. Illinois Power Co.*[1249] A Missouri court in *Dawson v. Dawson*[1250] similarly found the demand futility issue "largely mooted" by the making of a demand and accordingly stayed proceedings in that case pending the corporation's response to a demand.[1251]

A North Carolina court rejected the Delaware approach in *Alford v. Shaw.*[1252] The *Alford* court stated that "[w]e see no reason" why rules governing cases in which demand is excused "should not apply to cases . . . where demand was made although it could legitimately have been excused."[1253] A federal court construing Colorado law in *Bach v. National Western Life Insurance Co.*[1254] also rejected the Delaware approach. The *Bach* court reasoned that "the Delaware rule . . . discourages the making of demands and the delegation of investigative duties to the most independent directors."[1255] The court stated that "[i]n this sense, the Delaware rule is hostile to business judgment and is an unlikely

---

1246. *Chicago Stock Exch.*, 701 A.2d at 71.

1247. *Id.*

1248. *Blasband v. Rales*, 971 F.2d 1034, 1051 (3d Cir. 1992).

1249. [1990-1991 Transfer Binder] Fed. Sec. L. Rep. (CCH) ¶ 95,747, at 98,588 (C.D. Ill. Sept. 17, 1990).

1250. 645 S.W.2d 120 (Mo. Ct. App. 1982).

1251. *Id.* at 127-28.

1252. 324 S.E.2d 878 (N.C. Ct. App. 1985), *aff'd and modified on other grounds*, 358 S.E.2d 323 (N.C. 1987).

1253. *Id.* at 883 n.2

1254. 810 F.2d 509 (5th Cir. 1987).

1255. *Id.* at 513.

candidate for adoption by jurisdictions in which business judgment is more warmly embraced."[1256] The court concluded that "[i]n our view, Colorado is such a jurisdiction, and we are persuaded that it would not subscribe to a theory of waiver."[1257]

The Second Circuit in *Joy v. North*,[1258] construing Connecticut law, stated that "[d]emand was made in the present case but was not required," but the court did not address any contention that the making of a demand had an effect upon the standard by which the conduct challenged in the case should be judged.[1259] The Seventh Circuit in *Kamen v. Kemper Financial Services, Inc.*[1260] held that the question whether the making of a demand constitutes a concession that demand is required is governed by federal law, and that under federal law, unlike Delaware law, the making of a demand does not constitute a concession that demand is required.[1261] *Kemper* was reversed by the Supreme Court on the ground that state law governs the demand requirement where state law does not conflict with federal policy.[1262]

Two pre-*Kemper* federal district court decisions, *Mozes v. Welch*[1263] and *Allison v. General Motors Corp.*[1264] (the latter of which was affirmed in an unpublished opinion that did not address this issue) declined to reach the question whether the making of a demand waived any claim that demand was excused.[1265]

---

1256. *Id.*

1257. *Id.*

1258. 692 F.2d 880 (2d Cir. 1982), *cert. denied*, 460 U.S. 1051 (1983).

1259. *Id.* at 888 n.7.

1260. 908 F.2d 1338 (7th Cir. 1990), *rev'd on other grounds*, 500 U.S. 90 (1991).

1261. *Id.* at 1334-44.

1262. *See Kamen v. Kemper Fin. Servs., Inc.*, 500 U.S. 90 (1991); *see also* Chapter III, Sections B 4 a-b (discussing this aspect of the *Kemper* decision).

1263. 638 F. Supp. 215 (D. Conn. 1986).

1264. 604 F. Supp. 1106 (D. Del.), *aff'd mem.*, 782 F.2d 1026 (3d Cir. 1985).

1265. *Mozes*, 638 F. Supp. at 218; *Allison*, 604 F. Supp. at 1116.

Both of these courts concluded that it was unnecessary to decide this question because demand would have been required even if it had not been made.[1266]

A New York court addressed a related issue in a case where a plaintiff made a demand and was advised that his demand would be considered at the board's next regular meeting, which was scheduled to occur in two weeks.[1267] The court held that the plaintiff in this case "satisfactorily complied" with the demand requirement. The court stated that "a factor which should be considered in determining whether plaintiff was justified in deeming the response to his demand unsatisfactory" is the fact that "[a]lthough plaintiff chose to make a demand upon the board, the complaint reveals that in view of the nature of the action, charging an overwhelming majority of the directors with breach of their fiduciary duties, such a demand was not necessary."[1268]

Courts following the Delaware approach are divided with respect to whether a demand by one shareholder precludes another shareholder (acting separately) from alleging that demand is excused and/or that the corporation's directors are not sufficiently disinterested and independent to act upon a demand. The Delaware Court of Chancery in *Avacus Partners, L.P. v. Brian*,[1269] a federal district court construing Delaware law in *Miller v. Loucks*[1270] and a New Jersey court in *In re Prudential Insurance Co. Derivative Litigation*[1271] have held that a demand by one shareholder has no effect upon the rights of other shareholders.[1272] By con-

---

1266. *Id.*

1267. *MacKay v. Pierce*, 86 A.D.2d 655, 446 N.Y.S.2d 403 (N.Y. App. Div. 2d Dep't 1982).

1268. *Id.* at 655, 446 N.Y.S.2d at 404.

1269. [1991 Transfer Binder] Fed. Sec. L. Rep. (CCH) ¶ 96,232 (Del. Ch. Oct. 24, 1990).

1270. 1992 U.S. Dist. LEXIS 16966, 1992 WL 329313 (N.D. Ill. Nov. 5, 1992).

1271. 659 A.2d 961 (N.J. Super. Ct. Ch. Div. 1995).

1272. *Avacus*, [1991 Transfer Binder] Fed. Sec. L. Rep. (CCH) at 91,216; *Miller*, 1992 U.S. Dist. LEXIS 16966, at *22, 1992 WL 329313, at *6; *Prudential*, 659 A.2d at 969-70.

trast, the Eleventh Circuit in a case construing Delaware law, *Stepak v. Addison*,[1273] noted a district court ruling in the case before it holding that one shareholder's demand precluded any other shareholder from contending that demand was excused, and stated that "[o]n appeal, Mondschein does not address the district court's holding that his claim of demand futility is mooted by Stepak's demand; the issue is therefore waived."[1274] An Illinois court in *Schnitzer v. O'Connor*[1275] similarly concluded that the dismissal of a derivative claim alleging wrongful refusal of demand bars a derivative claim in a second action challenging the same wrongdoing but alleging that demand is excused.[1276] The fact that a demand has been made upon a board has been held not to concede disinterestedness and independence where there is a change in the membership of the board between the time the demand is made and the time a derivative action is filed.[1277]

The Delaware rule that a demand concedes disinterestedness and independence does not necessarily apply in derivative actions brought on behalf of limited partnerships.[1278] This issue is discussed later in this Chapter.[1279]

*(ii) Board Delegation of Decision-Making Authority.* A second important waiver issue is whether a board delegation of decision-making authority in connection with a shareholder demand to a committee of disinterested directors waives any right the board otherwise would have to argue that demand was required and that the board as a whole is sufficiently disinterested and independent to act upon the demand.

---

1273. 20 F.3d 398 (11th Cir. 1994).

1274. *Id.* at 412.

1275. 653 N.E.2d 825 (Ill. App. Ct. 1995).

1276. *Id.* at 827, 831, 833.

1277. *Abrams v. Koether*, 766 F. Supp. 237, 257 (D.N.J. 1991).

1278. *See Seaford Funding L.P. v. M & M Assocs. II, L.P.*, 672 A.2d 66, 71-72 (Del. Ch. 1995).

1279. *See* Chapter IV, Section D 2.

The Delaware Court of Chancery's 1983 decision in *Abbey v. Computer & Communications Technology Corp.*[1280] involved a demand that was referred by a board to a special litigation committee having "full and final authority" to act on behalf of the corporation with respect to the demand.[1281] Before the committee responded to the demand, the shareholder who had made the demand filed a derivative action.[1282] The court stated that demand is excused "where, because of some alleged self-interest, the board of directors is disqualified from acting itself," and "[o]therwise, but for the disqualifying, self-interest factor, the board could make its decision for itself, whether it chose to do so through a committee or not."[1283] The court then stated that "[u]nder the facts of this matter" the board's determination to delegate the demand to a special litigation committee having the power to determine the corporation's position "in effect" conceded that the board was disqualified from acting and that demand thus was excused.[1284]

The court in *Abbey* added, however, that a board may appoint a committee "to investigate . . . allegations and to report back to the board" without conceding interest or lack of independence.[1285] *Abbey* thus has been distinguished in cases where it has not been alleged that a board "delegated the power to assume its litigation posture,"[1286] and where the committee had investigating authority but "no authority to act on the plaintiff's demand."[1287] "The 'waiver' rationale for which *Abbey* stands" also was distin-

---

1280. 457 A.2d 368 (Del. Ch. 1983).

1281. *Id.* at 374.

1282. *Id.* at 370.

1283. *Id.* at 373.

1284. *Id.*

1285. *Id.* at 374.

1286. *Allison v. General Motors Corp.*, 604 F. Supp. 1106, 1121 n.16 (D. Del.), *aff'd mem.*, 782 F.2d 1026 (3d Cir. 1985).

1287. *Scattered Corp. v. Chicago Stock Exch., Inc.*, 1996 Del. Ch. LEXIS 79, at *10 n.4, 1996 WL 417507, at *3 n.4 (Del. Ch. July 12, 1996), *aff'd on other grounds*, 701 A.2d 70 (Del. 1997).

guished in *Kaplan v. Peat, Marwick, Mitchell & Co.*,[1288] a case
where a board received two demands: one related to claims against
the corporation's directors and officers and one related to claims
against the corporation's accountants, Peat, Marwick, Mitchell &
Co. ("PMM"). The demand with respect to the corporation's directors and officers was referred by the board to a special committee
formed for that purpose, and the demand with respect to PMM was
referred by the board to senior management.[1289] The court held
that the board "cannot be said to have conceded any disqualification
. . . to decide whether or not PMM should be sued."[1290]

Other decisions have distinguished *Abbey* where a motion to
dismiss is filed before decision-making authority is delegated to a
special committee. The Delaware Court of Chancery relied upon
this distinction in *Richardson v. Graves*,[1291] a case decided
shortly after *Abbey* was decided. The court in *Richardson* explained
that in *Richardson* the board filed a motion to dismiss for non-compliance with the demand requirement, and only then did the corporation's board appoint a special litigation committee to investigate
and make a determination.[1292] The court concluded that the facts
in *Richardson* "do not support a finding of concession on the part
of the Defendants or divestment of their power at the time they
moved to dismiss. The Defendants here filed a proper motion to
dismiss and . . . must in the first instance be afforded the opportunity to control the litigation."[1293]

The Delaware Supreme Court's 1990 decision in *Spiegel v.
Buntrock*[1294] also involved a case that, like *Richardson*, involved
a board that "*first* filed a motion to dismiss" a complaint due to the
plaintiff's failure to make a demand, "and *later*, after [the plaintiff]

---

1288. 529 A.2d 254 (Del. Ch. 1987), *aff'd in part and rev'd in part
on other grounds*, 540 A.2d 726 (Del. 1988).
1289. *Id.* at 263.
1290. *Id.*
1291. 1983 Del. Ch. LEXIS 466, 1983 WL 21109 (Del. Ch. June
17, 1983).
1292. 1983 Del. Ch. LEXIS 466, at *11, 1983 WL 21109, at *4.
1293. *Id.*
1294. 571 A.2d 767 (Del. 1990).

did make a demand, appointed a special litigation committee to respond to that demand."[1295] The court noted "[t]he significance of th[e] procedural distinction" between these facts and the facts in *Abbey*, where the board "did not file a motion to dismiss . . . until *after* it had surrendered exclusive control of the derivative action to a special litigation committee."[1296] Relying upon this distinction, the Supreme Court in *Spiegel* rejected the contention that "*Abbey* stands for the proposition that a board of directors, *ipso facto*, waives its right to challenge a shareholder plaintiff's allegation that demand is excused by the act of appointing a special litigation committee and delegating to that committee the authority to act on the demand."[1297] The court in *Spiegel* added that "[n]ot only are the facts in *Abbey* procedurally different from those of the present case, but *Abbey* itself specifically recognizes" (in language quoted in the discussion of *Abbey* above) "the right of a board of directors to appoint committees to address derivative litigation" without "automatically" conceding that demand is excused.[1298] Thus, the Supreme Court in *Spiegel* concluded, "the decision of a board of directors to appoint a special litigation committee, with a delegation of complete authority to act on a demand, is not, *in all instances*, an acknowledgement that demand was excused and *ergo* that a shareholder's lawsuit was properly initiated as a derivative action."[1299]

The Delaware Court of Chancery's decision in *Seminaris v. Landa*[1300] read the Supreme Court's discussion in *Spiegel* concerning the timing of motions to dismiss and board delegations of authority as not establishing "a generally applicable procedural rule."[1301] The court in *Seminaris* explained that the Supreme Court in *Spiegel* "did not rely on a presumption or a legal standard to distinguish *Abbey*. The Supreme Court was affirming the Chan-

---

1295. *Id.* at 777.
1296. *Id.* at 776-77.
1297. *Id.* at 777.
1298. *Id.*
1299. *Id.*
1300. 662 A.2d 1350 (Del. Ch. 1995).
1301. *Id.* at 1353.

cery Court's finding that the facts in *Spiegel* did not support an inference that the board had conceded demand futility."[1302] Therefore, to demonstrate that a board has conceded that demand is excused, the court in *Seminaris* held, a plaintiff "must allege particularized facts to support a factual determination that the board intended to concede demand."[1303]    In other words, "[f]or this Court to find that a board of directors conceded the futility of demand, a derivative plaintiff must allege particularized facts that support a factual finding that the board made the concession."[1304]

Applying this standard, the court in *Seminaris* held that the board in that case did not concede that it was unable to act in a disinterested and independent manner by forming a special committee of outside directors to investigate misrepresentations in the corporation's financial statements, and then, after a derivative complaint was filed three weeks later, delegating the board's decision-making authority with respect to the derivative complaint to this already existing special committee.[1305] The court pointed to the fact that the board in *Abbey*, which had been found to have conceded interestedness, had reacted to the filing of the derivative complaint in that case by adding a new independent director to the board and designating him a one member special committee, while in *Seminaris*, by contrast, the board appointed current board members to the special committee.[1306]    The court added that the plaintiff in *Seminaris* alleged facts demonstrating "an apparent interest for some board members, but not for members of the special committee."[1307]

A federal court construing Illinois law in *Weiland v. Illinois Power Co.*[1308] similarly held that under *Spiegel* a board's delega-

---

1302. *Id.*
1303. *Id.*
1304. *Id.*
1305. *Id.*
1306. *Id.*
1307. *Id.*
1308. [1990-1991 Transfer Binder] Fed. Sec. L. Rep. (CCH) ¶ 95,747 (C.D. Ill. Sept. 17, 1990).

tion of full decision-making authority to a special litigation committee does not "automatically" constitute a concession of interest or lack of independence on the part of the board.[1309] The court reached this determination despite the fact that the delegation of decision-making authority was not preceded, as in *Richardson* and *Spiegel*, by a motion to dismiss.[1310]

The Eleventh Circuit in *Peller v. Southern Co.*,[1311] a case involving a parent corporation whose conduct was governed by Delaware law and a subsidiary corporation whose conduct was governed by Georgia law, followed *Abbey* under circumstances in which "the order of events" was "completely different from the order in *Spiegel* and virtually identical to the order in *Abbey*."[1312] The court reasoned as follows:

> When confronted with Peller's complaint, the Companies did not pursue a motion to dismiss. Rather, they appointed the Committee and delegated to it the sole authority to evaluate the merits of the suit and determine the Companies' response. The Companies then waited for the Committee to make its report and, upon the Committee's negative recommendation, filed a motion to dismiss with the district court. Like the board in *Abbey*, the Companies did not seek a motion to dismiss until *after* they had delegated sole authority to the Committee. Because the Companies, like the board in *Abbey*, did not file a motion to dismiss until after they appointed the Committee and delegated to it the sole authority to evaluate the Peller suit, we find that the district court did not abuse its discretion when it found that the Companies effectively acknowledged that Peller was excused from making a demand.[1313]

In light of cases such as *Abbey* and *Peller*, "[b]oards often are reluctant to create special litigation committees with full power to determine the company's response" to a demand "because there is

---

1309. *Id*. at 98,588-89.
1310. *Id*. at 98,583-84.
1311. 911 F.2d 1532 (11th Cir. 1990).
1312. *Id*. at 1537.
1313. *Id*. at 1537-38.

a risk that such action might be deemed an admission of demand futility."[1314]

*j. The Effect of Dismissal for Failure to Make a Demand.* The rules vary from forum to forum with respect to whether dismissal of a complaint for failure to make a pre-litigation demand should be with or without leave to file an amended complaint if a demand subsequently is made and refused. If leave to file an amended complaint is not granted, then the plaintiff is required to commence a new action if demand is made and refused. The rationale for requiring a new action in the jurisdictions that follow this rule is that "[t]he suit's pendency while intracorporate remedies are being exhausted would itself be contrary to the principle that the directors ordinarily have the responsibility of making the initial decision about whether to bring suit."[1315] "[R]equiring demand before the filing of suit affords directors 'the opportunity to decide in the first instance whether and in what manner action should be taken.' A demand after suit is filed would usurp this prerogative."[1316] The difference in rules can have dispositive significance where, for example, the statute of limitations precludes the filing of a new suit.[1317]

The First and Third Circuits have required the filing of new complaints.[1318] District courts in California and New York have divided on this question, with one decision requiring the filing of a

---

1314. *Stoner v. Walsh*, 772 F. Supp. 790, 800 (S.D.N.Y. 1991).

1315. *Weiss v. Temporary Inv. Fund, Inc.*, 520 F. Supp. 1098, 1100 (D. Del. 1981), *aff'd*, 692 F.2d 928 (3d Cir. 1982), *vacated and remanded on other grounds*, 465 U.S. 1001 (1984).

1316. *Weiss v. Temporary Inv. Fund, Inc.*, 692 F.2d 928, 943 (3d Cir. 1982), *vacated and remanded on other grounds*, 465 U.S. 1001 (1984).

1317. *Temporary Inv. Fund*, 520 F. Supp. at 1100 & n.2.

1318. *See Temporary Inv. Fund*, 520 F. Supp. at 1100 and 692 F.2d at 943; *Grossman v. Johnson*, 674 F.2d 115, 125-26 (1st Cir.), *cert. denied*, 459 U.S. 838 (1982); *Shlensky v. Dorsey*, 574 F.2d 131, 141-42 (3d Cir. 1978); *Recchion v. Kirby*, 637 F. Supp. 284, 287 (W.D. Pa. 1985); *Smachlo v. Birkelo*, 576 F. Supp. 1439, 1445 (D. Del. 1983).

new complaint[1319] and other decisions granting leave to re-
plead.[1320] The Seventh Circuit in one case held that a district
court's dismissal of a complaint due to the plaintiff's failure to
make a demand was without prejudice and therefore that the plaintiff in that case could have made a demand and amended his complaint after the board considered the demand, but that the plaintiff
lost this right by appealing the district court's decision.[1321] The
only reference to this issue in a Delaware decision is a footnote in
the Delaware Supreme Court's decision in *Spiegel v. Buntrock*.[1322] This footnote states that "[a]lthough the Court of Chancery held that a pre-suit demand was required and not made, it did
not dismiss Spiegel's complaint on that basis alone. Thereafter, it
re-examined Spiegel's complaint, following the rejection of his
post-suit demand."[1323]

### 6.    The Response to a Demand

*a. The Board's Options.* "The effect of a demand is to place
control of the derivative litigation in the hands of the board of
directors."[1324] The corporation's directors "can exercise their discretion to accept the demand and prosecute the action, to resolve

---

1319. *See Fox v. Reich & Tang, Inc.*, 94 F.R.D. 94, 99
(S.D.N.Y.), *rev'd on other grounds*, 692 F.2d 250 (2d Cir. 1982), *aff'd
on other grounds sub nom. Daily Income Fund, Inc. v. Fox*, 464 U.S. 523
(1984).

1320. *See Lewis v. Sporck*, 646 F. Supp. 574, 577 (N.D. Cal.
1986); *Stein v. Bailey*, 531 F. Supp. 684, 685 (S.D.N.Y. 1982);
*Abramowitz v. Posner*, 513 F. Supp. 120, 121 (S.D.N.Y. 1981), *aff'd on
other grounds*, 672 F.2d 1025 (2d Cir. 1982); *Markowitz v. Brody*, 90
F.R.D. 542, 563 (S.D.N.Y. 1981); *see also Tarlov v. PaineWebber
Cashfund, Inc.*, 559 F. Supp. 429, 434 & n.5 (D. Conn. 1983) (declining
to resolve issue but collecting cases).

1321. *Boland v. Engle*, 113 F.3d 706, 714-15 (7th Cir. 1997).

1322. 571 A.2d 767 (Del. 1990).

1323. *Id.* at 778 n.21.

1324. *Levine v. Smith*, 591 A.2d 194, 212 (Del. 1991) (quoting
*Spiegel v. Buntrock*, 571 A.2d at 767, 775 (Del. 1990)).

the grievance internally without resort to litigation, or to refuse the demand."[1325] The demand requirement thus

> affords the directors an opportunity to exercise their reasonable business judgment and "waive a legal right vested in the corporation in the belief that its best interests will be promoted by not insisting on such right. They may regard the expense of enforcing the right or the furtherance of the general business of the corporation in determining whether to waive or insist upon the right." On the other hand, if, in the view of the directors, "litigation is appropriate, acceptance of the demand places the resources of the corporation, including its information, personnel, funds, and counsel, behind the suit."[1326]

The directors also may determine not to commence litigation on behalf of the corporation but to allow the shareholder to commence and pursue the action on the corporation's behalf.[1327] The board, however, must "affirmatively object to or support" the commencement and maintenance of derivative litigation by the shareholder.[1328] The board cannot "assume a position of neutrality and take no position in response to the demand."[1329] A position of neutrality, if taken by the board, is "viewed as tacit approval for the continuation of the litigation."[1330] A failure to consider the possibility of "remaining neutral" in response to a shareholder

---

1325. *Rales v. Blasband*, 634 A.2d 927, 935 (Del. 1993) (quoting *Weiss v. Temporary Inv. Fund, Inc.*, 692 F.2d 928, 941 (3d Cir. 1982), *vacated and remanded on other grounds*, 465 U.S. 1001 (1984)).

1326. *Daily Income Fund, Inc. v. Fox*, 464 U.S. 523, 532-33 (1984) (quoting *Corbus v. Alaska Treadwell Gold Mining Co.*, 187 U.S. 455, 463 (1903), and Note, *The Demand and Standing Requirements in Stockholder Derivative Actions*, 44 U. Chi. L. Rev. 168, 171-72 (1976)).

1327. *See Halprin v. Babbitt*, 303 F.2d 138, 142 (1st Cir. 1962); *Sohland v. Baker*, 141 A. 277 (Del. 1927).

1328. *Spiegel*, 571 A.2d at 775 (quoting *Kaplan v. Peat, Marwick, Mitchell & Co.*, 540 A.2d 726, 731 (Del. 1988)).

1329. *Scattered Corp. v. Chicago Stock Exch., Inc.*, 701 A.2d 70, 78 (Del. 1997); *Grimes v. Donald*, 673 A.2d 1207, 1218 (Del. 1996); *Spiegel*, 571 A.2d at 775.

1330. *Peat Marwick*, 540 A.2d at 731.

demand thus does not render a board's consideration of the demand uninformed.[1331]

"[T]he directors must determine the best method to inform themselves of the facts relating to the alleged wrongdoing and the considerations, both legal and financial, bearing on a response to the demand."[1332] "There is no prescribed procedure that a Board must follow when investigating a demand."[1333] "In most instances, a factual investigation is appropriate so that the board can be fully informed about the validity, if any, of the claims of wrong-doing contained in the demand letter. Nevertheless, a formal inves-tigation will not always be necessary because the directors may already have sufficient information regarding the subject of the demand to make a decision in response to it."[1334]

The board may act on its own knowledge of the facts or upon the advice and recommendation of the corporation's general coun-sel, some other officer or agent of the corporation, or a committee appointed by the board.[1335] There is no requirement that a board

---

1331. *In re Consumers Power Co. Derivative Litig.*, 132 F.R.D. 455, 486-88 (E.D. Mich. 1990).

1332. *Rales*, 634 A.2d at 935.

1333. *Baron v. Siff*, 1997 Del. Ch. LEXIS 152, at *10, 1997 WL 666973, at *3 (Del. Ch. Oct. 17, 1997).

1334. *Rales*, 634 A.2d at 935 n.11.

1335. *See* Dooley & Veasey, *The Role of the Board in Derivative Litigation: Delaware Law and the Current ALI Proposals Compared*, 44 Bus. Law. 503, 508 (1989); Hamermesh, *Responding to Shareholder Demands in Derivative Litigation*, 2 Insights: The Corporate & Securities Law Advisor No. 7, July 1988, at 15; Williams, *Advising Committees of Boards of Directors Formed to Investigate Stockholder Demands*, LXII Prentice Hall Law & Business Corporation Bulletin No. 6, Mar. 19, 1991, at 1. *But see In re Oracle Sec. Litig.*, 829 F. Supp. 1176, 1187-90 (N.D. Cal. 1993) (refusing to approve settlement of a derivative action pursuant to the recommendation of a committee of directors who were not defen-dants in the action because the litigation involved claims against other directors and officers and the committee was advised by the corporation's general counsel rather than independent counsel; in-house attorneys, the court stated, are "inevitably subservient to the interests of the defendant

(continued...)

establish a committee to make a recommendation or determine the corporation's response to a demand.[1336] Where a committee is formed to make a recommendation and has no authority to act on the demand, the committee may include persons who are not board members.[1337] "[I]t is unquestionably the board's prerogative" "to entrust its investigation to a law firm," but entrustment of an investigation to a law firm that represents corporate directors and officers against whom wrongdoing has been alleged in criminal proceedings involving the same subject matter as the demand constitutes gross negligence and thus "strips a board's rejection of a shareholder demand of the protection of the business judgment rule."[1338] Potential waivers of board authority that may result from a board's delegation of its decision-making authority—as opposed to the boards's authority to investigate—are discussed earlier in this Chapter.[1339]

*b. The Board's Entitlement to Adequate Time.* "[A] stockholder who makes a demand is entitled to know promptly what action the board has taken in response to the demand."[1340] The board, however, is entitled to "an adequate and reasonable amount of time" to respond to the demand.[1341] As one court has

---

1335. (...continued)
directors and officers whom they serve"), *subsequent proceedings*, 852 F. Supp. 1437, 1440-45 (N.D. Cal. 1994) (approving same settlement, this time pursuant to the recommendation of a new committee acting with the advice of independent counsel); Ocampo & Small, *General Counsel's Role in Resolving Derivative Litigation: A Personal Perspective*, ACCA Docket, Vol. 13, No. 2, Mar./Apr. 1995, at 50 (criticism of *Oracle* decision by Oracle's general counsel).

1336. *In re General Motors Class E Stock Buyout Sec. Litig.*, 694 F. Supp. 1119, 1134 (D. Del. 1988), *reargument granted and decision rev'd on other grounds*, 790 F. Supp. 77, 81 n.5 (D. Del. 1992).

1337. *Scattered Corp. v. Chicago Stock Exch., Inc.*, 1996 Del. Ch. LEXIS 79, at *10 n.4, 15, 1996 WL 417507, at *3 n.4, 4 (Del. Ch. July 12, 1996), *aff'd on other grounds*, 701 A.2d 70 (Del. 1997).

1338. *Stepak v. Addison*, 20 F.3d 398, 404-11 (11th Cir. 1994).

1339. *See* Chapter IV, Section B 5 i (ii).

1340. *Grimes v. Donald*, 673 A.2d 1207, 1218 (Del. 1996).

1341. *Smachlo v. Birkelo*, 576 F. Supp. 1439, 1445 (D. Del. 1983)
(continued...)

explained: "Because the purpose of a demand upon the board of directors is to alert the board of directors so that it can take corrective action, if it feels any is merited, the shareholder should allow sufficient time for the directors to act upon the demand before instituting a derivative action."[1342]

Where a shareholder commences litigation before receiving a response to a demand, "no magical period of time exists by which to measure whether suit was filed prematurely."[1343] "[N]o formula exists by which the Court may determine if a 'reasonable' investigation period has elapsed."[1344] Rather, the amount of time that is reasonable "will vary depending upon the complexity of the issues" underlying the demand.[1345] Accordingly, "[t]here can be no precise rule as to how much time a Board must be given to respond to a demand," and "the question in premature filing cases is not how much time is needed to respond to the demand, but whether the time between demand and filing of suit was sufficient to permit the Board of Directors to discharge its duty to consider the demand."[1346] As several courts have stated, the "amount of time needed for a response will vary in direct proportion to the

---

1341. (...continued)
(quoting *Mills v. Esmark, Inc.*, 91 F.R.D. 70, 73 (N.D. Ill. 1981)).

1342. *Stallworth v. AmSouth Bank*, 1997 Ala. LEXIS 483, at *13, 1997 WL 778838, at *4 (Ala. Dec. 19, 1997); *see also Recchion v. Kirby*, 637 F. Supp. 1309, 1319 (W.D. Pa. 1986) ("[a]dequate time should be allowed for a response"); *Charal Inv. Co. v. Rockefeller*, [1995-1996 Transfer Binder] Fed. Sec. L. Rep. (CCH) ¶ 98,979, at 93,762 (Del. Ch. Nov. 7, 1995) ("the shareholder must allow the board a reasonable time to investigate and respond to the claim").

1343. *Rubin v. Posner*, 701 F. Supp. 1041, 1045 (D. Del. 1988), *quoted in BTZ, Inc. v. National Intergroup, Inc.*, 1993 Del. Ch. LEXIS 58, at *8, 1993 WL 133211, at *3 (Del. Ch. Apr. 7, 1993).

1344. *Charal*, [1995-1996 Transfer Binder] Fed. Sec. L. Rep. (CCH) at 93,762.

1345. *Recchion*, 637 F. Supp. at 1319.

1346. *Allison v. General Motors Corp.*, 604 F. Supp. 1106, 1117-18 (D. Del.), *aff'd mem.*, 782 F.2d 1026 (3d Cir. 1985), *quoted in Mozes v. Welch*, 638 F. Supp. 215, 220 (D. Conn. 1986).

complexity of the technological, quantitative, and legal issues raised by the demand."[1347]

Numerous decisions illustrate this principle. In *Allison v. General Motors Corp.*,[1348] for example, a federal court construing Delaware and federal law held that two and one-half months was not adequate time to investigate a demand asserting that the braking system in a particular car model was defective.[1349] The court reasoned as follows:

> Immediately, the GM Board, which was not necessarily composed of persons knowledgeable about automobiles, much less brake systems, was faced with the necessity of gaining some minimal understanding of the technology of automobile braking systems. The Board also had to determine what and when the six individuals named in the demand knew or should have known about the alleged brake system defect, and whether any of the six named persons were responsible for alleged incomplete and false information being supplied to the government. In addition, the GM Board had to investigate the extent of the damages GM incurred because of the defective braking system. The alleged source of these damages was varied. As a consequence, there had to be an investigation of government litigation efforts to secure a mandatory recall, over fifty personal injury lawsuits, and the other unidentified "numerous accidents" and settlements by General Motors.[1350]

---

1347. *Id.; Baron v. Siff*, 1997 Del. Ch. LEXIS 152, at *11, 1997 WL 666973 at *3 (Del. Ch. Oct. 17, 1997); *Charal*, [1995-1996 Transfer Binder] Fed. Sec. L. Rep. (CCH) at 93,762; *see also* Chapter IV, Section C 3 a (discussing this issue in special litigation committee context). *But see* Ill. Bus. Corp. Act § 5/7.80(b) ("If a demand for action was made and the corporation's investigation of the demand is in progress when the proceeding is filed, the court may stay the suit for thirty days or until the investigation is completed, whichever is less.").

1348. 604 F. Supp. 1106 (D. Del.), *aff'd mem.*, 782 F.2d 1026 (3d Cir. 1985).

1349. *Id.* at 1118.

1350. *Id.*

In *Recchion v. Kirby*,[1351] similarly, a federal court construing Pennsylvania law held that two months was insufficient time to complete an adequate investigation of alleged violations of federal securities laws, breaches of fiduciary duty and common law fraud by 23 individuals or entities, including a public accounting firm.[1352]

Likewise, in *Mozes v. Welch*,[1353] a federal court construing federal law dismissed a complaint filed on November 22, 1985, approximately eight months after a March 29, 1985 demand sent to the board of General Electric Company involving an indictment of GE and two former GE employees for submitting false time and labor charges to the United States Government.[1354] The court held that the eight month period was not "of sufficient duration for the Board to respond to the demand," and that the board and a special board committee formed to investigate the facts underlying the demand "were not afforded adequate time under the circumstances of this complex case to complete their investigation."[1355] The court explained that the committee's investigation was "extensive" in scope but faced "temporary impediments" caused by an "ongoing grand jury investigation and criminal proceedings," and that the committee "anticipated rendering its final report two months after the completion of all criminal proceedings."[1356] In the court's words:

> The Special Committee's investigation was proceeding on a parallel course with a continuing grand jury inquiry as to the individuals responsible for the very conduct for which the plaintiff demanded that action be taken. The pendency of the grand jury proceedings impeded the speed of the Special Committee's progress in two respects. First, it inhibited Committee counsel's access to grand jury materials which the Committee believed might prove to be of assistance in its

---

1351. 637 F. Supp. 1309 (W.D. Pa. 1986).
1352. *Id*. at 1319.
1353. 638 F. Supp. 215 (D. Conn. 1986).
1354. *Id*. at 217-18, 220.
1355. *Id*. at 220, 221.
1356. *Id*. at 221.

task. Second, interviews of GE employees, also believed to be imperative to the Committee's investigation, could not take place while the criminal proceedings were underway. Therefore, in order to not interfere with the criminal proceedings and in order to obtain full advantage of what those proceedings revealed, the Committee had determined, and advised plaintiff of said determination, that the investigation could not be completed until approximately two months after the completion of all criminal proceedings. . . .

Plaintiff's demand letter instructed the Board to take action against, *inter alia*, "those persons responsible for making, presenting and supervising false labor cost claims to the government." It is therefore beyond cavil that the Special Litigation Committee should have awaited the final results of the government's investigations before issuing a final report and recommendation to the full Board in order to fully comply with plaintiff's demand. The court would be remiss in its duties if it did not encourage, indeed require, the Special Litigation Committee to conduct the most thorough investigation under the circumstances.[1357]

The Delaware Court of Chancery reached the same result in *Charal Investment Co. v. Rockefeller*.[1358] This case challenged "highly complex" transactions over an eight year period involving hundreds of millions of dollars, including "the (1) negotiation of $400 million in letters of credit; (2) non-renewal of the letters of credit; (3) use of short-term borrowing of over $217 million over several years to repurchase convertible debentures; (4) making of capital distributions of $90 million over four years; (5) entering into interest rate swaps; and (6) borrowing of $225 million for purposes of debt restructuring."[1359] Plaintiff made its demand on February 3, 1995, a board committee was formed to investigate plaintiff's claims on February 21, and the committee advised plaintiff on May 31 that the committee expected to complete its investi-

---

1357. *Id.* at 221-22.
1358. [1995-1996 Transfer Binder] Fed. Sec. L. Rep. (CCH) ¶ 98,979 (Del. Ch. Nov. 7, 1995).
1359. *Id.* at 93,762.

gation by the fall.[1360] Given the "complexity" of plaintiff's allegations and the fact that "the committee established a time schedule for completing the investigation," the court concluded that "I cannot find that the length of time involved is unreasonable."[1361] The court also held that an alleged risk that the corporation might become insolvent during the pendency of the investigation did not change this result.[1362] The court stated that "regardless of whether the Corporation becomes bankrupt, its claim against the directors "will continue to exist as a corporate asset" and that "[p]laintiff does not allege that the directors will be judgment-proof."[1363] Thus, the court concluded, "I do not find the Corporation's financial position persuasive on the issue of whether I should infer that the board refused demand in this case."[1364]

Similar results have been reached by federal courts in *Mills v. Esmark, Inc.*,[1365] *In re E.F. Hutton Banking Practices Litigation*[1366] and *Smachlo v. Birkelo*[1367] and by the Delaware Court of Chancery in *BTZ, Inc. v. National Intergroup, Inc.*[1368] These cases held that periods of three days, ten days, two weeks and eight days, respectively, were insufficient periods of time for boards to respond to demands.[1369]

Other courts in cases involving circumstances different from the circumstances in the cases discussed above have concluded that demands were not responded to in adequate amounts of time.

---

1360. *Id.* at 93,761.

1361. *Id.* at 93,762.

1362. *Id.* at 93,762-63.

1363. *Id.* at 93,763.

1364. *Id.*

1365. 91 F.R.D. 70 (N.D. Ill. 1981) .

1366. 634 F. Supp. 265 (S.D.N.Y. 1986).

1367. 576 F. Supp. 1439 (D. Del. 1983).

1368. 1993 Del. Ch. LEXIS 58, 1993 WL 133211 (Del. Ch. Apr. 7, 1993).

1369. *See Mills*, 91 F.R.D. at 71, 73; *E.F. Hutton*, 634 F. Supp. at 272; *Smachlo*, 576 F. Supp. at 1445; *BTZ*, 1993 Del. Ch. LEXIS 58, at *8, 1993 WL 133211, at *3.

In *Rubin v. Posner*,[1370] for example, a complaint filed 27 days after a demand letter was mailed was held by a federal court construing Delaware law not to be premature where the corporation did not respond in any way to the letter and the issues raised were "straightforward and revolve almost entirely around . . . a single alleged agreement."[1371] In *Platt v. Richardson*,[1372] a federal court construing Delaware law held that two months was sufficient time for the board of a corporation with five principal stockholders to respond to a demand letter asserting that a board member was responsible for waste and mismanagement.[1373] In *Lewis v. Sporck*,[1374] a federal court construing federal law held that three months was sufficient time for a board to respond to a demand, in a case where the board had had knowledge of trade secret thefts underlying the demand for three years prior to the demand and had planned but not yet begun an investigation concerning whether to commence litigation.[1375]

A comparable result was reached by the Delaware Court of Chancery in *Thorpe v. CERBCO, Inc.*,[1376] a case where a demand was made in May 1990, a special committee consisting of two directors was formed in July 1990 to review the demand, litigation was commenced in August 1990, the members of the committee reported its findings to the board in late 1990 and then resigned from the board, and the board neither acted on the report nor disclosed the contents of the report to shareholders who had requested this information.[1377] In subsequent proceedings not involving this ruling, the Delaware Supreme Court stated that "the Chancellor was not satisfied that the entire board had conducted a reasonable review of the shareholder demand, so the claim was not

---

1370. 701 F. Supp. 1041 (D. Del. 1988).
1371. *Id.* at 1046.
1372. [1989-1990 Transfer Binder] Fed. Sec. L. Rep. (CCH) ¶ 94,786 (M.D. Pa. June 6, 1989).
1373. *Id.* at 94,233.
1374. 646 F. Supp. 574 (N.D. Cal. 1986).
1375. *Id.* at 578.
1376. 611 A.2d 5 (Del. Ch. 1991).
1377. *Id.* at 11.

subject to dismissal."[1378] The Court of Chancery has distinguished *Thorpe* in other cases on the ground that *Thorpe* involved "unusual" and "egregious" facts.[1379]

A New York court in *MacKay v. Pierce*[1380] held that a shareholder "satisfactorily complied" with the demand requirement by making a demand and commencing litigation after being advised that his demand letter would be considered at the board's next meeting, which was scheduled to occur in two weeks.[1381] The court reasoned that "a factor which should be considered in determining whether plaintiff was justified in deeming the response to his demand unsatisfactory" is the fact that "[a]lthough plaintiff chose to make a demand upon the board, the complaint reveals that in view of the nature of the action, charging an overwhelming majority of the directors with breach of their fiduciary duties, such a demand was not necessary."[1382]

Until a board responds to a demand or fails to respond to the demand within an adequate period of time, "the shareholder generally may not move forward with a derivative action."[1383] If a derivative action is filed by a shareholder who has made a demand before the corporation's board has had adequate time to respond to the demand, the court either will dismiss the action as premature (generally with leave to amend)[1384] or stay proceedings until the

---

1378. *Thorpe v. CERBCO, Inc.*, 676 A.2d 436, 440 (Del. 1996).

1379. *Scattered Corp. v. Chicago Stock Exch., Inc.*, 23 Del. J. Corp. L. 355, 363 n.1 (Del. Ch. Apr. 7, 1997), *aff'd on other grounds*, 701 A.2d 70 (Del. 1997); *Boeing Co. v. Shrontz*, 1994 Del. Ch. LEXIS 14, at *11, 1994 WL 30542, at *4 (Del. Ch. Jan. 19, 1994).

1380. 86 A.D.2d 655, 446 N.Y.S.2d 403 (N.Y. App. Div. 2d Dep't 1982).

1381. *Id.* at 655, 446 N.Y.S.2d at 404.

1382. *Id.*

1383. *Charal*, [1995-1996 Transfer Binder] Fed. Sec. L. Rep. (CCH) at 93,762.

1384. *See, e.g.*, *Mozes*, 638 F. Supp. at 222; *Esmark*, 91 F.R.D. at 73; *Stallworth*, 1997 Ala. LEXIS 483, at *18 n.2, 1997 WL 778838, at *5 n.2; *Charal*, [1995-1996 Transfer Binder] Fed. Sec. L. Rep. at 93,763;

(continued...)

board has had adequate time to respond to the demand.[1385] One court that determined to dismiss a case and not retain jurisdiction explained that "the Court cannot presume whether Plaintiff is certain to make a challenge to the committee's decision" and that retaining jurisdiction over the corporation "would be unduly burdensome and, thus, inequitable to defendants."[1386] The motion to dismiss accordingly was granted without prejudice to refiling should plaintiff "wish to challenge the Special Committee's report after it is issued or should the Special Committee fail to provide the report within the time frame established."[1387]

The court in *Gagliardi v. Tri-Foods International, Inc.*[1388] concluded that an allegation that a demand was refused by a corporate officer and attorney without board involvement does not create a factual issue with respect to the effectiveness of the refusal of the demand or require denial of a motion to dismiss.[1389] The court explained that the shareholder "made a pre-suit demand, that the corporation did not institute the suit, that plaintiff did and that the corporation has moved to dismiss . . . . These undisputed facts establish the board's official response to the demand and make irrelevant the issue that plaintiff seeks to explore through discovery."[1390] The court in *Baron v. Siff*[1391] similarly concluded that the fact that a letter refusing a demand "was drafted and signed by counsel does not suggest that the Board did not address plain-

---

1384. (...continued)
*National Intergroup*, 1993 Del. Ch. LEXIS 58, at *8, 1993 WL 133211, at *3.

    1385. *See, e.g., Dawson v. Dawson*, 645 S.W.2d 120, 128 (Mo. Ct. App. 1982).

    1386. *Charal*, [1995-1996 Transfer Binder] Fed. Sec. L. Rep. (CCH) at 93,763.

    1387. *Id.*

    1388. 683 A.2d 1049 (Del. Ch. 1996) (published in part, complete text available at 1996 Del. Ch. 87 and 1996 WL 422330).

    1389. *Id.* at 1055 n.7.

    1390. *Id.*

    1391. 1997 Del. Ch. LEXIS 152, 1997 WL 666973 (Del. Ch. Oct. 17, 1997).

tiff's demand."[1392] The court stated that there was "no indication that counsel wrote the letter without the Board's input or authorization."[1393] Indeed, the court continued, "[i]t is understandable that a busy board of directors would . . . have counsel draft and sign a letter undoubtedly written with an eye toward complying" with the rules governing the demand requirement.[1394] The court added that the shareholder who made the demand also had counsel draft and sign the shareholder's demand letter.[1395]

   c. *The Wrongful Refusal Doctrine.* "[O]nce a demand has been made, absent a wrongful refusal, the stockholder's ability to initiate a derivative suit is terminated."[1396] The determination whether a refusal of a demand is a wrongful refusal turns upon the same "deferential 'business judgment rule' standard of review" pursuant to which all business judgments are tested.[1397]

   This principle first was stated by the United States Supreme Court in 1881 in *Hawes v. City of Oakland*,[1398] a shareholder action on behalf of a water company seeking to enjoin the corporation's supply of water at no cost to the city of Oakland. The court concluded that the board's decision to refuse a demand and not

---

1392. 1997 Del. Ch. LEXIS 152, at *8, 1997 WL 666973, at *3.

1393. 1997 Del. Ch. LEXIS 152, at *10, 1997 WL 666973, at *3.

1394. 1997 Del. Ch. LEXIS 152, at *9, 1997 WL 666973, at *3.

1395. 1997 Del. Ch. LEXIS 152, at *11, 1997 WL 666973, at *3.

1396. *Spiegel v. Buntrock*, 571 A.2d 767, 775 (Del. 1990); *Stotland v. GAF Corp.*, 469 A.2d 421, 422 (Del. 1983); *Charal Inv. Co. v. Rockefeller*, [1995-1996 Transfer Binder] Fed. Sec. L. Rep. (CCH) ¶ 98,979, at 93,761 (Del. Ch. Nov. 7, 1995).

1397. *Kamen v. Kemper Fin. Servs., Inc.*, 500 U.S. 90, 101 (1991); *see also, e.g., RCM Sec. Fund, Inc. v. Stanton*, 928 F.2d 1318, 1326 (2d Cir. 1991) ("[j]udicial review of a corporate decision to bring, not to bring, or to terminate a lawsuit is . . . governed by the business judgment rule"); 13 William M. Fletcher, *Cyclopedia of the Law of Private Corporations* § 5969, at 160 (1995 & Supp. 1997) ("the directors' determination that the maintenance of a derivative proceeding is not in the best interest of the corporation is presumptively protected by the business judgment rule if they acted in good faith after conducting a reasonable inquiry").

1398. 104 U.S. 450 (1881).

pursue the action could not be challenged in court. The court explained that the city "conferred on the company valuable rights by special ordinance; namely, the use of the streets for laying its pipes, and the privilege of furnishing water to the whole population."[1399] The court stated that "[i]t may be the exercise of the highest wisdom to let the city use the water in the manner complained of" and that "the directors are better able to act understandingly on this subject than a stockholder."[1400]

The Supreme Court next considered this issue in 1903 in *Corbus v. Alaska Treadwell Gold Mining Co.*,[1401] a case involving a shareholder's effort on behalf of a corporation to enjoin an allegedly illegal license fee. The court determined that the action could not proceed due to the shareholder's failure to make a prelitigation demand on the board.[1402] The court added that "mere technical compliance" with the demand requirement is not sufficient and does not "preclude[ ] all inquiry as to the right of the stockholder to maintain a bill against the corporation."[1403] The court continued as follows:

> The directors represent all the stockholders, and are presumed to act honestly and according to their best judgment for the interests of all. Their judgment as to any matter lawfully confided to their discretion may not lightly be challenged by any stockholder or at his instance submitted for review to a court of equity. The directors may sometimes properly waive a legal right vested in the corporation in the belief that its best interests will be promoted by not insisting on such right. They may regard the expense of enforcing the right or the furtherance of the general business of the corporation in determining whether to waive or insist upon the right. And a court of equity may not be called upon at the appeal of any single stockholder to compel the directors or the corporation to enforce every right which it may possess, irrespective of other considerations. It is not a trifling thing

1399. *Id.* at 462.
1400. *Id.*
1401. 187 U.S. 455 (1903)
1402. *Id.* at 465.
1403. *Id.* at 463.

for a stockholder to attempt to coerce the directors of a corporation to an act which their judgment does not approve, or to substitute his judgment for theirs.[1404]

The Supreme Court in 1917 in *United Copper Securities Co. v. Amalgamated Copper Co.*[1405] affirmed the dismissal of an antitrust suit filed by a shareholder on behalf of a corporation against competitors of the corporation following the board's refusal of a pre-litigation demand.[1406] Justice Louis D. Brandeis, writing for a unanimous Court, stated that "[w]hether or not a corporation shall seek to enforce in the courts a cause of action for damages is, like other business questions, ordinarily a matter of internal management and is left to the discretion of the directors."[1407] Justice Brandeis added that "[c]ourts interfere seldom to control such discretion *intra vires* the corporation, except where the directors are guilty of misconduct equivalent to a breach of trust, or where they stand in a dual relation which prevents an unprejudiced exercise of judgment."[1408]

The Supreme Court's 1936 decision in *Ashwander v. Tennessee Valley Authority*[1409] involved a challenge by a shareholder to a contract entered into by a corporation with a federal agency, the Tennessee Valley Authority, pursuant to legislation that a shareholder contended was unconstitutional.[1410] According to the shareholder, the contract not only was "injurious to the interests of the corporation" but also was an illegal transaction because the Tennessee Valley Authority allegedly acted "under color of the statute, . . . beyond the powers which the Congress could validly confer," and the corporation's directors "yield[ed], without appropriate resistance, to governmental demands which are without warrant of law or are in violation of constitutional restrictions."[1411]

---

1404. *Id.*
1405. 244 U.S. 261 (1917).
1406. *Id.* at 262-63.
1407. *Id.* at 263.
1408. *Id.* at 263-64.
1409. 297 U.S. 288 (1936).
1410. *Id.* at 316-17.
1411. *Id.* at 318-19.

The court—in an opinion written by Chief Justice Charles E. Hughes, speaking for a total of four justices—held that "[t]he fact that the directors in the exercise of their judgment, either because they were disinclined to undertake a burdensome litigation or for other reasons which they regarded as substantial, resolved to comply with the legislative or administrative demands, has not been deemed an adequate ground for denying to the stockholders an opportunity to contest the validity of the governmental requirements to which the directors were submitting."[1412] The court accordingly reached the merits of the case, and held that the challenged legislation was constitutional.[1413]

An often cited concurring opinion by Justice Brandeis, also speaking for a total of four justices, held that it was not necessary to reach the constitutional issue. Relying upon the principles announced in *Corbus* and *United Cooper*, Justice Brandeis stated that "[c]ourts may not interfere with the management of the corporation, unless there is bad faith, disregard of the relative rights of its members, or other action seriously threatening their property rights."[1414] According to Justice Brandeis, "[t]his rule applies . . . where the mistake alleged is the refusal to assert a seemingly clear cause of action, or the compromise of it."[1415] In Justice Brandeis' words: "If a stockholder could compel the officers to enforce every legal right, courts, instead of chosen officers, would be the arbiters of the corporation's fate."[1416]

Disagreeing with Chief Justice Hughes, Justice Brandeis stated that the fact that a shareholder "calls for an enquiry into the legality of the transaction does not overcome the obstacle that ordinarily stockholders have no standing to interfere with the management" of the corporation.[1417] To the contrary, Justice Brandeis stated, "[m]ere belief that corporate action, taken or con-

---

1412. *Id.* at 320.
1413. *Id.* at 324-40.
1414. *Id.* at 343 (Brandeis, J. concurring).
1415. *Id.*
1416. *Id.*
1417. *Id.*

templated, is illegal gives the stockholder no greater right to interfere than is possessed by any other citizen. Stockholders are not guardians of the public. The function of guarding the public against acts deemed illegal rests with the public officials."[1418]

*Hawes*, *Corbus*, *United Copper* and *Ashwander* all construe federal common law. The Supreme Court's subsequent decision in 1938 in *Erie Railroad Co. v. Tompkins*[1419] holds that federal courts deciding diversity cases must apply the substantive law of the state where the federal court is sitting.[1420] Subsequent decisions have concluded that director authority to control derivative litigation is a substantive issue governed by the law of the state of incorporation, except to the extent that state law is inconsistent with federal policy.[1421] Courts construing state law since *Erie* have adopted and followed the principles stated in *Hawes*, *Corbus*, *United Copper* and *Ashwander*.

The Delaware courts, for instance, have held that a board's decision to refuse a demand is "subject to 'judicial review according to the traditional business judgment rule,'"[1422] that "the board rejecting the demand is entitled to the presumption of the business judgment rule,"[1423] and that "[a]bsent an abuse of discretion, if the requirements of the traditional business judgment rule are met, the board of directors' decision not to pursue the derivative claim will be respected by the courts."[1424] In other words:

> The board's response, like other decisions affecting the management and affairs of the corporation, is protected by the business judgment rule, a rule which recognizes that the board, not the Court, is in the best position to manage the corporation's affairs. Business decisions by an informed,

---

1418. *Id.; see also* Chapter IV, Section 6 h (discussing board refusals of demands in cases alleging unlawful conduct).

1419. 304 U.S. 64 (1938).

1420. *Id.* at 71-80.

1421. *See* Chapter IV, Sections B 4 a-b.

1422. *Levine v. Smith*, 591 A.2d 194, 212 (Del. 1991) (quoting *Spiegel v. Buntrock*, 571 A.2d 767, 776 (Del. 1990)).

1423. *Grimes v. Donald*, 673 A.2d 1207, 1219 (Del. 1996).

1424. *Spiegel*, 571 A.2d at 777.

disinterested, independent board will be respected by this Court.[1425]

Accordingly, "the simple expedient of naming a majority of otherwise disinterested and well motivated directors as defendants and charging them with laxity or conspiracy etc., will not itself . . . override a board decision not to litigate a corporate claim."[1426] A long line of decisions by Delaware courts[1427] and courts in other jurisdictions construing Delaware law[1428] have reiterated this

---

1425. *In re Fuqua Indus., Inc. Shareholder Litig.*, 1997 Del. Ch. LEXIS 72, at *48, 1997 WL 257460, at *12 (Del. Ch. May 13, 1997).

1426. *Gagliardi v. TriFoods Int'l, Inc.*, 683 A.2d 1049, 1054 (Del. Ch. 1996) (published in part, complete text available at 1996 Del. Ch. LEXIS 87 and 1996 WL 422330).

1427. *See Rales v. Blasband*, 634 A.2d 927, 932-33 (Del. 1993); *Aronson v. Lewis*, 473 A.2d 805, 813 (Del. 1984); *Zapata Corp. v. Maldonado*, 430 A.2d 779, 784 & n.10 (Del. 1981); *Boeing Co. v. Shrontz*, 1994 Del. Ch. LEXIS 14, at *5, 1994 WL 30542, at *2 (Del. Ch. Jan. 19, 1994); *Mount Moriah Cemetery v. Moritz*, [1990-1991 Transfer Binder] Fed. Sec. L. Rep. (CCH) ¶ 95,900, at 99,442 (Del. Ch. Apr. 4, 1991), *aff'd*, 599 A.2d 413 (unpublished opinion, text available at 1991 Del. LEXIS 244 and 1991 WL 165558) (Del. Aug. 12, 1991); *Caruana v. Saligman*, [1990-1991 Transfer Binder] Fed. Sec. L. Rep. (CCH) ¶ 95,889, at 99,378 (Del. Ch. Dec. 21, 1990); *Cottle v. Standard Brands Paint Co.*, [1990 Transfer Binder] Fed. Sec. L. Rep. (CCH) ¶ 95,306, at 96,432 (Del. Ch. Mar. 22, 1990); *In re NVF Co. Litig.*, 16 Del. J. Corp. L. 361, 372-73 (Del. Ch. Nov. 21, 1989); *Brook v. Acme Steel Co.*, 15 Del. J. Corp. L. 149, 154-55 (Del. Ch. May 11, 1989); *Spiegel v. Buntrock*, 1988 Del. Ch. LEXIS 160, at *3, 4, 1988 WL 135509, at *1 (Del. Ch. Dec. 14, 1988), *aff'd*, 571 A.2d 767, 778 (Del. 1990); *Lewis v. Hett*, 10 Del. J. Corp. L. 240, 244-45 (Del. Ch. Sept. 4, 1984).

1428. *See Stepak v. Addison*, 20 F.3d 398, 402, 403 (11th Cir. 1994); *Litton Indus., Inc. v. Hoch*, 996 F.2d 1225 (unpublished opinion, text available at 1993 U.S. App. LEXIS 16992, at *3 and 1993 WL 241549, at *1) (9th Cir. July 2, 1993); *Abramowitz v. Posner*, 672 F.2d 1025, 1030, 1033-34 (2d Cir. 1982); *Levner v. Prince Alwaleed Bin Talal Bin Abdulaziz Al Saud*, 903 F. Supp. 452, 456 (S.D.N.Y. 1994), *aff'd*, 61 F.3d 8, 8-9 (2d Cir. 1995) (affirming "on the carefully reasoned opinion" of the district court); *Abrams v. Koether*, 766 F. Supp. 237, 249, 254

(continued...)

statement of the law.

The business judgment rule similarly governs board decisions to refuse demands in numerous other jurisdictions that have addressed the issue, including Alabama,[1429] Arkansas,[1430] California,[1431] Colorado,[1432] Connecticut,[1433] the District of Columbia,[1434] Florida,[1435] Illinois,[1436] Massachusetts,[1437] Michigan,[1438] Minnesota,[1439] Missouri,[1440] Montana,[1441] New Jer-

---

1428. (...continued)
(D.N.J. 1991) and [1992 Transfer Binder] Fed. Sec. L. Rep. (CCH) ¶ 96,995, at 94,338-39 (D.N.J. Aug. 7, 1992); *Lewis v. Hilton*, 648 F. Supp. 725, 727 (N.D. Ill. 1986); *Allison v. General Motors Corp.*, 604 F. Supp. 1106, 1122-23 (D. Del.), *aff'd mem.*, 782 F.2d 1026 (3d Cir. 1985); *Varian Assocs., Inc. v. Superior Court*, No. H011025, slip op. at 11-13 (Cal. Ct. App. Aug. 31, 1993).

1429. *See Roberts v. Alabama Power Co.*, 404 So. 2d 629, 632, 636 (Ala. 1981).

1430. *See Red Bud Realty Co. v. South*, 131 S.W. 340, 345 (Ark. 1910).

1431. *See Lewis v. Anderson*, 615 F.2d 778, 781-82 (9th Cir. 1979), *cert. denied*, 449 U.S. 869 (1980); *Country Nat'l Bank v. Mayer*, 788 F. Supp. 1136, 1144 (E.D. Cal. 1992); *Findley v. Garrett*, 109 Cal. App. 2d 166, 174, 240 P.2d 421, 426 (Cal. Dist. Ct. App. 1952).

1432. *See Bach v. National W. Life Ins. Co.*, 810 F.2d 509, 510, 514 (5th Cir. 1987).

1433. *See Joy v. North*, 692 F.2d 880, 888 (2d Cir. 1982), *cert. denied*, 460 U.S 1051 (1983).

1434. *See Woodward & Lothrop, Inc. v. Schnabel*, 593 F. Supp. 1385, 1399 (D.D.C. 1984).

1435. *See Orlando Orange Groves Co. v. Hale*, 161 So. 284, 289 (Fla. 1935); *James Talcott, Inc. v. McDowell*, 148 So. 2d 36, 38 (Fla. Dist. Ct. App. 1962).

1436. *See Swanson v. Traer*, 249 F.2d 854, 858-59 (7th Cir. 1957); *Weiland v. Illinois Power Co.*, [1990-1991 Transfer Binder] Fed. Sec. L. Rep. (CCH) ¶ 95,747, at 98,589 (C.D. Ill. Sept. 17, 1990).

1437. *See S. Solomont & Sons Trust v. New England Theatres Operating Corp.*, 93 N.E.2d 241, 248 (Mass. 1950); *Bartlett v. New York, New Haven & Hartford R.R.*, 109 N.E. 452, 456 (Mass. 1915); *Dunphy v. Travelers' Newspaper Ass'n*, 16 N.E. 426, 431 (Mass. 1888).

1438. *See In re Consumers Power Co. Derivative Litig.*, 132
(continued...)

sey,[1442] New York,[1443] Ohio,[1444] Tennessee,[1445] Texas[1446] and Washington.[1447]

The rationale underlying the deference all of these courts have given board decisions to refuse demands is the same rationale underlying the demand requirement: (1) directors, not minority shareholders, should determine whether litigation of a claim belonging to the corporation should be pursued on behalf of the corporation, (2) directors should be permitted an opportunity to pursue remedies other than litigation and thus avoid unnecessary litigation,

---

1438. (...continued)
F.R.D. 455, 469 (E.D. Mich. 1990); *Futernick v. Statler Builders, Inc.*, 112 N.W.2d 458, 462 (Mich. 1961).

1439. *See Skoglund v. Brady*, 541 N.W.2d 17, 20 (Minn. Ct. App. 1995); *Black v. NuAire, Inc.*, 426 N.W.2d 203, 209-10 (Minn. Ct. App. 1988).

1440. *See McLeese v. J.C. Nichols Co.*, 842 S.W.2d 115, 120 (Mo. Ct. App. 1992); *Merrill v. Davis*, 225 S.W.2d 763, 768 (Mo. 1950).

1441. *See Brooks v. Brooks Pontiac, Inc.*, 389 P.2d 185, 187 (Mont. 1964); *Noble v. Farmers Union Trading Co.*, 216 P.2d 925, 936 (Mont. 1950).

1442. *See Groel v. United Elec. Co.*, 61 A. 1061, 1063 (N.J. Ch. 1905).

1443. *See Stoner v. Walsh*, 772 F. Supp. 790, 800 (S.D.N.Y. 1991); *Rosengarten v. International Tel. & Tel. Corp.*, 466 F. Supp. 817, 822 (S.D.N.Y. 1979); *Gall v. Exxon Corp.*, 418 F. Supp. 508, 515-18 (S.D.N.Y. 1976); *Klotz v. Consolidated Edison Co.*, 386 F. Supp. 577, 581-82 (S.D.N.Y. 1974); *Auerbach v. Bennett*, 47 N.Y.2d 619, 623-24, 630-35, 393 N.E.2d 994, 996, 1000-03, 419 N.Y.S.2d 920, 922, 926-29 (1979); *Syracuse Television, Inc. v. Channel 9, Syracuse, Inc.*, 51 Misc. 2d 188, 194, 273 N.Y.S.2d 16, 25 (N.Y. Sup. Ct. Onondaga 1966).

1444. *See Cooper v. Central Alloy Steel Corp.*, 183 N.E. 439, 441 (Ohio Ct. App. 1931); *Rice v. Wheeling Dollar Sav. & Trust Co.*, 130 N.E.2d 442, 448-49 (Ohio Ct. Common Pleas 1954).

1445. *See Lewis v. Boyd*, 838 S.W.2d 215, 222 (Tenn. Ct. App. 1992); *Wallace v. Lincoln Sav. Bank*, 15 S.W. 448, 449-50 (Tenn. 1891).

1446. *See Zauber v. Murray Sav. Ass'n*, 591 S.W.2d 932, 936 (Tex. Civ. App. 1979), *error refused*, 601 S.W.2d 940 (Tex. 1980).

1447. *See Goodwin v. Castleton*, 144 P.2d 725, 732 (Wash. 1944).

and (3) directors should be protected from the harassment of costly, baseless "strike suit" litigation.[1448]

As stated 40 years ago by the Seventh Circuit in *Swanson v. Traer*[1449]:

> It is obvious that the requirement that a stockholder, before filing a derivative action on behalf of his corporation, must first demand of its board of directors that it cause such an action to be instituted, does not mean that the board's refusal on demand to act, *ipso facto*, clears the way for a suit by the demanding stockholder on behalf of the corporation. If it were so, the making of the demand would become a meaningless mechanical operation.[1450]

In other words: "If a plaintiff only needed to plead generally that the board wrongfully rejected the presuit demand," the demand requirement "would be substantially undermined, allowing even the most frivolous of suits to proceed following the board's refusal."[1451] "If Courts would not respect the directors' decision not to file suit, then demand would be an empty formality."[1452]

*d. Motions to Dismiss: The Delaware Standard.* On a motion to dismiss a case in which a pre-litigation demand is alleged to have been wrongfully refused, Delaware courts apply the "reasonable doubt" standard utilized in cases where demand is alleged to be excused as futile,[1453] with one exception: in the demand refused context, the shareholder's making of a demand is a concession that a demand was required and that a majority of the corporation's directors are disinterested and independent with respect to the subject matter of the demand.[1454] As a result, the only issues to be

---

1448. *See* Chapter IV, Section B 2 (discussing rationale for demand requirement).

1449. 249 F.2d 854 (7th Cir. 1957).

1450. *Id.* at 858.

1451. *Lewis v. Hilton*, 648 F. Supp. 725, 727 (N.D. Ill. 1986).

1452. *Spiegel v. Buntrock*, 571 A.2d 767, 777-78 (Del. 1990) (quoting *Starrels v. First Nat'l Bank*, 870 F.2d 1168, 1174 (7th Cir. 1989) (Easterbrook, J., concurring)).

1453. *See* Chapter IV, Section B 5 b.

1454. *Scattered Corp. v. Chicago Stock Exch., Inc.*, 701 A.2d 70,

(continued...)

examined by the court in a demand refused case are "the good faith and reasonableness" of the board's investigation of the claims in the demand.[1455] Thus, to survive a motion to dismiss, plaintiffs must raise a reasonable doubt as to the directors' "good faith and/or the reasonableness of their investigation."[1456]

The determinative question on a motion to dismiss therefore is the "application of the traditional business judgment rule to the Board's refusal of the demand"[1457]—in other words, whether facts have been alleged "with particularity which create a reasonable doubt that the directors' action was entitled to the protections of the business judgment rule."[1458] As stated by the Delaware Supreme Court in *Levine v. Smith,*[1459] *Grimes v. Donald*[1460] and *Scattered Corp. v. Chicago Stock Exchange, Inc.*[1461]:

> [I]n a case of demand refused, director independence and lack of self-interest is conceded. Therefore, the trial court reviews the board's decision only for compliance with the

---

1454. (...continued)
74 (Del. 1997); *Grimes v. Donald,* 673 A.2d 1207, 1218-19 (Del. 1996); *Rales v. Blasband,* 634 A.2d 927, 935 n.12 (Del. 1993); *Levine v. Smith,* 591 A.2d 194, 212-13 (Del. 1991); *Spiegel v. Buntrock,* 571 A.2d 767, 775 (Del. 1990); *Boeing Co. v. Shrontz,* 1994 Del. Ch. LEXIS 14, at *5-6, 1996 WL 30542, at *2 (Del. Ch. Jan. 19, 1994); *Thorpe v. CERBCO, Inc.,* 611 A.2d 5, 10-11 (Del. Ch. 1991); *see also* Chapter IV, Section B i (i) (discussing this issue in greater detail); *Abrams v. Koether,* 766 F. Supp. 237, 254-55 (D.N.J. 1991) (wrongful refusal claim dismissed where plaintiffs contended only that a board was not disinterested in the conduct underlying litigation).
    1455. *Levine,* 591 A.2d at 212; *Spiegel,* 571 A.2d at 777.
    1456. *Boeing,* 1994 Del. Ch. LEXIS 14, at *6, 1994 WL 30542, at *2; *see also Charal Inv. Co. v. Rockefeller,* [1995-1996 Transfer Binder] Fed. Sec. L. Rep. (CCH) ¶ 98,979, at 93,761 (Del. Ch. Nov. 7, 1995); *CERBCO,* 611 A.2d at 10-11.
    1457. *Levine,* 591 A.2d at 212.
    1458. *Levine,* 591 A.2d at 210 (quoting *Aronson v. Lewis,* 473 A.2d 805, 808 (Del. 1984)).
    1459. 591 A.2d 194 (Del. 1991).
    1460. 673 A.2d 1207 (Del. 1996).
    1461. 701 A.2d 70 (Del. 1997).

traditional business judgment rule. The only relevant question is whether the directors acted in an informed manner and with due care, in a good faith belief that their action was in the best interest of the corporation. . . .

> The Court of Chancery in the exercise of its sound discretion must be satisfied that a plaintiff has alleged facts with particularity which, taken as true, support a reasonable doubt that the challenged transaction was the product of a valid exercise of business judgment.[1462]

*     *     *

If a demand is made and rejected, the board rejecting the demand is entitled to the presumption of the business judgment rule unless the stockholder can allege facts with particularity creating a reasonable doubt that the board is entitled to the benefit of the presumption.[1463]

As stated by the Delaware Court of Chancery:

> In determining whether a demand was wrongly refused, this court reviews the board's decision under traditional business judgment rule standards, which are the board's disinterest and independence and the good faith and reasonableness of its investigation. . . . By making a demand, a shareholder-plaintiff tacitly concedes the disinterest and independence of the board. . . . Therefore, in that particular context the only issues to be decided are the good faith and reasonableness of the board's investigation of the claims articulated in the demand. . . . A plaintiff claiming wrongful refusal has the burden to plead particularized facts that create a reasonable doubt . . . whether the board conducted its investigation of the claims set forth in the Demand reasonably and in good faith.[1464]

---

1462. *Levine*, 591 A.2d at 197-98, 210 (quoting *Aronson*, 473 A.2d at 815), *quoted in Chicago Stock Exch.*, 701 A.2d at 73.

1463. *Grimes*, 673 A.2d at 1219.

1464. *Chicago Stock Exch.*, 701 A.2d at 72-73 (quoting Court of Chancery decision in *Scattered Corp. v. Chicago Stock Exch.*, 1996 Del. Ch. LEXIS 79, at *9-11, 1996 WL 417507, at *3 (Del. Ch. July 12, 1996), *aff'd*, 701 A.2d 70 (Del. 1997), and stating that "[t]hese statements of law essentially follow the rubric of Delaware Supreme Court cases").

\*          \*          \*

It is settled law that directors, as part of their managerial responsibility, ordinarily make the decision whether to prosecute a corporate claim. Thus, a stockholder wishing to bring a derivative action must overcome the presumptions accorded by the business judgment rule. . . . This can be accomplished, in the demand refused context, by alleging facts with particularity that create a reasonable doubt as to whether demand was wrongfully refused. By making demand, plaintiffs concede the independence and disinterestedness of a majority of the Boeing board. Accordingly, in order to prevail, plaintiffs must raise a reasonable doubt as to the directors' good faith and/or the reasonableness of their investigation.[1465]

\*          \*          \*

Stated another way, in deciding a motion to dismiss, this Court accepts the well-pled allegations in the complaint as being true, and then applies the business judgment rule to determine whether the board's rejection of the pre-suit demand is protected from further judicial scrutiny. . . . In other words, the complaint must have alleged facts sufficient to rebut the presumption that the business judgment rule protects the decision of the board in rejecting his demand.[1466]

\*          \*          \*

The refusal of a demand is reviewed under the business judgment rule. . . . The presumption can be rebutted only if the party alleging wrongful refusal creates a reasonable doubt that the decision was a valid exercise of business judgment. By making a pre-suit demand, a plaintiff concedes the independence and disinterestedness of the board. Thus, to establish wrongful refusal, a plaintiff must plead with particularity facts that create a reasonable doubt as to the good faith or reasonableness of a board's investigation. Mere conclusory allegations are insufficient.[1467]

---

1465. *Boeing*, 1994 Del. Ch. LEXIS 14, at \*5-6, 1994 WL 30542, at \*1 (citations omitted).

1466. *Szeto v. Schiffer*, 19 Del. J. Corp. L. 1310, 1319-20 (Del. Ch. Nov. 24, 1993).

1467. *Baron v. Siff*, 1997 Del. Ch. LEXIS 152, at \*5, 1997 WL

(continued...)

"Failure to carry that burden will result in the complaint's dismissal."[1468]

While the making a demand is a concession that a majority of the corporation's directors are disinterested and independent, the making of a demand is not necessarily a concession that the directors will act in a disinterested and independent manner in response to the demand.[1469] Thus "[i]t is not correct that a demand concedes independence 'conclusively' and *in futuro* for all purposes relevant to the demand."[1470] The Delaware Supreme Court has noted that there is nothing inconsistent (1) with the proposition that "in assessing whether a demand has been wrongfully refused, the court looks only to good faith and the reasonableness of the investigation" and (2) the proposition that "a board that appears independent *ex ante* may not necessarily act independently *ex post* in rejecting a demand."[1471] The court explained that the "[f]ailure of an otherwise independent-appearing board or committee to act independently is a failure to carry out its fiduciary duties in good faith or to conduct a reasonable investigation," and "[s]uch a failure could constitute wrongful refusal."[1472]

In sum, "[i]f there is reason to doubt that the board acted independently or with due care in responding to the demand, the stockholder may have the basis *ex post* to claim wrongful refusal. The stockholder then has the right to bring the underlying action with the same standing which the stockholder would have had, *ex ante*, if demand had been excused as futile."[1473]

---

1467. (...continued)
666973, at *2 (Del. Ch. Oct. 17, 1997) (footnotes omitted).

    1468. *Chicago Stock Exch.*, 1996 Del. Ch. LEXIS 79, at *11, 1996 WL 417507, at *3.

    1469. *Chicago Stock Exch.*, 701 A.2d at 74; *Grimes*, 673 A.2d at 1219.

    1470. *Chicago Stock Exch.*, 701 A.2d at 74.

    1471. *Id.*

    1472. *Id.*

    1473. *Id.; Grimes*, 673 A.2d at 1219.

Where a committee is formed to investigate issues raised by a demand and recommend a course of action to the board, "the good faith and reasonableness of both groups must be considered."[1474] "[P]articularized allegations that the Special Committee (as the investigating committee) or the Executive Committee (as the decisionmaking committee) was biased, lacked independence, or failed to conduct a reasonable investigation" may create "a reasonable doubt that demand was properly refused."[1475]

Finally, where a copy of a board's letter refusing a shareholder demand is attached to a complaint, the court may consider the contents of the board's letter in deciding a motion to dismiss a complaint filed by a shareholder alleging a wrongful refusal of the demand.[1476] With respect to any statement in the board's letter, the court "must presume it to be true absent a particularized allegation rebutting this statement."[1477]

*e. Motion to Dismiss Decisions by Delaware Courts.* The Delaware Supreme Court's decisions in *Levine v. Smith*,[1478] *Grimes v. Donald*[1479] and *Scattered Corp. v. Chicago Stock Exchange, Inc.*[1480] provide three examples of cases applying the standard summarized above.[1481]

---

1474. *Boeing*, 1994 Del. Ch. LEXIS 14, at *6, 1994 WL 30542, at *2.

1475. *Chicago Stock Exch.*, 701 A.2d at 75.

1476. *See, e.g., Chicago Stock Exch.*, 701 A.2d at 76 n.24; *Levine*, 591 A.2d at 214; *Mount Moriah Cemetary v. Moritz*, [1990-1991 Transfer Binder] Fed. Sec. L. Rep. (CCH) ¶ 95,900, at 99,443 (Del. Ch. Apr. 4, 1991), *aff'd*, 599 A.2d 413 (unpublished opinion, text available at 1991 Del. LEXIS 244 and 1991 WL 165558) (Del. Aug. 12, 1991); *In re General Motors Class E Stock Buyout Sec. Litig.*, 790 F. Supp. 77, 81 (D. Del. 1992); *see also* Fed. R. Civ. P. 10(c) ("[a] copy of any written instrument which is an exhibit to a pleading is a part thereof for all purposes").

1477. *Chicago Stock Exch.*, 701 A.2d at 76 n.24.

1478. 591 A.2d 194 (Del. 1991).

1479. 673 A.2d 1207 (Del. 1996).

1480. 701 A.2d 70 (Del. 1997).

1481. *See* Chapter IV, Section B 6 d.

The court in *Levine v. Smith*[1482] rejected a shareholder plaintiff's contention that a refusal of a demand by the board of General Motors Corporation ("GM") was wrongful. The refusal of the demand allegedly was wrongful because, according to the plaintiff, the board (1) did not permit plaintiff's counsel to make an oral presentation to the board concerning his demand, and (2) failed to undertake any investigation of the demand and instead "did nothing" following receipt of the demand.[1483] The court stated that a board's determination not to permit a shareholder or his counsel to make an oral presentation to the board in connection with a demand the shareholder has made does not render the board's refusal of the shareholder's demand uninformed or unreasonable.[1484] The court explained as follows:

> A board of directors is not legally obligated to permit a demanding shareholder to make an oral presentation at a meeting. Corporate directors normally have only limited available time to deliberate, and a determination of what matters will (and will not) be considered must necessarily fall within the board's discretion. A ruling that, as a practical matter, would require GM's Board to hear the plaintiff's oral presentation, would place directors in the untenable position of having to entertain presentations by any shareholder who threatens to file a derivative action.[1485]

The court similarly concluded that the plaintiff's allegations that the board failed to undertake an investigation of his demand and "did nothing" following receipt of the demand failed on two grounds. First, the allegations were conclusory in nature and "[t]he business judgment rule accords directors the presumption that they acted on an informed basis." Second, the allegations were contrary to the pleading record because the board's letter refusing the plaintiff's demand (a copy of which was attached to plaintiff's com-

---

1482. 591 A.2d 194 (Del. 1991).

1483. *Id.* at 213.

1484. *Id.* at 214.

1485. *Id.* (quoting *Levine v. Smith*, 16 Del. J. Corp. L. 333, 349 (Del. Ch. Nov. 27, 1989), *aff'd*, 591 A.2d 194 (Del. 1991) (citing Manning, *The Business Judgment Rule and the Director's Duty of Attention: Time for Reality*, 39 Bus. Law. 1477, 1485 (1984)).

plaint) expressly referred to the board's "review of the matters" set forth in the shareholder's demand letter.[1486] The court stated that the "only reasonable inference to be drawn from this document is that the GM Directors did act in an informed manner in addressing Levine's demand."[1487]

A federal court in *In re General Motors Class E Stock Buyout Securities Litigation*[1488] followed *Levine* in a case arising out of the same facts and raising the same issue as *Levine*.[1489] The *General Motors* decision granted a motion for reargument of and reversed an earlier decision by the federal court denying a motion to dismiss.[1490] The Delaware Supreme Court's decision in *Levine* stated that the federal court's first decision in *General Motors* was "premised on a serious misunderstanding of the controlling Delaware law."[1491]

The Delaware Supreme Court in *Grimes v. Donald*[1492] dismissed a complaint alleging wrongful refusal of demand on the grounds that the plaintiff disagreed with the board's determination to refuse the demand in that case and alleged that "the refusal could not have been the result of an adequate, good faith investigation since the Board decided not to act on the demand."[1493] The court described "[s]uch conclusory, *ipse dixit*, assertions" as inconsistent with the requirement that particularized allegations be pleaded that, if true, "would raise a reasonable doubt that the Board's decision to reject the demand was the product of a valid business judgment."[1494]

---

1486. 591 A.2d at 214, *quoted in Chicago Stock Exch.*, 701 A.2d at 76 n.24.

1487. *Id.*

1488. 790 F. Supp. 77 (D. Del. 1992).

1489. *Id.* at 78-81.

1490. *In re General Motors Class E Stock Buyout Litig.*, 694 F. Supp. 1119 (D. Del. 1988), *reargument granted and decision rev'd*, 790 F. Supp. 77 (D. Del. 1992).

1491. *Levine*, 591 A.2d at 211.

1492. 673 A.2d 1207 (Del. 1996).

1493. *Id.* at 1220.

1494. *Id.*

The Delaware Supreme Court reached the same result in *Scattered Corp. v. Chicago Stock Exchange, Inc.*,[1495] a case where a demand by Scattered Corporation, a registered broker-dealer and a member of the Chicago Stock Exchange, a Delaware non-stock corporation, was refused by the Executive Committee of the Chicago Stock Exchange. The determination was made by the Executive Committee pursuant to a provision in the Chicago Stock Exchange's Constitution that permitted "the Executive Committee 'to exercise all the rights, powers, authority, duties and obligations of the Board . . .' between meetings of the full Board."[1496] A letter written by Erwin E. Schulze, the Chairman of the Exchange, and a copy of which was attached to the complaint in the case, advised Scattered Corporation that its demand had been refused and stated the following:

> (i) the Executive Committee of the Board has full authority to act for the Board between meetings of the full Board, and it appointed the Special Committee of past and current Board members to investigate the allegations contained in Scattered's demand; (ii) the Special Committee had retained independent counsel; (iii) the Special Committee and its counsel had interviewed over 25 individuals, including the individuals Scattered identified as having knowledge of the demand allegations; (iv) the chairman of the Special Committee had advised the Executive Committee that the allegations in Scattered's demand could not be substantiated; and (v) after careful consideration, the Executive Committee had determined that there was no basis upon which to take further action with respect to Scattered's demand.[1497]

"It later developed that the statement in Mr. Schulze's letter that the Executive Committee appointed the Special Committee was in error, and that the full Board, in fact, appointed the Special Committee. It was the Executive Committee, however, meeting between Board meetings, that ultimately made the decision 'after careful consideration' (according to Mr. Schulze's letter . . . ) to refuse the

---

1495. 701 A.2d 70 (Del. 1997).
1496. *Id.* at 74.
1497. *Id.*

demand, presumably based on the Special Committee's conclusion that the allegations were 'unsubstantiated.'"[1498]

Plaintiffs (which included Scattered and another member of the Exchange) contended that they had satisfied their pleading burden by alleging the following:

> (a) that Messrs. Schulze, Livingston and Fletcher were all members of the Executive Committee at the time the demand was made, that they are each accused by the plaintiffs of wrongdoing and that these three individuals "had the ability to dominate and control the ten-member Executive Committee;" (b) that five members constituted a quorum of the Executive Committee, and that, although plaintiffs do not know who actually voted to reject their demand, Schulze, Livingston and Fletcher could have constituted a majority of that quorum and thereby unduly influenced the vote; and (c) the Executive Committee told plaintiffs of its decision not to pursue their demand on the same day that the Executive Committee received the investigatory report from the Special Committee, such quick action raising a reasonable doubt that the Executive Committee adequately considered the matter.[1499]

The court held that "plaintiffs' 'facts' creating a reasonable doubt about the disinterestedness and independence of the Executive Committee are not facts at all. Rather, they are conclusory and speculative statements, suffering fatally from a paucity of particularization."[1500]

Citing *Levine*, the Supreme Court pointed to the statement in Schulze's letter that the Executive Committee refused Scattered's demand after "careful consideration" of the special committee's investigation.[1501] Because a copy of that letter was attached to the complaint, the Supreme Court stated, "we must presume it to be true absent a particularized allegation rebutting this state-

---

1498. *Id.* at 72 n.1.
1499. *Id.* at 73-74.
1500. *Id.* at 75.
1501. *Id.* at 76.

ment."[1502] The Supreme Court then pointed to the following facts noted by the Court of Chancery in considering "the good faith and reasonableness of the investigation into plaintiffs' complaint":

> (a) the creation of the Special Committee; (b) the fact that it interviewed 25 people as well as other people the plaintiffs had suggested would corroborate their claims of wrongful conduct; (c) the findings by the Special Committee that claims made in the demand were unsubstantiated; and (d) the conclusion by the Executive Committee, after "careful consideration" of the Special Committee's investigation, that there is no basis on which it could or should take action with respect to plaintiffs' allegations.[1503]

Based upon these facts, the Supreme Court stated, the Court of Chancery concluded as follows:

> "[N]one of the particularized pleaded facts supports the plaintiffs' claim that the Executive Committee violated its duty of care by relying upon the Special Committee's investigation. . . . To the contrary, the pleaded facts confirm that the Executive Committee's decision was the product of a valid exercise of business judgment."[1504]

The Supreme Court also noted the Court of Chancery's conclusion—"after it became known that the full Board rather than the Executive Committee appointed the Special Committee to conduct the investigation into plaintiffs' complaint"—that this new fact was "immaterial to the reasoning or result."[1505] The court explained:

> That is because on the dismissal motion the only legal issue was whether the complaint alleged particularized facts creating a reason to doubt that the investigation of the demand was reasonable and conducted in good faith. The investigation was conducted by the Special Committee. Whether the Special Committee was created by the Executive Committee

---

1502. *Id.* at 76 n.24.

1503. *Id.* at 76 (footnotes omitted).

1504. *Id.* at 76.

1505. *Id.* (quoting *Scattered Corp. v. Chicago Stock Exch., Inc.*, 23 Del. J. Corp. L. 355, 360 (Del. Ch. Apr. 7, 1997), *aff'd*, 701 A.2d 70 (Del. 1997)).

(as originally assumed) or by the full Board (the "new fact") has no logical or legal bearing on that issue.[1506]

*          *          *

There is no basis to infer from that single fact, or from the timing or other circumstances of its disclosure, that it exemplified a larger group of other misrepresented facts. . . . If plaintiffs had a factual basis to dispute Mr. Schulze's statements [made in the letter refusing plaintiffs' demand], their obligation was to plead those facts in their complaint and rely on them when opposing defendant's motion to dismiss. If plaintiffs had no such contrary facts, they cannot fill the gap by offering up improper inferences as a substitute.[1507]

The Supreme Court described these conclusions by the Court of Chancery as "well-reasoned and firmly rooted in settled law" and stated that there was "no basis for disturbing" these conclusions.[1508]

As discussed later in this Chapter, the Delaware Supreme Court in both *Levine* and *Chicago Stock Exchange* also held that discovery is not available to shareholders in cases alleging that a demand has been wrongfully refused before the complaint survives a motion to dismiss.[1509]

A series of Delaware Court of Chancery decisions also illustrate the principles applied in cases involving motions to dismiss claims that demands have been wrongfully refused. These decisions all reach the same result reached by the Delaware Supreme Court in *Levine*, *Grimes* and *Chicago Stock Exchange*.

The Court of Chancery in *Mount Moriah Cemetery v. Moritz*,[1510] for example, granted a motion to dismiss in a case where the plaintiff alleged that a board committee formed to inves-

---

1506. *Id.*

1507. *Id.* at 77 (quoting 23 Del. J. Corp. L. at 361).

1508. *Id.* at 77.

1509. *See* Chapter IV, Section B 7.

1510. [1990-1991 Transfer Binder] Fed. Sec. L. Rep. (CCH) ¶ 95,900 (Del. Ch. Apr. 4, 1991), *aff'd*, 599 A.2d 413 (unpublished opinion, text available at 1991 Del. LEXIS 244 and 1991 WL 165558) (Del. Aug. 12, 1991).

tigate a shareholder demand had not interviewed everyone who the shareholder believed the committee should have interviewed, had not reviewed documents from a time period that the shareholder believed should have been considered by the committee, and had not obtained expert assistance or investigated general industry practices.[1511]

Holding that these allegations failed to state a cause of action, the court in *Mount Moriah* explained that "[i]n deciding whether directors have made an informed decision, the standard is gross negligence."[1512] As a result, according to the court, the alleged deficiencies in the corporation's investigation "must rise to the level of gross negligence if the directors' decision is to be condemned as uninformed."[1513] "In any investigation," the court continued, "the choice of people to interview or documents to review is one on which reasonable minds may differ."[1514] The court described this as "especially so" in a case such as the case before the court, "where the challenged conduct covers a period of more than ten years."[1515] Under the circumstances, the court stated, "[i]nevitably, there will be potential witnesses, documents and other leads that the investigator will decide not to pursue."[1516]

Here, the court stated, the committee's investigation spanned more than six months, the committee reviewed over 167,000 pages of documents, interviewed the senior officers accused of wrongdoing and their immediate subordinates, met several times with counsel for the shareholder who had made the demand underlying the investigation, and "compiled enough information to produce a 163 page Report."[1517] Moreover, the court added, the issues underlying the demand were "well known" to the corporation's directors even before the shareholder's demand was received due to

---

1511. *Id.* at 99,442.

1512. *Id.*

1513. *Id.; see also* Chapter I, Section D 3 and Chapter II, Section A 4 a (discussing gross negligence standard).

1514. *Id.* at 99,442.

1515. *Id.*

1516. *Id.*

1517. *Id.* at 99,442-43.

two class actions, numerous individual suits, and widespread media attention involving the issues raised in the demand.[1518]

The court also rejected an allegation that the corporation's board had accepted the committee's recommendation "without serious deliberation, question or request for any further inquiry" and thus "failed to bring their business judgment to bear on this question."[1519] The court stated that this allegation was "conclusory" and "unsupported by any specific factual allegations."[1520] The court also pointed to the fact that the corporation's letter refusing the demand, which was attached to the complaint, stated that there had been a "full discussion" of the committee's report by the full board.[1521] The court acknowledged that "plaintiff may not agree with this description" but concluded that "there is nothing in its complaint to contradict it."[1522]

The Delaware Supreme Court affirmed the Court of Chancery's decision in *Mount Moriah* in an unpublished decision stating that "it is manifest on the face of appellant's brief that the appeal is without merit."[1523] The Supreme Court in *Chicago Stock Exchange* cited *Mount Moriah* in support of the proposition that "conclusory statements will not suffice to cast a reasonable doubt upon the disinterestedness, good faith or reasonableness" of a board or committee acting on a demand."[1524] The court in *Chicago Stock Exchange* described *Mount Moriah* as holding that a claim for wrongful refusal is "not properly stated where plaintiffs could only quibble with the method of the committee's investigation and could only state in conclusory terms that the investigation was inadequate."[1525]

---

1518. *Id.*

1519. *Id.* at 99,442, 99,443.

1520. *Id.* at 99,443.

1521. *Id.*

1522. *Id.*

1523. *Mount Moriah Cemetery v. Moritz*, 599 A.2d 413 (unpublished opinion, text available at 1991 Del. LEXIS 244, 1991 WL 165558, at *1) (Del. Aug. 12, 1991).

1524. 701 A.2d at 74-75 n.23.

1525. *Id.*

Another Court of Chancery decision dismissing a complaint alleging wrongful refusal of a demand is *Boeing Co. v. Shrontz*.[1526] This case involved the refusal of a demand alleging that directors "failed to prevent and/or correct a pattern of misconduct, including criminal activity, by officers and employees in connection with various government contracts."[1527] The shareholder who made the demand was informed that a committee of outside board members had been established to review the demand and that the committee was represented by counsel, and the shareholder's counsel was asked to meet with the committee's counsel and provide the committee any information counsel had concerning the allegations made in the demand.[1528] A meeting between the shareholder's counsel and the committee's counsel was held, and the shareholder's counsel asked at that meeting and in two letters written after the meeting that the shareholder's counsel be permitted to address the committee directly and be given copies of any report or recommendation prepared by the committee.[1529] These requests were denied.[1530]

After the shareholder's demand was refused, the shareholder who made the demand and another shareholder commenced a derivative action. The court rejected several challenges to the good faith and reasonableness of the special committee's consideration and refusal of the demand.

First, the court rejected a contention that the special committee acted in bad faith and unreasonably by not meeting with the shareholder's counsel during their investigation. The court cited the rejection by the Delaware Supreme Court in *Levine* of the argument in that case that a special committee must allow shareholders an opportunity to make an oral presentation to a board considering a demand.[1531] The court stated that the obligation of a board or a

---

1526. 1994 Del. Ch. LEXIS 14, 1994 WL 30542 (Del. Ch. Jan. 19, 1994).

1527. 1994 Del. Ch. LEXIS 14, at *2, 1994 WL 30542, at *1.

1528. 1994 Del. Ch. LEXIS 14, at *2-4, 1994 WL 30542, at *1-2.

1529. 1994 Del. Ch. LEXIS 14, at *4, 1994 WL 30542, at *1.

1530. *Id*.

1531. 1994 Del. Ch. LEXIS 14, at *7, 1994 WL 30542, at *2.

board committee investigating a demand is to be informed and that correspondence attached to plaintiffs' complaint established that "the special committee sought out any relevant information plaintiffs might have had" by meeting with plaintiffs' counsel and making "several written requests" to plaintiffs' counsel for information.[1532] The court accordingly held that "the failure to interview plaintiffs or meet with plaintiffs' counsel does not create a reasonable doubt as to the quality of the special committee's investigation."[1533]

Second, the court rejected a contention that the special committee acted in bad faith and unreasonably allegedly by changing its position with respect to whether to schedule a face-to-face meeting between the committee and plaintiffs' counsel. The plaintiffs relied upon a letter written by the committee's counsel at the beginning of its investigation stating that the members of the committee "believe that, given the fact that our investigation is still in its early stages, it would be premature to meet with you at this time" and that "[a]t the appropriate stage of the investigation, we will further discuss with the Special Committee the advisability of having you or one of your colleagues address the Committee on the matters you have mentioned."[1534] According to plaintiffs, "the 'clear import' of this letter was that the special committee would meet with plaintiffs' counsel as some future time."[1535] According to the court, however, plaintiffs "read far too much" into the letter.[1536] The court explained that the letter "says only that the special committee will consider the advisability of having a face-to-face meeting with plaintiffs' counsel" and that at the end of its investigation the committee "apparently decided that such a meeting was not advisable."[1537] The court stated that "nothing about this process . . . suggests the absence of due care or bad faith" because the commit-

---

1532. *Id.*
1533. *Id.*
1534. 1994 Del. Ch. LEXIS 14, at *7-8, 1994 WL 30542, at *3.
1535. 1994 Del. Ch. LEXIS 14, at *8, 1994 WL 30542, at *3.
1536. *Id.*
1537. 1994 Del. Ch. LEXIS 14, at *8-9, 1994 WL 30542, at *3.

tee "sought out information from plaintiffs and their counsel to the extent and in the manner that the committee felt appropriate."[1538]

Third, the court rejected a contention that the committee acted in bad faith and unreasonably allegedly by misleading plaintiffs' counsel concerning the status of the committee's investigation. Plaintiffs alleged that during a telephone conversation on the day that the committee planned to (and did) present its recommendation to the corporation's board the committee's counsel told plaintiffs' counsel that the committee "would make a determination sometime in the near future[ ] and . . . that he could not be more specific."[1539] Plaintiffs' contention that these facts suggested bad faith, the court stated, was a "grasping at phrases here and there as suggesting some sinister motivation."[1540] According to the court, "plaintiffs were not given any inaccurate information"; "[t]hey simply were not given all the information they would have liked with respect to the workings of the special committee."[1541] The court held that "[w]ithout more," these alleged facts "do not create a reasonable doubt as to the good faith of the Special Committee."[1542]

Fourth, the court rejected the following additional allegations as insufficient to raise a reasonable doubt concerning the good faith and reasonableness of the board's consideration of the demand: (1) the corporation's general counsel waited three days to notify plaintiffs of the board's determination to refuse demand, (2) the corporation's general counsel then notified plaintiffs concerning the board's decision by sending a letter to the shareholder who had made the demand rather than to his counsel, and (3) the corporation refused to identify the members of the committee that had considered the demand or give plaintiffs a copy of the committee's report.[1543] The court stated that "there appears to be nothing unusual about the special committee's investigation, its report or the board's decision

1538. 1994 Del. Ch. LEXIS 14, at *9, 1994 WL 30542, at *3.
1539. 1994 Del. Ch. LEXIS 14, at *4-5, 1994 WL 30542, at *1.
1540. 1994 Del. Ch. LEXIS 14, at *9, 1994 WL 30542, at *3.
1541. 1994 Del. Ch. LEXIS 14, at *9-10, 1994 WL 30542, at *3.
1542. 1994 Del. Ch. LEXIS 14, at *10, 1994 WL 30542, at *3.
1543. 1994 Del. Ch. LEXIS 14, at *10, 1994 WL 30542, at *3-4.

following review of that report."[1544] The court also pointed to the Delaware Supreme Court's decision in *Levine* holding that discovery is not available before a motion to dismiss is decided in cases alleging wrongful refusal of a demand.[1545]

The Court of Chancery in *Baron v. Siff*[1546] reached the same result in a case where a shareholder alleged that the corporation's directors "purposefully and knowingly" breached their fiduciary duty by refusing a demand.[1547] Pointing to the Supreme Court's rejection as conclusory of the allegation in *Grimes* that a "refusal could not have been the result of an adequate, good faith investigation since the Board decided not to act on the demand," the court rejected the allegation in *Baron* as "not a particularized fact; it is a conclusory allegation of the type that has been rejected by the Supreme Court."[1548]

The court also rejected a contention that the board's letter refusing the demand, which was incorporated by reference in and attached to the complaint, established the wrongfulness of the board's refusal. The letter, plaintiff contended, "(1) was drafted and signed by counsel, (2) does not state that the Directors held a meeting to discuss the demand letter, (3) does not respond to each allegation in the demand letter, (4) does not mention the Board until the second to the last line, and (5) is dated nine days after the demand letter."[1549] Based upon these facts, plaintiff contended, "defendants either failed to investigate the demand letter altogether or inappropriately delegated the investigation to counsel."[1550]

These five facts, the court held, did not establish that the Board failed to investigate plaintiff's demand, for the following reasons:

---

1544. 1994 Del. Ch. LEXIS 14, at *10-11, 1994 WL 30542, at *4.
1545. 1994 Del. Ch. LEXIS 14, at *11-12, 1994 WL 30542, at *4.
1546. 1997 Del. Ch. LEXIS 152, 1997 WL 666973 (Del. Ch. Oct. 17, 1997).
1547. 1997 Del. Ch. LEXIS 152, at *3, 1997 WL 666973, at *1.
1548. 1997 Del. Ch. LEXIS 152, at *6, 1997 WL 666973, at *2.
1549. 1997 Del. Ch. LEXIS 152, at *7, 1997 WL 666973, at *2.
1550. *Id.*

- "That the refusal letter was drafted and signed by defendants' counsel does not suggest that the Board did not address plaintiff's demand. . . . It is understandable that a busy board of directors would, as plaintiff did, have counsel draft and sign a letter undoubtedly written with an eye toward complying with [the demand requirement]."[1551]

- "That the Board itself is not mentioned until the end of the letter is of no moment because the first sentence of the letter indicates that counsel was writing in his capacity as CDI's representative. There is no indication that counsel wrote the letter without the Board's input or authorization."[1552]

- "The refusal letter's failure to state that the Board held a meeting and failure to contain a point-by-point response to all allegations in the demand letter does not stand for the proposition that the Board did not consider the demand before refusing it."[1553]

- "That the refusal letter is dated nine days after the demand letter is also insufficient to rebut the presumption that the Board adequately investigated the demand."[1554] The court pointed to the board's "familiarity with the issues plaintiff raised" and stated that "plaintiff's own demand letter must be read to conclude that no more than ten days was necessary to investigate his demand. It stated: 'If you do not commence these actions within ten (10) days of receipt of this letter, we will consider these demands rejected.'"[1555]

The court added that even if the board's letter refusing demand did, "as plaintiff contends, 'facially establish[ ]' that the Board failed to investigate plaintiff's demand altogether . . . the mere allegation

---

1551. 1997 Del. Ch. LEXIS 152, at *8-9, 1997 WL 666973, at *3.
1552. 1997 Del. Ch. LEXIS 152, at *9, 1997 WL 666973, at *3.
1553. 1997 Del. Ch. LEXIS 152, at *10, 1997 WL 666973, at *3.
1554. 1997 Del. Ch. LEXIS 152, at *11, 1997 WL 666973, at *3.
1555. *Id.*

that a board did not investigate a demand is insufficient to rebut the presumption of the business judgment rule."[1556]

   *f. Motion to Dismiss Decisions by Courts Construing Delaware Law Outside of Delaware.* Courts construing Delaware law outside of Delaware have reached the same result reached in the *Levine v. Smith,*[1557] *Grimes v. Donald,*[1558] *Scattered Corp. v. Chicago Stock Exchange, Inc.,*[1559] *Mount Moriah Cemetery v. Moritz,*[1560] *Boeing Co. v. Shrontz*[1561] and *Baron v. Siff*[1562] decisions discussed above.[1563]

   *Litton Industries, Inc. v. Hoch,*[1564] a federal court decision in California that was affirmed by the Ninth Circuit, provides one example. The court in *Litton* explained that the plaintiffs in this case had not demonstrated that an investigation by a special litigation committee, which had recommended that the corporation's board refuse the demand in the case, was "not thorough and complete" or that the board "acted outside the bounds of reasonable judgment" in adopting the committee's recommendation.[1565] The court stated that plaintiffs had not identified any witness willing to be questioned by the committee who had information concerning the subject matter of plaintiffs' demand but was not interviewed by

---

1556. 1997 Del. Ch. LEXIS 152, at *12, 1997 WL 666973, at *3.

1557. 591 A.2d 194 (Del. 1991).

1558. 673 A.2d 1207 (Del. 1996).

1559. 701 A.2d 70 (Del. 1997).

1560. [1990-1991 Transfer Binder] Fed. Sec. L. Rep. (CCH) ¶ 95,900 (Del. Ch. Apr. 4, 1991), *aff'd,* 599 A.2d 413 (unpublished opinion, text available at 1991 Del. LEXIS 244 and 1991 WL 165558) (Del. Aug. 12, 1991).

1561. 1994 Del. Ch. LEXIS 14, 1994 WL 30542 (Del. Ch. Jan. 19, 1994).

1562. 1997 Del. Ch. LEXIS 152, 1997 WL 666973 (Del. Ch. Oct. 17, 1997).

1563. *See* Chapter IV, Section B 6 e.

1564. No. 89-1967 RG (C.D. Cal. Oct. 30, 1991), *aff'd,* 996 F.2d 1225 (unpublished opinion, text available at 1993 U.S. App. LEXIS 16992 and 1993 WL 241549) (9th Cir. July 2, 1993).

1565. *Id.,* slip op. at 9.

the committee or its counsel.[1566] The court also stated that plaintiffs had not identified any documents that the committee should have considered but did not consider.[1567] The court acknowledged that plaintiffs had "suggested ways" that the committee "might have conducted its investigation differently" but had "not introduced any evidence to show that the investigation was conducted in a grossly negligent manner, or to show that any of their suggested alternatives would have changed the outcome of the investigation in any way."[1568] The Ninth Circuit affirmed the district court's decision, stating that "directors need not show that they performed a perfect investigation."[1569] The Ninth Circuit concluded that the committee's "investigatory procedure were adequate," and that "[n]othing more was required."[1570]

The same result was reached in *Varian Associates, Inc. v. Superior Court,*[1571] a California state court decision construing Delaware law. The court reasoned as follows:

> The substantive effect of the business judgment rule . . . is to provide corporate directors a complete defense to a shareholder derivative lawsuit unless the shareholder can point to specific facts showing either lack of independence of the directors or "wrongful refusal" of the demand. . . .
>
> Plaintiff has not met this burden. He attacks the committee's investigation on procedural grounds, arguing that it was short, cursory, and hidden from public scrutiny. However, that investigation had actually been going on for a long time before plaintiff made his demand to pursue litigation. . . . [P]laintiff must make a particularized showing of wrongful refusal or of bias of the decision makers before the court will proceed further to a factual inquiry into the decisional process. . . . The attack on the procedures is wholly conclusion-

---

1566. *Id.*

1567. *Id.*

1568. *Id.* at 10.

1569. *Litton Indus., Inc. v. Hoch,* 996 F.2d 1225 (unpublished opinion, text available at 1993 U.S. App. LEXIS 16992, at *8 and 1993 WL 241549, at *3) (9th Cir. July 2, 1993).

1570. *Id.*

1571. No. H011025 (Cal. Ct. App. Aug. 31, 1993).

ary; there is nothing inherently imperfect in an investigation which lasts two years, instead of three, or fills four rather than six three ring binders. There is no showing at all of any specific infirmity in the committee's investigative procedures such as would result in harm to the corporation or its shareholders.

Also, he has made no showing whatsoever of harm to the corporation resulting from that decision; the only harms he has alleged are the past harms done to the corporation by the malefactors, not any present cost/benefit analysis showing that it will profit the corporation more to pursue the litigation than to take the measures it has instead elected. In short, there is nothing specific in plaintiff's presentation showing that the instant decision not to pursue litigation was "wrongful." It has not even been shown to be "harmful." . . .

Plaintiff's demonstration here has been mainly concerned with showing the undeniable existence of much past wrongdoing by Varian employees and officers. Those are regrettable conditions but they are not necessarily dispositive of the decision whether such wrongdoers should be subjected to a lawsuit. To impugn the presumed business judgment of the corporate Board and its committee, the minority shareholder must show clearly that it is in the corporation's best interests to pursue the litigation and that the decision not to do so is corrupt or patently ill advised. He has not even begun to do so.[1572]

A summary judgment dismissal of the litigation therefore was appropriate, the court concluded, because the corporation had established "a complete affirmative defense of proper exercise of its business judgment, and plaintiff has produced no specific facts rebutting that exercise of corporate management prerogative."[1573]

A federal court in New York applying Delaware law reached the same result in *Levner v. Prince Alwaleed Bin Talal Bin Abdulaziz Al Saud*,[1574] a case involving a shareholder demand asking

---

1572. *Id.*, slip op. at 18-20.
1573. *Id.* at 20.
1574. 903 F. Supp. 452 (S.D.N.Y. 1994), *aff'd*, 61 F.3d 8 (2d Cir. 1995).

that litigation be commenced concerning trading in Citicorp's stock by Prince Alwaleed and a board refusal of the demand "on the basis of a letter issued by Alwaleed's attorneys."[1575] The court held that this allegation was insufficient to state a claim that the board's refusal of the demand was wrongful because there were no allegations "as to what was in this letter, whether the board relied on the letter, or why any such reliance would be inappropriate."[1576] The court added that "from the face of the amended complaint, it is evident that the Citicorp board did not make an uninformed decision to refuse to take action and, in fact, did initiate an investigation into this matter."[1577]

The court also denied leave to amend. Plaintiff's proposed amended complaint alleged that plaintiff's counsel had met with Citicorp's attorneys and "disclosed confidential information" and that "the directors did not, and could not have made an adequate investigation of the information given Citicorp by plaintiff's counsel as required by Delaware law."[1578] The court stated that "bare conclusory allegations of wrongful refusal" of this nature were insufficient.[1579] Comparing plaintiff's original allegations with his new allegations, the court stated that the new allegations, while "more *lengthy*" than his prior allegations, were "no more particular."[1580] "Instead," the court concluded, "once again, the allegations are conclusory and not supported by specific facts sufficient to create a reasonable doubt that Citicorp acted in an informed manner."[1581]

The Second Circuit affirmed "on the carefully reasoned opinion" of the district court.[1582]

---

1575. *Id.* at 457.
1576. *Id.*
1577. *Id.*
1578. *Id.* at 458.
1579. *Id.*
1580. *Id.*
1581. *Id.*
1582. *Levner v. Prince Alwaleed Bin Talal Bin Abdulaziz Al Saud*, 61 F.3d 8, 8-9 (2d Cir. 1995).

*g. Decisions Construing New York, Illinois and Michigan Law.* Federal court decisions in *Stoner v. Walsh*,[1583] *In re Consumers Power Co. Derivative Litigation*[1584] and *Weiland v. Illinois Power Co.*[1585] illustrate the law in New York, Michigan and Illinois, respectively.

The court in *Stoner v. Walsh*[1586] relied principally upon the New York Court of Appeals' decision in *Auerbach v. Bennett*,[1587] a case discussed later in this Chapter that involved a special litigation committee decision to terminate a derivative action in which there was no claim that demand was required or wrongfully refused.[1588] Briefly, *Auerbach* permits judicial review of determinations by special litigation committees that pursuit of derivative claims would not serve the best interest of the corporation. This judicial review, however, is limited to the "disinterested independence of the members of that committee" and "the appropriateness and sufficiency of the investigative procedures chosen and pursued by the committee."[1589] By contrast, "the substantive aspects" of the decision, the court in *Auerbach* held, "are beyond judicial inquiry."[1590]

The court in *Stoner* described *Auerbach*'s limitation of judicial review to the decision-making directors' "disinterested independence" and the "appropriateness and sufficiency" of the committee's "investigative procedures" as "simply an application of the general business judgment rule to the particular situation of a board's decision to prevent shareholder litigation of a corporate

---

1583. 772 F. Supp. 790 (S.D.N.Y. 1991).

1584. 132 F.R.D. 455 (E.D. Mich. 1990).

1585. [1990-1991 Transfer Binder] Fed. Sec. L. Rep. (CCH) ¶ 95,747 (C.D. Ill. Sept. 17, 1990).

1586. 772 F. Supp. 790 (S.D.N.Y. 1991).

1587. 47 N.Y.2d 619, 393 N.E.2d 994, 419 N.Y.S.2d 920 (1979).

1588. *See* Chapter IV, Section C 1 a & 2 a.

1589. 47 N.Y.2d at 623-24, 393 N.E.2d at 996, 419 N.Y.S.2d at 922.

1590. *Id.* at 623, 393 N.E.2d at 996, 419 N.Y.S.2d at 922; *see also* Chapter IV, Section C 2 a (discussing *Auerbach* standard in more detail).

cause of action."[1591] This standard, the court in *Stoner* stated, governs "whenever a board or a committee of the board is charged with wrongfully preventing shareholder litigation of a corporate cause of action, whether the purportedly wrongful action was termination of an existing suit, as alleged in *Auerbach*, or rejection of a demand."[1592]

Therefore, the court in *Stoner* stated, "the issues to be determined when a shareholder alleges wrongful rejection is whether the body having the power to prevent shareholder litigation, and which did in fact prevent it, was disinterested and whether it employed sufficient and appropriate procedures."[1593] "Where both factors are present, the business judgment doctrine forecloses further judicial review."[1594] To satisfy this standard, a shareholder plaintiff "must show facts that would lead a reasonable person to infer that a *majority* of the Directors were not disinterested or that a *majority* of the Directors failed to employ appropriate and sufficient investigative procedures in rejecting the demand."[1595]

Applying this standard, the court in *Stoner* dismissed the complaint before it "because plaintiff fails to plead facts from which a reasonable person could infer that a majority of the Board was other than disinterested or that a majority of the Board failed to employ appropriate and sufficient investigative procedures."[1596] The court noted plaintiff's pleading "in conclusory terms that there was a grand design and conspiracy to conceal the truth" but held that once these allegations are "shorn of rhetoric and such devices as the word 'purported' and quotation marks to suggest sinister meaning in otherwise neutral words, plaintiff alleges no fact that would suggest the existence of such a conspiracy other than the naked fact that her demand was rejected."[1597] Even under notice

---

1591. 772 F. Supp. at 800.
1592. *Id.* at 800-01.
1593. *Id.* at 801.
1594. *Id.*
1595. *Id.*
1596. *Id.*
1597. *Id.* at 802.

pleading requirements, the court concluded, "[t]hat is simply not enough."[1598]

The court rejected plaintiff's "shotgun tactic" of demanding that the company commence litigation against all board members because each "would seem to have been responsible" for alleged waste and mismanagement. If this type of pleading were sufficient to allege a wrongful refusal of a demand, the court explained, plaintiffs in any derivative suit "could always preclude any board from rejecting a demand by simply making blunderbuss allegations against every current board member."[1599] The court rejected plaintiff's contention that "a director's desire to continue receiving general director's fees or other benefits is sufficient to imply that he or she was not disinterested when rejecting demand."[1600] "By plaintiff's logic," the court stated, "no paid director could ever vote properly to reject a demand."[1601] The court also held that an "insured versus insured" provision in the corporation's directors and officers liability insurance policy that excluded coverage of claims by the corporation against corporate directors did not render the directors interested in the subject matter of the demand. The court explained that New York law "explicitly recognizes the propriety of indemnifying officers and directors for their litigation costs by means of insurance" and that the insured versus insured exclusion is a standard provision in director and officer insurance policies.[1602] Plaintiff's contention regarding this exclusion, the court stated, would "preclude rejection of a demand whenever the standard exclusion exists" and "finds no support in either case authority or logic."[1603]

---

1598. *Id.*

1599. *Id.* at 805.

1600. *Id.*

1601. *Id.*

1602. *Id.* at 805 (citing N.Y. Bus. Corp. Law § 726(e)).

1603. *Id.* at 805; *see also* Chapter IV, Section B 5 c (i) (citing additional cases holding that demand is not excused by the presence of an "insured versus insured" provision in a directors' and officers' liability insurance policy); Chapter V, Section B 9 c (discussing insured versus insured provisions).

The court also rejected plaintiff's contention that an investigation by a three director committee upon which the board relied in rejecting plaintiff's demand was a "sham," a "cover-up" and a "whitewash."[1604] This contention, the court stated, was unsupported by any factual allegations in plaintiff's complaint. The court acknowledged that "bad faith in investigating a demand . . . would take the Board's decision outside the protection of the business judgment doctrine" but stated that "simply adding the words 'bad faith,' or a synonym, to a complaint is not sufficient to withstand a motion to dismiss."[1605]

*In re Consumers Power Co. Derivative Litigation*[1606] involved allegations of mismanagement, misrepresentation, corporate waste and breach of fiduciary duty in connection with the construction by a utility company, Consumers Power Company, of a nuclear power plant. Plaintiffs alleged that this misconduct resulted in shareholders paying billions of dollars in construction costs for a nuclear power plant that never would be completed, litigation against the corporation by Dow Chemical Company, a securities fraud class action naming the corporation and certain of the corporation's directors and officers as defendants, a Securities and Exchange Commission investigation and a Michigan Public Service Commission rate proceeding.[1607]

Following dismissal of plaintiffs' original complaint due to plaintiffs' failure to make a demand,[1608] plaintiffs made a demand and the corporation's board referred the demand to a special advisory committee. This committee consisted of four directors who had joined the corporation's board after the challenged events and who had not been identified as wrongdoers by the plaintiffs. Two months later, the committee recommended that the demand be refused. The committee assumed for purposes of its investigation

---

1604. *Id.* at 805-07.

1605. *Id.* at 806.

1606. 132 F.R.D. 455 (E.D. Mich. 1990).

1607. *Id.* at 457, 459.

1608. *See In re Consumers Power Co. Derivative Litig.*, 111 F.R.D. 419 (E.D. Mich. 1986).

that the corporation could prevail on the claims against the directors and officers charged with wrongdoing and recover $50 million in directors' and officers' liability insurance. The committee concluded, however, that this benefit to the corporation would be outweighed by the derivative action's negative impact upon the corporation's financial and business plans and the corporation's positions in the *Dow* and securities class action litigations, the SEC investigation and the Michigan rate proceeding. The board determined to follow the committee's recommendation and refused the demand.[1609]

Plaintiffs challenged the determination to refuse the demand on several grounds, including a contention that the committee's investigation was inadequate because the committee relied too extensively upon biased information from counsel for the committee and counsel for the defendants in the *Dow* and other litigations, investigations and proceedings.

The plaintiffs' primary attack upon the committee's counsel was the fact that the same law firm that was advising the committee regarding the allegations in plaintiffs' demand letter was also defending the corporation in the *Dow* litigation. The court acknowledged that "the integrity of a special litigation committee can be undermined if the attorneys representing and advising it have a sufficient conflict of interest to taint the committee's investigation and decision-making" but held that this was not the case here.[1610] The court explained that the committee counsel's client in both representations—the corporation in the *Dow* litigation and the committee in connection with the demand—was "one and the same— Consumers Power" and that the committee counsel "does not represent any of the individual director defendants in the present case or any other matters."[1611] "As corporate counsel," the court stated, counsel's "allegiance is to the corporate entity, not to its individual officers and directors."[1612]

---

1609. 132 F.R.D. at 457-59, 470-71, 473.
1610. *Id.* at 474.
1611. *Id.* at 476-77.
1612. *Id.* at 477; *cf. Stepak v. Addison*, 20 F.3d 398, 404-11 (11th
(continued...)

The court also stated that plaintiffs had "not presented the court a scintilla of factual evidence" suggesting that counsel "has, in the handling of the *Dow* case or in the representation of the Advisory Committee, violated any professional obligation to . . . his sole client, Consumers Power."[1613] The court added that plaintiffs' contention that counsel's "vigorous defense against claims of director mismanagement in the *Dow* case precluded him from giving unbiased advice to the Advisory Committee or adequately representing the committee" was undermined by the committee's determination "not to consider the merits of the case, but rather only the effect of the derivative action on the position of Consumers in the *Dow* case and other matters."[1614] Thus, according to the court, even if counsel "had an inappropriate bias in favor of the individual directors, the fact that the committee chose to presume the legitimacy of the merits of the claims against the directors blunted any effect such a bias would have."[1615] The court also stated that while counsel "may have been biased in favor of defending his client, Consumers Power, in the *Dow* litigation, it comes as little surprise—and can hardly be said to be a product infected by bias—to say that Consumers would be harmed in the *Dow* litigation by doing a complete about-face in pursuing a claim of fraud and mismanagement against its officers and directors."[1616]

The court similarly rejected the plaintiffs' challenge to the committee's consultation with the attorneys representing both the corporation and its directors and officers in the related securities

---

1612. (...continued)
Cir. 1994) (holding that a delegation of an investigation concerning a shareholder demand to a law firm that represented the directors and officers against whom wrongdoing was alleged in criminal proceedings involving the same subject matter as the demand constituted gross negligence and thus "strips a board's rejection of a shareholder demand of the protection of the business judgment rule").

1613. *Id.* at 478.
1614. *Id.*
1615. *Id.*
1616. *Id.*

class action and SEC proceedings. The court stated that there was nothing improper about consulting with opposing counsel concerning the merits of a case even in the most hostile of adversarial litigation.[1617] Here, moreover, the court explained, the directors' counsel was consulted not about the merits of the derivative claim against the corporation's directors and officers but only about the effect prosecution of that claim would have upon the corporation's position in the class action and SEC proceedings.[1618] The court added that even if plaintiffs could demonstrate a conflict caused by representation by the same counsel of the corporation and the corporation's directors and officers in the class action and SEC proceedings (the court emphasized, however, that plaintiffs had failed to do so), this would not affect the special committee's investigation because the committee was represented by separate counsel acting "as a filter and independent advisor."[1619]

Plaintiffs also contended that the committee's investigation was inadequate due to the committee's determination not to consider the merits of the alleged claims or perform a damage analysis. The court rejected this contention as follows:

> In arriving at a decision on whether to bring an independent action against its officers and directors, two areas of consideration are relevant: (1) Are the merits of the case strong enough to make it likely that the corporation could maintain a successful action against its officers and directors for wrongdoing? If there is not a winnable lawsuit, a corporation should reject a derivative stockholder's demand. (2) Even if there is a meritorious suit against the directors of a corporation, should such an action be maintained in light of other factors? In other words, once other factors are evaluated, might bringing the derivative action work a potentially greater harm to the corporation than any possible gain from that action?[1620]

---

1617. *Id.* at 479.
1618. *Id.*
1619. *Id.*
1620. *Id.* at 485.

Here, the court stated, the committee had proceeded upon the assumption that the answer to the first consideration was yes—the corporation[ could successfully maintain an action against its directors and officers and recover $50 million in directors' and officers' insurance.[1621] The court then focused its time and effort upon the second consideration—whether such a litigation would serve the best interests of the corporation.[1622]

The court described this methodology as "a common and acceptable method in decision theory for performing cost-benefit analysis" that "reasonable board members could find acceptable."[1623] The court explained that this decision-making process avoided the enormous time and expense that review of years of related litigation and hundreds of thousands of pages of documents would have entailed.[1624] The court also explained that this course would have risked disclosure of negative facts that might have been uncovered by the committee to the corporation's adversaries in the related litigation if the committee's report was released to the public in a subsequent judicial proceeding.[1625] The court also observed that a damage analysis would have been an enormous task and had not yet even been undertaken by either party in the related securities class action, which was in its sixth year of litigation. The court added that the plaintiffs' demand letter had "insisted upon a 'prompt[ ]' reply" within "thirty (30) days from the date of this letter."[1626] This time limitation, the court stated, made completion of "a sophisticated damage study . . . to say the least, . . . diffi-

---

1621. *Id.* at 473, 486.

1622. *Id.* at 485.

1623. *Id.*

1624. *Id.* at 483-85.

1625. *Id.* at 462-63 n.20 & 485 (citing *In re Continental Ill. Sec. Litig.*, 732 F.2d 1302, 1308-16 (7th Cir. 1984), a case requiring, based upon the facts before the court in that case, that a committee report used to support a motion to terminate a derivative action be made available to the public); *see also* Chapter IV, Section E 2 (discussing this issue and the *Continental* decision).

1626. *Id.* at 484.

cult."[1627] Accordingly, the court concluded, "[u]nder the totality of the circumstances, the failure of the Advisory Committee to undertake a damage study could not be found an unreasonable lack of thoroughness by any reasonable factfinder."[1628]

The court also pointed to the reasonableness of the directors' determination that the $50 million in insurance payments that might be obtained by the corporation if the corporation successfully prosecuted the derivative claim against the corporation's directors and officers was outweighed by the losses—possibly in excess of $1 billion—that the corporation might suffer in the *Dow* and securities class action proceedings as a result of success on the derivative claim. The court acknowledged that different decision-makers could view this decision differently but concluded that it was "not for this Court to decide who is right, nor to second-guess the special Advisory Committee" on this subject.[1629] Rather, the court explained, the court's responsibility was "only to consider whether the plaintiffs have evidence that would support a determination that the decision-making procedures were so uninformed and curtailed as to lie beyond the parameters of behavior that would be acceptable to reasonable business people."[1630]

The court acknowledged that "an ideal investigation and evaluation of the plaintiffs' demand would have involved an independent counsel who could make a thorough and independent investigation of the merits of the claim against the directors and an analysis of its impact on the liability and damages issues" in all of the related litigations.[1631] The court similarly acknowledged that "in a perfect world, where time and expense were no object, the Advisory Committee might even have chosen the ultimate in decision-making objectivity and thoroughness—the adversary system— with separate independent counsel to investigate and present argument on both sides of the issue before the neutral Advisory Com-

---

1627. *Id.*
1628. *Id.* at 485.
1629. *Id.* at 486.
1630. *Id.*
1631. *Id.* at 483.

mittee, who could decide the issue like a tribunal."[1632] The court concluded, however, that "for the business judgment rule to apply, a corporation is not required to undertake the ideal or perfect investigation—one that can anticipate all suggestions and withstand any criticism of derivative plaintiffs or of future court review. What is required is that the corporation makes a *reasonable* effort to reach an informed business decision."[1633]

Applying this standard, the court held that "no evidence or argument" had been presented from which a fact-finder could conclude that the board's advisory committee "ignored material information, including a review of the merits, 'reasonably' available to them," or that the committee's inquiry was "'so restricted and so shallow in execution, or otherwise so *pro forma* and half-hearted as to constitute a pretext or sham.'"[1634] Accordingly, the court held, a reasonable fact-finder could not conclude that the board's rejection of the shareholder demand was wrongful.[1635]

*Weiland v. Illinois Power Co.*[1636] also involved a demand that litigation be commenced on behalf of a utility company, Illinois Power Company, against directors and officers "for failing to properly exercise their duties in connection with the planning, construction and licensing" of a nuclear power plant, Clinton Power Station.[1637] As in *Consumers Power*, Illinois Power faced related litigation, including an appeal of an Illinois Commerce Commission determination (1) that approximately $665 million in construction costs were "unreasonably and imprudently incurred" by Illinois Power and (2) to disallow 72.8 percent of Illinois Power's invest-

---

1632. *Id.*

1633. *Id.*

1634. *Id.* at 486 (quoting *Auerbach v. Bennett*, 47 N.Y.2d 619, 634, 393 N.E.2d 994, 1003, 419 N.Y.S.2d 920, 929 (1979)); *see also* Chapter IV, Section C 2 a (discussing *Auerbach*).

1635. *Id.* at 486, 488.

1636. [1990-1991 Transfer Binder] Fed. Sec. L. Rep. (CCH) ¶ 95,747 (C.D. Ill. Sept. 17, 1990).

1637. *Id.* at 98,583.

ment as not "useful in providing electric utility service to Illinois Power's rate payers."[1638]

The demand was referred to a special committee for an investigation and determination.[1639] During a 13 month investigation, the committee met 39 times and the three directors who served on the committee collectively spent more than 700 hours in meetings and 72 interviews of 65 individuals.[1640] Following the investigation, a 236 page report concluded that the directors fulfilled their fiduciary responsibilities to the corporation in connection with the construction of Clinton and that the best interests of the corporation required that no claims be instituted or maintained against the corporation's directors and officers.[1641] More specifically, the committee found the following:

> a. That there is no reasonable possibility of any liability being effectively asserted against the Illinois Power officers and directors because they acted in good faith, on an informed basis with due care, and in the reasonable belief that they were acting in the best interests of Illinois Power.
>
> b. That even if the case were submitted to a jury, the result would be the imposition of substantial expenses upon Illinois Power with a very remote possibility that a jury would award damages to Illinois Power.
>
> c. That pursuit of the claims asserted by Plaintiff would cause great harm to Illinois Power operationally, financially, in its dealings with regulators and actual and potential adversaries, in the value and ratings of its securities, and in its ability to conduct its business.[1642]

The shareholder who made the demand conceded that the members of the special committee were "persons of character and integrity" and that the committee's investigation was "thorough."[1643]

---

1638. *Id.*
1639. *Id.* at 98,583-84.
1640. *Id.* at 98,585.
1641. *Id.* at 98,586-87.
1642. *Id.* at 98,587.
1643. *Id.* at 98,585, 98,586.

The court held that the committee's determination was "subject to review according to the traditional business judgment rule" and "protected by the business judgment rule."[1644] The court stated that "[u]nder the business judgment rule, the only issues are the independence of the Directors of the Special Committee, the reasonableness of its investigation, and its good faith."[1645]

With respect to the independence of the committee, the court rejected plaintiff's reliance upon claimed "structural" and inherent bias of any special committee in favor of board colleagues. The court explained that "[t]he majority view recognizes that independent directors are capable of rendering an unbiased decision though they were appointed by the defendant directors and share a common experience with the defendants."[1646] The court also rejected a contention that the determination that litigation of claims on behalf of a corporation would not serve the best interests of the corporation was "entitled to no weight because it would have been a breach of a fiduciary duty of the committee to find any other way as prosecuting the claims against the directors and officers would have an adverse impact upon the corporation in other proceedings and relationships," including, most significantly, the corporation's appeal of the Illinois Commerce Commission decision.[1647] To the contrary, the court concluded, "the future impact a derivative action will have on a corporation is a relevant consideration in addition to the consideration of the likelihood of the success of the claims against the directors and officers."[1648]

With respect to the reasonableness of the committee's investigation, the court stated that the committee's conclusion that Illinois Power's directors were "reasonably informed and reasonably responded to problems" was "amply supported by the record of the

---

1644. *Id.* at 98,589.

1645. *Id.* at 98,590.

1646. *Id.; see also* Chapter IV, Section C 2 f (discussing structural bias theory).

1647. *Id.* at 98,591.

1648. *Id.*

investigation."[1649] The court stated that the committee "inquired into the Board's level of involvement with Clinton and the extent to which the Directors were informed about Clinton matters."[1650] The court pointed to the committee's review of documents, interviews of directors, auditors retained by the Illinois Commerce Commission to audit Clinton, former Nuclear Regulatory Commission officials and others.[1651] The court also stated that the committee's report was "extensive, comprehensive, thorough, and well-reasoned."[1652]

With respect to the committee's good faith, the court stated that "there are no indications that the decision of the Special Committee lacked good faith."[1653] The court rejected a contention that "the fact that the Special Committee found that there was not even a remote possibility of any wrongful conduct on the part of any of the directors and officers of Illinois Power defies reason and implies bad faith"; to the contrary, the court explained, "the Committee's decision was reasonable" and there was "no evidence which shows or suggests that the members of the independent litigation committee were not unbiased or independent in their decision-making."[1654] The court rejected a contention that the committee did not act in good faith because it was "mindful that even a hint or suggestion of liability on the part of any of the Directors" would have a "detrimental impact" upon other pending litigation" and, according to the plaintiff, this concern by the committee "was too significant to allow for a fair and unbiased investigation."[1655] The court explained that "concerns about the detrimental impact that the litigation would have on the corporation" is "a legitimate consideration" in determining whether litigation will serve the best interests of the corporation.[1656] The court recognized that "[o]f course, the

---

1649. *Id.* at 98,592.
1650. *Id.* at 98,593.
1651. *Id.*
1652. *Id.*
1653. *Id.*
1654. *Id.*
1655. *Id.*
1656. *Id.*

Committee must consider other factors" but concluded that in this case it was "clear from the analysis of the Special Committee that the detrimental impact that the litigation would have on the corporation" was "only one of the many considerations it analyzed."[1657]

*h. Cases Involving Unlawful Conduct.* As noted above,[1658] the United States Supreme Court's decision in *Ashwander v. Tennessee Valley Authority*,[1659] construing federal law in a pre-*Erie Railroad Co. v. Tompkins*[1660] opinion, held that a board's refusal of a demand that the corporation challenge legislation alleged to be unconstitutional does not constitute an "adequate ground for denying to the stockholders an opportunity to contest the validity of the governmental requirements to which the directors were submitting."[1661] The Supreme Court's decision in *Ashwander* was written by Chief Justice Charles E. Hughes and was joined by a total of four justices. An often cited concurring opinion in *Ashwander* by Justice Louis D. Brandeis, also joined by a total of four justices, stated that the fact that a shareholder "calls for an enquiry into the legality of the transaction does not overcome the obstacle that ordinarily stockholders have no standing to interfere with the management" of the corporation.[1662] To the contrary, Justice Brandeis stated, "[m]ere belief that corporate action, taken or contemplated, is illegal gives the stockholder no greater right to interfere than is possessed by any other citizen. Stockholders are not guardians of the public. The function of guarding the public against acts deemed illegal rests with the public officials."[1663]

Subsequent decisions elaborate upon the rules governing board decisions to refuse demands involving conduct alleged to be unlawful.

---

1657. *Id.*

1658. *See* Chapter IV, Section B 6 c.

1659. 297 U.S. 288 (1936).

1660. 304 U.S. 64 (1938).

1661. 297 U.S. at 320; *see also* Chapter IV, Section B 6 c (discussing *Ashwander* in more detail).

1662. 297 U.S. at 343 (Brandeis, J., concurring).

1663. *Id.*

The Third Circuit in *Miller v. American Telephone & Telegraph Co.*,[1664] construing New York law, held that a board may not determine not to pursue a claim where the decision not to pursue the claim itself constitutes an illegal act or results in the continuation of an on-going illegal act. The shareholder plaintiffs in *AT&T* sought reimbursement on behalf of AT&T from the Democratic National Committee of $1.5 million in expenses incurred by AT&T during the 1968 Democratic National Convention.[1665] The failure to collect this debt, the shareholders alleged, constituted a breach of AT&T's directors' fiduciary duty to the corporation and a violation of a federal prohibition on corporate campaign spending.[1666]

The court stated that "[h]ad plaintiffs' complaint alleged only failure to pursue a corporate claim, application of the sound business judgment rule would support the district court's ruling that a shareholder could not attack the directors' decision."[1667] The court held, however, that where "the decision not to collect a debt owed the corporation is itself alleged to have been an illegal act, different rules apply."[1668] Under these circumstances, the court concluded, "[t]he business judgment rule cannot insulate the defendant directors from liability" if they did in fact act in violation of federal campaign spending laws, as plaintiffs alleged.[1669]

A similar conclusion was reached by the Delaware Court of Chancery in *Szeto v. Schiffer*.[1670] "Certainly," the court stated in that case, if the directors violated Section 271 of the Delaware General Corporation Law by transferring all or substantially all of the corporation's assets without shareholder approval, then "the

---

1664. 507 F.2d 759 (3d Cir. 1974).
1665. *Id*. at 761.
1666. *Id*.
1667. *Id*. at 762.
1668. *Id*.
1669. *Id*.
1670. 19 Del. J. Corp. L. 1310 (Del. Ch. Nov. 24, 1993).

directors' refusal to take action to rectify this violation could not be protected by the business judgment rule."[1671]

The opposite result was reached by federal district courts in New York in *Klotz v. Consolidated Edison Co.*,[1672] *Gall v. Exxon Corp.*[1673] and *Rosengarten v. International Telephone & Telegraph Corp.*[1674]

*Klotz v. Consolidated Edison Co.*[1675] involved a claim that the directors of Consolidated Edison followed "a long standing and continuing policy of quiet accommodation and appeasement of state and local officials" and "yielded without resistance" to "illegal confiscatory rate-making policies and procedures" by the Public Service Commission of the State of New York (the "PSC") and the Finance Administrator of the City of New York.[1676] The challenged rate-making policies and procedures allowed Con Edison to charge customers rates that allegedly were "inadequate" to allow Con Edison "to earn a reasonable rate of return on the value of its property" and that thus imposed an "unidentified tax" that "affects only Con Edison, is invidiously discriminatory, and therefore deprives Con Edison of property without due process of law."[1677]

The court rejected plaintiff's reliance upon Chief Justice Hughes' opinion in *Ashwander* for the proposition that shareholders may bring actions against public officials.[1678] The court explained that "[h]appily, it is not here necessary to choose between the wisdom of Chief Justice Hughes and that of Mr. Justice Brandeis" in his dissent.[1679] Even "[a]ccepting the Chief Justice's view as correct, it is not applicable to this action," the court explained, because "the essence of his holding is quite simple: to wit, a stock-

---

1671. *Id.* at 1320.
1672. 386 F. Supp. 577 (S.D.N.Y. 1974).
1673. 418 F. Supp. 508 (S.D.N.Y. 1976).
1674. 466 F. Supp. 817 (S.D.N.Y. 1979).
1675. 386 F. Supp. 577 (S.D.N.Y. 1974).
1676. *Id.* at 580.
1677. *Id.*
1678. *Id.* at 582.
1679. *Id.* at 583.

holder has standing to prevent his corporation from surrendering its property to public officials acting pursuant to a statute which is challenged as unconstitutional."[1680] The court stated that "[i]n *Ashwander*, the action of the TVA were not attacked as unreasonable"; "[r]ather, the stockholders challenged the authority's right to act at all."[1681] The court thus held that "[w]here the question is that of unlawful usurpation of regulatory control *as distinguished from the reasonableness of regulatory action by an agency with conceded jurisdiction*, a stockholder has standing to attack an administrative order in which the corporate management has acquiesced even though he cannot show an interest other than a derivative one on behalf of the corporation."[1682]

Applying this rule, the court in *Con Edison* held that "there is no contention that there has been 'usurpation of regulatory control' by officials purporting to act pursuant to an unconstitutional statute."[1683] To the contrary, the court concluded, "the question here" is whether the public authorities were "exercising their 'conceded jurisdiction' in an unlawful manner."[1684] "It follows," the court stated, "that *Ashwander* is inapplicable, and thus that plaintiff is without standing to maintain this action."[1685]

*Gall v. Exxon Corp.*[1686] involved allegations that Exxon Corporation utilized $59 million in corporate funds "as bribes or political payments, which were improperly contributed to Italian political parties and others during the period 1963-1974, in order to secure special political favors as well as other allegedly illegal commitments."[1687] As in *Con Edison*, the court noted the competing views expressed by Chief Justice Hughes and Justice Brandeis in *Ashwander*, and, as in *Con Edison*, stated that "*Ashwander* may be

---

1680. *Id.*

1681. *Id.*

1682. *Id.* (quoting *Breswick & Co. v. United States*, 134 F. Supp. 132, 139 (S.D.N.Y. 1955), *rev'd on other grounds*, 353 U.S. 151 (1957).

1683. *Id.* at 584.

1684. *Id.*

1685. *Id.*

1686. 418 F. Supp. 508 (S.D.N.Y. 1976).

1687. *Id.* at 509.

read quite narrowly as holding that a shareholder may sue on behalf of his corporation where the corporation has declined to bring an action, in order to prevent the corporation from surrendering its property pursuant to statutory or regulatory controls which are challenged as unconstitutional."[1688] Here, the court stated, "[s]ince no 'usurpation of regulatory control' is at issue . . . , the rule in *Ashwander* is inapplicable."[1689]

The court also distinguished *Ashwander* on the ground that *Ashwander* involved a request for injunctive relief "preventing the corporation from continuing to participate in allegedly illegal activity," while in the case before the court Exxon had determined to end its previous practice of making illegal political payments and had stopped making such payments.[1690] The court reasoned as follows:

> The decision not to bring suit with regard to past conduct which may have been illegal is not itself a violation of law and does not result in the continuation of the alleged violation of law. Rather, it is a decision by the directors of the corporation that pursuit of a cause of action based on acts already consummated is not in the best interest of the corporation. Such a determination, like any other business decision, must be made by the corporate directors in the exercise of their sound business judgment.[1691]

The court stated that "[t]he conclusive effect of such a judgment cannot be affected by the allegedly illegal nature of the initial action which purportedly gives rise to the cause of action."[1692] The court added that a decision "not to sue does not constitute the ratification of an illegal act" because "[t]he question of the good faith exercise of sound business judgment is entirely separate from the question of ratification."[1693]

---

1688. *Id*. at 518.
1689. *Id*.
1690. *Id*.
1691. *Id*.
1692. *Id*.
1693. *Id*. at 518 n.18.

The court distinguished *AT&T* based upon the court's statement in *AT&T* had observed that "had plaintiff's complaint alleged only a failure to pursue a corporate claim, application of the business judgment rule" would preclude a shareholder attack upon the board's decision, but "where the decision not to collect the debt owed to the corporation was itself alleged to be an illegal act, a different rule would apply."[1694] Here, the court in *Exxon* stated, the decision not to sue "is not itself an illegal act or the perpetuation of an illegal act."[1695]

The court in *Rosengarten v. International Telephone & Telegraph Corp.*[1696] similarly rejected a contention that "the business judgment rule does not permit ratification of illegal acts."[1697] "This argument," the court stated, "misses the point."[1698] The court quoted from the *Exxon* decision and added the following: "A derivative action is designed to redress wrongs to the corporation and not wrongs to the public. If the directors legitimately determine that such an action will not benefit the corporation, then, regardless of the illegality of the underlying transaction, the business judgment rule permits termination of the suit."[1699]

Conflicting results were reached by a federal court construing Delaware law in *Miller v. Loucks*[1700] and the Delaware Court of Chancery in *Cohan v. Loucks*.[1701] These two cases arose out of the same "allegations of egregious criminal conduct": a hospital supply company had "embarked on a crusade, a reckless one," to remove its name from an Arab League boycott blacklist of companies doing business with Israel.[1702] The alleged wrongdoing

---

1694. *Id.* at 518 n.19.

1695. *Id.*

1696. 466 F. Supp. 817 (S.D.N.Y. 1979).

1697. *Id.* at 824.

1698. *Id.*

1699. *Id.*

1700. 1992 U.S. Dist. LEXIS 16966, 1992 WL 329313 (N.D. Ill. Nov. 5, 1992).

1701. [1993 Transfer Binder] Fed. Sec. L. Rep. (CCH) ¶ 97,698, at 97,241 (Del. Ch. June 11, 1993).

1702. 1992 U.S. Dist. LEXIS 16966, at *1, 31, 1992 WL 329313,

(continued...)

included "a litany of . . . wrongful acts" such as "affiliation with alleged Syrian terrorists and anti-semites, complicity and encouragement of a terrorist country, attempted construction of [a] Syrian intravenous fluid factory with chemical warfare capabilities, and bribery of Syrian officials."[1703] The court in *Miller* held on a motion to dismiss that this alleged conduct, if proven, would be sufficiently "egregious on its face" to render the business judgment rule inapplicable to a board decision not to pursue claims against present or former corporate officers alleged to be responsible for this conduct.[1704] The court in *Cohan*, in the context of approving a settlement of the litigation, stated that "the evidence suggests that the business judgment rule ultimately would protect the board's decision not to pursue claims against present or former officers."[1705]

The Delaware Court of Chancery in *Weinberger v. Bankston*[1706] held that the business judgment rule protects a decision to settle litigation.[1707] According to the court in *Weinberger*, "[t]he fact that the underlying claim may have involved illegal activity does not deprive the directors of their power to settle the claim and does not make the settlement unlawful."[1708]

*i. The Model Business Corporation Act and Statutory Provisions Similar to the Model Act.* The Model Business Corporation Act codifies the business judgment rule standard of review of board decisions to refuse shareholder demands. Different language is used in the Model Act than in the case law that has evolved in Delaware

---

1702. (...continued)
at *1, 8.
    1703. 1992 U.S. Dist. LEXIS 16966, at *28-29, 1992 WL 329313, at *8.
    1704. 1992 U.S. Dist. LEXIS 16966, at *29, 1992 WL 329313, at *8.
    1705. [1993 Transfer Binder] Fed. Sec. L. Rep. (CCH) at 97,241.
    1706. [1987-1988 Transfer Binder] Fed. Sec. L. Rep. (CCH) ¶ 93,539 (Del. Ch. Nov. 19, 1987).
    1707. *Id.* at 97,418.
    1708. *Id.*

and the other jurisdictions discussed above,[1709] however, because
the Model Act—unlike Delaware—requires a "universal demand" in
all cases.[1710]

Within this universal demand framework, the Model Act
seeks to "carry forward the distinction" recognized in Delaware
between demand required cases (where determinations to refuse
demands by boards consisting of a majority of disinterested and
independent directors are protected by the business judgment rule)
and demand excused cases (where demand cannot be refused).[1711]
The Model Act does this "by establishing pleading rules and allocating the burden of proof" depending upon the composition of the
board—i.e., whether the board consists of a majority of disinterested and independent directors—at the time the determination
is made that the maintenance of a derivative proceeding would not
serve the best interests of the corporation.[1712]

Section 7.44 of the Model Act provides that a derivative proceeding "shall be dismissed" if a majority of the corporation's
independent directors (if the independent directors constitute a
quorum) or a majority of a committee consisting of two or more
independent directors (appointed by majority vote of independent
directors, whether or not the independent directors making the
appointment constitute a quorum) has determined "in good faith
after conducting a reasonable inquiry upon which its conclusions
are based that the maintenance of the derivative proceeding is not in
the best interests of the corporation."[1713] The plaintiff is required
to allege "with particularity facts establishing" either (1) that "a
majority of the board of directors did not consist of independent
directors at the time the determination was made" or (2) that the
determination by the decision-making group that maintenance of the
derivative proceeding would not be in the best interests of the cor-

---

1709. *See* Chapter IV, Section B 6 c-h.

1710. *See* Chapter IV, Section B 5 g.

1711. 2 Model Bus. Corp. Act Annotated § 7.44 & Official Comment at 7-351 (3d ed. 1996).

1712. *Id.*

1713. *Id.* §§ 7.44(a), (b).

poration was not made "in good faith after conducting a reasonable inquiry upon which its conclusions are based."[1714]

A court therefore initially must decide whether a shareholder plaintiff has alleged (and ultimately proves) particularized facts that establish that a majority of the corporation's board did not consist of independent directors at the time that the determination to refuse demand was made.[1715] Where the plaintiff does not allege (or prove) particularized facts that establish that a majority of the board did not consist of independent directors at the time the demand was refused, the plaintiff has the burden of alleging (and proving) particularized facts that establish that the directors who determined to refuse the demand did not act in good faith or on the basis of a reasonable inquiry.[1716] Where the plaintiff does allege (and prove) particularized facts that establish that a majority of the board did not consist of independent directors at the time the demand was refused, the corporation has the burden of proving that the directors who determined to refuse demand acted in good faith and on the basis of a reasonable inquiry.[1717]

The Model Act states that "[n]one of the following shall by itself cause a director to be considered not independent":

(1) the nomination or election of the director by persons who are defendants in the derivative proceeding or against whom action is demanded;

(2) the naming of the director as a defendant in the derivative proceeding or as a person against whom action is demanded; or

(3) the approval by the director of the act being challenged in the derivative proceeding or demand if the act resulted in no personal benefit to the director.[1718]

The Model Act's Official Comment adds that "[d]iscovery is available to the plaintiff only after the plaintiff successfully has stated a

---

1714. *Id.* § 7.44(d).

1715. *Id.* §§ 7.44(d), (e) & Official Comment at 7-356.

1716. *Id.* §§ 7.44(d), (e) & Official Comment at 7-354.

1717. *Id.*

1718. *Id.* § 7.44(c).

cause of action."[1719]

Section 7.44 also provides that the court "may appoint a panel of one or more independent persons upon motion by the corporation to make a determination whether the maintenance of the derivative proceeding is in the best interests of the corporation."[1720] In such a case, the plaintiff has the burden of proving that a determination by the committee that the derivative proceeding is not in the best interests of the corporation was not made in good faith or on the basis of a reasonable inquiry.[1721]

As discussed earlier in this Chapter,[1722] fourteen states— Arizona, Connecticut, Florida, Georgia, Maine, Michigan, Mississippi, Montana, Nebraska, New Hampshire, North Carolina, Texas, Virginia and Wisconsin—have adopted statutes implementing a universal demand requirement mandating a demand in all cases.[1723] Six of these fourteen states—Connecticut, Mississippi, Montana, Nebraska, New Hampshire and Wisconsin—have enacted statutes identical to Section 7.44 of the Model Act to govern board decisions to refuse a universal demand.[1724] The remaining eight states—Arizona, Florida, Georgia, Maine, Michigan, North Carolina, Texas and Virginia—have enacted statutes similar to the Model Act but with the differences summarized below.

---

1719. *Id.* § 7.44 Official Comment at 7-356.

1720. *Id.* § 7.44(f).

1721. *Id.* §§ 7.44(a), (f).

1722. *See* Chapter IV, Section B 5 g.

1723. *See* Ariz. Bus. Corp. Act § 10-742; Conn. Bus. Corp. Act § 33-722; Fla. Bus. Corp. Act § 607.07401(2); Ga. Bus. Corp. Code § 14-2-742; Me. Bus. Corp. Act § 630; Mich. Bus. Corp. Act § 450.1493a(a); Miss. Bus. Corp. Act § 79-4-7.42; Mont. Bus. Corp. Act § 35-1-543; Neb. Bus. Corp. Act § 21-2072; N.H. Bus. Corp. Act § 293-A:7.42; N.C. Bus. Corp. Act § 55-7-42; Tex. Bus. Corp. Act § 5.14(C); Va. Stock Corp. Act § 13.1-672.1B(1); Wis. Bus. Corp. Law § 180.0742.

1724. *See* Conn. Bus. Corp. Act § 33-724; Miss. Bus. Corp. Act § 79-4-7.44; Mont. Bus. Corp. Act § 35-1-545; Neb. Bus. Corp. Act § 21-2074; N.H. Bus. Corp. Act § 293-A:7.44; Wis. Bus. Corp. Law § 180.0744.

Arizona's statute provides that a derivative proceeding "may" —not "shall," as in the Model Act—be dismissed based upon "a determination by a panel of one or more "independent persons" appointed by the court that "has determined in good faith after conducting a reasonable inquiry on which its conclusions are based that the maintenance of the derivative proceeding is not in the best interests of the corporation."[1725] The term "independent person" is defined to mean "a person with no personal interest in the transaction and no personal or other relationship which influences the person."[1726] The plaintiff has the "burden of proving by clear and convincing evidence" that the statutory requirements have not been met.[1727]

The Florida and Georgia statutes contain five noteworthy additions or differences from the Model Act.

First, the Florida and Georgia statutes provide that a derivative proceeding "may"—rather than "shall"—be dismissed if the prerequisites for dismissal set forth in the respective statutes are satisfied.[1728]

Second, the Florida and Georgia statutes require a determination "in good faith after conducting a reasonable *investigation*" rather than a "reasonable *inquiry*."[1729] The drafters of the Model Act explain the difference between the terms "investigation" and "inquiry" and why the Model Act utilizes the term "inquiry" rather than "investigation" as follows:

> The word "inquiry" rather than "investigation" has been used to make it clear that the scope of the inquiry will depend upon the issues raised and the knowledge of the group making the determination with respect to the issues. In some cases, the issues may be so simple or the knowledge of the group so extensive that little additional inquiry is required. In other cases, the group may need to engage counsel and other

---

1725. Ariz. Bus. Corp. Act §§ 10-744 (A), (B).

1726. *Id.* § 10-740(2).

1727. *Id.* § 10-744(B).

1728. Fla. Bus. Corp. Act § 607.07401(3); Ga. Bus. Corp. Code § 14-2-744(a).

1729. *Id.* (emphasis added).

professionals to make an investigation and assist the group in
its evaluation of the issues.[1730]

Third, the Florida and Georgia statutes place upon the corporation the burden of establishing the independence and good faith of
the directors making the determination that litigation will not serve
the best interests of the corporation and the reasonableness of the
investigation underlying this determination.[1731] The Model Act,
as explained above, places this burden upon the corporation only
where the shareholder plaintiff establishes that a majority of the
corporation's board lacked independence at the time of the determination that litigation would not serve the best interests of the corporation.[1732]

Fourth, the Florida statute does not include the Model Act
provision specifying that a shareholder plaintiff cannot establish a
lack of independence on the part of a particular director simply by
alleging that the director (1) was nominated or elected by persons
against whom action is demanded or who have been named as
defendants in a derivative proceeding, (2) is a person against whom
action is demanded or who has been named as a defendant in the
proceeding, or (3) approved the act being challenged in the demand
or derivative proceeding if the act resulted in no personal benefit to
the director.[1733] The Georgia statute does include this Model Act
provision.[1734]

Fifth, the Florida and Georgia statutes provide that the same
rules govern judicial review of determinations by directors and
determinations by court-appointed panels of independent persons
concerning whether maintenance of derivative litigation will serve
the best interests of the corporation.[1735]

---

1730. Model Bus. Corp. Act Annotated § 7.44(a) & Official
Comment 7-351.

1731. Fla. Bus. Corp. Act § 607.07401(3); Ga. Bus. Corp. Code
§ 14-2-744(a).

1732. Model Bus. Corp. Act Annotated § 7.44(e).

1733. *Id.* § 7.44(c) (quoted in full above).

1734. Ga. Bus. Corp. Code § 14-2-744(c).

1735. Fla. Bus. Corp. Act § 607.07401(3)(c); Ga. Bus. Corp. Code
§ 14-2-744(b)(3).

Maine's statute states that a derivative proceeding "must"—rather than "shall"—be dismissed if the prerequisites for dismissal stated in the statute are satisfied.[1736]

Michigan's statute requires dismissal of derivative litigation on the same basis as the Model Act but utilizes the "reasonable investigation" language used in Florida and Georgia rather than the "reasonable inquiry" language used in the Model Act.[1737] The Michigan statute also uses the word "disinterested" rather than "independent," defines a "disinterested person" as a person "who is not a party to a derivative proceeding" or "is a party if the corporation demonstrates that the claim asserted against the person is frivolous or insubstantial," and places upon the corporation the burden of proving the good faith and reasonableness of the directors' investigation concerning whether litigation will serve the best interests of the corporation.[1738] In addition, the Michigan statute allows the determination to refuse a demand to be made by "all disinterested independent directors."[1739] The term "independent director" is defined to include a director meeting the following requirements:

(a) Is elected by the shareholders.

(b) Is designated as an independent director by the board or the shareholders.

(c) Has at least 5 years of business, legal, or financial experience, or other equivalent experience. For a corporation with securities registered under section 12 of the securities exchange act of 1934, . . . "experience" shall mean experience as a senior executive, director, or attorney, or other equivalent experience, for a corporation with registered securities.

(d) Is not and during the 3 years prior to being designated as an independent director has not been any of the following:

(i) An officer or employee of the corporation or any affiliate of the corporation.

---

1736. Me. Bus. Corp. Act § 632(1).
1737. Mich. Bus. Corp. Act §§ 450.1495(1), (2)(a)-(c).
1738. *Id*. §§ 450.1491a(c), 450.1495(1), (2)(a)-(c).
1739. *Id*. § 450.1495(2)(d).

(ii) Engaged in any business transaction for profit or series of transactions for profit, including banking, legal, or consulting services, involving more than $10,000.00 with the corporation or any affiliate of the corporation.

(iii) An affiliate, executive officer, general partner, or member of the immediate family of any person that had the status or engaged in a transaction described in subparagraph (i) or (ii).

(e) Does not propose to enter into a relationship or transaction described in subdivision (d)(i) through (iii).

(f) Does not have an aggregate of more than 3 years of service as a director of the corporation, whether or not as an independent director.[1740]

Where the determination is made by such "independent directors," the plaintiff bears the burden of proving that the determination that litigation will not serve the best interests of the corporation was not made in good faith or that the independent directors' investigation was not reasonable.[1741]

North Carolina's statute requires dismissal of derivative litigation on the same basis as the Model Act but states that prior to the court's ruling on a motion to dismiss based upon the statute's pleading requirements "the plaintiff shall be entitled to discovery only with respect to the issues presented by the motion and only if and to the extent that the plaintiff has alleged such facts with particularity."[1742] This "preliminary discovery," according to North Carolina's statute, shall be limited solely to matters germane and

---

1740. *Id.* §§ 450.1107(3), 450.1505(3); *see also* Moscow, Lesser & Schulman, *Michigan's Independent Director*, 46 Bus. Law. 57, 59-61, 62-63 (1990) (discussing this statute); *Kearney v. Jandernoa*, 934 F. Supp. 863, 865-67 (W.D. Mich. 1996), *subsequent proceedings*, 949 F. Supp. 510 (W.D. Mich. 1996) and 979 F. Supp. 1156 (W.D. Mich. 1997), *mandamus granted sub nom. In re Perrigo Co.*, 128 F.3d 430 (6th Cir. 1997) (discussing this statute and requiring production of report by an independent director to a shareholder-plaintiff challenging an independent director's decision that litigation would not serve the best interests of the corporation); Chapter IV, Section E 3 (discussing *Kearney* and *Perrigo* decisions).

1741. Mich. Bus. Corp. Act §§ 450.1495(1), (2)(d).

1742. N.C. Bus. Corp. Act § 55-7-44(d).

necessary to support the facts alleged with particularity relating solely to the requirements" for dismissal.[1743]

The Texas statute requires dismissal of derivative litigation on the same basis as the Model Act with five additions or differences.

First, while the Model Act uses the term "independent" to describe the directors who may make the determination that derivative litigation would not serve the best interest of the corporation, the Texas statute states that the decision-making directors must be "independent and disinterested"[1744] and defines those terms.[1745] The statute also specifies that the vote of independent and disinterested directors at a board meeting must be taken at a time when interested directors are not present.[1746]

Second, the Model Act and the Texas statute require a determination by the decision-making directors "in good faith" and "after conducting a reasonable inquiry"; the Texas statute adds that the "reasonable inquiry" is to be "based on the factors" that the decision-making group "deems appropriate under the circumstances."[1747]

Third, the Texas statute states the burden of proof in a manner similar to the Model Act and then adds that "if the corporation presents prima facie evidence that demonstrates" that directors appointed to a committee consisting of two or more independent and disinterested directors are independent and disinterested, then "the burden of proof is on the plaintiff shareholder."[1748]

Fourth, the Texas statute states that "[i]f a derivative proceeding is commenced after a demand is rejected, the petition must allege with particularity facts that establish that the rejection was not made in accordance with the requirements" of the statute.[1749]

---

1743. *Id.*

1744. Tex. Bus. Corp. Act §§ 5.14(H)(1), (2).

1745. *Id.* §§ 1.02(12), 1.02(15) (defining these terms); Chapter I, Section D 2 h (quoting the definitions of these terms).

1746. *Id.* § 5.14(H)(1).

1747. *Id.* § 5.14(F).

1748. *Id.* § 5.14(F)(2).

1749. *Id.* § 5.14(G).

Fifth, the Texas statute states that if a corporation "proposes to dismiss a derivative proceeding" pursuant to the statute, discovery "shall be limited" to facts relating to whether the decision-making directors are independent and disinterested, the good faith of the inquiry and review, and the reasonableness of the procedures followed in conducting the review.[1750] Discovery "will not extend to any facts or substantive mattes with respect to the act, omission, or other matter that is the subject matter of the action in the derivative proceeding."[1751] The scope of discovery may be expanded if the court determines after notice and hearing that a good faith review of the allegations . . . has not been made by an independent and disinterested person or group."[1752]

Virginia's statute requires that a derivative proceeding be dismissed if a committee consisting of two or more independent directors

> 1. Conducted a review and evaluation, adequately informed in the circumstances, of the allegations made in the demand or complaint;
>
> 2. Determined in good faith on the basis of that review and evaluation that the maintenance of the derivative proceeding is not in the best interests of the corporation; and
>
> 3. Submitted in support of the motion a short and concise statement of the reasons for [their] determination.[1753]

If a derivative proceeding is commenced after a determination has been made to refuse a shareholder demand, the statute requires that "the complaint shall allege with particularity facts establishing that the requirements" quoted above "have not been met."[1754] The shareholder plaintiff is "entitled to discovery with respect to the issues presented by the motion only if and to the extent that the complaint alleges such facts with particularity."[1755] Unlike the

---

1750. *Id.* § 5.14(D)(2).
1751. *Id.*
1752. *Id.*
1753. Va. Stock Corp. Act § 13.1-672.4(A).
1754. *Id.* § 13.1-672.4(D).
1755. *Id.*

Model Act, the burden of establishing that the decision-making directors have acted in accordance with the required standard of conduct does not turn upon whether the board includes a majority of independent directors. Instead, in all cases the plaintiff has the burden of proving that the requirements quoted above have not been met but with one exception: the burden with respect to the independence of the decision-making directors shifts to the corporation "if the complaint alleges with particularity facts raising a substantial question as to such independence."[1756]

An Alaska statute codifies the business judgment rule standard of review without creating a universal demand requirement. The Alaska statute states that a shareholder's right to bring a derivative action "terminates" where a board of directors refuses a shareholder demand because "in its business judgment, the litigation would not be in the best interest of the corporation."[1757]

*j. Principles of Corporate Governance.* Standing in contrast to the Model Business Corporation Act approach is Principles of Corporate Governance: Analysis and Recommendations and *Cuker v. Mikalauskas*,[1758] a decision by the Pennsylvania Supreme Court adopting the Principles of Corporate Governance approach as the law of Pennsylvania.[1759] Like the Model Act, Principles of Corporate Governance requires a universal demand,[1760] but, unlike the Model Act, Principles of Corporate Governance rejects the distinction that has evolved in Delaware and other jurisdictions between demand required and demand excused cases.[1761] Instead of focusing, as does the Model Act and Delaware, upon whether a board has a majority of independent directors, Principles of Corporate Governance sets forth "an elaborate set of standards that calibrates the deference afforded the decision of the directors to the

---

1756. *Id.* § 13.1-672.4(E).
1757. Alaska Corp. Code § 10.06.435(e).
1758. 692 A.2d 1042 (Pa. 1997).
1759. *Id.* at 1048-55.
1760. *See* Chapter IV, Section B 5 g.
1761. *See* 2 Principles of Corporate Governance: Analysis and Recommendations § 7.03 Comment at 58, § 7.10 Comment at 134-35 (1994).

character of the claim being asserted by the derivative plain-tiff."[1762]

Section 7.05 of Principles of Corporate Governance provides the corporation two types of motions to dismiss separate and apart from any motions that would be available in a litigation that is not a shareholder derivative action: (1) a motion to dismiss the action due to plaintiff's failure to comply with pleading requirements, and (2) a motion to dismiss the action as contrary to the best interests of the corporation. The first type of motion is governed by Section 7.04 of Principles of Corporate Governance. The second type of motion is governed by Sections 7.07 through 7.13 of Principles of Corporate Governance. The following discussion focuses upon Section 7.04 and Section 7.07 through 7.13 motions in cases involving claims against directors, officers and controlling shareholders:

*(i) Section 7.04 Motions.* Section 7.04(a) states the following pleading requirements for cases in which shareholders challenge the refusal by a corporation of a demand, which is required by Section 7.03 in all cases:

§ 7.04.   Pleading, Demand Rejection, Procedure, and Costs in a Derivative Action

The legal standards applicable to a derivative action should provide that:

(a)   *Particularity; demand rejection.*

(1)   *In general.* The complaint shall plead with particularity facts that, if true, raise a significant prospect that the transaction or conduct complained of did not meet the applicable requirements of Parts IV (Duty of Care and the Business Judgment Rule), V (Duty of Fair Dealing), or VI (Role of Directors and Shareholders in Transactions in Control and Tender Offers), in light of any approvals of the transaction or conduct communicated to the plaintiff by the corporation.

(2)   *Demand rejection.* If the corporation rejects the demand made on the board pursuant to § 7.03, and if, at or following the rejection, the corporation delivers to the plain-

---

1762. *Kamen v. Kemper Fin. Servs., Inc.*, 500 U.S. 90, 104 (1991).

tiff a written reply to the demand which states that the demand was rejected by directors who were not interested in the transaction or conduct described in and forming the basis for the demand and that those directors constituted a majority of the entire board and were capable as a group of objective judgment in the circumstances, and provides specific reasons for those statements, then the complaint shall also plead with particularity facts that, if true, raise a significant prospect that either:

(A)  The statements in the reply are not correct;

(B)  If Part IV, V or VI provides that the underlying transaction or conduct would be reviewed under the standard of the business judgment rule, that the rejection did not satisfy the requirements of the business judgment rule as specified in § 4.01(c); or

(C)  If Part IV, V, or VI provides that the underlying transaction or conduct would be reviewed under a standard other than the business judgment rule, either (i) that the disinterested directors who rejected the demand did not satisfy the good faith and informational requirements (§ 4.01(c)(2)) of the business judgment rule or (ii) that disinterested directors could not reasonably have determined that rejection of the demand was in the best interests of the corporation.

If the complaint fails to set forth sufficiently such particularized facts, defendants shall be entitled to dismissal of the complaint prior to discovery.[1763]

The following commentary accompanying Section 7.04 is significant:

A motion to dismiss under § 7.04(a)(2) is a motion on the pleadings, and in part for that reason, discovery is not available. Correspondingly, § 7.04(a)(2) does not contemplate a mini-trial, and the court's attention should be limited to the complaint (including any documents incorporated in the complaint) and the reply to the demand. Accordingly, in proceedings pursuant to a motion to dismiss under § 7.04(a)(2) the plaintiff may not supplement the complaint with factual asser-

---

1763. Principles of Corporate Governance § 7.04 (a reference to a definition of the term "interested" is omitted).

tions not in the complaint, and the corporation and the defendants may not supplement the reply to the demand with factual assertions not in the reply.

Section 7.04(a)(2) does not require the reply to state the reasons why the disinterested directors rejected the demand. Nevertheless, if reasons are provided in the reply the court should determine a motion under § 7.04(a)(2) by focusing on those stated reasons, not on the basis of different reasons that might have conceivably motivated a rejection. If no reasons are stated in the reply the corporation may not advance reasons in the hearing on the motion.[1764]

*(ii) Section 7.07 Through 7.13 Motions.* Section 7.07 authorizes dismissal of a derivative action against directors, officers and controlling shareholders "in the best interests of the corporation" if "the conditions specified in § 7.08 . . . are satisfied."[1765] Section 7.08, in turn, provides for dismissal if

> (a) The board of directors or a properly delegated committee thereof (either in response to a demand or following commencement of the action) has determined that the action is contrary to the best interests of the corporation and has requested dismissal of the action;

> (b) The procedures specified in § 7.09 (Procedures for Requesting Dismissal of a Derivative Action) for the conduct of a review and evaluation of the action were substantially complied with (either in response to a demand or following commencement of the action), or any material departures therefrom were justified under circumstances; and

> (c) The determinations of the board or committee satisfy the applicable standard of review set forth in § 7.10(a) (Standard of Judicial Review with Regard to a Board of Committee Motion Requesting Dismissal of a Derivative Action Under § 7.08).[1766]

Section 7.09 sets forth the following procedures for requesting dismissal of a derivative action:

---

1764. *Id.* § 7.04 comment at 75.
1765. *Id.* § 7.07(a)(2).
1766. *Id.* §§ 7.08(a), (b), (c).

(a) The following procedural standards should apply to the review and evaluation of a derivative action by the board or committee under § 7.08 (Dismissal of a Derivative Action Against Directors, Senior Executives, Controlling Persons, or Associates Based on a Motion Requesting Dismissal by the Board or a Committee) . . . :

(1) The board or a committee should be composed of two or more persons, no participating member of which was interested in the action, and should as a group be capable of objective judgment in the circumstances;

(2) The board or committee should be assisted by counsel of its choice and such other agents as it reasonably considers necessary;

(3) The determinations of the board or committee should be based upon a review and evaluation that was sufficiently informed to satisfy the standards applicable under § 7.10(a); and

(4) If the board or committee determines to request dismissal of the derivative action, it shall prepare and file with the court a report or other written submission setting forth its determinations in a manner sufficient to enable the court to conduct the review required under § 7.10 (Standard of Judicial Review with Regard to a Board or Committee Motion Requesting Dismissal of a Derivative Action Under § 7.08).

(b) If the court is unwilling to grant a motion to dismiss under § 7.08 . . . because the procedures followed by the board or committee departed materially from the standards specified in § 7.09(a), the court should permit the board or committee to supplement its procedures, and make such further reports or other written submissions, as will satisfy the standards specified in § 7.09(a), unless the court decides that (i) the board or committee did not act on the basis of a good faith belief that its procedures and report were justified in the circumstances; (ii) unreasonable delay or prejudice would result; or (iii) there is no reasonable prospect that such further steps would support dismissal of the action.[1767]

---

1767. *Id*. §§ 7.09(a), (b) (a reference to a definition of the term "interested" is omitted).

Section 7.10(a) then defines the standard of judicial review as follows:

(a) *Standard of Review.* In deciding whether an action should be dismissed under § 7.08 (Dismissal of a Derivative Action Against Directors, Senior Executives, Controlling Persons, or Associates Based on a Motion Requesting Dismissal by the Board or a Committee), the court should apply the following standards of review:

(1) If the gravamen of the claim is that the defendant violated a duty set forth in Part IV (Duty of Care and the Business Judgment Rule), other than by committing a knowing and culpable violation of law that is alleged with particularity, or if the underlying transaction or conduct would be reviewed under the business judgment rule under § 5.03, § 5.04, § 5.05, § 5.06, § 5.08, or § 6.02, the court should dismiss the claim unless it finds that the board's or committee's determinations fail to satisfy the requirements of the business judgment rule as specified in § 4.01(c).

(2) In other cases governed by Part V (Duty of Fair Dealing) or Part VI (Role of Directors and Shareholders in Transactions in Control and Tender Offers), or to which the business judgment rule is not applicable, including cases in which the gravamen of the claim is that defendant committed a knowing and culpable violation of law in breach of Part IV, the court should dismiss the action if the court finds, in light of the applicable standards under Part IV, V, or VI that the board or committee was adequately informed under the circumstances and reasonably determined that dismissal was in the best interests of the corporation, based on grounds that the court deems to warrant reliance.

(3) In cases arising under either Subsection (a)(1) or (a)(2), the court may substantively review and determine any issue of law.[1768]

Section 7.10(b) prohibits dismissal of any action "if the plaintiff establishes that dismissal would permit a defendant . . . to retain a significant improper benefit" where

---

1768. *Id.* §§ 7.10(a)(1), (2), (3).

(1) The defendant, either alone or collectively with others who are also found to have received a significant improper benefit arising out of the same transaction, possesses control of the corporation; or

(2) Such benefit was obtained:

(A) As the result of a knowing and material misrepresentation or omission or other fraudulent act; or

(B) Without advance authorization or the requisite ratification of such benefit by disinterested directors (or, in the case of a non-director senior executive, advance authorization by a disinterested superior), or authorization or ratification by disinterested shareholders, and in breach of § 5.02 (Transactions with the Corporation) or § 5.04 (Use by a Director or Senior Executive of Corporate Property, Material Non-Public Corporate Information, or Corporate Position);

unless the court determines, in light of specific reasons advanced by the board or committee, that the likely injury to the corporation from continuation of the action convincingly outweighs any adverse impact on the public interest from dismissal of the action.[1769]

Section 7.13 addresses judicial procedures on motions to dismiss pursuant to Sections 7.07 through 7.13 with respect to three issues: the filing of a report by the board or committee, discovery, and burdens of proof.

Section 7.13(a) requires that the corporation "file with the court a report or other written submission setting forth the procedures and determinations of the board or committee."[1770] A copy of this report or other written submission also must be provided to the plaintiff's counsel.[1771]

Section 7.13(c) provides for discovery or an evidentiary hearing in connection with a motion pursuant to Sections 7.07

---

1769. *Id.* §§ 7.10(b)(1), (2) (references to definitions of the terms "control", "disinterested director" and "disinterested shareholders" are omitted).

1770. *Id.* § 7.13(a).

1771. *Id.*

through 7.13 "if the plaintiff has demonstrated that a substantial issue exists whether the applicable standards of § 7.08, § 7.09, § 7.10, § 7.11, or § 7.12 have been satisfied and if the plaintiff is unable without undue hardship to obtain the information by other means."[1772] Under these circumstances, "the court may order such limited discovery or limited evidentiary hearing, as to issues specified by the court, as the court finds to be (i) necessary to enable it to render a decision on the motion under the applicable standards . . . , and (ii) consistent with an expedited resolution of the motion."[1773]

Section 7.13(d) imposes burdens of proof as follows:

> The plaintiff has the burden of proof in the case of a motion . . . under § 7.08 where the standard of judicial review is determined under § 7.10(a)(1) because the basis of the claim involves a breach of a duty set forth in Part IV (Duty of Care and the Business Judgment Rule) or because the underlying transaction would be reviewed under the business judgment rule. . . . The corporation has the burden of proof in the case of a motion under § 7.08 where the standard of judicial review is determined under § 7.10(a)(2) because the underlying transaction would be reviewed under a standard other than the business judgment rule, except that the plaintiff retains the burden of proof in all cases to show (i) that a defendant's conduct involved a knowing and culpable violation of law, (ii) that the board or committee as a group was not capable of objective judgment in the circumstances as required by § 7.09(a)(1), and (iii) that dismissal of the action would permit a defendant or an associate thereof to retain a significant improper benefit under § 7.10(b). The corporation shall also have the burden of proving under § 7.10(b) that the likely injury of the corporation from continuation of the action convincingly outweighs any adverse impact on the public interest from dismissal of the action.[1774]

---

1772. *Id.* § 7.13(c).

1773. *Id.*

1774. *Id.* § 7.13(d) (a reference to a definition of the term "associate" is omitted).

Like the Model Business Corporation Act, Principles of Corporate Governance provides for court appointment of a committee but with more specificity than the Model Act: "On motion made by a corporation in whose name or right a derivative action is brought or upon which a demand has been made, the court may appoint one or more individuals to serve as a panel in lieu of a committee of directors for purposes of § 7.08 . . . , none of whom should be interested in the action or have a significant relationship with a senior executive of the corporation or a similar relationship with any defendant or plaintiff."[1775] Any report or other written submission prepared by such a panel has "the same status . . . as a report or other written submission of the board or a properly delegated committee thereof."[1776]

## 7.   Discovery on the Demand Issue

"A plaintiff's standing to sue in a derivative suit, whether based on demand-refused or demand-excused, must be determined on the basis of the well-pleaded allegations of the complaint."[1777] Plaintiffs "are not entitled to discovery to assist their compliance with the particularized pleading requirement."[1778] Numerous cases stand for this proposition both in the context of claims that demand is excused as futile[1779] and in the context of claims that

---

1775. *Id.* § 7.12(a) (references to definitions of the terms "interested", "significant relationship" and "senior executive" are omitted).

1776. *Id.* For a detailed discussion and analysis of the derivative litigation provisions in Principles of Corporate Governance, see Block, Radin & Maimone, *Derivative Litigation: Current Law Versus the American Law Institute*, 48 Bus. Law. 1443 (1993), and Dooley & Veasey, *The Role of the Board in Derivative Litigation: Delaware Law and the Current ALI Proposals Compared*, 44 Bus. Law. 503 (1989).

1777. *Scattered Corp. v. Chicago Stock Exch., Inc.*, 701 A.2d 70, 77 (Del. 1997).

1778. *Id.*

1779. *See, e.g., Gonzalez Turul v. Rogatol Distribs., Inc.*, 951 F.2d 1, 3 (1st Cir. 1991); *Cramer v. General Tel. & Elecs. Corp.*, 582 F.2d 259, 277 (3d Cir. 1978), *cert. denied*, 439 U.S. 1129 (1979); *In re Kauffman Mut. Fund Actions*, 479 F.2d 257, 263 (1st Cir.), *cert. denied*, 414
(continued...)

demand has been wrongfully refused.[1780]

The Delaware Supreme Court's decision in *Levine v. Smith*[1781] explains the rationale underling this rule: the pleading requirements imposed upon a shareholder plaintiff by the demand requirement—i.e., the plaintiff must plead particularized facts demonstrating either that demand is excused as futile or that a demand has been made and wrongfully refused—constitute "a recognition of the board's duty to manage the business and affairs of the corporation" and "an exception to the general notice pleading standard" applied in other contexts.[1782] Allowing a shareholder

---

1779. (...continued)
U.S. 857 (1973); *Grimes v. Donald*, 673 A.2d 1207, 1218 n.22 (Del. 1996); *Levine v. Smith*, 591 A.2d 194, 210 (Del. 1991); *Grobow v. Perot*, No. 8759, Tr. at 80-83 (Del. Ch. Jan. 12, 1987); *Good v. Getty Oil Co.*, 514 A.2d 1104, 1109 (Del. Ch. 1986); *Kaufman v. Belmont*, 479 A.2d 282, 289 (Del. Ch. 1984); *Lewis v. Hett*, 10 Del. J. Corp. L. 240, 245-46 (Del. Ch. Sept. 4, 1984); *Good v. Texaco, Inc.*, 9 Del. J. Corp. L. 461, 465-66 (Del. Ch. May 14, 1984); *Stotland v. GAF Corp.*, 1983 Del. Ch. LEXIS 477, at *7, 1983 WL 21371, at *3 (Del. Ch. Sept. 1, 1983), *appeal dismissed*, 469 A.2d 421 (Del. 1983); *Weinstock v. Bromery*, No. 100151/95 (N.Y. Sup. Ct. N.Y. Co. Oct. 30, 1996), *aff'd sub nom. Teachers' Retirement Sys. v. Welch*, --- A.D.2d ---, 664 N.Y.S.2d 38 (N.Y. App. Div. 1st Dep't 1997); *see also Harris v. Insuranshares of Am., Inc.*, 1988 Del. Ch. LEXIS 145, at *7-9, 1988 WL 119409, at *3-4 (Del. Ch. Nov. 7, 1988) (denying defendants' motion to compel answers to interrogatories seeking facts underlying plaintiff's allegations that a demand was excused as futile because defendants previously had moved to dismiss for failure to comply with the demand requirement).

1780. *See, e.g., Stepak v. Addison*, 20 F.3d 398, 410 (11th Cir. 1994); *Stoner v. Walsh*, 772 F. Supp. 790, 796, 807 (S.D.N.Y. 1991); *Lewis v. Hilton*, 648 F. Supp. 725, 727 n.1 (N.D. Ill. 1986); *Allison v. General Motors Corp.*, 604 F. Supp. 1106, 1120-21 (D. Del.), *aff'd mem.*, 782 F.2d 1026 (3d Cir. 1985); *Chicago Stock Exch.*, 701 A.2d at 77-79; *Grimes*, 673 A.2d at 1218 n.22; *Levine*, 591 A.2d at 210; *Boeing Co. v. Shrontz*, 1994 Del. Ch. LEXIS 14, at *11-12, 1994 WL 30542, at *4 (Del. Ch. Jan. 19, 1994); *Szeto v. Schiffer*, 19 Del. J. Corp. L. 1310, 1315, 1317-18, 1319-20 (Del. Ch. Nov. 24, 1993); *McLeese v. J.C. Nichols Co.*, 842 S.W.2d 115, 121 (Mo. Ct. App. 1992).

1781. 591 A.2d 194 (Del. 1991).

1782. *Id.* at 210; *see also* Chapter IV, Sections B 1 & 2 (citing
(continued...)

plaintiff discovery before the plaintiff survives a motion to dismiss premised upon the plaintiff's failure to comply with the demand requirement, the court thus held, would constitute a "complete abrogation" of these principles.[1783] Discovery thus is permitted only after the plaintiff has established the legal sufficiency of his claim.[1784] A shareholder plaintiff thus may not plead compliance with the demand requirement "in general terms, hoping that, by discovery or otherwise, [s]he can later establish a case. Indeed, if the requirement could be met otherwise, it would be meaningless."[1785]

Similarly, the failure to provide a form of discovery such as the identity of the membership of a committee that has recommended refusal of a demand and a copy of such a committee's report does not provide evidence of a wrongful refusal of demand.[1786] Likewise, a refusal to disclose "information relating to the independence, good faith and reasonableness" of a board or a board committee's investigation of the facts underlying a demand that has been refused—including the identities of all persons interviewed, the identities of the decision-making individuals, "all reports or summaries" of the investigation, and "any other documents that would verify the impartiality and reasonableness of that investigation"—does not constitute "bad faith" and "does nothing to advance the analysis."[1787] Any argument to the contrary "turns the law on its head, because the argument is premised upon a claimed right to discovery that is contrary to Delaware law."[1788]

---

1782. (...continued)
additional cases).
    1783. *Id.*
    1784. *Id.*
    1785. *Gonzalez Turul*, 951 F.2d at 3 (quoting *Kauffman*, 479 F.2d at 263).
    1786. *Boeing*, 1994 Del. Ch. LEXIS 14, at 11-12, 1994 WL 30542, at *4.
    1787. *Scattered Corp. v. Chicago Stock Exch., Inc.*, 1996 Del. Ch. 79, at *6, 15, 1996 WL 417507, at *2, 4 (Del. Ch. July 12, 1996), *aff'd*, 701 A.2d 70 (Del. 1997).
    1788. 1996 Del. Ch. LEXIS 79, at *15, 1996 WL 417507, at *4.

New York courts similarly have held that "discovery is not permitted in shareholder derivative suits unless plaintiff has presented factual allegations of evidentiary value to establish charges of improper conduct."[1789]

As discussed earlier in this Chapter, the Model Business Corporation Act and statutes enacted in Arizona, Connecticut, Florida, Georgia, Maine, Michigan, Mississippi, Montana, Nebraska, New Hampshire, North Carolina, Texas, Virginia and Wisconsin have adopted universal demand requirements[1790] and authorize the refusal of shareholder demands and the termination of derivative litigation by boards or board committees.[1791] The Official Comment to the Model Business Corporation Act states that "[d]iscovery is available to the plaintiff only after the plaintiff has successfully stated a cause of action."[1792] To the extent that the state statutes identified above include additional (or different) rules governing discovery, those rules are discussed above.[1793]

Different rules govern where a motion to dismiss goes beyond the four corners of the complaint. In *Kahn v. Tremont Corp.*,[1794] for example, the Delaware Court of Chancery held that "[a]t least when plaintiff can allege with sufficient particularity that a transaction with an arguably controlling shareholder was authorized by a board composed predominately of persons with a conflicting inter-

---

1789. *Teachers' Retirement Sys. v. Welch*, --- A.D.2d ---, ---, 664 N.Y.S.2d 38, 39 (N.Y. App. Div. 1st Dep't 1997); *see also Stepak v. Alexander's Inc.*, 58 A.D.2d 520, 521, 395 N.Y.S.2d 173, 174 (N.Y. App. Div. 1st Dep't), *modified on other grounds*, 58 A.D.2d 754, 404 N.Y.S.2d 538 (N.Y. App. Div. 1st Dep't 1977); *Nomako v. Ashton*, 20 A.D.2d 331, 333-34, 247 N.Y.S.2d 230, 233 (N.Y. App. Div. 1st Dep't 1964).

1790. *See* Chapter III, Section B 5 g.

1791. *See* Chapter IV, Section B 6 i.

1792. 2 Model Bus. Corp. Act Annotated § 7.44 Official Comment at 7-356 (3d ed. 1996).

1793. *See* Chapter IV, Section B 6 i.

1794. 18 Del. J. Corp. L. 723 (Del. Ch. Aug. 21, 1992), *subsequent proceedings*, 1996 Del. Ch. LEXIS 40, 1996 WL 145452 (Del. Ch. Mar. 21, 1996), *rev'd on other grounds*, 694 A.2d 422 (Del. 1997).

est, and an independent committee's action is set forth as an answer to that claim of interest, fairness to plaintiff and due regard for the proper administration of the derivative remedy dictates, in my opinion, that limited discovery into the independence of the committee is appropriate."[1795] The court reasoned as follows:

> Without prejudging the merits of defendants' motion to dismiss, I am able to say that that motion appears to raise one or more factual questions not raised by the complaint. The complaint appears to plead a transaction authorized by a board that is predominantly subject to a conflicting interest. The answer made to that point appears to be that the board in fact took action at the recommendation of a disinterested committee and by a vote that was not numerically dominated by those with an interest.
>
> This may be so, and, if so, those facts may have the legal effect that defendants assert, but unquestionably in advancing this position defendants seek to rely upon facts beyond those pleaded in the complaint. It would, in my view, be an affront to very basic standards of our system of justice to accept the few additional facts that defendants present as being not only true, but as being the only facts relevant to the question of the actual independence of the Special Committee.[1796]

The Delaware Supreme Court stated in *Rales v. Blasband*[1797] in 1993 and in *Grimes v. Donald*[1798] in 1996 that "[a]lthough derivative plaintiffs may believe it is difficult to meet the particularization requirement . . . because they are not entitled to discovery" prior to pleading compliance with the demand requirement, shareholders in fact have "many avenues available to obtain information bearing on the subject of their claims."[1799] The court explained that there are "a variety of public sources from which the details of a corporate act may be discovered, including the media and governmental agencies such as the Securities and Exchange

---

1795. *Id.* at 730.
1796. *Id.* at 728-29.
1797. 634 A.2d 927 (Del. 1993).
1798. 673 A.2d 1207 (Del. 1996).
1799. *Rales*, 634 A.2d at 934 n.10, *quoted in Grimes*, 673 A.2d at 1216 n.11.

Commission."[1800] Additionally, "a stockholder who has met the procedural requirements and has shown a specific proper purpose may use the summary procedure" provided for in Section 220 of the Delaware General Corporation Law, which allows stockholders to inspect corporate books and records, "to investigate the possibility of corporate wrongdoing."[1801] Thus, the Court stated in *Grimes* and in 1997 in *Scattered Corp. v. Chicago Stock Exchange, Inc.*,[1802] "[a] stockholder who makes a serious demand and receives only a peremptory refusal has the right to use the 'tools at hand' to obtain the relevant corporate records, such as reports or minutes, reflecting the corporate action and related information in order to determine whether or not there is a basis to assert that demand was wrongfully refused."[1803]

The Delaware Supreme Court stated its view in both *Rales* and *Grimes* that "[s]urprisingly, little use has been made of section 220 as an information-gathering tool in the derivative context."[1804] The Delaware Supreme Court similarly observed in *Security First Corp. v. U.S. Die Casting & Development Co.*[1805] in 1997 that "[t]his Court has encouraged the use of Section 220 as an 'information-gathering tool in the derivative context,' provided a proper purpose is shown," and that "[i]t is well established that investigation of mismanagement is a proper purpose for a Section 220 books and records inspection."[1806] The court in *Security First* added that "a Section 220 proceeding may serve a salutary mission as a prelude to a derivative suit."[1807] The court in *Chicago Stock Exchange* noted that the shareholder plaintiffs in that case "inexplicably" did not commence a Section 220 action to

---

1800. *Id.*

1801. *Id.*

1802. 701 A.2d 70 (Del. 1997).

1803. *Grimes*, 673 A.2d at 1218, *quoted in Chicago Stock Exch.*, 701 A.2d at 78.

1804. *Rales*, 634 A.2d at 934 n.10, *quoted in Grimes*, 673 A.2d at 1216 n.11.

1805. 687 A.2d 563 (Del. 1997).

1806. *Id.* at 567 & n.3.

1807. *Id.* at 571.

obtain "necessary information" before filing their derivative action and had "not taken advantage of the opportunity to bring an action under . . . § 220 to inspect minutes, reports and other books and records . . . *targeted* at the process and findings" of the board and board committees that acted upon plaintiffs' demand.[1808]

The court in *Security First* emphasized, however, that a "proper balance" must be struck because it "would invite mischief to open corporate management to indiscriminate fishing expeditions."[1809] This "proper balance" is determined, the court explained, by assessing whether the shareholder seeking inspection of books and records establishes by a preponderance of the evidence "a credible basis to find probable wrongdoing on the part of corporate management."[1810] Actual wrongdoing itself, however, need not be proved.[1811] The court described the burden that this standard places upon a shareholder as "not insubstantial" and stated that "the threshold may be satisfied by a credible showing, through documents, logic, testimony or otherwise, that there are legitimate issues of wrongdoing."[1812] "Mere curiosity or a desire for a fishing expedition will not suffice."[1813] The court in *Security First* also emphasized that discovery permitted under Section 220 and discovery permitted in the context of a shareholder derivative action are "not the same and should not be confused."[1814] Section 220 discovery, the court stated, is "circumscribed with rifled precision," while discovery in other contexts "may often be broader" in scope.[1815] The court stated again in *Chicago Stock Exchange* that discovery in a Section 220 proceeding should be "circumscribed with rifled precision."[1816]

---

1808. *Chicago Stock Exch.*, 701 A.2d at 78-79.
1809. *Security First Corp.*, 687 A.2d at 571.
1810. *Id.* at 567.
1811. *Id.*
1812. *Id.* at 568.
1813. *Id.*
1814. *Id.* at 570.
1815. *Id.*
1816. 701 A.2d at 78 n.37; *see also Thomas & Betts Corp. v. Levi-*
(continued...)

Principles of Corporate Governance: Analysis and Recommendations provides that a letter refusing a demand must state that "the demand was rejected by directors who were not interested in the transaction or conduct described in and forming the basis for the demand and that those directors constituted a majority of the entire board and were capable as a group of objective judgment in the circumstances."[1817] According to Principles of Corporate Governance, a letter refusing a demand also must provide "specific reasons for those statements."[1818] If the letter refusing a demand contains this information and a plaintiff fails to allege the facts required by Principles of Corporate Governance discussed earlier in this Chapter,[1819] then "defendants shall be entitled to dismissal of the complaint prior to discovery."[1820] Pennsylvania has adopted

---

1816. (...continued)
*ton Mfg. Co.*, 681 A.2d 1026, 1031 n.3 (Del. 1996) ("this Court in *Grimes* did not suggest that its reference to a Section 220 demand as one of the 'tools at hand' was intended to eviscerate or modify the need for a stockholder to show a proper purpose under Section 220"), *quoted in Security First*, 687 A.2d at 571 n.36; *Berkowitz v. Legal Sea Foods, Inc.*, 1997 Del. Ch. LEXIS 35, at *6 n.4, 1997 WL 153815, at *2 n.4 (Del. Ch. Mar. 24, 1997) (inspection of books and records for use in a litigation seeking to vindicate a shareholder's individual interests rather than derivative interests benefitting all shareholders is not a proper purpose); *Weiland v. Central & S.W. Corp.*, 15 Del. J. Corp. L. 273, 275-76 (Del. Ch. May 9, 1989) (granting a motion to dismiss an action to inspect corporate books and records pursuant to Del. Gen. Corp. Law § 220 in order to determine whether the corporation's board had wrongfully refused a pre-litigation demand, the court concluded as follows: "Pursuant to . . . § 220, a stockholder must establish that he has a proper purpose, which is defined as a 'purpose reasonably related to such person's interest as a stockholder.' It is well settled that one proper purpose is to investigate corporate mismanagement. However, it is not enough for a stockholder merely to state that he suspects corporate mismanagement. There must be some factual basis for that suspicion; he is not entitled to engage in a fishing expedition.") (citations omitted).

1817. 2 Principles of Corporate Governance: Analysis and Recommendations § 7.04(a)(2) (1994).

1818. *Id.*

1819. *See* Chapter IV, Section B 5 j (i).

1820. Principles of Corporate Governance § 7.04(a)(2).

the Principles of Corporate Governance formulation by judicial decision.[1821]

## 8.   Standing to Raise Demand as a Defense

An issue that may arise in litigation is the standing of parties other than the corporation on whose behalf a derivative action is brought and the corporation's directors to raise a plaintiff's failure to comply with the demand requirement as a defense to the action.

The Third Circuit held in *Shlensky v. Dorsey*[1822] that "it is well settled . . . that defendants other than the corporation whose rights the shareholder plaintiffs are seeking to vindicate may successfully raise the defense of failure to comply" with the demand requirement.[1823] The court cited five cases in support of this statement, each of which appear to have allowed defendants other than the corporation to raise the demand issue as a defense but none of which directly discussed the standing question.[1824] *Shlensky* has been followed by two district courts in the Third Circuit,[1825]

---

1821. *See Cuker v. Mikalauskas*, 692 A.2d 1042, 1048-55 (Pa. 1997).

1822. 574 F.2d 131 (3d Cir. 1978).

1823. *Id.* at 142.

1824. *See Brody v. Chem. Bank*, 517 F.2d 932 (2d Cir. 1975); *Landy v. Federal Deposit Ins. Corp.*, 486 F.2d 139 (3d Cir. 1973), *cert. denied*, 416 U.S. 960 (1974); *In re Kauffman Mut. Fund Actions*, 479 F.2d 257 (1st Cir.), *cert. denied*, 414 U.S. 857 (1973); *Ash v. International Bus. Machs., Inc.*, 353 F.2d 491 (3d Cir. 1965), *cert. denied*, 384 U.S. 927 (1966); *Meyers v. Keeler*, 414 F. Supp. 935 (W.D. Okla. 1976); *see also Colan v. Monumental Corp.*, 524 F. Supp. 1023, 1028 n.5 (N.D. Ill. 1981) (stating that the *Shlensky* decision "provided no reasons for allowing defendants other than the corporation standing to raise the failure of demand defense" and "cited authorities for this 'well settled' rule which do not directly discuss the question").

1825. *See Recchion v. Westinghouse Elec. Corp.*, 606 F. Supp. 889, 896 (W.D. Pa. 1985); *Weiss v. Temporary Inv. Fund, Inc.*, 516 F. Supp. 665, 667 n.4 (D. Del. 1981), *reargument denied*, 520 F. Supp. 1098 (D. Del. 1981), *aff'd on other grounds*, 692 F.2d 928 (3d Cir. 1982), *vacated and remanded on other grounds*, 465 U.S. 1001 (1984).

a district court in the Second Circuit[1826] and the Supreme Court of Washington.[1827]

The Delaware Supreme Court held in *Kaplan v. Peat, Marwick, Mitchell & Co.*[1828] that defendants other than the corporation and its directors may assert non-compliance with the demand requirement as a defense. The court in *Peat Marwick* reasoned that "the very nature of the demand requirement recognizes the 'fundamental precept that directors manage the business and affairs of the corporation.'"[1829] The court concluded that "[a]n expansive standing rule furthers this goal by increasing the class of defendants available to raise the demand issue, and as such, assures that the decision as to whether to proceed with the litigation is made by the appropriate party, i.e., the directors."[1830] The court also stated that "[a]llowing a third party to assert demand related defenses simply provides the defendant with the opportunity to challenge the shareholder plaintiff's capacity to act on behalf of the subject corporation."[1831] The Delaware Court of Chancery's decision in *Peat Marwick* also relied upon "Chancery Rule 9(a), which permits defendants (without distinctions) to challenge a plaintiff's capacity to sue."[1832]

Standing in contrast to *Shlensky* and *Peat Marwick* is *Markowitz v. Brody*,[1833] a case brought under Section 36(b) of the Investment Company Act of 1940[1834] and decided by a federal

---

1826. *See Lou v. Belzberg*, 728 F. Supp. 1010, 1019 (S.D.N.Y. 1990).

1827. *Haberman v. Washington Public Power Supply Sys.*, 744 P.2d 1032, 1060-61 (Wash. 1987), *appeal dismissed*, 488 U.S. 805 (1988).

1828. 540 A.2d 726 (Del. 1988).

1829. *Id*. at 730 (quoting *Aronson v. Lewis*, 473 A.2d 805, 812 (Del. 1984)).

1830. *Id*. at 730.

1831. *Id*.

1832. *Kaplan v. Peat, Marwick, Mitchell & Co.*, 529 A.2d 254, 259 (Del. Ch. 1987), *aff'd*, 540 A.2d 726 (Del. 1988); *see also* Fed. R. Civ. P. 9(a) (same as Del. Ch. Ct. R. 9(a)).

1833. 90 F.R.D. 542 (S.D.N.Y. 1981).

1834. 15 U.S.C. § 80a-35(b). After *Markowitz* was decided, United

(continued...)

court in New York. The *Markowitz* court adopted as a "general principle" the rule that "only the part(ies) for whose benefit a defense (to a shareholder derivative action) is intended should be permitted to raise the defense."[1835] The court explained that the demand requirement is intended to benefit the corporation and parties having a fiduciary relationship with the corporation.[1836] As a result, the court concluded, "fiduciaries of a derivative corporation, but not strangers" have standing "to complain of the plaintiff's failure to make a demand."[1837] Two New York state courts—*Ripley v. International Railways of Central America*[1838] and *Lazar v. Merchants' National Properties, Inc.*[1839]—likewise have "question[ed]"[1840] and "seriously questioned"[1841] the ability of defendants other than the corporation and its directors to raise the demand issue as a defense. The court in *Ripley* also observed that "[c]ertainly the alleged wrongdoer ought not to be able to dictate whether the injured corporation or minority stockholders in a derivative capacity should bring the suit."[1842]

Neither *Markowitz*, *Ripley* nor *Lazar*, however, held that the defendants raising the demand issue in those cases lacked standing

---

1834. (...continued)
States Supreme Court ruled that shareholder actions brought under Section 36(b) of the Investment Company Act are not derivative in nature and therefore are not subject to the pre-litigation demand requirement. *See Daily Income Fund, Inc. v. Fox*, 464 U.S. 523 (1984).

1835. 90 F.R.D. at 561 (quoting Note, *Defenses in Shareholders' Derivative Suits—Who May Raise Them*, 66 Harv. L. Rev. 342, 346 (1952)).

1836. *Id.* at 561.

1837. *Id.*

1838. 8 A.D.2d 310, 188 N.Y.S.2d 62 (N.Y. App. Div. 1st Dep't 1959), *aff'd on other grounds*, 8 N.Y.2d 430, 171 N.E.2d 443, 209 N.Y.S.2d 289 (1960).

1839. 45 Misc. 2d 235, 256 N.Y.S.2d 514 (N.Y. Sup. Ct. N.Y. Co. 1964), *aff'd mem.*, 23 A.D.2d 630, 256 N.Y.S.2d 542 (N.Y. App. Div. 1st Dep't 1965).

1840. *Ripley*, 8 A.D.2d at 317, 188 N.Y.S.2d at 72.

1841. 45 Misc. 2d at 236-37, 256 N.Y.S.2d at 517.

1842. 8 A.D.2d at 317, 188 N.Y.S.2d at 72.

to raise the demand issue. The moving defendants in *Markowitz* were an underwriter and an investment advisor who were found to have a fiduciary relationship with the corporation and therefore were held to have standing.[1843] *Ripley* was decided on the ground that demand was excused,[1844] and *Lazar* held that the corporation's board had wrongfully refused the demand in that case.[1845]

## 9.  Section 16(b) Cases

Section 16(b) of the Securities Exchange Act of 1934 authorizes a corporation or any security holder suing on the corporation's behalf to recover any profit realized by any officer, director or 10 percent shareholder from any purchase and sale (or sale and purchase) of an equity security of the corporation within a six month period.[1846] The statute includes a demand requirement permitting a security holder to sue only "if the issuer shall fail or refuse to bring such suit within sixty days after request."[1847]

Section 16(b) "authorizes shareholder suits to recover insider 'short swing' profits on behalf of the company notwithstanding the decision of the board of directors not to sue."[1848] Standing requirements for shareholder derivative actions therefore "are not applicable to a § 16(b) plaintiff."[1849]

---

1843. 90 F.R.D. at 547, 561.
1844. 8 A.D.2d at 317, 188 N.Y.S.2d at 72.
1845. 45 Misc. 2d at 237, 256 N.Y.S.2d at 517.
1846. 15 U.S.C. § 78p(b).
1847. *Id.*
1848. *Burks v. Lasker*, 441 U.S. 471, 484 n.13 (1979).
1849. *Mendell v. Gollust*, 909 F.2d 724, 728 (2d Cir. 1990), *aff'd*, 501 U.S. 115 (1991) (discussing Section 16(b) standing requirements generally); *see also Cramer v. General Tel. & Elecs. Corp.*, 582 F.2d 259, 276 n.22 (3d Cir. 1978), *cert. denied*, 439 U.S. 1129 (1979) ("[A] stockholder may maintain an action against a corporate insider under § 16(b) of the 1934 Act, 15 U.S.C. § 78p(b), 'if the issuer shall fail or refuse to bring such suit within sixty days after request or shall fail diligently to prosecute the same thereafter. . . .' Thus, although a derivative action under § 16(b) cannot be brought unless the shareholder has first made a demand on the directors, the directors' decision not to prosecute the suit

(continued...)

The Delaware Court of Chancery's decision in *Kaplan v. Peat, Marwick, Mitchell & Co.*[1850] noted this distinction between a shareholder demand in an action under Section 16(b) and a shareholder demand in other contexts and pointed specifically to the "unique" and "paramount Congressional policy of deterring statutory insiders from 'short swing' trading in the corporation's securities."[1851] Section 16(b) effectuates this policy, the court added, by being "a statute that, as a general matter, imposes liability without fault. Once a transaction proscribed by that statute has occurred, liability is imposed without regard to whether the profiting insider actually used inside information or even intended to engage in short-term trading."[1852] The court accordingly rejected the applicability of Section 16(b) decisions—including decisions holding that defendants other than the corporation do not have standing to raise the demand issue in actions brought under Section 16(b)[1853]—in contexts other than Section 16(b) cases.[1854] The

---

1849. (...continued)
does not preclude a subsequent action by the shareholder himself."); *Levner v. Prince Alwaleed Bin Talal Bin Abdulaziz Al Saud*, 903 F. Supp. 452, 455 n.2 (S.D.N.Y. 1994) ("Section 16(b) has been held to create a private right of action notwithstanding a decision of the board of directors not to sue"), *aff'd*, 61 F.3d 8, 8-9 (2d Cir. 1995) (affirming "on the carefully reasoned opinion" of the district court); *Markowitz v. Brody*, 90 F.R.D. 542, 563 n.20 (S.D.N.Y. 1981) ("[t]he Rule 23.1 demand or excuse requirement does not apply to Section 16(b) actions, because that section contains its own demand requirement, which permits a security holder to sue only 'if the issuer shall fail or refuse to bring such suit within sixty days after request.' 15 U.S.C. § 78p(b)").

1850. 529 A.2d 254 (Del. Ch. 1987), *aff'd*, 540 A.2d 726 (Del. 1988).

1851. *Id.* at 261.

1852. *Id.* (citing 15 U.S.C. § 78p(b) and *Burks v. Lasker*, 441 U.S. 471, 484 n.13 (1979)).

1853. *See Colan v. Monumental Corp.*, 524 F. Supp. 1023, 1028 (N.D. Ill. 1981); *Prager v. Sylvestri*, 449 F. Supp. 425, 429 (S.D.N.Y. 1978); *Morales v. Mylan Lab., Inc.*, 443 F. Supp. 778, 779 (W.D. Pa. 1978); *Schur v. Salzman*, 365 F. Supp. 725, 732-33 & n.30 (S.D.N.Y. 1973); *Grossman v. Young*, 72 F. Supp. 375, 380 (S.D.N.Y. 1947); *see*

(continued...)

Congressional policy underlying Section 16(b) cases, the Court of Chancery concluded in *Peat Marwick*, is not present in derivative actions brought under state law, where the demand requirement is intended to enable the corporation's board of directors to determine whether pursuit of litigation would serve the best interests of the corporation.[1855]

## 10. Demand on Shareholders

Rule 23.1 of the Federal Rules of Civil Procedure provides that demand must be made not merely upon the corporation's directors but also—"if necessary"—upon the corporation's shareholders.[1856] The "if necessary" reservation reflects the fact that the need for a demand on shareholders is governed by state law. If the applicable state law requires a demand on shareholders, then a demand on shareholders is "necessary" under Rule 23.1.[1857] In jurisdictions where a demand on shareholders is required, an action will be dismissed where a shareholder pleads facts demonstrating that a demand upon the board is excused but fails to plead facts demonstrating that a demand upon shareholders is excused.[1858]

---

1853. (...continued)
*also Markowitz*, 90 F.R.D. at 563 n.20 ("[a]n unbroken line of cases has held, on the theory that the Section 16(b) demand requirement is intended to benefit only the defendant derivative corporation, and not corporate insiders, that defendant corporate insiders have no standing to complain of a Section 16(b) plaintiff's failure to make a demand").

1854. 529 A.2d at 261.

1855. *Id.; see also* Chapter IV, Section B 2 (discussing the rationale for the demand requirement).

1856. Fed. R. Civ. P. 23.1.

1857. *See, e.g., Allright Mo., Inc. v. Billeter*, 829 F.2d 631, 639 (8th Cir. 1987); *Wolgin v. Simon*, 722 F.2d 389, 392 (8th Cir. 1983); *Jacobs v. Adams*, 601 F.2d 176, 179-80 (5th Cir. 1979); *Brody v. Chemical Bank*, 482 F.2d 1111, 1114 (2d Cir.), *cert. denied*, 414 U.S. 1104 (1973); *In re Midlantic Corp. Shareholder Litig.*, 758 F. Supp. 226, 239 (D.N.J. 1990).

1858. *See, e.g., Abraham v. Parkins*, 36 F. Supp. 238, 240-41 (W.D. Pa. 1940).

"[T]he shareholder demand rule has been widely criticized,"[1859] and a demand upon shareholders is not a prerequisite to the commencement of a derivative action in California,[1860] Delaware or New York.[1861] A demand on shareholders also is not required by the Model Business Corporation Act[1862] or Principles of Corporate Governance: Analysis and Recommendations.[1863]

Nevertheless, a substantial minority of jurisdictions continues to require that a demand be made on shareholders.[1864] This requirement allows shareholders to weigh the benefits of litigation against "the costs, divisiveness and other detriments involved."[1865] Another rationale for requiring demand on shareholders is the fact that the challenged conduct may be subject to ratification by a majority of the corporation's shareholders.[1866]

Like demand upon directors, demand upon shareholders is excused where it would be futile. The most prominent examples of such futility are cases where defendant directors are large share-

---

1859. *Strougo v. Scudder, Stevens & Clark, Inc.*, 964 F. Supp. 783, 795 (S.D.N.Y. 1997).

1860. Cal. Gen. Corp. Law § 800(b)(2).

1861. N.Y. Bus. Corp. Law § 626(c); *Syracuse Television, Inc. v. Channel 9, Syracuse, Inc.*, 51 Misc. 2d 188, 193, 273 N.Y.S.2d 16, 24 (N.Y. Sup. Ct. Onondaga Co. 1966).

1862. 2 Model Bus. Corp. Act Annotated § 7.42 (3d ed. 1996).

1863. 2 Principles of Corporate Governance: Analysis and Recommendations § 7.03(c) (1994).

1864. *See Allright Mo.*, 829 F.2d at 639 (Missouri law); *Wolgin*, 722 F.2d at 392 (Missouri law); *Strougo*, 964 F. Supp. at 795 (Maryland law); *Grill v. Hoblitzell*, 771 F. Supp. 709, 713 n.5 (D. Md. 1991) (Maryland law); *Bell v. Arnold*, 487 P.2d 545, 547-48 (Colo. 1971) (Colorado law); *New Crawford Valley, Ltd. v. Benedict*, 847 P.2d 642, 646 (Colo. Ct. App. 1993) (Colorado law); *Skolnik v. Rose*, 55 N.Y.2d 964, 965, 434 N.E.2d 251, 252, 449 N.Y.S.2d 182, 183 (1982) (Massachusetts law); *McLeese v. J.C. Nichols Co.*, 842 S.W.2d 115, 119 (Mo. Ct. App. 1992) (Missouri law); *Burdon v. Erskine*, 401 A.2d 369, 370-71 (Pa. Super. Ct. 1979) (Pennsylvania law).

1865. *Grill*, 771 F. Supp. at 712 n.5.

1866. *Wolgin*, 722 F.2d at 392.

holders (although, in some jurisdictions, not necessarily majority shareholders).[1867] Some courts also have excused demand on shareholders in cases where the number of shareholders in a publicly held corporation would make the demand a costly and time-consuming procedure,[1868] or where the practical likelihood of replacing directors or achieving an intracorporate settlement is minimal.[1869] Other courts, however, have rejected contentions that demand on shareholders may be excused on these grounds.[1870] Some courts have excused demand on shareholders where the alleged wrong cannot be ratified by shareholders[1871] or where shareholders have refused to ratify the alleged wrong.[1872] Other courts have held that demand on shareholders is required even where alleged wrongs are not subject to shareholder ratification.[1873] Some courts have excused demand on shareholders

---

1867. *See Meltzer v. Atlantic Research Corp.*, 330 F.2d 946, 949 (4th Cir.) (40 percent shareholder), *cert. denied*, 379 U.S. 841 (1964); *Gottesman v. General Motors Corp.*, 268 F.2d 194, 197 (2d Cir. 1959) (23 percent shareholder); *Treves v. Servel, Inc.*, 244 F. Supp. 773, 778 (S.D.N.Y. 1965) (55 percent shareholder); *Pupecki v. James Madison Corp.*, 382 N.E.2d 1030, 1034 (Mass. 1978) (90 percent shareholder).

1868. *See Levitt v. Johnson*, 334 F.2d 815, 818 (1st Cir. 1964) (contacting 48,000 stockholders labeled "a pointless or, alternatively, impossibly burdensome act"), *cert. denied*, 379 U.S. 961 (1965); *Meltzer*, 330 F.2d at 949; *Midlantic*, 758 F. Supp. at 239; *Weiss v. Sunasco Inc.*, 316 F. Supp. 1197, 1206-07 (E.D. Pa. 1970); *Elgin v. Alfa Corp.*, 598 So. 2d 807, 817-18 (Ala. 1992); *New Crawford*, 847 P.2d at 646.

1869. *See Gottesman*, 268 F.2d at 197; *Sunasco*, 316 F. Supp. at 1207.

1870. *See Wolgin*, 722 F.2d at 392; *Zimmerman v. Bell*, 585 F. Supp. 512, 516 (D. Md. 1984).

1871. *See Wolgin*, 722 F.2d at 392; *Mayer v. Adams*, 141 A.2d 458, 465 (Del. 1958); *McLeese*, 842 S.W.2d at 119-20.

1872. *Allright Mo.*, 829 F.2d at 639.

1873. *See Bell*, 487 P.2d at 547-48; *Claman v. Robertson*, 128 N.E.2d 429, 436 (Ohio 1955); *cf. Rogers v. American Can Co.*, 305 F.2d 297, 317-19 (3d Cir. 1962) (construing New Jersey law to grant shareholders standing to pursue a derivative action alleging illegal conduct not subject to ratification after a demand on shareholders had been made and refused during the course of a proxy contest).

where even if the shareholders wanted to act they would be unable to do so in time to prevent the alleged wrong.[1874] Some courts also have excused demand on shareholders where shareholders would be demanding that directors sue themselves or remove themselves from office.[1875]

## C. Termination by Special Litigation Committees

The business judgment rule provides a means by which directors under appropriate circumstances can secure the dismissal of derivative litigation not only in actions where a pre-litigation demand is made and refused but also in actions where a pre-litigation demand is excused. In actions where demand is excused, the corporation can create a special litigation committee—often referred to as an "SLC"—composed solely of disinterested and independent directors who are vested with full authority to act on behalf of the corporation with respect to the litigation. The special litigation committee then determines whether pursuit of litigation will serve the best interests of the corporation and thus should be continued or whether pursuit of the litigation will not serve the best interests of the corporation and thus should be terminated. The committee may determine "to terminate the litigation, to take it over, or to permit the plaintiff's action to continue."[1876] In this manner, the board "delegate[s] to a committee of disinterested directors the board's power to control corporate litigation."[1877] "[A] mere advisory role of the Special Litigation Committee fails to bestow sufficient legitimacy on the Board's decision to warrant deference to the Board" by a court.[1878]

This special litigation committee termination procedure need not be utilized where demand is required because if demand is

---

1874. *See, e.g., Campbell v. Loew's Inc.*, 134 A.2d 565, 567 (Del. Ch. 1957).

1875. *Strougo*, 964 F. Supp. at 796; *Zimmerman*, 585 F. Supp. at 516.

1876. *Strougo v. Padegs*, 986 F. Supp. 812, 814 (S.D.N.Y. 1997).

1877. *Kamen v. Kemper Fin. Servs., Inc.*, 500 U.S. 90, 102 (1991).

1878. *In re Par Pharmaceutical, Inc. Derivative Litig.*, 750 F. Supp. 641, 647 (S.D.N.Y. 1990).

required the board as a whole may act in a manner that will be judged pursuant to the business judgment rule.[1879] Thus, "only in 'extraordinary circumstances'" is it "appropriate for a board to delegate its 'fundamental responsibility and authority for corporate management' to 'individuals wholly separate and apart from the board.'"[1880] The Delaware Supreme Court accordingly stated in *Grimes v. Donald*[1881] that where a demand is required "[t]he use of a committee of the board formed to respond to a demand or to advise the board on its duty in responding to a demand is not the same as the SLC process."[1882] "It is important that these discrete and quite different processes not be confused."[1883]

## 1.  The Power to Terminate

*a. Gall, Auerbach and Zapata.* The first decision expressly recognizing the power of special litigation committees consisting of a minority of the corporation's directors to terminate derivative actions naming a majority of the corporation's directors as defendants was a decision by a federal court construing New York law in *Gall v. Exxon Corp.*[1884] (An earlier decision by another federal court construing New York law, *Lasker v. Burks*,[1885] approved the use of a quorum of disinterested directors to determine the posi-

---

1879. *See* Chapter IV, Section B 6 c-j; *Stoner v. Walsh*, 772 F. Supp. 790, 796 (S.D.N.Y. 1991); *Spiegel v. Buntrock*, 571 A.2d 767, 778 (Del. 1990); *Aronson v. Lewis*, 473 A.2d 805, 813 (Del. 1984); *Zapata Corp. v. Maldonado*, 430 A.2d 779, 784 n.10 (Del. 1981); *Powell v. Western Ill. Elec. Coop.*, 536 N.E.2d 231, 234 (Ill. App. Ct.), *appeal denied*, 545 N.E.2d 129 (Ill. 1989), *cert. denied*, 493 U.S. 1079 (1990).

1880. *Stoner*, 772 F. Supp. at 803 (quoting *Auerbach v. Bennett*, 47 N.Y.2d 619, 633, 393 N.E.2d 994, 1002, 419 N.Y.S.2d 920, 928 (1979)).

1881. 673 A.2d 1207 (Del. 1996).

1882. *Id*. at 1216 n.13.

1883. *Id*.

1884. 418 F. Supp. 508 (S.D.N.Y. 1976).

1885. 404 F. Supp. 1172 (S.D.N.Y. 1975), *subsequent proceedings*, 426 F. Supp. 844 (S.D.N.Y. 1977), *rev'd*, 567 F.2d 1208 (2d Cir. 1978), *rev'd*, 441 U.S. 471 (1979).

tion the corporation should take in a derivative action and, if appropriate, to seek to terminate the action.[1886])

The shareholder plaintiff in *Exxon* alleged that improper foreign payments by Exxon Corporation from 1963 through 1974 constituted a breach of fiduciary duty by the corporation's directors and a waste of corporate assets and that the nondisclosure of these payments violated federal securities laws.[1887] Exxon's board appointed a special litigation committee consisting of one director who was a member of the corporation's management and two outside directors. All three of these directors had been elected to the board after the alleged improper payments had ended.[1888] Following an investigation conducted with the assistance of special counsel, the committee determined that the prospects for success by the corporation in any litigation challenging the alleged improper payments were unfavorable and that any such litigation would be costly to pursue, would interrupt corporate business and would undermine morale within the corporation. The committee accordingly concluded that litigation by the corporation or shareholders acting on the corporation's behalf would be contrary to the corporation's best interests and directed the appropriate officers of the corporation to seek dismissal of the litigation.[1889]

On a motion for summary judgment, the court stated that "[t]here is no question that the rights sought to be vindicated in this lawsuit are those of Exxon and not those of the plaintiff suing derivatively on the corporation's behalf."[1890] The court then discussed decisions such as *Hawes v. City of Oakland*,[1891] *Corbus v. Alaska Treadwell Gold Mining Corp.*[1892] and *United Copper Securities Co. v. Amalgamated Copper Co.*[1893]—cases discussed earlier in this Chapter in the context of board refusals of shareholder

---

1886. *Id.* at 1175, 1179.
1887. 418 F. Supp. at 509.
1888. *Id.* at 510 & n.2.
1889. *Id.* at 514 & nn. 12, 13.
1890. *Id.* at 514.
1891. 104 U.S. 450 (1881).
1892. 187 U.S. 455 (1903).
1893. 244 U.S. 261 (1917).

demands.[1894] Based upon these decisions, the court explained that "it is the interests of the corporation which are at stake" and therefore it is "the responsibility of the directors of the corporation to determine, in the first instance, whether an action should be brought on the corporation's behalf."[1895] Accordingly, the court continued, "[i]t follows that the decision of corporate directors whether or not to assert a cause of action held by the corporation rests within the sound business judgment of the management."[1896] The court thus concluded that "absent allegations of fraud, collusion, self-interest, dishonesty or other misconduct of a breach of trust nature, and absent allegations that the business judgment exercised was grossly unsound, the court should not . . . interfere with the judgment of the corporate officers."[1897] The court refused, however, to grant summary judgment until after plaintiff had been given an opportunity "to test the bona fides and independence of the Special Committee through discovery and, if necessary, at a plenary hearing."[1898]

The court acknowledged that "the legality and morality of foreign political contributions, bribes and other payments by American corporations has been widely debated" but stated that "[t]he issue before me for decision . . . is not whether the payments made . . . were proper or improper."[1899] Rather, "the issue is whether the Special Committee, acting as Exxon's Board of Directors and in the sound exercise of their business judgment, may determine that a suit against any present or former director or officer would be contrary to the best interests of the corporation."[1900]

The first decision by the highest court of any state to consider whether special litigation committees consisting of a minority of a

---

1894. *See* Chapter IV, Section B 6 c.
1895. 418 F. Supp. at 515.
1896. *Id.*
1897. *Id.* at 516.
1898. *Id.* at 520.
1899. *Id.* at 519.
1900. *Id.*

corporation's directors have the power to terminate derivative actions naming directors as defendants was the New York Court of Appeals' 1979 decision in *Auerbach v. Bennett*.[1901] The facts in *Auerbach* were similar to those in *Exxon*. A shareholder alleged that various past and present members of the corporation's board were liable for breach of their fiduciary duties to the corporation as a result of bribes and kickbacks paid by the corporation.[1902] The board appointed a special litigation committee consisting of three directors who had joined the board after the challenged payments had occurred and "all of the authority of the Board of Directors to determine, on behalf of the Board, the position that the Corporation shall take" with respect to the litigation was delegated to the committee.[1903] Following an investigation conducted with the assistance of independent outside counsel, the committee determined that the claims asserted by the shareholder lacked merit, that litigation costs would be high, and that the publicity surrounding such a litigation could be damaging to the corporation.[1904] The committee accordingly instructed the corporation's general counsel to move to dismiss the litigation.[1905]

The court rejected plaintiff's contention that "any committee authorized by the board of which defendant directors were members must be held legally infirm and may not be delegated power to terminate a derivative action.[1906] The court explained that "[i]n the very nature of the corporate organization it was only the existing board of directors which had authority on behalf of the corporation to direct the investigation and to assure the cooperation of corporate employees.[1907] The court also explained that "it is only that same board by its own action—or as here pursuant to authority duly delegated by it—which had authority to decide whether to prosecute the

---

1901. 47 N.Y.2d 619, 393 N.E.2d 994, 419 N.Y.S.2d 920 (1979).

1902. *Id*. at 624, 393 N.E.2d at 997, 419 N.Y.S.2d at 923.

1903. *Id*. at 625, 632, 393 N.E.2d at 997, 1001, 419 N.Y.S.2d at 923, 927.

1904. *Id*. at 625-26, 393 N.E.2d at 997, 419 N.Y.S.2d at 923.

1905. *Id*. at 626, 393 N.E.2d at 997, 419 N.Y.S.2d at 923-24.

1906. *Id*. at 632, 393 N.E.2d at 1001, 419 N.Y.S.2d at 927.

1907. *Id*. at 632, 393 N.E.2d at 1001, 419 N.Y.S.2d at 927-28.

claims against defendant directors."[1908] Here, the court concluded, the corporation's board, "with slight adaption, followed
prudent practice in observing the general policy that when individual members of a board of directors prove to have personal
interests which may conflict with the interests of the corporation,
such interested directors must be excluded while the remaining
members of the board proceed to consideration and action."[1909]
The court stated that "[c]ourts have consistently held that the business judgment rule applies where some directors are charged with
wrongdoing, so long as the remaining directors making the decision
are disinterested and independent."[1910]

The Delaware Supreme Court reached the same conclusion in
*Zapata Corp. v. Maldonado.*[1911] Previously, however, the Delaware Court of Chancery in *Maldonado v. Flynn*[1912] had concluded that where demand is not required directors "do not have
the right to compel the dismissal of a derivative suit brought by a
stockholder to rectify an apparent breach of fiduciary duty by the
directors to the corporation and its stockholders."[1913] Rather, the
Court of Chancery had held, a shareholder in such a case possesses
an "independent right to redress the wrong by bringing a derivative
suit."[1914] The Delaware Supreme Court reversed the Court of
Chancery's decision and held that where demand is not required
shareholders have a right to commence a derivative action but do
not have an absolute right to pursue the action to its conclusion.[1915] Any other rule, the court reasoned, would "automatically result in the placement in the hands of the litigating stockholder sole control of the corporate right throughout the litigation"

---

1908. *Id.* at 632, 393 N.E.2d at 1001, 419 N.Y.S.2d at 928.
1909. *Id.* at 632, 393 N.E.2d at 1001, 419 N.Y.S.2d at 928.
1910. *Id.* at 632, 393 N.E.2d at 1001-02, 419 N.Y.S.2d at 928.
1911. 430 A.2d 779 (Del. 1981).
1912. 413 A.2d 1251 (Del. Ch. 1980), *rev'd sub nom. Zapata Corp. v. Maldonado*, 430 A.2d 779 (Del. 1981).
1913. *Id.* at 1262.
1914. *Id.* at 1263.
1915. 430 A.2d at 784.

and thus promote "the interest of one person or group to the exclusion of all others within the corporate entity."[1916]

The overwhelming majority of courts that have considered the issue, including state courts in Alabama,[1917] Massachusetts,[1918] Minnesota,[1919] North Carolina[1920] and Ohio[1921] and federal courts construing the laws of California,[1922] Colorado,[1923] Connecticut,[1924] Georgia,[1925] Illinois,[1926] Maryland,[1927] Massachusetts,[1928] Michi-

---

1916. *Id.* at 784-85.

1917. *See Stallworth v. AmSouth Bank*, 1997 Ala. LEXIS 483, at *19, 1997 WL 778838, at *6 (Ala. Dec. 19, 1997); *Roberts v. Alabama Power Co.*, 404 So. 2d 629, 632, 636 (Ala. 1981).

1918. *See Houle v. Low*, 556 N.E.2d 51, 57 (Mass. 1990).

1919. *See Skoglund v. Brady*, 541 N.W.2d 17, 20-21 (Minn. Ct. App. 1995); *Black v. NuAire, Inc.*, 426 N.W.2d 203, 209-10 (Minn. Ct. App. 1988).

1920. *See Alford v. Shaw*, 358 S.E.2d 323, 325-28 (N.C. 1987), *subsequent proceedings*, 398 S.E.2d 445 (N.C. 1990).

1921. *See Miller v. Bargaheiser*, 591 N.E.2d 1339, 1341-43 (Ohio Ct. App. 1990).

1922. *See Gaines v. Haughton*, 645 F.2d 761, 770-72 (9th Cir. 1981), *cert. denied*, 454 U.S. 1145 (1982); *Lewis v. Anderson*, 615 F.2d 778, 781-83 (9th Cir. 1979), *cert. denied*, 449 U.S. 869 (1980); *Will v. Engebretson & Co.*, 213 Cal. App. 3d 1033, 1042, 261 Cal. Rptr. 868, 873 (1989).

1923. *See Bach v. National W. Life Ins. Co.*, 810 F.2d 509, 511-12 (5th Cir. 1987).

1924. *See Joy v. North*, 692 F.2d 880, 887-93 (2d Cir. 1982), *cert. denied*, 460 U.S. 1051 (1983).

1925. *See Peller v. Southern Co.*, 911 F.2d 1532, 1536 (11th Cir. 1990).

1926. *See Weiland v. Illinois Power Co.*, [1990-1991 Transfer Binder] Fed. Sec. L. Rep. (CCH) ¶ 95,747, at 98,589-90 (C.D. Ill. Sept. 17, 1990).

1927. *See Strougo v. Padegs*, 986 F. Supp. 812, 814 (S.D.N.Y. 1997); *Rosengarten v. Buckley*, 613 F. Supp. 1493, 1498-1500 (D. Md. 1985); *Grossman v. Johnson*, 89 F.R.D. 656, 662-63 (D. Mass. 1981), *aff'd on other grounds*, 674 F.2d 115 (1st Cir.), *cert. denied*, 459 U.S. 838 (1982).

1928. *See Hasan v. CleveTrust Realty Investors*, 729 F.2d 372,
(continued...)

gan,[1929] New Jersey,[1930] Ohio,[1931] Pennsylvania[1932] and Virginia,[1933] agree that special litigation committees acting on behalf of corporate boards have the power to terminate derivative litigation against directors. As discussed below, statutes now have been enacted in several of these states.[1934]

   *b. Model and Statutory Provisions.* As discussed earlier in this Chapter in connection with board refusals of shareholder demands, statutes enacted in Arizona, Connecticut, Florida, Georgia, Maine, Michigan, Mississippi, Montana, Nebraska, New Hampshire, North Carolina, Texas, Virginia and Wisconsin and model formulations proposed by the Model Business Corporation Act and Principles of Corporate Governance: Analysis and Recommendations have adopted universal demand requirements[1935] and authorize the refusal of shareholder demands and the termination of derivative litigation by boards or board committees.[1936] Pennsylvania has adopted the Principles of Corporate Governance formulation by judicial decision.[1937]

---

1928. (...continued)
375-77 (6th Cir. 1984).

   1929. *See Genzer v. Cunningham*, 498 F. Supp. 682, 686-87 (E.D. Mich. 1980).

   1930. *See In re Par Pharmaceutical, Inc. Derivative Litig.*, 750 F. Supp. 641, 646 n.11 (S.D.N.Y. 1990).

   1931. *See In re General Tire & Rubber Co. Sec. Litig.*, 726 F.2d 1075, 1082-83 (6th Cir.), *cert. denied*, 469 U.S. 858 (1984); *Holmstrom v. Coastal Indus., Inc.*, 645 F. Supp. 963, 966 (N.D. Ohio 1984).

   1932. *See Cuker v. Mikalauskas*, 692 A.2d 1042, 1045, 1048-49 (Pa. 1997).

   1933. *See Abella v. Universal Leaf Tobacco Co.*, 546 F. Supp. 795, 798-800 (E.D. Va. 1982), *reconsidering and rev'g* 495 F. Supp. 713 (E.D. Va. 1980).

   1934. *See* Chapter IV, Section C 1 b.

   1935. *See* Chapter IV, Section B 5 g.

   1936. *See* Chapter IV, Sections 6 i-j.

   1937. *See Cuker v. Mikalauskas*, 692 A.2d 1042, 1048-55 (Pa. 1997).

As also discussed earlier in this Chapter,[1938] an Alaska statute provides that a shareholder's right to bring a derivative action "terminates" where a board of directors refuses a shareholder demand because "in its business judgment, the litigation would not be in the best interest of the corporation."[1939] A separate provision of the statute provides that where dismissal is not available by means of a board refusal of a demand (because, for example, demand is excused), the following alternative procedure is available:

> [D]isinterested, noninvolved directors acting as the board or a duly charged board committee may petition the court to dismiss the plaintiff's action on grounds that in their independent, informed business judgment the action is not in the best interest of the corporation. The petitioners shall have the burden of establishing to the satisfaction of the court their disinterest, independence from any direct or indirect control of defendants in the action, and the informed basis on which they have exercised their asserted business judgment. If the court is satisfied that the petitioners are disinterested, independent, and informed it shall then exercise an independent appraisal of the plaintiff's action to determine whether, considering the welfare of the corporation and relevant issues of public policy, it should dismiss the action.[1940]

An additional statute dealing solely with termination by board committees has been enacted in Indiana. The Indiana statute authorizes the creation of a committee that consists of three or more disinterested directors or other persons and that is "not subject to the direction or control of or termination by the board."[1941] The committee's responsibility under the statute is to determine "whether the corporation has a legal or equitable right or remedy" and "whether it is in the best interests of the corporation to pursue that right or remedy, if any, or to dismiss a proceeding that seeks to assert the right or remedy on behalf of the corporation."[1942] The

---

1938. *See* Chapter IV, Section B 6 i.
1939. Alaska Corp. Code § 10.06.435(e).
1940. *Id*. § 10.06.435(f).
1941. Ind. Bus. Corp. Law § 23-1-32-4(a).
1942. *Id*.

statute provides that if the committee determines that pursuit of the right or remedy is not in the best interests of the corporation, then "the merits of that determination shall be presumed to be conclusive" unless a shareholder plaintiff demonstrates that the committee was not disinterested or the committee's determination was "not made after an investigation conducted in good faith."[1943] The statute defines a disinterested director or other person as an individual who is "able under the circumstances to render a determination in the best interests of the corporation" and who is not a party to the action or who has been named as a party "but only on the basis of a frivolous or insubstantial claim or for the sole purpose of seeking to disqualify the director or other person from serving on the committee."[1944] An officer, employee or agent of the corporation or a related corporation may be a member of the committee, according to the Indiana statute, only in cases "in which the right or remedy under scrutiny is not assertable against a director or officer of the corporation or a related corporation."[1945]

Minnesota and North Dakota have enacted statutes that provide simply that

> Committees having the authority of the board in the management of the business of the corporation . . . may include a special litigation committee consisting of one or more independent directors or other independent persons to consider legal rights or remedies of the corporation and whether those rights and remedies should be pursued. Committees other than special litigation committees . . . are subject at all times to the direction and control of the board.[1946]

Until 1989, Minnesota's statute provided as follows:

> Unless prohibited by the articles or bylaws, the board may establish a committee composed of two or more disinterested directors or other disinterested persons to determine whether it is in the best interests of the corporation to pursue a partic-

---

1943. *Id.* § 23-1-32-4(c).
1944. *Id.* § 23-1-32-4(d)(1), (2).
1945. *Id.* § 23-1-32-4(d)(3).
1946. Minn. Bus. Corp. Act § 302A.241(1); N.D. Bus. Corp. Act § 10-19.1-48.

ular legal right or remedy of the corporation and whether to cause the dismissal or discontinuance of a particular proceeding that seeks to assert a right or remedy on behalf of the corporation. For purposes of this section, a director or other person is "disinterested" if the director or other person is not the owner of more than one percent of the outstanding shares of, or a present or former officer, employee, or agent of, the corporation or of a related corporation and has not been made or threatened to be made a party to the proceeding in question. The committee, once established, is not subject to the direction or control of, or termination by, the board. A vacancy on the committee may be filled by a majority vote of the remaining members. The good faith determinations of the committee are binding upon the corporation and its directors, officers, and shareholders. The committee terminates when it issues a written report of its determination to the board.[1947]

That statute was repealed in 1989 but "[t]he legislature expressly stated that repealing section 302A.243 was not intended to convey any legislative intent with regard to the substance of the repealed section."[1948]

   *c. Miller and Alford.* Standing in contrast to the case law and statutes discussed in the preceding sections of this Chapter[1949] is the Iowa Supreme Court's 1983 decision in *Miller v. Register & Tribune Syndicate, Inc.*[1950] *Miller* holds that interested directors may not under any circumstances confer the power to terminate a derivative action upon a special litigation committee consisting of less than a majority of a corporation's directors. *Miller* involved a derivative action commenced against all four of a corporation's directors. The plaintiff alleged that the corporation had sold its stock at fraudulently low prices to the directors and had overcompensated the directors.[1951] The four directors on the board expanded the board to include two new directors and then created a

---

1947. Former Minn. Bus. Corp. Act § 302A.243.
1948. *Skoglund v. Brady*, 541 N.W.2d 17, 21 (Minn. Ct. App. 1995) (quoting 1989 Minn. Laws ch. 172, § 12).
1949. *See* Chapter IV, Sections C 1 a and b.
1950. 336 N.W.2d 709 (Iowa 1983).
1951. *Id.* at 710.

special litigation committee consisting of these two new directors.[1952] The court rejected this procedure on the ground that the selection of the new directors by interested persons tainted the disinterestedness and independence of the new directors.[1953]

The *Miller* court principally relied upon Tentative Draft No. 1 of the American Law Institute's corporate governance project, then called Principles of Corporate Governance and Structure: Restatement and Recommendations, which proposed precluding the selection of committee members by interested directors.[1954] Section 7.08 of the final version of Principles of Corporate Governance, however, rejects *Miller*.[1955]

*Miller* was followed by a lower appellate court in North Carolina in 1985 in *Alford v. Shaw*.[1956] There, following demands by minority shareholders regarding "wrongful, unlawful and fraudulent transactions" by a majority of the corporation's directors, the board appointed two new directors and created a special litigation committee consisting of these two new directors.[1957] Before the committee completed its investigation, the shareholders commenced a derivative action.[1958] The committee then completed its investigation and recommended that two of the

---

1952. *Id.*

1953. *Id.* at 718.

1954. *Id.* at 717 (citing *Principles of Corporate Governance and Structure: Restatement and Recommendations* § 7.03 (Tentative Draft No. 1 Apr. 1, 1982)).

1955. *See* 2 Principles of Corporate Governance: Analysis and Recommendations § 7.05 Comment at 103 (1994) ("this Chapter . . . does not adopt the . . . rule announced" in *Miller*); *id.* § 7.09 Comment at 121 (stating the *Miller* rule and that "Section 7.09 does not adopt this sweeping a rule").

1956. 324 S.E.2d 878 (N.C. Ct. App. 1985), *rev'd*, 349 S.E.2d 41 (N.C. 1986), *withdrawn to affirm and modify*, 358 S.E.2d 323 (N.C. 1987).

1957. 349 S.E.2d at 42-43; 358 S.E.2d at 324-25.

1958. 349 S.E.2d at 43; 358 S.E.2d at 325.

plaintiffs' claims be settled and that the remainder of the claims be dismissed.[1959]

The court acknowledged that "[t]he cases rejecting the special committee device are few" and cited only *Miller*.[1960] The court, however, determined to follow *Miller* and held that "directors . . . who are parties to a derivative action may not confer upon a special committee of the board of directors the power to bind the corporation as to its conduct of the litigation."[1961] The court pointed to what it described as North Carolina's public policy favoring suits by minority shareholders and concluded that permitting corporations to utilize the special litigation committee device impermissibly shifts the burden "to plaintiff stockholders to show interest, a most difficult task in view of the stockholders' lack of access to corporate records and information, and the many levels of financial, social, occupational, and psychological pressures that a corporation's board may be in a position to exert."[1962] According to the *Alford* court, judicial intervention in the special litigation committee process (such as placing the burden of proof upon the corporation, allowing discovery of committee members, requiring the corporation to consult with plaintiffs regarding selection of committee members and counsel, or requiring the committee to explain with particularity the facts and assumptions underlying its decision) provides "too many complications and possibilities for litigation-extending error."[1963]

The North Carolina Supreme Court rejected the lower appellate court's "*per se* rule prohibiting disqualified directors from delegating litigation decisions to a special litigation committee."[1964] According to the Supreme Court, the rule adopted in *Miller* and by the lower court in *Alford* would not "serve the best

---

1959. *Id.*
1960. 324 S.E.2d at 884.
1961. *Id.* at 886.
1962. *Id.* at 881-82, 886.
1963. *Id.* at 885-86.
1964. *Alford v. Shaw*, 349 S.E.2d 41, 50 (N.C. 1986), *withdrawn to affirm and modify*, 358 S.E.2d 323 (N.C. 1987).

interests of all segments of the corporate community in North Carolina, including minority stockholders, majority stockholders, officers, directors and the corporate entity."[1965] The Supreme Court later withdrew this opinion after reconsidering the standard of judicial review to be applied to a special litigation committee recommendation (this aspect of the *Alford* decision is discussed later in this Chapter)[1966] but left intact its rejection of the *per se* rule adopted by the lower court.[1967] Termination of derivative litigation by special litigation committees in North Carolina now is governed by statute.[1968]

The approach adopted in *Miller* and by the lower court in *Alford* has been rejected by federal courts construing Illinois, Maryland and Massachusetts law in *Weiland v. Illinois Power Co.*,[1969] *Rosengarten v. Buckley*[1970] and *Houle v. Low*,[1971] respectively and by a state court in Minnesota in *Black v. NuAire, Inc.*[1972]

## 2. The Scope of Judicial Review—Auerbach Versus Zapata

Assuming the power to terminate does exist, the scope of judicial review of a special litigation committee's determination that derivative litigation will not serve the best interests of the corporation and therefore should be terminated becomes important. Two competing philosophies have developed. Under the first view, exemplified by the New York Court of Appeals' decision in *Auerbach v. Bennett*,[1973] disinterested directors can and should be trusted to decide whether to pursue derivative claims. Judicial review is limited to the issues of good faith, the independence of

---

1965. *Id.*

1966. *See* Chapter IV, Section C 2 d.

1967. *Alford v. Shaw*, 358 S.E.2d 323, 326 (N.C. 1987).

1968. *See* Chapter IV, Sections B 6 i and C 1 b.

1969. [1990-1991 Transfer Binder] Fed. Sec. L. Rep. (CCH) ¶ 95,747, at 98,591 (C.D. Ill. Sept. 17, 1990).

1970. 613 F. Supp. 1493, 1498-99 (D. Md. 1985).

1971. 556 N.E.2d 51, 54-57 (Mass. 1990).

1972. 426 N.W.2d 203, 210 n.3 (Minn. Ct. App. 1988).

1973. 47 N.Y.2d 619, 393 N.E.2d 994, 419 N.Y.S.2d 920 (1979).

the members of the committee and the sufficiency of the committee's investigation. Judicial review of the merits of the committee's decision is precluded.[1974]

The contrary view is exemplified by the Delaware Supreme Court's decision in *Zapata Corp. v. Maldonado.*[1975] *Zapata* provides for a two-step test in cases where demand is excused. The first step of this test requires an examination of the good faith, independence and thoroughness of the special litigation committee's investigation. The second step, which is discretionary and need not be reached, allows the court to exercise its own "independent business judgment" by reviewing the merits of the committee's decision.[1976]

While the standards of review applied by different courts "differ as to the degree of deference a court should afford to a special litigation committee's conclusions," the competing approaches "all require that the committee, upon whose recommendation the court is asked to base its dismissal, make a reasonable, good faith inquiry into the merits of the claims alleged by the shareholder(s)."[1977]

*a. The Auerbach Approach.* The New York Court of Appeals' decision in *Auerbach v. Bennett*[1978] bases its analysis upon the following basic principles underlying derivative litigation:

> Derivative claims against corporate directors belong to the corporation itself. As with other questions of corporate policy and management, the decision whether and to what extent to explore and prosecute such claims lies within the judgment and control of the corporation's board of directors. Necessarily such decision must be predicated on the weighing and balancing of a variety of disparate considerations to reach a considered conclusion as to what course of action or inaction

---

1974. *See* Chapter IV, Section C 2 a.

1975. 430 A.2d 779 (Del. 1981).

1976. *See* Chapter IV, Section C 2 b.

1977. *Ostrowski v. Avery*, 1996 Conn. Super. LEXIS 2557 at *11, 1996 WL 580981, at *4 (Conn. Super. Ct. Sept. 30, 1996), *rev'd on other grounds*, 703 A.2d 117 (Conn. 1997).

1978. 47 N.Y.2d 619, 393 N.E.2d 994, 419 N.Y.S.2d 920 (1979).

is best calculated to protect and advance the interests of the corporation. This is the essence of the responsibility and role of the board of directors, and courts may not intrude to interfere.[1979]

In accordance with these principles, the court limited judicial review of a special litigation committee decision by distinguishing between "the selection of procedures" by a committee consisting of disinterested directors and "the ultimate substantive decision" by the committee.[1980] Judicial review is allowed with respect to the "disinterested independence" of committee members and "the appropriateness and sufficiency of the investigative procedures chosen and pursued by the committee."[1981] "[T]he substantive aspects of a decision to terminate a shareholders' derivative action against defendant corporate directors made by a committee of disinterested directors appointed by the corporation's board of directors are beyond judicial inquiry under the business judgment doctrine."[1982]

The court explained that the substantive decision not to pursue a derivative action "falls squarely within the embrace of the business judgment doctrine" because it involves "the weighing and balancing of legal, ethical, commercial, promotional, public relations, fiscal and other factors familiar to the resolution of many if not most corporate problems."[1983] "To permit judicial probing of such issues," the court stated, "would be to emasculate the business judgment doctrine as applied to the actions and determinations of the special litigation committee."[1984] By contrast, the court continued, "courts are well equipped by long and continuing experience" to make decisions regarding the "methodologies and procedures best suited to the conduct of an investigation of facts and the

---

1979. *Id.* at 631, 393 N.E.2d at 1000-01, 419 N.Y.S.2d at 927, *quoted in part in Marx v. Akers*, 88 N.Y.2d 189, 194, 666 N.E.2d 1034, 1037, 644 N.Y.S.2d 121, 124 (1996).

1980. *Id.* at 633, 393 N.E.2d at 1002, 419 N.Y.S.2d at 928.

1981. *Id.* at 623-24, 393 N.E.2d at 996, 419 N.Y.S.2d at 922.

1982. *Id.* at 623, 393 N.E.2d at 996, 419 N.Y.S.2d at 922.

1983. *Id.* at 633-34, 393 N.E.2d at 1002, 419 N.Y.S.2d at 928.

1984. *Id.* at 634, 393 N.E.2d at 1002, 419 N.Y.S.2d at 928.

determination of legal liability."[1985] "[T]he determinations to be made in the adoption of procedures partake of none of the nuances or special perceptions . . . of business judgment or corporate activities or interests. The question is solely how appropriately to set about to gather the pertinent data."[1986]

The court cautioned that "[w]hile the court may properly inquire as to the adequacy and appropriateness of the committee's investigative procedures and methodologies, it may not under the guise of consideration of such factors trespass in the domain of business judgment."[1987] To the contrary, the court stated, "[w]hat has been uncovered and the relative weight accorded in evaluating and balancing the several factors and considerations are beyond the scope of judicial concern."[1988] The court added, however, that proof that "the investigation has been so restricted in scope, so shallow in execution, or otherwise so *pro forma* or halfhearted as to constitute a pretext or sham, consistent with the principles underlying the application of the business judgment doctrine, would raise questions of good faith or conceivably fraud which would never be shielded by that doctrine."[1989]

A federal court in New York in *Stoner v. Walsh*,[1990] a case discussed earlier in this Chapter that involved the refusal of a demand,[1991] described *Auerbach*'s limitation of judicial review to the decision-making directors' "disinterested independence" and the "appropriateness and sufficiency" of the committee's "investigative procedures"[1992] as "simply an application of the general business judgment rule to the particular situation of a board's decision to prevent shareholder litigation of a corporate cause of action."[1993]

---

1985. *Id*. at 634, 393 N.E.2d at 1002, 419 N.Y.S.2d at 929.

1986. *Id*.

1987. *Id*.

1988. *Id*. at 634, 393 N.E.2d at 1003, 419 N.Y.S.2d at 929.

1989. *Id*. at 634-35, 393 N.E.2d at 10-03, 419 N.Y.S.2d at 929

1990. 772 F. Supp. 790 (S.D.N.Y. 1991).

1991. *See* Chapter IV, Section B 6 g.

1992. 47 N.Y.2d at 623-24, 393 N.E.2d at 996, 419 N.Y.S.2d at 922.

1993. 772 F. Supp. at 800.

This rule, the court in *Stoner* stated, governs the conduct of either a board or a board committee "charged with wrongfully preventing shareholder litigation of a corporate cause of action, whether the purportedly wrongful action was termination of an existing suit, as alleged in *Auerbach*, or rejection of demand," as alleged in *Stoner*.[1994]

Applying the standard established in *Auerbach*, the court in *Auerbach* stated that "[t]he selection of appropriate investigative methods must always turn on the nature and characteristics of the particular subject being investigated" and found nothing in the record requiring a trial of any material issue of fact concerning "the sufficiency or appropriateness of the procedures chosen by this special litigation committee."[1995] The court explained that the committee "promptly engaged eminent special counsel to guide its deliberations and to advise it," reviewed the work that already had been completed by the corporation's audit committee, tested the "completeness, accuracy and thoroughness" of that work, interviewed the audit committee's counsel, reviewed transcripts of testimony by corporate officers and employees before the Securities and Exchange Commission, studied documents collected and prepared by the audit committee's counsel, interviewed directors found to have participated in any way in the questioned payments, and sent questionnaires to each of the corporation's nonmanagement directors.[1996] On the basis of this record, the court stated that "we do not find either insufficiency or infirmity as to the procedures and methodologies chosen and pursued by the special litigation committee."[1997] Nor, the court concluded, was there anything in the record raising a triable issue of fact concerning the good faith pur-

---

1994. *Id.*

1995. 47 N.Y.2d at 636, 393 N.E.2d at 1003, 419 N.Y.S.2d at 930.

1996. *Id.* at 635, 393 N.E.2d at 1003, 419 N.Y.S.2d at 929-30.

1997. 47 N.Y.2d at 635, 393 N.E.2d at 1003, 419 N.Y.S.2d at 929.

suit of the committee's investigation.[1998] Summary judgment therefore was granted in the corporation's favor.[1999]

The same result has been reached by federal courts applying the *Auerbach* standard in *Stoner v. Walsh*[2000] and *Levit v. Rowe.*[2001] As noted above, *Stoner*, unlike *Auerbach*, was a case where a demand was made and refused.[2002] *Levit*, like *Auerbach*, was a case where a special litigation committee moved to terminate litigation.[2003] An intermediate appellate court in New York, *Rosen v. Bernard*,[2004] affirmed a trial court's denial of a corporation's motion to dismiss pursuant to a special litigation committee decision on the ground—according to the trial court—that "two of the three members of the special litigation committee may not have been truly independent and the methods of investigation of the special litigation committee were 'somewhat suspect.'"[2005] The appellate court in *Rosen,* however, reversed the trial court's denial of the corporation's subsequent request for "a limited issue hearing" on these issues.[2006] The appellate court explained that "the issues of the independence of the special litigation committee and the methods of its investigation are potentially dispositive of the lawsuit, and a hearing of these issues should be held."[2007]

The *Auerbach* approach limiting judicial review of a special litigation committee decision to seek termination to the "disinterested independence" of the committee members and the "appropri-

---

1998. *Id.*

1999. *Id.* at 635-36, 393 N.E.2d at 1003, 419 N.Y.S.2d at 929-30.

2000. 772 F. Supp. 790 (S.D.N.Y. 1991).

2001. 1992 U.S. Dist. LEXIS 15036, 1992 WL 277997 (E.D. Pa. Sept. 30, 1992).

2002. 772 F. Supp. at 798-807; *see also* Chapter IV, Section B 6 g (discussing *Stoner*).

2003. 1992 U.S. Dist. LEXIS 15036, at *9-23, 1992 WL 277997, at *3-8.

2004. 108 A.D.2d 906, 485 N.Y.S.2d 791 (N.Y. App. Div. 2d Dep't 1985).

2005. *Id.* at 906, 485 N.Y.S.2d at 792.

2006. *Id.* at 906-07, 485 N.Y.S.2d at 792.

2007. *Id.* at 907, 485 N.Y.S.2d at 793.

ateness and sufficiency" of the committee's investigation has been followed by state courts in Alabama[2008] and Ohio[2009] and by federal courts construing the law of California,[2010] Michigan,[2011] Minnesota[2012] and Ohio.[2013] The North Carolina Supreme Court adopted the *Auerbach* approach in one case[2014] but reversed course and withdrew that opinion less than a year later.[2015] Two federal courts have reached different conclusions concerning whether Maryland courts would follow the *Auerbach* approach.[2016]

---

2008. *See Stallworth v. AmSouth Bank*, 1997 Ala. LEXIS 483, at *19, 1997 WL 778838, at *6 (Ala. Dec. 19, 1997); *Roberts v. Alabama Power Co.*, 404 So. 2d 629, 632, 636 (Ala. 1981).

2009. *See Miller v. Bargaheiser*, 591 N.E.2d 1339, 1343 (Ohio Ct. App. 1990).

2010. *See Gaines v. Haughton*, 645 F.2d 761, 770-72 (9th Cir. 1981), *cert. denied*, 454 U.S. 1145 (1982); *Lewis v. Anderson*, 615 F.2d 778, 782-83 (9th Cir. 1979), *cert. denied*, 449 U.S. 869 (1980).

2011. *See Genzer v. Cunningham*, 498 F. Supp. 682, 687-89 (E.D. Mich. 1980).

2012. *See Skoglund v. Brady*, 541 N.W.2d 17, 20 (Minn. Ct. App. 1995); *Black v. NuAire, Inc.*, 426 N.W.2d 203, 209-11 (Minn. Ct. App. 1988).

2013. *See Holmstrom v. Coastal Indus., Inc.*, 645 F. Supp. 963, 966, 972 (N.D. Ohio 1984); *see also In re General Tire & Rubber Co. Sec. Litig.*, 726 F.2d 1075, 1083 (6th Cir.) (construing Ohio law, the court found it unnecessary to choose between the *Auerbach* approach and the *Zapata* approach because the district court's acceptance of a special litigation committee's determination to settle a derivative suit was premised upon the more stringent *Zapata* approach), *cert. denied*, 469 U.S. 858 (1984).

2014. *See Alford v. Shaw*, 349 S.E.2d 41, 52, 56 (N.C. 1986), *withdrawn*, 358 S.E.2d 323 (N.C. 1987).

2015. *See Alford v. Shaw*, 358 S.E.2d 323, 326-27 (N.C. 1987) (adopting *Zapata* approach and expanding *Zapata* approach to govern not only cases where demand is excused but also cases where demand is required and is refused); *see also* Chapter IV, Section C 2 b (discussing *Alford*).

2016. *Compare Grossman v. Johnson*, 89 F.R.D. 656, 662-63 (D. Mass. 1981) (following *Auerbach*), *aff'd on other grounds*, 674 F.2d 115 (1st Cir.), *cert. denied*, 459 U.S. 838 (1982) *with Rosengarten v. Buckley*, 613 F. Supp. 1493, 1499-1500 (D. Md. 1985) (following *Zapata*).

As discussed above, statutes now have been enacted in Michigan and North Carolina.[2017]

*Miller v. Bargaheiser*,[2018] an Ohio decision that adopted the *Auerbach* approach, offers the following noteworthy description of the role of a special litigation committee and the role of the courts in reviewing a special litigation committee recommendation that a lawsuit should be terminated:

> [E]vidence of some slight misconduct or the appearance of an impropriety on the part of one or more of the named defendants does not preclude the committee from returning a recommendation to terminate the lawsuit and such a recommendation will not be viewed as a coverup or evidence of wrongdoing on the part of the committee.
>
> This is not a perfect world. To expect an SLC to inquire into the activities of the defendants named in a derivative action and find absolutely no evidence of misconduct or not even the appearance of impropriety is not realistic. Indeed there are few among us who never make a misstep, who never have a momentary lapse and then in hindsight realize that what was done was not entirely appropriate. However, it is not the job of this committee to sniff out every particle of misconduct attributable to these named defendants and submit all to the court and jury for final evaluation. The committee must determine what is in the best interests of the corporation and then recommend a course of action to the trial court for the disposition of the derivative action. If the committee determines that certain misconduct should be corrected by action within the corporation rather than in the public arena of the courtroom, then a recommendation to dismiss the lawsuit should be made and such action will not be seen as a cover-up or as evidence of an incomplete or a bad faith investigation.
>
> *       *       *
>
> The issue before the trial court was the reliability of the SLC report and recommendation. If the trial court finds the report to be reliable then as a matter of law summary judgment

---

2017. *See* Chapter IV, sections B 6 i and C 1 b.
2018. 591 N.E.2d 1339 (Ohio Ct. App. 1990).

should be granted for each of the named defendants. To be
sure, there are facts in dispute between the parties; however,
these facts are not material. What is material is the reliability
of the committee's report and recommendation. We have
already said that there is insufficient evidence to undermine
the committee report. That report recommends the termination of the derivative action, not with respect to some of the
defendants but as to all defendants. Thus, the court was correct to grant summary judgment in favor of all the individual
defendants as a matter of law.[2019]

The Pennsylvania Supreme Court in *Cuker v. Mikalauskas*,[2020] while not adopting *Auerbach* as the standard for cases
governed by Pennsylvania law, pointed to the same considerations
that underlie the *Auerbach* decision. The court reasoned as follows:

> Assuming that an independent board of directors may termi-
> nate shareholder derivative actions, what is needed is a pro-
> cedural mechanism for implementation and judicial review of
> the board's decision. Without considering the merits of the
> action, a court should determine the validity of the board's
> decision to terminate the litigation; if that decision was made
> in accordance with the appropriate standards, then the court
> should dismiss the derivative action prior to litigation on the
> merits.
>
> The business judgment rule should insulate officers and direc-
> tors from judicial intervention in the absence of fraud or self-
> dealing, if challenged decisions were within the scope of the
> directors' authority, if they exercised reasonable diligence,
> and if they honestly and rationally believed their decisions
> were in the best interests of the company. It is obvious that a
> court must examine the circumstances surrounding the deci-
> sions in order to determine if the conditions warrant appli-
> cation of the business judgment rule. If they do, the court
> will never proceed to an examination of the merits of the
> challenged decisions, for that is precisely what the business
> judgment rule prohibits. In order to make the business judg-
> ment rule meaningful, the preliminary examination should be
> limited and precise so as to minimize judicial involvement

---

2019. *Id.* at 1344-45.
2020. 692 A.2d 1042 (Pa. 1997).

when application of the business judgment rule is warranted.[2021]

The court in *Cuker* then adopted the rules recommended by Principles of Corporate Governance: Analysis and Recommendations—discussed elsewhere in this Chapter[2022]—and noted that "New York law parallels Pennsylvania law in many respects" but "does not set forth any procedures to govern the review of corporate decisions relating to derivative litigation" in the manner done in Principles of Corporate Governance.[2023] The court in *Cuker* expressly rejected the *Zapata Corp. v. Maldonado*[2024] approach used in Delaware, pursuant to which a court is permitted "in some cases ('demand excused' cases) to apply its own business judgment in the review process when deciding to honor the directors' decision to terminate derivative litigation."[2025] "In our view," the court in *Cuker* stated, "this is a defect which could eviscerate the business judgment rule and contradict a long line of Pennsylvania precedents."[2026]

   *b. The Zapata Approach.* In *Zapata Corp. v. Maldonado*,[2027] the Delaware Supreme Court adopted a less deferential approach than the *Auerbach v. Bennett*[2028] approach adopted in New York.[2029] The judicial scrutiny provided for by *Zapata* differentiates between (1) cases where demand upon the corporation's directors is required and refused and (2) cases where demand is excused or has been wrongfully refused, and applies only in the second category of cases—where demand is excused or has been wrongfully refused.[2030] As the Delaware Supreme Court accord-

---

2021. *Id.* at 1048.
2022. *See* Chapter IV, Sections B 6 j and C 2 i.
2023. *Cuker*, 692 A.2d at 1049.
2024. 430 A.2d 779 (Del. 1981).
2025. *Cuker*, 692 A.2d at 1049; *see also* Chapter IV, Section C 2 b (discussing *Zapata* approach).
2026. *Id.*
2027. 430 A.2d 779 (Del. 1981).
2028. 47 N.Y.2d 619, 393 N.E.2d 994, 419 N.Y.S.2d 920 (1979).
2029. *See* Chapter IV, Section C 2 a.
2030. *See, e.g., Spiegel v. Buntrock*, 571 A.2d 767, 778 (Del.
(continued...)

ingly stated in *Grimes v. Donald*,[2031] "[t]he use of a committee of the board formed to respond to a demand or to advise the board on its duty in responding to a demand is not the same as the SLC process contemplated by *Zapata*."[2032] "It is important that these discrete and quite different processes not be confused."[2033] Thus, where a shareholder can allege facts excusing demand, a special litigation committee's prior recommendation that an earlier shareholder demand in connection with the same transaction should be refused does not require dismissal of the second shareholder's claim because different standards govern the two claims.[2034]

Where demand is required and is refused, the board's decision that pursuit of litigation will not serve the best interests of the corporation is protected by the business judgment rule.[2035]

Where demand is excused because it would be futile (or has been wrongfully refused), *Zapata* sets forth a two-step test permitting, but not requiring, judicial examination of the merits of a special litigation committee's decision that pursuit of litigation will not serve the best interests of the corporation and the exercise of the court's "independent business judgment":

*Step One:* Under step one, the court reviews the "independence and good faith of the committee and the bases supporting its conclusions."[2036] Unlike review under the business judgment rule, there is no presumption in favor of the conduct of the directors serving on the special litigation committee. To the contrary, the corporation (acting through its special litigation committee) has the burden of proving the independence, good faith and reasonable-

---

2030. (...continued)

1990); *Aronson v. Lewis*, 473 A.2d 805, 813 (Del. 1984); *Zapata*, 430 A.2d at 784 & n.10.

    2031. 673 A.2d 1207 (Del. 1996).

    2032. *Id.* at 1216 n.13.

    2033. *Id.*

    2034. *Avacus Partners, L.P. v. Brian*, [1991 Transfer Binder] Fed. Sec. L. Rep. (CCH) ¶ 96,232, at 91,216 (Del. Ch. Oct. 24, 1990).

    2035. *See* Chapter IV, Sections B 6 c-j.

    2036. *Zapata*, 430 A.2d at 788.

ness of the committee's determination.[2037] If the corporation meets this burden, the court may "in its discretion" (1) grant the motion and dismiss the derivative action, or (2) proceed to step two of the test.[2038]

*Step Two:* Under step two, the court may "in its discretion" exercise its own "independent business judgment" concerning whether the action should be dismissed. Directors sitting on a special litigation committee, the court explained in *Zapata*, are passing judgment on fellow directors—often, indeed, the directors who designated them to serve as directors and committee members. Accordingly, "[t]he question naturally arises whether a 'there but for the grace of God go I' empathy might not play a role. And the further question arises whether inquiry as to independence, good faith and reasonable investigation is sufficient safeguard against abuse, perhaps subconscious abuse."[2039] *Zapata* thus "recognizes a special consideration when a derivative suit has been *properly* instituted, and thereafter the board, acting through a special committee of independent directors, seeks its dismissal. In that situation, where the board had already either wrongfully refused a demand to sue or was not in a position to exercise a binding judgment on that question, . . . 'some tribute must be paid to the fact that the lawsuit *was properly initiated.*'"[2040] In this setting, the court must "steer a middle course" between yielding "to the independent business judgment of a board committee" and yielding "to unbridled plaintiff stockholder control."[2041]

The *Zapata* court accordingly stated the following concerning the second step of the *Zapata* test:

---

2037. *Id.*

2038. *Id.* at 789.

2039. *Id.* at 787.

2040. *Spiegel v. Buntrock*, 1988 Del. Ch. LEXIS 149, at *7, 1988 WL 124324, at *3 (Del. Ch. Nov. 17, 1988) (quoting *Zapata*, 430 A.2d at 787 (emphasis added by *Spiegel* court), *aff'd*, 571 A.2d 767 (Del. 1990).

2041. *Zapata*, 430 A.2d at 788.

The second step is intended to thwart instances where corporate actions meet the criteria of step one, but the result does not appear to satisfy its spirit, or where corporate actions would simply prematurely terminate a stockholder grievance deserving of further consideration in the corporation's interest. The Court of Chancery of course must carefully consider and weigh how compelling the corporate interest in dismissal is when faced with a non-frivolous lawsuit. The Court of Chancery should, when appropriate, give special consideration to matters of law and public policy in addition to the corporation's best interests.[2042]

According to the *Zapata* court, the second step of the *Zapata* test envisions discretionary consideration not only of legal and public policy questions, but also ethical, commercial, promotional, public relations, employee relations and fiscal factors.[2043]

The *Zapata* court also stated that the context for the *Zapata* determination by the Court of Chancery is a "pretrial motion to dismiss" that includes "a thorough written record of the investigation and its findings and recommendations."[2044] The court explained that "[u]nder appropriate Court supervision, akin to proceedings on summary judgment, each side should have an opportunity to make a record on the motion."[2045] "[A]s to the limited issues presented by the motion . . . , the moving party should be prepared to meet the normal burden" imposed on a motion for summary judgment of showing that "there is no genuine issue as to any material fact and that the moving party is entitled to dismissal as a matter of law."[2046] The court added that "[w]e do not foreclose a discretionary trial of factual issues"—an issue "not presented in this appeal."[2047] The case was remanded to the Court of Chancery for further proceedings, but the litigation was resolved in related

---

2042. *Id.* at 789.
2043. *Id.* at 788.
2044. *Id.*
2045. *Id.*
2046. *Id.*
2047. *Id.* at 788 n.15.

actions in New York and Texas prior to a decision in the Court of Chancery.[2048]

The Delaware Court of Chancery in *Kaplan v. Wyatt*[2049]—in an analysis labeled "excellent" and "accurate" by the Delaware Supreme Court[2050]—reduced *Zapata*'s "general guidelines" to the following "step-by-step procedure."[2051] The references to Rules 12(b), 23.1, 41(a)(2) and 56 are to Delaware Court of Chancery Rules 12(b), 23.1, 41(a)(2) and 56, which are substantively the same as Federal Rules of Civil Procedure 12(b), 23.1, 41(a)(2) and 56.[2052]

> [W]here a derivative action is brought pursuant to Rule 23.1 without a demand first being made upon the board of directors because of reasons set forth in the complaint, the board, if it so desires, may appoint an independent committee to investigate the allegations of wrongdoing against the corporation as contained in the complaint.
>
> After a thorough and objective investigation, the independent committee appointed by the board of directors—otherwise referred to herein as the Special Litigation Committee—may cause the corporation to file a pretrial motion to dismiss a derivative suit brought on the corporation's behalf.
>
> The basis for the motion is the best interests of the corporation, as determined by the independent Special Litigation Committee.

---

2048. *See Maher v. Zapata Corp.*, 714 F.2d 436 (5th Cir. 1983) (summarizing the Delaware, New York and Texas litigations and upholding settlement of Texas action); *Maldonado v. Flynn*, 573 F. Supp. 684, 686 (S.D.N.Y. 1983) (dismissing New York litigation on res judicata grounds due to Texas settlement but making "a further finding based upon my independent business judgement that it is in the best interest of the Zapata Corporation that the action be dismissed").

2049. 484 A.2d 501 (Del. Ch. 1984), *aff'd*, 499 A.2d 1184 (Del. 1985).

2050. *Kaplan v. Wyatt*, 499 A.2d 1184 (Del. 1985).

2051. 484 A.2d at 506.

2052. *See* Del. Ch. R. 12(b), 23.1, 41(a)(2), 56; Fed. R. Civ. P. 12(b), 23.1, 41(a)(2), 56.

The motion must be supported by a thorough written record. The written record must speak to three separate elements, namely, (1) the investigation made by the Committee; (2) the findings of the Committee; and (3) the recommendation of the Committee.

. . . [T]he motion itself is neither a motion to dismiss under Rule 12(b), nor is it a motion for summary judgment pursuant to Rule 56. This is because it is not addressed to the adequacy of the cause of action alleged in the complaint, on the one hand, nor, on the other, is it addressed to the merits of the issues joined by the pleadings. Rather, the motion is a hybrid one, derived by analogy to a motion to dismiss a derivative suit based upon a voluntary settlement reached between the parties and to a motion brought pursuant to Rule 41(a)(2) whereby a plaintiff unilaterally seeks a voluntary dismissal of the complaint subsequent to the filing of an answer by the defendant. As such, it is addressed necessarily to the reasonableness of dismissing the complaint prior to trial without any concession of liability on the part of the defendants and without adjudicating the merits of the cause of action itself.

Despite the fact, however, that the motion is not strictly one for summary judgment pursuant to Rule 56, *Zapata* says that it is to be handled procedurally in a manner akin to proceedings on summary judgment in two separate respects:

(1) Each side (and as to the motion this means the plaintiff on the one hand and the corporation through its representative, the Special Litigation Committee—and not the other defendants—on the other) shall have an opportunity to make a record on the motion. (Presumably, this means by supplementing the pleadings with affidavits and/or verified documents, and, as hereafter noted, by such other discovery as may be permitted by the Court).

(2) As to the limited issues presented by the motion, the corporation (through the Committee), as the moving party, has the normal burden imposed on a moving party under a Rule 56 motion of demonstrating that there is no genuine issue as to any material fact and that the corporation is entitled to dismiss the complaint as a matter of law.

\* \* \*

The issues to be considered by the Court on the motion are
. . . limited and they are to be addressed by the Court in a
two-step analysis. In order, the issues for determination are:

(1)  The independence and good faith of the Committee in
     making its investigation plus the reasonableness of the
     bases relied upon by the Committee in concluding and
     recommending that the cause of action on behalf of the
     corporation be dismissed.

(2)  The interests of the corporation in having the litigation
     continued by one of its shareholders on its behalf
     despite the fact that the Committee has proven to the
     satisfaction of the Court that it was independent and
     that its investigation and recommendation was made in
     good faith and supported by a reasonable basis in fact
     and law.

With regard to the first step, the burden is on the Corporation to prove the independence of the Special Litigation Committee and to prove also that it conducted a reasonable investigation of the matters alleged in the complaint in good faith.
For purposes of the motion the Committee is entitled to no
presumption of independence, good faith and reasonableness.

If, after the motion has been argued or submitted for decision, the Court

(1)  is satisfied on the record presented by the motion that
     there is a genuine issue as to one or more material
     facts, or

(2)  determines on the undisputed material facts that the
     Committee is not independent, or

(3)  determines on the undisputed material facts that the
     Committee has not shown reasonable bases for its con-
     clusions, or

(4)  is not satisfied on the undisputed material facts that the
     Committee has acted in good faith, or

(5)  is satisfied for other reasons relating to the investiga-
     tive process engaged in by the Committee that it has
     failed to carry its burden of proving its independence,
     good faith and a reasonable basis for its recommenda-
     tion,

then the Court shall deny the motion for such reason and need go no farther, the result being that the shareholder plaintiff may resume immediate control of the litigation with a view toward prosecuting it to a conclusion regardless of the position taken by the special investigating committee appointed by the corporation's board of directors.

If, however, after the motion has been argued or submitted for decision, the Court

(1)    is satisfied that there is no genuine issue as to any material fact presented by the record made on the motion, *and*

(2)    is further satisfied on the undisputed facts of record pertaining to the motion that the Committee is independent of the corporation's board of directors, that it has made a reasonable investigation and has shown reasonable bases for its findings and recommendations, and that they were made in good faith,

then the Court may do either of two things, namely, (1) grant the motion, order a dismissal of the suit and end the litigation, or (2) *in its discretion*, proceed to the second-step analysis before rendering a decision on the motion. . . .

In proceeding to this discretionary, second-step analysis, it is important to note two things. Again, as a precondition, the Court must be satisfied from the record presented by the motion that the Committee was, in fact independent, that it acted in good faith in making its investigation, that it conducted a reasonable investigation under the circumstances, and that it had a reasonable basis for making its recommendation that the derivative action be dismissed. Second, the Court must proceed on the premise that the cause of action alleged on behalf of the corporation in the derivative complaint is a "legitimate" one, i.e., presumably one that states on its face a legally cognizable wrong against the corporation which, once the proof is in, may well result in a judgment in favor of the corporation. . . .

The discretionary second-step analysis thus contemplates the balancing of two potentially off-setting premises, namely, the good faith and reasonably supported view of an independent Committee, as factually established, that it would be in the best interests of the corporation and its shareholders to dismiss the derivative action without asking the Court to address the merits of the matter, versus a theoretically valid cause of action which may well result in a recovery on behalf of the corporation if it is permitted to go to trial or final disposition on the merits.

In applying its own independent business judgment to this second-step analysis, should the Court choose in its discretion to make one, it is necessary that the Court, in addition to considering matters of law and public policy, consider also such ethical, commercial, promotional, public relations, employee relations and fiscal factors as may be involved in a given situation.

If the Court is satisfied as a result of its own independent, second-step analysis that the derivative suit should go forward despite the good faith and reasonably supported recommendation by the Special Litigation Committee that it be dismissed, then, again, the motion to dismiss initiated on behalf of the corporation by the independent Committee will be denied and immediate active control of the suit will be returned to the plaintiff shareholder.

Finally, if the Court is itself satisfied after this second-step analysis that it is in the best interests of the corporation to dismiss the suit, as recommended by the Special Litigation Committee, it may grant the motion and do so, subject to such equitable terms or conditions as the Court may find to be appropriate as a result of its second-step analysis.[2053]

---

2053. 484 A.2d at 506-09; *see also Johnson v. Hui*, 811 F. Supp. 479, 485 (N.D. Cal. 1991) (noting that on a motion for summary judgment under Federal Rule of Civil Procedure 56 the court "does not make determinations of credibility or weigh conflicting evidence," but "determinations of credibility are essential to the first step of a *Zapata* review, which requires the Court to consider the biases, interests, independence, and good faith" of the committee, and the court "must weigh conflicting evidence to conduct the discretionary second step of a *Zapata* review, which requires the Court to apply its own independent business judgment in light of the entire evidentiary record"); *Katell v. Morgan Stanley Group, Inc.*, [1995 Transfer Binder] Fed. Sec. L. Rep. (CCH) ¶ 98,861, at 93,169 (Del. Ch. June 15, 1995) ("In evaluating the Special Committee under the *Zapata* standard, I employ a standard akin to a motion for summary judgment"); *id.* at 93,173 (special committee must "show that Plain-

(continued...)

The Delaware Court of Chancery's decision in *Carlton Investments v. TLC Beatrice International Holdings, Inc.*[2054] described
the second step of *Zapata* as "difficult to rationalize in principle."[2055] The court in *TLC Beatrice* stated that the second step
"must have been designed to offer protection for cases in which,
while the court could not consciously determine on the first leg of
the analysis that there was no want of independence or good faith,
it nevertheless 'felt' that the result reached was 'irrational' or 'egregious' or some other such extreme word."[2056] The court stated its
view that "[t]he idea suggested in *Zapata* that the court may—for
reasons of public policy—require the board to continue a litigation
even though an independent committee determined in good faith
and on appropriate information that a proposed settlement is advantageous to the corporation, is difficult to understand."[2057] The
court asked "on what basis may a court legitimately impose the cost
and risk of litigation on a party in order to achieve only a perceived
public benefit?," and answered that "[i]n other contexts the constitution explicitly protects against such exactions (i.e., takings clause
of U.S. constitution)."[2058]

An article published shortly after *Zapata* was decided offered
the views of one commentator—who now is the Chief Justice of the
Delaware Supreme Court—concerning the second step of *Zapata*:

> The adjective *business* used as a modifier to describe the
> court's judgment imparts a direction to the court to exercise
> discretion in evaluating all factors, including the impact on
> the corporation's business as well as the merits of the under-

---

2053. (...continued)
tiffs do not dispute the existence of information or evidence relied on by
the Special Committee" but need not "show that the parties do not dispute
material facts regarding Plaintiffs' allegations").
    2054. 1997 Del. Ch. LEXIS 86, 1997 WL 305829 (Del. Ch. May
30, 1997).
    2055. 1997 Del. Ch. LEXIS 86, at *7, 1997 WL 305829, at *2.
    2056. *Id.*
    2057. 1997 Del. Ch. LEXIS 86, at *7 n.4, 1997 WL 305829, at *2
n.4.
    2058. *Id.*

lying cause of action. Presumably, the committee will have made those judgments. The crucial question is how much deference the court will pay to the committee's determination. In the settlement context the court weighs the value of the cause of action and the probable recovery against the downside to the corporation—expense, distraction, uncertainty, and other business questions. Applying the same analysis in the termination context, the court should decide whether or not the committee acted reasonably in terminating. This scope of judicial review is consistent with the observation by some scholars that the *Zapata* court may have intended only a half-step requiring the court of chancery to invoke its "independent discretion to analyze the reasonableness of the business judgment reached by the independent board committee (as opposed to superimposing its own business judgment)."[2059]

The *Zapata* approach has been followed by federal courts construing Connecticut,[2060] Georgia,[2061] Illinois[2062] and Virginia[2063] law. Two federal courts have reached different conclusions concerning whether Maryland courts would follow the *Zapata* approach.[2064] The Fifth and Sixth Circuits have found it unneces-

---

2059. Veasey, *Seeking a Safe Harbor from Judicial Scrutiny of Directors' Business Decisions—An Analytical Framework for Litigation Strategy and Counselling Directors*, 37 Bus. Law. 1247, 1267-68 (1982) (footnotes omitted) (quoting Hinsey & Dreizen, *Delaware Court Addresses Business Judgment Rule*, Legal Times of Washington, June 8, 1981, at 15).

2060. *See Joy v. North*, 692 F.2d 880, 891 (2d Cir. 1982), *cert. denied*, 460 U.S. 1051 (1983).

2061. *See Peller v. Southern Co.*, 911 F.2d 1532, 1536, 1538 (11th Cir. 1990).

2062. *See Weiland v. Illinois Power Co.*, [1990-1991 Transfer Binder] Fed. Sec. L. Rep. (CCH) ¶ 95,747, at 98,589-90 (C.D. Ill. Sept. 17, 1990).

2063. *Abella v. Universal Leaf Tobacco Co.*, 546 F. Supp. 795, 797-800 (E.D. Va. 1982), *reconsidering and rev'g* 495 F. Supp. 713 (E.D. Va. 1980).

2064. *Compare Grossman v. Johnson*, 89 F.R.D. 656, 662-63 (D. Mass. 1981) (following *Auerbach*), *aff'd on other grounds*, 674 F.2d 115 (1st Cir.), *cert. denied*, 459 U.S. 838 (1982) *with Rosengarten v. Buckley*, 613 F. Supp. 1493, 1499-1500 (D. Md. 1985) (following *Zapata*).

sary to decide whether courts in Colorado and Massachusetts, respectively, would adopt the *Auerbach* or *Zapata* approach.[2065] The Sixth Circuit reached this same conclusion with respect to Ohio law,[2066] but an Ohio court later adopted the *Auerbach* approach.[2067] As discussed above, statutes now have been enacted in Connecticut, Georgia and Virginia.[2068]

    *c. Applications of Zapata. Kaplan v. Wyatt*[2069]—the first case in Delaware to reach the point of a judicial decision on a special litigation committee motion to terminate pursuant to the principles announced in *Zapata Corp. v. Maldonado*[2070]—involved allegations that Oscar S. Wyatt, Jr., the chairman of the board and chief executive officer of Coastal Corporation, (1) "interpositioned" himself in the oil spot market to profit personally from corporate opportunities, (2) wrongfully caused Coastal to enter into a sale and leaseback transaction on unfair terms with an entity controlled by Wyatt's son, and (3) received excessive compensation by leasing his personal airplane to Coastal.[2071] A special litigation

---

    2065. *See Bach v. National W. Life Ins. Co.*, 810 F.2d 509, 512-14 (5th Cir. 1987) (construing Colorado law, the court concluded that it was unnecessary to choose between *Auerbach* and *Zapata* because demand was not excused and thus a Delaware court would not apply *Zapata*); *Hasan v. CleveTrust Realty Investors*, 729 F.2d 372, 375-80 (6th Cir. 1984) (construing Massachusetts law, the court concluded that the district court's acceptance of a special litigation committee recommendation was erroneous under both *Auerbach* and *Zapata*).

    2066. *See In re General Tire & Rubber Co. Sec. Litig.*, 726 F.2d 1075, 1083 (6th Cir.), *cert. denied*, 469 U.S. 858 (1984) (finding it unnecessary to choose between *Auerbach* and *Zapata* because the district court's acceptance of a special litigation committee's determination to settle a derivative suit was premised upon the more stringent *Zapata* approach).

    2067. *See Miller v. Bargaheiser*, 591 N.E.2d 1339, 1343 (Ohio Ct. App. 1990); *see also* Chapter IV, Section C 2 a (discussing *Bargaheiser*).

    2068. *See* Chapter IV, Sections B 6 i and C 1 b.

    2069. 499 A.2d 1184 (Del. 1985).

    2070. 430 A.2d 779 (Del. 1981).

    2071. 499 A.2d at 1186-88.

committee was created, and following an investigation the committee moved to terminate the litigation.[2072]

With respect to the first step of the *Zapata* test, the Delaware Supreme Court held that the committee operated independently of both Wyatt and Coastal's board. The court reached this determination notwithstanding challenges to the committee's composition (discussed later in this Chapter),[2073] the scheduling of committee interviews by representatives of the corporation's management and the presence of the corporation's in-house counsel at these interviews.[2074] The court acknowledged that these practices are "not recommended" but concluded that they were "not fatal" because the plaintiff had failed to present evidence demonstrating that these practices "influenced those being interviewed, altered the outcome of the investigation, or impaired the independence of the Committee in making its report."[2075]

The court also found that the committee acted in good faith and that the committee's investigation adequately supported its recommendation. The court rejected the plaintiff's reliance upon the following "allegations and innuendos"[2076]:

- the committee's counsel had been held liable for a portion of a $50 million recovery in an earlier, unrelated class action brought by the attorneys representing the plaintiff in the case under consideration by the committee (the court found that the allegation that the committee's counsel "must be hostile" to the plaintiff as a result of the outcome of that prior action was "without merit");[2077]

- the committee had destroyed handwritten notes taken during the course of its interviews (the court observed that the destruction of notes is routinely engaged in by law

---

2072. *Id.* at 1186, 1188.

2073. *Id.* at 1188-89; *see also* Chapter IV, Section C 2 e (discussing this aspect of *Kaplan* decision).

2074. *Id.* at 1190.

2075. *Id.*

2076. *Id.*

2077. *Id.*

enforcement agencies, and has been sanctioned by the courts);[2078] and

- the committee, once it had determined that Wyatt had purposely remained out of negotiations involving one of the challenged transactions, focused its investigation on the fairness of that transaction rather than the family and business relationships between the various participants in the transaction (the court concluded that in light of the committee's finding regarding Wyatt's lack of participation in the negotiations, "it was unnecessary . . . to examine more fully the relationships between the parties to the transaction").[2079]

With respect to the second step of the *Zapata* test, the Delaware Supreme Court affirmed the Court of Chancery's conclusion that the facts in this case made it unnecessary to proceed to the discretionary second-step analysis because the dismissal of the action "does not disturb the spirit of *Zapata*."[2080] The Court of Chancery had noted the plaintiff's failure, with regard to the misappropriation of corporate opportunities allegations, to provide "any indication—let alone any evidence—of any specific transaction in which Wyatt personally 'skimmed' anything rightfully belonging to Coastal" despite requests by the committee for such information.[2081] "In view of this status of affairs," the Court of Chancery stated, "I fail to see how I could reasonably conclude that the . . . grievance . . . is deserving of further consideration in the corporation's interest."[2082]

A similar result was reached in *Spiegel v. Buntrock*,[2083] a case in which the Delaware Court of Chancery held that demand

---

2078. *Id.*

2079. *Id.* at 1191.

2080. *Id.* at 1191-92.

2081. *Kaplan v. Wyatt*, 484 A.2d 501, 521 (Del. Ch. 1984), *aff'd*, 499 A.2d 1184 (Del. 1985).

2082. *Id.*

2083. 1988 Del. Ch. LEXIS 149, 1988 WL 124324 (Del. Ch. Nov. 17, 1988), *aff'd*, 571 A.2d 767 (Del. 1990).

was not excused either by the facts pled in the complaint regarding the challenged transaction[2084] or by the board's appointment of a special litigation committee having full authority to act on behalf of the board in connection with the demand.[2085] The court accordingly approved the committee's determination to seek dismissal of the action pursuant to a business judgment rule analysis.[2086] As an alternative holding, however, the court added the following:

> [W]hile I would not tend to share the view of the special committee—that the chances of ultimate success on these claims, if litigated, is utterly bleak—I do see, based upon their investigation, substantial difficulties with respect to the claims. However, that different professional view would not lead me to conclude that the present motion should be denied, even were I of the view that the *Zapata* form of judicial review applied to a matter of this type. Thus, were I to be required to pass upon the reasonableness or fairness of the decision not to sue, I could not find it to be unreasonable considering all of the circumstances.[2087]

The Delaware Supreme Court affirmed the Court of Chancery's decision in *Spiegel* without addressing this alternative holding.[2088]

The Delaware Court of Chancery in *Katell v. Morgan Stanley Group, Inc.*[2089] expressed a similar view in a case involving a special litigation committee formed by a limited partnership pursuant to the governing partnership agreement. The court stated that it would "not linger over all the details criticized by Plaintiffs" but would base its decision "on my overall impression" of the committee's good faith and the reasonableness of its investigation.[2090]

---

2084. 1988 Del. Ch. LEXIS 149, at *11-12, 1988 WL 124324, at *4.

2085. 1988 Del. Ch. LEXIS 149, at *8-10, 1988 WL 124324, at *3; *see also* Chapter IV, Section B 4 h (i) (discussing this aspect of the *Spiegel* decision).

2086. 1988 Del. Ch. LEXIS 149, at *12, 1988 WL 124324, at *4.

2087. 1988 Del. Ch. LEXIS 149, at *13, 1988 WL 124324, at *4.

2088. *Spiegel v. Buntrock*, 571 A.2d 767 (Del. 1990).

2089. [1995 Transfer Binder] Fed. Sec. L. Rep. (CCH) ¶ 98,861 (Del. Ch. June 15, 1995).

2090. *Id*. at 93,171.

The court added that "[i]n reviewing the Special Committee's conclusions, the Court does not take an independent look at the merits" of a lawsuit but must determine only whether the special committee's "consideration of the merits of the claims was reasonable."[2091] The court concluded that "I decline to undertake an independent review of the merits of Plaintiffs' claims" pursuant to the discretionary second step of *Zapata* because "I am satisfied that the Special Committee's decision to dismiss this lawsuit is the product of the procedure envisioned by the Supreme Court in *Zapata*."[2092]

The Delaware Court of Chancery's decision in *Carlton Investments v. TLC Beatrice International Holdings, Inc.*[2093] arose in the context of a motion seeking approval of a settlement of a derivative action proposed by a special litigation committee. The case involved allegations by Carlton Investments, "a very substantial stockholder" of TLC Beatrice International Holdings, Inc., that present and past directors of TLC Beatrice had breached their fiduciary duties by approving an approximately $19.5 million compensation package for the corporation's former chief executive officer, Reginald F. Lewis, who at the time of the court's decision was deceased.[2094] After more than a year of motion practice and extensive discovery in the case, TLC's Beatrice added two new directors to the board, and formed a special litigation committee consisting of these two new directors.[2095]

The committee conducted a five month investigation and was assisted in this investigation by counsel, an executive compensation expert and accountants.[2096] The committee and its counsel began by determining that Carlton had eleven principal claims and then met with representatives of Carlton, the Lewis estate and the corpo-

---

2091. *Id.* at 93,173.

2092. *Id.* at 93,174.

2093. 1997 Del. Ch. LEXIS 86, 1997 WL 305829 (Del. Ch. May 30, 1997).

2094. 1997 Del. Ch. LEXIS 86, at *2-3, 1997 WL 305829, at *1.

2095. 1997 Del. Ch. LEXIS 86, at *3-4, 26-27, 1997 WL 305829, at *1, 6.

2096. 1997 Del. Ch. LEXIS 86, at *27, 1997 WL 305829, at *6.

ration to confirm that all claims had been identified and to ensure that the committee understood the parties' positions concerning these claims.[2097] The committee and its counsel then "determined the applicable legal standards" and conducted "an intensive factual investigation regarding the validity and probability of recovery in litigation for each claim."[2098]

With respect to the applicable legal standards, the court found that the committee and its counsel "comprehensively researched the appropriate legal tests and diligently applied them to the facts."[2099] With respect to the committee's factual investigation, the court found that "it appears to have been comprehensive as well": either the committee or its counsel reviewed 100,000 pages of documents that had been produced in the litigation (plus documents in the corporation's possession that were privileged or protected by the work product doctrine), attended or reviewed the transcripts of depositions of 59 witnesses who testified for a total of 77 days, interviewed 23 witnesses, obtained expert analyses concerning compensation and expenses reimbursement issues, and participated in meetings with each other, Carlton and most of the directors named as defendants in the case.[2100]

The committee reached conclusions concerning the validity and settlement value of each of the eleven claims and determined that the eleven claims had a total settlement value of $12,450,000. The committee then (1) increased this amount to $14,932,000 to reflect an 8 percent annual rate of interest to be paid for the four year period that had passed since the disputed compensation had been paid and (2) decreased this amount by $2 million to reflect litigation expenses that the committee estimated the corporation would save as a result of the settlement.[2101] The committee then met with representatives of Carlton and the defendants in the case

---

2097. *Id.*

2098. 1997 Del. Ch. LEXIS 86, at *31, 1997 WL 305829, at *7.

2099. *Id.*

2100. 1997 Del. Ch. LEXIS 86, at *32 & nn. 36, 37, 1997 WL 305829, at *8 & nn. 36, 37.

2101. 1997 Del. Ch. LEXIS 86, at *39, 1997 WL 305829, at *9.

and negotiated a settlement with defendants.[2102] During those negotiations, the committee refused requests by the estate that the amount sought by the committee be lowered.[2103] The committee did agree, however, to the estate's insistence that payments could be spread over a seven year period (with a sufficient number of shares pledged to cover the full value of the settlement).[2104] This term was insisted upon because the Lewis family did not want to lose control over the corporation and the estate's assets other than the corporation's stock were insufficient to fund the settlement.[2105]

Carlton opposed the settlement. Because the settlement had been negotiated by a special litigation committee, the court utilized the *Zapata* approach to assess the fairness and reasonableness of the settlement.[2106]

The court began with the first step of the *Zapata* test—the requirement that "the court must analyze the 'independence and good faith of the committee and the bases supporting its conclusions.'"[2107] The court concluded that the committee and its counsel had "proceeded in good faith throughout its investigation and negotiation of the proposed settlement," that the committee's conclusions, "which formed the basis for the amount of the proposed settlement, were well informed by the existing record," and that the proposed settlement fell "within a range of reasonable solutions to the problem presented."[2108]

---

2102. 1997 Del. Ch. LEXIS 86, at *33-34, 39-40, 1997 WL 305829, at *8.

2103. 1997 Del. Ch. LEXIS 86, at *39, 1997 WL 305829, at *9.

2104. 1997 Del. Ch. LEXIS 86, at *40-41, 46, 1997 WL 305829, at *10.

2105. 1997 Del. Ch. LEXIS 86, at 40, 46, 1997 WL 305829, at *10, 11.

2106. 1997 Del. Ch. LEXIS 86, at *5, 1997 WL 305829, at *2; *see also* Chapter IV, Section A 7 (discussing standard governing judicial review of settlements of derivative actions).

2107. 1997 Del. Ch. LEXIS 86, at *5-6, 1997 WL 305829, at *2 (quoting *Zapata*, 430 A.2d at 788).

2108. 1997 Del. Ch. LEXIS 86, at *6-7, 1997 WL 305829, at *2.

The court rejected a claim by Carlton that the committee and its counsel were not independent because, according to Carlton, the committee had been "hand-picked" by the Lewis family "in an attempt to engineer a settlement" that would permit the family "to maintain control of the company."[2109] The court also rejected a claim that the committee "did not conduct a reasonable investigation" due to an alleged "over-reliance on the research and conclusions of counsel."[2110] These portions of the court's decision are discussed later in this Chapter.[2111]

The court rejected a claim that the committee, even if independent, did not seek to maximize TLC Beatrice's recovery in the proposed settlement. According to Carlton, "by seeking a settlement that would be fair to all parties, the SLC could not fulfill its obligation to maximize value for the company and its shareholders."[2112] The court explained that a special litigation committee "is not required to attempt to maximize returns from the lawsuit."[2113] To the contrary, "[t]he whole point of recognizing the board's authority and responsibility in this context is to allow the board's judgment concerning what is in the long-run best interest of the corporation to be acted upon," and this "may not be the same as maximizing the return from the lawsuit."[2114] Special litigation committees thus "can legitimately sacrifice present compensation in the settlement if its good faith, informed judgment indicates to it that that course is best for the corporation."[2115] The court also rejected objections by Carlton (1) to the committee's deduction of $2 million from the committee's valuation of the case to reflect litigation expenses saved as a result of the settlement and (2) to the committee's agreement to accept delayed payment terms. The court explained that "those decisions were but part of a complex of nego-

---

2109. 1997 Del. Ch. LEXIS 86, at *43, 1997 WL 305829, at *11.

2110. 1997 Del. Ch. LEXIS 86, at *46, 1997 WL 305829, at *12.

2111. *See* Chapter IV, Sections C 2 e & h.

2112. 1997 Del. Ch. LEXIS 86, at *44-45, 1997 WL 305829, at *11.

2113. 1997 Del. Ch. LEXIS 86, at *45, 1997 WL 305829, at *11.

2114. *Id.*

2115. *Id.*

tiating decisions that resulted in the proposed 'deal.'"[2116] The court stated that "[i]t is the deal itself that the court must evaluate for fairness and reasonableness, not each part of it."[2117]

The court then stated that "[a]lthough the merits of Carlton's claims are not to be adjudicated on a motion to approve a proposed settlement, the second prong of the *Zapata* test requires that this court exercise its own business judgment with respect to the reasonableness of the settlement."[2118] Against this backdrop, the court reviewed the "four areas" of the special litigation committee's conclusions concerning the adequacy of the proposed settlement that "appeared most susceptible to possible challenge."[2119] On the basis of this review, the court "determined in my own business judgment that the SLC's investigation and conclusions concerning the proper settlement value for the compensation claim fell within a range which reasonable minds might accept."[2120] The court stated that "[a]lthough the SLC's investigation and conclusions are not free from criticism, the SLC's good faith efforts achieved a settlement which I believe can reasonably be thought as fair, and adequate, recovery for the company."[2121]

The court concluded as follows:

> [T]o the extent I am required by the second step of *Zapata*, uncomfortably, to exercise some form of independent judgment concerning the merits of the settlement, I cannot conclude that it is badly off the mark. It is true that in some respects the claims that Carlton asserts on behalf of TLC Beatrice appear strong. But the settlement proposed offers substantial consideration for their release. As to the conceptually difficult second step of the *Zapata* technique, it is difficult to rationalize in principle; but it must have been

---

2116. 1997 Del. Ch. LEXIS 86, at *45, 1997 WL 305829, at *11.
2117. 1997 Del. Ch. LEXIS 86, at *45-46, 1997 WL 305829, at *11.
2118. 1997 Del. Ch. LEXIS 86, at *49, 1997 WL 305829, at *13.
2119. 1997 Del. Ch. LEXIS 86, at *48, 1997 WL 305829, at *12.
2120. 1997 Del. Ch. LEXIS 86, at *68, 1997 WL 305829, at *19.
2121. 1997 Del. Ch. LEXIS 86, at *68-69, 1997 WL 305829, at *19.

designed to offer protection for cases in which, while the court could not consciously determine on the first leg of the analysis that there was no want of independence or good faith, it nevertheless "felt" that the result reached was "irrational" or "egregious" or some other such extreme word. . . . But if I am directed to exercise my own "business judgment" by the second step of *Zapata*, I must conclude that this settlement represents one reasonable compromise of the claims asserted.[2122]

\*            \*            \*

This settlement process and result, although not perfect, is in my opinion an example of a fair and reasonable settlement achieved by an independent SLC with the assistance of experienced counsel. While reasonable minds might differ over any number of decisions (and I would) I conclude that the result as a whole is reasonable and the product of independent, informed action of directors acting in good faith. Therefore, I will approve the proposed settlement.[2123]

Several cases decided outside of Delaware by federal courts construing Delaware law also are worthy of note.

*In re Oracle Securities Litigation,*[2124] a decision by a federal court in California construing Delaware law, involved a determination by a committee of disinterested directors appointed to consider whether the corporation should accept a proposed settlement of a derivative litigation pursuant to terms agreed upon by the plaintiffs and defendants in the action.[2125] *Oracle* thus differs from *TLC Beatrice* because the committee in *Oracle* was formed only after the parties had agreed to a settlement of the litigation and only for the purpose of assessing the settlement. The court rejected the committee's recommendation that the settlement should be accepted. The court based its determination upon the fact that the committee was represented by the corporation's general counsel.

---

2122. 1997 Del. Ch. LEXIS 86, at *7-8, 1997 WL 305829, at *2.

2123. 1997 Del. Ch. LEXIS 86, at *71-72, 1997 WL 305829, at *20.

2124. 829 F. Supp. 1176 (N.D. Cal. 1993), *subsequent proceedings*, 852 F. Supp. 1437 (N.D. Cal. 1994).

2125. *Id.* at 1186-87.

According to the court, "in-house attorneys are inevitably subservient" to the interests of directors and officers, and in this case directors and officers were named as defendants in the litigation that the committee was recommending should be settled.[2126] The court directed the corporation to "retain independent counsel having no prior relationship with the corporation or the individual defendants."[2127] At that point, the court stated, "the corporation would seem to have three options for resolution of the derivative suit: settlement, termination, or trial.[2128] "A final decision on these issues," the court also stated, "depends in large part on the business judgment of the independent directors, after they have persuaded the court that they carried out a good faith investigation into the merits of the derivative action."[2129]

A new committee was formed and the committee retained independent counsel. This new committee then concluded in a 67 page report that settlement of the action pursuant to the agreed upon terms would serve the best interests of the corporation.[2130] This time, the court concluded that the committee's conclusions were "well reasoned and supported by the record" and "therefore satisfy the business judgment standard."[2131]

The Eleventh Circuit's decision in *Peller v. Southern Co.*[2132] involved Southern Company, a Delaware corporation, and Georgia Power Company, a wholly-owned subsidiary of Southern and a Georgia corporation. A shareholder of Georgia Power commenced a derivative action on behalf of both corporations. This shareholder contended that the directors of both corporations had breached their fiduciary duties during a 16 year period in connection with the construction of the Alvin W. Vogtle nuclear power

---

2126. *Id.* at 1187-90.

2127. *Id.* at 1190.

2128. *Id.*

2129. *Id.*

2130. *In re Oracle Sec. Litig.*, 852 F. Supp. 1437, 1440-41 (N.D. Cal. 1994).

2131. *Id.* at 1444.

2132. 911 F.2d 1532 (11th Cir. 1990).

plant.[2133] The district court and the Eleventh Circuit held that Delaware law governed the action with respect to Southern, that Georgia law governed the action with respect to Georgia Power, and that Georgia would follow Delaware law.[2134]

At the same time that an independent litigation committee (called the "ILC" by the court) was conducting its investigation, the Georgia Public Service Commission (the "PSC") was considering whether to allow Georgia Power to recover the costs of constructing the plant by increasing customer rates. By statute, the PSC was required to make this decision by October 2, 1987. On that day, the PSC "found a number of imprudent management decisions by the Companies and disallowed approximately 300 million dollars from inclusion in the ratebase."[2135] One day before the PSC was scheduled to make this decision, the committee issued a report concluding that "all of the challenged decisions were either correct or at least reasonable business judgments at the times they were made."[2136] The committee accordingly determined that "as a matter of business judgment, the derivative action was neither in the best interests of the Companies nor their shareholders and should be dismissed."[2137] "By issuing its report on October 1, 1987, just one day before the PSC's decision and well before the November 30 deadline imposed by the district court, the Committee deliberately chose not to wait for the PSC's outcome."[2138]

The district court determined "to reject the recommendation of the Committee and permit the derivative suit to proceed."[2139] The district court found that "the Committee's conclusions were not reasonable" for the following three reasons:

---

2133. *Id.* at 1534.

2134. *Id.* at 1536; *Peller v. Southern Co.*, [1987-1988 Transfer Binder] Fed. Sec. L. Rep. (CCH) ¶ 93,714, a 98,310-11 (N.D. Ga. Mar. 25, 1988), *aff'd*, 911 F.2d 1532 (11th Cir. 1990).

2135. 911 F.2d at 1535.

2136. *Id.*

2137. *Id.*

2138. *Id.*

2139. *Id.* at 1536.

- "by issuing its report only one day before the PSC's decision, the Committee rejected without adequate explanation the findings, made by technical consultants employed by the PSC, that several key decisions during the construction of the Vogtle plant were imprudent and cost the Companies several hundred million dollars,"[2140]

- "the Committee had implausibly blamed 'middle management' personnel for the crucial decisions which cost the Companies hundreds of millions of dollars,"[2141] and

- "the Committee . . . failed to conduct an adequate investigation of the damages sustained by the Companies."[2142]

The district court accordingly concluded that "it is not satisfied that defendants have met their burden of establishing the good faith and reasonableness of the ILC," and that "[t]here exist too many troubling aspects about the manner in which the ILC conducted its investigation."[2143]

Additionally, the court continued, "the district court invoked the 'second step' of *Zapata* to hold that 'even if . . . defendants had met their burden [as to independence, good faith and reasonableness], the items enumerated above would be sufficiently troubling' to warrant denial of the Companies' motion to dismiss."[2144]

The Eleventh Circuit affirmed. The Eleventh Circuit acknowledged that the district court's decision erroneously stated that "[the Companies] have not persuaded the court that the [Committee], as opposed to the PSC, arrived at the correct conclusion."[2145] The Eleventh Circuit, however, concluded that the district court used

---

2140. *Id.* at 1538.
2141. *Id.*
2142. *Id.; see also Peller v. Southern Co.*, 707 F. Supp. 525, 529-30 (N.D. Ga. 1988), *aff'd*, 911 F.2d 1532 (11th Cir. 1990).
2143. 707 F. Supp. at 530.
2144. 911 F.2d at 1538 (quoting 707 F. Supp. at 530-31).
2145. *Id.* at 1538 (quoting 707 F. Supp. at 529-30).

the word "correct" only in passing."[2146] The Eleventh Circuit explained that "the district court noted that the Committee had implausibly charged middle management for decisions costing the Companies several hundred million dollars and failed to investigate adequately the damages suffered by the Companies before the court held that the Companies had not 'met their burden of establishing the good faith and reasonableness of the [Committee].'"[2147]

The Eleventh Circuit concluded that "[t]he Companies' arguments . . . largely come down to the contention that under the traditional 'plain vanilla' business-judgment standard, the Committee's recommendation should not be disturbed."[2148] The court stated that "[t]he Companies are obviously correct that if the proper standard was the 'plain vanilla' business judgment rule, the district court would be obligated to defer to the Committee's judgment."[2149] *Zapata*, however, and not the business judgment rule, the court held, was the governing standard.[2150]

*Weiland v. Illinois Power Co.*[2151]—a case discussed earlier in this Chapter in which a federal court construing Illinois law upheld a determination by a board committee to refuse a demand that litigation be commenced on behalf of a utility company against its directors "for failing to properly exercise their duties in connection with the planning, construction and licensing" of a nuclear power plant[2152]—also held that the result would have been the same even if *Zapata* provided the appropriate standard of review for the committee's determination.[2153] The court's reasoning with respect to the committee's independence, the reasonableness of its decision and its good faith is addressed in the section of this

---

2146. *Id.* at 1538-39.

2147. *Id.* at 1539 (quoting 707 F. Supp. at 530-31).

2148. *Id.* at 1539.

2149. *Id.* (citation omitted).

2150. *Id.*

2151. [1990-1991 Transfer Binder] Fed. Sec. L. Rep. (CCH) ¶ 95,747 (C.D. Ill. Sept. 17, 1990).

2152. *See* Chapter IV, Section B 6 g.

2153. [1990-1991 Transfer Binder] Fed. Sec. L. Rep. (CCH) at 98,590-93.

Chapter discussing the board committee's refusal of the demand in the case.[2154] The court distinguished the *Peller* case, stating that "one of the fundamental concerns of the court in *Peller* was that the special committee deliberately released its report the day before the Georgia Public Service Commission's decision disallowing certain plant costs from the ratebase was expected."[2155] By contrast, the court stated, in *Illinois Power* "the Special Committee had the full benefit of the completed record" in an Illinois Commerce Commission proceeding "and had analyzed carefully all aspects of that record."[2156]

With respect to the second step of *Zapata*, the court in *Illinois Power* stated that "the results of the findings of the special independent litigation committee satisfy the spirit of the business judgment rule and that this stockholder grievance does not deserve further consideration in the corporation's interest."[2157] Thus, the court concluded, "this Court, in its own discretion, believes that it is unnecessary to apply its own independent business judgment to the facts of this case."[2158]

*Mills v. Esmark, Inc.*[2159] and *In re Continental Illinois Securities Litigation*,[2160] decided by courts sitting in the Northern District of Illinois in 1982 and 1983, respectively, reject or fail to focus upon the distinction stated in *Zapata* between cases where demand is required and cases where demand is excused. *Esmark* involved a decision by a special litigation committee, to which the board had delegated its authority in connection with a demand, that litigation would not serve the best interests of the corporation.[2161] The court acknowledged that the business judgment rule rather than

---

2154. *See* Chapter IV, Section B 6 g.

2155. [1990-1991 Transfer Binder] Fed. Sec. L. Rep (CCH) at 98,591.

2156. *Id*. at 98,591-92.

2157. *Id*. at 98,593.

2158. *Id*.

2159. 544 F. Supp. 1275 (N.D. Ill. 1982).

2160. 572 F. Supp. 928 (N.D. Ill. 1983).

2161. 544 F. Supp. at 1281; *Mills v. Esmark, Inc.*, 91 F.R.D. 70, 71-72 (N.D. Ill. 1981).

the *Zapata* test governs cases where demand is required, but the court nevertheless rejected any "bright line" distinction between cases where demand is required and cases where demand is excused.[2162] The court explained that "the existence of the demand on the board, although certainly relevant to the *level* of the appropriate substantive review, does not itself bar all such review in this Court under Delaware law."[2163] The court stated:

> The limited scope of inquiry permitted in this context under Delaware law and the business judgment rule does not . . . bar all substantive review of the SLC's conclusions and recommendations. In cases where, as here, the shareholder plaintiffs articulate specific grounds on which to question the good faith of a special litigation committee's investigation, the Court must examine the committee's treatment of the merits of the shareholders' underlying claims in order to determine the appropriate weight to be given to the committee's recommendations. To shield our eyes entirely from the merits would prevent us from evaluating the underlying independence of the committee.[2164]

The *Continental Illinois* court similarly concluded that the *Zapata* test applied both in cases where demand is required and in cases where demand is excused.[2165] The court explained:

> In *Zapata*, there was no demand, so the court discussed the significance of that fact. I do not interpret that discussion (430 A.2d at 784) read in the context of the entire opinion, as holding that the merits of the corporate decision are beyond judicial review in a case where a demand is not excused. So simplistic a view is inconsistent with the tenor of the court's discussion at pp. 787-789 of the opinion. For instance, the court's discussion of the possibility of a "'. . . there but for the grace of God go I'" attitude on the part of even innocent directors (p. 787) seems applicable to any

---

2162. 544 F. Supp. at 1282-83, 1283 n.4.
2163. *Id.* at 1283 n.4.
2164. *Id.* at 1283.
2165. 572 F. Supp. at 929.

decision on whether to bring suit against fellow directors, including the demand-required situation.[2166]

In subsequent proceedings on an appeal to the Seventh Circuit of another issue in the case, a majority opinion expressed no view on this issue.[2167] One judge, however, stated in a dissenting opinion that *Zapata* applied only in cases where demand is excused.[2168]

The Delaware Supreme Court's subsequent decision in *Aronson v. Lewis*[2169] made clear that under Delaware law the *Zapata* test applies only where demand is excused.[2170] *Lewis v. Hilton*[2171]—a more recent case in the Northern District of Illinois by the same judge that decided *Esmark*—relied upon *Aronson* to hold that the *Zapata* test has no applicability in cases where demand is required.[2172] *Esmark* and *Continental Illinois* thus can no longer be viewed as authoritative even within the court that decided those cases. As the Delaware Supreme Court stated in *Levine v. Smith*,[2173] "[t]his Court's decision in *Aronson*, which followed *Continental Illinois*, demonstrates that the *Continental Illinois* court misapplied Delaware law."[2174]

    *d. Variations of the Zapata Standard of Review by Courts Construing Connecticut, Massachusetts and North Carolina Law.* A more expansive application of Delaware's *Zapata Corp. v. Maldonado*[2175] standard of review[2176] can be found in *Joy v. North*,[2177] a 1982 Second Circuit decision construing Connecticut

---

2166. *Id.*

2167. *In re Continental Ill. Sec. Litig.*, 732 F.2d 1302, 1305 n.3, 1309 n.12 (7th Cir. 1984).

2168. *Id.* at 1316-19 (Pell, J., dissenting).

2169. 473 A.2d 805 (Del. 1984).

2170. *Id.* at 813-14.

2171. 648 F. Supp. 725 (N.D. Ill. 1986).

2172. *Id.* at 727.

2173. 591 A.2d 194 (Del. 1991).

2174. *Id.* at 210.

2175. 430 A.2d 779 (Del. 1981).

2176. *See* Chapter IV, Sections C 2 b & c.

2177. 692 F.2d 880 (2d Cir. 1982), *cert. denied*, 460 U.S. 1051 (1983).

law. The court in *Joy* stated "guidelines" for "[i]ndependent judicial scrutiny" of a special litigation committee's motion to terminate cases where demand is excused and plaintiffs allege "direct economic injury to the corporation . . . as a consequence of fraud, mismanagement or self-dealing."[2178] These guidelines identify a series of costs to the corporation that may arise in the context of litigation and provide that these costs may be taken into account in the balancing process only to the following extent:

- Attorney's fees and other out-of-pocket expenses related to time spent by corporate personnel in litigation-oriented activities and the applicability of mandatory indemnification may be considered (insurance, the court stated, is relevant to the calculation of potential benefits but not costs because premiums already have been paid),[2179]

- The distraction of key personnel and damage caused by adverse publicity may be considered only if, after allowing for the out-of-pocket costs specified above, the court concludes that a small net benefit might result from the litigation,[2180] and

- Other intangible costs, such as injury to employee morale and the corporate image, may not be considered.[2181]

The *Joy* approach differs significantly from the approach in *Zapata* because *Joy* limits the extent to which disinterested and independent directors may consider factors that may counsel against litigation, such as distraction of key personnel, adverse publicity and negative impact upon employee morale and corporate image.

Applying the guidelines it had established, the *Joy* court determined not to defer to a special litigation committee's recommendation that the action in *Joy* should be dismissed. The court found that the plaintiff's likelihood of success in the case was "rather high" because a trier of fact "might easily find liability . . .

---

2178. *Id.* at 891-92.
2179. *Id.*
2180. *Id.*
2181. *Id.*

resulting in a return of several million dollars . . . or perhaps 10% or more of the shareholder equity."[2182] This return, the court concluded, "far exceeds the potential cost of the litigation to the corporation."[2183]

The *Joy* approach has been replaced by statute in Connecticut.[2184]

The Sixth Circuit's decision construing Massachusetts law in 1984 in *Hasan v. CleveTrust Realty Investors*[2185] offers another example of an expansive application of the *Zapata* standard of review. The court in *Hasan* stated its view that "the policies of the business judgment rule do not create a presumption in favor of the good faith of a special committee and . . . the realities of corporate life militate against any such presumption."[2186] The court concluded that "[u]nder the particular facts" of the case before it, a one member special litigation committee had not demonstrated its disinterestedness and independence and the adequacy of the committee's investigation.[2187] The court's conclusions concerning the interestedness and lack of independence on the part of the committee are discussed later in this Chapter;[2188] the court's conclusion that the committee had not demonstrated an adequate investigation centered around the committee's failure to interview representatives of two firms that had acquired 22.4 percent of the corporation's stock and then resold the stock to the corporation "at a price exceeding the fair market value" of the stock in one of the transactions challenged in the litigation.[2189] Interviews of representatives of those two firms, the court stated, "could have provided crucial evidence of the purpose of that challenged transaction," the

---

2182. *Id*. at 896-897.
2183. *Id*. at 897.
2184. *See* Chapter IV, Sections B 6 i and C 1 b.
2185. 729 F.2d 372 (6th Cir. 1984).
2186. *Id*. at 377.
2187. *Id*. at 379.
2188. *See* Chapter IV, Section C 2 e.
2189. 729 F.2d at 373.

value of certain corporate assets, and "concrete evidence" of "possible self-interested motivation for the transaction."[2190]

The Massachusetts Supreme Judicial Court adopted a different rule in 1990 in *Houle v. Low*.[2191] Following *Houle*, courts in Massachusetts "determine, on the basis of the evidence presented, whether the committee reached a reasonable and principled decision," or whether "the committee's decision is contrary to the great weight of evidence."[2192] This review of the committee's decision, the court stated, should look to factors such as "the likelihood of a judgment in the plaintiff's favor, the expected recovery as compared to out-of-pocket costs, whether the corporation itself took corrective action, whether the balance of corporate interests warrants dismissal, and whether dismissal would allow any defendant who has control of the corporation to retain a significant improper benefit."[2193] This "limited review," the court explained, "will avoid the problem in the second level of the *Zapata* test, which requires the judge to exercise his or her own business judgment."[2194] The court stated that "courts are better able to determine the merits of a law suit than whether a decision is correct based on a subjective evaluation of the business policies involved."[2195]

The North Carolina Supreme Court's 1987 decision in *Alford v. Shaw*[2196] adopted the *Zapata* standard of review, but expanded its scope to reach not only cases where demand is excused but also cases where demand is required and refused[2197]—a view explicitly rejected in Delaware.[2198] The court in *Alford* acknowledged that "[t]he *Zapata* Court limited its two-step judicial inquiry to

---

2190. *Id.* at 379.

2191. 556 N.E.2d 51 (Mass. 1990).

2192. *Id.* at 59.

2193. *Id.* (citing *Principles of Corporate Governance: Analysis and Recommendations* § 7.08 (Tentative Draft No. 8 Apr. 15, 1988)).

2194. *Id.* at 59.

2195. *Id.*

2196. 358 S.E.2d 323 (N.C. 1987).

2197. *Id.* at 326-27.

2198. *See* Chapter IV, Sections C Introduction and C 2 c.

cases in which demand upon the corporation was futile and therefore excused."[2199] To support its determination to expand *Zapata* to cases where demand is not excused, the court in *Alford* relied upon what it viewed as a "growing concern" in other jurisdictions "about the deficiencies inherent in a rule giving great deference to the decisions of a corporate committee whose institutional symbiosis with the corporation necessarily affects its ability to render a decision that fairly considers the interest of plaintiffs forced to bring suit on behalf of the corporation."[2200] The court stated that North Carolina's Business Corporation Act reflects a "policy of protecting minority shareholders" and contains "liberal provisions which do not impose many of the restrictions upon derivative actions encountered in other jurisdictions."[2201] The court pointed to a provision in North Carolina's Business Corporation Act stating that a shareholder derivative action "shall not be discontinued, dismissed, compromised or settled without the approval of the court"[2202] and reasoned as follows:

> The plain language of the statute requires thorough judicial review of suits initiated by shareholders on behalf of a corporation: the court is directed to determine whether the interest of any shareholder will be substantially affected by the discontinuance, dismissal, compromise, or settlement of a derivative suit. Although the statute does not specify what test the court must apply in making this determination, it would be difficult for the court to determine whether the interests of shareholders or creditors would be substantially affected by such discontinuance, dismissal, compromise, or settlement without looking at the proposed action substantively. . . . To rely blindly on the report of a corporation-appointed committee . . . is to abdicate the judicial duty to consider the interests of shareholders imposed by the statute. This abdication is particularly inappropriate in a case such as this one, where

---

2199. *Id.* at 327.

2200. *Id.* at 326.

2201. *Id.*

2202. *Id.* (quoting Former N.C. Bus. Corp. Act § 55-55(c), which now is N.C. Bus. Corp. Act § 55-7-40(d)).

> shareholders allege serious breaches of fiduciary duties owed
> to them by the directors controlling the corporation.[2203]

This statutory provision, the court concluded, "is inclusive and draws no distinctions between demand-excused and other types of cases."[2204] The court accordingly adopted a "modified *Zapata* rule, requiring judicial scrutiny of the merits of the litigation committee's recommendation" in all cases.[2205] A later opinion by the court upheld a trial court's determination to accept a special litigation committee's recommendation that several of the claims in the case should be settled and that the remainder of the claims should be dismissed.[2206]

Termination of derivative litigation by special litigation committees in North Carolina now is governed by statute.[2207]

Both the *Houle* and the *Alford* courts hold that the *Zapata* analysis is to be made by the court rather than a jury.[2208] That is, of course, also the rule in Delaware, where the determination is made by the Court of Chancery, an equity court in which there is no jury. A New York decision, *Rosen v. Bernard*,[2209] similarly provided for a limited hearing on "the issue of the independence of the special litigation committee and the methods of its investigation."[2210] By contrast, a California court in *Will v. Engebretson & Co.*[2211]—a decision not reaching the appropriateness of the *Zapata* procedure[2212]—reversed a trial court determination to conduct a limited hearing on interestedness and sufficiency of investi-

---

2203. *Id.* at 326-27.

2204. *Id.* at 327.

2205. *Id.* at 326.

2206. *Alford v. Shaw*, 398 S.E.2d 445, 447, 452-53, 457-60 (N.C. 1990).

2207. *See* Chapter IV, Sections B 6 i and C 1 b.

2208. *See Houle*, 556 N.E.2d at 59; *Alford*, 398 S.E.2d at 457.

2209. 108 A.D.2d 906, 485 N.Y.S.2d 791 (N.Y. App. Div. 2d Dep't 1985).

2210. *Id.* at 907, 485 N.Y.S.2d at 793; *see also* Chapter IV, Section C 2 a (discussing *Rosen*).

2211. 213 Cal. App. 3d 1033, 261 Cal. Rptr. 868 (1989).

2212. *Id.* at 1042 n.5, 261 Cal. Rptr. at 873 n.5.

gation issues. Instead, this court held, a plaintiff who establishes a
material issue of fact on a corporation's motion for summary judgment based upon a special litigation committee report is entitled to
a full trial on the merits.[2213]

*e. Director Disinterestedness and Independence.* As is the
case with directors determining whether to refuse a demand, directors serving on a special litigation committee in cases where
demand is excused must be disinterested and independent with
respect to the subject matter of the allegations being considered by
the committee. A determination of disinterestedness and independence typically is made by the courts only if and when the committee recommends that the litigation not be pursued.[2214]

While it is of course preferable that special litigation committee members be directors who were not directors at the time of the
challenged conduct or transaction and who are not defendants in the
action, this is not required as a matter of law because shareholders
trying to elude the demand requirement and/or a motion to terminate frequently attempt to disqualify all of the corporation's directors simply by naming all directors as defendants. By itself, the fact
that a director has been named as a defendant therefore is insufficient to disqualify the director from considering a demand or from
serving on a special litigation committee; "[t]o hold otherwise
would allow a small number of shareholders to 'incapacitate an

---

2213. *Id.* at 1039-44, 261 Cal. Rptr. at 871-74.

2214. *See Strougo v. Padegs,* 986 F. Supp. 812, 815 (S.D.N.Y.
1997) ("more appropriate" to address independence of committee when
court reviews the committee's recommendations because then "the full
facts of the Committee's procedures and investigation would be available
for review"); *Katell v. Morgan Stanley Group, Inc.,* 19 Del. J. Corp. L.
797, 801-04 (Del. Ch. Sept. 27, 1993); *Pompeo v. Hefner,* 1983 Del. Ch.
LEXIS 506, at *2-5, 1983 WL 20284, at *1-3 (Del. Ch. Mar. 23, 1983).
*But see International Broadcasting Corp. v. Turner,* 734 F. Supp. 383,
393 (D. Minn. 1990) (refusing to stay discovery while committee conducted its investigation because the committee was not "sufficiently independent and disinterested . . . to warrant the granting of the requested
stay").

entire board of directors' merely by naming the entire board as defendants."[2215]

A director also does not become interested in the conduct or transaction challenged in a litigation merely by authorizing a motion seeking dismissal of the action on the ground that the plaintiff failed to make a pre-litigation demand because a vote on such a motion does not "manifest any prejudgment of the merits" of a case.[2216] Voting to indemnify or advance litigation expenses to directors named as defendants also does not establish a disabling interest.[2217] Disinterestedness also has been found in a case where one member of a special litigation committee appeared on a radio show

---

2215. *Mills v. Esmark, Inc.*, 544 F. Supp. 1275, 1283 (N.D. Ill. 1982) (quoting *Zapata Corp. v. Maldonado*, 430 A.2d 779, 785 (Del. 1981)); *see also Johnson v. Hui*, 811 F. Supp. 479, 487 (N.D. Cal. 1991) ("Teal's nominal appearance as a defendant does not undermine his ability to operate as an independent and unbiased member of the SLC"); *Weiland v. Illinois Power Co.*, [1990-1991 Transfer Binder] Fed. Sec. L. Rep. (CCH) ¶ 95,747, at 98,589 (C.D. Ill. Sept. 17, 1990) (rejecting claim that "the fact that a majority of the Board of Directors have been named in the Complaint is sufficient to allege self-interest" because if that were the law "a plaintiff could effectively undermine the authority of the Board of Directors by merely naming a majority of the Board in a complaint").

2216. *Esmark*, 544 F. Supp. at 1283 n.5; *see also Blecker v. Araskog*, No. 21946-80, slip op. at 37 (N.Y. Sup. Ct. N.Y. Co. June 3, 1987) (bad faith or improper motive cannot be inferred from the fact that a special litigation committee was not formed until after the denial of a motion to dismiss the action on the ground that the action was barred by the result of a prior litigation).

2217. *See Bach v. National W. Life Ins. Co.*, 810 F.2d 509, 512 (5th Cir. 1987) (finding disinterestedness where special litigation committee members voted prior to their investigation in favor of a resolution authorizing advancement of the litigation expenses incurred by directors named as defendants in the litigation); *Kaplan v. Wyatt*, 499 A.2d 1184, 1189 (Del. 1985) (finding disinterestedness where special litigation committee member voted to indemnify the chairman of the corporation's board and chief executive officer, who was a defendant in the litigation, in connection with expenses incurred in connection with the chairman's guilty plea to a misdemeanor charge that was related to the allegations in the litigation).

prior to his appointment to the committee and stated his "respect for his fellow board members and his opinion that a lawsuit is generally an undesirable mechanism for effecting a creative social change in one's community."[2218]

Instead, the Delaware courts and a majority of the courts in other jurisdictions that have considered the disinterestedness and independence of special litigation committee members have focused upon whether, considering the totality of the circumstances, the members of the committee base their decision "on the merits of the issue rather than . . . extraneous considerations or influences."[2219] Significant factors that the courts have considered in deciding whether committee members are disinterested and independent include, but are not limited to, the following:

- whether committee members are defendants in the litigation;[2220]

---

2218. *Miller v. Bargaheiser*, 591 N.E.2d 1339, 1343 (Ohio Ct. App. 1990).

2219. *Kaplan*, 499 A.2d at 1189; *see also In re Oracle Sec. Litig.*, 852 F. Supp. 1437, 1441 (N.D. Cal. 1994); *Carlton Invs. v. TLC Beatrice Int'l Holdings, Inc.*, 1997 Del. Ch. LEXIS 86, at *42, 1997 WL 305829, at *10 (Del. Ch. May 30, 1997); *Katell v. Morgan Stanley Group, Inc.*, [1995 Transfer Binder] Fed. Sec. L. Rep. (CCH) ¶ 98,861, at 93,170 (Del. Ch. June 15, 1995).

2220. *Compare Lewis v. Anderson*, 615 F.2d 778, 780 (9th Cir. 1979), *cert. denied*, 449 U.S. 869 (1980) (finding disinterestedness where one of three committee members was a defendant), *Oracle*, 852 F. Supp. at 1441-42 (noting this factor and finding disinterestedness where committee members were not defendants), *Levit v. Rowe*, 1992 U.S. Dist. LEXIS 15036, at *10, 1992 WL 277977, at *3 (E.D. Pa. Sept. 30, 1992) (finding disinterestedness where one of three committee members was a defendant), *Johnson v. Hui*, 811 F. Supp. 479, 486-87 (N.D. Cal. 1991) (finding disinterestedness despite "nominal appearance as a defendant" by one of two committee members), *Esmark*, 544 F. Supp. at 1283-84 (finding disinterestedness where committee members were defendants but were not alleged to have participated in wrongdoing), *Genzer v. Cunningham*, 498 F. Supp. 682, 693 (E.D. Mich. 1980) (finding disinterestedness where committee members were not defendants), *Rosengarten v. International Tel. & Tel. Corp.*, 466 F. Supp. 817, 821 (S.D.N.Y. 1979)

(continued...)

- whether committee members have direct and substantial (as opposed to merely indirect or nominal) exposure to liability;[2221]

- whether committee members are outside, non-management directors;[2222]

---

2220. (...continued)
(finding disinterestedness where committee members were not defendants) *and Katell*, [1995 Transfer Binder] Fed. Sec. L. Rep. (CCH) at 93,170 (finding disinterestedness where the single member of a committee was a defendant) *with International Broadcasting Corp. v. Turner*, 734 F. Supp. 383, 393 (D. Minn. 1990) (finding lack of disinterestedness where two members of three member committee were defendants and the third member of the committee was a designee to the board of a party involved in the alleged wrongdoing) *and Lewis v. Fuqua*, 502 A.2d 962, 966 (Del. Ch. 1985) (finding lack of disinterestedness where the single member of a committee was a defendant), *appeal refused*, 504 A.2d 571 (unpublished opinion, text available at 1986 Del. LEXIS 1027 and 1986 WL 16292) (Del. Jan. 24, 1986).

2221. *Compare In re General Tire & Rubber Co. Sec. Litig.*, 726 F.2d 1075, 1084 (6th Cir.), *cert. denied*, 469 U.S. 858 (1984) (finding disinterestedness where committee members were "not charged . . . with direct liability"), *Anderson*, 615 F.2d at 780 (finding disinterestedness where one committee member was a "named defendant, but . . . did not benefit from the challenged transactions"), *Oracle*, 852 F. Supp. at 1441-42 (noting this factor and finding disinterestedness), *Johnson*, 811 F. Supp. at 486-87 (same), *Esmark*, 544 F. Supp. at 1283 (finding disinterestedness where the committee's two members were not alleged to have participated in the challenged decisions or received any payment or benefit challenged in the litigation) *and Katell*, [1995 Transfer Binder] Fed. Sec. L. Rep. (CCH) at 93,170 (finding disinterestedness where the single member of a committee approved the challenged transaction and noting that "potential liability for approving a transaction, standing alone," does not establish interestedness) *with Abbey v. Control Data Corp.*, 603 F.2d 724, 727 (8th Cir. 1979), *cert. denied*, 444 U.S. 1017 (1980) (stating that "where the directors, themselves, are subject to personal liability in the action," they "cannot be expected to determine impartially whether it is warranted," but finding disinterestedness), *and Galef v. Alexander*, 615 F.2d 51, 60-61 (2d Cir. 1980) (quoting *Abbey* but not deciding disinterestedness issue).

2222. *See Oracle*, 852 F. Supp. at 1441-42 (finding disinterested-
(continued...)

- whether committee members were members of the corporation's board at the time of the alleged wrongdoing;[2223]

---

2222. (...continued)
ness where committee consisted of outside, non-management directors); *Levit*, 1992 U.S. Dist. LEXIS 15036, at \*10, 1992 WL 277997, at \*3 (same); *IT&T*, 466 F. Supp. at 821 (same); *Carlton Invs.*, 1997 Del. Ch. LEXIS 86, at \*26-27, 1997 WL 305829, at \*6 (same).

2223. *Compare Anderson*, 615 F.2d at 780 (finding disinterestedness where two of three committee members had joined the board after the challenged transactions), *Levit*, 1992 U.S. Dist. LEXIS 15036, at \*10, 16 n.2, 1992 WL 277997, at \*4, 13 n.2 (finding disinterestedness where one member of committee joined the board after the alleged misconduct, one member of the committee served on the board during part of the alleged misconduct, and one member of the committee served on the board for the entire period of the alleged misconduct), *Oracle*, 852 F. Supp. at 1441-42 (noting this factor and finding disinterestedness); *Johnson*, 811 F. Supp. 486-87 (finding disinterestedness where one of two committee members joined the board after the challenged transactions), *Genzer*, 498 F. Supp. at 684-85, 693 (finding disinterestedness where both members of a two member committee joined the board after the alleged wrongdoing), *IT&T*, 466 F. Supp. at 821 (finding disinterestedness where all three committee members were "not affiliated with the corporation at the time of the wrongs complained of"), *Kaplan*, 499 A.2d at 1189 (finding disinterestedness despite the "mere fact" that a committee member—in this case, one of two members of a committee—"was on the Board at the time of the acts alleged in the complaint"), *TLC Beatrice*, 1997 Del. Ch. LEXIS 86, at \*26-27, 43, 1997 WL 305829, at \*6, 11 (finding disinterestedness where both members of a two member committee joined the board after the challenged conduct), *Auerbach v. Bennett*, 47 N.Y.2d 619, 625, 393 N.E.2d 994, 997, 419 N.Y.S.2d 920, 923 (1979) (finding disinterestedness where "[t]he special committee comprised three disinterested directors who had joined the board after the challenged transactions had occurred") *and Blecker*, slip op. at 38 (finding disinterestedness where both members of a two member committee had not been directors at the time of the alleged wrongdoing) *with Fuqua*, 502 A.2d at 966 (finding lack of disinterestedness where only member of committee had been a member of the corporation's board at the time of the challenged conduct).

- whether committee members participated in the alleged wrongdoing;[2224]

- whether committee members approved conduct or a transaction involving the alleged wrongdoing;[2225]

- whether committee members (or firms with which the committee members are affiliated) have had business dealings with the corporation other than as directors of the

---

2224. *Compare Oracle*, 852 F. Supp. at 1441-42 (finding disinterestedness where committee members did not participate in alleged wrongdoing), *Johnson*, 811 F. Supp. at 486-87 (same), *Esmark*, 544 F. Supp. at 1283-84 (same) *and Blecker*, slip op. at 37-38 (same) *with Grynberg v. Farmer*, [1980 Transfer Binder] Fed. Sec. L. Rep. (CCH) ¶ 97,683, at 98,586 (D. Colo. Oct. 8, 1980) (finding lack of disinterestedness where corporation did not offer proof demonstrating that committee members did not have "personal financial interests" with respect to options that they had received that were "substantially identical" to options challenged in the litigation); *cf. De Moya v. Fernandez*, 559 So. 2d 644, 644-45 (Fla. Dist. Ct. App. 1990) (finding question of fact concerning interestedness requiring an evidentiary hearing in a case where the court had appointed the receiver of a bankrupt corporation—the receiver also was the corporation's principal creditor—to act as a special litigation committee in a suit involving allegations of wrongdoing against the corporation's directors and the receiver).

2225. *Compare Oracle*, 852 F. Supp. at 1441-42 (finding disinterestedness where committee members did not approve the alleged wrongdoing), *Johnson*, 811 F. Supp. at 486-87 (same); *Kaplan*, 499 A.2d at 1189 (finding disinterestedness despite the fact that one of two committee members had approved the challenged transaction) *and Katell*, [1995 Transfer Binder] Fed. Sec. L. Rep. (CCH) at 93,170 (finding disinterestedness where the single member of a committee approved the challenged transaction) *with Esmark*, 544 F. Supp. at 1283-84 (finding interestedness since "[a]s a practical matter, neither Dr. Dykes nor Admiral Zumwalt can be expected to exercise truly independent judgment in evaluating the propriety of their own decision to approve the proxy statement"); *cf. IT&T*, 466 F. Supp. at 825 (finding disinterestedness where two of three committee members allegedly participated at other corporations in the same type of wrongdoing—questionable foreign payments—that were the subject of the committee's investigation, and where one of these committee members was named as a defendant in an action alleging this conduct at another corporation).

corporation,[2226] including, for example, service as an outside counsel[2227] or a consultant;[2228] and

- whether committee members have or have had business or social relationships with one or more of the defendants in the litigation.[2229]

---

2226. *See Kaplan*, 499 A.2d at 1189 (finding disinterestedness in case where committee member had various investments and affiliations with the corporation; discussed in text later in this Section); *Oracle*, 852 F. Supp. at 1441-42 (noting this factor and finding disinterestedness in case where one of two committee members had had dealings with the corporation; discussed in text later in this section); *Kaplan*, 499 A.2d at 1189 (same); *TLC Beatrice*, 1997 Del. Ch. LEXIS 86, at *43, 1997 WL 305829, at *11 (finding disinterestedness where committee members did not have "any prior affiliation" with the corporation); *Skoglund v. Brady*, 541 N.W.2d 17, 19 (Minn. Ct. App. 1995) (finding disinterestedness where committee member did not have "any prior relationship" with corporation); *Auerbach*, 47 N.Y.2d at 632, 393 N.E.2d at 1001, 419 N.Y.S.2d at 927 (finding disinterestedness where none of three committee members "had had any . . . affiliation with the corporation" other than as directors after the alleged wrongdoing).

2227. *See General Tire*, 726 F.2d at 1084 (finding disinterestedness despite the fact that one member of a four member committee was an attorney who had served as outside counsel to the corporation for many years and whose law firm had been retained to investigate the corporate practices challenged in the litigation).

2228. *See General Tire*, 726 F.2d at 1084 (finding disinterestedness despite the fact that one member of committee had served the corporation as an "independent consultant" who "participated in the corporation's attempt to scrutinize" the alleged misconduct being investigated by the committee); *Genzer*, 498 F. Supp. at 693-94 (finding disinterestedness despite service by one of two committee members as a consultant to the corporation).

2229. *Compare Oracle*, 852 F. Supp. at 1441-43 (noting this factor and finding disinterestedness; discussed in text later in this Section); *Levit*, 1992 U.S. Dist. LEXIS 15036, at *12, 16, 1992 WL 277997, at *5, 6 (finding disinterestedness, and holding that committee member's independence was not undermined by fact that the committee member and a defendant "sit together as directors on another board"), *Johnson*, 811 F. Supp. at 486-87 (finding disinterestedness; discussed in text later in this

(continued...)

Courts also consider

- the nature of the alleged wrongdoing (where the alleged wrongdoing is egregious in nature, courts are less likely to find disinterestedness and independence on the part of committee members who recommend termination of litigation);[2230]

---

2229. (...continued)
Section), *Rosengarten v. Buckley*, 613 F. Supp. 1493, 1500 (D. Md. 1985) (finding disinterestedness; discussed in text later in this Section), *TLC Beatrice*, 1997 Del. Ch. LEXIS 86, at *43, 1997 WL 305829, at *11 (finding disinterestedness where committee members did not have "any prior affiliation" with any parties in the action); *Katell*, [1995 Transfer Binder] Fed. Sec. L. Rep. (CCH) at 93,170 (finding disinterestedness where the "relationship" between the single member of a committee with the principal defendant in the case consisted of "arm's-length trading and two limited partnerships in the process of liquidating their portfolio" and where the committee member had "shown that it can and will oppose" that defendant), *Skoglund*, 541 N.W.2d at 19 (finding disinterestedness where the single member of a committee did not have "any prior relationship" with defendants) *and Bargaheiser*, 591 N.E.2d at 1344 (finding disinterestedness where there were no business and social contacts between committee members and defendants) *with Hasan v. CleveTrust Realty Investors*, 729 F.2d 372, 378-79 (6th Cir. 1984) (finding lack of disinterestedness where the only member of a committee had a "close business relationship" with a defendant), *Grynberg v. Farmer*, [1980 Transfer Binder] Fed. Sec. L. Rep. (CCH) at 98,586 (finding lack of disinterestedness where one member of committee was counsel to one of the directors named as a defendant in the case and thus "may have a professional duty not to undertake any activity adverse to his client") *and Fuqua*, 502 A.2d at 966-67 (finding lack of disinterestedness; discussed in text later in this Section); *cf. Houle v. Low*, 556 N.E.2d 51, 58-59 (Mass. 1990) (finding question of fact regarding interestedness requiring an evidentiary hearing where the "professional advancement" of the only member of a committee "appears to be dependent on the individual defendants"); *Blecker*, slip op. at 37-38 (rejecting challenge to disinterestedness of a committee member who had had contact as a government official on an unrelated matter with a member of a special litigation committee that previously had investigated and recommended termination of a related litigation).

2230. *See Fuqua*, 502 A.2d at 972 (discussed in text later in this Section).

- the number of directors on the committee: the more directors on the committee, the less weight courts tend to assign to a particular disabling interest affecting a single member of the committee[2231] (it has been said that "[i]f a single member committee is to be used, the member should, like Caesar's wife, be above reproach;"[2232] it also has been said that "[t]he procedure created in *Zapata* is very fact

---

2231. *See Oracle*, 852 F. Supp. at 1441-42 (noting this factor; discussed in text later in this section); *Johnson*, 811 F. Supp. at 486-87 (same); *Houle*, 556 N.E.2d at 58-59 ("[w]e decline to adopt a per se rule that special litigation committees should have more than one director, but we think that the number of committee members should be a factor in determining the committee's ability to act independently"). *Compare Hasan*, 729 F.2d at 378-79 *and Fuqua*, 502 A.2d at 966-67 (finding lack of disinterestedness in cases involving one member committees) *with General Tire*, 726 F.2d at 1083-84, *Oracle*, 852 F. Supp. at 1441-42, *Johnson*, 811 F. Supp. 486-87, *Buckley*, 613 F. Supp. at 1500-01 *and Kaplan*, 499 A.2d at 1189-90 (finding disinterestedness in cases involving two, three and four member committees notwithstanding challenges to two of four committee members in *General Tire*, one of two committee members in *Oracle* and *Johnson*, one of three committee members in *Buckley*, and one of two committee members in *Kaplan*).

2232. *Fuqua*, 502 A.2d at 967; *cf. Kahn v. Tremont Corp.*, 694 A.2d 422, 429-30 (Del. 1997) (quoting *Fuqua* in context of a three member committee formed to negotiate and determine whether a transaction should be entered into by a corporation and a controlling shareholder, where two members of the committee "abdicated their responsibility as committee members" by failing "to fully participate in an active process" and permitting a third member of the committee—the member of the committee "whose independence was most suspect"—to perform the committee's "essential functions," thus making the committee's third member "*de facto*, a single member committee"; discussed in Chapter II, Section B 3 i); *Kahn v. Dairy Mart Convenience Stores, Inc.*, 21 Del. J. Corp. L. 1143, 1157 (Del. Ch. Mar. 29, 1996) (quoting *Fuqua* in context of a two member committee formed in connection with a leveraged buyout transaction pursuant to which the corporation would be merged into an entity controlled by the corporation's majority shareholder, where one of the two members of the committee could not be deemed independent for the purpose of a motion for summary judgment; discussed in Chapter II, Section B 3 j).

specific" and "cannot be cabined into all purpose rules like 'no one member special committees'"[2233]); and

- whether the committee received advice from independent counsel and, where appropriate, other independent professional advisors.[2234]

---

2233. *Katell*, [1995 Transfer Binder] Fed. Sec. L. Rep. (CCH) at 93,171 (rejecting challenge to one member committee); *Skoglund*, 541 N.W.2d at 19 (finding disinterestedness in case involving one member committee, without discussion of this specific issue).

2234. *See General Tire*, 726 F.2d at 1084 (noting use of "independent counsel"); *Andersen*, 615 F.2d at 780 (committee "retained independent legal counsel"); *Oracle*, 852 F. Supp. at 1442 (committee retained "independent outside counsel"); *Johnson*, 811 F. Supp. at 482-83 (committee hired its counsel); *Skoglund*, 541 N.W.2d at 19 (committee retained accounting firm); *Auerbach*, 47 N.Y.2d at 635, 393 N.E.2d at 1003, 419 N.Y.S.2d at 929 (committee "promptly engaged eminent special counsel"); *TLC Beatrice*, 1997 Del. Ch. LEXIS 86, at *27, 1997 WL 305829, at *6 (committee worked "with the assistance of counsel, an executive compensation expert, and accountants"); *Katell*, [1995 Transfer Binder] Fed. Sec. L. Rep. (CCH) at 93,171 (committee "hired its own counsel"); *Blecker*, slip op. at 38 (committee "was advised of its responsibilities by highly respected independent outside counsel of its own choosing"). *Compare Levit*, 1992 U.S. Dist. LEXIS 15036, at *17-18 & n.3, 1992 WL 277997, at *6, 13 n.3 (upholding choice by a General Electric special litigation committee of a law firm that represented GE "in significant matters" but that received "less than one percent of the money GE paid for outside legal services" and that derived no more than one half of one percent of its total annual revenues from GE; the court stated that "GE is one of the largest companies in the world and has 19 directors who sit on various other boards and are often officers of other major entities. Given these realities, there are probably few firms capable of supervising a special litigation committee in a matter like this that have not had some contact with GE or its directors"), *In re Consumers Power Co. Derivative Litig.*, 132 F.R.D. 455, 478-79 (E.D. Mich. 1990) (dismissing action pursuant to the recommendation of an advisory committee formed in a case where a demand had been made and that is discussed in Chapter IV, Section B 6 g, where counsel to the committee also was counsel to the corporation but not the corporation's directors in related litigation) *and Bargaheiser*, 591 N.E.2d at 1343 (dismissing action pursuant to special

(continued...)

Retention by a committee of a law firm of which a committee member is a partner or with which a committee member is or has been affiliated does not demonstrate interestedness or a lack of independence. The court in *Maldonado v. Flynn*[2235] rejected a contention that a committee member whose law firm was retained to act as the committee's counsel was "somehow predisposed to a particular determination" because his firm was paid for the legal work it performed and thus the director "'personally' profited from the investigation."[2236] The court called this contention "a non sequitur" that was "hardly worthy of comment."[2237] The court in *Carlton Investments v. TLC Beatrice International Holdings, Inc.*[2238] described the use by a special litigation committee mem-

---

2234. (...continued)
litigation committee determination where counsel to the committee also was counsel to the corporation) *with In re Oracle Sec. Litig.*, 829 F. Supp. 1176, 1187-90 (N.D. Cal. 1993) (refusing to approve settlement pursuant to the recommendation of a committee of non-defendant directors because the committee was advised by the corporation's general counsel rather than independent counsel; in-house attorneys, the court stated, are "inevitably subservient to the interests of the defendant directors and officers whom they serve"), *subsequent proceedings*, 852 F. Supp. 1437, 1440-45 (N.D. Cal. 1994) (approving same settlement but this time on the basis of a recommendation by a newly constituted special litigation committee acting with the advice of independent counsel), *In re Par Pharmaceutical Inc. Derivative Litig.*, 750 F. Supp. 641, 644 (S.D.N.Y. 1990) (refusing to dismiss action in accordance with recommendation of committee where the committee "did not obtain independent legal counsel but instead relied upon the firm of Solin & Breindel, attorneys for Par and its Board in this litigation") and *Ostrowski v. Avery*, 1996 Conn. Super. LEXIS 2557, at *10-19, 1996 WL 580981, at *3-6 (Conn. Super. Ct. Sept. 30, 1996), *rev'd on other grounds*, 703 A.2d 117 (Conn. 1997) (refusing to dismiss action where counsel did not act independently; discussed in Chapter IV, Section C 2 h).

2235. 485 F. Supp. 274 (S.D.N.Y. 1980), *aff'd in part and rev'd in part on other grounds*, 671 F.2d 729, 732 (2d Cir. 1982).

2236. *Id.* at 283.

2237. *Id.*

2238. 1997 Del. Ch. LEXIS 86, 1997 WL 305829 (Del. Ch. May 30, 1997).

ber of "his highly reputable firm to assist him in the process" as "efficient, rather than culpable."[2239]

Courts typically look at all of the factors listed above together. As a general rule, only one of these factors may in and of itself be dispositive against a special litigation committee member: direct participation in the conduct or transaction underlying the litigation. Where the committee member has not participated in the alleged wrongdoing, the courts typically are reluctant to find that director to be interested[2240] and will do so only where a substantial disabling interest can be demonstrated.[2241] Courts recognize that a "totality of the circumstances" test does not require "the complete absence of any facts which might point to non-objectivity" because "[b]usiness dealings seldom take place between complete strangers and it would be a strained and artificial rule which required a director to be unacquainted or uninvolved with fellow directors in order to be regarded as independent."[2242] To the contrary, as the Delaware Supreme Court stated in *Kaplan v. Wyatt*,[2243] the plaintiff must show that the committee member "based his conclusions . . . on . . . outside influences rather than the merits of the issues."[2244]

*Kaplan* involved a derivative action brought on behalf of Coastal Corporation and a special litigation committee consisting of

---

2239. 1997 Del. Ch. LEXIS 86, at *44, 1997 WL 305829, at *11.

2240. *See General Tire*, 726 F.2d at 1083-84; *Anderson*, 615 F.2d at 780; *Levit*, 1992 U.S. Dist. LEXIS 15036, at *15-16, 1992 WL 277977, at *5; *Oracle*, 852 F. Supp. at 1441-42; *Johnson*, 811 F. Supp. at 486-87; *Buckley*, 613 F. Supp. at 1500-01; *Esmark*, 544 F. Supp. at 1281-88; *Genzer*, 498 F. Supp. at 693-94; *Kaplan*, 499 A.2d at 1189-90; *TLC Beatrice*, 1997 Del. Ch. LEXIS 86, at *42-48, 1997 WL 305829, at *10-12; *Blecker*, slip op. at 36-44; *Bargaheiser*, 591 N.E.2d at 1342-43.

2241. *See Hasan*, 729 F.2d at 378-79; *Fuqua*, 502 A.2d at 965.

2242. *Oracle*, 852 F. Supp. at 1442.

2243. 499 A.2d 1184 (Del. 1985).

2244. *Id.* at 1190; *see also Bargaheiser*, 591 N.E.2d at 1344 ("a lack of independence could be found, for example, if a business or family relationship existed between a named defendant and a committee member which would compel a report supporting the named defendant, the facts of the investigation to the contrary notwithstanding").

two directors, one of whom died following the completion of the committee's report but prior to the taking of any discovery concerning the disinterestedness and independence of the two members of the committee.[2245] The disinterestedness and independence of the second director, J. Howard Marshall, II, was challenged on several grounds. Marshall, in addition to serving on Coastal's board at the time of the events underlying the litigation, had the following investments and affiliations with companies conducting substantial business with Coastal:

- Marshall was a director and, with his family, a 16 percent shareholder of Koch, a corporation that did $100 million worth of business with Coastal during the year prior to the formation of the committee and $266 million worth of business during the year the committee filed its report ($266 million of business, the court noted, constituted less than 2 percent of Koch's sales);[2246]

- Marshall had, at the time of the events underlying the litigation, been a 50 percent owner of Petco, a corporation that acted as a general partner of limited partnerships engaged in oil and gas exploration programs, and Coastal had been a limited partner in at least three of these programs, involving millions of dollars in both program costs and distributions;[2247] and

- Petco had owned 38 percent (which, in turn, had made Marshall a 19 percent owner) of IRC, a corporation that had engaged in certain of the transactions with Coastal challenged in the litigation (Petco, the court noted, had sold its interest in IRC prior to the appointment of the special litigation committee).[2248]

None of this, the court concluded, established interestedness or a lack of independence because there was no evidence of any "per-

---

2245. *Id.* at 1186; *Kaplan v. Wyatt*, 484 A.2d 501, 512 (Del. Ch. 1984), *aff'd*, 499 A.2d 1184 (Del. 1985).

2246. 499 A.2d at 1187; 484 A.2d at 513.

2247. *Id.*

2248. *Id.*

sonal dealings" between Marshall and Coastal or any defendant with respect to the transactions challenged in the litigation.[2249] Likewise, there was no showing how any of "these connections impair" Marshall's "ability to make an independent decision."[2250]

The Delaware Court of Chancery in *Carlton Investments v. TLC Beatrice International Holdings, Inc.*[2251] similarly rejected a claim that a special litigation committee and its counsel were not independent on the ground, according to the plaintiff, that the committee had been "hand-picked" by the family of Reginald F. Lewis, the principal defendant in the case, who was deceased, "in an attempt to engineer a settlement" that would allow the family "to maintain control of the company."[2252] In support of this contention, the plaintiff pointed to the fact that a Lewis family attorney had suggested one of the two members of the committee, and the fact that the committee retained that committee member's law firm, where the Lewis family attorney previously had been a partner, to represent the committee.[2253] The court described this fact as "circumstantial evidence" and concluded that there was "no reason to believe that either the members of the SLC or their counsel accepted their appointments in bad faith or behaved in any improper manner during the investigation."[2254] To the contrary, the court stated, "[t]he strong career records of both men appointed to the SLC are the more probable justification of why they were chosen" (one was a former federal court judge and a former director of the Central Intelligence Agency, and the other was a former Secretary of the Army).[2255] The fact that one of them "chose to use members of his highly reputable firm to assist him in the process," the court stated, as noted above, "seems efficient, rather

---

2249. 499 A.2d at 1189.

2250. *Id.*

2251. 1997 Del. Ch. LEXIS 86, 1997 WL 305829 (Del. Ch. May 30, 1997).

2252. 1997 Del. Ch. LEXIS 86, at *43, 1997 WL 305829, at *11.

2253. *Id.*

2254. 1997 Del. Ch. LEXIS 86, at *44, 1997 WL 305829, at *11.

2255. 1997 Del. Ch. LEXIS 86, at *26-27, 44, 1997 WL 305829, at *6, 11.

than culpable."[2256] The court also relied upon the fact that the plaintiff in the litigation was "a very substantial stockholder" of the corporation who had a representative on the corporation's board, and that this board member had voted in favor of the election of the members of the committee and voiced no objection concerning the interestedness or independence of these new directors until after the committee had reached its determination.[2257]

The same result was reached in *Johnson v. Hui*,[2258] a case involving alleged insider trading. A special litigation committee consisting of two directors, Robert Louthan and Robert Teal, was formed. The court rejected a challenge to Louthan, who had become a director after the litigation was commenced.[2259] At the time of the alleged wrongdoing, Louthan "had no identified business or personal relationship" with the corporation or any of the defendants in the action.[2260] According to the plaintiff in the action, however, Louthan had "discussed an unidentified business arrangement with certain of the defendants roughly two months before he was appointed to the SLC."[2261] The court held that there was "no evidence . . . that this alleged business arrangement ever moved beyond the stage of speculative discussion, or, more significantly, that the success or failure of this venture is an any way connected with Louthan's performance as a member of the SLC."[2262]

The court also rejected the plaintiff's challenge to the other member of the committee, Robert Teal. Teal was a director of the corporation at the time of the alleged wrongdoing and a defendant in the litigation. As a director, according to the court, Teal "presumably has business and personal contacts with other defendant

---

2256. 1997 Del. Ch. LEXIS 86, at *44, 1997 WL 305829, at *11.
2257. 1997 Del. Ch. LEXIS 86, at *3, 44, 1997 WL 305829, at *1, 11.
2258. 811 F. Supp. 479 (N.D. Cal. 1991).
2259. *Id.* at 482-83, 486-87.
2260. *Id.* at 486.
2261. *Id.* at 486-87.
2262. *Id.* at 487.

directors."[2263] The court held that these facts "do not demonstrate the sort of substantial bias or interest which would cause the Court to question the SLC's ability 'to base [its] decision on the merits of the issue rather than . . . extraneous considerations or influences.'"[2264] To the contrary, the court stated, Teal had not sold stock during the period of time during which insider trading allegedly had occurred or "otherwise actively participated in the pattern of misconduct alleged by plaintiff."[2265] Moreover, the court added, "even if the evidence suggests that Teal is tainted to some degree, this taint does not rise to the level where the Court should conclude that the SLC is tainted. Teal is not the only member of the SLC, and there is no indication that the objectivity of Louthan or committee counsel were overborne by the arguments or conduct of Teal."[2266]

The court in *In re Oracle Securities Litigation*,[2267] another case involving alleged insider trading, also found that both members of a special litigation committee were disinterested "in the sense that they are in a position to base their decisions on the merits of the issues rather than extraneous considerations or influences."[2268]

The court acknowledged that one of the committee members, Joseph Costello, had had "extensive prior contacts" with some of the defendants in the case and the corporation prior to joining the corporation's board, including service with one defendant as directors of the corporation, service with a second defendant as officers of another corporation, and a purchase of a real estate investment with a third defendant.[2269] The court stated that these contacts "admittedly implicate some of the factors that courts have used to identify lack of independence" because Costello's past business

---

2263. *Id.*
2264. *Id.* (quoting *Kaplan*, 499 A.2d at 1189).
2265. *Id.*
2266. *Id.*
2267. 852 F. Supp. 1437 (N.D. Cal. 1994).
2268. *Id.* at 1441.
2269. *Id.*

dealings with these three defendants "may arguably predispose him to a position favoring their interests."[2270] The court, however, held that the requirement of independence does not "necessitate the complete absence of any facts which might point to non-objectivity."[2271] The court explained:

> In any business setting, associations and contacts of the type which Costello has had with some of the individual defendants and Oracle are certainly neither inappropriate nor such as to suggest that Costello would not faithfully discharge his obligations to Oracle's shareholders. Business dealings seldom take place between complete strangers and it would be a strained and artificial rule which required a director to be unacquainted or uninvolved with fellow directors in order to be regarded as independent. Costello's contacts, alone, do not demonstrate an interest or bias that would compromise Costello's objectivity.[2272]

The court also relied upon the fact that Costello was not the only member of the committee and the absence of evidence that the objectivity of the other committee member was affected by Costello's participation in the committee's work.[2273] The court also pointed to the committee's independent counsel and stated that "independent counsel, and their obvious interest in their reputation, acted as a further safeguard against any improper influence which Costello's associations . . . might exert."[2274] The court added that "[t]here is nothing before the court to indicate that the SLC conducted its investigation improperly."[2275]

Another illustrative case is *Rosengarten v. Buckley*.[2276] The court in *Buckley* upheld the independence of a special litigation committee formed by McCormick & Company, Incorporated, consisting of three directors, none of whom "was a board member or

---

2270. *Id.* at 1442.
2271. *Id.*
2272. *Id.* (citation omitted).
2273. *Id.*
2274. *Id.*
2275. *Id.*
2276. 613 F. Supp. 1493 (D. Md. 1985).

had any connection with the Company at the time of the transaction attacked in the . . . action."[2277] The court rejected a challenge to the committee's disinterestedness premised upon the fact that one of the committee's members, George V. McGowan, was president and chief operating officer of Baltimore Gas and Electric Company ("BG&E"). According to the plaintiffs in the case, McGowan was not disinterested and independent because Harry K. Wells, a defendant in the litigation and thus one of the McCormick directors whose conduct was being investigated by the committee, was a member of BG&E's management committee, which made recommendations concerning executive compensation at BG&E, including McGowan's compensation.[2278] The court explained that McGowan met with BG&E's chairman and chief executive officer and not Wells concerning compensation issues and that the BG&E management committee "simply makes recommendations to the full board" of BG&E regarding compensation.[2279] The court also stated that the actions of Wells with respect to the conduct investigated by the committee did not differ from the actions of the committee's other two members.[2280]

Similarly, in *Rosengarten v. International Telephone & Telegraph Corp.*,[2281] a case involving allegations of bribes, kickbacks and other questionable corporate payments, the court upheld the independence of two committee members who had not been on the corporation's board at the time of the alleged wrongdoing but who had been on other corporate boards at times when those corporations allegedly had made similar questionable payments.[2282] The court stated that the plaintiffs had had "extensive opportunity to examine both men" but had "failed to establish that either man was personally involved in the payments or even knew that they had been made prior to public disclosure."[2283]

---

2277. *Id.* at 1494-95.
2278. *Id.* at 1500.
2279. *Id.*
2280. *Id.*
2281. 466 F. Supp. 817 (S.D.N.Y. 1979).
2282. *Id.* at 819-21, 823.
2283. *Id.* at 825.

*Lewis v. Fuqua*,[2284] a case where fourteen of Fuqua Industries' fifteen directors were alleged to have breached their fiduciary duty to the corporation by diverting a corporate opportunity to purchase stock in Triton Group Limited to themselves, illustrates a case where a substantial disabling interest or lack of independence was found. The court held that a committee consisting of the one Fuqua director not alleged to have purchased Triton stock for himself—Terry Sanford, then the President of Duke University and a former Governor of North Carolina—did not possess the requisite independence to constitute a one member special litigation committee. The court found several bases upon which to question Mr. Sanford's independence:

> He was a member of the Board of Directors of Fuqua Industries at the time the challenged actions took place; he is one of the defendants in this suit; he has had numerous political and financial dealings with J.B. Fuqua who is the chief executive officer of Fuqua Industries and who allegedly controls the Board; he is President of Duke University which is a recent recipient of a $10 million pledge from Fuqua Industries and J.B. Fuqua; and J.B. Fuqua has, in the past, made several contributions to Duke University and is a Trustee of that University.[2285]

The court expressed particular concern with both the egregious nature of the alleged breach of fiduciary duty (the court stated if the claim that "the directors diverted an opportunity of the corporation to purchase Triton common stock to themselves for their own personal financial gain . . . is true, it is difficult to imagine a more egregious breach of fiduciary duty")[2286] and the fact that the special litigation committee included only one member: "If a single member committee is to be used," the court stated, "the member should, like Caesar's wife, be above reproach."[2287]

---

2284. 502 A.2d 962 (Del. Ch. 1985), *appeal refused*, 504 A.2d 571 (unpublished opinion, text available at 1986 Del. LEXIS 1027 and 1986 WL 16292) (Del. Jan. 24, 1986).

2285. *Id*. at 966-67.

2286. *Id*. at 972.

2287. *Id*. at 967; *see also id*. at 972.

Interestedness and a lack of independence also was found in *Davidowitz v. Edelman*,[2288] a decision by a trial court in New York in a case involving a four member special litigation committee. The court held that "close business and personal relations" between committee members and Asher B. Edelman, the corporation's controlling shareholder and the chairman of the corporation's board, "preclude this court from finding that the committee possessed the required disinterested independence" with respect to transactions involving Edelman and the corporation.[2289] Three of four members of the committee, the court explained, had participated in "takeover" and other "investment groups" with Edelman, and the fourth member of the committee was Edelman's tax attorney and personal friend.[2290] The trial court's decision was affirmed by an intermediate appellate court for the reasons stated by the trial court.[2291]

The court in *Ostrowski v. Avery*,[2292] a decision by a trial court in Connecticut, reached a similar conclusion, in this case because the special litigation committee's counsel, a former probate judge, "did not approach his duties independently, but rather, adopted the posture of an advocate for the defendants."[2293] This bias, the court stated, "tainted" the committee's recommendation that litigation not be pursued.[2294] The court also stated that counsel's investigation "was not so thorough as to allow the committee to rely substantially" upon counsel's report because counsel

---

2288. 153 Misc. 2d 853, 583 N.Y.S.2d 340 (N.Y. Sup. Ct. Kings Co. 1992), *aff'd*, 203 A.D.2d 234, 612 N.Y.S.2d 882 (N.Y. App. Div. 2d Dep't 1994).

2289. *Id.* at 857, 583 N.Y.S.2d at 343.

2290. *Id.* at 856, 583 N.Y.S.2d at 343.

2291. *Davidowitz v. Edelman*, 203 A.D.2d 234, 612 N.Y.S.2d 882 (N.Y. App. Div. 2d Dep't 1994).

2292. 1996 Conn. Super. LEXIS 2557, 1996 WL 580981 (Conn. Super. Ct. Sept. 30, 1996), *rev'd on other grounds*, 703 A.2d 117 (Conn. 1997).

2293. 1996 Conn. Super. LEXIS 2557, at *17, 1996 WL 580981, at *5.

2294. 1996 Conn. Super. LEXIS 2557, at *10-11, 17-18, 1996 WL 580981, at *3, 6.

did not determine whether the defendants in the case had breached their fiduciary duty to the corporation "pursuant to any recognized legal authority" or "legal standards."[2295]

Another decision that is worthy of note is *Mills v. Esmark, Inc.*[2296] The court in *Esmark* upheld the independence of a special litigation committee consisting of two outside directors, both of whom were named as defendants in an action alleging that compensation awards to corporate officers violated the fiduciary duty owed by the corporation's directors to its shareholders and that material misrepresentations in the corporation's proxy material concerning the compensation plan constituted violations of Section 14(a) of the Securities Exchange Act of 1934.[2297] All of the corporation's directors were named as defendants in the case, including the two directors who were appointed to the special litigation committee after the suit was brought.[2298]

The court found that the committee members were nominal defendants and thus were disinterested for the purpose of evaluating plaintiffs' state law claims because they had not received any payment or benefit challenged in the lawsuit and had not participated in the decisions to award the challenged payments made by the board committees responsible for these decisions.[2299] By contrast, however, the court found that the two directors did participate in the alleged wrongdoing to the extent that they, as directors sitting on the board, approved the alleged misrepresentations in the corporation's proxy statement and thus could not "be expected to exercise truly independent judgment in evaluating the propriety of their own decision to approve the proxy statement."[2300] The court noted the dichotomy it had created but concluded that the committee members' "interest in the resolution of plaintiffs' section 14

---

2295. 1996 Conn. Super. LEXIS 2557, at *13-15, 1996 WL 580981, at *4-5.

2296. 544 F. Supp. 1275 (N.D. Ill. 1982).

2297. 15 U.S.C. § 78n(a).

2298. 544 F. Supp. at 1281, 1283.

2299. *Id.* at 1283, 1284 n.7.

2300. *Id.* at 1283-84.

claim does not establish a lack of independence or disinterestedness as to plaintiffs' other claims."[2301]

*Katell v. Morgan Stanley Group, Inc.*[2302] illustrates these principles in the context of a special litigation committee formed by a limited partnership and is discussed in that context later in this Chapter.[2303]

*f. The Structural Bias Theory.* A minority of cases approach the issue of director disinterestedness and independence from a "structural bias" viewpoint. These cases hold that the judgment of seemingly disinterested directors—who are not defendants in a litigation or participants in wrongdoing alleged in a litigation—is inherently corrupted by the "common cultural bond" and "natural empathy and collegiality" shared by most directors.[2304] As several commentators have observed:

- Board members are "persons who are economically or psychologically dependent upon or tied to the corporation's executives, particularly its chief executive."[2305]

- The "process of director selection and socialization, which incumbent management dominates, may cause even the outside director to perceive his role, once litigation is commenced, as that of a buffer by which to shelter and protect management from hostile and litigious stockholders."[2306]

---

2301. *Id.* at 1284 n.7.

2302. [1995 Transfer Binder] Fed. Sec. L. Rep. (CCH) ¶ 98,861 (Del. Ch. June 15, 1995).

2303. *See* Chapter IV, Section D.

2304. Cox, *Searching for the Corporation's Voice in Derivative Litigation: A Critique of Zapata and the ALI Project*, 1982 Duke L.J. 959, 962, 1008 (1982).

2305. Melvin A. Eisenberg, *The Structure of the Corporation: A Legal Analysis* 145 (1976).

2306. Coffee & Schwartz, *The Survival of the Derivative Suit: An Evaluation and a Proposal for Legislative Reform*, 81 Colum. L. Rev. 261, 283 (1981).

- "[P]sychological mechanisms can be expected to generate subtle, but powerful, biases which result in the independent directors' reaching a decision insulating colleagues on the board from legal sanctions."[2307]

- "Most outside directors share similar social and professional backgrounds and general attitudes with their inside director colleagues. Most are themselves corporate executives, often with firms that do business with the corporation, and thus are unlikely to look favorably on shareholder interference with management generally, or on derivative suits seeking to foist liability on corporate directors. Outside directors are often friends of high executives in the corporation before becoming directors, and even if not, friendships among directors naturally grow during their tenures on the board. Furthermore, the outside director is indebted to his fellow directors for the income and prestige he derives from his position, and he depends on those same directors for the continued receipt of these benefits."[2308]

This view accordingly holds that courts must scrutinize the purported independence of special litigation committee members carefully. Taken to its extreme—as illustrated by *Miller v. Register & Tribune Syndicate, Inc.*,[2309] a case discussed earlier in this Chapter—the structural bias view may preclude even the creation of a special litigation committee.[2310]

The Second Circuit twice has embraced the structural bias point of view. First, in *Lasker v. Burks*,[2311] a derivative action

---

2307. Cox & Munsinger, *Bias in the Boardroom: Psychological Foundations and Legal Implications of Corporate Cohesion*, 48 L. & Contemp. Probs. 83, 85 (Summer 1985).

2308. Dent, *The Power of Directors to Terminate Shareholder Litigation: The Death of the Derivative Suit?*, 75 Nw. U. L. Rev. 96, 112-13 (1980) (footnotes omitted).

2309. 336 N.W.2d 709 (Iowa 1983).

2310. *See* Chapter IV, Section C 1 c.

2311. 567 F.2d 1208 (2d Cir. 1978), *rev'd*, 441 U.S. 471 (1979).

on behalf of an investment trust alleging violations of Sections 13(a)(3) and 36 of the Investment Company Act of 1940[2312] and Section 206 of the Investment Advisers Act of 1940[2313] and breach of fiduciary duty, the court concluded that independent directors do not have the power to terminate "nonfrivolous litigation" brought by shareholders against a majority of the corporation's directors.[2314] The court reasoned as follows:

> In the ordinary routine of running an investment trust, the disinterested directors must constantly deal with interested directors in a spirit of accommodation. Indeed, they are compelled for the most part to rely on the information and expert advice provided by the adviser and the majority directors. The continued service of the statutorily disinterested directors, for which in this case they were paid from $11,000 to $13,000 *per annum*, depends almost entirely on the establishment of satisfactory working arrangements between them and the majority responsible for their selection. It is asking too much of human nature to expect that the disinterested directors will view with the necessary objectivity the actions of their colleagues in a situation where an adverse decision would be likely to result in considerable expense and liability for the individuals concerned.[2315]

The court stated that its decision was based upon the "unique nature of the investment company," and that its decision did not "reach questions of the exercise of similar power by directors of other types of corporations."[2316]

The Supreme Court in *Burks v. Lasker*[2317] reversed the Second Circuit's decision on the ground that "the structure and purpose" of the Investment Company Act "indicate that Congress entrusted to the independent directors of investment companies, exercising the authority granted to them by state law, the primary

---

2312. 15 U.S.C. §§ 80a-13(a)(3), 80a-35.
2313. 15 U.S.C. §§ 80b-1--80b-21.
2314. 567 F.2d at 1212.
2315. *Id.* (footnotes omitted).
2316. *Id.* at 1212 n.14.
2317. 441 U.S. 471 (1979).

responsibility for looking after the interests of the funds' share-holders."[2318] The court continued:

> There may well be situations in which the independent direc-tors could reasonably believe that the best interests of the shareholders call for a decision not to sue—as, for example, where the costs of litigation to the corporation outweigh any potential recovery. In such cases, it would certainly be con-sistent with the Act to allow the independent directors to terminate a suit, even though not frivolous. Indeed, it would have been paradoxical for Congress to have been willing to rely largely upon "watchdogs" to protect shareholder inter-ests and yet, where the "watchdogs" have done precisely that, require that they be totally muzzled.[2319]

Three years later, in *Joy v. North*,[2320] the Second Circuit, construing the law of Connecticut, which now is governed by stat-ute,[2321] addressed a determination by a special litigation commit-tee that a derivative action should be terminated. The committee consisted of directors appointed to the corporation's board after the alleged wrongdoing had occurred and who were not defen-dants.[2322] The court rejected the corporation's contention that the business judgment rule should play a "major role" in a case where a demand upon the board of directors is not required.[2323] The court explained:

> As a practical matter, new board members are selected by incumbents. The reality is, therefore, that special litigation committees created to evaluate the merits of certain litigation are appointed by the defendants to that litigation. It is not cynical to expect that such committees will tend to view derivative actions against the other directors with skepticism. Indeed, if the involved directors expected any result other

---

2318. *Id*. at 484-85.
2319. 441 U.S. at 485 (citations omitted).
2320. 692 F.2d 880 (2d Cir. 1982), *cert. denied*, 460 U.S. 1051 (1983).
2321. *See* Chapter IV, Sections B 6 j and C 1 b.
2322. 692 F.2d at 883-84.
2323. *Id*. at 888.

than a recommendation of termination at least as to them, they would probably never establish the committee.[2324]

Accordingly, the court concluded, "[t]he conflict of interest which renders the business judgment rule inapplicable in the case of directors who are defendants is hardly eliminated by the creation of a special litigation committee."[2325] One judge dissented on the ground that "[o]ur court has been down this path before" and was reversed.[2326] As the dissenting opinion explained:

> When *Burks* was before us we took the same position that the majority now does, i.e., that directors could never be wholly disinterested in deciding whether to pursue claims against fellow directors. On appeal that view was rejected by the Supreme Court which concluded that lack of impartiality of disinterested directors is not a determination to be made as a matter of law.[2327]

The Sixth Circuit expressed a view similar to that of the Second Circuit in *Burks* and *Joy* in *Hasan v. CleveTrust Realty Investors*.[2328] In *Hasan*, shareholders sued the corporation and eight of the corporation's nine directors. The ninth director, who joined the board after the challenged conduct had ended but who had a long history of business dealings with the corporation and the chairman of the corporation's board, was appointed as a one member special litigation committee.[2329] The court concluded that the committee member's business affiliations with the corporation and the chairman of the corporation's board demonstrated a lack of disinterestedness on the part of the committee member.[2330] The court endorsed the structural bias theory, explaining as follows:

> The problems of peer pressure and group loyalty exist *a fortiori* where the members of a special litigation committee are not antagonistic, minority directors, but are carefully

---

2324. *Id.*

2325. *Id.*

2326. *Id.* at 900 (Cardamone, J., dissenting).

2327. *Id.* (citations omitted).

2328. 729 F.2d 372 (6th Cir. 1984).

2329. *Id.* at 373, 378-79.

2330. *Id.* at 377.

selected by the majority directors for their advice. Far from
supporting a presumption of good faith, the pressures placed
upon such a committee may be so great as to justify a presumption against independence.[2331]

The court stopped short of relying upon such a "conclusive presumption against good faith."[2332] Instead, the court held only that
in this case the "personal interests and prior affiliation with the corporation" of the special litigation committee member "preclude any
affirmative demonstration of disinterest."[2333]

The structural bias theory is a minority view that has been
accepted by the courts only to the extent described above. The
Delaware Supreme Court rejected the theory in 1984 in *Aronson v.
Lewis*[2334] in the context of a determination that demand was not
excused by allegations concerning a consulting agreement entered
into by the corporation and a 75 year old retiring director who also
was a 47 percent shareholder.[2335] The court stated the following:

> We recognize that drawing the line at a majority of the board
> may be an arguably arbitrary dividing point. Critics will
> charge that we are ignoring the structural bias common to
> corporate boards throughout America, as well as the other
> unseen socialization processes cutting against independent
> discussion and decision-making in the boardroom. The diffi-
> culty with structural bias in a demand futile case is simply
> one of establishing it in the complaint . . . . We are satisfied
> that discretionary review by the Court of Chancery of com-
> plaints alleging specific facts pointing to bias on a particular
> board will be sufficient for determining demand futility.[2336]

Some observers have dismissed the "broad brush attribution
of character traits and feelings to masses of strangers" reflected by
the structural bias view as "pop psychology, the logic of which is

---

2331. *Id.*
2332. *Id.* at 379.
2333. *Id.*
2334. 473 A.2d 805 (Del. 1984).
2335. *See* Chapter IV, Section B 5 c (i).
2336. 473 A.2d at 815 n.8.

irrefutable only because it is unprovable."[2337] Other observers who are willing to concede (for purposes of discussing the theory) that strangers are probably less susceptible to bias than colleagues still find the theory "not only unconvincing but positively mischievous on policy grounds."[2338] This is because, as Professor Michael P. Dooley and E. Norman Veasey, then of the Delaware bar and now Chief Justice of the Delaware Supreme Court, correctly observed in 1989, the theory has no logical finishing point, and thus can be carried to an endless extreme:

> If familiarity breeds acquiescence in litigation matters, will it not do so in other contexts as well? If so, does this not suggest a wholesale abandonment of the business judgment rule in favor of judicial review of every board approval of a management proposal that turns out badly?

As Chief Justice Veasey observed in 1997:

> Friendship, golf companionship, and social relationships are not factors that necessarily negate independence. There is no place in corporate America today for empty formalities, adversarial boards, chilly boardroom atmospheres, timidity or risk-averseness. Likewise, there is nothing to suggest that, on the issue of questioning the loyalty of the CEO, the bridge partner of the CEO cannot act independently as a director. To make a blanket argument otherwise would create a dubious presumption that the director would sell his or her soul for friendship.[2339]

"The majority view" thus "recognizes that independent directors are capable of rendering an unbiased decision though they were appointed by the defendant directors and share a common experience with the defendants,"[2340] and that "[a]llegations of natural

---

2337. Dooley & Veasey, *The Role of the Board in Derivative Litigation: Delaware Law and the Current ALI Proposals Compared*, 44 Bus. Law. 503, 534 (1989).

2338. *Id.* at 534-35.

2339. Veasey, *The Defining Tension in Corporate Governance in America*, 52 Bus. Law. 393, 406 (1997).

2340. *Weiland v. Illinois Power Co.*, [1990-1991 Transfer Binder] Fed. Sec. L. Rep. (CCH) ¶ 95,747, at 98,590 (C.D. Ill. Sept. 17, 1990)
(continued...)

bias not supported by tangible evidence of an interest" by decision making directors in the outcome of the decision "do not demonstrate a lack of independence."[2341] The courts have recognized that "if independent litigation committees are to be utilized, courts must accept the likelihood that members of an independent litigation committee will have experience like that of the defendant directors" because appointment of persons with no background in a corporation's business or corporate management as directors of the corporation "would probably be irresponsible."[2342] As one court has stated:

> It must be remembered that the SLC was composed of members of the board of the FHA. It therefore follows that the members of the SLC had known the five named defendants over a period of time and had worked with them from time to time on other hospital business. We conclude that these relationships are incidental to board membership and are unavoidable. These incidental relationships do not necessarily prevent the members of the SLC from being independent in their evaluation of the facts presented to them. To find otherwise would make the use of an SLC practically impossible. On the record in this case we find no evidence that these incidental relationships prejudiced the work of the SLC.[2343]

In short, if special litigation committees "are all viewed as inherently biased then the purpose of the *Zapata* rule . . . will be frustrated entirely."[2344]

Nevertheless, some courts that have rejected the structural bias view as a means in and of itself by which the independence of a special litigation committee can be challenged have identified

---

2340. (...continued)
(citing *Peller v. Southern Co.*, 707 F. Supp. 525, 527 (N.D. Ga. 1988), *aff'd*, 911 F.2d 1532 (11th Cir. 1990)).

    2341. *Kaplan v. Wyatt*, 499 A.2d 1184, 1189-90 (Del. 1985).

    2342. *Illinois Power*, [1990-1991 Transfer Binder] Fed. Sec. L. Rep. (CCH) at 98,590 (citing *Peller*, 707 F. Supp. at 527).

    2343. *Miller v. Bargaheiser*, 591 N.E.2d 1339, 1343 (Ohio Ct. App. 1990).

    2344. *Johnson v. Hui*, 811 F. Supp. 479, 486 n.6 (N.D. Cal. 1991).

structural bias as one consideration that a court may consider in evaluating the totality of the circumstances surrounding the independence of a special litigation committee.[2345] According to this view, one consideration relevant to determining the totality of the circumstances surrounding the independence of a special litigation committee is whether the "manner in which the SLC was appointed and proceeded was one which was inevitably bound to be empathetic to defendants, and, therefore, biased in favor of terminating the litigation."[2346] As stated by the Massachusetts Supreme Judicial Court in *Houle v. Low*,[2347] a case describing the "structural bias" concern as "not unfounded," "[t]he real danger of taint lies in whether the particular committee chosen is independent and unbiased."[2348] According to this court, "judicial scrutiny of the committee's independence, in each case, should purge the danger of taint."[2349]

*g. Effect of Procedural Context on the Level of Interest Required to Disqualify Directors.* Several courts have considered whether different levels of interestedness or lack of independence are required in the context of a claim that demand is excused as futile, in the context of a refusal of a demand and/or in the context of a special litigation committee motion to terminate a pending action where demand is excused. The Delaware Supreme Court in *Kaplan v. Wyatt*[2350] concluded that the distinction between a determination whether to commence a litigation in response to a demand and a determination to terminate an already pending litigation is "irrelevant" to the ability of directors to make an independent business judgment.[2351] The Third Circuit similarly con-

---

2345. *In re Oracle Sec. Litig.*, 852 F. Supp. 1437, 1441 (N.D. Cal. 1994); *Illinois Power*, [1990-1991 Transfer Binder] Fed. Sec. L. Rep. (CCH) at 94,850; *Peller*, 707 F. Supp. at 528; *Houle v. Low*, 556 N.E.2d 51, 54-57 (Mass. 1990).

2346. *Johnson*, 811 F. Supp. at 486.

2347. 556 N.E.2d 51 (Mass. 1990).

2348. *Id.* at 54.

2349. *Id.* at 57.

2350. 499 A.2d 1184 (Del. 1985).

2351. *Id.* at 1189 n.1.

cluded in *Lewis v. Curtis*[2352] that "we do not think that we should apply different standards of 'interestedness' to cases in which plaintiff has made no demand and to those in which a demand has been made and rejected."[2353] At least two federal district courts have followed *Curtis*.[2354]

In decisions that pre-date *Kaplan* and *Curtis*, the First, Second and Fifth Circuits in *Heit v. Baird*,[2355] *Galef v. Alexander*,[2356] and *Clark v. Lomas & Nettleton Financial Corp.*,[2357] respectively, have suggested that directors may be sufficiently disinterested and independent to require demand but might not be sufficiently disinterested and independent to refuse demand or move to terminate the action.[2358] These courts have suggested that the showing of interest or lack of independence that is required to excuse a demand is "more rigorous" than the showing that is necessary "to vitiate subsequent director action."[2359] Thus, according to this view, a showing of disinterestedness or lack of independence "that is insufficient to excuse a demand may nonetheless disqualify directors from barring a derivative suit."[2360] The rationale offered by these courts is similar to the rationale offered for the universal demand requirement discussed earlier in this Chapter[2361]—i.e., that the demand "permits the company an opportunity to put its own house in order before resort to the courts" and "might cause the corporation to pursue the suit," even where the

---

2352. 671 F.2d 779 (3d Cir.), *cert. denied*, 459 U.S. 880 (1982).
2353. *Id.* at 786.
2354. *See Feinberg v. Carter*, 652 F. Supp. 1066, 1073 n.3 (S.D.N.Y. 1987); *Vanderbilt v. Geo-Energy Ltd.*, 590 F. Supp. 999, 1001 n.2 (E.D. Pa. 1984).
2355. 567 F.2d 1157 (1st Cir. 1977).
2356. 615 F.2d 51 (2d Cir. 1980).
2357. 625 F.2d 49 (5th Cir. 1980), *cert. denied*, 450 U.S. 1029 (1981).
2358. *Clark*, 625 F.2d at 54 n.5; *Galef*, 615 F.2d at 59-60; *Heit*, 567 F.2d at 1162 n.6.
2359. *Clark*, 625 F.2d at 54 n.5.
2360. *Heit*, 567 F.2d at 1162 n.6.
2361. *See* Chapter IV, Section B 5 g.

directors making this determination would not be permitted to preclude litigation either by refusing demand or moving to terminate the action.[2362]

*h. Considerations Involving Counsel.* Several courts have considered objections to special litigation committee or SLC investigations based upon what plaintiffs have described as "over-reliance"[2363] or "excessive reliance"[2364] upon committee counsel and the utilization of procedures by counsel that shield substantial portions of the committee's investigation from scrutiny pursuant to the attorney-client and work product privileges. The courts typically have defined the relevant issue in these cases to be "not whether the SLC's reliance on counsel was substantial, but whether the SLC's reliance upon counsel amounts to an abdication by the SLC of its investigative role, or renders the SLC's conclusions unreasonable or unreliable."[2365] The courts generally have considered "the use of capable counsel" an "indicia of good faith and reasonableness" in a special litigation committee investigation.[2366]

The court in *Carlton Investments v. TLC Beatrice International Holdings, Inc.*,[2367] for example, rejected a claim of "over-reliance" upon counsel in a case where "due to the vast amount of information that required review, the two members of the SLC delegated a large percentage of this work to its counsel and their expert assistants."[2368] As a result, "counsel performed the vast preponderance of the legal and factual research" completed by the

---

2362. *Heit*, 567 F.2d at 1162 n.6; *Galef*, 615 F.2d at 59.

2363. *Carlton Invs. v. TLC Beatrice Int'l Holdings, Inc.*, 1997 Del. Ch. LEXIS 86, at *46, 1997 WL 305829, at *12 (Del. Ch. May 30, 1997).

2364. *Johnson v. Hui*, 811 F. Supp. 479, 488 (N.D. Cal. 1991).

2365. *Id.* at 489.

2366. *Grafman v. Century Broadcasting Corp.*, 762 F. Supp. 215, 220 (N.D. Ill. 1991); *see also, e.g., Kaplan v. Wyatt*, 499 A.2d 1184, 1191 (Del. 1985); *Rosengarten v. Buckley*, 613 F. Supp. 1493, 1503 (D. Md. 1985).

2367. 1997 Del. Ch. LEXIS 86, 1997 WL 305829 (Del. Ch. May 30, 1997).

2368. 1997 Del. Ch. LEXIS 86, at *32, 1997 WL 305829, at *8.

committee: "Whereas the SLC's counsel spent over 4000 hours reviewing the facts and then presenting the information to the SLC, each of the SLC members themselves estimated that he spent approximately 100 hours prior to the proposed settlement."[2369]

The court concluded that there was no reason to believe that the committee's reliance upon counsel "was inappropriate or constituted a relinquishment of their duties."[2370] The court explained that "[w]hile the directors bear ultimate responsibility for making informed judgments, good faith reliance by a SLC on independent, competent counsel to assist the SLC in investigating claims is legally acceptable, practical, and often necessary."[2371] The court found "[t]hroughout the process, the SLC met with its counsel to be updated on its findings, personally reviewed transcripts on documents relating to important or unclear issues, and appear to have made the final substantive judgments concerning the proper settlement values for each claim."[2372] The court stated that the members of the committee "exhibited an understanding of their role, a familiarity with the record, and confidence that the decisions they made were in the best interests of the company."[2373]

The court concluded that "[w]here there is no evidence of overreaching by counsel or neglect by the SLC, the court ought not second guess the SLC's decisions regarding the role which counsel played in assisting them in their task."[2374] Here, the court held, "working together, the SLC and its counsel performed a good faith review and analysis of the factual and legal underpinnings of the claims."[2375]

---

2369. 1997 Del. Ch. LEXIS 86, at *32, 46, 1997 WL 305829, at *8, 12.

2370. 1997 Del. Ch. LEXIS 86, at *46, 1997 WL 305829, at *12.

2371. *Id.*

2372. 1997 Del. Ch. LEXIS 86, at *47, 1997 WL 305829, at *12.

2373. *Id.*

2374. *Id.*

2375. *Id.*

The court in *Johnson v. Hui*[2376] reached the same result. This court held that the "substantial reliance" by the committee in that case upon counsel "to gather documents and interview witnesses does not appear to have affected the independence of the SLC, the reliability of the SLC's evidence gathering, or the reasonability of the SLC's analysis."[2377] The court added that the plaintiff's objection that witness interviews were too short and were not transcribed was not dispositive because

> [o]f course, long transcribed interviews might provide both substantive support for the SLC's conclusions and evidence of the SLC's good faith. But the absence of long transcribed interviews does not undermine the undisputed facts which the SLC has managed to prove without the aid of long transcribed interviews. . . . While the record could be longer, it is now long enough to support Everex's motion to terminate the present litigation.[2378]

The court in *Litton Industries, Inc. v. Hoch*[2379] similarly rejected a claim (in the context of a case where a demand was made and refused) that a special litigation committee improperly relied upon oral summaries of witness interviews conducted by the committee's counsel because "plaintiffs have not suggested why reliance on summaries of testimony was unreasonable or constituted bad faith."[2380] The *Litton* court also rejected a contention that the committee's investigation was not objective because inside counsel interviewed senior management. The court reasoned that "plaintiffs failed to show how participation by inside counsel either adversely affected the investigation or demonstrated bad faith."[2381]

---

2376. 811 F. Supp. 479 (N.D. Cal. 1991).

2377. *Id.* at 489.

2378. *Id.*

2379. 996 F.2d 1225 (unpublished opinion, text available at 1993 U.S. App. LEXIS 16992 and 1993 WL 241549) (9th Cir. July 2, 1993).

2380. 1993 U.S. App. LEXIS 16992, at *8, 1993 WL 241549, at *3.

2381. 1993 U.S. App. LEXIS 16992, at *8-9, 1993 WL 241549, at *3.

The court in *Varian Associates, Inc. v. Superior Court*[2382] reached the same result (also in the context of a case where a demand was made and refused). The court explained that a "purely conclusory assertion that the law firm relied on tainted sources is not enough to constitute a particularized showing of taint of the decisional process," and that "there is nothing necessarily pernicious about delegating a decision whether or not to sue to a law firm; that seems the sort of business they are particularly trained to resolve."[2383] Accordingly, the court concluded, if a plaintiff "cannot show some corruption" in the choice of a law firm, then "he cannot, we believe, call into question the business judgment of the committee to give consideration to the advice of this law firm in making the decision whether or not to pursue litigation."[2384]

The court in *Miller v. Bargaheiser*[2385] also rejected a claim that an investigation was not conducted in good faith because "the committee members did not conduct the investigation but rather relied on counsel for that purpose."[2386] The *Miller* court stated that there is nothing "inherently wrong with using counsel to assist the committee with its work."[2387] The court in *Katell v. Morgan Stanley Group, Inc.*[2388] reached the same conclusion. The court in *Katell* stated that there is "nothing unreasonable" about "heavy reliance" by a special litigation committee "on its competent attorneys."[2389] The court added that "[p]laintiffs have not asserted that LCF's counsel had an improper conflict of interest or incompetently conducted the interviews."[2390]

---

2382. No. H011025 (Cal. Ct. App. Aug. 31, 1993).

2383. *Id.*, slip op. at 19.

2384. *Id.*

2385. 591 N.E.2d 1339 (Ohio Ct. App. 1990).

2386. *Id.* at 1344.

2387. *Id.*

2388. [1995 Transfer Binder] Fed. Sec. L. Rep. (CCH) ¶ 98,861 (Del. Ch. June 15, 1995).

2389. *Id.* at 93,172.

2390. *Id.; see also Rosengarten v. Buckley*, 613 F. Supp. 1493, 1500-03 (D. Md. 1985) (rejecting several challenges to a special litigation

(continued...)

By contrast, the court in *Peller v. Southern Co.*[2391]—a case declining to accept a special litigation committee recommendation that a litigation be terminated[2392]—acknowledged that a special litigation committee's reliance upon counsel "is an accepted practice" but concluded that it was "troubled" in this case by the fact that the committee "relied almost exclusively" on its counsel "to conduct the substantive aspects of the investigation."[2393] The court explained that by "relying on counsel to outline and to conduct all interviews and then prepare interview summaries that contain 'privileged information,'" the committee had "insulated its investigation from scrutiny" and thus left the plaintiff and the court with no way to determine whether the committee "pursued its charge with diligence and zeal, or whether it played softball with critical players."[2394] "This is not good faith," the court concluded.[2395] The court later modified this finding to state that the court "did not determine that the failure of defendants to provide [Peller] with the [Committee's] interview notes constituted a lack of good faith in the [Committee's] investigation. Rather, the court was concerned with the [Committee's] conducting its investigation in

---

2390. (...continued)
committee's investigation, including the committee's formation of a tentative conclusion prior to interviewing plaintiff's counsel, the committee's failure to interview certain witnesses until after such interviews were suggested by plaintiff's counsel, revisions to drafts of committee minutes prior to their publication as part of the committee's report, the committee's failure to keep a stenographic record of committee meetings, and the conduct of certain witness interviews by counsel alone); *Kaplan v. Wyatt*, 499 A.2d 1184, 1190-91 (Del. 1984) (rejecting challenges to special litigation committee procedures, including the presence of the corporation's in-house counsel at committee interviews of corporate officials and the destruction of handwritten interview notes, discussed in Chapter IV, Section C 2 e).

2391. 707 F. Supp. 525 (N.D. Ga. 1988), *aff'd*, 911 F.2d 1532, 1538 (11th Cir. 1990).

2392. *See* Chapter IV, Section C 2 c.

2393. 707 F. Supp. at 529.

2394. *Id.*

2395. *Id.*

such a way that the only record prepared was considered 'privileged.'"[2396]

The Eleventh Circuit affirmed the district court's decision. The Eleventh Circuit stated that "regardless of whether the district court renounced its earlier bad faith finding, it was clearly still concerned, in *Zapata*'s words, 'for other reasons relating to the process, including but not limited to . . . good faith.'"[2397] The court in *Weiland v. Illinois Power Co.*[2398]—a case discussed earlier in this Chapter[2399]—distinguished the district court's decision in *Peller* in part on the ground that the committee in *Illinois Power* had "planned and executed" its investigation itself and included memoranda summarizing all interviews in a report filed with the court rather than "shielding or withholding information."[2400]

The court in *Zitin v. Turley*,[2401] like the court in *Peller*, concluded that a determination to "specifically set up the investigation so that all of the communications and underlying information" upon which a committee's report was based "would be either privileged or work product" was "an indication of the lack of good faith of the Committee and Counsel in investigating the allegations" made in that case.[2402]

The same result was reached in *Davidowitz v. Edelman*,[2403] a case where the court concluded that a special litigation committee

---

2396. *Peller v. Southern Co.*, 911 F.2d 1532, 1538 n.6 (11th Cir. 1990).

2397. *Id.* (quoting *Zapata*, 430 A.2d at 789).

2398. [1990-1991 Transfer Binder] Fed. Sec. L. Rep. (CCH) ¶ 95,747 (C.D. Ill. Sept. 17, 1990)

2399. *See* Chapter IV, Sections B 6 g and C 2 c.

2400. [1990-1991 Transfer Binder] Fed. Sec. L. Rep. (CCH) at 98,586, 98,592.

2401. [1991 Transfer Binder] Fed. Sec. L. Rep. (CCH) ¶ 96,123 (D. Ariz. June 20, 1991), *interlocutory appeal denied*, [1991 Transfer Binder] Fed. Sec. L. Rep. (CCH) ¶ 96,284 (D. Ariz. Sept. 19, 1991).

2402. Id. at 90,684.

2403. 153 Misc. 2d 853, 583 N.Y.S.2d 340 (N.Y. Sup. Ct. Kings Co. 1992), *aff'd*, 203 A.D.2d 234, 612 N.Y.S.2d 882 (N.Y. App. Div. 2d Dep't 1994).

"did not join in their counsel's investigation or review, save in the most perfunctory manner" and thus the investigation "did not fulfill the requirements of a thorough and reasonable inquiry."[2404] The court also found that counsel "approached the investigation having determined that the actions of the board were shielded by the business judgment doctrine and their inquiry consequently was limited."[2405] The court stated that "[t]he erroneous use by the committee of a court's limited standard of review rather than the careful, diligent and meticulous standard required of a committee scrutinizing a possible breach of fiduciary duty vitiates the usefulness of the committee's findings as a defense to this action."[2406] The court accordingly held that "[t]he report of the special litigation committee is not entitled to this court's deference as a genuine business judgment."[2407] The trial court's decision was affirmed by an intermediate appellate court for the reasons stated by the trial court.[2408]

*i. Model and Statutory Provisions.* As discussed earlier in this Chapter, the Model Business Corporation Act and Principles of Corporate Governance: Analysis and Recommendations have proposed a universal demand requirement mandating demand in all cases except those where requiring a demand would cause irreparable injury to the corporation.[2409]

The Model Act provisions governing a board or special litigation committee refusal of such a universal demand or a motion to terminate a derivative action brought after a universal demand has been refused "carry forward the distinction" drawn under present law between cases where demand is required and cases where demand is excused "by establishing pleading rules and allocating the burden of proof" depending upon the composition of the board

---

2404. *Id.* at 857, 583 N.Y.S.2d at 344.

2405. *Id.* at 858, 583 N.Y.S.2d at 344.

2406. *Id.* at 857-88, 583 N.Y.S.2d at 344.

2407. *Id.* at 858, 583 N.Y.S.2d at 344.

2408. *Davidowitz v. Edelman*, 203 A.D.2d 234, 612 N.Y.S.2d 882 (N.Y. App. Div. 2d Dep't 1994).

2409. *See* Chapter IV, Section B 5 g.

—i.e., whether the board consists of a majority of independent
directors—at the time a determination is made that the maintenance
of a derivative action would not serve the best interests of the
corporation.[2410] Where a shareholder plaintiff alleges facts demonstrating that a majority of the board lacks disinterestedness or independence (and thus that demand would be excused under present
law), the corporation has the burden of proving that a determination
that litigation would not serve the best interests of the corporation
was made in good faith and on the basis of a reasonable
inquiry.[2411] Where a shareholder plaintiff fails to allege facts
demonstrating that a majority of the board lacks disinterestedness or
independence, the shareholder plaintiff has the burden of proving
that a determination that litigation would not serve the best interests
of the corporation was not made in good faith and on the basis of a
reasonable inquiry.[2412]

Principles of Corporate Governance, by contrast, rejects the
demand required versus demand excused distinction and the principles underlying that distinction. Instead, Principles of Corporate
Governance states detailed standards providing for differing levels
of judicial review depending upon the nature of the claim (duty of
care claims, for example, are treated differently than duty of loyalty
claims).[2413]

The Model Act and Principles of Corporate Governance provisions, statutes in Alaska, Arizona, Connecticut, Florida, Georgia,
Maine, Michigan, Mississippi, Montana, Nebraska, New Hampshire, North Carolina, Texas, Virginia and Wisconsin stating rules
governing board and special litigation committee decisions concerning derivative litigation, and a Pennsylvania decision adopting the
Principles of Corporate Governance approach—*Cuker v. Mikalauskas*[2414]—are discussed in detail earlier in this Chapter.[2415]

---

2410. 2 Model Bus. Corp. Act Annotated § 7.44 Official Comment
at 7–93-94 (3d ed. 1996).

2411. *Id.* §§ 7.44(a), (d), (e) & Official Comment at 7–93-94.

2412. *Id.* Official Comment at 7-94.

2413. *See* 2 Principles of Corporate Governance: Analysis and
Recommendations §§ 7.04–7.13 (1994).

2414. 692 A.2d 1042, 1048-55 (Pa. 1997).

Additional statutes enacted in Indiana, Minnesota and North Dakota dealing solely with special litigation committee decisions regarding derivative litigation also are discussed earlier in this Chapter.[2416]

## 3. Discovery on the Termination Issue

The scope of discovery that is permitted before a motion to terminate pursuant to a special litigation committee or SLC determination is decided is as important a consideration as the standard of judicial review and the definition of disinterestedness and independence used by the courts in evaluating the committee's recommendation. The more discovery plaintiff is permitted, the closer the motion to terminate comes to being the costly and time-consuming review of the merits that the motion is designed to avoid. As one federal court has noted, "strict limitation on the plaintiff's ability to take discovery regarding the SLC's report arises as an essential corollary of *Zapata*'s efficiency rationale" because "[a]llowing adversarial discovery on the merits would eviscerate the SLC's power."[2417]

*a. After the Committee is Formed, But Before its Recommendation.* The Delaware Court of Chancery stated in *Kaplan v. Wyatt*[2418] that after a special litigation committee is formed but before the committee completes its work it is "a foregone conclusion" that a stay of discovery "must be granted."[2419] "Otherwise," the court continued, "the entire rationale of *Zapata*, i.e., the inherent right of the board of directors to control and look to the well-being of the corporation in the first instance, collapses."[2420] Thus, once a special litigation committee is formed, "Delaware law

---

2415. (...continued)

    2415. *See* Chapter IV, Sections B 6 i and j.

    2416. *See* Chapter IV, Section C 1 b.

    2417. *Johnson v. Hui*, 811 F. Supp. 479, 490 n.9 (N.D. Cal. 1991).

    2418. 484 A.2d 501 (Del. Ch. 1984), *aff'd*, 499 A.2d 1184 (Del. 1985).

    2419. *Id.* at 510.

    2420. *Id.*

requires that all proceedings . . . be stayed pending the Committee's investigation."[2421]

Two federal courts construing Maryland law—*Burt v. Danforth*[2422] and *Strougo v. Padegs*[2423]—have followed the Delaware rule. In both cases, stays were ordered for three month periods, although in *Strougo* the three month stay, combined with the three months that the committee had had before the court ruled on the issue, provided the committee a total of six months to complete its work.[2424]

A federal court construing Delaware law in *Grafman v. Century Broadcasting Corp.*[2425] held that "the corporation itself has the initial, preemptive opportunity to investigate derivative claims, and to determine whether the corporation should pursue them," but "the corporation's power to investigate derivative claims does not translate into an absolute right to halt all related proceedings."[2426] Rather, the court explained, "[i]t is the duty of the courts to ensure that the corporation's investigation is not a mere artifice for delay." In order to carry out this duty, the court continued, a court must ascertain how long an investigation by a special litigation committee will take, what discovery the plaintiff seeks in the interim, and whether such discovery would interfere with the committee's investigation.[2427] The court stated that "[t]he parties do not discuss these matters in their briefs, and so the court will postpone its decision on the defendants' motion for a stay."[2428]

---

2421. *Katell v. Morgan Stanley Group, Inc.*, 19 Del. J. Corp. L. 797, 804 (Del. Ch. Sept. 27, 1993); *see also Pompeo v. Hefner*, 1983 Del. Ch. LEXIS 506, at *2-5, 1983 WL 20284, at *1-3 (Del. Ch. Mar. 23, 1983)

2422. No. 89-1276C(1) (E.D. Mo. Nov. 28, 1990).

2423. 986 F. Supp. 812 (S.D.N.Y. 1997).

2424. *Burt*, slip op. at 2-3; *Strougo*, 986 F. Supp. at 815.

2425. 743 F. Supp. 544 (N.D. Ill. 1990).

2426. *Id*. at 547, 548.

2427. *Id*.

2428. *Id*.

Another federal court, construing Minnesota law, denied a motion seeking a stay of proceedings pending a determination by a special litigation committee in *International Broadcasting Corp. v. Turner*[2429] because, the court found, the committee was not "sufficiently independent and disinterested . . . to warrant the granting of the requested stay."[2430] Discovery also was allowed by the Delaware Court of Chancery in *Szeto v. Schiffer*,[2431] a case where a special litigation committee was not empowered to act on behalf of the corporation and the stay of discovery was sought by the defendants in the litigation and the corporation rather than by the committee.[2432]

The Model Business Corporation Act provides that once an inquiry is commenced by a special litigation committee "the court may stay any derivative proceeding for such period as the court deems appropriate."[2433] The Model Act also states that "it is expected that the court will monitor the course of the inquiry to ensure that it is proceeding expeditiously and in good faith."[2434] Principles of Corporate Governance: Analysis and Recommendations provides that "the court should stay discovery and all further proceedings by the plaintiff in a derivative action on the motion of the corporation and upon such conditions as the court deems appropriate pending the completion within a reasonable period of any review and evaluation undertaken and diligently pursued" by a special litigation committee.[2435]

---

2429. 734 F. Supp. 383 (D. Minn. 1990).

2430. *Id.* at 393.

2431. 19 Del. J. Corp. L. 1310 (Del. Ch. Nov. 24, 1993).

2432. *Id.* at 1318-19; *see also Carlton Invs. v. TLC Beatrice Int'l Holdings, Inc.*, 22 Del. J. Corp. L. 1165, 1171 (Del. Ch. Jan. 28, 1997) (noting that court had "declined to stay plaintiff's opportunity to take discovery").

2433. 2 Model Bus. Corp. Act Annotated § 7.43 (3d ed. 1996).

2434. *Id.* § 7.43 Official Comment at 7-346; *see also* Chapter IV, Section B 6 b (discussing this issue in context of demand requirement).

2435. 2 Principles of Corporate Governance: Analysis and Recommendations § 7.06 (1994); *see also Cuker v. Mikalauskas*, 692 A.2d 1042, 1048 (Pa. 1997) (adopting Principles of Corporate Governance rule, but stating that "a court might stay the derivative action").

*b. After the Committee's Recommendation.* Two lines of cases, one in Delaware and one in New York, consider the appropriateness of discovery following a special litigation committee or "SLC" recommendation that a litigation should be terminated. This question also is addressed in the Model Business Corporation Act, Principles of Corporate Governance and various state statutes.

*(i) The Delaware Approach.* Once a motion to terminate is filed, according to the Delaware Supreme Court in *Zapata Corp. v. Maldonado*,[2436] "[l]imited discovery may be ordered" regarding the independence and good faith of the committee and the bases supporting its conclusions (i.e., step one of the two-step *Zapata* test)[2437] and "each side should have an opportunity to make a record on the motion."[2438] Post-*Zapata* decisions make clear that discovery on special litigation committee motions to terminate will be kept under relatively strict control and "may be undertaken only if first authorized by the court."[2439] As the Delaware Court of Chancery twice has noted, "if a derivative plaintiff is to be permitted full discovery of his case under the guise of making a record in opposition to a motion to dismiss brought by a special litigation committee, what would be the need for having the special litigation committee procedure to begin with?"[2440] To the contrary, "[t]he efficiency of the utilization of a special litigation committee would be defeated, at least in part, by permitting full discovery on the merits by a party objecting to the committee's recommendation, without any showing of evidence that the committee did not proceed in good faith."[2441]

---

2436. 430 A.2d 779 (Del. 1981).

2437. *See* Chapter IV, Section C 2 b.

2438. 430 A.2d at 788.

2439. *Kaplan v. Wyatt*, 484 A.2d 501, 507 (Del. Ch. 1984), *aff'd*, 499 A.2d 1184 (Del. 1985).

2440. *Abbey v. Computer & Communications Tech. Corp.*, 1983 Del. Ch. LEXIS 511, at *6, 1983 WL 18005, at *2 (Del. Ch. Apr. 13, 1983), *quoted in Carlton Invs. v. TLC Beatrice Int'l Holdings, Inc.*, 1997 Del. Ch. LEXIS 4, at *10 n.4 (Del. Ch. Jan. 28, 1997).

2441. *TLC Beatrice*, 1997 Del. Ch. LEXIS 4, at *10 n.4.

The Delaware Court of Chancery in *Kaplan v. Wyatt*[2442] explained the following:

> The decision in *Zapata* makes clear that the function of the Court . . . is to inquire into the independence and good faith of the committee and reasonableness of the bases for its conclusion that the derivative action should be dismissed. Limited discovery may be permitted by the Court, in its discretion, to facilitate its inquiries into this limited area. Thus, the purpose of any discovery at this stage is to aid the Court in evaluating the motion to dismiss under the aforesaid guidelines more so than to aid the plaintiff in developing facts which would support the merits of his case.[2443]

"[W]hat the Committee did or did not do, and the actual existence of the documents and persons purportedly examined by it, should constitute the factual record on which the decision as to the independence and good faith of the Committee, and the adequacy of its investigation in light of the derivative charges made, must be based."[2444]

The Court of Chancery in *Kaplan* accordingly required the production of four categories of documents related to the independence of the special litigation committee members in that case and refused to require the production of dozens of categories of documents used by the committee in its investigation. The court explained that "the total production of all other documents reviewed and relied upon by the Committee in compiling its report" is neither "necessary" nor "warranted" by "the plaintiff's right to challenge the good faith of the Committee or the reasonableness of the bases for its conclusion that the derivative action should be dismissed."[2445] The court stated that it was "mindful of the fact that the plaintiff has set forth no particulars in his complaint of any specific misconduct . . . to support his general charges of wrongdoing" by the defendants in the case, while the committee, by con-

---

2442. 9 Del. J. Corp. L. 205 (Del. Ch. Jan. 18, 1984), *aff'd*, 499 A.2d 1184 (Del. 1985).

2443. 9 Del. J. Corp. L. at 209 (citation omitted).

2444. 484 A.2d at 519.

2445. 9 Del. J. Corp. L. at 210.

trast, had "filed a lengthy and detailed report setting forth numerous findings as well as the factual basis relied upon by it in reaching each such conclusion."[2446] The court stated that the committee's report "discloses in detail the breadth of the Committee's investigation and the reasons for its recommendation," that "Plaintiff has the Committee's position and its bases therefore," and that "[t]here is no doubt" where the committee "stands on the plaintiff's charges, or why."[2447] The court stated that if plaintiff "has evidentiary matter which tends to contradict the facts relied upon and disclosed by the Committee in reaching its conclusions, or facts which would tend to indicate that the Committee did not conduct its investigation in good faith, then I think that the time has come for the plaintiff to bring them forth and develop them on his own as opposed to culling through hundreds or thousands of documents previously reviewed by the Committee on the pretense of attempting to satisfy himself that the Committee has done a good faith job and that its report and recommendation are warranted based on that which it had before it."[2448]

The court did grant the plaintiff in *Kaplan* the right to take a deposition of one member of the special committee, and stated that a deposition of the second member of the committee would have been allowed if the second member of the committee had not died.[2449] In light of the death of the second member of the committee and "[i]n view of the scope of the report and the length of the Committee's investigation," the court continued, "I do not think it would be fair to limit the plaintiff to the deposition of only one person who participated in the enterprise."[2450] The court therefore also permitted a deposition of the member of the law firm that represented the committee who was "most knowledgeable of the facts" underlying the committee's investigation and the manner in which the investigation was conducted.[2451] The court rejected a

---

2446. *Id.* at 210-11.
2447. *Id.* at 211.
2448. *Id.*
2449. *Id.*
2450. *Id.*
2451. *Id.*

request that depositions be permitted of all members of the law firm that assisted in the investigation.[2452]

In a later decision, the court noted the rationale underlying the plaintiff's extensive discovery requests in *Kaplan*:

> [E]xperience shows (as it did here) that the plaintiff will attempt to seek all the discovery that he could possibly hope to obtain if he were seeking discovery on the merits of the allegations of the complaint. And why not? He certainly has nothing to lose by asking. And he has arguable justification. How can he test fully the reasonableness and good faith of the Committee's investigation unless he looks at each and every document reviewed by the Committee and unless he takes his own deposition of each person interviewed by the Committee so as to compare the Committee's findings with his own? And why should he not have access even to documents that were not examined by the Committee? Certainly, if he can turn up something of substance that was ignored by the Committee, it will support his argument that the recommendation of the Committee should not be honored.[2453]

"Of course," the court concluded, "such all-encompassing discovery is not within the spirit of *Zapata* since its mandate contemplates only such discovery as fits the occasion in the view of the Court."[2454]

On appeal, the Delaware Supreme Court rejected plaintiff's contention that discovery had been improperly restricted as "totally without merit."[2455] The Supreme Court stated that "discovery is not by right, but by order of the Court, with the type and extent of discovery left totally to the discretion of the Court."[2456] The Supreme Court held that plaintiff "was not entitled to discover all the information relating to the Committee's report" and that the Court of Chancery provided plaintiff "with sufficient means to dis-

---

2452. *Id.* at 208.
2453. *Kaplan v. Wyatt*, 484 A.2d 501, 510-11 (Del. Ch. 1984), *aff'd*, 499 A.2d 1184 (Del. 1985).
2454. *Id.* at 511.
2455. *Kaplan v. Wyatt*, 499 A.2d 1184, 1192 (Del. 1985).
2456. *Id.*

cover and examine the independence and good faith of the Committee's investigation."[2457]

The Delaware Court of Chancery followed *Kaplan* in *Carlton Investments v. TLC Beatrice International Holdings, Inc.*,[2458] a case where a shareholder plaintiff, Carlton Investments, made "an extensive document request" seeking "all of the documents" reviewed by a special litigation committee that had recommended a settlement of litigation and all "documents regarding the manner" in which the committee "was assisted by its counsel and other expert advisors."[2459] Carlton also sought to take depositions of both members of the committee, the committee's counsel, and an expert retained by the committee to assist it in its investigation.[2460]

The court rejected Carlton's attempt to distinguish *Kaplan* on the ground that Carlton was "not seeking merits discovery" because Carlton already had spent "eighteen months doing extensive discovery on the merits" and already possessed "practically the entire universe of merits-related documents and testimony that the 'SLC or its counsel' reviewed."[2461] According to the court, "[t]he fact that Carlton has already had an opportunity to do such discovery in this case does not, in my opinion, entitle Carlton to do the type of discovery denied to the *Kaplan* plaintiff."[2462] Rather, the court continued, "to avoid further wasted resources and delay, Carlton should be similarly limited in its discovery at this time.[2463] Quoting *Kaplan*, the court stated that if Carlton

> has evidentiary matter which tends to contradict the facts relied upon and disclosed by the Committee in reaching its conclusions, or facts which would tend to indicate that the Committee did not conduct its investigation in good faith, then I think the time has come for the plaintiff to bring them

---

2457. *Id.*
2458. 22 Del. J. Corp. L. 1165 (Del. Ch. Jan. 28, 1997).
2459. *Id.* at 1169, 1172.
2460. *Id.* at 1169.
2461. *Id.* at 1173.
2462. *Id.*
2463. *Id.*

> forth and develop them on his own as opposed to culling through hundreds or thousands of documents previously reviewed by the Committee on the pretense of attempting to satisfy himself that the Committee had done a good faith job and that its report and recommendation are warranted based upon that which it had before it.[2464]

According to the court, "[a]fter almost two years of discovery in this matter, Carlton should be well-equipped without further discovery to evaluate the independence, good faith, and reasonableness" of the committee's investigation.[2465]

The court therefore required production only of documents related to the creation of the committee and the appointment of its two members, retention letters between the committee and its counsel and between counsel and the committee's compensation expert, and communications between the committee and defendants relating to "the case or its settlement."[2466]

The court also held that Carlton could not take the deposition of the committee's counsel. The court again relied upon *Kaplan*, stating that "[i]n *Kaplan*, the Court made it clear that under normal circumstances it would not allow a derivative plaintiff to depose counsel for a special litigation committee" and that an exception was made in *Kaplan* only because a committee member had died prior to being deposed concerning the committee's investigation.[2467] Here, the court explained, "[w]hat is important at this stage in the proceedings" is what the committee "knew and did during the investigation and in reaching their conclusions."[2468] This information, the court stated, can be obtained by deposing the committee members.[2469] The court acknowledged that a different circumstance would be present if there were "grounds to think that counsel himself acted in bad faith—manipulating the process" in an attempt to affect the committee's deliberations, but stated that

---

2464. *Id.* at 1173-74.
2465. *Id.* at 1174.
2466. *Id.*
2467. *Id.*
2468. *Id.* at 1175.
2469. *Id.*

"[t]here is no ground to suspect that here . . . or to assume such a fact, and no fishing expedition into that terrain will be permitted at this point."[2470]

Other courts applying the *Zapata* approach similarly have permitted the depositions of committee members and production of some documents considered during the committee's investigation, but not merits discovery or documents prepared or reviewed by the committee's counsel that were not provided to committee members. Examples include the following cases:

- *Watts v. Des Moines Register & Tribune*,[2471] ("[P]laintiff shareholders are entitled to limited discovery into the bases supporting the committee's conclusions in order to challenge the reasonableness of such conclusions. . . . [P]laintiffs may inquire into *what* factors entered into the committee's decision, but not *why* such factors were considered or not considered.");[2472]

- *Abbey v. Computer & Communications Technology Corp.*[2473] ("[P]laintiff will be limited to taking the deposition of the Special Litigation Committee with a view toward establishing just what was done in the course of its investigation, and why. This will include production of the documentary materials utilized or relied upon by the Committee during its investigation.");[2474]

- *Peller v. Southern Co.*[2475] (limiting discovery to depositions of committee members, production of a list of documents reviewed by the committee, production of

---

2470. *Id.*

2471. 525 F. Supp. 1311 (S.D. Iowa 1981).

2472. *Id.* at 1329.

2473. 1983 Del. Ch. LEXIS 511, 1983 WL 18005 (Del. Ch. Apr. 13, 1983).

2474. 1983 Del. Ch. LEXIS 511, at *8, 1983 WL 18005, at *3.

2475. [1987-1988 Transfer Binder] Fed. Sec. L. Rep. (CCH) ¶ 93,714 (N.D. Ga. Mar. 25, 1988), *aff'd on other grounds*, 911 F.2d 1532 (11th Cir. 1990).

notes taken by committee members during interviews and production of minutes or notes taken during committee meetings, and in each case only with respect to the following issues "specified" as "particular concerns" to the court and "no others": (1) the committee's focus upon "the overall decisions" to finish construction of a nuclear power plant rather than "specific decisions regarding the plant's construction" and the committee's failure to address "specific findings" of imprudence by a regulatory agency's consultants, and (2) the adequacy of the committee's investigation of "damage to the corporation and collectability of damages," in light of the committee's statement that "because it found the allegations of the complaint to be without merit, it accorded little weight to the issue of damages and collectability" and the fact that the committee "appears to have relied solely upon a letter from the insurance carrier stating that the carrier believed, based upon its reading of the complaint, that insurance was not available");[2476]

- *Farber v. Public Service Co.*[2477] (limiting discovery to "documents that were reviewed and relied on by the SLC which have not already been produced" and not requiring production of "notes of the SLC and its members," "communications of the SLC to and from third parties including persons interviewed, consultants, business people, etc." and "reports or communications to the committee by the committee's experts and consultants"; the court stated that "[t]his exclusion is being made either on the basis of work product or applicable privilege, or in the proper exercise of my discretion considering the purposes of a special litigation commit-

---

2476. *Id.* at 98,312.

2477. [1991 Transfer Binder] Fed. Sec. L. Rep. (CCH) ¶ 96,106 (D.N.M. Apr. 4, 1991).

tee, the relationship of the parties, and the nature of the respective law suits");[2478]

- *Johnson v. Hui*[2479] (limiting discovery to the depositions of committee members and the production of documents relied upon by the committee, including notes taken by committee members and documents prepared or reviewed by counsel that were considered or relied upon by the committee and drafts of the committee's final report that were reviewed by the committee but excluding documents prepared or reviewed by the committee's counsel that were not provided to committee members, and not allowing a deposition of the committee's counsel);[2480] and

- *Litton Industries, Inc. v. Hoch*[2481] (affirming rulings limiting discovery to the committee report, board minutes and committee minutes, and not permitting discovery of notes taken by the committee's counsel during witness interviews conducted by counsel and various other documents; the court explained: "The SLC relied on oral summaries of witness interviews, rather than the written notes of counsel. Thus counsel's notes of witness interviews are not relevant to the good faith and reasonableness of the SLC's investigation and the Board's decision. In the absence of a reason to suspect the reliability of the lawyers' work in preparing the summaries, the SLC had no obligation to read the lawyers' notes of the witness interviews to make sure that the summaries provided to the SLC reflected those notes. Thus, the district court did not abuse its discre-

---

2478. *Id*. at 90,597-98.
2479. No. C-90-1863 DLJ (N.D. Cal. June 27, 1991), *subsequent proceedings*, 811 F. Supp. 479 (N.D. Cal. 1991).
2480. No. C-90-1863 DLJ, slip op. at 2-4; 811 F. Supp. at 483.
2481. 996 F.2d 1225 (unpublished opinion, text available at 1993 U.S. App. LEXIS 16992 and 1993 WL 241549) (9th Cir. July 2, 1993).

tion in denying the plaintiffs' motion to compel production of the witness notes or any other documents.").[2482]

One court has suggested that its potential need to exercise independent business judgment under the second step of the *Zapata* test may be considered in formulating an appropriate discovery order.[2483] Another court has concluded that it was required to "rely upon the record generated by the Committee" in determining whether to exercise its discretion under the second step of the *Zapata* test.[2484]

*(ii) The New York Approach.* Unlike the *Zapata Corp. v. Maldonado*[2485] standard of review provided for by Delaware law,[2486] the *Auerbach v. Bennett*[2487] standard of review provided for by New York law[2488] limits judicial review to the "disinterested independence" of committee members and "the appropriateness and sufficiency of the investigative procedures chosen and pursued by the committee."[2489] "[T]he substantive aspects of a decision to terminate a shareholders' derivative action against defendant corporate directors made by a committee of disinterested directors appointed by the corporation's board of directors are beyond judicial inquiry under the business judgment doc-

---

2482. 1993 U.S. App. LEXIS 16992, at *5-6, 1993 WL 241549, at *3. *But see Zitin v. Turley*, [1991 Transfer Binder] Fed. Sec. L. Rep. (CCH) ¶ 96,123, at 90,683 (D. Ariz. June 20, 1991) (permitting discovery of 16 categories of documents, including drafts of a committee report, documents reviewed by the committee or its counsel, documents "made regarding and communications between" the committee and its counsel and any individuals interviewed by the committee or counsel, and communications between the committee and its counsel and any defendant or defendant's counsel), *interlocutory appeal denied*, [1991 Transfer Binder] Fed. Sec. L. Rep. (CCH) ¶ 96,284 (D. Ariz. Sept. 19, 1991).

2483. *Kaplan*, 484 A.2d at 510.

2484. *Rosengarten v. Buckley*, 613 F. Supp. 1493, 1503 (D. Md. 1985).

2485. 430 A.2d 779 (Del. 1981).

2486. *See* Chapter IV, Section C 2 b.

2487. 47 N.Y.2d 619, 393 N.E.2d 994, 419 N.Y.S.2d 920 (1979).

2488. *See* Chapter IV, Section C 2 a.

2489. *Id.* at 623-24, 393 N.E.2d at 996, 419 N.Y.S.2d at 922.

trine."[2490] No discovery was allowed in *Auerbach* because there had been no request for discovery at trial court level and no identification at the appellate level by the party seeking discovery of "any particulars as to which he desires discovery relating to the disinterestedness of the members of the special litigation committee or to the procedures followed by that committee."[2491]

The New York Court of Appeals in *Parkoff v. General Telephone & Electronics Corp.*[2492] (in dictum, because the case was decided pursuant to res judicata principles)[2493] stated that discovery should be permitted in connection with the issues upon which judicial inquiry is permitted under *Auerbach.*[2494] The court in *Parkoff* rejected a claim that "recognition of a generalized demand for disclosure as sufficient to cause postponement of a motion for summary judgment might be thought to authorize and countenance fishing expeditions."[2495] The court explained that "in this type of case the plaintiff must necessarily be given more latitude to discover than in most and that the appropriate counterbalance lies in the vigilance of the court in its oversight of disclosure devices to issue appropriate protective orders so as to forestall their employment as instruments of corporate harassment without frustrating the legitimate interests of the shareholder plaintiffs."[2496]

In *Levit v. Rowe,*[2497] a federal court construing New York law and following the *Parkoff* guidelines denied plaintiffs' request

---

2490. *Id.* at 623, 393 N.E.2d at 996, 419 N.Y.S.2d at 922.

2491. *Id.* at 636, 393 N.E.2d at 1003-04, 419 N.Y.S.2d at 930.

2492. 53 N.Y.2d 412, 425 N.E.2d 820, 442 N.Y.S.2d 432 (1981).

2493. *Id.* at 418-23, 425 N.E.2d at 822-25, 442 N.Y.S.2d at 435-38.

2494. *Id.* at 417-18, 425 N.E.2d at 822, 442 N.Y.S.2d at 434; *see also Byers v. Baxter*, 69 A.D.2d 343, 348-50, 419 N.Y.S.2d 497, 500-01 (N.Y. App. Div. 1st Dep't 1979) (pre-*Auerbach* and *Parkoff* decision permitting discovery).

2495. 53 N.Y.2d at 418 n.2, 425 N.E.2d at 822 n.2, 442 N.Y.S.2d at 434 n.2.

2496. *Id.*

2497. 1991 U.S. Dist. LEXIS 8314, 1991 WL 111173 (E.D. Pa. June 18, 1991).

for "essentially every document connected with or considered" during a special litigation committee's investigation.[2498] With respect to the disinterestedness and independence of the committee members, the court stated that plaintiffs had not alleged any impropriety in the choice of special litigation committee members and therefore were not entitled to any discovery on this issue.[2499] With respect to the committee's methodology, the court limited discovery by permitting plaintiff only "enough discovery . . . to learn whether the committee selected procedures that were appropriate to its charge."[2500]

To accomplish this, the court directed the corporation "to collect the materials used or consulted in connection with the special committee's investigation and divide them into four groups."[2501] The four groups consisted of the following:

A. The first group shall contain all documents and materials concerning solely matters of procedure and methodology.

B. The second group shall contain all documents and materials concerning a combination of procedural, methodological, and substantive matters.

C. The third group shall include all documents concerning purely substantive matters.

D. The fourth group shall include all privileged materials not falling into any other category.[2502]

The term "substantive matters" as used in these four groups was defined to "include things relating to 'the ultimate substantive

---

2498. 1991 U.S. Dist. LEXIS 8314, at *2, 1991 WL 111173, at *1.

2499. 1991 U.S. Dist. LEXIS 8314, at *6, 1991 WL 111173, at *3.

2500. 1991 U.S. Dist. LEXIS 8314, at *6-7, 1991 WL 111173, at *3.

2501. 1991 U.S. Dist. LEXIS 8314, at *7, 1991 WL 111173, at *3.

2502. 1991 U.S. Dist. LEXIS 8314, at *8, 1991 WL 111173, at *3.

decision . . . not to pursue the claims'" advanced by the shareholder plaintiffs in the case.[2503]

    The court ordered the corporation to produce the documents in the first group to the plaintiffs in the case and to produce a list of each document in the second, third and fourth groups to the court for an in camera inspection.[2504] The court stated that it would "entertain further discovery requests" if plaintiffs' "examination of the methodological materials reveal the special committee's work was not reasonably complete," or that the committee "failed to make a good faith pursuit of inquiry into all relevant areas."[2505] In this way, the court concluded, "plaintiffs will be able to pursue specific areas if they have legitimate questions, and I will maintain the control *Parkoff* contemplates."[2506] Following a request by plaintiff for further discovery, the court stated that "my order left the door open for future discovery if the plaintiffs could identify specific areas of inquiry based on the materials they received" and then denied further discovery because plaintiffs failed to "identify specific areas of inquiry and appropriate justification."[2507]

    *(iii) Model and Statutory Provisions.* As discussed earlier in this Chapter, statutes enacted in Arizona, Connecticut, Florida, Georgia, Maine, Michigan, Mississippi, Montana, Nebraska, New Hampshire, North Carolina, Texas, Virginia and Wisconsin and model formulations proposed by the Model Business Corporation Act and Principles of Corporate Governance: Analysis and Recom-

---

2503. 1991 U.S. Dist. LEXIS 8314, at *7, 1991 WL 111173, at *3 (quoting *Auerbach*, 47 N.Y.2d at 633, 393 N.E.2d at 1002, 419 N.Y.S.2d at 928).

2504. 1991 U.S. Dist. LEXIS 8314, at *7-8, 1991 WL 111173, at *3.

2505. 1991 U.S. Dist. LEXIS 8314, at *8, 1991 WL 111173, at *3.

2506. 1991 U.S. Dist. LEXIS 8314, at *8, 1991 WL 111173, at *3.

2507. *Levit v. Rowe*, 1992 U.S. Dist. LEXIS 15036, at *22, 1992 WL 277997, at *8 (E.D. Pa. Sept. 30, 1992).

mendations have adopted universal demand requirements[2508] and authorize the refusal of shareholder demands[2509] and the termination of derivative litigation by boards or board committees.[2510] Pennsylvania has adopted the Principles of Corporate Governance formulation by judicial decision.[2511] As also discussed earlier in this Chapter, Alaska, Indiana, Minnesota and North Dakota have enacted additional statutes governing termination of derivative litigation by board committees.[2512]

The Model Business Corporation Act permits discovery only after a shareholder plaintiff states a cause of action by pleading particularized facts that, if true, would demonstrate that directors who have determined that derivative litigation would not serve the best interests of the corporation either are not independent or did not make their determination in good faith after conducting a reasonable inquiry.[2513] Principles of Corporate Governance states that the court may order "limited discovery" or a "limited evidentiary hearing" if the plaintiff demonstrates that "a substantial issue exists" concerning the special litigation committee's decision that litigation would not serve the best interests of the corporation and "if the plaintiff is unable without undue hardship to obtain the information by other means."[2514] The scope of this discovery or evidentiary hearing is limited to issues the court finds "necessary to enable it to render a decision on the motion" seeking dismissal of the action and must be "consistent with an expedited resolution of the motion."[2515] The Pennsylvania Supreme Court states in its decision adopting the Principles of Corporate Governance approach

---

2508. *See* Chapter IV, Section B 5 g.

2509. *See* Chapter IV, Section B 6 i-j.

2510. *See* Chapter IV, Section C 1 b.

2511. *See Cuker v. Mikalauskas*, 692 A.2d 1042, 1048-55 (Pa. 1997).

2512. *See* Chapter IV, Section C 1 b.

2513. 2 Model Bus. Corp. Act Annotated § 7.44(a) & Official Comment at 7-95 (3d ed. 1996).

2514. 2 Principles of Corporate Governance: Analysis and Recommendations § 7.13(c) (1994).

2515. *Id.*

that "[t]he court might order limited discovery or an evidentiary hearing to resolve issues respecting the board's decision."[2516]

To the extent that the state statutes identified above include additional (or different) rules governing discovery, those rules are discussed above.[2517]

## 4.  The Special Litigation Committee— Some Practical Considerations

Former Delaware Chancellor Grover C. Brown observed in *Kaplan v. Wyatt*[2518] that the entire special litigation committee procedure provided for in *Zapata v. Maldonado Corp.*[2519] and its progeny is "fraught with practical complications at the trial court level."[2520] Chancellor Brown stated that the procedure "certainly does not speed up the course of derivative litigation" and that it is "doubtful" whether it "reduces the expense or inconvenience of derivative litigation to the corporation."[2521]   In Chancellor Brown's words:

> Experience since *Zapata*, including the activities in this case, indicates that procedurally the Special Litigation Committee approach has added at least three new hearings to a derivative suit brought by a shareholder in the absence of demand on the board of directors. The first thing that takes place is that the Special Litigation Committee, upon being appointed, promptly moves on the corporation's behalf for a stay of all discovery by the plaintiff pending the investigation and report of the Committee. It is a foregone conclusion that such a stay must be granted. Otherwise, the entire rationale of *Zapata*, i.e., the inherent right of the board of directors to control and look to the well-being of the corporation in the first instance, collapses.

---

2516. *Cuker*, 692 A.2d at 1048.
2517. *See* Chapter IV, Section B 6 i.
2518. 484 A.2d 501 (Del. Ch. 1984), *aff'd*, 499 A.2d 1184 (Del. 1985).
2519. 430 A.2d 779 (Del. 1981).
2520. 484 A.2d at 509.
2521. *Id.*

The practical problem comes, however, with the length of the stay. This, in turn, must be measured against the complexities of the plaintiff's allegations since the nature of the wrongs alleged will naturally have a bearing on the extent of the investigation to be made. The Committee generally will seek a stay of many months so that it will have ample time to be thorough in its task. (*Zapata* specifically requires that the investigation be thorough.) The plaintiff naturally thinks that a far shorter time, say 60 to 90 days, will be adequate. Thus the conflicting contentions of the parties, and their reasons, must be heard and the Court must issue a ruling setting a timetable for the extra-judicial investigation to be performed by the Committee.

Secondly, it would seem that there always exists at least a reasonable likelihood that the Committee will come back with a report recommending that the suit be dismissed. . . . In that event, the plaintiff then moves . . . to take discovery of the Special Litigation Committee so as to examine into its independence and good faith, the reasonableness of its investigation given the circumstances, and the justification for its conclusions and recommendations. . . . [S]ince such discovery is not afforded to the plaintiff as a matter of right but only to such extent as the Court deems necessary for the purpose of facilitating its inquiries, and since each case will naturally vary according to its facts, it necessarily follows that the Court is first required to read and digest the report of the Special Litigation Committee before determining the extent of the discovery to be permitted. This discovery exercise under the *Zapata* procedure has its drawbacks.

To begin with, the developing rule of thumb in this jurisdiction would appear to be that a report by a Special Litigation Committee recommending dismissal of a derivative suit must be at least 150 pages in length, exclusive of appendices and attachments. Presumably, length is thought to be supportive of thoroughness and good faith on the part of the Committee. Correspondingly, it is apparently feared that a shorter report might be thought to be indicative of the converse. In any event, it then becomes the task of the Court to review the report for the purpose of ruling on the plaintiff's pending discovery request, keeping in mind that at the same time the Court is laying a foundation for the possible exercise of its business judgment in the event that it should feel the need, in its discretion, to go to the second step of the *Zapata* test in ultimately passing on the motion to dismiss.

Also as a practical matter, experience shows (as it did here) that the plaintiff will attempt to seek all the discovery that he could possibly hope to obtain if he were seeking discovery on the merits of the allegations of the complaint. And why not? He certainly has nothing to lose by asking. And he has arguable justification. How can he test fully the reasonableness and good faith of the Committee's investigation unless he looks at each and every document reviewed by the Committee and unless he takes his own deposition of each person interviewed by the Committee so as to compare the Committee's findings with his own? And why should he not have access even to documents that were not examined by the Committee? Certainly, if he can turn up something of substance that was ignored by the Committee, it will support his argument that the recommendation of the Committee should not be honored. Of course, such all encompassing discovery is not within the spirit of *Zapata* since its mandate contemplates only such discovery as fits the occasion in the view of the Court.

In any event, the "limited discovery" request of the plaintiff takes on particular significance since that which he gets— which in all probability will be something less than all he wants—will constitute the framework on which he must defend the motion initiated by the Special Litigation Committee to have his derivative suit dismissed. Again, after assimilating a lengthy factual report, the Court must hear the parties on this issue and make the appropriate ruling.

Finally, we come to the third hearing, namely, the hearing on the motion sponsored by the Special Litigation Committee to dismiss the suit. By that time, . . . the shareholder plaintiff has his back to the wall. He is about to be put out of court unless he can establish that there is a genuine dispute of material fact with regard to the investigation and effort of the Committee or unless it can be made to appear from the record on the motion that for some reason the Committee is not an independent one, or that it did not act in good faith, or that there are no reasonable bases to support its conclusions and recommendation. This naturally causes the plaintiff to pull out all stops and to throw every possible argument imaginable into the controversy, no matter how minor or pica-yune.

The facts of this case are indicative of the breadth that the scope of such a hearing can take on. In this case the Special Litigation Committee represents that it has interviewed more than 140 persons at various locations throughout the world during the course of its investigation. . . . The law firm retained by the Special Litigation Committee to assist it in its investigation is said to have expended more than 2,000 hours on the matter so far (this is plaintiff's figure—the Committee says the hours are 5,000 in number) and has received fees and reimbursements in the vicinity of $500,000 for its efforts. The report itself is 156 pages in length, exclusive of attachments.

When the results of such an all-out effort by the Committee are set against an all-out attack by the plaintiff on each and every item on which he can arguably base a claim of lack of independence, bad faith or questionable investigatory proce dure or conclusion on the part of the Committee, the complexity of the adjudicatory task becomes apparent.

In short, the new *Zapata* procedure, while perhaps laudatory in legal concept, has the pragmatic effect of setting up a form of litigation within litigation. (At this point in this case, we are some three years after the amended complaint was filed, we have had three full-scale, briefed arguments, we have had all of the investigation and activity previously mentioned, and as yet we have not reached the point of any of the normal discovery and motion practice permitted by the Court Rules.) The *Zapata* procedure adds, in effect, a new party to derivative litigation—the Special Litigation Committee—and a new battery of lawyers—counsel for the Committee—with the attendant expense to the corporation. It sidetracks derivative litigation as we have heretofore known it for approximately two years at a minimum while the Committee goes through its functions and while the plaintiff passively awaits his chances to resist them. And in the process the *Zapata* procedure has imposed substantial additional burdens at the trial court level in each such derivative suit in which it has been employed.[2522]

## D.  The Limited Partnership Context

As outlined in the preceding sections of this Chapter, the 1980s and 1990s have witnessed tremendous developments in the law governing shareholder derivative litigation on behalf of corporations. Until the early 1990s, however, there was only sparse law involving derivative litigation brought by limited partners on behalf of limited partnerships.[2523] Decisions in the Delaware Court of Chancery during the early and mid 1990s—two in *Litman v. Prudential-Bache Properties, Inc.*,[2524] four in *Katell v. Morgan Stanley Group, Inc.*[2525] and one in *Seaford Funding LP v. M & M Associates II, LP*[2526]—expand the law in this area considerably.

---

2522. *Id.* at 510-12; *see also Katell v. Morgan Stanley Group, Inc.*, [1995 Transfer Binder] Fed. Sec. L. Rep. (CCH) ¶ 98,861, at 93,171 (Del. Ch. June 15, 1995) ("the *Zapata* procedure encourages Plaintiffs to bring an all out attack against the details of the Special Committee's investigation"); Lewis, *In Restrained Praise of the Derivative Suit*, 12 Litigation No. 1, Fall 1985, at 3 (criticizing entire special litigation committee procedure).

2523. *See, e.g., Allright Mo., Inc. v. Billeter*, 829 F.2d 631, 635-38 (8th Cir. 1987) (holding that limited partners have standing to assert derivative claims on behalf of limited partnerships and rejecting a minority line of cases "barring in at least some instances a limited partner from bringing a derivative suit").

2524. 611 A.2d 12 (Del. Ch. 1992) *("Litman I")*, *subsequent proceedings*, [1992-1993 Transfer Binder] Fed. Sec. L. Rep. (CCH) ¶ 97,313 (Del. Ch. Jan. 4, 1993) *("Litman II")*.

2525. [1992-1993 Transfer Binder] Fed. Sec. L. Rep. (CCH) ¶ 97,437 (Del. Ch. Jan. 14, 1993) *("Katell I")*, *subsequent proceedings*, 1993 Del. Ch. LEXIS 92, 1993 WL 205033 (Del. Ch. June 8, 1993) *("Katell II")*, *subsequent proceedings*, 19 Del. J. Corp. L. 797 (Del. Ch. Sept. 27, 1993) *("Katell III")*, *subsequent proceedings*, [1995 Transfer Binder] Fed. Sec. L. Rep. (CCH) ¶ 98,861 (Del. Ch. June 15, 1995) *("Katell IV")*.

2526. 672 A.2d 66 (Del. 1995).

## 1. The Demand Requirement

The Court of Chancery's decision in *Litman v. Prudential-Bache Properties, Inc. ("Litman I")*[2527] holds that the determination whether a fiduciary duty lawsuit is derivative in nature—and thus subject to the pre-litigation demand requirement—is "substantially the same" in limited partnership cases as it is in corporate cases.[2528] The *Litman* case involved allegations that general partners had breached their fiduciary duties to limited partners by inadequately investigating and monitoring investments and placing their interest in obtaining fees for themselves above the interests of limited partners. The court held that the complaint alleged a claim that was derivative in nature and that plaintiff's failure to bring the suit derivatively and to comply with the pre-litigation demand requirement required dismissal of the action.[2529]

Plaintiffs amended their complaint and alleged in *Litman v. Prudential-Bache Properties, Inc. ("Litman II")*[2530] that demand was excused on the ground (among others) that "a corporation and its directors have the prerogative of controlling derivative litigation, while general partners do not."[2531] The court rejected this contention on the ground that the statutory rules requiring a demand in the corporate context and in the limited partnership context are "almost identical."[2532] The rules in both contexts, the court stated, require that "a plaintiff plead 'with particularity' those facts which warrant a suit."[2533]

---

2527. 611 A.2d 12 (Del. Ch. 1992).

2528. *Id.* at 15 & n.3; *see also* Chapter IV, Section A 8 (discussing distinction between derivative and non-derivative actions).

2529. *Id.* at 17; *see also* Chapter IV, Section B (discussing demand requirement).

2530. [1992-1993 Transfer Binder] Fed. Sec. L. Rep. (CCH) ¶ 97,313 (Del. Ch. Jan. 4, 1993).

2531. *Id.* at 95,583.

2532. *Id.*

2533. *Id.* (citing Del. Ch. R. 23.1 and 6 Del. C. §§ 17-1001, 17-1003); *see also* Chapter IV, Section B 5 (discussing rules governing demand futility).

Applying these principles to the allegations regarding demand futility in *Litman II*, the court held that demand was not excused.[2534] Plaintiffs appealed the *Litman II* decision, and the Delaware Supreme Court, without addressing the pre-litigation demand requirement, remanded the case to determine an issue not reached by the Court of Chancery in *Litman I* or *II*: whether plaintiffs' claims were time-barred.[2535] On remand, the Court of Chancery dismissed the case on that ground.[2536] Plaintiffs appealed again, and the Supreme Court affirmed "on the basis of and for the reasons stated in the Court of Chancery's well-reasoned Memorandum Opinion."[2537]

The Court of Chancery re-affirmed the principles stated in *Litman I* and *II* concerning the demand requirement in derivative litigation on behalf of limited partnerships in *Katell v. Morgan Stanley Group, Inc.*[2538] Unlike the case in *Litman II*, the court in *Katell* held that the allegations in that case did excuse demand.[2539]

## 2. The Wrongful Refusal of Demand Doctrine

The Court of Chancery's decision in *Seaford Funding LP v. M & M Associates II, LP*[2540] holds that the rules governing judi-

---

2534. [1992-1993 Transfer Binder] Fed. Sec. L. Rep. (CCH) at 95,583.

2535. *Litman v. Prudential-Bache Properties, Inc.*, 1993 WL 603303, at *1 (Del. Nov. 18, 1993).

2536. *Litman v. Prudential-Bache Properties, Inc.*, 19 Del. J. Corp. L. 1260 (Del. Ch. Jan. 14, 1994), *aff'd*, 642 A.2d 837 (unpublished opinion, text available at 1994 Del. LEXIS 125 and 1994 WL 144297) (Del. Apr. 21, 1994).

2537. *Litman v. Prudential-Bache Properties, Inc.*, 642 A.2d 837 (unpublished opinion, text available at 1994 Del. LEXIS 125, at *1 and 1994 WL 144297, at *7) (Del. Apr. 21, 1994).

2538. [1992-1993 Transfer Binder] Fed. Sec. L. Rep. (CCH) ¶ 97,437 (Del. Ch. Jan. 14, 1993).

2539. *Id*. at 96,441.

2540. 672 A.2d 66 (Del. Ch. 1995).

cial review of refusals of pre-litigation demands by directors in the context of corporations also govern refusals of pre-litigation demands in the context of limited partnerships.[2541]

The court, however, also held that the rule in the corporate context that a shareholder who makes a demand concedes the disinterestedness and independence of a majority of the corporation's board[2542] does not necessarily apply in the limited partnership context. The court explained that "[t]he demand rules assume the existence of an effective dispute resolution mechanism shareholders concede should be in the hands of an independent and effective board of managers elected to decide corporate policy," and that "submitting the dispute first to the board, reasoned persons acting in an environment constituting a more practical alternative than the Courts, promotes judicial efficiency."[2543] The rule in the corporate context that a shareholder who makes a demand concedes board disinterestedness and independence, the court continued, "requires a further leap of faith—that logic as well as judicial economy support the conclusion that submission of the demand for action to the board requires one to conclude the decision making authority is capable of acting independently and without self-interest."[2544] The court stated that "[h]ow well this rule functions . . . is a question beyond our responsibility to answer," but that "in the limited partnership context, the doctrine fails to promote judicial efficiency at least when there is a single general partner."[2545]

In the *Seaford Funding* case, the court continued, the rule did not apply. The court explained that the partnership on whose behalf the litigation was brought had only one general partner, Thomas R. Mullen, and the limited partners who brought the litigation had pleaded facts that, if true, would demonstrate self-dealing and

2541. *Id.* at 70; *see also* Chapter IV, Sections B 6 c-j (discussing refusals of demands).
2542. *See* Chapter IV, Section B 5 i (i) and 6 d.
2543. *Id.* at 71.
2544. *Id.*
2545. *Id.*

personal interest on the part of Mullen.[2546] Under these circumstances, the court reasoned as follows:

> The limited partners, understanding Mullen's self-interested conflict, simply requested Mullen do what he personally obligated himself to do in a way that made sense from a practical point of view. Basically they asked the one individual empowered to act to do so in the obvious best interest of the limited partnership he controlled. This gave Mullen an opportunity to do the right thing under uncontrovertible circumstances. A rule punishing plaintiffs using intrapartnership remedies to avoid litigation flatly and illogically conflicts with any rational view of the concept of judicial efficiency. Parties attempting to avoid rushing to the courthouse should be rewarded, not penalized. A court of equity ought not blindly apply a corporate rule which is premised upon a reasoned vote of a majority of individuals constituting a board of directors, to a one person general partner enveloped in a self-spun web of conflicting interests.[2547]

In short, the court concluded, "[t]here are no Delaware cases extending the innovative corporate concession rule to limited partnerships," and "I will not do so on these facts."[2548]

## 3.  Special Litigation Committees

Four decisions in *Katell v. Morgan Stanley Group, Inc.* *("Katell I",*[2549] *"Katell II",*[2550] *"Katell III"*[2551] and *"Katell IV")*[2552] explore the applicability of corporate special litigation committee concepts in the limited partnership context. The case involved claims brought on behalf of the Morgan Stanley Lever-

---

2546. *Id.*

2547. *Id.*

2548. *Id.*

2549. [1992-1993 Transfer Binder] Fed. Sec. L. Rep. (CCH) ¶ 97,437 (Del. Ch. Jan. 14, 1993).

2550. 1993 Del. Ch. LEXIS 92, 1993 WL 205033 (Del. Ch. June 8, 1993).

2551. 19 Del. J. Corp. L. 797 (Del. Ch. Sept. 27, 1993).

2552. [1995 Transfer Binder] Fed. Sec. L. Rep. (CCH) ¶ 98,861 (Del. Ch. June 15, 1995).

aged Equity Fund, L.P. (the "Fund") by two limited partners, Gerald Katell and Desert Equities, Inc. The Fund had two general partners having equal voting power: Morgan Stanley LCF and CIGNA LCF, which were affiliates of Morgan Stanley & Co. and CIGNA Corporation, respectively.[2553]

Disagreements arose between Morgan Stanley and CIGNA, and they determined to wind up the Fund's affairs and sell the Fund's assets to Morgan Stanley affiliates. These sales, principally involving investments in leveraged buy-outs of Container Corporation of America ("CCA") and Silgan Corporation, proved "very lucrative" and produced "handsome profits" for all of the Fund's partners. Plaintiffs, however, alleged breaches of fiduciary duty by Morgan Stanley LCF and CIGNA LCF because, according to plaintiffs, the returns from these sales could have been even greater if Morgan Stanley affiliates had not stood on both sides of the transactions.[2554] The court held in *Katell I* that demand was excused due to the absence of a disinterested and independent majority of general partners because Morgan Stanley LCF had 50 percent of voting power and thus there was no majority of disinterested and independent general partners.[2555]

The general partners of the Fund then determined to create a special litigation committee consisting of CIGNA LCF. The court in *Katell II*, however, held that the special litigation committee procedure provided for in the corporate context pursuant to the doctrine announced in *Zapata Corp. v. Maldonado*[2556] is not necessarily applicable in the limited partnership context. The court reasoned that unlike the demand requirement, which is "easily applied to partnership law because the organic language, in each instance, is almost identical,"[2557] the special litigation committee concept

---

2553. [1995 Transfer Binder] Fed. Sec. L. Rep. (CCH) at 93,166.

2554. *Id*. at 93,166-67.

2555. [1992-1993 Transfer Binder] Fed. Sec. L. Rep. (CCH) at 96,441.

2556. 430 A.2d 779 (Del. 1981); *see also* Chapter IV, Section C (discussing *Zapata* doctrine).

2557. 1993 Del. Ch. LEXIS 92, at *6, 1993 WL 205033, at *2

(continued...)

"is derived from corporate origins not mirrored in our partnership law."[2558] The court explained that "the *Zapata* special committee procedure is premised on the express provisions of § 141," which "provides for the delegation of managerial decision-making power."[2559] This includes, under Section 141(a), "delegation under a corporation's certificate of incorporation," and, under Section 141(c), the designation of committees to "exercise all the powers and authority of the board of directors in the management of the business and affairs of the corporation."[2560]

Delaware law with respect to limited partnerships is different, the court continued, because the Delaware statute authorizing the creation of limited partnerships "does not contain an express provision allowing general partners to delegate their authority to a committee."[2561] "Rather, the specific rights and responsibilities of parties in a general or limited partnership are determined by the parties' particular partnership agreement."[2562] To illustrate this, the court pointed to the following provisions of the Delaware statute authorizing the creation of limited partnerships:

- "Except as provided in this chapter *or in the partnership agreement*, a general partner of a limited partnership has the rights and powers and is subject to the restrictions of a partner in a partnership without limited partners."[2563]

- "It is the policy of this chapter to give maximum effect to the principle of freedom of contract and to the

---

2557. (...continued)
(citing 6 Del. C. §§ 17-1001 and 1003 (limited partnerships) and Del. Ch. R. 23.1 (corporations)).

2558. 1993 Del. Ch. LEXIS 92, at *6, 1993 WL 205033, at *2.

2559. 1993 Del. Ch. LEXIS 92, at *6-7, 1993 WL 205033, at *2 (citing *Aronson v. Lewis*, 473 A.2d 805, 813 (Del. 1984)).

2560. *Id.* (citing *Zapata*, 430 A.2d at 785, and Del. Gen. Corp. Law §§ 141(a), (c)).

2561. 1993 Del. Ch. LEXIS 92, at *7, 1993 WL 205033, at *2 (citing 6 Del. Ch. §§ 1501 to 1543 and 6 Del. C. §§ 17-101 to 17-1109).

2562. 1993 Del. Ch. LEXIS 92, at *7-8, 1993 WL 205033, at *2.

2563. 6 Del. C. § 17-403(a) (emphasis added by court).

enforceability of partnership agreements."[2564]

- "The rights and duties of the partners in relation to the partnership shall be determined, subject to any agreement between them, by the following rules: [rules omitted]."[2565]

For these reasons, the court stated, "[i]n order to extend the *Zapata* doctrine to our partnership law, one must determine on a case-by-case basis whether the general partners created a valid special litigation committee in accordance with the terms of their particular partnership agreement."[2566]

The court then examined the partnership agreement establishing the Fund and the agreement pursuant to which the Fund's general partners had delegated their authority to the special litigation committee in the *Katell* litigation. The court held that the agreement delegating the general partners' authority to the special litigation committee was invalid because the effect of that agreement was to amend the partnership agreement establishing the Fund without complying with a provision in the partnership agreement requiring that amendments to the agreement be approved by a majority of limited partners.[2567]

In response, the general partners obtained the approval of over 80 percent of the Fund's limited partners (including all limited partners other than the two plaintiffs in the litigation) of an amendment to the partnership agreement authorizing the creation of a special litigation committee consisting of CIGNA LCF. In *Katell III*, the court held that the amended partnership agreement validly authorized the creation of a special litigation committee consisting of CIGNA LCF.[2568]

CIGNA LCF then appointed three senior managing directors of CIGNA LCF's parent corporation, CIGNA, to act as the com-

---

2564. *Id.* § 17-1101(c).

2565. *Id.* § 1518.

2566. 1993 Del. Ch. LEXIS 92, at *8-9, 1993 WL 205033, at *3.

2567. 1993 Del. Ch. LEXIS 92, at *9-16, 1993 WL 205033, at *3-5.

2568. 19 Del. J. Corp. L. at 801.

mittee. The committee retained counsel, counsel conducted interviews of the persons involved in the challenged transactions, and the committee reviewed documentation. At the end of this process, the committee issued "a detailed, 126 page report" that concluded that continuing the litigation would not serve the best interests of the Fund and recommended dismissal. A motion to dismiss accordingly was filed.[2569]

The court in *Katell IV* tested the special litigation committee's conclusions by applying the *Zapata* test, pursuant to which, as discussed earlier in this Chapter,[2570] (1) "the corporation must prove that the committee is independent, and conducted a good faith, reasonable investigation," and (2) "[i]n its discretion" the court "can undertake its own independent review of the merits of the derivative claim before sanctioning the Special Committee's recommendation of dismissal."[2571] The court addressed each of these elements in turn: (1) independence, the good faith and reasonableness of the committee's investigation, the reasonableness of the basis for the committee's conclusion, and (2) *Zapata*'s discretionary second step.

*Independence.* Under Delaware law, the court stated, "[a] special committee is independent when it can base its decision on 'the merits of the issue rather than being governed by extraneous considerations or influences.'"[2572] The court acknowledged that CIGNA LCF was a defendant in the action and had "played a crucial role" in the challenged transactions, but held that "the undisputed facts . . . conclusively support CIGNA LCF's independence."[2573]

First, the court explained, "the overwhelming majority of the limited partners approved CIGNA LCF's appointment as Special

---

2569. [1995 Transfer Binder] Fed. Sec. L. Rep. (CCH) at 93,169.
2570. *See* Chapter IV, Section C 2 b.
2571. [1995 Transfer Binder] Fed. Sec. L. Rep. (CCH) at 93,169, 93,174.
2572. *Id.* at 93,170 (quoting *Kaplan v. Wyatt*, 499 A.2d 1184, 1189 (Del. 1985)).
2573. [1995 Transfer Binder] Fed. Sec. L. Rep. (CCH) at 93,170.

Committee."[2574] This vote, "while not dispositive," the court reasoned, reduced the concern noted in *Zapata* (in the corporate context) that "a special committee handpicked by a corporation's board of directors may suffer from a "there but for the grace of God go I' empathy" for the defendants in the case.[2575]

Second, the court stated, in both of the challenged transactions, CIGNA LCF was in "the same economic position as the limited partners" because if Morgan Stanley unfairly transferred profits from the Fund to another Morgan Stanley entity, "it did so at the expense of the limited partners *and* CIGNA LCF."[2576]

Third, the court rejected as "contrary to well-settled Delaware law" plaintiffs' contention that while CIGNA LCF "may not have obtained any illicit profit" by approving the challenged transactions, its "potential liability" for approving the transactions would affect its decision whether to pursue this litigation.[2577] The court explained that just as "potential liability" on the part of corporate directors for approving a transaction does not by itself excuse demand, so too "[a] general partner's potential liability for approving a transaction, standing alone, does not preclude it from deciding whether the limited partnership should pursue claims against the general partners."[2578] Likewise, the court continued, CIGNA LCF's status as a defendant in the litigation "does not render it incapable of deciding whether to pursue this litigation."[2579]

Fourth, the court rejected plaintiffs' claim that CIGNA LCF's ongoing business relationship with Morgan Stanley rendered CIGNA LCF an interested party and/or cast doubt upon its independence.[2580] The court explained that CIGNA and Morgan Stanley's relationship was a "rather limited" one that consisted of nothing more than "arm's-length trading and two limited partner-

---

2574. *Id.*
2575. *Id.* (quoting *Zapata*, 430 A.2d at 787).
2576. *Id.* at 93,170.
2577. *Id.*
2578. *Id.*
2579. *Id.*
2580. *Id.*

ships in the process of liquidating their portfolios."[2581] As a result, the court stated, it was "nearly impossible" for Morgan Stanley "to influence CIGNA LCF's decision in this matter."[2582] To the contrary, the court continued, CIGNA LCF had shown "a willingness to stand up to Morgan Stanley" and had challenged Morgan Stanley "when CIGNA LCF disagreed with Morgan Stanley LCF's plans for managing the limited partnership."[2583] The court thus concluded that "I strongly doubt that the Special Committee took Morgan Stanley's interests into account when it decided to recommend dismissing this lawsuit."[2584]

Fifth, the court rejected plaintiffs' reliance upon *Lewis v. Fuqua*[2585] for the proposition that one member special litigation committees are disfavored.[2586] "Plaintiffs' attempt to find 'rules' in the previous special litigation committee decisions of this Court is misguided," the court stated, because "[t]he procedure created in *Zapata* is very fact specific" and "cannot be cabined into all purpose rules like 'no one member special committees.'"[2587]

Here, the court continued, "[d]efendants have shown that only one *independent* general partner is available" because the Fund had two general partners and one of those two general partners had a disabling self-interest in the disputed transactions.[2588] The court acknowledged that the independence of a special committee of a limited partnership cannot be established simply by a "best available general partner" test, but concluded that under the circumstances in the case before the court, where there was "only one *independent* general partner available," "I find nothing insidious

---

2581. *Id.*

2582. *Id.*

2583. *Id.*

2584. *Id.* at 93,171.

2585. 502 A.2d 962 (Del. Ch. 1985), *appeal refused*, 504 A.2d 571 (unpublished opinion, text available at 1986 Del. LEXIS 1027 and 1986 WL 16292) (Del. Jan. 24, 1986).

2586. [1995 Transfer Binder] Fed. Sec. L. Rep. (CCH) at 93,171.

2587. *Id.*

2588. *Id.*

about leaving the decision to pursue this litigation to that one general partner."[2589]

*Good Faith and Reasonableness of Investigation.* The court turned next to the special litigation committee's good faith and the reasonableness of its investigation. The court found that the committee had carried its burden with respect to both of these issues.

The court began by noting the observation in *Kaplan v. Wyatt*[2590] that "the *Zapata* procedure encourages Plaintiffs to bring an all out attack against the details of the Special Committee's investigation."[2591] Here, plaintiffs' "all out attack" included the following allegations:

- the committee "sought to uncover as little evidence as possible, and then reach the predetermined conclusion to dismiss the lawsuit";[2592]

- CIGNA LCF "chose three CIGNA employees who worked closely with the persons involved in the disputed transaction to conduct the affairs of the Special Committee";[2593]

- in order to recommend continuing the litigation, these three CIGNA employees "would have to criticize their superiors at CIGNA";[2594]

- these three CIGNA employees by their own admission "had heard favorable statements about the disputed transactions prior to their appointment to conduct the affairs of the Special Committee";[2595]

---

2589. *Id.*

2590. 484 A.2d 501 (Del. Ch. 1984), *aff'd*, 499 A.2d 1184 (Del. 1985).

2591. [1995 Transfer Binder] Fed. Sec. L. Rep. (CCH) at 93,171 (quoting *Kaplan*, 484 A.2d at 517).

2592. [1995 Transfer Binder] Fed. Sec. L. Rep. (CCH) at 93,171.

2593. *Id.*

2594. *Id.*

2595. *Id.*

- these three CIGNA employees "never attempted to independently value" CCA or Silgan, and "[w]ithout an independent analysis of the transactions . . . the Special Committee could not reasonably investigate the claims";[2596]

- the committee delegated attendance at interviews to counsel;[2597] and

- the three members of the committee "spared . . . from an interview" Arthur C. Reeds, III, the chief executive officer of CIGNA's Investment Management Division, "because he is their boss" and notwithstanding his involvement in the Fund's decision to invest in CCA and Silgan.[2598]

The court stated that it would "not linger over all the details criticized by Plaintiffs."[2599] Instead, the court determined to base its decision "on my overall impression" of the committee's good faith and the reasonableness of its investigation.[2600] Applying this standard, the court held that CIGNA LCF "demonstrated its good faith by selecting . . . three qualified people with little or no prior contact with the transactions to be investigated, to conduct its affairs as Special Committee."[2601] These were, the court stated, "fresh sets of eyes previously unaffiliated with CIGNA LCF."[2602] The fact that these individuals worked in the same division of CIGNA as the persons involved in CIGNA LCF, the court stated, "does not reflect that CIGNA LCF selected them in bad faith."[2603]

The court similarly held that the committee undertook a reasonable investigation. The court stated that capable counsel was

---

2596. *Id.*
2597. *Id.*
2598. *Id.*
2599. *Id.*
2600. *Id.*
2601. *Id.* at 93,172.
2602. *Id.*
2603. *Id.*

selected to assist the investigation, and there was "nothing unreasonable" about the committee's "heavy reliance on its competent attorneys."[2604] The court added that "[p]laintiffs have not asserted that LCF's counsel had an improper conflict of interest or incompetently conducted the interviews."[2605]

*Reasonableness of Basis for Conclusion.* The court then turned to the special committee's "last burden": "to demonstrate a reasonable basis for its conclusion to dismiss the lawsuit."[2606] Plaintiffs' "chief criticism" of the committee's reasoning challenged the committee's conclusion that CIGNA LCF had the "ability to effectively bargain with Morgan Stanley over the price of the CCA and Silgan stock" because, according to the committee, CIGNA LCF "was in the same position" as all limited partners and thus had "a strong incentive to maximize the return" for the Fund.[2607] The court rejected this criticism of the committee's work. The court explained that "Delaware law presumes that investors act to maximize the value of their own investments," that plaintiffs provided no "plausible reason why CIGNA LCF would not seek a fair price for its own investments," and that the special committee's conclusion that CIGNA LCF's decision to approve the challenged transactions was "free from any improper influence" and "not unreasonable."[2608]

The court then focused upon four legal conclusions reached by the special committee: (1) limited partnership agreements can modify the extent of a general partner's fiduciary duties, (2) the Fund's partnership agreement did so by requiring a showing of gross negligence by a general partner who voted to approve a challenged transaction in order to establish liability (CIGNA LCF had voted to approve the challenged transaction) and willful misconduct by a general partner who did not vote to approve a challenged

---

2604. *Id.*

2605. *Id.; see also* Chapter IV, Section C 2 h (also discussing this portion of decision).

2606. *Id.*

2607. *Id.* at 93,173.

2608. *Id.*

transaction (Morgan Stanley LCF had not voted to approve the transaction due to its conflict of interest), (3) plaintiffs bore the burden of proving the conduct required by the partnership agreement to establish liability, and (4) although "Plaintiffs may be able to prove that the prices . . . received . . . were unfair," plaintiffs were "unlikely to prove CIGNA LCF's gross negligence or Morgan Stanley's willful misconduct."[2609] The court acknowledged plaintiffs' contentions that the special committee had misconstrued Delaware law and the partnership agreement and had improperly assigned to plaintiff the burden of proving CIGNA LCF's gross negligence and Morgan Stanley's willful misconduct, but held that "[i]n reviewing the Special Committee's conclusions" the court determines only whether the special committee's "consideration of the merits of the claims was reasonable" and "does not take an independent look at the merits of a lawsuit."[2610]

The committee met this burden, the court concluded, because "the legal analysis in the Special Committee's report provides a reasonable prediction of how this Court might rule on the issues in this case."[2611] The court stated that although the Special Committee's report "does touch upon unsettled issues regarding the fiduciary duties of general partners of limited partnerships . . . it provides a careful and reasonable analysis of each of these issues."[2612] Thus, the court held, the special committee had demonstrated "a reasonable basis for its determination that the Plaintiffs are unlikely to recover money damages for the limited partnership."[2613]

*The Zapata Second Step.* The court concluded its analysis with an examination of the second step of *Zapata*, pursuant to which "[i]n its discretion" the court "can undertake its own independent review of the merits of the derivative claim before sanctioning the Special Committee's recommendation of dismissal"—a

---

2609. *Id.*
2610. *Id.*
2611. *Id.*
2612. *Id.*
2613. *Id.* at 93,173-74.

step "designed to prevent situations where the Special Committee complied with all the technical requirements of *Zapata*, but the outcome violates the spirit of that procedure."[2614]

The court stated that it was "satisfied" that the special committee's decision to dismiss this lawsuit was "the product of the procedure envisioned by the Supreme Court in *Zapata* and by the limited partners when they approved the Amendment," and therefore "I decline to undertake an independent review of the merits of Plaintiffs' claims."[2615] The court explained that the committee "conducted a thorough evaluation" of plaintiffs' claims and "reasonably concluded" that the claims should not be pursued by the Fund.[2616] The court noted the committee's acknowledgment that because the Fund was winding up its affairs the lawsuit would "not distract the general partners from more important affairs," but agreed with the committee that "that does not mean that this lawsuit has no costs to the limited partners," including the possibility that the Fund would be required to indemnify the general partners for potentially more than $1 million in attorneys fees in a case in which the committee believed plaintiffs were unlikely to recover damages.[2617]

## E. Privilege and Work Product Considerations

Unique privilege issues arise where a shareholder purports to act on behalf of a corporation in a shareholder derivative litigation. These issues include (1) the applicability of the attorney-client privilege and the work product doctrine in shareholder derivative litigation generally, (2) the applicability of the attorney-client privilege and the work product doctrine in the specific context of a board or board committee investigation of a shareholder demand or, in a case where demand is excused, a special litigation committee investigation of claims asserted in a shareholder derivative action, (3) waiver of the protection provided by the attorney-client privi-

---

2614. *Id.* at 93,174.
2615. *Id.*
2616. *Id.*
2617. *Id.*

lege and the work product doctrine in a shareholder derivative action when a report prepared in response to a shareholder demand or by a special litigation committee is used to seek dismissal or termination of the derivative action, (4) waiver of the protection provided by the attorney-client privilege and the work product doctrine in litigation other than the shareholder derivative action where the other litigation arises out of the same facts that underlie the shareholder demand or derivative action, and (5) the public's right of access to board or committee reports that are used to seek dismissal of derivative litigation.

## 1. The Garner Doctrine

The Fifth Circuit's 1970 decision in *Garner v. Wolfinbarger*[2618] illustrates a potential exception to the attorney client privilege in shareholder derivative litigation. *Garner* holds that there are cases where a shareholder plaintiff—who, in any derivative action, purports to represent the corporation and thus purports to have a "mutuality of interest" with the corporation—is entitled to discovery of legal advice provided to the corporation by the corporation's counsel.[2619] The shareholder has the burden of showing "good cause" why the privilege should not protect the particular information at issue.[2620] The determination whether such "good cause" exists requires a balancing of numerous factors:

> There are many indicia that may contribute to a decision of presence or absence of good cause, among them the number of shareholders and the percentage of stock they represent; the bona fides of the shareholders; the nature of the shareholders' claim and whether it is obviously colorable; the apparent necessity or desirability of the shareholders having the information and the availability of it from other sources; whether, if the shareholders' claim is of wrongful action by the corporation, it is of action criminal, or illegal but not criminal, or of doubtful legality; whether the communication

---

2618. 430 F.2d 1093 (5th Cir. 1970), *cert. denied*, 401 U.S. 974 (1971).

2619. *Id*. at 1101, 1103-04.

2620. *Id*. at 1104.

related to past or to prospective actions; whether the communication is of advice concerning the litigation itself; the extent to which the communication is identified versus the extent to which the shareholders are blindly fishing; the risk of revelation of trade secrets or other information in whose confidentiality the corporation has an interest for independent reasons.[2621]

Examples of cases finding good cause in derivative actions and piercing the privilege include *In re Fuqua Industries, Inc. Shareholder Litigation*,[2622] *Cole v. Wilmington Materials, Inc.*,[2623] *Lee v. Engle*[2624] and *In re Dairy Mart Convenience Stores, Inc. Derivative Litigation*.[2625] Examples of cases finding an absence of good cause in derivative actions and refusing to pierce the privilege include *Ohio-Sealy Mattress Manufacturing Co. v. Kaplan*,[2626] *Tabas v. Bowden*[2627] and *Gerrits v. Brannen Banks, Inc.*[2628]

Courts also have construed and applied the *Garner* doctrine in class actions, although the court in *Garner* recognized that the reasoning underlying the *Garner* doctrine might not apply where the corporation is defending a suit brought by shareholders on behalf of the suing shareholders rather than on behalf of the corporation, and "whose interests or intention may be inconsistent with those of other shareholders."[2629] Some courts accordingly have barred the use of *Garner* in any non-derivative action[2630] or at least any

2621. *Id.*

2622. 1992 Del. Ch. LEXIS 204, at *10, 1992 WL 296448, at *3 (Del. Ch. Oct. 8, 1992).

2623. 1993 Del. Ch. LEXIS 106, at *7, 1993 WL 257415, at *2-3 (Del. Ch. July 1, 1993).

2624. 1995 Del. Ch. LEXIS 149, at *8-11, 1995 WL 761222, at *3-4 (Del. Ch. Dec. 15, 1995).

2625. 1997 Del. Ch. LEXIS 173, at *5-7, 1997 WL 732467, at *1-2 (Del. Ch. Nov. 13, 1997).

2626. 90 F.R.D. 21, 31 (N.D. Ill. 1980).

2627. 1982 WL 17820, at *3 (Del. Ch. Feb. 16, 1982) (also available on LEXIS without file number)

2628. 138 F.R.D. 574, 578-79 (D. Colo. 1991).

2629. 430 F.2d at 1101 n.17.

2630. *See, e.g.*, *Weil v. Investment/Indicators, Research & Manage-
(continued...)*

non-derivative action in which plaintiffs were not shareholders during the period in which the challenged communications were made (and thus no fiduciary duty exists between the corporation's management and the shareholder seeking discovery).[2631] Courts that have allowed the use of the *Garner* doctrine in non-derivative actions have heightened the burden in such cases upon plaintiffs attempting to show the "good cause" required by *Garner*.[2632]

The courts uniformly have refused to extend the *Garner* doctrine to work product.[2633] This is because "[u]nlike the attorney-client privilege, which serves only the client's interest, the work product privilege also operates to protect *counsel* from unfair and intrusive disclosure."[2634] As two courts have explained:

---

2630. (...continued)
*ment, Inc.*, 647 F.2d 18, 23 (9th Cir. 1981).

2631. *See, e.g., Moskowitz v. Lopp*, 128 F.R.D. 624, 637 (E.D. Pa. 1989); *In re Atlantic Fin. Management Sec. Litig.*, 121 F.R.D. 141, 146 (D. Mass. 1988); *Quintel Corp. N.V. v. Citibank, N.A.*, 567 F. Supp. 1357, 1363-64 (S.D.N.Y. 1983).

2632. *See, e.g., Fausek v. White*, 965 F.2d 126, 130 (6th Cir.), *cert. denied*, 506 U.S. 1034 (1992); *Ward v. Succession of Freeman*, 854 F.2d 780, 786 (5th Cir. 1988), *cert. denied*, 490 U.S. 1065 (1989); *Picard Chem. Inc. Profit Sharing Plan v. Perrigo Co.*, 951 F. Supp. 679, 687 (W.D. Mich. 1996); *Miller v. Genesco, Inc.*, 1994 Del. Ch. LEXIS 17771, at *2-3, 1994 WL 698287, at *1 (S.D.N.Y. Dec. 13, 1994).

2633. *See, e.g., Cox v. Administrator U.S. Steel & Carnegie*, 17 F.3d 1386, 1423 (11th Cir.), *modified on other grounds*, 30 F.3d 1347 (11th Cir. 1994), *cert. denied*, 513 U.S. 1110 (1995); *Sandberg v. Virginia Bankshares, Inc.*, 979 F.2d 332, 355 n.22 (4th Cir. 1992); *In re International Sys. & Controls Corp. Sec. Litig.*, 693 F.2d 1235, 1239 (5th Cir. 1982); *Picard Chem.*, 951 F. Supp. at 687; *In re Pfizer Inc. Sec. Litig.*, 1993 U.S. Dist. LEXIS 18215, at *47-48, 1993 WL 561125, at *14 (S.D.N.Y. Dec. 23, 1993); *In re Rospatch Sec. Litig.*, 1991 U.S. Dist. LEXIS 3270, at *41-42, 1991 WL 574963, at *13 (W.D. Mich. Mar. 14, 1991); *Helt v. Metropolitan Dist. Comm'n*, 113 F.R.D. 7, 11 (D. Conn. 1986); *In re Dayco Corp. Derivative Sec. Litig.*, 99 F.R.D. 616, 620 (S.D. Ohio 1983); *Donovan v. Fitzsimmons*, 90 F.R.D. 583, 587 (N.D. Ill. 1981).

2634. *Pfizer*, 1993 U.S. Dist. LEXIS 18215, at *47, 1993 WL 561125, at *14.

The *Garner* rule forecloses the use of attorney-client privilege, itself intended for the ultimate benefit of the *client*, to prevent disclosure of a breach of the client's trust. Shareholders or beneficiaries, however, do not stand in the same position with respect to the *attorney*, for whom the work product rule is designed to benefit, as they do to their own trustees. And as a result, the *Garner* analysis cannot be readily applied to defeat the work product rule.[2635]

*Principles of Corporate Governance: Analysis and Recommendations* has reached the same conclusion.[2636]

There is little case law addressing the applicability of the *Garner* doctrine to legal advice received by a board or board committee considering a shareholder demand or determining whether to move to terminate a derivative action that already has been filed. Section 7.13(e) of Principles of Corporate Governance does address this issue and proposes the following rule:

The plaintiff's counsel should be furnished a copy of related legal opinions received by the board or committee if any opinion is tendered to the court . . . . Subject to that requirement, communications, both oral and written, between the board or committee and its counsel with respect to the subject matter of the action do not forfeit their privileged character, and documents, memoranda, or other material qualifying as attorney's work product do not become subject to discovery, on the grounds that the action is derivative or that the privilege was waived by the production to the plaintiff or the filing with the court of a report, other written submission or supporting documents.[2637]

The commentary accompanying Section 7.13(e) explains the following:

Submission of the board's or committee's report or other written submission to the court waives the privilege as to such documents and, to a more limited extent, as to the proc-

---

2635. *Donovan*, 90 F.R.D. at 588, *quoted in Pfizer*, 1993 U.S. Dist. LEXIS 18215, at *47-48, 1993 WL 561125, at *14.

2636. 2 Principles of Corporate Governance: Analysis and Recommendations § 7.13 Comment at 178 (1994).

2637. *Id.* § 7.13(e).

ess of their preparation. The established law of the attorney-client privilege has long provided that invocation of the reliance-on-counsel defense waives the privilege. Thus, it would be unfair if the board or committee could rely on legal advice from its counsel that the action was not meritorious as a ground for dismissing the action and then deny plaintiff access to the substance of that advice. Accordingly, § 7.13(e) requires the disclosure of any formal opinion (including an oral opinion summarizing written advice) or other written legal advice given by counsel to the board or to the committee with regard to the action if any legal opinion is tendered to the court. The decision belongs to the corporation whether to submit such an opinion to the court, but once one is tendered, all other formal legal opinions (including those in draft or oral form) given to the board or committee and pertaining to the same general subject matter must be given to the plaintiff. This rule is intended to discourage opinion shopping without chilling the board's or committee's access to confidential legal advice. Otherwise, absent special circumstances, the plaintiff should not be permitted to depose the counsel or to reconstruct the dialogue between the board or the committee and its counsel.[2638]

The commentary accompanying Section 7.13(e) also explains that two of the *Garner* factors are "'whether the communication is of advice concerning the litigation itself' and 'whether the communication related to past or prospective actions.'"[2639] "Those decisions that have found 'good cause' to pierce the veil of the attorney-client privilege," the commentary states, "have involved communications that were roughly contemporaneous with the events giving rise to the litigation."[2640] The commentary states that

> the position of counsel to a board or a litigation committee considering a demand or a derivative action is substantially different from that of a general counsel or other corporate attorney who is giving advice with respect to a prospective transaction. The special counsel has undertaken to serve only a narrowly defined client—the disinterested members of the

---

2638. *Id.* § 7.13 Comment at 175 (citation omitted).
2639. *Id.* at 174 (quoting 430 F.2d at 1104).
2640. *Id.*

board, or a litigation committee—and counsel's communications uniquely relate to the appraisal of the pending litigation. Moreover, the functioning of the disinterested members of the board or the litigation committee might be severely hampered if communication between them and their counsel could not be conducted with reasonable candor and confidence on both sides.[2641]

The commentary accompanying Section 7.13(e) also explains the following:

> In the typical internal corporate investigation that is conducted with respect to a derivative action, the special counsel to the litigation committee may interview dozens of witnesses. If the resulting interview notes and other memoranda were subject to discovery (subject only to the attorney/client privilege), the special counsel would be severely hampered in gathering or reporting facts to the litigation committee or in estimating the probable value of the litigation. For the litigation committee to conduct a thorough investigation, it must of necessity rely on its counsel, and counsel's effectiveness depends in substantial measure on the availability of the work product doctrine. Thus, counsel's notes, internal drafts, correspondence with witnesses, and similar materials should normally be protected from disclosure under the work product doctrine, regardless of the availability of the attorney-client privilege.[2642]

The Second Circuit in *Joy v. North*,[2643] construing Connecticut law, took a very different view of these issues. The Second Circuit held that a motion to terminate a derivative action pursuant to a special litigation committee recommendation waives the attor-

---

2641. *Id.* at 175; *see also Zitin v. Turley*, [1991 Transfer Binder] Fed. Sec. L. Rep. (CCH) ¶ 96,123, at 90,683 n.1 (D. Ariz. June 20, 1991) (declining to follow *Garner* where the attorney-client communications at issue related to a board committee's investigation of shareholder demands and not to the conduct underlying the demands), *interlocutory appeal on different grounds denied*, [1991 Transfer Binder] Fed. Sec. L. Rep. (CCH) ¶ 96,284 (D. Ariz. Sept. 19, 1991).

2642. Principles of Corporate Governance § 7.13 Comment at 178.

2643. 692 F.2d 880 (2d Cir. 1982), *cert. denied*, 460 U.S. 1051 (1983).

ney-client privilege with respect to both the committee's report and "all underlying data."[2644] The Second Circuit also held that a motion to terminate a derivative action waives the work product doctrine to the extent that "working papers of the committee's counsel" are communicated to the committee.[2645] Once communicated to the committee, the *Joy* court held, "the immunity may not be claimed, since the papers may be part of the basis for the committee's recommendations."[2646]

The Sixth Circuit's view of these issues in *In re Perrigo Co.*,[2647] a case construing Michigan law, is discussed later in this Chapter.[2648]

## 2.   Public Access to Court Filings

A related issue is the public's right to documents presented to a court by a corporation or directors in support of a motion to dismiss or terminate a derivative action. The Second Circuit in *Joy v. North*[2649] held that "[a]n adjudication is a formal act of government, the basis of which should, absent exceptional circumstances, be subject to public scrutiny."[2650] The court stated that "[w]e simply do not understand the argument that derivative actions may be routinely dismissed on the basis of secret documents."[2651] The court added that "[w]e cannot say what the effect on investor confidence would be if special litigation committees were routinely allowed to do their work in the dark of night."[2652]

---

2644. *Id.* at 893.

2645. *Id.* as 893-94.

2646. *Id.* at 894.

2647. 128 F.3d 430 (6th Cir. 1997).

2648. *See* Chapter IV, Sections E 3 b and c.

2649. 692 F.2d 880 (2d Cir. 1982), *cert. denied*, 460 U.S. 1051 (1983).

2650. *Id.* at 893.

2651. *Id.*

2652. *Id.*

The Seventh Circuit in *In re Continental Illinois Securities Litigation*[2653] declined to go as far as the Second Circuit concerning public access to reports prepared in support of motions to dismiss or terminate derivative litigation. The Seventh Circuit held only that "when the report is used in an adjudicative procedure to advance the corporate interest, there is a strong presumption that confidentiality must be surrendered."[2654] The court then held that the district court in the *Continental* case had not abused its discretion in ordering disclosure to the public of the special litigation committee report in that case. Like the *Joy* court, the *Continental* court stated that "[c]ertainly, an open airing of the issues surrounding the litigation would be more conducive to public confidence than a secret report which led to dismissal of several claims."[2655]

The Seventh Circuit in *Continental*, however, recognized that "the device of a special litigation committee to conduct an investigation and make a report may be useful in handling derivative litigation" and that "confidentiality may advance this process."[2656] To the extent that public disclosure imposes burdens upon corporations "attempting to evaluate the merits of derivative suits," the court stated, "procedures can be developed whereby these interests can be accommodated."[2657] One such procedure, the court suggested, would be "editing out portions of the Report that might be particularly sensitive."[2658]

The Sixth Circuit's view of these issues in *In re Perrigo Co.*,[2659] a case construing Michigan law, is discussed later in this Chapter.[2660]

Principles of Corporate Governance contains no black letter provision on this point, but the commentary in Principles of Corpo-

---

2653. 732 F.2d 1302 (7th Cir. 1984).
2654. *Id.* at 1315.
2655. *Id.* at 1316.
2656. *Id.* at 1315.
2657. *Id.* at 1316.
2658. *Id.* at 1315 n.21.
2659. 128 F.3d 430 (6th Cir. 1997).
2660. *See* Chapter IV, Sections E 3 b and c.

rate Governance states its agreement with the Seventh Circuit's position in *Continental* that "[t]he court could excise confidential matter . . . but still disclose the substance of it on a 'generic' basis."[2661] The commentary also notes that "greater information" can be given to the plaintiff than the public "because the plaintiff has a direct interest and because the plaintiff can be made subject to a protective order."[2662]

A North Carolina statute provides that "[i]n any derivative proceeding, no shareholder shall be entitled to obtain or have access to any communication within the scope of the corporation's attorney-client privilege that could not be obtained by or would not be accessible to a party in an action other than on behalf of the corporation."[2663]

## 3. Perrigo

A series of district court decisions in related shareholder derivative and class actions arising out of the same underlying allegations of wrongdoing, *Kearney v. Jandernoa*[2664] and *Picard Chemical Inc. Profit Sharing Plan v. Perrigo Co.*,[2665] and a Sixth Circuit decision granting in part and denying in part a petition for a writ of mandamus in the shareholder derivative action, *In re Perrigo Co.*,[2666] explore several of the issues discussed above.[2667]

---

2661. 2 Principles of Corporate Governance: Analysis and Recommendations § 7.13 Comment at 177 (1994).

2662. *Id.*

2663. N.C. Bus. Corp. Act § 55-7-49.

2664. 934 F. Supp. 863 (W.D. Mich.), *subsequent proceedings*, 949 F. Supp. 510 (W.D. Mich. 1996) and 979 F. Supp. 1156 (W.D. Mich.), *mandamus granted sub nom. In re Perrigo Co.*, 128 F.3d 430 (6th Cir. 1997).

2665. 951 F. Supp. 679 (W.D. Mich. 1996).

2666. 128 F.3d 430 (6th Cir. 1997).

2667. *See* Chapter IV, Sections E 1 and 2.

*a. The District Court Decisions. Kearney v. Jandernoa*[2668] involved a demand by shareholders that Perrigo Company, a Michigan corporation, commence litigation against directors and officers of the corporation in connection with conduct claimed to be wrongful or improper in a class action alleging securities fraud entitled *Picard Chemical Inc. Profit Sharing Plan v. Perrigo Co.*[2669] Perrigo's board appointed Peter Formanek, who according to Perrigo was the corporation's only disinterested independent director, to investigate the facts underlying the demand and determine "whether it would be in the best interest of Perrigo to bring, on behalf of the corporation, the claims raised by the plaintiffs in the instant case."[2670] Formanek, with the assistance of counsel, prepared a report concluding that "it would not be in Perrigo Company's best interest, at this time, to pursue any of the three derivative claims described in the Demand."[2671] The report contained a detailed factual and legal analysis of the securities fraud claims alleged in the *Picard Chemical* action, discussed interviews with Perrigo employees, and discussed legal theories relevant to the *Picard Chemical* action.[2672]

The shareholders who had made the demand responded by commencing a derivative action, and the corporation moved to dismiss the action pursuant to Section 495 of the Michigan Business Corporation Act, which provides that "[t]he court shall dismiss a derivative proceeding if, on motion by the corporation, the court finds" that "all disinterested independent directors" have made "a determination in good faith after conducting a reasonable investiga-

---

2668. 934 F. Supp. 863 (W.D. Mich.), *subsequent proceedings*, 949 F. Supp. 510 (W.D. Mich. 1996) and 979 F. Supp. 1156 (W.D. Mich.), *mandamus granted sub nom. In re Perrigo Co.*, 128 F.3d 430 (6th Cir. 1997).

2669. *Id.* at 865; *Picard Chem. Inc. Profit Sharing Plan v. Perrigo*, 951 F. Supp. 679 (W.D. Mich. 1996).

2670. 934 F. Supp. at 865; *see also* Chapter IV, Sections B 6 i and C 2 i (discussing definition in Mich. Bus. Corp. Act § 450.1107(3) of an independent director).

2671. 934 F. Supp. at 865.

2672. *Id.*

tion upon which its conclusions are based that the maintenance of the derivative proceeding is not in the best interests of the corporation."[2673]

This motion, the court stated, raised "the following legal and factual issues: whether Mr. Formanek was independent; whether Mr. Formanek was disinterested, whether Mr. Formanek was 'all disinterested independent directors;' whether Mr. Formanek made a determination; whether Mr. Formanek acted in good faith; and whether Mr. Formanek conducted a reasonable investigation upon which his conclusions were based."[2674] The court permitted discovery concerning these issues, and plaintiffs sought production of Formanek's report.[2675] The corporation contended that there could be adequate discovery concerning the issues identified by the court without permitting plaintiffs access to the report.[2676] The court disagreed and ordered production of the report. The court stated that "the report will probably be the best evidence of Mr. Formanek's good faith and the adequacy of his investigation, or lack thereof," "[c]ertainly, this Court will want to have the report before it when it rules upon Perrigo's motion to dismiss," and "this Court will not rule on the motion to dismiss in reliance upon the determination contained in the report unless plaintiffs have had the opportunity to read and comment upon the report."[2677]

With respect to the attorney-client privilege, the court explained that "the determination contained in the report is being submitted *to the Court* under Section 495 as a complete and substantive defense to the derivative claims," and not simply to the corporation or an independent committee of the corporation's board "in order to enable it or them to make a recommendation or decision."[2678] The court held that "if a corporation . . . relies upon Section 495 in moving to dismiss a shareholders derivative claim,

---

2673. *Id.*; Mich. Bus. Corp. Act § 450.1495.
2674. 934 F. Supp. at 866.
2675. *Id.*
2676. *Id.*
2677. *Id.*
2678. *Id.*

that corporation thereby waives any attorney-client privilege which attached to the report containing the disinterested independent directors' determination."[2679]

The court rejected the corporation's attempt to distinguish between the contents of the report and the determination itself. The court stated that "if a disinterested independent director makes a determination and a report, the report and determination are one and the same" because "the determination is not simply the final conclusion but also embodies independent, specific conclusions regarding specific claims and the rationale for those conclusions."[2680] The court stated that "without access to the report" there is "no practical way" for plaintiffs to carry "the burden of proving that the determination was not made in good faith or that the investigation was not reasonable," as required by Section 495.[2681] The court added that it "does not believe that the Michigan Legislature intended to bar a derivative claim upon the mere statement that a determination was made" pursuant to Section 495.[2682]

With respect to the work product doctrine, the court stated that "even if there is work product protection for the report, there is good cause to disclose the report to the derivative plaintiffs during discovery so that the derivative plaintiffs can properly prepare their response to Perrigo's motion to dismiss under Section 495."[2683]

The court summarized these rulings in a later opinion as follows:

> Section 495(1) and (2)(d) of the MBCA, the subsections upon which Perrigo relies, clearly and specifically mandate that, prior to dismissing a derivative proceeding, this Court *must find* that Formanek, as "*all disinterested independent directors,*" made a *determination in good faith* and after conduct-

---

2679. *Id.*
2680. *Id.*
2681. *Id.* at 865, 866.
2682. *Id.* at 866-67.
2683. *Id.* at 866.

ing a *reasonable investigation*, upon which Formanek's *conclusions are based*, that maintenance of the derivative proceeding is not in Perrigo's best interest. Perrigo is correct that Plaintiffs have the burden of proving these elements. *See* M.C.L. § 450.1495(1) and (2). This Court, however, had made it clear that Plaintiffs would be unable to present facts essential to justify their opposition to Perrigo's motions unless they had access to the Formanek Report. In essence, Perrigo is asking the Court to make findings of fact in favor of a defendant based solely upon the defendant's conclusions and assurances, without more, that the facts are indeed true. Moreover, Perrigo is asking the Court to make these findings even when a Plaintiff has no fair opportunity to respond to the motion. No court would hold that Section 495 of the MBCA would allow a court to find facts in favor of a defendant, upon a defendant's motion, based on conclusions and assurances by the defendant of the truth of facts asserted, especially without a response from the plaintiff.

If Perrigo expects the Court to rule in its favor on its motion at this point in time, based only upon Perrigo's conclusions and assurances that the facts it asserts are true, it is mistaken.[2684]

The court recognized that the report "might be of substantial assistance" to the plaintiffs in the *Picard Chemical* securities fraud class actions against Perrigo. The court accordingly held that Perrigo's waiver of the attorney-client privilege and work product doctrine by using the report to seek a dismissal of the action "does not extend to any person other than the parties in the derivative case."[2685] The court acknowledged that "[o]ne could reason that, if there is a waiver, waiver is total" but concluded that "such simplistic reasoning overlooks the unique position of a derivative plaintiff" who is "in effect, acting on behalf of the corporation in that such a plaintiff is seeking recovery on behalf of the corporation."[2686] The court explained the dilemma created by the nature

---

2684. *Kearney v. Jandernoa*, 979 F. Supp. 1156, 1158 (W.D. Mich.), *mandamus granted sub nom. In re Perrigo Co.*, 128 F.3d 430 (6th Cir. 1997).

2685. 934 F. Supp. at 867.

2686. *Id.*

of a derivative action—an action on behalf of the corporation—where pursuit of the action might harm the corporation's interests in another legal proceeding. In the court's words:

> Logically, the best result that can be achieved by a corporate defendant in a securities fraud case is to avoid a judgment for securities fraud in the first instance. Derivative plaintiffs asserting the corporation's interests, therefore, should not be permitted to disrupt or direct the corporation's defense of the securities fraud claims by forcing the corporation to give up any claim it has to attorney-client privilege or protection of attorneys work product. Such disruption or direction would not be in the best interest of the corporation—the very interest the derivative plaintiffs claim to represent. In other words, derivative plaintiffs' right to the Formanek report derives from their seeking to represent the best interest of the corporation and cannot be used to injure the corporation by waiving any privilege, protection, or defense possessed by the corporation.[2687]

Therefore, the court concluded, "any right which the derivative plaintiffs have to the Formanek report is limited to the right to use the report to respond to Perrigo's motion to dismiss under Section 495."[2688] The court specifically prohibited "the derivative plaintiffs and their attorneys and all other parties in the derivative case . . . from delivering the report, or any portion thereof, to, or discussing the report, or any portion thereof, with, any other person, including securities fraud plaintiffs or their attorneys, until further Order of this Court."[2689]

The plaintiffs in the *Picard Chemical* securities fraud class action then moved to compel production of the report in that case. Perrigo once again asserted that the report was protected by the attorney-client privilege and the work product doctrine.[2690] In the context of the *Picard Chemical* class action litigation against the corporation—as opposed to the *Kearney* derivative action litigation

---

2687. *Id.*

2688. *Id.*

2689. *Id.* at 867.

2690. *Picard Chem. Inc. Profit Sharing Plan v. Perrigo Co.*, 951 F. Supp. 679, 684 (W.D. Mich. 1996).

on behalf of the corporation—the court held that the attorney-client privilege and the work product doctrine had not been waived.

With respect to attorney-client privilege, the court held that the privilege was not waived for the purpose of the *Picard Chemical* class action by placing the report "at issue" in the derivative action. The court explained that "[i]n its motion to dismiss, Perrigo did not reveal any of the Report, nor did it summarize evidence contained in the Report."[2691] To the contrary, the court stated, "[t]he references to the Report were general in nature and lacking substantive content."[2692] Moreover, the court continued, "the policy behind the 'at-issue' waiver is that it would be inherently unfair for one party to rely on a document in a dispositive motion without the other party having access to it in order to respond appropriately."[2693] This concern was not implicated in the *Picard Chemical* securities fraud class action, the court reasoned, because "[t]he derivative plaintiffs in *Kearney* needed to review the Report . . . in order to refute Perrigo's motion to dismiss," but the plaintiffs in *Picard Chemical* were "unable to show that they are prejudiced in any way in the class action suit now before the Court."[2694]

With respect to the work product doctrine, the court held that work product protection was not waived for the purpose of the *Picard Chemical* class action by the fact that the report was disclosed in the derivative action. The court reasoned that the disclosure had been compelled after the corporation "took reasonable steps" to insure that the report would be protected, including objecting to disclosure of the report and submitting it to the court for in camera review.[2695] The court also held that the work product doctrine was not waived for the purpose of the *Picard Chemical* class action by disclosure of the report to the corporation's directors because the corporation and its directors had similar interests:

---

2691. *Id*. at 688-89.
2692. *Id*. at 689.
2693. *Id*.
2694. *Id*.
2695. *Id*.

they all were potential defendants in the *Picard Chemical* class action lawsuit.[2696]

Because—unlike the case in the *Kearney* derivative action— the court in the *Picard Chemical* class action found no waiver of the attorney-client privilege or attorney work product protection, the court was required to address two threshold issues not addressed in the court's derivative action decision: whether, separate and apart from the claimed waiver, the report constituted a protected attorney-client communication and work product.

With respect to the attorney-client privilege, the court held that failure to provide the report attorney-client privilege protection would undermine the policy underlying the privilege. The court explained that "[i]f the confidentiality of an internal investigation is not protected, especially for use in class actions, the corporation would be far less likely to allow the investigation to take place or would be far more likely to limit the scope of the investigation."[2697]

The court rejected a contention that "the communications made to counsel were not made in confidence" because, according to plaintiffs, "Perrigo knew that the Report would be admitted into evidence in a motion to dismiss the derivative suit."[2698] The court explained that "[w]hen Formanek's investigation began, the possibility existed that he would recommend that Perrigo take the steps requested" in the demand letter that had prompted the investigation.[2699] In that case, the court stated, no motion to dismiss in reliance upon the report ever would have been filed.[2700] Additionally, the court continued, even if an independent director recommended the filing of a motion to dismiss, the corporation still would not have been required to so do.[2701] Accordingly, the court concluded, "absent a motion to dismiss, the corporation has

---

2696. *Id.* at 690.
2697. *Id.* at 685.
2698. *Id.*
2699. *Id.*
2700. *Id.*
2701. *Id.*

every reason to believe that its internal report will remain confidential."[2702]

The court also rejected a contention that the attorney-client privilege did not protect the report because, according to plaintiffs, the report concerned a business decision rather than a legal decision. The court explained that the report contained "a legal analysis of the securities fraud claims" and "discusses legal theories which are relevant to the securities fraud action," and that "'[t]he mere fact that business considerations are weighed in the rendering of legal advice does not vitiate the attorney-client privilege.'"[2703] The court also rejected a contention that Perrigo could not invoke the attorney-client privilege because Formanek rather than Perrigo was the client. To the contrary, the court stated, "Formanek was a director at Perrigo acting on behalf of the Board and not in his individual capacity."[2704] Accordingly, "Perrigo was the client and can invoke the privilege."[2705]

With respect to the work product doctrine, the court held that the report constituted work product because the report was "prepared in anticipation of litigation or for trial," including "the prospect of litigation."[2706] Consistent with its attorney-client privilege ruling, the court held that "[t]he fact that both business and legal interests are reflected in the Report does not prevent the Report from being immune" from discovery under the work product doctrine.[2707] The court stated that "[a]lthough the Report in the case at bar was prepared in anticipation of litigation in the derivative suit, work product immunity applies in the class action suit as well" because "work product immunity applies to material prepared in anticipation of other litigation."[2708]

---

2702. *Id.*
2703. *Id.* at 685-86 (quoting *Coleman v. American Broadcasting Co.*, 106 F.R.D. 201, 206 (D.D.C. 1985)).
2704. *Id.* at 686.
2705. *Id.*
2706. *Id.*
2707. *Id.*
2708. *Id.*

The court turned to the fiduciary exception to the attorney-client privilege (but not the work product doctrine) created by the *Garner v. Wolfinbarger*[2709] doctrine, pursuant to which a shareholder may overcome the attorney-client privilege by showing "good cause" why an attorney-client communication should not be protected by the privilege.[2710] The court noted, however, that the attorney work product doctrine also applied and that the attorney work product doctrine can be overcome only by a showing of "substantial need and undue hardship."[2711] "Since both the attorney-client privilege and work product immunity apply," the court stated, "plaintiffs will have to satisfy the test of substantial need and undue hardship."[2712] The court held that the plaintiffs in the *Picard Chemical* class action had not met their burden with respect to this test.[2713] Contrasting the *Kearney* derivative action where disclosure of the report had been ordered, the court reasoned as follows:

> Unlike the derivative action in *Kearney*, the class action securities fraud plaintiffs have no need to rebut the presumption that Formanek acted in good faith and made a reasonable investigation. In addition, these plaintiffs have not shown that the information is not available through other means. Thus, although the plaintiffs in the derivative suit in *Kearney* were able to establish that there was substantial need for the Report, plaintiffs in this class action securities fraud suit have not done so.[2714]

The court thus held that disclosure in the *Kearney* derivative action did not require disclosure in the *Picard Chemical* securities fraud class action.[2715]

---

2709. 430 F.2d 1093 (5th Cir. 1970), *cert. denied*, 401 U.S. 974 (1971).

2710. 951 F. Supp. at 686-87; *see also* Chapter IV, Section E 1 (discussing *Garner* doctrine).

2711. 951 F. Supp. at 687.

2712. *Id.; see also id.* at 684.

2713. *Id.* at 687.

2714. *Id.* at 687-88 (citations omitted).

2715. *Id.* at 688.

Finally, the court held that once the report became part of the court record in the derivative action, the public, including the securities fraud class action plaintiffs in the *Picard Chemical* action, would have access to the report pursuant to the "common law right of access to judicial records allowing public inspection and copying."[2716] The court recognized that "[t]he right to inspect and copy judicial records . . . is not absolute" and that "district courts have the discretion to deny or permit access to judicial records," but the court also stated that "only the most compelling reasons justify the non-disclosure of judicial records."[2717]

Here, the court found, Perrigo had not directed the court's attention to anything in the report that would be "damaging to Perrigo in the conduct of its business of manufacturing and marketing" or that would harm Perrigo's competitive standing.[2718] Instead, the court stated, Perrigo relied upon harm that disclosure of the report would cause to the corporation's reputation.[2719] This type of harm, the court held, does not constitute a "compelling reason for the Court to deny the public access to the Report."[2720] The court added, however, that "[i]f a special litigation report is clearly and significantly damaging to a corporation, then there may be greater reluctance to require disclosure."[2721]

The court acknowledged that "[a]lmost any corporate misjudgment or misfortune can serve as a fertile ground in which disgruntled stockholders could sprout claims of a breach of the duties of due care."[2722] The court recognized that if shareholders who make a demand in these types of cases can "threaten public disclosure of the corporation's special and confidential reports" following a refusal of the demand, then "this would strengthen the stockholders' hand and bargaining power because of the potential risk of

---

2716. *Id*. at 690.

2717. *Id*. at 691.

2718. *Id*.

2719. *Id*.

2720. *Id*. at 692.

2721. *Id*. at 691.

2722. *Id*. (quoting *In re Consumers Power Co. Derivative Litig*., 132 F.R.D. 455, 463 n.20 (E.D. Mich. 1990)).

embarrassment or actual harm to the corporation."[2723] The court also stated that the "threat of likely public disclosure increases the 'settlement value' of marginal derivative suits" and would "likely lead to an increase in derivative 'strike suits' intended to leverage a quick settlement."[2724] Another result, the court stated, would be to "limit internal corporate reviews in scope and in documentation, making them a less effective instrument of corporate policy."[2725] Nevertheless, the court concluded, "the importance of public access to judicial records is more important than any potential consequences that might result from disclosure" because "if derivative actions were routinely dismissed on the basis of 'secret documents,' confidence in the administration of justice would be severely weakened."[2726]

The court accordingly held that "at that point in time when Perrigo submits the Report to this Court in support of its motion to dismiss, which must occur at some point before this Court rules on Perrigo's motion, the submission of the Report in order to induce this Court's reliance upon the good faith and reasonable investigation of Formanek will make the Report part of this Court's judicial records."[2727] The court concluded as follows:

> This Court finds that once the Report is submitted to this Court to induce reliance upon the Report, the public interest in open adjudication outweighs the interests underlying the attorney-client privilege and work product immunity. Therefore, although the Report is protected by both the attorney-client privilege and work product immunity, the Report will have to be disclosed to the public once the Report is submitted to the Court for this Court's determination of whether Formanek made a good faith judgment after a reasonable investigation.[2728]

---

2723. *Id.*
2724. *Id.*
2725. *Id.*
2726. *Id.* at 692.
2727. *Id.* at 691.
2728. *Id.* at 692.

The court stated that this ruling "gives Perrigo control of whether and when the Report will be submitted and become part of the public record."[2729] "Perrigo may withdraw its motion to dismiss in *Kearney* if it does not wish to have the Report become part of the judicial records to which the public will have access," or "Perrigo may wait until the conclusion of all discovery in *Kearney* before submitting the Report to the Court."[2730] The court added that "[i]t is also possible that after some discovery the derivative plaintiffs may conclude that they have no case."[2731]

A short time later, and "for the reasons set forth in this Court's Opinion . . . in *Picard Chemical*," the court vacated the portion of its prior decision in *Kearney* "referring to waiver of the attorney-client privilege and waiver of work product immunity."[2732] The court then ruled as follows with respect to the plaintiffs in the *Kearney* derivative action:

> 1) the Report is protected by the attorney-client privilege and work product immunity;
>
> 2) plaintiffs have established that there is substantial need for their access to the Report and that undue hardship would result from the Court denying them the Report;
>
> 3) it is not necessary for the Court to determine if Perrigo waived the attorney-client privilege or work product immunity since plaintiffs have established substantial need and undue hardship.
>
> 4) at this time, only the plaintiffs have established substantial need and undue hardship; thus, until further order of this Court, only plaintiffs are entitled to the Report; and
>
> 5) . . . Perrigo's request to redact portions of the Report will be denied.[2733]

---

2729. *Id.*

2730. *Id.*

2731. *Id.*

2732. *Kearney v. Jandernoa*, 949 F. Supp. 510, 511 (W.D. Mich. 1996), *subsequent proceedings*, 979 F. Supp. 1156 (W.D. Mich.), *mandamus granted sub nom. In re Perrigo Co.*, 128 F.3d 430 (6th Cir. 1997).

2733. *Id.*

The court subsequently denied a motion for reconsideration and added the following to its prior holding:

> Once Plaintiffs obtain the Formanek Report, they will determine whether or not the Report will be submitted to the Court with their response to either or both of Perrigo's pending motions [to dismiss]. However, there are still open questions of whether this case will be resolved between the parties after Plaintiffs have seen the Formanek Report or whether the Report will be submitted by either side. In any event, if and when the Report is submitted by either side in order to induce reliance by this Court, it will become a public record for the reasons previously stated by this Court.[2734]

The court then denied a motion to certify an interlocutory appeal or to stay proceedings pending a petition for a writ of mandamus.[2735] Perrigo sought a writ of mandamus, and the Sixth Circuit stayed the district court's order requiring production of the report pending a ruling on the merits of the petition.[2736]

*b. The Sixth Circuit Decision.* In its decision on the merits in *In re Perrigo Co.*,[2737] the Sixth Circuit began by observing that the district court "gave Perrigo the benefit of considerable doubt in holding that the Report was protected, in its entirety, by Perrigo's corporate attorney-client privilege and work product immunity," and stated that "we need not decide if this constituted error."[2738] The court also made "no judgment at this juncture about the district court's actual function under the Michigan statute" or "whether Formanek permissibly constituted 'all disinterested independent directors' within the meaning of the Michigan statute."[2739]

---

2734. *In re Perrigo Co.*, 128 F.3d 430, 434 (6th Cir. 1997).

2735. *Kearney v. Jandernoa*, 979 F. Supp. 1156, 1159 (W.D. Mich.), *mandamus granted sub nom. In re Perrigo Co.*, 128 F.3d 430 (6th Cir. 1997).

2736. 128 F.3d at 434.

2737. 128 F.3d 430 (6th Cir. 1997)

2738. *Id.* at 438 n.3.

2739. *Id.* at 438 & n.3.

The Sixth Circuit then held that mandamus relief was inappropriate "with respect to the district court's finding that the derivative plaintiffs are entitled to the Report based on substantial need and undue hardship only for purposes of responding to Perrigo's motion to dismiss."[2740] The Sixth Circuit explained that "the purposes of the Michigan statute will be furthered by allowing the plaintiffs access to the Report" because "[a]s a matter of fairness and practicality, the derivative plaintiffs (unlike the class action plaintiffs) will need the Report in order 'rebut the presumption that Formanek acted in good faith and made a reasonable investigation.'"[2741] The court stated that "[e]ven if Perrigo were correct that the court's only function under the Michigan statute is to determine whether Formanek's recommendation of dismissal represents a good faith determination based upon a reasonable investigation by all disinterested independent directors of Perrigo, the court must have the Report before it can properly rule on Perrigo's motion and perform its judicial function."[2742]

The Sixth Circuit, however, held that mandamus relief was appropriate with respect to the district court's ruling requiring public disclosure of the report once it was submitted to the court. This ruling by the district court, the Sixth Circuit explained, left Perrigo with "the choice of waiving the protection of the Report or withdrawing its motion to dismiss."[2743] This result, the Sixth Circuit stated, "certainly could not have been intended" by a statute "designed specifically to allow the disinterested independent directors to determine whether a derivative suit would be in the corporation's best interest."[2744]

The Sixth Circuit acknowledged that the statute "does not require that the disinterested independent director issue a report with its recommendation" or "consult with counsel."[2745] Never-

---

2740. *Id.* at 437-38.
2741. *Id.* at 438 (quoting *Picard Chem.*, 951 F. Supp. at 687).
2742. *Id.*
2743. *Id.*
2744. *Id.*
2745. *Id.* at 438-39.

theless, the court stated, "in order to perform a meaningful investigation, particularly in large corporations, consultations with counsel and exchanging of documents" are "commonplace."[2746] As a result, "automatic public disclosure of the Report upon the filing of a motion to dismiss under the Michigan statute will hinder further communications between the independent directors and attorneys reviewing whether a derivative action is in the corporation's interest" and "cause future disinterested independent directors in Michigan reviewing whether a derivative litigation is in the corporate interest not to produce extensive written materials."[2747] The court stated that "Michigan would surely not wish to discourage disinterested independent directors from working candidly with counsel in discharging their duties under the statute."[2748]

The Sixth Circuit added that the district court's order had "the effect of giving the derivative plaintiffs, representing a tiny fraction of Perrigo's shareholders, the untrammeled power to waive Perrigo's protections in the Report if Perrigo does not first do so" because if Perrigo pursued a motion to dismiss and did not submit the report in defense of the motion, plaintiffs had the option of doing so.[2749] Plaintiffs, the court stated, "could reveal the entire Report, which may contain highly confidential information, business trade practices or secrets, or other materials helpful to competitors and prejudicial to Perrigo itself."[2750] In connection with this point, the court noted the district court's discussion "recognizing the probable consequences of a ruling that the public should have access to the Report, including the potential for increased bargaining leverage for stockholders, invitation of unscrupulous attempts to 'graymail' the corporation into settlement, and misuse of the derivative action by attorneys who hope to gain handsome fees."[2751]

---

2746. *Id*. at 439.
2747. *Id*.
2748. *Id*.
2749. *Id*. at 439-40.
2750. *Id*. at 440.
2751. *Id*. at 439 n.6 (citing *Picard Chem.*, 951 F. Supp. at 692).

The Sixth Circuit also noted the district court's denial of Perrigo's request that Perrigo "be allowed to submit a redacted version of the Report" in order to "support its claim that Formanek's recommendation was made in good faith or that his investigation was reasonable."[2752] The court stated that it "cannot discern" why the district court "would not allow Perrigo voluntarily to waive its rights to portions of the Report."[2753]

For all of these reasons, the Sixth Circuit concluded that "[w]e do not deem, at this juncture of the proceedings, that Perrigo has utterly waived its privilege from public disclosure under Michigan law."[2754]

The Sixth Circuit then turned to the public's right of access to a report by a disinterested independent director once the report has been filed in court. The court recognized that "the public has a right to copy and inspect judicial records" but stated that this right "is not absolute" and that "district courts have the discretion to deny or permit access to judicial records."[2755] Here, the court recognized, the public included the plaintiffs in the *Picard Chemical* securities fraud litigation against the corporation. The court held that "[w]e see no need at this stage" to give confidential information not just to plaintiffs in a derivative action on behalf of the corporation, but also to "plaintiffs in a hostile securities action" against the corporation.[2756] The Sixth Circuit thus held that the district court "may study, examine, interpret, and inspect the report" in connection with Perrigo's motion to dismiss "without making it public property."[2757]

The court also held that the report "should not become a part of the 'judicial record' until the district court has read the Report and has adequately weighed the interests of the public against the interests of Perrigo in maintaining its privilege as to all or part of

---

2752. *Id.* at 438.
2753. *Id.* at 438 n.4.
2754. *Id.* at 439.
2755. *Id.* at 440.
2756. *Id.*
2757. *Id.* at 441.

the Report."[2758] This balancing process, the court stated, should include "a hearing regarding whether the Report or parts thereof should be disclosed to the public, or whether that information should remain sealed."[2759] The court offered the following guidelines to be used in the course of this balancing:

> [A] court "should begin its analysis with a presumption in favor of preserving the privilege." Accordingly, the burden of establishing a waiver under the balancing approach rests on the party seeking discovery. . . . [D]iscovery, if allowed, should be narrowly limited to those portions of the privileged material that bear directly on the issues at hand. . . . [T]he need to pierce the veil of confidentiality "does not mean that [parties] should receive wholesale access to the confidential records of others."[2760]

The Sixth Circuit thus held that the district court committed "clear error" by holding that submitting a report of a disinterested independent director "in purported compliance with the Michigan statute, to 'induce reliance' by the court (which will undoubtedly occur), automatically places it in the public domain."[2761] The court acknowledged that "[i]t may be that for good and sufficient reasons at some point in the proceedings, after a full hearing on the matter, the district court may conclude that public disclosure of the Report or certain portions thereof is necessary and appropriate for limited purposes."[2762] Nevertheless, the court stated, to reach that point simply because the report has been submitted to the court and to plaintiff in a derivative action in an effort to dismiss the derivative action might "'. . .have the effect of thwarting the developing procedure of corporations to employ independent out-

---

2758. *Id.* at 440.

2759. *Id.*

2760. *Id.* (quoting *Howe v. Detroit Free Press, Inc.* 487 N.W.2d 374, 383 (Mich. 1992)).

2761. *Id.* at 441.

2762. *Id.*

side counsel to investigate and advise them in order to protect stockholders, potential stockholders and customers.'"[2763]

*c. The Sixth Circuit Dissent.* Judge Karen Nelson Moore concurred and dissented. Like the majority, Judge Moore assumed that the Formanek Report constituted an attorney-client communication and work product.[2764] Like the majority, Judge Moore agreed with the district court that a shareholder plaintiff in a derivative action must have access to a report by a disinterested independent director in order to respond meaningfully to a motion to dismiss by that director.[2765] Judge Moore also agreed that the court must have access to the report to undertake a considered examination of the motion "even assuming that the court's inquiry under the Michigan Business Corporation Act is limited to ascertaining whether Formanek's recommendation represents a good faith determination based upon reasonable investigation."[2766]

Judge Moore, however, was "not convinced that the Report should remain inaccessible to the public if either party uses any portion of the Report in the ensuing litigation."[2767] According to Judge Moore, Perrigo's motion to dismiss constituted an implied waiver of the attorney-client privilege and the work product doctrine. "Once Perrigo moved for dismissal based upon Formanek's investigation and determination, the company lost its ability to conceal the Report from the derivative plaintiff, the court, and presumably the public; it was as if Perrigo had actually attached the Report to its own court filing."[2768]

Judge Moore criticized the majority's decision to permit the derivative plaintiff access to the report as "the carving out of an exception to the attorney-client privilege based on the plaintiff's

---

2763. *Id.* (quoting *Diversified Indus., Inc.* v. *Meredith*, 572 F.2d 596, 611 (8th Cir. 1978) *(en banc))*.
2764. *In re Perrigo Co.*, 128 F.3d 430, 442 (6th Cir. 1997) (Moore, J., concurring and dissenting).
2765. *Id.*
2766. *Id.*
2767. *Id.*
2768. *Id.* at 446.

substantial need for the Report and the undue hardship he would experience were he denied access to the Report."[2769] Under the majority's view, according to Judge Moore, the privilege was left "intact with respect to other individuals and the public-at-large."[2770] Judge Moore, by contrast, believed that Perrigo's reference to and reliance upon the Report in its motion to dismiss required the court to find a waiver of the privilege with respect to plaintiffs and the public—including the plaintiffs in the *Picard Chemical* securities fraud class action. Accordingly, Judge Moore concluded, "the majority is wrong when it asserts that the plaintiff has the power to waive Perrigo's privilege by submitting the Report to the court."[2771] Judge Moore reached the same conclusion with respect to the work product doctrine.[2772]

Judge Moore acknowledged Perrigo's protest that "it will face a Hobson's choice if it is held to have impliedly waived disclosure protections—either the corporation moves to dismiss, relies on the Report, and thereby forfeits protections for the Report, or the corporation suffers through potentially unmeritorious litigation but protects the confidentiality of the Report."[2773] Judge Moore responded that "Perrigo has assumed this risk by moving to dismiss on the basis of Formanek's investigation and conclusions, and certainly cannot claim to be surprised by such a dilemma."[2774] Perrigo's board, Judge Moore continued, "could anticipate from the outset that any report produced by the disinterested independent director would in all likelihood eventually underlie a motion to dismiss and thus become enmeshed in a dispositive court ruling. This, in itself, largely undermines any expectation of perpetual confidentiality."[2775] Judge Moore acknowledged that "if my position were to prevail, in the future disinterested independent directors in Michigan reviewing whether a derivative litigation is in

---

2769. *Id.* at 444 n.2.
2770. *Id.*
2771. *Id.*
2772. *Id.* at 445.
2773. *Id.*
2774. *Id.*
2775. *Id.*

the corporate interest may not be inclined to produce extensive written materials."[2776] Judge Moore cautioned, however, that a board nevertheless

> will be well-advised to ascertain for itself that the disinterested independent directors acted in good faith and conducted a reasonable investigation. At minimum, the board should seek assurances that the corporation has a legitimate basis for moving to dismiss in compliance with Rule 11 of the Federal Rules of Civil Procedure or its state law equivalent. This evaluation will be best undertaken with all of the requisite facts and supporting documentation before the board.[2777]

Judge Moore then turned to the public's right of access to judicial records. Judge Moore stated her view that "[t]he majority wrongly begins with a presumption favoring Perrigo" and that "[b]y instructing the district court to 'study, examine, interpret, and inspect the Report without making it public property in connection with the disposition of the motion to dismiss,' the majority conceals the record of the court behind a veil of secrecy, thereby threatening to undermine public confidence in our judicial system."[2778] Judge Moore contended that sealing court records is "a drastic step" that only can be justified by "the most compelling reasons."[2779] In Judge Moore's view, Perrigo had "not made a persuasive case that overriding confidentiality concerns should prevent the public from having access to the Formanek Report should it become part of the judicial record."[2780] According to Judge Moore, "[t]he potent presumption favoring open access to the courtroom and court documents should not yield to Perrigo's desire to conceal the Report absent Perrigo demonstrating a compelling reason, such as an actual trade-secret, to set aside the presumption."[2781] In other words, Judge Moore concluded, "[s]hould Perrigo claim a need for special protection of specific segments of the Report . . . , for example if

---

2776. *Id.* at 445-46.
2777. *Id.* at 446.
2778. *Id.* at 446 n.5.
2779. *Id.* at 446.
2780. *Id.*
2781. *Id.* at 446 n.5.

actual trade secrets might be revealed, then the district judge remains free to order particularized protection."[2782]

Judge Moore acknowledged that "it may be true that the Michigan legislature would be concerned about promoting candor between independent directors and attorneys assisting with internal investigations."[2783] According to Judge Moore, however, "the Michigan legislature has an explicit policy favoring open judicial proceedings."[2784] Judge Moore stated that "[n]owhere do the provisions of the Michigan Business Corporation Act mention the importance of the attorney-client privilege held by corporations, let alone indicate that it is essential to fulfillment of the statutory goal of promoting effective monitoring of management by independent directors."[2785] Judge Moore therefore saw "no reason to assume that the Michigan legislature intended to abandon the compelling public policies furthered by open adjudicative proceedings in favor of the policies served by candid discussions between independent directors and hired counsel."[2786]

---

2782. *Id.* at 448.
2783. *Id.*
2784. *Id.*
2785. *Id.*
2786. *Id.*

# CHAPTER V

# Indemnification and Insurance

Indemnification refers to reimbursement by the corporation of liabilities, including judgments, amounts paid in settlement, expenses and attorneys' fees, incurred by directors and officers in the course of their service to the corporation. Insurance, commonly called directors' and officers' liability insurance or "D & O" insurance, is carried both to reimburse the corporation for indemnification payments made to directors and officers and to cover the directors and officers in circumstances where indemnification from the corporation is unavailable.

Indemnification and insurance of corporate directors and officers are directly related to the courts' utilization (or non-utilization) of the business judgment rule as a means of reviewing alleged wrongdoing by directors and officers. The more likcly it is that directors may be held liable for money damages, the more likely it also is that indemnification may be required and/or insurers will have exposure under D & O policies. The more likely it is that lawsuits against directors will not be resolved in favor of directors at an early stage of litigation, the more likely it is that indemnifiable and/or insured against defense costs (particularly attorneys' fees) will be high, even in cases where directors and officers ultimately prevail. As exposure under D & O policies for monetary damages and defense costs increases, of course, the premiums charged for D & O policies also increase.[1]

---

1. *See generally Dynamics Corp. of Am. v. CTS Corp.*, 794 F.2d
(continued...)

During the mid-1980s a widespread perception arose that corporate directors and officers faced an increased likelihood of being held liable for money damages. Combined with other factors, this perception led D & O insurers to raise the premiums charged for policies, to cut back their business to a fraction of previous capacity, and in some cases to stop writing D & O policies altogether. The steps taken by corporations and state legislatures during the mid-to-late 1980s in response to the decreased availability of D & O insurance remain important aspects of the current legal environment.

# A.  Indemnification

## 1.  Underlying Policy Considerations

Under the common law, courts were divided over the right of a corporate director or officer to receive indemnification from the corporation for liabilities arising out of service to the corporation.[2] This uncertainty, together with "increasing legislative acceptance of the idea as reasonable and normal," ultimately led to the enactment of statutes authorizing indemnification in all fifty states.[3]

---

1. (...continued)
250, 256 (7th Cir. 1986), *rev'd on other grounds*, 481 U.S. 69 (1987):

> [A] more searching judicial review of corporate decisions concerning defensive measures to takeovers than of decisions concerning ordinary business decisions . . . is not without its costs. It makes directors overcautious, makes people reluctant to serve as directors, drives up directors' fees and officers' and directors' liability insurance rates, and leads boards of directors to adopt ponderous, court-like procedures. But the price is one the courts have been willing to pay.

2. *Compare, e.g.*, *New York Dock Co. v. McCollom*, 173 Misc. 106, 109-11, 16 N.Y.S.2d 844, 847-49 (N.Y. Sup. Ct. Onondaga Co. 1939) *and Griesse v. Lang*, 175 N.E. 222, 222-23 (Ohio Ct. App. 1931) (indemnification not permitted) *with In re E.C. Warner Co.*, 45 N.W.2d 388, 393-94 (Minn. 1950) *and Solimine v. Hollander*, 19 A.2d 344, 348 (N.J. Ch. 1941) (indemnification permitted).

3. Joseph W. Bishop, Jr., *The Law of Corporate Officers and Directors: Indemnification and Insurance* ¶ 6.02, at 6–4-5 (1981 & Supp. 1997); *see also Western Fiberglass, Inc. v. Kirton, McConkie & Bushnell*,

(continued...)

A broad right of indemnification is necessary, and courts have interpreted indemnification rights "very broadly,"[4] in order

> to "promote the desirable end that corporate officials will resist what they consider" unjustified suits and claims, "secure in the knowledge that their reasonable expenses will be borne by the corporation they have served if they are vindicated." Beyond that, its larger purpose is "to encourage capable men to serve as corporate directors, secure in the knowledge that expenses incurred by them in upholding their honesty and integrity as directors will be borne by the corporation they serve."[5]

As stated by the Delaware Court of Chancery in *Scharf v. Edgcomb Corp.*[6]:

> Delaware's corporation code authorizes liberal indemnification provisions for officers and directors of its corporations for sound policy reasons that benefit all of a corporation's constituencies. Indemnification provisions authorized by statute and

---

3. (...continued)
789 P.2d 34, 37-38 (Utah Ct. App. 1990) (discussing history of these statutes); John F. Olson & Josiah O. Hatch III, *Director and Officer Liability: Indemnification and Insurance* §§ 4.05 - 4.11 (1997) (same).

4. *Witco Corp. v. Beekhuis*, 38 F.3d 682, 691 (3d Cir. 1994).

5. *Hibbert v. Hollywood Park, Inc.*, 457 A.2d 339, 343-44 (Del. 1983) (quoting Ernest L. Folk, *The Delaware General Corporation Law* 98 (1st ed. 1972), *Mooney v. Willys-Overland Motors, Inc.*, 204 F.2d 888, 898 (3d Cir. 1953), and *Essential Enters. Corp. v. Automatic Steel Prods., Inc.*, 164 A.2d 437, 441-42 (Del. Ch. 1960)); *see also Witco*, 38 F.3d at 691; *Heffernan v. Pacific Dunlop GNB Corp.*, 965 F.2d 369, 375 (7th Cir. 1992); *United States v. Weissman*, 1997 U.S. Dist. LEXIS 8540, at *52-53, 1997 WL 334966, at *17 (S.D.N.Y. June 16, 1997), *subsequent proceedings*, 1997 U.S. Dist. LEXIS 12975, at *28-29, 1997 WL 539774, at *9-10 (S.D.N.Y. Aug. 28, 1997); *Megeath v. PLM Int'l, Inc.*, No. 930369, slip op. at 18-19 (Cal. Super. Ct. Mar. 18, 1992), *reprinted in* Corp. Officers & Directors Liability Litig. Rep. 11791 (Apr. 8, 1992); *Mayer v. Executive Telecard, Ltd.*, 705 A.2d 220, 223 (Del. Ch. 1997); *MCI Telecommunications Corp. v. Wanzer*, 1990 Del. Super. LEXIS 222, at *1, 22, 1990 WL 91100, at *1, 8-11 (Del. Super. June 19, 1990); *Western Fiberglass*, 789 P.2d at 37-38.

6. 1997 Del. Ch. LEXIS 169, 1997 WL 762656 (Del. Ch. Dec. 2, 1997).

incorporated into bylaws by shareholder action demonstrate
the desire to broaden the flexibility of decision making by
eliminating the chilling effect of potential personal liability on
the part of officers and directors. Shareholder democracies
want directors and officers to engage in broadly based decision making in order to enhance shareholder value by encouraging prudent risk taking to their and the other corporate constituencies' advantage. Indemnification for officers and directors should be seen as less an individual benefit arising from
personal employment than as a desirable underwriting of risk
by the corporation in anticipation of greater corporate-wide
rewards. Analyzing director and officer indemnification provisions as if they were salary, company cars or other personal
corporate perquisites simply makes no sense. More simply
put, director and officer indemnification benefits the corporation more than the director or the officer covered.[7]

There is disagreement, however, concerning how to ensure
that the right to indemnification does not become too broad. The
drafters of the Model Business Corporation Act have stated the problem as follows:

The fundamental issue that must be addressed by an indemnification statute is . . . to ensure that indemnification is permitted only where it will further sound corporate policies and to
prohibit indemnification where it might protect or encourage
wrongful or improper conduct. As phrased by one commentator, the goal of indemnification is to "seek the middle ground
between encouraging fiduciaries to violate their trust, and discouraging them from serving at all." The increasing number
of suits against directors, the increasing cost of defense, and
the increasing emphasis on diversifying the membership of
boards of directors all militate in favor of workable arrangements to protect directors against liability to the extent consistent with established principles.[8]

---

7. 1997 Del. Ch. LEXIS 169, at *14-15, 1997 WL 762656, at *4.
8. 2 Model Bus. Corp. Act Annotated §§ 8.50-8.59 Introductory
Comment at 8-290 (3d ed. 1996) (quoting Johnston, *Corporate Indemnification and Liability Insurance for Directors and Officers*, 33 Bus. Law.
1993, 1994 (1978)); *see also* J. Olson & J. Hatch § 4.04[1].

As courts in the Fourth Circuit and California have observed:

> Indemnification, if permitted too broadly, may violate . . . basic tenets of public policy. It is inappropriate to permit management to use corporate funds to avoid the consequences of wrongful conduct or conduct involving bad faith. A director, officer, or employee who acted wrongfully or in bad faith should not expect to receive assistance from the corporation for legal or other expenses and should be required to satisfy not only any judgment entered against him but also expenses incurred in connection with the proceeding from his personal assets. Any other rule would tend to encourage socially undesirable conduct.[9]

The following discussion focuses upon the efforts of various jurisdictions to balance these competing interests. Particular attention is devoted to statutes enacted in Delaware, California and New York and to the approaches taken in the Model Business Corporation Act and Principles of Corporate Governance: Analysis and Recommendations.[10] Other state statutes and federal regulations governing federal savings associations[11] are noted where they illustrate particular points.

## 2.    Directors, Officers, Employees and Agents

Some statutes, such as the California and Delaware statutes, specifically authorize indemnification of directors, officers, employ-

---

9. *In re Landmark Land Co.*, 76 F.3d 553, 562 (4th Cir.), *cert. dismissed*, 518 U.S. 1034 (1996) (quoting *Plate v. Sun-Diamond Growers*, 225 Cal. App. 3d 1115, 1124, 275 Cal. Rptr. 667, 672 (Cal. Ct. App. 1990)); *see also Weissman*, 1997 U.S. Dist. LEXIS 8540, at *52-53, 1997 WL 334966, at *17 and 1997 U.S. Dist. LEXIS 12975, at *29-30, 1997 WL 539774, at *10 (noting competing policy considerations, and deciding the policy considerations presented by the case before the court pursuant to the choices made by New York in adopting its statute and by the corporation in drafting its bylaws); Chapter V, Section A 5 b (discussing *Weissman*).

10. *See* Cal. Gen. Corp. Law § 317; Del. Gen. Corp. Law § 145; N.Y. Bus. Corp. Law §§ 721-726; Model Bus. Corp. Act Annotated §§ 8.50-8.59; 2 Principles of Corporate Governance: Analysis and Recommendations § 7.20 (1994).

11. 12 C.F.R. § 545.121.

ees and agents,[12] although the term "agent" is subject to different interpretations.[13] Other statutes, such as the New York statute, specifically authorize indemnification only of directors and officers.[14] The Model Business Corporation Act distinguishes between officers who are directors and officers who are not directors. Like the New York statute, the Model Act does not address employees and agents.[15] The drafters of the Model Act explain that

> the concerns of self-dealing that arise when directors provide for their own indemnification and expense advance (and sometimes for senior executive officers) are not present when directors (or officers) provide for indemnification and expense advance for employees and agents who are not directors or officers. Moreover, the rights of employees and agents to indemnification and advance for expenses derive from principles of agency, the doctrine of respondeat superior, collective bargaining, or other contractual arrangements rather than from a corporation statute.[16]

---

12. *See* Cal. Gen. Corp. Law § 317; Del. Gen. Corp. Law § 145.

13. *See APSB Bancorp v. Grant*, 26 Cal. App. 4th 926, 931, 934, 31 Cal. Rptr. 2d 736, 739, 740-41 (Cal. Ct. App. 1994) (holding that the term "agent" means "one who represents another, called the principal, in dealings with third persons," and that a certified public accounting firm was not an agent for the purpose of California's indemnification statute: "Appellant's business is to conduct, among other things, independent audits for corporations. . . . [A]ppellant was sued to recover losses directly resulting from the failure of appellants to recognize and warn the corporation of the defalcations of Vassegh. Appellant was not being sued by third persons for losses occasioned by appellant's representation of the corporation or for taking action on behalf of the corporation in the classical sense of agency."); *Western Fiberglass*, 789 P.2d at 38-39 (holding that "the words 'director, officer, employee or agent'" in such a statute "have synonymous underlying meanings," and that the term "agent" applies only to "corporate personnel who exercise management discretion and who have authority to bind the corporation," and not to "someone like Kirton [an attorney] having any type of agency relationship with the corporation").

14. *See* N.Y. Bus. Corp. Law §§ 721-726.

15. 2 Model Bus. Corp. Act Annotated § 8.56 (3d ed. 1996).

16. *Id.* § 8.56 Official Comment at 8-369.

The Model Act thus "intends to leave a corporation free, subject only to principles of agency and contract law, to provide for indemnification and expense advancement for employees and agents in whatever manner the corporation chooses."[17]

Principles of Corporate Governance: Analysis and Recommendations likewise does not address the issue of indemnification of employees and agents who are not directors or officers of the corporation. Instead, Principles of Corporate Governance states, "[e]ntitlement of such persons to indemnification is covered by the law of agency and contracts."[18]

## 3. Mandatory Indemnification

Indemnification may be mandatory pursuant to the governing corporation law statute, or pursuant to a charter, bylaw or contract provision.

*a. Statutory Provisions.* The Delaware and New York statutes state that indemnification is mandatory where the person to be indemnified has been "successful on the merits or otherwise."[19] These provisions grant "an absolute right of indemnification in such situations."[20] This indemnification obligation is imposed "upon the corporation whether or not the corporation is a losing party (or even a party at all) in the underlying action."[21] California's statute requires that in order to be entitled to mandatory indemnification the person to be indemnified must be successful "on the merits" rather than "on the merits or otherwise."[22] The Model Business Corpora-

---

17. Committee on Corporate Laws, *Changes in the Model Business Corporation Act—Amendments Pertaining to Indemnification and Advance for Expenses*, 49 Bus. Law. 741, 747 (1994).

18. 2 Principles of Corporate Governance: Analysis and Recommendations § 7.20 Comment at 265 (1994).

19. Del. Gen. Corp. Law § 145(c); N.Y. Bus. Corp. Law § 723(a).

20. *Witco Corp. v. Beekhuis*, 38 F.3d 682, 691 (3d Cir. 1994).

21. *Mayer v. Executive Telecard, Ltd.*, 705 A.2d 220, 223 (Del. Ch. 1997).

22. Cal. Gen. Corp. Law § 317(d); *see also American Nat'l Bank & Trust Co. v. Schigur*, 83 Cal. App. 3d 790, 793, 148 Cal. Rptr. 116, 117-

(continued...)

tion Act and Principles of Corporate Governance: Analysis and Recommendations provide for mandatory indemnification where the person to be indemnified has been "wholly successful, on the merits or otherwise."[23]

None of these formulations require any of the elements required for permissive indemnification that are discussed later in this Chapter—typically, a determination by disinterested directors, an independent counsel or shareholders that the person to be indemnified acted in good faith and in a manner he reasonably believed to be in the best interests of the corporation.[24] One court construing Michigan's indemnification statute—*Stoddard v. Michigan National Corp.*[25]—has held that mandatory indemnification also differs from permissive indemnification because mandatory indemnification is permitted only for conduct by "directors, officers, employees, and agents of the corporation from which mandatory indemnification is sought," and not for conduct by persons "serving in other corporations at the request of the corporation from which mandatory indemnification is sought."[26] Thus, according to the *Stoddard* court, an officer of a bank holding corporation was not entitled to mandatory indemnification from the corporation for conduct by the officer as an officer of a bank owned by the corporation.[27]

---

22. (...continued)
18 (Cal. Ct. App. 1978) (the omission of the expression "or otherwise" suggests "a legislative intent that mandatory indemnification should depend upon a judicial determination of the actual merits of the agent's defense").

23. 2 Model Bus. Corp. Act Annotated § 8.52 (3d ed. 1996); 2 Principles of Corporate Governance: Analysis and Recommendations § 7.20(a)(3)(A) (1994).

24. *Green v. Westcap Corp.*, 492 A.2d 260, 264-65 (Del. Super. 1985); *Stoddard v. Michigan Nat'l Corp.*, No. 125352, slip op. at 3 (Mich. Ct. App. Apr. 8, 1992), *appeal denied*, 497 N.W.2d 184 (Mich. 1993); *see also* Chapter V, Sections A 3 a and b (discussing permissive indemnification).

25. No. 125352 (Mich. Ct. App. Apr. 8, 1992), *appeal denied*, 497 N.W.2d 184 (Mich. 1993).

26. *Id.*, slip op. at 3.

27. *Id.* at 3-4.

The Delaware, New York, Model Act and Principles of Corporate Governance "on the merits *or otherwise*" requirement recognizes that although an "occasional defendant" who has in fact done something wrong may become "entitled to indemnification because of procedural defenses not related to the merits, e.g., the statute of limitations or disqualification of the plaintiff, it is unreasonable to require a defendant with a valid procedural defense to undergo a possibly prolonged and expensive trial on the merits in order to establish eligibility for mandatory indemnification."[28] Thus, indemnification is required where a case is dismissed for insufficient service of process.[29] Similarly, the fact that an action brought as a class action is dismissed before a class is certified and as a result "there is the possibility out there that someone else may file a lawsuit" has no bearing upon the right of a defendant to indemnification because "[c]learly" he won "a victory . . . on the merits or otherwise."[30] "This avoids forcing on a director or officer (and ultimately on the indemnifying corporation) the additional expense of litigating an issue on the merits where a preliminary technical defense will suffice."[31]

The Second Circuit, construing Delaware law in *Waltuch v. Conticommodity Services, Inc.*,[32] thus stated the governing rule as follows: "'[S]uccess' . . . does not mean moral exoneration. Escape from an adverse judgment or other detriment, for whatever reason,

---

28. Model Bus. Corp. Act Annotated § 8.52 Official Comment at 8-343.

29. *Waltuch v. Conticommodity Servs., Inc.*, 833 F. Supp. 302, 310, 311 (S.D.N.Y. 1993), *aff'd and rev'd on other grounds*, 88 F.3d 87 (2d Cir. 1996).

30. *Mayer v. Executive Telecard, Ltd.*, No. 14459, Tr. at 2-3 (Del. Ch. Apr. 19, 1996), *subsequent proceedings*, 705 A.2d 220, 223 (Del. Ch. 1997) (noting prior ruling granting "indemnification of the fees and expenses [Mayer] incurred in successfully defending a federal securities action brought against him").

31. 1 Ernest L. Folk, Rodman Ward, Jr. and Edward P. Welch, *Folk on the Delaware Corporation Law* § 145.4, at 145:11 (3d ed. 1998).

32. *Waltuch v. Conticommodity Servs., Inc.*, 88 F.3d 87 (2d Cir. 1996).

is determinative. . . . [T]he only question a court may ask is what the result was, not why it was."[33] Applying this standard, the court in *Waltuch* held that a $35 million settlement of lawsuits against a corporation and a former officer of the corporation, Norton D. Waltuch, paid for entirely by the corporation, without the former officer assuming any liability, constitutes "success on the merits or otherwise" and entitled Waltuch to mandatory indemnification.[34] The court rejected the corporation's contention that "because of its $35 million settlement payments, Waltuch's settlement without payment should not really count as a settlement without payment."[35] According to the court, "[w]hatever the impetus for the plaintiffs' dismissal of their claims" against Waltuch, "he still walked away without liability and without making a payment. This constitutes a success that is untarnished by the process that achieved it."[36] The court added that "Delaware law cannot allow an indemnifying corporation to escape . . . mandatory indemnification . . . by paying a sum in settlement on behalf of an unwilling indemnitee."[37]

Another federal court construing Delaware law, *Mayer v. Executive Telecard, Ltd.*,[38] stated that *Waltuch* requires indemnification "whenever a party escapes from an adverse judgment or other detriment 'for whatever reason' and that "'the only question a court may ask is what the result was, not why it was.'"[39] Applying this standard, the court held that "[t]he litigation underlying this case settled and was dismissed with prejudice. This dismissal applied to all claims, including those against Mayer. As a result, Mayer escaped adverse judgment and detriment. Clearly, therefore, indemnification is appropriate."[40] As stated by a New York court con-

---

33. *Id.* at 96.
34. *Id.* at 89, 95-97.
35. *Id.* at 96.
36. *Id.* at 97.
37. *Id.*
38. 1997 U.S. Dist. LEXIS 317, 1997 WL 16669 (S.D.N.Y. Jan. 17, 1997).
39. 1997 U.S. Dist. LEXIS 317, at *7, 1997 WL 16669, at *3 (quoting *Waltuch*, 88 F.3d at 96).
40. 1997 U.S. Dist. LEXIS 317, at *7-8, 1997 WL 16669, at *3;

(continued...)

struing Delaware law in *Stewart v. Continental Copper & Steel Industries, Inc.*,[41] "any result . . . other than indictment" in the context of a grand jury proceeding "should be considered success for purposes of the mandatory indemnification statute."[42]

The Ninth Circuit, construing Maryland law, which, like Delaware, New York, the Model Act and Principles of Corporate Governance, requires "success on the merits or otherwise,"[43] similarly concluded in *Safeway Stores, Inc. v. National Union Fire Insurance Co.*[44] that "[p]resumably, a 'successful defense' in a settlement . . . occurs where no liability is conceded."[45] The court accordingly held that directors who "denied any liability whatsoever" in a settlement agreement pursuant to which the corporation but not the directors paid money were "successful 'on the merits or otherwise.'"[46]

Courts construing Illinois and Pennsylvania statutes, both of which also require success "on the merits or otherwise,"[47] likewise have held that a settlement pursuant to which there is no payment or assumption of liability by the person to be indemnified "surely" constitutes success "on the merits or otherwise."[48] The Fourth Circuit in *In re Landmark Land Co.*,[49] construing Louisiana law, which also requires success "on the merits or otherwise,"[50] stated that the

---

40. (...continued)
*see also Mayer v. Executive Telecard, Ltd.*, No. 95 Civ. 5403 (BSJ) (S.D.N.Y. Apr. 30, 1997), *reprinted in* Corporate Officers and Directors Liability Litig. Rptr. 21230 (May 14, 1997) (determining amount owed).

41. 67 A.D.2d 293, 414 N.Y.S.2d 910 (N.Y. App. Div. 1st Dep't 1979).

42. *Id.* at 301-02, 414 N.Y.S.2d at 915.

43. Md. Gen. Corp. Law § 2-418(b).

44. 64 F.3d 1282 (9th Cir. 1995).

45. *Id.* at 1290 n.24.

46. *Id.*

47. Ill. Bus. Corp. Act § 8.75(c); Pa. Bus. Corp. Law § 1743.

48. *Wisener v. Air Express Int'l Corp.*, 583 F.2d 579, 583 (2d Cir. 1978) (applying Illinois law); *B & B Inv. Club v. Kleinert's Inc.*, 472 F. Supp. 787, 789-91 (E.D. Pa. 1979) (applying Pennsylvania law).

49. 76 F.3d 553 (4th Cir.), *cert. dismissed*, 518 U.S. 1034 (1996).

50. La. Bus. Corp. Law § 12:83(B).

terms of a settlement agreement between a director and the Office of Thrift Supervision (the "OTS") that confirmed that the director committed no intentional wrongful act and acted in good faith, and pursuant to which the director signed a cease and desist order prohibiting breaches of fiduciary duty in the future, "would likely" constitute success "on the merits or otherwise" in defense of OTS charges.[51] The court also held that a regulatory agency's failure to file charges against a group of corporate employees after investigating the employees' conduct, issuing subpoenas to the employees and making the employees appear at depositions "under circumstances that were clearly adversarial" constituted success requiring mandatory indemnification.[52] By contrast, the court in *Landmark* held that another group of corporate employees, who had entered into a settlement agreement stating that these employees continued to dispute the OTS charges against them but accepted prohibition from practicing in the affairs of any insured depository institution and debarment from practicing before the OTS, were not successful "on the merits or otherwise" in defense of the OTS charges.[53]

California law, as noted above, differs from Delaware, New York, the Model Act and Principles of Corporate Governance by requiring that the director be successful "on the merits" rather than "on the merits or otherwise."[54] *Dalany v. American Pacific Holding Corp.*[55] involved a former corporate director and officer, Michael D. Delany, who sued the corporation to collect $165,000 in loans he had advanced to the corporation. The corporation filed a counterclaim alleging breaches of fiduciary duty by Delany. The case was settled by a payment of $105,000 by the corporation to Delany.[56] The court held that Delany was not "successful on the

---

51. 76 F.3d at 565-66.

52. *Id*. at 567.

53. *Id*.

54. Cal. Gen. Corp. Law § 317(d).

55. 42 Cal. App. 4th 822, 50 Cal. Rptr. 2d 13 (Cal. Ct. App. 1996).

56. *Id*. at 825-26, 50 Cal. Rptr. 2d at 14.

merits" in defending the claim asserted against him by the corporation.[57] The court reasoned as follows:

> Delany cannot establish APHC's cross-complaint was terminated in his favor. The lengthy negotiations between counsel for Delany and counsel for APHC leave no doubt the stipulation for entry of judgment and the judgment were entered as a result of settlement negotiations between Delany and APHC. Moreover the terms of the stipulation and judgment, which allowed APHC to discharge its liability to Delany for substantially less than the face amount of his loans to the corporation, demonstrate the judgment was the product of compromise by the parties and not any determination of the merits by the parties or the trial court.[58]

Delaware's statute, which provides for mandatory indemnification "[t]o the extent that" the person to be indemnified has been "successful on the merits or otherwise,"[59] requires partial indemnification in cases of partial success. The meaning of partial success has been the subject of substantial litigation.

In *Merritt-Chapman & Scott Corp. v. Wolfson ("Wolfson I")*,[60] for example, the Delaware Supreme Court held that a court's determination to remove a Rule 10b-5 element of a conspiracy count alleging "perjury, filing false statements with the SEC, obstruction of justice, and fraud upon the corporate shareholders in violation of SEC Rule 10b-5" did not constitute partial success.[61] In a later proceeding, *Merritt-Chapman & Scott Corp. v. Wolfson ("Wolfson II")*,[62] however, the court awarded partial indemnification to two defendants who, pursuant to a plea bargain, were successful on one count of a criminal indictment (conspiracy to violate federal securities laws) but unsuccessful on a related count—in one defendant's case, perjury; in the other defendant's case, filing false annual

---

57. *Id.* at 830, 50 Cal. Rptr. 2d at 17.
58. *Id.* at 828, 50 Cal. Rptr. 2d at 16.
59. Del. Gen. Corp. Law § 145(c).
60. 264 A.2d 358 (Del. Super. 1970).
61. *Id.* at 359.
62. 321 A.2d 138 (Del. Super. 1974).

reports with the Securities and Exchange Commission and the New York Stock Exchange.[63]

The Delaware Supreme Court in *Green v. Westcap Corp.*[64] reached a result similar to the result in *Wolfson II* and ordered a corporation to indemnify a former corporate officer for legal expenses incurred in successfully defending a criminal action in which the officer was alleged to have defrauded and embezzled funds from the corporation.[65] The corporation unsuccessfully argued that any decision regarding indemnification should await the conclusion of related civil litigation because the judge who directed the judgment of acquittal had stated that "not guilty" did not imply innocence and that he believed the officer seeking indemnification would be punished in a civil court.[66] The court in *Westcap* relied upon the fact that indemnification was sought only for the successful defense of the criminal charge and that a grant of such indemnification would not establish any right to indemnification in any other litigation.[67]

The Delaware Superior Court in *MCI Telecommunications Corp. v. Wanzer*[68] ordered partial indemnification in a case where a corporation sued a former corporate officer for breach of fiduciary duty, fraud, conspiracy to defraud and conversion, and the jury returned a verdict (1) in favor of the corporation on the breach of fiduciary duty claim and awarded $1 million in damages, and (2) in favor of the corporate employee on the fraud, conspiracy to defraud and conversion counts.[69] The Fifth Circuit, construing Delaware law in *McLean v. International Harvester Co.*,[70] ordered indemnification of expenses incurred by a former corporate officer in an action seeking expungement of the officer's name from the records

---

63. *Id.* at 141.
64. 492 A.2d 260 (Del. Super. 1985).
65. *Id.* at 262.
66. *Id.* at 265.
67. *Id.* at 265-66.
68. 1990 Del. Super. LEXIS 222, 1990 WL 91100 (Del. Super. June 19, 1990).
69. 1990 Del. Super. LEXIS 222, at *1-3, 27-37, 1990 WL 91100, at *1, 8-11.
70. 902 F.2d 372 (5th Cir. 1990).

of corporation's guilty plea even though expungement was denied. The court reasoned that the expungement action was "part and parcel" of the corporate officer's "successful criminal defense."[71] A federal district court construing Delaware law in *Galdi v. Berg*[72] held that "dismissal without prejudice solely because the same charge is being litigated in other presently pending actions" does not constitute partial success and does not entitle the defendant to mandatory indemnification.[73]

The Model Business Corporation Act rejects Delaware's partial success rule by requiring that the person to be indemnified must have been "*wholly* successful, on the merits or otherwise."[74] According to the drafters of the Model Act, "[a] defendant is 'wholly successful' only if the entire proceeding is disposed of on a basis which does not involve a finding of liability."[75] New York amended its indemnification statute in 1986 to delete a "wholly successful" requirement and thus made mandatory indemnification available, as in Delaware, in cases where the director has been "successful."[76] The California statute, like the Delaware and New York statutes, is worded in terms of the person seeking indemnification being "successful" rather than "wholly successful," although (as noted above) California's statute does not include the "on the merits *or otherwise*" language found in the Delaware and New York statutes.[77]

---

71. *Id.* at 374.

72. 359 F. Supp. 698 (D. Del. 1973).

73. *Id.* at 702.

74. Model Bus. Corp. Act Annotated § 8.52 (emphasis added).

75. *Id.* Official Comment at 8-343.

76. N.Y. Bus. Corp. Law § 723(a); Former N.Y. Bus. Corp. Law § 724(a).

77. Cal. Gen. Corp. Law § 317(d); *see also Harris v. Resolution Trust Corp.*, 939 F.2d 926, 928-29 (11th Cir. 1991) (federal banking regulation providing for mandatory indemnification if there is a "final judgment on the merits" held to require indemnification only where the person to be indemnified "has received a final judgment on the merits in his or her favor in the entire action for which indemnification is sought," and that a director acquitted on one count of a two count indictment therefore was not entitled to mandatory indemnification); *Tomash v. Midwest Tech-*

(continued...)

As discussed above, the Model Act distinguishes between officers who are directors and officers who are not directors.[78] For purposes of mandatory indemnification, however, the same rules govern officers who are directors and officers who are not directors.[79]

The terms "successful" and "wholly successful" have been construed by courts in Hawaii and New York, respectively, to require finality. This means that where the person to be indemnified obtains a favorable result in a trial court but an appeal is pending, the person is not yet successful for the purpose of mandatory indemnification.[80]

Different rules govern mandatory indemnification in the context of federal savings associations. In that context, mandatory indemnification is required where a director, officer or employee obtains a "final judgment on the merits . . . in his or her favor, provided that the Office of Thrift Supervision is given at least 60 days' notice of a determination to grant indemnification, and provided that indemnification is not granted if the OTS objects to the indemnification.[81]

While the Delaware statute addresses indemnification of directors, officers, employees and agents, the statutory provision pro-

---

77. (...continued)

*nical Dev. Corp.*, 160 N.W.2d 273, 275-76 (Minn. 1968) (construing pre-statutory case law providing for mandatory indemnification for directors "vindicated on the merits" and holding that directors who had been found not guilty of "gross abuse of trust" but had been held to have violated Section 17(d) of the Investment Company Act of 1940, 15 U.S.C. § 80a-17(d), were not "completely vindicated" and therefore were not entitled to mandatory indemnification).

78. *See* Chapter V, Section A 2.

79. Model Bus. Corp. Act Annotated § 8.56(c).

80. *See Lussier v. Mau-Van Dev., Inc.*, 667 P.2d 830, 832-34 (Haw. Ct. App. 1983) (construing Hawaii's "successful" requirement); *Haenel v. Epstein*, 88 A.D.2d 652, 653, 450 N.Y.S.2d 536, 537 (N.Y. App. Div. 2d Dep't 1982) (construing "wholly successful" requirement in New York statute, which, as noted in the text above, has been amended and is now a "successful" rather than a "wholly successful" requirement).

81. 12 C.F.R. § 545.121(c)(1).

viding for mandatory indemnification applies only to directors and officers.[82] This provision does not apply "with respect to employees and agents of the corporation who are neither officers nor directors of the corporation."[83] The California statute addresses indemnification of directors, officers, employees and agents and does not distinguish between directors and officers on one hand and employees and agents on the other hand for the purpose of mandatory indemnification.[84] The New York statute, the Model Act and Principles of Corporate Governance address indemnification only of directors and officers.[85]

*b. Charter, Bylaw and Contract Provisions.* Indemnification also may be mandatory where charter, bylaw or contractual provisions provide that indemnification that otherwise would be permissive "shall"—as opposed to "may"—be granted "to the full extent permitted by law." As stated in the Model Business Corporation Act, "[a] corporation may, by a provision in its articles of incorporation or bylaws or in a resolution adopted or a contract approved by its board of directors or shareholders, obligate itself in advance of the act or omission giving rise to a proceeding to provide indemnification."[86] Examples of cases enforcing such provisions include *Heffernan v. Pacific Dunlop GNB Corp.*,[87] *Mitrano v. Total Pharmaceutical Care, Inc.*,[88] *B & B Investment Club v. Kleinert's Inc.*,[89]

---

82. Del. Gen. Corp. Law § 145(c).

83. *Id.* Ch. 120, L. '97 Synopsis of Section 145.

84. Cal. Gen. Corp. Law § 317(d).

85. *See* Chapter V, Section A 2.

86. 2 Model Bus. Corp. Act Annotated § 8.58(a) (3d ed. 1996); *see also* 2 Principles of Corporate Governance: Analysis and Recommendations § 7.20(a)(3)(B) (1994) (indemnification is mandatory where "the corporation properly obligates itself to so indemnify the director or officer . . . by a provision in its charter documents or by contract").

87. 965 F.2d 369, 371-72 (7th Cir. 1992), *subsequent proceedings*, 1993 U.S. Dist. LEXIS 5, at *25-30, 1993 WL 3553, at *8-10 (N.D. Ill. Jan. 5, 1993) (Delaware law).

88. 75 F.3d 72, 73-74 (1st Cir. 1996) (California law).

89. 472 F. Supp. 787, 793 (E.D. Pa. 1979) (Pennsylvania law).

*Citadel Holding Corp. v. Roven,*[90] and *Warde v. Bayly, Martin & Fay International, Inc.*[91] and *Jackson v. Turnbull.*[92]

The Delaware Court of Chancery observed in 1992 in *Advanced Mining Systems, Inc. v. Fricke*[93] that "most corporations and virtually all public corporations" have bylaw provisions that "mandate the extension of indemnification rights in circumstances in

---

90. 603 A.2d 818, 820-24 (Del. 1992) (Delaware law).

91. No. G008209, slip op. at 9-10, 16-17 (Cal. Ct. App. May 22, 1990), *review denied*, 1990 Cal. LEXIS 3474 (Cal. Aug. 1, 1990) (Delaware law).

92. No. 13042, Tr. at 3-10 (Del. Ch. May 22, 1995) (Delaware law); *see also Anglo Am. Ins. Group, P.L.C. v. CalFed Inc.*, 899 F. Supp. 1070, 1075-81 (S.D.N.Y. 1995) (denying motion to dismiss indemnification claim under English law in case involving a mandatory indemnification provision); *Scharf v. Edgcomb Corp.*, 1997 Del. Ch. LEXIS 169, at *8 n.7, 12-16, 1997 WL 762656, at *3 n.7, 4-5 (Del. Ch. Dec. 2, 1997) (claim for mandatory indemnification pursuant to a charter, bylaw or contract provision is governed by the three year statute of limitations applicable under 10 Del. C. § 8106 to breach of contract claims and not the one year statute of limitations applicable under 10 Del. C. § 8111 to "a claim for wages, salary or overtime for work, labor or personal service performed . . . or for any other benefits arising from such work" because "[i]ndemnification for officers and directors should be seen as less an individual benefit arising from personal employment than as a desirable underwriting of risk by the corporation in anticipation of greater corporate-wide rewards"); *see also* Chapter V, Section A 1 (quoting *Edgcomb* decision at greater length); *cf. Boston Children's Heart Found. Inc. v. Nadal-Ginard*, 73 F.3d 429, 436-37 & n.8 (1st Cir. 1996) (indemnification not required where bylaw requiring indemnification contained an exception for "any matter as to which [the person to be indemnified] shall have been adjudicated in any proceeding not to have acted in good faith in the reasonable belief that his action was in the best interests of the Corporation," and where there had been an adjudication finding such conduct); *In re P.J. Keating Co.*, 180 B.R. 18, 22 n.1, 23 (Bankr. D. Mass. 1995) (indemnification not required where bylaw provided that indemnification "shall" be granted except that in the event of a settlement a vote of disinterested directors was required following "receipt of a written opinion of corporate counsel opining the director or officer has not been guilty of acts which would prohibit indemnification," and where there had been no such vote by disinterested directors).

93. 623 A.2d 82 (Del. Ch. 1992).

which indemnification" otherwise would be permissible but not mandatory.[94] These provisions, one court has held, apply prospectively and not retroactively absent evidence of an intent to the contrary.[95]

Where charter, bylaw or contract provisions requiring indemnification are adopted, the only business judgment the corporation's board may make upon a request for indemnification is whether the person seeking indemnification has met the standard of conduct set forth in the charter, bylaw or contract provision. The corporation's board is not entitled to make a business judgment concerning the wisdom of indemnification under the circumstances as the circumstances then exist.[96] Mandatory indemnification charter, bylaw and contract provisions thus create problems where former directors and officers (and employees, where they are protected by mandatory indemnification provisions) seek indemnification for the defense of claims asserted against them—sometimes by the corporation itself— for conduct that the corporation's board has determined to be contrary to the best interests of the corporation. This issue arises most frequently in the context of requests for advancement of legal expenses and is discussed in that context later in this Chapter.[97]

---

94. *Id.* at 83.

95. *First Chicago Int'l v. United Exch. Co.*, 125 F.R.D. 55, 59 (S.D.N.Y. 1989); *cf. Salaman v. National Media Corp.*, 1992 Del. Super. LEXIS 564, at *15-16, 1992 WL 808095, at *6 (Del. Super. Oct. 8, 1992) (holding that bylaw provision mandating advancement applied retroactively to require advancement for conduct that primarily occurred prior to the adoption of the bylaw, where the bylaw defined an indemnified event as "a claim asserted against the executive by reason of his service or actions in his position," and where the claim was asserted after the adoption of the bylaw).

96. *Pacific Dunlop*, 1993 U.S. Dist. LEXIS 5, at *27-28, 1993 WL 3553, at *9.

97. *See* Chapter V, Section A 5 b; *see also Jett v. Kidder Peabody & Co.*, N.Y.L.J., Dec. 23, 1997, at 30 (N.Y. Sup. Ct. N.Y. Co.) and No. 94-01696 (NASD Regulation, Inc. Jan. 26, 1998); Siconolfi, *GE's Kidder Wins Round in Dispute with Joseph Jett*, Wall St. J., Oct. 7, 1994, at C17 (each discussing effort by Orlando Joseph Jett, a former Kidder Peabody & Co. trader alleged by Kidder to have created $350 million in false profits, to obtain indemnification and advancement pursuant to a
(continued...)

Corporations also can adopt charter, bylaw or contract provisions that require indemnification that otherwise would be permissive unless the corporation's directors make an affirmative finding that the applicable statutory standards for permissive indemnification have not been met.[98] Such a provision also can require that any such finding be made by the board either within a specified time period or "reasonably and promptly" following a request for advancement.[99]

Another possibility is a charter or bylaw indemnification provision that adds that the indemnification and advancement rights provided for in the charter or bylaw constitute a "contract" between the directors and officers and the corporation.[100] Separate indemnifica-

---

97. (...continued)
corporate indemnification policy requiring "prompt" payment and reimbursement by Kidder of defense costs incurred by any past or present Kidder director, officer or employee); Arkin, *Should Kidder Advance Jett's Defense Costs?*, Nat'l L.J., Oct. 10, 1994, at A21 ("[a]s more scenarios unravel and spell possible dilemmas for corporate management, the language chosen for indemnification agreements should become more specific").

98. *See, e.g., PepsiCo, Inc. v. Continental Casualty Co.*, 640 F. Supp. 656, 661 (S.D.N.Y. 1986) (noting PepsiCo bylaw providing that "[u]nless the Board of Directors shall determine otherwise, the Corporation shall indemnify, to the full extent permitted by law"); *Lipson v. Supercuts, Inc.*, No. 15074, Tr. op. at 97-98 (Del. Ch. Dec. 10, 1996) (charter provision placing burden upon corporation to prove that person seeking indemnification was not entitled to indemnification); *see also* John F. Olson & Josiah O. Hatch III, *Director and Officer Liability: Indemnification and Insurance* § 7.10, at 7–15-16 (1997).

99. *See* J. Olson & J. Hatch § 7.10, at 7-16.

100. *See, e.g., Warde v. Bayly, Martin & Fay Int'l, Inc.*, No. G008209, slip op. at 9-10, 16-17 (Cal. Ct. App. May 22, 1990), *petition for review denied*, 1990 Cal. LEXIS 3474 (Cal. Aug. 1, 1990) (enforcing charter provision providing for indemnification of corporate directors, officers, employees and agents "to the fullest extent authorized by the Delaware General Corporation Law" and stating that "[t]he right to indemnification conferred in this Article shall be a contract right"); *Murphee v. Federal Ins. Co.*, 1997 Miss. LEXIS 145, at *24-25, 29-32 & n.6, 36, 1997 WL 167002, at *9, 11 & n.6 (Miss. Apr. 10, 1997) (in

(continued...)

tion contracts also can be entered into by a corporation with individual directors and officers.[101] Commentators have suggested that an indemnification contract may be more readily enforceable than a charter or bylaw provision because a contract reflects individual, bargained for consideration in the form of the beneficiary's agreement to accept or continue employment—a factor that at least arguably makes unilateral modification or repeal by the corporation more difficult following, for example, the beneficiary's termination or a change in control.[102] Indemnification contracts also may include provisions prohibiting the corporation from agreeing to a merger or

---

100. (...continued)
case involving a charter provision that stated that "all the rights" in the charter requiring indemnification and advancement "shall be deemed a contract between the corporation and the Indemnified Representative pursuant to which the corporation and each Indemnified Representative intend to be legally bound," the court held that the corporation's refusal to pay advancement constituted a breach of contract and raised a material issue of fact with respect to whether the corporation's breach constituted bad faith or intentional, grossly negligent or reckless conduct warranting punitive damages; discussed in Chapter V, Section A 5 b).

101. *See, e.g., Citadel Holding Corp. v. Roven*, 603 A.2d 818, 820-24 (Del. 1992) (enforcing contract provision requiring advancement); *Megeath v. PLM Int'l, Inc.*, No. 930369 (Cal. Super. Ct. Mar. 18, 1992), *reprinted in* Corp. Officers and Directors Liability Litig. Rep. 11791 (Apr. 8, 1992) (same).

102. *See* J. Olson & J. Hatch §§ 8.01-8.07; Robbins & Cohen, *Ensuring Mandatory Indemnification of Corporate Officers and Directors*, 8 Insights: The Corporate & Securities Law Advisor No. 10, Oct. 1994, at 14; *but cf. Beneficial Indus. Loan Corp. v. Smith*, 170 F.2d 44, 50 (3d Cir. 1948) ("[t]he right of the officers and directors . . . to indemnification under the bylaw is analogous to a contract right"), *aff'd on other grounds sub nom. Cohen v. Beneficial Indus. Loan Corp.*, 337 U.S. 541 (1949); *B & B Inv. Club v. Kleinert's Inc.*, 472 F. Supp. 787, 793 (E.D. Pa. 1979) ("since § 7-1 of Kleinert's bylaws uses the mandatory word 'shall' I find that Stephens may have a contractual right to indemnification"); *Salaman v. National Media Corp.*, 1992 Del. Super. LEXIS 564, at *17-18, 1992 WL 808095, at *6 (Del. Super. Oct. 8, 1992) (describing bylaw mandating indemnification and advancement as having "the force of a contract" and granting "a vested contract right which cannot be unilaterally terminated").

other business combination unless the surviving corporation agrees to indemnify directors and maintain insurance at a specified level.[103] If these contracts are approved by shareholders, the corporation and the directors can avoid questions concerning interestedness on the part of the directors receiving the contracts.[104] Charter, bylaw and contract provisions would not ensure indemnification rights in the event of an adverse change in state law because "[p]rivate parties may not circumvent the legislative will simply by agreeing to do so."[105]

## 4.  Permissive Indemnification

Where indemnification is not mandatory, corporation statutes provide for permissive indemnification of corporate directors and officers where specified standards of conduct are met. Most statutes provide separate but similarly worded standards for permissive indemnification in third party actions, on the one hand, and actions brought by or in the right of the corporation, on the other hand. Exceptions—most important in the context of actions by or in the right of the corporation—then are added.[106] The Model Business Corporation Act and Principles of Corporate Governance, by contrast, state a single set of standards for permissive indemnification and then identify situations in which permissive indemnification is not permitted in actions by or in the right of the corporation.[107]

While the corporation is *permitted* to indemnify directors and officers whose conduct falls within the bounds stated in these statutes and model provisions, this indemnification is not mandatory (except in a small minority of states, including Minnesota, North

---

103. *See From Simple to Bizarre: Ten Ways to Cope with D & O Insurance Crisis*, Corporate Control Alert, May 1986, at 1, 6.

104. J. Olson & J. Hatch §§ 7.05, 8.03; Robbins & Cohen, Insights, Oct. 1994, at 14.

105. *Citadel*, 603 A.2d at 823.

106. *See, e.g.*, Cal. Gen. Corp. Law §§ 317(b), (c); Del. Gen. Corp. Law §§ 145(a), (b); N.Y. Bus. Corp. Law §§ 722(a), (c).

107. 2 Model Bus. Corp. Act Annotated § 8.51 (3d ed. 1996); 2 Principles of Corporate Governance: Analysis and Recommendations §§ 7.20(a)(1), (b)(1)(D) (1994).

Dakota and Wisconsin).[108] To the contrary, a statute authorizing permissive indemnification does nothing more than "permit a corporation to make discretionary payments . . . should the corporation so desire."[109] Directors determining to award permissive indemnification must act in accordance with the same fiduciary obligations required of directors in the context of any other board action. Accordingly, "an act of indemnification, like any other exercise by a corporation of one or more of its powers, is subject to challenge . . . in the same way that other corporate actions may be reviewed."[110] A board that grants indemnification where indemnification is not permitted by law does so "at the risk of a derivative lawsuit."[111]

As explained in the preceding section of this Chapter, a corporation may by charter, bylaw or contract mandate the payment of indemnification that otherwise would be permissive but not mandatory.[112] One court—the Delaware Court of Chancery in *Mayer v. Executive Telecard, Ltd.*[113]—has held that Delaware's statutory provision permitting indemnification of expenses incurred in con-

---

108. Minn. Bus. Corp. Act § 302A.521(2); N.D. Bus. Corp. Act § 10-19.1-91(2); Wis. Bus. Corp. Law § 180.0851(1), (2); *see also Barry v. Barry*, 28 F.3d 848, 851 (8th Cir. 1994) (noting that "Delaware's statute provides that a corporation may choose both whether to indemnify and whether to provide advances," but "[u]nder the Minnesota statute, indemnification and advances are mandatory unless the corporation chooses to alter this scheme").

109. *McLean v. International Harvester Co.*, 817 F.2d 1214, 1223 (5th Cir. 1987); *see also Qantel Corp. v. Niemuller*, 771 F. Supp. 1372, 1374 (S.D.N.Y. 1991) (N.Y. Bus. Corp. Law §§ 722 and 723, which provide for permissive indemnification, "merely *permit* the indemnification of directors and officers. Section 724, in contrast, specifies the standards and procedures by which a court may *order* such indemnification").

110. *Petty v. Bank of N.M. Holding Co.*, 787 P.2d 443, 450 (N.M. 1990).

111. *Thorpe v. CERBCO, Inc.*, 1996 Del. Ch. LEXIS 110, at *9, 1996 WL 560173, at *3 (Del. Ch. Sept. 13, 1996), *aff'd*, 703 A.2d 645 (unpublished opinion, text available at 1997 Del. LEXIS 438 and 1997 WL 776169) (Del. Dec. 3, 1997).

112. *See* Chapter V, Section A 3 b.

113. 705 A.2d 220 (Del. Ch. 1997).

nection with an action, suit or proceeding does not permit indemnification of expenses incurred in connection with obtaining this indemnification. Accordingly, a bylaw provision requiring the payment of indemnification that otherwise would be permissive does not require the indemnification of expenses incurred in a proceeding seeking to enforce the bylaw provision. The court reasoned as follows:

> § 145(a) . . . encompasses the expenses incurred as a result of having been made a *party* to *any* action by reason of the claimant's status as an officer, director, employee or agent. . . .

> Does § 145(a) . . . include in addition to the expenses incurred in the underlying action, the expenses incurred in the indemnification action? . . . Concededly, the language of § 145(a) permitting indemnification to a party in *any* action could be read literally to encompass the indemnification action. Nonetheless, I am persuaded that § 145(a) addresses only the indemnification of fees incurred in the underlying action, not "fees for fees."

> Section 145(a) permits indemnification of the indemnification claimant's expenses where the claimant "acted in good faith and in a manner he reasonably believed to be in or not opposed to the best interests of the corporation." Were the Court to find that § 145(a) permits indemnification of "fees for fees," it would be required to apply the "good faith/reasonable belief" standard to the conduct underlying the bringing of the indemnification claim. Otherwise, that standard would be without any legal effect. But to do that would be a pointless exercise that would make the "good faith/reasonable belief" requirement meaningless surplusage. That is because it is difficult to imagine how a director could ever be said to have acted in bad faith in enforcing his contractual right to indemnification, or to construct a case where the director's successful prosecution of an indemnification action would be found to disserve the best interests of the corporation.

> The only sensible construction of § 145(a) is one that would avoid imposing a requirement that would be meaningless because it would invariably be satisfied. Therefore, the appropriate construction is to interpret § 145(a) as referring to the fees incurred in the underlying action, and to its requirement that the fee claimant must have acted in good faith and in the reasonable belief that it was in the corporation's best interests,

as applicable to the claimant's conduct that is the basis for the underlying action. To adopt [plaintiff's] proposed reading of 145(a) as including "fees for fees" would require an analytical process so awkward, that it leads to the conclusion that the General Assembly cannot have had the subject of "fees for fees" in mind when it enacted § 145(a).[114]

The court noted, however, that Section 145(f) of Delaware's statute, which "provides that the statutory indemnification provisions shall not be deemed exclusive of any other indemnification rights established by bylaw or other agreement," "[a]rguably would permit a bylaw that explicitly allows indemnification of 'fees for fees.'"[115] The court stated that it "need not reach that issue" because the bylaw underlying the litigation provided for mandatory indemnification *"to the fullest extent permissible under subsections (a) through (e) of Section 145 of the General Corporation Law of Delaware* or the indemnification provisions of any successor statute."[116] "Therefore, the bylaw as written limits indemnification to that which is explicitly permitted in those sections, which this Court has found do not include 'fees for fees.'"[117]

As discussed earlier in this Chapter, the Model Act distinguishes between officers who are directors and officers who are not directors.[118] Permissive indemnification may be granted both to officers who are directors and to officers who are not directors pursuant to the rules stated below.[119] Permissive indemnification of an officer who is not a director and who is made a party to a proceeding on the basis of "an act or omission solely as an officer" also may be authorized

> to such further extent as may be provided by the articles of incorporation, the bylaws, a resolution of the board of directors, or contract except for (A) liability in connection with a proceeding by or in the right of the corporation other than for

---

114. *Id.* at 224-25 (citations and footnotes omitted).
115. *Id.* at 225 n.7.
116. *Id.* (emphasis added).
117. *Id.*
118. *See* Chapter V, Section A 2.
119. *See* Chapter V, Sections A 4 a-c.

reasonable expenses incurred in connection with the proceeding or (B) liability arising out of conduct that constitutes (i) receipt by him of a financial benefit to which he is not entitled, (ii) an intentional infliction of harm on the corporation or the shareholders, or (iii) an intentional violation of criminal law.[120]

*a. Third Party Actions.* Most statutes authorize permissive indemnification in third party actions of judgments, fines, penalties, amounts paid in settlement and reasonable expenses, including attorneys' fees.[121] The termination of an action by judgment, order, settlement, conviction or plea of *nolo contendere* or its equivalent does not by itself create a presumption that the standard of conduct required for permissive indemnification has not been satisfied.[122]

The standard for permissive indemnification in most statutes (including Delaware's statute) permits indemnification in third party actions if the director or officer to be indemnified "acted in good faith and in a manner the person reasonably believed to be in or not opposed to the best interests of the corporation, and, with respect to any criminal action or proceeding, had no reasonable cause to believe the person's conduct was unlawful."[123] New York's statute is similar, except it permits indemnification where the person to be indemnified acted "for a purpose which he reasonably believed to be in . . . the best interests of the corporation" but adds that conduct undertaken on behalf of the corporation for any entity other than the

---

120. Model Bus. Corp. Act Annotated §§ 8.56(a)(2), (b).

121. *See* Cal. Gen. Corp. Law § 317(b); Del. Gen. Corp. Law § 145(a); N.Y. Bus. Corp. Law § 722(a); 2 Model Bus. Corp. Act Annotated §§ 8.50(4), (5), 8.51(a) (3d ed. 1996); *cf.* 2 Principles of Corporate Governance: Analysis and Recommendations § 7.20(a)(1) & Comment at 266 (1994) (providing for indemnification of "liabilities and reasonable expenses," with the term "liabilities" defined to include "amounts paid in settlement, judgments, fines and civil penalties, subject to the limitations of Section 7.20(b)," which are set forth in the text below); *Anglo Am. Ins. Group, P.L.C. v. CalFed Inc.*, 899 F. Supp. 1070, 1075-81 (S.D.N.Y. 1995) (discussing English law).

122. *See* Cal. Gen. Corp. Law § 317(b); Del. Gen. Corp. Law § 145(a); N.Y. Bus. Corp. Law § 722(b); Model Bus. Corp. Act Annotated § 8.51(c).

123. Del. Gen. Corp. Law § 145(a).

corporation (for example, another corporation, a partnership, a joint venture, a trust or an employee benefit plan) need only be "not opposed to . . . the best interests of the corporation."[124] California's statute also is similar to Delaware's statute but requires conduct "in the best interests of the corporation" rather than conduct "in or not opposed to the best interests of the corporation."[125]

The Model Business Corporation Act requires that the person to be indemnified "reasonably believed: (A) in the case of conduct in his official capacity, that his conduct was in the best interests of the corporation; and (B) in all other cases, that his conduct was at least not opposed to the best interests of the corporation."[126] The Model Act specifies that "[a] director's conduct with respect to an employee benefit plan for a purpose he reasonably believed to be in the interests of the participants in, and beneficiaries of, the plan" is conduct that satisfies the standard required for permissive indemnification.[127]

---

124. N.Y. Bus. Corp. Law § 722(a); *see also Kaufman v. CBS Inc.*, 135 Misc. 2d 64, 64-65, 514 N.Y.S.2d 620, 620-21 (N.Y. Civ. Ct. N.Y. Co. 1987) (corporate officer who "grabbed a piece of a subordinate . . . employee's clothing and made a lewd remark about her in public" acted in "an obvious deviation" from his duties and outside of the scope of his employment," and by no "stretch of the imagination can it be said that he acted in good faith for a purpose reasonably believed to be in the best interests of the corporation").

125. Cal. Gen. Corp. Law § 317(b); *see also In re Landmark Land Co.*, 76 F.3d 553, 562-63 (4th Cir.) (holding, in case construing California law, that the issue of good faith is for the court to decide, and that the court's role in reviewing a finding of good faith by the corporation is not limited to ensuring that the corporation utilized proper procedures in making its finding of good faith), *cert. dismissed*, 518 U.S. 1034 (1996); *Slottow v. American Casualty Co.*, 10 F.3d 1355, 1358 (9th Cir. 1993) (concluding, in case construing California law, that "[b]ecause Slottow's duties at FNT were performed at the bank's behest, it was perfectly appropriate for the bank to indemnify him for liability incurred in discharging those duties, even though he served a subsidiary corporation as well.").

126. Model Bus. Corp. Act Annotated §§ 8.51(a)(1)(ii)(A), (B).

127. *Id.* § 8.51(b).

The Model Act also authorizes permissive indemnification where the person to be indemnified has "engaged in conduct for which broader indemnification has been made permissible or obligatory under a provision of the articles of incorporation" authorized by Section 2.02(b)(5) of the Model Act.[128] As discussed in Chapter II,[129] Section 2.02(b)(5) permits the adoption of articles of incorporation provisions "permitting or making obligatory indemnification of a director for liability . . . to any person for any action taken, or any failure to take any action, as a director, except liability for (A) receipt of a financial benefit to which he is not entitled, (B) an intentional infliction of harm on the corporation or its shareholders, (C) a violation of Section 8.33 [of the Model Act, which imposes liability upon directors for unlawful distributions], or (D) an intentional violation of criminal law."[130] Indemnification is prohibited for conduct for which the person to be indemnified has been "adjudged liable on the basis that he received a financial benefit to which he was not entitled."[131] This is true "even if, for example, he acted in a manner not opposed to the best interests of the corporation."[132] According to the Model Act, a settlement is not to be construed as an adjudication of liability, even where the settlement creates an obligation to pay money.[133]

Section 7.20(a)(1) of Principles of Corporate Governance contains a somewhat different formulation. Section 7.20(a)(1) authorizes permissive indemnification in connection with an action where a director or officer is or may be required to appear in a judicial proceeding:

> (A) Because such person was acting in his or her capacity as a director or officer of the corporation, or acting in some capacity on behalf of a third party at the request of the corporation, if such person was acting in good faith or otherwise engaged in good faith conduct in such capacity, or

---

128. *Id.* § 8.51(a)(2).
129. *See* Chapter II, Section A 8.
130. 1 Model Bus. Corp. Act Annotated § 2.02(b)(5).
131. 2 Model Bus. Corp. Act Annotated § 8.51(d)(2).
132. *Id.* Official Comment at 8-339.
133. *Id.*

(B) Solely because of the fact that such person is or was a director or officer.[134]

The commentary accompanying Section 7.20 explains the differences between this formulation and most statutory formulations and the distinction between Sections 7.20(a)(1)(A) and (B) as follows:

> Most indemnification statutes expressly require as a condition to securing indemnification in either third party or derivative actions that a director or officer has acted in good faith and in a manner the director or officer reasonably believed to be in or not opposed to the best interests of the corporation. Section 7.20(a)(1)(A) contains only the requirement that the director or officer has acted in good faith when acting in the capacity of a director or officer of the corporation or in some capacity on behalf of a third party at the request of the corporation.
>
> *              *              *
>
> Section 7.20(a)(1)(B) extends indemnification to directors or officers who have been made parties to a proceeding or who are otherwise required to appear therein solely because of their status as directors or officers of the corporation, even though they were not in fact acting within the scope of their duties as directors or officers. On the other hand, § 7.20(a)(1)(B) would not apply to proceedings brought against directors or officers in which recovery is not dependent on their status as directors or officers. If a proceeding is based on the fact that a person was acting within the scope of the person's duties as a director or officer, § 7.20(a)(1)(A), rather than § 7.20(a)(1)(B), will apply.[135]

Indemnification is not permitted, according to Section 7.20(b)(1) of Principles of Corporate Governance,

> (A) if the conduct for which indemnification is sought directly involved a knowing and culpable violation of law or a significant pecuniary benefit was obtained to which the director or officer was not legally entitled;
>
> (B) to the extent that the indemnification would involve any amount paid in satisfaction of a fine, civil penalty, or similar

---

134. Principles of Corporate Governance: Analysis and Recommendations § 7.20(a)(1).

135. *Id.* § 7.20(a) Comment at 266-67 (citations to Illustrations in Principles of Corporate Governance omitted).

judgment as a result of violation of statutory law the policy of which clearly precludes indemnification;

(C) if the indemnification would involve any amount paid in settlement of the proceeding and the conduct directly involved a violation of statutory law, the policy of which clearly precludes indemnification . . . .[136]

Different rules govern permissive indemnification in the context of federal savings associations. Permissive indemnification may be granted to a director, officer or employee of a federal savings association where the person to be indemnified has acted "in good faith within the scope of his or her employment or authority as he or she could reasonably have perceived it under the circumstances and for a purpose he or she could reasonably have believed under the circumstances was in the best interests of the savings association."[137] This includes cases where there has been a final judgment against the director, officer or employee, or a settlement (a term defined to include "entry of a judgment by consent or confession or a plea of guilty or *nolo contendere*").[138] The Office of Thrift Supervision must be given at least 60 days' notice of a determination to grant indemnification, and indemnification may not be granted if the OTS objects to the indemnification.[139]

    *b. Actions by or in the Right of the Corporation.* As noted above, most statutes utilize similarly worded standards to define the bounds of permissive indemnification in both third party actions and actions by or in the right of the corporation.[140] In the context of actions by or in the right of the corporation, however, exceptions are added that are tailored to the specialized nature of actions by or in the right of the corporation.[141] No distinction is made between

---

136. *Id.* § 7.20(b)(1).

137. 12 C.F.R. § 545.121(c)(2).

138. *Id.*

139. *Id.*

140. *See* Chapter V, Section A 4 Introduction.

141. *See* Cal. Gen. Corp. Law §§ 317(b), (c); Del. Gen. Corp. Law §§ 145(a), (b); N.Y. Bus. Corp. Law §§ 722(a), (c); 2 Model Bus. Corp. Act Annotated §§ 8.51(a)-(d) (3d ed. 1996); 2 Principles of Corpo-

(continued...)

actions by the corporation and actions in the right of the corporation (i.e., shareholder derivative actions).[142]

One exception governing actions by or in the right of the corporation found in most statutes precludes indemnification of directors or officers adjudged liable to the corporation.[143] The Model Act provides that the adjudication of liability must be on the basis that the person to be indemnified "received a financial benefit to which he was not entitled" in order for indemnification to be precluded.[144] Under most statutes, a judicial determination that a duty to the corporation has been breached, without an adjudication of liability, is not enough to preclude indemnification.[145] Many juris-

---

141. (...continued)
rate Governance: Analysis and Recommendations §§ 7.20(a)(1), (b)(1)(D) (1994).

142. *See MCI Telecommunications Corp. v. Wanzer*, 1990 Del. Super. LEXIS 222, at *9-26, 1990 WL 91100, at *3-8 (Del. Super. June 19, 1990) (rejecting contention that the reference in Del. Gen. Corp. Law § 145(b) to actions "by or in the right of the corporation" provides for indemnification only in shareholder derivative actions brought in the right of the corporation, and does not apply in actions brought directly by the corporation).

143. *See* Cal. Gen. Corp. Law § 317(c)(1) ("adjudged to be liable to the corporation"); Del. Gen. Corp. Law § 145(b) ("adjudged to be liable to the corporation"); N.Y. Bus. Corp. Law § 722(c) ("adjudged to be liable to the corporation"); Principles of Corporate Governance § 7.20(b)(1)(D) ("adjudged liable to the corporation").

144. Model Bus. Corp. Act Annotated § 8.51(d)(2).

145. Until a 1986 amendment of the New York statute, New York required only a judicial determination that a duty had been breached—not an adjudication of liability. *See* Former N.Y. Bus. Corp. Law § 722(a). This former provision reflected the denials of indemnification on public policy grounds in *Diamond v. Diamond*, 307 N.Y. 263, 120 N.E.2d 819 (1954), and *People v. Uran Mining Corp.*, 13 A.D.2d 419, 216 N.Y.S.2d 985 (N.Y. App. Div. 4th Dep't 1961). In *Diamond*, one of two sole shareholders, both of whom "were equally guilty of flagrant and continued wrongdoing," sued the other. The court affirmed the trial court's dismissal of the complaint on the ground that the plaintiff was "estopped by knowledge, ratification and participation" from proceeding with a stockholder's action and reversed an award of legal expenses for the defendant (based
(continued...)

dictions, including California, Delaware and New York, provide for an exception to the exception precluding indemnification of directors or officers adjudged liable to the corporation. This exception to the exception permits the court in which an action by or in the right of a corporation is pending to determine, in view of all the circumstances of the particular action, that a director or officer "adjudged to be liable to the corporation" nevertheless is "fairly and reasonably entitled" to indemnification of expenses.[146] Similar provisions are included in the Model Business Corporation Act and Principles of Corporate Governance.[147] A settlement or consent decree does not

---

145. (...continued)
upon the defendant's "success" in the action) because "[s]o unconscionable a result . . . should not be countenanced if there be any escape therefrom." 307 N.Y. at 266-67, 120 N.E.2d at 820-21. *Uran Mining* held that a director and officer who "did nothing whatsoever to correct misstatements or misrepresentations" utilized by other corporate officials to sell stock fraudulently (but against whom a complaint was dismissed because "[t]he acts and representations attributed to . . . [him] . . . were honestly made in complete good faith") was not entitled to "a portion of the fund being preserved for defrauded stockholders." 13 A.D.2d at 423-24, 216 N.Y.S.2d at 989-90. No New York court has considered the continued viability of *Diamond* and *Uran Mining* following the 1986 amendment of New York's statute.

146. *See* Cal. Gen. Corp. Law § 317(c)(1); Del. Gen. Corp. Law § 145(b); N.Y. Bus. Corp. Law § 722(c); *see also Yiannatsis v. Stephanis*, 653 A.2d 275, 280-81 (Del. 1995) (finding that under the circumstances in this case a director was not "fairly and reasonably entitled to indemnity"); *Thorpe v. CERBCO, Inc.*, 1996 Del. Ch. LEXIS 110, at *8-9, 1996 WL 560173 at *3 (Del. Ch. Sept. 13, 1996) (noting statutory right under Delaware law to apply to the court for indemnification in an action by or on behalf of the corporation despite an adjudication of liability where "in view of all of the circumstances of the case" the person seeking indemnification "is fairly and reasonably entitled to indemnification"), *aff'd*, 703 A.2d 645 (unpublished opinion, text available at 1997 Del. LEXIS 438 and 1997 WL 776169) (Del. Dec. 3, 1997).

147. Model Bus. Corp. Act Annotated § 8.54(a)(3); Principles of Corporate Governance § 7.20(c)(2); *see also* Chapter V, Section A 6 (discussing court-ordered indemnification).

result in an adjudication against the party consenting to it and therefore does not preclude indemnification.[148]

Another exception historically found in most statutes precludes indemnification of judgments and amounts paid in settling or otherwise disposing of actions by or in the right of the corporation. Delaware follows the historical rule: Section 145(a) of the Delaware statute authorizes indemnification in third party actions for "expenses (including attorneys' fees), judgments, fines and amounts paid in settlement," and Section 145(b) authorizes indemnification in actions by or in the right of the corporation only for "expenses (including attorneys' fees)."[149] According to the drafters of the statute, the omission in Section 145(b) of the words "judgments, fines and amounts paid in settlement" was intentional.[150]

The basis for this rule is a belief that it would be circular if funds received by the corporation (the ultimate plaintiff on whose behalf an action by or in the right of a corporation is brought) were returned to the director who paid them. As explained by the Delaware Supreme Court in *Arnold v. Society for Savings Bancorp, Inc.*,[151] indemnification of judgments or amounts paid to settle a derivative action is "discredited" and "circular" because "the corporation would simply be paying itself for injury caused to it by the very directors being indemnified by the corporation. Stockholders would not benefit, and the result would be expensive since the corporation would be saddled with both plaintiff's and defendant's attorney fees."[152] In the words of the drafters of the Model Act:

> Permitting indemnification of settlements and judgments in derivative proceedings would give rise to a circularity in

---

148. *See Raychem Corp. v. Federal Ins. Co.*, 853 F. Supp. 1170, 1177 (N.D. Cal. 1994); *Cambridge Fund, Inc. v. Abella*, 501 F. Supp. 598, 617 (S.D.N.Y. 1980).

149. Del. Gen. Corp. Law §§ 145(a), (b).

150. *See* Arsht & Stapleton, *Delaware's New General Corporation Law: Substantive Changes*, 23 Bus. Law. 75, 79-80 (1967); Sebring, *Recent Legislative Changes in the Law of Indemnification of Directors, Officers and Others*, 23 Bus. Law. 95, 103 (1967).

151. 678 A.2d 533 (Del. 1996).

152. *Id.* at 540 n.18.

which the corporation receiving payment of damages by the
director in the settlement or judgment (less attorneys' fees)
would then immediately return the same amount to the director (including attorneys' fees) as indemnification. Thus, the
corporation would be in a poorer economic position than if
there had been no proceeding.[153]

Delaware continues to follow this historical rule, with a proposal to amend Section 145(b) of Delaware's statute to allow indemnification of judgments and amounts paid in settlement of derivative
actions having been rejected by the General Corporation Law Section of the Delaware Bar Association in 1986.[154] The trend in
legislative enactments during the mid-to-late 1980s and the 1990s,
however, has been to permit indemnification to one extent or
another in actions by or in the right of the corporation of amounts
paid to settle and/or judgments (but typically judgments only in
cases where there has been no adjudication of liability to the corporation). In some states only indemnification of amounts paid to settle
is permitted, and in other states indemnification of amounts paid to
settle or judgments is permitted. In some states court approval is
required, and in other states court approval is not required. New
York, for example, amended its indemnification statute in 1986 to
permit indemnification of amounts paid to settle actions by or in the
right of the corporation where court approval is obtained.[155] Until
1987, California's statute barred indemnification of amounts paid to
settle an action by or in the right of the corporation "*with or* without
court approval."[156] California amended its statute in 1987 to bar
indemnification of amounts paid to settle an action by or in the right
of the corporation "without court approval."[157] The obvious impli-

---

153. Model Bus. Corp. Act Annotated § 8.51 Official Comment at
8–337-38.

154. *See Arnold*, 678 A.2d at 540 n.18; 1 R. Franklin Balotti &
Jesse A. Finkelstein, *The Delaware Law of Corporations and Business
Organizations* § 4.29, at 4-108 (3d ed. 1998); Veasey & Finkelstein, *New
Delaware Statute: Allows Limits on Director Liability and Modernizes
Indemnification Protection*, 6 Bus. Law. Update 1, 2 (July/Aug. 1986).

155. N.Y. Bus. Corp. Law § 722(c).

156. Former Cal. Gen. Corp. Law § 317(c)(2) (emphasis added).

157. Cal. Gen. Corp. Law § 317(c)(2).

cation is that indemnification is available where court approval is obtained.[158]

The Model Business Corporation Act was amended in 1994 to permit indemnification of amounts paid to settle (but not judgments) in actions by or in the right of the corporation if court approval is obtained.[159] The drafters of the Model Act explained that in determining to limit indemnification in this way they were "influenced by the fact that Delaware prohibits indemnification for derivative suit settlements and no major problems are perceived to have been encountered there."[160] The drafters also explained that their determination to allow indemnification with court approval of amounts paid to settle derivative actions is intended to provide an "escape hatch" for the "unusual situation."[161] As stated in the Model Act's Official Comment:

> The discretionary authority of the court to order indemnification of a derivative proceeding settlement under section 8.54(a)(3) contrasts with the denial of similar authority under section 145(b) of the Delaware General Corporation Law. A director seeking court-ordered indemnification or expense advance under section 8.54(a)(3) must show that there are facts peculiar to his situation that make it fair and reasonable to both the corporation and to the director to override an intra-corporate declination or any otherwise applicable statutory prohibition against indemnification.[162]

Principles of Corporate Governance permits indemnification of amounts paid to settle (but not judgments) in actions by or in the right of the corporation where court approval is obtained and the

---

158. *See generally* Kuykendall, *A Neglected Policy Option: Indemnification of Directors for Amounts Paid to Settle Derivative Suits—Looking Past "Circularity" to Context and Reform*, 32 San Diego L. Rev. 1063 (1995).

159. Model Bus. Corp. Act Annotated §§ 8.51(d)(1), 8.54(a)(3).

160. Committee on Corporate Laws, *Changes in the Model Business Corporation Act—Amendments Pertaining to Indemnification and Advance for Expenses*, 49 Bus. Law. 741, 743 (1994).

161. *Id.* at 743-44.

162. Model Bus. Corp. Act Annotated § 8.54 Official Comment at 8-358.

court does not find "a substantial likelihood that the director or officer received a significant pecuniary benefit to which the director or officer was not legally entitled."[163]

In the federal savings association context, one court has held that indemnification is not permitted in an action against directors by a government agency—in that case, the Resolution Trust Corporation.[164] Any other result, the court stated, "would lead to the absurd result that the RTC could succeed in a suit against the perfidious directors, and then recover from itself."[165]

As discussed later in this Chapter, some state indemnification statutes include non-exclusivity provisions that permit corporations to provide indemnification under circumstances not specifically provided for by statute.[166] These statutes arguably permit indemnification in actions by or in the right of the corporation beyond the indemnification for such actions specifically authorized by statute. The Second Circuit in *Waltuch v. Conticommodity Services, Inc.*[167] held that the non-exclusivity provision in Section 145(f) of Delaware's statute does not permit indemnification "inconsistent with the substantive statutory provisions of § 145" and that a corporation "has no power to transgress the indemnification limits set out in the substantive provisions of § 145."[168]

A small number of statutes specifically address whether the non-exclusivity provisions in these statutes permit indemnification in actions by or in the right of the corporation under circumstances where indemnification is not specifically provided for by statute. Virginia's non-exclusivity provision, for example, states that indem-

---

163. Principles of Corporate Governance §§ 7.20(b)(1)(D)(i), (c)(2); *see also* Chapter V, Section A 6 b (discussing this provision in greater detail).

164. *Adams v. Resolution Trust Corp.*, 831 F. Supp. 1471, 1478 & n.15 (D. Minn. 1993), *aff'd sub nom. Adams v. Greenwood*, 10 F.3d 568 (8th Cir. 1993).

165. *Id.* at 1478.

166. *See* Chapter V, Section A 10.

167. 88 F.3d 87 (2d Cir. 1996).

168. *Id.* at 91, 94; *see also* Chapter V, Section A 10 (discussing *Waltuch* decision).

nification granted pursuant to that provision may include indemnification arising out of an action by or in the right of the corporation.[169] Pennsylvania's statute goes one step further and declares that indemnification arising out of an action by or in the right of the corporation is "consistent with the public policy of this Commonwealth."[170] The non-exclusivity provision in California's statute, by contrast, expressly prohibits indemnification for any breach of duty to the corporation and its shareholders in "circumstances in which indemnity is expressly prohibited" by specific provisions in the statute.[171]

The Model Business Corporation Act states that indemnification is allowed "only as permitted" in specific provisions of the Model Act.[172] Principles of Corporate Governance contains a non-exclusivity provision that is "[s]ubject to the limitations" that otherwise govern indemnification.[173]

*c. Authorization.* The decision to authorize permissive indemnification involves two questions. The first question is whether the person seeking permissive indemnification has met the applicable standard of conduct.[174] The second question, which only needs to be addressed if the person seeking indemnification has met the applicable standard conduct and a charter, bylaw or contract provision does not mandate indemnification whenever indemnification is permitted by law,[175] is whether granting permissive indemnification constitutes an appropriate exercise of business judgment based upon the circumstances of the particular case. "This decision includes a review of the reasonableness of the expenses, the financial ability of the corporation to make the payment, and the judgment whether limited financial resources should be devoted to this or some other

---

169. Va. Stock Corp. Act § 13.1-704(B).

170. Pa. Bus. Corp. Law § 1746(c); Pa. Corp. Law § 518(c).

171. Cal. Gen. Corp. Law §§ 317(g), 204(a)(11).

172. Model Bus. Corp. Act Annotated § 8.59.

173. Principles of Corporate Governance § 7.20(e).

174. *See* Chapter V, Sections A 4 a-b.

175. *See* Chapter V, Section A 3 b (discussing charter, bylaw and contract provisions that mandate indemnification whenever indemnification is permitted by law).

use by the corporation."[176] The determination that indemnification is permissible "is a separate decision from the actual decision to indemnify and must be made even if the by-laws provide for mandatory indemnification to the extent allowed" by law.[177]

The determinations required by the two questions identified above typically are made by the board of directors, independent counsel or shareholders.[178] Delaware also permits the determination to be made by a committee consisting of directors who are not parties to the proceeding, where the committee is designated by a majority vote of directors who are not parties to the proceeding.[179] There is no requirement that either the committee or the directors designating the committee constitute a quorum.[180] A charter or bylaw provision, however, may restrict the manner of authorization by, for example, requiring that the determination be made only by a specified percentage of the corporation's shareholders.[181]

A board determination authorizing indemnification must be made, according to the Delaware statute, by a majority vote of directors who are not parties to the proceeding (or, as noted above, a committee consisting of directors who are not parties to the proceeding), whether or not the decision-making directors constitute a quorum.[182] These rules, however, apply only with respect to "a person who is a director or officer at the time of such determina-

---

176. 2 Model Bus. Corp. Act Annotated § 8.55 Official Comment at 8-363 (3d ed. 1996).

177. *Havens v. Attar*, 22 Del. J. Corp. L. 1230, 1258 (Del. Ch. Jan. 30, 1997), *subsequent proceedings*, 1997 Del. Ch. LEXIS 164, 1997 WL 770670 (Del. Ch. Sept. 22, 1997) and 1997 Del. Ch. LEXIS 147, 1997 WL 695579 (Del. Ch. Nov. 5, 1997).

178. Cal. Gen. Corp. Law § 317(e); Del. Gen. Corp. Law § 145(d); N.Y. Bus. Corp. Law § 723(b); Model Bus. Corp. Act Annotated § 8.55(a).

179. Del. Gen. Corp. Law § 145(d)(2).

180. *Id.*

181. *See, e.g., Danaher Corp. v. Chicago Pneumatic Tool Co.*, 1986 Dist. LEXIS 24022, 1986 WL 7001, at *11 (S.D.N.Y. June 18, 1986).

182. Del. Gen. Corp. Law § 145(d).

tion."[183] There is no requirement in Delaware that indemnification of employees and agents who are not directors or officers be authorized by directors, independent counsel or shareholders.[184] Indemnification of former directors and officers and of present or former employees and agents may be authorized by "any person or persons having corporate authority to act on the matter, including those persons who are authorized by statute to determine whether to indemnify directors and officers."[185]

A board determination that indemnification is permissible in California and New York must be made by a majority vote of a quorum consisting of directors who are not parties to the proceeding.[186] The Model Business Corporation Act provides that a board having two or more disinterested directors may determine that indemnification is permissible by "a majority vote of all the disinterested directors (a majority of whom shall for such purpose constitute a quorum), or by a majority of the members of a committee of two or more disinterested directors appointed by such a vote."[187] As discussed earlier in this Chapter, the California statute addresses indemnification of directors, officers, employees and agents, and the New York statute and the Model Act address indemnification only of directors and officers.[188] No distinction is drawn in California, New York or the Model Act between granting indemnification to present directors and officers and granting indemnification to former directors and officers.[189]

The term "disinterested director" is defined for this purpose in the Model Act to mean a director who at the time of the vote "is not (i) a party to the proceeding, or (ii) an individual having a familial, financial, professional or employment relationship with the director

---

183. Del. Gen. Corp. Law § 145(d).

184. Ch. 120, L. '97 Synopsis of Section 145.

185. *Id.*

186. Cal. Gen. Corp. Law § 317(e)(1); N.Y. Bus. Corp. Law § 723(b)(1).

187. Model Bus. Corp. Act Annotated § 8.55(b)(1).

188. *See* Chapter V, Section A 2.

189. Cal. Gen. Corp. Law § 317(e); N.Y. Bus. Corp. Law § 723(b); Model Bus. Corp. Act Annotated §§ 8.55(b), (c).

whose indemnification . . . is the subject of the decision being made, which relationship would, in the circumstances, reasonably be expected to exert an influence on the director's judgment when voting on the decision being made."[190] "The fact that a director was nominated for the board by directors who are parties to the proceeding or are interested in the request or is a director of another corporation of which the director who is a party to the proceeding or is interested in the request is also a director should not, absent unusual circumstances, constitute a disqualifying relationship."[191]

A federal court in New York construing Delaware law has held that where the determination that indemnification is permissible is made by directors, the merits of the directors' determination is subject to *de novo* review—not business judgment review—in an action challenging the directors' determination.[192] The court, however, certified this question for an interlocutory appeal on the ground that "a broader view of the scope of the business judgment rule is possible."[193] The court's decision certifying this question for an interlocutory appeal explained that "[t]here is apparently no Delaware case law precluding a broader reading and it is true, as the defendants point out, that there is little point to indemnity decisions made by the corporation pursuant to Section 145(d) of the Delaware statute unless disgruntled claimants are precluded by the business judgment rule from obtaining *de novo* review of the corporation's decision."[194] The Second Circuit denied leave for an interlocutory appeal,[195] and in an appeal following the conclusion of district court proceedings this question was not raised.[196]

---

190. *Id.* § 8.50(3).

191. *Id.* Official Comment at 8–295-96.

192. *Waltuch v. Conticommodity Servs., Inc.*, 833 F. Supp. 302, 305-06 (S.D.N.Y. 1993), *aff'd and rev'd on other grounds*, 88 F.3d 87 (2d Cir. 1996).

193. *Waltuch v. Conticommodity Servs., Inc.*, 1994 U.S. Dist. LEXIS 1392, at *5, 1994 WL 48841, at *2 (S.D.N.Y. Feb. 10, 1994).

194. 1994 U.S. Dist. LEXIS 1392, at *5-6, 1994 WL 48841, at *2.

195. *Waltuch v. Conticommodity Servs., Inc.*, Nos. 94-8003, 94-8004 (2d Cir. Mar. 22, 1994).

196. *Waltuch v. Conticommodity Servs., Inc.*, 88 F.3d 87, 89 n.3 (2d Cir. 1996).

A federal court in California, also construing Delaware law, did apply business judgment rule principles in this context. According to this court, a decision to authorize indemnification by directors not named as defendants in the lawsuit for which indemnification was sought should be upheld unless the party contesting the authorization of indemnification demonstrated that the decision to grant indemnification had not been made in good faith.[197]

"Independent" or "special" legal counsel is permitted by most states (including California, Delaware and New York) to determine whether indemnification is permissive under the applicable standard of conduct where the board of directors does not have the requisite number of non-defendant directors or (in Delaware and New York, but not California) if a quorum of non-party or disinterested directors asks independent or special counsel to do so.[198] Under the Model Act, if a corporation has two or more disinterested directors, then special legal counsel may be selected by the board of directors in the same manner that the directors themselves could determine to authorize indemnification.[199] If a corporation has fewer than two disinterested directors, then the Model Act permits special legal counsel to be selected by the board of directors as a whole, with directors who do not qualify as disinterested directors allowed to participate in the selection.[200]

Most statutes do not define what constitutes "independent" or "special" legal counsel. The drafters of the Model Act explain the term (and the lack of a precise definition for the term in the Model Act) as follows:

> "Special legal counsel" normally should be counsel having no prior professional relationship with those seeking indemnification, should be retained for the specific occasion, and should not be or have been either inside counsel or regular outside counsel to the corporation. Special legal counsel should also

---

197. *Raychem Corp. v. Federal Ins. Co.*, 853 F. Supp. 1170, 1178, 1185, 1186 (N.D. Cal. 1994).

198. Cal. Gen. Corp. Law § 317(e)(2); Del. Gen. Corp. Law § 145(d); N.Y. Bus. Corp. Law § 723(b)(2)(A).

199. Model Bus. Corp. Act Annotated § 8.55(b)(2)(i).

200. *Id.* § 8.55(b)(2)(ii)

not have any familial, financial, or other relationship with any of those seeking indemnification that would, in the circumstances, reasonably be expected to exert an influence on counsel in making the determination. It is important that the process be sufficiently flexible to permit selection of counsel in light of the particular circumstances and so that unnecessary expense may be avoided. Hence the phrase "special legal counsel" is not defined in the statute.[201]

Statutes enacted in Minnesota, North Dakota, Ohio and Vermont do define the term "independent" or "special" legal counsel. The Minnesota and North Dakota statutes provide that "'[s]pecial legal counsel' means counsel who has not represented the corporation or a related organization, or a director, officer, member of a committee of the board, or employee whose indemnification is in issue."[202] Ohio, which uses the term "independent counsel", requires the passage of five years from the independent counsel's previous association with the corporation and the person to be indemnified.[203] The Vermont statute provides that "[s]pecial legal counsel means counsel that has never been an employee of the corporation and who has not, and whose firm has not, performed legal services for the corporation pertaining to the matter for which indemnification is sought for a period of at least two years before retention as special counsel."[204]

A shareholder determination that indemnification is permissible, under most statutes—including the Delaware and New York statutes—is based upon a vote of all shareholders.[205] California, however, does not allow the voting of shares owned by the person

---

201. *Id.* § 8.55 Official Comment at 8-364; *see also Schmidt v. Magnetic Head Corp.*, 97 A.D.2d 151, 161-62, 468 N.Y.S.2d 649, 656-57 (N.Y. App. Div. 2d Dep't 1983) (an "independent legal counsel" is "an attorney who is free from past connections with the corporation or the persons to be indemnified").

202. Minn. Bus. Corp. Act § 302A.521(1)(e); N.D. Bus. Corp. Act § 10-19.1- 91(1)(d).

203. Ohio Gen. Corp. Law § 1701.13(E)(4)(b).

204. Vt. Bus. Corp. Act § 8.50(8).

205. Del. Gen. Corp. Law § 145(d)(3); N.Y. Bus. Corp. Law § 723(b)(2)(B).

seeking indemnification.[206] The Model Act precludes voting of shares owned by or voted under the control of a director who at the time does not qualify as a disinterested director (as that term is defined in the Model Act definition discussed above).[207]

In California, the determination also may be made by the court in which the action or proceeding is pending.[208]

The California, Delaware and New York statutes defining how permissive indemnification may be authorized do not differentiate between the determination that indemnification is permissive and the determination that permissive indemnification should be authorized. The Model Act specifies that "[a]uthorization of indemnification shall be made in the same manner as the determination that indemnification is permissible, except that if there are fewer than two disinterested directors or if the determination is made by special legal counsel, authorization of indemnification shall be made by those entitled . . . to select special legal counsel."[209] The drafters of the Model Act explain that "[d]irectors who do not qualify as disinterested directors may . . . participate in the decision to 'authorize' indemnification on the basis of a favorable 'determination'" that indemnification is permissive "if necessary to permit action by the board of directors."[210] The drafters of the Model Act reason that "[t]his limited participation of interested directors in the authorization decision is justified by the principle of necessity."[211]

Principles of Corporate Governance provides that the determination that the corporation has authority to award permissive indemnification may be made by "disinterested directors, disinterested shareholders, or independent counsel" but contains no specific requirements of the type found in the California, Delaware and New York statutes and the Model Act.[212] Principles of Corporate Gov-

---

206. Cal. Gen. Corp. Law § 317(e)(3).

207. Model Bus. Corp. Act Annotated § 8.55(b)(3).

208. Cal. Gen. Corp. Law § 317(e)(4).

209. Model Bus. Corp. Act Annotated § 8.55(c).

210. *Id.* § 8.55 Official Comment at 8-364.

211. *Id.*

212. 2 Principles of Corporate Governance: Analysis and Recommendations § 7.20(b) (1994).

ernance does, however, include a provision granting a director or officer "standing to seek a *de novo* court determination" if one of the groups authorized to make the decision—disinterested directors, disinterested shareholders or independent counsel—concludes that the director or officer is ineligible for indemnification because the conduct at issue is conduct for which indemnification is not permitted.[213]

In the context of a federal savings association, a determination to indemnify must be made by "a majority of the disinterested directors of the savings association."[214] At least 60 days' notice of the determination must be given to the Office of Thrift Supervision, and indemnification is not permitted if the OTS objects to indemnification.[215]

## 5. Advancement

Most statutes authorize, but do not require, corporations to advance expenses incurred by directors in litigation or other proceedings. Permitting advancement is considered "sound public policy" because "a person who serves an entity in a representative capacity should not be required to finance his own defense. Moreover, adequate legal representation often requires substantial expenses during the proceeding and many individuals are willing to serve as directors only if they have the assurance that the corporation has the power to advance these expenses. In fact, many corporations contractually obligate themselves (by a provision in the articles or bylaws or otherwise) to advance expenses for directors."[216]

---

213. *Id.*
214. 12 C.F.R. § 545.121(c)(2).
215. *Id.*
216. 2 Model Bus. Corp. Act Annotated § 8.53 Official Comment at 8–348-49 (3d ed. 1996); *United States v. Weissman*, 1997 U.S. Dist. LEXIS 8540, at *52-53, 1997 WL 334966, at *17 (S.D.N.Y. June 16, 1997) (stating that "[a]dvancement of attorneys' fees may be 'necessary for the executive to wage a vigorous defense'" and that "[i]ndemnification agreements assist corporations in securing qualified officers by assuring that, if the officer is subject to a civil or criminal action, he will be given the means to contest it"), *subsequent proceedings*, 1997 U.S. Dist. LEXIS

(continued...)

There is, of course, an "importance difference" between indemnification and advancement of expenses: "Indemnification is retrospective and, therefore, enables the persons determining whether to indemnify to do so on the basis of known facts, including the outcome of the proceeding."[217] Advancement, by contrast, "is necessarily prospective and the individuals making the decision whether to advance expenses generally have fewer known facts on which to base their decision."[218]

*a. Permissive Advancement.* Absent a charter, bylaw or contract provision to the contrary, advancement of expenses, including attorneys fees, prior to the "final disposition" of a proceeding is permissive, not mandatory.[219] The term "final disposition" refers not

---

216. (...continued)
12975, as *28, 1997 WL 539774, at *9 (S.D.N.Y. Aug. 28, 1997) ("advancement provisions ensure that qualified officers will not be deterred from accepting employment by the possibility of civil or criminal litigation arising out of their employment" and "'enhance the reliability of litigation-outcomes involving directors and officers of corporations by assuring a level playing field'") (quoting *Ridder v. Cityfed Fin. Corp.*, 47 F.3d 85, 87 (3d Cir. 1995)); *1997 Watson Wyatt Worldwide D & O Liability Survey Report* 42, 47-48 (1997) (average defense cost for 914 claims made over the approximately nine year period beginning in 1988 and ending in mid-1997 was approximately $920,000; "[o]f these, three-fifths were closed as of the date the survey form was completed" and thus the $920,000 average claim calculation does "not reflect the possibility that the open claims may eventually close for greater amounts, on average. Thus the ultimate cost in today's dollars could be substantially higher.").

217. Model Bus. Corp. Act Annotated § 8.53 Official Comment at 8-348.

218. *Id.*

219. *See* Cal. Gen. Corp. Law § 317(f) ("[e]xpenses . . . may be advanced"); Del. Gen. Corp. Law § 145(e) ("[e]xpenses . . . may be paid . . . in advance"); N.Y. Bus. Corp. Law § 723(c) ("[e]xpenses . . . may be paid . . . in advance"); 2 Model Bus. Corp. Act Annotated § 8.53(a) (3d ed. 1996) ("[a] corporation may pay for or reimburse . . . expenses . . . in advance"); 2 Principles of Corporate Governance: Analysis and Recommendations § 7.20(a)(2) (1994) ("[a] corporation should have the power to pay expenses . . . in advance"); *Citadel Holding Corp. v. Roven*, 603 A.2d 818, 823 (Del. 1992) ("The General Corporation Law of
(continued...)

to a "final judgment" but to the point in time when "all avenues of appeal are exhausted."[220]

Section 145(e) of the Delaware statute is typical. Until 1986, this provision—like most indemnification statutes until that time—permitted advancement of expenses only *"as authorized by the board of directors in the specific case* upon receipt of an undertaking . . . to repay . . . *unless* it shall ultimately be determined" that the person to whom expenses are advanced "is entitled to be indemnified."[221] This provision was amended in 1986. The words "as authorized by the board of directors in the specific case" were deleted, and the words "unless it shall ultimately be determined . . ." were changed to *"if* it shall ultimately be determined" that the person to whom expenses are advanced "is *not* entitled to be indemnified."[222]

---

219. (...continued)
Delaware expressly allows a corporation to advance the costs of defending a suit to a director. 8 *Del. C.* § 145(e). The authority conferred is permissive. The corporation 'may' pay an officer or director's expense in advance."); *cf. Barry v. Barry*, 28 F.3d 848, 851 (8th Cir. 1994) (noting that "Delaware's statute provides that a corporation may choose both whether to indemnify and whether to provide advances" but "[u]nder the Minnesota statute, indemnification and advances are mandatory unless the corporation chooses to alter this scheme").

220. *Theriot v. Bourg*, 691 So. 2d 213, 227-28 (La. Ct. App.), *writ denied*, 696 So. 2d 1008 (La. 1997).

221. Former Del. Gen. Corp. Law § 145(e) (emphasis added).

222. Del. Gen. Corp. Law § 145(e) (emphasis added); *see also Stephanis v. Yiannatsis*, 20 Del. J. Corp. L. 440, 445-46 (Del. Ch. May 9, 1994) (requiring reimbursement of amounts advanced where corporate officer had been adjudged liable for usurping a corporate opportunity), *aff'd*, 653 A.2d 275, 280-81 (Del. 1995); *Waltuch v. Conticommodity Servs., Inc.*, 833 F. Supp. 302, 318 (S.D.N.Y. 1993) ("since it has been determined that Waltuch is entitled to be indemnified for the legal expenses actually and reasonably incurred by him in defending the *Michaelson* action, Conti cannot recoup the monies advanced for that action"; "since there has been no final decision as to Waltuch's entitlement to indemnity for his remaining legal expenses, the question of recoupment must await that determination"), *aff'd and rev'd on other grounds*, 88 F.3d 87 (2d Cir. 1996).

One court has held that an action by shareholders challenging advancement is premature until the action for which advancement is sought is completed.[223] The same court, in a later decision, rejected a claim that the damages assessed following an adjudication of liability on a breach of fiduciary duty claim should include reimbursement of the amounts advanced to the defendants in the case. The court stated that the determination whether to seek repayment of amounts advanced—even following an adjudication of liability in an action by or in the right of the corporation—"is, in the first instance, a question for the company's board."[224] Thus, the court concluded, the question whether amounts advanced should be returned to the corporation as part of the damages suffered by the corporation in a case where there has been an adjudication of liability to the corporation is "premature" until the corporation's board addresses the question.[225]

The court explained that "[a] board decision not to indemnify and to seek repayment of funds advanced" would render the question moot.[226] The court also explained that even if the board were to decide to authorize indemnification, judicial review of a shareholder challenge to that determination would require an inquiry concerning issues with respect to which there was not yet a record and that the court accordingly was "not now in a position responsibly to make."[227] These issues included the question whether the defendants who had been found liable to the corporation had acted "in good faith and in a manner he reasonably believed to be in or not opposed to the best interest of the corporation," the question

---

223. *Thorpe v. CERBCO, Inc.*, 611 A.2d 5, 9 n.4 (Del. Ch. 1991); *see also Thorpe v. CERBCO, Inc.*, 1996 Del. Ch. LEXIS 110, at *7, 1996 WL 560173, at *3 (Del. Ch. Sept. 13, 1996), *aff'd*, 703 A.2d 645 (unpublished opinion, text available at 1997 Del. LEXIS 438 and 1997 WL 776169) (Del. Dec. 3, 1997) ("I have declined to adjudicate this matter in this litigation previously, finding that before a final judgment is rendered the matter is premature").

224. *CERBCO*, 1996 Del. Ch. LEXIS 110, at *7, 1996 WL 560173, at *3.

225. *Id.*

226. *Id.*

227. 1996 Del. Ch. LEXIS 110, at *7-8, 1996 WL 560173, at *3.

whether "despite the adjudication of liability, but in view of all of the circumstances of the case, such person is fairly and reasonably entitled to indemnification," and the appropriate apportionment of expenses among issues.[228]

Unlike the case with permissive indemnification, there is no requirement in Delaware conditioning the advancement of expenses upon a finding that a particular standard of conduct has been met.[229] This rule reflects the fact that "the propriety of the person's conduct may not be ascertainable in the early stages of the action, suit, or proceeding."[230] Also unlike the case with permissive indemnification, there is no requirement that the decision to advance expenses be made by disinterested directors, independent counsel or shareholders.[231] This is because advances "only become permanent obligations of the company if indemnification is later determined to be proper. Rather than director self-dealing, the primary risk posed to the company by such advances is that the officials to whom the advances are paid will be unable to repay the company if they are not ultimately indemnified. The requirement that company officials undertake to repay the advances for litigation expenses is an attempt to minimize this risk."[232]

---

228. 1996 Del. Ch. LEXIS 110, at *8-9, 1996 WL 560173, at *3.

229. *Ridder v. CityFed Fin. Corp.*, 47 F.3d 85, 87 (3d Cir. 1995) ("[u]nder Delaware law, appellants' right to receive the costs of defense in advance does not depend upon the merits of the claims asserted against them, and is separate and distinct from any right of indemnification they may later be able to establish"); *Lipson v. Supercuts, Inc.*, No. 15074, Tr. op. at 98 (Del. Ch. Dec. 10, 1996) (person seeking advancement need not show that he has "met the applicable standard of conduct required for indemnification"); *Johnson v. Gene's Supermarket, Inc.*, 453 N.E.2d 83, 87-89 (Ill. App. Ct. 1983) (construing Illinois statute "copied directly from the Delaware statute").

230. Monteleone & Conca, *Directors and Officers Indemnification and Liability Insurance: An Overview of Legal and Practical Issues*, 51 Bus. Law. 573, 581 (1996).

231. *Security Am. Corp. v. Walsh, Case, Coale, Brown & Burke*, 1985 U.S. Dist. LEXIS 23482, at *9, 1985 WL 225, at *3 (N.D. Ill. Jan. 11, 1985) (construing Delaware law).

232. 1985 Del. LEXIS 23482, at *10-11, 1985 WL 225, at *4.

Delaware's statute thus "leaves to the business judgment of the board the task of determining whether the undertaking proffered in all of the circumstances is sufficient to protect the corporation's interest in repayment and whether, ultimately, advancement of expenses would on balance be likely to promote the corporation's interests."[233] "Simply put, a board's decision to accept an undertaking and to advance expenses is left to the business judgment of the board in the absence of a by-law specifically providing for mandatory advancement."[234]

The Delaware Court of Chancery in *Havens v. Attar*[235] preliminarily enjoined advancement in a case where plaintiffs alleged that directors breached their duty of care by awarding advancement without considering "the potential magnitude of expenses or damages or the ability of the defendant directors to repay any funds ultimately advanced" if the directors ultimately were found not to be entitled to indemnification.[236] The court stated that "in the absence of a by-law specifically providing for mandatory advancement," the decision to accept an undertaking and to advance expenses is a business judgment that must be made (and tested by the courts) in the same manner as any other business judgment.[237] Here, the court found, the directors "point to no evidence rebutting plaintiffs' claim" that the defendant directors "failed to obtain or consider any information pertaining to the decision" to advance, or "that would allow me to conclude . . . that plaintiffs would face even a remote chance of failing on the merits."[238] The court accordingly concluded that "plaintiffs have demonstrated that they will be likely to rebut the presumptions of the business judgment rule and that defen-

---

233. *Advanced Mining Sys., Inc. v. Fricke*, 623 A.2d 82, 84, (Del. Ch. 1992), *quoted in Havens v. Attar*, 22 Del. J. Corp. L. 1230, 1254 (Del. Ch. Jan. 30, 1997), 1997 Del. Ch. LEXIS 164, at *1-2, 1997 WL 770670, *1 (Del. Ch. Sept. 22, 1997), and 1997 Del. Ch. LEXIS 147, at *2, 1997 WL 695579, at *1 (Del. Ch. Nov. 5, 1997).

234. *Havens*, 22 Del. J. Corp. L. at 1256.

235. 22 Del. J. Corp. L. 1230 (Del. Ch. Jan. 30, 1997).

236. *Id.* at 1257.

237. *Id.* at 1256.

238. *Id.* at 1256-57.

dants, unable to provide evidence that they considered any details of
the decisions they were about to make, will be unable to show that
the decision was entirely fair."[239]

The court's decision did not reach a contention that the directors also breached their duty of loyalty by voting to advance
expenses to themselves in votes in which the majority of voting
directors were interested directors.[240] The court stated that "[i]t is
clear" that the rules in Section 145(d) of Delaware's statute that govern decisions to grant indemnification (requiring that the determination to grant indemnification be made by a majority vote of directors
who are not parties, a committee of directors who are not parties,
independent legal counsel in a written opinion, or shareholders")[241] do not apply to decisions to advance expenses.[242] The
court added, however, that "[i]t is also clear . . . that the statute
does not provide a shield to directors that would protect them from
plaintiffs' successful rebuttal of the presumption of the business
judgment rule."[243]

On a motion seeking to dissolve the preliminary injunction, the
court re-stated its prior conclusion that "the determination of whether to advance expenses, in the absence of a bylaw clearly mandating such an advancement, is left to the business judgment of the
board," and that in making this determination the board must consider the two factors noted above: (1) "whether the undertaking proffered . . . is sufficient to protect the corporation's interest in
repayment," and (2) "whether, ultimately, advancement of expenses
would on balance be likely to promote the corporation's interests."[244] Here, however, the court stated, "[t]he Board has presented no evidence . . . that this second factor was at all con-

---

239. *Id.* at 1257.
240. *Id.*
241. Del. Gen. Corp. Law § 145(d); *see also* Chapter V, Section
A 4 c (discussing this provision).
242. 22 Del. J. Corp. L. at 1257 n.58.
243. *Id.*
244. *Havens v. Attar*, 1997 Del. Ch. LEXIS 164, at *1-2, 1997
770670, at *1 (Del. Ch. Sept. 22, 1997).

sidered."[245]

On a motion seeking reconsideration of the court's ruling refusing to dissolve the injunction, the court rejected a contention that it had held the board's decision to advance expenses "to any greater scrutiny than that required by the business judgment rule, although I have determined preliminarily that plaintiffs will be able to rebut the presumption of the business judgment rule."[246] The court stated that the business judgment rule applies only where a decision has been made. Here, the court concluded, the defendants failed to show that they had made the decision they were required to make before authorizing advancement: "whether, ultimately, advancement of expenses would on balance be likely to promote the corporation's interests."[247] Indeed, the court added, the defendants had failed to show even "that they were aware of the need to consider the interests of the corporation."[248]

The court also addressed the duty of loyalty issue the court had not ruled upon in its initial decision and rejected a contention that its ruling imposed "a virtual per se rule precluding advancement absent a binding contract or bylaw provision whenever directors are the subject of a shareholder (or other) action."[249] The court acknowledged that interested directors do not have "absolute authority to advance expenses to themselves pursuant to a vote taken after their interest is established" but explained that advancement for interested directors may be approved by disinterested directors or shareholders or by an opinion by an independent counsel.[250] Here, however, the court explained, the directors faced "circumstances that are most uncommon": (1) the corporation's bylaws "do not provide for mandatory advancement," (2) "every member of the Board is apparently

---

245. *Id.* at 2.

246. *Havens v. Attar*, 1997 Del. Ch. LEXIS 147, at *6, 1997 WL 695579, at *2 (Del. Ch. Nov. 5, 1997).

247. 1997 Del. Ch. LEXIS 147, at *2, 5-6, 1997 WL 695579, at *1, 2.

248. 1997 Del. Ch. LEXIS 147, at *6, 1997 WL 695579, at *2.

249. 1997 Del. Ch. LEXIS 147, at *10, 1997 WL 695579, at *3.

250. 1997 Del. Ch. LEXIS 147, at *12 n.18, 1997 WL 695579, at *3 n.18.

interested in the decision to advance expenses," and (3) "it appears as if the plaintiffs (who represent one of the four directors and who own 28% of the outstanding shares) have negotiated a supermajority voting provision that allows them to block certain actions by the Board including the defendant directors' attempt to secure advancement by amending the Certificate or by obtaining the requisite shareholder approval."[251] The court added that interested directors also have the option of granting themselves advancement and showing that the decision to advance was fair to the corporation.[252]

*Service Corp. International v. H.M. Patterson & Son, Inc.*,[253] a decision construing Georgia law, reflects a different view. The court in *Service*, construing an advancement statute similar in all relevant respects to the Delaware advancement statute,[254] held that a determination to grant advancement in a case where all board members are named as defendants is not subject to the rules governing conflict of interest transactions. The court reasoned that the advancement procedure is intended "to expedite the advancement of expenses and minimize the cost involved in approving such payments."[255]

A determination by a corporate officer to refuse advancement offered on terms that are unsatisfactory to the officer does not waive the officer's entitlement to mandatory indemnification if he ultimately is "successful in defending himself."[256]

Like the post-1986 Delaware statute, the current New York statute (which, like Delaware's statute, was amended in 1986) does not condition advancement upon authorization "in the specific case" and does not require a determination that the standard for permissive indemnification has been met.[257] California's statute similarly does

---

251. 1997 Del. Ch. LEXIS 147, at *12, 1997 WL 695579, at *3.

252. 1997 Del. Ch. LEXIS 147, at *12, 1997 WL 695579, at *3.

253. 434 S.E.2d 455 (Ga. 1993).

254. Ga. Bus. Corp. Code § 14-2-853.

255. 434 S.E.2d at 458.

256. *McLean v. International Harvester Co.*, 817 F.2d 1214, 1223 (5th Cir. 1987).

257. N.Y. Bus. Corp. Law §§ 723(c), 725(a). Until 1986, the New
(continued...)

not condition advancement upon authorization "in the specific case."[258] One court construing California law has rejected a contention that directors and officers must "show that they will be entitled to indemnification *prior* to any advancement of defense costs."[259] "Such an interpretation," the court stated, "is not only illogical but clearly contrary to the legislative intent."[260] This court also upheld a determination made by a majority of interested directors to grant advancement. The court explained that "a contract between a corporation and one or more of its financially interested directors is lawful as long as the contract is 'just and reasonable to the corporation at the time it was authorized.'"[261] According to the court, "if an adequate bond were posted, the contract for advancement . . . would be 'just and reasonable' . . . because the corporation's financial interests would be protected."[262]

The Model Business Corporation Act also does not condition advancement upon authorization "in the specific case."[263] The Model Act does, however, require that the person receiving advancement furnish the corporation "a written affirmation of his good faith belief" that he has acted in accordance with the standard of conduct required for permissive indemnification.[264] A 1994 amendment to the Model Act deleted a previous Model Act requirement that a determination be made pursuant to the procedures applied in the permissive indemnification context that "the facts then known to those making the determination" do not preclude indemnification.[265] The drafters of the Model Act explained that this

---

257. (...continued)
York statute permitted advancement of expenses only as authorized in the same manner as permissive indemnification. *See* Former N.Y. Bus. Corp. Law § 724(c).

258. Cal. Gen. Corp. Law § 317(f).

259. *O'Brien v. Murphy*, No. A069128, slip op. at 11 (Cal. Ct. App. June 18, 1996).

260. *Id.*

261. *Id.* at 11-12 (quoting Cal. Gen. Corp. Law § 310(a)(3)).

262. *Id.* at 12.

263. Model Bus. Corp. Act Annotated § 8.53(a)(1).

264. *Id.*

265. Former Model Bus. Corp. Act § 8.53(a)(1).

change was made "because the facts known at the time of the determination usually consist of not very informative pleadings and very little other information."[266] "If the corporation believes a director is not entitled to an advance for expenses, notwithstanding delivery of the affirmation and undertaking," the drafters continued, "then the corporation may refuse to advance expenses and the director may seek relief" pursuant to the Model Act's provision providing for court-ordered indemnification and advancement where "fair and reasonable."[267]

The Model Act also provides that in the absence of a charter, bylaw or contract provision mandating advancement of expenses, advancement must be authorized by directors or shareholders.[268] If a board includes fewer than two disinterested directors—a circumstance under which board authorization of permissive indemnification is not an available option[269]—then advancement may be authorized by the affirmative vote of a majority of directors constituting a quorum unless the corporation's articles of incorporation or bylaws require the vote of more than a majority.[270] Directors who do not qualify as disinterested directors may participate in this vote.[271] The Model Act thus differs from Delaware law by allowing "[a]dvancement of funds by interested directors to themselves . . . even without a by-law or a contractual provision mandating advances."[272]

The drafters of the Model Act note that the decision to advance is governed by the standard of conduct provided for in

---

266. Committee on Corporate Laws, *Changes in the Model Business Corporation Act—Amendments Pertaining to Indemnification and Advance for Expenses*, 49 Bus. Law. 741, 745 (1994).

267. *Id.*; Model Bus. Corp. Act Annotated § 8.54(a)(3); *see also* Chapter V, Section A 6 b (discussing § 8.54(a)(3)).

268. *See* Model Bus. Corp. Act Annotated § 8.53(c).

269. *Id.* § 8.55(b); *see also* Chapter V, Section A 4 c (discussing § 8.55(b)).

270. Model Bus. Corp. Act Annotated §§ 8.53(c)(1)(ii), 8.24(c).

271. *Id.* § 8.53(c)(1)(ii).

272. *Havens v. Attar*, 1997 Del. Ch. LEXIS 147, at *12 n.18, 1997 WL 695579, at *3 n.18 (Del. Ch. Nov. 5, 1997).

Section 8.30 of the Model Act that ordinarily governs decisions by directors.[273] According to the drafters:

> Directors normally meet the standards of section 8.30 in approving an advance for expenses if they limit their consideration to the financial ability of the corporation to pay the amounts in question and do not have actual knowledge of facts sufficient to cause them to believe that [the affirmation by the person receiving advancement that he has acted in accordance with the standard of conduct required for permissive indemnification] was not made in good faith. The directors are not required by section 8.30 to make any inquiry into the merits of the proceeding or the good faith of the belief stated in that affirmation. Thus, in the great majority of cases, no special inquiry will be required. The directors acting on a decision to advance expenses may, but are not required to, consider any additional matters they deem appropriate and may condition the advance of expenses upon compliance with any additional requirements they desire to impose.[274]

The drafters of the Model Act also state that directors are free to reconsider a decision to advance expenses at any time during the course of the proceedings for which expenses are being advanced, including, for example, following a change in the corporation's financial ability to pay the amounts requested.[275] While the proceeding for which expenses are being advanced "will often terminate without a judicial or other determination of whether the director's conduct met that standard," the drafters state, the board "should make or cause to be made, an affirmative determination of entitlement to indemnification at the conclusion of the proceeding."[276]

Principles of Corporate Governance authorizes advancement of expenses but "does not require any specific procedure that must be

---

273. Model Bus. Corp. Act Annotated § 8.53 Official Comment at 8-349; *see also* Chapter I Introduction and Chapter II, Section A 3 (discussing Model Act § 8.30).

274. *Id.* § 8.53 Official Comment at 8–349-50.

275. *Id.* at 8-350.

276. *Id.* at 8-352.

followed by the corporation in authorizing payment of expenses."[277]

Standing in contrast to the Delaware, California, New York, Model Act and Principles of Corporate Governance approaches to advancement are the rules governing advancement in federal savings associations. In that context, a majority of the directors of the savings association may authorize advancement if they conclude that the person to whom advancement is being granted "ultimately may become entitled to indemnification."[278]

Like the advancement provisions in the post-1986 Delaware statute, the advancement provisions in the current California and New York statutes, in Principles of Corporate Governance, and in the federal savings association context, all require an undertaking to repay amounts that are advanced if the person receiving advancement ultimately is determined not to be entitled to indemnification.[279] The Model Act requires a "written undertaking to repay any funds advanced" if the person receiving advancement is "not entitled to mandatory indemnification" and "it is ultimately determined . . . that he has not met the relevant standard of conduct" required for permissive indemnification.[280]

The term "undertaking" is not defined in most statutes, but there is general agreement that it means nothing more than an unsecured promise to repay.[281] The Model Act's "undertaking" require-

---

277. Principles of Corporate Governance: Analysis and Recommendations § 7.20(a)(2) & Comment at 267.

278. 12 C.F.R. § 545.121(e).

279. Cal. Gen. Corp. Law § 317(f); N.Y. Bus. Corp. Law §§ 723(c), 725(a); Principles of Corporate Governance § 7.20(a)(2); 12 C.F.R. § 545.121(e).

280. Model Bus. Corp. Act Annotated § 8.53(a)(2).

281. *See Fidelity Federal Sav. & Loan Ass'n v. Felicetti*, 830 F. Supp. 262, 267-68 (E.D. Pa. 1993); *Megeath v. PLM Int'l, Inc.*, No. 930369, slip op. at 27 (Cal. Super. Ct. Mar. 18, 1992), *reprinted in* Corp. Officers & Directors Liability Litig. Rep. 11791 (Apr. 8, 1992); *In re Central Banking Sys., Inc.*, 1993 WL 183692, at *3-4 (Del Ch. May 12, 1993); Comment, *Law for Sale: A Study of the Delaware Corporation Law of 1967*, 117 U. Pa. L. Rev. 861, 883 (1969) (citing interview with Ernest L. Folk, one of the drafters of the Delaware statute).

ment specifies that the undertaking is an "unlimited general obligation" that "need not be secured and may be accepted without reference to the financial ability of the director to make repayment."[282] The rationale underlying this rule is that "wealthy directors should not be favored over directors whose financial resources are modest."[283] The Model Act also states that the undertaking "must be made by the director and not by a third party."[284]

Delaware's advancement statute applies only to "an officer or director" and not, as in the case of indemnification, to "a director, officer, employee or agent."[285] This difference is intentional. Until 1983, Delaware's advancement provision did not include the phrase "an officer or director."[286] The addition of the phrase "an officer or director" to the statute, according to the drafters, "eliminates the requirement that an employee or agent to whom expenses of defending a civil or criminal action, suit or proceeding are paid by the corporation in advance furnish an undertaking to the corporation to repay such advances."[287] Instead, the drafters stated, "the board of directors may determine the terms and conditions, if any, that should be imposed in connection with the making of such advances."[288] California's statute does not distinguish for the purpose of advancement between directors and officers on one hand, and employees and agents on the other hand.[289] As discussed above, the indemnification provisions in the New York statute and the Model Business Corporation Act and Principles of Corporate Governance do not address employees at all.[290]

---

282. Model Bus. Corp. Act Annotated § 8.53(b).

283. *Id.* § 8.53 Official Comment at 8-349.

284. *Id.*

285. *Compare* Del. Gen. Corp. Law § 145(e) (advancement) *with* Del. Gen. Corp. Law §§ 145(a)-(d) (indemnification).

286. Former Del. Gen. Corp. Law § 145(e).

287. 1983 Legislative History, *printed in* 2 R. Franklin Balotti & Jesse A. Finkelstein, *The Delaware Law of Corporations and Business Organizations* IV-40 (3d ed. 1998).

288. *Id.*

289. Cal. Gen. Corp. Law § 317(f).

290. *See* Chapter V, Section A 2.

Delaware's advancement statute also distinguishes between advancement to present directors and officers and advancement to former directors and officers. Advancement to former directors and officers, like advancement to present or former employees and agents, may be paid "upon such terms and conditions, if any, as the corporation deems appropriate."[291] Advancement to former directors and officers, like advancement to present or former employees and agents, may be authorized by "any person or persons having corporate authority to act on the matter, including those persons who are authorized by statute to determine whether to indemnify directors and officers."[292] The California and New York statutes, the Model Act and Principles of Corporate Governance do not distinguish between advancement to present directors and officers and advancement to former directors or officers.[293]

As discussed earlier in this Chapter, the Model Act distinguishes between officers who are directors and officers who are not directors.[294] Advancement may be granted both to officers who are directors and to officers who are not directors pursuant to the rules stated in the preceding paragraphs. Advancement to officers who are not directors and who are made a party to a proceeding on the basis of "an act or omission solely as an officer" also may be authorized in the same additional manner that permissive indemnification of officers who are not directors may be authorized—i.e.,

> to such further extent as may be provided by the articles of incorporation, the bylaws, a resolution of the board of directors, or contract except for (A) liability in connection with a proceeding by or in the right of the corporation other than for reasonable expenses incurred in connection with the proceeding or (B) liability arising out of conduct that constitutes (i) receipt by him of a financial benefit to which he is not entitled, (ii) an intentional infliction of harm on the corporation or

---

291. Del. Gen. Corp. Law § 145(e).

292. Ch. 120, L. '97 Synopsis of Section 145.

293. Cal. Gen. Corp. Law §§ 317(a), (f); N.Y. Bus. Corp. Law § 723(c); Model Bus. Corp. Act Annotated §§ 8.50(2), 8.53(a), 8.56(a); Principles of Corporate Governance § 7.20(a)(1).

294. *See* Chapter V, Section A 2.

the shareholders, or (iii) an intentional violation of criminal law.[295]

*b. Mandatory Advancement.* Charter, bylaw or contract provisions may mandate advancement that otherwise would be permissive by providing that advancement "shall"—as opposed to "may"—be granted to the full extent permitted by law. As stated in the Model Business Corporation Act, "[a] corporation may, by a provision in its articles of incorporation or bylaws or in a resolution adopted or a contract approved by its board of directors or shareholders, obligate itself in advance of the act or omission giving rise to a proceeding to . . . advance funds to pay for or reimburse expenses."[296] Examples of cases enforcing such provisions include *Heffernan v. Pacific Dunlop GNB Corp.,*[297] *Ridder v. CityFed Financial Corp.,*[298] *Mitrano v. Total Pharmaceutical Care, Inc.,*[299] *United States v. Weissman,*[300] *Megeath v. PLM International, Inc.,*[301] *Citadel Holding Corp. v. Roven,*[302] *Fujisawa Pharmaceutical Co. v.*

---

295. Model Bus. Corp. Act Annotated §§ 8.56(a)(2), (b); *see also* Chapter V, Section A 4 c (discussing authorization of permissive indemnification).

296. 2 Model Bus. Corp. Act Annotated § 8.58(a) (3d ed. 1996); *see also Fidelity Federal Sav. & Loan Ass'n v. Felicetti*, 830 F. Supp. 262, 268 (E.D. Pa. 1993) ("while the Pennsylvania law establishes a floor for when expenses may be advanced, there is nothing to preclude a corporation from contracting through its bylaws, articles of incorporation or by private contract to provide for mandatory advancements" to the full extent allowed by Pennsylvania law).

297. 965 F.2d 369, 371 n.2 (7th Cir. 1992), *subsequent proceedings*, 1993 U.S. Dist. LEXIS 5, at *20-24, 1993 WL 3553, at *6-8 (N.D. Ill. Jan. 5, 1993) (Delaware law).

298. 47 F.3d 85, 87-88 (3d Cir. 1995) (Delaware law).

299. 75 F.3d 72, 73-74 (1st Cir. 1996) (California law).

300. 1997 U.S. Dist. LEXIS 8540, at *1-8, 27-54, 1997 WL 334966, at *1-3, 9-18 (S.D.N.Y. June 16, 1997), *subsequent proceedings*, 1997 U.S. Dist. LEXIS 12975, at *23-37, 1997 WL 539774, at *8-12 (S.D.N.Y. Aug. 28, 1997) (New York law).

301. No. 930369 (Cal. Super. Ct. Mar. 18, 1992), *reprinted in* Corp. Officers & Directors Liability Litig. Rep. 11791 (Apr. 8, 1992) (Delaware law).

302. 603 A.2d 818, 820-24 (Del. 1992) (Delaware law).

*Kapoor,*[303] *In re Central Banking System, Inc.,*[304] *Lipson v. Supercuts, Inc.*[305] and *Neal v. Neumann Medical Center.*[306] The Delaware Superior Court in *Salaman v. National Media Corp.*[307] refused to set aside a jury verdict awarding a former director $387,887.70 in compensatory damages and $1,550,000 in punitive damages for failure to comply with a bylaw provision mandating indemnification and advancement.[308] Shortly after the *Salaman* decision, a new provision was added to the Delaware statute granting exclusive jurisdiction to the Court of Chancery "to hear and determine all

---

303. 655 A.2d 307 (unpublished opinion, text available at 1995 Del. LEXIS 25, at *5-10 and 1995 WL 24906, at *2-3) (Del. Jan. 17, 1995), *aff'g* 1994 Del. Super. LEXIS 233, at *3-13, 19-20, 1994 WL 233947, at *1-5, 7-8 (Del. Super. May 10, 1994) (Delaware law).

304. 1993 WL 183692, at *3 (Del. Ch. May 12, 1993) (Delaware law).

305. No. 15074, Tr. op. at 95-113 (Del. Ch. Dec. 10, 1996).

306. 667 A.2d 479, 480-83 (Pa. Commw. Ct. 1995), *appeal denied*, 694 A.2d 624 (Pa. 1996) (Pennsylvania law); *cf. VonFeldt v. Stifel Fin. Corp.*, 1997 Del. Ch. LEXIS 108, at *5-11, 1997 WL 525878, at *2-3 (Del. Ch. Aug. 18, 1997) (advancement not required where director had not signed an indemnification agreement; the court rejected a contention that the director was entitled to indemnification because before he became a director the corporation had entered into indemnification agreements with the persons then serving as directors, summarized the terms of these agreements and included an unsigned sample copy of the agreement in a public filing, and included a statement in the public filing that the corporation had entered into agreements modeled upon the sample agreement with each of its directors; the court held that the statement in the public filing, which was repeated in later years, did not establish the existence of a contract to indemnify the director seeking advancement according to the sample copy of the agreement); *Shearin v. E.F. Hutton Group, Inc.*, 652 A.2d 578, 593-95 (Del. Ch. 1994) (advancement not required pursuant to a bylaw mandating advancement to the full extent permitted by Delaware law where person seeking indemnification had commenced the litigation for which she sought advancement and the suit was not brought as part of her duties to the corporation and its shareholders; discussed in Chapter V, Section A 7).

307. 1994 Del. Super. LEXIS 353, 1994 WL 465534 (Del. Super. July 22, 1994).

308. *Id.*

actions for advancement of expenses or indemnification brought under this section or under any bylaw, agreement, vote of stockholders or disinterested directors, or otherwise."[309] The Court of Chancery lacks jurisdiction to award punitive damages.[310]

The adoption of a mandatory advancement provision requires a business judgment. "Mandatory advances, like indemnification, serve the salutary purpose of encouraging qualified persons to become or remain as directors . . . , by assuring them . . . that they may resist lawsuits that they consider meritless, free of the burden of financing (at least initially) their own legal defense."[311] As a result, "[m]any corporations have adopted such provisions, often with shareholder approval."[312]

Also in accordance with the purpose of mandatory advancement provisions, Section 141(k) of the Delaware General Corporation Law, which was enacted in 1994, grants the Delaware Court of Chancery the authority to "summarily determine a corporation's obligation to advance expenses."[313] The Court of Chancery has observed that "[b]y its very nature, a proceeding of this kind must be summary in character, because if advance indemnification is to have any utility or meaning, a claimant's entitlement to it must be decided relatively promptly."[314] The Court of Chancery also has observed that "a claim for advanced indemnification occupies a special status in our corporate law. It is . . . by legislative fiat, a summary proceeding. It requires expedition because of the very nature of the claim and the predicament of the claimant."[315] In

---

309. Del. Gen. Corp. Law § 145(k).
310. *See Pacific Ins. Co. v. Higgins*, 1993 Del. Ch. LEXIS 68, at *17, 1993 WL 133181, at *6 (Del. Ch. Apr. 15, 1993); *Beals v. Washington Int'l, Inc.*, 386 A.2d 1156, 1157-60 (Del. Ch. 1978).
311. *In re Central Banking Sys., Inc.*, 1993 WL 183692, at *3 (Del. Ch. May 12, 1993).
312. Model Bus. Corp. Act Annotated § 8.58 Official Comment at 8-380.
313. Del. Gen. Corp. Law § 145(k).
314. *Lipson v. Supercuts, Inc.*, 1996 Del. Ch. LEXIS 108, at *4, 1996 WL 560191, at *2 (Del. Ch. Sept. 10, 1996).
315. *Lipson v. Supercuts, Inc.*, No. 15074, Tr. op. at 95 (Del. Ch.
(continued...)

such a proceeding, as a result, "[t]he normally uncontroversial right to pre-summary judgment discovery may, in limited instances, have to give way."[316]

Summary proceedings are not required, however, where the action for which advancement is sought has ended with a dismissal in favor of the person seeking advancement. Under this circumstance, the court is not "confronted with the sort of situation demanding the rapid resolution contemplated by § 145(k)."[317] Rather, the person seeking advancement "faces no imminent trial, there is no pressing need to forego the defendant's customary right to take discovery in preparing a defense to plaintiff's motion for summary judgment, and any discovery-induced delay will not be significant."[318] Discovery will not be limited in such a case in the manner it may be limited in a summary proceeding under Section 145(k), especially where "the critical facts on which the plaintiff relied in claiming his right to advance indemnification" are disputed.[319]

---

315. (...continued)
Dec. 10, 1996).

316. *Supercuts*, 1996 Del. Ch. LEXIS 108, at *5, 1996 WL 560191, at *2, *quoted in Chamison v. Healthtrust, Inc.—The Hospital Co.*, 1997 Del. Ch. LEXIS 154, at *5 n.8, 1997 WL 695576, at *1 n.8 (Del. Ch. Oct. 29, 1997).

317. *Chamison*, 1997 Del. Ch. LEXIS 154, at *5-6, 1997 WL 695576, at *2.

318. 1997 Del. Ch. LEXIS 154, at *6, 1997 WL 695576, at *2.

319. 1997 Del. Ch. LEXIS 154, at *7, 1997 WL 695576, at *2. *Compare Supercuts*, 1996 Del. Ch. LEXIS 108, at *4-6, 1997 WL 560191, at *2 (discovery not permitted where the proceedings for which advancement was sought were on-going and the pending motion for partial summary judgment sought a ruling only upon the right to advancement (and not what amount of advancement was merited) that "rest[ed] upon a few undisputed material facts" and the discovery sought did not relate to those undisputed material facts) *with Chamison*, 1997 Del. Ch. LEXIS 154, at *6-8, 1997 WL 695576, at *2 (discovery permitted where the proceedings for which advancement was sought had concluded, the defendant "sharply contests the facts alleged by the plaintiff in support of his right to advance indemnification (the liability issue)" and the discovery sought

(continued...)

The cases noted above in which advancement has been ordered illustrate the problems that mandatory advancement provisions may create for corporations where former directors and officers (and employees, where they are protected by mandatory advancement provisions) seek advancement for the defense of claims asserted against them—sometimes by the corporation itself—for conduct that the corporation's board has determined to be contrary to the best interests of the corporation. *Citadel*, *Lipson* and *Salaman*, for instance, involved claims by corporations that corporate officers had engaged in illegal trading of the stock of the corporations involved in those cases.[320] *Neumann* involved a claim by a corporation that former corporate officers committed negligence, breach of fiduciary duty and tortious interference with contract.[321] *Megeath* involved a claim by a corporation against a former officer for breaches of fiduciary duty and defamation.[322] *CityFed* involved a similar type of claim—a suit by the Resolution Trust Corporation, as receiver for an insolvent financial institution, alleging that former corporate officials committed fraud and breaches of their fiduciary duties to the corporation.[323]

The drafters of the Model Act thus have observed that "a corporation should consider whether obligatory expense advance is intended for direct suits by the corporation as well as for derivative suits by shareholders in the right of the corporation," because if an obligatory advancement provision does not distinguish between these two types of actions "the corporation could be required to fund the defense of a defendant director even where the board of

---

319. (...continued)
"goes to the heart of the summary judgment motion—information that will show whether the plaintiff has satisfied all the preconditions for indemnification under the Merger Agreement and, thus, whether HealthTrust has an obligation to provide advance indemnification").

320. *Citadel*, 603 A.2d at 820-21; *Lipson*, No. 15074, Tr. op. at 96,105; *Salaman*, 1994 Del. Super. LEXIS 353, at *2-3, 1994 WL 465534, at *1.

321. 667 A.2d at 480 n.1.

322. *Megeath*, slip op. at 6, *reprinted in* Corp. Officers & Directors Liability Litig. Rep. at 11793.

323. *CityFed*, 47 F.3d at 86.

directors has already concluded that he has engaged in significant wrongdoing."[324] Other commentators similarly have stated that in determining whether to grant directors and officers the protection of mandatory advancement, a board "should give consideration to the fact that mandatory advancement provisions not qualified as discussed above may sometimes compel the corporation to advance expenses under circumstances in which it would have preferred not to do so."[325] The Delaware Court of Chancery in *Advanced Mining Systems, Inc. v. Fricke*[326] stated that "I assume" that a bylaw mandating advancement would be valid but observed that this type of bylaw "deprives the board of an opportunity to evaluate the important credit aspects of a decision with respect to advancing expenses."[327] According to the *Advanced Mining* court, "the better policy, more consistent with the provisions of Section 145(e) [of the Delaware statute], is to require any such by-law expressly to state its intention to mandate the advancement by the corporation of arguably indemnifiable expenses."[328]

The courts in cases where advancement is mandatory pursuant to charter, bylaw or contract provisions that do not include qualifications such as those suggested by the drafters of the Model Act and in *Advanced Mining* have rejected the contention that advancement should not be required where there is a likelihood that indemnification ultimately will not be allowed.

The leading case is the Delaware Supreme Court's decision in *Citadel Holding Corp. v. Roven*,[329] a case involving "but one chapter in a continuing fight for control" of Citadel Holding Corporation between two Citadel directors—James J. Cotter and Alfred

---

324. Model Bus. Corp. Act Annotated § 8.58 Official Comment at 8-381.

325. John F. Olson & Josiah O. Hatch III, *Director and Officer Liability: Indemnification and Insurance* § 5.03[3], at 5-20 (1997).

326. 623 A.2d 82 (Del. Ch. 1992).

327. *Id.* at 84; *see also Security Am. Corp. v. Walsh, Case, Coale, Brown & Burke*, 1985 U.S. Dist. LEXIS 23482, 1985 WL 225 (N.D. Ill. Jan. 11, 1985) (discussed in Chapter V, Section A 12).

328. 623 A.2d at 84.

329. 603 A.2d 818 (Del. 1992).

Roven.[330] Citadel contended that Roven violated Section 16(b) of
the Securities Exchange Act of 1934,[331] that Roven had no right
to indemnification in light of the nature of the corporation's allegations against Roven, and thus "he has no right to advances."[332]
The court explained that the advancement provision in that case
stated that "costs and expenses (including attorneys' fees) incurred
. . . shall be paid by the Corporation in advance of the final disposition of such matter."[333] This language, according to the court,
in no way renders the right to advances dependent upon the right to
indemnity."[334] Limitations upon rights to indemnification, the
court stated, are "irrelevant to the scope of" rights to advancement.[335] The Third Circuit in *Ridder v. CityFed Financial
Corp.*[336] likewise stated that "[u]nder Delaware law, appellants'
right to receive the costs of defense in advance . . . is separate and
distinct from any right of indemnification they may later be able to
establish."[337] Accordingly, as the Delaware Court of Chancery
stated in *Lipson v. Supercuts, Inc.*,[338] "it is no defense . . . in the
advancement context" that the person seeking advancement "has not
met the applicable standard of conduct required for indemnification."[339] As the Court of Chancery stated in *Delphi Easter Partners Limited Partnership v. Spectacular Partners, Inc.*,[340] "[t]he
public policy of Delaware is to allow advancement" even in cases
alleging breach of fiduciary duty, and "[t]his regularly has been
done under corporate indemnification provisions."[341]

---

330. *Id.* at 821.

331. 15 U.S.C. § 78p(b).

332. *Id.* at 822.

333. *Id.* at 820.

334. *Id.*

335. *Id.*

336. 47 F.3d 85 (3d Cir. 1995).

337. *Id.* at 87.

338. No. 15074 (Del. Ch. Dec. 10, 1996).

339. *Id.*, Tr. op. at 98.

340. 19 Del. J. Corp. L. 722 (Del. Ch. Aug. 6, 1993).

341. *Id.* at 735; *see also Christman v. Brauvin Realty Advisors, Inc.*, 1997 U.S. Dist. LEXIS 19563, at *5, 1997 WL 797685, at *1 (N.D.
(continued...)

The courts also have rejected arguments that mandatory advancement obligations need not be met in the absence of an undertaking that is secured in some manner. To the contrary, mandatory advancement obligations apply even where it is clear that the person seeking advancement lacks the financial means to repay the amounts advanced and thus that advancement for all practical purposes would constitute indemnification.

In *In re Central Banking Systems, Inc.*,[342] for example, the Delaware Court of Chancery held that public policy considerations do not justify requiring "the furnishing of security" or "a demonstration that the officer or director-recipient has the monetary resources to satisfy his or her undertaking" in cases where advancement is mandatory.[343] The court explained that the policy underlying mandatory advancement—"encouraging qualified persons to become or remain as directors of Delaware corporations, by assuring them, ex ante, that they may resist lawsuits that they consider meritless, free of the burden of financing (at least initially) their own legal defense"—"would be undermined if the corporation is permitted to rewrite its mandatory advance indemnification contract to condition such advances" upon a financial ability to repay the amounts advanced.[344] The court stated that absent a charter, bylaw or contract provision mandating advancement, corporations have the power to require as a condition of advancement that persons receiving advances provide security or demonstrate financial ability to repay the amounts advanced.[345] Here, however, the court continued, the corporation did not condition the receipt of

---

341. (...continued)
Ill. Dec. 3, 1997) ("indemnification of legal expenses is a separate issue from advancement of these expenses"); *Delphi Easter*, 19 Del. J. Corp. L. at 729 (indemnification and advancement are "separate" questions); J. Olson & J. Hatch § 5.03[2], at 5-16 n.29 (1997) ("indemnification and advancement of expenses are treated as distinct rights under Delaware law"); *id.* § 7.11, at 7-18 ("advancement of litigation expenses may be allowed even where indemnification would not be").
    342. 1993 WL 183692 (Del. Ch. May 12, 1993).
    343. *Id.* at *3.
    344. *Id.*
    345. *Id.* at *4.

advancement upon the providing of security or the demonstration of an ability to repay.[346] To the contrary, "[b]y approving the mandatory Indemnification By-law and the Indemnification Agreement, CBSI's shareholders contracted away the corporation's right to demand security in these circumstances. As a consequence, CBSI cannot be permitted to do retrospectively what it has precluded itself from doing *ex ante*."[347]

A California court construing Delaware law in *Megeath v. PLM International, Inc.*[348] reached the same conclusion. The court stated that "to suggest that PLMI has the right to insist that Megeath demonstrate that he has the monetary resources to satisfy any undertaking before he may receive advancement of fees is . . . chilling and effectively negates any real benefit to the mandatory advancement provisions."[349] In other words, "[w]hen mandatory advancement is contractually provided, . . . a board may not change the terms of 'mandatory' advancement by later conditioning that advancement upon a showing of financial responsibility."[350]

*Lipson v. Supercuts, Inc.*[351] involved a lawsuit by the former chairman and chief executive officer of Supercuts, Inc. against Supercuts and counterclaims by Supercuts. Pursuant to a certificate of incorporation provision mandating advancement where permitted by law, the court required advancement for expenses incurred in defending the counterclaim. The court stated that the expenses incurred in defending the counterclaims were the only subject of the advancement claim and that "[t]here is nothing" in the certificate provision supporting the argument that "if an indemnification claimant initiates a lawsuit against the corporation,

---

346. *Id.*

347. *Id.*

348. No. 930369 (Cal. Super. Ct. Mar. 18, 1992), *reprinted in* Corp. Officers & Directors Liability Litig. Rep. 11791 (Apr. 8, 1992).

349. *Id.*, slip op. at 27, *quoted in Central Banking*, 1993 WL 183692, at *4.

350. *Havens v. Attar*, 22 Del. J. Corp. L. 1230, 1256 (Del. Ch. Jan. 30, 1997); *see also* Chapter V, Section A 5 a (citing additional authorities stating that undertakings need not be secured).

351. No. 15074 (Del. Ch. Dec. 10, 1996).

that operates as a waiver of all claims for indemnification or advancement for expenses that relate to any counterclaims asserted by the corporation in response to the claim initiated by the indemnitee."[352]

*United States v. Weissman*[353] involved bylaw provisions requiring (1) indemnification "unless prohibited by applicable law" and unless "a judgment or other final adjudication" establishes that "acts were committed in bad faith or were the result of active and deliberate dishonesty,"[354] and (2) advancement of expenses "upon receipt of an undertaking by or on behalf of such director or officer to repay such amount if it shall ultimately be determined that he or she is not entitled to be indemnified by the Corporation."[355] Following the conviction by a jury of Jerry Weissman, the former chief financial officer of Empire Blue Cross/Blue Shield, a not-for-profit corporation, on two counts of perjury and one count of obstruction of justice, Empire stopped advancing the attorneys' fees and other expenses incurred by Weissman in defending the case. This included amounts incurred before the jury verdict that had not yet been paid, and amounts that might be incurred in future legal proceedings, including post-trial motions and appeals.[356] Weissman sought an order requiring Empire to continue advancing defense costs.[357]

The court held that Weissman's conviction for perjury "was necessarily premised on a finding by the jury that he engaged in 'deliberate dishonesty.'"[358] The court also held, however, that the

---

352. *Id.*, Tr. at 106-07.
353. 1997 U.S. Dist. LEXIS 8540, 1997 WL 334966 (S.D.N.Y. June 16, 1997), *subsequent proceedings*, 1997 U.S. Dist. LEXIS 12975, 1997 WL 539774 (S.D.N.Y. Aug. 28, 1997).
354. 1997 U.S. Dist. LEXIS 8540, at *2-3, 1997 WL 334966, at *1; 1997 U.S. Dist. LEXIS 12975, at *24, 1997 WL 539744, at *8.
355. 1997 U.S. Dist. LEXIS 8540, at *4, 1997 WL 334966, at *2; 1997 U.S. Dist. LEXIS 12975, at *24-25, 1997 WL 539744, at *8.
356. 1997 U.S. Dist. LEXIS 8540, at *1, 6, 1997 WL 334966, at *1, 2.
357. 1997 U.S. Dist. LEXIS 8540, at *1, 1997 WL 334966, at *1.
358. 1997 U.S. Dist. LEXIS 8540, at *27, 1997 WL 334966, at *9

jury's verdict against Weissman did not itself constitute a "judgment or other final adjudication" because a convicted defendant may seek a new trial or challenge the sufficiency of the evidence supporting a verdict.[359] The court stated that "either the By-Laws or the statute under which they were promulgated could have provided that indemnification would cease following a 'conviction'; instead, they employed the term 'judgment.' They could have made reference to an 'adjudication'; instead, they used the phrase 'final adjudication.'"[360]

The court thus concluded that the bylaw was ambiguous and, because courts construe ambiguities in an insurance contract against the drafter and against the insurer, the court construed the bylaw in Weissman's favor.[361] On this basis, the court held that "a jury's verdict alone is not 'final adjudication,' terminating Empire's obligation to advance funds for Weissman's defense. Finality is achieved only after the court has decided defendant's post-trial motions, at which point the defendant's guilt is established to the same degree as it will be on entry of judgment."[362] Thus, the court stated, "Empire's obligation to advance the costs of Weissman's legal fees will terminate upon an adverse resolution of his post-trial motions challenging the jury's verdict."[363]

Here, however, the court continued, the court lacked jurisdiction to hear post-trial motions challenging the jury's verdict because the court, with the consent of all parties, had approved a request for an extension of the deadline for post-trial motions in a manner not permitted by the Federal Rules of Criminal Procedure, which

---

359. 1997 U.S. Dist. LEXIS 8540, at *28-29, 1997 WL 334966, at *9.

360. 1997 U.S. Dist. LEXIS 8540, at *40, 1997 WL 334966, at *13.

361. 1997 U.S. Dist. LEXIS 8540, at *28-29, 40, 1997 WL 334966, at *9, 13.

362. 1997 U.S. Dist. LEXIS 8540, at *40, 1997 WL 334966, at *13.

363. 1997 U.S. Dist. LEXIS 8540, at *54, 1997 WL 334966, at *18.

are jurisdictional in nature.[364] The court stated that "[a] trial court's approval of an extension request cannot give rise to an exception to or enlargement of time limits proscribed in the rules of procedure" because "the burden of complying with time restrictions ultimately falls not on the court, but on the parties."[365] Nor, the court continued, "does the government's consent to the request alter this outcome."[366] (The court nevertheless noted that "[t]he result might well be different if the Court specifically advised a party as to the timeliness of a filing."[367]) As a result, the court concluded, a "final adjudication" of Weissman's guilt occurred on the date his time for filing a post-trial motion challenging the verdict expired, and Empire's obligation to advance funds for Weissman's defense ended at the same time.[368]

With respect to attorneys' fees and expenses incurred prior to the date upon which Weissman's time for filing a post-trial motion challenging the verdict expired, the court held that Empire was required to pay these amounts despite the fact that a final adjudication against Weissman now had been made. The court stated that it did not believe that this result "undermines the intent or violates the language of the By-Laws" because "Empire was required under those provisions . . . to advance him the costs of his defense until such time as a final adjudication established his guilt."[369] The court added that "Empire ceased to meet that obligation before any such adjudication was in place."[370] "If Empire were permitted to

364. 1997 U.S. Dist. LEXIS 8540, at *42-43, 1997 WL 334966, at *14; 1997 U.S. Dist. LEXIS 12975, at *4-6, 14-15, 1997 WL 539774, at *2, 5.

365. 1997 U.S. Dist. LEXIS 12975, at *21, 1997 WL 539774, at *7.

366. 1997 U.S. Dist. LEXIS 12975, at *19, 1997 WL 539774, at *6.

367. 1997 U.S. Dist. LEXIS 12975, at 21 n.5, 1997 WL 539774, at *7 n.5.

368. 1997 U.S. Dist. LEXIS 8540, at *45, 1997 WL 334966, at *14; 1997 U.S. Dist. LEXIS 12975, at *23, 1997 WL 539774, at *8.

369. 1997 U.S. Dist. LEXIS 8540, at *49-50, 1997 WL 334966, at *16; 1997 U.S. Dist. LEXIS 12975, at *26-27, 1997 WL 539774, at *9.

370. 1997 U.S. Dist. LEXIS 8540 at *50, 1997 WL 334966, at
(continued...)

benefit from this breach," the court stated, "its undertaking to 'advance' Weissman his legal fees would be rendered a nullity" because "Empire could simply wait out the results of an action before deciding whether to pay the requisite costs; if the ultimate judgment was adverse to the defendant, Empire could claim that it was no longer required to pay the expenses previously incurred."[371]

The court stated that advancement "does not simply insure a corporate officer that he will recover outlays for his defense if vindicated."[372] To the contrary, advancement also "protects his ability to mount such a defense in the first instance, by safeguarding his ability to meet his expenses at the time they arise, and to secure counsel on the basis of such an assurance."[373] Here, the court stated, "Empire promised to provide its officers in general, and Weissman in particular, with this benefit."[374] The court held that Empire could not "shirk its responsibilities thereunder, and then seek to evade them altogether as soon as the guilt of the indemnified officer has been established. Rather, it had to pay Weissman's expenses as they were incurred, and may seek reimbursement of this money from Weissman once a final adjudication establishes his guilt."[375]

Indeed, the court stated, "I cannot envision an alternative."[376] "If all this court may do, at the close of a criminal proceeding, is to leave the indemnifying employer and the employee defendant as the court found them, it would be in that employer's financial interest to use all means at its disposal so as to avoid

---

370. (...continued)
*16; 1997 U.S. Dist. LEXIS 12975, at *27, 1997 WL 539774, at *9.
    371. *Id.*
    372. 1997 U.S. Dist. LEXIS 8540, at *50, 1997 WL 334966, at *16.
    373. *Id.*
    374. *Id.*
    375. 1997 U.S. Dist. LEXIS 8540, at *50-51, 1997 WL 334966, at *16.
    376. 1997 U.S. Dist. LEXIS 12975, at *27, 1997 WL 539774, at *9.

advancing expenses during trial."[377] Any such rule, the court reasoned, would undermine the following purposes of the advancement agreement: to protect the ability of a corporate official to mount a defense "by safeguarding his ability to meet his expenses at the time they arise, and to secure counsel on the basis of such an assurance," to "ensure that qualified officers will not be deterred from accepting employment by the possibility of civil or criminal litigation arising out of their employment," to "assist corporations in securing qualified officers by assuring that, if the officer is subject to a civil or criminal action, he will be given a means to contest it," and to "enhance the reliability of litigation-outcomes involving directors and officers of corporations by assuring a level playing field."[378] These values would not be served, the court stated, "by an advancement regime which ties the degree of advancement to the timing of the proceedings' conclusion and the employer's alacrity in turning over funds. Such an uncertain framework for securing payment of attorneys' fees would hardly enhance the ability of a corporate officer to obtain counsel."[379]

The court recognized that "[a] corporation may, of course, determine that other concerns outweigh the goals promoted by advancing expenses, and that advancement should be made optional, or should not be permitted at all."[380] The court also acknowledged that "there is a public policy rationale for permitting a non-profit corporation to cease advancing funds for the defense of one of its officers when that officer has been found guilty of a crime involving deliberate dishonesty."[381] The court defined "the difficult question" to be "[a]t what point it becomes sufficiently clear that the officer has engaged in dishonest conduct, and thus is

---

377. *Id.*

378. 1997 U.S. Dist. LEXIS 8540, at *50, 52-53, 1997 WL 334966, at *16, 17; 1997 U.S. Dist. LEXIS 12975, at *28, 1997 WL 539774, at *9.

379. 1997 U.S. Dist. LEXIS 12975, at *29, 1997 WL 539774, at *10.

380. 1997 U.S. Dist. LEXIS 12975, at *29-30, 1997 WL 539774, at *10.

381. 1997 U.S. Dist. LEXIS 8540, at *52, 1997 WL 334966, at *17.

no longer entitled to the corporation's assistance in presenting his defense."[382]

The answer to this question, the court stated, was for "Empire, in its drafting of the By-Laws, and for the New York State legislature, in its promulgation of rules establishing the contours for indemnification of corporate officers, to decide."[383] Here, "Empire chose to provide such fees until there was a 'judgment or after final adjudication' against the officer. It did not, under New York law, need to use this formulation. Having done so, it must be bound by what is at least a reasonable construction thereof: 'a judgment or other final adjudication' occurs, in a criminal case, when the defendant has exhausted his post-trial motions, either because the court denied them, or because the time for making them has elapsed."[384]

The court acknowledged that Empire's filings "amply support its contention that it is unlikely to retrieve the vast sums of money it has advanced for Weissman's defense" but stated that "the issue before me does not concern Weissman's ultimate liability for these funds."[385] According to the court, the "risk in the event Weissman will be unable to repay these advances . . . should lie with Empire" because "[b]y agreeing to advance funds for an officer's defense, Empire took upon itself the risk that these funds might not be repaid in the event of an adverse verdict."[386]

Another decision, this one by the Mississippi Supreme Court in *Murphree v. Federal Insurance Co.*,[387] addressed Institute for Technology Development ("ITD") certificate of incorporation pro-

---

382. *Id.*

383. 1997 U.S. Dist. LEXIS 8540, at *53, 1997 WL 334966, at *17.

384. 1997 U.S. Dist. LEXIS 8540, at *53-54, 1997 WL 334966, at *17.

385. 1997 U.S. Dist. LEXIS 8540, at *52, 1997 WL 334966, at *17; 1997 U.S. Dist. LEXIS 12975, at *31, 1997 WL 539774, at *10.

386. 1997 U.S. Dist. LEXIS 12975, at *32, 1997 WL 539774, at *10.

387. 1997 Miss. LEXIS 145, 1997 WL 167002 (Miss. Apr. 10, 1997).

visions requiring advancement. Notwithstanding these provisions, ITD, with the advice of counsel, determined not to advance expenses to David L. Murphree, a former director and officer of ITD, who had been indicted for embezzlement.[388]   Murphree was acquitted, and ITD then indemnified Murphree for the full amount of attorney's fees and expenses he had incurred, $270,817.01.[389] Murphree filed a bad faith suit against ITD. Murphree acknowledged ITD's full payment of Murphree's defense costs after his acquittal but contending that "his need for an advancement had placed him in a position of hardship" and had forced him to cash in a retirement fund.[390]

The court held that ITD had breached a contractual obligation to advance the cost of Murphree's defense, that Murphree had raised material issues of fact concerning ITD's motivation for breaching that contractual obligation, and that these material issues of fact required the denial of a motion for summary judgment by ITD on Murphree's bad faith claim.

The court explained that Mississippi law barred indemnification where a director or officer is "adjudged liable on the basis that personal benefit was improperly received by him," but that here "Murphree was not convicted. Therefore he was not adjudged liable."[391] The court recognized that under Mississippi law advancement was permitted only upon "[a] determination . . . that the facts then known to those making the determination would not preclude indemnification" but stated that the mere indictment of Murphree was not enough to preclude indemnification under this standard.[392] The court held that the statute "clearly calls for the director to be adjudged liable before indemnification can be denied" and that an indictment is not the same as being "adjudged liable."[393] To the contrary, the court labeled ITD's suggestion that an indictment was the same as an adjudication of liability "a

---

388. 1997 Miss. LEXIS 145, at *2-3, 1997 WL 167002, at *1.

389. 1997 Miss. LEXIS 145, at *10-12, 1997 WL 167002, at *4.

390. 1997 Miss. LEXIS 145, at *12, 1997 WL 167002, at *4.

391. 1997 Miss. LEXIS 145, at *26, 1997 WL 167002, at *10.

392. 1997 Miss. LEXIS 145, at *27, 1997 WL 167002, at *10.

393. *Id.*

blatant disregard for clear legislative intent."[394]

The court also held that ITD's reliance upon advice of counsel was not "a valid excuse" because, the court stated—quoting a decision involving insurance—"[i]t is simply not enough for the carrier to say it relied on advice of counsel, however unfounded, and then expect that valid claims for coverage can be denied with impunity pursuant to such advice. . . . [W]here, through verbal sleight of hand, the advising attorney concocts an imagined loophole in a policy whose plain language extends coverage, such advice is heeded as the carrier's risk."[395] The court stated that "[t]he attorneys misread the plain language of the statute and wrongly instructed ITD as to whether it should grant Murphree's claim," and "ITD 'heeded' the attorneys' advice at its own risk."[396]

Against this backdrop of a breach of contract, the court defined the question before the court in Murphree's bad faith suit to be whether ITD's determination that indemnification was precluded by the facts known to ITD at the time of Murphree's request for advancement—was a determination made in good faith.[397] The court held that ITD's actions "give rise to questions that could cause reasonable minds to differ as to ITD's motives in denying indemnification."[398] The court stated that it was not holding that ITD's actions did in fact constitute bad faith; rather, it held only that a jury should "determine whether the acts of ITD constituted either bad faith in delay of payments or a breach of contract that was intentional, grossly negligent, or in reckless disregard for the rights of Murphree."[399] The court stated that if a jury found that

---

394. *Id.*

395. 1997 Miss. LEXIS 145, at *28, 1997 WL 167002, at *10 (quoting *Szumigala v. Nationwide Mut. Ins. Co.*, 853 F.2d 274, 282 (5th Cir. 1988)).

396. 1997 Miss. LEXIS 145, at *28-29, 1997 WL 167002, at *11.

397. 1997 Miss. LEXIS 145, at *29, 1997 WL 167002, at *11.

398. 1997 Miss. LEXIS 145, at *36, 1997 WL 167002, at *13.

399. *Id.*

ITD's acts "constituted either of these heightened torts, then punitive damages should be awarded."[400]

One court—*Fidelity Federal Savings & Loan Association v. Felicetti*[401]—held in an action governed by Pennsylvania law that expenses need not be advanced where a bylaw provision mandates advancement of expenses if the corporation's directors determine that granting advancement would conflict with the directors' fiduciary obligation to act as they believe will serve the best interests of the corporation.[402] Applying this principle, the court upheld a decision by the board in this case not to advance expenses in a lawsuit by the corporation against former officers of the corporation alleging breach of fiduciary duty, fraud, conspiracy and racketeering.[403] The Third Circuit in *Ridder v. CityFed Financial Corp.*[404] held that the reasoning of the court in *Felicetti* is contrary to Delaware law.[405] The Third Circuit in *CityFed* also described the reasoning of the court in *Felicetti* as "unpersuasive" because "[r]arely, if ever, could it be a breach of fiduciary duty on the part of corporate directors to comply with the requirements of the corporation's by-laws, as expressly authorized by statute."[406] An intermediate appellate court in Pennsylvania in *Neal v. Neumann Medical Center*[407] also declined to follow *Felicetti*. The court in *Neal* stated that "it would appear that Neumann's directors can only act in the corporation's best interests by implementing the mandatory advancement provision, since the bylaws which contain it were presumably adopted for Neumann's benefit."[408]

---

400. *Id.*

401. 830 F. Supp. 262 (E.D. Pa. 1993).

402. *Id.* at 270.

403. *Id.*

404. 47 F.3d 85 (3d Cir. 1995).

405. *Id.* at 87.

406. *Id.*

407. 667 A.2d 479 (Pa. Commw. Ct. 1995), *appeal denied*, 694 A.2d 624 (Pa. 1996).

408. *Id.* at 482.

The Third Circuit's decision in *Ridder v. CityFed Financial Corp.*[409] and the District of Columbia Circuit's decision in *CityFed Financial Corp. v. Office of Thrift Supervision*[410]—related cases involving the same corporation, CityFed Financial Corporation, and the same factual setting—offer conflicting views of mandatory advancement requirements in the context of failed financial institutions. The right to advancement, the Third Circuit stated in its *CityFed* decision, "does not depend upon the merits of the claims asserted" and is "separate and distinct from any right of indemnification" that later may be established.[411] The fact that a corporation is in receivership and there is a public interest in assuring equal treatment to all creditors rather than according priority to the directors, the Third Circuit held, has no bearing on the right to advancement where a charter or bylaw provision mandates advancement.[412] The court explained that

> [t]he statutory provisions authorizing the advancement of defense costs, conditioned upon an agreement to repay if a right of indemnification is not later established, plainly reflect a legislative determination to avoid deterring qualified persons from accepting responsible positions with financial institutions for fear of incurring liabilities greatly in excess of their means, and to enhance the reliability of litigation-outcomes involving directors and officers of corporations by assuring a level playing field.[413]

According to the Third Circuit, "[i]t is not the province of judges to second-guess these policy determinations."[414]

A short time later, the District of Columbia Circuit, in its *CityFed* decision, refused to overturn a temporary cease and desist order issued by the Office of Thrift Supervision (the "OTS") against CityFed that froze most of the corporation's assets.[415] The

---

409. 47 F.3d 85 (3d Cir. 1995).
410. 58 F.3d 738 (D.C. Cir. 1995).
411. 47 F.3d at 87.
412. *Id.*
413. *Id.*
414. *Id.*
415. 58 F.3d at 740.

District of Columbia Circuit rejected CityFed's claim that the cease and desist order precluded compliance by CityFed with the Third Circuit's ruling requiring advancement. The District of Columbia Circuit reasoned that the OTS had "agreed to allow CityFed to advance fees to the directors as long as they agree to return the fees should CityFed lose" in the administrative proceeding brought by the OTS against the directors (an offer the directors had refused), that the district court had concluded that the directors had sufficient personal assets to meet their legal needs, and that even if the directors did not have sufficient assets the OTS's order allowed CityFed to request "hardship" relief from the OTS.[416] The District of Columbia Circuit added that "[e]ven if OTS refuses to grant City-Fed's 'hardship' request, the company could still petition the Third Circuit for a stay" of the advancement obligations ordered by the Third Circuit pending resolution of OTS's cease and desist proceedings.[417] "At the very least," the District of Columbia Circuit stated, that a request "would present the Third Circuit with a new issue because its decision—which was based on a state law interpretation of the indemnity agreement that CityFed has with those officers—did not consider the OTS order."[418]

The Official Comment to the Model Business Corporation Act states that any charter, bylaw or contract provision mandating advancement must comply with the Model Act's provisions requiring that the person receiving advancement provide the corporation with (1) an affirmation stating that he has a good faith belief that he has acted in a manner entitling him to indemnification, and (2) a written undertaking to repay the advancement if it ultimately is determined that he is not entitled to mandatory indemnification and did not act in accordance with the standard of conduct required for permissive indemnification.[419]

*c. Does "Indemnification" Include "Advancement"?* Charter, bylaw or contract provisions sometimes permit or mandate indemni-

---

416. *Id.* at 746-47.
417. *Id.* at 747.
418. *Id.*
419. Model Bus. Corp. Act Annotated § 8.53 Official Comment at 8-349.

fication but are silent with respect to advancement. Different views have been expressed with respect to whether a permissive or mandatory indemnification provision that is silent concerning advancement permits and/or mandates advancement.

The Delaware Court of Chancery in *Advanced Mining Systems, Inc. v. Fricke*[420] held that charter and bylaw provisions stating that the corporation "shall indemnify" its directors and officers "to the extent permitted" by Delaware law mandated indemnification but not advancement.[421] The court explained that "indemnification rights and rights to advancement of possibly indemnifiable expenses" are two "quite distinct types of legal rights," and that Delaware law at the time the bylaw was adopted provided that advancement decisions were to be made "in the specific case" and that it therefore was "extremely unlikely that a reasonable person could then have assumed that a right to advancement in every case had been created by the . . . by-law."[422] The court added that even after the deletion of the words "in the specific case" from Delaware's statute in 1986,[423] a narrow reading of the corporation's indemnification provision to exclude advancement is "more in keeping with the tenor" of Delaware's advancement statute "than the alternative interpretation would be."[424] Thus, the court concluded, "the better policy . . . is to require any such by-law expressly to state its intention to mandate advancement by the corporation of arguably indemnifiable expenses."[425] The Delaware Court of Chancery in *Havens v. Attar*[426] reaffirmed this principle: "advancement is not mandatory absent a clearly worded by-law or contract making it mandatory."[427]

---

420. 623 A.2d 82 (Del. Ch. 1992).

421. *Id*. at 84.

422. *Id*. at 84-85.

423. *See* Chapter V, Section 4 a.

424. 623 A.2d at 85.

425. *Id*. at 84.

426. 1997 Del. Ch. LEXIS 147, 1997 WL 695579 (Del. Ch. Nov. 5, 1997).

427. 1997 Del. Ch. LEXIS 147, at *12, 1997 WL 695579, at *3.

A federal court in Illinois construing Delaware law also followed *Advanced Mining* in *Heffernan v. Pacific Dunlop GNB Corp.*[428] The court in *Heffernan* held that a bylaw provision requiring that the corporation "shall indemnify . . . to the extent permitted by the law of Delaware" "did not wrest from a corporation the ability, granted by § 145(e), to refuse advance payments."[429] Another federal court in Illinois construing Delaware law followed *Advanced Mining* in *Christman v. Brauvin Realty Advisors, Inc.*[430] in the context of a limited partnership.[431]

A federal court in Kansas construing Delaware law before *Advanced Mining* reached the opposite conclusion in *TBG Inc. v. Bendis.*[432] The bylaw in the *TBG* case provided that advancement "may"—not shall—"be paid . . . as authorized . . . in the specific case."[433] The *TBG* court concluded that this bylaw was "impliedly amended" by the 1986 revision of Delaware's statute to delete the board authorization requirement for advancement because another bylaw stated that the corporation "shall indemnify . . . to the full extent permitted" by Delaware law "as the same now exists or may hereafter be amended."[434] The *TBG* court pointed to the specific references to the advancement of litigation expenses in Delaware's indemnification statute and the charter and bylaw provisions in the *TBG* case and concluded that the purpose of the statute and charter and bylaw provisions "was to include such pre-adjudication expenses within the scope of permissible 'indemnifica-

---

428. 1992 U.S. Dist. LEXIS 14809, 1992 WL 275573 (N.D. Ill. Oct. 1, 1992).

429. 1992 U.S. Dist. LEXIS 14809, at *6, 8, 1992 WL 275573, at *2, 3.

430. 1997 U.S. Dist. LEXIS 19563, 1997 WL 797685 (N.D. Ill. Dec. 3, 1997).

431. 1997 U.S. Dist. LEXIS 19563, at *4-12, 1997 WL 797685, at *1-3.

432. 1991 U.S. Dist. LEXIS 2765, 1991 WL 34199 (D. Kan. Feb. 19, 1991).

433. 1991 U.S. Dist. LEXIS 2765, at *6, 1991 WL 34199, at *2.

434. 1991 U.S. Dist. LEXIS 2765, at *8, 15, 1991 WL 34199, at *3, 4.

tion.'"[435] The *Advanced Mining* court explicitly rejected the *TBG* court's reasoning.[436]

The Model Business Corporation Act rejects the holding in *Advanced Mining*.[437] According to the Model Act, "[a]ny . . . provision that obligates the corporation to provide indemnification to the fullest extent permitted by law shall be deemed to obligate the corporation to advance funds to pay for or reimburse expenses."[438]

The court in *Fidelity Federal Savings & Loan Ass'n v. Felicetti*[439] held that the term "indemnification" in the federal regulations governing indemnification in federal savings associations includes advancement of expenses.[440] The court pointed to the purpose of indemnification—"to encourage capable individuals to serve as corporate directors, secure in the knowledge that expenses incurred by them in upholding their honesty and integrity as directors will be borne by the corporation they serve," and to ensure that "people who serve as corporate directors and officers, absent fraud or breach of fiduciary duties," can "perform their jobs free of the fear that they will be saddled with personal liability for corpo-

---

435. 1991 U.S. Dist. LEXIS 2765, at *16-17, 1991 WL 34199, at *5.

436. *See Advanced Mining*, 623 A.2d at 85 ("I cannot accept the reasoning of that case as correct"); *see also Pacific Dunlop*, 1992 U.S. Dist. LEXIS 14809, at *10 n.6, 1992 WL 275573, at *5 n.6 (noting the *Advanced Mining* court's rejection of the *TBG* court's analysis).

437. 2 Model Bus. Corp. Act Annotated § 8.58 Official Comment at 8-381 (3d ed. 1996).

438. *Id.* § 8.58(a); *see also Barry v. Barry*, 28 F.3d 848, 851 (8th Cir. 1994) (noting different result under Minnesota law than under Delaware law, because Minnesota statute, Minn. Bus. Corp. Act §§ 302A.521(2) & (3), provides that "indemnification and advances are mandatory unless the corporation chooses to alter this scheme"; thus "[b]y providing for indemnification to the extent of the Minnesota statute, the parties included the mandatory payment of advances as provided for in subdivision 3 of Section 302A.521").

439. 830 F. Supp. 262 (E.D. Pa. 1993).

440. *Id.* at 266.

rate acts."[441] The court stated that "[w]hether the monetary obligations commensurate with being personally liable for corporate acts arise up-front by way of defensive and litigation costs and expenses or whether they appear at the back-end by way of damages seems to be of no moment."[442] The court also pointed to the text of the federal savings association regulation, which the court stated "itself indicates that the term indemnification is meant to be inclusive of advancement of expenses."[443] The court reasoned as follows:

> First, the entire regulation is entitled "Indemnification of directors, officers and employees." Rather than promulgating two separate regulations, one relating to reimbursement of expenses after final judgment and the other relating to payment of expenses as they accrue, the drafters chose to include the advance payment provision as a subsection of the general regulation entitled "indemnification." Furthermore, in the "Exclusiveness of provisions" section, the drafters explicitly made compliance with the regulation's insurance provisions mandatory regardless of existing bylaws. In contrast, there is no such restriction regarding advancements. If the drafters intended to restrict the applicability of existing bylaws by prohibiting advancements except under the terms of the regulations, it could have specifically so stated in the "exclusiveness of provisions" section as it did in regard to insurance.

Accordingly, the court held, a regulation stating that a savings association that "has a bylaw in effect relating to indemnification of its personnel shall be governed solely by that bylaw" should be construed to include advancement as well as indemnification.[444]

## 6. Court-Ordered Indemnification and Advancement

The judiciary's power to order indemnification and advancement may arise in two contexts: (1) court-ordered indemnification or advancement enforcing an entitlement by statute, charter, bylaw

---

441. *Id.*
442. *Id.*
443. *Id.*
444. *Id.* at 265-66 (quoting 12 C.F.R. § 545.121(f)).

or contract provision to mandatory indemnification or advancement, and (2) court-ordered indemnification or advancement under circumstances where the person seeking indemnification or advancement (i) is not eligible for mandatory or permissive indemnification or (ii) is eligible for permissive indemnification or advancement but the corporation has determined not to grant indemnification or advancement.

*a. Enforcement of Mandatory Indemnification or Advancement Obligations.* A director or officer may seek to enforce an entitlement to mandatory indemnification or advancement, whether mandatory pursuant to statute[445] or mandatory pursuant to a charter, bylaw or contract provision.[446] The Delaware Court of Chancery has stated that a proceeding seeking to enforce a mandatory advancement obligation "must be summary in character, because if advance indemnification is to have any utility or meaning, a claimant's entitlement to it must be decided relatively promptly."[447] The cases discussed and cited earlier in this Chapter in which courts have ordered mandatory indemnification and advancement all involve examples of court-ordered indemnification and advancement.[448]

A charter, bylaw or contract provision may require payment of expenses and attorneys' fees in enforcing a right to mandatory indemnification or advancement.[449] In the absence of a charter, bylaw or contract provision requiring payment of expenses and attorneys' fees incurred in enforcing a right to mandatory indem-

---

445. *See* Chapter V, Sections A 3 a and 5 a.

446. *See* Chapter V, Sections A 3 b and 5 b.

447. *Lipson v. Supercuts, Inc.*, 1996 Del. Ch. LEXIS 108, at *4, 1996 WL 560191, at *2 (Del. Ch. Sept. 10, 1996).

448. *See* Chapter V, Sections A 3 and 5.

449. *See Mayer v. Executive Telecard, Ltd.*, 705 A.2d 220, 224-25 (Del. Ch. 1997) (finding that bylaw did not cover fees incurred in obtaining mandatory indemnification); *Lipson v. Supercuts, Inc.*, No. 15074, Tr. at 113 (Del. Ch. Dec. 10, 1996) (enforcing charter provision providing for indemnification of amounts incurred in obtaining mandatory advancement); *Jackson v. Turnbull*, No. 13042, Tr. at 11 (Del. Ch. May 22, 1995) (stating that a bylaw can require indemnification of fees incurred in obtaining mandatory indemnification).

nification or advancement, the courts are divided with respect to whether expenses and attorneys' fees incurred in enforcing such a right are recoverable.

Construing Delaware law, the courts in *Davis & Cox v. Summa Corp.*,[450] *Mayer v. Executive Telecard, Ltd.*,[451] *Jackson v. Turnbull*[452] and *MCI Telecommunications Corp. v. Wanzer*[453] have held that expenses and attorneys fees incurred in enforcing an entitlement to mandatory indemnification are not recoverable.[454] These cases have relied upon the general rule that attorneys' fees are not recoverable in the absence of an express statutory or contract provision requiring payment of attorneys' fees and the absence of any such requirement in Delaware's statute, which provides that "[t]o the extent that a director . . . has been successful on the merits or otherwise in defense of any action, suit or proceeding . . . he shall be indemnified against expenses . . . incurred by him in connection therewith."[455] This provision does not, according to these courts, include expenses incurred in pursuit of indemnification.[456] As stated in *Mayer*, "the term 'in connection therewith' refers to the expenses in the original underlying action in which the claimant prevailed on the merits" and "not this Delaware indemnification proceeding."[457] "To read 'in connection therewith' more broadly," the court continued, "would stretch those words beyond

---

450. 751 F.2d 1507 (9th Cir. 1985).

451. 705 A.2d 220 (Del. Ch. 1997) and No. 95 Civ. 5403 (BSJ), slip op. at 2 (S.D.N.Y. Apr. 30, 1997), *reprinted in* Corporate Officers and Directors Liability Litig. Rptr. 21230 (May 14, 1997).

452. No. 13042 (Del. Ch. May 22, 1995).

453. 1990 Del. Super. LEXIS 222, 1990 WL 91100 (Del. Super. June 19, 1990).

454. *Summa*, 751 F.2d at 1527-28, *Mayer*, 705 A.2d at 221-23; *Jackson*, Tr. at 10-11; *MCI*, 1990 Del. Super. LEXIS 222, at *42-43, 1990 WL 91100, at *14.

455. Del. Gen. Corp. Law § 145(c).

456. *Summa*, 751 F.2d at 1527-28 & n.11; *Mayer*, 705 A.2d at 221; *Jackson*, Tr. at 10-11; *MCI*, 1990 Del. Super. LEXIS 222, at *42, 1990 WL 91100, at *14.

457. *Mayer*, 705 A.2d at 221.

their common and ordinary meaning.[458] According to this view, Delaware's General Assembly could have "included language explicitly granting a successful claimant 'fees for fees,' as other states have done in their statutes" but "chose not to include such language."[459] According to these courts, "the absence of explicit language evidences an intent *not* to provide for such fees."[460]

The *Mayer* court acknowledged as "not without force" the contention by the director seeking recovery of his expenses in *Mayer* that "requiring a director to pay the costs of vindicating his indemnification right would undercut" the legislative purpose underlying Delaware's indemnification statute—to encourage competent people to serve Delaware corporations—"by encouraging corporations routinely to oppose indemnification claims, and thereby coerce indemnification claimants to settle for less than their full entitlement."[461] This argument, the *Mayer* court stated, "suggests that the sounder public policy may be for such fees to be made recoverable as a matter of right."[462] The *Jackson* court similarly stated that "I have no reason to doubt that a fairness argument could be made for why repayment of the cost of seeking indemnification should be allowed" because "[t]he argument that the director would not be made whole if that director were required to pay the costs of this motion out of his own pocket has a certain appeal."[463]

These decisions also recognize, however, that this argument "has appeal in every case in which a plaintiff has to go to court in order to vindicate a right, even a clear right, whether it's a right

---

458. *Id.*

459. *Id.* at 222 (citing Ga. Bus. Corp. Code § 14-2-854(b), Ind. Bus. Corp. Law § 23-1-37-11 and Model Bus. Corp. Act Annotated § 8.54(b) (3d ed. 1996)).

460. *Id.; see also Summa*, 751 F.2d at 1528 n.11 ("the absence of such a provision in the Delaware code suggests that Delaware law does not require corporations to reimburse those who incur expenses in establishing their right to indemnification").

461. *Mayer*, 705 A.2d at 222.

462. *Id.*

463. *Jackson*, Tr. at 10.

that arises under the corporation law, contract law or tort law."[464]
This equitable principle, these courts continue, "has not been
viewed, at least by our courts, as sufficient to create a right to be
reimbursed, to be made whole, in that sense."[465] In other words,
"it is not the province of this Court to create an entitlement that the
General Assembly has elected not to provide."[466] In short:

> [T]he purpose of § 145 . . . is to encourage capable persons
> to serve as officers, directors, employees or agents of
> Delaware corporations, by assuring that their reasonable legal
> expenses will be paid. To that end, the Delaware General
> Assembly apparently has concluded that allowing mandatory
> indemnification for fees incurred in the underlying action is
> an adequate incentive, without also requiring indemnification
> of the fees incurred by the claimant in the indemnification
> action itself. Reasonable persons may disagree with that judg-
> ment, i.e., whether "fees for fees" is also needed as a further
> incentive for capable persons to serve as directors or officers
> of Delaware corporations. In the end, however, that judg-
> ment is legislative, not judicial.[467]

Two courts—*Professional Insurance Co. v. Barry*[468] and
*Sierra Rutile Ltd. v. Katz*[469]—have required indemnification in the
context of a New York statute providing that "[w]here indemnification is sought by judicial action, the court may allow a person such
reasonable expenses . . . during the pendency of the litigation as
are necessary in connection with his defense therein."[470] The
court in *Barry* explained that "where the corporation has failed to
provide indemnification . . . it makes no difference whether the
allowance is sought within the ambit" of the case being defended or

---

464. *Id.*

465. *Id.* at 10-11.

466. *Mayer*, 705 A.2d at 222.

467. *Id.* at 223.

468. 60 Misc. 2d 424, 303 N.Y.S.2d 556 (N.Y. Sup. Ct. N.Y.
Co.), *aff'd mem.*, 32 A.D.2d 898, 302 N.Y.S.2d 722 (N.Y. App. Div.
1st Dep't 1969).

469. 1997 U.S. Dist. LEXIS 11018, 1997 WL 431119 (S.D.N.Y.
July 31, 1997).

470. N.Y. Bus. Corp. Law § 724(c).

in a separate action seeking indemnification "as long as such allowance is necessary in connection with the defense in the litigation."[471] The court stated that this interpretation of New York's statute was supported by the need "to encourage directors and officers to assume stewardship responsibilities."[472] The same relief was granted by the court in *Sierra Rutile*.[473] The *Barry* decision has been rejected in Delaware.[474]

California's indemnification statute expressly provides for the recovery of "any expenses of establishing a right to indemnification,"[475] a point that the court in *Summa* noted in support of its conclusion that there is no such right under Delaware law.[476] Another court construing California law—*Mitrano v. Total Pharmaceutical Care, Inc.*[477]—required indemnification of amounts incurred seeking mandatory indemnification based upon a bylaw provision requiring indemnification of "expenses relating to obtaining a determination" that a director or officer was "entitled to indemnification."[478]

The Model Business Corporation Act "requires, rather than just permits" court-ordered indemnification of expenses incurred "in connection with obtaining court-ordered indemnification or advance for expenses."[479] Principles of Corporate Governance: Analysis and Recommendations also provides that directors are

---

471. 60 Misc. 2d at 428, 303 N.Y.S.2d at 561.

472. *Id.* at 428, 303 N.Y.S.2d at 561.

473. 1997 U.S. Dist. LEXIS 11018, at *7-8, 11, 1997 WL 431119, at *1, 2.

474. *See MCI*, 1990 Del. Super. LEXIS 222, at *42-43, 1990 WL 91100, at *14.

475. Cal. Gen. Corp. Law § 317(a).

476. *Summa*, 751 F.2d at 1527-28 & n.11.

477. 75 F.3d 72 (1st Cir. 1996).

478. *Id.* at 74.

479. 2 Model Bus. Corp. Act Annotated § 8.54(b) (3d ed. 1996); Committee on Corporate Laws, *Changes in the Model Business Corporation Act—Amendments Pertaining to Indemnification and Advance for Expenses*, 49 Bus. Law. 741, 745 (1994).

entitled to indemnification of expenses and attorneys' fees incurred in obtaining mandatory indemnification.[480]

*b. Court-Ordered Indemnification Where Indemnification Is Not Otherwise Required.* Within limitations stated in particular statutes, courts also may order indemnification notwithstanding a director's ineligibility for mandatory or permissive indemnification under the standards governing mandatory and permissive indemnification.[481]

The Model Business Corporation Act, for example, authorizes court-ordered indemnification in cases where "the court determines, in view of all the relevant circumstances, that it is fair and reasonable" to do so.[482] The Model Act states specifically that indemnification may be "fair and reasonable" even if the standard the corporation is required to apply in determining whether to grant indemnification prohibits indemnification.[483] The only limitation placed upon the court's power by the Model Act is that indemnification is limited to reasonable expenses where the director has been "adjudged liable" in a proceeding by or in the right of the corporation or in a proceeding where there has been an adjudication of liability based upon the receipt by the director of a financial benefit to which he was not entitled.[484] Indemnification with court approval of amounts paid to settle actions by or in the right of the corporation thus is permitted.[485]

The Official Comment to the Model Act states that the question whether indemnification is "fair and reasonable" is committed to the court's discretion.[486] "Among the factors a court may want

---

480. 2 Principles of Corporate Governance: Analysis and Recommendations § 7.20(c)(1) (1994).

481. Cal. Gen. Corp. Law §§ 317(c)(1), (e)(4); Del. Gen. Corp. Law § 145(b); N.Y. Bus. Corp. Law §§ 722(c), 724(a); 2 Model Bus. Corp. Act Annotated § 8.54(a) (3d ed. 1996); 2 Principles of Corporate Governance: Analysis and Recommendations § 7.20(c)(2) (1994).

482. Model Bus. Corp. Act Annotated § 8.54(a)(3).

483. *Id.*

484. *Id.* §§ 8.54(a)(3), 8.51(d)(1),(2).

485. *Id.* § 8.54 Official Comment at 8-358.

486. *Id.*

to consider" in exercising this discretion "are the gravity of the offense, the financial impact upon the corporation, the occurrence of a change in control or, in the case of an advance for expenses, the inability of the director to finance his defense."[487] The Official Comment states that in determining whether indemnification is fair and reasonable "a court should give appropriate deference to an informed decision of a board or committee made in good faith and based upon full information."[488]

With the exception relating to actions by or in the right of the corporation discussed in the next paragraph, the California and New York statutes permit court awards of non-mandatory indemnification only in cases where the corporation itself could grant indemnification.[489]

Delaware's statute explicitly authorizes court-ordered non-mandatory indemnification only for expenses and only in actions by or in the right of the corporation in which the person seeking indemnification has been "adjudged to be liable to the corporation" and in which the court determines that "in view of all the circumstances of the case, such person is fairly and reasonably entitled to indemnity."[490] Provisions permitting court-ordered indemnification of expenses in actions by or in the right of the corporation similar to the Delaware provision are included in the California and New York statutes.[491] New York's statute, unlike the Delaware and California statutes, permits the court to order indemnification under these circumstances not just for expenses, but also for amounts paid in settlement.[492] As noted in the preceding paragraph, however, the California and New York statutes also contain separate court-ordered indemnification provisions that limit awards

---

487. *Id.*

488. *Id.* at 8-357.

489. Cal. Gen. Corp. Law § 317(e)(4); N.Y. Bus. Corp. Law § 724(a).

490. Del. Gen. Corp. Law § 145(b).

491. Cal. Gen. Corp. Law § 317(c)(1); N.Y. Bus. Corp. Law § 722(c).

492. N.Y. Bus. Corp. Law § 722(c).

of non-mandatory indemnification to cases in which the corporation itself could grant indemnification.[493]

Principles of Corporate Governance authorizes court-ordered non-mandatory indemnification where the court determines that it is "fair and reasonable, in whole or in part, in view of all the circumstances."[494] This indemnification, however, is limited to

- "amounts paid in settlement of an action brought by or in the right of the corporation (other than amounts paid in settlement of an action in which the court determines that there was a substantial likelihood that the director or officer received a significant pecuniary benefit to which the director or officer was not legally entitled),"[495]

- expenses in any proceeding where there is a judgment or settlement of an action brought by or in the right of the corporation,[496] and

- expenses in any proceeding where "the conduct for which indemnification is sought directly involved a knowing and culpable violation of law or a significant pecuniary benefit was obtained to which the director or officer was not legally entitled."[497]

*c. Court-Ordered Advancement Where Advancement Is Not Otherwise Required.* The Delaware and California statutes do not authorize court-ordered advancement of expenses during the pendency of a litigation where advancement is not mandatory pursuant to a charter, bylaw or contract provision. Section 724(c) of the New York statute authorizes the court in which an action is pending to grant advancement if the court finds that the person to be indemnified "has by his pleadings or during the course of the litigation raised genuine issues of fact or law."[498]

---

493. Cal. Gen. Corp. Law § 317(c)(4); N.Y. Bus. Corp. Law § 724(a).

494. Principles of Corporate Governance § 7.20(c)(2).

495. *Id.* § 7.20(c)(2).

496. *Id.* §§ 7.20(c)(2), 7.20(b)(1)(A).

497. *Id.* § 7.20(c)(2), 7.20(b)(1)(D).

498. N.Y. Bus. Corp. Law § 724(c).

An intermediate appellate court decision in New York in *Bear, Stearns & Co. v. D.F. King & Co.*[499] illustrates this distinction between Delaware and New York law. The issue in this decision was whether a Delaware corporation, D.F. King & Co., "should be obliged, over its objection, to provide interim indemnification" pursuant to New York law to an employee alleged to have improperly obtained information concerning Bear, Stearns & Co. customers during the term of his employment at D.F. King.[500]

The court acknowledged the authority under New York law of "a *court* to grant indemnification for legal expenses during the pendency of an action," but stated that this authority was limited "with regard to a foreign corporation where such award 'would be inconsistent with the law of the jurisdiction of incorporation of a foreign corporation which prohibits or otherwise limits such indemnification.'"[501] The court stated that Section 145(e) of Delaware's statute "provides for interim indemnification at the corporation's discretion . . . but contains no provision for court-ordered interim indemnification analogous to BCL § 724(c)," and "Delaware case law reads § 145(e) as providing that, absent contractual agreement, the question of interim indemnification lies solely within the corporation's discretion."[502]

The court rejected as "without merit" a contention that "Delaware law and New York law on this issue are different, but not inconsistent."[503] To the contrary, the court concluded, "[i]n this instance, the law of the two States are incompatible, since New York's policy gives priority to the individual at the expense of the corporation and Delaware's policy gives priority to the corporation at the expense of the individual."[504] Accordingly, the court found that "the policy of this State is inconsistent with that of Delaware

---

499. --- A.D.2d ---, 663 N.Y.S.2d 12 (N.Y. App. Div. 1st Dep't 1997).

500. --- A.D.2d at ---, 663 N.Y.S.2d at 13.

501. *Id.* (quoting N.Y. Bus. Corp. Law § 725(b)(1)).

502. --- A.D.2d at ---, 663 N.Y.S.2d at 13 (citations omitted).

503. --- A.D.2d at ---, 663 N.Y.S.2d at 13.

504. *Id.*

on this issue and that, pursuant to BCL § 725(b)(1), the former must defer to the latter."[505]

Three decisions—*Professional Insurance Co. v. Barry*,[506] *Sequa Corp. v. Gelmin*[507] and *Sierra Rutile Ltd. v. Katz*[508]—illustrate the operation of Section 724(c) of New York's statute where it does govern.

*Professional Insurance Co. v. Barry*[509] involved an action commenced by a corporation, Professional Insurance, against a former director of the corporation, Robert Chaut, for an accounting and damages arising from alleged breaches of fiduciary duties by the former director.[510] Chaut served a third party complaint against a second corporation, Schapiro, upon whose behalf Chaut contended that he had served Professional Insurance. Chaut's third party complaint sought "his reasonable expenses, including attorneys' fees, during the pendency of the litigation as are necessary in connection with his defense."[511]

The court rejected the contention that Chaut had failed to raise the "genuine issues of fact or law" required by Section 724(c) in order to permit advancement (the statute was at that time numbered Section 725(c)) as "untenable."[512] The court reasoned as follows:

> In essence Chaut maintains that at all relevant times he was an officer of Schapiro and served as a director of plaintiff, Professional, at the request of and for the benefit of Scha-

---

505. *Id.*

506. 60 Misc. 2d 424, 303 N.Y.S.2d 556 (N.Y. Sup. Ct. N.Y. Co.), *aff'd mem.*, 32 A.D.2d 898, 302 N.Y.S.2d 722 (N.Y. App. Div. 1st Dep't 1969).

507. 828 F. Supp. 203 (S.D.N.Y. 1993).

508. 1997 U.S. Dist. LEXIS 11018, 1997 WL 431719 (S.D.N.Y. July 31, 1997).

509. 60 Misc. 2d 424, 303 N.Y.S.2d 556 (N.Y. Sup. Ct. N.Y. Co.), *aff'd mem.*, 32 A.D.2d 898, 302 N.Y.S.2d 722 (N.Y. App. Div. 1st Dep't 1969).

510. *Id.* at 425, 303 N.Y.S.2d at 558.

511. *Id.* at 424-25, 303 N.Y.S.2d at 557-58.

512. *Id.* at 427, 303 N.Y.S.2d at 560.

piro; that at all such times he acted in good faith for a purpose he reasonably believed to be in the best interest of Schapiro. Schapiro admits that Chaut was an officer but denies that he served as a director of Professional, at the request of or for the benefit of Schapiro. Clearly a genuine issue of fact is raised by these pleadings.[513]

The court also rejected the contention that Chaut was obligated by Section 724(c) to establish a "reasonable probability of success."[514]

Accordingly, in view of "all of the aforesaid and the circumstances herein," including the legal fees that had been incurred as of that point in the litigation by Chaut and an affidavit by Chaut describing his financial condition, the court determined "to exercise its discretion" under Section 724(c) and award Chaut his reasonable expenses, including attorneys fees.[515] This determination, however, was conditioned upon an agreement by Chaut to "provide sufficient undertaking to repay the whole or such portion of said amount together with interest at the legal rate as the court may ultimately determine to be reimbursable."[516]

*Sequa Corp. v. Gelmin*[517] involved a motion pursuant to Section 724(c) of New York's statute by a former corporate officer seeking a court order requiring the corporation to advance him litigation expenses, including attorneys' fees, in a litigation brought against him and others by the corporation involving claims under the Racketeer Influenced and Corrupt Practices Act ("RICO"),[518] fraud and breach of fiduciary duties.[519]

The court rejected the corporation's contention that the filing of a federal claim such as the RICO claim asserted by the corporation against the former officer deprived the former officer of any right he otherwise would have had under state law to ask the court

---

513. *Id.*
514. *Id.* at 427-28, 303 N.Y.S.2d at 560.
515. *Id.* at 428-29, 303 N.Y.S.2d at 561.
516. *Id.* at 429, 303 N.Y.S.2d at 561.
517. 828 F. Supp. 203 (S.D.N.Y. 1993).
518. 18 U.S.C. §§ 1961-1968.
519. 828 F. Supp. at 204-05.

to order that the corporation pay him litigation expenses during the pendency of the litigation.[520] The court also held that the former officer's "protestations of innocence" in affidavits were sufficient to raise "genuine issues of fact" and that there was no requirement that the former officer make "a showing comparable to that required to obtain summary judgment."[521]

The court in *Sequa* also rejected the corporation's request that the former officer be required to post a bond to secure repayment in the event that the former officer ultimately was found not to be entitled to indemnification. The court held that the requirement in Section 723(c) of the New York statute that a director or officer receiving advancement of expenses from the corporation provide "an undertaking . . . to repay" pursuant to Section 725(a) if the director or officer ultimately is found not to be entitled to indemnification "has no relevance" to a motion seeking court-ordered advancement of expenses from the court pursuant to Section 724.[522] Section 723, the court explained, "refers to the payment of indemnification other than by court award," and "Section 724 contains no language requiring the giving of security by an officer or director who successfully invokes its provisions."[523]

The corporation in *Sequa* responded to the court's decision by dismissing without prejudice the claims asserted against the former officer seeking indemnification and then noticing the former officer's deposition in the case. The court rejected the corporation's claim that under these circumstances the corporation no longer was required to advance the officer's legal expenses under Section 724 because, according to the corporation, the officer no longer was a party and the corporation was "unlikely" to reassert its claims against the officer at a later time.[524] The court explained that "if

---

520. *Id.* at 206.

521. *Id.* at 206-07.

522. *Id.* at 207.

523. *Id.; see also* Chapter V, Section A 5 a (discussing advancement by the corporation pursuant to N.Y. Bus. Corp. Law §§ 723(c) and 725(a)).

524. *Sequa Corp. v. Gelmin*, 1993 U.S. Dist. LEXIS 16253, at *1, 1993 WL 481346, at *1 (S.D.N.Y. Nov. 17, 1993).

Sequa has in mind submitting O'Brien to a deposition undefended by counsel and then using perceived admissions to sue him again, the question arises whether O'Brien remains a defendant in the substantive if not the technical sense."[525] The court accordingly ordered that the corporation either consent that its prior dismissal of the former officer would be with prejudice or brief the question identified by the court.[526]

*Sierra Rutile Ltd. v. Katz*[527] also involved a motion under Section 724(c) of New York's statute. The court stated that if a director or officer satisfies the requirements in Section 724(c), "the Court may order their corporation to advance litigation expenses, notwithstanding the corporation's allegations that the director or officer engaged in wrongdoing against the corporation."[528] The two corporations from whom indemnification was sought did "not dispute for purposes of these motions that their articles of association provide for the indemnification" sought by the former officers or that the former officers had raised "genuine issues of fact as to liability in this action."[529] The court therefore ordered advancement of the "reasonable expenses and attorneys' fees for the making of these motions and for expenses and fees incurred from the date the motions were fully submitted and henceforth."[530]

The court noted that the corporations from whom indemnification was sought were Cayman Islands corporations but rejected a contention that these corporations were exempted from New York law by Sections 725(f) and 1320 of New York's statute, pursuant to which a foreign corporation authorized to do business in New York

---

525. 1993 U.S. Dist. LEXIS 16253, at *2, 1993 WL 481346, at *1.

526. *Id.*

527. 1997 U.S. Dist. LEXIS 11018, 1997 WL 431119 (S.D.N.Y. July 31, 1997).

528. 1997 U.S. Dist. LEXIS 11018, at *8, 1997 WL 431119, at *1.

529. 1997 U.S. Dist. LEXIS 11018, at *9, 1997 WL 431119, at *1.

530. 1997 U.S. Dist. LEXIS 11018, at *11, 1997 WL 431119, at *2.

is excused from New York's indemnification requirements if the corporation's shares are listed on a national securities exchange or less than half of the corporation's income is allocable to New York for franchise tax purposes.[531] This exemption did not apply, the court held, because there was no proof offered to the court that the corporations "are or were authorized to do business in New York."[532] The court also concluded that Section 725(b)(1) of New York's statute, which provides that indemnification and advancement are not permitted under New York law where indemnification "would be inconsistent with the law of the jurisdiction of incorporation of a foreign corporation which prohibits or otherwise limits such indemnification," did not preclude advancement because an advance of expenses under § 724(c) would not be inconsistent with the law of the Cayman Islands.[533]

The Model Act permits court-ordered advancement of expenses pursuant to the same rules governing court-ordered indemnification, except in the advancement context consideration must be given to the ability of the director to finance his defense without advancement.[534] Like the Delaware and California statutes and unlike the New York statute and the Model Act, Principles of Corporate Governance does not authorize court-ordered advancement of expenses during the pendency of a litigation.

## 7.   Types of Proceedings Covered

Assuming the applicable statutory requirements are satisfied, Sections 145(a) and (b) of Delaware's statute and most other state statutes permit corporations to indemnify "any person who was or is a party or is threatened to be made a party to any threatened, pending or completed action, suit or proceeding, whether civil,

---

531. N.Y. Bus. Corp. Law §§ 725(f), 1320; 1997 U.S. Dist. LEXIS 11018, at *9, 1997 WL 431119, at *2.

532. 1997 U.S. Dist. LEXIS 11018, at *10, 1997 WL 431119, at *2.

533. N.Y. Bus. Corp. Law § 725(b)(1); 1997 U.S. Dist. LEXIS 11018, at *8, 10-11, 1997 WL 431119, at *1, 2.

534. Model Bus. Corp. Act Annotated § 8.54(a)(3) & Official Comment at 8-358.

criminal, administrative or investigative."[535] This language is broad enough to cover the expenses incurred by a director or officer in connection with internal investigations, including investigations by a board or board committee with respect to a pre-litigation shareholder demand or a shareholder derivative action.[536]

The Model Business Corporation Act similarly permits indemnification of amounts incurred in "any threatened, pending, or completed action, suit, or proceeding, whether civil, criminal, administrative, arbitrative, or investigative and whether formal or informal."[537] Principles of Corporate Governance permits indemnification of amounts incurred in "any threatened, pending, or completed action, suit, or other proceeding, formal or informal, whether civil, criminal, administrative, or investigative."[538]

## 8. Expenses Incurred Other Than as a Defendant

As noted in the preceding section, most statutes providing for permissive indemnification refer to directors or officers who are or who may become a "party" to an action or proceeding.[539] These

---

535. Del. Gen. Corp. Law §§ 145(a), (b); *see also* Cal. Gen. Corp. Law §§ 317(a), (b), (c) (similar language); N.Y. Bus. Corp. Law §§ 722(a), (c) (referring to "an action or proceeding, . . . whether civil or criminal"); *Citadel Holding Corp. v. Roven*, 603 A.2d 818, 823 n.6 (Del. 1992) (stating that "we can think of no legal matter in which a director would incur costs" under the governing contractual "any action, suit, proceeding or investigation" standard but not under the Delaware statutory "any civil, criminal, administrative or investigative action, suit or proceeding" formulation, and therefore construing "the two phrases to be legal equivalents").

536. *See* John F. Olson & Josiah O. Hatch III, *Director and Officer Liability: Indemnification and Insurance* § 5.03[1][b], at 5-14 (1997).

537. 2 Model Bus. Corp. Act. Annotated § 8.50(8) (3d ed 1996).

538. 2 Principles of Corporate Governance: Analysis and Recommendations § 7.20(a)(1) (1994).

539. Cal. Gen. Corp. Law §§ 317 (b), (c), ("a party"); Del. Gen. Corp. Law §§ 145(a), (b) ("a party"); N.Y. Bus. Corp. Law §§ 722(a), (c) ("a party"); 2 Model Bus. Corp. Act Annotated § 8.51(a) (3d ed. 1996) ("a party"); 2 Principles of Corporate Governance: Analysis and

(continued...)

statutes include "the expenses incurred as a result of having been made a *party* to *any* action by reason of the claimant's status" as director or officer.[540] These statutes therefore have been interpreted "to encompass (for example) a case where the directors are the plaintiffs in the underlying action."[541]

The Delaware Supreme Court's decision in *Hibbert v. Hollywood Park, Inc.*,[542] a case where directors sought and were awarded indemnification for litigation expenses incurred as a plaintiff during a proxy contest, illustrates this principle. The court explained that the litigation sought to compel other directors to attend board meetings and to protect the independence of the board's internal auditing procedures and thus was not "entirely initiated without regard to any duty the plaintiffs might have had as directors."[543] The court held that a corporate bylaw authorized indemnification of expenses incurred by directors in litigation regardless of the director's role in the litigation in language "broad enough to include an individual who acts as an intervenor or *amicus curiae* in any particular case."[544] The court also held that "indemnification here is consistent with current Delaware law" because Sections 145(a) and (b) of the Delaware statute permit indemnification of "any person who was or is a party or is threatened to be made a party" in any litigation.[545] "By this language," the court concluded, "indemnity is not limited to only those who stand as a defendant in the main action."[546]

---

539. (...continued)
Recommendations § 7.20(a) (1994) ("a party"). *But see* Mass. Bus. Corp. Law § 67; Tex. Bus. Corp. Act 2.02-1(B) (both limiting indemnification to amounts incurred in defending an action or proceeding).

540. *Mayer v. Executive Telecard, Ltd.*, 705 A.2d 220, 224 (Del. Ch. 1997).

541. *Id.*

542. 457 A.2d 339 (Del. 1983).

543. *Id.* at 344.

544. *Id.* at 343.

545. *Id.* at 344.

546. *Id.*

A California court construing Delaware law in *Megeath v. PLM International, Inc.*[547] stated that "*Hibbert* expressly permits indemnity for expenses in suing the corporation one serves or served."[548] The court accordingly enforced bylaw and indemnification agreement provisions providing for indemnification and advancement in an action filed by former corporate official alleging wrongful discharge, defamation, invasion of privacy and severe emotional distress.[549]

The Delaware Court of Chancery in *Shearin v. E.F. Hutton Group, Inc.*[550] again stated the principle that "in Delaware, . . . a plaintiff may . . . be entitled to indemnification" when a suit is brought "as part of the claimant's duties to the corporation."[551] The court in *Shearin*, however, denied indemnification because the case involved lawsuits brought by a former corporate officer after she was terminated raising "purely . . . personal rights (defamation, breach of contract)."[552] The court held that the lawsuits "plainly sought to advance her own interest, not the interest of the corporation," and that none of her claims were "in any part motivated by a fiduciary or other obligation to the corporation."[553] Accordingly, the court concluded, the former officer's "demand that the corporation bear her expenses is without merit."[554]

Another issue that has been litigated is whether the statutory grant of the power to indemnify "any person who was or is a party or is threatened to be made a party" to an action or proceeding includes expenses incurred as a witness.

The court in *Lipson v. Supercuts, Inc.*[555] required advancement pursuant to a mandatory advancement provision for the for-

---

547. No. 930369 (Cal. Super. Ct. Mar. 18, 1992), *reprinted in* Corp. Officers and Directors Liability Litig. Rep. 11791 (Apr. 8, 1992).

548. *Id.*, slip op. at 11-13, 29.

549. *Id.* at 29.

550. 652 A.2d 578 (Del. Ch. 1994).

551. *Id.* at 594.

552. *Id.* at 581, 594.

553. *Id.* at 594-95.

554. *Id.* at 595.

555. No. 15074 (Del. Ch. Dec. 10, 1996).

mer chairman and chief executive officer of Supercuts, Inc., David E. Lipson, for expenses incurred as a witness in a Securities and Exchange Commission investigation. The investigation involved allegations by Supercuts that Lipson traded Supercuts stock "based on confidential information acquired during the time that he was an officer and/or director of Supercuts" and thus violated his duties to the corporation.[556] The court reasoned that a certificate of incorporation provision requiring advancement was "not altogether clear" with respect to whether expenses incurred as a witness in such a proceeding were covered by the provision, that the provision placed the burden of showing non-entitlement to advancement upon the corporation, and that not requiring advancement "would defeat the broad purpose" of the provision, which "by its own language in different places evidences an attempt to create very broad indemnification rights, and advancement rights as well."[557]

The court added that "even if this interpretation were incorrect," the court was satisfied that the Lipson was "defending" a proceeding.[558] The court explained:

> To the extent that the term "defend" has any meaning in the SEC investigatory context, it must cover the situation where a witness, although complying with his or her legal obligations to testify and to produce documents, will conduct himself so as to avoid becoming a target or, worse, charged with federal securities violations. That is a risk that is inherent in anyone being called to testify, at least with respect to a stated concern about trading on inside information, and where the person who is the witness is the person who was doing the trading.[559]

The court rejected a claim that the challenged conduct did not occur in Lipson's official capacity. The court stated that the SEC was focusing upon trading by Lipson while he was chairman and chief executive officer of the corporation and based upon informa-

---

556. *Id.*, Tr. at 96, 105.
557. *Id.* at 100-01.
558. *Id.* at 102.
559. *Id.*

tion provided to him in that position.[560] The court also stated that the certificate provision mandating advancement "covers proceedings whose basis is not only action by the indemnitee in an official capacity, but also in any other capacity while serving as an officer or director."[561] The court also rejected a claim that some of the challenged conduct occurred after Lipson left the corporation. The court stated that "nothing in the certificate or the case law . . . supports an argument that that circumstance alone defeats an entitlement to advancement."[562] "At most," the court stated, "it might trigger an obligation . . . to refund a portion of the advanced costs" if the post-employment conduct is found not to be indemnifiable.[563] The court noted, however, that this possibility "seems remote, in view of the fact that the company itself has taken the position that Mr. Lipson's post-termination conduct involved an alleged violation of duties owed to the corporation by Mr. Lipson by virtue of his position as an officer and director."[564]

By contrast, the court in *Heffernan v. Pacific Dunlop GNB Corp.*[565] denied a request for indemnification of expenses incurred by a former director in responding to subpoenas in lawsuits in which the former director was not named as a party, and a corporate bylaw provided that the corporation "'shall indemnify' its directors to the extent 'permitted' by Delaware law."[566] The court reasoned that "[i]n order to qualify for indemnification under § 145(a) of the Delaware General Corporation Law, Heffernan must either be a party or be threatened with suit. Heffernan's amended complaint is devoid of any allegation that he is, or has been threatened to be named, a party in the Gould or Barosh suits.

---

560. *Id.* at 103.

561. *Id.* at 103-04.

562. *Id.* at 104.

563. *Id.*

564. *Id.* at 104-05.

565. 1992 U.S. Dist. LEXIS 14809, 1992 WL 275573 (N.D. Ill. Oct. 1, 1992).

566. 1992 U.S. Dist. LEXIS 14809, at *1, 5, 1992 WL 275573, at *1, 2.

Indeed, Heffernan's amended complaint states that he is not a party to either suit."[567]

The Model Business Corporation Act provides for indemnification of a "party to a proceeding" and defines a "party" as "an individual who was, is, or is threatened to be made, a defendant or respondent in a proceeding."[568] The Official Comment states that "[a]n individual who is only called as a witness is not a 'party' within this definition."[569] A separate provision of the Model Act states that the Model Act's provisions concerning indemnification do "not limit a corporation's power to pay or reimburse expenses incurred" by a person in connection with "appearance as a witness in a proceeding at a time when he is not a party."[570] Principles of Corporate Governance refers to liabilities and expenses "incurred in connection with any threatened, pending, or completed action, suit or other proceeding" to which a person "is or may be made a party or in connection with which" the person "is or may be otherwise required to appear."[571]

Indemnification that is mandatory by statute (as opposed to indemnification that is mandatory due to a charter, bylaw or contract provision) is limited in most jurisdictions to conduct "in defense of any action, suit or proceeding."[572]

## 9.  Types of Conduct Covered

Most statutes, including the California, Delaware and New York statutes, allow indemnification for conduct by the person to

---

567. 1992 U.S. Dist. LEXIS 14809, at *4, 13-14, 1992 WL 275573, at *1, 4.

568. Model Bus. Corp. Act Annotated §§ 8.51(a), 8.50(7).

569. *Id*. § 8.50 Official Comment at 8-297.

570. *Id*. § 8.58(d).

571. Principles of Corporate Governance § 7.20(a)(1).

572. Del. Gen. Corp. Law § 145(c); *see also Mayer v. Executive Telecard, Ltd.*, 705 A.2d 220, 224 (Del. Ch. 1997) ("[i]n contrast to § 145(c), § 145(a) is not limited to expenses incurred 'in connection with the defense of any action'"); Cal. Gen. Corp. Law § 317(d); N.Y. Bus. Corp. Law § 723(a); Model Bus. Corp. Act Annotated § 8.52; Principles of Corporate Governance § 7.20(a)(3).

be indemnified that arises "by reason of the fact" the person is or was a director or officer of the corporation.[573] The Model Business Corporation provides for indemnification for liabilities and expenses incurred by a director or officer made a party to a proceeding "because" he is a director or officer.[574] Principles of Corporate Governance provides for indemnification for liabilities and expenses incurred in a proceeding to which a director or officer is or may be required to appear "[b]ecause such person was acting in his or her capacity as a director or officer of the corporation" or "[s]olely because of the fact that such person is or was a director or officer.[575]

"[M]any courts have interpreted" the "by reason of the fact" language in the California, Delaware and New York statutes with "breadth."[576] In *Witco Corp. v. Beekhuis*,[577] for example, the Environmental Protection Agency (the "EPA") and the surviving corporation in a merger brought allegations under the Comprehensive Environmental Response, Compensation and Liability Act ("CERCLA")[578] against the estate of a former director, who also had been a director, officer and majority shareholder of the corporation that had been acquired in the merger. The surviving corporation entered into a consent decree with the EPA that required expenditures by the corporation, and then sought contribution from the estate of the former director. The estate won the action. Because the liabilities of the acquired corporation, including indemnification obligations, had been assumed by the surviving corporation, the estate sought indemnification pursuant to the provision in

---

573. Cal. Gen. Corp. Law §§ 317(b), (c); Del. Gen. Corp. Law §§ 145(a), (b); N.Y. Bus. Corp. Law §§ 722(a), (c).
574. 2 Model Bus. Corp. Act Annotated §§ 8.51(a), 8.56(a)(1) (1994).
575. 2 Principles of Corporate Governance: Analysis and Recommendations § 7.20(a)(1) (1994).
576. *United States v. Lowe*, 29 F.3d 1005, 1010-11 (5th Cir. 1994); *see also Grove v. Daniel Valve Co.*, 874 S.W. 2d 150, 156 (Tex. Ct. App. 1994) (noting in this context "the generous parameters the Delaware statute intended").
577. 38 F.3d 682 (3d Cir. 1994).
578. 42 U.S.C. §§ 9601 et seq.

Delaware's indemnification statute making indemnification mandatory where a director (or his heirs, executors or administrators) is "successful on the merits or otherwise."[579]

The Third Circuit held that the case involved both personal and corporate conduct because the director could be found personally liable as an "operator" within the meaning of CERCLA.[580] The court concluded, however, that indemnification is mandatory whenever a director "successfully defends against claims of personal liability that arise from or have a nexus to his corporate position."[581] The claims against the director in this case, the court held, arose by virtue of his activities as a director and officer of the corporation acquired in the merger. Indemnification therefore was required.[582]

The Seventh Circuit's decision in *Heffernan v. Pacific Dunlop GNB Corp.*[583] also illustrates this principle. The plaintiff in *Heffernan* was Daniel E. Heffernan, a former director and 6.7 percent of shareholder of GNB Holdings, Inc. ("Holdings") and its wholly-owned subsidiary, GNB Inc. ("GNB"). Heffernan was sued by Pacific Dunlop Holdings, Inc. after Pacific acquired control of a majority of Holdings' shares and then acquired Heffernan's shares pursuant to a stock purchase agreement.[584] Pacific Dunlop alleged violations of Section 12(2) of the Securities Act of 1933[585] and sought "to rescind its purchase of Heffernan's shares on the ground that the Stock Purchase Agreement was materially misleading in regard to its disclosure of certain liabilities facing Holdings and GNB."[586] Prior to the stock purchase agreement, Heffernan also

---

579. 38 F.3d at 684-86, 691; *see also* Del. Gen. Corp. Law § 145(c); Chapter V, Section A 3 a (discussing Del. Gen. Corp. Law § 145(c)).

580. 38 F.3d at 692.

581. *Id.*

582. *Id.* at 692-93.

583. 965 F.2d 369 (7th Cir. 1992).

584. *Id.* at 371.

585. 15 U.S.C. § 77*l*(2).

586. 965 F.2d at 371.

had been an officer of Holdings' investment banker, which owned 20 percent of the corporation's stock.[587]

Heffernan requested indemnification and advancement pursuant to bylaw provisions requiring indemnification and advancement "to the fullest extent permitted by the Delaware General Corporation Law."[588] The Seventh Circuit reversed a decision by the district court granting a motion to dismiss.

The Seventh Circuit explained that Section 145(a) of Delaware's statute provides that "a corporation may indemnify any person who was or is a party to any [suit] by reason of the fact that he is or was a director" and that the corporation's bylaw quoted above made such indemnification mandatory.[589] The court acknowledged that the director seeking indemnification "wore three hats—director, shareholder and investment banker—" and that "his director status may not be the *only* reason that he was sued."[590] The court concluded, however, that "at this stage of the litigation, we cannot, as a matter of law, rule out the fact that it may have been *one* reason."[591] The court added its view that "Delaware is no neophyte in corporate law matters," and "[h]ad it desired to limit permissible indemnification solely to those suits in which a director is sued for breaching a duty of his directorship or for certain enumerated causes of action, it would have jettisoned the supple 'by reason of the fact that' phrase in favor of more specific language."[592] Instead, according to the court, Delaware's statute utilizes "by reason of the fact that" language that "is broad enough to encompass suits against a director in his official capacity as well as suits against a director that arise more tangentially from his role, position or status as a director."[593] The court emphasized that "our inquiry in this case has been a narrow one, confined to whether Heffernan's indemnification . . . claim . . . should be allowed to

---

587. *Id.*
588. *Id.* at 371-72 & n.2.
589. *Id.* at 371-72.
590. *Id.* at 375.
591. *Id.*
592. *Id.*
593. *Id.*

proceed. . . . We hold only that his suit was prematurely dismissed under an unduly restrictive reading of Delaware's indemnification law. Holdings' by-laws have numerous prerequisites that a director must meet before being entitled to indemnification. Those remain to be explored in the district court."[594]

On a subsequent motion for summary judgment by the corporation, the district court—in "a review guided by the Seventh Circuit's opinion"—concluded that the former director had in fact been sued by the corporation "by reason of the fact that" he was a director of the corporation.[595] The district court pointed in particular to the corporation's complaint in the underlying litigation, which, the court stated, repeatedly alleged that the former director's "status as a director placed him in a position 'where, in the performance of his duties as a director, he either learned or should have learned of those liabilities'" facing Holdings and GNB.[596]

The Eighth Circuit in *Barry v. Barry*,[597] another case involving alleged actions taken by directors and officers in both their official corporate capacities and as controlling shareholders, similarly held that "the mere fact that the Swartzes wore two hats in their dealings . . . does not compel the conclusion that they were not sued, at least in part, because of their official status."[598] The court, construing Minnesota law, accordingly held that advancement was required.[599]

The Delaware Superior Court in *Salaman v. National Media Corp.*[600] likewise held that a determination regarding the capacity in which a director who also was the corporation's largest shareholder had been sued is premature in the context of a request for

---

594. *Id.* at 376.

595. *Heffernan v. Pacific Dunlop GNB Corp.*, 1993 U.S. Dist. LEXIS 5, at *27, 1993 WL 3553, at *9 (N.D. Ill. Jan. 5, 1993).

596. *Id.*

597. 28 F.3d 848 (8th Cir. 1994).

598. *Id.* at 851.

599. *Id.*

600. 1992 Del. Super. LEXIS 564, 1992 WL 808095 (Del. Super. Oct. 8, 1992).

advancement.[601] The court stated that it was "entirely possible" that a director had been "sued because of his acts as a director," even though the allegations in the case involved the sale by the director of much of his stock during a period in which the corporation was alleged to have artificially inflated the value of its stock.[602] Moreover, the court continued, "[t]he fact that Salaman may be found not to be entitled to indemnification does not prevent him from receiving advancements of his expenses. . . . If it is determined . . . that Salaman was sued because of his personal dealings, not his actions as a director, National Media may recover the advancement pursuant to Salaman's undertaking."[603] The same result also was reached by the Delaware Superior Court in *Kapoor v. Fujisawa Pharmaceutical Co.*[604]

A New Mexico court in *Petty v. Bank of New Mexico Holding Co.*,[605] by contrast, reversed a decision granting a motion to dismiss a shareholder derivative action alleging that the corporation's board of directors improperly authorized the advancement of litigation expenses to directors and officers.[606] The court explained that the governing New Mexico statute, like Delaware's statute, "empowers a corporation to indemnify a person made a party to a proceeding 'by reason of the fact that the person is or was a director.'"[607] In this case, the court explained, however, the directors and officers that had been indemnified had been sued "by reason of the fact that they are shareholders . . . and signatories to [a] buy-sell and voting trust agreement."[608]

---

601. 1992 Del. Super. LEXIS 564, at *14, 1992 WL 808095, at *5.

602. *Id.*

603. 1992 Del. Super. LEXIS 564, at *15, 1992 WL 808095, at *5.

604. 1994 Del. Super. LEXIS 233, at *16-19, 1994 WL 233947, at *6-7 (Del. Super. May 10, 1994) (same result), *aff'd on other grounds*, 655 A.2d 307 (unpublished opinion, text available at 1995 Del. LEXIS 25 and 1995 WL 24906) (Del. Jan. 17, 1995).

605. 787 P.2d 443 (N.M. 1990).

606. *Id.* at 444-45.

607. *Id.* at 447.

608. *Id.*

A bankruptcy court in Massachusetts in *In re P.J. Keating Co.*,[609] construing Massachusetts law, reached the same conclusion. The court in this case held that causes of action alleging that a controlling shareholder had induced minority shareholders to enter into a shareholder's agreement and wrongfully terminated minority shareholders' employment by the corporation "were based, at least primarily, upon the fiduciary obligations owed by a controlling stockholder . . . to his fellow stockholders."[610] Consequently, the court concluded, the allegations "did not arise from . . . services as an officer or director" and were not subject to indemnification.[611] The same result was reached by a California court construing California law in *Plate v. Sun-Diamond Growers*,[612] a case where corporate employees were sued because of activity undertaken to establish their own business, independent of the corporation that employed them, for their own personal benefit and not in furtherance of the corporation's policies or objectives.[613] Likewise, the Eleventh Circuit in *National Union Fire Insurance Co. v. Emhart Corp.*[614] held that no provision in Virginia law permitted indemnification for actions taken prior to the time an individual became an officer or employee of Emhart Corporation and "relating to a separate company as to which Emhart had no interest or involvement."[615]

Most statutes, including the California, Delaware and New York statutes, allow indemnification not just for conduct by the person to be indemnified that arises "by reason of the fact" the person is or was a director of officer of the corporation, but also "by reason of the fact" that the person "is or was serving at the request of the corporation as a director, officer, employee or agent"

---

609. 180 B.R. 18 (Bankr. D. Mass. 1995).

610. *Id.* at 23.

611. *Id.*

612. 225 Cal. App. 3d 1115, 275 Cal. Rptr. 667 (Cal. Ct. App. 1990).

613. *Id.* at 1126, 275 Cal. Rptr. at 673.

614. 11 F.3d 1524 (11th Cir. 1993).

615. *Id.* at 1530.

of another entity.[616] The Model Business Corporation Act provides for indemnification for conduct by the person to be indemnified "because he is a director," with the term "director" defined as a person "who, while a director of the corporation, is or was serving at the corporation's request as a director, officer, partner, trustee, employee, or agent" of another entity.[617] Principles of Corporate Governance uses the formulation "acting in some capacity on behalf of a third party at the request of the corporation."[618]

## 10. Exclusivity and Non-Exclusivity Provisions

Most statutory indemnification provisions state that "[t]he corporation may provide greater protection than that granted by the statute,"[619] and thus do "not mark the exclusive ambit of indemnification rights."[620]

Section 145(f) of the Delaware General Corporation Law, for example, states that any indemnification provided by or granted pursuant to other provisions of Section 145 "shall not be deemed exclusive of any other rights to which those seeking indemnification or advancement of expenses may be entitled under any bylaw, agreement, vote of stockholders or disinterested directors or otherwise, both as to action in such person's official capacity and as to action in another capacity while holding such office."[621]

New York's statute provides as follows:

The indemnification and advancement of expenses granted pursuant to, or provided by, this article shall not be deemed exclusive of any other rights to which a director or officer seeking indemnification or advancement of expenses may be

---

616. Cal. Gen. Corp. Law §§ 317(b), (c); Del. Gen. Corp. Law §§ 145(a), (b); N.Y. Bus. Corp. Law §§ 722(a), (c).

617. Model Bus. Corp. Act Annotated §§ 8.51(a), 8.50(2).

618. Principles of Corporate Governance § 7.20(a)(1)(A).

619. *Salaman v. National Media Corp.*, 1992 Del. Super. LEXIS 564, at *11, 1992 WL 808095, at *4 (Del. Super. Oct. 8, 1992).

620. *Heffernan v. Pacific Dunlop GNB Corp.*, 1993 U.S. Dist. LEXIS 5, at *15, 1993 WL 3553, at *5 (N.D. Ill. Jan. 5, 1993).

621. Del. Gen. Corp. Law § 145(f).

entitled, whether contained in the certificate of incorporation or the by-laws or, when authorized by such certificate of incorporation or by-laws, (i) a resolution of shareholders, (ii) a resolution of directors, or (iii) an agreement providing for such indemnification.[622]

New York's statute, however, adds an important qualification:

[N]o indemnification may be made to or on behalf of any director or officer if a judgment or other final adjudication adverse to the director or officer establishes that his acts were committed in bad faith or were the result of active and deliberate dishonesty and were material to the cause of action so adjudicated, or that he personally gained in fact a financial profit or other advantage to which he was not legally entitled.[623]

California allows broader indemnification than that otherwise permitted in its statute to the extent authorized by a charter provision. Indemnification is not permitted, however, for breaches of duty to the corporation involving circumstances in which indemnification is expressly prohibited by specific provisions of the statute or for liability:

(i) for acts or omissions that involve intentional misconduct or a knowing and culpable violation of law, (ii) for acts or omissions that a director believes to be contrary to the best interests of the corporation or its shareholders or that involve the absence of good faith on the part of the director, (iii) for any transaction from which a director derived an improper personal benefit, (iv) for acts or omissions that show a reckless disregard for the director's duty to the corporation or its shareholders in circumstances in which the director was aware, or should have been aware, in the ordinary course of performing a director's duties, of a risk of serious injury to the corporation or its shareholders, (v) for acts or omissions that constitute an unexcused pattern of inattention that amounts to an abdication of the director's duty to the corporation or its shareholders, (vi) under Section 310 [interested

---

622. N.Y. Bus. Corp. Law § 721.
623. *Id.*

director transactions], or (vii) under Section 316 [illegal distributions].[624]

The indemnification provisions in Principles of Corporate Governance are not exclusive, but any indemnification granted pursuant to the non-exclusivity provision in Principles of Corporate Governance is "[s]ubject to the limitations" that otherwise govern indemnification.[625] The Model Business Corporation Act permits indemnification and advancement "only as permitted" by the specific terms of the Model Act.[626] The Model Act, however, "does not preclude provisions in articles of incorporation, bylaws, resolutions, or contracts designed to provide procedural machinery in addition to (but not inconsistent with)" specific Model Act provisions.[627] "For example, a corporation may properly obligate the board of directors to consider and act expeditiously on an application for indemnification or advance for expenses or to cooperate in the procedural steps required to obtain a judicial determination" in an application by a director for court-order indemnification or advancement.[628]

---

624. Cal. Gen. Corp. Law §§ 204(a)(10), (11), 317(g); *see also Johnston v. Lindblade*, 1995 Minn. App. LEXIS 695, at *4-5, 1995 WL 311617, at *2 (Minn. Ct. App. May 23, 1995) (construing non-exclusivity provision in Minn. Bus. Corp. Act § 302A.521(9), which states that "nothing in [§ 302A.521] shall be construed to limit the power of the corporation to indemnify other persons by contract or otherwise," and rejecting contention that this provision permits indemnification only of agents of the corporation: "The plain meaning of Minn. Stat. § 302A.521, subd. 9, is that Minn. Stat. § 302A.521 does not limit the authority of a corporation to choose to indemnify a person who is not eligible for indemnification under the other provisions of Minn. Stat. § 302A.521. Subdivision 9 does not require a person to be an agent of the corporation to be eligible for indemnification. Johnston is a person the corporation chose to indemnify. Thus, the indemnification is authorized by Minn. Stat. § 302A.521, subd.9.").

625. 2 Principles of Corporate Governance: Analysis and Recommendations § 7.20(e) (1994).

626. 2 Model Bus. Corp. Act Annotated § 8.59 (3d ed. 1996).

627. *Id.* Official Comment at 8-384.1.

628. *Id.*

Prior to 1994, the Model Act allowed indemnification of directors only where "consistent" with the Act.[629] The change from only where "consistent" to only where "permitted" was made in light of other amendments to the Model Act in 1994 that expanded the corporation's power to grant permissive indemnification and advancement and the court's power to order indemnification and advancement.[630] The Model Act permits corporations to enact charter provisions that limit any right to indemnification or advancement that a director otherwise would have.[631]

In the federal savings association context, the regulations governing indemnification are exclusive.[632] A federal savings association that "has a bylaw in effect relating to indemnification of its personnel," however, is "governed solely by that bylaw."[633]

There is general agreement that a non-exclusivity provision is subject to at least some public policy limitations. This is particularly true with respect to indemnification expressly prohibited by statutory provisions other than the non-exclusivity provision. The leading case is *Waltuch v. Conticommodity Services, Inc.*,[634] a Second Circuit decision construing Delaware law. *Waltuch* involved a former corporate officer who did not contend that he had acted in good faith[635] and thus did not contend that he had acted in accordance with Section 145(a) of Delaware's statute, which, as discussed earlier in this Chapter,[636] permits indemnification where the person to be indemnified has "acted in good faith and in a manner the

---

629. Former Model Bus. Corp. Act § 8.58(a).

630. *Changes in the Model Business Corporation Act—Amendments Pertaining to Indemnification and Advance for Expenses*, 49 Bus. Law. 741, 748 (1994).

631. Model Bus. Corp. Act Annotated § 8.58(c).

632. 12 C.F.R. § 545.121(f).

633. *Id.; see also Fidelity Federal Sav. & Loan Ass'n v. Felicetti*, 830 F. Supp. 262, 265 (E.D. Pa. 1993) ("while the OTS regulations are exclusive, if an association . . . has a bylaw which governs indemnification, the association is bound by the bylaw rather than the OTS regulation").

634. 88 F.3d 87 (2d Cir. 1996).

635. *Id.* at 95.

636. *See* Chapter V, Section A 4 a.

person reasonably believed to be in or not opposed to the best interests of the corporation."[637] Indemnification was sought solely pursuant to the non-exclusivity provision in Section 145(f) of Delaware's statute and a certificate of incorporation provision providing in relevant part—and with no requirement of "good faith"—as follows:

> The Corporation shall indemnify and hold harmless each of its incumbent or former directors, officers, employees and agents . . . against expenses actually and necessarily incurred by him in connection with the defense of any action, suit or proceeding threatened, pending or completed, in which he is made a party, by reason of his serving in or having held such position or capacity, except in relation to matters as to which he shall be adjudged in such action, suit or proceeding to be liable for negligence or misconduct in the performance of duty.[638]

The court held that Section 145(f) permits indemnification rights "broader than those set out in the statute," but that indemnification under Section 145(f) "cannot be inconsistent with the 'scope' of the corporation's power to indemnify, as delineated in the statute's substantive provisions."[639] The court accordingly held that by requiring indemnification even where the person to be indemnified acted in bad faith, the certificate provision relied upon by the former officer seeking indemnification was "inconsistent with § 145(a) and thus exceeds the scope of a Delaware corporation's power to indemnify."[640]

The court explained that Sections 145(a) and (b), which govern permissive indemnification, grant corporations the power to indemnify, while Section 145(f)'s non-exclusivity provision grants "rights" to directors, officers and others but does not provide the corporation "power" to indemnify that the corporation does not otherwise possess. In the court's words:

637. Del. Gen. Corp. Law § 145(a).
638. 88 F.3d at 89.
639. *Id.* at 92.
640. *Id.* at 95.

Subsections (a) (indemnification for third-party actions) and (b) (similar indemnification for derivative suits) expressly grant a corporation the power to indemnify directors, officers, and others, if they "acted in good faith and in a manner reasonably believed to be in or not opposed to the best interest of the corporation." These provisions thus limit the scope of the power that they confer. They are permissive in the sense that a corporation may exercise less than its full power to grant the indemnification rights set out in these provisions. By the same token, subsection (f) permits the corporation to grant additional rights: the rights provided in the rest of § 145 "shall not be deemed exclusive of any other rights to which those seeking indemnification may be entitled." But crucially, subsection (f) merely acknowledges that one seeking indemnification may be entitled to "other rights" (of indemnification or otherwise); it does not speak in terms of corporate power, and therefore cannot be read to free a corporation from the "good faith" limit explicitly imposed in subsections (a) and (b).[641]

The court stated that any other construction of Sections 145(a), (b) and (f) "would effectively force us to ignore certain explicit terms of the statute."[642] According to the court, Section 145(a) empowers corporations to indemnify directors and officers who act "in good faith and in a manner reasonably believed to be in or not opposed to the best interest of the corporation," and "[t]his statutory limit must mean that there is no power to indemnify" where the person to be indemnified did not act in good faith.[643] "Otherwise, . . . § 145(a)—and its good faith clause—would have no meaning: a corporation could indemnify whomever and however it wished regardless of the good faith clause or anything else the Delaware Legislature wrote into § 145(a)."[644]

The court also pointed to Section 145(g) of Delaware's statute, pursuant to which, as discussed later in this Chapter,[645] corporations are granted corporate power to "circumvent the 'good

---

641. *Id.* at 92-93 (citation and footnote omitted).
642. *Id.* at 93.
643. *Id.*
644. *Id.*
645. *See* Chapter V, Section B 1.

faith' clause of subsection (a) by purchasing a directors and officers liability insurance policy."[646] Section 145(g), the court stated, "is framed as a grant of corporate power":

> A corporation shall have power to purchase and maintain insurance on behalf of any person who is or was a director, officer, employee or agent of the corporation . . . against any liability asserted against him and incurred by him in any such capacity, or arising out of his status as such, *whether or not the corporation would have the power to indemnify him against such liability under this section.*[647]

The court stated that the language in Section 145(g) italicized above demonstrates that "corporations have the power under § 145 to indemnify in some situations and not in others":

> Since § 145(f) is neither a grant of corporate power nor a limitation on such power, subsection (g) must be referring to the limitations set out in § 145(a) and the other provisions of § 145 that describe corporate power. If § 145 (through subsection (f) or another part of the statute) gave corporations unlimited power to indemnify directors and officers, then the final clause of subsection (g) would be unnecessary: that is, its grant of "power to purchase and maintain insurance" (exercisable regardless of whether the corporation itself would have the power to indemnify the loss directly) is meaningful only because, in some insurable situations, the corporation simply lacks the power to indemnify its directors and officers directly.[648]

The court also pointed to legislative history demonstrating that the drafters of Section 145 believed that revision of Delaware's statutory authorization of indemnification "was appropriate with respect to the limitations which must necessarily be placed on the power to indemnify in order to prevent the statute from undermining the substantive provisions of the criminal law and corporation law."[649] There was a need, the drafters stated, for Section 145

---

646. 88 F.3d at 93.

647. *Id.* (quoting Del. Gen. Corp. Law § 145(g); emphasis added by court).

648. *Id.* at 93.

649. *Id.* at 94 (quoting Arsht & Stapleton, *Delaware's New General*
(continued...)

"to protect the corporation law's requirement of loyalty to the corporation," and "[u]ltimately it was decided that the power to indemnify should not be granted unless it appeared that the person seeking indemnification had 'acted in good faith and in a manner reasonably believed to be in or not opposed to the best interest of the corporation.'"[650] This legislative history, the court stated, "makes clear that a corporation has no power to transgress the indemnification limits set out in the substantive provisions of § 145."[651]

The court rejected the contention by the former corporate officer who sought indemnification that "reading § 145(a) to bar the indemnification of officers who acted in bad faith would render § 145(f) meaningless."[652] The court explained that Section 145(f) refers to "any other rights to which those seeking indemnification or advancement of expenses may be entitled," and there are "various indemnification rights that are 'beyond those provided by statute' and that are at the same time consistent with the statute."[653] Quoting an article co-authored by E. Norman Veasey, then a member of the Delaware bar and now the Chief Justice of the Delaware Supreme Court, the court stated as follows:

> Subsection (f) provides general authorization for the adoption of various procedures and presumptions making the process of indemnification more favorable to the indemnitee. For example, indemnification agreements or by-laws could provide for: (i) mandatory indemnification unless prohibited by statute; (ii) mandatory advancement of expenses, which the indemnitee can, in many instances, obtain on demand; (iii) accelerated procedures for the "determination" required by section 145(d) to be made in the "specific case"; (iv) litigation "appeal" rights of the indemnitee in the event of an unfavorable determination; (v) procedures under which a

---

649. (...continued)

*Corporation Law: Substantive Changes*, 23 Bus. Law. 75, 77-78 (1967)).

    650. *Id.*

    651. *Id.* at 94.

    652. *Id.*

    653. *Id.* (quoting *Hibbert v. Hollywood Park, Inc.*, 457 A.2d 339, 344 (Del. 1983)).

favorable determination will be deemed to have been made under circumstances where the board fails or refuses to act; [and] (vi) reasonable funding mechanisms.[654]

The Delaware Court of Chancery in *Mayer v. Executive Telecard, Ltd.*[655] has stated that "[t]his Court agrees with the Second Circuit's construction of § 145 that a Delaware corporation lacks the power to indemnify a party who did not act in good faith."[656] Another federal court construing Delaware law, in *Choate, Hall & Stewart v. SCA Services, Inc.*,[657] similarly has observed that "it is generally accepted that an agreement to indemnify within § 145(f), to survive into enforceability, must be able to withstand an attack on grounds of policy or basic equity, that is, a defense amounting to illegality."[658] Numerous commentators agree that there are public policy limitations upon non-exclusivity provisions.[659]

A pre-*Waltuch* decision by a federal district court within the Second Circuit—*PepsiCo, Inc. v. Continental Casualty Co.*[660]—

---

654. *Id.* at 94 (quoting Veasey, Finkelstein & Bigler, *Delaware Supports Directors with a Three-Legged Stool of Limited Liability, Indemnification and Insurance*, 42 Bus. Law. 399, 415 (1987)); *see also Mayer v. Executive Telecard, Ltd.*, 705 A.2d 220, 225 (Del. Ch. 1997) ("[a]rguably, § 145(f), which provides that the statutory indemnification provisions shall not be deemed exclusive of any other indemnification rights established by bylaw or other agreement, would permit a bylaw that explicitly allows indemnification of 'fees for fees'" incurred in enforcing a right to indemnification); Model Bus. Corp. Act Annotated § 8.59 Official Comment at 8-384.1 (discussed above).

655. 705 A.2d 220 (Del. Ch. 1997).

656. *Id.* at 224 n.6.

657. 495 N.E.2d 562 (Mass. App. Ct. 1986).

658. *Id.* at 566.

659. *See* 1 R. Franklin Balotti & Jesse A. Finkelstein, *The Delaware Law of Corporations and Business Organizations* § 4.26 (3d ed. 1998); John F. Olson & Josiah O. Hatch III, *Director and Officer Liability: Indemnification and Insurance* § 5.04[5], at 5–40-42 (1997); Arsht & Stapleton, 23 Bus. Law. at 79-80; Sebring, *Recent Legislative Changes in the Law of Indemnification of Directors, Officers and Others*, 23 Bus. Law. 95, 105 (1967); Veasey, Finkelstein & Bigler, 42 Bus. Law. at 413-15.

660. 640 F. Supp. 656 (S.D.N.Y. 1986).

held that the Delaware statute's non-exclusivity provision permits corporations to grant indemnification without adherence to any of the procedural requirements otherwise governing permissive indemnification, and characterized Sections 145(a) and (b) of Delaware's statute as "'backstop' provisions."[661] The Second Circuit in *Waltuch* expressed its disagreement with the decision in *PepsiCo*.[662] Delaware observers likewise have concluded that although Delaware's non-exclusivity provision "does provide support for wideranging agreements or by-laws that broaden upon indemnification rights granted in the other subsections" of Delaware's indemnification statute, "[i]t is questionable whether a Delaware court would be quite" as "sweeping" as the *PepsiCo* court "in its language in a case . . . involving the outer limits" of the authority provided in Section 145(f).[663] Rather, these commentators—like the Second Circuit in *Waltuch*—conclude that indemnification provisions that "are contrary to the limitations or prohibitions set forth in other section 145 subsections, other statutes, court decisions, or public policy may be unenforceable."[664]

Pennsylvania's non-exclusivity statute eliminates the issue of public policy constraints by providing that indemnification authorized by a corporation pursuant to a non-exclusivity provision is permitted "whether or not the corporation would have the power to indemnify the person under any other provision of law."[665] Except in the case of willful misconduct or recklessness, the Pennsylvania statute states, indemnification granted pursuant to a non-exclusivity provision that the corporation would not have the

---

661. *Id.* at 660-61; *see also* Chapter V, Sections A 3 a-b (discussing procedural requirements governing permissive indemnification).

662. *Waltuch*, 88 F.3d at 94-95 n.8.

663. Veasey, Finkelstein & Bigler, 42 Bus. Law. at 415; *see also* R. Balotti & J. Finkelstein § 4.26, at 4-100.

664. Veasey, Finkelstein & Bigler, 42 Bus. Law. at 415; *see also* R. Balotti & J. Finkelstein § 4.26, at 4-100 ("provisions in . . . a by-law or agreement which are contrary to limitations or prohibitions set forth in the other subsections [of Section 145] may be held to be unenforceable if they violate other statutes, court decisions or public policy").

665. Pa. Bus. Corp. Law §§ 1746(b), (c); Pa. Corp. Law §§ 518 (b), (c).

power to grant under any other provision of law is "consistent with the public policy of this Commonwealth."[666] Several other non-exclusivity statutes deal directly with the question whether indemnification of judgments and/or amounts paid to settle actions by or in the right of the corporation not otherwise permitted by the statute may be permitted pursuant to a non-exclusivity provision. These statutes are discussed earlier in this Chapter.[667]

## 11. Public Policy Limitations

"Basic tenets of public policy"[668] (beyond the public policy issues raised by non-exclusivity provisions)[669] also may limit indemnification. As explained by the drafters of the Model Business Corporation Act:

> It is inappropriate to permit management to use corporate funds to avoid the consequences of certain conduct. For example, a director who intentionally inflicts harm on the corporation should not expect to receive assistance from the corporation for legal or other expenses and should be required to satisfy from his personal assets not only any adverse judgment but also expenses incurred in connection with the proceeding. Any other rule would tend to encourage socially undesirable conduct.[670]

The drafters of the Model Act add that "[a] further policy issue is raised in connection with indemnification against liabilities or sanctions imposed under state or federal civil or criminal statutes."[671] "A shift of the economic cost of these liabilities from the individual director to the corporation by way of indemnification," the drafters explain, "may in some instances frustrate the public policy of those statutes."[672]

---

666. *Id.*

667. *See* Chapter V, Section A 4 b.

668. 2 Model Bus. Corp. Act Annotated §§ 8.50-8.59 Introductory Comment at 8-289 (3d ed. 1996).

669. *See* Chapter V, Section A 10.

670. Model Bus. Corp. Act Annotated §§ 8.50-8.59 Introductory Comment at 8–289-90.

671. *Id.* at 8-290.

672. *Id.; see also* 41 American Jurisprudence 2d *Indemnity* §§ 1, 8-

(continued...)

The leading case is the Second Circuit's decision in *Globus v. Law Research Service, Inc.*[673] In *Globus*, indemnification was not allowed in an action under Section 10(b) of the Securities Exchange Act of 1934[674] where an issuer and an underwriter were found liable for misconduct involving "actual knowledge" and "wanton indifference" to legal obligations.[675] The Second Circuit stated that "one cannot insure himself against his own reckless, willful or criminal misconduct."[676]

Several courts have extended the *Globus* principle to reach conduct less culpable than willful or reckless conduct and claims, including under Section 11 and 12(2) of the Securities Act of 1933.[677] The Third Circuit in *Eichenholtz v. Brennan*,[678] for example, found an indemnification agreement between an issuer and an underwriter to be contrary to public policy and unenforceable with respect to claims arising under Sections 11 and 12.[679] The Fourth Circuit in *Baker, Watts & Co. v. Miles & Stockbridge*[680] dismissed indemnification claims by a corporation found to have violated Section 12(2) against a law firm that represented the corporation in connection with the offering underlying the Section 12(2) claims.[681] The court stated that "[a]lthough a right to indemnification may not be preempted in each and every circumstance, we reject plaintiff's assertion that federal policy against indemnification extends only to intentional wrongdoing. The goal of the 1933

---

672. (...continued)
9, 11, 12, 25 (1995 & Supp. 1998) (indemnification under the common law or pursuant to an express or implied contract for intentional wrongdoing or illegal conduct generally is contrary to public policy); 42 Corpus Juris Secundum *Indemnity* §§ 2, 3, 13a, 29 (1991 & Supp. 1997) (same).

673. 418 F.2d 1276 (2d Cir. 1969), *cert. denied*, 397 U.S. 913 (1970).

674. 15 U.S.C. § 78j(b).

675. *Id.* at 1288.

676. *Id.*

677. 15 U.S.C. §§ 77k, 77l(2).

678. 52 F.3d 478 (3d Cir. 1995).

679. *Id.* at 483-85.

680. 876 F.2d 1101 (4th Cir. 1989).

681. *Id.* at 1108.

and 1934 Acts is preventative as well as remedial, and 'denying indemnification encourages the reasonable care required by the federal securities provisions.'" The Ninth Circuit in *Laventhol, Krekstein, Horwath & Horwath v. Horwitch*[682] dismissed indemnification claims by an underwriter and an accountant against an issuer and officers of the issuer for Section 11 liability. As in *Baker*, the court stated that "permitting indemnity would undermine the statutory purpose of assuring diligent performance of duty and deterring negligence."[683] The Fifth and Seventh Circuits in *Stowell v. Ted S. Finkel Investment Services, Inc.* [684] and *Heizer Corp. v. Ross*[685] similarly stated that "[a] securities wrongdoer should not be permitted to escape loss by shifting his entire responsibility to another party," and that the 1933 and 1934 Securities Acts "do not provide anywhere for indemnification under any circumstances."[686]

Other courts, including courts addressing indemnification of directors and officers (rather than indemnification of underwriters, law firms and accountants, as in cases such as *Globus, Eichenholtz, Baker* and *Laventhol*), have construed the *Globus* principle much more narrowly. The Second Circuit—the court that decided *Globus* —in *Wisener v. Air Express International Corp.*,[687] a case construing Illinois law, stated that "a corporation may commit itself to

---

682. 637 F.2d 672 (9th Cir. 1980), *cert. denied*, 452 U.S. 963 (1981).

683. *Id.* at 676; *see also In re Crazy Eddie Sec. Litig.*, 740 F. Supp. 149, 151 (E.D.N.Y. 1990) ("Peat Marwick argues that indemnification is available for merely negligent violations of the Securities Act. A number of courts have rejected this argument as inconsistent with the purpose of the Act"); *Odette v. Shearson, Hammill & Co.*, 394 F. Supp. 946, 956-57 (S.D.N.Y. 1975) (no indemnification permitted for Section 12(2) claims or claims under Section 10(b)); *Kennedy v. Josepthal & Co.*, [1982-1983 Transfer Binder] Fed. Sec. L. Rep. (CCH) ¶ 99,204, at 95,821-22 (D. Mass. May 9, 1983) ("it is the purpose of the federal securities laws to deter conduct that is merely negligent").

684. 641 F.2d 323 (5th Cir. 1981).

685. 601 F.2d 330 (7th Cir. 1979).

686. *Heizer*, 601 F.2d at 334, *quoted in Stowell*, 641 F.2d at 325.

687. 583 F.2d 579 (2d Cir. 1978).

indemnify its officers and directors for litigation expenses incurred in defending against liability for actions taken in carrying out corporate responsibilities, even though negligent, if the corporation finds it in the corporate interest to undertake such a commitment."[688]

The court in *Raychem Corp. v. Federal Insurance Co.*[689] distinguished *Globus* and its progeny in the context of a federal securities law action that was settled without a finding or admission of liability. According to the court in *Raychem*, a corporation may voluntarily determine to indemnify its officers and directors for settlement payments and defense costs in such a case.[690] The court in *Raychem* stated that "allowing a corporation to indemnify its officers and directors for settlement payments and defense costs supports two competing public policies: encouraging qualified individuals to serve as corporate officers and directors, and encouraging settlement . . . . Thus, federal law does not prohibit Raychem's indemnification of its officers and directors for settlement payments and defense costs."[691]

The court in *Steinberg v. Pargas, Inc.*[692] likewise stated that "[s]urely, an agreement providing for the payment of an officer's or director's legal expenses resulting from meritless claims . . . is enforceable. In fact, in *Globus*, the Second Circuit expressly left open the possibility that an indemnity agreement could be enforced where the corporate official's liability arises from mere negligence."[693] In the words of the court in *Cambridge Fund, Inc. v. Abella*[694]: "Read *most liberally*," *Globus* and its progeny "stand for the proposition that it is against public policy to allow a party who has been adjudicated to have been engaged in reckless, wilful

---

688. *Id.* at 581.

689. 853 F. Supp. 1170 (N.D. Cal. 1994).

690. *Id.* at 1177.

691. 853 F. Supp. at 1177.

692. [1984-1985 Transfer Binder] Fed. Sec. L. Rep. (CCH) ¶ 91,979 (S.D.N.Y. Mar. 18, 1985).

693. *Id.* at 90,882.

694. 501 F. Supp. 598 (S.D.N.Y. 1980).

or criminal conduct to shift his liability to others."[695] The court in *Cambridge Fund* thus held that indemnification of corporate agents was not barred by public policy because there had been "no adjudication of willfulness—only the entry of a consent order with such findings."[696]

*Commodity Futures Trading Commission v. Richards*[697] illustrates these principles in the context of a decision denying a motion to dismiss an indemnification claim based upon a bylaw provision requiring indemnification of corporate officers for fines and amounts paid to settle claims provided that the officer acted in good faith and in a manner reasonably believed to be in or not opposed to the corporation's best interests.[698] The case involved (1) an investigation of Thomas Richards and Kemper Financial Services, Inc. by the Commodity Futures Trading Commission concerning conduct by Richards as a Kemper officer and (2) administrative and civil proceedings brought by the Commission against Richards and Kemper. Prior to the resolution of the Commission's proceedings, Richards and Kemper entered into a settlement agreement resolving claims Richards had asserted against Kemper. As part of the settlement agreement, Kemper acknowledged that it had reviewed the circumstances of the Commission's investigation and "had determined that Richards at all times acted in good faith and

---

695. *Id.* at 618-19.

696. *Id.* at 619; *see also Heffernan v. Pacific Dunlop GNB Corp.*, 965 F.2d 369 (7th Cir. 1992) (rejecting contention that public policy bars indemnification of a settlement of claims alleging violations of Section 12(2), without consideration of *Globus*); *PepsiCo, Inc. v. Continental Casualty Co.*, 640 F. Supp. 656, 660 (S.D.N.Y. 1986) (same as *Heffernan*, with respect to alleged violations of Section 10(b)); *Sequa Corp. v. Gelmin*, 828 F. Supp. 203, 206-07 (S.D.N.Y. 1993) (rejecting contention that the filing of a claim under the Racketeer Influenced and Corrupt Organizations Act ("RICO"), 18 U.S.C. §§ 1961-1968, against a former corporate officer deprived the former officer of any right he otherwise would have had under state law to ask the court to order that the corporation advance litigation expenses).

697. 1996 U.S. Dist. LEXIS 5359, 1996 WL 199729 (N.D. Ill. Apr. 23, 1996).

698. 1996 U.S. Dist. LEXIS 5359, at *2, 1996 WL 199729, at *1.

in a manner reasonably believed to be in or not opposed to the best interest of Kemper."[699] A short time later, Richards entered into a settlement agreement with the Commission "without any adjudication on the merits" and agreed to pay a civil penalty of $200,000. Richards then sought indemnification from Kemper for the $200,000 owed to the Commission.[700]

The court denied Kemper's motion to dismiss Richard's indemnification claim. The court distinguished cases that have refused to allow indemnification on the ground that those cases involved individuals found to have violated the securities laws.[701] The court also pointed to the distinction in *Raychem* of cases denying indemnification claims on the ground that those cases did not involve "a corporation indemnifying its officers and directors for settlement payments and defense costs."[702] The court rejected a contention that even if indemnification were allowed for settlement payments, civil penalties should be treated differently. At least for the purpose of deciding a motion to dismiss, the court explained, "Richards may be able to establish that he entered into a settlement with the Commission and that the $200,000 is a settlement payment."[703]

The court in *Heffernan v. Pacific Dunlop GNB Corp.*[704] rejected a claim that non-exclusivity provisions were unenforceable because they "seemingly indemnify directors for violations of federal securities laws in certain circumstances."[705] The court acknowledged that "there is some question" regarding whether indemnification can be obtained for a securities law violation but concluded that the corporation that was seeking to avoid paying

---

699. 1996 U.S. Dist. LEXIS 5359, at *3, 1996 WL 199729, at *1.
700. 1996 U.S. Dist. LEXIS 5359, at *4, 1996 WL 199729, at *2.
701. 1996 U.S. Dist. LEXIS 5359, at *10, 1996 WL 199729, at *4.

702. *Id.*
703. 1996 U.S. Dist. LEXIS 5359, at *13, 1996 WL 199729, at *5.

704. 1993 U.S. Dist. LEXIS 5, 1993 WL 3553 (N.D. Ill. Jan. 5, 1993).
705. 1993 U.S. Dist. LEXIS 5, at *17, 1993 WL 3553, at *6.

indemnification "provides no authority for the proposition that a court should strike as invalid a duly adopted bylaw provision that purports to permit such indemnification."[706]

The Securities and Exchange Commission's long-standing view is that an issuer's indemnification of directors or officers for liability for any claim under the Securities Act of 1933 is contrary to public policy.[707] The SEC enforces this view by threatening to deny acceleration to registrants who fail to disclose the SEC's policy and do not undertake that if a claim for indemnification against liability under the 1933 Act is made, "the registrant will, unless in the opinion of its counsel the matter has been settled by controlling precedent, submit to a court of appropriate jurisdiction the question whether such indemnification by it is against public policy as expressed in the Act and will be governed by the final adjudication of such issue."[708] As one commentator has explained the practical effect of the SEC's policy:

> [M]ost public offerings would be impossible if the registrant, after filing its "price amendment" (i.e., setting the price at which the issue will be sold), had to wait while the statutory [twenty-day] period, which starts afresh after every amendment, ran again. The market will not hold still that long. It is the general policy of the commission, however, upon request, to permit acceleration of the effective date of the registration statement as soon as possible after the filing of appropriate amendments. The power to grant or deny acceleration has thus been an effective club to insure respect for a number of the SEC's policies, including that with respect to indemnification.[709]

Wisconsin's indemnification and insurance statute explicitly permits "indemnification, allowance of expenses and insurance for any liability incurred in connection with . . . any proceeding involving a federal or state statute, rule or regulation regulating the

---

706. 1993 U.S. Dist. LEXIS 5, at *17-18, 1993 WL 3553, at *6.

707. 17 C.F.R. §§ 229.510, 229.512(h)(3).

708. *Id.* § 229.512(h)(3).

709. Joseph W. Bishop, Jr., *Law of Corporate Officers and Directors: Indemnification and Insurance* ¶ 9.08, at 9-16 (1981 & Supp. 1997).

offer, sale or purchase of securities, security brokers or dealers, or investment companies or investment advisors."[710]

## 12. Funding Mechanisms

Corporations also have sought to maximize indemnification rights by establishing funding mechanisms that segregate indemnification and advancement funds and that require the automatic release of these funds whenever certain procedures are followed. One example of such a funding mechanism is a letter of credit requiring a bank or other party to take the risk that the corporation will not pay the indemnification (for example, because of bankruptcy or a new board's refusal to pay following a change in control). Another example is a trust fund structured to release assets upon a determination by an independent trustee that a claimant is entitled to indemnification. Care should be taken in establishing trusts of this type in order to ensure that creditors and receivers cannot reach trust assets in the event of insolvency.[711]

Such care was not taken by the drafters of the directors and officers liability trust in *Askanase v. LivingWell, Inc.*[712] The trust in this case provided that "[c]hanges to this Trust Agreement may be made at any time or from time to time by the Company by resolution of its Board of Directors, and that in no case shall an amendment affect the rights, duties or responsibilities of the Trustee or the Administrator without its consent."[713] This language, the court stated, granted the corporation's board of directors "a nearly unlimited power of amendment" and thus permitted a "bankruptcy trustee, who succeeded to the rights of the board of directors of the

---

710. Wis. Bus. Corp. Law § 180.0859.

711. *See* John F. Olson & Josiah O. Hatch III, *Director and Officer Liability: Indemnification and Insurance* §§ 7.16, 9.02, 9.05-9.07 (1997); Johnston, *D & O Insurance Crisis: How to Fund Indemnification Arrangements*, 1 Insights: The Corporate & Securities Law Advisor No. 2, Aug. 1987, at 3; Polance & Graul, *Indemnification Trusts: Tax and Accounting Implications*, Insights: The Corporate & Securities Law Advisor, July 1988, at 19.

712. 45 F.3d 103 (5th Cir. 1995).

713. *Id.* at 106-07.

corporation" following the corporation's bankruptcy, to amend the trust fund to terminate the fund and then commence litigation against former directors and officers.[714] The court noted, however, that upon termination the amounts held by the trust fund were to be distributed "to the Company."[715] "Because LivingWell's bylaws provided for indemnification (independent of the insurance trust) of officers and directors to the maximum extent permissible under the laws of Delaware," the court stated, "claims for indemnification of the former officers or directors not covered by the trust as terminated" can "be pursued as claims against the bankruptcy estate."[716]

A federal court applying Delaware law—*Security America Corp. v. Walsh, Case, Coale, Brown & Burke*[717]—has upheld irrevocable and unamendable trusts established in the face of an imminent change of control in order to provide for advancement of expenses to the corporation's outgoing directors.[718] The court acknowledged contentions by the corporation's new board that "the trusts disable the corporation from reviewing a discretionary decision on a continuing basis and that there is no guarantee that the defendants can ever repay," that the trusts "put beyond the reach of the present management the decision not to advance expenses, a decision which is normally reviewable," and that there was no certainty of repayments.[719] The court concluded, however, that the corporation's bylaws, "adopted long before this dispute arose, contemplated such advances and the directors accepted their positions with that knowledge."[720] The court also concluded that "the present management had the pronounced intention not to exercise discretion but to terminate litigation support," and that the likelihood that the corporation "would in the future be able to respond

---

714. *Id.* at 106, 107.

715. *Id.* at 107.

716. *Id.* at 107 n.4.

717. 1985 U.S. Dist. LEXIS 23482, 1985 WL 225 (N.D. Ill. Jan. 11, 1985).

718. 1985 U.S. Dist. LEXIS 23482 at *12, 1985 WL 225 at *4.

719. *Id.*

720. *Id.*

to a legal obligation to indemnify was far more questionable than the likelihood that defendants, collectively, could repay."[721] The court stated that for these reasons and in light of the strong public policy supporting indemnification under Delaware law, "this court is persuaded that the trusts, in the circumstances presented here, were permissible."[722]

A small number of states have enacted statutes that specifically authorize outside funding arrangements of this type.[723] Two of these statutes also provide that in the absence of fraud a board decision concerning the terms and conditions of outside funding arrangements is "conclusive" and that no director can be held liable

---

721. *Id.*

722. *Id.; cf. Hills Stores Co. v. Bozic,* 23 Del. J. Corp. L. 230 (Del. Ch. Mar. 25, 1997) (denying motion to dismiss a complaint alleging that the establishment and funding of a trust providing for the immediate payment of "golden parachute" severance agreements constituted a breach of fiduciary duty); *see also* Chapter III, Section H 2 d (discussing *Hills Stores* decision).

723. *See* Ala. Bus. Corp. Act § 10-2B-8.57 (authorizing insurance or "similar protection (including but not limited to trust funds, self-insurance reserves or the like")); La. Bus. Corp. Law § 12:83(F)(1) ("a corporation may create a trust fund or other form of self-insurance arrangement for the benefit of persons indemnified by the corporation"); Md. Gen. Corp. Law 2-418(k)(2) (authorizing protection "including a trust fund, letter of credit, or surety bond"); Nev. Gen. Corp. Law § 78.752(2) (authorizing the creation of a trust fund, the "securing of [the corporation's] obligation of indemnification by granting a security interest or other lien on any assets of the corporation," and the "establishment of a letter of credit, guaranty or surety"); N.M. Bus. Corp. Act § 53-11-4.1(J) (authorizing a trust fund or letter of credit); Ohio Gen. Corp. Law § 1701.13(E)(7) (authorizing protection "including but not limited to trust funds [and] letters of credit"); Pa. Bus. Corp. Law § 1746(a), Pa. Corp. Law § 518(a) ("[a] corporation may create a fund of any nature, which may, but need not be, under the control of a trustee, or otherwise secure or insure in any manner its indemnification obligations"); Tex. Bus. Corp. Act § 2.02-1(R) ("a corporation may, for the benefit of persons indemnified by the corporation, (1) create a trust fund; (2) establish any form of self-insurance; (3) secure its indemnity obligation by grant of a security interest or other lien on the assets of the corporation; or (4) establish a letter of credit, guaranty, or surety arrangement").

for the adoption of such funding arrangements, even where the director is a beneficiary of the arrangement.[724]

## 13. Notice to Shareholders

The Delaware and California indemnification provisions do not require shareholder notification of indemnification payments. The New York statute, by contrast, requires that a corporation report to shareholders the purchase or maintenance of D & O insurance and any indemnification or insurance payments that are made.[725] These notification provisions do not expressly apply to advancement, but commentators have suggested that "New York corporations may find it prudent to notify stockholders generally that expenses are being advanced for defense of pending actions rather than reporting retroactively that such advancements have evolved into a sizeable indemnification obligation."[726]

Principles of Corporate Governance requires the reporting of indemnification or advancement in connection with a proceeding by or in the right of the corporation.[727] The Model Business Corporation Act requires notice "in writing" to shareholders "with or before the notice of the next shareholders' meeting" of indemnification or advancement to directors in connection with a proceeding by or in the right of the corporation.[728] The drafters of the Model Act explain that "[s]ome academic criticism of earlier versions of the Model Act pointed out the possible evil of secret payments of indemnification which may or may not be consistent with the standards set forth in the Act."[729] The drafters add that

---

724. Nev. Gen. Corp. Law § 78.752(4); Tex. Bus. Corp. Act § 2.02-1(R).

725. N.Y. Bus. Corp. Law §§ 725(c), 726(d).

726. John F. Olson & Josiah O. Hatch III, *Director and Officer Liability: Indemnification and Insurance* § 5.04[5], at 5-42 (1997).

727. 2 Principles of Corporate Governance: Analysis and Recommendations § 7.20(d) (1994).

728. 4 Model Bus. Corp. Act Annotated § 16.21(a) (3d. ed. 1996).

729. *Id.* Official Comment at 16-86.

"the use of corporate funds for this purpose is a legitimate matter of interest to shareholders."[730]

## B.  Insurance

### 1.  Statutory Provisions Authorizing Insurance

The overwhelming majority of indemnification statutes authorize corporations to purchase and maintain insurance for directors, officers, employees and agents for both indemnifiable and non-indemnifiable liabilities. Delaware's statute is typical:

> A corporation shall have power to purchase and maintain insurance on behalf of any person who is or was a director, officer, employee or agent of the corporation . . . against any liability asserted against such person and incurred by such person in any such capacity, or arising out of such person's status as such, whether or not the corporation would have the power to indemnify such person against such liability under this section.[731]

The Model Business Corporation Act is worded similarly but adds the words "or advance expenses" after the words "power to indemnify."[732]

Limitations on the extent of insurance coverage may be supplied by insurance law or by public policy considerations. In the words of one of the Delaware statute's drafters:

> Those who criticize this subsection believe that it permits a corporation to insure its directors at the corporation's expense for all sorts of wrongdoing, intentional or otherwise, and thereby insulate them from the consequences of their misdeeds. Nothing is further from the truth. The section does not purport to do that, and I think it cannot fairly be read to authorize that, since subsection (g) is a corporation law, not an insurance law. When we drafted the subsection, we did not purport to restate what we knew the insurance law to be

---

730. *Id.*

731. Del. Gen. Corp. Law § 145(g); *see also* Cal. Gen. Corp. Law § 317(i) (similar language).

732. 2 Model Bus. Corp. Act Annotated § 8.57 (3d ed. 1996).

and what we knew the invariable practices of insurance companies to be. We knew that insurance is not obtainable against the kind of wrongdoing that the critics conjure up. We knew that it is against public policy to insure a director against liability for his own deliberate wrongdoing of the kind the critics describe. We also knew that no insurance company would write such a policy even if the law itself did not prohibit it. Therefore, we did not think that it was necessary to write into this corporation law a provision to the effect that no insurance company shall write a policy which purports to insure a person against the consequences of his deliberate wrongdoing. D & O liability policies are not obtainable for anything more serious than negligent misconduct.[733]

The drafters of the Model Business Corporation Act state that the Model Act's provision authorizing insurance "is not intended to set the outer limits on the type of insurance which a corporation may maintain or the persons to be covered. Rather, it is included to remove 'any doubt as to the power to carry insurance and to maintain it on behalf of directors, officers, employees and agents.'"[734]

New York's statute is more specific than the Delaware statute and the Model Act. New York's statute authorizes corporations to provide insurance for corporate directors and officers in "instances in which they may not otherwise be indemnified," provided that the insurance policy contains retention and co-insurance provisions "acceptable to the superintendent of insurance."[735] The New York statute explicitly bars insurance against liability for payments other

---

733. Arsht, *Indemnification Under Section 145 of the Delaware General Corporation Law*, 3 Del. J. Corp. L. 176, 179-80 (1978); *see also* Klink, Chalif, Bishop & Arsht, *Liabilities Which Can Be Covered Under State Statutes and Corporate By-Laws*, 27 Bus. Law. 109, 127 (1972) (Del. Gen. Corp. Law § 145(g) "is a corporation law, not an insurance law. . . . If a risk were not insurable before Subsection (g), the subsection's enactment did not make it so.").

734. Model Bus. Corp. Act Annotated § 8.57 Official Comment at 8-376 (quoting Sebring, *Recent Legislative Changes in the Law of Indemnification of Directors, Officers and Others*, 23 Bus. Law. 95, 106 (1967)).

735. N.Y. Bus. Corp. Law § 726(a)(3).

than defense costs whenever (1) "a judgment or other final adjudication" establishes that the insured committed "acts of active and
deliberative dishonesty" or "personally gained . . . a financial
profit or other advantage to which he was not legally entitled," or
(2) the insurance relates "to any risk the insurance of which is prohibited under the insurance law of this state."[736]

Underlying these limitations is a declaration in the New York
statute that it is "the public policy of this state to spread the risk of
corporate management, notwithstanding any other general or special
law of this state or of any other jurisdiction including the federal
government."[737] New York's only reported decision discussing
the validity of a directors and officers liability insurance policy,
*Flintkote Co. v. Lloyd's Underwriters*,[738] relied upon this expression of public policy and upheld the propriety of insurance for legal
fees and expenses—not fines or penalties—incurred by two officer-
directors who pleaded *nolo contendere* after being indicted for
criminal violations of the Sherman Act.[739]

Principles of Corporate Governance: Analysis and Recommendations utilizes language similar to the Delaware model.[740]
Principles of Corporate Governance, however, adds that "[a] corporation should not be entitled to purchase insurance . . . to the extent
that the insurance would furnish protection against liability for
conduct directly involving a knowing and culpable violation of law
or involving a significant pecuniary benefit obtained by an insured
person to which the person is not legally entitled."[741]

In the federal savings association context, insurance may not
be obtained that "provides for payment of losses of any person

---

736. *Id.* § 726(b).

737. *Id.* § 726(e).

738. 1976 WL 16591 (N.Y. Sup. Ct. N.Y. Co. July 27, 1976),
*aff'd mem.*, 56 A.D.2d 743, 391 N.Y.S.2d 1005 (N.Y. App. Div. 1st
Dep't 1977).

739. 1976 WL 16591, at *5.

740. 2 Principles of Corporate Governance: Analysis and Recommendations § 7.20(a)(4) (1994).

741. *Id.* § 7.20(b)(2).

incurred as a consequence of his or her willful or criminal misconduct."[742]

## 2. The Need for Insurance

D & O insurance provides a means by which corporations can be reimbursed for indemnification and advancement payments to directors and officers. D & O insurance also protects directors and officers from at least four potential gaps in the availability of indemnification.

First, as discussed earlier in this Chapter, there are statutory limitations upon indemnification.[743] Most significantly, a substantial number of jurisdictions, including Delaware, either do not permit or limit indemnification of judgments and amounts paid to settle actions by or in the right of the corporation and indemnification of expenses incurred by persons adjudged liable to the corporation in such actions.[744]

Second, and also as discussed earlier in this Chapter, public policy limitations upon indemnification may preclude indemnification.[745] Unlike indemnification, the SEC does not regard the maintenance of D & O insurance to be contrary to public policy, even if the corporation pays the cost of the insurance.[746]

Third, corporations may refuse to indemnify certain directors or officers for certain conduct. This problem may be a particularly important problem following an unfriendly change in control of the corporation.

Fourth, corporations may be unable to pay indemnification due to bankruptcy or other financial difficulties. "The commencement of a bankruptcy case obviously adversely affects the ability of creditors generally to enforce their rights against a debtor corporation, and this is no less so in the case of officers and directors who

---

742. 12 C.F.R. § 121(f).
743. *See* Chapter V, Sections A 1-10.
744. *See* Chapter V, Section A 4 b.
745. *See* Chapter V, Sections A 10 and 11.
746. 17 C.F.R. § 230.461(c).

have indemnification claims against the corporation."[747] Two commentators have described the effect of bankruptcy upon directors and officers who have claims for indemnification against a corporation as follows:

> Commencement of a case under the Bankruptcy Code will, at least as to legal actions arising out of prebankruptcy events, often impair and possibly destroy the ability of directors and officers to secure the timely payment of defense costs from the debtor corporation. Such claims often will be treated as ordinary prepetition claims for which payment can be made only pursuant to a confirmed Chapter 11 plan. While some courts permit the debtor to advance litigation defense costs in limited circumstances, these courts require as a precondition to payment of such costs that the debtor demonstrate that such payment is necessary to induce officers and directors to continue to perform services for the debtor-in-possession and that such services will confer a postpetition benefit on the debtor-in-possession commensurate with the cost of honoring the claims. Worse still from the standpoint of officers and directors is the fact that in many cases indemnification claims of directors and officers (including claims for the defense costs incurred prior to entry of a judgment adjudicating such directors' and officers' liability) may be subordinated to the claims of all other creditors under Section 510(b) of the Bankruptcy Code (which may result in no distribution of any kind being made under the plan in respect of such claims) and, to the extent such indemnification claims are contingent or unliquidated at the time of allowance by the Bankruptcy Court, they will likely be disallowed under Section 502(e)(1) of the Bankruptcy Code.[748]

---

747. John F. Olson & Josiah O. Hatch III, *Director and Officer Liability: Indemnification and Insurance* § 6B.01, at 6B-3 (1997).

748. *Id.* (footnotes omitted); *see also* Bailey & Lane, *The Impact of Bankruptcy Issues on D & O Insurance and Indemnification, in Directors' and Officers' Liability Insurance 1994* 253-340 (Practising Law Institute 1994); *Directors' and Officers' Liability Insurance 1993: Impact of the Bankruptcy Laws* (Practising Law Institute 1993); Wander & Jerue, *Indemnification and Securities Litigation, in* 7 *Securities Law Techniques* § 121.03[3], at 121–1-2 (A.A. Sommer, Jr. ed. 1998); Comment, *Direc-*

(continued...)

## 3. Public Policy Limitations

As noted above, insurance law principles impose public policy limitations upon insurance.[749] Most important, insurance cannot be obtained for losses that the insured "may purposefully and wilfully cause, or which may arise from his immoral, fraudulent, or felonious conduct."[750] This generally includes criminal fines and penalties but has been held not to include attorneys' fees incurred "in defense of a criminal matter, at least where the insured is acquitted"[751] or attorneys' fees incurred in a proceeding where directors and officers plead *nolo contendere* after being indicted for criminal violations of the Sherman Act.[752]

At least one court—the Second Circuit in the *Globus* v. *Law Research Service, Inc.*[753] case discussed earlier in this Chap-

---

748. (...continued)
*tors and Officers Insurance Proceeds in Bankruptcy: The Impact on an Estate and its Claimants*, 13 Bankr. Dev. J. 235 (1996).

749. *See* Chapter V, Section B 1.

750. 7 Lee R. Russ & Thomas F. Segalla, *Couch on Insurance 3d* § 101:22, at 101–79-82 (1997); *see also Industrial Sugars, Inc. v. Standard Accident Ins. Co.*, 338 F.2d 673, 676 (7th Cir. 1964) ("A contract of insurance to indemnify a person for damages resulting from his own intentional misconduct is void as against public policy and the courts will not construe a contract to provide such coverage"); *Sheehan v. Goriansky*, 72 N.E.2d 538, 541 (Mass. 1947) ("an insurance policy indemnifying an insured against liability due to his wilful wrong is void as against public policy"); *Public Serv. Mut. Ins. Co. v. Goldfarb*, 53 N.Y.2d 392, 399, 425 N.E.2d 810, 814, 442 N.Y.S.2d 422, 426 (1981) ("[o]ne who intentionally injures another may not be indemnified for any civil liability thus incurred"). *But see National Union Fire Ins. Co. v. Seafirst Corp.*, 662 F. Supp. 36, 39 (W.D. Wash. 1986) (holding that public policy considerations do not bar insurance of bank personnel against liability for deliberate wrongdoing or dishonesty).

751. *See Polychron v. Crum & Forster Ins. Co.*, 916 F.2d 461, 463-64 (8th Cir. 1990).

752. *See Flintkote Co. v. Lloyd's Underwriters*, 1976 WL 16591, at *5 (N.Y. Sup. Ct. N.Y. Co. July 27, 1976), *aff'd mem.*, 56 A.D.2d 743, 391 N.Y.S.2d 1005 (N.Y. App. Div. 1st Dep't 1977).

753. 418 F.2d 1276 (2d Cir. 1969), *cert. denied*, 397 U.S. 913
(continued...)

ter[754]—has stated that reckless conduct also falls within this public policy exclusion: "It is well established," the *Globus* court stated, "that one cannot insure himself against his own reckless, wilful or criminal misconduct."[755] *Globus* appears to stand alone in stating that reckless conduct, causing an unintended result, precludes insurance.[756]

The courts are divided with respect to whether punitive damages are insurable.[757] There are fewer cases dealing with the mul-

---

753. (...continued)
(1970).

754. *See* Chapter V, Section A 11.

755. 418 F.2d at 1288.

756. *See, e.g., Allstate Ins. Co. v. Patterson*, 904 F. Supp. 1270, 1284 n.12 (D. Utah 1995) (collecting cases from numerous jurisdictions); *Raychem Corp. v. Federal Ins. Co.*, 853 F. Supp. 1170, 1179-80, 1185-86 (N.D. Cal. 1994) (holding that an insurer is liable for negligent or reckless conduct but not for willful conduct and allowing discovery concerning whether insureds who had settled claims under Section 10(b) of the Securities Exchange Act of 1934, 15 U.S.C. § 78j(b), had acted willfully); *Allstate Ins. Co. v. Zuk*, 78 N.Y.2d 41, 574 N.E.2d 1035, 571 N.Y.S.2d 429 (1991) (reversing grant of summary judgment in favor of insurer in case involving the insured's criminally reckless shooting of another person); *International Surplus Lines Ins. Co. v. Princehorn*, 1994 Ohio App. LEXIS 2039, at *2-8, 1994 WL 175672, at *1-3 (Ohio Ct. App. May 11, 1994) (holding that a corporate officer's liability under state law for the corporation's failure to pay taxes is not uninsurable on public policy grounds where the liability does not arise from intentional conduct by the officer), *appeal not allowed*, 639 N.E.2d 795 (Ohio 1994).

757. *Compare Aetna Cas. & Sur. Co. v. Marion Equip. Co.*, 894 P.2d 664, 671 (Alaska 1995), *Whalen v. On-Deck, Inc.*, 514 A.2d 1072, 1074 (Del. 1986), *Greenwood Cemetery, Inc. v. Travelers Indem. Co.*, 232 S.E.2d 910, 913-14 (Ga. 1977), *Lunceford v. Peachtree Cas. Ins. Co.*, 495 S.E.2d 88, 91-92 (Ga. Ct. App. 1997), *Federal Ins. Co. v. National Distrib. Co.*, 417 S.E.2d 671, 674 (Ga. Ct. App. 1992), *cert. denied*, 1992 Ga. LEXIS 665 (Ga. July 16, 1992), *South Carolina State Budget & Control Bd. v. Prince*, 403 S.E.2d 643, 648 (S.C. 1991) *and American Home Assurance Co. v. Safway Steel Prods. Co.*, 743 S.W.2d 693, 704-05 (Tex. Ct. App. 1987) (punitive damages are insurable) *with United States Fire Ins. Co. v. Goodyear Tire & Rubber Co.*, 920 F.2d 487

(continued...)

tiplied portion of multiplied damage awards than with punitive damages, but at least one court has held that the multiplied portion of multiple damage awards is not insurable.[758]

As noted above,[759] the SEC does not regard the maintenance of directors and officers insurance to be contrary to public policy. This is true even if the corporation pays the cost of the insurance.[760]

## 4. Typical Policy Structure and Terms

Historically, the typical D & O policy has followed a two-part structure.

One part—the Company Reimbursement Part—insures the corporation for indemnification payments the corporation makes to insured directors and officers. The corporation's own liability and defense costs are not covered. Even though the corporation's own liability and defense costs are not covered, the corporation still is an insured party and the insurer accordingly has a duty to treat the corporation as an insured party.[761] The fact that the corporation is

---

757. (...continued)
(8th Cir. 1990) (Minnesota law), *PPG Indus., Inc. v. Transamerica Ins. Co.*, 49 Cal. App. 4th 1120, 1126, 56 Cal. Rptr. 2d 889, 892 (Cal. Ct. App.), *petition for review granted*, 927 P.2d 1174, 59 Cal. Rptr. 2d 670 (Cal. 1996), *Country Manors Ass'n v. Master Antenna Sys., Inc.*, 534 So. 2d 1187, 1195-96 (Fla. Dist. Ct. App. 1988), *Johnson & Johnson v. Aetna Casualty & Surety Co.*, 667 A.2d 1087, 1091 (N.J. 1995), *Soto v. State Farm Ins. Co.*, 83 N.Y.2d 718, 722, 724-25, 635 N.E.2d 1222, 1223, 1224-25, 613 N.Y.S.2d 352, 353, 354-55 (1994) *and National Union Fire Ins. Co. v. Ambassador Group, Inc.*, 157 A.D.2d 293, 299, 556 N.Y.S.2d 549, 553 (N.Y. App. Div. 1st Dep't 1990) (punitive damages are not insurable), *motion for leave to appeal dismissed*, 77 N.Y.2d 873, 571 N.E.2d 85, 568 N.Y.S.2d 915 (1991).

758. *See Country Manors*, 534 So. 2d at 1195-96.

759. *See* Chapter V, Section B 2.

760. 17 C.F.R. § 230.461(c).

761. *American Med. Int'l, Inc. v. National Union Fire Ins. Co.*, 54 F.3d 785 (unpublished opinion, text available at 1995 U.S. App. LEXIS 11808, at *9 and 1995 WL 299851, at *3) (9th Cir. May 17, 1995), *cert. granted and case remanded*, 516 U.S. 984 (1995).

entitled to payments under the policy only if the corporation is required to indemnify a director or officer does not relieve the insurer of its duty of good faith and fair dealing with respect to the corporation.[762]

Another part—the Directors and Officers Reimbursement Part —insures directors and officers in situations where they are not indemnified by the corporation—either because indemnification is not permitted by law, because indemnification is not practical or possible due to the corporation's financial condition, or because the corporation for some other reason elects not to grant indemnification.[763] Many policies are drafted to provide for insurance payments for directors and officers pursuant to the Directors and Officers Reimbursement Part only when indemnification is not legally permitted or the corporation is the subject of bankruptcy proceedings because as a general rule retention and deductible levels are much higher for the Company Reimbursement Part of the policy than for the Director and Officers Reimbursement Part of the policy.[764] Some insurers have written "entity" policies that provide coverage for corporate entity liability as well as coverage for corporate indemnification payments and director and officer liability.[765]

---

762. *Id.*, 1995 U.S. App. LEXIS 11808, at *9-10, 1995 WL 299851, at *3 (affirming jury verdict finding breach of duty by insurer).

763. *See* John F. Olson & Josiah O. Hatch III, *Director and Officer Liability: Indemnification and Insurance* § 10.05, at 10-13 (1997); Johnston, *Directors' and Officers' and Related Forms of Liability Insurance, in 7 Securities Law Techniques* § 122.03[2][a] (A.A. Sommer, Jr. ed. 1998); Hinsey, *The New Lloyd's Policy Form for Directors and Officers Liability Insurance—An Analysis*, 33 Bus. Law. 1961, 1962-63 (1978); Mallen & Evans, *Surviving the Directors' and Officers' Liability Crisis: Insurance and the Alternatives*, 12 Del. J. Corp. L. 439, 444 (1988); Monteleone & Conca, *Directors and Officers Indemnification and Liability Insurance: An Overview of Legal and Practical Issues*, 51 Bus. Law. 573, 587-88 (1996).

764. Johnston §§ 122.03[2][a]; Monteleone & Conca, 51 Bus. Law. at 587.

765. Monteleone & Conca, 51 Bus. Law. at 620; Monteleone,
(continued...)

D & O policies generally consist of declarations (including the policy period, an identification (either with names or corporate titles) of the insured parties (some policies cover subsidiaries in existence at the start of the policy period and/or subsidiaries created or acquired during the policy period, and some do not—a particular concern to corporations engaged in mergers and acquisitions activity),[766] the insurer's limit of liability, retentions, deductibles and the policy premium, insuring clauses, exclusions, general terms and conditions (typically describing the procedures that the insureds must follow when making a claim and the insurer's rights regarding issues such as advancement) and endorsements ("side agreements" between the insureds and the carrier changing terms of the insurer's printed form).[767] It has been said that some policies "are so heavily endorsed that the actual contract issued is very often a substantially different document from the unendorsed specimen form."[768] One or more excess policies, often adopting the terms and conditions of the underlying policy or policies and in some cases adding additional provisions, may provide additional layers of coverage.[769]

---

765. (...continued)
*D & O Allocation: Problems and Solutions*, XVIII The Risk Report No. 8, Apr. 1996, at 6-8, *reprinted in Securities Litigation 1996* 997, 1002-04 (Practising Law Institute 1996); Weiss, *Filling the Gaps in D & O Insurance*, 6 Bus. Law Today No. 3, Jan./Feb. 1997, at 44.
766. Weiss, 6 Bus. Law Today No. 3 at 44-45.
767. J. Olson & J. Hatch § 10.05, at 10–14-15.
768. Monteleone & Conca, 51 Bus. Law. at 620.
769. Weiss, *Doing D & O Insurance Right*, 4 Bus. Law Today No. 2, Nov./Dec. 1994, at 50, 54; *see also Koppers Co. v. Aetna Cas. & Surety Co.*, 98 F.3d 1440, 1454 (3d Cir. 1996) (stating the following: "a true excess or secondary policy is not 'triggered' or required to pay until the underlying primary coverage has been exhausted"; "[t]his remains true even . . . if the underlying primary insurer is insolvent"; and "if the underlying primary insurer is solvent but the policyholder settles its claim against the primary insurer for less than policy limits, . . . the policyholder may recover on the excess policy for a proven loss to the extent it exceeds the primary policy's limits").

In order to recover under a typical D & O policy, (1) a claim must be made against insured directors and/or officers, (2) notice of the claim must be given to the insurer in accordance with the policy's requirements, (3) the claim must be for wrongful acts committed by these directors and officers in their capacity as directors and officers, (4) the directors and officers must have suffered a loss, and (5) the claim must not be subject to a coverage exclusion.[770] These five requirements are discussed in the following sections of this Chapter.[771]

Ambiguities in D & O policies, as in other kinds of insurance policies, generally are construed against the insurer, and in favor of the insureds.[772] Legal expenses typically are payable only as part of the stated limit of liability and not in addition to the limit.[773] Most D & O policies do not impose an obligation upon the insurer to provide a defense for the insureds but do require reimbursement of expenses incurred by the insureds in the defense of the

---

770. J. Olson & J. Hatch §§ 10.06, at 10-16 & 10.06[5], at 10-27.

771. *See* Chapter V, Sections B 5-9.

772. *See, e.g., Caterpillar, Inc. v. Great Am. Ins. Co.*, 62 F.3d 955, 966 (7th Cir. 1995); *Slottow v. American Casualty Co.*, 10 F.3d 1355, 1361 (9th Cir. 1993); *Federal Deposit Ins. Corp. v. American Casualty Co.*, 998 F.2d 404, 408 (7th Cir. 1993); *American Casualty Co. v. Federal Deposit Ins. Corp.*, 958 F.2d 324, 326 (10th Cir. 1992); *McCuen v. American Casualty Co.*, 946 F.2d 1401, 1406 (8th Cir. 1991); *Little v. MGIC Indem. Corp.*, 836 F.2d 789, 793 (3d Cir. 1987); *Okada v. MGIC Indem. Corp.*, 823 F.2d 276, 281 (9th Cir. 1987); *Abifadel v. Cigna Ins. Co.*, 8 Cal. App. 4th 145, 159-60, 9 Cal. Rptr. 2d 910, 919 (Cal. Ct. App. 1992).

773. *See* Johnston § 122.03[2][b][iii]; *Continental Ins. Co. v. Superior Court*, 37 Cal. App. 4th 69, 83, 43 Cal. Rptr. 2d 374, 381-82 (Cal. Ct. App. 1995); *Helfand v. National Union Fire Ins. Co.*, 10 Cal. App. 4th 869, 879-84, 13 Cal. Rptr. 2d 295, 298-302 (Cal. Ct. App. 1992), *petition for review denied*, 1993 Cal. LEXIS 716 (Cal. Feb. 11, 1993), *cert. denied*, 510 U.S. 824 (1993); *Harbor Ins. Co. v. Superior Court*, No. E006522, slip op. at 1 (Cal. Ct. App. May 12, 1989), *reprinted in* Corp. Officers & Directors Liability Litig. Rep. 6,130 (May 24, 1989), *petition for review denied*, 1989 Cal. LEXIS 4084 (Cal. Aug. 10, 1989).

claim.[774] Communications between insureds and D & O insurers concerning claims may not be protected by any privilege or the work product doctrine.[775]

Policies also generally include both a per loss or per occurrence limit and an aggregate limit on potential liability.[776] Litigation has been required in several cases to resolve disputes concerning whether different claims are based upon the same or different occurrences and thus whether a per occurrence limit applies to each claim separately or to all of the claims together.

The Ninth Circuit in *Okada v. MGIC Indemnity Corp.*,[777] for example, rejected an insurer's contention that multiple individual losses culminated in the failure of a savings and loan association and thus that the individual losses should be aggregated into

---

774. *See, e.g., Valassis Communications, Inc. v. Aetna Cas. & Sur. Co.*, 97 F.3d 870, 876 (6th Cir. 1996); *Federal Deposit Ins. Corp. v. Booth*, 824 F. Supp. 76, 79-80 (M.D. La. 1993), *subsequent decision aff'd on other grounds*, 82 F.3d 670 (5th Cir. 1996); *Continental*, 37 Cal. App. 4th at 82, 43 Cal. Rptr. 2d at 381-83; *Helfand*, 10 Cal. App. 4th at 879, 13 Cal. Rptr. at 298-99; *First State Bank v. American Casualty Co.*, 1994 Minn. App. LEXIS 448, at *4, 1994 WL 193751, at *1 (Minn. Ct. App. May 17, 1994); *National Union Fire Ins. Co. v. Ambassador Group, Inc.*, 157 A.D.2d 293, 299, 556 N.Y.S.2d 549, 553 (N.Y. App. Div. 1st Dep't 1990), *motion for leave to appeal dismissed*, 77 N.Y.2d 873, 571 N.E.2d 85, 568 N.Y.S.2d 915 (1991); *cf. Hotel des Artistes, Inc. v. Transamerica Ins. Co.*, 1994 U.S. Dist. LEXIS 7800, at *2, 7-18, 1994 WL 263429, at *1, 3-6 (S.D.N.Y. June 13, 1994) (requiring insurer to defend claims where policy granted insurer "the right and duty to defend").

775. *See Linde Thomson Langworthy Kohn & Van Dyke, P.C. v. Resolution Trust Corp.*, 5 F.3d 1508, 1514-15 (D.C. Cir. 1993); *In re Imperial Corp. of Am.*, 167 F.R.D. 447, 451-57 (S.D. Cal. 1995).

776. *See* Johnston § 122.03[2][b][iii]; Mallen & Evans, 12 Del. J. Corp. L. at 448-49; *see also Gilliam v. American Casualty Co.*, 735 F. Supp. 345, 346, 349-53 (N.D. Cal. 1990) (holding that a policy's annual limit of liability applied not to each of the two policy years during which wrongful acts allegedly occurred but to the single policy year in which notice of a claim was made, and thus that the insured had $100 million rather than $200 million in coverage).

777. 823 F.2d 276 (9th Cir. 1987).

one overall loss to determine the applicable policy limit.[778] The Ninth Circuit reached a similar conclusion in *Eureka Federal Savings & Loan Association v. American Casualty Co.*,[779] a case holding that "the fact that all loan losses arguably originated from one loan policy"—"an aggressive lending strategy adopted by Eureka in 1983 to reverse chronic operating losses"—"does not require finding only one 'loss.'"[780] To the contrary, the court stated, "there were numerous intervening business decisions that took place after the loan policy was initiated that required the exercise of independent business judgment. . . . [T]he decision to implement the aggressive loan policy did not cause the losses, rather it was the alleged negligence on the part of the . . . defendants in making or approving the individual transactions."[781] The Eighth Circuit similarly found in favor of the insureds in *McCuen v. American Casualty Co.*,[782] a case holding that each of 17 loans was "a separate act" and thus that the insurer was liable for 17 losses.[783] The court rejected the insurer's contention in that case that there were only three potential losses because, according to the insurer, the insured "made all of the loans in question in reliance on, though maybe not directly to, three borrowers."[784]

The opposite result was reached by the Fourth Circuit in *Atlantic Permanent Federal Savings & Loan Association v. American Casualty Co.*,[785] a case rejecting an insurer's claim, for the purpose of calculating a deductible, that seven causes of action, each of which was asserted by nine different customers against a savings and loan association, constituted a total of 63 separate

---

778. *Id.* at 283.

779. 873 F.2d 229 (9th Cir. 1989).

780. *Id.* at 234-35.

781. *Id.* at 235.

782. 946 F.2d 1401 (8th Cir. 1991).

783. *Id.* at 1407-08.

784. *Id.* at 1407; *see also Federal Sav. & Loan Ins. Corp. v. Burdette*, 718 F. Supp. 649, 657-60 (E.D. Tenn. 1989) (finding multiple losses); *North River Ins. Co. v. Huff*, 628 F. Supp. 1129, 1133-34 (D. Kan. 1985) (finding multiple losses).

785. 839 F.2d 212 (4th Cir.), *cert. denied*, 486 U.S. 1056 (1988).

losses.[786] The court held that "when the claims asserted against the insureds arise out of a series of interrelated acts—here, the planning and carrying out of Atlantic's home improvement loan program—they should be treated as a single 'loss.'"[787]

A similar conclusion was reached by a state court in Colorado in *Barr v. Colorado Insurance Guarantee Association,*[788] a case construing an insurance policy stating that "a single loss results from 'Losses arising out of the same Wrongful Act . . . or interrelated Wrongful Acts' by one or more plaintiffs."[789] Directors and officers were alleged to have approved a $5 million loan without first researching the borrower's background or the value of the collateral.[790] The case was settled for $371,000, and each director submitted a claim to a state insurance entity formed to pay claims of up to $50,000 per claim where, as in this case, insurance carriers were insolvent.[791] The court held that the policy language required the aggregation of losses incurred by the directors and officers into one claim, and the state insurance entity therefore was acquired to pay one claim for $50,000 and not $50,000 per insured director or officer. In the court's words: "Since plaintiff's action, as the Board of Directors, to approve the loan was made in concert, they are deemed to have committed the same wrongful act. Thus, pursuant to the policy terms, any loss is a 'single loss.'"[792] In sum: "The policy here is clear and unambiguous in providing that losses arising out of the same wrongful act shall be considered to be a single loss. Therefore, since there was a single act, there was only a single loss, and there can be only a single covered claim."[793]

---

786. *Id.* at 219.
787. *Id.* at 219-20.
788. 926 P.2d 102 (Colo. Ct. App. 1995).
789. *Id.* at 104.
790. *Id.* at 103, 104.
791. *Id.* at 103-04.
792. *Id.* at 104.
793. *Id.* at 105.

The insurer's consent to a settlement sought by the insureds typically is required but cannot unreasonably be withheld. *First Fidelity Bancorporation v. National Union Fire Insurance Co.*[794] illustrates litigation that has arisen in this context. There, First Fidelity and its directors and officers were sued by shareholders in a class action alleging that First Fidelity and its directors and officers had failed to disclose information concerning First Fidelity's loan portfolio, credit practices, the inadequacy of loan loss reserves.[795] The governing policy permitted the insureds to conduct the defense of the case, required the insurer to pay the costs of this defense to the extent that the insurer consented to these costs, prohibited the unreasonable withholding of consent to defense costs or a settlement, and provided that the insurer was "entitled to full information and all particulars it may request in order to reach a decision as to reasonableness."[796] The parties in the litigation agreed to a $30 million settlement, but First Fidelity's primary insurance carrier refused to consent to the settlement on the ground, according to the insurer, that the proposed settlement was "premature and excessive."[797] An excess carrier agreed to contribute $14.75 million to the settlement pursuant to a provision requiring the excess carrier to "drop down" "[i]n the event that the Underlying Insurance . . . fails or refuses to indemnify all or any portion of the Damages or Defense Costs associated with a Claim."[798] Following a trial, a jury determined that the primary carrier unreasonably withheld consent to the settlement, that the insureds complied with their obligation to cooperate with the primary carrier, and that the excess carrier therefore was entitled to recovery from

---

794. 1994 U.S. Dist. LEXIS 3977, 1994 WL 111363 (E.D. Pa. Mar. 30, 1994).

795. 1994 U.S. Dist. LEXIS 3977, at *4-5, 11, 1994 WL 111363, at * 1, 4.

796. 1994 U.S. Dist. LEXIS 3977, at *20-21, 1994 WL 111363, at *7.

797. 1994 U.S. Dist. LEXIS 3977, at *9-10, 1994 WL 111363, at *3.

798. 1994 U.S. Dist. LEXIS 3977, at *9-10, 28, 1994 WL 111363, at *3, 9.

the primary carrier.[799] The court denied a motion by the primary carrier to set aside the jury award.[800]

The failure by insureds to obtain the insurer's consent in connection with a settlement may constitute a failure to satisfy a condition precedent to coverage and thus void coverage for the settlement. This is true in some jurisdictions even where the insurer is not prejudiced.[801] Unless the governing policy provides otherwise, a requirement that insurers must consent to a settlement before the settlement is completed does not require that insurers be advised concerning (or consent to) settlement offers made by the insured parties before the offers are made.[802] Collusive settlements need not be consented to by the insurer.[803]

The insureds' consent to a settlement sought (and to be paid for) by the insurer also typically is required and also typically cannot unreasonably be withheld. Some policies provide that "[i]f any insured withholds"—some policies say "unreasonably withholds"—"consent to a settlement, the insurer's liability for all loss

---

799. 1994 U.S. Dist. LEXIS 3977, at *17-19, 1994 WL 111363, at *6.

800. 1994 U.S. Dist. LEXIS 3977, at *12-30, 1994 WL 111363, at *4-10.

801. *Compare, e.g.*, *Central Bank v. St. Paul Fire & Marine Ins. Co.*, 929 F.2d 431, 434 (8th Cir. 1991) *and Apollo Indus., Inc. v. Associated Int'l Ins. Co.*, No. 89-908715-CK, slip op. at 3-7 (Mich. Cir. Ct. Oct. 31, 1990), *reprinted in* Corp. Officers & Directors Litig. Rptr. 9059, 9060-62 (Nov. 14, 1990) (prejudice not required) *with Public Utility Dist. No. 1 v. International Ins. Co.*, 881 P.2d 1020, 1028 (Wash. 1994) (prejudice required).

802. *See, e.g.*, *Caterpillar, Inc. v. Great Am. Ins. Co.*, 62 F.3d 955, 966 (7th Cir. 1995), *aff'g* 864 F. Supp. 849, 857-61 (N.D. Ill. 1994).

803. *See, e.g.*, *Beck v. American Casualty Co.*, 1990 U.S. Dist. LEXIS 13756, at *42-50, 1990 WL 598573, at *15-18 (W.D. Tex. Apr. 12, 1990); *National Union Fire Ins. Co. v. Continental Ill. Group*, 1987 U.S. Dist. LEXIS 11785, at *3-4, 1987 WL 28297, at *1 (N.D. Ill. Dec. 14, 1987); *Xebec Dev. Partners, Ltd. v. National Union Fire Ins. Co.*, 12 Cal. App. 4th 501, 550-52, 15 Cal. Rptr. 2d 726, 753-54 (Cal. Ct. App. 1993).

on account of such claim shall not exceed the amount for which the Insurer could have settled such claim plus defense costs incurred as of the date such settlement was proposed in writing by the insurer."[804] This is known as a "hammer clause" because of the power such a clause provides an insurer to force a settlement.[805]

Policies also often contain cancellation provisions. The decision in *American Casualty Co. v. Federal Deposit Insurance Corp.*[806] illustrates the care with which cancellation provisions and cancellation notices must be read. The court held that a December 13 notice to an insurer of occurrences that could give rise to claims under the policy was timely notwithstanding an October 23 notice from the insurer that stated that coverage "would terminate thirty days from receipt of the notice at 12:00 noon standard time."[807] The court explained that the notice was not received until November 14 because the insured had moved its offices.[808]

At least one court has held that D & O carriers "do not have an unfettered right to cancel coverage, notwithstanding mutual cancellation clauses to that effect" because "[a]n arbitrary cancellation is a breach of the covenant of good faith and fair dealing."[809] This court found that the attempted cancellation in the case before the court was "without legal justification."[810]

---

804. Weiss, 6 Bus. Law Today No. 3 at 46.

805. Monteleone & McCarrick, *D & O Insurance: Settlement Issues in Securities Litigation Involving Directors and Officers*, 10 Insights: The Corporate & Securities Advisor No. 9, Sept. 1996, at 7, 8; Weiss, 6 Bus. Law Today No. 3 at 46.

806. 999 F.2d 480 (10th Cir. 1993).

807. *Id.* at 481.

808. *Id.* at 481, 483.

809. *Helfand v. National Union Fire Ins. Co.*, 10 Cal. App. 4th 869, 903-06, 13 Cal. Rptr. 2d 295, 315-17 (Cal. Ct. App. 1992), *petition for review denied*, 1993 Cal. LEXIS 716 (Cal. Feb. 11, 1993), *cert. denied*, 510 U.S. 824 (1993), *subsequent proceedings sub nom. McLaughlin v. National Union Fire Ins. Co.*, 23 Cal. App. 4th 1132, 1152-60, 29 Cal. Rptr. 2d 559, 570-75 (Cal. Ct. App. 1994).

810. *Helfand*, 10 Cal. App. 4th at 905, 13 Cal. Rptr. 2d at 316; *see*

(continued...)

Once a D & O claim is resolved, one of three types of releases must be given by the insured to the insurer: a litigation release, a claim release, or a policy release. A litigation release provides the insurer a release from liability only for the settled litigation. A claim release provides the insurer a release from liability for both the settled claim and any pending or future claims arising out of the conduct underlying the settled claim. A policy release provides the insurer a release from liability for all claims, whether related or unrelated to the conduct underlying the settled claim.[811]

## 5. The Claim Made Requirement

Most D & O policies are "claim made" policies.[812] Claim made policies cover claims made during the period specified in the policy, no matter when the occurrence giving rise to the claim took place. "Occurrence" policies cover claims arising out of an occurrence that takes place during the period specified in the policy, no

---

810. (...continued)

*also Unocal Corp. v. Superior Court*, 198 Cal. App. 3d 1245, 1250-52, 244 Cal. Rptr. 540, 542-43 (Cal. Ct. App. 1988) (denying motion to dismiss RICO mail fraud claim), *petition for review denied but Reporter of Decisions directed not to publish opinion*, 1988 Cal. LEXIS 135 (Cal. June 1, 1988); Victor, *D & O Canceled and Unocal Sues*, Legal Times, July 29, 1985, at 1 (reporting one D & O insurer's cancellation of Unocal Corporation's D & O policy one day after T. Boone Pickens announced in 1985 that Pickens had acquired 7.9 percent of Unocal's stock, and a suit filed by Unocal against the insurer alleging that the insurer had engaged in a pattern of cancelling D & O policies upon learning of contests for control of insured corporations).

811. Monteleone & McCarrick, 10 Insights No. 9, at 11.

812. John F. Olson & Josiah O. Hatch III, *Director and Officer Liability: Indemnification and Insurance* § 10.06[1], at 10-16 (1997); Monteleone & Conca, *Directors and Officers Indemnification and Liability Insurance: An Overview of Legal and Practical Issues*, 51 Bus. Law. 573, 588 (1996); Johnston, *Directors' and Officers' and Related Forms of Liability Insurance, in 7 Securities Law Techniques* § 122.03[2][c] (A.A. Summer, Jr. ed. 1998).

matter when a claim is made.[813] "Therefore, claims-made policies theoretically provide unlimited retroactive coverage, whereas occurrence policies offer unlimited prospective coverage."[814]

Particular policies may be written to vary these definitions in any manner agreed upon by the insurer and the insured. Some claims made policies thus provide for "coverage for potential claims provided [the insurer] receives, within the policy period, notice of the occurrence of a specified wrongful act."[815] Other policies provide for coverage for actual and/or potential claims reported to the insurer during the policy period or during a post-policy discovery "tail" period.[816] The post-policy discovery tail

---

813. *See, e.g., Township of Center v. First Mercury Syndicate, Inc.*, 117 F.3d 115, 118 (3d Cir. 1997); *Aetna Casualty & Surety Co. v. Lindner*, 92 F.3d 1191 (unpublished opinion, text available at 1996 U.S. App. LEXIS 18541, at *2-3 and 1996 WL 413621, at *1) (9th Cir. July 22, 1996); *LaForge v. American Casualty Co.*, 37 F.3d 580, 583 (10th Cir. 1994); *Resolution Trust Corp. v. Ayo*, 31 F.3d 285, 288 (5th Cir. 1994); *Federal Deposit Ins. Corp. v. Mijalis*, 15 F.3d 1314, 1330 (5th Cir. 1994); *Burns v. International Ins. Co.*, 929 F.2d 1422, 1424 n.3 (9th Cir. 1991); *Helfand v. National Union Fire Ins. Co.*, 10 Cal. App. 4th 869, 885 n.8, 13 Cal. Rptr. 2d 295, 303 n.8 (Cal. Ct. App. 1992), *petition for review denied*, 1993 Cal. LEXIS 716 (Cal. Feb. 11, 1993), *cert. denied*, 510 U.S. 824 (1993); *Klein v. Fidelity & Deposit Co. of Am.*, 700 A.2d 262, 263 n.1 (Md. Ct. Spec. App. 1997).

814. *Gilliam v. American Casualty Co.*, 735 F. Supp. 345, 349 & n.4 (N.D. Cal. 1990).

815. *See, e.g., Ayo*, 31 F.3d at 288; *Federal Deposit Ins. Corp. v. Interdonato*, 988 F. Supp. 1, 3 (D.D.C. 1997); *American Casualty Co. v. Federal Deposit Ins. Corp.*, 1990 U.S. Dist. LEXIS 6065, at *6 n.5, 1990 WL 66505, at *2 n.5 (N.D. Iowa Feb. 26, 1990), *aff'd in part and rev'd in part*, 944 F.2d 455 (8th Cir. 1991); *Federal Sav. & Loan Ins. Corp. v. Burdette*, 718 F. Supp. 649, 651-52 & n.2 (E.D. Tenn. 1989).

816. *Compare Baker*, 22 F.3d at 888-92, *American Casualty Co. v. Federal Deposit Ins. Corp.*, 999 F.2d 480, 481-82 (10th Cir. 1993), *American Casualty Co. v. Federal Deposit Ins. Corp.*, 958 F.2d 324, 327-28 (10th Cir. 1992), *American Casualty Co. v. Resolution Trust Corp.*, 845 F. Supp. 318, 325 & 326 n.8 (D. Md. 1993) *and Federal Deposit Ins. Corp. v. American Casualty Co.*, 528 N.W.2d 605, 607-09 (Iowa

(continued...)

period typically applies only where the policy is not renewed and a successor policy (on the same or different terms) is not agreed upon by the insurer and the insured.[817] A runoff policy covers claims "on a claims made basis, but only . . . claims for wrongful acts allegedly occurring prior to [a particular date]."[818] Without a provision expressly limiting coverage to claims "first made" during the policy period, the fact that a prior claim has been made in a prior policy period does not preclude coverage for a new claim made during a new policy period.[819] The fact that discrete claims for damages are brought together in one lawsuit or consolidated in one lawsuit does not alter the status of the claims as separate claims that may have been "first made" during different policy periods.[820]

"Where the term 'claim' is defined in D & O policies, it may be narrowly defined to include only litigation or it may be broadly defined to include other less formal proceedings" such as an informal investigation by an administrative, regulatory or governmental

---

816. (...continued)
1995) (each construing identical policy language to require either notice of actual or potential claims within the policy period or notice of actual claims within the discovery period) *with McCuen v. American Casualty Co.*, 946 F.2d 1401, 1404-06 (8th Cir. 1991), *American Casualty Co. v. Sentry Fed. Sav. Bank*, 867 F. Supp. 50, 60-61 (D. Mass. 1994), *Slaughter v. American Casualty Co.*, 842 F. Supp. 371, 374-76 (E.D. Ark.), *subsequent proceedings*, 842 F. Supp. 376, 377-78 (E.D. Ark. 1993), *rev'd on other grounds*, 37 F.3d 385 (8th Cir. 1994) *and United States Fire Ins. Co. v. Fleekop*, 682 So. 2d 620, 625-28 (Fla. Dist. Ct. App. 1996) (each interpreting similar policy language to require notice of actual or potential claims within policy period or discovery period).

817. *See American Casualty Co. v. Baker*, 22 F.3d 880, 892-94 (9th Cir. 1994) (citing cases).

818. *See Old Republic Ins. Co. v. Rexene Corp.*, 1990 Del. Ch. LEXIS 187, at *4-5, 1990 WL 176791, at *1-2 (Del. Ch. Nov. 5, 1990).

819. *Apollo Indus., Inc. v. Associated Int'l Ins. Co.*, No. 153902, slip op. at 3 (Mich. Ct. App. Apr. 13, 1995).

820. *Home Ins. Co. v. Spectrum Info. Techs., Inc.*, 930 F. Supp. 825, 845-48 (E.D.N.Y. 1996).

agency or a demand by a shareholder."[821] Often, however, the term "claim" is not defined in D & O policies.[822] Without a definition, "the determination of whether a given demand is a 'claim' within the meaning of a claims made policy requires a fact-specific analysis to be conducted on a case-by-case basis."[823] The term "may be something other than a formal lawsuit, such as a letter demanding money or other relief as a result of specific wrongdoing."[824] Beyond that general observation, the courts have reached a wide variety of results.

On one side of the spectrum are cases such as the following:

• *Polychron v. Crum & Forster Insurance Co.*[825] (holding that a grand jury investigation and questioning by an Assistant United States Attorney constituted a claim),[826]

• *International Insurance Co. v. Peabody International Corp.*[827] (holding that a letter insisting that a corporation "take immediate steps to remedy contractual shortcomings" constituted a claim),[828]

---

821. Monteleone & McCarrick, *Practical Concerns Involving Directors' and Officers' Liability Litigation*, 7 Insights: The Corporate & Securities Law Advisor No. 11, Nov. 1993, at 15; *see also D & O Policy Addition Covers Investigation of Claims Against Officers and Board*, Corp. Officers & Directors Liability Litig. Rptr. 21182 (May 14, 1997) (reporting policy provision offered by one insurer paying up to $250,000 for lawyers, auditors and other experts to advise the board in connection with investigations of shareholder demands); Weiss, *Doing D & O Insurance Right*, 4 Bus. Law Today No. 2, Nov./Dec. 1994, at 53.

822. Monteleone & Conca, 51 Bus. Law. at 588; Weiss, *Filling the Gaps in D & O Insurance*, 6 Bus. Law Today No. 3, Jan./Feb. 1997, at 50.

823. *Federal Deposit Ins. Corp. v. Mijalis*, 15 F.3d 1314, 1331 (5th Cir. 1994).

824. Monteleone & Conca, 51 Bus. Law. at 589.

825. 916 F.2d 461 (8th Cir. 1990).

826. *Id.* at 462-64.

827. 747 F. Supp. 477 (N.D. Ill. 1990).

828. *Id.* at 480-81.

- *Harbor Insurance Co. v. Continental Illinois Corp.*[829] (holding that a threatened Securities and Exchange Commission enforcement proceeding constituted a claim),[830] and

- *John Hancock Healthplan, Inc. v. Lexington Insurance Co.*[831] (holding that a threat to file a lawsuit constituted a claim).[832]

On the other side of the spectrum are cases including the following:

- *MGIC Indemnity Corp. v. Home State Savings Association*[833] (holding that a letter from an Assistant United States Attorney identifying corporate officials as targets of a grand jury investigation did not constitute a claim, even where the corporation had accepted a settlement of criminal charges against the corporation in substantial part in order to protect the corporate officials from having criminal charges brought against them),[834]

- *Bendis v. Federal Insurance Co.*[835] (holding that a statement by an attorney that his client had a "strong case" against two corporate officers, W. Terrence Schreier and Richard Bendis, "and possibly others, including other directors, attorneys and accountants, for fraud and/or negligent misrepresentation" but that his client "was not going to pursue these claims against Schreier and Bendis alone because they did not believe

---

829. 1989 U.S. Dist. LEXIS 14300, 1989 WL 152648 (N.D. Ill. Nov. 27, 1989), *rev'd on other grounds*, 922 F.2d 357 (7th Cir. 1990).

830. 1989 U.S. Dist. LEXIS 14300, at *11, 1989 WL 152648, at *4.

831. 1989 U.S. Dist. LEXIS 11019, 1989 WL 106992 (E.D. Pa. Sept. 8, 1989).

832. 1989 U.S. Dist. LEXIS 11019, at *9-13, 1989 WL 106992, at *4-5.

833. 797 F.2d 285 (6th Cir. 1986).

834. *Id.* at 286-88.

835. 958 F.2d 960 (10th Cir. 1991).

either gentleman had a 'deep enough pocket'" did not
constitute a claim),[836]

- *Winkler v. National Union Fire Insurance Co.*[837]
  (holding that threats "to take whatever legal action"
  was necessary to recoup alleged losses constituted
  "potential claims" but not "claims"; the court stated
  that "'[n]otice that it is [someone's] intention to hold
  the insureds responsible for a Wrongful Act' is an event
  commonly antecedent to and different in kind from a
  'claim'"),[838]

- *Evanston Insurance Co. v. Security Assurance Co.*[839]
  (holding that communications not constituting a
  "demand for money or property" did not constitute a
  claim),[840]

- *Abifadel v. Cigna Insurance Co.*[841] (holding that a
  demand against a majority shareholder is not a claim
  against individual directors and officers,[842] and that a
  cease and desist order issued by a regulatory agency to
  the corporation that did not threaten formal consequences against the directors and officers and that did
  not state that the directors and officers would be held
  liable for the regulatory violations identified in the
  order did not constitute a claim against directors and
  officers),[843]

- *Klein v. Fidelity & Deposit Co. of America*[844] (holding that letters threatening litigation against directors

---

836. *Id.* at 962-63.

837. 930 F.2d 1364 (9th Cir. 1991).

838. *Id.* at 1366-67.

839. 715 F. Supp. 1405 (N.D. Ill. 1989).

840. *Id.* at 1412-13.

841. 8 Cal. App. 4th 145, 9 Cal. Rptr. 2d 910 (Cal. Ct. App.
1992).

842. *Id.* at 160-64, 9 Cal. Rptr. 2d at 920-22.

843. *Id.* at 164-67, 9 Cal. Rptr. 2d at 922-24.

844. 700 A.2d 262 (Md. Ct. Spec. App. 1997).

and officers of a savings and loan association did not constitute a "claim" and thus that monies spent in the negotiation and sale of the savings and loan association to another financial institution and an agreement by a state regulatory agency not to assert civil actions against the directors and officers (at least for a certain period to time) were not covered claims; the court explained that the ordinary meaning of the word "claim" requires "a demand for something due or believed to be due" "as one's own or as one's right" and that the letters threatening litigation "at most, simply warn that claims were likely to be filed"),[845] and

- *Safeco Title Insurance Co. v. Gannon*[846] (distinguishing a "claim"—a term that "ordinarily means a demand on the insured for damages resulting from the insured's alleged negligent act or omission"—from "facts and circumstances that later gave rise" to a claim, and holding that facts and circumstances that later gave rise to a claim did not themselves constitute a claim).[847]

Much of the case law construing the term "claim" where the term is not defined in the governing insurance policy has arisen in the context of regulatory actions involving banking and financial institutions. The Fifth Circuit's decisions in *Federal Deposit Insurance Corp. v. Barham*,[848] *Federal Deposit Insurance Corp. v. Mijalis*[849] and *Federal Deposit Insurance Corp. v. Booth*[850] appear to represent the majority view. These cases hold that "when the terms 'claim' and 'loss' are intimately connected in a policy"— as is the case when, for example, a policy provides insurance for "claim(s) made . . . for loss"—"then a 'claim' is a 'demand which

---

845. *Id.* at 271.
846. 774 P.2d 30 (Wash. Ct. App.), *petition for review denied*, 782 P.2d 1069 (Wash. 1989).
847. *Id.* at 32-33.
848. 995 F.2d 600 (5th Cir. 1993).
849. 15 F.3d 1314 (5th Cir. 1994).
850. 82 F.3d 670 (5th Cir. 1996).

if sustained necessarily results in a loss.'"[851] Accordingly, "general demands for regulatory compliance" by regulatory authorities and "[e]ven specific formal demands" by regulatory authorities "for corrective action do not rise to the level of 'claims' unless coupled with indications that demands for payment will be made."[852]

*Federal Deposit Insurance Corp. v. Barham*[853] involved a letter agreement between an insured bank, First National Bank of Boston ("FNBR"), and the Office of the Comptroller of the Currency, pursuant to which the bank agreed to "adopt and implement policies and procedures to prevent future violations of law and regulation."[854] The court held that this did not constitute a claim. To the contrary, the court stated, an insurer that had been provided a copy of this letter "at most, possessed information that regulators had disapproved and criticized some of FNBR's banking relationships and loan transactions."[855]

*Federal Deposit Insurance Corp. v. Mijalis*[856] involved letters sent by the Federal Deposit Insurance Corporation to a bank's board of directors advising the board of the FDIC's concern with respect to certain lending practices by the bank, insisting that the bank cease these practices, and stating that "'unsafe and unsound conditions may exist' that, unless addressed, could impair the bank's future viability, threaten the interests of the Bank's depositors and 'pose a potential for disbursement of funds by the insuring agency.'"[857] The court concluded that the communication of these letters to an insurer was insufficient to establish that a claim had been made because "the appropriate inquiry is whether these communications referred to demands that would necessarily result in losses to the directors as a result of their failure to comply

---

851. *Booth*, 82 F.3d at 675 & n.11; *Mijalis*, 15 F.3d at 1332; *Barham*, 995 F.2d at 604.

852. *Mijalis*, 15 F.3d at 1333.

853. 995 F.2d 600 (5th Cir. 1993).

854. *Id.* at 604.

855. *Id.* at 604, 605.

856. 15 F.3d 1314 (5th Cir. 1994).

857. *Id.* at 1332-33.

with the relevant banking regulations."[858] The answer to this question in the *Mijalis* case, according to the court, was no, except arguably with respect to a letter warning board members that civil money penalties "would be considered if prompt good faith efforts were not made to correct the Bank's violations of federal banking regulations."[859] The court found it unnecessary to decide this final question, however, because the governing insurance policy excluded civil money penalties from the policy's definition of loss.[860]

*Federal Deposit Insurance Corp. v. Booth*[861] involved letters sent by the FDIC to directors of a bank summarizing and enclosing an FDIC Report of Examination of the Bank and "reminding the Directors of their obligations and warning them that 'failure to take corrective action . . . could result in civil money penalties being recommended and/or more severe enforcement actions being recommended to the FDIC Board of Directors."[862] The court explained that the governing policy defined a claim as a demand that if complied with "necessarily results in a loss" and that the FDIC's letter in this case did not state a demand that if complied with "necessarily results in a loss" because the language used by the FDIC "indicates that even the FDIC considered the correspondence only a warning of 'potential liability,' making it more akin to a potential claim than a true claim."[863] The court stated that "[e]quating the mere threat of a claim with an actual claim negates the 'necessarily' element in the very definition of claim'" and "would contradict the intentions of the insurance contract."[864]

The same result was reached by the Ninth Circuit in *California Union Insurance Co. v. American Diversified Savings Bank,*[865]

---

858. *Id*. at 1332.
859. *Id*. at 1333.
860. *Id*. at 1333-34.
861. 82 F.3d 670 (5th Cir. 1996).
862. *Id*. at 675.
863. *Id*. at 676.
864. *Id*.
865. 914 F.2d 1271 (9th Cir. 1990), *cert. denied*, 498 U.S. 1088

(continued...)

a case involving a series of letters from regulatory authorities, including the Federal Savings and Loan Insurance Corporation (the "FSLIC") and the California Department of Savings and Loan (the "CDSL"), to American Diversified Savings Bank ("ADSB"). These letters detailed deficiencies and requested immediate action by ADSB's directors.[866] In an action brought by Ranbir S. Sahni, a former director seeking to hold an insurer liable for amounts Sahni might be found to owe to FSLIC, ADSB's receiver, the court held that these letters did not constitute claims within the meaning of the bank's insurance policies. The court reasoned as follows:

> The CDSL management order of July 6, 1984, and the two letters of April 6 and October 6, 1984 pertaining to CDSL's cease-and-desist orders do not assert claims because they neither threatened formal proceedings against Sahni as a consequence of failure to comply nor propose to hold the officers and directors personally liable for the deficiencies. CDSL's cease-and-desist order did not state any formal consequences for ADSB's failure to comply with the order. Similarly, CDSL's order requiring ADSB to submit to a management audit stated that the audit's purpose was to aid ADSB's compliance with the necessary regulations, and did not threaten any formal consequences for failure to comply. Finally, although the FSLIC agreement stated that the Board had agreed to take certain actions in return for FSLIC's "forbearance" from formal cease-and-desist proceedings against the institution, no formal action was threatened against the officers or directors as a consequence of breaching the agreement.[867]

The same result also was reached by district courts in *American Casualty Co. v. Rahn*[868] and *In re Ambassador Group, Inc. Litigation*.[869] The court in *Rahn* held that the entry by a savings association and the Federal Home Loan Bank Board into a Supervi-

---

865. (...continued)
(1991).
  866. *Id.* at 1275-76.
  867. *Id.* at 1276.
  868. 854 F. Supp. 492 (W.D. Mich. 1994).
  869. 830 F. Supp. 147 (E.D.N.Y. 1993).

sory Agreement stating that the FHLBB was of the opinion that the savings association had violated certain statutes and regulations and had engaged in unsafe or unsound business practices, and pursuant to which the savings association agreed to take several actions in order to avoid the initiation of cease-and-desist proceedings, did not constitute a claim.[870] The court in *Ambassador Group* likewise held that a letter written by a state regulatory authority to an insurer containing a "general assertion" of wrongdoing by directors and officers but that "lacks a specific demand for relief" and "any enumeration of Wrongful Acts" did not constitute a claim.[871]

Even assuming agreement or a court determination that a claim has been made, the date upon which the claim is made, and thus whether it is a covered claim (or under which of multiple policies it is covered) still may be unclear. Possibilities in the case of a lawsuit include the date the complaint is filed, the first date service is made upon an insured party, the first date an insured party learns of the complaint (whether by service or in some other manner, such as a news report or the delivery of a "courtesy copy" of the complaint to the insured's counsel).[872] Some policies address this issue directly; other policies do not.[873] The court in *Aetna Casu-*

---

870. 854 F. Supp. at 494, 496-97.

871. 830 F. Supp. at 155-56.

872. Monteleone & Conca, *Directors and Officers Indemnification and Liability Insurance: An Overview of Legal and Practical Issues*, 51 Bus. Law. 573, 589 (1996).

873. *See* Monteleone & McCarrick, *Practical Concerns Involving Directors' and Officers' Liability Litigation*, 7 Insights: The Corporate & Securities Law Advisor, Nov. 1993, at 16 (noting policy provision stating that a claim "shall be deemed to have been first made against a Director and/or Officer on the date that a summons or similar document is first served upon such Director and/or Officer"); *Ameriwood Indus. Int'l Corp. v. American Casualty Co.*, 840 F. Supp. 1143, 1149, 1152 (W.D. Mich. 1993) (stating that "Clause 4(b) of the policies . . . sets forth that a claim is made 'at the date notice is given to the Insurer pursuant to Clause 6(a) or 6(b), or at the date a suit is brought against the Directors and Officers, whichever shall occur first," and holding that "[a] suit begins in federal court with the filing of a complaint" and that the amendment of a com-
(continued...)

*alty & Surety Co. v. Lindner*[874] held in a case where a complaint was filed during a policy period but not served until after the policy period, and where the insurer was not notified of the complaint until after service, that no claim was made during the policy period.[875] An additional issue may arise where a complaint is filed against insured parties during one policy period and an amended complaint, adding a new insured party and new factual allegations and/or legal claims, is filed during a later policy period. The court in *Informix Corp. v. Lloyd's of London*[876] held under these circumstances that the amended complaint was "part of the same claim initiated by the filing of the original complaint" and that "[a]ny loss sustained by plaintiffs . . . is covered, if at all, under the policy in effect during the first policy period.[877]

## 6.   The Notice Requirement

Assuming that the "claim made" requirement is satisfied, notice of the claim must be given to the insurer in the manner and in the form required by the policy and within the period specified in the policy. The required time for the notice often is "as soon as practicable" and sometimes must precede the expiration of the policy period.[878]

---

873. (...continued)
plaint therefore constitutes a claim made on the date the initial complaint in the case was filed); *cf. Safeco Surplus Lines Co. v. Employers Reinsurance Corp.*, 11 Cal. App. 4th 1403, 1407, 15 Cal. Rptr. 2d 58, 60 (Cal. Ct. App. 1992) (non-D & O insurance policy case holding that a claim is made on the date that the insured receives a demand letter and not on the date that the letter is mailed).

874. 92 F.3d 1191 (unpublished opinion, text available at 1996 U.S. App. LEXIS 18541 and 1996 WL 413621) (9th Cir. July 22, 1996).

875. 1996 U.S. App. LEXIS 18541, at *2, 3, 1996 WL 413621, at *1.

876. 1992 U.S. Dist. LEXIS 16836, 1992 WL 469802 (N.D. Cal. Oct. 16, 1992).

877. 1992 U.S. Dist. LEXIS 16836, at *3, 6, 1992 WL 469802, at *1, 2.

878. John F. Olson & Josiah O. Hatch III, *Director and Officer Liability: Indemnification and Insurance* § 10.06[6], at 10-41 (1997).

Failure to provide notice in the required manner and form may jeopardize coverage, as demonstrated by a California court in *Helfand v. National Union Fire Insurance Co.*[879] The court in *Helfand* construed a policy to require both a claim made and notice to the insurer during the policy year.[880] Notice was not given during the policy year, and the claim accordingly was held not to be a covered claim.[881] The court rejected a contention that an insurer should not be permitted to avoid coverage due to insufficient notice absent a demonstration of actual and substantial prejudice arising from the delay in receipt of notice. According to the court, notice was an element of coverage in the governing policy, and "[t]he hallmark of a 'claims made' policy is that exposure for claims terminates with expiration or termination of the policy, thereby providing certainty in gauging potential liability."[882]

The Seventh Circuit, construing Illinois law in *Harbor Insurance Co. v. Continental Bank Corp.*[883] reached the same conclusion. The insurance policy in this case required notice of "any occurrence that may later give rise to a claim" and "if and when a claim against the director or officer is actually made, the insured 'shall as a condition precedent to its rights under this policy give to the [insurance] company notice as soon as practicable in writing of any such claim.'"[884] The court rejected a contention that "occurrence notice and claim notice are alternative rather than sequential requirements" as "contrary to the language and evident purpose of the requirement."[885] With respect to the purpose, the court explained, "[t]he insurer wants to know whether there is a possibility that it will be receiving a claim after the policy period, but of

---

879. 10 Cal. App. 4th 869, 13 Cal. Rptr. 2d 295 (Cal. Ct. App. 1992), *petition for review denied*, 1993 Cal. LEXIS 716 (Cal. Feb. 11, 1993), *cert. denied*, 510 U.S. 824 (1993).

880. *Id.* at 886-87, 13 Cal Rptr. 2d at 303-04.

881. *Id.* at 885, 13 Cal. Rptr. 2d at 303.

882. *Id.* at 888, 13 Cal. Rptr. 2d at 304-05.

883. 922 F.2d 357 (7th Cir. 1990).

884. *Id.* at 369.

885. *Id.*

course it also wants to receive notice of that claim when and if it materializes."[886]

Similar policy language, however, was construed by the Ninth Circuit in *Continental Insurance Co. v. Metro-Goldwyn-Mayer, Inc.*[887] as "alternative rather than sequential notice requirements."[888] According to the Ninth Circuit, "the contract treats 'occurrence' notice as a claim made; it is an alternative to claim notice."[889] As a result, "[n]otice of claims or potential claims is all that is required by the insuring agreement."[890] The Ninth Circuit in *Metro-Goldwyn-Mayer* pointed to the statement by the Seventh Circuit in *Harbor* that "[t]he insurer wants to know whether there is a possibility that it will be receiving a claim after the policy period, but of course it also wants to receive notice of the claim if and when it materializes" and responded that the insurer "obviously wants to receive notice, and that is not an unreasonable expectation, but the contract in this case does not explicitly require this second notice.[891]

Additional decisions of note include the following:

- *American Casualty Co. v. Federal Deposit Ins. Corp.*[892] (holding that communications between an insured and an insurer that did not conform to policy requirements —specifically, that "[n]otice of occurrences that might lead to claims had to be specific and in writing"—were insufficient);[893]

- *American Casualty Co. v. Rahn*[894] (denying coverage where notice was given to an independent insurance agent rather than an insurance agent having authority to

---

886. *Id.*
887. 107 F.3d 1344 (9th Cir. 1997).
888. *Id.* at 1347.
889. *Id.*
890. *Id.*
891. *Id.*
892. 944 F.2d 455 (8th Cir. 1991).
893. *Id.* at 460.
894. 854 F. Supp. 492 (W.D. Mich. 1994).

act on the insurer's behalf and the notice was not communicated to the insurer);[895]

- *RHI Holdings, Inc. v. National Union Fire Ins. Co.*[896] (denying coverage for claims asserted in an amended complaint where the amended complaint was not sent to the insurer until two years after the amendment was filed and four years after the expiration of the policy period);[897]

- *In re Kenai Corp.*[898] (rejecting insurer's contention that a letter to the insurer did not constitute sufficient notice because, according to the insurer, the letter was "insufficiently detailed"; the court stated that "as the drafter" the insurer "could have defined the relevant terms in the policy and provided for the construction of those terms it urges on this motion," and "[h]aving failed to do so, it should not now be permitted to avoid responsibility for coverage").[899]

Several courts, including the Third Circuit in *American Casualty Co. v. Continisio*,[900] the Eighth Circuit in *American Casualty Co. v. Federal Deposit Insurance Corp.*[901] and *Federal Deposit Insurance Corp. v. St. Paul Fire & Marine Insurance Co.*,[902] and the Tenth Circuit in *LaForge v. American Casualty Co.*[903] have rejected efforts by insureds (1) to argue that information provided to an insurer's underwriting department in a renewal application placed the insurer's claims department on notice of a potential

---

895. *Id.* at 497-98.

896. [1994-1995 Transfer Binder] Fed. Sec. L. Rep. (CCH) ¶ 98,315 (E.D. Pa. May 4, 1994), *aff'd mem.*, 47 F.3d 1161 (3d Cir. 1995).

897. *Id.* at 90,197.

898. 136 B.R. 59 (S.D.N.Y. 1992).

899. *Id.* at 62.

900. 17 F.3d 62 (3d Cir. 1994).

901. 944 F.2d 455 (8th Cir. 1991).

902. 993 F.2d 155 (8th Cir. 1993).

903. 37 F.3d 580 (10th Cir. 1994).

claim, and/or (2) to "deny knowledge of potential claims in their renewal application and rely on information submitted with the same application to support an argument that the insurer should have known a claim could be made."[904]

The court in *Continisio* explained that "[b]ecause the notice of claim provision defines coverage under this policy, the only reasonable interpretation of the policy provision is that the insureds must regard the information they possess as a potential claim and formally notify their insurer through its claims liability department that a claim may be asserted."[905] This notice, the court continued, "must be given through formal claims channels" and not simply to an insurer's underwriting department in a renewal application because "the information needed, or at least the perspective utilized in reviewing it, varies when predicting the probability of future losses and recognizing the need to investigate a claim that may be made based on past occurrences."[906] An insured, the court thus concluded, is prohibited from "insisting that its insurer's underwriting department sift through a renewal application and decide what should be forwarded to the claims department on the insured's behalf."[907]

The court in *LaForge* similarly concluded that information in a renewal application did not provide the required notice in that case "in part, because of the context in which the information was provided"—"an application form designed to seek a continuation of coverage from the insurer's underwriters, rather than in a document designed to seek recovery under the policy in effect at the time through American Casualty's claims mechanism."[908] "Although that fact would not by itself necessarily be fatal," the court stated, "it requires an unmistakably clear, unequivocal, and conspicuous statement of a claim in such a context to satisfy the notice require-

---

904. *Continisio*, 17 F.3d at 69, *quoted in LaForge*, 37 F.3d at 584.
905. *Continisio*, 17 F.3d at 69.
906. *Id*.
907. *Id*.
908. *LaForge*, 37 F.3d at 584.

ments of the insurance contract."[909] Here, the court found, no such "unmistakably clear, unequivocal, and conspicuous statement of a claim" had been made.[910] To the contrary, the court stated, the application claimed lack of knowledge of "any possible violations of laws or regulations."[911] Thus "[f]ar from intending to put the insurer on notice of past problems likely to lead to claims against the directors, the application played down any problems."[912] The court in *St. Paul* similarly stated that "[n]otice that would cause one to investigate a renewal for insurance must surely be different than notice to investigate potential claims under a 'claims made' policy."[913]

The Fifth Circuit's decisions in *Federal Deposit Insurance Corp. v. Barham*,[914] *McCullough v. Fidelity & Deposit Co.*,[915] *Federal Deposit Insurance Corp. v. Mijalis*,[916] *Resolution Trust Corp. v. Ayo*[917] and *Federal Deposit Insurance Corp. v. Booth*[918] and the Eleventh Circuit's decision in *Resolution Trust Corp. v. Artley*[919] also reject efforts by insureds to contend that "constructive notice of wrongful acts" to insurers constitutes sufficient notice of a claim for the purpose of triggering policy coverage where the policy requires written notice of a claim or a specific act or acts that might give rise to a claim. Where such notice is required by the policy, these courts hold, it is not enough to give an insurer

- notice of "general bad practices . . . disapproved and criticized" by regulators or of a letter agreement between the insured and regulators pursuant to which the insured agreed to "adopt and implement policies

909. *Id.*
910. *Id.*
911. *Id.*
912. *Id.*
913. *St. Paul*, 993 F.2d at 160.
914. 995 F.2d 600 (5th Cir. 1993).
915. 2 F.3d 110 (5th Cir. 1993).
916. 15 F.3d 1314 (5th Cir. 1994).
917. 31 F.3d 285 (5th Cir. 1994).
918. 82 F.3d 670 (5th Cir. 1996).
919. 24 F.3d 1363 (11th Cir. 1994).

and procedures to prevent future violations of law and regulation,"[920]

- notice of an FDIC cease and desist order that does not identify specific wrongful acts or unsound practices,[921]

- notice of an FDIC cease and desist order and a listing of classified loans,[922]

- copies of regulatory reports issued by the Federal Home Loan Bank Board, reports prepared by an independent auditing agency, and copies of complaints and other materials concerning two lawsuits (not the lawsuits for which coverage was at issue) filed against a savings and loan association and one of its directors,[923]

- general financial regulatory material, including copies of FDIC regulatory examinations, a loan watch list and a Report of Examination by a state Commissioner of Financial Institutions that identified as an "asset listed for special mention" one of the loans that later became the subject of litigation between the bank and the insurer,[924] or

- information demonstrating that the bank's loan portfolio was "troubled," and that regulatory authorities were concerned about the bank's lending practices.[925]

In short, the *Artley* court held, "notice of an institution's worsening financial condition is not notice of an officer's or director's act, error, or omission."[926] To the contrary, the *Artley* court stated, "[s]uch a view, we believe, would destroy the notification requirements at the heart of a claims made policy—that coverage

---

920. *Barham*, 995 F.2d at 604-05.
921. *McCullough*, 2 F.3d at 112-13.
922. *Mijalis*, 15 F.3d at 1334-37.
923. *Ayo*, 31 F.3d at 290-91.
924. *Booth*, 82 F.3d at 677-78.
925. *Artley*, 24 F.3d at 1367.
926. *Id.*

triggers only upon notice of the wrongful act."[927] As observed by the court in *Ayo*: "Insurance companies may limit their liability through clear and unambiguous notice provisions, and impose any reasonable conditions they wish upon the insureds under the contract. The purpose of the reporting requirement is to define the scope of coverage by providing a certain date after which an insurer knows it is no longer liable under the policy, and for this reason such reporting requirements are strictly construed."[928] As the court in *Booth* explained further: "In occurrence based policies, the notice requirement is generally included to aid the insurer in administration of its coverage of claims; in claims-made policies, the notice requirement actually serves to aid the insured by extending claims-made coverage beyond the policy period. As such, we believe it should be strictly construed."[929]

The Ninth Circuit in *Continental Insurance Co. v. Metro-Goldwyn-Mayer, Inc.*[930] reached a different result. The insured in this case, Metro-Goldwyn Mayer ("MGM"), sent its insurer, Continental Insurance Company, notice on September 20, 1990 of several claims and potential claims arising out of a merger between MGM and Pathe Communications, including a class action complaint by producers alleging "that the Pathe acquisition . . . will render MGM/UA insolvent and therefore unable to satisfy its obligations to the class" (the Grimaldi complaint).[931] The notice also included a "laundry list" of potential claims that contained the following statement: "There is a potential that producers other than Grimaldi may contend that MGM/UA does not have the right to

---

927. *Id*. at 1368.

928. 31 F.3d at 289.

929. 82 F.3d at 678; *see also American Casualty Co. v. Wilkinson*, 1990 U.S. Dist. LEXIS 20153, at *11-12, 1990 WL 302175, at *4 (N.D. Okla. Dec. 21, 1990) (insurer's "general knowledge about the financial condition of the savings and loan industry does not constitute notice of a specific claim or occurrence"), *aff'd on other grounds sub nom. American Casualty Co. v. Federal Deposit Ins. Corp.*, 958 F.2d 324, 328 (10th Cir. 1992).

930. 107 F.3d 1344 (9th Cir. 1997).

931. *Id*. at 1345.

transfer distribution rights to Warner Bros. under the pending Pathe acquisition."[932]

The court held that this notice triggered coverage for a complaint filed on February 14, 1991 by a producer of motion pictures alleging that MGM engaged in fraudulent leveraged buy-out transactions in connection with the merger of MGM and Pathe Communications (the *Danjaq* complaint).[933] The court explained that the governing insurance policy required that a notice "must state: (1) the date or dates when the wrongful act occurred and (2) the specific nature of the wrongful act."[934] The court continued:

> On September 20, 1990, MGM sent Continental a list of pending or potential litigation in order "to put [Continental] on notice that claims involving one or more of [MGM's] Directors and Officers may rise out of the legal actions or claims shown thereon." MGM sent a copy of the *Grimaldi* complaint, which sought relief on behalf of a class of producers with respect to the MGM-Pathe merger. This complaint set forth the details of the merger and some of its potential consequences. MGM also stated in the "laundry list" of potential claims that other producers might contend that the transfer of distribution rights pursuant to the Pathe merger was improper.
>
> The combination of these documents provided Continental with all the information required by the notice provisions of the insurance contract. Additionally, Continental should be held to the language of endorsement 7, which states:
>
> > . . . any series of continuous, repeated, connected, related or interrelated wrongful acts shall for the purposes of the application of this insurance constitute a single wrongful act which shall be deemed to have taken place at the date of the initial wrongful act.
>
> If the initial wrongful act is the MGM-Pathe merger and the related distribution agreements, Continental had notice of these wrongful acts from a variety of sources, including the

---

932. *Id.*
933. *Id.*
934. *Id.* at 1348.

*Grimaldi* complaint and several entries on the "laundry list." They also had explicit notice from MGM that this merger agreement might result in claims against MGM and the directors and officers of MGM.[935]

In sum, the court concluded, "MGM provided sufficient notice to Continental. Continental knew of the transaction that was expected to give rise to claims against MGM and its directors and officers, and this notice was sufficiently specific to satisfy the terms of the policy."[936]

*Federal Deposit Insurance Corp. v. Interdonato*[937] provides another example of a court finding that notice of an occurrence was sufficient to trigger coverage for a later claim involving the occurrence. The court reasoned as follows:

> To trigger coverage under the D & O Policy, UNB had to provide notice to VSC during the policy period of an "occurrence" that might subsequently give rise to a claim. The policy period commenced on March 15, 1985 and concluded on March 15, 1988. During this policy period, UNB provided sufficiently particular information to VSC to satisfy the notice provisions of the policy under existing caselaw. UNB affirmatively undertook to notify VSC of a potential "occurrence" under the policy as opposed to merely expecting the insurer to discover from information UNB routinely submitted that an occurrence existed that might give rise to a claim. One of UNB's letters to VSC alerted VSC that it was intended by UNB to provide notice under the D & O policy. This "actual notice" by UNB is in sharp contrast to the constructive notice relied upon by the insureds in many of the cases cited by VSC. *See infra*, discussion of case law regarding notice. UNB's letters indicated that a loss had been suffered by UNB, identified that the APA loans might give rise to a claim, and described how the APA loans were made. The letters further indicated how and why violations of law might have occurred, notifying VSC of possible loan policy violations, unsafe lending practices, and fraud with

---

935. *Id.*
936. *Id.*
937. 988 F. Supp. 1 (D.D.C. 1997).

regard to the APA loans. Samuel Foggie's October 13, 1987 letter described the following APA loan problems: (1) violations of UNB's loan policy, (2) inadequate financial support, (3) violation of sound credit principles, (4) loans made on false representations by APA, (5) disbursement of funds despite defects in title documentation and despite the failure of the customer to receive the automobiles, and (6) the misapplication of loans made to fund the resale of repossessed automobiles, with the effect that two loans were secured by the same automobile. UNB's letters also explained how and why these problems were discovered.

These letters were not a mere recital of policy language or a laundry list of possible errors by the bank. These letters targeted a particular situation or in the language of the policy, "occurrence," and indicated why these loans might give rise to claims. In two separate letters to VSC, UNB specifically mentioned the possibility of director liability, at one point identifying Interdonato as a director. Collectively, the letters sent by UNB to VSC during the policy period would have led a reasonable insurer to be aware of an "occurrence" that could give rise to a later claim under the policy for a wrongful act.[938]

The court in *Resolution Trust Corp. v. American Casualty Co.*[939] reached the same result in a case where letters were sent to an insurer stating "the identity of a potential claimant and very vague descriptions of the circumstances under which the insureds became aware of a potential claim and the nature of the claim."[940] The court reasoned that the "required content of notice" under the policy was ambiguous and that ambiguous provisions in an insurance contract are construed in favor of the insured.[941] The court distinguished the *Barham, McCullough* and *Ayo* line of cases discussed above on the ground that those cases involved "more demanding notice provisions" requiring a "specified Wrongful Act" and "constructive notice issues unlike the instant suit," where the

---

938. *Id*. at 7.
939. 874 F. Supp. 961 (E.D. Mo. 1995).
940. *Id*. at 965.
941. *Id*.

insured corporation "attempted to comply with notice provisions" by sending the insurer a letter on behalf of its directors and officers.[942]

The same result was reached in *Slaughter* v. *American Casualty Co.*,[943] a case where a banking corporation, Independence Federal Bank, notified its insurer, American Casualty Company ("ACC"), that directors and officers were aware of "certain losses . . . which may subsequently give rise to a claim being made against them" and of "rumors and allegations existing within their own community concerning financial problems . . . which may subsequently give rise to a claim."[944] The court held that this notification constituted a claim. The court reasoned as follows:

> Independence sent a letter, the sole purpose of which was to put ACCO on notice of potential claims. . . . Independence sent a specific letter notifying ACCO of potential claims pursuant to the policy. While the letter may not have been as specific as ACCO wanted, it certainly put ACCO on notice of possible claims.[945]

The court in *American Casualty Co. v. Sentry Federal Savings Bank*[946] similarly held that a letter advising an insurer of potential claims involving malfeasance by directors and officers was sufficient and timely notice where it "described the potential defendants, plaintiffs, and circumstances from which claims may arise."[947] The court in *Sentry* distinguished the notice held insufficient in *American Casualty Co. v. Wilkinson*,[948] which the court in *Sentry* described as a "'laundry list' of fifty potential claimants without

---

942. *Id*. at 965-66.

943. 842 F. Supp. 376 (E.D. Ark. 1993), *rev'd on other grounds*, 37 F.3d 385 (8th Cir. 1994).

944. *Id*. at 378.

945. *Id*. at 379.

946. 867 F. Supp. 50 (D. Mass. 1994).

947. *Id*. at 60.

948. 1990 U.S. Dist. LEXIS 20153, 1990 WL 302175 (N.D. Okla. Dec. 21, 1990), *aff'd on other grounds sub nom. American Casualty Co. v. Federal Deposit Ins. Corp.*, 958 F.2d 324, 328 (10th Cir. 1992).

explanation of the surrounding circumstances or alleged Wrongful Act."[949]

The court in *Continental Insurance Co. v. Superior Court*[950] also held that a notice was adequate. The notice "identified a number of events and circumstances which had occurred during the policy period" as "potential claims" in an "extensive and detailed" manner.[951] With respect to the subject matter of a claim asserted at a later date, the notice identified certain acquisitions that the insured, Winn Enterprises, had entered into and stated that "[c]laims in the future may be asserted challenging the wisdom of these acquisitions or the management of these businesses after they were acquired, or the distribution of the assets of these companies upon their sale, liquidation, ceasing to do business or other disposition."[952]

The court pointed to the policy's notice provision, which required notice that

> (1) the insureds had received written notice or oral notice that a third party intended to hold them responsible for the results of *any specified wrongful act* committed by the insureds or (2) the insureds had become aware of an occurrence which *might subsequently* give rise to a claim against the insureds "in respect of *any such wrongful act.*"

The court stated that the second clause of this provision expressly permitted "notices of 'occurrences' which may lead to a future claim."[953] The court also stated that "plaintiffs had provided all of the information they had; that is, they provided the best notice they could. The notice clearly spelled out imprudence, negligence and mismanagement as possible allegations which were likely, if not anticipated, in connection with the acquisition by Winn

---

949. 867 F. Supp. at 60; *see also* 1990 U.S. Dist. LEXIS 20153, at *12, 1990 WL 302175, at *4-5.

950. 37 Cal. App. 4th 69, 43 Cal. Rptr. 2d 374 (Cal. Ct. App. 1995).

951. *Id.* at 76, 43 Cal. Rptr. at 377.

952. *Id.* at 76, 43 Cal. Rptr. at 378.

953. *Id.* at 79-80, 43 Cal. Rptr. at 380.

Enterprises of certain corporate subsidiaries."[954] Under these circumstances, the court stated, the insurer "cannot avoid coverage by claiming that plaintiffs' description of possible future events was not more specific. Plaintiffs provided all of the information they had as well as all they were likely to have until a specific complaint was actually filed.[955] In sum, the court concluded, "[t]he policy could not reasonably require more."[956]

## 7. The Wrongful Act Requirement

The definition of "wrongful act" varies from policy to policy but generally includes "any breach of duty, neglect, error, misstatement, misleading statement, omission or act by the Directors or Officers of the Company in their respective capacities as such, or any matter claimed against them solely by reason of their status as Directors or Officers of the Company."[957] The term "Wrongful Act" thus is "defined broadly," and it is "hard to think of any act or omission by a director or officer, acting as such, which would not be covered by this definition."[958]

Where a director or officer has relationships with a corporation other than his service as a director or officer, disputes may arise concerning whether a claim is the result of conduct as a

---

954. *Id.* at 80, 43 Cal. Rptr. at 380.

955. *Id.* at 81, 43 Cal. Rptr. at 380.

956. *Id.*

957. *See* John F. Olson & Josiah O. Hatch III, *Director and Officer Liability: Indemnification and Insurance* § 10.06[3], at 10-21 (1997); Johnston, *Directors' and Officers' and Related Forms of Liability Insurance, in 7 Securities Law Techniques* § 122.03[2][f] (A.A. Sommer, Jr. ed. 1998); Monteleone & Conca, *Directors and Officers Indemnification and Liability Insurance: An Overview of Legal and Practical Issues*, 51 Bus. Law. 573, 599 (1996).

958. *Reliance Group Holdings, Inc. v. National Union Fire Ins. Co.*, 188 A.D.2d 47, 53, 594 N.Y.S.2d 20, 23-24 (N.Y. App. Div. 1st Dep't), *motion for leave to appeal dismissed in part and denied in part*, 82 N.Y.2d 704, 619 N.E.2d 656, 601 N.Y.S.2d 578 (1993) (quoting Johnston, *Corporate Indemnification and Liability Insurance for Directors and Officers*, 33 Bus. Law. 1993, 2017 (1978)).

director or officer. This issue has been litigated in several cases and the results vary with the particular facts in each case.

*Continental Copper & Steel Industries, Inc. v. Johnson,*[959] for example, involved directors of Continental Copper & Steel Industries who were insured in that capacity and who served as Continental's designees on the board of International Halliwell Mines, Ltd.[960] The court held that these directors were entitled to insurance in connection with a litigation alleging that they had mismanaged Halliwell. The court explained that these directors were sued both "for breach of their duties as Halliwell directors" and "for wrongful acts committed in their capacities as directors and officers of Continental in mismanaging Halliwell for the benefit of Continental."[961] In short, the court concluded, the directors "were allegedly acting on behalf of Continental in looting Halliwell for Continental's benefit. They thus allegedly committed wrongful acts on behalf of the insured corporation.[962]

Similarly, in *Ratcliffe v. International Surplus Lines Insurance Co.,*[963] the court held that directors and officers who were insured in their capacity as directors and officers of a corporation were entitled to insurance for a litigation alleging wrongful conduct by the directors and officers in their dual capacities as directors and officers of the corporation and trustees of trusts because the corporation had been established for the purpose of servicing the trusts.[964] The same result was reached in *Raychem Corp. v. Federal Insurance Co.,*[965] a case involving allegations by shareholders that corporate officials had made false and misleading statements in corporate press releases, quarterly and annual SEC filings and at an analysts' meeting. According to plaintiffs, these false and misleading statements were made in order to facilitate an

---

959. 641 F.2d 59 (2d Cir. 1981).
960. *Id.* at 60.
961. *Id.*
962. *Id.*
963. 550 N.E.2d 1052 (Ill. App. Ct. 1990).
964. *Id.* at 1059-60.
965. 853 F. Supp. 1170 (N.D. Cal. 1994).

exercise of options held by the corporate officials to acquire common stock at favorable prices.[966] The court held that the plaintiffs complained of the "official conduct" of making allegedly false and misleading statements—conduct that occurred in the defendants' official capacities as officers and directors—and not the exercise of options.[967] The exercise of options, the court stated, "merely provided a possible basis for defendants' alleged scienter."[968]

By contrast, coverage was denied in *Bowie v. Home Insurance Co.*,[969] where the insureds were sued for conduct as directors of one corporation—Transit Casualty Company—but sought coverage pursuant to a policy insuring them as directors of another corporation—DMT Financial Group.[970] The court reasoned as follows:

> The insurers have not unqualifiedly covered Bowie and Gregory, but rather only have covered them in their capacities as DMT officials. The California action names them as defendants only in their capacities as Transit officials. The mere fact that Bowne and Gregory are named in the California action is not controlling. The directors of Transit and the directors of DMT may as well have been completely different people. What is important is not their identities but their capacities. Here the insured capacities are not implicated in the California action.[971]

The same result was reached in *Aetna Casualty & Surety Co. v. Lindner*,[972] a case in which two directors, Carl and Keith Lindner, (1) were named in a complaint as defendants in their capacity as individuals and as controlling shareholders, and, (2) after their

---

966. *Id.* at 1173-74, 1184.

967. *Id.* at 1184.

968. *Id.*

969. 923 F.2d 705 (9th Cir. 1991).

970. *Id.* at 706.

971. *Id.* at 708 (citations omitted).

972. No. Civ. 90-1221-PHX-PGR (D. Ariz. Dec. 12, 1994), *aff'd on other grounds*, 92 F.3d 1191 (unpublished opinion, text available at 1996 U.S. App. LEXIS 18541 and 1996 WL 413621) (9th Cir. July 22, 1996).

insurance policy expired, were named in an amended complaint in their capacity as directors. The court explained that the governing policy required allegations of wrongdoing by directors in their capacity as directors, and that the naming of the directors "as defendants during the term of the policy for alleged wrongdoing unrelated to their positions" as directors was insufficient.[973] The court stated that "[t]he action triggering coverage is not merely the filing of a lawsuit but the filing of a specific type of lawsuit and here there was simply no lawsuit pending during the policy period that fell within the express terms of the policy—i.e. one against the Lindners arising from their actions as Circle K directors."[974]

Likewise, in *Snokist Growers v. Washington Insurance Guaranty Ass'n*,[975] the court held that claims by U-Haul Company of Inland Northwest for the cost of environmental cleanup of U-Haul's property against directors of Snokist Growers were not covered by a Snokist director and officer insurance policy. The court found that these individuals were sued as owners, officers and/or directors of Yakima Valley Spray Company ("YVS") and that even if their service as YVS directors and officers was within the scope of their duties as Snokist directors and officers, their conduct as YVS directors and officers was not within the scope of their duties as Snokist directors and officers "and consequently the policies do not provide coverage."[976] According to the court, U-Haul sued those individuals "in their capacities as officers, directors, and owners of YVS" and did not allege facts that "would indicate Snokist controlled" these individuals "in their service on the YVS board."[977]

Coverage similarly was denied in *Beck v. American Casualty Co.*[978] because the claims asserted in that case did not arise out of actions taken in the insureds' "sole capacity as officers or direc-

---

973. *Id.*, slip op. at 2-3.
974. *Id.* at 3.
975. 922 P.2d 821 (Wash. Ct. App. 1996).
976. *Id.* at 823-24.
977. *Id.* at 825.
978. 1990 U.S. Dist. LEXIS 13756, 1990 WL 598573 (W.D. Tex. Apr. 12, 1990).

tors," as required by the policy in that case.[979] Coverage also was denied in *Olson v. Federal Insurance Co.*[980] a case involving a series of actions commenced by one director against other directors arising out of intra-board disputes. The court stated that the conduct at issue was "outside the reasonable parameters of the policy issued."[981]

## 8.  Losses Covered

"Loss" typically is defined to include any amount an insured is obligated to pay—including damages, judgments, settlements and costs and expenses incurred in defense of an action—arising out of a "claim made" for a "wrongful act."[982] The inclusion of judgments and settlements is significant because state indemnification statutes often preclude indemnification of judgments and amounts paid to settle actions by or in the right of the corporation.[983]

For the corporation, the term loss generally encompasses indemnification payments by the corporation to directors and officers. For directors and officers, the term loss generally encompasses amounts the directors and officers are legally obligated to pay and for which they have not been—and, in some policies, cannot be—indemnified.[984]

---

979. 1990 U.S. Dist. LEXIS 13756, at *39-42, 1990 WL 598573, at *14-15.

980. 219 Cal. App. 3d 252, 268 Cal. Rptr. 90 (Cal. Ct. App. 1990).

981. *Id.* at 256-64, 268 Cal. Rptr. at 91-96.

982. John F. Olson & Josiah O. Hatch III, *Director and Officer Liability: Indemnification and Insurance* § 10.06[3], at 10-21 (1996); Johnston, *Directors' and Officers' and Related Forms of Liability Insurance, in 7 Securities Law Techniques* § 122.03[2][c], [e] (A.A. Sommer, Jr. ed. 1998); Monteleone & Conca, *Directors and Officers Indemnification and Liability Insurance: An Overview of Legal and Practical Issues*, 51 Bus. Law. 573, 598-99 (1996).

983. *See* Chapter V, Sections A 4 b and B 2.

984. J. Olson & J. Hatch § 10.06[4], at 10-24.

Where the governing policy covers only "[l]oss for which the Insured Organization grants indemnification . . . as permitted or required by law" and no indemnification has been granted by the corporation pursuant to the terms of the governing indemnification statute or a charter, bylaw or contract provision, an insurer has no obligation to reimburse the corporation for payments "advanced" by the corporation on behalf of directors and officers.[985] By contrast, a grant of indemnification is not required in order to trigger the insurer's obligation to pay for a loss where the governing policy covers losses for which the corporation "is required to indemnify" pursuant either to a statute or to a charter, bylaw or contract provision.[986]

Settlements naming the insured corporation rather than directors or officers as payer are not *"per se* excluded from coverage where the policy require[s] indemnification or an obligation to indemnify."[987] This is because "it is a detail whether the director or officer first incurs an expense to a plaintiff which [the corporation] then reimburses or [the corporation] pays the plaintiff directly. The latter route is merely more direct; it cuts out the middleman."[988] Under this circumstance, it has been said, "[i]nsistence on a meaningless formality of having the directors and officers pay

---

985. *See Macmillan, Inc. v. Federal Ins. Co.*, 741 F. Supp. 1079, 1082 (S.D.N.Y. 1990); *see also Atlantic Permanent Fed. Sav. & Loan Ass'n v. American Casualty Co.*, 839 F.2d 212, 215 & n.5 (4th Cir.) (where corporation failed to comply with Federal Home Loan Bank Board procedures governing indemnification and advancement, corporation was not entitled to insurance for losses "for which [it] is *required to indemnify,* or for which [it] *has, to the extent permitted by law, indemnified* the Directors and Officers"; corporation, however, was entitled to proceed against insurer as subrogee to the rights of the insured directors and officers whose defense and settlement costs had been paid by the corporation) (quoting policy, emphasis added by court), *cert. denied*, 486 U.S. 1056 (1988).

986. *Ameriwood Indus. Int'l Corp. v. American Casualty Co.*, 840 F. Supp. 1143, 1158-59 (W.D. Mich. 1993).

987. *Id.* at 1158.

988. *Harbor Ins. Co. v. Continental Bank Corp.*, 922 F.2d 357, 366 (7th Cir. 1990).

initially and then be indemnified from the assets of [the corporation] should not be required to secure the coverage . . . sold to [the corporation] and [the insurer's] other customers."[989]

The court in *First State Underwriters Agency v. Public Utility District No. 1*[990] held that there had been no indemnification and thus that a corporation was not entitled to insurance in a case where directors settled securities fraud claims by assigning their rights under insurance policies to the plaintiffs in the case, and the plaintiffs later assigned those rights to the corporation in return for a settlement payment by the corporation. The court explained that the governing policy insured the corporation when it indemnified its officers or directors "for damages, judgments, settlements, costs, charges, or expenses" relating to a covered claim, and that in this case there was no such loss by directors or officers that the corporation had repaid.[991]

The term "loss" has been construed—sometimes as a result of explicit policy language, and sometimes as a matter of law on public policy grounds—not to include losses arising out of an insured's intentional or criminal conduct.[992] Similarly, the return by insured directors or officers of money or property wrongfully taken from the corporation was held not to constitute a "loss" in *Reliance Group Holdings, Inc. v. National Union Fire Insurance Co.*[993]

---

989. *Safeway Stores, Inc. v. National Union Fire Ins. Co.*, 64 F.3d 1282, 1290 (9th Cir. 1995); *see also Vitkus v. Beatrice Co.*, 127 F.3d 936, 944 (10th Cir. 1997) (quoting *Safeway* and stating that "it is irrelevant that National Union paid the $10 million on Vitkus's behalf in the first instance" because the policy "only required that Vitkus incur an obligation to pay in order to be entitled to indemnification").

990. 41 F.3d 1513 (unpublished opinion, text available at 1994 U.S. App. LEXIS 31307 and 1994 WL 637139) (9th Cir. Nov. 7, 1994), *cert. denied*, 516 U.S. 822 (1995).

991. 1994 U.S. App. LEXIS 31307, at *6, 1994 WL 637139, at *2.

992. *See* Chapter V, Section B 3.

993. 188 A.D.2d 47, 594 N.Y.S.2d 20 (N.Y. App. Div. 1st Dep't), *motion for leave to appeal dismissed in part and denied in part*, 82 N.Y.2d 704, 619 N.E.2d 656, 601 N.Y.S.2d 578 (1993).

*Reliance* involved a settlement of an action—*Heckmann v. Ahmanson*,[994] a case discussed in Chapter III[995]—pursuant to an agreement requiring defendants to return $21.1 million to Walt Disney Productions, Inc. that defendants had received in "greenmail" proceeds.[996] The court in *Reliance* held that this settlement was "essentially equivalent to a determination, reached through agreement of the parties, that Reliance had been unjustly enriched in the amount of $21.1 million through its actions in connection with the Disney takeover attempt" and therefore did not constitute a "loss" as defined in the policy.[997] To the contrary, the court stated, the defendants "realized a profit of approximately $74 million in connection with its Disney takeover attempt" even after the $21.1 million payment pursuant to the *Heckmann* settlement.[998]

The court also pointed to the following hypothetical fact pattern that "illustrates the untenability" of the contention by the insureds in *Reliance* that the term "loss" should be construed to "cover any settlement, whether for damages, or for restitution of property wrongfully acquired":

> Assume that by embezzlement or fraud a corporation obtains title to stock worth $60 million. The rightful owner sues to impress a trust on the proceeds of the sale of the stock, and after the court imposes a temporary constructive trust the action is settled by a payment of $20 million, which would undoubtedly constitute partial restitution to the rightful owner. Under the construction urged by Reliance and Steinberg, if an officer or director was sued together with the corporation, the corporation could make full or partial restitution of the embezzled or fraudulently obtained funds purportedly on behalf of its officer, adopt a resolution indemnifying the officer, and then successfully make claim against its D & O insurer for the full amount of the settlement. Surely the corporation's disgorgement of such wrong-

---

994. 168 Cal. App. 3d 119, 214 Cal. Rptr. 177 (Cal. Ct. App. 1985).

995. *See* Chapter III, Section I 1 b.

996. 188 A.D.2d at 51-52, 594 N.Y.S.2d at 22-23.

997. *Id.* at 55, 594 N.Y.S.2d at 25.

998. *Id.*

fully acquired property would not be recognized as an insurable loss.[999]

*Safeway Stores, Inc. v. National Union Fire Insurance Co.*[1000] involved an $11.5 million dividend Safeway determined to pay to Safeway shareholders before rather than after a 1986 leveraged buyout of Safeway by Kravis, Kohlberg & Roberts ("KKR") as part of a settlement of lawsuits by shareholders alleging that Safeway's directors and officers had breached their fiduciary duties to Safeway and Safeway's shareholders by approving an earlier KKR offer.[1001] The court held that this payment did not constitute a "loss" within the meaning of Safeway's D & O policy. The court explained:

> It is difficult to see how a corporation's payment of a dividend could ever be a "loss" under the terms of an insurance policy. Neither the owners of that corporation nor its directors suffered a loss. The effect of a dividend is simply to transfer corporate profits from one part of the corporation to another, that is, from the purse of the corporate entity into the pockets of the corporation's owners, the shareholders. . . . Safeway is not entitled to reimbursement for a payment made, in essence, to itself.
>
> Furthermore, the fact that Safeway, by action of its directors, arranged to pay the dividend to its shareholders, rather than to KKR as originally anticipated, is of no relevant consequence. It could make no difference to the "corporate personality" Safeway who received the dividend; once the dividend was declared, it became a corporate obligation that Safeway had to meet in any event. In effect, therefore, the settlement did not—and could not—result in an $11.5 million loss because Safeway was obliged to pay out the dividend in due course, without the settlement. Only Safeway's shareholders could have complained had they established that the directors sold their assets too cheaply. This possibility was forestalled by paying them the $11.5 million dividend.

---

999. *Id*. at 54, 594 N.Y.S.2d at 24.
1000. 64 F.3d 1282 (9th Cir. 1995).
1001. *Id*. at 1284-85.

. . . [T]he early payout of the dividend essentially amounted to KKR's upping its purchase price for Safeway by $11.5 million. Under the explicit terms of the settlement agreement, "the plaintiff shareholders released their claims against [Safeway and KKR] in consideration of a direct benefit provided to them by KKR's acceptance of a detrimental change to its merger agreement with Safeway." Under this view, the dividend, if a "loss" to anyone, was KKR's, not Safeway's, and could not be claimed under Safeway's insurance policy.[1002]

The court did hold, however, that approximately $1.8 million paid by Safeway in attorneys' fees to the shareholder plaintiffs' counsel in the litigation and $230,000 in defense costs incurred by Safeway's directors and officers in the litigation constituted losses within the meaning of the policy. "Unlike the dividend," the court stated, these costs "were an actual out-of-pocket loss to Safeway incurred in defense of its directors and officers."[1003]

## 9.  Exclusions

*a. Common Exclusions.* Certain losses are excluded from coverage either in exclusions that are "so generally applied as to have become part of the printed policy form" or in endorsements "more fitted to the particular circumstances and risks of the individual company" obtaining the insurance.[1004] Examples of losses that often—but not always—are excluded from coverage include dishonesty, awards of punitive damages or treble damages,[1005] the receipt of a personal profit or advantage to which an insured is not legally entitled, illegal remuneration, short-swing profit liability under Section 16(b) of the Securities Exchange Act of 1934,[1006] violations of the Employment Retirement Income Security Act

---

1002. *Id.* at 1286.

1003. *Id.* at 1285, 1287.

1004. John F. Olson & Josiah O. Hatch III, *Director and Officer Liability: Indemnification and Insurance* § 10.06[5][d], at 10-39 (1997).

1005. *See* Chapter V, Section B 3 (noting different views in different jurisdictions concerning whether awards of punitive damages and treble damage are insurable).

1006. 15 U.S.C. § 78p(b).

("ERISA")[1007] or similar provisions of any comparable state or local statutory or common law, employment practice claims, libel or slander claims, claims based upon bodily or physical injury or death, damage or destruction of tangible property or emotional distress, and claims based upon pollution or other environmental damage and/or nuclear accidents.[1008]

The dishonesty exclusion is a particularly important exclusion because this exclusion "potentially has application to almost every claim under a D & O policy."[1009] Many—but not all—policies require "a judgment or other final adjudication" adverse to an insured person in order to trigger the dishonesty exclusion.[1010] Courts have held that where a policy requires "a judgment or other final adjudication" an insurer may not litigate whether the insured acted dishonestly for the purpose of determining the applicability of the exclusion after the underlying litigation is concluded (for example, by a settlement in which money is paid but there is no finding of wrongdoing).[1011] "In other words," these courts hold, "the dis-

---

1007. 29 U.S.C. §§ 1001-1461.

1008. *See* J. Olson & J. Hatch §§ 10.06[5][a], [b], [d], at 10–27-32, 10–39-40; Johnston, *Directors' and Officers' and Related Forms of Liability Insurance, in 7 Securities Law Techniques* § 122.03[2][g] (A.A. Sommer, Jr. ed. 1998); Mallen & Evans, *Surviving the Directors' and Officers' Liability Crisis: Insurance and the Alternatives*, 12 Del. J. Corp. L. 439, 454-57 (1988); Monteleone & Conca, *Directors and Officers Indemnification and Liability Insurance: An Overview of Legal and Practical Issues*, 51 Bus. Law. 573, 600-04 (1996); Weiss, *Filling the Gaps in D & O Insurance*, 6 Bus. Law Today No. 3, Jan./Feb. 1997, at 44, 47.

1009. Monteleone & Conca, 51 Bus. Law. at 601.

1010. Johnston § 122.03[2][g][iv]; Monteleone & Conca, 51 Bus. Law. at 601; *see also First Nat'l Bank Holding Co. v. Fidelity & Deposit Co.*, 885 F. Supp. 1533, 1537-38 (N.D. Fla. 1995) (guilty plea to counts alleging bank fraud, conspiracy to commit bank fraud, making a false statement on a bank document and violation of currency reporting requirements held to constitute dishonesty).

1011. *See Atlantic Permanent Fed. Sav. & Loan Ass'n v. American Casualty Co.*, 839 F.2d 212, 216-17 (4th Cir.), *cert. denied*, 486 U.S. 1056 (1988); *In re Donald Sheldon & Co.*, 186 B.R. 364, 370 (S.D.N.Y.

(continued...)

honesty must be adjudicated in the context of the underlying claim or not at all."[1012]

The reasoning in *In re Donald Sheldon & Co.*[1013] is illustrative. There, two directors and officers of a broker-dealer were found liable for breaches of fiduciary duty in connection with transactions that violated the Securities and Exchange Commission's net capital rules and that caused customers to lose securities and the corporation to liquidate under the Securities Investors Protection Act.[1014] The applicable policy provision excluded losses "brought about or contributed to by the dishonesty of such Insured Person if a judgment or other final adjudication adverse to such Insured Person established that the acts of active and deliberate dishonesty were committed or attempted by such Insured Person with actual dishonest purpose and intent and were material to the cause of action so adjudicated."[1015] The court held that this provision did not exclude coverage. The court reasoned as follows:

> The explicit language of the provision excludes coverage if actively dishonest acts and actual dishonest purpose and intent both are established by adjudication. As the exclusion requires that actual dishonest purpose and intent be "established" by adjudication, the exclusion certainly is susceptible to the interpretation, well developed in the law of collateral estoppel, that the judgment establishes dishonesty under the exclusion only if a finding of dishonesty was necessary to the judgment, which in this case it was not. The fact that this interpretation of the exclusion gives the parties to the underlying action some control over the insurer's liability—to the extent that the parties can affect the jury charge and evidence

---

1011. (...continued)
1995); *National Union Fire Ins. Co. v. Continental Ill. Corp.*, 666 F. Supp. 1180, 1197-99 (N.D. Ill. 1987); *National Union Fire Ins. Co. v. Seafirst Corp.*, 662 F. Supp. 36, 38-39 (W.D. Wash. 1986); *PepsiCo, Inc. v. Continental Casualty Co.*, 640 F. Supp. 656, 659-60 (S.D.N.Y. 1986).

1012. Monteleone & Conca, 51 Bus. Law. at 601.

1013. 186 B.R. 364 (S.D.N.Y. 1995).

1014. *Id.* at 365-67.

1015. *Id.* at 367-68.

received—is not unfair to insurers. Contracts routinely have conditions of performance contingent on the behavior or conduct of only one of the contracting parties or of strangers to the contract. The insurance company, which drafts, markets and prices its policies, is capable of ameliorating this risk either through its pricing of the policy or by redrafting the relevant exclusions.[1016]

"A number of insurers have reacted" to decisions such as *Sheldon* "by dropping the adjudication requirement and requiring only dishonesty 'in fact.'"[1017]

Dishonesty, it should be noted, may trigger coverage for the corporation under a fidelity bond protecting the corporation for dishonest acts by directors, officers and/or employees.[1018] The Fifth Circuit in *Eglin National Bank v. Home Indemnity Co.*[1019] held that the D & O insurance policy and the fidelity bond at issue in that case were mutually exclusive: once a loss was proven for the purpose of recovery under the fidelity bond, the dishonesty exclusion in the D & O policy was triggered.[1020]

Another common exclusion excludes coverage for circumstances for which notice has been given under a prior policy and for claims arising from litigation filed prior to the policy's effective date.[1021]

In *Ameriwood Industries International Corp. v. American Casualty Co.*,[1022] for example, the court granted summary judgment in favor of an insurer where the governing policy excluded claims "made against the Directors or Officers based upon or attributable to litigation prior to or pending at the inception date of this policy . . . or arising out of the facts or circumstances under-

---

1016. *Id.* at 370 (citations omitted).

1017. Monteleone & Conca, 51 Bus. Law. at 601.

1018. *Id.* at 602.

1019. 583 F.2d 1281 (5th Cir. 1978).

1020. *Id.* at 1288.

1021. J. Olson & J. Hatch § 10.06[5][b], at 10-30; Johnston § 122.03[2][g][xi]; Monteleone & Conca, 51 Bus. Law. at 606-07.

1022. 840 F. Supp. 1143 (W.D. Mich. 1993).

lying or alleged in any such prior or pending litigation."[1023] The court held that "[e]ven if the naming of a new target of allegedly unlawful proxy solicitation in Count II were to differentiate the second amended complaint from the original complaint in *Alizac*, the second amended complaint, including Count II, is undeniably 'based upon or attributable to' the lawsuit of which it is part. Because *Alizac* was filed on April 21, 1988, it was 'prior to or pending at' the beginning of the 88/89 policy in October, 1988. Therefore, Count II of the second amended complaint in *Alizac* falls squarely under the Prior or Pending litigation endorsement, and is not covered under the 88/89 policy."[1024] The court also held that a second action by the same plaintiff against the same defendants asserting the same wrongful acts and legal violations asserted in the plaintiff's first action but attributing a different harmful effect to the conduct "'[arose] out of the facts or circumstances underlying or alleged in' the earlier suit" and therefore was barred by the prior or pending litigation exclusion.[1025]

In *Anglo-American Insurance Co. v. Molin*,[1026] the court held that two actions by the Pennsylvania Insurance Commissioner against the directors and officers of Corporate Life Insurance Co. involved "distinct claims alleging different wrongs to different people."[1027] As a result, the second action constituted a claim that was separate from the claim submitted for the first action and was not excluded from coverage by a new policy that had become effective between the dates of the two actions and that excluded any loss in connection with any claim

> based upon, arising out of, directly or indirectly resulting from or in consequence of, or in any way involving:
>
> (1) any Wrongful Act or any fact, circumstance or situation, event or transaction which has been the subject of any notice

---

1023. *Id.* at 1152.
1024. *Id.*
1025. *Id.* at 1153.
1026. 673 A.2d 986 (Pa. Cmmw. Ct. 1996), *rev'd*, 691 A.2d 929 (Pa. 1997).
1027. *Id.* at 993.

given prior to the effective date of this Policy under any prior policy, or

(2) any other Wrongful Act whenever occurring, which, together with a Wrongful Act which has been the subject of such notice, would constitute Interrelated Wrongful Acts.[1028]

The policy stated that

More than one Claim involving the same Wrongful Act or Interrelated Wrongful Acts of one or more of the Directors and Officers shall be deemed to constitute a single Claim and such single Claim shall be deemed to have been made at the earlier of the following times:

(1) the time the earliest of any Claim within such single Claim was first made; or

(2) the earliest time at which notice was given under any policy of insurance of any Wrongful Act or any fact, circumstance, situation, event, or transaction which underlies any Claim within such single Claim.[1029]

"Interrelated Wrongful Acts" were defined as "Wrongful Acts which have as a common nexus any fact, circumstance, situation, event, transaction or series of facts, circumstances, situations, events or transactions."[1030]

The court explained that one of the actions was filed by the Insurance Commissioner "acting in the capacity as a regulator of insurance companies under Pennsylvania insurance law and regulations," while the other action was filed by the Insurance Commissioner "acting in her capacity as the Statutory Liquidator of Corporate Life"—a capacity in which "the Statutory Liquidator is seeking to enforce the rights of Corporate Life's insureds, creditors and shareholders."[1031] The court added that there were "numerous allegations" in the second action that were not raised in the first action, including allegations that directors acted wrongfully "in

---

1028. *Id.* at 989.
1029. *Id.*
1030. *Id.*
1031. *Id.* at 993.

placing unqualified individuals on Corporate Life's board of directors, in using Corporate Life's assets to purchase overvalued and
substandard mortgages, in using Corporate Life's assets in effect to
purchase itself, in delegating Corporate Life's powers to other
companies, and in causing other transactions to occur for their own
personal benefits."[1032]

This decision was reversed on the ground that it arose in the
procedural context of a motion for a preliminary injunction, where
relief can be granted only upon a showing that the right to relief is
"clear."[1033] The court reasoned that a "viable argument" could
be made that both cases involved "a common nexus of facts,
circumstances, situations, events and transactions"—allegations that
the defendants "were raping the insurance company and that their
conduct involved fraud and numerous violations of law."[1034] The
court acknowledged that the defendants "may, in fact, prevail in
their claim" that they are entitled to insurance coverage for two
years rather than one year "after the case has been fully litigated"
but held that "we cannot say that their right to relief, on this
record, is clear."[1035]

---

1032. *Id.*

1033. *Anglo-American Ins. Co. v. Molin*, 691 A.2d 929, 933-34
(Pa. 1997).

1034. *Id.* at 934.

1035. *Id.; see also Home Ins. Co. v. Spectrum Info. Tech. Inc.*, 930
F. Supp. 825, 848-49 (E.D.N.Y. 1996) (holding in favor of insureds
following a bench trial on the ground that "wrongs which are factually and
legally distinct" from prior claims are not covered by an exclusion for
"prior and/or pending litigation which was reported during and/or covered
by a pre-existing policy); *David v. American Home Assurance Co.* 1997
U.S. Dist. LEXIS 4177, at *8, 1997 WL 160367, at *3 (S.D.N.Y. Apr.
3, 1997) (denying motion to dismiss claim challenging reliance by insurer,
American Home Assurance Co., upon exclusions for conduct concerning
which a claim was asserted or litigation was filed in a prior policy period,
and stating that "[t]he examination and comparison of the relevant complaints to determine their similarities and distinctions involve issues of fact
that are not properly resolved on a motion to dismiss. In fact, counsel for
defendant has been unable to point to a single case resolving the applica-
(continued...)

Another issue that may arise in the context of a policy provision excluding coverage for acts that occurred prior to a particular date is whether the policy excludes coverage for all insured directors and officers due to a prior act by any one insured director and officer or whether the policy excludes coverage only with respect to insured directors and officers who themselves have committed a prior act. The court in *Federal Deposit Insurance Corp. v. Interdonato*[1036] held that the prior acts exclusion in that case only excluded claims by particular directors and officers who had committed acts prior to the date specified in the policy.[1037] The court reasoned that the policy contained a severability clause making the policy a contract with each insured director and officer and "does not contain any reference to indicate to whom the prior acts exclusion applies."[1038] The court stated that "[i]n the absence of a phrase expanding the clause's scope . . . the prior acts exclusion, read in conjunction with the severability clause," should only exclude coverage for prior acts by directors and officers who themselves committed prior acts.[1039]

Additional "non-standard" exclusions such as antitrust exclusions or discrimination exclusions sometimes are added as endorsements to particular D & O policies by insurers depending upon their assessment of the risks faced by particular insureds.[1040] Some policies also exclude claims arising out of securities law claims or comparable common law claims.

---

1035. (...continued)

bility of a prior litigation exclusion in the context of a motion to dismiss; the cases upon which American Home relies instead all involve motions for summary judgment. . . . The presence of a significant degree of ambiguity requires that the parties at least be permitted to conduct some discovery into the meaning of the exclusion at issue before I determine the question of coverage.").

1036. 988 F. Supp. 1 (D.D.C. 1997).

1037. *Id.* at 12.

1038. *Id.*

1039. *Id.*

1040. Johnston § 122.03[2][g][xvii].

*Bendis v. Federal Insurance Co.*,[1041] for example, involved a policy provision that excluded claims "directly or indirectly, based on, attributable to, arising out of, resulting from or in any manner related to any actual or alleged violation" of any securities law.[1042] Based upon this policy language, the court found that the common law claims in that case arose out of the same factual allegations that formed the basis of alleged violations of securities laws and thus were excluded from coverage.[1043] The court in *RHI Holdings, Inc. v. National Union Fire Insurance Co.*[1044] similarly concluded that a policy provision excluded coverage for claims relating to the filing of a registration statement with the Securities and Exchange Commission and that the claims in that case fell within this exclusion.[1045]

The court in *Ross Stores, Inc. v. Certain Underwriters at Lloyd's, London*[1046] reached a different result in a case involving a policy provision that the court referred to as an "S.E.C. Exclusion" and that excluded coverage for conduct involving "the offering or sale of securities of the Company."[1047] The case involved alleged misrepresentations and omissions in connection with an initial public offering and subsequent "aftermarket" statements concerning the insured's financial condition.[1048] The court concluded that the insurer "knew perfectly well how to draft an exclusion as broad as it argues the S.E.C. Exclusion is intended to be."[1049] The court added that "the 'aftermarket' statements did not directly involve the sale of . . . stock."[1050] Rather, the court

---

1041. 958 F.2d 960 (10th Cir. 1991).

1042. *Id.* at 961.

1043. *Id.* at 963.

1044. [1994-1995 Transfer Binder] Fed. Sec. L. Rep. (CCH) ¶ 98,315 (E.D. Pa. May 4, 1994), *aff'd mem.*, 47 F.3d 1161 (3d Cir. 1995).

1045. *Id.* at 90,196-97.

1046. No. C 88 20344 RPA (N.D. Cal. Mar. 7, 1989).

1047. *Id.*, slip op. at 6.

1048. *Id.* at 2-3.

1049. *Id.* at 8.

1050. *Id.* at 10.

stated, "[t]he claims are based on misrepresentations and omissions regarding Ross' past performance and future prospects. The purchase of Ross' stock at inflated prices is merely the damage that resulted from the statements. Thus, the acts giving rise to liability are statements regarding the company's financial status and not the sale of securities."[1051]

Underlying many of these exclusions is the principle that D & O insurance is not "a substitute for the corporation's normal liability and property insurance coverage" or for other types of insurance that can be purchased by the corporation.[1052] To the contrary, it has been said, "[i]f a corporation can purchase another type of insurance to cover a specific D & O risk, the D & O insurer expects that other insurance to be purchased and therefore the D & O policy will not cover that risk."[1053] This principal is illustrated by the Ninth Circuit's decision in *Olympic Club v. Those Interested Underwriters at Lloyd's London*.[1054] The court in this case denied coverage for conduct resulting from corporate policies and practices (specifically, discrimination by a social club against blacks and women) where the corporation, not any insured directors or offices, had been sued, and it could not reasonably be said that the suit against the corporation was based upon wrongful acts of directors and officers that could be imputed to the corporation as their principal.[1055] The court reasoned as follows:

> Stripped to its essentials, the issue in this case is whether the underlying lawsuits are against the Club for the Club's own policies, or are against the Club because of "wrongful acts" of its directors and employees that are "imputed to [the Club] as their principal." In our view, the City's claims for injunctive and declarative relief are clearly based on the Club's own policies; it is the policies of the Club itself that are

---

1051. *Id.*

1052. Johnston § 122.03[2][g][vi].

1053. Monteleone & McCarrick, *D & O Insurance: Settlement Issues in Securities Litigation Involving Directors and Officers*, 10 Insights: The Corporate & Securities Advisor No. 9, Sept. 1996 at 7, 8.

1054. 991 F.2d 497 (9th Cir. 1993).

1055. *Id.* at 498-500.

sought to be enjoined and declared unlawful. It is the Club that is claimed to have breached its lease. The Club is not being sued for some "wrongful act" of its directors or employees that is "imputed to the [Club] as principal." Accordingly, the defense costs for the state litigation do not qualify as "losses" covered by Endorsement # 2 of the policy. The policy, after all, is a Directors' and Officers' liability policy with an endorsement protecting the Club; it is not an expanded comprehensive liability policy insuring the Club against liability for everything it does.

*          *          *

The Club's argument reduces to the assertion that the policy covers the Club's wrongful acts, as though the Club were the directors' agent. If this interpretation governed, the Club's directors, officers, and employees would be liable for *every* corporate act undertaken by the Club and Lloyd's would be obligated to pay defense costs for every suit against the Club. This argument defies any reasonable interpretation of Endorsement # 2 and the unmistakable purpose of a directors and officers liability insurance policy.[1056]

The following discussion addresses three exclusions that began appearing in policies in the mid to late 1980s and that quickly became the subject of extensive case law: the takeover exclusion, the insured versus insured exclusion, and the regulatory exclusion.[1057]

   *b. The Contest for Control Exclusion.* In the mid-1980s, insurers began adding exclusions to their policies for claims arising out of contests for corporate control—sometimes known as "take-over" exclusions.[1058] "[T]here are a number of different takeover

---

1056. *Id.* at 500-01.

1057. *See* Chapter V, Sections B 9 b-g.

1058. *See* John F. Olson & Josiah O. Hatch III, *Director and Officer Liability: Indemnification and Insurance* § 10.06[5][c][iii] (1997); Johnston, *Directors' and Officers' and Related Forms of Liability Insurance, in 7 Securities Law Techniques* § 122.03[2][g][v] (A.A. Sommer, Jr. ed. 1998); Bader, *Takeover and Personal Profit Exclusions in Directors' and Officers' Liability Insurance, in Directors' and Officers' Liability*

(continued...)

exclusions which vary in the breadth of activities they purport to cover," and "[i]t is not always clear from the language employed what takeover activities, or responses to those activities, fall within these provisions."[1059] Some policies include exclusions terminating coverage altogether in the event of a change in control.[1060]

Contest for control exclusions have been construed narrowly in the three cases where their reach has been litigated: *KDT Industries, Inc. v. Home Insurance Co.*,[1061] *Ameriwood Industries International Corp. v. American Casualty Co.*,[1062] and *Lynott v. National Union Fire Insurance Co.*[1063]

The court in *KDT Industries, Inc. v. Home Insurance Co.*[1064] construed a policy provision excluding coverage for losses "directly or indirectly arising from any attempt to gain control or from any gaining of control of the Company."[1065] The court construed this provision narrowly to allow coverage of two derivative actions in which the "primary allegation" was that the corporation paid too high a price for assets purchased from a shareholder who recently had taken control of the corporation.[1066] The court held that "only those claims by minority shareholders . . . arising from the acquisition of control are excluded from coverage under the policy."[1067] The court rejected the insurer's reliance

---

1058. (...continued)
*Insurance 1989* 195, 197-210 (Practising Law Institute 1989); Mallen & Evans, *Surviving the Directors' and Officers' Liability Crisis: Insurance and the Alternatives*, 12 Del. J. Corp. L. 439, 456 (1988); Hertzberg, *Insurers Beginning to Refuse Coverage on Directors, Officers in Takeover Cases*, Wall St. J., Jan. 20, 1986, at 3.

1059. Bader, at 203; *see also* J. Olson & J. Hatch § 10.06[5][b][iii] (including examples).

1060. Bader, at 206.

1061. 603 F. Supp. 861 (D. Mass. 1985).

1062. 840 F. Supp. 1143 (W.D. Mich. 1993).

1063. 871 P.2d 146 (Wash. 1994).

1064. 603 F. Supp. 861 (D. Mass. 1985).

1065. *Id*. at 862.

1066. *Id*. at 863-65, 868-69.

1067. *Id*. at 867.

upon the word "indirectly" because the insurer's construction of "indirectly" "suggests that if a person gained control of KDT, and at some later point exercised that control to the detriment of the company, then a stockholder suit challenging the detrimental exercise of control would arise indirectly from the gaining of control and would be barred."[1068] The court stated that it "cannot approve such a sweeping interpretation," which "would render the policy a nullity, for KDT would have paid substantial premiums for insubstantial coverage."[1069] Under the circumstances," the court concluded, "a limiting construction is required."[1070] The court also stated that liability "hinged on the fairness of the challenged transaction," that "[a]lthough control was an issue, it was only incidental," and that the shareholder plaintiffs in the case "would have been upset about this particular sale of assets even if there had been no preceding takeover."[1071]

The court in *Ameriwood Industries International Corp. v. American Casualty Co.*[1072] addressed a policy insuring directors and officers of Rospatch Corporation that excluded liability for any loss in connection with any claim "based upon or attributable to" (1) "any attempts, whether alleged or actual, successful or unsuccessful, by persons or entities to acquire securities of the Company against the opposition of the Company and/or the Directors of the Company," or (2) "any claims arising from, attributable to or involving efforts, whether alleged or actual, successful or unsuccessful, by the Company and/or its Directors to resist such attempts."[1073]

On a motion for summary judgment, the court held that the plaintiffs in the litigations underlying the insurance dispute alleged that the corporation's directors had "attempted to prevent third parties from acquiring control" of Rospatch" but did not allege

---

1068. *Id.* at 868.
1069. *Id.*
1070. *Id.*
1071. *Id.* at 869.
1072. 840 F. Supp. 1143 (W.D. Mich. 1993).
1073. *Id.* at 1156.

"attempts by the officers and directors to prevent acquisition of Rospatch securities."[1074] The court explained that "'control' of a corporation has long been defined by legislatures, courts and the Securities and Exchange Commission to be obtainable through a variety of means, and not necessarily to require ownership of a particular number of shares of the corporation's stock."[1075] Rather, the court stated, the SEC has defined control as "the possession, direct or indirect, of the power to direct or cause the direction of the management and policies of a person, whether through the ownership of voting securities, by contract, or otherwise."[1076] Construing the allegations against Rospatch's directors "in the light of these definitions" and in accordance "with the general rule requiring construction of an ambiguous exclusion in favor of the insured," the court found that the exclusion did not cover the allegations concerning the attempts by Rospatch directors and officers to prevent third parties from acquiring control of Rospatch.[1077] To the contrary, the court concluded, "[t]hose allegations cannot be interpreted as necessarily including assertions that Rospatch's officers and directors were attempting to prevent the purchase of its securities by third parties who sought control of Rospatch. The third parties could have been seeking control by any of a number of means other than the purchase of securities."[1078] The court therefore held that the alleged wrongdoing did "not fit squarely into the exclusion" and "as a matter of law, the Securities Acquisition endorsement does not prevent coverage."[1079]

The court in *Lynott v. National Union Fire Insurance Co.*[1080] construed a policy excluding coverage for claims "arising out of any merger, acquisition or divestiture or any merger, acquisition or divestiture negotiations or any attempted merger,

---

1074. *Id*. at 1157.
1075. *Id*.
1076. *Id*.
1077. *Id*. at 1157-58.
1078. *Id*.
1079. *Id*. at 1157, 1158.
1080. 871 P.2d 146 (Wash. 1994).

acquisition or divestiture negotiations involving the insured."[1081] The case involved stock sales by Tacoma Boatbuilding Company to 21 separate investors. Together, these 21 separate investors acquired a total of 61 percent of the stock of Tacoma Boatbuilding Company, with no single investor acquiring more than 14.9 percent of Tacoma's stock. The investors later commenced litigation against Tacoma's directors and officers and others. This litigation alleged wrongful acts and omissions in connection with the stock sales.[1082]

The court concluded that the word "acquisition" was ambiguous and that there was no evidence of "an objective manifestation of mutual intent as to the meaning of 'acquisition' or that the January 1985 purchases were specifically excluded from coverage."[1083] The court construed this ambiguity strictly against the insurer because "[e]xclusions of coverage will not be extended beyond their 'clear and unequivocal' meaning."[1084] This was especially true here, the court stated, where the insurer did not define the term acquisition even though it was aware of the pending negotiations at the time the policy was negotiated and had "a standard form clause which would have excluded specifically the subject transaction by merely inserting a description of the potential investors or the transaction in general."[1085]

   *c. The Insured Versus Insured Exclusion.* Insurers also began adding exclusions in the mid-1980s for claims brought by corporations against their own directors and officers.[1086] This exclusion

---

1081. *Id.* at 148.
1082. *Id.*
1083. *Id.*
1084. *Id.* at 154.
1085. *Id.*

1086. *See* John F. Olson & Josiah O. Hatch III, *Director and Officer Liability: Indemnification and Insurance* § 10.06[5][c][i], at 10–33-37 (1997); Johnston, *Directors' and Officers' and Related Forms of Liability Insurance, in* 7 *Securities Law Techniques* § 122.03[2][g][ix] (A.A. Sommer, Jr. ed. 1998); Monteleone & Conca, *Directors and Officers Indemnification and Liability Insurance: An Overview of Legal*
(continued...)

was prompted by lawsuits such as those brought by Seattle-First National Bank, Bank of America and Chase Manhattan Bank against their own directors and/or officers for negligence in connection with losses by these financial institutions in the 1980s[1087] and the belief by D & O insurers that the corporate policy holder should not be allowed "to cash in on D & O policies by suing its own directors and officers."[1088] The exclusion thus arose from attempts to use "Director and Officer policies to recoup operational losses," and "[t]he primary focus of the exclusion is to prevent collusive suits in which an insured company might seek to force its insurer to pay for the poor business decisions of its officers or managers."[1089] This exclusion often is called an "insured versus

---

1086. (...continued)
*and Practical Issues*, 51 Bus. Law. 573, 604-05 (1996); Sloane, *Insurer-Management Liability Rift Seen Growing*, N.Y. Times, Dec. 19, 1985, at D8.

1087. *See Seafirst Corp. v. Jenkins*, 644 F. Supp. 1152, 1158-59 (W.D. Wash. 1986) (denying motion for summary judgment by directors and officers sued by corporation for negligent mismanagement); *National Union Fire Ins. Co. v. Seafirst Corp.*, 662 F. Supp. 36, 37-38 (W.D. Wash. 1986) (summarizing litigation between Seafirst and its insurer regarding coverage issues), *subsequent proceedings*, No. C85-396R, slip op. at 9-16 (W.D. Wash. Mar. 19, 1986) (available on LEXIS without file number) (holding that the governing insurance policy covered actions by the corporation against its directors and officers), *aff'd mem.*, 804 F.2d 146 (9th Cir. 1986), *subsequent proceedings*, 1987 U.S. Dist. LEXIS 14284, at *2-17 (W.D. Wash. Mar. 25, 1987) (denying insurer's motion to dismiss breach of contract, bad faith, breach of fiduciary trust, fraud and unfair insurance practice claims brought by corporation), *subsequent proceedings*, 1987 U.S. Dist. LEXIS 14394, at *22-31 (W.D. Wash. Dec. 28, 1987) (denying corporation's motion for summary judgment on its claim seeking payment of all or part of $110 million settlement); *Bank of Am. v. Powers* (Cal. Super. Ct. complaint filed Mar. 1, 1985), *reprinted in Directors' and Officers' Liability Insurance 1987* 247-83 (Practising Law Institute 1987); *Fox v. Chase Manhattan Corp.*, 11 Del. J. Corp. L. 888 (Del. Ch. Dec. 6, 1985) (approving $32.5 million settlement).

1088. J. Olson & J. Hatch § 10.06[5][c][i], at 10-33.

1089. *Township of Center v. First Mercury Syndicate, Inc.*, 117 F. 3d 115, 119 (3d Cir. 1997).

insured" or a "one versus one" or "1 vs. 1" (the "one" or "1" being used in place of the "I" in "Insured") exclusion.[1090]

Most insured versus insured exclusions used in policies today create an exception for shareholder claims that have not been asserted in collusion with an insured party. Some insured versus insured exclusions also add an exception for wrongful discharge or termination claims against the corporation by former corporate officers. One common provision states as follows:

> The Insurer shall not be liable to make any payment for Loss in connection with any claim or claims made against the Directors or Officers . . . which are brought by any Insured or the Company; or which are brought by any security holder of the Company, whether directly or derivatively, unless such claim(s) is instigated and continued totally independent of, and totally without the solicitation of, or assistance of, or active participation of, or intervention of, any Insured or the Company; provided, however, this exclusion shall not apply to wrongful termination of employment claims brought by a former employee other than a former employee who is or was a Director of the Company.[1091]

This type of exclusion "screens out the possibility of suits by the company or individual or corporate proxies for the company, while presumably still permitting noncollusive derivative actions to be covered."[1092] Some insured versus insured provisions also carve out employment practices claims.[1093]

---

1090. Monteleone & Conca, 51 Bus. Law. at 605.

1091. J. Olson & J. Hatch § 10.06[5][c][i], at 10-39.

1092. *Id.* at 10–39-40; *see also International Ins. Co. v. Morrow, Inc.*, No. 86-1247-JU, slip op. at 8-12 (D. Or. Oct. 23, 1987) (policy provided that if notice is given to insurer of an occurrence that may subsequently give rise to a claim against the insureds for a wrongful act, then any claim that may subsequently be made arising out of that wrongful act shall be treated as a claim made during the policy year when notice of the occurrence was provided to the insurer; court held that an amendment of the policy to include an insured versus insured exclusion did not exclude coverage of a later filed action for conduct arising out of a previously reported occurrence).

1093. Weiss, *Filling the Gaps in D & O Insurance*, 6 Bus. Law

(continued...)

Insured versus insured exclusions have been enforced by the courts in several cases, including the Second Circuit in *Levy v. National Union Fire Insurance Co.*,[1094] the Fifth Circuit in *Fidelity & Deposit Co. v. Conner*[1095] and *Voluntary Hospitals of America, Inc. v. National Union Fire Insurance Co.*[1096] and the Ninth Circuit in *LaFon v. American Casualty Co.*[1097]

The Second Circuit in *Levy v. National Union Fire Insurance Co.*[1098] stated that the insured versus insured exclusion in the policy litigated in that case "self-evidently excludes claims arising from suits brought by 'one or more past, present or future Directors . . . and/or the Company,'" that the action for which coverage was sought was indisputably an action by "the Company," and that the insured's effort to obtain coverage was "totally frivolous."[1099] The Ninth Circuit in *LaFon v. American Casualty Co.*[1100] similarly found that an insured versus insured provision (this one in a professional liability insurance policy) was unambiguous. In the court's words: "Appellant falls squarely within the policy's definition of insured. . . . Appellant is an insured, and the exclusion applies."[1101]

The Fifth Circuit in *Fidelity & Deposit Co. v. Conner*[1102] likewise held that an insured versus insured provision excluding

---

1093. (. . .continued)
Today No. 3, Jan./Feb. 1997, at 44, 47; *Weiss, Doing D & O Insurance Right*, 4 Bus. Law Today No. 2, Nov./Dec. 1994, at 50, 53.

1094. 889 F.2d 433 (2d Cir. 1989).

1095. 973 F.2d 1236 (5th Cir. 1992).

1096. 859 F. Supp. 260 (N.D. Tex. 1993), *aff'd mem.*, 24 F.3d 239 (5th Cir. 1994).

1097. 73 F.3d 369 (unpublished opinion, text available at 1995 U.S. App. LEXIS 37741 and 1995 WL 759454) (9th Cir. Dec. 22, 1995).

1098. 889 F.2d 433 (2d Cir. 1989).

1099. *Id.* at 434.

1100. 73 F.3d 369 (unpublished opinion, text available at 1995 U.S. App. LEXIS 37741 and 1995 WL 759454) (9th Cir. Dec. 22, 1995).

1101. 1995 U.S. App. LEXIS 37741, at *4-5, 1995 WL 759454, at *2.

1102. 973 F.2d 1236 (5th Cir. 1992).

"[l]oss in connection with any claim made against the Directors and Officers by any other Director or Officer of the Bank/Association or by the Bank/Association" was unambiguous.[1103] As the district court stated in the *Conner* case:

> [T]here is only one logical interpretation of the Insured v. Insured Exclusion Clause. That is, losses incurred from a claim made by one director or officer of the Bank against another are excluded from coverage. The intention of the parties is clear. There is no ambiguity in this exclusion clause. Consequently, the Insured v. Insured Exclusion Clause is unambiguous as a matter of law.[1104]

The Fifth Circuit in *Conner*, however, did not bar coverage on the basis of this provision because the court already had determined to bar coverage pursuant to a regulatory exclusion in the policy.[1105]

The Fifth Circuit in *Voluntary Hospitals of America, Inc. v. National Union Fire Insurance Co.*[1106] affirmed without opinion a district court decision that held that an insured versus insured exclusion was unambiguous. The court thus held that the policy did not provide coverage for a shareholder derivative action commenced by shareholders "with the active assistance of Thomas Reed, a former officer and director of VHA Enterprises," against VHA, VHA Enterprises and several of VHA's directors and officers.[1107] The court reasoned as follows:

> The parties do not dispute that Reed assisted [the shareholder plaintiffs in the shareholder action]; nor do they dispute that Reed was a former director and officer of a VHA subsidiary as contemplated by the policy's language. Because the insured v. insured exclusion is reasonably susceptible of only

---

1103. *Id.* at 1244-45.

1104. *Fidelity & Deposit Co. v. Conner*, 1991 U.S. Dist. LEXIS 11874, at *14, 1991 WL 229954, at *5 (S.D. Tex. June 3, 1991), *aff'd*, 973 F.2d 1236 (5th Cir. 1992).

1105. 973 F.2d at 1245 & n.27 (discussed in Chapter V, Sections B 9 f-g).

1106. 859 F. Supp. 260 (N.D. Tex. 1993), *aff'd mem.*, 24 F.3d 239 (5th Cir. 1994).

1107. *Id.* at 261, 262-63.

one meaning and is therefore unambiguous, National Union
has demonstrated the applicability of that exclusion and therefore its entitlement to summary judgment.[1108]

The court added that "[t]o read the language otherwise would be to
adopt the textual methodology of the protodeconstructionist Humpty
Dumpty, for whom words meant what he wanted them to. However, the body of anti-Humpty Dumpty jurisprudence is now well
established in the courts."[1109]

The same result has been reached by federal district courts in
*Bendis v. Federal Insurance Co.*,[1110] *Parker v. Watts*[1111] and
*Foster v. Kentucky Housing Corp.*[1112] A state court in Washington in *Frank and Rose Steele Foundation v. Tudor Insurance
Co.*[1113] also has concluded that the "plain language" of an
insured versus insured exclusion was clear and ambiguous.[1114]
The court rejected a claim that the exclusion's applicability was
altered by the fact that the insured had filed for reorganization
under the United States Bankruptcy Code and the Bankruptcy Court
had confirmed a reorganization plan calling for liquidation of
assets, including "claims against former Officers and Directors
having an unknown value" and the disbursement of the proceeds to
creditors.[1115]

A federal district court in Iowa also enforced an insured
versus insured exclusion in *American Casualty Co. v. Federal
Deposit Insurance Corp.*,[1116] but only with respect to insureds

---

1108. *Id.* at 263.

1109. *Id.*

1110. 1989 U.S. Dist. LEXIS 15930, at *7, 1989 WL 161437, at
*3 (D. Kan. Dec. 4, 1989), *aff'd on other grounds*, 958 F.2d 960 (10th
Cir. 1991).

1111. 1987 U.S. Dist. LEXIS 6862, at *8-9, 1987 WL 7450, at *3
(E.D. La. Feb. 27, 1987).

1112. 850 F. Supp. 558, 561 (E.D. Ky. 1994).

1113. No. 12891-11 (Wash. Ct. App. June 7, 1994).

1114. *Id.*

1115. *Id.*

1116. 1990 U.S. Dist. LEXIS 6065, 1990 WL 66505 (N.D. Iowa
(continued...)

who were not "unfairly surprised" by the existence and meaning of the exclusion.[1117] Insureds who did not understand the existence and meaning of the exclusion, the court held, were not bound by the exclusion because the insurer had been "less than open and candid" in notifying the insureds regarding the exclusion and because the corporate officer with whom the insurer had dealt was not authorized to accept new policy terms such as the insured versus insured exclusion.[1118] Under these circumstances, the court concluded, the exclusion was "unconscionable and violates the insureds' reasonable expectations of insurance coverage and an implied warranty of fitness"[1119] On appeal, the Eighth Circuit did not reach this finding by the district court.[1120]

Insured versus insured exclusions were construed narrowly and held not to bar coverage of wrongful discharge claims in *Township of Center v. First Mercury Syndicate, Inc.*[1121] and *Conklin Co. v. National Union Fire Insurance Co.*[1122] The insured versus

---

1116. (...continued)
Feb. 26, 1990), *aff'd in part and rev'd in part*, 944 F.2d 455 (8th Cir. 1991).

    1117. 1990 U.S. Dist. LEXIS 6065, at *59-60, 1990 WL 66505, at *16.

    1118. 1990 U.S. Dist. LEXIS 6065, at *17-35, 1990 WL 66505, at *5-9.

    1119. 1990 U.S. Dist. LEXIS 6065, at *58-59, 1990 WL 66505, at *15.

    1120. *See American Casualty Co. v. Federal Deposit Ins. Corp.*, 944 F.2d 455, 457 n.1 (8th Cir. 1991). The Eighth Circuit did, however, reverse the district court's conclusion that a regulatory exclusion was unconscionable and violated the insurer's reasonable expectations and the insured's implied warranty of fitness. *See id.* at 459-60 (discussed in Chapter V, Section B 9 f). Because the district court based its invalidation of the insured versus insured and regulatory exclusions on the same rationale, the Eighth Circuit's reasoning reversing the invalidation of the regulatory exclusion would appear to be equally applicable to the district court's analysis of the insured versus insured exclusion.

    1121. 117 F.3d 115 (3d Cir. 1997).

    1122. 1987 U.S. Dist. LEXIS 12337, 1987 WL 108957 (D. Minn. Jan. 28, 1987).

insured provisions in these cases did not say anything about wrongful discharge claims; as noted above, insured versus insured provisions in some policies deal explicitly with wrongful discharge claims.[1123]

*Township of Center v. First Mercury Syndicate*,[1124] which arose in the context of a public officials' liability insurance policy, involved wrongful discharge claims by former employees of an insured township.[1125] An insured versus insured provision excluded coverage for claims "by an 'insured' against another 'insured,'" and the term "insured" was defined to include "[a]ll persons acting within the scope of their official duties who were, now are or shall be lawfully elected or lawfully appointed officials and members of the 'Governmental Entity.'"[1126] The court held that "because the policy here is a 'claims made' policy . . . the determination of the status of the injured party must be made as of the time that the claim is made," and at the time the claim was made in this case the injured parties were not insured parties.[1127] The court stated that the fact that the injured parties were insured parties at the time of the alleged wrongful conduct was "irrelevant."[1128]

The court found "further support" for its conclusion "in the policy underlying the 'insured v. insured' exclusion"—"to prevent collusive suits in which an insured company might seek to force its insurer to pay for the poor business decisions of its officers or managers."[1129] The court stated that "[w]here . . . it is clear that the underlying action is not collusive, the exclusion has not prevented coverage."[1130] Here, the court found, "there is no contention that the underlying actions are collusive," and "the discharged

---

1123. J. Olson & J. Hatch § 10.06[5][c][i], at 10-34.
1124. 117 F.3d 115 (3d Cir. 1997).
1125. *Id.* at 116.
1126. *Id.* at 117.
1127. *Id.* at 118.
1128. *Id.*
1129. *Id.* at 119.
1130. *Id.*

employees are not seeking coverage under the policy."[1131] Indeed, the court stated, "[i]t is difficult to imagine a circumstance, short of a conspiracy to defraud, in which a wrongful discharge suit, brought by a former employee, could be perceived as constituting a collusive act."[1132] The court thus held that "under the facts of this case the ex-employees/plaintiffs are not insured within the meaning of the policies's exclusion."[1133]

*Conklin Co. v. National Union Fire Insurance Co.*[1134] involved a wrongful discharge claim by a former corporate officer. The court rejected the insurer's contention that coverage was excluded because the former corporate officer was "potentially an 'insured' under the D & O policy."[1135] The court explained that the purpose of an insured versus insured exclusion is "to prevent collusive or friendly lawsuits, where, for example, the insured company sues its directors or officers for their wrongful acts and both parties seek coverage under the D & O policy."[1136] Accordingly, the court stated, "[t]he exclusionary endorsement . . . prevents a corporation from suing its own directors or officers to obtain the benefits of its own D & O policy coverage."[1137] By contrast, the court continued, the wrongful discharge cause of action at issue in *Conklin* was not a collusive or friendly claim. Rather, the cause of action was a claim by an officer who was suing as an employee rather than as an officer and who "neither seeks nor is subject to coverage under the policy for his wrongful discharge claims."[1138]

---

1131. *Id.*

1132. *Id.*

1133. *Id.*

1134. 1987 U.S. Dist. LEXIS 12337, 1987 WL 108957 (D. Minn. Jan. 28, 1987).

1135. 1987 U.S. Dist. LEXIS 12337, at *6, 1987 WL 108957, at *2.

1136. *Id.*

1137. *Id.*

1138. 1987 U.S. Dist. LEXIS 12337, at *7, 1987 WL 108957, at *2.

The reasoning by the court in *Conklin* was rejected by the court in *Foster v. Kentucky Housing Corp.*,[1139] a case where insureds "urged the Court to declare that there is an ambiguity" concerning whether the policy in that case was "intended to cover the breach of contract/wrongful discharge claim of a former director/officer" and whether the policy was intended to exclude "merely collusive and friendly suits."[1140] The court reasoned as follows:

> The Policy clearly defines "directors/officers" as "any persons who *were*, now are, or shall be: . . . directors of officers of the Organization." . . . [T]he Policy explicitly defines "officers/directors" as those persons who *were* employed as officers and directors and excludes them from coverage when sued by another insured.[1141]

The court therefore concluded that it "finds no ambiguity in the exclusion provision and declines to rewrite the insurance contract to enlarge the risk of the insurer."[1142]

*Howard Savings Bank v. Northland Insurance Co.*[1143] involved coverage under an insured versus insured exclusion for claims asserted against Howard Savings Bank by John Prodromos, the holder of 40 percent of the outstanding stock of the bank and a former director and officer of the bank. Prodromos asserted claims on his own behalf against the bank and its directors for failing to credit interest to his Individual Retirement Account. Prodromos also asserted claims derivatively on behalf of the bank against the bank's directors for breach of fiduciary duty.[1144] Wrongful discharge claims also were asserted by Prodromos, but the parties

---

1139. 850 F. Supp. 558 (E.D. Ky. 1994).

1140. *Id.* at 561 & n.2.

1141. *Id.* at 561.

1142. *Id.*

1143. 1997 U.S. Dist. LEXIS 11857, 1997 WL 460973 (N.D. Ill. Aug. 11, 1997).

1144. 1997 U.S. Dist. LEXIS 11857, at *2, 11-12, 1997 WL 460973, at * 1, 5.

agreed that those claims were excluded from coverage by the terms of the insured versus insured provision.[1145]

With respect to the claims that the parties disputed, the court held that the governing policy language in the case "unambiguously defined an insured person as a 'past, present or future director or officer of the Insured Financial Institution, while acting solely in the capacity of director or officer of the Insured Financial Institution."[1146] The court explained that this policy, unlike the policies in most other cases construing insured versus insured provisions, defined an insured person not merely as "a past, present or future director or officer" but as "a past, present or future director or officer . . . while acting solely in the capacity of director or officer."[1147] The court found that claims asserted by Prodromos were not asserted by Prodromos "as a former officer or director acting solely in the capacity of director or officer."[1148] The court therefore held that "applying the Policy's unambiguous definition of an insured person, John Prodromos is not an insured person under defendant's Policy."[1149] The court stated that "if the insurer "really meant for all past, present or future officers and directors to be considered insured persons under its Policy," then it "should have drafted its Policy to define an insured person as a past, present or future officer or director."[1150]

*d. The Insured Versus Insured Exclusion in the Regulatory Context.* Much of the litigation construing the insured versus insured exclusion has involved actions brought by regulatory agencies against or on behalf of failed banking institutions. Since

---

1145. 1997 U.S. Dist. LEXIS 11857, at *6, 11, 1997 WL 460973, at *3, 5.

1146. 1997 U.S. Dist. LEXIS 11857, at *10, 1997 WL 460973, at *4.

1147. *Id.*

1148. 1997 U.S. Dist. LEXIS 11857, at *11-12, 1997 WL 460973, at *5.

1149. 1997 U.S. Dist. LEXIS 11857, at *11, 1997 WL 460973, at *5.

1150. 1997 U.S. Dist. LEXIS 11857, at *12, 1997 WL 460973, at *5.

the enactment of the Financial Institutions Reform, Recovery and Enforcement Act of 1989 ("FIRREA"),[1151] these cases generally have been brought by the Federal Deposit Insurance Corporation (the "FDIC") or the Resolution Trust Corporation (the "RTC") (which ceased its existence at the end of 1995). Prior to FIRREA, the cases generally were brought by the FDIC, the Federal Home Loan Bank Board (the "FHLBB") or the Federal Savings and Loan Insurance Corporation (the "FSLIC").

The insurers in these cases typically argue that the regulatory agency that has commenced the action "stands in the shoes" of the failed banking institution, and thus is itself an insured within the meaning of the exclusion. The regulatory agencies bringing these suits, by contrast, typically argue that they represent other entities, including depositors, shareholders and/or creditors and thus are not subject to the insured versus insured exclusion. The regulatory agencies also argue that insured versus insured provisions are intended to protect insurers from collusive suits by a corporation against its own directors and that these provisions should not be utilized outside of that context. The results have varied.

On one side of the spectrum are the majority of cases, in which the courts have held as a matter of law that insured versus insured exclusions do not apply to actions by regulatory agencies against the directors and officers of failed banking institutions and thus do not protect insurers from claims by regulatory agencies. These cases include federal district court decisions[1152] and a deci-

---

1151. Pub. L. 101-73, 103 Stat. 183 (1989) (codified primarily in 12 U.S.C., but portions also codified in numerous other titles of U.S.C.).

1152. *See American Casualty Co. v. Sentry Fed. Sav. Bank*, 867 F. Supp. 50, 59-60 (D. Mass. 1994); *Slaughter v. American Casualty Co.*, 842 F. Supp. 371, 374 (E.D. Ark. 1993), *rev'd on other grounds*, 37 F.3d 385 (8th Cir. 1994); *Federal Deposit Ins. Corp. v. Mijalis*, 800 F. Supp. 397, 403 (W.D. La. 1992), *aff'd in part and rev'd on other grounds*, 15 F.3d 1314 (5th Cir. 1994); *American Casualty Co. v. Federal Deposit Ins. Corp.*, 791 F. Supp. 276, 278 (W.D. Okla. 1992); *Federal Deposit Ins. Corp. v. Zaborac*, 773 F. Supp. 137, 144 (C.D. Ill. 1991), *aff'd on other grounds sub nom. Federal Deposit Ins. Corp. v. American*
(continued...)

sion by the Maryland Court of Appeals[1153] and have utilized several lines of reasoning.

First, the courts in several of these cases have concluded that regulatory agencies such as the FDIC and the FSLIC do not "stand in the shoes" of a failed bank in a suit by the agency on behalf of the bank. Rather, these courts hold, these agencies represent both the failed institution's depositors, shareholders and creditors and federal insurance funds. These agencies, according to these courts, thus are not insureds, and their suits against insured banking institutions thus are not suits by insureds against insureds. In the words of these courts:

- "the RTC does not stand in the shoes of a failed institution";[1154]

- "the FDIC in its receivership capacity represents the interests of uninsured shareholders as well as the bank";[1155]

- "the FDIC does not merely stand in the shoes of Grove, it can also stand in the shoes of the shareholders; therefore, as a shareholder, it has the independent

---

1152. (...continued)
*Casualty Co.*, 998 F.2d 404 (7th Cir. 1993); *St. Paul Fire & Marine Ins. Co. v. Federal Deposit Ins. Co.*, 765 F. Supp. 538, 548 (D. Minn. 1991), *aff'd on other grounds*, 968 F.2d 695 (8th Cir. 1992); *American Casualty Co. v. Baker*, 758 F. Supp. 1340, 1349 (C.D. Cal. 1991), *aff'd on other grounds*, 22 F.3d 880 (9th Cir. 1994); *Federal Deposit Ins. Corp. v. American Casualty Co.*, 814 F. Supp. 1021, 1027 (D. Wyo. 1991); *Fidelity & Deposit Co. v. Zandstra*, 756 F. Supp. 429, 433-34 (N.D. Cal. 1990); *Branning v. CNA Ins. Cos.*, 721 F. Supp. 1180, 1184 (W.D. Wash. 1989); *American Casualty Co. v. Federal Sav. & Loan Ins. Corp.*, 704 F. Supp. 898, 899-902 (E.D. Ark. 1989); *Federal Sav. & Loan Ins. Corp. v. Mmahat*, 1988 U.S. Dist. LEXIS 1825, at *3, 1988 WL 19304, at *1 (E.D. La. Mar. 3, 1988).

1153. *See Finci v. American Casualty Co.*, 593 A.2d 1069 (Md. 1991).

1154. *Slaughter*, 842 F. Supp. at 374.

1155. *American Casualty*, 791 F. Supp. at 278.

authority to bring a suit against American Casualty";[1156]

- the FDIC has "greater standing than the failed institution" because it is "authorized to bring suit not only as its successor, but as a creditor itself, on behalf of the creditors and shareholders of the institution, and as subrogee to the rights of depositors";[1157]

- "while the FDIC steps into the shoes of the predecessor bank, it is nonetheless in the unique position of representing the interests of itself, shareholder[s], and all other creditors. . . . The FDIC's role in acting as a receiver is much more expansive than that of either director, officer or bank";[1158]

- "FSLIC represents depositors, shareholders, creditors and the federal insurance fund as well as the failed institution";[1159]

- "because the FSLIC is required to marshall the assets of a failed institution for the benefit of its depositors and creditors and to minimize payouts from the insurance fund, it is motivated to bring suit by interests distinctly different from that of an institution which has remained solvent";[1160] and

- "FSLIC operates in several capacities in a context such as this").[1161]

---

1156. *Zaborac*, 773 F. Supp. at 144.

1157. *Baker*, 758 F. Supp. at 1350.

1158. *American Casualty*, 814 F. Supp. at 1026-27.

1159. *Branning*, 721 F. Supp. at 1184.

1160. *American Casualty*, 704 F. Supp. at 901.

1161. *Mmahat*, 1988 U.S. Dist. LEXIS 1825, at *3-4, 1988 WL 19304, at *1; *see also Cigna Ins. Co. v. Gulf USA Corp.*, No. CV 97-250-N-EJL, slip op. at 10-12 (D. Idaho Sept. 11, 1997) (using similar reasoning in decision construing insured versus insured provision in context of claims by a debtor-in-possession against insured directors); Chapter V, Section B 9 e (discussing *Gulf* decision).

Second, some of these courts have focused upon a provision found in many insured versus insured exclusions that denies coverage for claims against insured directors and officers by "any other Director or Officer or by the Institution"—or, in some policies, by "an insured or insureds . . . , including the company"—"except for stockholders derivative actions brought by a shareholder of the company."[1162] These courts reason that regulatory agencies bringing suits against financial institutions act "in part, as representative of the [corporation] in the nature of a stockholder's derivative action."[1163] According to these courts, the exclusion's exception for shareholder derivative actions demonstrates the insurers' intent "to place on itself the risk for actions against the directors and officers based upon allegations of mismanagement, waste, fraud, or abuse of the failed institution"—"precisely the claims" brought by the regulatory agencies against directors and officers in these cases.[1164] As explained by one court:

> The claim in a shareholder's derivative suit is a claim *of* the institution, but it is not asserted *by* the institution, although it is asserted on behalf of the institution. The recovery in a shareholder's derivative suit inures directly to the corporation, and indirectly to the shareholders. Here, the claim by [the Maryland Deposit Insurance Fund Corporation] in the underlying action sought a recovery which would inure to the benefit of [the failed institution, First Maryland Savings and Loan, Inc. ("FMSL")], in receivership. Out of that receivership estate, depositors and other creditors would benefit. Thus, if the purpose of the exclusion is satisfied even if a

---

1162. *Mijalis*, 800 F. Supp. at 403; *American Casualty*, 791 F. Supp. at 277-78; *Baker*, 758 F. Supp. at 1349; *Zandstra*, 756 F. Supp. at 431; *Finci*, 593 A.2d at 1081.

1163. *Mijalis*, 800 F. Supp. at 403.

1164. *Baker*, 758 F. Supp. at 1349-50; *Zandstra*, 756 F. Supp. at 431; *see also American Casualty*, 791 F. Supp. at 278 ("[t]he quoted endorsement shows that the insurer intended to assume the risk of mismanagement, waste, fraud or abuse, and these are precisely the claims brought by the FDIC").

shareholder's derivative suit is involved, the intent of the parties is not to exclude claims for the benefit of FMSL.[1165]

The court in another case reached the same conclusion even though the policy provision in that case did not expressly state an exception for shareholder derivative actions. The court described this distinction as having "little significance" because even without an express exclusion "a suit by shareholders, other than an Insured, clearly does not fall within the parameters of this endorsement."[1166]

Third, some of the courts in these cases have reasoned that the intent underlying the insured versus insured exclusion is to protect the insurer against collusive suits among the insured corporation and its directors and officers. According to these courts, "there can be no real dispute" that regulatory agencies are "genuinely adverse" to directors and officers named as defendants in suits by these agencies and that a regulatory agency's involvement in such a case is not collusive.[1167] As one court concluded, "[t]he obvious intent behind the 'insured vs. insured' exclusion is to protect the insurer from collusive suits among a bank and its directors and officers; but the FDIC's involvement is obviously not collusive."[1168] In the words of another court, "it is clear that the policy reasons for attaching such an endorsement do not apply in cases like the present. The potentiality which prompted the drafting of this exclusion, the directors and officers of the bank acting collusively and suing either themselves or the bank, does not exist once the FDIC has been appointed receiver. There is no dispute that the FDIC, as receiver, is a genuinely adverse party in this action."[1169] Another court similarly concluded that "the purpose

---

1165. *Finci*, 593 A.2d at 1082.

1166. *American Casualty*, 814 F. Supp. at 1025, 1026 & n.3; *see also Gulf*, slip op. at 12 (using similar reasoning in decision construing insured versus insured provision in context of claims by a debtor-in-possession against insured directors); Chapter V, Section B 9 e (discussing *Gulf* decision).

1167. *Baker*, 758 F. Supp. at 1350; *Zandstra*, 756 F. Supp. at 432.

1168. *American Casualty*, 791 F. Supp. at 278, *quoted in Sentry*, 867 F. Supp. at 60.

1169. *American Casualty*, 814 F. Supp. at 1026.

of the exclusion is to prevent collusive claims" and that the insurer "runs no risk of a collusive suit when a regulatory agency brings the underlying action as receiver."[1170] In sum, according to these courts, the insured versus insured exclusion is intended "to protect the insurer against collusive suits between the failed institution and its directors and officers" and therefore "does not apply to a suit brought by the RTC because the RTC is a genuinely adverse party to the defendant officers and directors."[1171]

One court that has reached the same result reached in these cases has rejected this reasoning. According to this court, "[c]ertainly, one of the purposes of the insured versus insured clause could be to prevent collusive lawsuits; however, that is not the only possibility. Before a court can start divining the intent behind a clause such as this one, the court must determine that the clause was ambiguous. This Court does not believe that the clause is in any way ambiguous."[1172]

Fourth, some of the courts in these cases have concluded that insured versus insured exclusions are ambiguous in the context of a regulatory agency takeover of a financial institution as a receiver and therefore should be construed against the insurer.[1173] As one of these courts has observed, "the stated purpose of the policy . . . to insure the officers and directors against loss from claims made for breach of duty . . . would be entirely defeated or very severely restricted if suits brought by the FSLIC were not covered. Therefore, it would not be unreasonable for such a broad exclusion, if intended, to be stated expressly."[1174] These courts have pointed to the fact that regulatory exclusions specifically precluding suits by

---

1170. *Finci*, 593 A.2d at 1082 (footnote omitted).

1171. *Slaughter*, 842 F. Supp. at 374; *see also Gulf*, slip op. at 13 (using similar reasoning in decision construing insured versus insured provision in context of claims by a debtor-in-possession against insured directors); Chapter V, Section B 9 e (discussing *Gulf* decision).

1172. *Zaborac*, 773 F. Supp. at 143.

1173. *St. Paul*, 765 F. Supp. at 548; *American Casualty*, 814 F. Supp. at 1026; *Zandstra*, 756 F. Supp. at 433; *American Casualty*, 704 F. Supp. at 902.

1174. *American Casualty*, 704 F. Supp. at 901.

regulatory agencies (regulatory exclusions are discussed later in this Chapter)[1175] demonstrate that "[a] regulatory agency assuming the claims of the bank could have been included in the endorsement,"[1176] that the insurers "kn[o]w what language to use to explicitly preclude such suits,"[1177] and that "[h]ad the insurer wanted to exclude actions against . . . directors or officers by a regulatory agency, 'it was well within [its] power and knowledge to clearly indicate any intent to include within the 'insured v. insured' exclusion actions maintained by FDIC or FSLIC.'"[1178]

Put another way, one court has stated, where a D & O policy contains a regulatory exclusion barring coverage for claims brought by regulatory agencies against insured directors and officers, "the mere existence of the Regulatory Exclusion" supports the conclusion that an insured versus insured exclusions does not cover regulatory agencies.[1179] To the contrary, this court asked, "[i]f the parties had intended" that an insured versus insured exclusion would "exclude coverage when the RTC and FDIC sued directors and officers," then "why was that language not specifically used as in the Regulatory Exclusion?"[1180]

The opposite result has been reached as a matter of law in a small group of federal district court cases that hold that insured versus insured exclusions do apply in the context of litigation commenced by regulatory agencies and that these exclusions therefore do protect insurers from claims by regulatory agencies. The leading case is *Gary v. American Casualty Co.*[1181] The *Gary* court rejected the view that claims by regulatory agencies are "brought for the benefit of depositors and creditors of the failed institution

---

1175. *See* Chapter V, Sections B 9 f-g.

1176. *American Casualty*, 814 F. Supp. at 1026.

1177. *St. Paul*, 765 F. Supp. at 548.

1178. *American Casualty*, 814 F. Supp. at 1026 (quoting *Zandstra*, 756 F. Supp. at 433); *see also American Casualty*, 704 F. Supp. at 902 (relying upon fact that "the FSLIC was expressly referred to" in a regulatory exclusion in the policy).

1179. *Sentry*, 867 F. Supp. at 60 n.14.

1180. *Id.*

1181. 753 F. Supp. 1547 (W.D. Okla. 1990).

and for the benefit of itself as a creditor" and not "merely in the capacity of the successor to a failed financial institution."[1182] According to the *Gary* court, "regardless of to whom the benefits of any recovery on a D & O policy by the FDIC or the FSLIC might indirectly or ultimately inure, their claims are claims of the financial institution which they acquired after failure of such financial institution by succession or purchase and are thus asserted in the capacity of assignee of the failed financial institution."[1183] Creditors of a failed bank who claim that they were damaged as a result of a wrongful act of a director or officer of the bank, the *Gary* court added, can prosecute their own claims against the director or officer, and obtain payment from the insurer.[1184]

Moreover, the *Gary* court continued, "regardless of whom the FDIC *may* represent and to whom the benefits of any claims asserted by it may inure, it is clear that in this case the FDIC is seeking a determination of coverage for claims previously owned by the bank and that the FDIC in its corporate capacity may assert them only because the FDIC as Liquidating Agent succeeded to the rights and assets of the bank and sold these particular rights or assets—claims against the bank directors and officers—to the FDIC in its corporate capacity."[1185] The court explained:

> In its Amended Complaint . . . , the FDIC, after reciting its purchase of certain bank assets, including claims against the bank's directors and officers, alleges that Defendant directors and officers breached their implied contractual obligations *to the bank*, resulting in losses to the bank; breached their fiduciary duties *to the bank*, causing the bank to sustain losses; breached their duty of due care owed *to the bank*, directly causing losses to the bank; and that the Defendant directors are personally liable for loans made by the bank in violation of the bank's legal lending limit while Defendants were bank directors. These allegations belie the assertion that the FDIC's claims for which a determination of insurance cover-

---

1182. *Id*. at 1555.
1183. *Id*. (footnote omitted).
1184. *Id*.
1185. *Id*.

age is sought herein are claims asserted on behalf of creditors or depositors.[1186]

The *Gary* court accordingly held that "the FDIC is standing in the shoes of the bank in prosecuting these claims. As such, the 'Insured vs. Insured' exclusion . . . applies to the FDIC's claims and precludes D & O insurance coverage therefor."[1187] Summary judgment therefore was granted in favor of the insurer and against the FDIC.[1188]

The courts in *National Union Fire Insurance Co. v. Resolution Trust Corp.*[1189] and *Evanston Insurance Co. v. Federal Deposit Insurance Corp.*[1190] followed the *Gary* court's reasoning,[1191] although the *Evanston* court later vacated its decision on another ground.[1192]

---

1186. *Id.* (citations to complaint omitted).

1187. *Id.* at 1554.

1188. *Id.* at 1556.

1189. 1992 U.S. Dist. LEXIS 14914, 1992 WL 611463 (S.D. Tex. Aug. 13, 1992).

1190. 1988 U.S. Dist. LEXIS 16263 (C.D. Cal. May 17, 1988), *vacated*, No. CV 88-0407 (C.D. Cal. July 1, 1988).

1191. *National Union*, 1992 U.S. Dist. LEXIS 14914, at *7, 1992 WL 611463, at *3 ("[b]ased upon the reasoning of *Gary*, this Court finds that the claims asserted by the RTC in this action are barred by the Insured v. Insured Exclusion"); *Evanston*, 1988 U.S. Dist. LEXIS 16263, at *4 (granting summary judgment in insurer's favor on the same ground as the *Gary* court: "The underlying action does not purport to enforce the rights of creditors. It is based on negligence, and it asserts that the directors breached the duty of care owed by them to the Bank. The FDIC is not attempting to enforce whatever rights the creditors may have against the directors; the claim is limited to the rights of the Bank acquired by assignment.").

1192. *Evanston Ins. Co. v. Federal Deposit Ins. Corp.*, No. CV 88-0407, slip op. at 1 (C.D. Cal. July 1, 1988) (order granting summary judgment to the insurer vacated on the ground that the insurer had not moved for summary judgment (the insureds had moved and the court had granted summary judgment to the insurer despite the absence of a cross-motion) and the insureds contended that this procedure deprived them of an opportunity to present extrinsic evidence on the subject of the parties' intent).

The court in *Mt. Hawley Insurance Co. v. Federal Savings &
Loan Insurance Corp.*[1193] likewise granted summary judgment in
favor of the insurer. This court relied upon its view that the insured
versus insured provision in this case unambiguously excluded
coverage for cases filed by the bank against bank officials and that
FSLIC as a receiver for a failed bank for "all intents and purposes
. . . stands in the place of the bank."[1194] The "plain terms of the
policy," the court thus concluded, barred "coverage for any claims
made against the D & O defendants" by the failed bank "through
the FSLIC as its receiver."[1195]

In an alternative holding, the *Mt. Hawley* court stated that
even if the reach of the insured versus insured exclusion were
ambiguous, summary judgment in favor of the insurer still would
be appropriate because D & O insurance is "meant to protect the
insureds against the hazards posed by 'unruly stockholders' and the
uncertainties created by 'fertile legal imaginations' conceiving
'novel and alarming theories of liability.'"[1196] D & O insurance,
the court continued, "is not meant to protect the insureds from
claims made against them by the corporation itself."[1197] The
court explained that "it is difficult to argue that it is within the reasonable expectations of the parties . . . that the corporation was
paying D & O insurance premiums to protect the directors and
officers from the consequences of breaching their duty to the
corporation."[1198] "If coverage for claims made by the corporation against the officers and directors does not fall within the scope
of the 'insured's reasonable expectation of coverage,'" the court
concluded, "there is no reason for the insureds to suppose that
these same claims would be covered if brought by the receiver for

---

1193. 695 F. Supp. 469 (C.D. Cal. 1987).

1194. *Id*. at 482.

1195. *Id*. at 485.

1196. *Id*. at 484 (quoting Bishop, *New Problems in Indemnifying
and Insuring Directors: Protection Against Liability under the Federal
Securities Laws*, 1972 Duke L.J. 1153, 1153 (1972)).

1197. *Id*. at 484.

1198. *Id*.

the corporation."[1199] The court stated that this interpretation of the policy in no way eviscerated coverage because the directors and officers still were insured against claims brought by employees, customers and government agencies suing on their own behalf rather than on behalf of the corporation.[1200]

Other courts—in decisions that for the most part predate most of the decisions discussed above—have refused to resolve the insured versus insured exclusion issue in the regulatory context one way or the other as a matter of law. Instead, these courts have required trials.

In *Federal Deposit Insurance Corp. v. National Union Fire Insurance Co.*,[1201] for example, the court held that "[t]o the extent that the FDIC represents the failed bank's shareholders, . . . it is suing in the same capacity as the failed bank" and thus is barred by the insured versus insured exclusion.[1202] The court continued, however, by recognizing that the FDIC also represents itself "as a creditor, as well as its predecessor's other creditors."[1203] The court stated that "insofar as the FDIC is suing to recoup its own losses, it is arguably like any other third party bringing action against the insurer and the insured, who would not be barred" by the insured versus insured exclusion.[1204] Likewise, "[i]nsofar as the agency represents the failed bank's depositors and other creditors, it is again in the capacity of a third party, rather than standing directly in the failed bank's shoes.[1205] The court held that these different FDIC roles resulted in ambiguity on the face of the insured versus insured provision regarding the application of the exclusion to claims brought by the FDIC, and thus the court needed to examine evidence beyond the four corners of the policy in order

---

1199. *Id.*
1200. *Id.* at 484-85.
1201. 630 F. Supp. 1149 (W.D. La. 1986).
1202. *Id.* at 1157.
1203. *Id.*
1204. *Id.*
1205. *Id.*

to establish the intent of the parties.[1206] Because the evidence offered by the parties in support of their respective positions regarding intent conflicted, the court denied the insurer's motion for summary judgment.[1207]

The court in *Federal Deposit Insurance Corp. v. National Union Fire Insurance Co.*[1208] likewise denied an insurer's motion for summary judgment on the ground that an insured versus insured exclusion was ambiguous in the regulatory context and raised issues of fact.[1209]

The district court in *American Casualty Co. v. Federal Deposit Insurance Corp.*[1210] reached the same conclusion on two motions for summary judgment by an insurer, albeit by a more circuitous path.[1211] The court then ruled in favor of the regulatory agency following a bench trial.[1212]

On the insurer's first motion for summary judgment, the court concluded that the insured versus insured provision in this case unambiguously excluded "any claim made against any Director or Officer by any other Director or Officer or by the Institution" and that this provision was triggered when the FDIC "stepped into the shoes" of the insured bank as receiver.[1213] The court nevertheless denied the insurer's summary judgment motion on the ground that the exclusion appeared contrary to the insureds' asserted intention and reasonable expectation in obtaining the policy

---

1206. *Id.*

1207. *Id.*

1208. 1989 WL 251473 (E.D. Tenn. Jan. 6, 1989).

1209. *Id.* at *4.

1210. 677 F. Supp. 600 (N.D. Iowa 1987), *subsequent proceedings*, 713 F. Supp. 311 (N.D. Iowa 1988).

1211. *Id.*

1212. *American Casualty Co. v. Federal Deposit Ins. Corp.*, 1990 U.S. Dist. LEXIS 6065, 1990 WL 66505 (N.D. Iowa Feb. 26, 1990), *aff'd in part and rev'd in part on other grounds*, 944 F.2d 455 (8th Cir. 1991).

1213. 677 F. Supp. at 604.

—i.e., to obtain insurance coverage for claims based on negligence in office.[1214]

The court reversed course on a second motion for summary judgment by the insurer. This second motion for summary judgment followed an amendment by the FDIC of its complaint "to clarify" that it had sued the insureds "on its own behalf as a creditor, as a representative of other creditors of the Bank, and on behalf of the shareholders of the Bank."[1215] This time, the court stated that "[c]ourts which have analyzed the role of FDIC . . . have recognized for over forty years that the FDIC does not strictly 'step into the shoes' of a failed bank" and that the insured versus insured provision accordingly was ambiguous.[1216] Summary judgment thus was denied due to the material issues of fact that surrounded the FDIC's role in the litigation.[1217]

Following a bench trial, the court reaffirmed its conclusion that the insured versus insured provision was ambiguous concerning the FDIC's status as an insured.[1218] The court then concluded that "the evidence at trial, specifically including insurance underwriter . . . testimony that the exclusion was not intended to bar claims by the FDIC and has no application to the FDIC," together with rules of contract construction requiring that ambiguous language be construed against the drafter (here, the insurer), "convince this Court that FDIC is not an 'insured' under such exclusion" and that claims by the FDIC therefore were not excluded from coverage.[1219] The Eighth Circuit affirmed and reversed other

---

1214. *Id*. at 605.

1215. *American Casualty Co. v. Federal Deposit Ins. Corp.*, 713 F. Supp. 311, 316 (N.D. Iowa 1988).

1216. *Id*.

1217. *Id*.

1218. *American Casualty Co. Federal Deposit Ins. Corp.*, 1990 U.S. Dist. LEXIS 6065, at *41, 1990 WL 66505, at *10-11 (N.D. Iowa Feb. 26, 1990), *aff'd in part and rev'd in part on other grounds*, 944 F.2d 455 (8th Cir. 1991).

1219. *Id*. (footnote and citations omitted).

aspects of the *American Casualty* district court's post-trial decision on various grounds but did not address this issue.[1220]

The court in *Continental Casualty Co. v. Allen*[1221] adopted the district court's initial reasoning in *American Casualty*—i.e., that an insured versus insured provision identical to the insured versus insured provision in *American Casualty* was unambiguous but that questions of fact surrounding the insureds' reasonable expectations in obtaining the policy precluded granting the insurer's motion for summary judgment.[1222] As in *American Casualty*, the court in *Continental Casualty* reconsidered its determination that the insured versus insured provision was ambiguous following a trial and concluded at that time that the provision was ambiguous and should be construed against the insurer.[1223]

A final insured versus insured exclusion issue that has been litigated in the regulatory context is whether enforcement of an insured versus insured exclusion against a regulatory agency is barred by public policy. This issue is litigated more frequently in regulatory exclusion cases and is discussed in that context later in this Chapter.[1224]

*e. The Insured Versus Insured Exclusion in the Bankruptcy Context.* Another insured versus insured exclusion issue that has been litigated—although less frequently than the insured versus insured exclusion in the regulatory context—is the insured versus insured exclusion in the context of bankruptcy. The results reached in these litigations have differed.

---

1220. *American Casualty Co. v. Federal Deposit Ins. Co.*, 944 F.2d 455, 457 n.1 (8th Cir. 1991).

1221. No. CA-5-86-252 (N.D. Tex. Feb. 16, 1988), *subsequent proceedings*, 710 F. Supp. 1088 (N.D. Tex. 1989).

1222. *Id.*, slip op. at 4-5.

1223. *Continental Casualty Co. v. Allen*, 710 F. Supp. 1088, 1097-98 (N.D. Tex. 1989).

1224. *See* Chapter V, Section B 9 g.

*Reliance Insurance Co. v. Weis*[1225] involved Bank Building and Equipment Corporation ("BBC"), a company in liquidation. A committee formed pursuant to the plan of liquidation brought an action against three former BBC officers. This action alleged breach of fiduciary duty and negligence by these former BBC officers.[1226]

A federal court in Missouri held that the claim asserted in this litigation constituted a claim by an insured against insureds and thus that no insurance was available pursuant to an insured versus insured exclusion. The court reasoned as follows:

> [W]hatever right of action BBC had against its former officers for mismanagement and breach of fiduciary duty was transferred to the bankruptcy estate upon the filing of its bankruptcy petition. Once BBC was liquidated, Agent Miller and the Plan Committee were obligated to pursue BBC's right of action in order to recover assets for BBC's estate. The purpose of the pending state court action is to recover all available funds for distribution to BBC's creditors. It is clear that the pending state court action was filed on behalf of BBC and its estate, although the benefits sought may eventually inure to the creditors. For purposes of this litigation, there is no significant legal distinction between BBC and its bankruptcy estate.[1227]

The court also relied upon the fact that the insurer drafted the policy and included other provisions in the policy addressing the parties' rights in the event of bankruptcy. For this reason, the court stated, "it appears reasonable to conclude" that if the insurer "had wanted to expressly address the issue of bankruptcy" in the policy's insured versus insured exclusion then "it would have done so."[1228]

---

1225. 148 B.R. 575 (E.D. Mo. 1992), *aff'd mem.*, 5 F.3d 532 (8th Cir. 1993), *cert denied*, 510 U.S. 1117 (1994).

1226. *Id.* at 577-78.

1227. *Id.* at 583.

1228. *Id.* at 580.

The opposite conclusion was reached in *Pintlar Corp. v. Fidelity & Casualty Co.*[1229] and *Cigna Insurance Co. v. Gulf Corp.*,[1230] two decisions arising out of the same dispute. These decisions involved claims by Gulf USA Corporation and Pintlar Corporation, as debtors-in-possession, against former directors and officers of Gulf and Pintlar following the filing of bankruptcy proceedings. After these claims were brought, they were assigned by the debtors-in-possession to litigation trusts "formed for the purpose of prosecuting the D & O claims 'on behalf, and for the sole benefit' of creditors designated in the plan of reorganization."[1231] These litigation trusts specifically excluded the debtors-in-possession as beneficiaries of the trusts.[1232]

In the first decision, *Pintlar Corp. v. Fidelity & Casualty Co.*,[1233] a bankruptcy court in Idaho held that the insured versus insured exclusion did not preclude coverage for this claim. The court reasoned that "Gulf and Pintlar, either in the capacities as pre-filing corporations or as debtors in possession are for all practical purposes nonexistent."[1234] The court explained that "[a]lthough Gulf and Pintlar have not been liquidated in the ordinary sense of the term, the assets and liabilities of these entities have, for the most part, been dedicated to the purpose of fulfilling the terms and conditions of the confirmed plan of reorganization," and "[t]he primary purpose of the plan is to marshal the remaining assets of Gulf and Pintlar for payment of creditors."[1235] Accordingly, the court stated, "[t]he claims against the officers and directors now belong to the creditors acting through the litigation trus-

---

1229. 205 B.R. 945 (Bankr. D. Idaho 1997), *aff'd sub nom. Cigna Ins. Co. v. Gulf USA Corp.*, No. CV 97-250-N-EJL (D. Idaho Sept. 11, 1997).

1230. No. CV 97-250-N-EJL (D. Idaho Sept. 11, 1997).

1231. 205 B.R. at 946; No. CV 9-250-N-EJL, slip op. at 3-4.

1232. 205 B.R. at 946; No. CV 9-250-N-EJL, slip op. at 4.

1233. 205 B.R. 945 (Bankr. D. Idaho 1997), *aff'd sub nom. Cigna Ins. Co. v. Gulf USA Corp.*, No. CV 97-250-N-EJL (D. Idaho Sept. 11, 1997).

1234. *Id.* at 947.

1235. *Id.* at 947-48.

tees."[1236] In other words, "the litigation trustees are not acting for the benefit of the corporation, but for the benefit of the corporation's creditors, including the shareholders."[1237]

The court added that the claims against former directors and officers at issue are "the same claims a shareholder could have pursued prior to the filing of the Chapter 11 petition."[1238] "[C]overage would have extended to these shareholder derivative actions," the court stated, because the insured versus insured provisions before the court provided coverage for "a claim brought derivatively by a shareholder who is acting 'totalling independent of, and totally without the solicitation of, or assistance of' the company."[1239]

In the second decision, the district court, in a proceeding now called *Cigna Insurance Co. v. Gulf USA Corp.*,[1240] affirmed the bankruptcy court's decision but pursuant to different reasoning.

The district court rejected the bankruptcy court's reliance upon the transfer of the claims asserted by the debtors-in-possession to litigation trusts. The court explained the "[t]he insurance policies at issue in this case were written on a 'claims made,' rather than an occurrence, basis."[1241] "Under a 'claims made' policy," the court stated, "the 'insured v. insured' exclusion is triggered at the time the claim is made."[1242] Accordingly, the court concluded, "the status of the party asserting the claim must be determined at that same time" and "[t]he status of the party asserting the claims cannot be altered by effectuating a transfer after the fact."[1243]

The district court thus analyzed the scope of the insured versus insured exclusions in the Gulf and Pintlar policies (the court referred to Gulf and Pintlar collectively as Gulf) "based on the

1236. *Id.* at 948.
1237. *Id.*
1238. *Id.*
1239. *Id.*; No. CV 97-250-N-EJL, slip op. at 3.
1240. No. CV 97-250-N-EJL (D. Idaho Sept. 11, 1997).
1241. *Id.*, slip op. at 7.
1242. *Id.*
1243. *Id.*

identity of the D & O plaintiff at the time the claims were made: Gulf as a debtor-in-possession."[1244] The court reasoned that once a corporation enters bankruptcy and assumes its status as debtor-in-possession its relationship to its creditors and shareholders becomes "subject to a different set of legal obligations" because "the Bankruptcy Code imposes the same duties on a debtor-in-possession as it does on a trustee," including "a fiduciary responsibility to the creditors" and "a duty to manage the property of the estate for the benefit of the 'entire community of interest in the corporation—creditors as well as stockholders.'"[1245] At the same time, "[a]ny claim that could have been brought pre-petition in a derivative action by shareholders or creditors becomes the property of the estate, and can only be asserted by the debtor-in-possession."[1246]

Accordingly, the court stated, "Gulf as debtor-in-possession is vested with the exclusive right to assert the D & O claims on behalf of shareholders and creditors, and under the Bankruptcy Code, Gulf as debtor-in-possession is obligated to pursue the claims for the benefit of those same interests."[1247] Under these circumstances, the court continued, the debtor-in-possession asserts claims "on behalf of and for the benefit of" shareholders and creditors, and not "'by,' or 'on behalf of,' or by 'successors'" to the corporation.[1248]

The court added that "the asserted claims are of the same type that could have been made pre-petition by the corporation's shareholders," and, as noted in the discussion of the bankruptcy court's ruling above, the insured versus insured exclusions in the governing policies "explicitly provide for insurance coverage for such claims."[1249] The court also added that its decision was "bolstered by the policy considerations underpinning the 'insured v.

---

1244. *Id.*
1245. *Id.* at 10.
1246. *Id.*
1247. *Id.*
1248. *Id.* at 12.
1249. *Id.* at 3, 12.

insured' exclusion."[1250] Quoting *Township of Center v. First Mercury Syndicate, Inc.*[1251]—a case discussed in the preceding Section of this Chapter[1252]—the court stated that "[t]he primary focus of the exclusion is to prevent collusive suits in which an insured company might seek to force its insurer to pay for poor business decisions of its officers and managers."[1253] The court stated that there was "no dispute that in this case the parties to the D & O action are truly adverse."[1254] Quoting *First Mercury* again, the court concluded that "[w]here . . . the underlying action is not collusive, the ['insured v. insured'] exclusion has not precluded coverage."[1255]

The court thus concluded that "the 'insured v. insured' exclusions do not apply" to claims by a debtor-in-possession against directors and officers.[1256] The district court acknowledged that its decision was "at odds with *Reliance*," the only published opinion construing an 'insured v. insured' exclusion in the bankruptcy context."[1257] The court stated its belief that "the *Reliance* opinion placed undue emphasis on the fact that the D & O claims could be viewed as 'belonging' to the bankrupt corporation, and ignored the fact that the claims actually were being asserted on behalf of creditors."[1258] The court stated that the *Reliance* court's "refusal to view the claims as 'belonging' to shareholders and creditors was based in part on the failure of the plaintiff" in the litigation underlying the *Reliance* decision to allege that the claims in that case were "derivatively asserted on behalf of . . . shareholders."[1259] The court noted that the complaint underlying the *Cigna* litigation did "state that the asserted D & O claims are 'derivative

---

1250. *Id.* at 13.
1251. 117 F.3d 115 (3d Cir. 1997).
1252. *See* Chapter V, Section B 9 d.
1253. Slip op. at 13 (quoting *First Mercury*, 117 F.3d at 119).
1254. *Id.* at 13.
1255. *Id.*
1256. *Id.* at 12.
1257. *Id.* at 12 n.6.
1258. *Id.* (citations omitted).
1259. *Id.* (citation omitted).

claims held by equity holders.'"[1260] The court added that "in several instances" the insurers in the *Cigna* case had "deemed certain D & O claims 'to have been made' in 1990 precisely because they were identical to claims asserted in a derivative shareholder action filed against Gulf's officers and directors in 1990."[1261]

 *f. The Regulatory Exclusion: Ambiguity Considerations.* Regulatory exclusions specifically withhold coverage for claims brought by regulatory agencies against insured directors and officers.[1262] Regulatory exclusions provide a more direct means of excluding coverage for claims by regulatory agencies than applying insured versus insured exclusions in regulatory actions.[1263]

 A substantial majority of the courts that have considered claims by regulatory agencies that regulatory exclusions are ambiguous have rejected these claims as a matter of law. The leading decision is the Eighth Circuit's decision in *St. Paul Fire & Marine Insurance Co. v. Federal Deposit Insurance Corp.*[1264] The court in this case held that an insurer was entitled to a summary judgment dismissal of a claim by the Federal Deposit Insurance Corporation where the policy stated that "there is no coverage for any claims made against the Directors and Officers of the Insured based upon or attributable to any claim, action or proceeding brought by or on behalf of the Federal Deposit Insurance Corporation . . . ."[1265] The Eighth Circuit stated that

---

1260. *Id.*

1261. *Id.*

1262. *See* John F. Olson & Josiah O. Hatch III, *Director and Officer Liability: Indemnification and Insurance* § 10.06[5][c][ii] (1997); Johnston, *Directors' and Officers' and Related Forms of Liability Insurance, in* 7 *Securities Law Techniques* § 122.03[2][g][xvi] (A.A. Sommer, Jr. ed. 1998); Monteleone & Conca, *Directors and Officers Indemnification and Liability Insurance: An Overview of Legal and Practical Issues*, 51 Bus. Law. 573, 605-06 (1996).

1263. *See* Chapter V, Section B 9 d.

1264. 968 F.2d 695 (8th Cir. 1992).

1265. *St. Paul Fire & Marine Ins. Co. v. Federal Deposit Ins. Corp.*, 765 F. Supp. 538, 548 (D. Minn. 1991), *aff'd*, 968 F.2d 695 (8th Cir. 1992).

[t]he plain language of the regulatory exclusion bars coverage for any claim against the directors and officers of the bank based on any action or proceeding brought by or on behalf of the FDIC. When read as a whole, the regulatory exclusion covers any claim, direct or secondary, brought against the directors and officers of the bank by the FDIC in any capacity.[1266]

The same result has been reached by the Fourth, Fifth, Sixth, Seventh and Tenth Circuits in *Federal Deposit Insurance Corp. v. American Casualty Co.*,[1267] *Fidelity & Deposit Co. v. Conner*,[1268] *American Casualty Co. v. Federal Deposit Insurance Corp.*,[1269] *Federal Deposit Insurance Corp. v. American Casualty Co.*,[1270] *American Casualty Co. v. Federal Deposit Insurance Corp.*[1271] and *Federal Deposit Insurance Corp. v. American Casualty Co.*[1272]

In the Fifth Circuit's words in *Conner*: "Although we construe ambiguity in policy language in favor of the insured, this court 'has no right to read an ambiguity into the plain language of an insurance contract in order to construe it against the insurer.' Accordingly, we will not read ambiguity into the language of the D & O policy exclusions."[1273] As the Seventh Circuit put it: the exclusion "fits like a glove."[1274] The Sixth Circuit decision arose in the context of a case brought by a shareholder derivatively, on behalf of a regulatory agency, rather than by the regulatory agency itself. The court stated that the derivative nature of the action did not change the result because the FDIC had the legal right to bring the action and "[p]ursuant to the unambiguous terms of the exclu-

---

1266. 968 F.2d at 701.

1267. 995 F.2d 471, 472-73 (4th Cir. 1993), *aff'g Federal Deposit Ins. Corp. v. Heidrick*, 812 F. Supp. 586, 588-89 (D. Md. 1991).

1268. 973 F.2d 1236, 1244-45 (5th Cir. 1992).

1269. 39 F.3d 633, 638 (6th Cir. 1994).

1270. 998 F.2d 404, 408 (7th Cir. 1993), *aff'g Federal Deposit Ins. Corp. v. Zaborac*, 773 F. Supp. 137, 141-42 (C.D. Ill. 1991).

1271. 16 F.3d 152, 153-54 (7th Cir. 1994).

1272. 975 F.2d 677, 680 (10th Cir. 1992).

1273. 973 F.2d at 1244-45 (quoting *St. Paul*, 968 F.2d at 701).

1274. *American Casualty*, 16 F.3d at 154.

sion itself, the policy provision included 'any type of legal action which such Agencies *have the legal right to bring* as receiver, conservator, liquidator or otherwise.'"[1275] In sum, in the Fourth Circuit's words, "[t]he plain language of the regulatory exclusion provision and the overwhelming weight of case law demonstrates that it is not ambiguous."[1276] In the Tenth Circuit's words, "[w]e agree . . . with the vast majority of courts to consider this question, that the FDIC's interpretation of the regulatory exclusion is strained."[1277]

The same result also has been reached by federal district courts in the context of pre-trial motions in numerous cases,[1278]

---

1275. *American Casualty*, 39 F.3d at 637.

1276. *American Casualty*, 995 F.2d at 472.

1277. *American Casualty*, 975 F.2d at 680.

1278. *See American Casualty Co. v. Sentry Fed. Sav. Bank*, 867 F. Supp. 50, 58 (D. Mass. 1994); *American Casualty Co. v. Resolution Trust Corp.*, 1994 U.S. Dist. LEXIS 9447, at *10-11 & n.5, 1994 WL 361508, at *3 & n.5 (E.D. Pa. July 7, 1994); *American Casualty Co. v. Rahn*, 854 F. Supp. 492, 499-500 (W.D. Mich. 1994); *Resolution Trust Corp. v. Moskowitz*, 1994 U.S. Dist. LEXIS 4049, at *11 (D.N.J. Mar. 30, 1994); *American Casualty Co. v. Resolution Trust Corp.*, 845 F. Supp. 318, 326-27 (D. Md. 1993); *American Casualty Co. v. Resolution Trust Corp.*, CV No. 92-10543-WF, slip op. at 29-30 (D. Mass. Oct. 19, 1993); *Benafield v. Continental Casualty Co.*, 1993 U.S. Dist. LEXIS 16887, at *4, 1993 WL 723510, at *2 (E.D. Ark. Oct. 1, 1993); *Chandler v. American Casualty Co.*, 833 F. Supp. 735, 738 (E.D. Ark. 1993); *American Casualty Co. v. Resolution Trust Corp.*, 839 F. Supp. 282, 290-93 (D.N.J. 1993); *American Casualty Co. v. Federal Deposit Ins. Corp.*, 1993 WL 610760, at *9-11 (S.D. Miss. Apr. 8, 1993); *American Casualty Co. v. Federal Deposit Ins. Corp.*, 1993 U.S. Dist. LEXIS 5853, at *8, 1993 WL 625521, at *3 (W.D. Mich. Jan. 8, 1993) and 1993 U.S. Dist. LEXIS 5853, at *15 (W.D. Mich. Jan. 8, 1993); *Bartley v. National Union Fire Ins. Co.*, 824 F. Supp. 624, 632-34 (N.D. Tex. 1992); *National Union Fire Ins. Co. v. Resolution Trust Corp.*, 1992 U.S. Dist. LEXIS 14914, at *5, 1992 WL 611463, at *2 (S.D. Tex. Aug. 13, 1992); *Federal Sav. & Loan Ins. Corp. v. Shelton*, 789 F. Supp. 1355, 1357-58 (M.D. La. 1992); *Powell v. American Casualty Co.*, 772 F. Supp. 1188, 1190-91 (W.D. Okla. 1991); *American Casualty Co. v. Baker*, 758 F. Supp. 1340,

(continued...)

as well as in cases decided by state courts in Colorado[1279] and Maryland.[1280]

One federal district court decision in Ohio—*American Casualty Co. v. Federal Savings & Loan Insurance Corp.*[1281]—found a regulatory provision clear and unambiguous but held that the exclusion did not apply where the action had been brought by a shareholder prior to insolvency, the FSLIC then was appointed as a receiver, and the FSLC then substituted itself as plaintiff.[1282] The court reasoned that "[t]o 'bring' an action or suit refers to the initiation, not the maintenance, of legal proceedings," and "a suit is 'brought' at the time it is commenced."[1283] The Seventh Circuit's decision in *Federal Deposit Insurance Corp. v. American Casualty Co.*[1284] rejected the distinction drawn in the Ohio *American Casualty* decision between suits "brought" by a regulatory agency and

---

1278. (...continued)
1344-48 (C.D. Cal. 1991), *aff'd on other grounds*, 22 F.3d 880 (9th Cir. 1994); *Federal Deposit Ins. Corp. v. Continental Casualty Co.*, 796 F. Supp. 1344, 1351 (D. Or. 1991); *Federal Deposit Ins. Corp. v. American Casualty Co.*, 814 F. Supp. 1021, 1024-25 (D. Wyo. 1991), *subsequent proceedings*, No. 90-CV-0265-J, slip op. at 13 (D. Wyo. Sept. 9, 1994); *Gary v. American Casualty Co.*, 753 F. Supp. 1547, 1550-51 (W.D. Okla. 1990); *International Ins. Co. v. McMullan*, 1990 U.S. Dist. LEXIS 19940, at *58-59, 1990 WL 483731, at *20-21 (S.D. Miss. Mar. 7, 1990); *McCuen v. International Ins. Co.* 1988 U.S. Dist. LEXIS 17624, at *13, 1988 WL 242680, at *6 (S.D. Iowa Sept. 29, 1988), *aff'd on other grounds sub nom. McCuen v. American Casualty Co.*, 946 F.2d 1401 (8th Cir. 1991); *cf. Mt. Hawley Ins. Co. v. Federal Sav. & Loan Ins. Corp.*, 695 F. Supp. 469, 482 (C.D. Cal. 1987) (stating that "if the regulatory endorsement had been a part of the policy, it would quite clearly have barred coverage").

1279. *See Federal Deposit Ins. Corp. v. American Casualty Co.*, 843 P.2d 1285, 1289-90 (Colo. 1992).

1280. *See Finci v. American Casualty Co.*, 593 A.2d 1069, 1074-76 (Md. 1991).

1281. 683 F. Supp. 1183 (S.D. Ohio 1988).

1282. *Id.* at 1184-85.

1283. *Id.* at 1185.

1284. 998 F.2d 404 (7th Cir. 1993).

suits "brought" by a shareholder and later "maintained" by the regulatory agency.[1285] The Sixth Circuit's decision in *American Casualty Co. v. Federal Deposit Insurance Corp.*[1286] distinguished the Ohio *American Casualty* decision on the ground that the Ohio decision involved litigation commenced by a shareholder on the corporation's behalf before a receiver was appointed and before the receiver substituted itself as plaintiff, while the case in the Sixth Circuit had been commenced by a shareholder on the FDIC's behalf after the FDIC had been appointed as receiver.[1287]

One federal district court in Arkansas—*American Casualty Co. v. Federal Savings & Loan Insurance Group.*[1288]—has held that a regulatory provision excluding coverage for "any claim made against the insured . . . based upon or attributable to: any action or proceeding resulting from violation of any laws, regulations, lending or reporting policy as promulgated by . . . any . . . national or state regulatory agency, . . . whether such action or proceeding is brought in the name of said Agencies or by or on behalf of such Agencies in the name of any other entity or solely in the name of any Third Party" excluded only "actions brought by a regulatory agency to enforce compliance with, or to exact civil penalties for the violation of laws and regulations."[1289] The exclusion, the court held, did not reach an FSLIC action alleging not that the directors violated federal regulations, but that the directors breached "a fiduciary duty to prevent those violations."[1290]

The court reasoned that "[n]early every imaginable breach of fiduciary duty, which American agreed to insure against, would involve conduct that would violate one or more federal regulations."[1291] The court continued:

---

1285. *Id.* at 407, 409.
1286. 39 F.3d 633 (6th Cir. 1994).
1287. *Id.* at 637.
1288. 704 F. Supp. 898 (E.D. Ark. 1989).
1289. *Id.* at 902-03.
1290. *Id.* at 903.
1291. *Id.*

American has cited 12 C.F.R. § 563.17(a) numerous times for the proposition that FSLIC's claims against the defendant officers and directors result from regulatory violations. That section requires savings and loan associations to "maintain safe and sound management" and to pursue safe financial policies. Essentially, § 563.17(a) is a codification of the fiduciary standard. It is preposterous to suggest that any institution would pay a substantial premium for a policy to insure against loss resulting from breach of fiduciary duty, but which at the same time excludes coverage for claims resulting from conduct inconsistent with the fiduciary standard.[1292]

The court stated it would "not construe an exclusion so broadly as to eviscerate the policy."[1293] For these reasons, the court concluded, the regulatory exclusion was "at best, ambiguous and it does not exclude coverage for actions brought by the FSLIC, as receiver, against former officers and directors of FirstSouth for breach of fiduciary duty."[1294]

A federal district court in Louisiana—*Federal Deposit Insurance Corp. v. Mijalis*[1295]—reached a similar conclusion. The court held that a regulatory provision excluding "all claims arising out of insolvency or financial impairment of the Bank made by, or on behalf of, any federal governmental agency" was ambiguous.[1296] The court reasoned that in bringing the action the FDIC acted "not only on its own behalf but also as representative of the failed bank's depositors and other creditors as well as shareholders," and that it was "unclear whether this exclusion was intended to apply to the FDIC when acting in multiple capacities, particularly a representative capacity."[1297] The court thus concluded that a "clearly worded regulatory exclusion, which would unmistakably exclude coverage for claims made by the FDIC in

---

1292. *Id.*

1293. *Id.*

1294. *Id.* at 904.

1295. 800 F. Supp. 397 (W.D. La. 1992), *aff'd in part and rev'd in part on other grounds*, 15 F.3d 1314 (5th Cir. 1994).

1296. *Id.* at 402.

1297. *Id.*

their present capacity, is not present in the instant case."[1298] The court accordingly held that the provision was "ambiguous as applied to the FDIC in this situation," and therefore "it must be construed in favor of the insured."[1299]

Several other federal district courts—in decisions pre-dating most of the decisions discussed above—have required trials on this issue. The most frequently cited example is *American Casualty Co. v. Federal Deposit Insurance Corp.*,[1300] a case involving a provision excluding claims "made against the Directors or Officers based upon or attributable to any action or proceeding brought by or on behalf of the Federal Deposit Insurance Corporation, the Federal Savings & Loan Insurance Corporation . . . or any other national or state regulatory agency."[1301]

The district court in this case initially held that this exclusion was ambiguous because it could be construed to apply (1) to any regulatory agency suit, or (2) only to what the court described as the "common occurrence" where "the FDIC sues a former bank customer, and then the customer sues an officer or director"—i.e., "only to 'secondary' suits occasioned by actions brought by the FDIC against third parties, not direct actions by the FDIC."[1302] Construing this ambiguity in favor of the insured, the court denied the insurer's motion for summary judgment. The court stated that if the insurer "had truly intended to exclude coverage for direct actions against the officers and directors by the FDIC, it would have been a simple matter to say so directly, rather than phrasing this exclusion in the cumbersome manner which it has."[1303] The court reached the same result on a renewed motion for summary

---

1298. *Id.*

1299. *Id.*

1300. 677 F. Supp. 600 (N.D. Iowa 1987), *subsequent proceedings*, 713 F. Supp. 311 (N.D. Iowa 1988), *subsequent proceedings*, 1990 U.S. Dist. LEXIS 6065, 1990 WL 66505 (N.D. Iowa Feb. 26, 1990), *aff'd in part and rev'd in part*, 944 F.2d 455 (8th Cir. 1991).

1301. 677 F. Supp. at 602.

1302. *Id.* at 603.

1303. *Id.* at 604.

judgment following the completion of discovery.[1304] The courts in *Federal Savings & Loan Insurance Corp. v. Heidrick*,[1305] *Federal Savings & Loan Insurance Corp. v. Mmahat*[1306] and *Continental Casualty Co. v. Allen*[1307] each followed the analysis in these *American Casualty* decisions, and each denied motions for summary judgment by insurers.[1308] The *Heidrick* court reversed course and granted the insurer's motion for summary judgment in that case eight months later, however, after the Maryland Supreme Court (the *Heidrick* case was governed by Maryland law) held in *Finci v. American Casualty Co.*[1309] that a virtually identical regulatory provision was unambiguous as a matter of law.[1310]

Following a bench trial in *American Casualty*, the *American Casualty* court reconsidered its earlier rulings "[b]ecause additional evidence and recent rulings from other courts were presented at trial."[1311] On the basis of this "additional evidence" and these "recent rulings from other courts," the court concluded that the regulatory exclusion at issue was not ambiguous and did exclude

---

1304. *American Casualty Co. v. Federal Deposit Ins. Corp.*, 713 F. Supp. 311, 314 (N.D. Iowa 1988), *subsequent proceedings*, 1990 U.S. Dist. LEXIS 6065, 1990 WL 66505 (N.D. Iowa Feb. 26, 1990), *aff'd in part and rev'd in part*, 944 F.2d 455 (8th Cir. 1991).

1305. 774 F. Supp. 352 (D. Md.), *motion for reconsideration granted sub nom. Federal Deposit Ins. Corp. v. Heidrick*, 812 F. Supp. 586 (D. Md. 1991), *aff'd sub nom. Federal Deposit Ins. Corp. v. American Casualty Co.*, 995 F.2d 471 (4th Cir. 1993).

1306. 1988 U.S. Dist. LEXIS 1825, 1988 WL 19304 (E.D. La. Mar. 3, 1988).

1307. No. CA-5-86-252 (N.D. Tex. Feb. 16, 1988).

1308. *Heidrick*, 774 F. Supp. at 359-61; *Mmahat*, 1988 U.S. Dist. LEXIS 1825, at *6, 1988 WL 19304, at *2; *Allen*, slip op. at 3-4.

1309. 593 A.2d 1069 (Md. 1991).

1310. *Federal Sav. & Loan Ins. Corp. v. Heidrick*, 812 F. Supp. 586, 588-89 (D. Md. 1991), *aff'd sub nom. Federal Deposit Ins. Corp. v. American Casualty Co.*, 995 F.2d 471 (4th Cir. 1993).

1311. *American Casualty Co. v. Federal Deposit Ins. Corp.*, 1990 U.S. Dist. LEXIS 6065, at *39, 1990 WL 66505, at *10 (N.D. Iowa Feb. 26, 1990), *aff'd in part and rev'd in part*, 944 F.2d 455 (8th Cir. 1991).

coverage of a claim by a regulatory agency.[1312] The same result was reached following a trial in *Continental Casualty Co. v. Allen*,[1313] one of the cases noted above in which the earlier decisions in *American Casualty* finding the exclusion ambiguous in the context of a motion for summary judgment had been followed.[1314]

The *American Casualty* court, however, held that to the extent that the insureds in the *American Casualty* case did not understand the existence and meaning of the exclusion, they were not bound by the exclusion. According to the district court, the corporate officer who agreed to the regulatory exclusion had not been authorized to accept policy terms of this type, and the insurer had been "less than open and candid" in the materials concerning the exclusion that were sent to the insureds. The district court accordingly concluded that the exclusion was unconscionable and a violation of the insureds' reasonable expectations of insurance coverage and the insurer's implied warranty of fitness.[1315]

The Eighth Circuit affirmed the district court's determination in *American Casualty* that the regulatory exclusion was not ambiguous and thus excluded coverage of a claim by a regulatory agency. In the Eighth Circuit's words: "We see no error of law or fact in the District Court's analysis and conclusions . . . . They are in line with the vast majority of courts which have considered this exclusion. No good purpose would be served by repeating those discussions."[1316] The Eight Circuit, however, reversed the district court's finding that insureds who did not understand the existence and meaning of the exclusion were not bound by the exclusion. The Eighth Circuit explained that the corporate officer who agreed to

---

1312. 1990 U.S. Dist. LEXIS 6065, at *40, 1990 WL 66505, at *10.

1313. 710 F. Supp. 1088 (N.D. Tex. 1989).

1314. *Id.* at 1098.

1315. 1990 U.S. Dist. LEXIS 6065, at *17-34, 50-58, 1990 WL 66505, at *5-9, 12-15.

1316. *American Casualty Co. v. Federal Deposit Ins. Corp.*, 944 F.2d 455, 460-61 (8th Cir. 1991).

the exclusion had apparent authority to bind the board.[1317] The Eighth Circuit also stated that it "cannot be reasonable for the Board to expect coverage clearly inconsistent with the actual knowledge of its own agent."[1318] The Eighth Circuit accordingly held that rather than being unconscionable, as the district court had concluded, the regulatory provision was "a bargain struck by adult business people. We have no reason to suppose that a better deal could have been gotten for the bank from any other insurer."[1319]

The Resolution Trust Corporation ("RTC"), which was created in 1989 (after many policies containing regulatory exclusions already had been drafted) and which ceased its existence at the end of 1995, contended in a series of cases that it is not a regulatory agency as that term is used in regulatory exclusions that do not specifically mention the RTC. The courts repeatedly have rejected this argument.[1320]

---

1317. *Id*. at 457-60.

1318. *Id*. at 460.

1319. *Id.; see also St. Paul Fire & Marine Ins. Co. v. Federal Deposit Ins. Corp.*, 968 F.2d 695, 700-01 (8th Cir. 1992) (rejecting contention that insureds were not given clear and conspicuous notice of changes in policy coverage, including regulatory exclusion); *American Casualty Co. v. Baker*, 1993 U.S. Dist. LEXIS 6981, at *8-9 (C.D. Cal. Apr. 29, 1993), *aff'd*, 22 F.3d 880, 891-92 (9th Cir. 1994) (same); *American Casualty Co. v. Rahn*, 854 F. Supp. 492, 500-03 (W.D. Mich. 1994) (declining to invalidate a regulatory exclusion added to policy by the insurer at the time the policy was renewed without alerting the insured that coverage was not substantially the same as in prior policy; the court relied upon the fact that the insured learned of the exclusion prior to the time of the claim at issue but did not "air its concerns within a reasonable time").

1320. *See American Casualty Co. v. Baker*, 22 F.3d 880, 895 (9th Cir. 1994) (noting that "[e]very other court to consider the issue has concluded that the RTC falls within the scope of the Regulatory Exclusion" and determining to "follow this overwhelming authority"); *Resolution Trust Corp. v. Hedden*, 879 F. Supp. 600, 601 (N.D. Miss. 1995); *American Casualty Co. v. Sentry Fed. Sav. Bank*, 867 F. Supp. 50, 58 (D. Mass. 1994); *American Casualty Co. v. Beranek*, 862 F. Supp. 322, 327-28 (D. Kan. 1994); *American Casualty Co. v. Resolution Trust Corp.*, 1994 U.S. Dist. LEXIS 9447, at *10-11 & n.5, 1994 WL 361508, at 3 &

(continued...)

    *g. The Regulatory Exclusion: Public Policy Considerations.* The majority of courts that have addressed regulatory exclusions (and not found them unenforceable on ambiguity grounds),[1321] including "every circuit court that has considered the exclusion," has found the exclusion "valid and not violative of public policy."[1322] Among these courts are the Fourth Circuit in *Federal Deposit Insurance Corp. v. American Casualty Co.*,[1323] the Fifth Circuit in *Fidelity & Deposit Co. v. Conner*,[1324] the Sixth Circuit in *American Casualty Co. v. Federal Deposit Insurance Corp.*,[1325] the Seventh Circuit in *Federal Deposit Insurance Corp. v. American Casualty Co.*,[1326] the Eighth Circuit in *Ameri-*

---

1320. (...continued)
n.5 (E.D. Pa. July 7, 1994); *Resolution Trust Corp. v. Moskowitz*, 1994 U.S. Dist. LEXIS 4049, at *7-11 (D.N.J. Mar. 30, 1994); *American Casualty Co. v. Resolution Trust Corp.*, 845 F. Supp. 318, 326-27 (D. Md. 1993); *American Casualty Co. v. Resolution Trust Corp.*, CV No. 92-10543-WF, slip op. at 25-29 (D. Mass. Oct. 19, 1993); *Benafield v. Continental Casualty Co.*, 1993 U.S. Dist. LEXIS 16887, at *4, 1993 WL 723510, at *2 (E.D. Ark. Oct. 1, 1993); *American Casualty Co. v. Resolution Trust Corp.*, 839 F. Supp. 282, 290-92 (D.N.J. 1993); *Adams v. Resolution Trust Corp.*, 1993 U.S. Dist. LEXIS 7496 at *23-27, 1993 WL 181303, at *6-7 (D. Minn. May 19, 1993), *aff'd on other grounds sub nom. Adams v. Greenwood*, 10 F.3d 568 (8th Cir. 1993); *Chandler v. American Casualty Co.*, 833 F. Supp. 735, 737-38 (E.D. Ark. 1993); *Resolution Trust Corp. v. Walke*, 1993 U.S. Dist. LEXIS 20095, at *4 n.2, 1993 WL 455195, at *2 n.2 (W.D. La. Apr. 15, 1993); *National Union Fire Ins. Co. v. Resolution Trust Corp.*, 1992 U.S. Dist. LEXIS 14914, at *2-6, 1992 WL 611463, at *1-2 (S.D. Tex. Aug. 13, 1992).
    1321. *See* Chapter V, Section B 9 f.
    1322. *American Casualty Co. v. Baker*, 22 F.3d 880, 894 (9th Cir. 1994).
    1323. 995 F.2d 471, 472-73 (4th Cir. 1993).
    1324. 973 F.2d 1236, 1241-44 (5th Cir. 1992).
    1325. 39 F.3d 633, 637-39 (6th Cir. 1994).
    1326. 998 F.2d 404, 409-10 (7th Cir. 1993), *aff'g Federal Deposit Ins. Corp. v. Zaborac*, 773 F. Supp. 137, 144-47 (C.D. Ill. 1991); *see also American Casualty Co. v. Federal Deposit Ins. Corp.*, 16 F.3d 152, 153-54 (7th Cir. 1994) (following Seventh Circuit *American Casualty* decision noted in text without referring to public policy issue).

*can Casualty Co. v. Federal Deposit Insurance Corp.*,[1327] *St. Paul Fire & Marine Insurance Co. v. Federal Deposit Insurance Corp.*[1328] and *Slaughter v. American Casualty Co.*,[1329] the Ninth Circuit in *American Casualty Co. v. Baker*[1330] and the Tenth Circuit in *Federal Deposit Insurance Corp. v. American Casualty Co.*[1331] The same result has been reached by numerous federal district courts[1332] and by the Maryland Supreme Court.[1333]

---

1327. 944 F.2d 455, 460-61 (8th Cir. 1991).

1328. 968 F.2d 695, 702 (8th Cir. 1992).

1329. 37 F.3d 385, 388 (8th Cir. 1994).

1330. 22 F.3d 880, 894-95 (9th Cir. 1994).

1331. 975 F.2d 677, 680-82 (10th Cir. 1992), *aff'g* 765 F. Supp. 538, 549-50 (D. Minn. 1991).

1332. *See Resolution Trust Corp. v. Hedden*, 879 F. Supp. 600, 601 (N.D. Miss. 1995); *American Casualty Co. v. Sentry Fed. Sav. Bank*, 867 F. Supp. 50, 58 (D. Mass. 1994); *American Casualty Co. v. Beranek*, 862 F. Supp. 322, 326 (D. Kan. 1994); *American Casualty Co. v. Resolution Trust Corp.*, 1994 U.S. Dist. LEXIS 9447, at *12, 1994 WL 361508, at *4 (E.D. Pa. July 7, 1994); *American Casualty Co. v. Rahn*, 854 F. Supp. 492, 500 (W.D. Mich. 1994); *Resolution Trust Corp. v. Moskowitz*, 1994 U.S. Dist. LEXIS 4049, at *11-18 (D.N.J. Mar. 30, 1994); *American Casualty Co. v. Resolution Trust Corp.*, 845 F. Supp. 318, 326-27 (D. Md. 1993); *American Casualty Co. v. Resolution Trust Corp.*, CV No. 92-10543-WF, slip op. at 22-23 (D. Mass. Oct. 19, 1993); *Benafield v. Continental Casualty Co.*, 1993 U.S. Dist. LEXIS 16887, at *4, 1993 WL 723510, at *2 (E.D. Ark. Oct. 1, 1993); *Chandler v. American Casualty Co.*, 833 F. Supp. 735, 738 (E.D. Ark. 1993); *American Casualty Co. v. Resolution Trust Corp.*, 839 F. Supp. 282, 286-89 (D.N.J. 1993); *American Casualty Co. v. Federal Deposit Ins. Corp.*, 1993 WL 610760, at *12-13 (S.D. Miss. Apr. 8, 1993); *Adams v. Resolution Trust Corp.*, 1993 U.S. Dist. LEXIS 7496, at *27 & n.24, 1993 WL 181303, at *7 & n.24 (D. Minn. May 19, 1993), *aff'd on other grounds sub nom. Adams v. Greenwood*, 10 F.3d 568 (8th Cir. 1993); *American Casualty Co. v. Federal Deposit Ins. Corp.*, 1993 U.S. Dist. LEXIS 5853, at *12 (W.D. Mich. Jan. 8, 1993); *Bartley v. National Union Fire Ins. Co.*, 824 F. Supp. 624, 634 (N.D. Tex. 1992); *Federal Sav. & Loan Ins. Corp. v. Shelton*, 789 F. Supp. 1355, 1358-59 (M.D. La. 1992); *Powell v. American Casualty Co.*, 772 F. Supp. 1188, 1190 (W.D. Okla. 1991); *Federal Deposit Ins. Corp. v. Continental Casualty Co.*, 796 F. Supp. 1344, 1350-

(continued...)

These courts have stated that "[c]ourts will not invalidate otherwise valid contracts on general public policy grounds."[1334] To the contrary, according to these courts, the power to refuse to enforce contracts on public policy grounds is "limited to situations in which the contract violates 'some explicit public policy'" that is "well defined and dominant, and is to be ascertained 'by reference to the laws and legal precedents and not from general considerations of supposed public interests.'"[1335] Public policy thus "opens only a narrow exception" to the general rule that "competent persons shall have the utmost liberty of contract."[1336] This exception is "applied cautiously and only in plain cases involving dominant public interests."[1337]

---

1332. (...continued)
51 (D. Or. 1991); *Federal Deposit Ins. Corp. v. American Casualty Co.*, 814 F. Supp. 1021, 1027-29 (D. Wyo. 1991), *subsequent proceedings*, No. 90-CV-0265-J, slip op. at 13 (D. Wyo. Sept. 9, 1994); *Gary v. American Casualty Co.*, 753 F. Supp. 1547, 1553 (W.D. Okla. 1990); *Continental Casualty Co. v. Allen*, 710 F. Supp. 1088, 1098-1100 (N.D. Tex. 1989); *McCuen v. International Ins. Co.*, 1988 U.S. Dist. LEXIS 17624, at *9, 13, 1988 WL 242680, at *4, 6 (S.D. Iowa Sept. 29, 1988), *aff'd on other grounds sub nom. McCuen v. American Casualty Co.*, 946 F.2d 1401 (8th Cir. 1991).

1333. *See Finci v. American Casualty Co.*, 593 A.2d 1069, 1074-75 (Md. 1991).

1334. *American Casualty*, 975 F.2d at 680-81.

1335. *American Casualty*, 39 F.3d at 638; *American Casualty*, 998 F.2d at 409; *American Casualty*, 995 F.2d at 473; *American Casualty*, 975 F.2d at 681; *Conner*, 973 F.2d at 1241-42; *St. Paul*, 968 F.2d at 702 (each quoting or citing one or more of *United Paperworkers Int'l Union v. Misco, Inc.*, 484 U.S. 29, 43 (1987), *W.R. Grace & Co. v. Rubber Workers*, 461 U.S. 757, 766 (1983), *Muschany v. United States*, 324 U.S. 49, 66 (1945), and *St. Paul Mercury Ins. Co. v. Duke Univ.*, 849 F.2d 133, 135 (4th Cir. 1988)).

1336. *Conner*, 973 F.2d at 1241.

1337. *Id; see also Zaborac*, 773 F. Supp. at 145; *Allen*, 710 F. Supp. at 1098 (each stating that "[f]or contractual provisions to be void for public policy reasons, they must be injurious to the public good or be subversive to sound morality," and each citing *Ritter v. Mutual Life Ins.*

(continued...)

Regulatory exclusions, these courts have concluded, do not rise to this level. These courts explain that directors' and officers' liability insurance is not required by any statute, rule or regulation,[1338] and "[s]ince universal coverage is not required by statute, policies which limit coverage . . . are not contrary to public policy."[1339] As two courts have reasoned:

> [I]f exclusions such as the regulatory exclusion herein 'would so seriously hamper . . . [the federal agency] in carrying out its duties that public policy prevents' enforcement, then a bank's failure to obtain directors' and officers' liability insurance would also violate public policy to the same extent because in that instance the FDIC would also have to look solely to the assets of the directors and officers to collect any judgment against them for breach of their statutory and common law duties. Yet there is no statutory or regulatory requirement that a bank . . . obtain or maintain officers' and directors' liability insurance. When directors' and officers' liability insurance is not required by statute, such that complete failure to obtain such insurance cannot be contrary to public policy, and there is no mandated form of coverage if coverage is obtained, certainly directors' and officers' lia-

---

1337. (...continued)
*Co.*, 169 U.S. 139, 154 (1898)); *Zaborac*, 773 F. Supp. at 146; *Baker*, 758 F. Supp. at 1347 (each stating that "[a]s the term 'public policy' is vague, there must be definite indications in the law of the sovereignty to justify the invalidation of a contract as contrary to that policy," and each citing *Muschany*, 324 U.S. at 66); *Finci*, 593 A.2d at 1078 ("the theory of public policy embodies a doctrine of vague and variable quality, and, unless deducible in the given circumstances from constitutional or statutory provisions, should be accepted as the basis of a judicial determination, if at all, only with the utmost circumspection").

1338. *Conner*, 973 F.2d at 1243; *Sentry*, 867 F. Supp. at 58; *Moskowitz*, 1994 U.S. Dist. LEXIS 4049, at *17; *American Cas. Co. v. Kirchner*, 1992 U.S. Dist. LEXIS 15879, at *19, 1992 WL 300843, at *6 (W.D. Wis. May 22, 1992), *aff'd sub nom. American Cas. Co. v. Federal Deposit Ins. Corp.*, 16 F.3d 152 (7th Cir. 1994); *Zaborac*, 773 F. Supp. at 144; *St. Paul*, 765 F. Supp. at 550; *Allen*, 710 F. Supp. at 1099.

1339. *Moskowitz*, 1994 U.S. Dist. LEXIS 4049, at *18.

bility insurance policies providing only limited coverage such as those herein are not contrary to public policy.[1340]

These decisions also state that the Financial Institutions Reform, Recovery and Enforcement Act ("FIRREA")[1341] grants regulatory agencies the right to enforce contracts entered into by a financial institution notwithstanding contractual provisions providing for termination of rights upon insolvency and appointment of a receiver, but provides an exception for directors' and officers' liability insurance contracts:

> (e) Provisions relating to contracts entered into before appointment of conservator or receiver
>
> \*          \*          \*
>
> (12) Authority to enforce contracts
>
> > (A)  In general
> >
> > The conservator or receiver may enforce any contract, other than a director's or officer's liability insurance contract or a depository institution bond, entered into by the depository institution notwithstanding any provision of the contract providing for termination, default, acceleration, or exercise of rights upon, or solely by reason of, insolvency or the appointment of a conservator or receiver.
> >
> > (B)  Certain rights not affected
> >
> > No provision of this paragraph may be construed as impairing or affecting any right of the conservator or receiver to enforce or recover under a directors or officers liability insurance contract or depository institution bond under other applicable law.[1342]

"In light of this express statutory provision exempting enforcement of D & O liability policies by a conservator or receiver," these courts have held, "we cannot see how enforcement of the

---

1340. *Gary*, 753 F. Supp. at 1553 (citations omitted), *quoted in American Casualty*, 814 F. Supp. at 1028.

1341. Pub. L. 101-73, 103 Stat. 183 (1989) (codified primarily in 12 U.S.C., but portions also codified in numerous other titles of U.S.C.).

1342. 12 U.S.C. § 1821(e)(12).

regulatory exclusion would violate public policy."[1343] Indeed, these courts have noted, FIRREA's legislative history demonstrates that Congress rejected proposed language that, if enacted, would explicitly have granted regulatory agencies the right to avoid regulatory (and insured versus insured) exclusions in D & O policies.[1344] As one of these courts explained:

> [B]y including a "regulatory exclusion" in its D & O policy, American Casualty is simply offering lesser insurance coverage, presumably at a lower price. Had the director defendants insisted upon insurance coverage without the "regulatory exclusion," they surely would have expected to pay more for such coverage. Recognition of a public policy against D & O liability insurance containing a "regulatory exclusion" would, in effect, either require a particular, high-quality form of D & O insurance, or else require insurers to furnish a level of insurance coverage for which they will not be paid. Neither result is supportable public policy.[1345]

As another of these courts has put it: "Stripped to its essentials," the argument that regulatory exclusions are contrary to public

---

1343. *St. Paul*, 968 F.2d at 702; *see also American Casualty*, 39 F.3d at 638 (in light of the explicit exception for D & O liability insurance contracts, "FIRREA cannot be relied upon to create or define a public policy against enforcement of a 'regulatory exclusion'"); *American Casualty*, 998 F.2d at 410 ("[t]he enactment of § 1821(e)(12) evidences Congress' intent to remain neutral on regulatory exclusions and completely rebuts the FDIC's argument that the enforcement of such clauses violates a public policy embodied in a different subsection of the same provision"); *American Casualty*, 995 F.2d at 473 ("[b]ecause FIRREA expressly exempts from enforcement by a receiver directors' and officers' liability policies, the regulatory exclusion provision does not violate any well established or dominant public policy"); *American Casualty*, 975 F.2d at 681; *Kirchner*, 1992 U.S. Dist. LEXIS 15879, at *18, 1992 WL 300843, at *6; *Powell*, 772 F. Supp. at 1190; *Baker*, 758 F. Supp. at 1347; *Finci*, 593 A.2d at 1077 n.8.

1344. *See American Casualty*, 39 F.3d at 638; *American Casualty*, 998 F.2d at 410; *American Casualty*, 995 F.2d at 473; *American Casualty*, 975 F.2d at 681-82; *Conner*, 973 F.2d at 1242 & n.15; *St. Paul*, 968 F.2d at 702.

1345. *American Casualty*, 39 F.3d at 639.

policy is that dollars which cannot be collected from insurance funds must be paid by taxpayers, and that it is "socially desirable" to reduce the amount that must be collected from taxpayers "to the maximum extent possible."[1346] This court stated that "[t]he citizens of this State, and this Court, certainly endorse that concept in the abstract," but "the problem presented here is the clash of that appealing result with the established policy of freedom of contract."[1347] Indeed, the court added, "if the regulatory exclusion is unenforceable because it prevents the State from collecting money, then the $3 million limit of D & O coverage in the [insurer's] policy is likewise invalid, and [the insurer] would stand with the promise to pay unlimited sums for which the directors and officers are liable."[1348]

Three courts have rejected public policy challenges to exclusions similar to regulatory exclusions. In *California Union Insurance Co. v. American Diversified Savings Bank*[1349] and *Federal Deposit Insurance Corp. v. Aetna Casualty & Surety Co.*,[1350] provisions in fidelity bonds terminating coverage "upon the taking over of the Insured by a receiver or other liquidator or by State or Federal officials" were upheld against public policy challenges.[1351] In *Federal Deposit Insurance Corp. v. Mijalis*,[1352] a classified loan exclusion, pursuant to which the insurer was not liable for losses in connection with any claim "arising out of the granting of any loan which shall be deemed classified by any regulatory body or authority," similarly was upheld against a public policy challenge.[1353]

---

1346. *Finci*, 593 A.2d at 1079.

1347. *Id.* at 1080.

1348. *Id.*

1349. 948 F.2d 556 (9th Cir. 1991).

1350. 903 F.2d 1073 (6th Cir. 1990).

1351. *California Union*, 948 F.2d at 560 n.4, 561-63; *Aetna*, 903 F.2d at 1077-78.

1352. 800 F. Supp. 397 (W.D. La. 1992), *aff'd in part and rev'd in part on other grounds*, 15 F.3d 1314 (5th Cir. 1994).

1353. *Id.* at 403.

The opposite result has been reached by federal district courts in *Branning v. CNA Insurance Cos.*,[1354] *Federal Savings & Loan Insurance Corp. v. Oldenburg*,[1355] *Federal Savings & Loan Insurance Corp. v. Mmahat*[1356] and *International Insurance Co. v. McMullan.*[1357] All four of these district court decisions predate the circuit court decisions and many of the district court decisions rejecting public policy challenges to regulatory exclusions discussed above.[1358]

The court in *Branning* reasoned as follows:

> The court finds that the clause substantially hinders FSLIC's exercise of its federal powers and therefore is contrary to federal policy. Under 12 U.S.C. § 1729(d), Congress explicitly authorized FSLIC to
>
>> collect all obligations to the insured institutions, to settle, compromise, or release claims in favor of or against the insured institutions, and to do all other things that may be necessary in connection therewith, *subject only to the regulation of the Federal Home Loan Bank Board . . .*
>
> 12 U.S.C. § 1729(d); *see also* 12 CFR § 549.3(a) (collect all obligations and money due). If the court were to enforce the FSLIC exclusion as written, all of FSLIC's claims, regardless of their origin or status under the policy, would not be covered simply because FSLIC rather than a shareholder, depositor, or third party prosecuted the claim. Private parties to an insurance contract may not frustrate the Congressional

---

1354. 721 F. Supp. 1180 (W.D. Wash. 1989).

1355. 671 F. Supp. 720 (D. Utah 1987).

1356. 1988 U.S. Dist. LEXIS 1825, 1988 WL 19304 (E.D. La. Mar. 3, 1988).

1357. 1990 U.S. Dist. LEXIS 19940, 1990 WL 483731 (S.D. Miss. Mar. 7, 1990).

1358. *See also American Casualty Co. v. Federal Deposit Ins. Corp.*, 1993 WL 610760, at *8 (S.D. Miss. Apr. 8, 1993) (declining to follow *McMullan*, a prior decision in the same district as the *American Casualty* case, because *McMullan* was not binding precedent and the court in *American Casualty* disagreed with the *McMullan* court's conclusion).

purpose behind receivership by annulling FSLIC's federal powers.[1359]

The court in *Oldenburg* similarly concluded that public policy considerations barred enforcement of a regulatory exclusion because enforcement "would so seriously hamper the FSLIC in carrying out its duties."[1360] The courts in *Oldenburg* and *Mmahat* similarly stated that public policy will not allow banks "to bargain away the rights of the FSLIC to carry out its statutory function."[1361]

The Colorado Supreme Court in *Federal Deposit Insurance Corp. v. American Casualty Co.*[1362] described "the validity of the regulatory exclusion" as "not settled under federal banking law" but "contrary to the public policy expressed in state banking law."[1363] The Colorado legislature overruled the *American Casualty* decision in a statute declaring that regulatory exclusions are "enforceable and are in conformity with the public policy of this state."[1364]

## 10.  Advancement

The advancement of litigation expenses by insurers often is as important to directors and officers as insurance for ultimate judgments or settlements. The reasons for this are the same reasons that advancement of litigation expenses is important in the indemnification context: protracted litigation is expensive, and many directors do not have the resources necessary or are unwilling to finance such litigation.[1365] Advancement of litigation expenses by insurers also is important because indemnification and/or advancement by the corporation may for one reason or another be unavailable:

---

1359. 721 F. Supp. at 1184.

1360. 671 F. Supp. at 724.

1361. 1988 U.S. Dist. LEXIS 1825, at *6, 1988 WL 19304, at *2 (quoting *Oldenburg*, 671 F. Supp. at 723).

1362. 843 P.2d 1285 (Colo. 1992).

1363. *Id.* at 1294-95.

1364. Colo. Rev. Stat. §§ 11-3-120(4)(a), 11-22-116(5)(a), 11-23-117.5(1), 11-41-134(2).

1365. *See* Chapter V, Section A 5 (discussing advancement in indemnification context).

perhaps due to state law restrictions upon indemnification (such as judgments in or amounts paid to settle derivative actions), perhaps due to a change in control, or perhaps due to financial difficulties on the part of the corporation.[1366] As commentators have noted, "[d]uring the course of protracted litigation, attorneys' fees may build to gigantic levels, creating stress on the individual insureds and a strain on the good conscience of any company which has decided to advance defense expenses."[1367]

Until the mid-to-late 1980s, many D & O policies either were silent or included language concerning advancement that did not definitively resolve the obligation to advance one way or the other.[1368] The question accordingly became the subject of a substantial body of case law that is more or less "evenly split" between decisions requiring advancement and decisions not requiring advancement.[1369] Making matters more confusing, courts have "interpreted virtually identical policy language in an inconsistent fashion."[1370] Policies today frequently address this issue in a definitive manner.[1371]

---

1366. *See* Chapter V, Section B 2 (discussing gaps in indemnification).

1367. John F. Olson & Josiah O. Hatch III, *Director and Officer Liability: Indemnification and Insurance* § 10.07[3], at 10-54 (1997).

1368. *Id.*

1369. Monteleone & Conca, *Directors and Officers Indemnification and Liability Insurance: An Overview of Legal and Practical Issues*, 51 Bus. Law. 573, 594 (1996).

1370. *Id.*

1371. J. Olson & J. Hatch § 10.07[3], at 10–54-55; Johnston, *Directors' and Officers' and Related Forms of Liability Insurance*, in 7 *Securities Law Techniques* § 122.03[2][j] (A.A. Sommer, Jr. ed. 1998); Monteleone & Conca, 51 Bus. Law. at 595-96 & nn. 112, 113; Monteleone, *D & O Allocation: Problems and Solutions*, XVIII The Risk Report No. 8 Apr. 1996, at 1, *reprinted in Securities Litigation 1996* 997 (Practising Law Institute 1996); Weiss, *Doing D & O Insurance Right*, 4 Bus. Law Today No. 2, Nov./Dec. 1994, at 50, 53; *see also Fight Against Coercive Tactics Network, Inc. v. Coregis Ins. Co.*, 926 F. Supp. 1426, 1433 (D. Colo. 1996) (insurers can use "language putting the matter

(continued...)

Much of the litigation described above—including, most prominently, the Third Circuit's decision in *Little v. MGIC Indemnity Corp.*[1372] and the Ninth Circuit's decision in *Okada v. MGIC Indemnity Corp.*[1373]—has involved policy provisions including the following language:

- "[t]he term 'Loss' shall mean any amount which the Directors and Officers are legally obligated to pay,"

- "[n]o costs, charges and expenses shall be incurred or settlements made without the Insurer's consent which consent shall not be unreasonably withheld; however, in the event such consent is given, the Insurer shall pay . . . such costs, charges and expenses," and

- "[t]he Insurer may at its option . . . advance on behalf of the Directors or Officers . . . expenses which they have incurred in connection with claims made against them."[1374]

The *Little* and *Okada* courts both held that this policy language mandates advancement of litigation costs.

These courts reasoned that this policy language is liability policy language (in a liability policy, the insurer's obligation to pay arises as soon as the insured incurs liability for a loss) rather than indemnity policy language (in an indemnity policy, the insurer is obligated only to reimburse the insured for a loss that the insured

---

1371. (...continued)

beyond reasonable question"); *American Casualty Co. v. Bank of Mont. Sys.*, 675 F. Supp. 538, 544 (D. Minn. 1987) ("[i]t is apparent that the insurance companies have no trouble making the policy language clear if they wish to do so"); *National Union Fire Ins. Co. v. Ambassador Group, Inc.*, 157 A.D.2d 293, 299, 556 N.Y.S.2d 549, 553 (N.Y. App. Div. 1st Dep't 1990) (determination whether insurer "is required to make interim advances of defense expenses . . . must depend upon the language of the policy involved"), *motion for leave to appeal dismissed*, 77 N.Y.2d 873, 571 N.E.2d 85, 568 N.E.2d 85, 568 N.Y.S.2d 915 (1991).

    1372. 836 F.2d 789 (3d Cir. 1987).

    1373. 823 F.2d 276 (9th Cir. 1987).

    1374. *Little*, 836 F.2d at 792-93; *Okada*, 823 F.2d at 278-79.

already has paid).[1375] The courts acknowledged that the policy
did not explicitly specify the timing of the insurer's duty to pay,
but stated that "[a] 'loss' is defined as an amount that the insured is
'legally obligated to pay'" and includes defense costs, that "the
only reasonable interpretation" is that the duty to pay defense costs
"arises at the time the insured becomes 'legally obligated to pay,'"
and that "[t]o infer any other, later time for the insurer's duty to
pay would be arbitrary because nothing" in the insurance policy
"gives any guidance as to when this later time might be."[1376] The
"may at its option . . . advance . . . expenses" clause did not
change this duty, these courts concluded, because "[o]ne could
reasonably understand the option clause . . . to apply only to one
type of expenditure"—expenses—"within the broader category of
'costs, charges, and expenses,' and because 'expenses' is not
defined, one could then conclude that defense costs do not fall within its meaning."[1377]

The *Little* and *Okada* courts each cited the general rule that
ambiguous provisions in insurance contracts are strictly construed
against insurers.[1378] According to these courts, the applicable
policy language was ambiguous because the "loss" provision
included defense costs within the insurer's duty of contemporaneous
payment but the "advancement option" provision did not clearly

1375. *Little*, 836 F.2d at 793; *Okada*, 823 F.2d at 280.

1376. *Little*, 836 F.2d at 793-94; *see also Okada*, 823 F.2d at 281
("Whenever 'loss' occurs (i.c., whenever the directors are 'legally
obligated to pay' on a covered claim), MGIC must pay that amount. The
policyholders thus are assured that they need not expend their own funds
in order to receive protection for liability.").

1377. *Little*, 836 F.2d at 795; *see also Okada*, 823 F.2d at 281
("[n]owhere does the policy define expenses, or explain how those
expenses differ from the broader language . . . which covers 'costs,
charges and expenses'"). *But see Little*, 836 F.2d at 797 (Stapleton, J.
dissenting) ("[b]ecause I can think of no 'expense incurred in connection
with a claim,' that would not also be a 'cost or charge incurred in connection with a claim,' Little's suggested distinction, for me, 'tortures the
language of the policy' and reads MGIC's option . . . out of the agreement of the parties").

1378. *Little*, 836 F.2d at 793; *Okada*, 823 F.2d at 281.

exclude advancement of defense costs from the scope of this duty. Advancement thus was held to be required by the policy.[1379]

The Eighth Circuit in *McCuen v. American Casualty Co.*[1380] and federal district courts in California,[1381] Minnesota[1382] and Tennessee[1383] have reached the same conclusions as the Third Circuit in *Little* and the Ninth Circuit in *Okada* in cases involving virtually identical policy language.[1384]

Federal district courts in California,[1385] Florida,[1386] Illinois,[1387] Iowa,[1388] Kentucky,[1389] Michigan,[1390] Ohio[1391] and Texas[1392]

---

1379. *Little*, 836 F.2d at 792-95; *Okada*, 823 F.2d at 280-81. *Okada* first was decided by the Ninth Circuit in favor of the insured on the ground that the policy imposed a duty to defend upon the insurer under Hawaii law, and consequently mandated immediate reimbursement of litigation costs. *See Okada v. MGIC Indem. Corp.*, 795 F.2d 1450, 1453-55 (9th Cir. 1986), *superseded*, 823 F.2d 276 (9th Cir. 1987). The court subsequently issued an amended opinion finding in favor of the insured for the reasons summarized in the text above.

1380. 946 F.2d 1401, 1406-07 (8th Cir. 1991).

1381. *See American Casualty Co. v. Sierra Chem. Co.*, 1989 U.S. Dist. LEXIS 7310, at *11-13 (N.D. Cal. Mar. 7, 1989); *National Union Fire Ins. Co. v. Federal Deposit Ins. Corp.*, No. CV 85-6860 RG, slip op. at 9-11 (C.D. Cal. Jan. 12, 1987).

1382. *See American Casualty Co. v. Bank of Mont. Sys.*, 675 F. Supp. 538, 540-44 (D. Minn. 1987).

1383. *See Federal Sav. & Loan Ins. Corp. v. Burdette*, 718 F. Supp. 649, 661 (E.D. Tenn. 1989).

1384. *See also American Casualty Co. v. Baker*, 22 F.3d 880, 885-86, 895-96 (9th Cir. 1994) (dismissing as moot an appeal from a district court decision—and vacating the district court decision—that questioned the reasoning in *Okada* but followed *Okada* because it was a controlling precedent).

1385. *See Clandening v. MGIC Indem. Corp.*, No. CV 83-2432-LTL, Tr. op. at 8 (C.D. Cal. May 23, 1983) (available on LEXIS without file number).

1386. *See Luther v. Fidelity & Deposit Co.*, 679 F. Supp. 1092, 1093 (S.D. Fla. 1986).

1387. *See Zaborac v. American Casualty Co.*, 663 F. Supp. 330, 334 (C.D. Ill. 1987).

1388. *See American Casualty Co. v. Federal Deposit Ins. Corp.*,

(continued...)

and a state court in Maryland[1393] have held that insurers are not obligated to advance defense costs under this policy language. According to these courts:

- "the policy clearly gives the insurer the option to advance defense costs prior to the conclusion of an action against a director or officer" and "[i]n no way . . . can . . . reasonably be construed as mandating such advance payment";[1394]

- the policy "does no more than acknowledge that at some time [the insurer] might be required to reimburse defendants for their legal fees and costs in defending the claims at issue but that it need not do so before the claim has been resolved";[1395]

- "[t]his clause gives [the insurer] the option, but not the obligation to advance defense costs as they are incurred";[1396]

- the policy "merely provides [the insurer] with the discretion to advance defense expenses, but it does not require this";[1397]

---

1388. (...continued)
677 F. Supp. 600, 605-06 (N.D. Iowa 1987).

1389. *See Enzweiler v. Fidelity & Deposit Co.*, 1986 U.S. Dist. LEXIS 25555, at *3, 1986 WL 20444, at *2 (E.D. Ky. May 13, 1986).

1390. *See American Casualty Co. v. Rahn*, 854 F. Supp. 492, 503-04 (W.D. Mich. 1994).

1391. *See Corabi v. CNA Ins. Cos.*, 1988 U.S. Dist. LEXIS 18424, at *4, 1988 WL 363612, at *2 (S.D. Ohio June 21, 1988).

1392. *See Continental Casualty Co. v. Allen*, No. CA-5-86-252, slip op. at 5-6 (N.D. Tex. Feb. 16, 1988).

1393. *See Faulkner v. American Casualty Co.*, 584 A.2d 734, 745 (Md. Ct. Spec. App.), *cert. denied*, 590 A.2d 158 (Md. 1991).

1394. *Corabi*, 1988 U.S. Dist. LEXIS 18424, at *4, 1988 WL 363612, at *2.

1395. *Allen*, slip op. at 6.

1396. *Zaborac*, 663 F. Supp. at 334.

1397. *American Casualty*, 677 F. Supp. at 605-06.

- the policy "clearly reflects that [the insurer], if it so chooses, *may* advance expenses including attorney's fees," but "it is equally clear that [the insurer] is not obligated to do so (prior to final disposition of any claim)";[1398]

- "[i]t is clear . . . upon a careful reading of the policy that the insurance company may elect . . . to wait the outcome of the underlying litigation against an insured before advancing any payments";[1399]

- "the policy expressly provides that the insurer may at its option advance defense costs prior to disposition of a claim," and "[s]ince payment of such costs is thus within the discretion of the insurer, [the insured] here has no right to such payments";[1400] and

- the policy "giv[es] the insurer the *option, but not the obligation* to advance expenses, including defense costs."[1401]

Courts in cases involving policies not including the "insurer may at its option . . . advance . . . expenses" language construed in *Little, Okada* and the other cases noted above also have reached differing results.

On one end of the spectrum are cases where advancement has been required. These cases include *Gon v. First State Insurance Co.,*[1402] *Mt. Hawley Insurance Co. v. Federal Savings & Loan Insurance Corp.,*[1403] *National Union Fire Insurance Co. v. Brown,*[1404] *Fight Against Coercive Tactics Network, Inc. v. Coregis*

---

1398. *Luther,* 679 F. Supp. at 1093.

1399. *Enzweiler,* 1986 U.S. Dist. LEXIS 25555, at *3, 1986 WL 20444, at *2.

1400. *Clandening,* Tr. op. at 8.

1401. *Faulkner,* 584 A.2d at 745.

1402. 871 F.2d 863 (9th Cir. 1989).

1403. 695 F. Supp. 469 (C.D. Cal. 1987).

1404. 787 F. Supp. 1424 (S.D. Fla. 1991), *aff'd mem.,* 963 F.2d 385 (11th Cir. 1992).

*Insurance Co.*,[1405] *PepsiCo, Inc. v. Continental Casualty Co.*,[1406] *Wedtech Corp. v. Federal Insurance Co.*[1407] and *Federal Deposit Insurance Corp. v. Booth.*[1408]

The Ninth Circuit in *Gon v. First State Insurance Co.*[1409] followed that court's earlier decision in *Okada*. The court stated that the policy in *Gon*—like the policy in *Okada*—required payment of all losses that the insureds became "legally obligated" to pay, including defense costs.[1410] The court in *Gon* then stated that "[t]his case is easier than *Okada* . . . because the policy in *Okada* . . . had a provision which sought to exclude legal expenses from expenses that were to be paid as incurred," but the policy in *Gon* included no such provision.[1411] The court in *Mt. Hawley Insurance Co. v. Federal Savings & Loan Insurance Corp.*[1412] also followed *Okada*. As in *Gon*, the court in *Mt. Hawley* pointed to the absence of a policy provision giving the insurer the option to advance expenses and concluded that "the policy at issue was a liability policy obligating the insurer to advance defense costs as they were incurred."[1413]

The court in *National Union Fire Insurance v. Brown*[1414] stated its agreement with the Third Circuit's reasoning in *Little* and the Ninth Circuit's reasoning in *Okada* and *Gon*.[1415] The court then distinguished between liability insurance policies and indemnity insurance policies as follows: liability policies obligate the insurer to pay "as soon as the insured incurs liability for the loss;

---

1405. 926 F. Supp. 1426 (D. Colo. 1996).

1406. 640 F. Supp. 656 (S.D.N.Y. 1986).

1407. 740 F. Supp. 214 (S.D.N.Y. 1990).

1408. 824 F. Supp. 76 (M.D. La. 1993), *subsequent decision aff'd on other grounds*, 82 F.3d 670 (5th Cir. 1996).

1409. 871 F.2d 863 (9th Cir. 1989).

1410. *Id.* at 868.

1411. *Id.*

1412. 695 F. Supp. 469 (C.D. Cal. 1987).

1413. *Id.* at 476.

1414. 787 F. Supp. 1424 (S.D. Fla. 1991), *aff'd mem.*, 963 F.2d 385 (11th Cir. 1992).

1415. *Id.* at 1432.

the insured need not pay the loss first," while indemnity policies obligate the insurer "only to reimburse the insured for [a] covered loss that the insured himself has already paid."[1416] Here, the court stated, the policy provision pursuant to which the insureds claimed a right to advancement was a liability provision. The court reasoned that the provision appeared in the "Directors and Officers Liability" part of the policy, where loss was defined as "any amount which the Insureds legally must pay."[1417] The court contrasted the "Corporation Reimbursement" part of the policy, which defined loss as "any amount the Company shall have paid to a Director or Officer as indemnity for a claim or claims against them."[1418]

The court concluded that the "only reasonable interpretation" of these definitions of loss is that the loss clause in the Directors and Officers Liability part of the policy obligates the insurer to pay "when the insured incurs the obligation, not after it has paid a judgment."[1419] Quoting *Little*, the court stated that "[t]o infer any other, later time for the insurer's duty to pay would be arbitrary because nothing" in the insurance policy "gives any guidance as to when this later time might be."[1420] The *Brown* court added that permitting an insurer to "wait on the sidelines" until the underlying litigation is resolved is "unreasonably harsh on the Insureds," who face defense costs that are "likely to be staggering" and that "could bring financial ruin upon a director or officer."[1421]

The court in *Fight Against Coercive Tactics Network, Inc. v. Coregis Insurance Co.*[1422] also concluded that the D & O policy in that case, which provided that the insurer "will pay on behalf of

---

1416. *Id.* at 1429.

1417. *Id.* at 1429-30.

1418. *Id.*

1419. *Id.* at 1430.

1420. *Id.* at 1432 (quoting *Little*, 836 F.2d at 794).

1421. *Id.* at 1433 (quoting *Little v. MGIC Indem. Corp.*, 649 F. Supp. 1460, 1468-69 (W.D. Pa. 1986), *aff'd*, 836 F.2d 789 (3d Cir. 1987)).

1422. 926 F. Supp. 1426 (D. Colo. 1996).

the Insureds all Loss which the Insureds shall be legally obligated to pay" and defined "Loss" as "any amount which the Insureds are legally obligated to pay," was a liability provision and not an indemnity provision.[1423] The court stated that "[a] reasonable interpretation of the 'Loss' clause is that [the insurer] has an obligation to pay expenses and costs when they are incurred and fees when they are billed, for in such instances, the Insureds have become legally obligated to pay them."[1424] The court also stated that if the insurer intended "to carve out an exception to its duty to pay for losses, including defense costs which the Insureds are legally obligated to pay, it could have used alternative language putting the matter beyond reasonable question."[1425] According to the court, other "seemingly conflicting provisions" in the policy "are to be construed against the insurer and in favor of the insured."[1426] The court added that the fact that "different courts have arrived at conflicting interpretations of similar clauses in other policies" also "is indicative of the Policy's ambiguity."[1427]

The court in *PepsiCo, Inc. v. Continental Casualty Co.*[1428] relied upon the fact that the policy in that case defined loss to include "amounts incurred in the defense of all allegations."[1429] The court stated that the insurer promised "to pay 'on behalf of' the directors and officers 'all loss which [they] shall become legally obligated to pay.' Thus, once the 'loss' or attorneys fees were incurred by the directors and officers, C.N.A.'s responsibility to reimburse the directors and officers attached."[1430] The court in *PepsiCo* also stated that "a liability insurer has a duty to pay all defense costs until it can confine its duty to pay only on those claims it has insured the policy holders against," and can "excuse itself from the contemporaneous duty" only by establishing "as a

---

1423. *Id.* at 1428, 1431, 1432-33, 1433-34.
1424. *Id.* at 1433.
1425. *Id.*
1426. *Id.*
1427. *Id.*
1428. 640 F. Supp. 656 (S.D.N.Y. 1986).
1429. *Id.* at 659.
1430. *Id.* (citation omitted).

matter of law that there was no possible factual basis on which it might be obligated to indemnify the directors and officers."[1431] The court in *Wedtech Corp. v. Federal Insurance Co.*[1432] cited *Okada*, *Little* and *PepsiCo* for the proposition that "[c]ourts have established" that policy provisions defining "loss" to include "defense costs" impose an obligation upon the insurer "to reimburse the directors . . . as soon as the attorneys' fees are incurred."[1433]

The court in *Federal Deposit Insurance Corp. v. Booth*,[1434] concluded that the policy in that case contained "no references whatsoever to defense costs" and thus "does not unambiguously negate a duty to pay defense costs as they are incurred."[1435] All ambiguities must be resolved in favor of the insured, the court stated, and advancement of legal fees therefore was required.[1436] The court certified this ruling for appeal, but the Fifth Circuit declined to hear the appeal.[1437]

The court in *Nu-Way Environmental, Inc. v. Planet Insurance Co.*,[1438] a case not involving a directors and officers insurance policy, stated that "some courts have found a duty to pay the defense costs as incurred" and that "others have held that no such duty exists," and that the "general rule" is as follows: "absent express language to the contrary, an insurer that does not undertake the duty to defend the insured has a duty to pay the insured's

---

1431. *Id.* at 660.

1432. 740 F. Supp. 214 (S.D.N.Y. 1990).

1433. *Id.* at 221 (also citing *McGinniss v. Employers Reins. Corp.*, 648 F. Supp. 1263, 1271 (S.D.N.Y. 1986), a decision following *Okada* and *PepsiCo* in the context of a publishers' libel and allied torts policy).

1434. 824 F. Supp. 76 (M.D. La. 1993), *subsequent decision aff'd on other grounds*, 82 F.3d 670 (5th Cir. 1996).

1435. *Id.* at 81.

1436. *Id.*

1437. *See Federal Deposit Ins. Corp. v. Booth*, 82 F.3d 670, 673 & n.3 (5th Cir. 1996).

1438. 1997 U.S. Dist. LEXIS 11884, 1997 WL 462010 (S.D.N.Y. Aug. 12, 1997).

defense costs as they come due."[1439] Therefore, "where the insurance policy does not impose a duty to defend, provides for the payment of defense costs, and is silent as to the timing of payment of such costs, the insurer has a duty of contemporaneous payment of defense costs."[1440] The court held that "[b]ecause the Policy is silent with respect to payment of defense costs, because other courts have held that a duty of contemporaneous payment exists under policy language similar to the language at issue here, and because to hold otherwise would not provide insureds with protection from financial harm that insurance policies are presumed to give, defendant has a duty under the Policy to reimburse plaintiff for its defense costs . . . on a contemporaneous basis."[1441]

On the other end of the spectrum are cases where advancement has not been required. These cases include *In re Ambassador Group, Inc. Litigation*,[1442] *In re Kenai Corp.*,[1443] *Harristown Development Corp. v. International Insurance Co.*[1444] and *National Union Fire Insurance Co. v. Goldman.*[1445]

The court in *In re Ambassador Group, Inc. Litigation*[1446] explicitly rejected the *Okada*, *Little* and *PepsiCo* decisions. The *Ambassador Group* court relied upon what it called "the pre-*Okada* consensus that director and officer liability policies . . . generally do not require the reimbursement of legal expenses until the legal liability of the Insureds has been established."[1447] The *Ambassador Group* court stated that under New York law, which gov-

---

1439. 1997 U.S. Dist. LEXIS 11884, at *6, 1997 WL 462010, at *2.

1440. 1997 U.S. Dist. LEXIS 11884, at *9, 1997 WL 462010, at *2.

1441. 1997 U.S. Dist. LEXIS 11884, at *9, 1997 WL 462010, at *3.

1442. 738 F. Supp. 57 (E.D.N.Y. 1990).

1443. 136 B.R. 59 (S.D.N.Y. 1992).

1444. 1988 U.S. Dist. LEXIS 12791, 1988 WL 123149 (M.D. Pa. Nov. 15, 1988).

1445. 548 So. 2d 790 (Fla. Dist. Ct. App. 1989).

1446. 738 F. Supp. 57 (E.D.N.Y. 1990).

1447. *Id.* at 61.

erned the *Ambassador Group* case, clear and unambiguous contracts "must be accorded their plain and ordinary meaning" and be "enforced as written," and that courts in New York view contracts such as D & O insurance contracts not from "the point of view of an easily befuddled or misled lay consumer" but "by the understanding of a person engaged in the insured's course of business."[1448] Applying this standard to the policy in *Ambassador Group*, the court stated that while "one could conceivably demonstrate the Policy's potential to confuse a layman," the court could not "accept the contention that persons . . . who are of sufficient sophistication to be in the market for this brand of insurance, would be misled" by the silence of the policy concerning the timing of the payment of legal expenses, or that the policy's silence concerning this issue created an ambiguity.[1449] To the contrary, the court stated, prior to decisions such as *Okada*, "there was never any doubt that legal expenses, while a covered loss, were not paid contemporaneously."[1450]

The *Ambassador Group* court also rejected the insured's contention that "[u]nless legal fees were reimbursed as billed . . . it would be impossible to sell a director and officer liability policy since the insureds would not truly be protected from harm."[1451] The court stated that the opposite conclusion was true: "judicial rewriting of policies for the benefit of insureds" would contribute to "an upward pressure on rates" and "could reduce the overall availability of coverage."[1452] According to the *Ambassador Group* court, the insured's argument also was "contrary to historical fact" because prior to decisions such as *Okada* "there was never any doubt that legal expenses, while a covered loss, were not paid contemporaneously."[1453]

---

1448. *Id*. at 63.
1449. *Id*.
1450. *Id*.
1451. *Id*. at 63 n.6.
1452. *Id*.
1453. *Id*.

The court in *Ambassador Group* also relied upon a provision in the policy in *Ambassador Group* requiring that the insurer pay 95 percent of all costs, charges and expenses, subject to the following:

1. If a payment not in excess of the Limit of Liability has to be made to dispose of a claim, costs, charges and expenses shall be payable up to the Limit of Liability applicable under this policy.

2. If the claim is successfully resisted by the Insureds, costs, charges and expenses shall be payable up to but not exceeding the Limit of Liability under this policy.[1454]

This provision, the court explained, made "claims of third parties for injuries caused by the acts or omissions of the insured officers and directors . . . superior to the Insureds' claims for legal fees" and thus was "easily and sensibly interpreted as precluding the contemporaneous payment of legal fees."[1455] Otherwise, the court continued, "the priority the endorsement gives to the claims of injured third parties could be defeated."[1456] "To be sure," the court acknowledged, "the endorsement is silent about the timing of the payment of legal expenses, but . . . there is only one reasonable interpretation of the provision, and thus only one reasonable answer to the contemporaneous fee payment question, and thus no ambiguity."[1457]

The court in *In re Kenai Corp.*[1458] followed *Ambassador Group* because it found "persuasive the reasoning adopted by the court in *Ambassador* as well as by other courts that have found that the insurer has no duty to advance defense costs."[1459] The court acknowledged that several of these decisions—citing the decisions rejecting the *Okada* and *Little* decisions discussed above—"attribute significance to the existence of an option clause allowing the insurer

---

1454. *Id*. at 60.
1455. *Id*. at 60, 63.
1456. *Id*. at 63.
1457. *Id*.
1458. 136 B.R. 59 (S.D.N.Y. 1992).
1459. *Id*. at 63.

to advance defense costs 'at its option'" and that "such a clause is not present here."[1460] "[I]n spite of the absence of an option clause in this case," the court stated, there were "strong independent reasons for finding that the issuer has no duty to advance defense costs."[1461] The court explained these reasons as follows:

> The D & O policy at issue here covers "losses", which are defined in the policy as "any amount which the Insureds are legally obligated to pay for a claim made against them for Wrongful Acts, and shall include damages, judgments, settlements, costs, charges, and expenses . . . incurred in the defenses of actions. . . ." Unlike duty to defend policies, which require the insurer to defend claims even if they are only *arguably* entitled to coverage, policies requiring the insurer to reimburse damages and defense costs related to wrongful acts entitle the insured to costs only when the underlying claims *are* covered by the policy. If this court were to require insurers to advance defense costs before resolution of the underlying action, insurers inevitably would pay some losses that are not covered by their policies. Insurers would be prejudiced by such a result, even if the insureds were required to reimburse the insurers for these costs once it was determined that the losses were not covered by the policy. Furthermore, as noted by the court in *Ambassador*, New York's rules of insurance contract construction favor deference to the plain meaning of such contracts. In the absence of a specific provision regarding the timing of defense cost reimbursement, D & O policy language defining losses in terms of wrongful acts suggests that the reimbursement should occur only after the losses have been determined to be covered by the contract.[1462]

The court in *Harristown Development Corp. v. International Insurance Co.*[1463] also rejected the *Okada*, *Little* and *PepsiCo* decisions. The court pointed to the absence in the policy in *Harristown* of a provision comparable to the provision in *Okada* and *Little*

---

1460. *Id*. at 64.
1461. *Id*.
1462. *Id*. (citations omitted).
1463. 1988 U.S. Dist. LEXIS 12791, 1988 WL 123149 (M.D. Pa. Nov. 15, 1988).

granting the insurer the option of paying "expenses" as expenses were incurred.[1464] The court also pointed to the fact that the *Okada*, *Little* and *PepsiCo* courts each interpreted policy provisions providing for direct payments to directors and officers—i.e., liability insurance requiring the insurer "to cover a loss which the officer or director may be 'legally obligated to pay'" once the loss was accrued, with the term "loss" including attorneys' fees.[1465] "The situation in the instant case is different," the court in *Harristown* explained, because the insureds in *Harristown* sought to recover amounts already paid by the corporation pursuant to "Company Reimbursement Liability" indemnity coverage.[1466] Absent specific policy language to the contrary, the court stated, the insurer's only duty pursuant to an indemnity provision is to reimburse the insured corporation for the total amount of attorneys' fees paid, without any requirement that this amount be paid as the insured becomes "legally obligated to pay."[1467]

The same result was reached in *National Union Fire Insurance Co. v. Goldman*.[1468] The court stated that the insurer's obligation to pay for a "loss" does not "ripen into a duty to pay until the loss can be determined with certainty."[1469] "Prior to judgment or settlement," the court concluded, "any claimed loss would be no more than speculation and guesswork."[1470]

The court in *Resolution Trust Corp. v. Ayo*[1471] also held that an insurer had no duty to advance or pay defense costs. The

---

1464. 1988 U.S. Dist. LEXIS 12791, at *29, 1988 WL 123149, at *10.

1465. 1988 U.S. Dist. LEXIS 12791, at *29-30, 1988 WL 123149, at *10.

1466. 1988 U.S. Dist. LEXIS 12791, at *30-31, 1988 WL 123149, at *11.

1467. 1988 U.S. Dist. LEXIS 12791, at *32-33, 1988 WL 123149, at *11.

1468. 548 So. 2d 790 (Fla. Dist. Ct. App. 1989).

1469. *Id.* at 792.

1470. *Id.* (quoting *Zaborac v. American Casualty Co.*, 663 F. Supp. 330, 332 (C.D. Ill. 1987)).

1471. 31 F.3d 285 (5th Cir. 1994).

court reached this conclusion, however, on a different ground. The court stated that an insurer is relieved of any duty to defend when there is no possibility of coverage.[1472] The court stated that the claims made in the case before the court were not made during the governing policy period, and the insurer "should not be called to foot the bill for ex-policy holders in their attempt to extend coverage."[1473]

As noted above, many insurance policies now resolve the advancement question by providing specifically that the insurer is or is not required to advance litigation costs, depending upon what the parties negotiate in each particular case. The district court in *Little* stated that a policy that unambiguously excludes advancement of defense costs would be unconscionable under Pennsylvania law;[1474] the Third Circuit expressly declined to address this issue.[1475] The court in *National Union Fire Insurance Co. v. Brown*[1476] quoted favorably from this passage of the district court's opinion in *Little* and added that "[w]hile the issue of the unconscionability of an option clause" granting an insurer the option of deferring payment for defense costs "is not before this court, the reasoning of the district court in *Little* demonstrates the unfairness" of not requiring advancement of defense costs by insurers.[1477] The district court in *Okada* made a similar observation:

> A directors' and officers' policy which did not provide, in the event of suit, for payment of the insureds' attorneys' fees until final judgment—when such suits can last for years and cost astronomical sums to defend—would be virtually impossible to sell to reasonable officers and directors, for it would not truly protect the insureds from financial harm caused by

---

1472. *Id.* at 293.

1473. *Id.*

1474. *See Little v. MGIC Indem. Corp.*, 649 F. Supp. 1460, 1468-69 (W.D. Pa. 1986), *aff'd on other grounds*, 836 F.2d 789 (3d Cir. 1987).

1475. 836 F.2d at 792 n.1.

1476. 787 F. Supp. 1424 (S.D. Fla. 1991), *aff'd mem.*, 963 F.2d 385 (11th Cir. 1992).

1477. *Id.* at 1433.

suits against them. An insurance policy should be construed according to the reasonable expectations of the insured.[1478]

## 11.  Allocation

An important problem arising where there are multiple defendants and/or multiple claims in a litigation and not all defendants and/or claims are insured is the allocation of loss, including, most often, settlements and defense costs. As explained below, allocation issues arise in two contexts: allocation between covered and non-covered defendants, and allocation between covered and non-covered claims.

*a. Allocation Between Defendants: The Larger Settlement and Proportional Fault/Relative Exposure Approaches.* As explained above, D & O policies typically cover only directors and officers. The corporation typically is an insured only to the extent that the corporation indemnifies its directors and officers and is not insured for its own liability or for the cost of its own defense, although there are exceptions—most notably, policies providing coverage for corporate entity liability payments.[1479] In the usual case where only directors and officers are insured but the defendants in the case include both (1) directors and officers and (2) the corporation and/or other parties, the insurer only is required to pay the loss that is attributable to the insured directors and officers. The insurer is not obligated to pay the portion of losses attributable to the corporation and to other uninsured defendants. A recent survey concluded that the corporation is a defendant in approximately 80 percent of the cases in which D & O claims are made.[1480] Of those cases where there was allocation, the average allocation percentage of judgments or settlement payments was 66 percent to the D & O insurer in 1996 and 53 percent to the D & O insurer in 1997.[1481]

---

1478. *Okada v. MGIC Indem. Corp.*, 608 F. Supp. 383, 387 (D. Haw. 1985), *aff'd in part and rev'd in part on other grounds*, 823 F.2d 276 (9th Cir. 1987).

1479. *See* Chapter V, Section B 4 & 11 d.

1480. *1997 Watson Wyatt Worldwide D & O Liability Survey Report* 5, 47 (1997).

1481. *Id.* at 5, 47.

The average allocation percentage of defense costs was 64 percent to the D & O insurer in 1996 and 58 percent to the D & O insurer in 1997.[1482]

The methodology used to allocate "has not been refined to an exact science."[1483] To the contrary, allocation has been the subject of considerable litigation. Resolution of this issue does not require judicial findings and conclusions with respect to "all fact and legal issues in the underlying case"; rather, it requires determination of what is "reasonable" in light of "uncertainties in both fact and law known at the time of the settlement."[1484]

The courts have suggested two methods by which settlement and defense costs may be allocated between insured directors and officers and uninsured defendants, including, in the typical case, the corporate entity: (1) a "larger settlement" approach, and (2) a "proportional fault" or "relative exposure" approach. The approach applied in a particular case may depend upon the governing policy language.[1485]

Under the "larger settlement" approach, settlement and defense costs are allocated to uninsured persons only where the loss incurred is "larger because of the activities of uninsured persons who were sued or persons who were not sued but whose actions may have contributed to the suit."[1486] In other words, "responsibility for any portion of the settlement should be allocated away from the insured party only if the acts of the uninsured party are

---

1482. *Id.*

1483. *Nodaway Valley Bank v. Continental Casualty Co.*, 715 F. Supp. 1458, 1467 (W.D. Mo. 1989), *aff'd*, 916 F.2d 1362 (8th Cir. 1990).

1484. *Nordstrom, Inc. v. Chubb & Son, Inc.*, 54 F.3d 1424, 1432 (9th Cir. 1995) (quoting *Nordstrom, Inc. v. Chubb & Son, Inc.*, 820 F. Supp. 530, 536 (W.D. Wash. 1992), *aff'd*, 54 F.3d 1424 (9th Cir. 1995), and *Nodaway Valley Bank*, 715 F. Supp. at 1465).

1485. *See, e.g., Safeway Stores, Inc. v. National Union Fire Ins. Co.*, 64 F.3d 1282, 1287, 1288 (9th Cir. 1995); *Caterpillar, Inc. v. Great Am. Ins. Co.*, 62 F.3d 955, 960 (7th Cir. 1995); *Nordstrom*, 54 F.3d at 1432 (9th Cir. 1995).

1486. *Caterpillar*, 62 F.3d at 960.

determined to have increased the settlement."[1487] Where the corporation is not insured, the larger settlement rule would require allocation of a portion of settlement and defense costs to the corporation only "if the corporate entity alone were liable for a particular claim, or if its liability would exceed that of the directors and officers on any claim for which the corporation was independently but jointly liable."[1488]

Under the "proportional fault" or "relative exposure" approach, settlement and defense costs are allocated "according to the relative exposures of the respective parties"—the "relative exposure" of insured officers and directors "vis a vis uninsured defendants."[1489] "[E]ven if the court determines that the directors and officers would be found liable on all claims," settlement and defense costs still are "allocated between the corporation and the directors and officers where there is some independent basis, not derivative of the officers' and directors' liability, for holding the corporate entity liable."[1490]

The factors that may be considered with respect to each beneficiary of a settlement pursuant to a "proportionate fault" or "relative exposure" analysis include but are not limited to the following:

(1) the identity, as an individual, an entity, or as a member of a group, of each beneficiary and the likelihood of an adverse judgment against each in the underlying action;

(2) the risks and hazards to which each beneficiary of the settlement was exposed;

(3) the ability of each beneficiary to respond to an adverse judgment;

(4) the burden of litigation on each beneficiary;

---

1487. *Nordstrom*, 54 F.3d at 1432.

1488. *Id.*

1489. *Caterpillar*, 62 F.3d at 961 (quoting *PepsiCo, Inc. v. Continental Casualty Co.*, 640 F. Supp. 656, 662 (S.D.N.Y. 1986), and *Safeway Stores, Inc. v. National Union Fire Ins.*, 1993 U.S. Dist. LEXIS 2006, at *12, 1993 WL 739643, at *5 (N.D. Cal. Feb. 4, 1993), *aff'd and rev'd*, 64 F.3d 1282 (9th Cir. 1995)).

1490. *Nordstrom*, 54 F.3d at 1432.

(5) the 'deep pocket' factor and its potential effect on the liability of each beneficiary;

(6) the funding of the defense activity in the litigation and the burden of such funding;

(7) the motivations and intentions of those who negotiated the settlement, as shown by their statements, the settlement documents and any other relevant evidence;

(8) the benefits sought to be accomplished and accomplished by the settlement as to each beneficiary, as shown by the statements of the negotiators, the settlement documents and any other relevant evidence;

(9) the source of the funds that paid the settlement sum;

(10) the extent to which any individual defendants are exempted from liability by state statutes or corporate charter provisions; and

(11) such other and similar matters as are peculiar to the particular litigation and settlement.[1491]

The proportionate fault or relative exposure approach thus "envisions a somewhat elaborate inquiry into what happened in a settlement and who really paid for what relief."[1492]

The larger settlement rule has been criticized as "an unfair rationing that allows uninsured defendants, usually the corporation, to piggy-back on D & O policies designed to insure only directors and officers" and because "directors and officers (and therefore

---

1491. *Caterpillar*, 62 F.3d at 961 (quoting *Safeway*, 1993 U.S. Dist. LEXIS 2006, at \*14-15, 1993 WL 739643, at \*5-6); *see also Perini Corp. v. National Union Fire Ins. Co.*, 1988 U.S. Dist. LEXIS 17442, at \*5-6, 1988 WL 192453, at \*2 (D. Mass. June 2, 1988), *quoted in John Hancock Healthplan, Inc. v. Lexington Ins. Co.*, No. 88-2308, slip op. at 16 (E.D. Pa. Feb. 5, 1991) (suggesting the following factors: "(a) are the claims directed principally against the corporation (e.g., breach of contract) or do they focus on officer/director wrongdoing (e.g., breach of fiduciary duty)?; (b) how many claims in the complaint are asserted against each defendant?; (c) what percentage of the total number of defendants are directors and officers?; and (d) which defendants will derive primary benefit from the resolution of the action?").

1492. *Caterpillar*, 62 F.3d at 961.

their insurers) should not have to subsidize" the benefits obtained by a corporation when litigation naming both the corporation and its directors and officers is settled.[1493] The proportional fault or relative exposure approach has been criticized on the ground that "a protracted pursuit of the motivations underlying a settlement . . . is not necessarily the best way to resolve coverage disputes: The question at issue is whether the insurance policy covered certain claims, not the metaphysical underpinnings of why a corporation or its directors and officers might have acted as they did."[1494]

*b. Allocation Between Defendants: The Case Law.* A total of six Court of Appeals decisions in the Seventh, Eighth, Ninth and Tenth Circuits have considered how settlement and defense costs should be allocated between insured directors and officers and uninsured corporations—in 1990, *Nodaway Valley Bank v. Continental Casualty Co.*[1495] and *Harbor Insurance Co. v. Continental Illinois Corp.*,[1496] in 1995, *Nordstrom, Inc. v. Chubb & Son, Inc.*,[1497] *Safeway Stores, Inc. v. National Union Fire Insurance Co.*[1498] and *Caterpillar, Inc. v. Great American Insurance Co.*,[1499] and, in 1997, *Vitkus v. Beatrice Co.*[1500] The first 1990 decision, *Nodaway*, and the 1997 decision, *Vitkus*, applied the proportionate fault or relative exposure approach. The second 1990 decision, *Harbor*, and the three 1995 decisions, *Nordstrom*, *Safeway* and *Caterpillar*, all applied the larger settlement rule.

The Eighth Circuit's 1990 decision in *Nodaway Valley Bank v. Continental Casualty Co.*[1501] involved an effort by United

---

1493. *Id.* at 960.

1494. *Id.* at 962; *see also Nordstrom*, 54 F.3d at 1433 n.2 (noting that "an analysis of factors other than liability, such as negative publicity, that might have had a practical effect on the amount of the settlement, . . . would likely lead to protracted discovery").

1495. 916 F.2d 1362 (8th Cir. 1990).

1496. 922 F.2d 357 (7th Cir. 1990).

1497. 54 F.3d 1424 (9th Cir. 1995).

1498. 64 F.3d 1282 (9th Cir. 1995).

1499. 62 F.3d 955 (7th Cir. 1995).

1500. 127 F.3d 936 (10th Cir. 1997).

1501. 916 F.2d 1362 (8th Cir. 1990).

Missouri Bank to acquire control of Nodaway Valley Bank, a corporation owned by a small number of descendants of the bank's founder and certain employees and their descendants. Nodaway responded to this takeover threat with a squeeze-out merger, pursuant to which all shareholders except United Missouri were permitted to exchange their Nodaway shares for shares in a holding company, Nodaway Valley Bancshares, Inc., which had been founded several years earlier as an entity that could purchase Nodaway stock that suddenly and unexpectedly become available and thus ensure maintenance of local control. United Missouri sued Nodaway Valley Bancshares, its directors and officers, and its shareholders. The case was settled for $500,000.[1502]

The issue before the Eighth Circuit in *Nodaway* was the district court's "evaluation of the comparative responsibilities of the particular parties and of their exposure to an award of damages in the underlying suit."[1503] The Eight Circuit summarized the district court's holding on this question as follows: "A realistic and fair appraisal, as of the time of settlement, would . . . have allocated about 10% of the exposure to the uninsured defendants . . . and 90% to the insured defendants."[1504]

The Eighth Circuit affirmed on the ground that the district court's "careful" and "comprehensive analysis" of the case was based upon its "thoroughly examining the nuances of the facts before it" and was not clearly erroneous, the standard required in cases where appellate courts are asked to overturn factual findings.[1505] The Eighth Circuit pointed to the district court's conclusion that "if the United Missouri suit had gone to trial, the defendants in that suit would probably have prevailed, and the district court's belief that "although it was 'difficult to allocate exposure in a defense that seemed probably headed for success,'" it

---

1502. *Id.* at 1363-64; *Nodaway Valley Bank v. Continental Cas. Co.*, 715 F. Supp. 1458, 1459, 1461-65 (W.D. Mo. 1989), *aff'd*, 916 F.2d 1362 (8th Cir. 1990).

1503. 916 F.2d at 1365.

1504. *Id.* at 1367 (quoting 715 F. Supp. at 1461).

1505. *Id.* at 1367.

believed that the greatest risk was borne by Nodaway Valley's directors."[1506] In reaching that conclusion, the Eighth Circuit stated, the district court was "not content to rely upon platitudes about the tendency of juries to attack corporate 'deep pockets.'"[1507] Instead, the district court reasoned that if the case had gone to trial, Nodaway Valley Bancshares "'would likely have been viewed by the jury as essentially a basket for holding stock or a collection of legal papers used by the leading individual defendants,'" and "'the jury probably would have understood'" that the corporation that "'held assets of many innocent shareholders (including aged and infirm persons) whose identity was dramatized by being present as defendants in the lawsuit.'"[1508]

*Nodaway* preceded any court's adoption of the larger settlement rule, but a portion of the district court's decision in *Nodaway*—which was not noted in the Eighth Circuit's affirmance of the district court's decision—reflects the reasoning underlying the larger settlement rule. This portion of the district court's opinion rejected the insurer's argument in *Nodaway* that the insurer "was liable for the conduct of insured directors and officers but not for the corporate liability created by their acts"[1509] According to the district court, this argument by the insurer came

> dangerously close to saying that D & O insurance is *never* adequate insurance, making whole the insureds, when the uninsured corporate employer is joined in litigation with insured officers and directors. This would defeat the reasonable expectations of insureds who have purchased insurance that supposedly gives full coverage for director and officer liability. It seems clear that merely derivative corporate liability should not cause an apportionment between the primary wrongdoer and a vicarious wrongdoer, where both are joined in litigation.[1510]

---

1506. *Id*. (quoting 715 F. Supp. at 1460).
1507. *Id*.
1508. *Id*.
1509. 715 F. Supp. at 1466.
1510. *Id*.

The district court in *Nodaway* stated that this conclusion does "not expand the insurance policy to unfairly create corporate coverage; it simply gives full effect to the D & O coverage."[1511] The court added that the insurer "would of course not be exposed to responsibility for corporate coverage where an uninsured employee creates corporate liability or even, apparently, where the corporation alone is sued."[1512]

The Seventh Circuit's 1990 decision in *Harbor Insurance Co. v. Continental Illinois Corp.*,[1513] issued two months after and not citing the Eighth Circuit's decision in *Nodaway*, arose out of a $17.5 million settlement of a class action naming both Continental Illinois and its directors and officers as defendants. Two insurers contended that Continental had entered into the settlement to protect its corporate reputation in the financial community rather than to protect its directors and officers. Continental, by contrast, contended that the entire settlement was covered by insurance because the corporation and its directors and officers were jointly liable for the settlement. A jury found in favor of the insurers and attributed none of the $17.5 million settlement to the directors and officers.[1514]

The Seventh Circuit reversed the judgment entered following the jury's verdict on the ground that the trial court improperly refused to admit into evidence the insurers' original pleading in the case. The insurers, the Seventh Circuit explained, had claimed in their original pleading that they were not liable to reimburse Continental under the terms of Continental's insurance policy because of the allegedly egregious nature of the directors' conduct.[1515] After the action had been settled, however, the insurers switched course and contended that Continental "had settled the cases prematurely; the directors had been guilty of no misconduct

---

1511. *Id.*

1512. *Id.*

1513. 922 F.2d 357 (7th Cir. 1990).

1514. *See* Adler, *D & O Insurers Are Not Liable for Bank's Settlement: Jury*, Bus. Ins., Jan. 23, 1989, at 2.

1515. 922 F.2d at 360.

at all!"[1516] Continental was entitled to a new trial, the Seventh Circuit held, with a jury instruction stating "that the insurance companies were not allowed to change the defense to liability presented in their original pleading unless the change was based on new information that could not have been obtained at the time of that pleading or on other changed circumstances to which the companies could properly respond without being deemed to violate their duty of dealing in good faith with their contractual partner, Continental."[1517]

The Seventh Circuit stated that if Continental "establishes liability in the new trial that we are ordering," then "it will be necessary for the district court to determine how much larger the settlement was by virtue of the activities of persons against whom no claim within the meaning of the policy was made, and to cut down Continental's $17.5 million claim against the insurance companies accordingly."[1518] The court stated that Continental was a proper defendant even if the five directors who were named as defendants in the settled suits were the sole participants in the alleged fraud but that any derivative liability assessed against Continental under those circumstances would be subject to full indemnification from the directors and thus would be a covered loss.[1519] Accordingly, the court concluded, "the entire $17.5 million of joint liability should be allocated to the directors and therefore that Continental is entitled to recover up to the insurance limits, except for the portion, if any, of Continental's derivative liability that was due to the conduct of other directors, officers, or employees, besides those directors against whom claims were made within the meaning of the policy."[1520] "To allow the insurance companies an allocation between the directors' liability and the corporation's derivative liability for the directors' acts," the court stated in a passage citing the district court's decision in *Nodaway*, "would rob

---

1516. *Id.*
1517. *Id.* at 365.
1518. *Id.* at 368.
1519. *Id.*
1520. *Id.*

Continental of the insurance protection that it sought and bought."[1521]

The Ninth Circuit's 1995 decision in *Nordstrom, Inc. v. Chubb & Son, Inc.*[1522] involved a dispute between an insured and an insurer concerning allocation of a $7.5 million settlement and the defense costs in a securities law class action against Nordstrom, Inc. and six Nordstrom directors and officers.[1523] The directors and officers were insured; the corporation was not insured.[1524]

The court considered both the larger settlement and proportional fault approaches and determined not to "decide whether any given rule is generally applicable to all settlement agreements under D & O insurance policies" where directors and officers but not corporate defendants are insured.[1525] Instead, the court determined to focus only upon "the particular policy in question to determine which rule best effectuates the reasonable expectations and intentions of the parties under the insurance contract."[1526]

The particular policy at issue, the court stated, provided coverage for "all loss . . . which the Insured Person has become legally obligated to pay on account of any claim . . . for a wrongful act committed . . . [by] such Insured Person(s)."[1527] The court reasoned that under this provision "the parties would expect" that the insurer "would be responsible for any amount of liability that is attributable in any way to the wrongful acts or omissions of the directors and officers, regardless of whether the corporation could be found concurrently liable on any given claim under an independent theory."[1528] Under these circumstances, the court held, "the larger settlement rule best effectuates the reasonable

---

1521. *Id.* (citing *Nodaway*, 715 F. Supp. at 1466).
1522. 54 F.3d 1424 (9th Cir. 1995).
1523. *Id.* at 1427.
1524. *Id.*
1525. *Id.* at 1432.
1526. *Id.*
1527. *Id.* at 1429, 1432-33.
1528. *Id.* at 1433.

expectations of the parties.[1529] The court accordingly held that "we will allocate only if there is some amount of corporate liability that is both independent of and not duplicated by liability against the directors and officers."[1530]

Applying this rule, the court concluded that Nordstrom's liability for the amount paid to settle the case was "wholly concurrent with D & O liability."[1531] The court rejected the insurer's contention that the corporation faced independent liability under the respondeat superior doctrine for actions taken by Nordstrom employees other than directors and officers. The court explained that "[e]ven if we were to find that persons other than the named directors and officers engaged in activity in furtherance of securities fraud, . . . the insured directors and officers would be liable for these same acts because they are 'controlling persons'" under the federal securities laws.[1532] The court acknowledged that respondeat superior liability was not necessarily the same as controlling person liability in all cases. In this case, the court concluded, however, the director and officer defendants indisputably were involved with and approved the issuance of the allegedly misleading statements challenged in the case, and there was no evidence that any conduct by any other corporate employees or agents increased the amount of the settlement.[1533]

The court also rejected the insurer's contention that the corporation might have direct corporate liability for securities fraud under a "collective scienter" theory. The court explained that the collective scienter theory had only limited case law support, and that in this case there was no evidence of collective scienter that did not also support a finding that one or more of the directors and officers named as defendants had the intent required to impose liability.[1534] Corporate scienter, the court stated, "relies heavily on

---

1529. *Id.*
1530. *Id.*
1531. *Id.*
1532. *Id.* at 1433.
1533. *Id.* at 1434.
1534. *Id.* at 1434-35.

the awareness of directors and officers" who—unlike, for example, members of public relations or personnel departments—"are necessarily aware of the requirements of SEC regulations and state law and of the 'danger of misleading buyers and sellers.'"[1535] On the record before it, the court accordingly concluded, "we see no way" that the insurer "could show that the corporation, but not any individual defendants, had the requisite intent to defraud. Thus, any direct corporate liability would be derivative of, or concurrent with, D & O liability."[1536]

The court reached the same result with respect to defense costs. The court stated that "we find that the corporate liability was concurrent with the directors' and officers' liability, and the attorneys' billing statements provide no basis for allocation."[1537] For these reasons, the court concluded, "the defense costs cannot reasonably be allocated."[1538]

The Ninth Circuit's 1995 decision in *Safeway Stores, Inc. v. National Union Fire Insurance Co.*,[1539] decided shortly after the Ninth Circuit decided *Nordstrom*, involved the allocation of an approximately $1.8 million settlement plus defense costs in a litigation challenging the approval by the directors of Safeway Stores, Inc. of a leveraged buyout of Safeway by Kravis, Kohlberg & Roberts ("KKR"). The shareholders who commenced the litigation alleged that Safeway's directors and officers breached their fiduciary duties to Safeway's shareholders and that KKR aided and abetted these breaches of fiduciary duties.[1540]

In accordance with its reasoning in *Nordstrom*, the Ninth Circuit found that the larger settlement rule "best effectuates the reasonable expectations and intentions" of the parties in agreeing to the policy at issue.[1541] The court explained that Safeway's D & O

---

1535. *Id.* at 1435.
1536. *Id.* at 1436.
1537. *Id.* at 1436 n.5.
1538. *Id.*
1539. 64 F.3d 1282 (9th Cir. 1995).
1540. *Id.* at 1284-85.
1541. *Id.* at 1288.

policy provided that "[t]his policy shall . . . pay on behalf of the Company . . . Loss . . . *arising from any claim* . . . against a Director or Officer . . . of the Company by reason of any Wrongful Act."[1542] According to the court in *Safeway*, "if anything" this language provided Safeway's directors "broader coverage than the policy in *Nordstrom*, which provided for "all loss . . . which the Insured Person has become *legally obligated to pay* on account of any claim . . . for a Wrongful Act . . . ."[1543]

Applying the larger settlement rule, the court held that "the settlement costs did not include any amount of independent liability" on the part of KKR. The court explained that the only allegation against KKR was that KKR aided and abetted breaches of fiduciary duty by Safeway directors and officers. Thus, "whatever liability KKR might have would be concurrent with the liability of Safeway's officers and directors: KKR could not be liable for aiding and abetting their breaches of fiduciary duty unless the Safeway officers and directors had indeed breached that duty."[1544]

The court rejected the insurer's contention that a provision in the governing policy requiring that the parties "use their best efforts to determine a fair and proper allocation of the settlement amount as between the Company and the Insureds" mandated allocation.[1545] The court explained that "[t]he language of . . . the policy is not mandatory; it . . . 'requires an allocation analysis,' but not necessarily an allocation."[1546]

The Seventh Circuit's 1995 decision in *Caterpillar, Inc. v. Great American Insurance Co.*,[1547] decided after the Ninth Circuit decided *Nordstrom* and before the Ninth Circuit decided *Safeway*, involved a dispute regarding the allocation of a settlement and defense costs in a securities law class action by Caterpillar, Inc.

---

1542. *Id.*
1543. *Id.*
1544. *Id.*
1545. *Id.* at 1289.
1546. *Id.*
1547. 62 F.3d 955 (7th Cir. 1995).

and five Caterpillar directors.[1548] The Seventh Circuit began its decision by stating that it had addressed the allocation issue in dicta in *Harbor* and had "counseled an allocation of a settlement only where that settlement is larger because of the activities of uninsured persons who were sued or persons who were not sued but whose actions may have contributed to the suit"—i.e., the larger settlement rule.[1549]

Like the Ninth Circuit in *Nordstrom* and *Safeway*, the Seventh Circuit in *Caterpillar* declined "to develop general canons of allocation for every conflict between D & O insurers and their insureds."[1550] Instead, the court read the parties' insurance agreement to determine "what method of allocation, if any, that contract envisions."[1551] The governing policy in *Caterpillar*, the court stated, provided coverage for "'all Loss which the Directors or Officers shall be legally obligated to pay' where 'any Claim is first made against the Directors or Officers, individually or collectively, for a Wrongful Act.'"[1552] This language, the court continued, "implies a complete indemnity for claims regardless of who else might be at fault for similar actions."[1553] "Thus, in the instant case," the court concluded, "we believe the larger settlement rule better suits the facts: the policy does not limit coverage because of the activities of others that might overlap the claims against the directors and officers."[1554] The court thus determined to "adopt *Harbor*'s dicta regarding the larger settlement rule as our holding today."[1555]

The court in *Caterpillar*, however, questioned what it described as the assumption in *Harbor* that "for almost any liability the corporation might have faced, it could have demanded reimburse-

---

1548. *Id.* at 956.
1549. *Id.* at 960.
1550. *Id.* at 961.
1551. *Id.*
1552. *Id.* at 962.
1553. *Id.*
1554. *Id.*
1555. *Id.*

ment from its directors and officers" and therefore that "any allocation between the directors' liability and corporate derivative liability 'would rob Continental of the insurance protection that it sought and bought.'"[1556] The court in *Caterpillar* explained that after *Harbor* was decided, the United States Supreme Court stated in *Musick, Peeler & Garrett v. Employers Insurance of Wausau*[1557] and *Central Bank v. First Interstate Bank*[1558] that corporations face direct liability under Section 10(b) of the Securities Exchange Act of 1934 and Rule 10b-5 promulgated thereunder.[1559] If a corporation's liability "is possibly direct and not merely derivative," the court stated, "then *Harbor*'s conjunction of officers and directors' liability and corporate liability loses some of its force."[1560]

The court in *Caterpillar* stated that "there are conceivable situations where the individual actors would not be liable but their corporate employer would be.[1561] As examples, the court pointed to cases that depend "on the collective scienter" of employees or "where defenses are available to individuals but not the corporation."[1562] The court also stated that "[c]orporate derivative liability, which would essentially be a form of respondeat superior for these cases, entitles a corporation to indemnification from its officers and directors for liability those persons bring upon the corporation," while "direct liability . . . ordinarily creates no such right of indemnification in the corporation."[1563] Caterpillar's policy, the court continued, expressly excluded coverage for "any claim made against the Directors or Officers . . . by or at the behest of the Company" and the "federal securities law contains no

---

1556. *Id.* (quoting *Harbor*, 922 F.2d at 368).

1557. 508 U.S. 286 (1993).

1558. 511 U.S. 164 (1994).

1559. 62 F.3d at 962 (citing *Musick*, 508 U.S. at 296-97 and *Central Bank*, 511 U.S. at 176-77); 15 U.S.C. § 78j(b); 17 C.F.R. § 240.10b-5.

1560. 62 F.3d at 962.

1561. *Id.*

1562. *Id.*

1563. *Id.* at 963.

implied right of indemnification."[1564] The court added, however, that there is "little case law supporting an independent corporate scienter theory."[1565] The court also stated that "regardless of whether corporate liability is legally direct or derivative, a corporation still must act through its agents" and "[i]f all those agents were directors and officers covered under the . . . policy, and Caterpillar incurred direct liability because of these individuals' actions, then perhaps the D & O policy should still cover claims based on those actions."[1566]

Turning to the allegations in the case, the court stated that direct liability against the corporation was "certainly a possibility": plaintiffs "alleged actions by Caterpillar as a whole and named Caterpillar in the complaint"; "the settlement contained language resolving any claims against the corporation and persons other than the directors and officers"; direct liability may have arisen "as the consequence of actions of persons other than officers and directors"; and direct liability may have arisen due to actions by corporate directors and officers "for which the directors and officers were themselves immune and could not have suffered any consequence."[1567] Accordingly, the court held, "[t]o the extent that the trier of fact determines that Caterpillar disposed of any direct action against it in settling the complaint and that that disposition increased the settlement figure, Caterpillar should not be entitled to recover from Great American Insurance Company, Caterpillar's insurer."[1568]

The court in *Caterpillar* concluded by observing that unlike the court in *Nordstrom* (as noted above, *Caterpillar* pre-dated *Safeway*), the court was not "able to look at the facts underlying the coverage" and determine that potential liability on the part of the corporation "was 'wholly concurrent with D & O liability.'"[1569]

---

1564. *Id.*
1565. *Id.*
1566. *Id.*
1567. *Id.*
1568. *Id.* at 963-64.
1569. *Id.* at 964 (quoting *Nordstrom*, 54 F.3d at 1433).

"That is not to say," the court in *Caterpillar* cautioned, "that such liability exists; it still ultimately must be proven that Caterpillar might have incurred an independent liability from these actions and that these actions increased the final settlement value."[1570]

The court in *Caterpillar* thus summarized its holdings as follows:

> Great American is entitled to attempt some measure of allocation . . . . That allocation may only reflect the extent to which the settlement was larger because of claims against uninsured persons or the actions of persons against whom no claims were made. Uninsured claims may include those made against the corporation for which the corporation would face direct liability and for which the insured directors and officers could not be held liable.[1571]

The Tenth Circuit's 1997 decision in *Vitkus v. Beatrice Co.*[1572] held that Beatrice Company was obligated to pay $10 million of a $26.5 million settlement resolving litigation brought by the Federal Deposit Insurance Corporation against several defendants associated with the failed Silverado Banking, Savings and Loan Association, which the FDIC seized in 1988. $10 million was the portion of the settlement allocated by the defendants to Richard Vitkus, an outside director of Silverado and an officer of Beatrice's predecessor, Beatrice Companies, Inc. ("BCI"), until BCI merged with Kohlberg, Kravis & Roberts in 1986.[1573] At the time of the merger, BCI had maintained a $10 million directors' and officers' liability policy with Lloyd's of London, and the merger agreement required Beatrice to maintain coverage for Vitkus at terms no less advantageous than the Lloyd's policy for six years. Beatrice failed to maintain insurance and thus, according to the court, "became a self-insurer, with the scope of its obligations measured by the Lloyd's policy."[1574] In 1988, Vitkus became an officer of Emhart Corporation. As an Emhart officer, Vitkus obtained excess cover-

---

1570. *Id.*
1571. *Id.*
1572. 127 F.3d 936 (10th Cir. 1997).
1573. *Id.* at 939-40.
1574. *Id.* at 939.

age to cover Vitkus's service on the Silverado board from National Union Fire Insurance Company.[1575]

After the FDIC seized Silverado, the FDIC commenced litigation against Vitkus, ten other Silverado directors and officers and Silverado's counsel. Beatrice refused to indemnify Vitkus under the terms of the merger agreement. National Union, which also insured Silverado's outside counsel, agreed to pay Vitkus's defense costs and to settle the litigation on behalf of all defendants in exchange for $26.5 million. The defendants agreed to an allocation agreement that allocated $10 million of the settlement amount to Vitkus and $16.5 million to Silverado's former counsel. Other defendants, who did not have insurance, each paid small amounts totaling approximately $300,000 to National Union. Vitkus and National Union sued Beatrice.[1576]

The court rejected each of the arguments offered by Beatrice in support of its claim that it was not required to pay the $10 million amount allocated by the defendants to Vitkus. The court acknowledged that it was "unclear whether the $10 million allocation to Vitkus of the total $26.5 million settlement accurately reflects his liability in the Silverado debacle."[1577] The court explained, however, that "[a]ctual liability . . . is not our guide in evaluating whether a settlement allocation is enforceable" because "[i]t would be wholly impracticable to charge the district court with trying the Silverado litigation after a successful settlement in order to ascertain Vitkus's and the other settling parties' relative culpabilities."[1578] Rather, the court held, the test was "whether the amount of the settlement allocation reasonably reflected Vitkus's potential exposure in the underlying litigation."[1579] More specifically, the court held, "where a reluctant insurer fails to participate in an insured's settlement discussions, and the insured becomes a party to a global settlement agreement, the insured may be indemni-

1575. *Id.* at 939-40.
1576. *Id.* at 940.
1577. *Id.* at 944.
1578. *Id.*
1579. *Id.*

fied for any amount of the total settlement package for which it can establish a reasonable anticipation of liability."[1580]

Here, the court concluded, "the potential exposure of the defendants exceeded $200 million."[1581] Even under a comparable fault analysis, the court stated, "Vitkus was still potentially liable for more than $10 million of the total judgment that the FDIC sought," and there was "strong evidence" that Vitkus's culpability was comparable to that of the other Silverado defendants."[1582] The court also stated that in assessing potential liability and the allocation of a settlement among multiple defendants, one relevant factor is the existence of insurance—i.e., "the 'deep pocket' factor."[1583] This factor, the court found, also supported the allocation to Vitkus of $10 million of the settlement payment.[1584]

*Slottow v. American Casualty Co.*,[1585] a Ninth Circuit decision pre-dating that court's 1995 decisions in *Nordstrom* and *Safeway*, involved a suit by Commercial Acceptance Corporation ("CAC") investors against CAC for fraud in a case involving loan pools underwritten by CAC. Plaintiffs also sued (1) Fidelity National Trust ("FNT"), the trustee for CAC's investors, (2) Fidelity Federal Bank ("FFB" or "the bank"), FNT's parent, and (3) Ralph S. Slottow, the president of FNT and a director and officer of FFB and who signed and supervised trust agreements.[1586] Plaintiffs alleged "lax enforcement" of the trust agreements and claims for breach of contract, negligence and breach of fiduciary duty."[1587]

The parties settled the action for $4.75 million and agreed to allocate 96 percent of this settlement to Slottow, an insured party, 4 percent to FNT, an uninsured party, and 0 percent to FFB, also an

---

1580. *Id.* at 945.
1581. *Id.* at 946.
1582. *Id.*
1583. *Id.*
1584. *Id.* at 946.
1585. 10 F.3d 1355 (9th Cir. 1993).
1586. *Id.* at 1357.
1587. *Id.*

uninsured party.[1588] The insurer refused to fund the settlement on the ground that too high a percentage of the settlement was allocated to Slottow.[1589] The district court found that the allocation "bore a reasonable relationship to the relative exposure of the parties to the underlying litigation," but adjusted the allocation slightly, to 93 percent (Slottow), 7 percent (FNT) and 0 percent (FFB).[1590]

The Ninth Circuit reversed. The Ninth Circuit stated that the parties and the district court "significantly over-estimated Slottow's personal exposure in the underlying litigation" and "probably underestimated FNT's potential liability and certainly underestimated the bank's."[1591] Indeed, the Ninth Circuit stated, "[w]ithout a doubt, the one party that faced the greatest exposure . . . was FNT."[1592] The Ninth Circuit acknowledged that the district court's ruling allocated liability against FNT equal to its net worth but held that "there was a strong likelihood" of recovery of "much more than that from the bank on an alter ego theory" and a piercing of the corporate veil theory.[1593] The court explained that FFB's initial capitalization of FNT was "woefully inadequate," there was a "unity of interest and ownership between the two corporations," and "an inequitable result would follow if the corporations were treated as separate entities."[1594] The court also reasoned that

> Slottow and the bank didn't have adverse interests; on the contrary, each had a strong incentive to structure the settlement precisely as it did. The bank faced liability as the alter ego of FNT; it knew it could avoid costly liability and public ignominy by allocating 0% of the liability to itself and 96% to Slottow. And the bank knew it could indemnify Slottow—who also sat on the bank's Board—while being fully

---

1588. *Id.* at 1357, 1358.
1589. *Id.* at 1358.
1590. *Id.*
1591. *Id.* at 1360.
1592. *Id.*
1593. *Id.*
1594. *Id.*

reimbursed by American under the terms of the policy. Slottow and the bank thus crafted a win-win solution for themselves, with the insurance company footing the bill.[1595]

For all of these reasons, the court concluded that the parties' allocation of the settlement did not reasonably reflect the parties' relative liabilities and thus was not entered into in good faith.[1596]

The case was remanded to the district court for a new allocation in light of the considerations stated by the Ninth Circuit, and on remand 55 percent of the settlement was allocated to Slottow.[1597] The Ninth Circuit's subsequent decision in *Nordstrom*—discussed above—rejected an insurer's claim that *Slottow* supports the proportional fault or relative exposure approach. The court in *Nordstrom* explained that the holding in *Slottow* "did not address an insurer's right to allocation on the basis of direct corporate liability;" rather, it held that "the settlement arrangement was not made in good faith because it did not reasonably reflect the relative liabilities of the parties."[1598]

Federal district courts in California, Colorado and Maryland and a state court in Michigan have utilized the larger settlement rule adopted by the Seventh and Ninth Circuits in *Harbor*, *Nordstrom*, *Safeway* and *Caterpillar*.

The California district court decision (which pre-dated the Ninth Circuit's decisions in *Nordstrom* and *Safeway*), *Raychem Corp. v. Federal Insurance Co.*,[1599] held that an insurer was liable for settlement payments and defense costs, except to the extent that (1) the actions of uninsured persons increased the settlement amount, or (2) defense costs were incurred for uninsured persons "independent of any reasonable relation to the defense of claims"

---

1595. *Id.* at 1359.

1596. *Id.*

1597. Monteleone & Conca, *Directors and Officers Indemnification and Liability Insurance: An Overview of Legal and Practical Issues*, 51 Bus. Law. 573, 618 (1996).

1598. 54 F.3d at 1435.

1599. 853 F. Supp. 1170 (N.D. Cal. 1994).

against insured directors and officers.[1600] On a motion for summary judgment, the court held that no evidence of either of these occurrences had been presented and therefore that "allocation in this case would be improper."[1601] *Vicorp Restaurants, Inc. v. Federal Insurance Co.*,[1602] the district court case in Colorado, held that allocation "is not appropriate when an uninsured corporation's liability is wholly derivative from the insured officer's or director's acts."[1603] *Federal Realty Investment Trust v. Pacific Insurance Co.*,[1604] the district court case in Maryland, utilized the following jury instruction:

> In order to determine the amount of damages in this case, you must decide what portion of the total fees and expenses incurred in the *ISM* action was reasonably related to the defense of the Trustees on claims by *ISM* covered by the insurance policy. . . .
>
> With respect to the contested items, a fee or expense is reasonably related to the defense of the Trustees on covered claims if an attorney hired to defend a suit against *only* the Trustees on *only* covered claims reasonably would have decided to perform the legal service applicable to the fee or expense.
>
> In deciding whether a fee or expense was reasonably related to the defense of the Trustees on covered claims, you *may not* consider whether the service associated with the expense or fee also aided in the defense of a party not covered by the insurance policy or a claim not covered by the insurance policy.[1605]

*Apollo Industries, Inc. v. Associated International Insurance Co.*,[1606] the appellate court decision in Michigan, allocated all

---

1600. *Id.* at 1183.

1601. *Id.* at 1183-84.

1602. 1993 U.S. Dist. LEXIS 20294, 1993 WL 736918 (D. Colo. June 30, 1993).

1603. 1993 U.S. Dist. LEXIS 20294, at *4, 1993 WL 736918, at *1.

1604. 760 F. Supp. 533 (D. Md. 1991).

1605. *Id.* at 537-38.

1606. No. 153902 (Mich. Ct. App. Apr. 13, 1995).

defense costs to the insured directors in the case. The court explained that all expenses incurred were "reasonably related to the defense" of insured directors because the focus of the suit was an alleged breach of fiduciary duty by the insured directors.[1607] The court relied upon an affidavit submitted by the attorney who represented the insured directors and the uninsured corporation. This affidavit stated that all amounts spent on defense would have been spent even if non-insured parties had not been named as defendants.[1608] The court stated that this affidavit had not been rebutted by evidence showing that any portion of defense expenses were incurred solely in defense of uninsured parties.[1609] The court thus concluded that the expenses could be allocated "wholly to the insured party."[1610]

A district court decision in Pennsylvania in *First Fidelity Bancorporation v. National Union Fire Insurance Co.*,[1611] another case pre-dating the Court of Appeals decisions in *Nordstrom, Safeway* and *Caterpillar*, upheld a jury verdict requiring an insurer to pay $14.8 million of a $30 million settlement in a case where the policy limit was $25 million. The court explained that insured directors and officers and the uninsured corporate entity each faced liability.[1612] The court rejected the corporation's contention that the corporation's liability arose exclusively from the conduct of the insured directors and officers and thus required the insurer to assume responsibility for the corporation's liability.[1613] The court pointed to claims under Section 11 of the Securities Act of 1933[1614] as an example:

1607. *Id.*, slip op. at 4.

1608. *Id.*

1609. *Id.*

1610. *Id.*

1611. 1994 U.S. Dist. LEXIS 3977, 1994 WL 111363 (E.D. Pa. Mar. 30, 1994).

1612. 1994 U.S. Dist. LEXIS 3977, at *38, 1994 WL 111363, at *12.

1613. *Id.*

1614. 15 U.S.C. § 77k.

> Section 11 of the Securities Act of 1933 provides separate
> standards of liability for issuers, such as First Fidelity, and
> individuals, such as directors and officers. . . . [A]n issuer is
> almost absolutely liable for any misstatements made in con-
> nection with the sale of securities, but the directors and
> officers are allowed a due diligence defense. The occasion
> could arise where liability results from the conduct of the
> insured directors and officers, but they are found not liable
> by way of the due diligence defense, but the issuing corpora-
> tion is found liable. In this instance, First Fidelity would
> contend that the D & O insurer should pay the damages on
> behalf of the issuing corporation, who is not insured under
> the policy. Such a result would be contrary to the purpose of
> the party's intent under the policy.[1615]

Even if this were not the case and an insurer was responsible
for corporate liability arising solely from the conduct of insured
directors and officers, the court continued, there was sufficient evidence in this case to support the jury's finding that conduct of uninsured individuals created liability for the corporation. Most significantly, the court explained, there was evidence that the underlying
action had been settled for business reasons rather than on the basis
of possible exposure to liability by insured directors and
officers.[1616] The court also relied upon a policy provision stating
that in the event of a settlement of a claim where the corporation
and directors and officers both were named as defendants, the
insurer and the insureds would use "their best efforts to determine
a fair and proper allocation of the settlement amount as between the
Company and the Insureds."[1617]

   *c. Allocation Between Defendants: The Burden of Proof.*
Courts have disagreed with respect to whether the insurer or the
insured bears the burden of proof when the allocation issue is
litigated. The Seventh Circuit in *Caterpillar, Inc. v. Great Ameri-*

---

1615. 1994 U.S. Dist. LEXIS 3977, at *38, 1994 WL 111363, at
*12.
   1616. 1994 U.S. Dist. LEXIS 3977, at *39-41, 1994 WL 111363,
at *12-13.
   1617. 1994 U.S. Dist. LEXIS 3977, at *11, 37, 1994 WL 111363,
at *3, 12.

*can Insurance Co.*[1618] summarized the respective arguments for imposing the burden of proof with respect to the allocation issue upon insurers and upon insureds as follows:

> On the one hand, insurers are normally obligated to pay for any settlements negotiated in good faith. However, under many D & O policies, . . . the insureds control the underlying litigation. That renders them not only in possession of most information regarding the suit, but also gives them the opportunity, and the perverse incentive, to structure the underlying litigation so as to place all the fault on the backs of officers and directors and thereby ensure complete coverage. Additionally, even if the insured is presumed covered for settlements negotiated in good faith, the insured should still have to show "the existence and extent of a loss covered by a policy."[1619]

The court in *Caterpillar* "express[ed] no view on the merits of this debate."[1620]

Cases placing the burden of proof upon the insurer include *PepsiCo, Inc. v. Continental Casualty Co.*[1621] and *Health-Chem Corp. v. National Union Fire Insurance Co.*[1622]

The court in *PepsiCo* stated that "[e]vidence of a good faith settlement of the underlying litigation . . . creates a presumption that the costs are covered by the policy" and thus places the "burden of proving what amount of the settlement cost should be excluded from the policy coverage" upon the insurer.[1623] The court in *Health-Chem* stated that "[o]nce prima facie proof that an expense was incurred in defense of a covered party has been introduced, the burden of showing that all or a specific portion of it was

---

1618. 62 F.3d 955 (7th Cir. 1995).
1619. *Id.* at 964 n.11 (citations omitted).
1620. *Id.*
1621. 640 F. Supp. 656 (S.D.N.Y. 1986).
1622. 148 Misc. 2d 187, 559 N.Y.S.2d 435 (N.Y. Sup. Ct. N.Y. Co. 1990).
1623. 640 F. Supp. at 662.

incurred in defense of a non-covered party" is upon the insurer."[1624]

Cases placing the burden of proof upon the insured include *John Hancock Healthplan, Inc. v. Lexington Insurance Co.*[1625] and *Raychem Corp. v. Federal Insurance Co.*[1626]

The court in *John Hancock* explicitly rejected the *PepsiCo* decision. The court in *John Hancock* explained that the court in *PepsiCo* incorrectly relied upon *H.S. Equities, Inc. v. Hartford Accident & Indemnity Co.*[1627] The *H.S. Equities* case, the *John Hancock* court stated, involved the issue whether an indemnitor "may challenge its *actual liability* under an indemnity clause where the indemnitee has settled the claims against it," and the *H.S. Equities* court held that the answer to this question was "no."[1628] According to the *John Hancock* court, the *H.S. Equities* court did not address the question whether an indemnitor "may challenge the amount *allocable* to those liabilities that it indemnified and which party has the burden of proving the proper allocation."[1629] The *John Hancock* court stated that placing the burden of proof upon the corporation seeking insurance coverage "comports with the general notion that the plaintiff has the burden of proving its case," and that in any event the corporation "is the party to this matter that settled the case and is in a better position to prove what part of the settlement amount represents the settlement of claims against the officers and directors."[1630]

---

1624. 148 Misc. 2d at 191, 559 N.Y.S.2d at 438.

1625. 1990 U.S. Dist. LEXIS 2450, 1990 WL 21137 (E.D. Pa. Mar. 6, 1990), *subsequent proceedings*, No. 88-2308 (E.D. Pa. Feb. 5, 1991).

1626. 853 F. Supp. 1170 (N.D. Cal. 1994).

1627. 661 F.2d 264 (2d Cir. 1981).

1628. 1990 U.S. Dist. LEXIS 2450, at *6, 1990 WL 21137, at *2.

1629. *Id.*

1630. 1990 U.S. Dist. LEXIS 2450, at *8, 1990 WL 21137, at *2; *see also John Hancock Healthplan, Inc. v. Lexington Ins. Co.*, No. 88-2308, slip op. at 14 (E.D. Pa. Feb. 5, 1991) (re-stating this holding).

The court in *Raychem* explained that "[t]he party seeking coverage must show the existence and extent of a loss covered by the policy."[1631] The court also explained that "the insured has better access to information relevant to allocation than does its insurer, particularly . . . where the insured chose counsel for itself and its officers and controlled the defense."[1632]

*d. Allocation Between Defendants: New Policy Approaches.* Recently drafted policy forms seek to avoid disputes concerning allocation in several ways. Some policies provide that insureds and insurers will use their "best efforts" to reach an allocation between covered and uncovered parties if a claim is made, arguably suggesting (at least according to insurers and one court[1633]) that some allocation is appropriate in all cases.[1634] Other policies provide for arbitration or other alternative dispute resolution mechanisms to resolve this issue in the event of a dispute.[1635]

Some policies go further by providing for pre-determined allocation percentages either for all claims or just for securities claims. The term "securities claims" is defined in one policy, for example, as "a Claim made against an Insured which alleges a violation of the Securities Act of 1933 or the Securities Exchange Act

---

1631. 853 F. Supp. at 1176.

1632. *Id.; see also Federal Realty Inv. Trust v. Pacific Ins. Co.*, 760 F. Supp. 533, 537 (D. Md. 1991); *Nodaway Valley Bank v. Continental Casualty Co.*, 715 F. Supp. 1458, 1467 (W.D. Mo. 1989) ("[t]reating the burden of proof and persuasion as being on plaintiff"—in *Nodaway*, the corporation seeking insurance—"both as to allocation of the settlement sum and of expenses"), *aff'd*, 916 F.2d 1362 (8th Cir. 1990).

1633. *See First Fidelity Bancorporation v. National Union Fire Ins. Co.*, 1994 U.S. Dist. LEXIS 3977 at *11, 37, 1994 WL 111363, at *3, 12 (E.D. Pa. Mar. 30, 1994); *see also* Chapter V, Section B 11 b (discussing *First Fidelity* case).

1634. Monteleone & Conca, *Directors and Officers Indemnification and Liability Insurance: An Overview of Legal and Practical Issues*, 51 Bus. Law. 573, 618 (1996); Monteleone, *D & O Allocation: Problems and Solutions*, XVIII The Risk Report No. 8, Apr. 1996, at 6 *reprinted in Securities Litigation 1996* 997, 1001 (Practising Law Institute 1996).

1635. Monteleone & Conca, 51 Bus. Law. at 618; Monteleone, The Risk Report, at 5, 6.

of 1934, rules or regulations promulgated thereunder, the securities laws of any state, or any foreign jurisdiction, and which alleges a Wrongful Act in connection with the claimant's purchase or sale of, or the offer to purchase or sell to the claimant, any securities of the Company, whether on the open market or arising from a public or private offering of securities by the Company."[1636]

Other policies provide coverage for corporate entity liability as well as coverage for corporate indemnification payments and director and officer liability.[1637] Still other policies provide for an exclusion from policy coverage for a specified but relatively small percentage of any "concurrent liability," a term defined as "damages, settlements and legal defense expenses incurred jointly by the corporation and its directors or officers."[1638]

*e. Allocation Between Claims.* Allocation between covered and non-covered claims—as opposed to covered and non-covered defendants—also often is required. An example would be a complaint alleging breach of fiduciary duty claims and a libel or slander claim where libel and slander are excluded from coverage.[1639]

The courts in *Harristown Development Corp. v. International Insurance Co.*[1640] and *Continental Casualty Co. v. Board of Education*[1641] have held that insureds are entitled to recover 100 percent of legal expenses incurred in defending a covered claim that also are necessary to defend a non-covered claim. An insurer is not entitled to apportionment between claims, these courts have con-

---

1636. Monteleone & Conca, 51 Bus. Law. at 618-20; Monteleone, The Risk Report, at 5-6, 7; 1997 Watson Wyatt Worldwide D & O Liability Survey Report 4 (1997).

1637. Monteleone & Conca, 51 Bus. Law. at 620; Monteleone, The Risk Report, at 6-8; Weiss, *Filling the Gaps in D & O Insurance*, 6 Bus. Law Today No. 3, Jan./Feb. 1997, at 44.

1638. Monteleone, The Risk Report, at 8-10.

1639. Monteleone & Conca, *Directors and Officers Indemnification and Liability Insurance: An Overview of Legal and Practical Issues*, 51 Bus. Law. 573, 608 (1996).

1640. 1988 U.S. Dist. LEXIS 12791, 1988 WL 123149 (M.D. Pa. Nov. 15, 1988).

1641. 489 A.2d 536 (Md. 1985).

cluded, "based simply on the fact that an item of legal service or expense would also be of use to counsel" in defending against an uncovered claim "in addition to its use" in defending against a covered claim.[1642] To the contrary: "Having purchased this form of litigation insurance, the Board is entitled to the full benefit of its bargain. So long as an item of service or expense is reasonably related to defense of a covered claim, it may be apportioned wholly to the covered claim."[1643]

A noteworthy illustration of this principle involves claims for punitive damages in jurisdictions where awards of punitive damages are not insurable on public policy grounds[1644] or where the governing policy excludes awards of punitive damages.[1645] Under these circumstances and under the reasoning in *Harristown* and *Continental Casualty*, an allegation in a complaint seeking punitive damages that did not affect defense strategy would not require allocation.[1646] Defense costs involving expert testimony proffered solely to establish the value of a defendant's assets as a measure for an award of punitive damages, however, arguably could be the subject of allocation.[1647]

*f. Allocation Where Some But Not All Claims are Covered and Advancement is Required.* The Ninth Circuit recognized in *Gon v. First State Insurance Co.*[1648] that the nature of the claims asserted in a complaint may not clearly indicate whether claims will be covered or uncovered claims. Under these circumstances, the court held, a policy requiring advancement requires advancement of all defense costs without allocation.[1649] The court explained that "some exclusions, such as libel or slander, are easy to distinguish

---

1642. *Harristown*, 1988 U.S. Dist. LEXIS 12791, at *35, 1988 WL 123149, at *12; *Continental Casualty*, 489 A.2d at 545.

1643. *Harristown*, 1988 U.S. Dist. LEXIS 12791, at *35-36, 1988 WL 123149, at *12; *Continental Casualty*, 489 A.2d at 544-45.

1644. *See* Chapter V, Section B 3.

1645. *See* Chapter V, Section B 9 a.

1646. Monteleone & Conca, 51 Bus. Law. at 609.

1647. *Id*.

1648. 871 F.2d 863 (9th Cir. 1989).

1649. *Id*. at 868-69.

from covered claims," but apportionment is much more difficult where, for example, a claim based upon an alleged act might be covered if the act were committed negligently, but not covered if committed intentionally.[1650] Apportionment in advance of a judgment in such a case is not required because it would be "very difficult, if not impossible."[1651] The court also stated that "the third party complainant, who may overstate the claims against the insured, should not be the arbiter of the policy's coverage" and that "apportioning legal expenses where coverage is not yet clear, because the facts are not fully developed, may deny the insureds the benefits of the protection they purchased."[1652]

The court acknowledged that the insurer may have "great difficulty in recovering should the court subsequently decide that a claim or individual was not covered by the policy."[1653] The court accordingly suggested that district courts "may well wish to consider the use of a master or other case management techniques to monitor the legal fees in order to keep track of those which are attributable to covered and uncovered matters, and to permit an earlier apportionment if it should develop that some portions of the incurred expenses prove to be uncovered and easily separable, without prejudice to the defense of covered claims."[1654]

The court in *Fight Against Coercive Tactics Network, Inc. v. Coregis Insurance Co.*[1655] followed *Gon*. The court held that "where the policy creates an obligation on the insurer to pay for defense costs as incurred, apart from those claims contained in the pleadings which are clearly excluded from coverage, . . . apportionment in advance of judgment is impractical" and not required.[1656] The court adopted the suggestion in *Gon* that a special master be appointed to monitor defense costs, keep track of

---

1650. *Id.* at 868.
1651. *Id.*
1652. *Id.* at 869.
1653. *Id.*
1654. *Id.*
1655. 926 F. Supp. 1426 (D. Colo. 1996).
1656. *Id.* at 1435.

defense costs attributable to covered and uncovered claims, and "permit early apportionment if it should emerge that some portion of the incurred expenses prove to be uncovered and easily severable, without prejudice to the defense of the covered aspects of the claims."[1657]

The court in *Anglo-American Insurance Co. v. Molin*[1658] similarly held that where "it is impossible" at a particular stage of proceedings to determine what claims in an action are covered claims and what claims in an action are not covered claims, an insurer is obligated to treat the entire action as a covered claim and reimburse all of the insureds' defense costs if the policy requires reimbursement of defense costs.[1659]

## 12. Misrepresentations in Policy Applications

D & O insurers, like other insurers, may deny liability due to misrepresentations or omissions of material facts in the insured's policy application.[1660] The application typically requests

> information concerning the corporation's business, including the corporation's (i) name, address, nature of business, and state of incorporation; (ii) assets, liabilities, and revenues; (iii) stock ownership information (i.e., the total shares outstanding, payment of dividends, and the number of shares held by directors and officers); (iv) subsidiary information (i.e., identity of all subsidiaries, dates of acquisition or creation, and percentage ownership); (v) plans for any extraordinary corporate transactions, such as a merger, divestiture, or acquisition; (vi) previous D & O insurance (i.e., limits of liability, deductibles, and premiums); (vii) previous claims experience; and (viii) present knowledge of any occur-

---

1657. *Id.* at 1436.

1658. 673 A.2d 986 (Pa. Cmmw. Ct. 1996), *rev'd on other grounds*, 691 A.2d 929 (Pa. 1997).

1659. *Id.* at 993-94.

1660. *See generally* 12A John A. Appleman, *Insurance Law & Practice* §§ 7291-7305 (1981 & Supp. 1998); 2 Lee R. Russ & Thomas F. Segalla, *Couch on Insurance 3d* § 31:10, at 31-19 (1997); John F. Olson & Josiah O. Hatch III, *Director and Officer Liability: Indemnification and Insurance* § 10.08[3][d], at 10-77 (1997).

rence or circumstance that may give rise to claims against the insured directors and officers.

The insured generally is also required to attach the following documents to the application: (i) a complete list of all the corporation's directors and officers, including their names, positions, terms of office, and affiliation with any other organizations; (ii) the most recent annual report; (iii) the most recent filings with the SEC (i.e., Form 10-K, Form 10-Q, Form 8K, etc.); (iv) the latest available interim financial statements; (v) proxy statements for the last and next annual meetings; and (vi) the most recent prospectus.[1661]

*a. General Principles.* Misrepresentations or omissions of material information may lead to denial of coverage for a particular claim, reformation of the policy (meaning "the 'rewriting' of the policy to reflect accurately what the terms of the policy would have been had the insured provided 'truthful' information in the policy application"), or rescission rendering the policy void *ab initio.*[1662] Whether particular alleged misrepresentations and/or omissions provide grounds for a denial of insurance depends upon the specific question asked by the insurer and the specific response provided by the insured.

Examples of cases resolving this question in favor of insurers include the following:

- *National Union Fire Insurance Co. v. Sahlen*[1663] (affirming grant of summary judgment in favor of insurer where insured attached false financial statements to policy application: "Misrepresentations and incorrect statements in a policy application bar recovery under the policy where, *inter alia*, they are material to the risk assumed by the insurer or the insurer would not have offered the same terms had it known the truth. . . .

---

1661. Monteleone & Conca, *Directors and Officers Indemnification and Liability Insurance: An Overview of Legal and Practical Issues*, 51 Bus. Law. 573, 584 (1996); *see also* J. Olson & J. Hatch § 10.08[3][d], at 10-77.

1662. Monteleone & Conca, 51 Bus. Law. at 584-85.

1663. 999 F.2d 1532 (11th Cir. 1993).

The actual, precarious state of SAI's financial health and the alleged criminal wrongdoing of certain of its high-level officers and employees quite obviously altered the risk assumed by the insurer."),[1664]

• *Republic Insurance Co. v. Masters, Mates & Pilots Pension Plan*[1665] (affirming grant of summary judgment where "Republic submitted evidence that, in their policy applications, the Plans falsely stated that Plan investments were under the control of an independent investment manager, when in fact certain Plan trustees were participating in investment decisions. In response to a question inquiring whether any Plan trustees were aware of potential claims, the Plans failed to disclose that they had made investments prohibited by Plan guidelines, and that they were under investigation by the Department of Labor. Republic also showed that the Plans failed to disclose an internal investigation to determine whether any investments violated ERISA. Republic contends that had the true information been disclosed, it would not have provided insurance.");[1666]

• *F/H Industries, Inc. v. National Union Fire Insurance Co.*[1667] (granting motion to dismiss by insurer against claim that insurer improperly refused coverage because the insurance application was "unequivocal in its exclusion of coverage for any claim about which the officers or directors of Scot Lad might have knowledge"),[1668]

• *Jaunich v. National Union Fire Insurance Co.*[1669] (granting partial summary judgment in favor of insurer

---

1664. *Id.* at 1534, 1536.
1665. 77 F.3d 48 (2d Cir. 1996).
1666. *Id.* at 52.
1667. 635 F. Supp. 60 (N.D. Ill. 1986), *vacated in part on other grounds*, 116 F.R.D. 224 (N.D. Ill. 1987).
1668. *Id.* at 61-63.
1669. 647 F. Supp. 209 (N.D. Cal. 1986).

where corporation neglected to communicate the corporation's awareness prior to the issuance of the policy
that the corporation's "financial situation was far worse
than had been previously reported to National Union,
making its earlier representations grossly misleading,"
and that "there existed a number of circumstances that
can lead to litigation . . . that had not been disclosed";
the court stated that "the financial health of a company
as well as the existence of circumstances that can lead
to litigation are material to an insurer's decision to
issue a directors and officers' liability policy" and are
"particularly material when the information has been
specifically requested as part of the insurance application, which was the case with respect to most of the
information at issue here"),[1670]

- *Chomat v. Spreckley*[1671] (granting summary judgment
  in favor of insurer where "(1) a misrepresentation was
  made where the insured failed to truthfully respond on
  the insurance application and (2) the insurer would not
  have in good faith issued the policy had the truth been
  known"),[1672]

- *Evanston Insurance Co. v. Security Assurance Co.*[1673]
  (granting summary judgment in favor of insurer where
  court found that insured had notice of a potential claim
  and thus that the insured's answers to particular questions on its policy application were false),[1674]

- *International Insurance Co. v. Peabody International
  Corp.*[1675] (granting summary judgment in favor of
  insurer where insured failed to disclose facts known to
  the insured that indicated the probability of a claim, and

---

1670. *Id*. at 210-11.
1671. 1989 U.S. Dist. LEXIS 8603 (S.D. Fla. Apr. 18, 1989).
1672. 1989 U.S. Dist. LEXIS 8603, at *5-6.
1673. 715 F. Supp. 1405 (N.D. Ill. 1989).
1674. *Id*. at 1415-16.
1675. 747 F. Supp. 477 (N.D. Ill. 1990).

where the policy application asked about "any circumstances, occurrence or condition . . . which may result
in the making or assertion of a claim"),[1676]

- *Association for Retarded Citizens - Santa Barbara
  Council v. North American Specialty Insurance
  Co.*[1677] (granting summary judgment in favor of insurer
  rescinding policy where corporate officials answered
  "no" to questions asking whether any employee had
  been dismissed within the previous 12 months, whether
  any claim had been made against the corporation or any
  other person proposed for insurance within the previous
  5 years, or whether any person proposed for insurance
  was "cognizant of any fact, circumstance or situation
  which may result" in a claim; in fact, an employee had
  been terminated two months earlier and had stated upon
  learning of the termination that she would be "getting
  Bill Gulje," one of the corporate officials who signed
  the application, "for sexual harassment," and the
  insurer submitted an affidavit stating that had this fact
  been disclosed the policy would not have been issued or
  would have excluded this claim),[1678]

- *First National Bank Holding Co. v. Fidelity & Deposit
  Co.*[1679] (granting summary judgment in favor of
  insurer seeking to void policy where bank chairman and
  president who had engaged in "an elaborate fraudulent
  scheme" in order to "far exceed" legal borrowing
  limits, and who later pleaded guilty to numerous banking code violations, answered "no" to a policy application question asking whether he had "knowledge or
  information of any act, error or omission which might
  give rise to a claim under the proposed policy," and it
  was undisputed that if he had answered that question

---

1676. *Id.* at 479-84.
1677. No. CV 94-4602 LGB (Ex) (C.D. Cal. Nov. 23, 1994).
1678. *Id.*, slip op. at 7-10.
1679. 885 F. Supp. 1533 (N.D. Fla. 1995).

truthfully the policy either would not have been issued
or would have been issued on different terms),[1680]

- *American International Specialty Lines Insurance Co. v.
  Towers Financial Corp.*[1681] (granting summary judgment in favor of insurer: "Barnes argues that Towers
  made no misrepresentations to AISLIC to induce
  AISLIC to issue the 1992 D & O Policy and thus that
  the 1992 AISLIC D & O Policy should not be
  rescinded. However, Towers reiterated the information
  contained in the 1992 financial statements on the
  AISLIC application. . . . The Insurers have presented
  (in the form of Ferro's deposition testimony) that this
  information was false, and Barnes has offered nothing
  to contradict this. Therefore, Towers provided false
  information to AISLIC in the application for the 1992
  Policy. . . . Towers' misrepresentations regarding
  Towers' financial condition clearly were material to
  AISLIC's decision to issue the 1992-93 D & O policy
  . . . .");[1682] and

- *National Union Fire Insurance Co. v. Federal Deposit
  Insurance Corp.*[1683] (affirming grant of summary
  judgment in favor of insurer rescinding policy where
  financial statements provided by a bank to the insurer
  contained material misrepresentations and the insurer's
  risk of loss was increased by those misrepresentations).[1684]

---

1680. *Id.* at 1534, 1535-36.

1681. 1997 U.S. Dist. LEXIS 22610, 1997 WL 906427 (S.D.N.Y.
Sept. 12, 1997).

1682. 1997 U.S. Dist. LEXIS 22610, at *26-28, 1997 WL 906427,
at *8.

1683. 1995 Tenn. App. LEXIS 69, 1995 WL 48462 (Tenn. Ct.
App. Feb. 8, 1995), *permission to appeal denied*, 1995 Tenn. LEXIS 295
(Tenn. May 30, 1995).

1684. 1995 Tenn. App. LEXIS 69, at *5-11, 1995 WL 48462, at
*2-4.

Examples of cases resolving this question in favor of insureds include the following:

- *Federal Insurance Co. v. Oak Industries, Inc.*[1685] (granting partial summary judgment in favor of insured where the insurer "did not inquire into" and the insured "was under no duty to disclose its knowledge of any facts or circumstances which would give rise to a claim"),[1686]

- *National Union Fire Insurance Co. v. Continental Illinois Corp.*[1687] (granting insured's motion for judgment on the pleadings where financial statements attached to policy renewal applications allegedly included materially false information because "[b]y the terms of their own forms, neither [insurer] asked [the insured] to represent or warrant the truth of the financial statements. They merely asked [that] the statements be 'attached.' [The insured] did that. . . . Its disclosure gave each insurer the opportunity to decide which (if any) of the items so disclosed would be requested as added representations or warranties (over and above the answers to specific application questions)"),[1688]

- *Harristown Development Corp. v. International Insurance Co.*[1689] (granting insured's motion for summary judgment because request for knowledge or information held by any director or officer concerning "any negligent act, error, omission or breach of duty which he reasonably should expect could give rise to a claim against him" did not "ask about facts or circumstances that could lead to litigation" and "there is no duty to

---

1685. [1985-1986 Transfer Binder] Fed. Sec. L. Rep. (CCH) ¶ 92,519 (S.D. Cal. Feb. 3, 1986).

1686. *Id.* at 93,120.

1687. 643 F. Supp. 1434 (N.D. Ill. 1986).

1688. *Id.* at 1438, 1441 (footnote omitted).

1689. 1988 U.S. Dist. LEXIS 12791, 1988 WL 123149 (M.D. Pa. Nov. 15, 1988).

provide information which goes beyond the questions asked"; the court stated that "a background against which liability could spring" due to an acrimonious relationship between a corporation and another corporate entity "are not matters which would have been responsive to the questions asked, which focused upon tortious acts"),[1690]

- *National Union Fire Insurance Co. v. Walker*[1691] (denying insurer's summary judgment motion where corporate representative correctly represented that he had no knowledge or information regarding any act, error or omission that might give rise to a claim under the proposed policy, because this "greatly limited representation" was not a "corporate warranty as to the knowledge of all officers and directors" of the corporation),[1692]

- *Federal Deposit Insurance Corp. v. Mijalis*[1693] (rejecting contention that insured misrepresented that insured had no claims as of the date that the policy was issued because (1) the policy application did not define the term claim, (2) the insured's belief that the term claim did not include FDIC statements that various deficiencies in identified lending practices must be corrected, while incorrect, was not unreasonable, and (3) "[i]t is obvious" by the terms and conditions of the policy that the insurer was aware of the problems facing the insured and "[i]t cannot, therefore, be stated that the failure of the directors and officers to list specifically

---

1690. 1988 U.S. Dist. LEXIS 12791, at *9-13, 1988 WL 123149, at *3-5.

1691. 1989 U.S. Dist. LEXIS 6079, 1989 WL 56164 (W.D. Mo. May 24, 1989).

1692. 1989 U.S. Dist. LEXIS 6079, at *2-7, 1989 WL 56164, at *1-2.

1693. 800 F. Supp. 397 (W.D. La. 1992), *aff'd in part and rev'd in part on other grounds*, 15 F.3d 1314 (5th Cir. 1994).

the claims facing them was a material misrepresenta-tion"),[1694] and

- *Home Insurance Co. v. Spectrum Information Technolo-gies, Inc.*[1695] (holding, following a bench trial, that insured's failure to disclose an informal inquiry by the Securities and Exchange Commission did not constitute a material misrepresentation because no question on the insurers' policy application required disclosure of the SEC inquiry, and that even if there was a duty to disclose the SEC inquiry the information not disclosed was not material to the insurers' underwriting decisions in light of the prior course of dealings between the insurer and the insureds, the insurers' "full awareness of the facts" underlying the SEC inquiry, "the likeli-hood of an SEC inquiry" under the circumstances pres-ent in the case, and the insurers' willingness to insure the insureds "notwithstanding several other substantial risk factors").[1696]

The courts have divided (principally in cases not involving D & O insurance policies) with respect to whether responses to

---

1694. *Id.* at 403.

1695. 930 F. Supp. 825 (E.D.N.Y. 1996).

1696. *Id.* at 835-43; *see also In re UFG Int'l, Inc.*, 207 B.R. 793, 799-801 (Bankr. S.D.N.Y. 1997) (denying summary judgment motion by insureds in case where insurer sought rescission of insurance policies due to an alleged misrepresentation on policy application because, according to the insureds, the insurer did not materially rely upon the answer to the question that allegedly was answered falsely; according to the court, the insureds "have failed to show that there are no genuine issues of fact concerning whether AESIC materially relied on the answer to Question #22"); *Old Republic Ins. Co. v. Rexene Corp.*, 1990 Del. Ch. LEXIS 187, at *13, 16-19, 1990 WL 176791, at *5, 6-7 (Del. Ch. Nov. 5, 1990) (denying summary judgment motion by insurers seeking rescission of insurance policies due to the insured's alleged misrepresentations on policy applications in response to questions seeking information concerning contemplated acquisitions, leveraged buyouts, tender offers or mergers because "the facts relating to the Application questions at issue must be developed").

policy application questions seeking the disclosure of facts that might give rise to a claim are to be evaluated objectively based upon what the applicant knew or should have known,[1697] or subjectively based upon what the applicant in fact believed,[1698] or whether "even an innocent material misrepresentation voids the policy."[1699]

An insurer may waive its right to rescind a policy by failing to make inquiries concerning information "distinctly implied" in facts that are disclosed.[1700] An insurer also may waive its right to rescind a policy by failing to seek rescission in a timely manner after learning of misstatements and/or omissions.[1701]

    *b. Innocent Director Cases.* Several courts have focused upon the effect of a material misrepresentation or omission made by one

---

1697. *See International Surplus Lines Ins. Co. v. Wyoming Coal Refining Sys., Inc.*, 52 F.3d 901, 903-04 (10th Cir. 1995); *Mt. Airy Ins. Co. v. Thomas*, 954 F. Supp. 1073, 1079 (W.D. Pa. 1997); *International Ins. Co. v. Peabody Int'l Corp.*, 747 F. Supp. 477, 483 (N.D. Ill. 1990); *Evanston Ins. Co. v. Security Assurance Co.*, 715 F. Supp. 1405, 1413-14 (N.D. Ill. 1989); *Smith v. Neumann*, 682 N.E.2d 1245, 1254-55 (Ill. App. Ct. 1997); *Ratcliffe v. International Surplus Lines Ins. Co.*, 550 N.E.2d 1052, 1057-58 (Ill. App. Ct. 1990).

1698. *See Citizens Bank v. Western Employers Ins. Co.*, 865 F.2d 964, 966 (8th Cir. 1989).

1699. *See Fabric v. Provident Life & Accident Ins. Co.*, 115 F.3d 908, 913 (11th Cir. 1997); *First Nat'l Bank Holding Co. v. Fidelity & Deposit Co.*, 885 F. Supp. 1533, 1536-37 (N.D. Fla. 1995).

1700. *See Jaunich v. National Union Fire Ins. Co.*, 647 F. Supp. 209, 211-15 (N.D. Cal. 1986); Cal. Ins. Code § 336 (providing that the "right to information of material facts may be waived . . . by neglect to make inquiries as to such facts, where they are distinctly implied in other facts of which information is communicated").

1701. *See Republic Ins. Co. v. Masters, Mates & Pilots Pension Plan*, 77 F.3d 48, 53 (2d Cir. 1996) (finding no waiver); *Walbrook Ins. Co. Ltd. v. Spiegel*, [1993-1994 Transfer Binder] Fed. Sec. L. Rep. (CCH) ¶ 98,020, at 98,306-08 (C.D. Cal. Aug. 6, 1993) (finding no waiver); *Federal Ins. Co. v. Oak Indus., Inc.*, [1985-1986 Transfer Binder] Fed. Sec. L. Rep. (CCH) ¶ 92,519, at 93,120 (S.D. Cal. Feb. 3, 1986) (finding waiver).

director or officer upon the insurance coverage of "innocent" directors or officers.

The leading case is *Bird v. Penn Central Co.*[1702] In that case, Lloyd's sought to rescind a $10 million policy obtained by Penn Central Company two years before Penn Central's collapse in 1970. Lloyd's contended that the chairman of Penn Central's finance committee falsely represented in Penn Central's policy application that none of the directors and officers applying for coverage knew of any acts or omissions that "might afford valid grounds for any future claim."[1703] The court, denying a motion for summary judgment by outside directors who had had no knowledge of any probable claims at the time the policy was obtained, held that Lloyd's would be entitled to rescind the policy if it demonstrated at trial the materiality of the misrepresentations and that it had relied upon the misrepresentations.[1704]

The court based its decision upon the status of the innocent directors as third party beneficiaries whose rights could be no greater than the rights of the corporation. Accordingly, if the finance chairman's application responses were fraudulent, the court reasoned, this fraud would be imputed to his principal—the corporation—regardless of the innocence of third party beneficiaries.[1705] Alternatively, the court viewed the innocent directors as individually contracting parties, with "each insured . . . considered a separate principal for the purposes of agency law."[1706] Under this analysis, a factual question requiring the denial of summary judgment was raised with respect to each insured director concerning whether the finance committee chairman was authorized within the meaning of agency law to act on behalf of that director when he completed the application, a sufficient ground upon which summary

1702. 334 F. Supp. 255 (E.D. Pa. 1971), *reargument granted and decision adhered to*, 341 F. Supp. 291 (E.D. Pa. 1972).
1703. 334 F. Supp. at 257; 341 F. Supp. at 292.
1704. 334 F. Supp. at 262; 341 F. Supp. at 295-96.
1705. 334 F. Supp. at 261; 341 F. Supp. at 292, 294-95.
1706. 334 F. Supp. at 262.

judgment could be denied.[1707] The *Bird* court observed that "[w]hile we sympathize with movants' position, and recognize that innocent officers and directors are likely to suffer if the entire policy is voidable because of one man's fraudulent response, it must be recognized that plaintiff insurers are likewise innocent parties."[1708]

The court in *Shapiro v. American Home Assurance Co.*[1709] similarly held that material misrepresentations by Jack H. Shapiro, the former president of an insured corporation—including overstatements of the corporation's earnings and false statements that the former president knew of no acts or omissions by officers or directors that might give rise to a claim under the policy—defeated coverage under the policy to all insureds, including those directors who had no knowledge of the misrepresentations.[1710] The court rejected the agency analysis relied upon by the *Bird* court, however, on the ground that "an innocent director or officer, particularly an 'outsider,' may have no control over the individual who applies for insurance coverage. Thus, binding the directors as principals is somewhat fictional."[1711] Instead, the court relied upon the particular misrepresentation made in the application by the corporation's president:

> The language in the application form, which was part of the insurance contract, is straightforward. The form, in Question No. 14, inquires about knowledge of *any* officer or director concerning facts which might give rise to claims under the policy. Because of the likelihood of joint and several liability being imposed on all directors for the wrongdoing of one, the facts known by Shapiro were highly material not only to his potential liability, but to that of all other directors. Since Shapiro's answer misrepresented the risk incurred in insuring all those covered by the policy, it follows that American

---

1707. *Id.*
1708. 341 F. Supp. at 294.
1709. 584 F. Supp. 1245 (D. Mass. 1984).
1710. *Id.* at 1249, 1252.
1711. *Id.* at 1251-52.

Home can avoid responsibility to all the insureds on the basis of that misrepresentation.[1712]

The *Shapiro* court suggested that policies could be negotiated that would protect innocent directors from misrepresentations by other directors in return for higher premiums.[1713] In a subsequent decision in the same case (involving Securities Act liability policies rather than D & O policies), the court held that two innocent directors and officers were protected by severability provisions stating that the policies were to be construed as "separate contract[s] with each Insured," and that references "to the Insured shall be construed as referring only to that particular Insured, and the liability of the Insurer to such Insured shall be independent of its liability to any other Insured."[1714]

The court in *Atlantic Permanent Federal Savings & Loan Association v. American Casualty Co.*[1715] construed a similar provision, which stated that "this policy shall not be voided or rescinded and coverage shall not be excluded as a result of any untrue statement in the [application] form, except as to those persons making such statement or having knowledge of its untruth."[1716] The court held that this provision "was plainly designed to prevent misrepresentations made by the particular officers responsible for preparing an application from depriving their innocent colleagues of coverage."[1717]

The court in *Wedtech Corp. v. Federal Insurance Co.*[1718] also held that a policy was not "void *ab initio* with respect to each and every director regardless of whether he participated in the alleged fraudulent inducement."[1719] In support of this conclusion,

---

1712. *Id*. at 1252.

1713. 584 F. Supp. at 1252.

1714. *Shapiro v. American Home Assurance Co.*, 616 F. Supp. 900, 902, 903-05 (D. Mass. 1984).

1715. 839 F.2d 212 (4th Cir.), *cert. denied*, 486 U.S. 1056 (1988).

1716. *Id*. at 215.

1717. *Id*.

1718. 740 F. Supp. 214 (S.D.N.Y. 1990).

1719. *Id*. at 219.

the court pointed to language in the policy application stating that "no statement in the application or knowledge on the part of one insured is to be imputed to another insured in determining the availability of coverage" and that "the written application for coverage is to be construed as a separate application by each insured."[1720]

The courts in *INA Underwriters Insurance Co. v. D.H. Forde & Co.*,[1721] *National Union Fire Insurance Co. v. Sahlen*,[1722] *Mazur v. Gaudet*,[1723] *American International Specialty Lines Insurance Co. v. Towers Financial Corp.*[1724] and *National Union Fire Insurance Co. v. Federal Deposit Insurance Corp.*[1725] each followed the *Bird* and the first *Shapiro* decision.[1726] The courts in *Sahlen*, *Mazur* and *Towers* each pointed to the absence in those cases of clear severability provisions comparable to the provisions in the second Shapiro decision, *Atlantic Permanent* and *Wedtech*.[1727] As stated by the courts in *INA*, *Sahlen*, *Mazur* and *Towers*, "this result may seem unfair to those defendants who find themselves without coverage through no fault of their own," but "an equally unjust result would occur if the insurance company were required to supply coverage for a risk it never intended to insure."[1728] The courts in *National*

---

1720. *Id.*

1721. 630 F. Supp. 76 (W.D.N.Y. 1985).

1722. 807 F. Supp. 743 (S.D. Fla. 1992), *aff'd on other grounds*, 999 F.2d 1532 (11th Cir. 1993).

1723. 826 F. Supp. 188 (E.D. La. 1992).

1724. 1997 U.S. Dist. LEXIS 22610, 1997 WL 906427 (S.D.N.Y. Sept. 12, 1997).

1725. 1995 Tenn. App. LEXIS 69, at *24-25, 1995 WL 48462, at *8 (Tenn. Ct. App. Feb. 8, 1995), *permission to appeal denied*, 1995 Tenn. LEXIS 295 (Tenn. May 30, 1995).

1726. *INA*, 630 F. Supp. at 77; *Sahlen*, 807 F. Supp. at 746-47; *Mazur*, 826 F. Supp. at 193-95; *Towers*, 1997 U.S. Dist. LEXIS 22610, at *30-33, 1997 WL 906427, at *9-10.

1727. *Sahlen*, 807 F. Supp. at 746; *Mazur*, 826 F. Supp. at 194-95; *Towers*, 1997 U.S. Dist. LEXIS 22610, at *32-33, 1997 WL 906427, at *10.

1728. *INA*, 630 F. Supp. at 77; *Sahlen*, 807 F. Supp. at 747; *Mazur*, 826 F. Supp. at 195; *Towers*, 1997 U.S. Dist. LEXIS 22610, at *30-31, 1997 WL 906427, at *9.

*Union Fire Insurance Co. v. Seafirst Co.,*[1729] *Federal Savings &
Loan Insurance Corp. v. Burdette*[1730] and *International Insurance
Co. v. McMullan*[1731] each reached the result reached in the second
*Shapiro* decision, *Atlantic Permanent* and *Wedtech.*[1732]

The Eleventh Circuit in *Pacific Insurance Co. v. General
Development Corp.*[1733] noted a district court ruling directing an
insurer who contended that the governing policy was void due to
misrepresentations and omissions by the insureds to "pay the
Insured Defendants' defense costs as they are incurred until fraud,
dishonesty or criminal acts are established by a judgment or other
final adjudication or there is a final adjudication voiding or rescinding the policy."[1734] The Eleventh Circuit dismissed an appeal of
that ruling as moot due to an intervening conviction of the insureds
for fraud and conspiracy.[1735]

## C. Self-Insurance and Insurance Pooling Arrangements

Self-insurance of directors and officers typically is in the
form of a wholly-owned "captive" insurance subsidiary.[1736] Cap-

---

1729. 1987 U.S. Dist. LEXIS 14394 (W.D. Wash. Dec. 28, 1987).

1730. 718 F. Supp. 649 (E.D. Tenn. 1989).

1731. 1990 U.S. Dist. LEXIS 19940, 1990 WL 483731 (S.D. Miss.
Mar. 7, 1990).

1732. *Seafirst,* 1987 U.S. Dist. LEXIS 14394, at *14-18; *Burdette,*
718 F. Supp. at 657; *McMullen,* 1990 U.S. Dist. LEXIS 19940, at *14-
25, 1990 WL 483731, at *6-9.

1733. 28 F.3d 1093 (11th Cir. 1994).

1734. *Id.* at 1095.

1735. *Id.* at 1096.

1736. *See* John F. Olson & Josiah O. Hatch III, *Director and
Officer Liability: Indemnification and Insurance* §§ 9.02, 9.03 (1997);
Brenner, *BankAmerica Captive Offshore Insurer Raises Legality and Pro-
priety Questions,* Am. Banker, Apr. 26, 1985, at 1; Johnston, *D & O
Insurance Crisis: How to Fund Indemnification Arrangements,* 1 Insights:
The Corporate & Securities Law Advisor No. 2, Aug. 1987, at 3, 30-31;
Rovner, *Banks Win Approval to Form Captives for Insurance,* Legal
(continued...)

tive insurance subsidiaries of this type sometimes will be reinsured for a large portion of potential liability.[1737] Until the mid-1980s, captive insurance subsidiaries often were domiciled in offshore locations such as Bermuda, the Cayman Islands, the Bahamas or Barbados, which are free from U.S. insurance regulations.[1738] The Tax Reform Act of 1986, however, eliminated the most important tax advantages of offshore captives, and the Liability Risk Retention Act of 1986 preempted certain burdensome state insurance regulation provisions.[1739] As a result, more captive insurance subsidiaries are being established in the United States.[1740]

Single parent captive insurance arrangements have drawbacks, including limited resources and a need to accept poorly distributed risks.[1741] Captive insurance arrangements also may not be "insurance" within the meaning of the applicable state statute.[1742] Reimbursement from a captive insurance company that insures only its parent corporation may be viewed as indemnification rather than insurance, and thus may be subject to public policy restrictions upon indemnification that do not apply to insurance, such as, for example, the prohibition in many states, including Delaware,

---

1736. (...continued)
Times, Mar. 3, 1986, at 1; Schauer, *Ailing D & O Insurance Market Looks for Cure*, 6 Bus. Law. Update 1, 2 (Mar./Apr. 1986); Note, *Protecting Corporate Directors and Officers: Insurance and Other Alternatives*, 40 Vand. L. Rev. 775, 797-801 (1987).

1737. Rubenstein, *Why General Mills Is Suing Its Own Captive Insurance Company: Chasing The Reinsurance Pot*, 2 U.S. Bus. Litig. No. 7, Feb. 1997, at 1.

1738. *See* J. Olson & J. Hatch § 9.03, at 9-8; Johnston, Insights, Aug. 1987, at 31.

1739. *Id.* at 9–8-8.1; *see also* Mallen & Evans, *Surviving the Directors' and Officers' Liability Crisis: Insurance and the Alternatives*, 12 Del. J. Corp. L. 439, 467-68 (1988).

1740. J. Olson & J. Hatch § 9.03, at 9-8.1; Johnston, Insights, Aug. 1987, at 31; *Vermont: Land of Green Mountains and Self-Insurance*, Bus. Wk., Aug. 21, 1989, at 77.

1741. J. Olson & J. Hatch § 9.03, at 9-8.1.

1742. *See* Chapter V, Section B 1 (discussing state statutes authorizing insurance).

against indemnification of amounts paid to settle derivative actions.[1743] As two commentators have observed with respect to the Delaware statute:

> For instance, Section 145(b) does not permit indemnification for judgments or amounts in settlement in derivative suits, but Section 145(g) permits insuring against those amounts. If an insurer-subsidiary reimburses its parent's directors dollar for dollar for a judgment or settlement in a derivative action, it can be argued that the parent has paid the judgment, a result not permitted by Section 145(b). Since the subsidiary looks to the parent for capitalization, ultimately the parent corporation will be reimbursing its directors for the derivative judgment in favor of the parent corporation. It also could be argued that the distinction between indemnification and insurance, as it is preserved in the statute, has been eliminated, at least in the absence of risk sharing.[1744]

These commentators have concluded that a "powerful argument in favor of the 'equities'" of a public policy permitting a captive insurance arrangement is that "the parent corporation is or may be on the verge of losing its directors as a result of the inability to obtain D & O insurance elsewhere."[1745]

Other commentators have recognized that despite being a wholly owned subsidiary a captive insurance company often is "managed by insurance brokers or other professional insurance managers who understand underwriting risks, advise as to reserve requirements, and assist in administering claims."[1746] A captive insurance company, these commentators continue, often "issues policies and charges the parent premiums based on actuarial estimates of the likely future costs of covered claims."[1747] A captive

---

1743. *See* Chapter V, Section A 4 b.

1744. 1 R. Franklin Balotti & Jesse A. Finkelstein, *The Delaware Law of Corporations and Business Organizations* § 4.28, at 4-107 (3d ed. 1998).

1745. *Id.; see also* Johnston, Insights, Aug. 1987, at 30 ("it is at least arguable that a properly organized captive . . . is an 'insurance company,' which is all the indemnification statute requires").

1746. J. Olson & J. Hatch § 9.03, at 9-3.

1747. *Id.*

insurance company also generally models "[p]olicy types and terms
. . . on those available in the commercial market, although exclusions and limitations which are objectionable to the parent may be
omitted."[1748] "Why, then," these commentators ask, "is such an
arrangement not the same as insurance?"[1749] These commentators
conclude as follows:

> If the captive is managed in a professional and actuarially
> sound manner, and the premiums paid to it and cost of capi-
> tal contributed do not greatly exceed the cost of comparable
> commercial insurance to the parent, then what public policy
> is violated if the broader statutory authorization for insurance
> coverage, such as Delaware Corporations Code § 145(g), is
> recognized as the relevant limitation? The case for referring
> to the broader insurance authority is particularly compelling
> where the captive reinsures a portion of its risks in the com-
> mercial insurance market or the captive insures a substantial
> amount of unrelated risks. Then, the key insurance element
> of risk sharing is clearly introduced.[1750]

California has addressed this issue by amending its indemnification and insurance statute to authorize corporations chartered in
that state to own "all or a portion" of a company issuing insurance
policies so long as (1) the corporation's charter authorizes indemnification pursuant to the statute's non-exclusivity provision and the
insurance is limited in the same ways that indemnification pursuant
to the non-exclusivity provision is required to be limited, or (2) the
insurance company is organized and regulated by the insurance
laws of the state of its organization, procedures for processing
claims are in place that do not permit the insurance company "to be
subject to the direct control of the corporation that purchased the
policy," and the policy provides for "some manner of risk sharing."[1751] A substantial number of other states also have enacted
statutes that in one form or another authorize alternatives to D & O

1748. *Id.*
1749. *Id.* at 9-4.
1750. *Id.* at 9-8.1.
1751. Cal. Gen. Corp. Law § 317(i).

insurance such as self-insurance.[1752] The General Corporation Law Section of the Delaware Bar Association rejected such a change in Delaware's statute in 1986 on the ground that "'insurance' without any genuine risk sharing" is "fundamentally circular."[1753]

The creation of a captive insurer also may have tax consequences. "Premiums" paid to a captive insurer typically are not deductible for federal income tax purposes because captive insurance arrangements generally do not involve an economic shift or distribution of risk.[1754] "Neither the Internal Revenue Code nor treasury regulations define the term 'insurance,' and the lack of a precise definition has resulted in extensive litigation concerning the proper tax treatment of payments made by parent corporations directly or indirectly to captive insurers."[1755] As discussed below, a series of decisions—most notably the Sixth Circuit's decision in *Humana Inc. v. Commissioner*,[1756] the Seventh Circuit's

---

1752. *See* Ala. Bus. Corp. Act § 10-2B-8.57; Ariz. Bus. Corp. Law § 10-857; Colo. Bus. Corp. Act § 7-109-108; Haw. Bus. Corp. Act § 415-35(h); La. Bus. Corp. Law § 12:83(F); Md. Gen. Corp. Law § 2-418(k); Nev. Gen. Corp. Law §§ 78.752(1), (2)(b); N.J. Bus. Corp. Act § 14A:3-5(9); N.M. Bus. Corp. Act § 53-11-4.1(J); Ohio Gen. Corp. Law § 1701.13(E)(7); Pa. Bus. Corp. Law § 1746(a), Pa. Corp. Law § 518(a); Tex. Bus. Corp. Act § 2.02-1(R); Utah Bus. Corp. Act § 16-10a-908.

1753. R. Balotti & J. Finkelstein § 4.28, at 4-107 n. 542, § 4.29, at 4-109; Veasey & Finkelstein, *New Delaware Statute: Allows Limits on Director Liability and Modernizes Indemnification Protection*, 6 Bus. Law. Update 1, 2 (July/Aug. 1986); *see also* Chapter V, Section A 4 b.

1754. *See* Rev. Rul. 77-316, 1977-2 C.B. 53; *Malone & Hyde, Inc. v. Commissioner*, 62 F.3d 835, 840-43 (6th Cir. 1995); *Gulf Oil Corp. v. Commissioner*, 914 F.2d 396, 411 (3d Cir. 1990); *Clougherty Packing Co. v. Commissioner*, 811 F.2d 1297, 1298-1307 (9th Cir. 1987); *Stearns-Roger Corp., Inc. v. United States*, 774 F.2d 414, 415-17 (10th Cir. 1985); *Carnation Co. v. Commissioner*, 640 F.2d 1010, 1012-13 (9th Cir.), *cert. denied*, 454 U.S. 965 (1981).

1755. *Kidde Indus., Inc. v. United States*, 40 Fed. Cl. 42, 46 (Fed. Cl. 1997).

1756. 881 F.2d 247 (6th Cir. 1989).

decision in *Sears, Roebuck & Co. v. Commissioner*[1757] and the Ninth Circuit's decision in *AMERCO, Inc. v. Commissioner*[1758]— illustrate that tax deductions will be allowed where an element of *insurance*—spreading of risk among unrelated parties—as opposed to simple *indemnification*" is present."[1759]

The court in *Humana Inc. v. Commissioner*[1760] held that premiums paid by Humana Inc. to a wholly-owned insurance subsidiary, Health Care Indemnity, did not constitute deductible insurance premiums, but that premiums paid by several operating subsidiaries of Humana to Health Care did involve sufficient risk shifting and risk distribution to constitute deductible insurance premiums on a consolidated tax return filed by Humana and its operating subsidiaries (but not Health Care).[1761] The court stated that Health Care was fully capitalized and recognized as an insurance company by Colorado, that Health Care received no capital from Humana or from Humana's operating subsidiaries (other than Health Care's initial capitalization), and that Humana and its operating subsidiaries had entered into bona fide arm's length contracts with Health Care. The court also stated that Health Care, although a captive insurer, was insuring several separate corporations within the affiliated group—an arrangement that permitted losses to be spread among distinct corporate entities.[1762] The court thus rejected the Internal Revenue Service's request that all of the Humana entities be treated as one "economic family" and stated that "[w]e . . . look solely to the relationship between the affiliates and Health Care" for purposes of assessing the deductibility of the affiliates' premiums to Health Care.[1763]

---

1757. 972 F.2d 858 (7th Cir. 1992).

1758. 979 F.2d 162 (9th Cir. 1992).

1759. Olson, *The D & O Insurance Gap: Strategies for Coping*, Legal Times, Mar. 3, 1986, at 25.

1760. 881 F.2d 247 (6th Cir. 1989).

1761. *Id*. at 251-57.

1762. *Id*. at 253, 257.

1763. *Id*. at 252.

The court in *Sears, Roebuck & Co. v. Commissioner*[1764] held that premiums paid by Sears, Roebuck & Co. to its Allstate Insurance Company subsidiary in return for insurance coverage constituted insurance for federal income tax purposes. The court explained that during the relevant time period 99.75 percent of Allstate's premiums came from customers other than Sears and that policies issued by Allstate to Sears were comparable to policies issued to insureds other than Sears. Premiums were calculated by Allstate for Sears in the same manner premiums were calculated by Allstate for other insureds.[1765]

The court rejected the Commissioner of Internal Revenue's contention that "'insurance' from a subsidiary is self-insurance by another name."[1766] The Commissioner reasoned as follows:

> Moving funds from one pocket to another does nothing, even if the pocket is separately incorporated. If Subsidiary pays out a dollar, Parent loses the same dollar. Nothing depends on whether Subsidiary has other customers; there is still a one-to-one correspondence between its payments and Parent's wealth. So although Allstate may engage in the pooling of risks, and thus *write* insurance, Sears did not purchase the shifting of risks, and thus did not *buy* insurance.[1767]

Instead, the court focused upon the pooling of risks by Allstate:

> Allstate puts Sear's risks in a larger pool, performing one of the standard insurance functions in a way that a captive insurer does not. More: Allstate furnishes Sears with the same hedging and administration services it furnishes to all other customers. It establishes reserves, pays state taxes, participates in state risk-sharing pools (for insolvent insurers), and so on, just as it would if Sears were an unrelated company. States recognize the transaction as "real" insurance for purposes of mandatory insurance laws (several of the policies were purchased to comply with such laws for Sear's auto fleet, and for worker's compensation in Texas). From Allstate's perspective this is real insurance in every way. It must

---

1764. 972 F.2d 858 (7th Cir. 1992).
1765. *Id*. at 860.
1766. *Id*. at 861.
1767. *Id*.

maintain the reserves required by state law (not to mention prudent management). Sears cannot withdraw these reserves on whim, and events that affect their size for good or ill therefore do not translate directly to Sear's balance sheet.[1768]

The court added that the transaction between Sears and Allstate has "substance independent of tax effects. It increases the size of Allstate's pool and so reduces the ratio between expected and actual losses; it puts Allstate's reserves at risk; it assigns claims administration to persons with a comparative advantage at that task."[1769]

*AMERCO, Inc. v. Commissioner*[1770] involved AMERCO, Inc. and approximately 250 subsidiaries that filed consolidated tax returns (the "AMERCO Group") and Republic Western Insurance Company, a wholly-owned AMERCO subsidiary that issued insurance policies at normal commercial rates to members of the AMERCO Group and to unrelated parties.[1771] The court allowed AMERCO to deduct the premiums it paid to Republic. The court explained that "we are satisfied that a parent and its subsidiaries can shift risk to a captive insurer, where that insurer has significant unrelated business"[1772] Here, the court stated, "if only AMERCO were looked at, its share of Republic's business was under one percent and if the whole AMERCO Group were considered, the share was from 26 percent to 48 percent of that business."[1773] The court concluded that this "left sufficient unrelated business to create a true pool and to allow for true risk-shifting."[1774]

---

1768. *Id.* at 863.

1769. *Id.* at 864.

1770. 979 F.2d 162 (9th Cir. 1992).

1771. *Id.* at 163-64.

1772. *Id.* at 168.

1773. *Id.*

1774. *Id.; see also Ocean Drilling & Exploration Co. v. United States*, 988 F.2d 1135, 1137, 1150-53 (Fed. Cir. 1993) (adopting Tax Court decision reprinted as Appendix to decision, which held that a wholly-owned insurer had "unrelated business of approximately 44 and 66 percent for the two years at issue" and that this unrelated business "suffi-

(continued...)

In light of the considerations summarized above, commentators have recommended that corporations that choose to utilize a captive insurance arrangement should take measures such as (1) maintaining separate corporate identities for the corporation and the captive insurer, (2) ensuring sufficient capitalization of the captive insurer so that the insurer can operate without periodically turning to its parent for funding over and above reasonable premiums, (3) placing independent professional managers in control of the insurer's business, (4) conducting the insurer's business in accordance with standard trade practices, including standard policy forms, premium charges, exclusions, claims determination procedures and limitations upon liability, (5) arranging for substantial third party ownership of the insurer, (6) obtaining reinsurance contracts from established reinsurers, and (7) insuring corporations other than just the captive insurer's parent.[1775]

Federal legislation was proposed in 1996 and again in 1997 with respect to taxation of captive insurance companies. The proposed legislation would require that premiums paid by a corporation to an insurer, 10 percent or more of whose voting stock is owned by the corporation, could not be deducted except to the extent that the insurance was reinsured with a third party insurer unrelated to the insured or the 10 percent or more owned insurer.[1776] Rather, the 10 percent or more owned insurer would

---

1774. (...continued)
ciently spreads risk so as to constitute risk distribution"); *Crawford Fitting Co. v. United States*, 606 F. Supp. 136, 137-39, 145-46 (N.D. Ohio 1985) (same result); *Hospital Corp. of Am. v. Commissioner*, 74 T.C.M. (CCH) 1020, 1033-42, T.C.M. (RIA) 97,482, 97-3232-43 (T.C. Oct. 27, 1997) (same result); *cf. Kidde Indus., Inc. v. United States*, 40 Fed. Cl. 42, 44-59, 67 (Fed. Cl. 1997) (reaching different conclusions with respect to different payments in different time periods).

1775. *See* R. Balotti & J. Finkelstein § 4.28, at 4-108; J. Olson & J. Hatch, *Director and Officer Liability: Indemnification and Insurance* § 9.03, at 9–7-8; Mallen & Evans, 12 Del. J. Corp. L. at 466-67; Note, 40 Vand. L. Rev. at 801.

1776. Joint Committee on Taxation Staff Description of Revenue Provisions Contained in President Clinton's Fiscal Year 1998 Budget
(continued...)

include in income the excess, if any, of the premiums received from the corporation and the claims paid to the corporation, and the corporation would include in income claims payments that exceeded premium payments.[1777]

Insurance pooling consortium arrangements solve many of the problems raised by captive insurance companies by spreading risk among a group of corporations that join together to form an insurance company to insure all members of the group.[1778] One prominent captive pooling arrangement formed in the mid-1980s was A.C.E. Insurance Co. Ltd., an entity organized by over 30 major United States corporations, including Chase Manhattan, Dow Chemical, Ford, General Electric, IBM, Shell Oil, U.S. Steel and Upjohn.[1779] Accounting firms, law firms, insurance brokerage and advisory firms and bank holding companies also have entered into similar captive pooling arrangements, often limited to a single industry or profession.[1780] Some of these arrangements offer pri-

---

1776. (...continued)
Proposal (JCS-10-97) (Apr. 16, 1997), *reprinted in* Daily Tax Report (BNA) No. 74, at L-30, L-59 (Apr. 17, 1997); Joint Committee on Taxation Staff Description of Revenue Provisions Contained in President Clinton's Fiscal Year 1997 Budget Proposal (JCS-2-96) (Mar. 27, 1996), *reprinted in* Daily Tax Report (BNA) No. 60, at L-1, L-33 (Mar. 28, 1996).

1777. *Id.*

1778. *See* J. Olson & J. Hatch § 9.03, at 9–8-8.3; Milligan, *The Return of the Captive*, Institutional Investor, Mar. 1986, at 187; Note, 40 Vand. L. Rev. at 801-03.

1779. *See* Hilder, *Big U.S. Firms Form Liability Insurer*, Wall St. J., Dec. 23, 1985, at 6; Milligan, Institutional Investor, Mar. 1986, at 187.

1780. *See* J. Olson & J. Hatch § 9.03, at 9-8.2 & n.17; Berton, *Group of 27 Medium-Sized Audit Firms Establishes an Offshore Liability Insurer*, Wall St. J., Aug. 15, 1986, at 36 (reporting on a captive insurer formed by a group of accounting firms); Rovner, *Banks Win Approval to Form Captives for Insurance*, Legal Times, Mar. 3, 1986, at 1 (reporting plans of two groups of bank holding companies to create captive insurance companies); Taravella, *Alternative Facilities Easing D & O Market*, Bus. Ins., Oct. 20, 1986, at 26 (listing nine captive insurance groups).

mary coverage, some offer only excess coverage, and some offer the directors and officers portion but not the corporate reimbursement portion of the typical D & O policy.[1781]

Consortium pooling arrangements "are not a funding panacea."[1782] "[T]hey are expensive to establish, carry some cost to operate, and, as a practical matter, are available primarily to well-established companies or members of well-organized industry and trade groups which have both substantial resources and good loss experience."[1783] Substantial up-front costs must be incurred by the organizers, adequate capital must be invested, and the owner/insureds generally must be willing to commit themselves to the pooling arrangement for an extended period of time during which market conditions may change and particular insureds in the consortium may have adverse law experiences. Consensus decision-making, which can be difficult in groups including multiple corporations, also is required.[1784] Finally, premiums paid to a consortium that produce benefits for the future (for example, by "front-loading" premium payments in order to establish a reserve) do not qualify as deductible business expenses in the tax year that these payments are made.[1785]

## D. The D & O Crisis of the Mid-1980s: The Crisis, the Responses and the Current Market

### 1. The Crisis

The market for directors and officers liability insurance reached a state of crisis in the mid-1980s.[1786] Premiums sky-

---

1781. *See* J. Olson & J. Hatch § 9.03, at 9-8.2.

1782. *Id.* at 9-8.3.

1783. *Id.*

1784. *Id.;* Milligan, Institutional Investor, Mar. 1986, at 187; Note, 40 Vand. L. Rev. at 802-03.

1785. *Black Hills Corp. v. Commissioner*, 73 F.3d 799, 803-07 (8th Cir. 1996); J. Olson & J. Hatch § 9.03, at 9-8.3.

1786. *See generally* John F. Olson & Josiah O. Hatch III, *Director and Officer Liability: Indemnification and Insurance* §§ 4.11, 10.02

(continued...)

rocketed,[1787] deductibles increased at an extraordinary rate,[1788] coverage shrank,[1789] and some insurance companies terminated their D & O programs.[1790] At the same time, policy durations became shorter,[1791] and the policies that were sold included new exclusions,[1792] including, for example, the takeover, insured versus insured and regulatory exclusions discussed earlier in this Chapter.[1793]

---

1786. (...continued)

(1997); Romano, *What Went Wrong with Directors' and Officers' Liability Insurance?*, 14 Del. J. Corp. L. 1, 1-9 (1989); *The Job Nobody Wants: Outside Directors Find That the Risks and Hassles Just Aren't Worth It*, Bus. Wk., Sept. 8, 1986, at 56; Barnhart & Hodge, *Gloomy News About 'D & O'*, Chi. Trib., Jan. 15, 1986, § 3, at 1; Fowler, *Scarce Corporate Directors*, N.Y. Times, Jan. 7, 1986, at D20; Galante, *Corporate Board-room Woes Grow*, Nat'l L.J., Aug. 4, 1986, at 1; Hilder, *Liability Insurance is Difficult to Find Now for Directors, Officers*, Wall St. J., July 10, 1985, at 1; Ipsen, *The Crisis in Directors and Officers Insurance*, Institutional Investor, Aug. 1985, at 231; Lewin, *Director Insurance Drying Up*, N.Y. Times, Mar. 7, 1986, at D1; Schatz, *Directors Feel the Legal Heat*, N.Y. Times, Dec. 15, 1985, § 3 at 12; Taravella & Shapiro, *Psst . . . Do You Know a D & O Insurer?*, Bus. Ins., July 29, 1985, at 1; Verespej, *Boardroom Roulette*, Ind. Wk., Aug. 10, 1987, at 47.

1787. *1985 Wyatt Directors and Officers Liability Survey* 17-20 (1985) *("1985 Wyatt Survey")*; *1984 Wyatt Directors and Officers Liability Survey* 31-37 (1984) *("1984 Wyatt Survey")*; Lyons, *Everybody Pays*, Forbes, Aug. 6, 1990, at 46 ("premiums rose almost thirteenfold between 1984 and 1988").

1788. *1985 Wyatt Survey* at 13-16; *1984 Wyatt Survey* at 22-24.

1789. *1985 Wyatt Survey* at 9-12; *1984 Wyatt Survey* at 18-21; Lewin, N.Y. Times, Mar. 7, 1986, at D1 ("[t]he amount of coverage [corporations] can get has been cut drastically, from as much as $50 million to $150 million last year to $10 million to $35 million").

1790. Hilder, Wall St. J., July 10, 1985, at 1; Ipsen, Institutional Investor, Aug. 1985, at 231; Taravella & Shapiro, Bus. Ins., July 29, 1985, at 1.

1791. *1985 Wyatt Survey* at 1.

1792. *1985 Wyatt Survey* at 21-25; *1984 Wyatt Survey* at 22-24.

1793. *See* Chapter V, Sections B 9 b-g.

Most troubling of all to directors and officers, D & O insurance in sufficient amounts and for reasonable premiums became unavailable for many corporations. As one commentator noted in 1985:

> For corporate risk managers, the D & O market has become nightmarishly treacherous. Luckier risk managers now face premiums that range from two to ten times what they were last year. If they aren't so lucky, they may not be able to find insurance at any price, or they may be handed a policy so riddled with exclusionary clauses as to be virtually worthless anyway. And just to keep everyone on their toes, not only are the once standard three-year policies a thing of the dim and delightful past, but in this fast-changing, fickle market, even a one year policy is, as one broker says, "only as good as its cancellation clause. These days, policies are good for 30, 60 or 90 days."[1794]

As another observer concluded in 1986, "[w]ith expanded exclusions, the new, larger deductible amounts, and vulnerability to early cancellation by a nervous insurer, even those corporations which do not 'go naked' may be clothed in no more than a D & O bikini."[1795]

The D & O crisis of the mid-1980s was the product of historically low D & O insurance premiums and claims payments and the increasing number and size of corporate and securities claims.[1796] One consulting firm discovered that 18.6 percent of

---

1794. Ipsen, Institutional Investor, Aug. 1985, at 231.

1795. Olson, *The D & O Insurance Gap: Strategies for Coping*, Legal Times, Mar. 3, 1986, at 25; *see also* J. Olson & J. Hatch § 10.02, at 10-5 n.11 ("[i]n 1984, insurance brokers could reportedly choose from well over 30 carriers, and limits of up to $200 million were available; by mid-1986, the number of insurers had shrunk to a handful and $50 million was a realistic maximum for a large company"); Mallen & Evans, *Surviving the Directors' and Officers' Liability Crisis: Insurance and the Alternatives*, 12 Del. J. Corp. L. 439, 439-41 (1988); Romano, 14 Del. J. Corp. L. at 1-2, 3-9; Note, *Protecting Corporate Directors and Officers: Insurance and Other Alternatives*, 40 Vand. L. Rev. 775, 775-82 (1987).

1796. *See* Romano, 14 Del. J. Corp. L. at 13-21; Hilder, Wall St.

(continued...)

the companies it surveyed for a 1984 survey had experienced claims against their directors—a 182 percent increase over the 7.1 percent figure this consulting firm had found in a 1974 survey. At the same time, according to this survey, the average cost of defending a claim rose from $181,500 per claim in 1974 to $461,000 in 1984, the percentage of claims paying over $1 million rose from 4.8 percent to 8.3 percent, and the average total cost per claim went from $586,500 to $1,044,000.[1797]

Following this survey's completion, the D & O insurance market was rocked by the Delaware Supreme Court's 1985 decision in *Smith v. Van Gorkom*,[1798] which held the directors of Trans Union Corporation liable for acting without due care when in good faith they agreed to sell Trans Union for a price representing an almost 50 percent premium over the prevailing market price of Trans Union stock.[1799] The case was settled for a $23.5 million payment, including a $10 million payment by either Trans Union's or the individual directors' insurance carrier and a $13.5 million payment by Trans Union's acquiror.[1800] A similar effect upon the D & O market was caused by suits such as those by Chase Manhattan and Seattle-First National Bank against their own corporate officers and employees for alleged wrongdoing that caused the corporation to suffer losses.[1801] The Chase action was settled in return

---

1796. (...continued)
J., July 10, 1985, at 1; *see also* Mallen & Evans, 12 Del. J. Corp. L. at 441-43 (discussing problems during this period in insurance industry as a whole).

1797. *1984 Wyatt Survey* at 4-15; Lewin, N.Y. Times, Mar. 7, 1986, at D4.

1798. 488 A.2d 858 (Del. 1985).

1799. *See* Chapter II, Section A 4 c.

1800. Perkins, *Proposed Trans Union Settlement: Directors to Contribute to $23.5 Million Settlement Fund*, Directorship, Sept. 1, 1985, at 1; Marsh, *Pritzkers Foot Directors' Bill for Trans Union Settlement*, Crain's Chi. Bus., Aug. 12, 1985, at 19.

1801. *See* Chapter V, Section B 9 c (discussing *Chase* and *Seafirst* lawsuits and the insured versus insured exclusion that developed as result of lawsuits such as the *Chase* and *Seafirst* lawsuits).

for a payment of $32.5 million by insurance carriers.[1802] The Sea-first action was settled for $110 million but with recovery limited to the amount that could be collected from the corporation's insurers.[1803]

D & O insurers' fears were fueled further by the many contests for corporate control that were fought during the 1980s because contests for control "typically spur a flurry of lawsuits by shareholders and others."[1804] The evolution of the Racketeer Influenced and Corrupt Organizations Act ("RICO"),[1805] particularly after the United States Supreme Court's 1985 decision in *Sedima, S.P.R.L. v. Imrex Co.*[1806] into a "tool for everyday fraud cases brought against 'respected and legitimate enterprises'" rather than the "archetypal, intimidating mobster,"[1807] also created potentially massive exposure for corporate directors.[1808]

## 2. Responses

Corporations and state legislatures developed several general approaches to the problems caused by the D & O insurance crisis of the mid 1980s. States adopted statutes that limit director liability and expand the power of corporations to grant indemnification and

---

1802. *See Fox v. Chase Manhattan Corp.*, 11 Del. J. Corp. L. 888, 889 (Del. Ch. Dec. 6, 1985); Sloane, *Insurer-Management Liability Rift Seen Growing*, N.Y. Times, Dec. 19, 1985, at D8.

1803. *See Seafirst Settles Suit Against Five*, N.Y. Times, July 9, 1986, at D4; Galante, *Corporate Boardroom Woes Grow*, Nat'l L.J., Aug. 4, 1986, at 1; *see also National Union Fire Ins. Co. v. Seafirst Corp.*, No. C85-396R, slip op. at 9-16 (W.D. Wash. Mar. 19, 1986) (available on LEXIS without file number) (holding that insurance policy covered actions by Seafirst against its directors and officers), *aff'd mem.*, 804 F.2d 146 (9th Cir. 1986); Parks, *Insurer Settles Seattle Bank's Liability Claim*, Am. Banker, Apr. 26, 1988, at 2.

1804. Hertzberg, *Insurers Beginning to Refuse Coverage on Directors, Officers in Takeover Cases*, Wall St. J., Jan. 20, 1986, at 3.

1805. 18 U.S.C. §§ 1961–1968.

1806. 473 U.S. 479 (1985).

1807. *Id.* at 499.

1808. *See* Galante, *Corporate Boardroom Woes Grow*, Nat'l L.J., Aug. 4, 1986, at 1.

purchase new alternatives to insurance. Corporations adopted certificate of incorporation, bylaw and contract provisions that maximize indemnification rights by requiring indemnification and advancement to the full extent permitted by law. Corporations also adopted funding mechanisms and entered into new types of self-insurance and insurance pooling arrangements.

These approaches to director protection constitute important elements of the legal environment in which directors serve today and are discussed in Chapter II and earlier sections of this Chapter. These approaches therefore are summarized only briefly below.

*a. Statutes Limiting Director Liability.* Since the mid-1980s, states have enacted statutes intended to protect directors from liability in certain situations. Most prominent among these statutes is Section 102(b)(7) of Delaware's General Corporation Law. As discussed more fully in Chapter II,[1809] Section 102(b)(7) authorizes the adoption by shareholders of certificate of incorporation provisions eliminating or limiting a director's liability to the corporation or its stockholders for money damages for breaches of fiduciary duty so long as such provisions do not apply to (1) any breach of the director's duty of loyalty, (2) "acts or omissions not in good faith or which involve intentional misconduct or a knowing violation of law," (3) unlawful payments of dividends or unlawful stock purchases or redemptions, and (4) "any transaction from which the director derived an improper personal benefit."[1810]

Many states have enacted statutes modeled to a greater or a lesser extent upon this Delaware statute.[1811] The statutes and similar provisions in the Model Business Corporation Act[1812] and Principles of Corporate Governance: Analysis and Recommendations[1813] are discussed in Chapter II.[1814] Another type of stat-

---

1809. *See* Chapter II, Section A 7.

1810. Del. Gen. Corp. Law § 102(b)(7).

1811. *See* Chapter II, Section A 7.

1812. 1 Model Bus. Corp. Act Annotated § 2.02(b)(4) (3d ed. 1996).

1813. 2 Principles of Corporate Governance: Analysis and Recommendations § 7.19 (1994).

ute adopted by some states tightens the standard of culpability for directors of all corporations chartered in these states. These statutes also are discussed in Chapter II.[1815]

On the federal level, the Private Securities Litigation Reform Act of 1995[1816] seeks to limit federal securities law claims against directors and officers. According to its drafters, this statute was "prompted by significant evidence of abuse in private securities lawsuits" and "implements needed procedural protections to discourage frivolous litigation."[1817] Among other things, the statute adopts a "uniform and more stringent pleading requirements to curtail the filing of meritless lawsuits."[1818]

*b. Statutes Increasing the Availability of Indemnification and Insurance.* Other statutes adopted by many states since the mid-1980s focus upon maximizing indemnification rights. These statutes do this by allowing corporations to indemnify amounts paid to settle and/or judgments in actions by or in the right of the corporation under certain circumstances and by expanding non-exclusivity provisions. These statutes are discussed earlier in this Chapter.[1819] Other statutes adopted since the mid-1980s protect directors by permitting outside funding arrangements and self-insurance and insurance pooling arrangements. These statutes also are discussed earlier in this Chapter.[1820]

*c. Charter, Bylaw and Contract Provisions Maximizing Indemnification Rights.* Corporations have sought to maximize indemnification rights by adopting charter, bylaw and contract provisions requiring mandatory indemnification and/or advancement

---

1814. (...continued)

1814. *See* Chapter II, Section A 7.

1815. *See* Chapter II, Section A 7.

1816. Pub. L. No. 104-67, 109 Stat. 737 (1995).

1817. H.R. Conf. Rep. No. 104-369, 104th Cong., 1st Sess. 31, 31 (1995), *reprinted in* 1995 U.S.C.C.A.N. 730, 730-31.

1818. H.R. Conf. Rep. No. 104-369 at 41, *reprinted in* 1995 U.S.C.C.A.N. at 740.

1819. *See* Chapter V, Sections A 4 b and A 10.

1820. *See* Chapter V, Sections A 12 and C.

whenever indemnification and/or advancement is permitted by law.[1821] Examples of cases requiring indemnification or advancement pursuant to such provisions are noted in the discussion of mandatory indemnification and advancement earlier in this Chapter.[1822] As noted following the discussions of those cases, care must be taken in adopting such provisions because corporations may find themselves in disputes with former directors and officers (and in some cases employees) seeking indemnification or advancement for the defense of claims asserted against them—sometimes by the corporation itself—for conduct that the corporation's board has determined to be contrary to the best interests of the corporation.[1823]

The practical value of charter, bylaw and contract provisions maximizing indemnification rights depends upon the corporation's financial resources: "For the established, financially solid corporation indemnification agreements afford meaningful and reliable protection for directors and officers. For the newly formed or thinly capitalized company, the protection of the indemnity agreement may be illusory."[1824] Thus, for corporations that are not financially capable of making indemnification payments, "indemnity agreements may not be a meaningful substitute for D & O liability insurance."[1825]

---

1821. *See* Chapter V, Section A 3 b and A 5 b.

1822. *Id.*

1823. *Id.*

1824. Mallen & Evans, *Surviving the Directors' and Officers' Liability Crisis: Insurance and the Alternatives*, 12 Del. J. Corp. L. 439, 466 (1988).

1825. *Id. See generally In re ENSTAR Group, Inc.*, 170 B.R. 173, 176-77 (Bankr. M.D. Ala. 1994) (where an indemnity agreement provided that the corporation was not liable to make any indemnification payment where a payment had been made under a valid and collectible insurance policy, and where the directors, following the corporation's bankruptcy, assigned their indemnification rights to the insurer in exchange for payment by the insurer, the insurer could not collect against the corporation's estate pursuant to charter and bylaw provisions providing for indemnification to the "fullest extent permitted by law" because such a charter and

(continued...)

*d. Funding Mechanisms.* Corporations also have sought to maximize indemnification rights by establishing outside funding mechanisms that segregate indemnification and advancement funds and automatically permit the release of these funds whenever certain procedures are followed. One example of this type of funding mechanism is a trust fund set up to release assets upon a determination by an independent trustee that a claimant is entitled to indemnification. Another example is a letter of credit that requires a bank or other third party to take the risk that the corporation will not pay the indemnification (for example, because of bankruptcy or a new board's refusal to pay following a change in control).[1826]

As with charter, bylaw and contract provisions maximizing indemnification rights, funding mechanisms dependent upon corporate assets provide directors and officers meaningful protection only if the corporation is financially capable of making indemnification payments.[1827]

*e. Self-Insurance and Insurance Pooling Arrangements.* Corporations also responded to the D & O crisis of the mid-1980s by developing alternatives to D & O insurance, such as self-insurance and insurance pooling arrangements.[1828] Like the other responses to the D & O crisis of the mid-1980s, these alternatives to traditional insurance are discussed earlier in this Chapter.[1829]

---

1825. (...continued)
bylaw provision "in no way prevents the directors and officers from specifically agreeing not to enforce the right against [the corporation] once the claim has been satisfied by a 'valid and collectible insurance policy'").

1826. *See* Chapter V, Section A 12.

1827. Mallen & Evans, *Surviving the Directors' and Officers' Liability Crisis: Insurance and the Alternatives*, 12 Del. J. Corp. L. 439, 466 (1988).

1828. *See* 1994 Wyatt Directors and Officers Liability Survey 3 (1994) ("Many companies reporting large commercial insurance deductibles used subsidiary insurance companies (captives) or other devices to finance a portion of the directors and officers liability risk").

1829. *See* Chapter V, Section C.

## 3.   The Current Market

D & O insurance has been somewhat more available since the late 1980s.[1830] One consulting firm's standardized premium index (established at a value of 100 for the average D & O policy, measured in terms of policy limits, corporate reimbursement deductibles and other coverage features) indicates the following leveling off of premiums:

### Historical Premium Index at the Median Level

| Year | Median |
|------|--------|
| 1974 | 100 |
| 1976 | 81 |
| 1978 | 103 |
| 1980 | 99 |
| 1982 | 71 |
| 1984 | 54 |
| 1986 | 682 |
| 1988 | 746 |
| 1990 | 704 |
| 1991 | 720 |
| 1992 | 720 |
| 1993 | 771 |
| 1994 | 806 |
| 1995 | 793 |
| 1996 | 726 |
| 1997 | 619[1831] |

As indicated in the chart above, 1996 witnessed an approximately 8 percent decline in the cost of D & O insurance and 1997 witnessed an approximately 15 percent decline in the cost of D & O insurance.[1832] This represented "a general softness in the marketplace"

---

1830. Weiss, *Filling the Gaps in D & O Insurance*, 6 Bus. Law Today No. 3, Jan./Feb. 1997, at 44; *Weiss, Doing D & O Insurance Right*, 4 Bus. Law Today No. 2, Nov./Dec. 1994, at 50.

1831. 1997 Watson Wyatt Worldwide D & O Liability Survey Report 3 (1997); 1996 Watson Wyatt Worldwide D & O Liability Survey Report 3 (1996).

1832. *Id.*

during a two year period that in 1996 saw about 30 percent of surveyed firms report premium increases, 38 percent report decreases and 32 percent report no change in premium, and in 1997 saw 29 percent of surveyed firms report premium increases, 49 percent report decreases and 22 percent report no change in premium.[1833] About half of those reporting premium increases obtained higher policy limits and improved coverage at favorable prices.[1834]

The D & O market nevertheless remains in a state of transition. High premiums and coverage shortages still pose substantial difficulties for some corporations—particularly high technology companies, initial public offering companies and firms having financial problems.[1835] Additionally, as D & O insurance companies have become more sophisticated in assessing and pricing risks and have gained access to increased information and used improved analytical tools, pricing has become more accurate. This accuracy has resulted in lower premiums for "top quality, well-positioned companies" but higher premiums for "companies with questionable financial strength, unrealistic stock prices compared to book value, or a weak economic region or industry."[1836]

Few corporate governance issues are more important than the availability of sufficient insurance at affordable prices. Without sufficient insurance, qualified individuals may decline service as

---

1833. *Id.*

1834. *Id.*

1835. 1997 Wyatt Survey at 2; 1996 Wyatt Survey at 2; *see also* Goldwasser, *Introduction to Directors' and Officers' Liability Insurance—1992, in Directors' and Officers' Liability Insurance* 9, 11, 27-28 (Practising Law Institute 1992); Harley, *Overview of the Directors' and Officers' Insurance Environment, in Directors' and Officers' Liability Insurance 1989* 11 (Practising Law Institute 1989); Hofmann, *Professional Perils: D & O Buyers Still Not Out of the Woods*, Bus. Ins., Oct. 10, 1988, at 3; *Long-Term Changes, Softening Seen in D & O Liability Markets*, 2 Liab. & Ins. Bull. (BNA) No. 38, at 6 (Apr. 11, 1988); Sills, *D & O Insurance: Special Risk, Special Protection*, Directorship, May 1988, at 1.

1836. 1997 Wyatt Survey at 2.

corporate directors because the potential for liability is so vastly disproportionate to the benefits directors typically receive in return for their service. The result could be an exodus of talented individuals from directorships of corporations unable to secure sufficient insurance[1837] (a phenomenon that was reported at the height of the D & O crisis of the mid-1980s)[1838] and an unhealthy over-cautiousness on the part of individuals who do remain in corporate directorships.[1839] As stated by the drafters of the Model Business

---

1837. *See* 1 Model Bus. Corp. Act Annotated § 2.02 Official Comment at 2-17 (3d ed. 1996) (noting the "increased costs and reduced availability of director and officer liability insurance" and "the resulting reluctance of qualified individuals to serve as directors"); Mallen & Evans, *Surviving the Directors' and Officers' Liability Crisis: Insurance and the Alternatives*, 12 Del. J. Corp. L. 439, 443-44, 461 (1988); Monteleone, *D & O Allocation: Problems and Solutions*, XVIII The Risk Report No. 8, Apr. 1996, at 11, *reprinted in Securities Litigation 1996* 997, 1007 (Practising Law Institute 1996); Note, *Statutory Responses to Boardroom Fears*, 1987 Colum. Bus. L. Rev. 749, 749-50 (1987).

1838. *See, e.g., Crutcher's Chairman and 3 Directors Quit; Lack of Insurance Cited*, Wall St. J., Feb. 12, 1986, at 21; Darlin, *Most of Armada's Directors Resign Over Insurance*, Wall St. J., Feb. 5, 1986, at 40; Hilder, *Liability Insurance is Difficult to Find Now for Directors, Officers*, Wall St. J., July 10, 1985, at 1 ("When Verna Corp., a Houston-based oil and gas drilling company, lost its $2 million directors' and officers' insurance coverage last month, four of its five directors quit"); Lewin, *Director Insurance Drying Up*, N.Y. Times, Mar. 7, 1986, at D4 ("Just in the last six months, the Control Data Corporation, the Continental Steel Corporation, the Lear Petroleum Corporation, South Texas Drilling and Exploration Inc. and Sykes Datatronics have all lost directors when their insurance ended"); Schares, *Directors Resigning Over Lost Insurance*, S.F. Chron., Sept. 9, 1985, at 23 ("Two of the five directors at Birmingham Federal Savings in Birmingham, Ala., quit recently when the association was unable to renew its $5 million directors and officers insurance policy").

1839. 1 Model Bus. Corp. Act Annotated § 2.02 Official Comment at 2-17; *see also* Herzel, *Law Should Allow Indemnity for Derivative Suits*, Legal Times, Mar. 31, 1986, at 11 ("Directors already have a bias toward being more cautious than is optimal for society—that is, they take less risk than owner-managers would. Directors have nothing personal to gain from

(continued...)

Corporation Act: "Developments in the mid- and late 1980s high-
lighted the need to permit reasonable protection of directors from
exposure to personal liability, in addition to indemnification, so that
directors would not be discouraged from fully and freely carrying
out their duties, including responsible entrepreneurial risk-taking."

---

1839. (...continued)
risky behavior. It is, therefore, in the interest of society not to force
on directors an added incentive to be too cautious. These undesirable
effects are greatest on new, growing companies."); Herzel & Harris,
*Uninsured Boards Mount Weak Defense*, Nat'l L.J., Apr. 21, 1986, at 19
("Target directors who are protected by liability insurance or indemnification may be willing to take the legal risks necessary to mount a strong
defense and secure the best possible price for shareholders. But directors
who lack protection may, in the moment of crisis, become paralyzed with
fear of ruinous personal liability."); Wriston, *"Risk," the American Law
Institute, and the Corporate Director*, *in* National Legal Center for the
Public Interest, *The American Law Institute and Corporate Governance:
An Analysis and Critique*, 7, 14 (1987) ("if directors are penalized for
taking business risks, our system is in jeopardy"); Mallen & Evans, 12
Del. J. Corp. Law at 443-44.

# Table of Authorities

**Cases:**                                                    **Page(s):**

A. Copeland Enterprises, Inc. v. Guste, 1989-2 Trade
Cas. (CCH) ¶ 68,712 (E.D. La. Nov. 28, 1988) . . . . . . . 1334

A. Copeland Enterprises, Inc. v. Guste, 706 F. Supp.
1283 (W.D. Tex. 1989) . . . . . . . . . . . . 687, 1096, 1107, 1154

A.D.M. Corp. v. Sigma Instruments, Inc., 628 F.2d
753 (1st Cir. 1980) . . . . . . . . . . . . . . . . . . . . . . . . . 1335

Abajian v. Kennedy, 18 Del. J. Corp. L. 179 (Del.
Ch. Jan. 17, 1992) . . . . . . . . . . . . . . . . . . . . . . . . . 1533

Abbey v. Computer & Communications Technology
Corp., 457 A.2d 368 (Del. Ch. 1983) . . . . . . . . . . . . . 1587

Abbey v. Computer & Communications Technology
Corp., 1983 Del. Ch. LEXIS 511, 1983 WL 18005
(Del. Ch. Apr. 13, 1983) . . . . . . . . . . . . . . . . . 1786, 1792

Abbey v. Control Data Corp., 603 F.2d 724 (8th Cir.
1979), cert. denied, 444 U.S. 1017 (1980) . . . . . . . 1466, 1747

Abbey v. E.W. Scripps Co., 1995 Del. Ch. LEXIS
94, 1995 WL 478957 (Del. Ch. Aug. 9, 1995)
. . . . . . . . . . . . . . . . . . . . . . . . . . . 497, 518, 527-28

Abbey v. Montedison S.P.A., 143 Misc. 2d 72, 539
N.Y.S.2d 862 (N.Y. Sup. Ct. N.Y. Co. 1989) . . 362, 521, 1347

In re Abbott Laboratories Derivative Litigation, 1994
U.S. Dist. LEXIS 938, 1994 WL 31034 (N.D. Ill.
Feb. 2, 1994) . . . . . . . . . . . . . . . . . . . . 1489, 1491, 1492

Abbot Redmont Thinlite Corp. v. Redmont, 475 F.2d
85 (2d Cir. 1973) . . . . . . . . . . . . . . . . . . . . . . . 297, 303-04

Abella v. Universal Leaf Tobacco Co., 495 F. Supp.
713 (E.D. Va. 1980), reconsidered and rev'd, 546 F.
Supp. 795 (E.D. Va. 1982) . . . . . . . . . . . . . . . . . . . 1696

Abella v. Universal Leaf Tobacco Co., 546 F. Supp.
795 (E.D. Va. 1982) . . . . . . . . . . . . . . . . . . . . . . . 1696

Abercrombie v. Davies, 123 A.2d 893 (Del. Ch.
1956), rev'd, 130 A.2d 338 (Del. 1957) . . . . . . . . . . 217, 218

Abifadel v. Cigna Insurance Co., 8 Cal. App. 4th
145, 9 Cal. Rptr. 2d 910 (Cal. Ct. App. 1992) . . . . 1990, 2002

Abraham v. Parkins, 36 F. Supp. 238 (W.D. Pa.
1940) . . . . . . . . . . . . . . . . . . . . . . . . . . . . . . . 1686

Abrahamson v. Waddell, 624 N.E.2d 1118 (Ohio Ct.
Common Pleas 1992) . . . . . . . . . . . . 24, 241, 667, 814, 1172

Abramowitz v. Posner, 513 F. Supp. 120 (S.D.N.Y.
1981), aff'd, 672 F.2d 1025 (2d Cir. 1982) . . . . . . 1466, 1593

Abramowitz v. Posner, 672 F.2d 1025 (2d Cir. 1982)
. . . . . . . . . . . . . . . . . . . . . . . . . . . . . . 1465, 1610

Abrams v. Allen, 297 N.Y. 52, 74 N.E.2d 305
(1947) . . . . . . . . . . . . . . . . . . . . . . . . . . . . . . 92

Abrams v. Donati, 66 N.Y.2d 951, 489 N.E.2d 751,
498 N.Y.S.2d 782 (1985) . . . . . . . . . . . . . . . . . . . . . 1414

Abrams v. Koether, 766 F. Supp. 237 (D.N.J. 1991)
. . . . . . . . . . . . . . . . . . . . . . . . . . 1586, 1610, 1614

Abrams v. Koether, [1992 Transfer Binder] Fed. Sec.
L. Rep. (CCH) ¶ 96,995 (D.N.J. Aug. 7, 1992)
. . . . . . . . . . . . . . . . . 1427, 1437, 1458, 1470, 1493, 1610

AC Acquisitions Corp. v. Anderson, Clayton & Co.,
519 A.2d 103 (Del. Ch. 1986)
. . . . . . 33, 44, 84, 264, 549, 550, 678-79, 683, 1011-13, 1550

A.C. Petters Co. v. St. Cloud Enterprises, 222
N.W.2d 83 (Minn. 1974) . . . . . . . . . . . . . . . . . . . . . 293

Adams v. Resolution Trust Corp., 1993 U.S. Dist.
LEXIS 7496, 1993 WL 181303 (D. Minn. May 19,
1993), aff'd sub nom. Adams v. Greenwood, 10 F.3d
568 (8th Cir. 1993) . . . . . . . . . . . . . . . . . . . . 2084, 2085

Adams v. Resolution Trust Corp., 831 F. Supp. 1471
(D. Minn.), aff'd sub nom. Adams v. Greenwood, 10
F.3d 568 (8th Cir. 1993) . . . . . . . . . . . . . . . . . . . . . 1886

Advanced Mining Systems, Inc. v. Fricke, 623 A.2d
82 (Del. Ch. 1992) . . . . . . . . 1868-69, 1899, 1914, 1929, 1931

Aetna Casualty & Surety Co. v. Lindner, No. Civ.
90-1221-PHX-PGR (D. Ariz. Dec. 12, 1994), aff'd,

92 F.3d 1191 (unpublished opinion, text available at
1996 U.S. App. LEXIS 18541 and 1996 WL 413621)
(9th Cir. July 22, 1996) . . . . . . . . . . . . . . . . . . . . . 2023-24

Aetna Casualty & Surety Co. v. Lindner, 92 F.3d
1191 (unpublished opinion, text available at 1996 U.S.
App. LEXIS 18541 and 1996 WL 413621) (9th Cir.
July 22, 1996) . . . . . . . . . . . . . . . . . . . . 1986, 1998, 2008

Aetna Casualty & Surety Co. v. Marion Equipment
Co., 894 P.2d 664 (Alaska 1995) . . . . . . . . . . . . . . . . 1986

AHI Metnall, L.P. v. J.C. Nichols Co., 891 F. Supp.
1352 (W.D. Mo. 1995) . . . . . 23, 663, 686, 804, 805, 1271-73

Ainscow v. Sanitary Co., 180 A. 614 (Del. Ch.
1935) . . . . . . . . . . . . . . . . . . . . . . . . . . . . . . . . . 1472

Air Line Pilots Ass'n v. UAL Corp., 717 F. Supp.
575 (N.D. Ill. 1989), aff'd, 897 F.2d 1394 (7th Cir.
1990) . . . . . . . . . . . . . . . . . . . . . . . . . . 12, 13, 654, 685

Air Line Pilots Ass'n v. UAL Corp., 897 F.2d 1394
(7th Cir. 1990) . . . . . . . . . . . . . . . . . . . . . 654-55, 685-86

Alabama By-Products Corp. v. Cede & Co., 657 A.2d
254 (Del. 1995) . . . . . . . . . . . . . . . . . . . . . . . . 477, 488-
89, 1380, 1381, 1382, 1386, 1389, 1390, 1412, 1426, 1444, 1455

Alabama By-Products Corp. v. Neal, 588 A.2d 255
(Del. 1991) . . . . . . . . . . . . . . . . . . . . 477, 484, 489, 1295

Alabama Farm Bureau Mutual Casualty Co. v.
American Fidelity Life Insurance Co., 606 F.2d 602
(5th Cir. 1979), cert. denied, 449 U.S. 820 (1980) . . . . . . . 526

Alexander & Alexander, Inc. v. Fritzen, 147 A.D.2d
241, 542 N.Y.S.2d 530 (N.Y. App. Div. 1st Dep't
1989) . . . . . . . . . . . . . . . . . . . . . . . . . . . . . 304

Alford v. Shaw, 324 S.E.2d 878 (N.C. Ct. App.
1985), rev'd, 349 S.E.2d 41 (N.C. 1986), withdrawn
to affirm and modify, 358 S.E.2d 323 (N.C. 1987)
. . . . . . . . . . . . . . . . . . . . . . . . . . . . . 1583, 1700-01

Alford v. Shaw, 349 S.E.2d 41 (N.C. 1986), withdrawn to affirm and modify, 358 S.E.2d 323 (N.C.
1987) . . . . . . . . . . . . . . . . . . . . . . . . . . . 1700-01, 1708

Alford v. Shaw, 358 S.E.2d 323 (N.C. 1987)
. . . . . . . . . . . . . . . . . . . 1695, 1700-02, 1708, 1741-43

Alford v. Shaw, 398 S.E.2d 445 (N.C. 1990)
. . . . . . . . . . . . . . . . . . . . . . . 1396, 1397, 1695, 1743

Alleghany Corp. v. Kirby, 218 F. Supp. 164
(S.D.N.Y. 1963) . . . . . . . . . . . . . . . . . . . . . . . . 1382

Allen v. Prime Computer, Inc., 540 A.2d 417 (Del.
1988) . . . . . . . . . . . . . . . . . . . . . . . . . . . . . 1274-76

Alliance Gaming Corp. v. Bally Gaming International,
Inc., 1995 Del. Ch. LEXIS 101, 1995 WL 523543
(Del. Ch. Aug. 11, 1995) . . . . . . . . . . . . . . . . 772, 774-77

Allison v. General Motors Corp., 604 F. Supp. 1106
(D. Del.), aff'd mem., 782 F.2d 1026 (3d Cir. 1985)
. . . . . . . . . . . . . . . . . . . . . . . . . 1427, 1428, 1429, 1457,
1460, 1466-67, 1492, 1494, 1584-85, 1587, 1597, 1598, 1610, 1674

Allright Missouri, Inc. v. Billeter, 829 F.2d 631 (8th
Cir. 1987) . . . . . . . . . 1399, 1428, 1438, 1443, 1686-88, 1804

Allstate Insurance Co. v. Patterson, 904 F. Supp.
1270 (D. Utah 1995) . . . . . . . . . . . . . . . . . . . . . . . . 1986

Allstate Insurance Co. v. Zuk, 78 N.Y.2d 41, 574
N.E.2d 1035, 571 N.Y.S.2d 429 (1991) . . . . . . . . . . . 1986

Alpert v. 28 Williams Street Corp., 63 N.Y.2d 557,
473 N.E.2d 19, 483 N.Y.S.2d 667 (1984)
. . . . . . . . . . . . . . . . . . . . . . . . . . 108, 369, 377-78, 469

Alta Health Strategies, Inc. v. Kennedy, 790 F. Supp.
1085 (D. Utah 1992) . . . . . . . . . . . . . . . . . . . . . . . . 112

Alvest, Inc. v. Superior Oil Corp., 398 P.2d 213
(Alaska 1965) . . . . . . . . . . . . . . . . . . . . . . . . . . 297, 304

Amalgamated Sugar Co. v. NL Industries, Inc., 644
F. Supp. 1229 (S.D.N.Y. 1986) . . . . . . . . . . 1098, 1099-1100

Amalgamated Sugar Co. v. NL Industries, Inc., 825
F.2d 634 (2d Cir.), cert. denied, 484 U.S. 992
(1987) . . . . . . . . . . . . . . . . . . . . . . . . . . . . . . . . . 1102

Amanda Acquisition Corp. v. Universal Foods Corp.,
708 F. Supp. 984 (E.D. Wis.), aff'd, 877 F.2d 496
(7th Cir.), cert. denied, 493 U.S. 955 (1989) . . . . . . . 180-81,
184, 187, 188, 190, 194, 668, 686, 810, 1090, 1096, 1098, 1179-80

Amanda Acquisition Corp. v. Universal Foods Corp.,
877 F.2d 496 (7th Cir.), cert. denied, 493 U.S. 955
(1989) . . . . . . . . . . . . . . . . . . . . . . . . . . . . . . . . . 1181

In re Ambassador Group, Inc. Litigation, 738 F.
Supp. 57 (E.D.N.Y. 1990) . . . . . . . . . . . . . . . . . . 2103-05

In re Ambassador Group, Inc. Litigation, 830 F.
Supp. 147 (E.D.N.Y. 1993) . . . . . . . . . . . . . . . . . 2006-07

Amdur v. Meyer, 15 A.D.2d 425, 224 N.Y.S.2d 440
(N.Y. App. Div. 3d Dep't 1962), appeal dismissed, 14
N.Y.2d 541, 198 N.E.2d 30, 248 N.Y.S.2d 639
(1964) . . . . . . . . . . . . . . . . . . . . . . . . 321, 322, 323, 341

AMERCO v. Shoen, 907 P.2d 536 (Ariz. Ct. App.
1995) . . . . . . . . . . . . . . . . . . . . . . . . . . . . . . 117, 299

AMERCO, Inc. v. Commissioner, 979 F.2d 162 (9th
Cir. 1992) . . . . . . . . . . . . . . . . . . . . . . . . . 2158, 2160

AmeriFirst Bank v. Bomar, 757 F. Supp. 1365 (S.D.
Fla. 1991) . . . . . . . . . . . . . . . . . . . . . . . . . . . . . . 98

American Casualty Co. v. Baker, 758 F. Supp. 1340
(C.D. Cal. 1991), aff'd, 22 F.3d 880 (9th Cir. 1994)
. . . . . . . . . . . . . 2056, 2057, 2058, 2059, 2076, 2087, 2089

American Casualty Co. v. Baker, 1993 U.S. Dist.
LEXIS 6981 (C.D. Cal. Apr. 29, 1993), aff'd, 22
F.3d 880 (9th Cir. 1994) . . . . . . . . . . . . . . . . . . . . 2083

American Casualty Co. v. Baker, 22 F.3d 880 (9th
Cir. 1994) . . . . . . . . . . . . . . . . 1998-99, 2083-85, 2096

American Casualty Co. v. Bank of Montana System,
675 F. Supp. 538 (D. Minn. 1987) . . . . . . . . . . . 2094, 2096

American Casualty Co. v. Beranek, 862 F. Supp. 322
(D. Kan. 1994) . . . . . . . . . . . . . . . . . . . . . . 2083, 2085

American Casualty Co. v. Continisio, 17 F.3d 62 (3d
Cir. 1994) . . . . . . . . . . . . . . . . . . . . . . . . . 2011, 2012

American Casualty Co. v. Federal Deposit Insurance
Corp., 677 F. Supp. 600 (N.D. Iowa 1987)
. . . . . . . . . . . . . . . . . . . . . . 2066, 2067, 2080, 2096-97

American Casualty Co. v. Federal Deposit Insurance
Corp., 713 F. Supp. 311 (N.D. Iowa 1988)
. . . . . . . . . . . . . . . . . . . . . . . . . . . . 2067, 2080, 2081

American Casualty Co. v. Federal Deposit Insurance
Corp., 1990 U.S. Dist. LEXIS 6065, 1990 WL 66505
(N.D. Iowa Feb. 26, 1990), aff'd in part and rev'd in
part, 944 F.2d 455 (8th Cir. 1991)
. . . . . . . . . . . . . . 1998, 2049-50, 2066, 2067, 2080, 2081-82

American Casualty Co. v. Federal Deposit Insurance
Corp., 944 F.2d 455 (8th Cir. 1991)
. . . . . . . . . . . . . . . . . . 2010-11, 2050, 2068, 2082-83, 2085

American Casualty Co. v. Federal Deposit Insurance
Corp., 791 F. Supp. 276 (W.D. Okla. 1992)
. . . . . . . . . . . . . . . . . . . . 2055, 2056, 2057, 2058, 2059

American Casualty Co. v. Federal Deposit Insurance
Corp., 958 F.2d 324 (10th Cir. 1992) . . . . . . . . . . 1990, 1998

American Casualty Co. v. Federal Deposit Insurance
Corp., 1993 U.S. Dist. LEXIS 5853, 1993 WL
625521 (W.D. Mich. Jan. 8, 1993) . . . . . . . . . . . 2076, 2085

American Casualty Co. v. Federal Deposit Insurance
Corp., 1993 WL 610760 (S.D. Miss. Apr. 8, 1993)
. . . . . . . . . . . . . . . . . . . . . . . . . . 2076, 2085, 2091

American Casualty Co. v. Federal Deposit Insurance
Corp., 998 F.2d 404 (7th Cir. 1993) . . . . . . . . . . . . . . 2089

American Casualty Co. v. Federal Deposit Insurance
Corp., 999 F.2d 480 (10th Cir. 1993) . . . . . . . . . . 1996, 1998

American Casualty Co. v. Federal Deposit Insurance
Corp., 39 F.3d 633 (6th Cir. 1994)
. . . . . . . . . . . . . . . . 2075, 2076, 2078, 2084, 2086, 2089

American Casualty Co. v. Federal Deposit Insurance
Corp., 16 F.3d 152 (7th Cir. 1994) . . . . . . . . . . 2075, 2084

American Casualty Co. v. Federal Savings & Loan
Insurance Corp., 683 F. Supp. 1183 (S.D. Ohio
1988) . . . . . . . . . . . . . . . . . . . . . . . . . . . . . . 2077

American Casualty Co. v. Federal Savings & Loan
Insurance Corp., 704 F. Supp. 898 (E.D. Ark. 1989)
. . . . . . . . . . . . . . . . . . 2056, 2057, 2060, 2061, 2078-79

American Casualty Co. v. Kirchner, 1992 U.S. Dist.
LEXIS 15879, 1992 WL 300843 (W.D. Wis. May 22,
1992), aff'd sub nom. American Casualty Co. v. Federal Deposit Insurance Corp., 16 F.3d 152 (7th Cir.
1994) . . . . . . . . . . . . . . . . . . . . . . . . . . . . . . 2089

American Casualty Co. v. Rahn, 854 F. Supp. 492
(W.D. Mich. 1994)
. . . . . . . . . . . . . 2006-07, 2010-11, 2076, 2083, 2085, 2097

American Casualty Co. v. Resolution Trust Corp., 839
F. Supp. 282 (D.N.J. 1993) . . . . . . . . . . . . . 2076, 2084-85

American Casualty Co. v. Resolution Trust Corp., 845
F. Supp. 318 (D. Md. 1993) . . . . . . . . . . 1998, 2076, 2084-85

American Casualty Co. v. Resolution Trust Corp., CV
No. 92-10543-WF (D. Mass. Oct. 19, 1993)
. . . . . . . . . . . . . . . . . . . . . . . . . . . . . 2076, 2084-85

American Casualty Co. v. Resolution Trust Corp.,
1994 U.S. Dist. LEXIS 9447, 1994 WL 361508 (E.D.
Pa. July 7, 1994) . . . . . . . . . . . . . . . . . . . . 2076, 2083-85

American Casualty Co. v. Sentry Federal Savings
Bank, 867 F. Supp. 50 (D. Mass. 1994)
. . . . . . . . 1999, 2019-20, 2055, 2059, 2061, 2076, 2083, 2085

American Casualty Co. v. Sierra Chemical Co., 1989
U.S. Dist. LEXIS 7310 (N.D. Cal. Mar. 7, 1989) . . . . . . 2096

American Casualty Co. v. Wilkinson, 1990 U.S. Dist.
LEXIS 20153, 1990 WL 302175 (N.D. Okla. Dec.
21, 1990), aff'd sub nom. American Casualty Co. v.
Federal Deposit Insurance Corp., 958 F.2d 324 (10th
Cir. 1992) . . . . . . . . . . . . . . . . . . . . . . . . . 2015, 2019

American General Corp. v. NLT Corp., [1982
Transfer Binder] Fed. Sec. L. Rep. (CCH) ¶ 98,808
(S.D. Tex. July 1, 1982) . . . . . . . . . . . . . . . . . . . . 1343

American General Corp. v. Torchmark Corp., 1990
WL 595282 (S.D. Tex. Apr. 11, 1990), preliminary
injunction stayed pending an expedited appeal, No.
90-2328 (5th Cir. Apr. 12, 1990), appeal dismissed,
903 F.2d 825 (5th Cir. 1990) . . . . . . . . . . . . . . 136, 1247

American General Corp. v. Texas Air Corp., 13 Del.
J. Corp. L. 173 (Del. Ch. Feb. 5, 1987) . . . . . . . . . . . . 462

American General Corp. v. Unitrin, Inc., [1994-1995
Transfer Binder] Fed. Sec. L. Rep. (CCH) ¶ 98,456
(Del. Ch. Aug. 26, 1994) . . . . . . . . . . . . . . . . . . . . 1025

American Home Assurance Co. v. Safway Steel Products Co., 743 S.W.2d 693 (Tex. Ct. App. 1987) . . . . . . 1986

American International Rent A Car, Inc. v. Cross, 9
Del. J. Corp. L. 144 (Del. Ch. May 9, 1984) . . . 1284-85, 1343

American International Specialty Lines Insurance Co.
v. Towers Financial Corp., 1997 U.S. Dist. LEXIS
22610, 1997 WL 906427 (S.D.N.Y. Sept. 12, 1997)
. . . . . . . . . . . . . . . . . . . . . . . . . . . . . . . 2144, 2152

American Medical International, Inc. v. National
Union Fire Insurance Co., 54 F.3d 785 (unpublished
opinion, text available at 1995 U.S. App. LEXIS
11808 and 1995 WL 299851) (9th Cir. May 17,
1995), cert. granted and case remanded, 516 U.S. 984
(1995) . . . . . . . . . . . . . . . . . . . . . . . . . . . . 1987-88

American National Bank & Trust Co. v. Schigur, 83
Cal. App. 3d 790, 148 Cal. Rptr. 116 (Cal. Ct. App.
1978) . . . . . . . . . . . . . . . . . . . . . . . . . . . . . 1857

American Pacific Corp. v. Super Food Services, Inc.,
8 Del. J. Corp. L. 320 (Del. Ch. Dec. 6, 1982) . . . . . 1285-86

Ameriwood Industries International Corp. v. American
Casualty Co., 840 F. Supp. 1143 (W.D. Mich. 1993)
. . . . . . . . . . . . . . . . . . . 2007-08, 2026, 2033-34, 2041-43

Amsellem v. Shopwell, Inc., 5 Del. J. Corp. L. 367
(Del. Ch. Sept. 6, 1979) . . . . . . . . . . . . . . . . . . . 1352

In re Amsted Industries, Inc. Litigation, 521 A.2d
1104 (Del. Ch. 1986) . . . . . . . . . . . . . . . . . . . . 1410

Anadarko Petroleum Corp. v. Panhandle Eastern
Corp., 545 A.2d 1171 (Del. 1988) . . . . . . . . . . . . 108, 376

Anago, Inc. v. Tecnol Medical Products, Inc., 976
F.2d 248 (5th Cir. 1992), cert. dismissed, 510 U.S.
985 (1993) . . . . . . . . . . . . . . . . . . . . . . . . . . . 1335, 1336

In re Anderson, Clayton Shareholders Litigation, 519
A.2d 669 (Del. Ch. 1986) . . . . . . . . . . . . . . . . . 509, 510

In re Anderson, Clayton Shareholders Litigation, 519
A.2d 680 (Del. Ch. 1986) . . . . . . . . . . . . . . . . . 507, 870

In re Anderson, Clayton Shareholders Litigation, 519
A.2d 694 (Del. Ch. 1986) . . . . . . . . . . . . . . . . . . . . . 698

Andreae v. Andreae, [1991-1992 Transfer Binder]
Fed. Sec. L. Rep. (CCH) ¶ 96,571 (Del. Ch. Mar. 3,
1992) . . . . . . . . . . . . 38-39, 43, 1495, 1498, 1501, 1527-28

Anglo American Insurance Group, P.L.C. v. CalFed
Inc., 899 F. Supp. 1070 (S.D.N.Y. 1995) . . . . . . . 1868, 1876

Anglo-American Insurance Co. v. Molin, 673 A.2d
986 (Pa. Cmmw. Ct. 1996), rev'd, 691 A.2d 929 (Pa.
1997) . . . . . . . . . . . . . . . . . . . . . . . . . . . . 2034-36, 2139

Anglo-American Insurance Co. v. Molin, 691 A.2d
929 (Pa. 1997) . . . . . . . . . . . . . . . . . . . . . . . . 2036, 2139

Ansell Inc. v. Schmid Laboratories, Inc., 757 F.
Supp. 467 (D.N.J.), aff'd mem., 941 F.2d 1200 (3d
Cir. 1991) . . . . . . . . . . . . . . . . . . . . . . . . . . . . . . 1338

AOC L.P. v. Horsham Corp., 1992 Del. Ch. LEXIS
131, 1992 WL 136474 (Del. Ch. June 17, 1992) . . 53, 184, 189

APL Corp. v. Johnson Controls, Inc., No. 85-C-990
(E.D.N.Y. Mar. 25, 1985) . . . . . . . . . . . . . . . . . . . 1096

Apollo Industries, Inc. v. Associated International
Insurance Co., No. 89-908715-CK (Mich. Cir. Ct.
Oct. 31, 1990), reprinted in Corp. Officers & Direc-
tors Litig. Rptr. 9059 (Nov. 14, 1990) . . . . . . . . . . . . 1995

Apollo Industries, Inc. v. Associated International
Insurance Co., No. 153902 (Mich. Ct. App. Apr. 13,
1995) . . . . . . . . . . . . . . . . . . . . . . . . . . . . . 1999, 2130-31

Aprahamian v. HBO & Co., 531 A.2d 1204 (Del. Ch.
1987) . . . . . . . . . . . . . . . . . . . . . . . . . . . . 802, 804, 1206-07

In re Appraisal of ENSTAR Corp., 604 A.2d 404
(Del. 1992) . . . . . . . . . . . . . . . . . . . . . . . . . . . . . . . . . 477

In re Appraisal of Ford Holdings, Inc. Preferred
Stock, 698 A.2d 973 (Del. Ch. 1997) . . . . . . . . . . 573, 575-76

In re Appraisal of Shell Oil Co., 1990 Del. Ch.
LEXIS 199, 1990 WL 201390 (Del. Ch. Dec. 11,
1990), aff'd, 607 A.2d 1213 (Del. 1992) . . . . . . 209, 486, 487

APSB Bancorp v. Grant, 26 Cal. App. 4th 926, 31
Cal. Rptr. 2d 736 (Cal. Ct. App. 1994) . . . . . . . . . . . . 1856

In re Arkla Exploration Co. Shareholders Litigation,
[1991-1992 Transfer Binder] Fed. Sec L. Rep. (CCH)
¶ 96,517 (Del. Ch. Jan. 14, 1992) . . . . . . . . . . . . . . . . 520

Armstrong v. Marathon Oil Co., 513 N.E.2d 776
(Ohio 1987) . . . . . . . . . . . . . . . . . . . . . . . . . . . . . . . . . 477

Arnold v. Society for Savings Bancorp, Inc., 19 Del.
J. Corp. L. 219 (Del. Ch. May 25, 1993) . . . . . . . . . 514, 515

Arnold v. Society for Savings Bancorp, Inc., [1993-
1994 Transfer Binder] Fed. Sec. L. Rep. (CCH)

¶ 98,006 (Del. Ch. Dec. 15, 1993), aff'd in part and
rev'd in part, 650 A.2d 1270 (Del. 1994) . . . . . .   514, 515, 711

Arnold v. Society for Savings Bancorp, Inc., 650
A.2d 1270 (Del. 1994) . . . . . . . .   107, 228-30, 490, 499, 501,
512, 514, 515, 518, 519, 522, 536, 695, 710, 711, 712, 721, 730

Arnold v. Society for Savings Bancorp, Inc., [1995
Transfer Binder] Fed. Sec. L. Rep. (CCH) ¶ 98,827
(Del. Ch. June 15, 1995), aff'd, 678 A.2d 533 (Del.
1996) . . . . . . . . . . . . . . . . . . . . . . . . . . . . . . . 508, 537

Arnold v. Society for Savings Bancorp, Inc., 678
A.2d 533 (Del. 1996)
. . . . . . .   1, 227-28, 499, 501, 508, 530, 536, 537, 1883, 1884

Aronoff v. Albanese, 85 A.D.2d 3, 446 N.Y.S.2d 368
(N.Y. App. Div. 2d Dep't 1982) . . . . . . . . . . . .  83, 226, 270

Aronson v. Crane, 145 A.D.2d 455, 535 N.Y.S.2d
417 (N.Y. App. Div. 2d Dep't 1988) . . . . . . . . . . . . . . 570

Aronson v. Lewis, 473 A.2d 805 (Del. 1984)
. . . . . .   20-21, 26, 39-45, 75, 81, 84, 124, 134, 146, 312, 346,
423, 424, 1381, 1443, 1447-48, 1473-75, 1479, 1482, 1483-85,
1504, 1530, 1549, 1572, 1610, 1614, 1615, 1690, 1738, 1770, 1810

Arthur Lipper Corp. v. Securities & Exchange Commission, 547 F.2d 171 (2d Cir. 1976), cert. denied,
434 U.S. 1009 (1978) . . . . . . . . . . . . . . . . . . . . . . . . 210

Asarco Inc. v. M.R.H. Holmes A Court, 611
F. Supp. 468 (D.N.J. 1985)
. . . . . . . . . . . . . . . .  24, 63, 1100, 1132, 1136-37, 1138-39

Ash v. Brunswick Corp., 405 F. Supp. 234 (D. Del.
1975) . . . . . . . . . . . . . . . . . . . . . . . . . . . . . . . . . . 327

Ash v. International Business Machines, Inc., 353
F.2d 491 (3d Cir. 1965), cert. denied, 384 U.S. 927
(1966) . . . . . . . . . . . . . . . . . . . . . . . . . . . .  1681

Ashburn v. Wicker, 381 S.E.2d 876 (N.C. Ct. App.
1989) . . . . . . . . . . . . . . . . . . . . . . . . . . . .  1390

Ashwander v. Tennessee Valley Authority, 297 U.S.
288 (1936) . . . . . . . . . . . . . . . . . . . . . . 1607-09, 1649

Askanase v. Fatjo, 1993 U.S. Dist. LEXIS 7911, 1993
WL 208440 (S.D. Tex. Apr. 22, 1993), aff'd, 130
F.3d 657 (5th Cir. 1997) . . . . . . . . . . . . . . . . . . . 627

Askanase v. Fatjo, 130 F.3d 657 (5th Cir. 1997) . . . . . 596, 600

Askanase v. LivingWell, Inc., 45 F.3d 103 (5th Cir.
1995) . . . . . . . . . . . . . . . . . . . . . . . . . . . 1976-77

Association for Retarded Citizens-Santa Barbara Council v. North American Specialty Insurance Co., No.
CV 94-4602 LGB (EX) (C.D. Cal. Nov. 23, 1994) . . . . . 2143

Atherton v. Federal Deposit Insurance Corp., 117 S.
Ct. 666 (1997) . . . . . . . . . . . . . . . . . . 2, 152, 226, 249-52

Atkins v. Tony Lama Co., 624 F. Supp. 250 (S.D.
Ind. 1985) . . . . . . . . . . . . . . . . . . . . . . . . 1492, 1495

In re Atlantic Financial Management Securities Litigation, 121 F.R.D. 141 (D. Mass. 1988) . . . . . . . . . . . . 1822

Atlantic Permanent Federal Savings & Loan Ass'n v.
American Casualty Co., 839 F.2d 212 (4th Cir.), cert.
denied, 486 U.S. 1056 (1988) . . . . . 1992-93, 2026, 2031, 2151

Auerbach v. Aldrich, N.Y.L.J. Dec. 23, 1977, at 13
(N.Y. Sup. Ct. Westchester Co. 1977) . . . . . . . . . . . .  1559

Auerbach v. Bennett, 47 N.Y.2d 619, 393 N.E.2d
994, 419 N.Y.S.2d 920 (1979) . . . . . . . . . . . . . . . . . 11, 15,
91, 272, 1380, 1381, 1444-45, 1450, 1612, 1636, 1645, 1690,
1693-94, 1702-08, 1711, 1721-22, 1748, 1750, 1753 1795-96, 1798

Avacus Partners, L.P. v. Brian, [1991 Transfer
Binder] Fed. Sec. L. Rep. (CCH) ¶ 96,232 (Del. Ch.
Oct. 24, 1990) . . . . . . . . . . . . . .  94, 1389, 1471, 1525, 1585

Aviall, Inc. v. Ryder Systems, Inc., 913 F. Supp. 826
(S.D.N.Y. 1996), aff'd, 110 F.3d 892 (2d Cir. 1997) . . . . . 376

Avon Products, Inc. v. Chartwell Associates L.P., 738
F. Supp. 686 (S.D.N.Y.), aff'd, 907 F.2d 322 (2d
Cir. 1990) . . . . . . . . . . . . . . . . . . . . . . . . . . . . . . 1098

Avon Products, Inc. v. Chartwell Associates L.P., 907
F.2d 322 (2d Cir. 1990) . . . . . . . . . . . . . . . . . . . . . 1098

Axis, S.p.A. v. Micafil, Inc., 870 F.2d 1105 (6th
Cir.), cert. denied, 493 U.S. 823 (1989) . . . . . . . . . . . 1338

AYR Composition, Inc. v. Rosenberg, 619 A.2d 592
(N.J. Super. 1993) . . . . . . . . . . . . . . . . . . . . . . . . . 598

B & B Investment Club v. Kleinert's Inc., 472 F.
Supp. 787 (E.D. Pa. 1979) . . . . . . . . . . . . 1861, 1867, 1871

In re B.S. Livingston & Co., 186 B.R. 841 (D.N.J.
1995) . . . . . . . . . . . . . . . . . . . . . . . . . . . . . . . . . 627

B.T.Z., Inc. v. Grove, 803 F. Supp. 1019 (M.D. Pa.
1992) . . . . . . . . . . . . . . . . . . . . . . . . 691, 1429-30, 1439

BTZ, Inc. v. National Intergroup, Inc., 1993 Del. Ch.
LEXIS 58, 1993 WL 133211 (Del. Ch. Apr. 7,
1993) . . . . . . . . . . . . . . . . . . . . . 1580, 1597, 1601, 1604

Bach v. National Western Life Insurance Co., 810
F.2d 509 (5th Cir. 1987)
. . . . . . . . . . . . . . . 1583-84, 1610, 1695, 1722, 1745, 1489

Bacine v. Scharffenberger, 10 Del. J. Corp. L. 603
(Del. Ch. Dec. 11, 1984) . . . . . . . . . . . . . . . . . . . . 1315

Bagdon v. Bridgestone/Firestone, Inc., 916 F.2d 379
(7th Cir. 1990), cert. denied, 500 U.S. 952 (1991) . . . . . . 1381

Baker, Watts & Co. v. Miles & Stockbridge, 876 F.2d
1101 (4th Cir. 1989) . . . . . . . . . . . . . . . . . . . . . . . 1970

Balin v. Amerimar Realty Co., 22 Del. J. Corp. L.
1115 (Del. Ch. Nov. 15, 1996) . . . . . . . . . . 1389, 1400, 1402

In re Bally's Grand Derivative Litigation, 1997 Del.
Ch. LEXIS 77, 1997 WL 305803 (Del. Ch. June 4,
1997) . . . . . . . . . . . . . 216, 217, 221-23, 224, 1474-75, 1572

In re Bally's Grand Derivative Litigation, No. 14644
(Del. Ch. Oct. 9, 1997) . . . . . . . . . . . . . . . . . . . . . 1409

Bagdon v. Bridgestone/Firestone, Inc., 916 F.2d 379
(7th Cir. 1990), cert. denied, 500 U.S. 952 (1991) . . . . . . . . 3

Balin v. Amerimar Realty Co., 22 Del. J. Corp. L.
1115 (Del. Ch. Nov. 15, 1996) . . . . . . . . . . . . . . . 31, 304

Bank Leumi-Le-Israel v. Sunbelt Industries Inc., 485
F. Supp. 556 (S.D. Ga. 1980) . . . . . . . . . . . . . . . . . 596

Bank of America v. Powers (Cal. Super. Ct. complaint filed Mar. 1, 1985), reprinted in Directors' and Officers' Liability Insurance 1987 247-83 (Practising Law Institute 1987) . . . . . . . . . . . . . . . . . . . . . . . . . . 2045

Bank of New York Co. v. Irving Bank Corp., 139 Misc. 2d 665, 528 N.Y.S.2d 482 (N.Y. Sup. Ct. N.Y. Co. 1988) . . . . . . . . . . . . . . . . . . . . . . . . . . 1184-86

Bank of N.Y. Co. v. Irving Bank Corp., 142 Misc. 2d 145, 536 N.Y.S.2d 923 (N.Y. Sup. Ct. N.Y. Co. 1988), subsequent proceedings, No. 10217/88, Order (N.Y. Sup. Ct. N.Y. Co. July 21, 1988), aff'd mem., 143 A.D.2d 1070, 533 N.Y.S.2d 411, and 143 A.D.2d 1073, 533 N.Y.S.2d 412, and 143 A.D.2d 1075, 533 N.Y.S.2d 412 (N.Y. App. Div. 1st Dep't Oct. 4, 1988) . . . . . . . . . . . . . . . . . . . . . . . . . . . . . . 1099

In re BankAmerica Securities Litigation, 636 F. Supp. 419 (C.D. Cal. 1986) . . . . . . . . . . . . . . . . . . . . . . . . 1456

Banks v. Whyte, 1994 U.S. Dist. LEXIS 11063, 1994 WL 418997 (E.D. Pa. Aug. 9, 1994) . . . . . . . . . . . . . 1399

Banner Industries, Inc. v. Schwartz, N.Y.L.J., Jan. 11, 1990, at 24 (N.Y. Sup. Ct. N.Y. Co.) . . . . . . . . . 736, 979

Banque Nationale de Paris S.A. v. Insurance Co. of North America, 896 F. Supp. 163 (S.D.N.Y. 1995) . . 15, 24, 42

Barkan v. Amsted Industries, Inc., 567 A.2d 1279 (Del. 1989) . . . . . . . . . . . . . . . . . . . . . . . . . . . . . . . . . . . 512, 513, 525, 526, 696, 700-03, 705, 707, 730-31, 765, 767, 939, 1147

Barnes v. Andrews, 298 F. 614 (S.D.N.Y. 1924) . . . . 88, 112

Baron v. Siff, 1997 Del. Ch. LEXIS 152, 1997 WL
666973 (Del. Ch. Oct. 17, 1997)
. . . . . . . . . 1455, 1582, 1595, 1598, 1604-05, 1616, 1630-32

Baron v. Strawbridge & Clothier, 646 F. Supp. 690
(E.D. Pa. 1986) . . . . . . . . . . . . . . . . . . 810, 1054, 1077-79

Barr v. Colorado Insurance Guarantee Ass'n, 926 P.2d
102 (Colo. Ct. App. 1995) . . . . . . . . . . . . . . . . . . . . . 1993

Barr v. Wackman, 36 N.Y.2d 371, 329 N.E.2d 180,
368 N.Y.S.2d 497 (1975)
. . . . . . . . . . . . . . 1445, 1447-49, 1547, 1543, 1544-46, 1558

Barrett v. Southern Connecticut Gas Co., 374 A.2d
1051 (Conn. 1977) . . . . . . . . . . . . . . . . . . . . . . . . . 1401

Barris Industries, Inc. v. Bryan, 686 F. Supp. 125
(E.D. Va. 1988) . . . . . . . . . . . . . . . . . . . . . 727, 1083-85

Barris Industries, Inc. v. Bryan, No. 88-0188-R (E.D.
Va. Aug. 15, 1988) . . . . . . . . . . . . . . . . . . . . 343, 349-50

Barry v. Barry, 28 F.3d 848 (8th Cir. 1994)
. . . . . . . . . . . . . . . . . . . . . . . . . 1873, 1896, 1931, 1956

Bartlett v. New York, New Haven & Hartford R.R.,
109 N.E. 452 (Mass. 1915) . . . . . . . . . . . . . . . . . . . 1611

Bartley v. National Union Fire Insurance Co., 824 F.
Supp. 624 (N.D. Tex. 1992) . . . . . . . . . . . . . . 2076, 2085

Basic Inc. v. Levinson, 485 U.S. 224 (1988) . . . . . . . 513, 538

Batchelor v. Oak Hill Medical Group, 870 F.2d 1446
(9th Cir. 1989) . . . . . . . . . . . . . . . . . . . . . . . . . 885, 886

Batra v. Investors Research Corp., [1992 Transfer
Binder] Fed. Sec. L. Rep. (CCH) ¶ 96,983 (W.D.
Mo. Apr. 2, 1992) . . . . . . . . . . . . . . . . 1458, 1496, 1497

In re Baxter International, Inc. Shareholders Litigation, 654 A.2d 1268 (Del. Ch. 1995)
. . . . . . . . . . . . . 43, 63, 128-29, 229, 1453, 1533, 1537-38

Beals v. Washington International, Inc., 386 A.2d
1156 (Del. Ch. 1978) . . . . . . . . . . . . . . . . . . . . . . . 1911

Bear, Stearns & Co. v. D.F. King & Co., --- A.D. 2d
---, 663 N.Y.S.2d 12 (N.Y. App. Div. 1st Dep't
1997) . . . . . . . . . . . . . . . . . . . . . . . . . . . . . 1941-42

Beard v. Elster, 160 A.2d 731 (Del. 1960)
. . . . . . . . . . . . 312, 321, 322, 324-25, 326, 327-28, 331-32

In re Beatrice Co. Litigation, 12 Del. J. Corp. L. 199
(Del. Ch. Apr. 16, 1986), aff'd, 522 A.2d 865 (unpublished opinion, text available at 1987 Del. LEXIS
1036 and 1987 WL 36708) (Feb. 20, 1987), cert.
denied, 484 U.S. 898 (1987) . . . . . . . . . . . . . . . . . . 1314

Beaumont v. American Can Co., 142 Misc. 2d 767,
538 N.Y.S.2d 136 (N.Y. Sup. Ct. N.Y. Co. 1988),
aff'd in part and rev'd in part, 160 A.D.2d 174, 553
N.Y.S.2d 145 (N.Y. App. Div. 1st Dep't 1990) . . . . . 568, 569

Beaumont v. American Can Co., 160 A.D.2d 174,
553 N.Y.S.2d 145 (N.Y. App. Div. 1st Dep't 1990) . . . . . . 569

Beaumont v. American Can Co., N.Y.L.J., May 20,
1991, at 25 (N.Y. Sup. Ct. N.Y. Co.) . . . . . . . . . . . . . . 569

Beaumont v. American Can Co., 215 A.D.2d 249,
626 N.Y.S.2d 201 (N.Y. App. Div. 1st Dep't), appeal

dismissed, 86 N.Y.2d 836, 658 N.E.2d 222, 634
N.Y.S.2d 444 (1995) . . . . . . . . . . . . . . . . . . . . . 569, 570

Beck v. American Casualty Co., 1990 U.S. Dist.
LEXIS 13756, 1990 WL 598573 (W.D. Tex. Apr. 12,
1990) . . . . . . . . . . . . . . . . . . . . . . . . . . . . 1995, 2024-25

Beebe v. Pacific Realty Trust, 578 F. Supp. 1128 (D.
Or. 1984) . . . . . . . . . . . . . . . . . . . . . . . . . . . . 972

Behrens v. United Investors Management Co., [1993
Transfer Binder] Fed. Sec. L. Rep. (CCH) ¶ 97,805
(Del. Ch. Oct. 1, 1993) . . . . . . . . . . . . . 188, 514, 516, 520

Belden Corp. v. InterNorth, Inc., 413 N.E.2d 98 (Ill.
App. Ct. 1980) . . . . . . . . . . . . . . . . . . . 994, 997-98, 1000

Bell Atlantic Corp. v. Bolger, 2 F.3d 1304 (3d Cir.
1993) . . . . . . . . . . . . . . . . . . . . . . . . . . . . . 1409

Bell v. Arnold, 487 P.2d 545 (Colo. 1971) . . . . . . . . . 1687-88

Bell v. Kirby Lumber Corp., 413 A.2d 137 (Del.
1980) . . . . . . . . . . . . . . . . . . . . . . . . . . . . 478, 479

Benafield v. Continental Casualty Co., 1993 U.S.
Dist. LEXIS 16887, 1993 WL 723510 (E.D. Ark.
Oct. 1, 1993) . . . . . . . . . . . . . . . . . . . . . . 2076, 2084-85

Bender v. Highway Truck Drivers & Helpers, 598 F.
Supp. 178 (E.D. Pa. 1984), aff'd mem., 770 F.2d
1066 (3d Cir. 1985) . . . . . . . . . . . . . . . . . . . . . . 1303

Bendis v. Federal Insurance Co., 1989 U.S. Dist.
LEXIS 15930, 1989 WL 161437 (D. Kan. Dec. 4,
1989), aff'd, 958 F.2d 960 (10th Cir. 1991) . . . . . . . . . . 2049

Bendis v. Federal Insurance Co., 958 F.2d 960 (10th
Cir. 1991) . . . . . . . . . . . . . . . . . . . . . . . 2001-02, 2038

Benedict v. Brennan, No. C-92-2236 (N.D. Cal. Sept.
3, 1993) . . . . . . . . . . . . . . . . . . . . . . . . 146, 1555-56

Beneficial Industrial Loan Corp. v. Smith, 170 F.2d
44 (3d Cir. 1948), aff'd sub nom. Cohen v. Beneficial
Industrial Loan Corp., 337 U.S. 541 (1949) . . . . . . . . . . 1871

Benerofe v. Cha, 1996 Del. Ch. LEXIS 115, 1996
WL 535405 (Del. Ch. Sept. 12, 1996)
. . . . . . . . . . . . . . . . 19, 45-46, 57, 94, 96, 1525, 1528-29

Benfield v. Steindler, No. C-1-92-729 (S.D. Ohio
May 3, 1993), appeal dismissed, No. 93-3652 (6th
Cir. Aug. 13, 1993) . . . . . . . . . . . . . . . . . . . . . . . 1560

Bennett v. Instrument Systems Corp., 66 A.D.2d 708,
411 N.Y.S.2d 287 (N.Y. App. Div. 1st Dep't 1978)
. . . . . . . . . . . . . . . . . . . . . . . . . . . . . . . 1471, 1559

Bennett v. Propp, 187 A.2d 405 (Del. 1962) . . . . . . 1005, 1351

Bennett v. Worden, 225 F. Supp. 42 (E.D. Ark.
1964) . . . . . . . . . . . . . . . . . . . . . . . . . . . . . . 1421

Bergstein v. Texas International Co., 453 A.2d 467
(Del. Ch. 1982), appeal denied, 461 A.2d 695 (Del.
1983) . . . . . . . . . . . . . . . . . . . . . . . . . . . 312, 1472

Berkowitz v. Legal Sea Foods, Inc., 1997 Del. Ch.
LEXIS 35, 1997 WL 153815 (Del. Ch. Mar. 24,
1997) . . . . . . . . . . . . . . . . . . . . . . . . . . . . . 1680

Berlin v. Emerald Partners, 552 A.2d 482 (Del.
1989) . . . . . . . . . . . . . . . . . . . . . . . . . . . . . 1247

Berman v. Gerber Products Co., 454 F. Supp. 1310
(W.D. Mich. 1978) . . . . . . . . . . . . . . . . . . . . . . . . . . . 1344

Bernstein v. Canet, 1996 Del. Ch. LEXIS 63, 1996
WL 342096 (Del. Ch. June 11, 1996) . . . . . . . . . . . . . . . 571

Bershad v. Curtiss-Wright Corp., 535 A.2d 840 (Del.
1987) . . . . . . . . . . . . . . . . . . . . . . . 349-50, 512, 528, 715-16

Bershad v. Hartz, 13 Del. J. Corp. L. 210 (Del. Ch.
Jan. 29, 1987) . . . . . . . . . . . . . . . . . . . . . . . . . . . . . . . 1299

Bevilacque v. Ford Motor Co., 125 A.D.2d 516, 509
N.Y.S.2d 595 (N.Y. App. Div. 2d Dep't 1986) . . . . . . . . . 108

Biesenbach v. Guenther, 588 F.2d 400 (3d Cir. 1978) . . . . . 526

Bildstein v. Atwater, 222 A.D.2d 545, 635 N.Y.S.2d
88 (N.Y. App. Div. 2d Dep't 1995)
. . . . . . . . . . . . . . . . . . . . . . 145, 232, 1491, 1550, 1552

Billman v. State of Maryland Deposit Insurance Fund
Corp., 593 A.2d 684 (Md. Ct. Spec. App.), cert.
denied, 599 A.2d 447 (Md. 1991) . . . . . . . . . . . . . . . 244-45

Bilunka v. Sanders, [1994-1995 Transfer Binder] Fed.
Sec. L. Rep. (CCH) ¶ 98,454 (N.D. Cal. Mar. 1,
1994) . . . . . . . . . . . . . . . . . . . . . . . . . . . . . . . . . . . 1477

Bird v. Penn Central Co., 334 F. Supp. 255 (E.D. Pa.
1971), reargument granted and decision adhered to,
341 F. Supp. 291 (E.D. Pa. 1972) . . . . . . . . . . . . . . . 2149-50

Black & Decker Corp. v. American Standard, Inc.,
682 F. Supp. 772 (D. Del. 1988)
. . . . . . . . . . 717-18, 753, 869-70, 1045, 1051, 1322, 1325-26

Black v. NuAire, Inc., 426 N.W.2d 203 (Minn. Ct.
App. 1988) . . . . . . . . . . . . . . . . 1612, 1695, 1702, 1705

Black Hills Corp. v. Commissioner, 73 F.3d 799 (8th
Cir. 1996) . . . . . . . . . . . . . . . . . . . . . . . . . . . . 2163

Blackwell v. Nixon, 17 Del. J. Corp. L. 1083 (Del.
Ch. Sept. 26, 1991), rev'd, 626 A.2d 1366 (Del.
1993) . . . . . . . . . . . . . . . . . . . . . . . . . . . . . . . 317

Blanchette v. Providence & Worcester Co., 428 F.
Supp. 347 (D. Del. 1977) . . . . . . . . . . . . . . . . . . . . . 526

Blasband v. Rales, 772 F. Supp. 850 (D. Del. 1991),
aff'd in part and rev'd in part, 971 F.2d 1034 (3d Cir.
1992) . . . . . . . . . . . . . . . . . . . . . . . . . . . 1427, 1437

Blasband v. Rales, 971 F.2d 1034 (3d Cir. 1992)
. . . . . . . . . . . . . . . . . . . . . . . . . . . . . 1394, 1415,
1416, 1426, 1441, 1458, 1491, 1494, 1495, 1533-34, 1573, 1583

Blasband v. Rales, 979 F.2d 324 (3d Cir. 1992) . . . . . . . 1394

Blasius Industries, Inc. v. Atlas Corp., 564 A.2d 651
(Del. Ch. 1988) . . . . . . . . . . 509, 637, 790, 791-92, 800, 804,
805-06, 813, 848, 1034, 1189, 1214, 1221, 1253-55, 1266, 1279

Blaustein v. Pan American Petroleum & Transport
Co., 293 N.Y. 281, 56 N.E.2d 705 (1944) . . . . . . . . . 297, 304

Blecker v. Araskog, No. 21946-80 (N.Y. Sup. Ct.
N.Y. Co. June 3, 1987) . . . . . 1745, 1748-49, 1751, 1753, 1755

Blish v. Thompson Automatic Arms Corp., 64 A.2d
581 (Del. 1948) . . . . . . . . . . . . . . 309, 314, 315, 335, 1382

Blosvern v. Fisher, 504 A.2d 571 (unpublished opinion, text available at 1986 Del. LEXIS 1030 and 1986 WL 16162) (Del. Jan. 30, 1986). . . . . . . . . . . . . 1435, 1492

Blumenthal v. Teets, 745 P.2d 181 (Ariz. Ct. App. 1987) . . . . . . . . . . . . . . . . . . . . . . . . . . . . . . 1459

BNS Inc. v. Koppers Co., 683 F. Supp. 458 (D. Del. 1988) . . . . . . . . . . . . . . . . . . . . . 1095, 1097, 1148, 1179

Bodkin v. Mercantile Stores Co., 22 Del. J. Corp. L. 1156 (Del. Ch. Nov. 1, 1996)
. . . . . . . . . . . . . . . . 43, 47, 66-67, 309, 314-15, 335, 1475

Boeing Co. v. Shrontz, 18 Del. J. Corp. L. 225 (Del. Ch. Apr. 20, 1992) . . . . . . . . . . . . 94, 131, 229, 1581, 1582

Boeing Co. v. Shrontz, 1994 Del. Ch. LEXIS 14, 1994 WL 30542 (Del. Ch. Jan. 19, 1994)
. . 1581, 1603, 1610, 1614, 1616, 1618, 1627-30, 1632, 1674-75

Bokat v. Getty Oil Co., 262 A.2d 246 (Del. 1970) . . . . . . 1391

Boland v. Engle, 113 F.3d 706 (7th Cir. 1997)
. . . . . . . . . . . . 4, 1442, 1457-58, 1478, 1489, 1569-70, 1593

Bomarko, Inc. v. International Telecharge, Inc., 1994 Del. Ch. LEXIS 51, 1994 WL 198726 (Del. Ch. May 16, 1994) . . . . . . . . . . . . . . . . . . . . . . . . . . . . . 484

Bonime v. Biaggini, 10 Del. J. Corp. L. 610 (Del. Ch. Dec. 7, 1984), aff'd mem., 505 A.2d 451 (Del. 1985) . . . . . . . . . . . . . . . . . . . . . . . . . . . . . . 1390

Boston Children's Heart Foundation, Inc. v. Nadal-Ginard, 73 F.3d 429 (1st Cir. 1996) . . . . . 123, 135, 282, 1868

Bouhayer v. Georgalis, 169 Misc. 2d 779, 645
N.Y.S.2d 1008 (N.Y. Sup. Ct. Queens Co. 1996) . . . . . . 1560

Bovay v. H.M. Byllesby & Co., 38 A.2d 808 (Del.
1944) . . . . . . . . . . . . . . . . . . . . . . . . . . . . . 598, 600, 622

Boyer v. Wilmington Materials, Inc., 1997 Del. Ch.
LEXIS 97, 1997 WL 382979 (Del. Ch. June 27,
1997) . . . . . . . . . . 182, 192, 206-07, 285, 287, 431, 499, 518

Bowerman v. Hamner, 250 U.S. 504 (1919) . . . . . . . . . . . 1

Bowie v. Home Insurance Co., 923 F.2d 705 (9th Cir.
1991) . . . . . . . . . . . . . . . . . . . . . . . . . . . . . . . . 2023

Braddock v. Citicorp, N.Y.L.J. Aug. 14, 1997, at 22
(N.Y. Sup. Ct. N.Y. Co.) . . . . . . . . . . . . . . . . . . . . . 1410

In re Brae Corp. Shareholders Litigation, [1991 Transfer Binder] Fed. Sec. L. Rep. (CCH) ¶ 96,004 (Del.
Ch. May 14, 1991) . . . . . . . . . . . . . . . . . . . . . . . . . 518

Bragger v. Budacz, 1994 Del. Ch. LEXIS 202, 1994
WL 698609 (Del. Ch. Dec. 7, 1994) . . . . . 503, 518, 521, 524

Brambles USA, Inc. v. Blocker, 731 F. Supp. 643 (D.
Del.), motion for reargument denied, 735 F. Supp.
1239 (D. Del. 1990) . . . . . . . . . . . . . . . . . . . . . . . 1386

Brandon v. Brandon Construction Co., 776 S.W.2d
349 (Ark. 1989) . . . . . . . . . . . . . . . . . . . . . . . . . 1401

Brane v. Roth, 590 N.E.2d 587 (Ind. Ct. App. 1992) . . 74, 172

Branning v. CNA Insurance Cos., 721 F. Supp. 1180
(W.D. Wash. 1989) . . . . . . . . . . . . 2056, 2057, 2091, 2092

Branson v. Exide Electronics Corp., 645 A.2d 568
(unpublished opinion, full text available at 1994 Del.
LEXIS 129 and 1994 WL 164084) (Del. Apr. 25,
1994) . . . . . . . . . . . . . . . . . . . . . . . . . . . . 517

Braunschweiger v. American Home Shield Corp.,
[1989-1990 Transfer Binder] Fed. Sec. L. Rep. (CCH)
¶ 94,779 (Del. Ch. Oct. 26, 1989) . . . . . . . . . . 754, 955, 972

Bray v. Oklahoma Publishing Co., 17 Del. J. Corp.
L. 1093 (Del. Ch. Sept. 24, 1991) . . . . . . . . . . . . . . 1083

Brazen v. Bell Atlantic Corp., 23 Del. J. Corp. L.
177 (Del. Ch. Mar. 19, 1997), aff'd, 695 A.2d 43
(Del. 1997) . . . . . . . . . . . . . . . . . . . . . . . . . . . 539, 543

Brazen v. Bell Atlantic Corp., 695 A.2d 43 (Del.
1997)
. . . . 20-22, 539, 540, 542-43, 642, 684, 958-62, 963, 972, 977

Breswick & Co. v. United States, 134 F. Supp. 132
(S.D.N.Y. 1955), rev'd, 353 U.S. 151 (1957) . . . . . . . . 1652

Briano v. Rubio, 46 Cal. App. 4th 1167, 54 Cal.
Rptr. 2d 408 (Cal. Ct. App. 1996) . . . . . . . . . . . . . . . . 22

Brickman v. Tyco Toys, Inc., 722 F. Supp. 1054
(S.D.N.Y. 1989) . . . . . . . . . . . . . . . . . . . . . . . . . . 1456

Brickman v. Tyco Toys, Inc., 731 F. Supp. 101
(S.D.N.Y. 1990) . . . . . . . . . . . . . . . . . . . . . . . . . . 342

Briggs v. Spaulding, 141 U.S. 132 (1891) . . . . . . 1, 12, 242-43

British Printing & Communication Corp. v. Harcourt
Brace Jovanovich, Inc., 664 F. Supp. 1519 (S.D.N.Y.
1987) . . . . . . . . . . . . . . . . . . . . . . . . . . . . . . . . . . . 181,
185, 186, 187, 191, 192, 194, 687, 870-72, 902-03, 1040, 1041-42

Broad v. Rockwell International Corp., 642 F.2d 929
(5th Cir.) (en banc), cert. denied, 459 U.S. 965
(1981) . . . . . . . . . . . . . . . . . . . . . . . . . . . . . . . . . . . 590

Broderick v. Marcus, 152 Misc. 413, 272 N.Y.S. 455
(N.Y. Sup. Ct. N.Y. Co. 1934) . . . . . . . . . . . . . . . . . . 244

Brody v. Chemical Bank, 482 F.2d 1111 (2d Cir.),
cert. denied, 414 U.S. 1104 (1973) . . . . . . . . . . . 1577, 1686

Brody v. Chemical Bank, 517 F.2d 932 (2d Cir.
1975) . . . . . . . . . . . . . . . . . . . . . . . . . . . . . . . . . . . 1681

Brody v. Zaucha, 697 A.2d 749 (Del. 1997)
. . . . . . . . . . . . . . . . . . . . . . . . 513, 521, 523, 524, 1206

Bronzaft v. Caporali, 162 Misc. 2d 281, 616
N.Y.S.2d 863 (N.Y. Sup. Ct. N.Y. Co. 1994) . . . . . . . . 1389

Brook v. Acme Steel Co, 15 Del. J. Corp. L. 149
(Del. Ch. May 11, 1989) . . . . . . . . . . . . . . . . . 1436, 1610

Brooks v. American Export Industries, 68 F.R.D. 506
(S.D.N.Y. 1975) . . . . . . . . . . . . . . . . . . . . . . . 1489, 1491

Brooks v. Brooks Pontiac, Inc., 389 P.2d 185 (Mont.
1964) . . . . . . . . . . . . . . . . . . . . . . . . . . . . . . . . . . . 1612

Brown v. Ferro Corp., 763 F.2d 798 (6th Cir.), cert.
denied, 474 U.S. 947 (1985) . . . . . . . . . . . 1298, 1301, 1319

Brown v. Halbert, 271 Cal. App. 2d 252, 76 Cal.
Rptr. 781 (Cal. Ct. App. 1969) . . . . . . . . . . . . . . . . . . 523

Brown v. Tenney, 532 N.E.2d 230 (Ill. 1988) . . . . . 1415, 1416

Broz v. Cellular Information Systems, Inc., 673 A.2d
148 (Del. 1996) . . . . . . . . . . . . . . . 294, 295, 301, 302, 304

In re Bruning, 143 B.R. 253 (D. Colo. 1992) . . . . . . . . . . 597

Brunswick Corp. v. Pueblo Bowl-O-Mat, Inc., 429
U.S. 477 (1977) . . . . . . . . . . . . . . . . . . . . . . . . . . . . . 1337

In re Buckhead America Corp., 178 B.R. 956 (D.
Del. 1994) . . . . . . . . . . . . . . . . . . . . . . . . . . . . . . . . . 626

Buckhorn, Inc. v. Ropak Corp., 656 F. Supp. 209
(S.D. Ohio), aff'd mem., 815 F.2d 76 (6th Cir.
1987) . . . . . . . . . . . . . . . . . . . . . . 179, 187, 191, 192, 640,
722, 869, 1091, 1121, 1126-31, 1302, 1303, 1304, 1315-18, 1320

In re Budget Rent A Car Corp. Shareholders Litigation, [1991 Transfer Binder] Fed. Sec. L. Rep. (CCH)
¶ 96,120 (Del. Ch. Mar. 15, 1991) . . . . . . . . 52, 371, 373-74

Buffalo Forge Co. v. Ogden Corp., 555 F. Supp. 892
(W.D.N.Y.), aff'd, 717 F.2d 757 (2d Cir.), cert.
denied, 464 U.S. 1018 (1983) . . . . . . . . . . . . . . . . . . . . 910

Buffalo Forge Co. v. Ogden Corp., 717 F.2d 757 (2d
Cir.), cert. denied, 464 U.S. 1018 (1983) . . . . . . . . . . 909-10

Burdon v. Erskine, 401 A.2d 369 (Pa. Super. Ct.
1979) . . . . . . . . . . . . . . . . . . . . . . . . . . . . . . . . . . . . . 1687

Burg v. Horn, 380 F.2d 897 (2d Cir. 1967) . . . . . . . . 297, 304

Burghart v. Landau, 821 F. Supp. 173 (S.D.N.Y.),
aff'd mem., 9 F.3d 1538 (2d Cir. 1993), cert. denied,
510 U.S. 1196 (1994) . . . . . . . . . . . . . . . . 312, 1412, 1458

Burks v. Lasker, 441 U.S. 471 (1979)
. . . . . . . . . . 3, 1406, 1407, 1450, 1460-62, 1684-85, 1767-68

Burlington Industries, Inc. v. Edelman, 666 F. Supp.
799 (M.D.N.C.), aff'd, [1987 Transfer Binder] Fed.
Sec. L. Rep. (CCH) ¶ 93,339 (4th Cir. June 22,
1987) . . . . . . . . . . . . . . . . . . . . . . . . . . . . . . 1336

Burlington Industries, Inc. v. Edelman, [1987 Transfer
Binder] Fed. Sec. L. Rep. (CCH) ¶ 93,339 (4th Cir.
June 22, 1987) . . . . . . . . . . . . . . . . . . . . . . . . 1335

Burns v. International Insurance Co., 929 F.2d 1422
(9th Cir. 1991) . . . . . . . . . . . . . . . . . . . . . . . . 1998

Burnup & Sims, Inc. v. Posner, 688 F. Supp. 1532
(S.D. Fla. 1988) . . . . . . . . . . . . . . . . . . . . 1335, 1336

Burt v. Danforth, 742 F. Supp. 1043 (E.D. Mo.
1990) . . . . . . . . . . . . . . . . . . . . . . . . . . . 136, 1456

Burt v. Danforth, No. 89-1276C (1) (E.D. Mo. Nov.
28, 1990) . . . . . . . . . . . . . . . . . . . . . . . . . . . 1784

Burton v. Exxon Corp., 583 F. Supp. 405 (S.D.N.Y.
1984) . . . . . . . . . . . . . . . . . . . . . . . . . . . 374-75

Business Roundtable v. Securities & Exchange Commission, 905 F.2d 406 (D.C. Cir. 1990) . . . . . . . . . 1060-63

Byers v. Baxter, 69 A.D.2d 343, 419 N.Y.S.2d 497
(N.Y. App. Div. 1st Dep't 1979) . . . . . . . . . . . . . . 1796

Byrne v. Lord, [1995-1996 Transfer Binder] Fed. Sec.
L. Rep. (CCH) ¶ 98,987 (Del. Ch. Nov. 9, 1995)
. . . . . . . . . . . . . . . . . . . . . . . . . 321, 322, 323, 337-40

C-T of Virginia, Inc. v. Barrett, 124 B.R. 689 (W.D.
Va. 1990) . . . . . . . . . . . . . . . . . . . . . . . . . . . 727, 812

California Union Insurance Co. v. American Diversified Savings Bank, 914 F.2d 1271 (9th Cir. 1990),
cert. denied, 498 U.S. 1088 (1991) . . . . . . . . . . . . . 2005-06

California Union Insurance Co. v. American Diversified Savings Bank, 948 F.2d 556 (9th Cir. 1991) . . . . . . 2090

Cambridge Fund, Inc. v. Abella, 501 F. Supp. 598
(S.D.N.Y. 1980) . . . . . . . . . . . . . . . . . . . . 1883, 1972-73

Campanelli v. Solomon, N.Y.L.J., Sept. 11, 1992, at
26 (N.Y. Sup. Ct. Nassau Co.) . . . . . . . . . . . . . . . . 1560

Campbell v. Loew's Inc., 134 A.2d 565 (Del. Ch.
1957) . . . . . . . . . . . . . . . . . . . . . . . . . . . . . 1689

Canada Southern Oils, Ltd. v. Manabi Exploration
Co., 96 A.2d 810 (Del. Ch. 1953) . . . . . . . . . . . . . . . 839

Canal Capital Corp. v. French, 18 Del. J. Corp. L.
611 (Del. Ch. July 2, 1992) . . . . . . 43, 94, 218, 223-24, 1495

In re Caremark International Inc. Derivative Litigation, 698 A.2d 959 (Del. Ch. 1996)
. . 15, 75, 86-88, 93, 112, 129-31, 134, 138, 141-43, 1408, 1409

Cargill, Inc. v. Montfort of Colorado, Inc., 479 U.S.
104 (1986) . . . . . . . . . . . . . . . . . . . . . . . . 1335, 1337

Carlton Investments v. TLC Beatrice International
Holdings, Inc., 21 Del. J. Corp. L. 1084 (Del. Ch.
Apr. 16, 1996) . . . . . . . . . . . . . . . . . . . . . . . . 114, 1416

Carlton Investments v. TLC Beatrice International
Holdings, Inc., 22 Del. J. Corp. L. 1165 (Del. Ch.
Jan. 28, 1997) . . . . . . . . . . . . . . 1410, 1785, 1786, 1790-92

Carlton Investments v. TLC Beatrice International
Holdings, Inc., 23 Del. J. Corp. L. 190 (Del. Ch.
Apr. 21, 1997) . . . . . . . . . . . . . . . . . . . . . . . . 1410, 1411

Carlton Investments v. TLC Beatrice International
Holdings, Inc., 1997 Del. Ch. LEXIS 86, 1997 WL
305829 (Del. Ch. May 30, 1997) . . 203, 211, 1408, 1409, 1451,
1720, 1726-31, 1746, 1748, 1750-51, 1753-55, 1757-58, 1775-76

Carnation Co. v. Commissioner, 640 F.2d 1010 (9th
Cir.), cert. denied, 454 U.S. 965 (1981) . . . . . . . . . . . 2157

Carret v. Western Nuclear, Inc., 436 F. Supp. 952
(S.D.N.Y. 1977) . . . . . . . . . . . . . . . . . . . . . . . . . . . 368

Carson Pirie Scott & Co. v. Gould, [1995 Transfer
Binder] Fed. Sec. L. Rep. (CCH) ¶ 98,831 (Del. Ch.
July 12, 1995) . . . . . . . . . . . . . . . . . . . . . . . 1003, 1030-33

Carter Hawley Hale Stores, Inc. v. The Limited, Inc.,
No. 84-2200-AWT (C.D. Cal. Apr. 17, 1984) . . . . 1335, 1336

Carter Hawley Hale Stores, Inc. v. The Limited, Inc.,
587 F. Supp. 246 (C.D. Cal. 1984) . . . . . . . . . . . . . . . 835

Caruana v. Saligman, [1990-1991 Transfer Binder]
Fed. Sec. L. Rep. (CCH) ¶ 95,889 (Del. Ch. Dec. 21,
1990) . . . . . . . . . . . . . . 94, 755, 759, 760, 1491, 1500, 1610

Caruso v. Metex Corp., [1992 Transfer Binder] Fed.
Sec. L. Rep. (CCH) ¶ 96,967 (E.D.N.Y. July 30,
1992) . . . . . . . . . . . . . . . . . . . . . . . . . 25, 43, 271

In re Castle & Cooke Derivative Shareholder Litigation, No. C-85-0663, EFL (N.D. Cal. June 28, 1985) . . . 918-19

Caterpillar, Inc. v. Great American Insurance Co.,
864 F. Supp. 849 (N.D. Ill. 1994), aff'd, 62 F.3d 955
(7th Cir. 1995) . . . . . . . . . . . . . . . . . . . . . . . . . 1995

Caterpillar, Inc. v. Great American Insurance Co., 62
F.3d 955 (7th Cir. 1995) . . 1990, 1995, 2110-13, 2121-25, 2133

Cato v. Mid-America Distribution Centers, Inc., 1996
Tenn. App. LEXIS 551, 1996 WL 502500 (Tenn. Ct.
App. Sept. 6, 1996) . . . . . . . . . . . . . . . . . . . . . 310, 311

Cavalier Oil Corp. v. Harnett, 564 A.2d 1137 (Del.
1989) . . . . . . . . . . . . . . . . . . . . 478, 479, 483, 489, 490

Cawley v. SCM Corp., 72 N.Y.2d 465, 530 N.E.2d
1264, 534 N.Y.S.2d 344 (1988) . . . . . . . . . . . . . . 478, 568

Cede & Co. v. Technicolor, Inc., 542 A.2d 1182
(Del. 1988) . . . . . . . . . . . . . 476-78, 483-84, 486, 489, 1413

Cede & Co. v. Technicolor, Inc., 634 A.2d 345 (Del.
1993)
     . . . . 19-20, 26-27, 29, 31-34, 39, 42, 45, 47-48, 51, 74-75, 98,
110, 112, 113-14, 124, 134, 146, 153, 186, 190, 194, 262, 263, 264,
267, 268, 271, 272, 273, 282, 284, 501, 521, 525, 735, 956, 1248

Cede & Co. v. Technicolor, Inc., No. 336, 1991 (Del.
Ch. Jan. 7, 1994), aff'd, No. 336, 1991 (Del. Jan. 18,
1994), reargument denied, 636 A.2d 956 (Del. 1994) . . 521, 525

In re Cencom Cable Income Partners, L.P. Litigation,
1996 Del. Ch. LEXIS 17, 1996 WL 74726 (Del. Ch.
Feb. 15, 1996) . . . . . . . . . . . . . . . . . . . . . . . . . . . . . . 581

Centaur Partners, IV v. National Intergroup, Inc., 582
A.2d 923 (Del. 1990) . . . . . . . . . . . . . . . . . 1245, 1247-48

Central Bank v. First Interstate Bank, 511 U.S. 164
(1994) . . . . . . . . . . . . . . . . . . . . . . . . . . . . . . . . . . . 2183

Central Bank v. St. Paul Fire & Marine Insurance
Co., 929 F.2d 431 (8th Cir. 1991) . . . . . . . . . . . . . . . 1995

In re Central Banking System, Inc., 1993 WL 183692
(Del. Ch. May 12, 1993) . . . . . . . . . . 1906, 1910-11, 1916-17

Central National Bank v. Rainbolt, 720 F.2d 1183
(10th Cir. 1983) . . . . . . . . . . . . . . . . . . . . . . . . . . . 1335

Central Trust Co., N.A. v. American Avents Corp.,
771 F. Supp. 871 (S.D. Ohio 1989) . . . . . . . . . . . . . . . 881

Chamison v. Healthtrust, Inc.—The Hospital Co.,
1997 Del. Ch. LEXIS 154, 1997 WL 695576 (Del.
Ch. Oct. 29, 1997) . . . . . . . . . . . . . . . . . . . . . . . . 1912-13

Chandler v. American Casualty Co., 833 F. Supp. 735
(E.D. Ark. 1993) . . . . . . . . . . . . . . . . . . . . . . 2076, 2084-85

Chapin v. Benwood Foundation Inc., 402 A.2d 1205
(Del. Ch. 1979), aff'd sub nom. Harrison v. Chapin,
415 A.2d 1068 (Del. 1980) . . . . . . . . . . . . . . . . . . 217, 218

Charal Investment Co. v. Rockefeller, [1995-1996
Transfer Binder] Fed. Sec. L. Rep. (CCH) ¶ 98,979
(Del. Ch. Nov. 7, 1995)
    . . . . 1455, 1581, 1597, 1598, 1600-01, 1603, 1604, 1605, 1614

Charitable Corp. v. Sutton, 2 Atk. 400 (1742) . . . . . . . . . . 1, 9

Chavin v. General Employment Enterprises, Inc., 584
N.E.2d 147 (Ill. App. Ct. 1991), appeal denied, 596
N.E.2d 626 (Ill. 1992) . . . . . . . . . . . . . . . . . . . . . . 1097

Cheff v. Mathes, 199 A.2d 548 (Del. 1964) . . . . . . 69, 1351-52

Chelrob, Inc. v. Barrett, 293 N.Y. 442, 57 N.E.2d
825 (1944) . . . . . . . . . . . . . . . . . . . . . . . . . . . . . 284

Chemetron Corp. v. Crane Co., 1977-2 Trade Cas.
(CCH) ¶ 61,717 (N.D. Ill. Sept. 8, 1977) . . . . . . . . . . 1335

Ches v. Arthur, 827 F. Supp. 159 (W.D.N.Y. 1993) . . . . . 882

In re Cheyenne Software, Inc. Shareholders Litigation,
22 Del. J. Corp. L. 1176 (Del. Ch. Nov. 7, 1996)
. . . . . . . . . . . . . 181, 185, 192, 203, 520, 755, 757, 758, 759

In re Chicago & Northwest Transportation Co. Shareholders Litigation, [1995 Transfer Binder] Fed. Sec.
L. Rep. (CCH) ¶ 98,823 (Del. Ch. June 26, 1995) . . . . . . . 209

Chicago Corp. v. Munds, 172 A. 452 (Del. Ch.
1934) . . . . . . . . . . . . . . . . . . . . . . . . . . . . . . . . 478

Choate, Hall & Stewart v. SCA Services, Inc., 495
N.E.2d 562 (Mass. App. Ct. 1986) . . . . . . . . . . . . . . 1967

Chomat v. Spreckley, 1989 U.S. Dist. LEXIS 8603
(S.D. Fla. Apr. 18, 1989) . . . . . . . . . . . . . . . . . . . . 2142

Christman v. Brauvin Realty Advisors, Inc., 1997
U.S. Dist. LEXIS 19563, 1997 WL 797685 (N.D. Ill.
Dec. 3, 1997) . . . . . . . . . . . . . . . . . . . . . 1915-16, 1930

Christopher v. Liberty Oil & Gas Corp., 665 So. 2d
410 (La. Ct. App. 1995) . . . . . . . . . . . . . . . . . . . . . 1390

In re Chrysler Corp. Shareholders Litigation, [1992
Transfer Binder] Fed. Sec. L. Rep. (CCH) ¶ 96,996
(Del. Ch. July 27, 1992) . . . . . . . . . 180, 1119, 1515-16, 1524

Chrysogelos v. London, 18 Del. J. Corp. L. 237 (Del.
Ch. Mar. 25, 1992) . . . . . . . . . . . 94, 116, 1118-19, 1516-17

Cigna Insurance Co. v. Gulf USA Corp., No. CV 97-
250-N-EJL (D. Idaho Sept. 11, 1997)
. . . . . . . . . . . . . . . . . . . . . . 2057, 2059, 2070, 2071-74

Cincinnati Bell Cellular Systems Co. v. Ameritech
Mobile Phone Services, Inc, 1996 Del. Ch. LEXIS
116, 1996 WL 506906 (Del. Ch. Sept. 3, 1996),
aff'd, 692 A.2d 411 (unpublished opinion, text available at 1997 Del. LEXIS 58 and 1997 WL 80058)
(Del. Feb. 11, 1997) . . . . . . . . . . 76, 139, 182, 186, 349, 358

Cinerama, Inc. v. Technicolor, Inc., 17 Del. J. Corp.
L. 551 (Del. Ch. June 21, 1991), aff'd in part and
rev'd in part sub nom. Cede & Co. v. Technicolor,
Inc., 634 A.2d 345 (Del. 1993)
. . 19, 30, 33, 35, 48-51 113, 153-57, 159, 347, 405, 521, 525, 956

Cinerama, Inc. v. Technicolor, Inc., 663 A.2d 1134
(Del. Ch. 1994), aff'd, 663 A.2d 1156 (Del. 1995)
. . 8, 34-35, 51, 64, 133, 138-39, 478, 153, 157, 160, 161, 162,
165, 166, 201, 203, 267, 272, 380, 499, 501, 525, 765, 943, 957

Cinerama, Inc. v. Technicolor, Inc., 663 A.2d 1156
(Del. 1995) . . . . . . . . . . . . . . . . . . . . . . . . 19-21, 26-27,
29-34, 47-48, 51, 74, 98, 107, 110, 111, 112, 114-16, 152, 153,
157, 158-62, 163-64, 165-67, 202, 203, 226, 230, 266, 267, 268,
270, 272, 275, 281, 282, 284, 412, 440, 478, 531, 731, 735, 957

Citadel Holding Corp. v. Roven, 603 A.2d 818 (Del.
1992) . . . . 1868, 1871, 1872, 1895, 1909, 1913, 1914-15, 1947

Citizens Bank v. Western Employers Insurance Co.,
865 F.2d 964 (8th Cir. 1989) . . . . . . . . . . . . . . . . . . 2148

Citron v. Burns, 10 Del. J. Corp. L. 830 (Del. Ch.
Feb. 4, 1985) . . . . . . . . . . . . . . . . . . . . . . . . . . . . 1352

Citron v. Daniell, 796 F. Supp. 649 (D. Conn. 1992)
. . . . . . . 62, 1458, 1467, 1489, 1493, 1496, 1497, 1498, 1501

Citron v. E.I. DuPont de Nemours & Co., 584 A.2d
490 (Del. Ch. 1990) . . . . . . . . . . . . . . . . . . . . . . . . 184,
185, 186, 190, 191, 194, 272, 375-76, 406, 407, 464-67, 521, 523

Citron v. Fairchild Camera & Instrument Corp.,
[1988-1989 Transfer Binder] Fed. Sec. L. Rep. (CCH)
¶ 93,915 (Del. Ch. May 19, 1988), aff'd, 569 A.2d
53 (Del. 1989) . . . . . . . . . . . . . . 78, 80-81, 755, 758, 759

Citron v. Fairchild Camera & Instrument Corp., 569
A.2d 53 (Del. 1989) . . . . . . . . . . 6, 19-21, 26-27, 63, 75, 77,
110, 134, 183, 193, 283, 344, 512, 521, 525, 643, 755, 757, 758, 759

Citron v. Steego Corp., 14 Del. J. Corp. L. 634 (Del.
Ch. Sept. 9, 1988) . . . . . . . . . . 77, 79, 188, 191-92, 346, 363

City Capital Associates L.P. v. Interco Inc., 551 A.2d
787 (Del. Ch. 1988), appeal dismissed, 556 A.2d
1070 (unpublished opinion, text available at 1988 Del.
LEXIS 408 and 1988 WL 149260) (Del. Nov. 17,
1988) . . . . . . . . . . . . . . . . . . . . . . . . . . . . . . . 645, 647,
667, 698, 720-21, 772, 832, 906-07, 1149, 1161, 1162-64, 1181

City Capital Associates L.P. v. Interco Inc., No.
10105 (Del. Ch. Nov. 3, 1988) . . . . . . . . . . 668, 1164, 1183

City Federal Savings & Loan Ass'n v. Mann, No.
84-4010 (D.N.J. Aug. 2, 1985), aff'd mem., 782 F.2d
1027 (3d Cir. 1986) . . . . . . . . . . . . . . . . . . . . . 1142, 1143

City Federal Savings & Loan Ass'n v. Mann, 782
F.2d 1027 (3d Cir. 1986) . . . . . . . . . . . . . . . . . . . . . 1143

City of Indianapolis v. Chase National Bank, 314 U.S.
63 (1941) . . . . . . . . . . . . . . . . . . . . . . . . . . . . . 1417

CityFed Financial Corp. v. Office of Thrift Supervision, 58 F.3d 738 (D.C. Cir. 1995) . . . . . . . . . . . 1927-28

Clagett v. Hutchison, 583 F.2d 1259 (4th Cir. 1978) . . . . . 363

Claman v. Robertson, 128 N.E.2d 429 (Ohio 1955) . . . . . 1688

Clandening v. MGIC Indemnity Corp., No. CV 83-
2432-LTL (C.D. Cal. May 23, 1983) . . . . . . . . . . 2096, 2098
Clarendon Group, Ltd. v. Smith Laboratories, Inc.,
741 F. Supp. 1449 (S.D. Cal. 1990) . . . . . . . . . . . . . 1102

Clark v. Lomas & Nettleton Financial Corp., 625
F.2d 49 (5th Cir. 1980), cert. denied, 450 U.S. 1029
(1981) . . . . . . . . . . . . . . . . . . . . . . . . . . . . . . 1774

Clarkson Co. v. Shaheen, 660 F.2d 506 (2d Cir.
1981), cert. denied, 455 U.S. 990 (1982) . . . . . . . . . 597, 605

Cline v. Commissioner, 34 F.3d 480 (7th Cir. 1994) . . . . 1320

Clougherty Packing Co. v. Commissioner, 811 F.2d
1297 (9th Cir. 1987) . . . . . . . . . . . . . . . . . . . . . . 2157

Coast Federal Savings & Loan Ass'n v. Culverhouse,
No. 89-1998-CA-01 (Fla. Cir. Ct. July 28, 1989) . . . . . . 1097

Coggins v. New England Patriots Football Club, Inc.,
492 N.E.2d 1112 (Mass. 1986) . . . . . . . . . . . . . 369, 469-70

Cohan v. Loucks, [1993 Transfer Binder] Fed. Sec. L.
Rep. (CCH) ¶ 97,698 (Del. Ch. June 11, 1993) . . . . 90, 1654-55

Cohen v. Ayers, 596 F.2d 733 (7th Cir. 1979)
. . . . . . . . . . . . . . . . 270, 271, 312, 323, 325, 327, 328, 341

Cohen v. Beneficial Industrial Loan Corp., 337 U.S.
541 (1949) . . . . . . . . . . . . . . 1380, 1381, 1398, 1404, 1406

Cohen v. Heussinger, 1994 U.S. Dist. LEXIS 7119,
1994 WL 240378 (S.D.N.Y. May 26, 1994) . . . . . . . . . . 1422

Colan v. Monumental Corp., 524 F. Supp. 1023
(N.D. Ill. 1981) . . . . . . . . . . . . . . . . . . . . . . . . 1681, 1685

Cole v. Wilmington Materials, Inc, 1993 Del. Ch.
LEXIS 106, 1993 WL 257415 (Del. Ch. July 1,
1993) . . . . . . . . . . . . . . . . . . . . . . . . . . . . . . . . . 1821

Coleman v. American Broadcasting Co., 106 F.R.D.
201 (D.D.C. 1985) . . . . . . . . . . . . . . . . . . . . . . . . . 1836

Coleman v. Plantation Golf Club Inc., 212 So. 2d 806
(Fla. Dist. Ct. App. 1968) . . . . . . . . . . . . . . . . . . . . . 312

Coleman v. Taub, 638 F.2d 628 (3d Cir. 1981) . . . . . . . . 108

Colonial Securities Corp. v. Allen, 1983 Del. Ch.
LEXIS 393, 1983 WL 19788 (Del. Ch. Apr. 18,
1983) . . . . . . . . . . . . . . . . . . . . . . . . . . . . . . . . . 1300

Columbia Pictures Industries, Inc. v. Kerkorian, No.
6334 (Del. Ch. Dec. 16, 1980) . . . . . . 521, 522, 524, 1346-47

Comeau v. Rupp, 810 F. Supp. 1127 (D. Kan. 1992) . . . 244-46

Commercial Cotton Co. v. United California Bank, 163 Cal. App. 3d 511, 209 Cal. Rptr. 551 (Cal. Ct. App. 1985) . . . . . . . . . . . . . . . . . . . . . . . . . . . . . . . 595

Committee of Unsecured Creditors of Specialty Plastic v. Doemling, 127 B.R. 945 (Bankr. W.D. Pa.), aff'd mem., 952 F.2d 1391 (3d Cir. 1991) . . . . . . . . . . . . . . 300

Commodity Futures Trading Commission v. Richards, 1996 U.S. Dist. LEXIS 5359, 1996 WL 199729 (N.D. Ill. Apr. 23, 1996) . . . . . . . . . . . . . . . . . . . . . . . . . 1973-74

Commonwealth Associates v. Providence Health Care, Inc., 19 Del. J. Corp. L. 704 (Del. Ch. Oct. 22, 1993) . . . . . . . . . . . . . . . . . . . . . . . . . . . . . . . 798-99

ConAgra, Inc. v. Cargill, Inc., 382 N.W.2d 576 (Neb. 1986) . . . . . . . . . . . . . . . . . . . . . 984, 989-91, 1000

Condec Corp. v. Lunkenheimer Co., 230 A.2d 769 (Del. Ch. 1967) . . . . . . . . . . . . . . . . . . . . . . . 635, 839

Conklin Co. v. National Union Fire Insurance Co., 1987 U.S. Dist. LEXIS 12337, 1987 WL 108957 (D. Minn. Jan. 28, 1987) . . . . . . . . . . . . . . . . . . . 2050, 2052

Consolidated Amusement Co. v. Rugoff, [1978 Transfer Binder] Fed. Sec. L. Rep. (CCH) ¶ 96,584 (S.D.N.Y. Oct. 6, 1978) . . . . . . . . . . . . . . . . . . . . 852-53

Consolidated Gold Fields PLC v. Minorco, S.A., 871 F.2d 252 (2d Cir.), cert. denied, 492 U.S. 939 (1989) . . . . . . . . . . . . . . . . . . . . . . . . . . . . . . . 1334

In re Consumers Power Co. Derivative Litigation, 111 F.R.D. 419 (E.D. Mich. 1986) . . . . . . 1456, 1489, 1492, 1639

In re Consumers Power Co. Derivative Litigation, 132 F.R.D. 455 (E.D. Mich. 1990) . . . . . . . . . 13, 15, 18, 23, 77-78, 143, 210, 1445, 1451, 1595, 1611, 1636, 1639-40, 1753, 1838

Continental Airlines Corp. v. American General Corp., 575 A.2d 1160 (Del.), cert. dismissed, 498 U.S. 953 (1990) . . . . . . . . . . . . . . . . . . . . . . . . . . . . . 463

Continental Casualty Co. v. Allen, No. CA-5-86-252 (N.D. Tex. Feb. 16, 1988) . . . . . . . . . . . . . . . 2081-82, 2097

Continental Casualty Co. v. Allen, 710 F. Supp. 1088 (N.D. Tex. 1989) . . . . . . . . . . . . . . . . . . . . . . . . . . . 2086

Continental Casualty Co. v. Board of Education, 489 A.2d 536 (Md. 1985) . . . . . . . . . . . . . . . . . . . . . . 2136-37

Continental Copper & Steel Industries, Inc. v. Johnson, 641 F.2d 59 (2d Cir. 1981) . . . . . . . . . . . . . . . . 2022

In re Continental Illinois Securities Litigation, 572 F. Supp. 928 (N.D. Ill. 1983) . . . . . . . . . . . . . . 1736-38, 1827

In re Continental Illinois Securities Litigation, 732 F.2d 1302 (7th Cir. 1984) . . . . . . . . . . . . 1643, 1738, 1827

Continental Insurance Co. v. Metro-Goldwyn-Mayer, Inc., 107 F.3d 1344 (9th Cir. 1997) . . . . . . . . . 2010, 2015-17

Continental Insurance Co. v. Superior Court, 37 Cal. App. 4th 69, 43 Cal. Rptr. 2d 374 (Cal. Ct. App. 1995) . . . . . . . . . . . . . . . . . . . . . . . . . . 1990-91, 2020-21

Cooke v. Oolie, 1997 Del. Ch. LEXIS 92, 1997 WL
367034 (Del. Ch. June 23, 1997)
. . . . . . . . . . . . . . . . . 65-66, 229, 272, 284-85, 304, 1470

Cookies Food Products, Inc. v. Lakes Warehouse Distributing, Inc., 430 N.W.2d 447 (Iowa 1988) . . . . . . . . . . . 23

Cooper v. Central Alloy Steel Corp., 183 N.E. 439
(Ohio Ct. App. 1931) . . . . . . . . . . . . . . . . . . . . . . . . 1612

Cooper v. Parsky, 1997 U.S. Dist. LEXIS 4391, 1997
WL 242534 (S.D.N.Y. Jan. 8, 1997), magistrate
judge's report and recommendation adopted by district
court, 1997 U.S. Dist. LEXIS 3665, 1997 WL 150934
(S.D.N.Y. Mar. 27, 1997) . . . . . . . . . . . . . . . . . . . . . 597

Cooper v. USCO Power Equipment Corp., 655 So. 2d
972 (Ala. 1995) . . . . . . . . . . . . . . . . . . . . . . . . . . . 1493

Corabi v. CNA Insurance Cos., 1988 U.S. Dist.
LEXIS 18424, 1988 WL 363612 (S.D. Ohio June 21,
1988) . . . . . . . . . . . . . . . . . . . . . . . . . . . . . . . . . 2097

Corbus v. Alaska Treadwell Gold Mining Co., 187
U.S. 455 (1903) . . . . . . . . . . . . . 1441, 1594, 1606-07, 1691

In re Corporate Software Inc. Shareholders Litigation
No. 13209 (Del. Ch. Nov. 23, 1993)
. . . . . . . . . . . . 520, 755, 757, 766-67, 769, 826, 946, 951-53

Corwin v. DeTrey, 16 Del. J. Corp. L. 267 (Del. Ch.
Dec. 4, 1989) . . . . . . . . . . . . . . . . 271, 274, 275-76, 1000

Cosmopolitan Trust Co. v. Mitchell, 136 N.E. 403
(Mass. 1922) . . . . . . . . . . . . . . . . . . . . . . . . . . . . . 244

Cottle v. Hilton Hotels Corp., 635 F. Supp. 1094
(N.D. Ill. 1986) . . . . . . . . . . . 1427, 1456, 1489, 1492, 1497

Cottle v. Standard Brands Paint Co., [1990 Transfer
Binder] Fed. Sec. L. Rep. (CCH) ¶ 95,306 (Del. Ch.
Mar. 22, 1990)
. . . . . . . 519, 522, 526, 539, 547, 550, 552, 1435, 1498, 1610

Cottle v. Storer Communication, Inc., 849 F.2d 570
(11th Cir. 1988)  . . 24, 756, 757, 759, 918, 928-31, 958, 968-69

Cottrell v. Pawcatuck Co., 128 A.2d 225 (Del. 1956),
appeal dismissed and cert. denied, 355 U.S. 12
(1957) . . . . . . . . . . . . . . . . . . . . . . . . . . . . . . . . . 1485

Country Manors Ass'n v. Master Antenna Systems,
Inc., 534 So. 2d 1187 (Fla. Dist. Ct. App. 1988) . . . . . . . 1987

Country National Bank v. Mayer, 788 F. Supp. 1136
(E.D. Cal. 1992) . . . . . . . . . . . . . . . . . . . . . 1460, 1611

Cox v. Administrator U.S. Steel & Carnegie, 17 F.3d
1386 (11th Cir.), modified, 30 F.3d 1347 (11th Cir.
1994), cert. denied, 513 U.S. 1110 (1995) . . . . . . . . . . 1822

Coyer v. Hemmer, 901 F. Supp. 872 (D.N.J. 1995)
. . . . . . . . . . . . . . . . . . . . 1426, 1458, 1482, 1495, 1502

Coyne & Delany Co. v. Selman, 98 F.3d 1457 (4th
Cir. 1996) . . . . . . . . . . . . . . . . . . . . . . . . . . . . . 886

In re CPC International Stock Repurchase Securities
Litigation, No. 87-40 (D. Del. Feb. 3, 1989) . . . . . . . . . 1456

Cramer v. General Telephone & Electronics Corp.,
582 F.2d 259 (3d Cir. 1978), cert. denied, 439 U.S.
1129 (1979) . . . . . . . . . 12-13, 85, 1445, 1448-49, 1673, 1684

Crane Co. v. Harsco Corp., 511 F. Supp. 294 (D. Del. 1981) . . . . . . . . . . . . . . . . . . . . . . . . . . . . . 1005

Crawford Fitting Co. v. United States, 606 F. Supp. 136 (N.D. Ohio 1985) . . . . . . . . . . . . . . . . . . . . . 2161

In re Crazy Eddie Securities Litigation, 740 F. Supp. 149 (E.D.N.Y. 1990) . . . . . . . . . . . . . . . . . . . . . 1971

Credit Lyonnais Bank Nederland, N.V. v. Pathe Communications Corp., 17 Del. J. Corp. L. 1099 (Del. Ch. Dec. 30, 1991) . . . . . . . . . . . . . . . . . . 603-04, 620-22

Crescott Investment Associates v. Davis, 16 Del. J. Corp. L. 274 (Del. Ch. Dec. 26, 1989) . . . . . . . . . . . . 1371

Crocker v. Federal Deposit Insurance Corp., 826 F.2d 347 (5th Cir. 1987), cert. denied, 485 U.S. 905 (1988) . . . . . . . . . . . . . . . . . . . . . . . . . . . . . 1381

In re Croton River Club, Inc., 52 F.3d 41 (2d Cir. 1995) . . . . . . . . . . . . . . . . . . . . 28, 44, 80, 82, 98, 282

Crouch v. French Riviera Health Spa, 1995 U.S. Dist. LEXIS 9869, 1995 WL 405700 (E.D. La. July 7, 1995) . . . . . . . . . . . . . . . . . . . . . . . . . . . . . 1421

Crouse-Hinds Co. v. InterNorth, Inc., 518 F. Supp. 390 (N.D.N.Y.), rev'd in part and appeal dismissed in part, 634 F.2d 690 (2d Cir. 1980) . . . . . . . . . . . . . . . 832

Crouse-Hinds Co. v. InterNorth, Inc., 634 F.2d 690 (2d Cir. 1980) . . . . . . . . . . . . . . . . . . 631, 687, 917, 1348

Crown Books Corp. v. Bookstop, Inc., [1990 Transfer
Binder] Fed. Sec. L. Rep. (CCH) ¶ 95,314 (Del. Ch.
Feb. 28, 1990) . . . . . . . . . . . . . . . . . . . . . . . . . . . . . 716

CRTF Corp. v. Federated Department Stores, Inc.,
No. 88 Civ. 487 (S.D.N.Y. Mar. 21, 1988) . . . . . . . . . . 1152

CRTF Corp. v. Federated Department Stores, Inc.,
683 F. Supp. 422 (S.D.N.Y. 1988)
. . . . . . . 640, 772, 942, 970, 1095, 1105, 1147, 1150-52, 1348

C-T of Virginia, Inc. v. Barrett, 124 B.R. 689 (W.D.
Va. 1990) . . . . . . . . . . . . . . . . . . . . . . . . . . . . . . 594

CTS Corp. v. Dynamics Corp. of America, 481 U.S.
69 (1987) . . . . . . . . . . . . . . . . . . . . . . . . . . . . . . . 3

Cuker v. Mikalauskas, 692 A.2d 1042 (Pa. 1997)
. . . . . . . . . . . . . . . . . . . . 5, 10, 12-13, 15-16, 24, 98, 106,
133, 1445, 1564, 1665, 1680, 1696-97, 1710-11, 1785, 1799, 1800

Curiale v. Reissman, N.Y.L.J., July 6, 1993 (N.Y.
Sup. Ct. N.Y. Co.), aff'd mem., 202 A.D.2d 201,
609 N.Y.S.2d 777 (N.Y. App. Div. 1st Dep't 1994) . . . 26, 601

Curreri v. Verni, 156 A.D.2d 420, 548 N.Y.S.2d 540
(N.Y. App. Div. 2d Dep't 1989) . . . . . . . . . . . . . . . . 1559

Cyprus Corp. v. Whitman, 93 F.R.D. 598 (S.D.N.Y.
1982) . . . . . . . . . . . . . . . . . . . . . . . . . . . . . . . . . 1348

D-Z Investment Co. v. Holloway, [1973-1974
Transfer Binder] Fed. Sec. L. Rep. (CCH) ¶ 94,588
(S.D.N.Y. June 11, 1974) . . . . . . . . . . . . . . . . . . . . 1346

Daily Income Fund, Inc. v. Fox, 464 U.S. 523
(1984) . . . . 1381, 1384, 1407, 1414, 1440-41, 1454, 1594, 1683

In re Dairy Mart Convenience Stores, Inc. Derivative Litigation, 1997 Del. Ch. LEXIS 173, 1997 WL 732467 (Del. Ch. Nov. 13, 1997) . . . . . . . . 1401, 1402, 1821

In re Daisy Systems Corp., [1993 Transfer Binder] Fed. Sec. L. Rep. (CCH) ¶ 97,729 (N.D. Cal. Feb. 3, 1993) . . . . . . . . . . . . . . . . . . . . . . . . . . . . . . . . 561

In re Daisy Systems Corp., 97 F.3d 1171 (9th Cir. 1996) . . . . . . . . . . . . . . . . . . . . . . . . . . . . . 254-55, 901

Dalany v. American Pacific Holding Corp., 42 Cal. App. 4th 822, 50 Cal. Rptr. 2d 13 (Cal. Ct. App. 1996) . . . . . . . . . . . . . . . . . . . . . . . . . . . . . 1862-63

In re Damon Corp. Stockholders Litigation, [1988-1989 Transfer Binder] Fed. Sec. L. Rep. (CCH) ¶ 94,040 (Del. Ch. Sept. 16, 1988)
. . . . . . . . . . . . . 181, 185-86, 189, 191, 520, 522, 523, 524, 846, 1095, 1106, 1148, 1177-78, 1277-78, 1302, 1303, 1304, 1305

Danaher Corp. v. Chicago Pneumatic Tool Co., 633 F. Supp. 1066 (S.D.N.Y. 1986) . . . 79, 181, 191, 854, 870-71

Danaher Corp. v. Chicago Pneumatic Tool Co., 635 F. Supp. 246 (S.D.N.Y. 1986) . . . . . . . . . . . . . . . . . . 882

Danaher Corp. v. Chicago Pneumatic Tool Co., 1986 U.S. Dist. LEXIS 24022, 1986 WL 7001 (S.D.N.Y. June 18, 1986) . . . . . . . . . . . . . . . . . . . . . . . 1217, 1888

Daniels v. Thomas, Dean & Hoskins, Inc., 804 P.2d 359 (Mont. 1990) . . . . . . . . . . . . . . . . . . . . . . . . . . . 15

Dann v. Chrysler Corp, 174 A.2d 696 (Del. Ch. 1961) . . . . . . . . . . . . . . . . . . . . . . . . . . . . . . . . . 1472

Dart v. Kohlberg, Kravis, Roberts & Co., 1985 Del. Ch. LEXIS 416, 1985 WL 21145 (Del. Ch. May 6, 1985), reargument denied, 11 Del. J. Corp. L. 602 (Del. Ch. June 25, 1985) . . . . . . . . . . . . . . . . . . . . . . 579

Data Probe, Inc. v. CRC Information Systems, Inc., N.Y.L.J., Dec. 28, 1984, at 7 (N.Y. Sup. Ct. N.Y. Co.) . . . . . . . . . . . . . . . . . . . . . . . . . . . . . . . . . . 916-17

Data Probe Acquisition Corp. v. Datatab, Inc., 568 F. Supp. 1538 (S.D.N.Y.), rev'd, 722 F.2d 1 (2d Cir. 1983), cert. denied, 465 U.S. 1052 (1984) . . . . . . . . . . 916-17

Data Probe Acquisition Corp. v. Datatab, Inc., 722 F.2d 1 (2d Cir. 1983), cert. denied, 465 U.S. 1052 (1984) . . . . . . . . . . . . . . . . . . . . . . . . . . . . . . . . . . 916

Datapoint Corp. v. Plaza Securities Co., 496 A.2d 1031 (Del. 1985) . . . . . . . . . . . . . . . . . . . . . . . . . . 1274-76

In re Dataproducts Corp. Shareholders Litigation, [1991 Transfer Binder] Fed. Sec. L. Rep (CCH) ¶ 96,227 (Del. Ch. Aug. 22, 1991) . . . . . . 230, 507, 508, 518

David v. American Home Assurance Co., 1997 U.S. Dist. LEXIS 4177, 1997 WL 160367 (S.D.N.Y. Apr. 3, 1997) . . . . . . . . . . . . . . . . . . . . . . . . . . . . . . . . 2036

Davidowitz v. Edelman, 153 Misc. 2d 853, 583 N.Y.S.2d 340 (N.Y. Sup. Ct. Kings Co. 1992), aff'd, 203 A.D.2d 234, 612 N.Y.S.2d 882 (N.Y. App. Div. 2d Dep't 1994) . . . . . . . . . . . . . . . . . . . . . 1763, 1780-81

Davidowitz v. Edelman, 203 A.D.2d 234, 612 N.Y.S.2d 882 (N.Y. App. Div. 2d Dep't 1994) . . . . 1763, 1781

Davis v. Comed, Inc., 619 F.2d 588 (6th Cir. 1980)
. . . . . . . . . . . . . . . . . . . . . . . . . . . . . 1399, 1402, 1403

Davis Acquisition, Inc. v. NWA, Inc., [1990 Transfer
Binder] Fed. Sec. L. Rep. (CCH) ¶ 95,434 (Del. Ch.
Apr. 25, 1989) . . . . . . . . . . . . . . . . . . . . . . . . 1190, 1349

Davis & Cox v. Summa Corp., 751 F.2d 1507 (9th
Cir. 1985) . . . . . . . . . . . . . . . . . . . . . . . . 1934-35, 1937

Davis-Eisenhart Marketing Co. v. Baysden, 539
N.W.2d 140 (Iowa 1995) . . . . . . . . . . . . . . . . . . . 343, 484

Dawson v. Dawson, 645 S.W.2d 120 (Mo. Ct. App.
1982) . . . . . . . . . . . . . . . . . . . . . . . . . . . . . 1583, 1603

Day v. Quotron Systems, Inc., 16 Del. J. Corp. L.
297 (Del. Ch. Nov. 20, 1989) . . . . . . . . . . . . 183, 185, 635

In re Dayco Corp. Derivative Securities Litigation, 99
F.R.D. 616 (S.D. Ohio 1983) . . . . . . . . . . . . . . . . . . 1822

In re Dayco Corp. Derivative Securities Litigation,
102 F.R.D. 624 (S.D. Ohio 1984) . . . . . . . . . . . . . . . 1402

De Moya v. Fernandez, 559 So. 2d 644 (Fla. Dist.
Ct. App. 1990) . . . . . . . . . . . . . . . . . . . . . . . . . . 1749

Dean v. Kellogg, 292 N.W. 704 (Mich. 1940) . . . . . . . . 1382

Decker v. Clausen, 15 Del. J. Corp. L. 1022 (Del.
Ch. Nov. 6, 1989) . . . . . . . . . . . 1488, 1494, 1496, 1500, 1502

In re Delaware Racing Association, 213 A.2d 203
(Del. 1965) . . . . . . . . . . . . . . . . . . . . . . . . . . . . . 478

Delphi Easter Partners L.P. v. Spectacular Partners, Inc., 19 Del. J. Corp. L. 722 (Del. Ch. Aug. 6, 1993) . . . . . . . . . . . . . . . . . . . . . . . . . . . . . . . 1915-16

Derouen v. Murray, 604 So. 2d 1086 (Miss. 1992) . . . . . . 307

Desert Equities, Inc. v. Morgan Stanley Leveraged Equity Fund, II, L.P., 624 A.2d 1199 (Del. 1993) . . . . . . . . 80

Desert Partners, L.P. v. USG Corp., 686 F. Supp. 1289 (N.D. Ill. 1988)
. . . . . . . . . . 181, 185, 189, 1095, 1097, 1104-05, 1147, 1177

Estate of Detwiler v. Offenbecher, 728 F. Supp. 103 (S.D.N.Y. 1989) . . . . . . . . . . . . . . . . . . . . . . . . . . . 4, 15, 78, 81, 98, 182, 184, 185, 186, 190, 191, 192, 510, 756, 757, 759

Diamond v. Diamond, 307 N.Y. 263, 120 N.E.2d 819 (1954) . . . . . . . . . . . . . . . . . . . . . . . . . . . . . . . 1881-82

Diduck v. Kaszycki & Sons Contractors, Inc., 737 F. Supp. 792 (S.D.N.Y. 1990), aff'd in part and rev'd in part, 974 F.2d 270 (2d Cir. 1992) . . . . . . . . . . 1440, 1466-67

DiRocco v. Roessner, 11 Del. J. Corp. L. 604 (Del. Ch. Aug. 12, 1985), interlocutory appeal refused, 505 A.2d 452 (Del. 1995) . . . . . . . . . . . . . . . . . 1142, 1143-44

District 65, UAW v. Harper & Row, Publishers, Inc., 670 F. Supp. 550 (S.D.N.Y. 1987) . . . . . . . . . . . . . . . 886

Diversified Industries, Inc. v. Meredith, 572 F.2d 596 (8th Cir. 1978) . . . . . . . . . . . . . . . . . . . . . . . . . . . 1846

DMG, Inc. v. Aegis Corp., 9 Del. J. Corp. L. 437 (Del. Ch. June 29, 1984) . . . . . . . . . . . . . . . . . . . . . . 931

Doctor v. Harrington, 196 U.S. 579 (1905) . . . . . . . . . . 1417

Dodge v. Ford Motor Co., 170 N.W. 668 (Mich. 1919) . . . . . . . . . . . . . . . . . . . . . . . . . . . . . . . . 7-8, 15

Dolgoff v. Projectavision, Inc., 21 Del. J. Corp. L. 1128 (Del. Ch. Feb. 29, 1996) . . . . . . . . 1235-38, 1346, 1347

In re Donald J. Trump Casino Securities Litigation, 7 F.3d 357 (3d Cir. 1993), cert. denied, 510 U.S. 1178 (1994) . . . . . . . . . . . . . . . . . . . . . . . . . . . . . . . . . . . 526

In re Donald Sheldon & Co., 186 B.R. 364 (S.D.N.Y. 1995) . . . . . . . . . . . . . . . . . . . . . . . . . . . . 2031, 2032-33

Donovan v. Bierwirth, 680 F.2d 263 (2d Cir.), cert. denied, 459 U.S. 1069 (1982) . . . . . . . . . . . . . . . . . . 880-82

Donovan v. Bierwirth, 754 F.2d 1049 (2d Cir. 1985) . . . . . 881

Donovan v. Fitzsimmons, 90 F.R.D. 583 (N.D. Ill. 1981) . . . . . . . . . . . . . . . . . . . . . . . . . . . . . . . . 1822-23

Doskocil Cos. v. Griggy, 14 Del J. Corp. L. 661 (Del. Ch. Aug. 4, 1988) . . . . . . . . . . . . . . . . . . . . . . 836

Doskocil Cos. v. Griggy, 14 Del. J. Corp. L. 668 (Del. Ch. Aug. 18, 1988) . . . . . . . . . . . . . . . . . 657, 836-37

Doskocil Cos. v. Griggy, 14 Del. J. Corp. L. 682 (Del. Ch. Oct. 7, 1988) . . . . . . . . . . . . . . . . . . . . . . 1153

Dover Diversified, Inc. v. Margaux, Inc., No. 13829 (Del. Ch. Nov 4, 1994) . . . . . . . 732-33, 767, 770, 937-38, 946

Dowling v. Narragansett Capital Corp., 735 F. Supp. 1105 (D.R.I. 1990) . . . . . . . . . . . . . . . . . . . . . . . . . . 497

Doyle v. Union Insurance Co., 277 N.W.2d 36 (Neb. 1979) . . . . . . . . . . . . . . . . . . . . . . . . . . . . . . 171-72

Drage v. Ameritrust Corp., 1988 Ohio App. LEXIS 3972, 1988 WL 113631 (Ohio Ct. App. Sept. 29, 1988), appeal dismissed, 550 N.E.2d 948 (Ohio 1990) . . . . . . . . . . . . . . . . . . . . . . . . . . . . 1356

Drage v. Procter & Gamble, No. A-9401998 (Ohio Ct. Comm. Pleas Jan. 19, 1996), aff'd, 694 N.E.2d 479 (Ohio Ct. App. 1997) . . . . . . . . . . . . 1427, 1445, 1469

Drage v. Procter & Gamble, 694 N.E.2d 479 (Ohio Ct. App. 1997)
. . 24, 1445, 1448, 1468-69, 1490, 1493, 1497, 1498, 1500, 1501

Drain v. Convenant Life Insurance Co., 685 A.2d 119 (Pa. Super. 1996), appeal granted, 698 A.2d 67 (Pa. 1997) . . . . . . . . . . . . . . . . . . . . . . . . . . . 1395, 1493

Draper v. Paul N. Gardner Defined Plan Trust, 625 A.2d 859 (Del. 1993) . . . . . . . . . . . . . . . . . 3, 1426, 1459

Duffey v. Wheeler, 820 F.2d 1161 (11th Cir. 1987) . . . . . 1421

Dunphy v. Travelers' Newspaper Ass'n, 16 N.E. 426 (Mass. 1888) . . . . . . . . . . . . . . . . . . . . . . . . . . . 1611

Durfee v. Durfee & Canning, Inc., 80 N.E.2d 522 (Mass. 1948) . . . . . . . . . . . . . . . . . . . . . . . . . 297, 304

Dynamics Corp. of America v. CTS Corp., 637 F. Supp. 406 (N.D. Ill.), aff'd, 794 F.2d 250 (7th Cir. 1986), rev'd, 481 U.S. 69 (1987) . . . . . . . . . . . 1097, 1108, 1111

Dynamics Corp. of America v. CTS Corp., [1986-
1987 Transfer Binder] Fed. Sec. L. Rep. (CCH)
¶ 92,765 (N.D. Ill. May 3, 1986) . . . . . . . . . . . . . . . 1126

Dynamics Corp. of America v. CTS Corp., 794 F.2d
250 (7th Cir. 1986), rev'd, 481 U.S. 69 (1987)
. . . . . 4, 12, 16, 179, 209, 830, 1091, 1108-11, 1123-24, 1852

Dynamics Corp. of America v. CTS Corp., 635 F.
Supp. 1174 (N.D. Ill. 1986), subsequent proceedings,
638 F. Supp. 802 (N.D. Ill. 1986), rev'd, 805 F.2d
705 (7th Cir. 1986) . . . . . . . . . . . . . . . . . . . . . . 1123-24

Dynamics Corp. of America v. CTS Corp., 638 F.
Supp. 802 (N.D. Ill. 1986), rev'd, 805 F.2d 705 (7th
Cir. 1986) . . . . . . . . . . . . . . . . . . . . . . . . . . . . 1123-24

Dynamics Corp. of America v. CTS Corp., 805 F.2d
705 (7th Cir. 1986)
. . . . . . . . . . . 191, 209, 686, 830, 1091, 1121, 1123-26, 1129

Dynamics Corp. of America v. WHX Corp., 967 F.
Supp. 59 (D. Conn. 1997)
. . . . 24, 185, 192, 631, 687, 958, 970-71, 983, 1190, 1191-93

In re E.C. Warner Co., 45 N.W.2d 388 (Minn.
1950) . . . . . . . . . . . . . . . . . . . . . . . . . . . . . . . . 1852

In re E.F. Hutton Banking Practices Litigation, 634 F.
Supp. 265 (S.D.N.Y. 1986)
. . . . . . . 62, 1451-52, 1456-57, 1491, 1496, 1497, 1499, 1601

EAC Industries, Inc. v. Frantz Manufacturing Co., 11
Del. J. Corp. L. 608 (Del. Ch. June 28, 1985), aff'd,
501 A.2d 401 (Del. 1985) . . . . . . . . . . . . . . . . . 179, 187

Ed Peters Jewelry Co. v. C & J Jewelry Co., 124
F.3d 252 (1st Cir. 1997) . . . . . . . . . . . . . . . . . . 596, 598

Edelman v. Authorized Distribution Network, Inc.,
1989 Del. Ch. LEXIS 156, 1989 WL 133625 (Del.
Ch. Nov. 3, 1989) . . . . . . . . . . . . . . . . . . . . . . . 1276-77

Edelman v. Fruehauf Corp., 798 F.2d 882 (6th Cir.
1986) . . 40, 74, 173, 175, 176, 178, 180, 726, 753, 974, 977-78

Edelman v. Phillips Petroleum Co., 10 Del. J. Corp.
L. 835 (Del. Ch. Feb. 12, 1985)
. . 95, 182, 184, 194, 853, 872, 1007-08, 1345, 1352, 1503, 1514

Edelman v. Phillips Petroleum Co., 1986 Del. Ch.
LEXIS 406 (Del. Ch. June 3, 1986) . . . . . . . . . . . . . . 1133

Edick v. Contran Corp., 12 Del. J. Corp. L. 244
(Del. Ch. Mar. 18, 1986) . . . . . . . . . . . . . . . . . . . . . 507

Eglin National Bank v. Home Indemnity Co., 583
F.2d 1281 (5th Cir. 1978) . . . . . . . . . . . . . . . . . . . . 2033

Eichenholtz v. Brennan, 52 F.3d 478 (3d Cir. 1995) . . . . . 1970

Eichorn v. Rexene Corp., 604 A.2d 416 (Del. Oct.
10, 1991) . . . . . . . . . . . . . . . . . . . . . . . . . . . . . . 1411

Eisenberg v. Chicago Milwaukee Corp., 537 A.2d
1051 (Del. Ch. 1987)
. . . . . . 181, 186-87, 189, 519, 527, 539, 544, 546-47, 578-79

Eldridge v. Tymshare, Inc., 186 Cal. App. 3d 767,
230 Cal. Rptr. 815 (Cal. Ct. App. 1986) . . . . . . . . . . 22, 631

Elfenbein v. Gulf & Western Industries, Inc., 590
F.2d 445 (2d Cir. 1978) . . . . . . . . . . . . . . . . . . . . . 1441

Elgin v. Alfa Corp., 598 So. 2d 807 (Ala. 1992)
. . . . . . . . . . . . . . . . . . . . . . . . . . 1402, 1445, 1688

Eliasberg v. Standard Oil Co., 92 A.2d 862 (N.J.
Super. Ct. Ch. Div. 1952), aff'd mem., 97 A.2d 437
(N.J. 1953) . . . . . . . . . . . . . . . . . . . . . . . . . . . 312, 341

Elster v. American Airlines, Inc., 100 A.2d 219 (Del.
Ch. 1953) . . . . . . . . . . . . . . . . . . . . . . . . . . . 1414

Elward v. Peabody Coal Co., 132 N.E.2d 549 (Ill.
App. Ct. 1956) . . . . . . . . . . . . . . . . . . . . . . . . . . 341

Emerald Partners v. Berlin, 564 A.2d 670 (Del. Ch.
1989) . . . . . . . . . . . . . . . . . . . . . . . . . . 1400, 1402, 1403

Emerald Partners v. Berlin, 19 Del. J. Corp. L. 1182
(Del. Ch. Dec. 23, 1993)
. . . . . . . . . . . . . . . 19, 94, 180, 1488, 1495, 1502, 1525-26

Emerald Partners v. Berlin, 21 Del. J. Corp. L. 221
(Del. Ch. Sept. 22, 1995), appeal dismissed, 676 A.2d
902 (unpublished opinion, text available at 1995 Del.
LEXIS 466 and 1995 WL 788603) (Del. Dec. 11,
1995) . . . . . . . . . . . . . . . . . . . . . . . . . . 82, 230, 508, 517

Emerson Radio Corp. v. International Jensen Inc.,
1996 Del. Ch. LEXIS 100, 1996 WL 483086 (Del.
Ch. Aug. 21, 1996), appeal refused, 683 A.2d 58 (unpublished opinion, text available at 1996 Del. LEXIS
311 and 1996 WL 526015) (Del. Aug. 23, 1996) . . . . 346, 349,
358, 520, 645, 723, 724, 755, 757, 758, 759, 773, 781-83, 833

Ench v. Breslin, 241 A.D.2d 475, 659 N.Y.S.2d 893
(N.Y. App. Div. 2d Dep't 1997) . . . . . . . . . . . . . 29, 287-88

Endervelt v. Nostalgia Network, Inc., [1991 Transfer Binder] Fed. Sec. L. Rep. (CCH) ¶ 96,249 (Del. Ch. July 23, 1991) . . . . . . . . . . . . . . . . . . . . . . . . . . . 304, 346

Ensign Corp. v. Interlogic Trace, Inc., [1990-1991 Transfer Binder] Fed. Sec. L. Rep. (CCH) ¶ 95,766 (S.D.N.Y. Dec. 19, 1990) . . . . . . . . . . . . . . . . . . . . 1388

In re ENSTAR Group, Inc., 170 B.R. 173 (Bankr. M.D. Ala. 1994) . . . . . . . . . . . . . . . . . . . . . . . . . 2170-71

Enterra Corp. v. SGS Associates, 600 F. Supp. 678 (E.D. Pa. 1985) . . . . . . . . . . 24, 810, 824, 1368-69, 1371-72

In re Envirodyne Industries, Inc. Shareholders Litigation, 15 Del. J. Corp. L. 175 (Del. Ch. Apr. 20, 1989) . . . . . . . . . . . . . . . . . . . . . . . . . . . . 756, 757, 758

Enzweiler v. Fidelity & Deposit Co., 1986 U.S. Dist. LEXIS 25555, 1986 WL 20444 (E.D. Ky. May 13, 1986) . . . . . . . . . . . . . . . . . . . . . . . . . . . . . . . 2097-98

Equity Corp. v. Milton, 221 A.2d 494 (Del. 1966) . . . . . . . . . . . . . . . . . . . . . . . . . . . . . 295, 297, 301, 304

Equity-Linked Investors, L.P. v. Adams, 705 A.2d 1040 (Del. Ch. 1997) . 571, 579-81, 603, 646, 695-97, 725, 732, 755, 757, 760, 783-90

ER Holdings, Inc. v. Norton Co., 735 F. Supp. 1094 (D. Mass. 1990), aff'd, No. 90-1314 (1st Cir. Apr. 18, 1990) . . . . . . . . . . . . . . . . . . . . . . . . . . . . . 1215-16

ER Holdings, Inc. v. Norton Co., No. 90-1314 (1st Cir. Apr. 18, 1990) . . . . . . . . . . . . . . . . . . . . . . . . 1216

Erie Railroad Co. v. Tompkins, 304 U.S. 64 (1938)
. . . . . . . . . . . . . . . . . . . . . . . . 250, 1419, 1649

Essential Enterprises Corp. v. Automatic Steel Products, Inc., 164 A.2d 437 (Del. Ch. 1960) . . . . . . . . . . 1853

Essex Universal Corp. v. Yates, 305 F.2d 572 (2d
Cir. 1962) . . . . . . . . . . . . . . . . . . . . . . . . . . 364-65

Eureka Federal Savings & Loan Ass'n v. American
Casualty Co., 873 F.2d 229 (9th Cir. 1989) . . . . . . . . . 1992

Evanston Insurance Co. v. Federal Deposit Insurance
Corp., 1988 U.S. Dist. LEXIS 16263 (C.D. Cal. May
17, 1988), vacated, No. CV 88-0407 (C.D. Cal. July
1, 1988) . . . . . . . . . . . . . . . . . . . . . . . . . . . 2063

Evanston Insurance Co. v. Federal Deposit Insurance
Corp., No. CV 88-0407 (C.D. Cal. July 1, 1988) . . . . . . 2063

Evanston Insurance Co. v. Security Assurance Co.,
715 F. Supp. 1405 (N.D. Ill. 1989) . . . . . . . 2002, 2142, 2148

Executive Leasing Co. v. Leder, 191 A.2d 199, 594
N.Y.S.2d 217 (N.Y. App. Div. 1st Dep't 1993) . . . . . . . 1383

F/H Industries, Inc. v. National Union Fire Insurance
Co., 635 F. Supp. 60 (N.D. Ill. 1986), vacated in
part, 116 F.R.D. 224 (N.D. Ill. 1987) . . . . . . . . . . . . 2141

Fabric v. Provident Life & Accident Insurance Co.,
115 F.3d 908 (11th Cir. 1997) . . . . . . . . . . . . . . . . 2148

Facet Enterprises, Inc. v. Prospect Group, Inc., 14
Del. J. Corp. L. 310 (Del. Ch. Apr. 15, 1988) . . . . . . . . 1153

Fair v. Fuchs, N.Y.L.J., Dec. 19, 1991 at 24 (N.Y.
Sup. Ct. N.Y. Co.) ......................... 1560

Faktor v. American Bromaterials Corp., 1991 U.S.
Dist. LEXIS 11927, 1991 WL 336922 (D.N.J. May
28, 1991) ............................... 1489

Farahpour v. DCX, Inc., 635 A.2d 894 (Del. 1994) ..... 1205

Farber v. Public Service Co., [1991 Transfer Binder]
Fed. Sec. L. Rep. (CCH) ¶ 96,106 (D.N.M. Apr. 4,
1991) ................................ 1793-94

Faulkner v. American Casualty Co., 584 A.2d 734
(Md. Ct. Spec. App.), cert. denied, 590 A.2d 158
(Md. 1991) ............................ 2097-98

Fausek v. White, 965 F.2d 126 (6th Cir.), cert.
denied, 506 U.S. 1034 (1992) ................. 1822

Fe Bland v. Two Trees Management Co., 66 N.Y.2d
556, 489 N.E.2d 223, 498 N.Y.S.2d 336 (1985) ........ 568

Federal Deposit Insurance Corp. v. Abel, 1995 U.S.
Dist. LEXIS 18159, 1995 WL 716729 (S.D.N.Y.
Dec. 6, 1995) ............................ 245

Federal Deposit Insurance Corp. v. Aetna Casualty &
Surety Co., 903 F.2d 1073 (6th Cir. 1990) ........... 2090

Federal Deposit Insurance Corp. v. American Casualty
Co., 814 F. Supp. 1021 (D. Wyo. 1991) subsequent
proceedings, No. 90-CV-0265-J (D. Wyo. Sept. 9,
1994) ......... 2056, 2057, 2059, 2060, 2061, 2077, 2086

Federal Deposit Insurance Corp. v. American Casualty
Co., 843 P.2d 1285 (Colo. 1992) ............ 2077, 2092

Federal Deposit Insurance Corp. v. American Casualty
Co., 975 F.2d 677 (10th Cir. 1992) . . . . . 2075, 2076, 2085-86

Federal Deposit Insurance Corp. v. American Casualty
Co., 995 F.2d 471 (4th Cir. 1993)
. . . . . . . . . . . . . . . . . 2075, 2076, 2081, 2084, 2086, 2089

Federal Deposit Insurance Corp. v. American Casualty
Co., 998 F.2d 404 (7th Cir. 1993)
. . . . . . . . . . . . . . . . . . 1990, 2075, 2077-78, 2084, 2086

Federal Deposit Insurance Corp. v. American Casualty
Co., 528 N.W.2d 605 (Iowa 1995) . . . . . . . . . . . . . 1998-99

Federal Deposit Insurance Corp. v. Barham, 995 F.2d
600 (5th Cir. 1993) . . . . . . . . . . . . . 2003-04, 2013, 2014

Federal Deposit Insurance Corp. v. Bates, 42 F.3d
369 (6th Cir. 1994) . . . . . . . . . . . . . . . . . . . . . . 249

Federal Deposit Insurance Corp. v. Benson, 867 F.
Supp. 512 (S.D. Tex. 1994) . . . . . . . . . . . . . 5, 19, 25, 243

Federal Deposit Insurance Corp. v. Bierman, 2 F.3d
1424 (7th Cir. 1993) . . . . . . . . . . . 112, 128, 168-69, 208, 242

Federal Deposit Insurance Corp. v. Booth, 824 F.
Supp. 76 (M.D. La. 1993) . . . . . . . . . 1991, 2013, 2099, 2102

Federal Deposit Insurance Corp. v. Booth, 82 F.3d
670 (5th Cir. 1996) . . . . . . . 2003-05, 2014, 2015, 2099, 2102

Federal Deposit Insurance Corp. v. Brown, 812 F.
Supp. 722 (S.D. Tex. 1992) . . . . . . . . . . 5, 12, 19, 24-25, 137

Federal Deposit Insurance Corp. v. Canfield, 967 F.2d
443 (10th Cir.), cert. dismissed, 506 U.S. 993 (1992) . . . . . 251

Federal Deposit Insurance Corp. v. Continental Casualty Co., 796 F. Supp. 1344 (D. Or. 1991) . . . . 2077, 2085-86

Federal Deposit Insurance Corp. v. Gonzalez-Gorrondona, 833 F. Supp. 1545 (S.D. Fla. 1993) . . . . . . . . . . . 239

Federal Deposit Insurance Corp. v. Harrington, 844 F. Supp. 300 (N.D. Tex. 1994) . . . . . . . 77, 84, 121, 136, 248

Federal Deposit Insurance Corp. v. Heidrick, 812 F. Supp. 586 (D. Md. 1991), aff'd sub nom. Federal Deposit Insurance Corp. v. American Casualty Co., 995 F.2d 471 (4th Cir. 1993) . . . . . . . . . . . . . . 2075, 2081

Federal Deposit Insurance Corp. v. Interdonato, 988 F. Supp. 1 (D.D.C. 1997) . . . . . . . . . . . 1998, 2017-18, 2037

Federal Deposit Insurance Corp. v. McSweeney, 976 F.2d 532 (9th Cir. 1992), cert. denied, 508 U.S. 950 (1993) . . . . . . . . . . . . . . . . . . . . . . . . . . . . . . . 136, 251

Federal Deposit Insurance Corp. v. Mijalis, 800 F. Supp. 397 (W.D. La. 1992), aff'd in part and rev'd in part, 15 F.3d 1314 (5th Cir. 1994)
. . . . . . . . . . . . . . . . . . . . . 2055, 2079-80, 2090, 2146-47

Federal Deposit Insurance Corp. v. Mijalis, 15 F.3d 1314 (5th Cir. 1994)
. . . . . . . . . . . . . 1998, 2000, 2003-05, 2013, 2014, 2146-47

Federal Deposit Insurance Corp. v. National Union Fire Insurance Co., 630 F. Supp. 1149 (W.D. La. 1986) . . . . . . . . . . . . . . . . . . . . . . . . . . . . . . . 2065-66

Federal Deposit Insurance Corp. v. National Union Fire Insurance Co., 1989 WL 251473 (E.D. Tenn. Jan. 6, 1989) . . . . . . . . . . . . . . . . . . . . . . . . . . . . 2066

Federal Deposit Insurance Corp. v. Raffa, 882 F.
Supp. 1236 (D. Conn. 1995) . . . . . . . . . . . . . . . . . . 136

Federal Deposit Insurance Corp. v. Schreiner, 892 F.
Supp. 869 (W.D. Tex. 1995) . . . . . . . . . . . . . 19, 76, 136

Federal Deposit Insurance Corp. v. Sea Pines Co.,
692 F.2d 973 (4th Cir. 1982), cert. denied, 461 U.S.
928 (1983) . . . . . . . . . . . . . . . . . . . . . . . . . . . . 596, 598

Federal Deposit Insurance Corp. v. St. Paul Fire &
Marine Insurance Co., 993 F.2d 155 (8th Cir. 1993) . . . . 2011

Federal Deposit Insurance Corp. v. Stahl, 854 F.
Supp. 1565 (S.D. Fla. 1994), aff'd in part and rev'd
in part, 89 F.3d 1510 (11th Cir. 1996) . . . . . 22-23, 99, 251-52

Federal Deposit Insurance Corp. v. Stahl, 89 F.3d
1510 (11th Cir. 1996) . . . . . . . . . . . . . . . . . . . . 5, 15, 91

Federal Deposit Insurance Corp. v. Wheat, 970 F.2d
124 (5th Cir. 1992) . . . . . . . . . . . . . . . . . . . . . . . . . 98

Federal Deposit Insurance Corp. v. Zaborac, 773 F.
Supp. 137 (C.D. Ill. 1991), aff'd sub nom. Federal
Deposit Insurance Corp. v. American Casualty Co.,
998 F.2d 404 (7th Cir. 1993) . . . . . . . . . . 2055, 2057, 2060

Federal Insurance Co. v. National Distributing Co.,
417 S.E.2d 671 (Ga. Ct. App. 1992), cert. denied,
1992 Ga. LEXIS 665 (Ga. July 16, 1992) . . . . . . . . . . 1986

Federal Insurance Co. v. Oak Industries, Inc.,
[1985-1986 Transfer Binder] Fed. Sec. L. Rep. (CCH)
¶ 92,519 (S.D. Cal. Feb. 3, 1986) . . . . . . . . . . . . 2145, 2148

Federal Realty Investment Trust v. Pacific Insurance Co., 760 F. Supp. 533 (D. Md. 1991) . . . . . . . . . 2130, 2135

Federal Savings & Loan Insurance Corp. v. Burdette, 718 F. Supp. 649 (E.D. Tenn. 1989)
. . . . . . . . . . . . . . . . . . . . . . . . . 1992, 1998, 2096, 2153

Federal Savings & Loan Insurance Corp. v. Heidrick, 774 F. Supp. 352 (D. Md.), reconsideration granted sub nom. Federal Deposit Insurance Corp. v. Heldrick 812 F. Supp. 586 (D. Md. 1991), aff'd sub nom. Federal Deposit Insurance Corp. v. American Casualty Co., 995 F.2d 471 (4th Cir. 1993) . . . . . . . . . . . . . . . 2081

Federal Savings & Loan Insurance Corp. v. Huff, 704 P.2d 372 (Kan. 1985) . . . . . . . . . . . . . . . . . . . . . . 246-47

Federal Savings & Loan Insurance Corp. v. Mmahat, 1988 U.S. Dist. LEXIS 1825, 1988 WL 19304 (E.D. La. Mar. 3, 1988)
. . . . . . . . . . . . . . . . . 2056, 2057, 2058, 2081, 2091, 2092

Federal Savings & Loan Insurance Corp. v. Musacchio, 695 F. Supp. 1053 (N.D. Cal. 1988) . . . . . . . . . . . . 28

Federal Savings & Loan Insurance Corp. v. Oldenburg, 671 F. Supp. 720 (D. Utah 1987) . . . . . . . . . 2091, 2092

Federal Savings & Loan Insurance Corp. v. Shelton, 789 F. Supp. 1355 (M.D. La. 1992) . . . . . . . . . . . 2076, 2085

Federal United Corp. v. Havender, 11 A.2d 331 (Del. 1940) . . . . . . . . . . . . . . . . . . . . . . . . . . . . . . 565

Feinberg v. Carter, 652 F. Supp. 1066 (S.D.N.Y. 1987) . . . . . . . . . . . . . . . . . . . . . . . 1357, 1361-63, 1774

Ferber v. Armstrong, No. 27878/91 (N.Y. Sup. Ct.
May 6, 1992) . . . . . . . . . . . . . . . . . . . . 1496, 1501, 1559

Ferris Elevator Co. v. Neffco, Inc., 674 N.E.2d 449
(Ill. App. Ct. 1996) . . . . . . . . . . . . . . . . . . . . . . 19, 23

Fidelity & Deposit Co. v. Conner, 1991 U.S. Dist.
LEXIS 11874, 1991 WL 229954 (S.D. Tex. June 3,
1991), aff'd, 973 F.2d 1236 (5th Cir. 1992) . . . . . . . . . . 2048

Fidelity & Deposit Co. v. Conner, 973 F.2d 1236 (5th
Cir. 1992) . . . . . . . . . . . . . 2047-48, 2075, 2084, 2086, 2089

Fidelity & Deposit Co. v. Zandstra, 756 F. Supp. 429
(N.D. Cal. 1990) . . . . . . . . . . . 2056, 2058, 2059, 2060, 2061

Fidelity Federal Savings & Loan Ass'n v. Felicetti,
830 F. Supp. 262 (E.D. Pa. 1993)
. . . . . . . . . . . . . . . . . . 1906, 1909, 1926, 1931-33, 1962

Field v. Trump, 850 F.2d 938 (2d Cir. 1988), cert.
denied, 489 U.S. 1012 (1989) . . . . . . . . . . . . . . . . . . 526

Fight Against Coercive Tactics Network, Inc. v. Coregis Insurance Co., 926 F. Supp. 1426 (D. Colo.
1996) . . . . . . . . . . . . . . . . . . 2093, 2098-2101, 2138-39

Finci v. American Casualty Co., 593 A.2d 1069 (Md.
1991) . . 1382, 2056, 2059, 2060, 2077, 2081, 2086-87, 2089-90

Findley v. Garrett, 109 Cal. App. 2d 166, 240 P.2d
421 (Cal. Ct. App. 1952) . . . . . . 1450-51, 1499, 1561-62, 1611

Fink v. Golenbock, 680 A.2d 1243 (Conn. 1996) . . . 1401, 1402

Firestone Tire & Rubber Co. v. Bruch, 489 U.S. 101
(1989) . . . . . . . . . . . . . . . . . . . . . . . . . . . . . . 879

First American Bank & Trust v. Frogel, 726 F. Supp. 1292 (S.D. Fla. 1989) . . . . . . . . . . . . . . . . . . . . . . . . . 1456

In re First Boston, Inc. Shareholders Litigation, [1990 Transfer Binder] Fed. Sec. L. Rep. (CCH) ¶ 95,322 (Del. Ch. June 7, 1990) . . . . . . . . . . . . 405, 409, 410, 825-26

First Chicago International v. United Exchange Co., 125 F.R.D. 55 (S.D.N.Y. 1989) . . . . . . . . . . . . . . . . . 1869

First Fidelity Bancorporation v. National Union Fire Insurance Co., 1994 U.S. Dist. LEXIS 3977, 1994 WL 111363 (E.D. Pa. Mar. 30, 1994)
. . . . . . . . . . . . . . . . . . . . . . . . . 1994-95, 2131-32, 2135

First National Bancshares of Beloit, Inc. v. Geisel, 853 F. Supp. 1333 (D. Kan. 1994) . . . . . . . . . . . . . . 1424-25

First New York Bank for Business v. Selzer, N.Y.L.J., July 11, 1990, at 21 (N.Y. Sup. Ct. N.Y. Co.) . . . . . . . . . . . . . . . . . . . . . . . . . . . . . . . . . . . 1559

First Options, Inc. v. Polonitza, 1989 U.S. Dist. LEXIS 13813, 1989 WL 153008 (N.D. Ill. Nov. 14, 1989) . . . . . . . . . . . . . . . . . . . . . . . . . . . . . . . . . . 597

First Options, Inc. v. Polonitza, 1990 U.S. Dist. LEXIS 9449, 1990 WL 114740 (N.D. Ill. July 31, 1990) . . . . . . . . . . . . . . . . . . . . . . . . . . . . . . . . 598, 604

First National Bank Holding Co. v. Fidelity & Deposit Co., 885 F. Supp. 1533 (N.D. Fla. 1995)
. . . . . . . . . . . . . . . . . . . . . . . . . 2031, 2143-44, 2148

First State Bank v. American Casualty Co., 1994
Minn. App. LEXIS 448, 1994 WL 193751 (Minn. Ct.
App. May 17, 1994) . . . . . . . . . . . . . . . . . . . . . . . . . 1991

First State Underwriters Agency v. Public Utility District No. 1, 41 F.3d 1513 (unpublished opinion, text
available at 1994 U.S. App. LEXIS 31307 and 1994
WL 637139) (9th Cir. Nov. 7, 1994), cert. denied,
516 U.S. 822 (1995) . . . . . . . . . . . . . . . . . . . . . . . . . 2027

Fischer v. CF & I Steel Corp., 599 F. Supp. 340
(S.D.N.Y. 1984) . . . . . . . . . . . . . . . . . . . . . . . . . . 1577-78

Fisher v. United Technologies Corp., 6 Del. J. Corp.
L. 380 (Del. Ch. May 12, 1981) . . . . . . . . . . . . . . . 519, 522

Fisher v. Weitzen, No. 28159/82 (N.Y. Sup. Ct. N.Y.
Co. May 26, 1983) . . . . . . . . . . . . . . . . . . . . . . 1300, 1301

Flanagan v. Bernstein, 1996 U.S. Dist. LEXIS 1915,
1996 WL 84184 (N.D. Ill. Feb. 22, 1996) . . . . . . . . . . 23, 28

Fleer v. Frank H. Fleer Corp., 125 A. 411 (Del. Ch.
1924) . . . . . . . . . . . . . . . . . . . . . . . . . . . . . . . . . . 1472

In re Fleet/Norstar Securities Litigation, 935 F. Supp.
99 (D.R.I. 1996) . . . . . . . . . . . . . . . . . . . . . . . . . . . . 98

Fleming v. International Pizza Supply Corp., 676
N.E.2d 1051 (Ind. 1997) . . . . . . . . . . . . . . . . . . . . . . 498

Fliegler v. Lawrence, 361 A.2d 218 (Del. 1976)
. . . . . . . . . . . . . . . . . . . . . . . . . . . . . . 270, 275, 529

Flintkote Co. v. Lloyd's Underwriters, 1976 WL
16591 (N.Y. Sup. Ct. July 27, 1976), aff'd mem., 56

A.D.2d 743, 391 N.Y.S.2d 1005 (N.Y. App. Div. 1st
Dep't 1977) . . . . . . . . . . . . . . . . . . . . . . . . . 1982, 1985

In re FLS Holdings, Inc. Shareholders Litigation, 19
Del. J. Corp. L. 270 (Del. Ch. Apr. 2, 1993), aff'd
sub nom. Sullivan Money Management, Inc. v. FLS
Holdings, Inc., 628 A.2d 84 (unpublished opinion,
text available at 1993 Del. LEXIS 251 and 1993 WL
245341) (Del. June 18, 1993) . . . . . . . . . . . . . 69, 395, 578

Flynn v. Bass Bros. Enterprises, Inc., 744 F.2d 978
(3d Cir. 1984) . . . . . . . . . . . . . . . . . . . . . . . . . . 506

FMA Acceptance Co. v. Leatherby Insurance Co.,
594 P.2d 1332 (Utah 1979) . . . . . . . . . . . . . . . . . . . 123

Forman v. Chesler, 167 A.2d 442 (Del. 1961) . . . . . . . . 327

In re Formica Corp. Shareholders Litigation, [1989
Transfer Binder] Fed. Sec. L. Rep. (CCH) ¶ 94,362
(Del. Ch. Mar. 22, 1989) . . 520, 756, 757, 769, 945, 948-49, 972

Fornaseri v. Cosmosart Realty & Building Corp., 96
Cal. App. 549, 274 P. 597 (Cal. Ct. App. 1929) . . . . . . . . . 22

In re Fort Howard Corp. Shareholders Litigation, 14
Del. J. Corp. L. 699 (Del. Ch. Aug. 8, 1988)
. . . . . . . . . . 702, 756, 757, 758, 769, 826, 945-48, 972, 982

In re Forum Group, Inc., 82 F.3d 159 (7th Cir.
1996) . . . . . . . . . . . . . . . . . . . . . . . . . . . . . . . . 1296

Foster v. Kentucky Housing Corp., 850 F. Supp. 558
(E.D. Ky. 1994) . . . . . . . . . . . . . . . . . . . . . . 2049, 2053

Fox v. Chase Manhattan Corp., 11 Del. J. Corp. L.
888 (Del. Ch. Dec. 6, 1985) . . . . . . . . . . . . . . . 2045, 2167

Fox v. Cosgriff, 159 P.2d 224 (Idaho 1945) . . . . . . . . . . 365

Fox v. Reich & Tang, Inc., 94 F.R.D. 94 (S.D.N.Y.), rev'd, 692 F.2d 250 (2d Cir. 1982), aff'd sub nom. Daily Income Fund, Inc. v. Fox, 464 U.S. 523 (1984) . . . . . . . . . . . . . . . . . . . . . . . . . . . . . 1593

Frances T. v. Village Green Owners Ass'n, 42 Cal. 3d 490, 723 P.2d 573, 229 Cal. Rptr. 456 (1986) . . . . . 15, 17

Francis v. United Jersey Bank, 432 A.2d 814 (N.J. 1981) . . . . . . . . . . . . . . . . . . . . . . . . . . . . . 595

Frank v. Arnelle, No. 15642 (Del. Ch. Apr. 22, 1997) . . . . . . . . . . . . . . . . . . . . . . . . . . . . . 520

Frank B. Hall & Co. v. Ryder System, Inc., No. 82, C 0092 (N.D. Ill. July 12, 1982) . . . . . . . . . . . . 1333, 1335

Frank Lerner & Associates, Inc. v. Vassy, 599 N.E.2d 734 (Ohio Ct. App. 1991) . . . . . . . . . . . . . 123, 241

Frank & Rose Steele Foundation v. Tudor Insurance Co., No. 12891-11 (Wash. Ct. App. June 7, 1994) . . . . . . 2049

Frankel v. Donovan, 120 A.2d 311 (Del. Ch. 1956) . . . . 325-26

In re Franklin National Bank Securities Litigation, 2 B.R. 687 (E.D.N.Y. 1979), aff'd mem. sub nom. Corbin v. Franklin National Bank, 633 F.2d 203 (2d Cir. 1980) . . . . . . . . . . . . . . . . . . . . . . . . 244, 283-84

Frantz Manufacturing Co. v. EAC Industries, 501 A.2d 401 (Del. 1985) . . . . . . . . . . . . . . . . . 635, 869, 1144

Freedman v. Barrow, 427 F. Supp. 1129 (S.D.N.Y. 1976) . . . . . . . . . . . . . . . . . . . . . . . . . . . . . 341

Freedman v. Braddock, N.Y.L.J., May 19, 1993, at 25 (N.Y. Sup. Ct. N.Y. Co.), aff'd mem., 202 A.D.2d 197, 609 N.Y.S.2d 777 (N.Y. App. Div. 1st Dep't 1994) . . . . . . . . . . . . . . . . . . . . . . . . . . . 231, 341

Freedman v. Restaurant Associates Industries, Inc., [1987-1988 Transfer Binder] Fed. Sec. L. Rep. (CCH) ¶ 93,502 (Del. Ch. Oct. 16, 1987) . . . . . . . . . . . . . . . . . . . . . 15, 69, 756, 757, 777-78, 824

Freedman v. Restaurant Associates Industries, Inc., [1990-1991 Transfer Binder] Fed. Sec. L. Rep. (CCH) ¶ 95,617 (Del. Ch. Sept. 21, 1990) . . . . . . . 349, 357, 431, 435-37, 716, 756, 759, 766, 772, 778

Friedman v. Baxter Travenol Laboratories, Inc., 1986 Del. Ch. LEXIS 367, 1986 WL 2254 (Del. Ch. Feb. 18, 1986) . . . . . . . . . . . . . . . . . . . . . . . . . . . . . . 973-74

Friedman v. Beningson, 21 Del. J. Corp. L. 659 (Del. Ch. Dec. 4, 1995), appeal refused, 676 A.2d 900 (unpublished opinion, text available at 1996 Del. LEXIS 11 and 1996 WL 33704) (Del. Jan. 10, 1996) . . . . . . . . . . . . . . . . . . . . . . . . . . . . . 59, 1511, 1520-21

Friedman v. Beway Realty Corp., 87 N.Y.2d 161, 661 N.E.2d 972, 638 N.Y.S.2d 399 (1995) . . . . . . . . 478, 479

Fry v. Trump, 681 F. Supp. 252 (D.N.J. 1988) . . . 1357, 1363

Fujisawa Pharmaceutical Co. v. Kapoor, 655 A.2d 307 (unpublished opinion, text available at 1995 Del. LEXIS 25 and 1995 WL 24906) (Del. Jan. 17, 1995) . . . . . . . . . . . . . . . . . . . . . . . . . . . 1910, 1957

Fuller v. American Machine & Foundry Co., 91 F. Supp. 710 (S.D.N.Y. 1950) . . . . . . . . . . . . . . . . . . . 1382

In re Fuqua Industries, Inc. Shareholder Litigation,
1992 Del. Ch. LEXIS 204, 1992 WL 296448 (Del.
Ch. Oct. 8, 1992) . . . . . . . . . . . . . . . . . . . . . . . . . . . . 1821

In re Fuqua Industries, Inc. Shareholder Litigation,
1997 Del. Ch. LEXIS 72, 1997 WL 257460 (Del. Ch.
May 13, 1997) . . . . . . . . . . . . . . . . . . . . . . . . . . . . 17, 26,
518, 524, 636, 657-58, 1381, 1426, 1511, 1530, 1532, 1574, 1610

Futernick v. Statler Builders, Inc., 112 N.W.2d 458
(Mich. 1961) . . . . . . . . . . . . . . . . . . . . . . . . . . . . . . . . 1612

GA Enterprises, Inc. v. Leisure Living Communities,
Inc., 517 F.2d 24 (1st Cir. 1975) . . . . . . . . . . . . . . . . 1399

Gabelli & Co. v. Liggett Group, Inc., 479 A.2d 276
(Del. 1984) . . . . . . . . . . . . . . . . . . . . . . . . . . . . . . . . 1039

Gabelli & Co. Profit Sharing Plan v. Liggett Group,
Inc., 444 A.2d 261 (Del. Ch. 1982) . . . . . . . . . . . . . . . . . 41

Gabelli & Co. Profit Sharing Plan v. Liggett Group,
Inc., 479 A.2d 276 (Del. 1984) . . . . . . . . . . . . . . . . . . . 375

Gabhart v. Gabhart, 370 N.E.2d 345 (Ind. 1977) . . . . . . . 1397

Gadd v. Pearson, 351 F. Supp. 895 (M.D. Fla.
1972) . . . . . . . . . . . . . . . . . . . . . . . . . . . . . . . . . . . . . 244

GAF Corp. v. Heyman, 724 F.2d 727 (2d Cir. 1983) . . . . . 526

GAF Corp. v. Union Carbide Corp., 624 F. Supp.
1016 (S.D.N.Y. 1985)
. . . . . . . . . . . 15, 687, 809-10, 1035, 1037-38, 1322, 1323-24

Gaff v. Federal Deposit Insurance Corp., 814 F.2d
311 (6th Cir.), vacated in part, 828 F.2d 1145 (6th
Cir. 1987) . . . . . . . . . . . . . . . . . . . . . . . . . . . 1381

Gaffin v. Teledyne, Inc., [1987-1988 Transfer Binder]
Fed. Sec. L. Rep. (CCH) ¶ 93,523 (Del. Ch. Oct. 9,
1987) . . . . . . . . . . . . . . . . . . . . . . . . . . . . . . 508

Gaffin v. Teledyne, Inc., 1990 Del. Ch. LEXIS 198,
1990 WL 195914 (Del. Ch. Dec. 4, 1990), aff'd in
part and rev'd in part, 611 A.2d 467 (Del. 1992) . . . . . . . . 532

Gaffin v. Teledyne, Inc., 611 A.2d 467 (Del. 1992)
. . . . . . . . . . . . . . . . . . . . . . . . . 508, 530, 532-33, 538

Gagliardi v. TriFoods International, Inc., 683 A.2d
1049 (Del. Ch. 1996) (published in part, complete text
available at 1996 Del. Ch. LEXIS 87 and 1996 WL
422330)
. . . . . 7, 13-14, 37, 81-82, 86-87, 89, 92-93, 95, 97, 152, 202,
312, 313, 316, 1384, 1385, 1427, 1448-49, 1490, 1514, 1604, 1610

Gaillard v. Natomas Co., 173 Cal. App. 3d 410, 219
Cal. Rptr. 74 (Cal. Ct. App. 1985) . . . . . . . . . . . 1300, 1396

Gaillard v. Natomas Co., 208 Cal. App. 3d 1250, 256
Cal. Rptr. 702 (Cal. Ct. App. 1989)
. . . 22, 131, 202, 1297, 1302, 1303, 1304, 1312-13, 1320, 1360

Gaines v. Haughton, 645 F.2d 761 (9th Cir. 1981)
cert. denied, 454 U.S. 1145 (1982) . . . . . . . . 1466, 1695, 1708

Galdi v. Berg, 359 F. Supp. 698 (D. Del. 1973) . . . . . . . 1865

Galef v. Alexander, 615 F.2d 51 (2d Cir. 1980)
. . . . . . . . . . . . . . . . . . . . 99, 1462-63, 1747, 1774, 1775

Gall v. Exxon Corp., 418 F. Supp. 508 (S.D.N.Y. 1976) . . . . . . . . . . 93, 1380, 1441, 1612, 1651-54, 1690-92

Gans v. MDR Liquidating Corp., 1990 Del. Ch. LEXIS 3, 1990 WL 2851 (Del. Ch. Jan. 10, 1990) . . . . . . . . . . . . . . . . . . . . . . . . . . . . . 597, 598, 599

Garber v. Lego, 1992 WL 554239 (W.D. Pa. Oct. 2, 1992), aff'd, 11 F.3d 1197 (3d Cir. 1993) . . . . . . . 1491, 1492

Garber v. Lego, 11 F.3d 1197 (3d Cir. 1993) . . . . . . . . . . . . . . . . . . . . . 7, 311, 313, 314, 1441, 1458

Garland's Inc. Profit Sharing Plan v. Pillsbury Co., No. 88-17834 (Minn. Dist. Ct. Dec. 16, 1988) . . . . . . . . 1165

Garner v. Wolfinbarger, 430 F.2d 1093 (5th Cir. 1970), cert. denied, 401 U.S. 974 (1971) . . . . . . 1820-21, 1837

Gary v. American Casualty Co., 753 F. Supp. 1547 (W.D. Okla. 1990) . . . . . . . . . . . . . . . 2061-63, 2077, 2086

Garza v. TV Answer, Inc., 19 Del. J. Corp. L. 290 (Del. Ch. Mar. 11, 1993) . . . . . . . . . . . . . . . . . . . . . . . 70

Gaubert v. Federal Home Loan Bank Board, 863 F.2d 59 (D.C. Cir. 1988) . . . . . . . . . . . . . . . . . . . . . . . 1456

In re Gaylord Container Corp. Shareholders Litigation, 22 Del. J. Corp. L. 1207 (Del. Ch. Dec. 19, 1996) . . . . . . . . . . . . . . . . 640, 644, 645, 1115-18, 1514

Gearhart Industries, Inc. v. Smith International, Inc., 592 F. Supp. 203 (N.D. Tex.), aff'd in part, rev'd in part and modified in part, 741 F.2d 707 (5th Cir. 1984) . . . . . . . . . . . . . . . . . . . . . . . . . . . . . . . 1334

Gearhart Industries, Inc. v. Smith International, Inc.,
741 F.2d 707 (5th Cir. 1984) . . . . . . . . . . . . . 136, 1144-46

Gelco Corp. v. Coniston Partners, 652 F. Supp. 829
(D. Minn. 1986), aff'd in part and vacated in part,
811 F.2d 414 (8th Cir. 1987) . . . . . . . . . . . . . . . . 23, 632,
686, 726-27, 810, 901-02, 1013-15, 1095, 1098, 1107, 1170, 1171

Gelco Corp. v. Coniston Partners, 811 F.2d 414 (8th
Cir. 1987) . . . . . . . . . . . . . . . . . . . . . . . . . . . 726, 1016

In re Genentech, Inc. Shareholders Litigation, [1990
Transfer Binder] Fed. Sec. L. Rep. (CCH) ¶ 95,317
(Del. Ch. June 6, 1990) . . . . . . . . . . . . . . . . . . . . . . . 520

General Electric Co. v. Welch, N.Y.L.J., Dec. 30,
1992, at 27 (N.Y. Sup. Ct. N.Y. Co.)
. . . . . . . . . . . . . . . . . . . . . 1492, 1495, 1498, 1500, 1501

Trustees of General Electric Pension Trust v. Leven-
son, 18 Del. J. Corp. L. 364 (Del. Ch. Mar. 3,
1992) . . . . . . . . . . . . . . . . . . . . . . . . . . . . . . . 464, 500

In re General Homes Corp., 199 B.R. 148 (S.D. Tex.
1996) . . . . . . . . . . . . . . . . . . . . . . . . . . . 311, 316, 600

In re General Motors Class E Stock Buyout Securities
Litigation, 694 F. Supp. 1119 (D. Del. 1988), reargu-
ment granted and decision rev'd, 790 F. Supp. 77 (D.
Del. 1992) . . . . . . . . . . . . . . . . . . . . . . . 1596, 1618, 1620

In re General Motors Class E Stock Buyout Securities
Litigation, 790 F. Supp. 77 (D. Del. 1992) . . . . . . 1428, 1620

General Portland, Inc. v. LaFarge Coppee S.A.,
[1982-1983 Transfer Binder] Fed. Sec. L. Rep. (CCH)
¶ 99,148 (N.D. Tex. Aug. 28, 1981) . . . . . . . . . . . . . 1370

In re General Tire & Rubber Co. Securities Litigation,
726 F.2d 1075 (6th Cir.), cert. denied, 469 U.S. 858
(1984) .... 1466, 1696, 1708, 1722, 1747, 1750, 1752-53, 1755

Genzer v. Cunningham, 498 F. Supp. 682 (E.D.
Mich. 1980) .......... 1696, 1708, 1746, 1748, 1750, 1755

Georgia-Pacific Corp. v. Great Northern Nekoosa
Corp., 727 F. Supp. 31 (D. Me. 1989) ............ 1090

Georgia-Pacific Corp. v. Great Northern Nekoosa
Corp., 728 F. Supp. 807 (D. Me. 1990) ........... 1097

Georgia-Pacific Corp. v. Great Northern Nekoosa
Corp., 731 F. Supp. 38 (D. Me. 1990) .......... 1289-90

Gerdes v. Reynolds, 28 N.Y.S.2d 622 (N.Y. Sup. Ct.
N.Y. Co. 1941) .............................. 366

Gerrits v. Brannen Banks Inc., 138 F.R.D. 574 (D.
Colo. 1991) ................................ 1821

Getty Oil Co. v. Skelly Oil Co., 267 A.2d 883 (Del.
1970) ............................. 350, 370, 373

Geyer v. Ingersoll Publications Co., 621 A.2d 784
(Del. Ch. 1992) ................ 597, 620, 622, 623-24

Giammalvo v. Sunshine Mining Co., 19 Del. J. Corp.
L. 1203 (Del. Ch. Jan. 31, 1994), aff'd, 651 A.2d
787 (unpublished opinion, text available at 1994 Del.
LEXIS 332 and 1994 WL 621998) (Del. Oct. 28,
1994) ...................... 39, 53, 82, 182, 188

Gibson v. BoPar Dock Co., 780 F. Supp. 371 (W.D.
Va. 1991) ........................... 1421, 1422

Gilbert v. Bagley, 492 F. Supp. 714 (M.D.N.C. 1980) . . . . . . . . . . . . . . . . . . . . . . . . . . . . . . . . . 28

Gilbert v. Burnside, 13 A.D.2d 982, 216 N.Y.S.2d 430 (N.Y. App. Div. 2d Dep't 1961), aff'd mem., 11 N.Y.2d 960, 183 N.E.2d 325, 229 N.Y.S.2d 10 (1962) . . . . . . . . . . . . . . . . . . . . . . . . . . . . . . . 203

Gilbert v. El Paso Co., 14 Del. J. Corp. L. 727 (Del. Ch. Nov. 21, 1988), aff'd, 575 A.2d 1131 (Del. 1990) . . . . . . . . . . . . . . . . . . . . . . . . . . . . . . 559

Gilbert v. El Paso Co., 490 A.2d 1050 (Del. Ch. 1984), aff'd, 575 A.2d 1131 (Del. 1990) . . . . . . . . . 252, 347

Gilbert v. El Paso Co., 575 A.2d 1131 (Del. 1990) . . . . 68-69, 560-61, 639, 641, 647, 649-50, 660, 663, 716-17, 755, 758, 908

Gilliam v. American Casualty Co., 735 F. Supp. 345 (N.D. Cal. 1990) . . . . . . . . . . . . . . . . . . . . . . 1991, 1998

Gimbel v. Signal Cos., 316 A.2d 599 (Del. Ch.), aff'd, 316 A.2d 619 (Del. 1974) . . . . . . . . . . . . . 88-89, 1485

Gintel v. XTRA Corp., No. 11422 (Del. Ch. Feb. 27, 1990) . . . . . . . . . . . . . . . . . . . . . . . . . . . . . 1207-08

Glaser v. Norris, [1990 Transfer Binder] Fed. Sec. L. Rep. (CCH) ¶ 95,433 (Del. Ch. July 13, 1989) . . . . . . . . . 109

Glassman v. Computervision Corp., 90 F.3d 617 (1st Cir. 1996) . . . . . . . . . . . . . . . . . . . . . . . . . . . . 506

Glassman v. Wometco Cable TV, Inc., 1989 Del. Ch.
LEXIS 1, 1989 WL 1160 (Del. Ch. Jan. 6, 1989)
. . . . . . . . . . . . . . . . . . . . . . . . . . . . 517, 518, 526

Glazer v. Pasternak, 693 A.2d 319 (Del. 1997) . . . . . . 1247-48

Glazer v. Zapata Corp., 658 A.2d 176 (Del. Ch.
1993) . . . . . . . . . . . . . . . . . . . . . . . . 96, 657-58, 837-39

Globus v. Law Research Service, Inc., 418 F.2d 1276
(2d Cir. 1969), cert. denied, 397 U.S. 913 (1970)
. . . . . . . . . . . . . . . . . . . . . . . . . . . . . 1970, 1985-86

Glosser v. Ketchum & Co., N.Y.L.J., May 9, 1991
(N.Y. Sup. Ct. N.Y. Co.) . . . . . . . . . . . . . . . . . . . . 469

GM Sub Corp. v. Liggett Group, Inc., 1980 Del. Ch.
LEXIS 581, 1980 WL 6430 (Del. Ch. Apr. 25,
1980) . . . . . . . . . . . . . . . . . . . . . . . . . . . 905-06, 1343

Godbold v. Branch Bank, 11 Ala. 191 (1847) . . . . . . . . 10, 12

Godley v. Crandall & Godley Co., 181 A.D. 75, 168
N.Y.S. 251 (N.Y. App. Div. 1st Dep't 1917), aff'd
mem., 227 N.Y. 656, 126 N.E. 907 (1920) . . . . . . . . . . 1383

Goldberg v. Meridor, 567 F.2d 209 (2d Cir. 1977),
cert. denied, 434 U.S. 1069 (1978) . . . . . . . . . . . . . . . 526

Goldsholl v. Shapiro, 417 F. Supp. 1291 (S.D.N.Y.
1976) . . . . . . . . . . . . . . . . . . . . . . . . . . . . . . 1410

Goldstein v. Groesbeck, 142 F.2d 422 (2d Cir.), cert.
denied, 323 U.S. 737 (1944) . . . . . . . . . . . . . . . . . . 1415

Gollust v. Mendell, 501 U.S. 115 (1991) . . . . . . . . . . . 1393

Golub v. PPD Corp., 576 F.2d 759 (8th Cir. 1978) . . . . . . 526

Gon v. First State Insurance Co., 871 F.2d 863 (9th
Cir. 1989) . . . . . . . . . . . . . . . . . . . . . . . 2098-99, 2137-38

Gonsalves v. Straight Arrow Publishers, Inc., 1996
Del. Ch. LEXIS 106, 1996 WL 483093 (Del. Ch.
Aug. 22, 1996), aff'd, 701 A.2d 357 (Del. 1997) . . . . . . . . 478

Gonsalves v. Straight Arrow Publishers, Inc., 22 Del.
J. Corp. L. 1215 (Del. Ch. Nov. 27, 1996), rev'd,
701 A.2d 357 (Del. 1997) . . . . . . . . . . . . . . . . . . . . 483

Gonsalves v. Straight Arrow Publishers, Inc., 701
A.2d 357 (Del. 1997) . . . . . . . . . . . . . . . . . 477, 479, 485

Gonzalez Turul v. Rogatol Distributors, Inc., 951
F.2d 1 (1st Cir. 1991) . . . . . . . . . . . 1458, 1470, 1673, 1675

Good v. Getty Oil Co., 514 A.2d 1104 (Del. Ch.
1986) . . . . . . . . . . . . . . . . . . . . . . . . 1454, 1498, 1674

Good v. Texaco, Inc., 9 Del. J. Corp. L. 461 (Del.
Ch. May 14, 1984) . . . . . . . . . . . . . . . . 1372, 1517-18, 1674

Goodman v. 225 East 74th Apartments Corp.,
N.Y.L.J., Aug. 19, 1997, at 22 (N.Y. Sup. Ct. N.Y.
Co. 1997) . . . . . . . . . . . . . . . . . . . . . . . . . . . . . 570

Goodwin v. Castleton, 144 P.2d 725 (Wash. 1944) . . . . . . 1612

Gottesfeld v. Richmaid Ice Cream Co., 115 Cal. App.
2d 854, 252 P.2d 973 (Cal. Ct. App. 1953) . . . . . . . . . . 1562

Gottesman v. General Motors Corp., 268 F.2d 194
(2d Cir. 1959) . . . . . . . . . . . . . . . . . . . . . . . . . . 1688

Gottlieb v. Heyden Chemical Corp., 90 A.2d 660
(Del.), reargument granted and denied, 91 A.2d 57
(Del.), decision adhered to on reargument, 92 A.2d
594 (Del. 1952) . . . . . . . . . . . . . . . 283, 329, 330-31, 332-33

Gottlieb v. Heyden Chemical Corp., 91 A.2d 57
(Del.), decision adhered to on reargument, 92 A.2d
594 (Del. 1952) . . . . . . . . . . . . . . . . . . . . . 275, 283, 328

Grace Bros., Ltd. v. Farley Industries, Inc., 450
S.E.2d 814 (Ga. 1994) . . . . . . . . . . . 485, 496, 1389, 1414

In re Grace Energy Corp. Shareholders Litigation, 18
Del. J. Corp. L. 690 (Del. Ch. June 26, 1992), appeal
denied, 610 A.2d 725 (unpublished opinion, text available at 1992 Del. LEXIS 246 and 1992 WL 153465)
(Del. June 26, 1992) . . . . . . . . . . . . . . . . . . . . . . . 65, 113

Grafman v. Century Broadcasting Corp., 743 F. Supp.
544 (N.D. Ill. 1990) . . . . . . . . . . . . . . . . . . . 1456, 1784

Grafman v. Century Broadcasting Corp., 762 F. Supp.
215 (N.D. Ill. 1991) . . . . . . . . . . . . . . . . . . . . . . . 1775

Graham v. Allis-Chalmers Manufacturing Co., 188
A.2d 125 (Del. 1963) . . . . . . . . . . . . 128, 203, 1537, 1538

Granada Investments, Inc. v. DWG Corp., 823 F.
Supp. 448 (N.D. Ohio 1993) . . . . . . . . . . . 12-13, 15-18, 24

Grand Council v. Owens, 620 N.E.2d 234 (Ohio Ct.
App. 1993) . . . . . . . . . . . . . . 1382, 1412, 1427, 1445, 1448

Grand Metropolitan PLC v. Pillsbury Co., No. 10319
(Del. Ch. Oct. 4, 1988) . . . . . . . . . . . . . . . . . . . . . 1344

Grand Metropolitan PLC v. Pillsbury Co., 14 Del. J.
Corp. L. 1042 (Del. Ch. Nov. 7, 1988) . . . . . . . 1180-81, 1344

Grand Metropolitan PLC v. Pillsbury Co., 558 A.2d
1049 (Del. Ch. 1988)
. . . . . . . 667, 668, 854, 907, 1162, 1164-65, 1181, 1183, 1344

Gray v. Zondervan Corp., 712 F. Supp. 1275 (W.D.
Mich. 1989)
. . . . . . . . 23, 756, 757, 758, 773-74, 913, 958, 966, 970, 982

Great Western Producers Co-Operative v. Great Western United Corp., 613 P.2d 873 (Colo. 1980)
. . . . . . . . . . . . . . . . . . . . . . . 984, 987-88, 1000, 1234

Green v. Phillips, 22 Del. J. Corp. L. 360 (Del. Ch.
June 19, 1996) . . . . . 43-44, 229, 230, 1473, 1475, 1495, 1497

Green v. Westcap Corp., 492 A.2d 260 (Del. Super.
1985) . . . . . . . . . . . . . . . . . . . . . . . . . . . . . 1858, 1864

Greenfield v. National Medical Care, Inc., 12 Del. J.
Corp. L. 737 (Del. Ch. June 6, 1986) . . . . . . . . . . . . 917-18

Greenfield Savings Bank v. Abercrombie, 97 N.E. 897
(Mass. 1912) . . . . . . . . . . . . . . . . . . . . . . . . . . . . . 244

Greenspun v. Del E. Webb Corp., 634 F.2d 1204 (9th
Cir. 1980) . . . . . . . . . . . . . . . . . . 1440, 1456, 1489, 1492

Greenwood Cemetery, Inc. v. Travelers Indemnity
Co., 232 S.E.2d 910 (Ga. 1977) . . . . . . . . . . . . . . . . 1986

Gregory v. Correction Connection, Inc. 1991 U.S.
Dist. LEXIS 3659, 1991 WL 42992 (E.D. Pa. Mar.
27, 1991), reconsideration denied, 1991 U.S. Dist.

LEXIS 6521, 1991 WL 83095 (E.D. Pa. May 15,
1991) . . . . . . . . . . . . . . . . . . . . . 721, 722, 799, 851-852

Griesse v. Lang, 175 N.E. 222 (Ohio Ct. App. 1931) . . . . 1852

Grill v. Hoblitzell, 771 F. Supp. 709 (D. Md. 1991)
. . . . . . . . . . . . . . . . . 1427, 1458, 1493, 1500, 1501, 1687

Grimes v. Donald, 20 Del. J. Corp. L. 757 (Del. Ch.
Jan. 11, 1995), aff'd, 673 A.2d 1207 (Del. 1996)
. . . . . . . . . . . . . . . . . . . . . . . . . 41, 215, 217, 219-21

Grimes v. Donald, 673 A.2d 1207 (Del. 1996)
. . . . . . 20-21, 26-28, 42, 216, 217, 219-21, 1301, 1412, 1413,
1415, 1426, 1443, 1447-48, 1455, 1473, 1475-77, 1479, 1482,
1488, 1490, 1493, 1504, 1563, 1579, 1582, 1594, 1596, 1609,
1614, 1615, 1617, 1618, 1620, 1673-74, 1677-78, 1680, 1690

Grimes v. Vitalink Communications Corp., 1997 Del.
Ch. LEXIS 124, 1997 WL 538676 (Del. Ch. Aug. 26,
1997) . . . . . . . . . . . . . . . . . . . . . . . . . . . . . . . . . . 481

Grobow v. Perot, No. 8759 (Del. Ch. June 12, 1987) . . . . 1674

Grobow v. Perot, 526 A.2d 914 (Del. Ch. 1987),
aff'd, 539 A.2d 180 (Del. 1988)
. . . . . . . . . . . 37, 1354, 1459, 1488, 1492, 1494, 1495, 1498

Grobow v. Perot, 539 A.2d 180 (Del. 1988)
. . . . . . . 20-21, 29, 44-45, 62, 94, 180, 184, 185, 1354, 1427,
1473-75, 1479, 1481-82, 1483, 1496, 1497, 1520, 1524, 1529, 1530

Grobow v. Perot, [1989-1990 Transfer Binder] Fed.
Sec. L. Rep. (CCH) ¶ 94,869 (Del. Ch. Jan. 2,
1990), aff'd sub nom. Levine v. Smith, 591 A.2d 194
(Del. 1991) . . . . . . . . . . . . . . . . . . . . . . . . . . . . . . 1498

Groel v. United Electric Co., 61 A. 1061 (N.J. Ch. 1905) . . . . . . . . . . . . . . . . . . . . . . . . . . . . . 1612

Grossman v. Johnson, 89 F.R.D. 656 (D. Mass. 1981), aff'd, 674 F.2d 115 (1st Cir.), cert. denied, 459 U.S. 838 (1982) . . . . . . . . . . . . . . . . . . . . 1708, 1721

Grossman v. Johnson, 674 F.2d 115 (1st Cir.), cert. denied, 459 U.S. 838 (1982) . . . . . . . . . . . . . . . 1592, 1695

Grossman v. Young, 72 F. Supp. 375 (S.D.N.Y. 1947) . . . . . . . . . . . . . . . . . . . . . . . . . . . . . 1685

Grove v. Daniel Valve Co., 874 S.W.2d 150 (Tex. Ct. App. 1994) . . . . . . . . . . . . . . . . . . . . . . . . 1953

Grumman Corp. v. LTV Corp., 665 F.2d 10 (2d Cir. 1981) . . . . . . . . . . . . . . . . . . . . . . . . . . . . . 1334

Grynberg v. Farmer, [1980 Transfer Binder] Fed. Sec. L. Rep. (CCH) ¶ 97,683 (D. Colo. Oct. 8, 1980) . . 1749, 1751

Guard-Life Corp. v. Parker Hardware Manufacturing Corp., 50 N.Y.2d 183, 406 N.E.2d 445, 428 N.Y.S.2d 628 (1980) . . . . . . . . . . . . . . . . . . . . . . 993

Gulf Oil Corp. v. Commissioner, 914 F.2d 396 (3d Cir. 1990) . . . . . . . . . . . . . . . . . . . . . . . . . . . 2157

Guth v. Loft, Inc., 5 A.2d 503 (Del. 1939) . . . . . . . . . . . . . . . . . . . . . . . . . . 262, 294-95, 297, 302

Guzewicz v. Eberle, 953 F. Supp. 108 (E.D. Pa. 1997) . . . . . . . . . . . . . . . . . . . . . . . . . . . . . 1382

H.F. Ahmanson & Co. v. Great Western Financial
Corp., 1997 Del. Ch. LEXIS 55, 1997 WL 225696
(Del. Ch. Apr. 25, 1997) . . . . . . . . . . . . . . . . . . . 1226-28

H.F. Ahmanson & Co. v. Great Western Financial
Corp., 1997 Del. Ch. LEXIS 84, 1997 WL 305824
(Del. Ch. June 3, 1997) . . . 802-03, 962, 972, 1222-26, 1229-35

H.S. Equities, Inc. v. Hartford Accident & Indemnity
Co., 661 F.2d 264 (2d Cir. 1981) . . . . . . . . . . . . . . 2134

Haber v. Bell, 465 A.2d 353 (Del. Ch. 1983)
. . . . . . . . . . . . . . . . . . . . . . . . . 43, 312, 327, 1489

Haberman v. Tobin, 466 F. Supp. 447 (S.D.N.Y.
1979) . . . . . . . . . . . . . . . . . . . . . . . . . . . . . . 1405

Haberman v. Washington Public Power Supply System, 744 P.2d 1032 (Wash. 1987), appeal dismissed,
488 U.S. 805 (1988) . . . . . . . . . . . . . . . . . . . . . . . 1682

Haenel v. Epstein, 88 A.D.2d 652, 450 N.Y.S.2d 536
(N.Y. App. Div. 2d Dep't 1982) . . . . . . . . . . . . . . . 1866

Haft v. Dart Group Corp., 1994 Del. Ch. LEXIS 200,
1994 WL 643185 (Del. Ch. Nov. 14, 1994) . . . . . . . . . . 323

Hagelberg v. Brunschwig, N.Y.L.J., June 29, 1977, at
15 (N.Y. Sup. Ct. Queens Co.) . . . . . . . . . . . . . . . . 1559

Hahn v. Carter-Wallace, Inc., 13 Del. J. Corp. L. 668
(Del. Ch. Oct. 9, 1987) . . . . . . . . . . . . . . 640, 826, 1074-75

Halifax Fund, L.P. v. Response U.S.A., Inc., 1997
Del. Ch. LEXIS 76 (Del. Ch. May 13, 1997) . . . . . . . . 577-78

Hall v. Aliber, 614 F. Supp. 473 (E.D. Mich. 1985)
. . . . . . . . . . . . . . . . . . . . . . 1399, 1457, 1489, 1491

Hall v. John S. Isaacs & Sons Farms, Inc., 146 A.2d
602 (Del. Ch. 1958), aff'd, 163 A.2d 288 (Del.
1960) . . . . . . . . . . . . . . . . . . . . . . . . . . . . . . . . 316

Hall v. Staha, 800 S.W.2d 396 (Ark. 1990) . . . . . . . . . . . 22

Hall v. Tennessee Dressed Beef Co., 1996 Tenn. App.
LEXIS 384, 1996 WL 355074 (Tenn. Ct. App. June
28, 1996), aff'd in part and rev'd in part, 957 S.W.2d
536 (Tenn. 1997) . . . . . . . . . . . . . . . . . . . . . . . . 24, 99

Halprin v. Babbitt, 303 F.2d 138 (1st Cir. 1962) . . . . . . . 1594

Hamilton v. Nozko, 1994 Del. Ch. LEXIS 139, 1994
WL 413299 (Del. Ch. July 26, 1994) . . . . . . . . . . . . . . 398

Hanson v. Ontario Milk Producers Cooperative, Inc.,
58 Misc. 2d 138, 294 N.Y.S.2d 936 (N.Y. Sup. Ct.
Oswego Co. 1968) . . . . . . . . . . . . . . . . . . . . . . . . . . 98

Hanson Trust PLC v. ML SCM Acquisition Inc., 781
F.2d 264 (2d Cir. 1986)
. . 24, 40, 74, 93, 110, 111, 113, 137, 173-75, 180, 186, 187, 192,
193, 194, 204-05, 215, 631, 687, 688, 918, 921, 925-28, 931, 1319

Harbor Finance Partners v. Sugarman, 1997 Del. Ch.
LEXIS 49, 1997 WL 162175 (Del. Ch. Apr. 3,
1997). . . . . . . . . . . . . . . . . . . . . . . . . . 60-61, 380, 399

Harbor Insurance Co. v. Continental Illinois Corp.,
1989 U.S. Dist. LEXIS 14300, 1989 WL 152648
(N.D. Ill. Nov. 27, 1989), rev'd, 922 F.2d 357 (7th
Cir. 1990) . . . . . . . . . . . . . . . . . . . . . . . . . . . . . 2001

Harbor Insurance Co. v. Continental Bank Corp., 922
F.2d 357 (7th Cir. 1990)
. . . . . . . . . . . . . . . 2001, 2009-10, 2026, 2113, 2116, 2123

Harbor Insurance Co. v. Superior Court, No.
E006522 (Cal. Ct. App. May 12, 1989), reprinted in
Corp. Officers & Directors Liability Litig. Rep. 6,130
(May 24, 1989), petition for review denied, 1989 Cal.
LEXIS 4084 (Cal. Aug. 10, 1989) . . . . . . . . . . . . . . . 1990

Harriman v. E.I. DuPont de Nemours & Co., 411 F.
Supp. 133 (D. Del. 1975) . . . . . . . . . . . . . . . . . . 346, 374

Harris v. Carter, 582 A.2d 222 (Del. Ch. 1990)
. . . . 366-67, 1412, 1468, 1473-75, 1527, 1532, 1572, 1573-74

Harris v. Insuranshares of America, Inc., 1988 Del.
Ch. LEXIS 145, 1988 WL 119409 (Del. Ch. Nov. 7,
1988) . . . . . . . . . . . . . . . . . . . . . . . . . . . . . . . . 1674

Harris v. Resolution Trust Corp., 939 F.2d 926 (11th
Cir. 1991) . . . . . . . . . . . . . . . . . . . . . . . . . . . . . 1865

Harristown Development Corp. v. International Insurance Co., 1988 U.S. Dist. LEXIS 12791, 1988 WL
123149 (M.D. Pa. Nov. 15, 1988)
. . . . . . . . . . . . . . . . . . 2103, 2106-07, 2136-37, 2145-46

Hart v. General Motors Corp., N.Y.L.J. Mar. 6,
1987, at 7 (N.Y. Sup. Ct. N.Y. Co.), rev'd, 129
A.D.2d 179, 517 N.Y.S.2d 490 (N.Y. App. Div. 1st
Dep't), leave to appeal denied, 70 N.Y.2d 608, 515
N.E.2d 910, 521 N.Y.S.2d 225 (1987) . . . . . . . . . . . 1459-60

Hart v. General Motors Corp., 129 A.D.2d 179, 517
N.Y.S.2d 490 (N.Y. App. Div. 1st Dep't), leave to

appeal denied, 70 N.Y.2d 608, 515 N.E.2d 910, 521
N.Y.S.2d 225 (N.Y. 1987) . . . . . . . . . . . . . . . . 3, 1459-60

Hartford Fire Insurance Co. v. Federated Department
Stores, Inc., 723 F. Supp. 976 (S.D.N.Y. 1989) . . . 592, 593-94

Harvard Industries, Inc. v. Tyson, [1986-1987 Transfer Binder] Fed. Sec. L. Rep. (CCH) ¶ 93,064 (E.D.
Mich. Nov. 25, 1986) . . . . . . . . . . . . . . . . . . . 1098, 1107

Hasan v. CleveTrust Realty Investors, 729 F.2d 372
(6th Cir. 1984)
. . . . . . . . . . 1695-96, 1722, 1740-41, 1751-52, 1755, 1769-70

Hastings-Murtagh v. Texas Air Corp., 649 F. Supp.
479 (S.D. Fla. 1986) . . . . . . . . . . . . . . . . . 910-11, 940-41

Havens v. Attar, 22 Del. J. Corp. L. 1230 (Del. Ch.
Jan. 30, 1997) . . 179, 182, 304, 354-55, 1888, 1899-1900, 1917

Havens v. Attar, 1997 Del. Ch. LEXIS 164, 1997 WL
770670 (Del. Ch. Sept. 22, 1997)
. . . . . . . . . . . . . . . . . . . . 179, 181, 1888, 1899, 1900-01

Havens v. Attar, 1997 Del. Ch. LEXIS 147, 1997 WL
695579 (Del. Ch. Nov. 5, 1997)
. . . . . . . . . . . . 179, 181, 1888, 1899, 1901-02, 1904, 1929

Hawes v. City of Oakland, 104 U.S. 450 (1881)
. . . . . . . . . . . . . . . 1380, 1381, 1407, 1447, 1605-06, 1691

Hayden v. Bardes Corp., 1989-1 Trade Cas. (CCH)
¶ 68,477 (W.D. Ky. Feb. 27, 1989) . . . . . . . . . . 1335, 1336

HB Korenvaes Investments, L.P. v. Marriott Corp.,
[1993 Transfer Binder] Fed. Sec. L. Rep. (CCH)
¶ 97,728 (Del. Ch. June 9, 1993) . . . . . . 571, 572, 574-75, 581

Health-Chem Corp. v. National Union Fire Insurance
Co., 148 Misc. 2d 187, 559 N.Y.S.2d 435 (N.Y. Sup.
Ct. N.Y. Co. 1990) . . . . . . . . . . . . . . . . . . . . . . . 2133-34

In re Healthco International, Inc., 195 B.R. 971
(Bankr. D. Mass. 1996) . . . . . . . . . . . . . . . . . 172, 597, 624

In re Healthco International, Inc., 203 B.R. 515
(Bankr. D. Mass. 1996) . . . . . . . . . . . . . . . . . . . . . . 345

In re Healthco International, Inc., 208 B.R. 288
(Bankr. D. Mass. 1997) . . . . . . . . . . . . . . . . . . . . . 67, 152,
207-08, 209, 226, 229, 605-16, 619, 624, 625-26, 724-25, 728

In re Healthco International, Inc., CA No. 97-40020
(D. Mass. June 2, 1997) . . . . . . . . . . . . . . . . . . . . . 616-18

In re Healthco International, Inc., CA No. 97-40020
(D. Mass. June 5, 1997) . . . . . . . . . . . . . . . . . . . . . . . 28,
42, 67, 83-84, 112, 208, 253, 254, 255-56, 618-19, 625, 725, 728

Hecco Ventures v. Sea-Land Corp., 12 Del. J. Corp.
L. 282 (Del. Ch. May 19, 1986) . . . . . . . . . 755, 758, 912-13

Heckmann v. Ahmanson, 168 Cal. App. 3d 119, 214
Cal. Rptr. 177 (Cal. Ct. App. 1985) . . . 1356, 1357-60, 1401, 2028

Heckmann v. Ahmanson, [1989 Transfer Binder] Fed.
Sec. L. Rep. (CCH) ¶ 94,447 (Cal. Super. Ct. Apr.
12, 1989) . . . . . . . . . . . . . . . . . . . . . . . 202, 1356, 1360-61

Hedberg v. Pantepec International, Inc., 645 A.2d 543
(Conn. App. Ct.), cert. granted, 648 A.2d 879 (Conn.
1994) . . . . . . . . . . . . . . . . . . . . . . . . . . . . 1302, 1311

Heffernan v. Heffernan, Ballinger, Pounds & Yarbrough, Inc., 1996 Tenn. App. LEXIS 567, 1996 WL 512639 (Tenn. Ct. App. Sept. 11, 1996) . . . . . . . . . . . . 263

Heffernan v. Pacific Dunlop GNB Corp., 965 F.2d 369 (7th Cir. 1992) . . . . . . . 1853, 1867, 1909, 1954-56, 1973

Heffernan v. Pacific Dunlop GNB Corp., 1992 U.S. Dist. LEXIS 14809, 1992 WL 275573 (N.D. Ill. Oct. 1, 1992) . . . . . . . . . . . . . . . . . . . . . . 1930-31, 1951-52

Heffernan v. Pacific Dunlop GNB Corp., 1993 U.S. Dist. LEXIS 5, 1993 WL 3553 (N.D. Ill. Jan. 5, 1993) . . . . . . . . . . 1867, 1869, 1909, 1956, 1959, 1974-75

Heine v. Signal Cos., [1976-1977 Transfer Binder] Fed. Sec. L. Rep. (CCH) ¶ 95,898 (S.D.N.Y. Mar 4, 1977) . . . . . . . . . . . . . . . . . . . . . . . . . . . . . . 1352

Heineman v. Datapoint Corp, [1990-1991 Transfer Binder] Fed. Sec. L. Rep. (CCH) ¶ 95,664 (Del. Ch. Oct. 9, 1990). . . . . . . . . . . . . . 94, 636, 1299, 1504-07, 1508

Heineman v. Datapoint Corp., 611 A.2d 950 (Del. 1992) . . . . . . . . . . . . . . . 1454, 1467, 1473, 1479, 1495

Heit v. Baird, 567 F.2d 1157 (1st Cir. 1977) . . . . . . . . . . . . . . . . . . 632, 1427, 1491, 1492, 1774, 1775

Heit v. Bixby, 276 F. Supp. 217 (E.D. Mo. 1967) . . . . . . . 171

Heizer Corp. v. Ross, 601 F.2d 330 (7th Cir. 1979) . . . . . 1971

Helfand v. Gambee, 136 A.2d 558 (Del. Ch. 1957) . . . . . 1391

Helfand v. National Union Fire Insurance Co., 10 Cal. App. 4th 869, 13 Cal. Rptr. 2d 295 (Cal. Ct.

App. 1992), petition for review denied, 1993 Cal.
LEXIS 716 (Cal. Feb. 11, 1993), cert. denied, 510
U.S. 824 (1993) . . . . . . . . . . . . 1990-91, 1996, 1998, 2009

Heller v. Boylan, 29 N.Y.S.2d 653 (N.Y. Sup. Ct.
N.Y. Co.), aff'd mem., 263 A.D. 815, 32 N.Y.S.2d
131 (N.Y. App. Div. 1st Dep't 1941) . . . . . . . . . . . . 311-12

Helt v. Metropolitan District Commission, 113 F.R.D.
7 (D. Conn. 1986) . . . . . . . . . . . . . . . . . . . . . . . . 1822

Henley Group Inc. v. Santa Fe Pacific Corp., 13 Del.
J. Corp. L. 1152 (Del. Ch. Mar. 11, 1988)
. . 504, 650, 651-52, 1040, 1042-45, 1095, 1097, 1113-14, 1250

Henry v. Frontier Industries, Inc., 863 F.2d 886 (unpublished opinion, text available at 1988 WL 132577)
(9th Cir. Dec. 1, 1988) . . . . . . . . . . . . . . . . . . . . . . 884

Herald Co. v. Seawell, 472 F.2d 1081 (10th Cir.
1972) . . . . . . . . . . . . . . . . . . . . . . . . . . . . . . 312, 810

Herd v. Major Realty Corp., [1990-1991 Transfer
Binder] Fed. Sec. L. Rep. (CCH) ¶ 95,772 (Del. Ch.
Dec. 21, 1990) . . . . 504, 516, 518, 524, 722, 766, 1428, 1436

Herman v. NationsBank Trust Co., 126 F.3d 1354
(11th Cir. 1997) . . . . . . . . . . . . . . . . . . . 892-93, 896-901

In re Hesston Corp., 870 P.2d 17 (Kan. 1994) . . . . . . . . . 468

H.F. Ahmanson & Co. v. Great Western Financial
Corp, 1997 Del. Ch. LEXIS 84, 1997 WL 305824
(Del. Ch. June 3, 1997) . . . . . . . . . . . . . . . . . 461, 543-44

Hibbert v. Hollywood Park, Inc., 457 A.2d 339 (Del.
1983) . . . . . . . . . . . . . . . . . . . . . . . . 1853, 1948, 1966

Highland Capital, Inc. v. Longview Fibre Co., 16
Del. J. Corp. L. 325 (Del. Ch. Jan. 22, 1990)
. . . . . . . . . . . . . . . . . . . . . . . . . . 520, 1240-41, 1288-89

Hills Stores Co. v. Bozic, 23 Del. J. Corp. L. 230
(Del. Ch. Mar. 25, 1997)
. . . . . . . . . . . . . 644, 651, 653, 1305, 1306, 1329-32, 1978

Hilton Hotels Corp. v. ITT Corp., 962 F. Supp. 1309
(D. Nev.), aff'd mem., 116 F.3d 1485 (9th Cir.
1997) . . . . . . . . . . . . . . . . . . . . . . . . . . . 1238-40, 1279

Hilton Hotels Corp. v. ITT Corp., 116 F.3d 1485
(unpublished opinion, text available at 1997 U.S. App.
LEXIS 14893 and 1997 WL 345963) (9th Cir. June
19, 1997) . . . . . . . . . . . . . . . . . . . . . . . . . . . . . . . 1240

Hilton Hotels Corp. v. ITT Corp., 978 F. Supp. 1342
(D. Nev. 1997) . . . . . . . . . . . . . . . . . . . . . 4, 18, 671-72,
681, 686, 729, 805-08, 813-14, 823-24, 1033, 1034-35, 1278-83

Hodges v. New England Screw Co., 1 R.I. 312
(1850) . . . . . . . . . . . . . . . . . . . . . . . . . . . . . . . . . . . 10

Hodges v. New England Screw Co., 3 R.I. 9 (1853) . . . . . . . 10

In re Hoffman Associates Inc., 194 B.R. 943 (Bankr.
D.S.C. 1995) . . . . . . . . . . . . . . . . . . . . . . . . . . . 597, 598

Hoffman v. Dann, 205 A.2d 343 (Del. 1964), cert.
denied, 380 U.S. 973 (1965) . . . . . . . . . . . . . . . . . . . . 326

Holland v. Stenhouse, 1991 U.S. Dist. LEXIS 2518,
1991 WL 30138 (N.D. Ill. Mar. 4, 1991) . . . . . . . . . 131, 209

Holloway v. Sharon Land Co., 3 Del. J. Corp. L. 578
(Del. Ch. Aug. 25, 1977) . . . . . . . . . . . . . . . . . . . . . . 302

In re Holly Farms Corp. Shareholders Litigation, [1988-1989 Transfer Binder] Fed. Sec. L. Rep. (CCH) ¶ 94,181 (Del. Ch. Dec. 30, 1988)
. . . . . . . . . . . . . . . . . . . . . 751-52, 925, 974-75, 1158, 1160

In re Holly Farms Corp. Shareholders Litigation, [1989 Transfer Binder] Fed. Sec. L. Rep. (CCH) ¶ 94,349 (Del. Ch. Mar. 22, 1989) . . . . . . . . . . . . . . . 752

In re Holly Farms Corp. Shareholders Litigation, [1989 Transfer Binder] Fed. Sec. L. Rep. (CCH) ¶ 94,443 (Del. Ch. May 18, 1989) . . . . . . . . . . . . . . . . 752

In re Holly Farms Corp. Shareholders Litigation, 564 A.2d 342 (Del. Ch. 1989) . . . . 712-13, 736, 752, 759, 1160-61

Holly Sugar Corp. v. Buchsbaum, [1981 Transfer Binder] Fed. Sec. L. Rep. (CCH) ¶ 98,366 (D. Colo. Oct. 28, 1981) . . . . . . . . . . . . . . . . . . . . . . . . . . . . . 1270-71

Holmstrom v. Coastal Industries, Inc., 645 F. Supp. 963 (N.D. Ohio 1984) . . . . . . . . . . . . . . . . . . . . . 1696, 1708

Holstein v. UAL Corp., 662 F. Supp. 153 (N.D. Ill. 1987) . . . . . . . . . . . . . . . . . . . . . . . . . . . . . . . . . . . . 1134

Home Insurance Co. v. Spectrum Information Technologies, Inc., 930 F. Supp. 825 (E.D.N.Y. 1996)
. . . . . . . . . . . . . . . . . . . . . . . . . . . . 1999, 2036, 2147

In re Home Shopping Network, Inc. Shareholders Litigation, [1993 Transfer Binder] Fed. Sec. L. Rep. (CCH) ¶ 97,619 (Del. Ch. May 19, 1993) . . . . . . . . . 520, 877

Honigman v. Green Giant Co., 309 F.2d 667 (8th Cir. 1962), cert. denied, 372 U.S. 941 (1963) . . . . . . . . . . . 363-64

Hornsby v. Lohmeyer, 72 A.2d 294 (Pa. 1950) . . . . . . . . 1383

Horton v. Benjamin, 1997 WL 778662 (Mass. Super.
Ct. Nov. 26, 1997) . . . . . . . . . . . . . . . . . . . . . . . . . . . . 470

Horwitz v. Southwest Forest Industries, Inc., 604 F.
Supp. 1130 (D. Nev. 1985) . . . . . . . . . . . . . . . . . 24, 1095

Hoschett v. TSI International Software, Ltd., 683
A.2d 43 (Del. Ch. 1996) . . . . . . . . . . . . . . . . . . . . . 1204

Hospital Corp. of America v. Commissioner, 74
T.C.M. (CCH) 1020, T.C.M. (RIA) 97,482 (T.C. Ct.
Oct. 27, 1997) . . . . . . . . . . . . . . . . . . . . . . . . . . . . . 2161

Hotel des Artistes, Inc. v. Transamerica Insurance
Co., 1994 U.S. Dist. LEXIS 7800, 1994 WL 263429
(S.D.N.Y. June 13, 1994) . . . . . . . . . . . . . . . . . . . . . 1991

Houle v. Low, 556 N.E.2d 51 (Mass. 1990)
. . . . . . . . . . 1445-46, 1695, 1702, 1741, 1743, 1751-52, 1773

Howard v. Carr, 222 A.D.2d 843, 635 N.Y.S.2d 326
(N.Y. App. Div. 3d Dep't 1995) . . . . . . . . . . . . . . . . . 304

Howard Savings Bank v. Northland Insurance Co.,
1997 U.S. Dist. LEXIS 11857, 1997 WL 460973
(N.D. Ill. Aug. 11, 1997) . . . . . . . . . . . . . . . . . . 2053-54

Howe v. Detroit Free Press, Inc., 487 N.W.2d 374
(Mich. 1992) . . . . . . . . . . . . . . . . . . . . . . . . . . . . . 1845

In re Howe Grain, Inc., 209 B.R. 496 (Bankr. D.
Neb. 1997) . . . . . . . . . . . . . . . . . . . . . . . . . . . 598, 599

Hoye v. Meek, 795 F.2d 893 (10th Cir. 1986) . . . . . . 127, 172

Hubbard v. Pape, 203 N.E.2d 365 (Ohio Ct. App.
1964) . . . . . . . . . . . . . . . . . . . . . . . . . . . . . . . 304

Hubbard v. Hollywood Park Realty Enterprises, Inc.,
17 Del. J. Corp. L. 238 (Del. Ch. Jan. 14, 1991) . . . . . . . 798

Hubbard v. Hollywood Park Realty Enterprises, Inc.,
No. 11902 (Del. Ch. Jan. 15, 1991) . . . . . . . . . 1219, 1292-95

Hubner v. Schoonmaker, 1991 U.S. Dist. LEXIS
4866, 1991 WL 60594 (E.D. Pa. Apr. 9, 1991) . . . . . . . . 1383

Huffington v. Enstar Corp., 9 Del. J. Corp. L. 185
(Del. Ch. Apr. 25, 1984) . . . . . . . . . . . . . . . . . . . . 1218

Humana Inc. v. Commissioner, 881 F.2d 247 (6th
Cir. 1989) . . . . . . . . . . . . . . . . . . . . . . . . . . . 2157-58

IBS Financial Corp. v. Seidman & Assocs., 954
F. Supp. 980 (D.N.J. 1997) . . . . . . . . . . 4, 805, 807, 1255-57

In re Imperial Corp. of America, [1992-1993 Transfer
Binder] Fed. Sec. L. Rep. (CCH) ¶ 97,271 (S.D. Cal.
Aug. 17, 1992) . . . . . . . . . . . . . . . . . . . . . . . . . . 627

In re Imperial Corp. of America, 167 F.R.D. 447
(S.D. Cal. 1995) . . . . . . . . . . . . . . . . . . . . . . . . . 1991

Imperial Group (Texas), Inc. v. Scholnick, 709
S.W.2d 358 (Tex. App. 1986, writ ref'd n.r.e.) . . . . . . . . 262

INA Underwriters Insurance Co. v. D.H. Forde &
Co., 630 F. Supp. 76 (W.D.N.Y. 1985) . . . . . . . . . . . 2152

Ince & Co. v. Silgan Corp., [1990-1991 Transfer
Binder] Fed. Sec. L. Rep. (CCH) ¶ 95,842 (Del. Ch.
Feb. 7, 1991) . . . . . . . . . . . . . . . . 468, 495, 517, 524, 526

Independent Cellular Telephone, Inc. v. Barker, 23
Del. J. Corp. L. 244 (Del. Ch. Mar. 21, 1997) . . . . . . . . . . 94

Industrial Indemnity Co. v. Golden State Co., 117
Cal. App. 2d 519, 256 P.2d 677 (Cal. Ct. App.
1953) . . . . . . . . . . . . . . . . . . . . . . . . . . . . . . . . 297

Industrial Sugars, Inc. v. Standard Accident Insurance
Co., 338 F.2d 673 (7th Cir. 1964) . . . . . . . . . . . . . . . 1985

Informix Corp. v. Lloyd's of London, 1992 U.S. Dist.
LEXIS 16836, 1992 WL 469802 (N.D. Cal. Oct. 16,
1992) . . . . . . . . . . . . . . . . . . . . . . . . . . . . . . . 2008

Insuranshares Corp. v. Northern Fiscal Corp., 35 F.
Supp. 22 (E.D. Pa. 1940) . . . . . . . . . . . . . . . . . . . 365-66

In re Interco, Inc., No. 91-4-0042-172 (E.D. Mo.
Oct. 23, 1991) (Report of Examiner Sandra E. Mayer-
son . . . . . . . . . . . . . . . . . . . . . . . . . . . . . . . . . 1164

Interco Inc. v. City Capital Associates L.P., 556 A.2d
1070 (unpublished opinion, text available at 1988 Del.
LEXIS 408, 1988 WL 149260) (Del. Nov. 17, 1988) . . . . 1164

International Association of Heat & Frost Insulators &
Asbestos Workers v. Absolute Environmental Ser-
vices, Inc., 814 F. Supp. 392 (D. Del. 1993) . . . . . . . . . . 98

International Banknote Co. v. Muller, 713 F. Supp.
612 (S.D.N.Y. 1989)
. . . . . . . . . . 179, 187, 189, 686, 687, 1269-70, 1273, 1278

International Broadcasting Corp. v. Turner, 734 F.
Supp. 383 (D. Minn. 1990) . . . . . . . . . . . 1744, 1747, 1785

International Brotherhood of Teamsters General Fund
v. Fleming Cos., No. CIV-96-1650 (W.D. Okla. Jan.
14, 1997), reprinted in The Word from Oklahoma,
Corporate Control Alert, Mar. 1997, at 11, certification granted, Nos. 97-6035, 97-6132 (10th Cir. Sept.
23, 1997), reprinted in 13 Corporate Officers &
Directors Liability Litig. Rptr. No. 7, Feb. 9, 1998, at
D1 . . . . . . . . . . . . . . . . . . . . . . . . . . . . . . . . . . 1196

International Brotherhood of Teamsters General Fund
v. Fleming Cos., No. CIV-96-1650, 1997 U.S. Dist.
LEXIS 2980 (W.D. Okla. Jan. 24, 1997), certification
granted, Nos. 97-6035, 97-6132 (10th Cir. Sept. 23,
1997), reprinted in 13 Corporate Officers & Directors
Liability Litig. Rptr. No. 7, Feb. 9, 1998, at D1. . . . . . . 1196

International Brotherhood of Teamsters General Fund
v. Fleming Cos., 1997 U.S. Dist. LEXIS 2979 (W.D.
Okla. Feb. 19, 1997) . . . . . . . . . . . . . . . . . . . . . . 1197

International Brotherhood of Teamsters General Fund
v. Fleming Cos., Nos. 97-6035, 97-6132 (10th Cir.
Sept. 23, 1997), reprinted in 13 Corporate Officers &
Directors Liability Litig. Rptr. No. 7, Feb. 9, 1998, at
D1 . . . . . . . . . . . . . . . . . . . . . . . . . . . . . 1196, 1198-99

International Equity Capital Growth Fund, L.P. v.
Clegg, 23 Del. J. Corp. L. 259 (Del. Ch. Apr. 21,
1997) . . . . . . . . . . . . . . . . . . . 61, 1386, 1389, 1482, 1512

International Insurance Co. v. Johns, 874 F.2d 1447
(11th Cir. 1989) . . . . . . . . . . . . . . . . . 15, 22-23, 91, 271,
312, 631, 659, 686, 1297, 1298, 1301, 1303, 1304, 1306-07, 1320

International Insurance Co. v. McMullan, 1990 U.S.
Dist. LEXIS 19940, 1990 WL 483731 (S.D. Miss.
Mar. 7, 1990) . . . . . . . . . . . . . . . . . . . . . 2077, 2091, 2153

International Insurance Co. v. Morrow, Inc., No. 86-1247-JU (D. Or. Oct. 23, 1987) . . . . . . . . . . . . . 2046

International Insurance Co. v. Peabody International Corp., 747 F. Supp. 477 (N.D. Ill. 1990) . . . 2000, 2142-43, 2148

In re International Jensen Inc. Shareholders Litigation, 1996 Del. Ch. LEXIS 77, 1996 WL 422345 (Del. Ch. July 16, 1996) . . . . . . . . . . . . . . . . . . . . . . . . . . . . . . . . 228

International Surplus Lines Insurance Co. v. Princehorn, 1994 Ohio App. LEXIS 2039, 1994 WL 175672 (Ohio Ct. App. May 11, 1994), appeal not allowed, 639 N.E.2d 795 (Ohio 1994) . . . . . . . . . . . . . . . . . . 1986

International Surplus Lines Insurance Co. v. Wyoming Coal Refining Systems, Inc., 52 F.3d 901 (10th Cir. 1995) . . . . . . . . . . . . . . . . . . . . . . . . . . . . . . . . . . . . 2148

In re International Systems & Controls Corp. Securities Litigation, 693 F.2d 1235 (5th Cir. 1982) . . . . . . . . . 1822

Invacare Corp. v. Healthdyne Technologies, Inc., 968 F. Supp. 1578 (N.D. Ga. 1997) . . . . 1089, 1186-89, 1199-1201

Ireland v. Wynkoop, 539 P.2d 1349 (Colo. Ct. App. 1975) . . . . . . . . . . . . . . . . . . . . . . . . . . . . . . . . . . . 1382

Irving Bank Corp. v. Board of Governors of the Federal Reserve System, 845 F.2d 1035 (D.C. Cir. 1988) . . . . . . . . . . . . . . . . . . . . . . . . . . . . . . . . . . . 595

Iseman v. Liquid Air Corp., 15 Del. J. Corp. L. 1041 (Del. Ch. Oct. 23, 1989) . . . . . . . . . . . . . . . . . . . . . . 463

Ivanhoe Partners v. Newmont Mining Corp., 13 Del. J. Corp. L. 673 (Del. Ch. Sept. 28, 1987) . . . . . . . . . . . 1373

Ivanhoe Partners v. Newmont Mining Corp., 533
A.2d 585 (Del. Ch.), aff'd, 535 A.2d 1334 (Del.
1987) . . . . . . . . . . 539, 547, 548, 549, 550, 553-56, 1373-74

Ivanhoe Partners v. Newmont Mining Corp., 535
A.2d 1334 (Del. 1987)
. . . . . . . 20-21, 272, 344, 346, 631, 635, 638, 641, 642, 643,
664, 713-14, 809, 823, 831-32, 844-45, 1040-41, 1371, 1372-76

Ivanhoe Partners v. Newmont Mining Corp., 1988
Del. Ch. LEXIS 48, 1988 WL 34526 (Del. Ch. Apr.
7, 1988) . . . . . . . . . . . . . . . . . . . . . . . . . . . . . . 1376

J.I. Case Co. v. Borak, 377 U.S. 426 (1964) . . . . . . . 1463-64

In re J.P. Stevens & Co. Shareholders Litigation, 542
A.2d 770 (Del. Ch. 1988), appeal refused, 540 A.2d
1088 (unpublished opinion, text available at 1988 Del.
LEXIS 102 and 1988 WL 35145) (Del. Apr. 12,
1988) . . . . . . . . . . . . . . . . . . . . . . . . . . . . . . . 15-16,
40, 82, 696, 736, 756, 757, 758, 759, 773, 826, 958, 963, 980-82

Jackson v. Turnbull, 1994 Del. Ch. LEXIS 25, 1994
WL 174668 (Del. Ch. Feb. 8, 1994), aff'd, 653 A.2d
306 (unpublished opinion, text available at 1994 Del.
LEXIS 382 and 1994 WL 693503) (Del. Dec. 7,
1994) . . . . . . . . . . . . . . . . . . . . . . . . . . . . . . . . 218

Jackson v. Turnbull, No. 13042 (Del. Ch. May 22,
1995) . . . . . . . . . . . . . . . . . . . . . . . . . . 1868, 1933-36

Jacobs v. Adams, 601 F.2d 176 (5th Cir. 1979) . . . . . . . . 1686

Jaffe Commercial Financial Co. v. Harris, 456 N.E.2d
224 (Ill. App. Ct. 1983) . . . . . . . . . . . . . . . . . . . . . 312

James Talcott, Inc. v. McDowell, 148 So. 2d 36 (Fla.
Dist. Ct. App. 1962) . . . . . . . . . . . . . . . . . . . . . . . . 1611

Jaunich v. National Union Fire Insurance Co., 647 F.
Supp. 209 (N.D. Cal. 1986) . . . . . . . . . . . . . 2141-42, 2148

Jedwab v. MGM Grand Hotels, Inc., 509 A.2d 584
(Del. Ch. 1986) . . . . . . . . 52, 371, 413, 429, 559, 572-73, 578

Jenkins v. Haworth, Inc., 572 F. Supp. 591 (W.D.
Mich. 1983) . . . . . . . . . . . . . . . . . . . . . . . . . . . . . 108

Jerozal v. Cash Reserve Management Inc., [1982-1983
Transfer Binder] Fed. Sec. L. Rep. ¶ 99,019
(S.D.N.Y. Aug. 10, 1982) . . . . . . . . . . . . . . . . . . . . 1489

Jett v. Kidder Peabody & Co., N.Y.L.J., Dec. 23,
1997, at 30 (N.Y. Sup. Ct. N.Y. Co.) . . . . . . . . . . . . . 1869

Jewel Cos. v. Pay Less Drug Stores Northwest, Inc.,
741 F.2d 1555 (9th Cir. 1984) . . . . . . 631, 729, 994-97, 1000

Jewel Recovery, L.P. v. Gordon, 196 B.R. 348 (N.D.
Tex. 1996) . . . . . . . . . . . . . . . . . . . . . . . . . . . . . . 626

Jewelcor Inc. v. Pearlman, 397 F. Supp. 221
(S.D.N.Y. 1975) . . . . . . . . . . . . . . . . . . . . . . . . . . 1346

John Hancock Capital Growth Management, Inc. v.
Aris Corp., 16 Del. J. Corp. L. 1515 (Del. Ch. Aug.
24, 1990) . . . . . . . . . . . . . . . . . . . . . . . . . . . . . . . 43

John Hancock Capital Growth Management, Inc. v.
Aris Corp., [1990 Transfer Binder] Fed. Sec. L. Rep.
(CCH) ¶ 95,461 (Del. Ch. Aug. 24, 1990) . . . . . . . . . . . 229

John Hancock Healthplan, Inc. v. Lexington Insurance
Co., 1989 U.S. Dist. LEXIS 11019, 1989 WL 106992
(E.D. Pa. Sept. 8, 1989) . . . . . . . . . . . . . . . . . . . . . . 2001

John Hancock Healthplan, Inc. v. Lexington Insurance
Co., 1990 U.S. Dist. LEXIS 2450, 1990 WL 21137
(E.D. Pa. Mar. 6, 1990) . . . . . . . . . . . . . . . . . . . . . . 2134

John Hancock Healthplan, Inc. v. Lexington Insurance
Co., No. 88-2308 (E.D. Pa. Feb. 5, 1991) . . . . . . . 2112, 2134

Johnson v. Gene's Supermarket, Inc., 453 N.E.2d 83
(Ill. App. Ct. 1983) . . . . . . . . . . . . . . . . . . . . . . . . . 1898

Johnson v. Hui, 752 F. Supp. 909 (N.D. Cal. 1990) . . . . . 1427

Johnson v. Hui, No. C-90-1863 DLJ (N.D. Cal. June
27, 1991) . . . . . . . . . . . . . . . . . . . . . . . . . . . . . . . . 1794

Johnson v. Hui, 811 F. Supp. 479 (N.D. Cal. 1991)
. . . . . . . . . . . . . . . . . . . . . . . . . . . . . . . . . . 1456, 1719,
1745-50, 1752-53, 1755, 1758-60, 1772, 1773, 1775, 1777, 1783

Johnson & Johnson v. Aetna Casualty & Surety Co.,
667 A.2d 1087 (N.J. 1995) . . . . . . . . . . . . . . . . . . . . . 1987

Johnston v. Greene, 121 A.2d 919 (Del. 1956)
. . . . . . . . . . . . . . . . . . . . . . . . . . . . . 295, 297, 302, 304

Johnston v. Lindblade, 1995 Minn. App. LEXIS 695,
1995 WL 311617 (Minn. Ct. App. May 23, 1995) . . . . . . 1961

Johnson v. Trueblood, 629 F.2d 287 (3d Cir. 1980),
cert. denied, 450 U.S. 999 (1981) . . . . . . . . . . . . . . . . 633

Jones v. Ellis, 551 So. 2d 396 (Ala. 1989) . . . . . . . . . . 22, 91

Jones v. H.F. Ahmanson & Co., 1 Cal. 3d 93, 460
P.2d 464, 81 Cal. Rptr. 592 (1969) . . . . . . . 1381, 1382, 1414

Jordon v. Bowman Apple Products Co., 728 F. Supp.
409 (W.D. Va. 1990) . . . . . . . . . . . . . . . . . . . 1399, 1456

Joseph v. Amrep Corp., 59 A.D.2d 841, 399
N.Y.S.2d 3 (N.Y. App. Div. 1st Dep't 1977) . . . . . . . . . 1559

Joseph E. Seagram & Sons, Inc. v. Abrams, 510 F.
Supp. 860 (S.D.N.Y. 1981) . . . . . . . . . . . . . . . . . 907-08

Joseph v. Shell Oil Co., 482 A.2d 335 (Del. Ch.
1984) . . . . . . . . . . . . . . . . . . . . . . . . . . . . . 361, 429, 519

Joy Manufacturing Corp. v. Pullman-Peabody Co.,
729 F. Supp. 449 (W.D. Pa. 1989) . . . . . . . . . . 1111, 1326-27

Joy v. North, 692 F.2d 880 (2d Cir. 1982), cert.
denied, 460 U.S. 1051 (1983) . . . . . . . . . . . . . . . . . 16-17,
84, 131, 133, 1584, 1610, 1695, 1721, 1738-40, 1768-69, 1825-26

Joyce v. Cuccia, 1997 Del. Ch. LEXIS 71, 1997 WL
257448 (Del. Ch. May 14, 1997) . . . . . . . . . . . 114, 265, 283

Judah v. Delaware Trust Co., 378 A.2d 624 (Del.
1977) . . . . . . . . . . . . . . . . . . . . . . . . . . . . . . . 571, 584

In re KDI Corp. Shareholders Litigation, [1990-1991
Transfer Binder] Fed. Sec. L. Rep. (CCH) ¶ 95,727
(Del. Ch. Dec. 13, 1990) . . . . . . . . . . 77, 180, 184, 185, 186

KDT Industries, Inc. v. Home Insurance Co., 603 F.
Supp. 861 (D. Mass. 1985) . . . . . . . . . . . . . . . . . 2041-42

Kademian v. Ladish Co., 792 F.2d 614 (7th Cir.
1986) . . . . . . . . . . . . . . . . . . . . . . . . . . . . . . . . . 526

Kahn v. Caporella, 1994 Del. Ch. LEXIS 29, 1994
WL 89016 (Del. Ch. Mar. 10, 1994)
. . . . . . . . . . 32, 520, 524, 712, 735, 753, 757, 770, 954-55

Kahn v. Dairy Mart Convenience Stores, Inc., 19 Del.
J. Corp. L. 1233 (Del. Ch. Mar. 1, 1994) . . . . . . 94, 442, 978

Kahn v. Dairy Mart Convenience Stores, Inc., 21 Del.
J. Corp. L. 1143 (Del. Ch. Mar. 29, 1996)
. . . . . . . . . . 59-60, 369, 404, 405, 431, 437-42, 978-79, 1752

Kahn v. Household Acquisition Corp., 591 A.2d 166
(Del. 1991) . . . . . . . . . . . . . . . . . . . . . . . . . . . . . . . 483, 512

Kahn v. Lynch Communication Systems, Inc., 19 Del.
J. Corp. L. 784 (Del. Ch. July 9, 1993), rev'd in part,
638 A.2d 1110 (Del. 1994), aff'd in part, 669 A.2d 79
(Del. 1995) . . . . . . . . . . . . . . . . . . . . . . . . . . . . . 521, 523

Kahn v. Lynch Communication Systems, Inc., 638
A.2d 1110 (Del. 1994) . . . . . . . . . . . . . . . 30, 33, 272, 278,
284, 343, 344, 348, 369, 378, 379-80, 401-12, 433-34, 438-39, 468

Kahn v. Lynch Communication Systems, Inc., 1995
Del. Ch. LEXIS 44, 1995 WL 301403 (Del. Ch. Apr.
17, 1995), aff'd, 669 A.2d 79 (Del. 1995) . . . . . . . . . 412, 523

Kahn v. Lynch Communication Systems, Inc., 669
A.2d 79 (Del. 1995)
. . . . . . . . . . . . 30-31, 163, 284, 343, 369, 378, 379-80, 402-
05, 406, 409, 411-12, 412-16, 434, 468, 499, 512-14, 521, 531

Kahn v. Roberts, [1993-1994 Transfer Binder] Fed.
Sec. L. Rep. (CCH) ¶ 98,201 (Del. Ch. Feb. 28,
1994) . . . . . . . . . . . . . . . . . . . . . . . . . . . . 44, 94, 172, 185,
189, 231, 505, 517, 1355-56, 1470-71, 1473, 1497, 1522-23, 1528

Kahn v. Roberts, 21 Del. J. Corp. L. 674 (Del. Ch.
Dec. 6, 1995), aff'd, 679 A.2d 460 (Del. 1996)
. . . . . 39, 76, 111, 195, 271, 282, 502-03, 517, 1355-56, 1523

Kahn v. Roberts, 679 A.2d 460 (Del. 1996)
. . . . . . . . . . . 20-21, 26, 182, 184, 185, 188, 189, 190, 191,
500, 502, 512, 519, 521, 635, 639, 641, 642, 644, 655-56, 1355

Kahn v. Sprouse, 842 F. Supp. 423 (D. Or. 1993)
. . . . . . . . . . . . . . . . . . . . . . . . . . . . . 648, 687, 1182

Kahn v. Sullivan, 594 A.2d 48 (Del. 1991)
. . . . . . . . . . . . . . . . . . 183, 184, 185, 1408, 1409, 1410

Kahn v. Tremont Corp., 18 Del. J. Corp. L. 723
(Del. Ch. Aug. 21, 1992), subsequent proceedings,
1996 Del. Ch. LEXIS 40, 1996 WL 145452 (Del. Ch.
Mar. 21, 1996), rev'd, 694 A.2d 422 (Del. 1997) . . . . 1676-77

Kahn v. Tremont Corp., 1994 Del. Ch. LEXIS 41,
1994 WL 162613 (Del. Ch. Apr. 21, 1994), subsequent proceedings, 21 Del. J. Corp. L. 1161 (Del.
Ch. Mar. 21, 1996), rev'd, 694 A.2d 422 (Del.
1997) . . . . . . . . . . . 94, 827-28, 1470, 1510, 1519-20, 1549

Kahn v. Tremont, 1996 Del. Ch. LEXIS 40, 1996 WL
145452 (Del. Ch. Mar. 21, 1996), rev'd, 694 A.2d
422 (Del. 1997) . . . . . . . . . . . . . . . . . . . . . . . . . . . 827

Kahn v. Tremont Corp., 21 Del. J. Corp. L. 1161
(Del. Ch. Mar. 21, 1996), rev'd, 694 A.2d 422 (Del.
1997) . . . . . . . . . . . . . . . . . 7, 342, 424, 440, 478-79, 525

Kahn v. Tremont Corp., 694 A.2d 422 (Del. 1997)
. . . . . . . . . . . . . . . . . . . . . . . . . . . . . 30-31, 46, 46, 53-
54, 342, 378, 379-80, 402, 402-05, 408, 416-27, 499, 513, 1752

Kahn v. Tremont Corp., 1997 Del. Ch. LEXIS 150,
1997 WL 689488 (Del. Ch. Oct. 27, 1997) . . . . . . 405, 427-28

Kahn v. United States Sugar Corp., 11 Del. J. Corp.
L. 908 (Del. Ch. Dec. 10, 1985) . . . . . . . . 361, 520, 527, 548

Kaiser Aluminum Corp. v. Matheson, 681 A.2d 392
(Del. 1996) . . . . . . . . . . . . . . . . . . . . . . . . . . . . . . . . 571

Kamen v. Kemper Financial Services, Inc., 659 F.
Supp. 1153 (N.D. Ill. 1987), aff'd, 908 F.2d 1338
(7th Cir. 1990), rev'd, 500 U.S. 90 (1991) . . . . . . . 1442, 1491

Kamen v. Kemper Financial Services, Inc., 908 F.2d
1338 (7th Cir. 1990), rev'd, 500 U.S. 90 (1991)
. . . . . . . . . . . . . . . . . . . 3, 16, 313, 1442, 1564-66, 1584

Kamen v. Kemper Financial Services, Inc., 500 U.S.
90 (1991) . . . . . . . . . . . . . . . . . . . . . . . . . . . . . . . 3,
1380, 1384, 1385, 1406, 1407, 1414, 1426, 1427, 1428, 1440-41,
1445, 1455, 1457, 1460, 1462, 1566-69, 1584, 1605, 1666, 1689

Kamen v. Kemper Financial Services, Inc., 939 F.2d
458 (7th Cir.), cert. denied, 502 U.S. 974 (1991)
. . . . . 62, 1468-69, 1489, 1490, 1494, 1495, 1496, 1501, 1569

Kamerman v. Steinberg, 891 F.2d 424 (2d Cir. 1989) . . . . 1356

Kamin v. American Express Co., 86 Misc. 2d 809,
383 N.Y.S.2d 807 (N.Y. Sup. Ct. N.Y. Co.), aff'd
mem., 54 A.D.2d 654, 387 N.Y.S.2d 993 (N.Y. App.
Div. 1st Dep't 1976) . . . . . . . . . . . . . . . . . . . . . . . . . 17

Kaplan v. Centex Corp., 284 A.2d 119 (Del. Ch.
1971) . . . . . . . . . . . . . . . . . . . . . . . . . . . . 41, 45, 98, 1484

Kaplan v. Fenton, 278 A.2d 834 (Del. 1971) . . . . . . . 295, 304

Kaplan v. Goldsamt, 380 A.2d 556 (Del. Ch. 1977) . . 225, 1352

Kaplan v. Peat, Marwick, Mitchell & Co., 529 A.2d
254 (Del. Ch. 1987), aff'd in part and rev'd in part,
540 A.2d 726 (Del. 1988) . . . . . . . . . . . . . . 1682, 1685-86

Kaplan v. Peat, Marwick, Mitchell & Co., 540 A.2d
726 (Del. 1988) . . . . . . . . . . . 1381, 1494, 1588, 1594, 1682

Kaplan v. Wyatt, 9 Del. J. Corp. L. 205 (Del. Ch.
Jan. 18, 1984) . . . . . . . . . . . . . . . . . . . . . . . . . 1787-89

Kaplan v. Wyatt, 484 A.2d 501 (Del. Ch. 1984),
aff'd, 499 A.2d 1184 (Del. 1985) . . . . . . . . . . . . . . . . 1715,
1719, 1724, 1756, 1783, 1786, 1787, 1789, 1795, 1800-04, 1815

Kaplan v. Wyatt, 499 A.2d 1184 (Del. 1985)
. . . . . . . . . . . . . . . . . . . . 1715, 1722-24, 1745-46, 1748,
1750, 1752, 1755-57, 1759, 1772, 1773, 1775, 1779, 1789-90, 1812

Kapoor v. Fujisawa Pharmaceutical Co., 1994 Del.
Super. LEXIS 233, 1994 WL 233947 (Del. Super.
May 10, 1994), aff'd, 655 A.2d 307 (unpublished
opinion, text available at 1995 Del. LEXIS 25 and
1995 WL 24906) (Del. Jan. 17, 1995) . . . . . . . . . 1910, 1957

Karasik v. Pacific Eastern Corp., 180 A. 604 (Del.
Ch. 1935) . . . . . . . . . . . . . . . . . . . . . . . . . . . . . 15

Karfunkel v. USLIFE Corp., 116 Misc. 2d 841, 455
N.Y.S.2d 937 (N.Y. Sup. Ct. N.Y. Co. 1982), aff'd
mem., 98 A.D.2d 628, 469 N.Y.S.2d 1020 (N.Y.
App. Div. 1st Dep't 1983) . . . . . . . . . . . . . . . . 1356, 1362

Kars v. Carey, 158 A.2d 136 (Del. Ch. 1960) . . . . . . . . . . 500

Kas v. Financial General Bancshares, Inc., 796 F.2d
508 (D.C. Cir. 1986) . . . . . . . . . . . . . . . . . . . . . . 526

Kaster v. Modification Systems, Inc., 731 F.2d 1014
(2d Cir. 1984) . . . . . . . . . . . . . . . . . . . . . . . . . 1456

Katell v. Morgan Stanley Group, Inc., [1992-1993
Transfer Binder] Fed. Sec. L. Rep. (CCH) ¶ 97,437
(Del. Ch. Jan. 14, 1993) . . . . . . 1477, 1804, 1806, 1808, 1809

Katell v. Morgan Stanley Group, Inc., 1993 Del. Ch.
LEXIS 92, 1993 WL 205033 (Del. Ch. June 8, 1993)
. . . . . . . . . . . . . . . . . . . . . . . . . . . . . . 1808, 1809-11

Katell v. Morgan Stanley Group, Inc., 19 Del. J.
Corp. L. 797 (Del. Ch. Sept. 27, 1993) . . 1744, 1784, 1808, 1811

Katell v. Morgan Stanley Group, Inc., [1995 Transfer
Binder] Fed. Sec. L. Rep. (CCH) ¶ 98,861 (Del. Ch.
June 15, 1995) . . . . . . . . . . . . . . . . . . 65, 1719, 1725-26,
1746-47, 1749, 1751, 1753, 1765, 1778, 1804, 1808-09, 1812-19

Katz v. Chevron Corp., 22 Cal. App. 4th 1352, 27
Cal. Rptr. 2d 681 (Cal. Ct. App. 1994)
. . . . . . . 52, 182, 184, 185, 191, 192, 1106, 1115, 1268, 1344

Katz v. Emmett, N.Y.L.J., Sept. 27, 1994, at 26
(N.Y. Sup. Ct. Westchester Co.), aff'd, 226 A.D.2d
588, 641 N.Y.S.2d 131 (N.Y. App. Div. 2d Dep't
1996) . . . . . . . . . . . . . . . . . 276, 314, 1453-54, 1492, 1500

Katz v. Emmett, 226 A.D.2d 588, 641 N.Y.S.2d 131
(N.Y. App. Div. 2d Dep't 1996) . . . . . . . . . . . . . . . . 1459

Katz v. Halperin, 21 Del. J. Corp. L. 690 (Del. Ch.
Feb. 5, 1996)
. . . . . 43, 46, 53, 504, 1475, 1478-79, 1488, 1495, 1501, 1572

Katz v. Oak Industries, Inc., 508 A.2d 873 (Del. Ch.
1986) . . . . . . . . . . . . . . . . . . . . . . . . . . 540, 591

Katz v. Pels, 774 F. Supp. 121 (S.D.N.Y. 1991) . . . . . . . 1458

Katz v. Plant Industries, Inc., 1981 Del. Ch. LEXIS
549, 1981 WL 15148 (Del. Ch. Oct. 27, 1981)
. . . . . . . . . . . . . . . . . . . . . . . . . . . 1400, 1402, 1403

Kauffman v. Dreyfus Fund, Inc., 434 F.2d 727 (3d
Cir. 1970), cert denied, 401 U.S. 974 (1971) . . . . . . . . . 1390

In re Kauffman Mutual Fund Actions, 479 F.2d 257
(1st Cir.), cert. denied, 414 U.S. 857 (1973)
. . . . . . . . . . . . . . . . . . . . . 1426, 1427, 1673-74, 1681

Kaufman v. Beal, 1983 Del. Ch. LEXIS 391, 1983
WL 20295 (Del. Ch. Feb. 25, 1983)
. . . . . . . . . . . . . . . 89, 95, 310, 312, 313, 1477, 1575-76

Kaufman v. Belmont, 479 A.2d 282 (Del. Ch. 1984)
. . . . . . . . . . . . . . . . . . . . . . . . . . . 1488, 1674-75

Kaufman v. CBS Inc., 135 Misc. 2d 64, 514 N.Y.S.
2d 620 (N.Y. Civ. Ct. N.Y. Co. 1987) . . . . . . . . . . . . 1877

Kaufman v. Kansas Gas & Electric Co., 634 F. Supp.
1573 (D. Kan. 1986) . . . . . . . . . . . . . . . . . . . . . 1489

Kaufman v. Safeguard Scientifics, Inc., 587 F. Supp.
486 (E.D. Pa. 1984) . . . . . . . . . . . . . . . . . . . . . 1494

Kaufman v. Shoenberg, 91 A.2d 786 (Del. Ch. 1952) . . 328, 341

Kaufman Malchman & Kirby, P.C. v. Hasbro, Inc.,
897 F. Supp. 719 (S.D.N.Y. 1995) . . . . . . . . . . . . . 1449

In re KDI Corp. Shareholders Litigation, 14 Del. J.
Corp. L. 759 (Del. Ch. Nov. 1, 1988) . . . . . . . . . . 755, 770

In re KDI Corp. Shareholders Litigation, [1990-1991
Transfer Binder] Fed. Sec. L. Rep. (CCH) ¶ 95,727
(Del. Ch. Dec. 13, 1990)
. . . . . . . . . . . . . . . . 755, 757, 758, 766, 769, 945-46, 951

Kearney v. Jandernoa, 934 F. Supp. 863 (W.D. Mich.
1996), subsequent proceedings 949 F. Supp. 510
(W.D. Mich. 1996) and 979 F. Supp. 1156 (W.D.
Mich.), mandamus granted sub nom. In re Perrigo
Co., 128 F.3d 430 (6th Cir. 1997) . . . . . . 1662, 1828, 1829-33

Kearney v. Jandernoa, 949 F. Supp. 510 (W.D. Mich.
1996), subsequent proceedings, 979 F. Supp. 1156
(W.D. Mich.), mandamus granted sub nom. In re Per-
rigo Co., 128 F.3d 430 (6th Cir. 1997) . . . . . . . . . . . . 1840

Kearney v. Jandernoa, 957 F. Supp. 116 (W.D. Mich.
1997) . . . . . . . . . . . . . . . . . . . . . . . . . . . . . 342, 346

Kearney v. Jandernoa, 979 F. Supp. 576 (W.D. Mich.
1997) . . . . . . . . . . . . . . . . . . . . . . . . . . . . . 342, 346

Kearney v. Jandernoa, 979 F. Supp. 1156 (W.D.
Mich.), mandamus granted sub nom. In re Perrigo
Co., 128 F.3d 430 (6th Cir. 1997) . . . . . . . . . . . 1832, 1841

Kelegian v. Mgrdichian, 33 Cal. App. 4th 982, 39
Cal. Rptr. 2d 390 (1995) . . . . . . . . . . . . . . . . . . 296, 304

Kells-Murphy v. McNiff, 17 Del. J. Corp. L. 632
(Del. Ch. July 12, 1991) . . . . . . . . . . . . . . . . . . . . 1509

Kelly v. Bell, 254 A.2d 62 (Del. Ch. 1969), aff'd,
266 A.2d 878 (Del. 1970) . . . . . . . . . . . . 99, 215, 504, 505

In re Kenai Corp., 136 B.R. 59 (S.D.N.Y. 1992)
. . . . . . . . . . . . . . . . . . . . . . . . . 2011, 2103, 2105-06

Kennecott Copper Corp. v. Curtiss-Wright Corp., 584
F.2d 1195 (2d Cir. 1978) . . . . . . . . . . . . . . . . . . . . . . 1347

Kennedy v. Josephal & Co., [1982-1983 Transfer
Binder] Fed. Sec. L. Rep. (CCH) ¶ 99,204 (D. Mass.
May 9, 1983) . . . . . . . . . . . . . . . . . . . . . . . . . . . . . 1971

Kennedy v. Titcomb, 553 A.2d 1322 (N.H. 1989) . . . . . . . 364

Kerbs v. California Eastern Airways, Inc., 90 A.2d
652 (Del.), reargument denied, 91 A.2d 62 (Del.
1952) . . . . . . . . . . . . . . . . . . . . . . . . 225, 329-30, 1274

Kerbs v. California Eastern Airways, Inc., 91 A.2d 62
(Del. 1952) . . . . . . . . . . . . . . . . . . . . . . . . . . . . . . 330

Kersten v. Pioneer Hi-Bred International, Inc., 626 F.
Supp. 647 (N.D. Iowa 1985) . . . . . . . . . . . . . . . . . . 1054

Kessler v. Sinclair, 641 N.E.2d 135 (Mass. App. Ct.
1994), review denied, 646 N.E.2d 409 (Mass. 1995)
. . . . . . . . . . . . . . . . . . . . . . . . . . . . 3, 1395, 1459

Keyser v. Commonwealth National Financial Corp.,
644 F. Supp. 1130 (M.D. Pa. 1986)
. . . . . . . . . . 24, 183, 185, 187, 189, 190, 193, 194, 810, 913

Keyser v. Commonwealth National Financial Corp.,
675 F. Supp. 238 (M.D. Pa. 1987)
. . . . . . . . . . . . . . . . 24, 172, 189, 190, 194, 195, 756, 810

Keyser v. Commonwealth National Financial Corp.,
120 F.R.D. 489 (M.D. Pa. 1988) . . . . . . . . . . . . . . . 1395

Kidde Industries, Inc. v. United States, 40 Fed. Cl. 42
(Fed. Cl. 1997) . . . . . . . . . . . . . . . . . . . . . . . . . 2157, 2161

Kidde Industries, Inc. v. Weaver Corp., 593 A.2d 563
(Del. Ch. 1991) . . . . . . . . . . . . . . . . . . . . . . . . . . . . . 597

Kidsco Inc. v. Dinsmore, 674 A.2d 483 (Del. Ch.
1995), aff'd, 670 A.2d 1338 (unpublished opinion,
text available at 1995 Del. LEXIS 426 and 1995 WL
715886) (Del. Nov. 29, 1995)
. . . . . . . . . . . . . 181, 187, 192, 676, 800-02, 1263-66, 1268

Kidsco Inc. v. Dinsmore, 670 A.2d 1338 (unpublished
opinion, text available at 1995 Del. LEXIS 426 and
1995 WL 715886) (Del. Nov. 29, 1995) . . . 52, 676, 802, 1268

King v. Douglass, 973 F. Supp. 707 (S.D. Tex.
1996) . . . . . . . . . . . . . . . . . . . . . . . . . . . . . . . 98, 1412

Kingsbridge Capital Group v. Dunkin' Donuts Inc., 15
Del. J. Corp. L. 663 (Del. Ch. Aug. 7, 1989) . . . . . . . . . . 846

Klang v. Smith's Food & Drug Centers, Inc., 1997
Del. Ch. LEXIS 73, 1997 WL 257463 (Del. Ch. May
13, 1997), aff'd, 702 A.2d 150 (Del. 1997) . . . . . . . . . . 511

Klang v. Smith's Food & Drug Centers, Inc., 702
A.2d 150 (Del. 1997) . . . . . . . . . . . . . . 203, 513, 521, 524

Klaus v. Hi-Shear Corp., 528 F.2d 225 (9th Cir.
1975) . . . . . . . . . . . . . . . . . . . . . . . . . . . . . . . . . . 869

Klein v. Fidelity & Deposit Co. of America, 700 A.2d
262 (Md. Ct. Spec. App. 1997) . . . . . . . . . . . 1998, 2002-03

Kleinhandler v. Borgia, [1989 Transfer Binder] Fed.
Sec. L. Rep. (CCH) ¶ 94,525 (Del. Ch. July 7,
1989) . . . . . . . . . . . . . . . . . . . . . . . . . . . 180, 188, 716

Klinicki v. Lundgren, 695 P.2d 906 (Or. 1985) . . . . . . . . . 307

KLM Royal Dutch Airlines v. Checchi, 698 A.2d 380
(Del. Ch. 1997) . . . . . . . . . . . . . . . . . . . . . . . . . . 1119-21

Klotz v. Consolidated Edison Co., 386 F. Supp. 577
(S.D.N.Y. 1974) . . . . . . . . . . . . . . . . . 1376, 1612, 1651-52

Klotz v. Warner Communications, Inc., 674 A.2d 878
(Del. 1995) . . . . . . . . . . . . . . . . . . . . . . . . . . . . . 477

Koenings v. Joseph Schlitz Brewing Co., 368 N.W.2d
690 (Wis. Ct. App.), rev'd, 377 N.W.2d 593 (Wis.
1985) . . . . . . . . . . . . . . . . . . . . . . . . . . . . 1297, 1310

Koenings v. Joseph Schlitz Brewing Co., 377 N.W.2d
593 (Wis. 1985) . . . . . . . . . . . . . 1297, 1302, 1304, 1309-11

Kolin v. American Plan Corp., [1984-1985 Transfer
Binder] Fed. Sec. L. Rep. ¶ 92,051 (E.D.N.Y. Apr.
30, 1985) . . . . . . . . . . . . . . . . . . . . . . . . . . . . 1489, 1491

Koos v. Central Ohio Cellular, Inc., 641 N.E.2d 265
(Ohio Ct. App. 1994) . . . . . . . . . . . . . . . . 13, 66, 312, 343

Koppers Co. v. Aetna Casualty & Surety Co., 98 F.3d
1440 (3d Cir. 1996) . . . . . . . . . . . . . . . . . . . . . . . 1989

Koppers Co. v. American Express Co., 121 F.R.D.
46 (W.D. Pa. 1988) . . . . . . . . . . . . . . . . . . . . . . . . 1348

Kors v. Carey, 158 A.2d 136 (Del. Ch. 1960) . . . . . . 500, 1351

Koster v. Lumbermens Casualty Mutual Co., 330 U.S.
518 (1947) . . . . . . . . . . . . . . . . . . . . . . . . . . . . . 1417

Kovacs v. NVF Co., 1987 Del. Ch. LEXIS 486, 1987
WL 17042 (Del. Ch. Sept. 10, 1987) . . . . . . . . . . . . 317-18

Kowal v. MCI Communications Corp., 16 F.3d 1271
(D.C. Cir. 1994) . . . . . . . . . . . . . . . . . . . . . . . . 506, 525

Kramer v. Western Pacific Industries, Inc., 12 Del. J.
Corp. L. 1087 (Del. Ch. Nov. 7, 1986) . . . . . . . 1302, 1314-15

Kramer v. Western Pacific Industries, Inc., 546 A.2d
348 (Del. 1988)
. . . . . . . . . . 1299, 1300, 1389, 1390, 1392, 1411, 1412, 1413

Krouner v. American Heritage Fund, 1997 U.S. Dist.
LEXIS 11445, 1997 WL 452021 (S.D.N.Y. Aug. 6,
1997) . . . . . . . . . . . . . . . . . . . . . . . . . . . . . . . . 1412

Krueger v. Cartwright, 996 F.2d 928 (7th Cir. 1993) . . . . 1417

Kumar v. Racing Corp. of America, Inc., [1990-1991
Transfer Binder] Fed. Sec. L. Rep. (CCH) ¶ 95,896
(Del. Ch. Apr. 26, 1991) . . . . . . . . 179, 184, 189, 191, 394-95

Kumpf v. Steinhaus, 779 F.2d 1323 (7th Cir. 1985) . . . . . . . 16

Kysor Industrial Corp. v. Margaux, Inc., 674 A.2d
889 (Del. Super. 1996) . . . . . . . . . . . . . . . . . . . 958, 964-65

LA Partners, L.P. v. Allegis Corp., [1987-1988 Transfer Binder] Fed. Sec. L. Rep. (CCH) ¶ 93,505 (Del.
Ch. Oct. 23, 1987) . . . . . . . . . . . . . . . . 252, 1515, 1518-19

Lacos Land Co. v. Arden Group, Inc., 517 A.2d 271
(Del. Ch. 1986) . . . . . . . . 540, 544-45, 1054, 1079, 1081-82

Lacos Land Co. v. Arden Group, Inc., 1986 Del. Ch.
LEXIS 495, 1986 WL 14525 (Del. Ch. Dec. 24,
1986) . . . . . . . . . . . . . . . . . . . . . . . . . . . 1083, 1356

LaFon v. American Casualty Co., 73 F.3d 369 (unpublished opinion, text available at 1995 U.S. App.
LEXIS 37741 and 1995 WL 759454 (9th Cir. Dec.
22, 1995) . . . . . . . . . . . . . . . . . . . . . . . . . . . . 2047

LaForge v. American Casualty Co., 37 F.3d 580 (10th
Cir. 1994) . . . . . . . . . . . . . . . . . . . . 1998, 2011, 2012-13

Laidlaw Acquisition Corp. v. Mayflower Group, Inc.,
636 F. Supp. 1513 (S.D. Ind. 1986) . . . . . . . . . . . . . . 1334

Lake Monticello Owners' Association v. Lake, 463
S.E.2d 652 (Va. 1995) . . . . . . . . . . . . . . . . . . 6, 25, 41

Lama Holding Co. v. Smith Barney Inc., 88 N.Y.2d
413, 668 N.E.2d 1370, 646 N.Y.S.2d 76 (1996) . . . . . . . . 343

In re Landmark Land Co., 76 F.3d 553 (4th Cir.),
cert. dismissed, 518 U.S. 1034 and cert. denied, 117
S. Ct. 59 (1996) . . . . . . . . . . . . 92, 1855, 1861, 1862, 1877

Landry v. Air Line Pilots Ass'n International, 901
F.2d 404 (5th Cir.), cert. denied, 498 U.S. 895
(1990) . . . . . . . . . . . . . . . . . . . . . . . . . . . . . . . 885

Landy v. Amsterdam, 815 F.2d 925 (3d Cir. 1987) . . . 3-4, 283

Landy v. Federal Deposit Insurance Corp., 486 F.2d
139 (3d Cir. 1973), cert. denied, 416 U.S. 960
(1974) . . . . . . . . . . . . . . . . . . . . . . . . . . . . 885, 1681

Langner v. Brown, 913 F. Supp. 260 (S.D.N.Y. 1996) . . . . . . . . . . 62, 1381, 1482, 1489, 1490, 1493, 1496

Lank v. Steiner, 224 A.2d 242 (Del. 1966) . . . . . . . . . . 500

Larson v. Dumke, 900 F.2d 1363 (9th Cir.), cert. denied, 498 U.S. 1012 (1990) . . . . . . . . . . . . . . 1399, 1402

Lasker v. Burks, 404 F. Supp. 1172 (S.D.N.Y. 1975), subsequent proceedings, 426 F. Supp. 844 (S.D.N.Y. 1977), rev'd, 567 F.2d 1208 (2d Cir. 1978), rev'd, 441 U.S. 471 (1979) . . . . . . . . . . . . . . . . . . . . . . . . 1690-91

Lasker v. Burks, 567 F.2d 1208 (2d Cir. 1978), rev'd, 441 U.S. 471 (1979) . . . . . . . . . . . . . . . . . 1766-67

Lauer v. Schoenholtz, 106 A.D.2d 551, 483 N.Y.S.2d 70 (N.Y. App. Div. 2d Dep't 1984), appeal dismissed, 64 N.Y.2d 610, 479 N.E.2d 826, 490 N.Y.S.2d 1023 (1985) . . . . . . . . . . . . . . . . . . . . . . . . . . . . . . . . . . 1559

Laventhol, Krekstein, Horwath & Horwath v. Horwitch, 637 F.2d 672 (9th Cir. 1980), cert. denied, 452 U.S. 963 (1981) . . . . . . . . . . . . . . . . . . . . . . . . . . 1971

Lazar v. Merchants' National Properties, Inc., 45 Misc. 2d 235, 256 N.Y.S.2d 514 (N.Y. Sup. Ct. N.Y. Co. 1964), aff'd mem., 23 A.D.2d 630, 256 N.Y.S.2d 542 (N.Y. App. Div. 1st Dep't 1965) . . . . . 1683-84

Lee v. Interinsurance Exchange, 50 Cal. App. 4th 694, 57 Cal. Rptr. 2d 798 (Cal. Ct. App. 1996) . . . . 6, 22, 26

Lee Builders v. Wells, 103 A.2d 918 (Del. Ch. 1954) . . . . . 960

Lee v. Engle, 1995 Del. Ch. LEXIS 149, 1995 WL 761222 (Del. Ch. Dec. 15, 1995) . . . . . . . . . . . . 1380, 1821

Leigh v. Engle, 727 F.2d 113 (7th Cir. 1984) . . . . . . . . 882-83

Leigh v. Engle, 669 F. Supp. 1390 (N.D. Ill. 1987),
aff'd, 858 F.2d 361 (7th Cir. 1988), cert. denied, 489
U.S. 1078 (1989) . . . . . . . . . . . . . . . . . . . . . . . . . 883

Leigh v. Engle, 858 F.2d 361 (7th Cir. 1988), cert.
denied, 489 U.S. 1078 (1989) . . . . . . . . . . . . . . . . . . 883

Lennane v. ASK Computer Systems, Inc., [1990-1991
Transfer Binder] Fed. Sec. L. Rep. (CCH) ¶ 95,674
(Del. Ch. Oct. 11, 1990), modified on reargument, 16
Del. J. Corp. L. 1538 (Del. Ch. Oct. 19, 1990)
. . . . . . . . . . . . . . . . . . . . . . . . . . . 795-97, 842-44

Lerman v. Diagnostic Data, Inc., 421 A.2d 906 (Del.
Ch. 1980) . . . . . . . . . . . . . . . . . 801, 804, 1257-59, 1261

Lerner v. Lerner, 511 A.2d 501 (Md. 1986) . . . . . . . . . . . 470

Leslie v. Telephonics Office Technologies, Inc., 19
Del. J. Corp. L. 1237 (Del. Ch. Dec. 30, 1993)
. . . . . . . . . . . . . . . . . . . . 229, 230, 1430, 1509, 1581

Levandusky v. One Fifth Avenue Apartment Corp., 75
N.Y.2d 530, 553 N.E.2d 1317, 554 N.Y.S.2d 807
(1990) . . . . . . . . . . . . . . . . . . . . . . . . . . . . . . 11

Levien v. Sinclair Oil Corp., 261 A.2d 911 (Del. Ch.
1969), aff'd in part and rev'd in part, 280 A.2d 717
(Del. 1971) . . . . . . . . . . . . . . . . . . . . . . . . . . 1386

Levin v. Mississippi River Corp., 59 F.R.D. 353
(S.D.N.Y.), aff'd mem., 486 F.2d 1398 (2d Cir.),
cert. denied, 414 U.S. 1112 (1973) . . . . . . . . . . . . . . . 13

Levine v. Bradlee, 248 F. Supp. 395 (E.D. Pa. 1965)
. . . . . . . . . . . . . . . . . . . . . . . . . . . . . . . . . 1405, 1407

Levine v. Milton, 219 A.2d 145 (Del. Ch. 1966) . . . . . . . 1415

Levine v. Prudential-Bache Properties, Inc., 855 F.
Supp. 924 (E.D. Ill. 1994) . . . . . . . . . 1458, 1492, 1494, 1499

Levine v. Smith, 16 Del. J. Corp. L. 333 (Del. Ch.
Nov. 27, 1989), aff'd, 591 A.2d 194 (Del. 1991) . 79, 1482, 1619

Levine v. Smith, 591 A.2d 194 (Del. 1991)
. . . . . . . . . . . . . . . . . . . . . . 20-21, 43, 75, 77, 144, 1354,
1380, 1381, 1426, 1427, 1443, 1473, 1475, 1479-81, 1483, 1524,
1579, 1593, 1609, 1614, 1615, 1618, 1619, 1620, 1632, 1674, 1738

Levit v. Rowe, 1991 U.S. Dist. LEXIS 8314, 1991
WL 111173 (E.D. Pa. June 18, 1991) . . . . . . . . . . . 1796-98

Levit v. Rowe, 1992 U.S. Dist. LEXIS 15036, 1992
WL 277997 (E.D. Pa. Sept. 30, 1992)
. . . . . . . . . . . . . 1707, 1746, 1748, 1750, 1753, 1755, 1798

Levitt v. Johnson, 334 F.2d 815 (1st Cir. 1964), cert.
denied, 379 U.S. 961 (1965) . . . . . . . . . . . . . . . . . . . 1688

Levner v. Prince Alwaleed Bin Talal Bin Abdulaziz Al
Saud, 903 F. Supp. 452 (S.D.N.Y. 1994), aff'd, 61
F.3d 8 (2d Cir. 1995)
. . . . . . . . . . . . . . 1427, 1431-33, 1458, 1610, 1634-35, 1685

Levner v. Prince Alwaleed Bin Talal Bin Abdulaziz Al
Saud, 61 F.3d 8 (2d Cir. 1995) . . . . . . . . . . . . . 1433, 1635

Levy v. Markal Sales Corp., 643 N.E.2d 1206 (Ill.
App. Ct. 1994), appeal denied, 649 N.E.2d 417 (Ill.),
cert. denied, 516 U.S. 861 (1995) . . . . . . . . . . . . . 304, 343

Levy v. National Union Fire Insurance Co., 889 F.2d
433 (2d Cir. 1989) . . . . . . . . . . . . . . . . . . . . . . . . . 2047

Levy v. Stern, No. 11955 (Del. Ch. Feb. 7, 1994),
reconsideration denied, 1996 Del. Ch. LEXIS 25,
1996 WL 118160 (Del. Ch. Mar. 12, 1996), rev'd,
687 A.2d 573 (unpublished opinion, text available at
1996 Del. LEXIS 468 and 1996 WL 742818) (Del.
Dec. 20, 1996) . . . . . . . . . . . . . . . . . . . . . . . . . . . 504

Levy v. Stern, 1996 Del. Ch. LEXIS 25, 1996 WL
118160 (Del. Ch. Mar. 12, 1996), rev'd, 687 A.2d
573 (unpublished opinion, text available at 1996 Del.
LEXIS 468 and 1996 WL 742818) (Del. Dec. 20,
1996) . . . . . . . . . . . . . . . . . . . . . . . . . . . . . . . . . 230

Lewis v. Akers, No. 13880/94 (N.Y. Sup. Ct. Kings
Co. Mar. 3, 1995), aff'd,    227 A.D.2d 595, 644
N.Y.S.2d 279 (N.Y. App. Div. 2d Dep't 1996) . . . . . . . . . 312

Lewis v. Akers, 227 A.D.2d 595, 644 N.Y.S.2d 279
(N.Y. App. Div. 2d Dep't), leave to appeal denied, 88
N.Y.2d 813, 672 N.E.2d 606, 649 N.Y.S.2d 380
(1996) . . . . . . . . . . . . . . . . . . . . . . . . 312, 314, 1491, 1559

Lewis v. Anderson, 615 F.2d 778 (9th Cir. 1979),
cert. denied, 449 U.S. 869 (1980) . . . . . . . . . . . . . . . 1386,
1389, 1390, 1391, 1392, 1464-65, 1611, 1708, 1746-48, 1755

Lewis v. Anderson, 477 A.2d 1040 (Del. 1984) . . . . . . . 1299

Lewis v. Aronson, 11 Del. J. Corp. L. 243 (Del. Ch.
May 1, 1985) . . 95, 1485-87, 1488, 1490, 1492, 1495, 1504, 1527

Lewis v. Bloomfield, 1983 Del. Ch. LEXIS 555, 1983
WL 103274 (Del. Ch. Jan. 11, 1983) . . 321, 322, 323, 341, 516

Lewis v. Boyd, 838 S.W.2d 215 (Tenn. Ct. App.
1992) . . . . . . . . . . . . . . . . . . . . . . . . . . . . 24, 1612

Lewis v. Brennan, No. 92 CH 58520 (Ill. Ch. Ct.
Feb. 15, 1995) . . . . . . . . . . . . . . 146, 1555, 1556-57, 1577

Lewis v. Celina Financial Corp., 655 N.E.2d 1333
(Ohio Ct. App. 1995) . . . . . . . . 377, 539, 664, 698, 730, 817

Lewis v. Charan Industries, Inc., 10 Del. J. Corp. L.
233 (Del. Ch. Sept. 20, 1984) . . . . . . . . . . . . . . . . . . . . 521

Lewis v. Curtis, 671 F.2d 779 (3d Cir.), cert. denied,
459 U.S. 880 (1982) . . . . . . . . . . . . . . . . 1491, 1492, 1774

Lewis v. Daum, 9 Del. J. Corp. L. 481 (Del. Ch.
May 24, 1984) . . . . . . . . . . . . . . . . . . . 1352, 1488, 1492

Lewis v. Fites, 18 Del. J. Corp. L. 1046 (Del. Ch.
Feb. 18, 1993) . . . . . . . . . . . . . 203, 1488, 1492, 1497, 1500

Lewis v. Fuqua, 502 A.2d 962 (Del. Ch. 1985),
appeal refused, 504 A.2d 571 (unpublished opinion,
text available at 1986 Del. LEXIS 1027 and 1986 WL
16292) (Del. Jan. 24, 1986)
    . . . . . . . . 405, 423, 424, 1747-48, 1751-52, 1755, 1762, 1814

Lewis v. General Employment Enterprises, Inc., 1991
U.S. Dist. LEXIS 950, 1991 WL 11383 (N.D. Ill.
Jan. 21, 1991), reconsideration denied, 1991 U.S.
Dist. LEXIS 1140, 1991 WL 10826 (N.D. Ill. Jan.
31, 1991) . . . . . . . . . . . . . . . . . . . . . . . . . . 519, 1251-53

Lewis v. Graves, 701 F.2d 245 (2d Cir. 1983)
    . . . . . . . . . . 1441, 1447, 1454, 1456, 1489, 1490, 1491, 1494

Lewis v. Hett, 10 Del. J. Corp. L. 240 (Del. Ch. Sept. 4, 1984) . . . . . . . . . . . . . . . . . . 1524-25, 1610, 1674

Lewis v. Hilton, 648 F. Supp. 725 (N.D. Ill. 1986) . . . . . . . . . . . . . . . . . . . . . . . . . . 1610, 1613, 1674, 1738

Lewis v. Hirsch, [1994-1995 Transfer Binder] Fed. Sec. L. Rep. (CCH) ¶ 98,382 (Del. Ch. June 1, 1994) . . . . . . . . . . . . . . . . . . . . . . . . . 312, 313, 1408-09

Lewis v. Hirsch, 1995 Del. LEXIS 62, 1995 WL 54419 (Del. Ch. Jan. 31, 1995) . . . . . . . . . . . . . . . . . 1410

Lewis v. Honeywell, Inc., [1987-1988 Transfer Binder] Fed. Sec. L. Rep. (CCH) ¶ 93,565 (Del. Ch. July 28, 1987) . . . . . . . . . . . . . . . . . . . . . . . . . 180, 188

Lewis v. Knutson, 699 F.2d 230 (5th Cir. 1983) . . . . . . . 1390

Lewis v. Kurshan, N.Y.L.J., Dec. 1, 1983 (N.Y. Sup. Ct. N.Y. Co.) . . . . . . . . . . . . . . . . . . . . . . 1356, 1362

Lewis v. Leaseway Transportation Corp., 13 Del. J. Corp. L. 738 (Del. Ch. June 12, 1987) . . . . . . . . . . . . . 181

Lewis v. Leaseway Transportation Corp., [1990 Transfer Binder] Fed. Sec. L. Rep. (CCH) ¶ 95,275 (Del. Ch. May 16, 1990) . . . . . . . . . . . . . . . 370, 510, 963

Lewis v. LFC Holding Corp., 11 Del. J. Corp. L. 254 (Del. Ch. Apr. 4, 1985) . . . . . . . . . . . . . . . . . . . 520

Lewis v. Odell, 503 F.2d 445 (2d Cir. 1974) . . . . . . . . . 1422

Lewis v. Playboy Enterprises, Inc., 664 N.E.2d 133
(Ill. App. Ct. 1996)
. . . . . . . . . 26, 29, 62, 183, 184, 186, 188, 189, 191, 1072-74

Lewis v. S.L.&E., Inc., 629 F.2d 764 (2d Cir. 1980)
. . . . . . . . . . . . . . . . . . . . . . . . . . . . 25, 28, 43-44, 282

Lewis v. Spencer, 577 A.2d 753 (unpublished opinion,
text available at 1990 Del. LEXIS 154 and 1990 WL
72615) (Del. May 11, 1990) . . . . . . . . . . . . . . . 1413, 1414

Lewis v. Sporck, 612 F. Supp. 1316 (N.D. Cal.
1985) . . . . . . . . . . . . . . . . . . . . . . . . . . 1491, 1494, 1499

Lewis v. Sporck, 646 F. Supp. 574 (N.D. Cal. 1986)
. . . . . . . . . . . . . . . . . . . . . . . . . . . . . . . . 1593, 1602

Lewis v. Straetz, 1986 Del. Ch. LEXIS 365, 1986
WL 2252 (Del. Ch. Feb. 12, 1986) . . 62, 1371, 1376-77, 1496

Lewis v. Vogelstein, 699 A.2d 327 (Del. Ch. 1997)
. . . . . . . . . . . . . . . . . . . . . . . . . . . . . . 95, 97, 225-26,
322, 327-28, 328-29, 332-33, 336-37, 505, 506, 517, 518, 528, 539

Lewis v. Welch, 126 A.D.2d 519, 510 N.Y.S.2d 640
(N.Y. App. Div. 2d Dep't 1987) . . . . 145, 1491, 1550, 1551-52

Liddy v. Urbanek, 707 F.2d 1222 (11th Cir. 1983)
. . . . . . . . . . . . . . . . . . . . . . . . . . . . . . . . 1382, 1421

Lieb v. Clark, 13 Del. J. Corp. L. 742 (Del. Ch. June
1, 1987) . . . . . . . . . . . . . . . . . . . 539, 540, 547, 548, 549

Lieberman v. Becker, 155 A.2d 596 (Del. 1959)
. . . . . . . . . . . . . . . . . . . . . . . . . . . 311, 321, 327, 328

Life Care Centers of America, Inc. v. Charles Town
Associates LP, 79 F.3d 496 (6th Cir. 1996) . . . . . . . . . . 123

Linde Thomson Langworthy Kohn & Van Dyke, P.C.
v. Resolution Trust Corp., 5 F.3d 1508 (D.C. Cir.
1993) . . . . . . . . . . . . . . . . . . . . . . . . . . . . . . . . . 1991

Linton v. Everett, 1997 Del. Ch. LEXIS 117, 1997
WL 441189 (Del. Ch. July 31, 1997) . . . 287, 315-16, 1259-62

Lipson v. Supercuts, Inc., 1996 Del. Ch. LEXIS 108,
1996 WL 560191 (Del. Ch. Sept. 10, 1996) . . . . 1911-12, 1933

Lipson v. Supercuts, Inc., No. 15074 (Del. Ch. Dec.
10, 1996) . . 1870, 1898, 1910-12, 1915, 1917-18, 1933, 1949-51

Lipton v. News International, Plc, 514 A.2d 1075
(Del. 1986) . . . . . . . . . . . . . . . . . . . . . . . 1411, 1412, 1414

Litman v. Prudential-Bache Properties, Inc., 611 A.2d
12 (Del. Ch. 1992) . . . . . . . . . . . . . . . . . . . . . . 1804, 1805

Litman v. Prudential-Bache Properties, Inc., [1992-
1993 Transfer Binder] Fed. Sec. L. Rep. (CCH)
¶ 97,313 (Del. Ch. Jan. 4, 1993)
. . . . . . . . . . . . . . . 1492, 1493, 1496, 1498, 1524, 1805-06

Litman v. Prudential-Bache Properties, Inc., 1993 WL
603303 (Del. Nov. 18, 1993) . . . . . . . . . . . . . . . . . . 1806

Litman v. Prudential-Bache Properties, Inc., 19 Del.
J. Corp. L. 1260 (Del. Ch. Jan. 14, 1994), aff'd, 642
A.2d 837 (unpublished opinion, text available at 1994
Del. LEXIS 125 and 1994 WL 144297) (Del. Apr. 21,
1994) . . . . . . . . . . . . . . . . . . . . . . . . . . . . . . . . 1806

Litman v. Prudential-Bache Properties, Inc., 642 A.2d
837 (unpublished opinion, text available at 1994 Del.
LEXIS 125 and 1994 WL 144297) (Del. Apr. 21,
1994) . . . . . . . . . . . . . . . . . . . . . . . . . . . . . . . . 1806

Little v. MGIC Indemnity Corp., 649 F. Supp. 1460
(W.D. Pa. 1986), aff'd, 836 F.2d 789 (3d Cir. 1987)
. . . . . . . . . . . . . . . . . . . . . . . . . . . . . . . . 2100, 2108

Little v. MGIC Indemnity Corp., 836 F.2d 789 (3d
Cir. 1987) . . . . . . . . . . . . . . . . 1990, 2094-96, 2100, 2108

Litton Industries, Inc. v. Hoch, 996 F.2d 1225 (unpublished opinion, text available at 1993 U.S. App.
LEXIS 16992 and 1993 WL 241549) (9th Cir. July 2,
1993) . . . . . . . . 1465-67, 1582, 1610, 1632-33, 1777, 1794-95

Litwin v. Allen, 25 N.Y.S.2d 667 (N.Y. Sup. Ct.
N.Y. Co. 1940) . . . . . . . . . . . . . . . . . . . . . . . . . . 244

In re Logue Mechanical Contracting Corp., 106 B.R.
436 (Bankr. W.D. Pa. 1989) . . . . . . . . . . . . . . . . . 604-05

Long v. Lampton, 922 S.W.2d 692 (Ark. 1996) . . 22, 66, 75, 98

Lorenz v. CSX Corp., 1 F.3d 1406 (3d Cir. 1993) . . . . . 591-92

Lou v. Belzberg, 728 F. Supp. 1010 (S.D.N.Y.
1990) . . . . . . . . . . . . . . . . . 1363, 1456, 1489, 1577, 1682

Loudon v. Archer-Daniels-Midland Co., 700 A.2d 135
(Del. 1997)
. . . . 510, 511, 513, 515, 518, 521, 523, 524, 530, 533-35, 536

In re Louisiana-Pacific Corp. Derivative Litigation,
705 A.2d 238 (Del. Ch. 1997) . . . . . . . . . . . . . . . . . 1410

Louisiana World Exposition v. Federal Insurance Co.,
864 F.2d 1147 (5th Cir. 1989) . . . . . . . . . . . . . . . . . 135

Lowry v. Lowry, 590 N.E.2d 612 (Ind. Ct. App.
1992) . . . . . . . . . . . . . . . . . . . . . . . . . . . . . . . . . 310

Lum v. Opticon, Inc., N.Y.L.J., Sept. 16, 1997, at 30
(N.Y. Sup. Ct. Nassau Co. 1997)
. . . . . . . . . . . . . . . . . . . . 29, 311, 343, 371, 375, 376-77

Lunceford v. Peachtree Casualty Insurance Co., 495
S.E.2d 88 (Ga. Ct. App. 1997) . . . . . . . . . . . . . . . . . 1986

Lussier v. Mau-Van Development, Inc., 667 P.2d 804
(Haw. Ct. App. 1983) . . . . . . . . . . . . . . . . . . . . . . . . 98

Lussier v. Mau-Van Development, Inc., 667 P.2d 830
(Haw. Ct. App. 1983) . . . . . . . . . . . . . . . . . . . . . . 1866

Luther v. Fidelity & Deposit Co., 679 F. Supp. 1092
(S.D. Fla. 1986) . . . . . . . . . . . . . . . . . . . . . . . . . 2096-97

Lutz v. Boas, 171 A.2d 381 (Del. Ch. 1961) . . . . . . . . 170-71

Lynch v. Vickers Energy Corp., 351 A.2d 570 (Del.
Ch. 1976), rev'd, 383 A.2d 278 (Del. 1977) . . . . . . . . . . 361

Lynch v. Vickers Energy Corp., 383 A.2d 278 (Del.
1977) . . . . . . . . . . . . . . . . . . . . . . . . . . . . . . . 499, 527

Lynott v. National Union Fire Insurance Co., 871
P.2d 146 (Wash. 1994) . . . . . . . . . . . . . . . . 2041, 2043-44

In re Lyondell Petrochemical Co. Securities Litigation,
984 F.2d 1050 (9th Cir. 1993) . . . . . . . . . . . . . . . . . 506

MacAndrews & Forbes Holdings, Inc. v. Revlon,
Inc., 1985 Del. Ch. LEXIS 545, 1985 WL 21129
(Del. Ch. Oct. 9, 1985) . . . . . . . . . . . . . . . . . . . . . . . . 1400

MacAndrews & Forbes Holdings, Inc. v. Revlon,
Inc., 501 A.2d 1239 (Del. Ch. 1985), aff'd, 506 A.2d
173 (Del. 1986) . . . . . . . . . . . . . . . . 927, 975, 1122, 1129

Macfadden Holdings, Inc. v. John Blair & Co., 12
Del. J. Corp. L. 773 (Del. Ch. July 2, 1986) . 539, 550-51, 756

MacFarlane v. North American Cement Corp., 157 A.
396 (Del. Ch. 1928) . . . . . . . . . . . . . . . . . . . . . . . . . 565

MacKay v. Pierce, 86 A.D.2d 655, 446 N.Y.S.2d 403
(N.Y. App. Div. 2d Dep't 1982) . . . . . . . . . . . . . 1585, 1603

MacLane Gas Co. v. Enserch Corp., 1992 Del. Ch.
LEXIS 260, 1992 WL 368614 (Del. Ch. Aug. 18,
1992) . . . . . . . . . . . . . . . . . . . . . . . . . . . . . . . 395, 520

Macmillan, Inc. v. Federal Insurance Co., 741 F.
Supp. 1079 (S.D.N.Y. 1990) . . . . . . . . . . . . . . . . . . 2026

Macmillan, Inc. v. Robert M. Bass Group, Inc., 548
A.2d 498 (unpublished opinion, text available at 1988
Del. LEXIS 276 and 1988 WL 101235) (Del. Sept.
14, 1988) . . . . . . . . . . . . . . . . . . . . . . . . . . . . 715, 735

Maher v. Zapata Corp., 714 F.2d 436 (5th Cir.
1983) . . . . . . . . . . . . . . . . . . . . . . . . . . . . . 1409, 1715

MAI Basic Four, Inc. v. Prime Computer, Inc.,
[1988-1989 Transfer Binder] Fed. Sec. L. Rep. (CCH)
¶ 94,179 (Del. Ch. Dec. 20, 1988) . . . . . . . . . . . 1178, 1219

MAI Basic Four, Inc. v. Prime Computer, Inc., 15
Del. J. Corp. L. 690 (Del. Ch. June 13, 1989) . . . . . . . . 1203

Mainiero v. Microbyx Corp., 1996 Del. Ch. LEXIS
107, 1996 WL 487939 (Del. Ch. Aug. 15, 1996) . . . . . . . 1203

Maldonado v. Flynn, 413 A.2d 1251 (Del. Ch. 1980),
rev'd sub nom. Zapata Corp. v. Maldonado, 430 A.2d
779 (Del. 1981) . . . . . . . . . . . . . . . . . . . . . . . . . . . . . 1694

Maldonado v. Flynn, 485 F. Supp. 274 (S.D.N.Y.
1980), aff'd in part and rev'd in part, 671 F.2d 729
(2d Cir. 1982) . . . . . . . . . . . . . . . . . . . . . . . . . . 1450, 1754

Maldonado v. Flynn, 671 F.2d 729 (2d Cir. 1982) . . 1465, 1754

Maldonado v. Flynn, 573 F. Supp. 684 (S.D.N.Y.
1983) . . . . . . . . . . . . . . . . . . . . . . . . . . . . . . . . . . . . 1715

Malone v. Brincat, 1997 Del. Ch. LEXIS 158, 1997
WL 697940 (Del. Ch. Oct. 30, 1997) . . . . . . . . . . . . . . 503

Malone & Hyde, Inc. v. Commissioner, 62 F.3d 835
(6th Cir. 1995) . . . . . . . . . . . . . . . . . . . . . . . . . . . . . 2157

Manacher v. Reynolds, 165 A.2d 741 (Del. Ch.
1960) . . . . . . . . . . . . . . . . . . . . . . . . . . . . . . . . 583, 584

Management Technologies, Inc. v. Morris, 961 F.
Supp. 640 (S.D.N.Y. 1997) . . . . . . . . . . . . . 270, 377, 626

Manbourne, Inc. v. Conrad, 796 F.2d 884 (7th Cir.
1986) . . . . . . . . . . . . . . . . . . . . . . . . . . . . 846-48, 1269

Manchester v. Narragansett Capital, Inc, 1989 Del.
Ch. LEXIS 141, 1989 WL 125190 (Del. Ch. Oct. 18,
1989) . . . . . . . . . . . . . . . . . . . . . . . . . . . . . . . . . . 1508

Marathon Oil Co. v. Mobil Corp., 669 F.2d 378 (6th Cir. 1981), cert. denied, 455 U.S. 982 (1982) . . . . . . . . . 1335

Marciano v. Nakash, 535 A.2d 400 (Del. 1987)
. . . . . . . . . . . . . . . . . . . . . . . . . . 43, 271, 274, 282

Marcus v. Otis, 168 F.2d 649 (2d Cir. 1948) . . . . . . . . . 1415

Margolies v. Pope & Talbot, Inc., 12 Del. J. Corp. L. 1092 (Del. Ch. Dec. 23, 1986) . . . . . . . . . . . . . . . 519, 524

Marhart, Inc. v. CalMat Co., [1991-1992 Transfer Binder] Fed. Sec. L. Rep. (CCH) ¶ 96,655 (Del. Ch. Apr. 22, 1992), reargument denied, 18 Del. J. Corp. L. 740 (Del. Ch. Aug. 19, 1992) . . . . . . . . . . . . . . . . . 504

Markowitz v. Brody, 90 F.R.D. 542 (S.D.N.Y. 1981) . . . . . . . . . . . . . . . . . . . . . . 1491, 1593, 1682-86

In re Marriott Hotel Properties II LP Unitholders Litigation, 22 Del. J. Corp. L. 373 (Del. Ch. June 12, 1996) . . . . . . . . . . . . 361, 363, 520, 523, 550, 556-58, 723

In re Marriott Hotel Properties II LP Unitholders Litigation, 1997 Del. Ch. LEXIS 128, 1997 WL 589028 (Del Ch. Sept. 17, 1997) . . . . . . . . . . . 360, 361, 723

Martin v. American Potash & Chemical Corp., 92 A.2d 295 (Del. 1952) . . . . . . . . . . . . . . . . . . . . . 1351

Martin v. Feilen, 965 F.2d 660 (8th Cir. 1992), cert. denied, 506 U.S. 1054 (1993) . . . . . . . . . . . . . . . . . 884-85

Martin v. Marlin, 529 So. 2d 1174 (Fla. Dist. Ct. App. 1988) . . . . . . . . . . . . . . . . . . . . . . . . . . . . . 364

Martin v. Nationsbank, N.A., 1993 U.S. Dist. LEXIS
6322, 1993 WL 345606 (N.D. Ga. Apr. 7, 1993) . . 879, 893-94

Martin Marietta Corp. v. Bendix Corp., No. 82 Civ.
6135 (S.D.N.Y. Sept. 16, 1982), appeal dismissed,
[1982-1983 Transfer Binder] Fed. Sec. L. Rep. (CCH)
¶ 99,067 (2d Cir. Sept. 21, 1982) . . . . . . . . . . . . . . . . 887

Martin Marietta Corp. v. Bendix Corp., No. 6942
(Del. Ch. Sept. 19, 1982), aff'd, No. 298, 1982 (Del.
Sept. 21, 1982) . . . . . . . . . . . . . . . . . . . . . . . . . . . 1341-42

Martin Marietta Corp. v. Bendix Corp., No. 298,
1982 (Del. Sept. 21, 1982) . . . . . . . . . . . . . . . . . . 1342-43

Martin Marietta Corp. v. Bendix Corp., [1982-1983
Transfer Binder] Fed. Sec. L. Rep. (CCH) ¶ 99,068
(S.D.N.Y. Sept. 22, 1982) . . . . . . . . . . . . . . . . . . . . . 887

Martin Marietta Corp. v. Bendix Corp., 549 F. Supp.
623 (D. Md. 1982) . . . . . . . . . . . . . . . . . . . . . . . . 1340-41

Marx v. Akers, 215 A.D.2d 540, 626 N.Y.S.2d 276
(N.Y. App. Div. 2d Dep't 1995), aff'd in part and
rev'd in part, 88 N.Y.2d 189, 666 N.E.2d 1034, 644
N.Y.S.2d 121 (1996) . . . . . . . . . . . . . . . . . . . 1380, 1704

Marx v. Akers, 88 N.Y.2d 189, 666 N.E.2d 1034,
644 N.Y.S.2d 121 (1996)
. . . . . . . . . 309, 315, 316-17, 1380, 1381, 1382, 1444, 1447-
49, 1475-76, 1543-44, 1546, 1547-49, 1551, 1557, 1558, 1572

Masi v. Ford City Bank & Trust Co., 779 F.2d 397
(7th Cir. 1985) . . . . . . . . . . . . . . . . . . . . . . . . . . . . 595

Maul v. Kirkman, 637 A.2d 928 (N.J. Super. Ct.
App. Div. 1994) . . . . . . . . . . . . . . . . . . . . . . . . . . . 24

Maurer v. Johnson, No. 9725 (Del. Ch. May 10, 1989) . . . . . . . . . . . . . . . . . . . . . . . . . . . . . 1494

Mautner v. Hirsch, 1992 U.S. Dist. LEXIS 6272, 1992 WL 106318 (S.D.N.Y. May 4, 1992) . . . . . . . . 82, 312

In re MAXXAM, Inc./Federated Development Shareholders Litigation, 659 A.2d 760 (Del. Ch. 1995) . . . . . . . . . . . . . . . . . . . . . . . 45, 58-59, 343, 447, 1410

In re MAXXAM, Inc./Federated Development Shareholders Litig., 698 A.2d 949 (Del. Ch. 1996) . . . . . 1380, 1389

In re MAXXAM, Inc./Federated Development Shareholders Litig., 23 Del. J. Corp. L. 277 (Del. Ch. Apr. 4, 1997) . . . . . . . . . . . . . . . 58-59, 342, 404, 432, 442-62

In re MAXXAM, Inc./Federated Development Shareholders Litigation, No. 12111 (Del. Ch. Aug. 20, 1997) . . . . . . . . . . . . . . . . . . . . . . . . . . . . . 461-62

Mayer v. Adams, 141 A.2d 458 (Del. 1958) . . . . . . . . . . 1688

Mayer v. Executive Telecard, Ltd., No. 14459 (Del. Ch. Apr. 19, 1996) . . . . . . . . . . . . . . . . . . . . . . 1859

Mayer v. Executive Telecard, Ltd., 705 A.2d 220 (Del. Ch. 1997) . . . . . . 1853, 1857, 1859, 1873-75, 1933-36, 1948, 1952, 1967

Mayer v. Executive Telecard, Ltd., 1997 U.S. Dist. LEXIS 317, 1997 WL 16669 (S.D.N.Y. Jan. 17, 1997) . . . . . . . . . . . . . . . . . . . . . . . . . . . . . 1860

Mayer v. Executive Telecard, Ltd., No. 95 Civ. 5403 (BSJ) (S.D.N.Y. Apr. 30, 1997), reprinted in Corpo-

rate Officers and Directors Liability Litig. Rptr. 21230
(May 14, 1997) . . . . . . . . . . . . . . . . . . . . . . 1861, 1934

Mazur v. Gaudet, 826 F. Supp. 188 (E.D. La. 1992) . . . . 2152

McClure v. Borne Chemical Co., 292 F.2d 824 (3d
Cir.), cert. denied, 368 U.S. 939 (1961) . . . . . . . . . . . 1407

McCuen v. American Casualty Co., 946 F.2d 1401
(8th Cir. 1991) . . . . . . . . . . . . . . . 1990, 1992, 1999, 2096

McCuen v. International Insurance Co., 1988 U.S.
Dist. LEXIS 17624, 1988 WL 242680 (S.D. Iowa
Sept. 29, 1988), aff'd sub nom. McCuen v. American
Casualty Co., 946 F.2d 1401 (8th Cir. 1991) . . . . . 2077, 2086

McCullough v. Fidelity & Deposit Co., 2 F.3d 110
(5th Cir. 1993) . . . . . . . . . . . . . . . . . . . . . . . 2013, 2014

McDaniel v. Painter, 418 F.2d 545 (10th Cir. 1969) . . . . . . 363

McDermott Inc. v. Lewis, 531 A.2d 206 (Del. 1987) . . . . . . 3

McDonald v. Williams, 174 U.S. 397 (1899) . . . . . . . . . . 623

McDonnell v. American Leduc Petroleums, Ltd., 491
F.2d 380 (2d Cir. 1974) . . . . . . . . . . . . . . . . . . . . 243

McGinniss v. Employers Reinsurance Corp., 648 F.
Supp. 1263 (S.D.N.Y. 1986) . . . . . . . . . . . . . . . . . 2102

McKee v. Rogers, 156 A. 191 (Del. Ch. 1931) . . . . . . . . 1472

McKnight v. Midwest Eye Institute, Inc., 799 S.W.2d
909 (Mo. Ct. App. 1990) . . . . . . . . . . . . . . . . . . . . 98

McLaughlin v. National Union Fire Insurance Co., 23
Cal. App. 4th 1132, 29 Cal. Rptr. 2d 559 (Cal. Ct.
App. 1994) . . . . . . . . . . . . . . . . . . . . . . . . . . . . . 1996

McLean v. International Harvester Co., 817 F.2d
1214 (5th Cir. 1987) . . . . . . . . . . . . . . . . . . . . 1873, 1902

McLean v. International Harvester Co., 902 F.2d 372
(5th Cir. 1990) . . . . . . . . . . . . . . . . . . . . . . . . . . 1864-65

McLeese v. J.C. Nichols Co., 842 S.W.2d 115 (Mo.
Ct. App. 1992) . . 183, 186, 189, 191, 194, 1612, 1674, 1687-88

MCI Telecommunications Corp. v. Wanzer, 1990 Del.
Super. LEXIS 222, 1990 WL 91100 (Del. Super. June
19, 1990) . . . . . . . . . . . . . . . . 1853, 1864, 1881, 1934, 1937

Mediators, Inc. v. Manney, 1996 U.S. Dist. LEXIS
14402, 1996 WL 554576 (S.D.N.Y. Sept. 30, 1996) . . . . . 597

In re Mediators, Inc., 105 F.3d 822 (2d Cir. 1997) . . . . . . 597

Medserv Corp. v. Nemnon, No. 1:95-cv-0462-TWT
(N.D. Ga. Sept. 23, 1997) . . . . . . . . . . . . . . . . . . . 98, 135

Megeath v. PLM International, Inc., No. 930369 (Cal.
Super. Ct. Mar. 18, 1992), reprinted in Corp. Officers
& Directors Liability Litig. Rep. 11791 (Apr. 8,
1992) . . . . . . . . . . 1853, 1871, 1906, 1909, 1913, 1917, 1949

Meimaris v. Hudner, 1995 U.S. Dist. LEXIS 9676,
1995 WL 413164 (S.D.N.Y. July 12, 1995) . . . . . . . . . . 1399

Meldrick Services, Inc. v. Ormes, No. 91-450-JJF (D.
Del. July 1, 1994) . . . . . . . . . . . . . . . . . . . . . . . . . 287

Meltzer v. Atlantic Research Corp., 330 F.2d 946 (4th
Cir.), cert. denied, 379 U.S. 841 (1964) . . . . . . . . 1456, 1688

Mendel v. Carroll, 651 A.2d 297 (Del. Ch. 1994)
. . . . . . . . . . . . . . . . . . . 349, 368, 716, 777, 779-81, 1039

Mendell v. Gollust, 909 F.2d 724 (2d Cir. 1990),
aff'd, 501 U.S. 115 (1991) . . . . . . . . . . . . . . . . . . . . 1684

Mendelovitz v. Vosicky, 1993 U.S. Dist. LEXIS
12936, 1993 WL 367091 (N.D. Ill. Sept. 16, 1993),
aff'd, 40 F.3d 182 (7th Cir. 1994) . . 1489, 1491, 1494, 1495, 1500

Meredith v. Camp Hill Estates, Inc., 77 A.D.2d 649,
430 N.Y.S.2d 383 (N.Y. App. Div. 2d Dep't 1980) . . . 96, 226

Merrill v. Davis, 225 S.W.2d 763 (Mo. 1950) . . . . . . . . 1612

Merritt v. Colonial Foods, Inc., 505 A.2d 757 (Del.
Ch. 1986) . . . . . . . . . . . . . . . . . . . . . . . . . 393-94, 1391

Merritt-Chapman & Scott Corp. v. Wolfson, 264 A.2d
358 (Del. Super. 1970) . . . . . . . . . . . . . . . . . . . . . 1863

Merritt-Chapman & Scott Corp. v. Wolfson, 321 A.2d
138 (Del. Super. 1974) . . . . . . . . . . . . . . . . . . . . 1863-64

Mesa Partners v. Phillips Petroleum Co., 488 A.2d
107 (Del. Ch. 1984) . . . . . . . . . . . . . . . . . . . . . . . 1370

Mesa Petroleum Co. v. Unocal Corp., 1985 Del. Ch.
LEXIS 461, 1985 WL 44692 (Del. Ch. Apr. 22,
1985) . . . . . . . . . . . . . . . . . . . . . . . . . . . . . 1262-63

Mesa Petroleum Co. v. Unocal Corp., 1985 Del. Ch.
LEXIS 411, 1985 WL 44691 (Del. Ch. May 13, 1985),
rev'd, 493 A.2d 946 (Del. 1985) . . . . . . 181-82, 186, 190, 191

In re Metropolitan Life Derivative Litigation, 935 F.
Supp. 286 (S.D.N.Y. 1996) . . . . . . . . . . . . . . . . . . . 1409

Metropolitan Life Insurance Co. v. RJR Nabisco, Inc.,
716 F. Supp. 1504 (S.D.N.Y. 1989) . . . . . . . . . 592, 593, 594

Metropolitan Securities v. Occidental Petroleum
Corp., 705 F. Supp. 134 (S.D.N.Y. 1989) . . . . . . . . . . 592-93

Meyer v. Alco Health Services Corp., [1990-1991
Transfer Binder] Fed. Sec. L. Rep. (CCH) ¶ 95,771
(Del. Ch. Jan. 17, 1991) . . . . . . . . . . . . . . 260-61, 519, 525

Meyers v. Keeler, 414 F. Supp. 935 (W.D. Okla.
1976) . . . . . . . . . . . . . . . . . . . . . . . . . . . . . . . . . 1681

Meyers v. Moody, 693 F.2d 1196 (5th Cir. 1982),
cert. denied, 464 U.S. 920 (1983) . . . . . . . . . . . . . . . . 123

MGIC Indemnity Corp. v. Home State Savings Ass'n,
797 F.2d 285 (6th Cir. 1986) . . . . . . . . . . . . . . . . . . . 2001

Michelson v. Duncan, 386 A.2d 1144 (Del. Ch.
1978), aff'd in part and rev'd in part, 407 A.2d 211
(Del. 1979) . . . . . . . . . . . . . . . . . . . . . . . . 323, 523, 524

Michelson v. Duncan, 407 A.2d 211 (Del. 1979)
. . . . . . . . . . . . 225, 274, 275, 276, 332, 323, 328, 333, 519

In re Midlantic Corp. Shareholder Litigation, 758 F.
Supp. 226 (D.N.J. 1990) . . . . . . . . . . . . . . . . . . . . . 1686

Miller v. American Telephone & Telegraph Co., 507
F.2d 759 (3d Cir. 1974) . . . . . . . . . . . . . . . . 91, 92, 1650

Miller v. Bargaheiser, 591 N.E.2d 1339 (Ohio Ct.
App. 1990) . . 24, 1695, 1708-10, 1722, 1745, 1751, 1753-56, 1778

Miller v. Genesco, Inc., 1994 Del. Ch. LEXIS 17771,
1994 WL 698287 (S.D.N.Y. Dec. 13, 1994) . . . . . . . . . 1822

Miller v. Kastner, 100 A.D.2d 728, 473 N.Y.S.2d
656 (N.Y. App. Div. 4th Dep't 1984) . . . . . . . . . . . . . 1559

Miller v. Loft, 153 A. 861 (Del. Ch. 1931) . . . . . . . . . . 1472

Miller v. Loucks, 1992 U.S. Dist. LEXIS 16966,
1992 WL 329313 (N.D. Ill. Nov. 5, 1992)
. . . 89-90, 1411, 1426, 1427, 1493, 1497, 1498, 1585, 1654-55

Miller v. Magline, Inc., 256 N.W.2d 761 (Mich. Ct.
App. 1977) . . . . . . . . . . . . . . . . . . . . . . . . . . . . . . 310

Miller v. Miller, 222 N.W.2d 71 (Minn. 1974) . . . 297, 298, 303

Miller v. Register & Tribune Syndicate, Inc., 336
N.W.2d 709 (Iowa 1983) . . . . . . . . . . . . . . . 1699-1700, 1766

Miller v. Schreyer, 200 A.D.2d 492, 606 N.Y.S.2d
642 (N.Y. App. Div. 1st Dep't 1994) . . . . . . . 1547, 1557-1558

Miller v. Schreyer, No. 29885/91 (Sup. Ct. N.Y. Co.
May 6, 1997) . . . . . . . . . . . . . . . . . . . . . . . . . . . . . 1558

Miller v. Steinbach, 268 F. Supp. 255 (S.D.N.Y.
1967) . . . . . . . . . . . . . . . . . . . . . . . . . . . . . . . . . 1395

Mills Acquisition Co. v. Macmillan, Inc., [1988-1989
Transfer Binder] Fed. Sec. L. Rep. (CCH) ¶ 94,071
(Del. Ch. Oct. 17, 1988), rev'd, 559 A.2d 1261 (Del.
1989) . . . . . . . . . . . . . . . . . . . . . . . . . . . . . 1158, 1159

Mills Acquisition Co. v. Macmillan, Inc., 559 A.2d
1261 (Del. 1989) . . . . . . . . . . . . . . . . . . . . . . . 20-21,

30, 33, 205, 282, 284, 631, 635, 638-39, 641, 642, 643, 666, 683, 694, 696, 707, 714, 715, 731, 734, 736, 737-43, 756, 757, 758, 809, 811, 827, 918, 921, 923-25, 928, 935-36, 1050, 1160, 1171

Mills v. Andreasen, No. 128824/93 (N.Y. Sup. Ct. Oct. 31, 1994) . . . . . . . . . . . . . . . . . . . . . . . . . . . . . 1559

Mills v. Electric Auto-Lite Co., 396 U.S. 375 (1970) . . . . . 512

Mills v. Esmark, Inc., 91 F.R.D. 70 (N.D. Ill. 1981) . . . . . . . . . . . . . . . . . . . . . . . . . . . . . 1597, 1601, 1603

Mills v. Esmark, Inc., 544 F. Supp. 1275 (N.D. Ill. 1982) . . . . 1301, 1462, 1736-37, 1745-47, 1749, 1755, 1764-65

Minstar Acquiring Corp. v. AMF Inc., 621 F. Supp. 1252 (S.D.N.Y. 1985) . . . . . . 633, 1100, 1121, 1131-32, 1133, 1139-40, 1322, 1325

Missouri Portland Cement Co. v. Cargill, Inc., 498 F.2d 851 (2d Cir.), cert. denied, 419 U.S. 883 (1974) . . . . . . . . . . . . . . . . . . . . . . . . . . . . . . 1338

Mitrano v. Total Pharmaceutical Care, Inc., 75 F.3d 72 (1st Cir. 1996) . . . . . . . . . . . . . . . . . 1867, 1909, 1937

Mlinarcik v. E.E. Wehrung Parking, Inc., 620 N.E.2d 181 (Ohio Ct. App. 1993) . . . . . . . . . . . . . . . . . . 310, 311

In re Mobile Communications Corp. of America, Inc., Consolidated Litigation, [1991-1992 Transfer Binder] Fed. Sec. L. Rep. (CCH) ¶ 96,558 (Del. Ch. Jan. 18, 1991), aff'd, 608 A.2d 729 (unpublished opinion, text available at 1992 Del. LEXIS 76 and 1992 WL 53379) (Del. Feb. 4, 1992), cert. denied, 505 U.S. 1221 (1992) . . . . . . . . . . . . . . . . . . . . . . . . . . . . . . . 63-64

Mobil Corp. v. Marathon Oil Co., [1981-1982 Transfer Binder] Fed. Sec. L. Rep. (CCH) ¶ 98,375 (S.D. Ohio Dec. 7, 1981), rev'd, 669 F.2d 366 (6th Cir. 1981), cert. denied, 455 U.S. 982 (1982) . . . . . . . . 913, 918-19

Moelis v. Schwab Safe Co., 706 F. Supp. 284 (S.D.N.Y. 1989) . . . . . . . . . . . . . . . . . . . . . . . . . . 1413

Mooney v. Willy's-Overland Motors, Inc., 204 F.2d 888 (3d Cir. 1953) . . . . . . . . . . . . . . . . . . . . . . . . . 1853

Moore v. 1600 Downing Street, Ltd., 668 P.2d 16 (Colo. Ct. App. 1983) . . . . . . . . . . . . . . . . . . . . . 1401, 1402

Moore Business Forms, Inc. v. Cordant Holdings Corp., 21 Del. J. Corp. L. 279 (Del. Ch. Nov. 2, 1995) . . . . . . . . . . . . . . . . . . . . . . . . . 570-71, 572, 576-78

Moore Business Forms, Inc. v. Cordant Holdings Corp., 1995 Del. Ch. LEXIS 155, 1995 WL 707877 (Del. Ch. Nov. 30, 1995) . . . . . . . . . . . . . . . . . . . . . . . 584

Moore Corp. v. Wallace Computer Services, Inc., 907 F. Supp. 1545 (D. Del. 1995) . . . . . . . . . . . . . . . 25, 29, 33, 642, 644, 659, 661, 664, 666, 674-75, 680-81, 684, 824, 1148, 1149, 1172-76, 1298, 1335, 1336

Morad v. Coupounas, 361 So. 2d 6 (Ala. 1978) . . . . . . . . . 304

Morales v. Mylan Laboratories, Inc., 443 F. Supp. 778 (W.D. Pa. 1978) . . . . . . . . . . . . . . . . . . . . . . . 1685

Moran v. Household International, Inc., 490 A.2d 1059 (Del. Ch.), aff'd, 500 A.2d 1346 (Del. 1985) . . 5, 62, 184, 823, 888, 1091, 1138, 1148, 1413, 1414, 1496, 1514

Moran v. Household International, Inc., 500 A.2d
1346 (Del. 1985) . . . . . 20-21, 183-84, 189, 631, 638, 640, 642,
643, 644, 664, 684, 1091-95, 1101-02, 1133, 1138, 1146, 1147, 1413

In re Mortgage & Realty Trust, 195 B.R. 740 (Bankr.
C.D. Cal. 1996) . . . . . . . . . . . . . . . . . . . 597, 598, 599

In re Mortgage & Realty Trust Securities Litigation,
787 F. Supp. 84 (E.D. Pa. 1991) . . . . . 1458, 1469, 1491, 1494

In re MortgageAmerica Corp., 714 F.2d 1266 (5th
Cir. 1983) . . . . . . . . . . . . . . . . . . . . . . . . . . . . . 596

Moskowitz v. Lopp, 128 F.R.D. 624 (E.D. Pa.
1989) . . . . . . . . . . . . . . . . . . . . . . . . . . . . . . . 1822

Mount Moriah Cemetery v. Moritz, [1990-1991 Transfer Binder] Fed. Sec. L. Rep. (CCH) ¶ 95,900 (Del.
Ch. Apr. 4, 1991), aff'd, 599 A.2d 413 (unpublished
opinion, text available at 1991 Del. LEXIS 244 and
1991 WL 165558) (Del. Aug. 12, 1991)
. . 76, 78, 180, 184, 185, 188, 1580, 1610, 1618, 1624-26, 1632

Mount Moriah Cemetery v. Moritz, 599 A.2d 413
(unpublished opinion, text available at 1991 Del.
LEXIS 244 and 1991 WL 165558) (Del. Aug. 12,
1991) . . . . . . . . . . . . . . . . . . . . . . . . . . . . . . . 1626

Mountain Manor Realty, Inc. v. Buccheri, 461 A.2d
45 (Md. Ct. Spec. App. 1983) . . . . . . . . . . . . . . . . . . . 867

Mozes v. Welch, 638 F. Supp. 215 (D. Conn. 1986)
. . . . . . . . 1489, 1491, 1494, 1584-85, 1597, 1599-1600, 1603

Mt. Airy Insurance Co. v. Thomas, 954 F. Supp.
1073 (W.D. Pa. 1997) . . . . . . . . . . . . . . . . . . . . . . 2148

Mt. Hawley Insurance Co. v. Federal Savings & Loan
Insurance Corp., 695 F. Supp. 469 (C.D. Cal. 1987)
. . . . . . . . . . . . . . . . . . . . . . . . 2064, 2077, 2098-99

In re Munford, Inc., 98 F.3d 604 (11th Cir. 1996)
. . . . . . . . . . . . . . . . . . . . . . . . . 98, 182, 185, 823

Munson v. Syracuse, Geneva & Corning Railroad
Co., 103 N.Y. 58, 8 N.E. 355 (1886) . . . . . . . . . . . . . . 265

Murphree v. Federal Insurance Co., 1997 Miss.
LEXIS 145, 1997 WL 167002 (Miss. Apr. 10, 1997)
. . . . . . . . . . . . . . . . . . . . . . . . . . 1870, 1923-26

Murray v. Miner, 876 F. Supp. 512 (S.D.N.Y. 1995) . . . . 1415

Murrell v. Elder-Beerman Stores Corp., 239 N.E.2d
248 (Ohio Ct. C.P. 1968) . . . . . . . . . . . . . . . . . . . . . 312

Muschany v. United States, 324 U.S. 49 (1945) . . . . . 2086-87

Muschel v. Western Union Corp., 310 A.2d 904 (Del.
Ch. 1973) . . . . . . . . . . . . . . . . . . . . . . . . . . . . 83

Musick, Peeler & Garrett v. Employers Insurance of
Wausau, 508 U.S. 286 (1993) . . . . . . . . . . . . . . . . . . 2123

N.V. Homes v. Ryan Homes, No. 86-2139 (W.D. Pa.
Oct. 24, 1986) . . . . . . . . . . . . . . . . . . . . . . 1095, 1114-15

Nagy v. Riblet Products Corp., 79 F.3d 572 (7th Cir.
1996) . . . . . . . . . . . . . . . . . . . . . . . . . . . . . 3, 362-63

National Bankers Life Insurance Co. v. Adler, 324
S.W.2d 35 (Tex. Civ. App. 1959) . . . . . . . . . . . . . . . 1383

National Education Corp. v. Bell & Howell Co., 1983
Del. LEXIS 408, 1983 WL 18035 (Del. Ch. Aug. 25,
1983) . . . . . . . . . . . . . . . . . . . . . . . . . . . . 1135, 1136

In re National Intergroup, Inc. Rights Plan Litigation,
[1990 Transfer Binder] Fed. Sec. L. Rep. (CCH)
¶ 95,355 (Del. Ch. July 3, 1990) . . . . . . . . . . . . . . . 1087

National Union Fire Insurance Co. v. Ambassador
Group, Inc., 157 A.D.2d 293, 556 N.Y.S.2d 549
(N.Y. App. Div. 1st Dep't 1990), motion for leave to
appeal dismissed, 77 N.Y.2d 873, 571 N.E.2d 85, 568
N.Y.S.2d 915 (1991) . . . . . . . . . . . . . . . . 1987, 1991, 2094

National Union Fire Insurance Co. v. Brown, 787 F.
Supp. 1424 (S.D. Fla. 1991), aff'd mem., 963 F.2d
385 (11th Cir. 1992) . . . . . . . . . . . . . . . . 2098-2100, 2108

National Union Fire Insurance Co. v. Continental
Illinois Corp., 643 F. Supp. 1434 (N.D. Ill. 1986) . . . . . . 2145

National Union Fire Insurance Co. v. Continental
Illinois Corp., 666 F. Supp. 1180 (N.D. Ill. 1987) . . . . . . 2032

National Union Fire Insurance Co. v. Continental
Illinois Group, 1987 U.S. Dist. LEXIS 11785, 1987
WL 28297 (N.D. Ill. Dec. 14, 1987) . . . . . . . . . . . . . 1995

National Union Fire Insurance Co. v. Emhart Corp.,
11 F.3d 1524 (11th Cir. 1993) . . . . . . . . . . . . . . . . 1958

National Union Fire Insurance Co. v. Federal Deposit
Insurance Corp., No. CV 85-6860 RG (C.D. Cal. Jan.
12, 1987) . . . . . . . . . . . . . . . . . . . . . . . . . . 2096

National Union Fire Insurance Co. v. Federal Deposit
Insurance Corp., 1995 Tenn. App. LEXIS 69, 1995

WL 48462 (Tenn. Ct. App. Feb. 8, 1995), permission
to appeal denied, 1995 Tenn. LEXIS 295 (Tenn. May
30, 1995) . . . . . . . . . . . . . . . . . . . . . . . . . . . 2144, 2152

National Union Fire Insurance Co. v. Goldman, 548
So. 2d 790 (Fla. Dist. Ct. App. 1989) . . . . . . . . . . 2103, 2107

National Union Fire Insurance Co. v. Resolution Trust
Corp., 1992 U.S. Dist. LEXIS 14914, 1992 WL
611463 (S.D. Tex. Aug. 13, 1992) . . . . . . . . 2063, 2076, 2084

National Union Fire Insurance Co. v. Sahlen, 807 F.
Supp. 743 (S.D. Fla. 1992), aff'd, 999 F.2d 1532
(11th Cir. 1993) . . . . . . . . . . . . . . . . . . . . . . . . . . 2152

National Union Fire Insurance Co. v. Sahlen, 999
F.2d 1532 (11th Cir. 1993) . . . . . . . . . . . . . 2140-41, 2152

National Union Fire Insurance Co. v. Seafirst Corp.,
662 F. Supp. 36 (W.D. Wash. 1986) . . . . . . 1985, 2032, 2045

National Union Fire Insurance Co. v. Seafirst Corp.,
No. C85-396R (W.D. Wash. Mar. 19, 1986), aff'd
mem., 804 F.2d 146 (9th Cir. 1986) . . . . . . . . . . 2045, 2167

National Union Fire Insurance Co. v. Seafirst Corp.,
1987 U.S. Dist. LEXIS 14284 (W.D. Wash. Mar. 25,
1987) . . . . . . . . . . . . . . . . . . . . . . . . . . . . . . 2045

National Union Fire Insurance Co. v. Seafirst Co.,
1987 U.S. Dist. LEXIS 14394 (W.D. Wash. Dec. 28,
1987) . . . . . . . . . . . . . . . . . . . . . . . . . . . 2045, 2152-53

National Union Fire Insurance Co. v. Walker, 1989
U.S. Dist. LEXIS 6079, 1989 WL 56164 (W.D. Mo.
May 24, 1989) . . . . . . . . . . . . . . . . . . . . . . . . . . 2146

Nault v. XTRA Corp., [1992 Transfer Binder] Fed.
Sec. L. Rep. (CCH) ¶ 97,022 (D. Mass. July 9,
1992) . . . . . . . . . . . . . . . 95, 341, 1297, 1302, 1303, 1318

NBT Bancorp Inc. v. Fleet/Norstar Financial Group,
Inc., 159 A.D.2d 902, 553 N.Y.S.2d 864 (N.Y. App.
Div. 3d Dep't), appeal dismissed, 76 N.Y.2d 886, 561
N.Y.S.2d 546, 562 N.E.2d 871 (1990) . . . . . 942, 985, 992-93

NBT Bancorp Inc. v. Fleet/Norstar Financial Group,
Inc., 87 N.Y.2d 614, 664 N.E.2d 492, 641 N.Y.S.2d
581 (1996) . . . . . . . . . . . . . . . . . . 983, 985, 991-94, 1000

NCR Corp. v. American Telephone & Telegraph Co.,
761 F. Supp. 475 (S.D. Ohio 1991)
. . . . . . . . . . . . . . . . . . . 4, 23, 111, 685, 853-54, 859-69

Neal v. Neumann Medical Center, 667 A.2d 479 (Pa.
Commw. Ct. 1995), appeal denied, 694 A.2d 624 (Pa.
1996) . . . . . . . . . . . . . . . . . . . . . . . . 1910, 1913, 1926

Nebel v. Southwest Bancorp, Inc., [1995 Transfer
Binder] Fed. Sec. L. Rep. (CCH) ¶ 98,846 (Del. Ch.
July 5, 1995) . . . . . . . . . . . . . . . . . . . . . . 490, 492, 517

Nebenzahl v. Miller, 1996 Del. Ch. LEXIS 113, 1996
WL 494913 (Del. Ch. Aug. 26, 1996)
. . . . . . . . . . . . . . . 26, 53, 253, 267, 268, 271, 272, 518

Needham v. Cruver, [1993 Transfer Binder] Fed. Sec.
L. Rep. (CCH) ¶ 97,673 (Del. Ch. May 12, 1993) . . . 305, 1575

Needham v. Cruver, 1995 Del. Ch. LEXIS 115, 1995
WL 510039 (Del. Ch. Aug. 16, 1995) . . . . . . . . . . . . . . 305

Nejmanowski v. Nejmanowski, 841 F. Supp. 864
(C.D. Ill. 1994) . . . . . . . . . . . . . . . . . . . . 1382, 1423-24

Nelson v. Martin, 958 S.W.2d 643 (Tenn. 1997) . . . . . . . . 343

Nelson v. Pacific Southwest Airlines, 399 F. Supp.
1025 (S.D. Cal. 1975) . . . . . . . . . . . . . . . . . . . . . . . . 1576

Nemo v. Allen, 466 F. Supp. 192 (S.D.N.Y. 1979) . . . . . 1405

New Crawford Valley, Ltd. v. Benedict, 847 P.2d 642
(Colo. Ct. App. 1993) . . . . . . . . . . . . . . 597, 1576, 1687-88

New York Credit Men's Adjustment Bureau, Inc. v.
Weiss, 305 N.Y. 1, 110 N.E.2d 397 (1953)
. . . . . . . . . . . . . . . . . . . . . . 597, 599-600, 601-02, 628

New York Dock Co. v. McCollom, 173 Misc. 106,
16 N.Y.S.2d 844 (N.Y. Sup. Ct. Onondaga Co.
1939) . . . . . . . . . . . . . . . . . . . . . . . . . . . . . . . . . 1852

Newell Co. v. Vermont American Corp., 725 F.
Supp. 351 (N.D. Ill. 1989)
. . . . . . . . . . . . . . 680, 841-42, 1022-24, 1103, 1154, 1402

Newkirk v. W.J. Rainey, Inc., 76 A.2d 121 (Del. Ch.
1950) . . . . . . . . . . . . . . . . . . . . . . . . . . . . . . . . . 1386

Newman v. Warren, 1996 Del. Ch. LEXIS 103, 1996
WL 487972 (Del. Ch. Aug. 19, 1996) . . . . . . . . . 515-16, 520

In re Newmont Mining Corp. Shareholders Litigation,
1988 Del. Ch. LEXIS 95, 1988 WL 73750 (Del. Ch.
July 15, 1988) . . . . . . . . . . . . . . . . . . . . . . . . . . . 1376

News International PLC v. Warner Communications,
Inc., 1984 Del. Ch. LEXIS 551, 1984 WL 21871
(Del. Ch. Jan. 12, 1984) . . . . . . . . . . . . . . . . . . . . 835-36

Newton v. Van Otterloo, 756 F. Supp. 1121 (N.D.
Ind. 1991) . . . . . . . . . . . . . . . . . . . . . . . . . . . . . 882, 886

Niehenke v. Right O Way Transportation, Inc., 1995
Del. Ch. LEXIS 159, 1995 WL 767348 (Del. Ch.
Dec. 28, 1995), reargument denied, 1996 Del. Ch.
LEXIS 22, 1996 WL 74724 (Del. Ch. Feb. 13, 1996) . . . . . 116

Niehenke v. Right O Way Transportation, Inc., 1996
Del. Ch. LEXIS 22, 1996 WL 74724 (Del. Ch. Feb.
13, 1996) . . . . . . . . . . . . . . . . . . . . . . . . . . . . . . . 116

Nixon v. Blackwell, 626 A.2d 1366 (Del. 1993)
. . . . . . . . . . . . 15, 29-30, 32-33, 41, 282, 284, 559, 562-63

Nixon v. Lichtenstein, 959 S.W.2d 854 (Mo. Ct. App.
1997) . . . . . . . . . . . . . . . . . . . . . . . . . . . . . . . . . . 98

Noble v. Baum, 1991 Conn. Super. LEXIS 1231,
1991 WL 101360 (Conn. Super. Ct. May 17, 1991) . . . . . 1493

Noble v. Farmers Union Trading Co., 216 P.2d 925
(Mont. 1950) . . . . . . . . . . . . . . . . . . . . . . . . . . . . . 1612

Nodaway Valley Bank v. Continental Casualty Co.,
715 F. Supp. 1458 (W.D. Mo. 1989), aff'd, 916 F.2d
1362 (8th Cir. 1990) . . . . . . . . . . . 2110, 2114-16, 2118, 2135

Nodaway Valley Bank v. Continental Casualty Co.,
916 F.2d 1362 (8th Cir. 1990) . . . . . . . . . . . . 2113-15, 2135

Noerr v. Greenwood, 1997 Del. Ch. LEXIS 121,
1997 WL 419633 (Del. Ch. July 16, 1997)
. . . . . . . . . . . . . . . . 60, 273-74, 517, 518, 525, 526, 1511

Nomako v. Ashton, 20 A.D.2d 331, 247 N.Y.S.2d
230 (N.Y. App. Div. 1st Dep't 1964) . . . . . . . . . . . . . 1676

Norberg v. Young's Market Co., [1990 Transfer
Binder] Fed. Sec. L. Rep. (CCH) ¶ 95,468 (Del. Ch.
Dec. 19, 1989) . . . . . . . . . . . . . . . . . . . . . . . . . . . 753-54

Norfolk Southern Corp. v. Conrail, Inc., No. 96-7167
(E.D. Pa. Nov. 19, 1996), aff'd mem., 111 F.3d 127
(3d Cir. 1997) . . . . . . . . . . . . . . . . . . . . . . . . 664, 691-92,
815, 914, 941, 958, 971, 984, 994, 998-99, 1102, 1193-94, 1209

Norfolk Southern Corp. v. Conrail, Inc., No. 96-7167
(E.D. Pa. Dec. 17, 1996) . . . . . . . . . . . . . . . . . . . . . . 1347

Norfolk Southern Corp. v. Conrail, Inc., No. 96-7167
(E.D. Pa. Jan. 9, 1997), aff'd mem., 111 F.3d 127
(3d Cir. 1997) . . . . . . . . . . . . . . . . . . . . . . . . . . 942, 984

Norlin Corp. v. Rooney, Pace Inc., 744 F.2d 255 (2d
Cir. 1984) . . . . . . . . . . . . 687, 688, 830, 853, 855-56, 1560

Nordstrom, Inc. v. Chubb & Son, Inc., 820 F. Supp.
530 (W.D. Wash. 1992), aff'd, 54 F.3d 1424 (9th
Cir. 1995) . . . . . . . . . . . . . . . . . . . . . . . . . . . . . 2110

Nordstrom, Inc. v. Chubb & Son, Inc., 54 F.3d 1424
(9th Cir. 1995) . . . . . . . . . . . 2110-11, 2113, 2118-20, 2129

Norfolk Southern Corp. v. Conrail, Inc., No. 96-7167
(E.D. Pa. Nov. 19, 1996 ), aff'd mem., 111 F.3d 127
(3d Cir. 1997) . . . . . . . . . . . . . . . . . . . . . 24, 203, 241-42,

Norlin Corp. v. Rooney, Pace Inc., 744 F.2d 255 (2d
Cir. 1984) . . . . . . . . . . . . . . . . . . . . . . . . 1, 28, 261, 282

Northeast Harbor Golf Club, Inc. v. Harris, 661 A.2d
1146 (Me. 1995) . . . . . . . . . . . . . . . . . . 294, 299, 305, 307

North River Insurance Co. v. Huff, 628 F. Supp.
1129 (D. Kan. 1985) . . . . . . . . . . . . . . . . . . . . . . . . 1992

NRG Barriers, Inc. v. Jelin, 1996 Del. Ch. LEXIS 99,
1996 WL 451319 (Del. Ch. Aug. 6, 1996) . . . . . 508, 522, 524

Nu-Way Environmental, Inc. v. Planet Insurance Co.,
1997 U.S. Dist. LEXIS 11884, 1997 WL 462010
(S.D.N.Y. Aug. 12, 1997) . . . . . . . . . . . . . . . . . . 2102-03

Nursing Center of Buckingham & Hampden, Inc. v.
Shalala, 990 F.2d 645 (D.C. Cir. 1993) . . . . . . . . . . . . . 983

In re Nuveen Fund Litigation, 1996 U.S. Dist. LEXIS
8062, 1996 WL 328001 (N.D. Ill. June 11, 1996) . . . . . . 1499

N.V. Homes v. Ryan Homes, No. 86-2139, Tr. op. at
5-6 (E.D. Pa. Oct. 24, 1986) . . . . . . . . . . . . . . . . . . . 810

In re NVF Co. Litigation, 16 Del. J. Corp. L. 361
(Del. Ch. Nov. 21, 1989)
  . . 62, 95, 172, 186, 187, 191, 193, 1496, 1508, 1523, 1527, 1610

O'Brien v. Murphy, No. A069128 (Cal. Ct. App.
June 18, 1996) . . . . . . . . . . . . . . . . . . . . . . . . . . . 1903

O'Neill v. Davis, 1990 U.S. Dist. LEXIS 1280, 1990
WL 16977 (N.D. Ill. Feb. 2, 1990) . . . . . . . . . 271, 274, 275

O'Neill v. Davis, 721 F. Supp. 1013 (N.D. Ill. 1989) . . 879, 882

Oberly v. Kirby, 592 A.2d 445 (Del. 1991) . . . . . . 30, 43, 63,
188, 266, 267, 268, 271, 275, 282, 284, 532, 703-04, 1245, 1355

In re Ocean Drilling & Exploration Co. Shareholders
Litigation, [1990-1991 Transfer Binder] Fed. Sec. L.
Rep. (CCH) ¶ 95,898 (Del. Ch. Apr. 30, 1991) . . . . . . . 360-61

Ocean Drilling & Exploration Co. v. United States, 988 F.2d 1135 (Fed. Cir. 1993) . . . . . . . . . . . . . . . 2160-61

Ocilla Industries, Inc. v. Katz, 677 F. Supp. 1291 (E.D.N.Y. 1987) . . . . . . . . 179, 1216-17, 1303, 1318-19, 1346

Odette v. Shearson, Hammill & Co., 394 F. Supp. 946 (S.D.N.Y. 1975) . . . . . . . . . . . . . . . . . . . . . . . . . 1971

Odyssey Partners, L.P. v. Fleming Cos., 1996 Del. Ch. LEXIS 91, 1996 WL 422377 (Del. Ch. July 24, 1996) . . . . . . . . . . . . . . . . . . . . . . . . . . . . . 350, 358-60

Ohio-Sealy Mattress Manufacturing Co. v. Kaplan, 90 F.R.D. 21 (N.D. Ill. 1980) . . . . . . . . . . . . . . . . . . . . 1821

Okada v. MGIC Indemnity Corp., 608 F. Supp. 383 (D. Haw. 1985), aff'd in part and rev'd in part, 823 F.2d 276 (9th Cir. 1987) . . . . . . . . . . . . . . . . . . . . . 2109

Okada v. MGIC Indemnity Corp., 795 F.2d 1450 (9th Cir. 1986), superseded, 823 F.2d 276 (9th Cir. 1987) . . . . 2096

Okada v. MGIC Indemnity Corp., 823 F.2d 276 (9th Cir. 1987) . . . . . . . . . . . . . . . . . . . . . . 1990-92, 2094-96

Old Republic Insurance Co. v. Rexene Corp., 1990 Del. Ch. LEXIS 187, 1990 WL 176791 (Del. Ch. Nov. 5, 1990) . . . . . . . . . . . . . . . . . . . . . . . . . 1999, 2147

Olesh v. Dreyfus Corp., [1995-1996 Transfer Binder] Fed. Sec. L. Rep. (CCH) ¶ 98,907 (E.D.N.Y. Aug. 8, 1995) . . . . . . . . . . . . . 62, 1426, 1470, 1489, 1493, 1496

Olson v. Federal Insurance Co., 219 Cal. App. 3d 252, 268 Cal. Rptr. 90 (Cal. Ct. App. 1990) . . . . . . . . . 2025

Olson Bros., Inc. v. Englehart, 211 A.2d 610 (Del.
Ch. 1965), aff'd, 245 A.2d 166 (Del. 1968) . . . . . . . . . 340-41

Olson Bros., Inc. v. Englehart, 245 A.2d 166 (Del.
1968) . . . . . . . . . . . . . . . . . . . . . . . . . . . . . 321, 322

In re Olympia & York Realty Corp., Nos. 92 B
42698-702 (JLG) (Bankr. S.D.N.Y. Jan. 10, 1995)
. . . . . . . . . 26, 184-85, 188-89, 190, 191, 194, 195, 312, 313

Olympic Club v. Those Interested Underwriters at
Lloyd's London, 991 F.2d 497 (9th Cir. 1993) . . . . . . 2039-40

Omnibank v. United Southern Bank, 607 So. 2d 76
(Miss. 1992) . . . . . . . . . . . . . . . . . . . . . . . . . . . 98

Ono v. Itoyama, 884 F. Supp. 892 (D.N.J. 1995);
aff'd mem., 79 F.3d 1138 (3d Cir. 1996) . . 1383, 1422, 1477-78

In re Oracle Securities Litigation, 829 F. Supp. 1176
(N.D. Cal. 1993) . . . . . . . . . . . . 210, 1595-96, 1731-32, 1754

In re Oracle Securities Litigation, 852 F. Supp. 1437
(N.D. Cal. 1994) . . . . . . . . . . . . . . . . . . 1595-96, 1731-32,
1746, 1747, 1748, 1749, 1750, 1752, 1753, 1754, 1755, 1759, 1773

Orban v. Field, 19 Del. J. Corp. L. 1275 (Del. Ch.
Dec. 30, 1993) . . . . . . . . . . . . . . . . . . . . . . . . . . 114

Orban v. Field, 23 Del. J. Corp. L. 335 (Del. Ch.
Apr. 1, 1997) . . . . . . . . 95, 271, 274, 312, 315, 582, 585-90

Orin v. Huntington Bancshares, Inc., Nos. 61129 &
61394 (Ohio Ct. Common Pleas Sept. 30, 1986), aff'd
sub nom. Worth v. Huntington Bancshares, Inc., 1987
Ohio App. LEXIS 9827, 1987 WL 25694 (Ohio Ct.

App. Nov. 25, 1987), aff'd in part and rev'd in part,
540 N.E.2d 249 (Ohio 1989) . . . . . . . . . . . . . . . . . . 1309

Orlando Orange Groves Co. v. Hale, 161 So. 284
(Fla. 1935) . . . . . . . . . . . . . . . . . . . . . . . . . . . . . 1611

Orlett v. Cincinnati Microwave, Inc., 953 F.2d 224
(6th Cir. 1990) . . . . . . . . . . . . . . . . . . . . . . . 123, 240-41

Ostrowski v. Avery, 1996 Conn. Super. LEXIS 2557,
1996 WL 580981 (Conn. Super. Ct. Sept. 30, 1996),
rev'd, 703 A.2d 117 (Conn. 1997) . . . . . . 1703, 1754, 1763-64

Ostrowski v. Avery, 703 A.2d 117 (Conn. 1997)
. . . . . . . . . . . . . . . . . . . . . 1, 28, 282, 301, 304, 307-08

Outen v. Mical, 454 S.E.2d 883 (N.C. Ct. App.
1995) . . . . . . . . . . . . . . . . . . . . . . . . . . . . . . . 1382

P.J. Acquisition Corp. v. Skoglund, 453 N.W.2d 1
(Minn. 1990) . . . . . . . . . . . . . . . . . . . . . . . . . . . . 298

In re P.J. Keating Co., 180 B.R. 18 (Bankr. D. Mass.
1995) . . . . . . . . . . . . . . . . . . . . . . . . . . . 1868, 1958

Pacific Insurance Co. v. General Development Corp.,
28 F.3d 1093 (11th Cir. 1994) . . . . . . . . . . . . . . . . . 2153

Pacific Insurance Co. v. Higgins, 1993 Del. Ch.
LEXIS 68, 1993 WL 133181 (Del. Ch. Apr. 15,
1993) . . . . . . . . . . . . . . . . . . . . . . . . . . . . . . 1911

Packer v. Yampol, 12 Del. J. Corp. L. 332 (Del. Ch.
Apr. 18, 1986), interlocutory appeal granted, Nos.
115, 116 & 117 (Del. Apr. 22, 1986)
. . . . . . . . . . . . . . . . . . . . . 839, 849-50, 1054, 1079-80

Palmer v. United States Savings Bank of America, 553
A.2d 781 (N.H. 1989) . . . . . . . . . . . . . . . . . . . . . . . . 1401

Panter v. Marshall Field & Co., 486 F. Supp. 1168
(N.D. Ill. 1980), aff'd, 646 F.2d 271 (7th Cir.), cert.
denied, 454 U.S. 1092 (1981) . . . . . . . . . . . . . . . . . . . . 632

Panter v. Marshall Field & Co., 646 F.2d 271 (7th
Cir.), cert. denied, 454 U.S. 1092 (1981)
. . . . . . . . . . . . . . . . 631, 633, 824, 830-31, 1332-33, 1344

Papilsky v. Berndt, [1976-1977 Transfer Binder] Fed.
Sec. L. Rep. (CCH) ¶ 95,627 (S.D.N.Y. June 24,
1976) . . . . . . . . . . . . . . . . . . . . . . . . . . . . . . . . . . . . 210-11

In re Par Pharmaceutical, Inc. Derivative Litigation,
750 F. Supp. 641 (S.D.N.Y. 1990)
. . . . . . . . . . . . . . . . . . . . . . . 1463-64, 1689, 1696, 1754

Para-Medical Leasing, Inc. v. Hangen, 739 P.2d 717
(Wash. Ct. App. 1987) . . . . . . . . . . . . . . . . . . . . . . . . 99

Paramount Communications Inc. v. QVC Network
Inc., [1993 Transfer Binder] Fed. Sec. L. Rep. (CCH)
¶ 98,000 (Del. Dec. 9, 1993) . . . . . . . . . . . . . . . . . 976-77

Paramount Communications Inc. v. QVC Network
Inc., 637 A.2d 34 (Del. 1994) . . . 20-21, 43, 75, 146, 179, 342,
343, 363, 631, 637, 639, 641, 642, 663, 681-82, 694, 706, 707-
10, 713, 721, 726, 730, 731, 733, 734, 735-36, 743, 744-45, 751,
756, 765, 771, 772, 783, 790, 914-15, 935-37, 939, 940, 963,
974-77, 984-85, 1000, 1149, 1150, 1171, 1172, 1176, 1177, 1205

Paramount Communications Inc. v. Time Inc., [1989
Transfer Binder] Fed. Sec. L. Rep. (CCH) ¶ 94,514
(Del. Ch. July 14, 1989), aff'd, 571 A.2d 1140 (Del.

1990) . . . . . . . . . . . . . . . . . . . . . . . . . . . 16, 37, 647-
48, 661, 679, 681, 710, 795, 911, 938, 1167, 1171, 1172, 1343

Paramount Communications Inc. v. Time Inc., 571
A.2d 1140 (Del. 1990) . . . . . . . . . . . . . . . . . . . . . . . 181
631, 639, 642, 643, 646, 648, 659, 660, 663, 666, 668-69, 672-
73, 679, 681, 683, 699-700, 705, 706, 710, 734, 794-95, 809,
811, 823, 876, 911, 938, 1029, 1149, 1165, 1166-67, 1176, 1177

Parker v. Watts, 1987 U.S. Dist. LEXIS 6862, 1987
WL 7450 (E.D. La. Feb. 27, 1987) . . . . . . . . . . . . . . 2047

Parkoff v. General Telephone & Electronics Corp, 53
N.Y.2d 412, 425 N.E.2d 820, 442 N.Y.S.2d 432
(1981) . . . . . . . . . . . . . . . . . . . . . . . . . . . . . . . 1796

Parnes v. Bally Entertainment Corp., 1997 Del. Ch.
LEXIS 70, 1997 WL 257435 (Del. Ch. May 12,
1997) . . . . . . . . . . . . . . . . . . . 26-28, 43, 62, 94, 96, 713

Paulman v. Kritzer, 219 N.E.2d 541 (Ill. App. Ct.
1966), aff'd, 230 N.E.2d 262 (Ill. 1967) . . . . . . . . . 297, 304

Peller v. Southern Co., [1987-1988 Transfer Binder]
Fed. Sec. L. Rep. (CCH) ¶ 93,714 (N.D. Ga. Mar.
25, 1988), aff'd, 911 F.2d 1532 (11th Cir. 1990)
. . . . . . . . . . . . . . . . . . . . . . . . . . . . 1733, 1792-93

Peller v. Southern Co., 707 F. Supp. 525 (N.D. Ga.
1988), aff'd, 911 F.2d 1532 (11th Cir. 1990)
. . . . . . . . . . . . . . . . . . . . . . . . 1734-35, 1772, 1779

Peller v. Southern Co., 911 F.2d 1532 (11th Cir.
1990) . . . . . . . . . . 3, 1591, 1695, 1721, 1732-35, 1772, 1780

Penington v. Commonwealth Hotel Construction
Corp., 155 A. 514 (Del. 1931) . . . . . . . . . . . . . . 559, 1039

In re Penn Central Securities Litigation, 335 F. Supp.
1026 (E.D. Pa. 1971) . . . . . . . . . . . . . . . . . . . . . . . . 1423

Penn Mart Realty Co. v. Perelman, 13 Del. J. Corp.
L. 369 (Del. Ch. Apr. 15, 1987), appeal dismissed,
529 A.2d 772 (Del. 1987) . . . . . . . . . . . . . . . . . . . . 1299

Pennzoil Co. v. Getty Oil Co., 1984 Del. Ch. LEXIS
418, 1984 WL 15664 (Del. Ch. Feb. 6, 1984) . . . . . . . 1001-02

People v. Uran Mining Corp., 13 A.D.2d 419, 216
N.Y.S.2d 985 (N.Y. App. Div. 4th Dep't 1961) . . . . . 1881-82

Pepper v. Litton, 308 U.S. 295 (1939) . . . . . . . . . . . 262, 342

PepsiCo, Inc. v. Continental Casualty Co., 640 F.
Supp. 656 (S.D.N.Y. 1986)
. . . . . . 1870, 1967-68, 1973, 2032, 2099, 2101-02, 2111, 2133

Percy v. Millaudon, 8 Mart. (n.s.) 68 (La. 1829) . . . . . 9-10, 12

Perini Corp. v. National Union Fire Insurance Co.,
1988 U.S. Dist. LEXIS 17442, 1988 WL 192453 (D.
Mass. June 2, 1988) . . . . . . . . . . . . . . . . . . . . . . . . 2112

Perlman v. Feldmann, 219 F.2d 173 (2d Cir.), cert.
denied, 349 U.S. 952 (1955) . . . . . . . . . . . . . . . . . . 367-68

In re Perrigo Co., 128 F.3d 430 (6th Cir. 1997)
. . . . . . . . . . . . . . . . . . . . . . . 1826, 1827, 1828, 1841-49

Persinger v. Carmazzi, 441 S.E.2d 646 (W. Va.
1994) . . . . . . . . . . . . . . . . . . . . . . . . . . . . . . . . . 468-69

Pessin v. Chris-Craft Industries, Inc., 181 A.D.2d 66,
586 N.Y.S.2d 584 (N.Y. App. Div. 1st Dep't 1992) . . . . . 1415

Petty v. Bank of New Mexico Holding Co., 787 P.2d
443 (N.M. 1990) . . . . . . . . . . . . . . . . . . . . . . . 1873, 1957

Petty v. Penntech Papers, Inc., 347 A.2d 140 (Del.
Ch. 1975) . . . . . . . . . . . . . . . . . . . . . . . . . . . . . 1005

In re Pfizer Inc. Securities Litigation, 1993 U.S. Dist.
LEXIS 18215, 1993 WL 561125 (S.D.N.Y. Dec. 23,
1993) . . . . . . . . . . . . . . . . . . . . . . . . . . . . . 1822, 1823

Phelps v. Burnham, 327 F.2d 812 (2d Cir. 1964) . . . . . . . 1406

Phillips v. Insituform of North America, Inc., 13 Del.
J. Corp. L. 774 (Del. Ch. Aug. 27, 1987)
 . . . . . . . . . . . . 565, 566-67, 568, 849, 1208, 1245, 1290-92

Phoenix Airline Services, Inc. v. Metro Airlines, Inc.,
397 S.E.2d 699 (Ga. 1990) . . . . . . . . . . . . . . . . . 298, 1382

Phototron Corp. v. Eastman Kodak Co., 842 F.2d 95
(5th Cir.), cert. denied, 486 U.S. 1023 (1988) . . . . . . . . . 1338

Picard Chemical Inc. Profit Sharing Plan v. Perrigo
Co., 951 F. Supp. 679 (W.D. Mich. 1996)
 . . . . . . . . . . . . . . . . . . . . . . 1822, 1828, 1829, 1833-40

Pintlar Corp. v. Fidelity & Casualty Co., 205 B.R.
945 (Bankr. D. Idaho 1997), aff'd sub nom. Cigna
Insurance Co. v. Gulf USA Corp., No. CV 97-250-N-
EJL (D. Idaho Sept. 11, 1997) . . . . . . . . . . . . . . . 2070-73

Pitman v. Aran, 935 F. Supp. 637 (D. Md. 1996) . . . . . . . 304

Pittelman v. Pearce, 6 Cal. App. 4th 1436, 8 Cal.
Rptr. 2d 359 (Cal. Ct. App. 1992) . . . . . . . . . . . . . . . 595

Pittiglio v. Michigan National Corp., 906 F. Supp.
1145 (E.D. Mich. 1995) . . . . . . . . . . . . . . . . . . . . . 726

Pittleman v. Tully, N.Y.L.J., July 18, 1996, at 22
(N.Y. Sup. Ct. N.Y. Co.) . . . . . . . . . . . . . . . . 145, 1543

Pittman v. American Metal Forming Corp., 649 A.2d
356 (Md. 1994) . . . . . . . . . . . . . . . . . . . . . 225, 300, 343

In re Pittsburgh & Lake Erie Railroad Co. Securities
& Antitrust Litigation, 543 F.2d 1058 (3d Cir. 1976) . . . . 1410

Pittsburgh Terminal Corp. v. Baltimore & Ohio Railroad, 680 F.2d 933 (3d Cir.), cert. denied, 459 U.S.
1056 (1982) . . . . . . . . . . . . . . . . . . . . . . . . . . . . . 123, 590

Pittsburgh Terminal Corp. v. Baltimore & Ohio Railroad, 875 F.2d 549 (6th Cir. 1989) . . . . . . . 28, 369, 399-400

Plate v. Sun-Diamond Growers, 225 Cal. App. 3d
1115, 275 Cal. Rptr. 667 (Cal. Ct. App. 1990) . . . . 1855, 1958

Platt v. Richardson, [1989-1990 Transfer Binder] Fed.
Sec. L. Rep. (CCH) ¶ 94,786 (M.D. Pa. June 6,
1989) . . . . . . . . . . . . . . . . . . . . . . . . 100, 172, 1383, 1602

Plaza Securities Co. v. Fruehauf Corp., 643 F. Supp.
1535 (E.D. Mich.), aff'd sub nom. Edelman v. Fruehauf Corp., 798 F.2d 882 (6th Cir. 1986)
. . . . . . . . . . . . . . . . . . . . 175-78, 186, 187, 189, 191, 686

Plaza Securities Co. v. Lucky Stores, Inc., No. C-86-
7016 (N.D. Cal. Dec. 22, 1986) . . . . . . . . . . . 558-59, 1252

Plaza Securities Co. v. Office, 12 Del. J. Corp. L.
1145 (Del. Ch. Dec. 15, 1986) . . . . . . . . . . . . . . . . 1348

Podesta v. Calumet Industries, Inc., [1978 Transfer Binder] Fed. Sec. L. Rep. (CCH) ¶ 96,433 (N.D. Ill. May 9, 1978) .............................. 869

Pogo Producing Co. v. Northwest Industries, Inc., No. H-83-2667 (S.D. Tex. May 24, 1983) .......... 1006

Pogostin v. Leighton, 523 A.2d 1078 (N.J. Super. Ct. App. Div.), cert. denied, 484 U.S. 964 (1987) ........ 1386

Pogostin v. Rice, 480 A.2d 619 (Del. 1984) .......... 312, 321, 322, 323, 326, 1448, 1473-74, 1479, 1481, 1488, 1490, 1572

Poland v. Caldwell, 1990 U.S. Dist. LEXIS 13634, 1990 WL 158479 (E.D. Pa. Oct. 12, 1990) ........ 62, 1439

Polaroid Corp. v. Disney, 862 F.2d 987 (3d Cir. 1988) ................................ 1010-11

Polk v. Good, 507 A.2d 531 (Del. 1986) ............... 643, 824, 1352-53, 1363, 1408, 1409

Pollitz v. Wabash Railroad Co., 207 N.Y. 113, 100 N.E. 721 (1912) .............................. 11

Polychron v. Crum & Forster Insurance Co., 916 F.2d 461 (8th Cir. 1990) ................ 1985, 2000

Pompeo v. Hefner, 1983 Del. Ch. LEXIS 506, 1983 WL 20284 (Del. Ch. Mar. 23, 1983) .......... 1744, 1784

Porter v. Texas Commerce Bancshares, Inc., 15 Del. J. Corp. L. 1113 (Del. Ch. Oct. 12, 1989) ...................... 370, 485, 490, 493, 517, 523

Potomac Capital Markets Corp. v. Prudential-Bache
Corporate Dividend Fund, Inc., 726 F. Supp. 87
(S.D.N.Y. 1989) . . . . . . . . . . . . . . . . . . . . . . . . . 136

Potter v. Pohlad, No. 95-3016 (Minn. Dist. Ct. Aug.
19, 1996), aff'd, 560 N.W.2d 389 (Minn. Ct. App.
1997), review denied, 1997 Minn. LEXIS 459 (Minn.
June 11, 1997) . . . . . . . . . . 7, 81, 99, 167-68, 203, 215, 216

Potter v. Pohlad, 560 N.W.2d 389 (Minn. Ct. App.
1997), review denied, 1997 Minn. LEXIS 459 (Minn.
June 11, 1997) . . 3, 7, 15, 19, 26-27, 76-77, 82, 183, 195-98, 504

Powell v. American Casualty Co., 772 F. Supp. 1188
(W.D. Okla. 1991) . . . . . . . . . . . . . . . . . . . . . 2076, 2085

Powell v. Gant, 556 N.E.2d 1241 (Ill. App. Ct.),
appeal denied, 564 N.E.2d 847 (Ill. 1990) . . . 1415, 1416, 1493

Powell v. Western Illinois Electric Cooperative, 536
N.E.2d 231 (Ill. App. Ct.), appeal denied, 545
N.E.2d 129 (Ill. 1989), cert. denied, 493 U.S. 1079
(1990) . . . . . . . . . . . . . . . . . . . . . . . . . . . . . . 23, 1690

PPG Industries, Inc. v. Transamerica Insurance Co.,
49 Cal. App. 4th 1120, 56 Cal. Rptr. 2d 889 (Cal. Ct.
App.), petition for review granted, 927 P.2d 1174, 59
Cal. Rptr. 2d 670 (Cal. 1996) . . . . . . . . . . . . . . . . . . 1987

Prager v. Sylvestri, 449 F. Supp. 425 (S.D.N.Y.
1978) . . . . . . . . . . . . . . . . . . . . . . . . . . . . . . . . 1685

Priddy v. Edelman, 883 F.2d 438 (6th Cir. 1989)
. . . . . . . . 23, 178-79, 182, 184, 185, 194, 345, 756, 757, 958

Pritchard v. Mead, 455 N.W.2d 263 (Wis. Ct. App.),
review denied, 458 N.W.2d 533 (Wis. 1990) . . . . . . . . . . 497

Professional Insurance Co. v. Barry, 60 Misc. 2d 424,
303 N.Y.S.2d 556 (N.Y. Sup. Ct. N.Y. Co.), aff'd
mem., 32 A.D.2d 898, 302 N.Y.S.2d 722 (N.Y. App.
Div. 1st Dep't 1969) . . . . . . . . . . . . . . . . . 1936-37, 1942-43

Providence & Worcester Co. v. Baker, 378 A.2d 121
(Del. 1977) . . . . . . . . . . . . . . . . . . . . . . 1054, 1097, 1140

In re Prudential Insurance Co. Derivative Litigation,
659 A.2d 961 (N.J. Super. Ct. Ch. Div. 1995)
. . . . . . . . . . . . . . . . . . . . . . . . . . . . 4, 41, 145, 1445,
1459, 1469-70, 1482, 1490, 1493, 1494, 1496, 1500, 1540-41, 1585

Public Investments Ltd. v. Bandeirante Corp., 740
F.2d 1222 (D.C. Cir. 1984) . . . . . . . . . . . . . . . . . . . . 98

Public Service Mutual Insurance Co. v. Goldfarb, 53
N.Y.2d 392, 425 N.E.2d 810, 442 N.Y.S.2d 422
(1981) . . . . . . . . . . . . . . . . . . . . . . . . . . . . . . 1985

Public Utility District No. 1 v. International Insurance
Co., 881 P.2d 1020 (Wash. 1994) . . . . . . . . . . . . . . . 1995

Pullman-Peabody Co. v. Joy Manufacturing Co., 662
F. Supp. 32 (D.N.J. 1986) . . . . . . . . . . . . . . . 1489, 1498

Puma v. Marriott, 283 A.2d 693 (Del. Ch. 1971)
. . . . . . . . . . . . . . . . . . . . . . . . . 26, 272, 283, 344-45

Pupecki v. James Madison Corp., 382 N.E.2d 1030
(Mass. 1978) . . . . . . . . . . . . . . . . . . . . . . . . . . 1688

Qantel Corp. v. Niemuller, 771 F. Supp. 1372
(S.D.N.Y. 1991) . . . . . . . . . . . . . . . . . . . . . . . . 1873

Quintel Corp., N.V. v. Citibank, N.A., 567 F. Supp.
1357 (S.D.N.Y. 1983) . . . . . . . . . . . . . . . . . . . . . 1822

Quirke v. St. Louis-San Francisco Railway Co., 277
F.2d 705 (8th Cir.), cert. denied, 363 U.S. 845
(1960) . . . . . . . . . . . . . . . . . . . . . . . . . . . . . . . . 1399

QVC Network Inc. v. Paramount Communications
Inc., 635 A.2d 1245 (Del. Ch. 1993), aff'd, 637 A.2d
34 (Del. 1994)
. . . . . . . . . 712, 719, 743, 745, 765, 915-16, 976, 1158, 1161

R-G Denver, Ltd. v. First City Holdings, 789 F.2d
1469 (10th Cir. 1986) . . . . . . . . . . . . 984-85, 988-89, 1000

R.C. Bigelow, Inc. v. Unilever N.V., 867 F.2d 102
(2d Cir.), cert denied, 493 U.S. 815 (1989) . . . . . . . . . . 1337

R.D. Smith & Co. v. Preway Inc., 644 F. Supp. 868
(W.D. Wis. 1986) . . . . . . . . . . . . . . . 1091, 1099, 1112-13

Rabkin v. Olin Corp., [1990 Transfer Binder] Fed.
Sec. L. Rep. (CCH) ¶ 95,255 (Del. Ch. Apr. 17,
1990), aff'd, 586 A.2d 1202 (unpublished opinion,
text available at 1990 Del. LEXIS 405 and 1990 WL
259720) (Del. Dec. 20, 1990) . . . 276, 283, 406, 409, 431, 433-34

Rabkin v. Olin Corp., 586 A.2d 1202 (unpublished
opinion, text available at 1990 Del. LEXIS 405 and
1990 WL 259720) (Del. Dec. 20, 1990) . . . . . . . . . . . . 434

Rabkin v. Philip A. Hunt Chemical Corp., 498 A.2d
1099 (Del. 1985) . . . . . . . . . . . . . . . . . . . . . . 431-32, 490

Rabkin v. Philip A. Hunt Chemical Corp., 547 A.2d
963 (Del. Ch. 1986), reargument denied, 13 Del. J.
Corp. L. 1210 (Del. Ch. Dec. 17, 1987)
. . . . . . . . . . . . . . . . . . . . 40, 172, 180, 184, 186, 191, 716

Rabkin v. Philip A. Hunt Chemical Corp., 13 Del. J.
Corp. L. 1210 (Del. Ch. Dec. 17, 1987) . . . . . . . . . . 140-41

Racine v. Weisflog, 477 N.W.2d 326 (Wis. Ct. App.
1991) . . . . . . . . . . . . . . . . . . . . . . . . . . . . . . . 298

In re Radiology Associates, Inc. Litigation, 1990 Del.
Ch. LEXIS 58, 1990 WL 67839 (Del. Ch. May 16,
1990) . . . . . . . . . . . . . . 169, 170, 209, 348, 468, 485, 526

Radol v. Thomas, 772 F.2d 244 (6th Cir. 1985), cert.
denied, 477 U.S. 903 (1986) . . . . . . . . . . . . . . . . . . . 631

Raese v. Kelly, 59 F.R.D. 612 (N.D. W. Va. 1973) . . . . . 1421

Raines v. Toney, 313 S.W.2d 802 (Ark. 1958) . . . . . . . . 297

Rales v. Blasband, 626 A.2d 1364 (Del. 1993) . . . . . . . . 1426

Rales v. Blasband, 634 A.2d 927 (Del. 1993) . . . . . . . . 19-21,
40, 42-45, 53, 56-57, 66, 1394, 1395, 1415, 1416, 1426, 1428,
1444, 1448, 1455, 1459, 1467, 1473-75, 1479, 1530-32, 1533-37,
1541, 1550, 1571, 1572, 1579, 1594, 1595, 1610, 1614, 1677-78

Rand v. Western Airlines, Inc., [1989-1990 Transfer
Binder] Fed. Sec. L. Rep. (CCH) ¶ 94,751 (Del. Ch.
Sept. 11, 1989) . . . . . . . . . . . . . . . . . . . . . . 912-13, 1300

Rand v. Western Air Lines, Inc., 19 Del. J. Corp. L.
1292 (Del. Ch. Feb. 25, 1994), aff'd, 659 A.2d 228
(unpublished opinion, text available at 1995 Del.
LEXIS 6 and 1995 WL 13432) (Del. Jan. 6, 1995)
. . . . . . . . . . . . . . . . . . . . . . . . . . . . 182, 184, 187, 189,
190, 194-95, 507, 519, 755, 757, 758, 766, 825, 912-13, 939-40

Rand v. Western Air Lines, Inc., 659 A.2d 228 (unpublished opinion, text available at 1995 Del. LEXIS 6 and 1995 WL 13432) . . . . . . . . . . . . . . . . . . . . . . . . . 940

Rankin v. Cooper, 149 F. 1010 (W.D. Ark. 1907) . . . . 128, 208

Rapid-American Corp. v. Harris, 603 A.2d 796 (Del. 1992) . . . . . . . . . . . . . . . . . . . . . . . . . . . . . . 478-79

Rapoport v. Schneider, 29 N.Y.2d 396, 278 N.E.2d 642, 328 N.Y.S.2d 431 (1972) . . . . . . . . . . . . . . . 270, 502

Raskin v. Birmingham Steel Corp., [1990-1991 Transfer Binder] Fed. Sec. L. Rep. (CCH) ¶ 95,668 (Del. Ch. Dec. 4, 1990) . . . . . . . . . . . . . . . . . . . . . . . . . 503

Ratcliffe v. International Surplus Lines Insurance Co., 550 N.E.2d 1052 (Ill. App. Ct. 1990) . . . . . . . . . . . . 2148

Raychem Corp. v. Federal Insurance Co., 853 F. Supp. 1170 (N.D. Cal. 1994) . . . . . . . . . . . . . 1883, 1891, 1972, 1986, 2129-30, 2134-35

RCM Securities Fund, Inc. v. Stanton, 928 F.2d 1318 (2d Cir. 1991) . . . . . 853, 856-58, 859, 1441, 1456, 1569, 1605

R.D. Smith & Co. v. Preway Inc., 644 F. Supp. 868 (W.D. Wis. 1986) . . . . . . . . . . . . . . . . . . . . . . . . . 25

In re Reading Co., 711 F.2d 509 (3d Cir. 1983) . . . . . . . . 342

Reading Co. v. Trailer Train Co., 9 Del. J. Corp. L. 223 (Del. Ch. Mar. 15, 1984) . . . . . . . . . . . . . . . . . . . 38

Realty Acquisition Corp. v. Property Trust of America, [1990 Transfer Binder] Fed. Sec. L. Rep. (CCH) ¶ 95,245 (D. Md. Oct. 27, 1989) . . . . . . . . . . . . . . . 1098

Recchion v. Kirby, 637 F. Supp. 284 (W.D. Pa. 1985) . . . . . . . . . . . . . . . . . . . . . . . . . . . . . . . 1457, 1592

Recchion v. Kirby, 637 F. Supp. 1309 (W.D. Pa. 1986) . . . . . . . . . . . . . . . . . . . . . . . . . 1489, 1597, 1599

Recchion v. Westinghouse Elec. Corp., 606 F. Supp. 889 (W.D. Pa. 1985) . . . . . . . . . . . . . . . . . . . . . . . 1681

Red Bud Realty Co. v. South, 131 S.W. 340 (Ark. 1910) . . . . . . . . . . . . . . . . . . . . . . . . . . . . . . . . 1611

Reed v. Norman, 152 Cal. App. 2d 892, 314 P.2d 204 (Cal. Ct. App. 1957) . . . . . . . . . . . . . . . . . . . . . 1562

Regal-Beloit Corp. v. Drecoll, 955 F. Supp. 849 (N.D. Ill. 1996) . . . . . . . . . . . . . . . . . . . . . . . . . . . . 304

Reich v. NationsBank, NA, 1995 U.S. Dist. LEXIS 5328, 1995 WL 316550 (N.D. Ga. Mar. 29, 1995), amended, 1995 WL 389614 (N.D. Ga. May 10, 1995), aff'd in part and rev'd in part sub nom. Herman v. NationsBank Trust Co., NA, 126 F.3d 1354 (11th Cir. 1997) . . . . . . . . . . . . . . . . . . . . . . . 879, 894-96

Reilly Mortgage Group, Inc. v. Mount Vernon Savings & Loan Ass'n, 568 F. Supp. 1067 (E.D. Va. 1983) . . . . . . . . . . . . . . . . . . . . . . . . . 1420, 1421, 1491

Reliance Group Holdings, Inc. v. National Union Fire Insurance Co., 188 A.D.2d 47, 594 N.Y.S.2d 20 (N.Y. App. Div. 1st Dep't), motion for leave to appeal dismissed in part and denied in part, 82 N.Y.2d 704, 619 N.E.2d 656, 601 N.Y.S.2d 578 (1993) . . . 2027, 2028-29

Reliance Insurance Co. v. Weis, 148 B.R. 575 (E.D. Mo. 1992), aff'd mem., 5 F.3d 532 (8th Cir. 1993), cert. denied, 510 U.S. 1117 (1994) . . . . . . . . . . . . . . . 2069

Remillard Brick Co. v. Remillard-Dandini Co., 109 Cal. App. 2d 405, 241 P.2d 66 (Cal. Ct. App. 1952) . . 270, 271

Remington Products, Inc. v. North American Philips, Corp., 755 F. Supp. 52 (D. Conn. 1991) . . . . . . . . . . . 1338

Renaissance Communications Corp. v. National Broadcasting Co., No. 14446 (Del. Ch. Aug. 1, 1995) . . . . . . . . . . . . . . . . . . . . . . . . . . . . . 986

Republic Insurance Co. v. Masters, Mates & Pilots Pension Plan, 77 F.3d 48 (2d Cir. 1996) . . . . . . . . 2141, 2148

Republic National Life Insurance Co. v. Beasley, 73 F.R.D. 658 (S.D.N.Y. 1977) . . . . . . . . . . . . . . . . . . 1408

Resolution Trust Co. v. Platt, 1992 U.S. Dist. LEXIS 21377, 1992 WL 672942 (S.D. Ill. Oct. 23, 1992) . . . . . . . . 98

Resolution Trust Corp. v. Acton, 844 F. Supp. 307 (N.D. Tex. 1994), aff'd, 49 F.3d 1086 (5th Cir. 1995) . . . . . . . . . . . . . . . . . . . . . . . . 77, 91, 137, 248

Resolution Trust Corp. v. American Casualty Co., 874 F. Supp. 961 (E.D. Mo. 1995) . . . . . . . . . . . . . . . 2018-19

Resolution Trust Corp. v. Artley, 24 F.3d 1363 (11th Cir. 1994) . . . . . . . . . . . . . . . . . . . . . . . 2013, 2014, 2015

Resolution Trust Corp. v. Ayo, 31 F.3d 285 (5th Cir. 1994) . . . . . . . . . . . . . . . . . 1998, 2013, 2014-15, 2107-08

Resolution Trust Corp. v. Blasdell, 930 F. Supp. 417
(D. Ariz. 1994)
. . . . . . . . . . 12, 14, 22, 39-40, 136, 139, 141, 168, 182, 190

Resolution Trust Corp. v. Bonner, 1993 U.S. Dist.
LEXIS 11107, 1993 WL 414679 (S.D. Tex. June 3,
1993) . . . . . . . . . . . . . . . . . . . . . . . . . . . . . . . 137, 376

Resolution Trust Corp. v. Bright, 872 F. Supp. 1551
(N.D. Tex. 1995) . . . . . . . . . . . . . . . . . . . . . . . . . . . 262

Resolution Trust Corp. v. Chapman, 29 F.3d 1120
(7th Cir. 1994) . . . . . . . . . . . . . . . . . . . 249, 250-52, 262

Resolution Trust Corp. v. CityFed Financial Corp., 57
F.3d 1231 (3d Cir. 1995), vacated and remanded sub
nom. Atherton v. Federal Deposit Insurance Corp.,
117 S. Ct. 666 (1997) . . . . . . . . . . . . . . . 152, 226, 250-51

Resolution Trust Corp. v. Dean, 854 F. Supp. 626 (D.
Ariz. 1994) . . . . . . . . . . . 136, 141, 172, 263, 270, 309, 311

Resolution Trust Corp. v. Eason, 17 F.3d 1126 (8th
Cir. 1994) . . . . . . . . . . . . . . . . . . . . . . . . . . . . . . . . 22

Resolution Trust Corp. v. Fleischer, 892 P.2d 497
(Kan. 1995) . . . . . . . . . . . . . . . . . . . . . . . . . . . . . . 248

Resolution Trust Corp. v. Frates, 52 F.3d 295 (10th
Cir. 1995) . . . . . . . . . . . . . . . . . . . . . . . . . . . . . . . 250

Resolution Trust Corp. v. Gallagher, 10 F.3d 416 (7th
Cir. 1993) . . . . . . . . . . . . . . . . . . . . . . . . . . . . 249, 250

Resolution Trust Corp. v. Gladstone, 895 F. Supp.
356 (D. Mass. 1995) . . . . . . . . . . . . . . . . . . . . . . . . . . 98

Resolution Trust Corp. v. Gregor, 872 F. Supp. 1140
(E.D.N.Y. 1994) . . . . . . . . . . . . . . . . . . . . . . . . 244-45

Resolution Trust Corp. v. Hays, 1993 WL 302150
(W.D. Tex. Mar. 29, 1993) . . . . . . . . . . . . . . . . . . . . 28

Resolution Trust Corp. v. Hedden, 879 F. Supp. 600
(N.D. Miss. 1995) . . . . . . . . . . . . . . . . . . . . . . 2083, 2085

Resolution Trust Corp. v. Heiserman, 839 F. Supp.
1457 (D. Colo. 1993) . . . . . . . . . . . . . . . . . . . . 136, 243

Resolution Trust Corp. v. Hess, 820 F. Supp. 1359
(D. Utah 1993) . . . . . . . . . . . . . . . . . . . . . . . . . . . 25

Resolution Trust Corp. v. Holmes, 1992 U.S. Dist.
LEXIS 18962, 1992 WL 533256 (S.D. Tex. Aug. 10,
1992) . . . . . . . . . . . . . . . . . . . . . . . . . . . . . . . 19, 25

Resolution Trust Corp. v. Hovnanian, 1994 U.S. Dist.
LEXIS 19359 (D.N.J. Oct. 11, 1994) . . . . . . . . . 18, 110, 136

Resolution Trust Corp. v. Miramon, 22 F.3d 1357
(5th Cir. 1994) . . . . . . . . . . . . . . . . . . . . . . 135, 249, 250

Resolution Trust Corp. v. Moskowitz, 1994 U.S. Dist.
LEXIS 4049 (D.N.J. Mar. 30, 1994) . . . . 2076, 2084, 2085, 2087

Resolution Trust Corp. v. Norris, 830 F. Supp. 351
(S.D. Tex. 1993) . . . . . . . . . . . . . . . . . . . . . . . . 12, 137

Resolution Trust Corp. v. Norris, No. H-92-748 (S.D.
Tex. Aug. 10, 1993) . . . . . . . . . . . . . . . . . . . . . . 19, 25

Resolution Trust Corp. v. Rahn, 854 F. Supp. 480
(W.D. Mich. 1994) . . . . . . . . . . . . . . . . 80, 136, 172, 208

Resolution Trust Corp. v. Scott, 887 F. Supp. 937
(S.D. Miss. 1995), rev'd, 125 F.3d 254 (5th Cir.
1997) . . . . . . . . . . . . . . . . . . . . . . . . . . . . . . . 248

Resolution Trust Corp. v. Scott, 929 F. Supp. 1001
(S.D. Miss. 1996), rev'd, 125 F.3d 254 (5th Cir.
1997) . . . . . . . . . . . . . . . . . . . . . . . . . . . . 76, 112, 248

Resolution Trust Corp. v. Walke, 1993 U.S. Dist.
LEXIS 20095, 1993 WL 455195 (W.D. La. Apr. 15,
1993) . . . . . . . . . . . . . . . . . . . . . . . . . . . . . . . 2084

Resolution Trust Corp. v. Wright, 868 F. Supp. 301
(W.D. Okla. 1993) . . . . . . . . . . . . . . . . . . . . . . . . 248

Revlon, Inc. v. MacAndrews & Forbes Holdings,
Inc., 506 A.2d 173 (Del. 1986)
. . 6, 20-21, 54, 152, 281, 590, 610, 631, 636, 638, 640, 641, 642,
643, 694, 698-99, 702, 706, 712, 713, 726, 730, 733, 735, 753,
778, 783, 790, 810-11, 813, 815-17, 824, 918, 921-23, 928,
930, 935-36, 974, 985, 1035, 1036, 1051, 1121-22, 1148, 1150, 1326

In re Rexene Corp. Shareholders Litigation, [1991
Transfer Binder] Fed. Sec. L. Rep. (CCH) ¶ 96,010
(Del. Ch. May 8, 1991), aff'd sub nom. Eichorn v.
Rexene Corp., 604 A.2d 416 (unpublished opinion,
text available at 1991 Del. LEXIS 333 and 1991 WL
210962) (Del. Oct. 10, 1991)
. . 65, 82, 94, 504, 505, 518, 523, 524, 1411, 1412, 1496, 1529

Reynolds v. Conger, 1995 U.S. Dist. LEXIS 17654,
1995 WL 686878 (E.D. La. Nov. 17, 1995) . . . . . 23, 687, 814

RHI Holdings, Inc. v. National Union Fire Insurance
Co., [1994-1995 Transfer Binder] Fed. Sec. L. Rep.
(CCH) ¶ 98,315 (E.D. Pa. May 4, 1994), aff'd mem.,
47 F.3d 1161 (3d Cir. 1995) . . . . . . . . . . . . . . . 2011, 2038

Rhone-Poulenc v. GAF Chemicals, 1993 Del. Ch.
LEXIS 59, 1993 WL 125512 (Del. Ch. Apr. 6,
1993) . . . . . . . . . . . . . . . . . . . . . . . . . . . . 283

Riblet Products Corp. v. Nagy, 683 A.2d 37 (Del.
1996) . . . . . . . . . . . . . . . . . . . . . . . . 362, 467-68, 501

Rice v. Wheeling Dollar Savings & Trust Co., 130
N.E.2d 442 (Ohio Ct. Common Pleas 1954) . . . . . . . . . . 1612

Richardson v. Graves, 1983 Del. Ch. LEXIS 466,
1983 WL 21109 (Del. Ch. June 17, 1983)
. . . . . . . . . . . . . . . . . . 1452-53, 1482, 1491, 1499, 1588

Richardson v. Gray, N.Y.L.J., Nov. 14, 1996, at 28
(N.Y. Sup. Ct. N.Y. Co.). . . . . . . . . . 396-97, 496, 519, 1393

Ridder v. CityFed Financial Corp., 47 F.3d 85 (3d
Cir. 1995) . . . . . . . . . 1895, 1898, 1909, 1913, 1915, 1926-27

Ripley v. International Railways of Central America, 8
A.D.2d 310, 188 N.Y.S.2d 62 (N.Y. App. Div. 1st
Dep't 1959), aff'd, 8 N.Y.2d 430, 171 N.E.2d 443,
209 N.Y.S.2d 289 (1960) . . . . . . . . . . . . . . . . . . . . 1683-84

Ritter v. Mutual Life Insurance Co., 169 U.S. 139
(1898) . . . . . . . . . . . . . . . . . . . . . . . . . . . . . . 2086-87

In re RJR Nabisco, Inc. Shareholders Litigation,
[1988-1989 Transfer Binder] Fed. Sec. L. Rep. (CCH)
¶ 94,194 (Del. Ch. Jan. 31, 1989), appeal refused,
556 A.2d 1070 (unpublished opinion, text available at
1989 Del. LEXIS 42 and 1989 WL 16907) (Del. Feb.
2, 1989) . . . . . . . . . . . . . . . . . . . . . . . . 78, 80, 86, 181,
184, 185, 193, 203, 696, 735, 754-55, 757, 759, 760-65, 812, 826

Robert A. Wachsler, Inc. v. Florafax International,
Inc., 778 F.2d 547 (10th Cir. 1985) . . . . . . . . . . . . . 3, 275

Robert M. Bass Group, Inc. v. Evans, 552 A.2d 1227
(Del. Ch. 1988), appeal dismissed sub nom. Macmillan, Inc. v. Robert M. Bass Group, Inc., 548 A.2d
498 (unpublished opinion, text available at 1988 Del.
LEXIS 276 and 1988 WL 101235) (Del. Sept. 14,
1988) . . . . . . . . . . . . . . 669-71, 714-15, 737, 827, 1045-50

Roberts v. Alabama Power Co., 404 So. 2d 629 (Ala.
1981) . . . . . . . . . . . . . . . . . . . . . . . . . . 1611, 1695, 1708

Roberts v. General Instrument Corp., [1990 Transfer
Binder] Fed. Sec. L. Rep. (CCH) ¶ 95,465 (Del. Ch.
Aug. 13, 1990) . . . . . . . . . . . . . . . . . . . . . . . . . . . 181,
184, 185, 194, 520, 735, 755-56, 765, 769, 826, 945, 949-51, 972

Robinson, Leatham & Nelson, Inc. v. Nelson, 109
F.3d 1388 (9th Cir. 1997) . . . . . . . . . . . . . . . . . . 296, 304

Rogers v. American Can Co., 305 F.2d 297 (3d Cir.
1962) . . . . . . . . . . . . . . . . . . . . . . . . . . . . . . . . 1688

Rogers v. Hill, 289 U.S. 582 (1933) . . . . . . . . . . . . 309, 312

Rogers v. Valentine, 426 F.2d 1361 (2d Cir. 1970) . . . . . 1420

Roland International Corp. v. Najjar, 407 A.2d 1032
(Del. 1979) . . . . . . . . . . . . . . . . . . . . . . . . . . . . 467

Romanik v. Lurie Home Supply Center, Inc., 435
N.E.2d 712 (Ill. App. Ct. 1982) . . . . . . . . . . . . . . 310, 311

Roney v. Joyner, 356 S.E.2d 401 (N.C. Ct. App.
1987) . . . . . . . . . . . . . . . . . . . . . . . . . . . . . . . 1494

Rosan v. Chicago Milwaukee Corp., 16 Del. J. Corp.
L. 378 (Del. Ch. Feb. 6, 1990) . . . . . . . . . . . 95, 577, 1527

Rosebud Corp. v. Boggio, 561 P.2d 367 (Colo. Ct.
App. 1977) . . . . . . . . . . . . . . . . . . . . . . . . . . . 597

Rosen v. Bernard, 108 A.D.2d 906, 485 N.Y.S.2d
791 (N.Y. App. Div. 2d Dep't 1985) . . . . . . . . . 1707, 1743

Rosen v. Burlington Industries, Inc., N.Y.L.J., June
3, 1988, at 22 (N.Y. Sup. Ct. N.Y. Co. 1988) . . . . . . . . 1018

Rosen v. Smith, 11 Del. J. Corp. L. 989 (Del. Ch.
Sept. 23, 1985) . . . . . . . . . . . . . . . . . . . . . . . . . . 1077

Rosenberg v. Oolie, 15 Del. J. Corp. L. 1140 (Del.
Ch. Oct. 16, 1989) . . . . . . . . . . . . . . . . . . . . . . . 181, 188

Rosenblatt v. Getty Oil Co., 493 A.2d 929 (Del.
1985) . . . . . . . . . . . . . . . . . . . . . . . . . . . . . . . 184,
185, 187, 189, 203, 216, 217, 273, 378, 400-02, 406, 409, 511, 521

Rosenblum v. Judson Engineering Corp., 109 A.2d
558 (N.H. 1954) . . . . . . . . . . . . . . . . . . . . . . . . . 297

Rosenfield v. Becor Western Inc., 1987 U.S. Dist.
LEXIS 14276 (E.D. Wis. Nov. 5, 1987) . . . . . . 756, 757, 758

Rosenfield v. Metals Selling Corp., 643 A.2d 1253
(Conn. 1994) . . . . . . . . . . . . . . . . . . 13, 16, 99, 133, 183

Rosengarten v. Buckley, 565 F. Supp. 193 (D. Md.
1982) . . . . . . . . . . . . . . . . . . . . . . . . . . . . . . . 1405

Rosengarten v. Buckley, 613 F. Supp. 1493 (D. Md.
1985) . . . . . . . . . . . . . . . . . . . . . . . . . . . . . . 1695,
1702, 1708-09, 1721, 1751, 1755, 1760-61, 1775, 1778, 1795

Rosengarten v. International Telephone & Telegraph
Corp., 466 F. Supp. 817 (S.D.N.Y. 1979)
. . . . . . . . . . . . . . . . . . . . 1612, 1651, 1654, 1746-49, 1761

Rosenstein v. CMC Real Estate Corp., 522 N.E.2d
221 (Ill. App. Ct. 1988) . . . . . . . . . . . . . . . . . . . . . . 468

Rosenthal v. Rosenthal, 543 A.2d 348 (Me. 1988) . . . . . . . . 23

In re Rospatch Securities Litigation, 1991 U.S. Dist.
LEXIS 3270, 1991 WL 574963 (W.D. Mich. Mar.
14, 1991) . . . . . . . . . . . . . . . . . . . . . . . . . . . . . . . 1822

Ross v. Bernhard, 396 U.S. 531 (1970) . . . . . 1380, 1381, 1382

Ross Stores, Inc. v. Certain Underwriters at Lloyd's,
London, No. C 8820344, RPA (N.D. Cal. Mar. 7,
1989) . . . . . . . . . . . . . . . . . . . . . . . . . . . . . . . . 2038-39

Roth v. Robertson, 64 Misc. 343, 118 N.Y.S. 351
(N.Y. Sup. Ct. Erie Co. 1909) . . . . . . . . . . . . . . . . . . 91-92

Rothenberg v. Santa Fe Pacific Corp., 18 Del. J.
Corp. L. 743 (Del. Ch. May 18, 1992) . . . . . . . . . . . . . 229

Rothenberg v. Santa Fe Pacific Corp., 21 Del. J.
Corp. L. 309 (Del. Ch. Sept. 5, 1995) . . . . . . 43, 51, 1526-27

Rothenberg v. Security Management Co., 667 F.2d
958 (11th Cir. 1982) . . . . . . . . . . . . . . . . . . . . . . . 1402

Rothenberg v. United Brands Co., [1977-1978
Transfer Binder] Fed. Sec. L. Rep. (CCH) ¶ 96,045
(S.D.N.Y. May 11, 1977), aff'd mem., 573 F.2d
1295 (2d Cir. 1977) . . . . . . . . . . . . . . . . . . . . . . . 1576

The Business Judgment Rule

Rothschild International Corp. v. Liggett Group, Inc.,

Rothschild International Corp. v. Liggett Group, Inc.,
474 A.2d 133 (Del. 1984) . . . . . . . . . . . . . . . . . . . . . . 571

Rottman v. Midway Airlines, Inc., 1987 U.S. Dist.
LEXIS 7073, 1987 WL 15401 (N.D. Ill. Aug. 5,
1987) . . . . . . . . . . . . . . . . . . . . . . . . . . . . . . 1097, 1134

Rovner v. Health-Chem Corp., 1996 Del. Ch. LEXIS
83, 1996 WL 377027 (Del. Ch. July 3, 1996) . . . . . . . . . . 228

Rowen v. Le Mars Mutual Insurance Co., 282
N.W.2d 639 (Iowa 1979) . . . . . . . . . . . . . . . . . . . . . . 203

Royal Crown Cos. v. McMahon, 359 S.E.2d 379 (Ga.
Ct. App. 1987), cert. denied (Ga. Sept. 8, 1987)
. . . . . . . . . . . . . . . . . . . . . . . . 1297, 1302, 1303, 1307

Royal Industries, Inc. v. Monogram Industries, Inc.,
[1976-1977 Transfer Binder] Fed. Sec. L. Rep. (CCH)
¶ 95,863 (C.D. Cal. Nov. 29, 1976) . . . . . . . . . . . . . . 1333

Rubin v. Posner, 701 F. Supp. 1041 (D. Del. 1988)
. . . . . . . . . . . . . . . . . . . . . . . . . . 1429, 1597, 1602

Rubinstein v. Catacosinos, 91 A.D.2d 445, 459
N.Y.S.2d 286 (N.Y. App. Div. 1st Dep't), aff'd, 60
N.Y.2d 890, 458 N.E.2d 1247, 470 N.Y.S.2d 570
(1983) . . . . . . . . . . . . . . . . . . . . . . . . . . . . . . . . 1389

Ryan v. Aetna Life Insurance Co., 765 F. Supp. 133
(S.D.N.Y. 1991) . . . . . . . . . . 79, 133, 180, 185, 1456, 1458

Ryan v. Tad's Enterprises, Inc., 709 A.2d 682 (Del.
Ch.), reargument denied, 709 A.2d 675 (Del. Ch.
June 13, 1996), aff'd, 693 A.2d 1082 (unpublished
opinion, text available at 1997 Del. LEXIS 120 and

1997 WL 188351) (Del. Apr. 10, 1997)
. . . . . . . . . . . . . . . . . . . . . . 34, 115, 383, 388-93, 430

Ryan v. Tad's Enterprises, Inc., 709 A.2d 675 (Del.
Ch. 1996), aff'd, 693 A.2d 1082 (unpublished opin-
ion, text available at 1997 Del. LEXIS 120 and 1997
WL 188351) (Del. Apr. 10, 1997) . . . . . . . . . . . . . . . 57-58

Ryan v. Tad's Enterprises, Inc., 693 A.2d 1082 (unpublished opinion, text available at 1997 Del. LEXIS
120 and 1997 WL 188351) (Del. Apr. 10, 1997) . . . . . . . . 393

S. Solomont & Sons Trust v. New England Theatres
Operating Corp., 93 N.E.2d 241 (Mass. 1950) . . . . . . . . 1611

Sachs v. R.P. Scherer Corp. 9 Del. J. Corp. L. 234
(Del. Ch. Apr. 2, 1984) . . . . . . . . . . . . . . . . . . . . . . 1077

Safeco Surplus Lines Co. v. Employers Reinsurance
Corp., 11 Cal. App. 4th 1403, 15 Cal. Rptr. 2d 58
(Cal. Ct. App. 1992) . . . . . . . . . . . . . . . . . . . . . . . . 2008

Safeco Title Insurance Co. v. Gannon, 774 P.2d 30
(Wash. Ct. App.) petition for review denied, 782 P.2d
1069 (Wash. 1989) . . . . . . . . . . . . . . . . . . . . . . . . 2003

In re Safety International Inc., 775 F.2d 660 (5th Cir.
1985) . . . . . . . . . . . . . . . . . . . . . . . . . . . . . . . . . 300

Safeway Stores, Inc. v. National Union Fire Insurance
Co., 1993 U.S. Dist. LEXIS 2006, 1993 WL 739643
(N.D. Cal. Feb. 4, 1993), aff'd and rev'd, 64 F.3d
1282 (9th Cir. 1995) . . . . . . . . . . . . . . . . . . . . . 2111-12

Safeway Stores, Inc. v. National Union Fire Insurance
Co., 64 F.3d 1282 (9th Cir. 1995)
. . . . . . . . . . . . . . . 3, 1861, 2027, 2029-30, 2113, 2120-21

Salaman v. National Media Corp., 1992 Del. Super.
LEXIS 564, 1992 WL 808095 (Del. Super. Oct. 8,
1992) . . . . . . . . . . . . . . . . . . 1869, 1871, 1956-57, 1959

Salaman v. National Media Corp., 1994 Del. Super.
LEXIS 353, 1994 WL 465534 (Del. Super. July 22,
1994) . . . . . . . . . . . . . . . . . . . . . . . . . . . . 1910, 1913

Salomon Bros. Inc. v. Interstate Bakeries Corp., 576
A.2d 650 (Del. Ch. 1989) . . . . . . . . . . . . . . . . . . . . 477

Salomon Brothers, Inc. v. Interstate Bakeries Corp.,
576 A.2d 650 (Del. Ch. 1989), appeal refused, 571
A.2d 787 (unpublished opinion, text available at 1990
Del. LEXIS 32 and 1990 WL 18152) (Del. Feb. 6,
1990) . . . . . . . . . . . . . . . . . . . . . . . . . . . . . . . . 1386

In re Salomon Inc. Shareholders' Derivative Litigation, [1994-1995 Transfer Binder] Fed. Sec. L. Rep.
(CCH) ¶ 98,454 (S.D.N.Y. Sept. 25, 1994) . . . . . . 1382, 1383

In re Salomon Inc. Shareholders' Derivative Litigation, 68 F.3d 554 (2d Cir. 1995) . . . . . . . . . . . . 1383, 1384

Saltzman v. Birrell, 78 F. Supp. 778 (S.D.N.Y.
1948) . . . . . . . . . . . . . . . . . . . . . . . . . . . . . . . 1415

Samjens Partners I v. Burlington Industries, Inc., 663
F. Supp. 614 (S.D.N.Y. 1987) . . . . . . . . . . . . . . 181, 184,
185, 190, 193, 194, 756, 757, 774, 944-45, 958, 969, 970, 1016-18

Sammis v. Strafford, 48 Cal. App. 4th 1935, 56 Cal.
Rptr. 2d 589 (Cal. Ct. App. 1996) . . . . . . . . . . . . . . . 276

Sandberg v. Virginia Bankshares, Inc., 891 F.2d 1112
(4th Cir. 1989), rev'd, 501 U.S. 1083 (1991)
. . . . . . . . . . . . . . . . . . . . . . . . . . . 169, 209, 234, 240

Sandberg v. Virginia Bankshares, Inc., 979 F.2d 332
(4th Cir. 1992), vacated, 1993 U.S. App. LEXIS
33286, 1993 WL 524680 (4th Cir. Apr. 7, 1993) . . . . 234, 1822

Sanders v. Devine, 1997 Del. Ch. LEXIS 131, 1997
WL 599539 (Del. Ch. Sept. 24, 1997) . . 109, 511, 518, 573-74

Sandfield v. Goldstein, 33 A.D.2d 376, 308 N.Y.S.2d
25 (N.Y. App. Div. 3d Dep't 1970), aff'd mem., 28
N.Y.2d 794, 270 N.E.2d 723, 321 N.Y.S.2d 904
(1971) . . . . . . . . . . . . . . . . . . . . . . . . . . . . 312

Sandoval v. Simmons, 622 F. Supp. 1174 (C.D. Ill.
1985) . . . . . . . . . . . . . . . . . . . . . . . . . . . . 885-86

Sanford Fork & Tool Co. v. Howe, Brown & Co.,
157 U.S. 312 (1895) . . . . . . . . . . . . . . . . . . . . 598, 628

In re Santa Fe Pacific Corp. Shareholder Litigation,
[1995 Transfer Binder] Fed. Sec. L. Rep. (CCH)
¶ 98,845 (Del. Ch. May 31, 1995), aff'd in part and
rev'd in part, 669 A.2d 59 (Del. 1995) . . . . . . . . . . 225, 280,
518, 659, 661, 666, 712, 755, 770-71, 958, 963, 1154-55, 1513

In re Santa Fe Pacific Corp. Shareholder Litigation,
669 A.2d 59 (Del. 1995) . . . 27, 252, 253, 280, 281, 282, 501,
512, 515, 518, 522, 631, 639, 642, 644, 684, 710, 711, 712, 721,
771, 790-91, 792-93, 800, 803, 807, 964, 1115, 1150, 1155, 1513

Sax v. World Wide Press, Inc., 809 F.2d 610 (9th
Cir. 1987) . . . . . . . . . . . . . . . . . . . . . . . . . . 1456

Saxe v. Brady, 184 A.2d 602 (Del. Ch. 1962) . . . . . . . 94, 1524

Scattered Corp. v. Chicago Stock Exchange, Inc.,
1996 Del. Ch. LEXIS 79, 1996 WL 417507 (Del. Ch.

July 12, 1996), aff'd, 701 A.2d 70 (Del. 1997)
· · · · · · · · · · · · · 185, 1400, 1587, 1596, 1615, 1617, 1675

Scattered Corp. v. Chicago Stock Exchange, Inc., 23
Del. J. Corp. L. 355 (Del. Ch. Apr. 7, 1997), aff'd,
701 A.2d 70 (Del. 1997) · · · · · · · · · · · · · · · · · 1603, 1623

Scattered Corp. v. Chicago Stock Exchange, Inc., 701
A.2d 70 (Del. 1997)
· · 20-21, 180, 185, 1448, 1455, 1579, 1582, 1583, 1594, 1613,
1614, 1615, 1617, 1618, 1621-23, 1624, 1632, 1673-74, 1678-79

Scattergood v. Perelman, 945 F.2d 618 (3d Cir.
1991) · · · · · · · · · · · · · · · · · · · · · · 1385, 1389, 1392, 1393

Scharf v. Edgcomb Corp., 1997 Del. Ch. LEXIS 169,
1997 WL 762656 (Del. Ch. Dec. 2, 1997) · · · 1853, 1854, 1868

Scheuer Family Foundation, Inc. v. 61 Associates,
179 A.D.2d 65, 582 N.Y.S.2d 662 (N.Y. App. Div.
1st Dep't 1992) · · · · · · · · · · · · · · · · · · · · · · · · · · · · 26

Schilling v. Belcher, 582 F.2d 995 (5th Cir. 1978) · · · · · · 1390

Schirmer v. Bear, 648 N.E.2d 1131 (Ill. App. Ct.
1995), aff'd, 672 N.E.2d 1171 (Ill. 1996) · · · · · · · · · · · · 98

Schlossberg v. First Artists Production Co., 12 Del. J.
Corp. L. 1173 (Del. Ch. Dec. 17, 1986) · · · · · · · · · · · · 183

Schmidt v. Magnetic Head Corp., 97 A.D.2d 151,
468 N.Y.S.2d 649 (N.Y. App. Div. 2d Dep't 1983) · · · · · 1892

Schmidt v. Magnetic Head Corp., 101 A.D.2d 268,
476 N.Y.S.2d 151 (N.Y. App. Div. 2d Dep't 1984) · · · · · 1559

Schneider v. Lazard Freres & Co., 159 A.D.2d 291,
552 N.Y.S.2d 571 (N.Y. App. Div. 1st Dep't 1990)
. . . . . . . . . . . . . . . . . . . . . . . . . . . . . . 257-59, 634-35

Schnell v. Chris-Craft Industries, Inc., 285 A.2d 437
(Del. 1971) . . . . . . . 635, 801, 804, 1204-05, 1218, 1242, 1257

Schnitzer v. O'Connor, 653 N.E.2d 825 (Ill. App. Ct.
1995) . . . . . . . . . . . . . . . . . . . . . . . . . . . . . . 1586

Schreiber v. Bryan, 396 A.2d 512 (Del. Ch. 1978)
. . . . . . . . . . . . . . . . . . . . . . . . . . . . 225, 302, 1386

Schreiber v. Burlington Northern, Inc., 731 F.2d 163
(3d Cir. 1984), aff'd, 472 U.S. 1 (1985) . . . . . . . . . . . 1319

Schreiber v. Burlington Northern, Inc., 472 U.S. 1
(1985) . . . . . . . . . . . . . . . . . . . . . . . . . . . 916, 1296

Schreiber v. Carney, 447 A.2d 17 (Del. Ch. 1982)
. . . . . . . . . . . . . . . . . . . . . . . . 95, 225, 1391, 1415

Schreiber v. Pennzoil Co., 419 A.2d 952 (Del. Ch.
1980) . . . . . . . . . . . . . . . . . . . . 225, 312, 371, 375, 402

Schur v. Salzman, 365 F. Supp. 725 (S.D.N.Y.
1973) . . . . . . . . . . . . . . . . . . . . . . . . . . . . . . 1685

Science Accessories Corp. v. Summagraphics Corp.,
425 A.2d 957 (Del. 1980) . . . . . . . . . . . . . . . . . 295, 304

Scopas Technology Co. v. Lord, 10 Del. J. Corp. L.
306 (Del. Ch. Nov. 20, 1984) . . . . . . . . . . . . . 1402, 1403

Scotts African Union Methodist Protestant Church v.
Conference of African Union First Colored Methodist

Protestant Church, 98 F.3d 78 (3d Cir. 1996), cert.
denied, 117 S. Ct. 688 (1997) . . . . . . . . . . . . . . . . . . . 1245

In re Sea-Land Corp. Shareholders Litigation,
[1988-1989 Transfer Binder] Fed. Sec. L. Rep. (CCH)
¶ 93,923 (Del. Ch. May 13, 1988) . . . . . . . . . . . . . . . . 346

In re Sea-Land Corp. Shareholders Litigation, 642
A.2d 792 (Del. Ch. 1993), aff'd, 633 A.2d 371 (unpublished opinion, text available at 1993 Del. LEXIS
362 and 1993 WL 385067) (Del. Sept. 21, 1993)
. . . . . . . . . . . . . . . . . . . . . . 63, 182-83, 185, 191, 193, 363,
559, 563-64, 570, 651, 652, 659, 743, 755, 757, 758, 770, 912-13

Seafirst Corp. v. Jenkins, 644 F. Supp. 1152 (W.D.
Wash. 1986) . . . . . . . . . . . . . . . . . . . . . . . . . . . . . 209, 2045

Seaford Funding L.P. v. M & M Assocs. II, L.P.,
672 A.2d 66 (Del. Ch. 1995) . . . . . . . . . 1586, 1804, 1806-08

Seagraves v. Urstadt Property Co., 16 Del. J. Corp.
L. 393 (Del. Ch. Nov. 13, 1989) . . . . . 429, 494, 517, 523, 524

Seagraves v. Urstadt Property Co., 1996 Del. Ch.
LEXIS 36, 1996 WL 159626 (Del. Ch. Apr. 1,
1996) . . . . . . . . . . . . . 188, 369, 395-96, 430, 494, 499, 518

Sealy Mattress Co. v. Sealy, Inc., 532 A.2d 1324
(Del. Ch. 1987) . . . . . . . 179, 192, 383-88, 429, 492, 493, 526

Sealy Mattress Co. v. Sealy, Inc., 1987 Del. Ch.
LEXIS 511, 1987 WL 15254 (Del. Ch. July 20,
1987) . . . . . . . . . . . . . . . . . . . . . . . . . . . . . . . . . 1507

Sears, Roebuck & Co. v. Commissioner, 972 F.2d
858 (7th Cir. 1992) . . . . . . . . . . . . . . . . . . . . . . . 2158-60

Securities & Exchange Commission v. Carter Hawley
Hale Stores, Inc., 760 F.2d 945 (9th Cir. 1985) . . . . . . . . . 835

Security America Corp. v. Walsh, Case, Coale,
Brown & Burke, 1985 U.S. Dist. LEXIS 23482, 1985
WL 225 (N.D. Ill. Jan. 11, 1985) . . . . . . . . . . 1898, 1977-78

Security First Corp. v. U.S. Die Casting & Development Co., 687 A.2d 563 (Del. 1997) . . . . . . . . . . . 1678-80

Sedima, S.P.R.L. v. Imrex Co., 473 U.S. 479 (1985) . . . . 2167

Seibert v. Gulton Industries, Inc., 5 Del. J. Corp. L.
514 (Del. Ch. June 21, 1979), aff'd mem., 414 A.2d
822 (Del. 1980) . . . . . . . . . . . . . . . . . . . . . . . 1250-51

Seibert v. Harper & Row, Publishers, Inc., 10 Del. J.
Corp. L. 645 (Del. Ch. Dec. 5, 1984)
. . . . . . . . . . . . . . . . . . . 363, 517, 523, 1436-37, 1518

Seibert v. Milton Bradley Co., 405 N.E.2d 131
(Mass. 1980) . . . . . . . . . . . . . . . . . . . . . . . . . . . 1251

Seinfeld v. Bays, 595 N.E.2d 69 (Ill. App. Ct. 1992) . . . . 1412

Seinfeld v. Robinson, 172 Misc. 2d 159, 656
N.Y.S.2d 707 (N.Y. Sup. Ct. N.Y. Co. 1997) . . . . . . . . 1410

Selcke v. Bove, 629 N.E.2d 747 (Ill. App. Ct. 1994) . . . . . . 99

Seltzer v. Krieger, N.Y.L.J., Aug. 1, 1996 at 24
(N.Y. Sup. Ct. N.Y. Co.) . . . . . . . . . . . . . 1495, 1498, 1501

Seminaris v. Landa, 662 A.2d 1350 (Del. Ch. 1995)
. . . . . . . . . . 145, 1492, 1494, 1537, 1538-40, 1572, 1589-90

Sequa Corp. v. Gelmin, 828 F. Supp. 203 (S.D.N.Y. 1993) . . . . . . . . . . . . . . . . . . . . . . . . . 1942-44, 1973

Sequa Corp. v. Gelmin, 1993 U.S. Dist. LEXIS 16253, 1993 WL 481346 (S.D.N.Y. Nov. 17, 1993) . . 1944-45

Service Corp. International v. H.M Patterson & Son, Inc., 434 S.E.2d 455 (Ga. 1993) . . . . . . . . . . . . . . . . 1902

7457 Partners v. Beck, 682 A.2d 160 (Del. 1996) . . . . . . 1386

Shamrock Holdings, Inc. v. Polaroid Corp., [1988-1989 Transfer Binder] Fed. Sec. L. Rep. (CCH) ¶ 94,185 (Del. Ch. Jan. 31, 1989) . . . . . . . . . . . . . . . 841

Shamrock Holdings, Inc. v. Polaroid Corp., 559 A.2d 257 (Del. Ch. 1989) . . . . . . . . 649, 853, 858, 868-69, 872-76

Shamrock Holdings, Inc. v. Polaroid Corp., 559 A.2d 278 (Del. Ch. 1989) . . . . . . . . . . . . . . . . . . . . . 181, 184, 185, 191, 667, 668, 677, 797, 839-41, 854, 878, 1020-22, 1029

Shanghai Power Co. v. Delaware Trust Co., 316 A.2d 589 (Del. Ch. 1974), aff'd in part and rev'd in part sub nom. Judah v. Delaware Trust Co., 378 A.2d 624 (Del. 1977) . . . . . . . . . . . . . . . . . . . . . . . . . . . . . 584

Shapiro v. American Home Assurance Co., 584 F. Supp. 1245 (D. Mass. 1984) . . . . . . . . . . . . . . . . . 2150-51

Shapiro v. American Home Assurance Co., 616 F. Supp. 900 (D. Mass. 1984) . . . . . . . . . . . . . . . . . . . 2151

Shapiro v. UJB Financial Corp., 964 F.2d 272 (3d Cir.), cert. denied, 506 U.S. 934 (1992) . . . . . . . . . . . 1491

Shaw v. Digital Equipment Corp., 82 F.3d 1194 (1st Cir. 1996) . . . . . . . . . . . . . . . . . . . . . . . . . . . 506

Shaw v. International Association of Machinists & Aerospace Workers Pension Plan, 563 F. Supp. 653 (C.D. Cal. 1983), aff'd, 750 F.2d 1458 (9th Cir.), cert. denied, 471 U.S. 1137 (1985) . . . . . . . . . . . . . . . . 886

Shearin v. E.F. Hutton Group, Inc., 652 A.2d 578 (Del. Ch. 1994) . . . . . . . . . . . . . . . . . . . . . . . . . 1910

Sheehan v. Goriansky, 72 N.E.2d 538 (Mass. 1947) . . . . . 1985

In re Shell Oil Co., 607 A.2d 1213 (Del. 1992) . . . . . . . . 478

Shell Petroleum, Inc. v. Smith, 606 A.2d 112 (Del. 1992) . . . . . . . . . . . . . . . . . . . . . 499-500, 512, 513, 519

Shelton v. Thompson, 544 So. 2d 845 (Ala. 1989) . . . . . . . . . . . . . . . . . . . . . . . . . . . . 1395, 1396, 1447

Shields v. Erickson, 710 F. Supp. 686 (N.D. Ill. 1989) . . . . . . . . . . . . . . . . . . . . . . . . 1467, 1495, 1499

Shields v. Erickson, [1989-1990 Transfer Binder] Fed. Sec. L. Rep. ¶ 94,723 (N.D. Ill. Aug. 24, 1989) . . . . . . . 1496

Shields v. Murphy, 116 F.R.D. 600 (D.N.J. 1987) . . . . . . . . . . . . . . . . . . . . . . . . . . . . . . 1456, 1491

Shields v. Singleton, 15 Cal. App. 4th 1611, 19 Cal. Rptr. 2d 459 (Cal. Ct. App. 1993). . . . . . . . . . 1490, 1560-61

Shingala v. Becor Western Inc., 13 Del. J. Corp. L.1232 (Del. Ch. Feb. 3, 1988) . . . . . . . . . . . . . . 756, 759

Shlensky v. Dorsey, 574 F.2d 131 (3d Cir. 1978)
. . . . . . . . . . . . . . . . . 1409, 1433-35, 1440, 1592, 1681

Shlensky v. Wrigley, 237 N.E.2d 776 (Ill. App. Ct.
1968) . . . . . . . . . . . . . . . . . . . . . . . . . . . . . . . . 8, 91

Shoaf v. Warlick, 380 S.E.2d 865 (S.C. Ct. App.
1989) . . . . . . . . . . . . . . . . . . . . . . . . . . . . . . . . 364

Shoen v. AMERCO, No. CV-N-94-0475-ECR (D.
Nev. July 20, 1994) . . . . . . . . . . . . . . . . . . 1209, 1211-12

Shoen v. AMERCO, 885 F. Supp. 1332 (D. Nev.
1994), modified, 1994 WL 904199 (D. Nev. Oct. 24,
1994), vacated pursuant to settlement, No. CV-N-
94-0475-ECR (D. Nev. Feb. 9, 1995) (WL Insta-cite
service) . . . . . . . . . . . . . . . . . . . . . . . . . . 4, 18, 21-22, 23-
24, 509, 510, 805-06, 853-54, 879-81, 888-91, 1209-10, 1212-14

Shoen v. Shoen, 804 P.2d 787 (Ariz. Ct. App. 1990),
review denied (Feb. 20, 1991) . . . . . . . . . . . . . . . . . . . 263

In re Shoe-Town, Inc. Stockholders Litigation, 16 Del.
J. Corp. L. 404 (Del. Ch. Feb. 12, 1990)
. . . . . . . . . . . . . . . . . . 252, 259, 345, 453, 486, 494, 495

Short v. McNatt, 17 Del. J. Corp. L. 649 (Del. Ch.
May 17, 1991) . . . . . . . . . . . . . . . . . . . . . . . . . . . . 26

In re Shultz, 208 B.R. 723 (Bankr. M.D. Fla. 1997) . . . 597, 600

SICPA Holding S.A. v. Optical Coating Laboratory,
Inc., 1997 Del. Ch. LEXIS 1, 1997 WL 10263 (Del.
Ch. Jan. 6, 1997) . . . . . . . . . . . . . . . . . . . . . 263, 283, 343

Siegman v. Columbia Pictures Entertainment, Inc.,
576 A.2d 625 (Del. Ch. 1989) . . . . . . . . . . . . . . . . . . 877

Siegman v. Tri-Star Pictures, Inc., 15 Del. J. Corp.
L. 218 (Del. Ch. May 5, 1989), aff'd in part and
rev'd in part sub nom. In re Tri-Star Pictures, Inc.,
Litig., 634 A.2d 319 (Del. 1993)
. . . . . . . . . . . . . . . . . . . . 227, 345, 1250, 1471, 1507-08

Sierra Rutile Ltd. v. Katz, 1997 U.S. Dist. LEXIS
11018, 1997 WL 431119 (S.D.N.Y. July 31, 1997)
. . . . . . . . . . . . . . . . . . . . . . . . . 1936-37, 1942, 1945-46

Sifferle v. Micom Corp., 384 N.W.2d 503 (Minn. Ct.
App. 1986) . . . . . . . . . . . . . . . . . . . . . . . . . . . . . . . . 468

In re Silicon Graphics, Inc. Securities Litigation,
[1996-1997 Transfer Binder] Fed. Sec. L. Rep. (CCH)
¶ 99,325 (N.D. Cal. Sept. 25, 1996) . . . . . . . . . . . 1458, 1492

Silver v. Farrell, 113 Misc. 2d 443, 450 N.Y.S.2d
938 (N.Y. Sup. Ct. Monroe Co. 1982) . . . . . . . . . . . . 1217

Silverman v. Schwartz, N.Y.L.J., Mar. 17, 1997, at
27 (N.Y. Sup. Ct. N.Y. Co.) . . . . . . . . . . . . . . . . 1307-08

Silverzweig v. Unocal Corp., 1989 Del. Ch. LEXIS 4,
1989 WL 3231 (Del. Ch. Jan. 19, 1989), aff'd, 561
A.2d 993 (unpublished opinion, text available at 1989
Del. LEXIS 151 and 1989 WL 68307) (Del. May 19,
1989) . . . . . . . . . . . . . . . . . . . . . . 1492, 1496, 1497, 1501

Simas v. Quaker Fabric Corp., 6 F.3d 849 (1st Cir.
1993) . . . . . . . . . . . . . . . . . . . . . . . . . . . . . . . . . . . 1328

Simons v. Cogan, 549 A.2d 300 (Del. 1988) . . . . . . . 343, 591

Sinclair Oil Corp. v. Levien, 280 A.2d 717 (Del.
1971) . . . . . . . . . . . . . . . . . . . . . . 21-22, 370-73, 377, 641

Singer v. Magnavox Co., 380 A.2d 969 (Del. 1977) . . . 343, 467

Siverio v. Lavergne, [1991-1992 Transfer Binder] Fed. Sec. L. Rep. (CCH) ¶ 96,427 (S.D.N.Y. Oct. 8, 1991) . . . . . . . . . . . . . . . . . . . . . . . . . . . . . . . . 191

Skoglund v. Brady, 541 N.W.2d 17 (Minn. Ct. App. 1995) . . . . . . . . .  15, 1612, 1695, 1699, 1708, 1750-51, 1753

Skolnik v. Rose, 55 N.Y.2d 964, 434 N.E.2d 251, 449 N.Y.S.2d 182 (1982) . . . . . . . . . . . . . . . . . . . . . . 1687

Slaughter v. American Casualty Co., 842 F. Supp. 371 (E.D. Ark. 1993), rev'd, 37 F.3d 385 (8th Cir. 1994) . . . . . . . . . . . . . . . . . . . . . 1999, 2055, 2056, 2060

Slaughter v. American Casualty Co., 842 F. Supp. 376 (E.D. Ark. 1993), rev'd, 37 F.3d 385 (8th Cir. 1994) . . . . . . . . . . . . . . . . . . . . . . . . . . . . . 1999, 2019

Slaughter v. American Casualty Co., 37 F.3d 385 (8th Cir. 1994) . . . . . . . . . . . . . . . . . . . . . . . . . . . . 1999, 2085

Slottow v. American Casualty Co., 10 F.3d 1355 (9th Cir. 1993) . . . . . . . . . . . . . . . . . . . . . 1877, 1990, 2127-29

Smachlo v. Birkelo, 576 F. Supp. 1439 (D. Del. 1983) . . . . . . . . . . . . . . . . . 1300, 1400, 1592, 1596, 1601

Smith v. Ayres, 977 F.2d 946 (5th Cir. 1992), cert. denied, 508 U.S. 910 (1993) . . . . . . . . . . . . . . . . . . . . 1399

Smith v. Gordon, 668 F. Supp. 520 (E.D. Va. 1987) . . . . 1456

Smith v. Leonard, 876 S.W.2d 266 (Ark. 1994) . . . . . . . . . 22

Smith v. Neumann, 682 N.E.2d 1245 (Ill. App. Ct. 1997) . . . . . . . . . . . . . . . . . . . . . . . . . . . . . . . 2147

Smith v. Shell Petroleum, Inc., [1990 Transfer Binder] Fed. Sec. L. Rep. (CCH) ¶ 95,316 (Del. Ch. June 19, 1990), aff'd, 606 A.2d 112 (Del. 1992) . . . . . . . . . . 209, 500

Smith v. Shell Petroleum, Inc., 1990 Del. Ch. LEXIS 190, 1990 WL 186446 (Del. Ch. Nov. 26, 1990), aff'd, 606 A.2d 112 (Del. 1992) . . . . . . . . . 486-88, 526, 531

Smith v. Sperling, 354 U.S. 91 (1957) . . . . . . . . . 1418, 1419

Smith v. SPNV Holdings, Inc., 13 Del. J. Corp. L. 1242 (Del. Ch. Oct. 28, 1987) . . . . . . . . . . . . . . . . . . 394

Smith v. SPNV Holdings, Inc., 15 Del. J. Corp. L. 244 (Del. Ch. Apr. 26, 1989) . . . . . . . . . . . . . 371, 394, 413

Smith v. Van Gorkom, 488 A.2d 858 (Del. 1985) . . . . . . . . . . . 20-21, 74-75, 111, 112, 124, 134, 146-51, 152, 153, 157, 163, 167, 179, 187-88, 203-04, 224, 225-26, 275, 276, 277, 281, 282, 516, 519, 528, 955-56, 987, 994, 999, 1522, 2166

Smith v. Van Gorkom, 11 Del. J. Corp. L. 1000 (Del. Ch. Oct. 11, 1985) . . . . . . . . . . . . . . . . . . . . . . . . . . . 151

Snokist Growers v. Washington Insurance Guaranty Ass'n, 922 P.2d 821 (Wash. Ct. App. 1996) . . . . . . . . . . 2024

Societe Holding Ray D'Albion S.A. v. Saunders Leasing System, Inc., 1981 Del. Ch. LEXIS 555, 1981 WL 15094 (Del. Ch. Dec. 16, 1981), appeal refused, 445 A.2d 338 (unpublished opinion) (Del. Dec. 24, 1981) . . . . . . . . . . . . . . . . . . . . . . . . . . . 1077

In re Sofamor Danek Group, Inc., 123 F.3d 394 (6th
Cir. 1997) . . . . . . . . . . . . . . . . . . . . . . . . . . 507

Sohland v. Baker, 141 A. 277 (Del. 1927) . . . . . . . 1471, 1594

Solash v. Telex Corp., [1987-1988 Transfer Binder]
Fed. Sec. L. Rep. (CCH) ¶ 93,608 (Del. Ch. Jan. 19,
1988) . . . . . 15-16, 19, 79, 181, 184, 186, 190, 191, 193, 263

Solfanelli v. Mainwaring, 1992 U.S. Dist. LEXIS
18883, 1992 WL 332223 (E.D. Pa. Nov. 4, 1992) . . . . . . . 499

Solimine v. Hollander, 19 A.2d 344 (N.J. Ch. 1941) . . . . 1852

Solomon v. Hall-Brooke Foundation, Inc., 1992 Conn.
Super. LEXIS 297, 1992 WL 31947 (Conn. Super.
Ct. Feb. 11, 1992), aff'd, 619 A.2d 863 (Conn. App.
Ct. 1993) . . . . . . . . . . . . . . . . . . . . . . . . . . . 22

Solomon v. Pathe Communications Corp., 20 Del. J.
Corp. L. 1123 (Del. Ch. Apr. 21, 1995), aff'd, 672
A.2d 35 (Del. 1996) . . . . . . . . . . . . . . . . . . . 283, 358-59

Solomon v. Pathe Communications Corp., 1995 Del.
Ch. LEXIS 46, 1995 WL 250374 (Del. Ch. Apr. 21,
1995), aff'd, 672 A.2d 35 (Del. 1996) . . . . . . . . . 550, 552-53

Solomon v. Pathe Communications Corp., 672 A.2d
35 (Del. 1996) . . . . . . . . . . . . . . . . . . . . . . 360, 362

Soto v. State Farm Insurance Co., 83 N.Y.2d 718,
635 N.E.2d 1222, 613 N.Y.S.2d 352 (1994) . . . . . . . . . 1987

South Carolina State Budget & Control Board v.
Prince, 403 S.E.2d 643 (S.C. 1991) . . . . . . . . . . . . . 1986

Southdown, Inc. v. Moore McCormack Resources,
Inc., 686 F. Supp. 595 (S.D. Tex. 1988)
. . . . . . . . . . . . . . . . . . . . . 1045, 1050-51, 1097, 1169-70

In re Southeast Banking Corp., 827 F. Supp. 742
(S.D. Fla. 1993) . . . . . . . . . . . . . . . . . . . . . . 22-23, 99

Southeast Consultants, Inc. v. McCrary Engineering
Corp., 273 S.E.2d 112 (Ga. 1980) . . . . . . . . . . . . . 298, 304

Southeastern Public Service Co. v. Graniteville Co.,
No. 83-1028-8 (D.S.C. May 25, 1983) . . . . . . . . . . . 1006-07

Southern Pacific Co. v. Bogert, 250 U.S. 483 (1919) . . . . . 342

Sperling's Appeal, 71 Pa. 11 (1872) . . . . . . . . . . . . . 10-11

Spiegel v. Buntrock, 1988 Del. Ch. LEXIS 149, 1988
WL 124324 (Del. Ch. Nov. 17, 1988), aff'd, 571
A.2d 767 (Del. 1990) . . . . . . . . . . . . . . . . . 1499, 1724-25

Spiegel v. Buntrock, 1988 Del. Ch. LEXIS 160, 1988
WL 135509 (Del. Ch. Dec. 14, 1988), aff'd, 571
A.2d 767 (Del. 1990) . . . . . . . . . . . . . . . . . . . 635, 1610

Spiegel v. Buntrock, 571 A.2d 767 (Del. 1990)
. . . . . . . . 12, 20-21, 26, 110, 1381, 1443-44, 1567, 1578-79,
1588-89, 1593, 1594, 1605, 1609, 1613, 1614, 1690, 1711-13, 1725

Spillyards v. Abboud, 662 N.E.2d 1358 (Ill. App. Ct.
1996) . . . . . . . . . . . . . . . . . . . . . . . . . . . . . . . 3,
28, 62, 95, 180, 184, 186, 187, 723, 846, 1412, 1496, 1497, 1519

Spinner Corp. v. Princeville Development Corp., No.
86-0701 (D. Haw. Oct. 31, 1986), vacated, [1987
Transfer Binder] Fed. Sec. L. Rep. (CCH) ¶ 93,157
(D. Haw. Jan. 30, 1987) . . . . . . . . . . . . . . . . 1095, 1098

Square D Co. v. Schneider S.A., 760 F. Supp. 362
(S.D.N.Y. 1991) . . . . . . . . . . . . . . . . . . . . . . . . . . . 1334

Square D Co. v. Schneider S.A., No. 91 Civ. 2928
(LBS) (S.D.N.Y. May 9, 1991) . . . . . . . . . . . . . . . . . 1334

St. Jude Medical, Inc. v. Medtronic, Inc., 536
N.W.2d 24 (Minn. Ct. App. 1995) . . . . . . . . . . . 958, 966-68

St. Paul Fire & Marine Insurance Co. v. Federal
Deposit Insurance Co., 765 F. Supp. 538 (D. Minn.
1991), aff'd, 968 F.2d 695 (8th Cir. 1992)
. . . . . . . . . . . . . . . . . . . . . 2056, 2060, 2061, 2074, 2075

St. Paul Fire & Marine Insurance Co. v. Federal
Deposit Insurance Corp., 968 F.2d 695 (8th Cir.
1992) . . . . . . . . . . . . . . . . . . . . . . . . . 2083, 2085, 2089

St. Paul Mercury Insurance Co. v. Duke University,
849 F.2d 133 (4th Cir. 1988) . . . . . . . . . . . . . . . . . . 2086

Staar Surgical Co. v. Waggoner, 588 A.2d 1130 (Del.
1991) . . . . . . . . . . . . . . . . . . . . . . . . . . . . . . . 1295-96

Stahl v. Apple Bancorp, Inc., 579 A.2d 1115 (Del.
Ch. 1990) . . . 33, 675, 797-98, 801, 803-05, 1219-22, 1267-68

Stahl v. Apple Bancorp, Inc. [1990 Transfer Binder]
Fed. Sec. L. Rep. (CCH) ¶ 95,412 (Del. Ch. Aug. 9,
1990). . . . . . . . . . . . . . . . . . . . . . . . . 798, 1094, 1156-58

Stallworth v. AmSouth Bank, 1997 Ala. LEXIS 483,
1997 WL 778838 (Ala. Dec. 19, 1997) . . . . . . . . . 289, 1427,
1428, 1438, 1445, 1447-48, 1468, 1489, 1597, 1603, 1695, 1708

Stamerman v. Ackerman, 184 A.2d 28 (Del. Ch. 1962) . . . . . . . . . . . . . . . . . . . . . . . . . . . . . . . . 327

Stamp v. Touche Ross & Co., 636 N.E.2d 616 (Ill. App. Ct. 1993) . . . . . . . . . . . . . . . . . . 23, 26, 74, 91, 123

Starkman v. Marathon Oil Co., 772 F.2d 231 (6th Cir. 1985), cert. denied, 475 U.S. 1015 (1986) . . . . . . . . . 507

Starrels v. First National Bank, 870 F.2d 1168 (7th Cir. 1989)
. . 180, 1426, 1442-43, 1447, 1449, 1456, 1475-76, 1569, 1613

State v. Rachmani Corp., 71 N.Y.2d 718, 525 N.E.2d 704, 530 N.Y.S.2d 58 (1988) . . . . . . . . . . . . . . . . . . . 513

Stearns-Roger Corp. v. United States, 774 F.2d 414 (10th Cir. 1985) . . . . . . . . . . . . . . . . . . . . . . . . . . . 2157

Stegemeier v. Magness, 1996 Del. Ch. LEXIS 122, 1996 WL 549832 (Del. Ch. Sept. 20, 1996), appeal refused, 687 A.2d 197 (unpublished opinion, text available at 1996 Del. LEXIS 408 and 1996 WL 637913) (Del. Oct. 31, 1996) . . . . . . . . . . . . . . . . . . . . . . . . 264

Stein v. Bailey, 531 F. Supp. 684 (S.D.N.Y. 1982) . . . . . . . . . . . . . . . . . . . . . . . . . . . . . . . . 1489, 1593

Stein v. Orloff, 11 Del. J. Corp. L. 312, (Del. Ch. May 30, 1985), appeal refused, 504 A.2d 572 (unpublished opinion, text available at 1986 Del. LEXIS 1024 and 1986 WL 16298) (Del. Jan. 28, 1986) . . . . . . . . . . . . . . . . . . . . . . . 95, 323, 1495, 1525

Steinberg v. Amplica, 42 Cal. 3d 1198, 729 P.2d 683, 233 Cal. Rptr. 249 (1986) . . . . . . . . . . . . . . . . . . . . 498

Steinberg v. Pargas, Inc., [1984-1985 Transfer Binder]
Fed. Sec. L. Rep. (CCH) ¶ 91,979 (S.D.N.Y. Mar.
18, 1985) . . . . . . . . . . . . . . . . . . . . . . . . . . . . . . . . 1972

Steiner v. Lozyniak, N.Y.L.J., June 19, 1997 at 29
(N.Y. Sup. Ct. N.Y. Co. 1997) . . . . . . . . . . . . . . 1190, 1191

Steiner v. Meyerson, [1995 Transfer Binder] Fed. Sec.
L. Rep. (CCH) ¶ 98,857 (Del. Ch. July 18, 1995)
. . . . 59, 94, 95, 96, 308-09, 312, 314, 316, 328, 333-34, 1548

Steiner v. Meyerson, 1997 Del. Ch. LEXIS 88, 1997
WL 349169 (Del. Ch. June 13, 1997)
. . . . . . . . . . . . . . . . . . . . . 1098, 1390, 1401, 1403, 1510

Steiner v. Milton Roy Co., 1989 Phila. Cty. Rptr.
LEXIS 58 (Pa. Ct. of Common Pleas Nov. 9, 1989) . . . . . 1098

Steiner v. Sizzler Restaurants International, Inc.,
[1990-1991 Transfer Binder] Fed. Sec. L. Rep. (CCH)
¶ 95,851 (Del. Ch. Mar. 19, 1991) . . . . . . . . . . . . . 361, 495

Steinkraus v. GIH Corp., 1991 Del. Ch. LEXIS 8,
1991 WL 3922 (Del. Ch. Jan. 16, 1991) . . . . . . . . . . . . 1289

Stepak v. Addison, 20 F.3d 398 (11th Cir. 1994) . . . . . . . . . 3,
77, 172, 205-06, 1454-55, 1500, 1586, 1596, 1610, 1640-45, 1674

Stepak v. Alexander's Inc., 58 A.D.2d 520, 395
N.Y.S.2d 173 (N.Y. App. Div. 1st Dep't), modified,
58 A.D.2d 754, 404 N.Y.S.2d 538 (N.Y. App. Div.
1st Dep't 1977) . . . . . . . . . . . . . . . . . . . . . . . . . . . . 1676

Stepak v. Schey, 553 N.E.2d 1072 (Ohio 1990)
. . . . . . . . . . . . . . . . . . . . . . 24, 497, 689, 690, 730, 817

Stephanis v. Yiannatsis, 20 Del. J. Corp. L. 440 (Del.
Ch. May 9, 1994), aff'd, 653 A.2d 275 (Del. 1995) . . . . . 1896

Stephenson v. Drever, 16 Cal. 4th 1167, 947 P.2d
1301, 69 Cal. Rptr. 2d 764 (Cal. 1997) . . . . . . . . . 108, 342-43

Sterling v. Mayflower Hotel Corp., 93 A.2d 107 (Del.
1952) . . . . . . . . . . . . . . . . . . . . . . . . . . . . . . . . . . 343, 369

Stern v. General Electric Co., 924 F.2d 472 (2d Cir.
1991) . . . . . . . . . . . . . . . . . . . . . . . . . . . . . . . . . . . . 81

Stern v. General Electric Co., 837 F. Supp. 72
(S.D.N.Y. 1993), aff'd, 23 F.3d 746 (2d Cir.), cert.
denied, 513 U.S. 916 (1994) . . . . . . . . . . . . . . . . . . . . . 93

Stern v. Lucy Webb Hayes National Training School,
381 F. Supp. 1003 (D.D.C. 1974) . . . . . . . . . . . . . . . . 171

Sternberg v. O'Neil, 550 A.2d 1105 (Del. 1988) . . . 1382, 1415

Stewart v. Continental Copper & Steel Industries,
Inc., 67 A.D.2d 293, 414 N.Y.S.2d 910 (N.Y. App.
Div. 1st Dep't 1979) . . . . . . . . . . . . . . . . . . . . . . . . . 1861

In re STN Enterprises, 779 F.2d 901 (2d Cir. 1985) . . . . . . 596

Stoddard v. Michigan National Corp., No. 125352
(Mich. Ct. App. Apr. 8, 1992), appeal denied, 497
N.W.2d 184 (Mich. 1993) . . . . . . . . . . . . . . . . . . . . . 1858

Stoner v. Walsh, 772 F. Supp. 790 (S.D.N.Y. 1991)
. . . . . . . . . . . . . . . . . . 24, 42, 62, 75, 81, 596, 1428, 1439-
40, 1496, 1500, 1559, 1592, 1612, 1636-39, 1674, 1690, 1705-07

Stotland v. GAF Corp., 1983 Del. Ch. LEXIS 477,
1983 WL 21371 (Del. Ch. Sept. 1, 1983), appeal dismissed, 469 A.2d 421 (Del. 1983) . . . . . . . . . . . .  1492, 1674

Stotland v. GAF Corp., 469 A.2d 421 (Del. 1983) . .  1578, 1605

Strasenburgh v. Straubmuller, 683 A.2d 818 (N.J.
1996) . . . . . . . . . . . . . . . . . . . . . . . . . . . . . . . . .  1381

Strawbridge v. Curtiss, 3 Cranch (7 U.S.) 267 (1806) . . . .  1417

Stroud v. Grace, 15 Del. J. Corp. L. 256 (Del. Ch.
Apr. 21, 1989) . . . . . . . . . . . . . . . . . . . . . . . . . . .  1240

Stroud v. Grace, 16 Del. J. Corp. L. 1588 (Del. Ch.
Nov. 1, 1990), aff'd in part and rev'd in part, 606
A.2d 75 (Del. 1992) . . . . . . . . . . . . . . . .  63, 183, 188, 191, 227

Stroud v. Grace, 606 A.2d 75 (Del. 1992) . . 278, 279, 349, 490,
499-501, 512, 524, 529, 530, 639, 640, 641, 642, 646, 655, 790,
792-93, 794, 799-800, 801, 803, 805, 807, 1273, 1286-87, 1296

Stroud v. Milliken Enterprises, Inc., 552 A.2d 476
(Del. 1989) . . . . . . . . . . . . . . . . . . . . . . . . . . . . . . .  501

Stroud v. Milliken Enterprises, Inc., 1988 Del. Ch.
LEXIS 38 (Del. Ch. Mar. 18, 1988) (published in part
at 585 A.2d 1306), vacated, 552 A.2d 476 (Del.
1989) . . . . . . . . . . . . . . . . . . . . . . . . . . . . . .  1502, 1503

Strougo v. Carroll, [1990-1991 Transfer Binder] Fed.
Sec. L. Rep. (CCH) ¶ 95,815 (Del. Ch. Jan. 29,
1991) . . . . . . . . . . . . . . . . . . . . . . . . . . . . . .  1508, 1529

Strougo v. Padegs, 986 F. Supp. 812 (S.D.N.Y.
1997) . . . . . . . . . . . . . . . . . . . . . . .  1689, 1695, 1744, 1784

Strougo v. Scudder, Stevens & Clark, Inc., 964 F.
Supp. 783 (S.D.N.Y. 1997), reargument denied, [1997
Transfer Binder] Fed. Sec. L. Rep. (CCH) ¶ 99,533
(S.D.N.Y. Aug. 18, 1997)
. . . . . . . . 62, 81, 1412, 1458, 1462, 1493, 1496, 1687, 1689

Stowell v. Ted S. Finkel Investment Services, Inc.,
641 F.2d 323 (5th Cir. 1981) . . . . . . . . . . . . . . . . . 1971

Stuart Silver Associates, Inc. v. Boca Development
Corp., --- A.D.2d ---, 665 N.Y.S.2d 415 (N.Y. App.
Div. 1st Dep't 1997) . . . . . . . . . . . . . . . . . . . . . . . . 37

Stuchen v. Duty Free International, Inc., 1996 Del.
Super. LEXIS 187 (Del. Super. Apr. 22, 1996) . . . . . . . 259-60

STV Engineers, Inc. v. Greiner Engineering, Inc., 861
F.2d 784 (3d Cir. 1988) . . . . . . . . . . . . . . . . . . . . . . 942

Sullivan v. Hammer, 1990 Del. Ch. LEXIS 20, 1990
WL 28020 (Del. Ch. Mar. 6, 1990), aff'd sub nom.
Kahn v. Sullivan, 594 A.2d 48 (Del. 1991) . . . . . . . . . 1410

Sullivan v. Hammer, [1990 Transfer Binder] Fed. Sec.
L. Rep. (CCH) ¶ 95,415 (Del. Ch. Aug. 7, 1990),
aff'd sub nom. Kahn v. Sullivan, 594 A.2d 48 (Del.
1991) . . . . . . . . . . . . . . . . . . . . . . . . . . . . . . 183, 312

Sumers v. Beneficial Corp., 1988 Del. Ch. LEXIS 35,
1988 WL 23948 (Del. Ch. Mar. 9, 1988) . . . . . . . . . . . . 180

Summa Corp. v. Trans World Airlines, Inc., 540
A.2d 403 (Del.), cert. denied, 488 U.S. 853 (1988)
. . . . . . . . . . . . . . . . . . . . . . . . . . . . . 369, 371, 375

Sundin v. Fisher, 10 Del. J. Corp. L. 917 (Del. Ch.
Feb. 15, 1985), aff'd sub nom. Blosvern v. Fisher,

504 A.2d 571 (unpublished opinion, text available at
1986 Del. LEXIS 1030 and 1986 WL 16162) (Del.
Jan. 30, 1986) . . . . . . . . . . . . . . . . . . . . . . . . . . . 1495, 1501

In re Sunrise Securities Litigation, 916 F.2d 874 (3d
Cir. 1990) . . . . . . . . . . . . . . . . . . . . . . . . . . . . 1411, 1412

Sutton Holding Corp. v. DeSoto, Inc., [1989-1990
Transfer Binder] Fed. Sec. L. Rep. (CCH) ¶ 94,964
(Del. Ch. Feb. 5, 1990) . . . . . . . . . . . . . 1095, 1106, 1167-69

Sutton Holding Corp. v. DeSoto, Inc., [1991 Transfer
Binder] Fed. Sec. L. Rep. (CCH) ¶ 96,012 (Del. Ch.
May 14, 1991) . . . . . . . . . . . . . . . . . . . . . . . . 1189, 1327

Swanson v. Traer, 249 F.2d 854 (7th Cir. 1957) . . . 1611, 1613

Swanson v. Traer, 354 U.S. 114 (1957) . . . . . . . . 1418, 1419

Swentzel v. Penn Bank, 23 A. 405 (Pa. 1892) . . . . . . . . . . . 11

Swinney v. Keebler Co., 480 F.2d 573 (4th Cir.
1973) . . . . . . . . . . . . . . . . . . . . . . . . . . . . . . . 366

Syphers v. Scardino, 1985 U.S. Dist. LEXIS 13161,
1985 WL 4283 (E.D. Pa. Dec. 5, 1985) . . . . . . . . . . . 1491

Syracuse Television, Inc. v. Channel 9, Syracuse,
Inc., 51 Misc. 2d 188, 273 N.Y.S.2d 16 (N.Y. Sup.
Ct. Onondaga Co. 1966) . . . . . . . . . . . . . . . . . 1612, 1687

Szeto v. Schiffer, 19 Del. J. Corp. L. 1310 (Del. Ch.
Nov. 24, 1993) . . . . . . . . . . . . . 1581, 1616, 1650-51, 1785

Szumigala v. Nationwide Mut. Ins. Co., 853 F.2d 274
(5th Cir. 1988) . . . . . . . . . . . . . . . . . . . . . . . . . . . 1925

Tabas v. Bowden, 1982 WL 17820 (Del. Ch. Feb. 16, 1982) . . . . . . . . . . . . . . . . . . . . . . . . . . . . 1821

Tabas v. Mullane, 608 F. Supp. 759 (D.N.J. 1985) . . . . . . . . . . . . . . . . . . . . . . . 19, 62, 1427, 1497, 1498

Tandycrafts, Inc. v. Initio Partners, 562 A.2d 1162 (Del. 1989) . . . . . . . . . . . . . . . . . . . . . 1412, 1426, 1503-04

Tanzer v. International General Industries, Inc., 379 A.2d 1121 (Del. 1977) . . . . . . . . . . . . . . . . . . . . . . 467

Tarlov v. PaineWebber Cashfund, Inc., 559 F. Supp. 429 (D. Conn. 1983) . . . . . . . . . . . . . . . . . . . . . 1593

Tate & Lyle PLC v. Staley Continental, Inc., [1987-1988 Transfer Binder] Fed. Sec. L. Rep. (CCH) ¶ 93,764 (Del. Ch. May 9, 1988) . . . . . . . . . . . . . . . . . . . . 832, 1153, 1302, 1303, 1304-05, 1321, 1322, 1323, 1328-29, 1348

Taylor v. Swirnow, 80 F.R.D. 79 (D. Md. 1978) . . . . . . 1423

TBG Inc. v. Bendis, 1991 U.S. Dist. LEXIS 2765, 1991 WL 34199 (D. Kan. Feb. 19, 1991) . . . . . . . . . 1930-31

TCG Securities, Inc. v. Southern Union Co., [1989-1990 Transfer Binder] Fed. Sec. L. Rep. (CCH) ¶ 94,928 (Del. Ch. Jan. 31, 1990) . . . . . . . 507, 515, 736, 756

Teachers' Retirement System v. Welch, No. 113271/94 (N.Y. Sup. Ct. N.Y. Co. Apr. 16, 1996), aff'd, --- A.D.2d ---, 664 N.Y.S.2d 38 (N.Y. App. Div. 1st Dep't 1997) . . . . . . . . . . . . 145, 232, 1550, 1552-53

Teachers' Retirement System v. Welch, --- A.D.2d ---, 664 N.Y.S.2d 38 (N.Y. App. Div. 1st Dep't 1997) . . . . . . . . . . . . . . . 232-33, 1459, 1543, 1553, 1676

Technicorp International II, Inc. v. Johnston, 1997
Del. Ch. LEXIS 127, 1997 WL 538671 (Del. Ch.
Aug. 22, 1997) . . . . . . . . . . . . . . . . . . . . . . . . . . . 315, 316

Teich v. National Castings Co., 201 F. Supp. 451
(N.D. Ohio 1962) . . . . . . . . . . . . . . . . . . . . . . . . . . 309

Telvest, Inc. v. Olson, 1979 Del. Ch. LEXIS 347,
1979 WL 1759 (Del. Ch. Mar. 8, 1979) . . . . . . . . . . . 1135

Tennessee Bearing & Supply, Inc. v. Parrish, 1988
Tenn. App. LEXIS 724, 1988 WL 122337 (Tenn. Ct.
App. Nov. 16, 1988) . . . . . . . . . . . . . . . . . . . . . . . 307

Tenney v. Rosenthal, 6 N.Y.2d 204, 160 N.E.2d 463,
189 N.Y.S.2d 158 (1959) . . . . . . . . . . . . . . . . . . . . . 1389

Terrydale Liquidating Trust v. Barness, 642 F. Supp.
917 (S.D.N.Y. 1986), aff'd, 846 F.2d 845 (2d Cir.),
cert. denied, 488 U.S. 927 (1988)
. . . . . . . . . . . . . . . . . . 183, 187-88, 191, 193, 194, 905

Terrydale Liquidating Trust v. Barness, 846 F.2d 845
(2d Cir.), cert. denied, 488 U.S. 927 (1988) . . . . . . 687, 904-05

Tessari v. Herald, 207 F. Supp. 432 (N.D. Ind.
1962) . . . . . . . . . . . . . . . . . . . . . . . . . . . . . . . . 1422-23

Texaco, Inc. v. Pennzoil, Co., 729 S.W.2d 768 (Tex.
App. 1987, writ ref'd n.r.e.), cert. denied, 485 U.S.
944 (1988) . . . . . . . . . . . . . . . . . . . . . . . . . . . . . 1001

In re The Times Mirror Co. Shareholders Litigation,
No. 13550 (Del. Ch. Nov. 30, 1994) . . . . . . . . . . . . . 1039

Theriot v. Bourg, 691 So. 2d 213 (La. Ct. App.), writ
denied, 696 So. 2d 1008 (La. 1997) . . . . . . . . 135, 170, 1896

Thomas & Betts Corp. v. Leviton Manufacturing Co.,
681 A.2d 1026 (Del. 1996) . . . . . . . . . . . . . . . . . 1679-80

Thomas v. Kempner, 1973 Del. Ch. LEXIS 154, 1973
WL 460 (Del. Ch. Mar. 22, 1973) . . . . . . . . . . . . . . . 698

Thompson v. Enstar Corp., 509 A.2d 578 (Del. Ch.
1984) . . . . . . . . . . . . . . . . . . . . . . . . . . . . . . 918, 920

Thompson v. Glenmede Trust Co., 1993 U.S. Dist.
LEXIS 7677, 1993 WL 197031 (E.D. Pa. June 8,
1993) . . . . . . . . . . . . . . . . . . . . . . . . . . . . . . . . 1412

Thompson v. Hambrick, 508 S.W.2d 949 (Tex. Ct.
App. 1974) . . . . . . . . . . . . . . . . . . . . . . . . . . . 364, 365

Thorpe v. CERBCO, Inc., 611 A.2d 5 (Del. Ch.
1991) . . . . . . . . . . . . . . . . . . . . . . . . . . . . . . . 1897

Thorpe v. CERBCO, Inc., 19 Del. J. Corp. L. 942
(Del. Ch. Oct. 29, 1993) . . . . . . . . . . . . . . . 302, 354, 367

Thorpe v. CERBCO, Inc., 21 Del. J. Corp. L. 339
(Del. Ch. Aug. 9, 1995), aff'd and rev'd, 676 A.2d
436 (Del. 1996) . . . . . . . . . . . . . . . . . . . . . 35, 265, 302

Thorpe v. CERBCO, Inc., 611 A.2d 5 (Del. Ch.
1991) . . . . . . . . . . . . . . . . . . . . . . . . 1580, 1602, 1614

Thorpe v. CERBCO, Inc., 676 A.2d 436 (Del. 1996)
. . . . . . . 35, 294, 295, 301, 304, 349, 350-54, 363, 365, 1604

Thorpe v. CERBCO, Inc., 1996 Del. Ch. LEXIS 110,
1996 WL 560173 (Del. Ch. Sept. 13, 1996), aff'd,

703 A.2d 645 (unpublished opinion, text available at
1997 Del. LEXIS 438 and 1997 WL 776169) (Del.
Dec. 3, 1997) . . . . . . . . . . . . . 355-56, 1873, 1882, 1897-98

Thorpe v. CERBCO, Inc., 703 A.2d 645 (unpublished
opinion, text available at 1997 Del. LEXIS 438 and
1997 WL 776169) (Del. Dec. 3, 1997) . . . . . . . . . . . . . 356

In re Times Mirror Co. Shareholders Litigation, No.
13,550 (Del. Ch. Nov. 30, 1994) . . . . . . . . . 349, 358, 564-65

Tobias v. Tobias, N.Y.L.J., Aug. 13, 1992, at 22
(N.Y. Sup. Ct. N.Y. Co.) . . . . . . . . . . . . . . . . . . . . 1560

Tomash v. Midwest Technical Development Corp.,
160 N.W.2d 273 (Minn. 1968) . . . . . . . . . . . . . . . . . 1866

Tomczak v. Morton Thiokol, Inc., 10 Del. J. Corp.
L. 921 (Del. Ch. Feb. 13, 1985) . . . . . . . . 182, 184, 186, 194

Tomczak v. Morton Thiokol, Inc., 12 Del. J. Corp.
L. 381 (Del. Ch. May 7, 1986) . . . . 172-73, 193, 652, 1521-22

Tomczak v. Morton Thiokol, Inc., [1990 Transfer
Binder] Fed. Sec. L. Rep. (CCH) ¶ 95,327 (Del. Ch.
Apr. 5, 1990) . . . . . . . . . . . . . . . . . . . . . . . . . . 76, 94, 135,
173, 183, 184, 185, 187, 190, 191, 194, 195, 345, 650, 722, 1522

Tong v. Hang Seng Bank, Ltd., 210 A.D.2d 99, 620
N.Y.S.2d 42 (N.Y. App. Div. 1st Dep't 1994) . . . . . . . . 1560

Topper Acquisition Corp. v. Emhart Corp., 1989 U.S.
Dist. LEXIS 9910, 1989 WL 513034 (E.D. Va. Mar.
23, 1989) . . . . . . . . . . . . . . . . . . . . . . . . . . . . . . 1099

Torchmark Corp. v. Bixby, 708 F. Supp. 1070 (W.D.
Mo. 1988)
. . 23, 181, 185, 187, 686, 727, 832-33, 1018-20, 1251-52, 1399

Tower Recreation, Inc. v. Beard, 231 N.E.2d 154
(Ind. Ct. App. 1967) . . . . . . . . . . . . . . . . . . . . . . . . . 297

Township of Center v. First Mercury Syndicate, Inc.,
117 F.3d 115 (3d Cir. 1997) . . 1998, 2045, 2050, 2051-52, 2073

In re Trans World Airlines, Inc. Shareholders Litigation, 14 Del. J. Corp. L. 870 (Del. Ch. Oct. 21,
1988) . . . . . . . . . . . . . . . . . . . . . . . . . 405, 431, 434-35

Traub v. Barber, N.Y.L.J., July 9, 1987, at 7 (N.Y.
Sup. Ct. N.Y. Co.) . . . . . . . . . . . . . . . . . . . . . . . . 1356

Treadway Cos. v. Care Corp., 638 F.2d 357 (2d Cir.
1980) . . . . . . . . . . . . . . . . . 187, 191, 194, 631, 687, 917

Treco, Inc. v. Land of Lincoln Savings & Loan, 749
F.2d 374 (7th Cir. 1984) . . . . . . . . . . . . . . . . 632, 1283-84

Treves v. Servel, Inc., 244 F. Supp. 773 (S.D.N.Y.
1965) . . . . . . . . . . . . . . . . . . . . . . . . . . . . . . . 1688

Tri-Continental Corp. v. Battye, 74 A.2d 71 (Del.
1950) . . . . . . . . . . . . . . . . . . . . . . . . . . . . . 478, 479

In re Tri-Star Pictures, Inc., Litigation, 634 A.2d 319
(Del. 1993) . . . . . . . . . . . . 29, 34, 53-56, 115, 227, 252, 343,
345, 347-48, 369, 397-98, 517, 530, 531, 532-33, 534, 1392, 1414

In re Tri-Star Pictures, Inc. Litigation, [1995 Transfer
Binder] Fed. Sec. L. Rep. (CCH) ¶ 98,818 (Del. Ch.
Mar. 9, 1995) . . . . . . . . . . . . . . . . . . . . . . . . . 56, 273

In re Triton Group Ltd. Shareholders Litigation,
[1990-1991 Transfer Binder] Fed. Sec. L. Rep. (CCH)
¶ 95,876 (Del. Ch. Feb. 22, 1991), aff'd sub nom.
Glinert v. Lord, 604 A.2d 417 (unpublished opinion,
text available at 1991 Del. LEXIS 315 and 1991 WL
235368) (Del. Sept. 27, 1991) . . . . . . . . . . . . 183, 185, 402

TSC Industries, Inc. v. Northway, Inc., 426 U.S. 438
(1976) . . . . . . . . . . . . . . . . . . . . . . . . . . . . . . 511, 514

In re Tufts Electronics, Inc., 746 F.2d 915 (1st Cir.
1984) . . . . . . . . . . . . . . . . . . . . . . . . . . . . . . . . . . 300

Tullos v. Parks, 915 F.2d 1192 (8th Cir. 1990) . . . . . . . . 1348

Turner Broadcasting System, Inc. v. CBS, Inc., 627
F. Supp. 901 (N.D. Ga. 1985) . . . . . . . . . 632, 1035, 1036-37

In re TW Services, Inc. Shareholder Litigation, [1989
Transfer Binder] Fed. Sec. L. Rep. (CCH) ¶ 94,334
(Del. Ch. Mar. 2, 1989) . . . . . . . . 648, 667, 811-12, 1181-83

In re UFG International, Inc., 207 B.R. 793 (Bankr.
S.D.N.Y. 1997) . . . . . . . . . . . . . . . . . . . . . . . . . . . . 2147

UIS, Inc. v. Walbro Corp., 13 Del. J. Corp. L. 806
(Del. Ch. Oct. 6, 1987) . . . . . . . . . . . . . . . . . . 698, 845-46

In re UJB Financial Corp. Shareholder Litigation,
1991 U.S. Dist. LEXIS 20710, 1991 WL 321909
(D.N.J. Jan. 22, 1991), aff'd sub. nom. Shapiro v.
UJB Financial Corp., 964 F.2d 272 (3d Cir.), cert.
denied, 506 U.S. 934 (1992) . . . . . . . . . . . . . . . . . . . . 1491

Uni-Marts, Inc. v. Stein, 1996 Del. Ch. LEXIS 95,
1996 WL 466961 (Del. Ch. Aug. 12, 1996) . . . . 94, 502, 1575

Unilever Acquisition Corp. v. Richardson-Vicks, Inc.,
618 F. Supp. 407 (S.D.N.Y. 1985) . . . . . . . . . . . . 1140-42

In re Unisys Savings Plan Litigation, 74 F.3d 420 (3d
Cir.), cert. denied, 117 S. Ct. 56 (1996) . . . . . . . . . . . . 879

In re Unisys Saving Plan Litigation, 1997 U.S. Dist.
LEXIS 19198, 1997 WL 732473 (E.D. Pa. Nov. 24,
1997) . . . . . . . . . . . . . . . . . . . . . . . . . . . . . 879

United Copper Securities Co. v. Amalgamated Copper
Co., 244 U.S. 261 (1917) . . . . . . . . . . . . . . 1607, 1691-92

United Paperworks International Union v. Misco, Inc.,
484 U.S. 29 (1987) . . . . . . . . . . . . . . . . . . . . . . . . 2086

United States Fire Insurance Co. v. Fleekop, 682 So.
2d 620 (Fla. Dist. Ct. App. 1996) . . . . . . . . . . . . . . 1999

United States Fire Insurance Co. v. Goodyear Tire &
Rubber Co., 920 F.2d 487 (8th Cir. 1990) . . . . . . . . . 1986-87

United States v. BNS Inc., 848 F.2d 945 (9th Cir.
1988) . . . . . . . . . . . . . . . . . . . . . . . . . . . . . 1338

United States v. BNS Inc., 858 F.2d 456 (9th Cir.
1988) . . . . . . . . . . . . . . . . . . . . . . . . . . . . . 1338

United States v. Lowe, 29 F.3d 1005 (5th Cir. 1994) . . . . 1953

United States v. Skeddle, 940 F. Supp. 1146 (N.D.
Ohio 1996) . . . . . . . . . . . . . . . . . . . . . . . . . 24, 43-44

United States v. Skeddle, 989 F. Supp. 873 (N.D.
Ohio 1997) . . . . . . . . . . . . . . . . . . . . . 269, 270, 282

United States v. Weissman, 1997 U.S. Dist. LEXIS
8540, 1997 WL 334966 (S.D.N.Y. June 16, 1997)
. . . . . . . . . . . . . . . . . . 1853, 1855, 1894, 1909, 1918-23

United States v. Weissman, 1997 U.S. Dist. LEXIS
12975, 1997 WL 539774 (S.D.N.Y. Aug. 28, 1997)
. . . . . . . . . . . . . . . 1853, 1855, 1894, 1909, 1918, 1920-23

United Teachers Associates Insurance Co. v. MacKeen
& Bailey Inc., 99 F.3d 645, 651 (5th Cir. 1996) . . . . . . . . 300

In re Unitrin, Inc. Shareholders Litigation, 1994 Del.
Ch. LEXIS 187, 1994 WL 698483 (Del. Ch. Oct. 13,
1994), rev'd sub nom. Unitrin, Inc. v. American General Corp., 651 A.2d 1361 (Del. 1995)
. . 182, 185, 645, 651, 653-54, 680, 718, 719, 1025, 1106, 1333

Unitrin, Inc. v. American General Corp., 651 A.2d
1361 (Del. 1995) . . . . . . . . . . . . . . . . . . . . . . 20-21, 26-27,
29-30, 33, 45, 62, 64, 282, 631, 632, 639, 641, 642, 643, 644,
645, 647, 648, 653-54, 664, 666, 673-74, 680, 681-83, 684, 720,
790, 792, 799-800, 803, 807, 1004, 1011, 1024, 1025, 1026-30,
1085, 1088, 1147-48, 1172, 1173, 1175, 1177, 1182, 1205-6, 1245-47

Universal Studios Inc. v. Viacom Inc., 705 A.2d 579
(Del. Ch. 1997), appeal dismissed, 698 A.2d 410
(unpublished opinion, text available at 1997 Del.
LEXIS 258 and 1997 WL 425504) (Del. July 21,
1997) . . . . . . . . . . . . . . . . . . . . . . . . . . . . . . . . . 114

Unocal Corp. v. Mesa Petroleum Co., 493 A.2d 946
(Del. 1985) . . . . . . . . . . . . . . . . . . . . . . . . . . . 20-21, 69,
281, 568, 631, 632, 635, 636, 638, 639, 640, 641, 642, 643, 644,
646, 649, 655, 659, 662, 663, 677, 681-82, 686, 697, 700, 719,
724, 727-28, 733, 790, 800, 809, 813, 823, 837, 923, 962, 1004,
1008-10, 1011, 1020, 1025, 1034, 1035, 1043, 1046, 1047, 1071,

1094, 1115, 1117, 1132, 1142, 1150, 1163, 1166, 1174, 1221-22, 1266, 1279, 1303, 1306, 1315, 1331, 1343, 1344, 1352, 1363, 1513

Unocal Corp. v. Pickens, 608 F. Supp. 1081 (C.D. Cal. 1985) . . . . . . . . . . . . . . . . . . . . . . . . . . . . 1010

Unocal Corp. v. Superior Court, 198 Cal. App. 3d 1245, 244 Cal. Rptr. 540 (Cal. Ct. App. 1988), review denied, 1988 Cal. LEXIS 135 (Cal. June 1, 1988) . . . . . . . . . . . . . . . . . . . . . . . . . . . . . 1997

U S WEST, Inc. v. Time Warner Inc., 22 Del. J. Corp. L. 447 (Del. Ch. June 6, 1996) . . . . . 262, 296, 302, 304

Untermeyer v. Valhi, Inc., 665 F. Supp. 297 (S.D.N.Y. 1987) . . . . . . . . . . . . . . . . . . . . . . . . . 1415

US Airways Group, Inc. v. British Airways, PLC, 989 F. Supp. 482 (S.D.N.Y. 1997) . . . . . . . . . . . . . . . 345

USACafes v. Office, 11 Del. J. Corp. L. 1034 (Del. Ch. Oct. 28, 1985) . . . . . . . . . . . . . . . . . . . . . . . . 1287

Valassis Communications, Inc. v. Aetna Casualty & Surety Co., 97 F.3d 870 (6th Cir. 1996) . . . . . . . . . . . 1991

Van de Walle v. Unimation, Inc., [1990-1991 Transfer Binder] Fed. Sec. L. Rep. (CCH) ¶ 95,834 (Del. Ch. Mar. 6, 1991) . . . . . . . . . . . . . . . . . . . . . . . . . 30, 51, 53, 70, 189, 191, 357-58, 369-70, 755, 757, 758, 760, 765-68

Van Gelder v. Taylor, 621 F. Supp. 613 (N.D. Ill. 1985) . . . . . . . . . . . . . . . . . . . . . . . . . 1419, 1420

Vanderbilt v. Geo-Energy Ltd., 590 F. Supp. 999 (E.D. Pa. 1984) . . . . . . . . . . . . . . . . . . . . . . . . . 1774

Varian Associates, Inc. v. Superior Court, No.
H011025 (Cal. Ct. App. Aug. 31, 1993)
. . . . . . . . . . . . . . . . 3, 19, 26, 1582, 1610, 1633-34, 1778

Velez v. Feinstein, N.Y.L.J., Oct. 18, 1981, at 7
(N.Y. Sup. Ct. N.Y. Co.) . . . . . . . . . . . . . . . . . . . . . 1559

In re VeriFone Securities Litigation, 11 F.3d 865 (9th
Cir. 1993) . . . . . . . . . . . . . . . . . . . . . . . . . . . . . 506

Viacom International Inc. v. Icahn, 747 F. Supp. 205
(S.D.N.Y. 1990), aff'd, 946 F.2d 998 (2d Cir. 1991),
cert. denied, 502 U.S. 1122 (1992) . . . . . . . . . . . . . . . 1356

Viacom International Inc. v. Tele-Communications,
Inc., 1994 U.S. Dist. LEXIS 14522, 1994 WL 561377
(S.D.N.Y. Oct. 12, 1994) . . . . . . . . . . . . . . . . . . . . . 983

Vicorp Restaurants, Inc. v. Federal Insurance Co.,
1993 U.S. Dist. LEXIS 20294, 1993 WL 736918 (D.
Colo. June 30, 1993) . . . . . . . . . . . . . . . . . . . . . . . 2130

Virginia Bankshares, Inc. v. Sandberg, 501 U.S. 1083
(1991) . . . . . . . . . . . . . . . . . . . . . . . . . . . . . . . 525

In re Vitalink Communications Corp. Shareholders
Litigation, [1991-1992 Transfer Binder] Fed. Sec. L.
Rep. (CCH) ¶ 96,585 (Del. Ch. Nov. 8, 1991), aff'd
sub nom. Grimes v. John P. McCarthy Profit Sharing
Plan, 610 A.2d 725 (unpublished opinion, text avail-
able at 1992 Del. LEXIS 162 and 1992 WL 115190)
(Del. Apr. 30, 1992), cert. denied, 506 U.S. 861
(1992) . . . . . . . . . . 183, 184, 185, 770, 912, 945, 953-54, 973

Vitkus v. Beatrice Co., 127 F.3d 936 (10th Cir.
1997) . . . . . . . . . . . . . . . . . . . . . . 2057, 2113, 2125-27

Vogt v. Empire Blue Cross & Blue Shield, No.
109450/96 (N.Y. Sup. Ct. N.Y. Co. Oct. 10, 1996) . . . . . . 309

Voluntary Hospitals of America, Inc. v. National
Union Fire Insurance Co., 859 F. Supp. 260 (N.D. Tex.
1993), aff'd mem., 24 F.3d 239 (5th Cir. 1994)
. . . . . . . . . . . . . . . . . . . . . . . . . . . . . 2047, 2048-49

VonFeldt v. Stifel Financial Corp., 1997 Del. Ch.
LEXIS 108, 1997 WL 525878 (Del. Ch. Aug. 18,
1997) . . . . . . . . . . . . . . . . . . . . . . . . . . . . . 1910

W & W Equipment Co. v. Mink, 568 N.E.2d 564
(Ind. App. 1991) . . . . . . . . . . . . . . . . . . . . . . . 363

Wacht v. Continental Hosts, Ltd., 12 Del. J. Corp. L.
418 (Del. Ch. Apr. 11, 1986) . . . . . . . . . . . . . . . . . 526

Wacht v. Continental Hosts, Ltd., [1994-1995 Transfer Binder] Fed. Sec. L. Rep. (CCH) ¶ 98,452 (Del.
Ch. Sept. 16, 1994) . . . . . . . . . . . . . . . . . 283, 385, 520

Walbrook Insurance Co. Ltd. v. Spiegel, [1993-1994
Transfer Binder] Fed. Sec. L. Rep. (CCH) ¶ 98,020
(C.D. Cal. Aug. 6, 1993) . . . . . . . . . . . . . . . . . . . 2148

Walden v. Elrod, 72 F.R.D. 5 (W.D. Okla. 1976) . . 1419, 1420

Wallace v. Lincoln Savings Bank, 15 S.W. 448 (Tenn.
1891) . . . . . . . . . . . . . . . . . . . . . . . . . . . . . 1612

In re Walt Disney Co. Derivative Litigation, 1997
Del. Ch. LEXIS 25, 1997 WL 118402 (Del. Ch. Mar.
13, 1997) . . . . . . . . . . . . . . . . . . . . . . . . . . . 1459

Walter J. Schloss Associates v. Arkwin Industries,
Inc., 90 A.D.2d 149, 455 N.Y.S.2d 844 (N.Y. App.

Div. 2d Dep't 1982), rev'd, 61 N.Y.2d 700, 460
N.E.2d 1090, 472 N.Y.S. 2d 605 (1984) . . . . . . . . . . . . 498

Walter J. Schloss Associates v. Arkwin Industries
Inc., 61 N.Y.2d 700, 460 N.E.2d 1090, 472
N.Y.S.2d 605 (1984) . . . . . . . . . . . . . . . . . . . . . . . 498

Walter J. Schloss Associates v. Chesapeake & Ohio
Railway Co., 536 A.2d 147 (Md. Ct. Spec. App.
1988) . . . . . . . . . . . . . . . . . . . . . . . . . . . . . . . . 470-71

Waltuch v. Conticommodity Services, Inc., 833 F.
Supp. 302 (S.D.N.Y. 1993), aff'd and rev'd, 88 F.3d
87 (2d Cir. 1996) . . . . . . . . . . . . . . 5, 18, 1859, 1890, 1896

Waltuch v. Conticommodity Services, Inc., 1994 U.S.
Dist. LEXIS 1392, 1994 WL 48841 (S.D.N.Y. Feb.
10, 1994) . . . . . . . . . . . . . . . . . . . . . . . . . . . . . . 1890

Waltuch v. Conticommodity Services, Inc., Nos.
94-8003, 94-8004 (2d Cir. Mar. 22, 1994) . . . . . . . . . . 1890

Waltuch v. Conticommodity Services, Inc., 88 F.3d
87 (2d Cir. 1996) . . . . . . . . . . . 1859-60, 1886, 1890, 1962-68

Wanvig v. Johnson Controls, Inc., No. 663-487 (Wis.
Cir. Ct. Mar. 29, 1985) . . . . . . . . . . . . . . . . . . . . . 25, 35

Ward v. Succession of Freeman, 854 F.2d 780 (5th
Cir. 1988), cert. denied, 490 U.S. 1065 (1989) . . . . . . . . 1822

Warde v. Bayly, Martin & Fay International, Inc.,
No. G008209 (Cal. Ct. App. May 22, 1990), review
denied, 1990 Cal. LEXIS 3474 (Cal. Aug. 1, 1990)
. . . . . . . . . . . . . . . . . . . . . . . . . . . . . . 1868, 1870

Warnaco Inc. v. Galef, No. B-86-146 (PCD) (D.
Conn. Apr. 25, 1986), aff'd mem., 800 F.2d 1129 (2d
Cir. 1986) . . . . . . . . . . . . . . . . . . . . . . . . . 1346

Warner Communications, Inc. v. Murdoch, 581 F.
Supp. 1482 (D. Del. 1984) . . . . . . . . . . . . . . . . . . . . 640

Warren v. Century Bankcorporation, Inc., 741 P.2d
846 (Okla. 1987) . . . . . . . . . . . . . . . . . . . . . . . . . . . . 24

Warshaw v. Calhoun, 221 A.2d 487 (Del. 1966) . . . . . . . . 269

Washington Bancorporation v. Said, 812 F. Supp.
1256 (D.D.C. 1993) . . . . . . . . . . . . . . . . . . . . . . . 4, 12,
19, 22, 25, 28, 39, 44, 81, 133, 136, 180, 185, 203, 247-48, 504

Washington Bancorporation v. Washington, [1989-
1990 Transfer Binder] Fed. Sec. L. Rep. (CCH)
¶ 94,893 (D.D.C. Sept. 26, 1989) . . . . . . . . . . . . . . . 1456

Watts v. Des Moines Register & Tribune, 525 F.
Supp. 1311 (S.D. Iowa 1981) . . . . . . . . . . . . . . . . . . 1792

Watts's Appeal, 78 Pa. 370 (1874) . . . . . . . . . . . . . . . 10-11

Wedtech Corp. v. Federal Insurance Co., 740 F.
Supp. 214 (S.D.N.Y. 1990) . . . . . . . . . . . 2099, 2102, 2151

Weigand v. Berry Petroleum Co., 1991 Del. Ch.
LEXIS 37, 1991 WL 45361 (Del. Ch. Mar. 27, 199) . . 394, 430

Weigel Broadcasting Co. v. Smith, 682 N.E.2d 745
(Ill. App. Ct. 1996) . . . . . . . . . . . . . . . . . . . . . . 477, 479

Weil v. Investment/Indicators, Research & Manage-
ment, Inc., 647 F.2d 18 (9th Cir. 1981) . . . . . . . . . . 1821-22

Weiland v. Central & South West Corp., 15 Del. J.
Corp. L. 273 (Del. Ch. May 9, 1989) . . . . . . . . . . . . .  1680

Weiland v. Illinois Power Co., [1990-1991 Transfer
Binder] Fed. Sec. L. Rep. (CCH) ¶ 95,747 (C.D. Ill.
Sept. 17, 1990)
        . . . . . . . 4, 7, 12, 91, 1456, 1491, 1502, 1583, 1590-91, 1611,
1636, 1645-49, 1695, 1702, 1721, 1735-36, 1745, 1771-72, 1780

Weinberger v. Bankston, [1987-1988 Transfer Binder]
Fed. Sec. L. Rep. (CCH) ¶ 93,539 (Del. Ch. Nov.
19, 1987) . . . . . . . . . . . . . . . . . . . . . . . . . . . . . . .  1655

Weinberger v. Lorenzo, 16 Del. J. Corp. L. 1647
(Del. Ch. Oct. 11, 1990) . . . . . . . . . . . . . . . . . . . . .  1382

Weinberger v. Rio Grande Industries, Inc., 519 A.2d
116 (Del. Ch. 1986) . . . . . . . . . . . . . . . . . . . . . . . 507, 527

Weinberger v. UOP, Inc., 457 A.2d 701 (Del. 1983)
 . . . . . . . . . . . . . . . . . . . . . . . . . . 29-31, 158, 160, 163,
269, 270, 272, 273, 283, 284, 343, 369, 375, 378-83, 400, 402,
404, 411, 432, 438-39, 466-68, 478-81, 483, 489, 520, 527, 528

Weinberger v. UOP, Inc., 10 Del. J. Corp. L. 945
(Del. Ch. Jan. 30, 1985), aff'd, 497 A.2d 792 (unpublished opinion, text available at 1985 Del. LEXIS 463
and 1985 WL 188543) (Del. Jul. 9, 1985) . . . . . . . . . 383, 531

Weinberger v. United Financial Corp., 1983 Del. Ch.
LEXIS 443, 1983 WL 20290 (Del. Ch. Oct. 13,
1983) . . . . . . . . . . . . . . . . . . . . . . . . . . . . . . . . 519, 524

Weinstock v. Bromery, N.Y.L.J., Mar. 28, 1996, at
29 (N.Y. Sup. Ct. N.Y. Co.), aff'd sub nom. Teachers' Retirement System v. Welch, --- A.D.2d ---, 664

N.Y.S.2d 38 (N.Y. App. Div. 1st Dep't 1997)
. . . . . . . . . . . . . . . . . . . 145, 1492, 1493, 1496, 1541-42

Weinstock v. Bromery, No. 100151/95, Order (N.Y.
Sup. Ct. N.Y. Co. Oct. 30, 1996), aff'd sub nom.
Teachers' Retirement System v. Welch, --- A.D.2d
---, 664 N.Y.S.2d 38 (N.Y. App. Div. 1st Dep't
1997) . . . . . . . . . . . . . . . . . . . . . . . . . . . 145, 1542

Weisbein v. Metrobank, 1992 U.S. Dist. LEXIS
20196, 1992 WL 398361 (E.D. Pa. Dec. 31, 1992) . . . . . 1492

Weisfeld v. Spartans Industries, Inc., 58 F.R.D. 570
(S.D.N.Y. 1972) . . . . . . . . . . . . . . . . . . . . . . . 1406

Weiss v. Kay Jewelry Stores, Inc., 470 F.2d 1259
(D.C. Cir. 1972) . . . . . . . . . . . . . . . . . . . . . . . 297

Weiss v. Leewards Creative Crafts, Inc., 19 Del. J.
Corp. L. 424 (Del. Ch. Apr. 29, 1993), aff'd, 633
A.2d 372 (unpublished opinion, text available at 1993
Del. LEXIS 396 and 1993 WL 476395) (Del. Oct. 20,
1993) . . . . . . . . . . . . . . . . . . . . . . . . . . . . . 109

Weiss v. Rockwell International Corp., No. 8811
(Del. Ch. Feb 6, 1987) . . . . . . . . . . . . . . . . 1054, 1075-76

Weiss v. Rockwell International Corp., 15 Del. J.
Corp. L. 777 (Del. Ch. July 19, 1989), aff'd, 574
A.2d 264 (unpublished opinion, text available at 1990
Del. LEXIS 74 and 1990 WL 38323) (Del. Mar. 14,
1990) . . . . . . . . . . . . . . 277, 519, 523, 1054, 1076, 1077

Weiss v. Rockwell International Corp., 574 A.2d 264
(unpublished opinion, text available at 1990 Del.
LEXIS 74, 1990 WL 38323) (Del. Mar. 14, 1990) . . . . . . 1077

Weiss v. Sunasco Inc., 316 F. Supp. 1197 (E.D. Pa. 1970) . . . . . . . . . . . . . . . . . . . . . . . . . . . 1688

Weiss v. Temporary Investment Fund, Inc., 516 F. Supp. 665 (D. Del.), reargument denied, 520 F. Supp. 1098 (D. Del. 1981), aff'd, 692 F.2d 928 (3d Cir. 1982), vacated and remanded, 465 U.S. 1001 (1984) . . . . . . . . . . . . . . . . . . . . . . . . . 1489, 1491, 1681

Weiss v. Temporary Investment Fund, Inc., 520 F. Supp. 1098 (D. Del. 1981), aff'd, 692 F.2d 928 (3d Cir. 1982), vacated and remanded on other grounds, 465 U.S. 1001 (1984) . . . . . . . . . . . . . . . . . . . . . . 1592

Weiss v. Temporary Investment Fund, Inc., 692 F.2d 928 (3d Cir. 1982), vacated and remanded, 465 U.S. 1001 (1984) . . . . . . . . . . . . . . . . . 12, 15, 1592, 1594

Wells Fargo & Co. v. First Interstate Bancorp, 21 Del. J. Corp. L. 818 (Del. Ch. Jan. 18, 1996) . . . . . . 517, 524, 644, 698, 712, 731, 913-14, 964, 1150, 1513

Wells v. Shearson Lehman/American Express, Inc., 127 A.D.2d 200, 514 N.Y.S.2d 1 (N.Y. App. Div. 1st Dep't 1987), rev'd, 72 N.Y.2d 11, 526 N.E.2d 8, 530 N.Y.S.2d 517 (1988) . . . . . . . . . . . . . . . . . . . . . 256

West Point-Pepperell, Inc. v. Farley Inc., 711 F. Supp. 1088 (N.D. Ga. 1988) . . . . . . . . . . . . . . 1098, 1370

West v. West, 825 F. Supp. 1033 (N.D. Ga. 1992) . . . . . . . . . . . . . . . . . . . . . . . . . . . . . . . . 1415, 1416

Western Fiberglass, Inc. v. Kirton, McConkie & Bushnell, 789 P.2d 34 (Utah Ct. App. 1990) . . 1852, 1853, 1856

In re Western World Funding, Inc., 52 B.R. 743
(Bankr. D. Nev. 1985), aff'd in part and rev'd in part
sub nom. Buchanan v. Henderson, 131 B.R. 859 (D.
Nev. 1990), rev'd, 985 F.2d 1021 (9th Cir. 1993) . . . . . . . 597

In re Westinghouse Securities Litigation, 832 F. Supp.
989 (W.D. Pa. 1993), aff'd mem., 92 F.3d 1175 (3d
Cir. 1996)
. . . . . 15, 37, 1404, 1426, 1464, 1489, 1491, 1492, 1496, 1500

In re Westinghouse Securities Litigation, No. 95-3079
(3d Cir. May 24, 1995) . . . . . . . . . . . . . . . . . . . . . 1404

Whalen v. On-Deck, Inc., 514 A.2d 1072 (Del.
1986) . . . . . . . . . . . . . . . . . . . . . . . . . . . . . . 1986

In re Wheelabrator Technologies Inc. Shareholders
Litigation, [1990 Transfer Binder] Fed. Sec. L. Rep.
(CCH) ¶ 95,489 (Del. Ch. Sept. 6, 1990) . . . . . 277, 521, 1076

In re Wheelabrator Technologics Inc. Shareholders
Litigation, 18 Del. J. Corp. L. 778 (Del. Ch. Sept. 1,
1992) . . . . . . . . . . . . . . . . . . . . . 229, 230, 508, 705-06

In re Wheelabrator Technologies, Inc. Shareholders
Litigation, 663 A.2d 1194 (Del. Ch. May 16, 1995)
. . 224, 225, 271, 274, 276-77, 278, 279-80, 346, 402, 519, 1076

White v. Banes Co., 866 P.2d 339 (N.M. 1993) . . . . . . . 1390

Whittaker Corp. v. Edgar, 535 F. Supp. 933 (N.D.
Ill. 1982), aff'd mem., Nos. 82-1305 & 82-1307 (7th
Cir. Mar. 5, 1982) . . . . . . . . . . . . . . . . . . . . 904, 1335

Wieboldt Stores, Inc. v. Schottenstein, 94 B.R. 488
(N.D. Ill. 1988) . . . . . . . . . . . . . . . . . 604, 686, 728-29

Wiegand v. Berry Petroleum Co., 1991 Del. Ch. LEXIS 37, 1991 WL 45361 (Del. Ch. Mar. 27, 1991). . . . . . . . . . . . . . . . . . . . . . . . . . . . . 394, 430

Wilderman v. Wilderman, 315 A.2d 610 (Del. Ch. 1974) . . . . . . . . . . . . . . . . . . . . . . . . . . 310, 317, 320

Wilkes v. Springside Nursing Home, Inc., 353 N.E.2d 657 (Mass. 1976) . . . . . . . . . . . . . . . . . . . . . . . . . 363

Will v. Engebretson & Co., 213 Cal. App. 3d 1033, 261 Cal. Rptr. 868 (1989) . . . . . . . . . . . . . . 1695, 1743-44

Williams v. First National Bank, 216 U.S. 582 (1910) . . . . . . . . . . . . . . . . . . . . . . . . . . . . . . 1409

Williams v. Geier, [1987 Transfer Binder] Fed. Sec. L. Rep. (CCH) ¶ 93,283 (Del. Ch. May 20, 1987) . . . . . . . . . . . . . . . . . . . . . . . . . . . . . 522, 524, 1054

Williams v. Geier, 1994 Del. Ch. LEXIS 165, 1994 WL 514871 (Del. Ch. Sept. 9, 1994), aff'd, 671 A.2d 1368 (Del. 1996) . . . . . . . . . . . . . . . . . . . . . . . . 522

Williams v. Geier, 671 A.2d 1368 (Del. 1996) . . . 20-21, 26-30, 39, 41, 45, 228, 267, 268, 275, 281, 284, 293, 342, 349, 500, 512, 528, 529, 530, 539, 540-42, 546, 631, 635, 639, 641, 642, 644, 655-56, 724, 791, 793-94, 1054, 1068-72, 1082, 1115, 1206

Willner's Fuel Distributors, Inc. v. Noreen, 882 P.2d 399 (Alaska 1994) . . . . . . . . . . . . . . . . . . . . . . . 597

Winkler v. National Union Fire Insurance Co., 930 F.2d 1364 (9th Cir. 1991) . . . . . . . . . . . . . . . . . . . . 2002

Winston v. Mandor, 1997 Del. Ch. LEXIS 82, 1997 WL 828776 (Del. Ch. May 12, 1997) . . . . . . . . . . . 574, 576

Wisener v. Air Express International Corp., 583 F.2d
579 (2d Cir. 1978) . . . . . . . . . . . . . . . . . . 1861, 1971-72

Witco Corp. v. Beekhuis, 38 F.3d 682 (3d Cir. 1994)
. . . . . . . . . . . . . . . . . . . . . . . . . . 1853, 1857, 1953-54

WLR Foods, Inc. v. Tyson Foods, Inc., 155 F.R.D.
142 (W.D. Va.), objections overruled, 857 F. Supp.
492 (W.D. Va. 1994), aff'd, 65 F.3d 1172 (4th Cir.
1995), cert. denied, 516 U.S. 1117 (1996) . . . . . . . . 728, 812

WLR Foods, Inc. v. Tyson Foods, Inc., 857 F. Supp.
492 (W.D. Va. 1994), aff'd, 65 F.3d 1172 (4th Cir.
1995), cert. denied, 516 U.S. 1117 (1996) . . 125, 1241, 1244-45

WLR Foods, Inc. v. Tyson Foods, Inc., 869 F. Supp.
419 (W.D. Va. 1994), aff'd, 65 F.3d 1172 (4th Cir.
1995), cert. denied, 516 U.S. 1117 (1996)
. . . . . . . . . . . . . . . . . . . . . . 169, 187, 189, 190, 194,
693, 1106, 1107, 1155, 1156, 1194, 1245, 1302, 1303, 1322, 1324

WLR Foods, Inc. v. Tyson Foods, Inc., 65 F.3d 1172
(4th Cir. 1995), cert. denied, 516 U.S. 1117 (1996)
. . . . . . . . . . . 124-25, 183, 185, 190, 1107, 1156, 1245, 1324

WNH Investments, LLC v. Batzel, [1995 Transfer
Binder] Fed. Sec. L. Rep. (CCH) ¶ 98,764 (Del. Ch.
Apr. 28, 1995) . . . . . . . . . . . . . . . . . . . . . . . . 636, 849

Wolfensohn v. Madison Fund, Inc., 253 A.2d 72
(Del. 1969) . . . . . . . . . . . . . . . . . . . . . . . . . . . . 304

Wolgin v. Simon, 722 F.2d 389 (8th Cir. 1983)
. . . . . . . . . . . . . . . . . . . . . . . . . . . 1300, 1686-87

Wood v. Coastal States Gas Corp., 401 A.2d 932
(Del. 1979) . . . . . . . . . . . . . . . . . . . . . . . . . . . . 571

Woodward & Lothrop, Inc. v. Schnabel, 593 F. Supp.
1385 (D.D.C. 1984) . . . . . . . . . . . . . . . . . . . . . . . 1611

In re Woolworth Corp. Shareholder Derivative Litigation, No. 109465/94 (N.Y. Sup. Ct. N.Y. Co. May 3,
1995), aff'd, 240 A.D.2d 189, 658 N.Y.S. 2d 869
(N.Y. App. Div. 1st Dep't 1997)
. . . . . . . . . . . . . 62, 146, 1496, 1500, 1501, 1551, 1553-54

In re Woolworth Corp. Shareholder Derivative Litiga-
tion, N.Y.L.J., Apr. 22, 1996, at 28 (Sup. Ct. N.Y.
Co.), aff'd, 240 A.D.2d 189, 658 N.Y.S.2d 869
(N.Y. App. Div. 1st Dep't 1997) . . . . . . . . . . . . . 146, 1554

In re Woolworth Corp. Shareholder Derivative Litigation, 240 A.D.2d 189, 658 N.Y.S.2d 869 (N.Y. App.
Div. 1st Dep't 1997) . . . . . . . . . . . . . . . . . 1548, 1554-55

In re Worlds of Wonder Securities Litigation, [1990-
1991 Transfer Binder] Fed. Sec. L. Rep. (CCH)
¶ 95,689 (N.D. Cal. Oct. 19, 1990) . . . . . . . . . . . . . . . 590

Worth v. Huntington Bancshares, Inc., 1987 Ohio
App. LEXIS 9827, 1987 WL 25694 (Ohio Ct. App.
Nov. 25, 1987), aff'd in part and rev'd in part, 540
N.E.2d 249 (Ohio 1989) . . . . . . . . . . . . . . . . . . . 85, 1320

Worth v. Huntington Bancshares, Inc., 540 N.E.2d
249 (Ohio 1989) . . . . . . . . . . . . . . . . 1297, 1302, 1308-09

W.R. Grace & Co. v. Rubber Workers, 461 U.S. 757
(1983) . . . . . . . . . . . . . . . . . . . . . . . . . . . . . . . . 2086

Wyles v. Campbell, 77 F. Supp. 343 (D. Del. 1948) . . . . . 309

Wyser-Pratte v. Smith, 23 Del. J. Corp. L. 369 (Del.
Ch. Mar. 18, 1997) . . . . . . . . . . . . . . . . . . . . . . 1241-43

Xebec Development Partners, Ltd. v. National Union
Fire Insurance Co., 12 Cal. App. 4th 501, 15 Cal.
Rptr. 2d 726 (Cal. Ct. App. 1993) . . . . . . . . . . . . . . 1995

In re Xonics, Inc., 99 B.R. 870 (Bankr. N.D. Ill.
1989) . . . . . . . . . . . . . . . . . . 597, 598, 599, 602-03, 628

Yampol v. Packer, Nos. 115, 116 (Del. Apr. 22,
1986) . . . . . . . . . . . . . . . . . . . . . . . . . . . . . . 1080

Yanow v. Scientific Leasing, Inc. [1987-1988 Transfer
Binder] Fed. Sec. L. Rep. (CCH) ¶ 93,660 (Del. Ch.
Feb. 5, 1988) . . . . . . . . . . 64, 755, 912-13, 943-44, 958, 963

Yanow v. Scientific Leasing, Inc., [1991 Transfer
Binder] Fed. Sec. L. Rep. (CCH) ¶ 96,189 (Del. Ch.
July 31, 1991) . . . . . . . . . . . . . . . . . . . . . . . . . 64,
651, 652, 734, 755, 757, 758, 759-60, 766, 768-69, 943-44, 983

Yaw v. Talley, 1994 Del. Ch. LEXIS 35, 1994 WL
89019 (Del. Ch. Mar. 2, 1994)
. . . . . . . . . . . . . 1428, 1430-31, 1455, 1509-10, 1523, 1581

Yiannatsis v. Stephanis, 653 A.2d 275 (Del. 1995)
. . . . . . . . . . . . . . . . . . . . . 275, 294, 295, 304, 528, 1882

Yost v. Early, 589 Λ.2d 1291 (Md. Ct. Spec. App.),
cert. denied, 596 A.2d 628 (Md. 1991) . . . . . . . . 4-5, 23, 111

Young v. Valhi, Inc., 382 A.2d 1372 (Del Ch. 1978) . . . . 1251

Youngman v. Tahmoush, 457 A.2d 376 (Del. Ch.
1983) . . . . . . . . . . . . . . . . . . . . . . . 1400, 1402, 1403

Zaborac v. American Casualty Co., 663 F. Supp. 330
(C.D. Ill. 1987) . . . . . . . . . . . . . . . . . . . . 2096-97, 2107

Zahn v. Transamerica Corp., 162 F.2d 36 (3d Cir.
1947) . . . . . . . . . . . . . . . . . . . . . . . . . . . . 582-83

Zapata Corp. v. Maldonado, 430 A.2d 779 (Del.
1981) . . . . . . . . . . . . . . . . . . . . . . . . . . 273, 1450,
1573, 1610, 1690, 1694-95, 1703, 1708, 1711, 1713-14, 1721-22,
1728, 1738, 1745, 1780, 1786, 1795, 1800, 1809, 1810, 1813

Zarowitz v. BankAmerica Corp, 866 F.2d 1164 (9th
Cir. 1989) . . . . . . . . . . . . . . . . . . . . . . . . . . 1399

Zauber v. Murray Savings Association, 591 S.W.2d
932 (Tex. Civ. App. 1979), error refused, 601
S.W.2d 940 (Tex. 1980) . . . . . . . . . . . . . . . 1450, 1612

ZB Holdings, Inc. v. White, 144 F.R.D. 42 (S.D.N.Y.
1992) . . . . . . . . . . . . . . . . . . . . . . . . . 1382, 1421, 1425

Zetlin v. Hanson Holdings, Inc., 48 N.Y.2d 684, 397
N.E.2d 387, 421 N.Y.S.2d 877 (1979) . . . . . . . . . . . . 364

Ziegler v. American Maize-Products Co., 658 A.2d
219 (Me. 1995) . . . . . . . . . . . . . . . . . . . . . . . . 850

Zimmerman v. Bell, 585 F. Supp. 512 (D. Md.
1984) . . . . . . . . . . . . . . . . . 1300, 1301, 1455, 1688-89

Zimmerman v. Bell, 800 F.2d 386 (4th Cir. 1986)
. . . . . . . . . . . . . . . . . . . . . . . 23, 1382, 1408, 1409

Zirn v. VLI Corp., [1990-1991 Transfer Binder] Fed.
Sec. L. Rep. (CCH) ¶ 95,862 (Del. Ch. Feb. 15,
1991) . . . . . . . . . . . . . . . . . . . . . . . . . . . . . 347

Zirn v. VLI Corp., 18 Del. J. Corp. L. 803 (Del. Ch.
June 10, 1992), rev'd, 621 A.2d 773 (Del. 1993) . . . . . . . . 347

Zirn v. VLI Corp., 621 A.2d 773 (Del. 1993) . . . . . 230, 512-14

Zirn v. VLI Corp., 1995 Del. Ch. LEXIS 74, 1995
WL 362616 (Del. Ch. June 12, 1995), aff'd, 681 A.2d
1050 (Del. 1996) . . . . . . . . . . . . . . . . . . . . . . . . . 514, 515

Zirn v. VLI Corp., 681 A.2d 1050 (Del. 1996)
. . . . . . . . . . . . . . . . . . . . . . . . . . 227, 278, 230, 347,
490, 499, 507, 508, 513, 516, 519, 521, 527, 530, 536-37, 538

Zitin v. Turley, [1991 Transfer Binder] Fed. Sec. L.
Rep. (CCH) ¶ 96,123 (D. Ariz. June 20, 1991), interlocutory appeal denied, [1991 Transfer Binder] Fed.
Sec. L. Rep. (CCH) ¶ 96,284 (D. Ariz. Sept. 19,
1991) . . . . . . . . . . . . . . . . . . . . . . . . . 1780, 1795, 1825

Zupnick v. Goizueta, 698 A.2d 384 (Del. Ch. 1997)
. . . . . . . . . . . 94, 96, 314, 315, 321, 323, 328, 333, 334-36

**Federal Statutes and Rules:**

Antitrust Procedures and Penalties Act, 15 U.S.C.
§ 16 . . . . . . . . . . . . . . . . . . . . . . . . . . . . . . . . . . . 1338

Clayton Act, 15 U.S.C. § 18 . . . . . . . . . . . . . . . . . . 1333

Comprehensive Environmental Response, Compensation and Liability Act (CERCLA), 42 U.S.C. §§ 9601
et seq. . . . . . . . . . . . . . . . . . . . . . . . . . . . . . . . . . . 1953

Defense Production Act of 1950, 50 U.S.C. App.
§§ 2061-2170 . . . . . . . . . . . . . . . . . . . . . . . . . . . . 1339

Deficit Reduction Act of 1984, 26 U.S.C. §§ 280G,
4999 . . . . . . . . . . . . . . . . . . . . . . . . . . . . . . 320-21, 1319

Employee Retirement Income Security Act of 1974
(ERISA), 29 U.S.C. §§ 1001-1461 . . . . . . . . . . . 878-80, 897

Employment Retirement Income Security Act
(ERISA), 29 U.S.C. §§ 1001-1461 . . . . . . . . . . . . . . 2031

Financial Institutions Reform, Recovery and Enforcement Act of 1989 (FIRREA), Pub. L. 101-73, 103
Stat. 183 (1989) . . . . . . . . . . . . . . . . . . . . . . . . 2055, 2088

Foreign Corrupt Practices Act of 1977, 15 U.S.C.
§§ 78a note, 78m, 78dd-1, 78dd-2, 78ff . . . . . . . . . . . . 1467

Hobbs Act, 18 U.S.C. § 1951 . . . . . . . . . . . . . . . . . 1356

Investment Advisers Act of 1940, 15 U.S.C.
§§ 80b-1–89b-21 . . . . . . . . . . . . . . . . . . . . . . . . . 1767

Investment Company Act of 1940, 15 U.S.C. §§ 80a-
1–80a-64 . . . . . . 1407, 1414, 1415, 1461, 1682-83, 1767, 1866

Omnibus Trade and Competitiveness Act of 1988,
Pub. L. No. 102-99, 105 Stat. 487 (1991) (amending
the Defense Production Act to permanently reauthorize
the Exon-Florio provision of the Act, 50 U.S.C. App.
§ 2170) . . . . . . . . . . . . . . . . . . . . . . . . . . . . . . 1339

Omnibus Trade and Competitiveness Act of 1988,
Pub. L. No. 100-418, 102 Stat. 1107 § 5021 (1988)
(amending the Defense Production Act of 1950, 50
U.S.C. App. §§ 2061-2170) . . . . . . . . . . . . . . . . . . 1339

Private Securities Litigation Reform Act of 1995, Pub.
L. No. 104-67, 109 Stat. 737 (1995) . . . . . . . . . . . . . 2169

H.R. Conf. Rep. No. 104-369, 104th Cong., 1st Sess.
31 (1995), reprinted in 1995 U.S.C.C.A.N. 730
. . . . . . . . . . . . . . . . . . . . . . . . . . . . . . . . . . . 2169-70

Racketeer Influenced and Corrupt Organizations Act
(RICO), 18 U.S.C. §§ 1961–1968
. . . . . . . . . . . . . . . . . 1356, 1429, 1463, 1943, 1973, 2167

Securities Act of 1933, 15 U.S.C. §§ 77a-77aa
. . . . . . . . . . . . . . . . . . . . . . . . . 704, 1954, 1970, 2131

Securities Exchange Act of 1934, 15 U.S.C. §§ 78a-mm
. . . . . . . . . . . . . . . . . . . . . . . . 916, 1061, 1062, 1213,
1350, 1393, 1415, 1462, 1684-85, 1764, 1915, 1970, 1986, 2030

11 U.S.C. § 101(32)(A) . . . . . . . . . . . . . . . . . . . . . . 619

11 U.S.C. § 502 . . . . . . . . . . . . . . . . . . . . . . . . . 1984

11 U.S.C. § 510 . . . . . . . . . . . . . . . . . . . . . . . . . 1984

11 U.S.C. § 523(a)(4) . . . . . . . . . . . . . . . . . . . . . . 626

12 U.S.C. § 1729 . . . . . . . . . . . . . . . . . . . . . . . . 2091

12 U.S.C. § 1821(k) . . . . . . . . . . . . . . . . . . . . 249, 2088

26 U.S.C. § 162(m) . . . . . . . . . . . . . . . . . . . . . . . 320

26 U.S.C. § 5881 . . . . . . . . . . . . . . . . . . . . . . . . 1368

28 U.S.C. § 1332 . . . . . . . . . . . . . . . . . . . . . 1416, 1417

28 U.S.C. § 2072 . . . . . . . . . . . . . . . . . . . . . . . . 1457

Fed. R. Evid. 301 . . . . . . . . . . . . . . . . . . . . . . . . 111

Federal Rule of Civil Procedure 9  . . . . . . . . . . . . . . .  1682

Federal Rule of Civil Procedure 10 . . . . . . . . . . . . . . .  1618

Federal Rule of Civil Procedure 11 . . . . . . . . . . . . . . .  1344

Federal Rule of Civil Procedure 12 . . . . . . . . . . .  1481, 1715

Federal Rule of Civil Procedure 23.1
. . . . . . . . . . . . . 1385, 1398, 1408, 1427, 1572, 1686, 1715

Federal Rule of Civil Procedure 41 . . . . . . . . . . . . . . .  1715

Federal Rule of Civil Procedure 56 . . . . . . . . . . . . . . .  1715

**Federal Regulations, Administrative Releases and No-Action Letters:**

Department of the Treasury, Internal Revenue Service,
Excise Tax Relating to Gain or Other Income Realized
By Any Person on Receipt of Greenmail, 56 Fed. Reg.
65685 (1991) (codified at 26 C.F.R. § 156.5881-1)  . . . . .  1368

Department of the Treasury, Internal Revenue Service,
Golden Parachute Payments, 26 C.F.R. Part 1 . . . . . . .  1319-20

ERISA Interpretive Bulletin 75-8, 29 C.F.R.
§ 2509.75  . . . . . . . . . . . . . . . . . . . . . . . . . . . . .  885

Joint Committee on Taxation Staff Description of
Revenue Provisions Contained in President Clinton's
Fiscal Year 1997 Budget Proposal (JCS-2-96) (Mar.
27, 1996), reprinted in Daily Tax Report (BNA) No.
60, at L-1, L-33 (Mar. 28, 1996) . . . . . . . . . . . . . . .  2162

Joint Committee on Taxation Staff Description of
Revenue Provisions Contained in President Clinton's

Fiscal Year 1998 Budget Proposal (JCS-10-97) (Apr. 16, 1997), reprinted in Daily Tax Report (BNA) No. 74, at L-30, L-59 (Apr. 17, 1997) . . . . . . . . . . . . . 2161-62

Letter from Department of Labor to Ian D. Lanoff (Sept. 28, 1995), reprinted in 22 Pens. & Ben. Rep. (BNA) 2249 (Oct. 9, 1995) . . . . . . . . . . . . 888-89, 892, 901

Letter from Department of Labor to Unnamed Corporation (Feb. 23, 1989), reprinted in 16 Pens. & Ben. Rep. (BNA) 390-91 (Mar. 6, 1989) and II Mergers & Acquisitions L. Rep. 426-27 (Apr. 1989) . . . . . . . . . 889, 891

Letter from Department of Labor to John Welch (Apr. 30, 1984), reprinted in 11 Pens. & Ben. Rep. (BNA) 633 (May 7, 1984) . . . . . . . . . . . . . . . . . . . . . . . . . . 888-89

Joint Department of Labor/Department of Treasury Statement on Pension Investments, 6 Pension Plan Guide (CCH) ¶ 23,770R (Jan. 31, 1989) . . . . . . . . . . . . 879

Securities & Exchange Commission v. Evans, SEC Litigation Release No. 12315 [1989-1990 Transfer Binder] Fed. Sec. L. Rep. (CCH) ¶ 94,802 (Dec. 6, 1989) . . . . . . . . . . . . . . . . . . . . . . . . . . . . . . . . . . . 855

Securities and Exchange Commission, Division of Corporate Finance, Registration of Rights Issuable Pursuant to Stockholder Rights Plans, [1987 Transfer Binder] Fed. Sec. L. Rep. (CCH) ¶ 78,411 (Jan. 7, 1987) . . . . . . . . . . . . . . . . . . . . . . . . . . . . . . . . . . 1134

Exchange Act Release No. 34-23421, 51 Fed. Reg. 25873 (July 17, 1986), reprinted in [1986-1987 Transfer Binder] Fed. Sec. L. Rep. (CCH) ¶ 84,016 . . . . . . . . 1010

Exchange Act Release No. 34-23951, 52 Fed. Reg.
1574 (Jan. 14, 1987) . . . . . . . . . . . . . . . . . . . . . . . . . 1057

Exchange Act Release No. 34-24623, 52 Fed. Reg.
23665 (June 24, 1987) . . . . . . . . . . . . . . . 1053, 1056, 1057

Exchange Act Release No. 34-25891, 53 Fed. Reg.
26376 (July 12, 1988) . . . . . . 1053, 1056, 1057, 1058, 1059-60

Exchange Act Release No. 34-34518, 59 Fed. Reg.
42614 (Aug. 18, 1994) . . . . . . . . . . . . . . . . . . . . . . . 1064

Exchange Act Release No. 34-35121, 59 Fed. Reg.
66570 (Dec. 19, 1994) . . . . . . . . . . . . 1064, 1065-68, 1135

Securities Act Release No. 33-6653, 51 Fed. Reg.
25873 (July 17, 1986), reprinted in [1986-1987 Transfer Binder] Fed. Sec. L. Rep. (CCH) ¶ 84,016 . . . . . . . . 1010

In re BF Goodrich Co., Exchange Act Release No.
34-22792, [1985-1986 Transfer Binder] Fed. Sec. L.
Rep. (CCH) ¶ 83,958 (Jan. 15, 1986) . . . . . . . . . . . . . 1350

Crane Co., SEC No-Action Letter, 1990 SEC No-Act
LEXIS 3, 1990 WL 286158 (S.E.C.) (Jan. 8, 1990) . . . . . 1322

Mobil Corp., SEC No-Action Letter, 1996 SEC
No-Act LEXIS 34, 1996 WL 15896 (Jan. 16, 1996) . . . . . 1195

Pittston Co., SEC No-Action Letter, 1990 SEC
No-Act LEXIS 328, 1990 WL 286484 (S.E.C.)
(Feb. 15, 1990) . . . . . . . . . . . . . . . . . . . . . . . . . . . 1322

PLM International, Inc., SEC No-Action Letter, 1997
SEC No-Act LEXIS 575, 1997 WL 219918 (Apr. 28,
1997) . . . . . . . . . . . . . . . . . . . . . . . . . . . . . . . . . . 1195

Rowan Cos., SEC No-Action Letter, 1995 SEC
No-Act LEXIS 995, 1995 WL 765431 (Dec. 28,
1995) ........................................ 1195

TPI Enterprises, Inc., SEC No-Action Letter,
1990 SEC No-Act LEXIS 480, 1990 WL 286197
(S.E.C.) (Mar. 13, 1990) ....................... 1322

Transamerica Corp., SEC No-Action Letter, 1990
SEC No-Act LEXIS 46, 1990 WL 285806 (S.E.C.)
(Jan. 10, 1990) ............................... 1322

Office of the Chief Economist of the Securities and
Exchange Commission, The Effects of Poison Pills on
the Wealth of Target Shareholders (Oct. 23, 1986) ...... 1086

Rev. Rul. 77-316, 1977-2 C.B. 53 ............... 2157

In re W.R. Grace & Co, Exchange Act Release Nos.
39156 & 39157 reprinted in [1997 Transfer Binder]
Fed. Sec. L. Rep. (CCH) ¶ 85,963 (Sept. 30, 1997) .... 211-14

12 C.F.R. § 121 ........................... 1983

12 C.F.R. § 545.121 .. 1855, 1866, 1880, 1894, 1906, 1932, 1962

12 C.F.R. § 549.3 .......................... 2091

12 C.F.R. § 563.17 ......................... 2079

17 C.F.R. § 229.510 ........................ 1975

17 C.F.R. § 229.512 ........................ 1975

17 C.F.R. § 230.144 ........................ 704

17 C.F.R. § 230.461 ........................ 1975

17 C.F.R. § 240.10b-5 . . . . . . . . . . . . . . . . . . 1983, 1987

17 C.F.R. § 240.13e-4 . . . . . . . . . . . . . . . . . . 1010, 1134

17 C.F.R. § 240.14a . . . . . . . . . . . . . . . . . . . . . 1213

17 C.F.R. § 240.14d-10 . . . . . . . . . . . . . . . . . . . 1134

17 C.F.R. § 240.19c-4 . . . . . . . . . . . . . . . . . . . 1058-59

**Stock Exchange Rules and Decisions:**

AMEX Company Guide § 712 . . . . . . . . . . . . . . . . . . 834

AMEX Company Guide § 713 . . . . . . . . . . . . . . . . . . 834

NASD Manual, Chapter Marketplace Rule 4460 . . . . . . . . 834

New York Stock Exchange Listed Company Manual
§ 312.03 . . . . . . . . . . . . . . . . . . . . . . . . . . . . 834

Jett v. Kidder Peabody & Co., No. 94-01696 (NASD
Regulation, Inc. Jan. 26, 1988) . . . . . . . . . . . . . . . . 1869

**State Statutes:**

Ala. Bus. Corp. Act § 10-2B-8.57 . . . . . . . . . . . . . . 2157

Alaska Corp. Code § 10.06.435 . . . . . . . . . . . . . 1665, 1697

Ariz. Bus. Corp. Act § 10-742 . . . . . . . . . . . . . . . . 1564

Ariz. Bus. Corp. Act § 10-744 . . . . . . . . . . . . . . 1658-59

Ariz. Bus. Corp. Law § 10-857 . . . . . . . . . . . . . . . . 2157

Ariz. Gen. Corp. Law § 10-2705 . . . . . . . . . . . . . . . 1321

Cal. Gen. Corp. Law § 204 . . . . . . . . . . . . 233, 1887, 1961

Cal. Gen. Corp. Law § 309 . . . . . . . . . . . . 2, 131, 199, 202

Cal. Gen. Corp. Law § 310 . . . . . . . . . . . . . 288, 289, 1903

Cal. Gen. Corp. Law § 317 . . . 1855, 1862, 1865, 1867, 1872, 1876, 1880, 1881, 1882, 1884, 1887, 1888, 1889, 1891, 1893, 1895, 1903, 1906, 1907, 1908, 1937-40, 1947, 1952-53, 1959, 1980, 2156

Former Cal. Gen. Corp. Law § 317 . . . . . . . . 1856, 1857, 1884

Cal. Gen. Corp. Code § 800
. . . . . . . . . . . . . . . . . . . . . . 1387, 1405, 1427, 1572, 1687

Cal. Ins. Code § 336 . . . . . . . . . . . . . . . . . . . . . . . . . 2148

Colo. Bus. Corp. Act § 7-106-205 . . . . . . . . . . . . . . . . . 1102

Colo. Bus. Corp. Act § 7-109-108 . . . . . . . . . . . . . . . . . 2157

Colo. Rev. Stat. § 11-3-120 . . . . . . . . . . . . . . . . . . . . . 2092

Colo. Rev. Stat. § 11-22-116 . . . . . . . . . . . . . . . . . . . . 2092

Colo. Rev. Stat. § 11-23-117.5 . . . . . . . . . . . . . . . . . . . 2092

Colo. Rev. Stat. § 11-41-134 . . . . . . . . . . . . . . . . . . . . 2092

Conn. Bus. Corp. Act § 33-636 . . . . . . . . . . . . . . . . . . . . 237

Conn. Bus. Corp. Act § 33-722 . . . . . . . . . . . . . . . 1564, 1658

Conn. Bus. Corp. Act § 33-724 . . . . . . . . . . . . . . . . . . 1658

Conn. Bus. Corp. Act § 33-756 . . . . . . . . . . . . . . . . 596, 816

Del. Gen. Corp. Law § 102
. . . . . . . . . . . . . . . . . 152, 167, 226-28, 231, 614, 1052, 2168

Del. Gen. Corp. Law § 109 . . . . . . . . . . . . . . . . . . . . . . 1245

Del. Gen. Corp. Law § 122 . . . . . . . . . . . . . . . . . . 321, 1485

Del. Gen. Corp. Law § 141 . . . . . . . . . 201, 208, 309, 614, 1810

Del. Gen. Corp. Law § 144 . . . . . . . . . . . . 268, 270, 276, 289

Del. Gen. Corp. Law § 151 . . . . . . . . . . . . . . . . . . 648, 1141

Del. Gen. Corp. Law § 145
. . . 1498, 1855, 1856, 1857, 1863, 1867, 1872, 1876, 1880, 1881,
1882, 1883, 1888-89, 1891, 1892, 1895, 1896, 1900, 1907,
1908, 1911, 1934, 1938-39, 1947, 1952-54, 1959, 1963, 1965, 1980

Del. Gen. Corp. Law Ch. 120, L. '97 Synopsis of
Section 145 . . . . . . . . . . . . . . . . . . . . . . . . . . . 1867, 1889

Former Del. Gen. Corp. Law § 145 . . . . . . . . . . . . . . . 1896

Del. Gen. Corp. Law § 151 . . . . . . . . . . . . . . . . . 648, 1141

Del. Gen. Corp. Law § 157 . . . . . . . . . . . . . . . . . . 321, 322

Del. Gen. Corp. Law § 160 . . . . . . . . . . . . . . . . . . . . 1004

Del. Gen. Corp. Law § 202 . . . . . . . . . . . . . . . . . . . . 1141

Del. Gen. Corp. Law § 203 . . . . . . . . . . . . . . . 875, 877-78

Del. Gen. Corp. Law § 211 . . . . . . . . . . . . . . . 1221, 1246

Del. Gen. Corp. Law § 212 . . . . . . . . . . . . . . . 1052, 1054

Del. Gen. Corp. Law § 213 . . . . . . . . . . . . . . . . . . . . 1241

Del. Gen. Corp. Law § 220 . . . . . . . . . . . . . . . . . . . . 1680

Del. Gen. Corp. Law § 222 . . . . . . . . . . . . . . . . . . . . 501

Del. Gen. Corp. Law § 226 . . . . . . . . . . . . . . . . . . . . 1289

Del. Gen. Corp. Law § 228 . . . . . . . . . . 396, 496, 1253, 1274

Del. Gen. Corp. Law § 242 . . . . . . . . . . . . . . 501, 529, 1052

Del. Gen. Corp. Law § 251 . . . . . . . . . . 218, 529, 983, 1182

Del. Gen. Corp. Law § 262 . . . . . . . . . . . . . . . . . . . . 478

Del. Gen. Corp. Law § 271 . . . . . . . . . . . . . . . . . . . . 529

Del. Gen. Corp. Law § 327 . . . . . . . . . . . . . . . . . . . . 1385

6 Del. C. § 1518 . . . . . . . . . . . . . . . . . . . . . . . . . . 1811

6 Del. C. § 17-403 . . . . . . . . . . . . . . . . . . . . . . . . . 1810

6 Del. C. § 17-1001 . . . . . . . . . . . . . . . . . . . . . 1805, 1810

6 Del. C. § 17-1003 . . . . . . . . . . . . . . . . . . . . . 1805, 1810

6 Del. C. § 17-1101 . . . . . . . . . . . . . . . . . . . . . . . . . 1811

10 Del. C. § 8106 . . . . . . . . . . . . . . . . . . . . . . . . . . 1868

10 Del. C. § 8111 . . . . . . . . . . . . . . . . . . . . . . . . . . 1868

Del. Ch. Ct. R. 9 . . . . . . . . . . . . . . . . . . . . . . . . . . 1682

Del. Ch. R. 12 . . . . . . . . . . . . . . . . . . . . . . . . . . . 1715

Del. Ch. R. 23.1 . . . . . . . . . . 1385, 1400, 1408, 1427, 1715

Del. Ch. R. 41 . . . . . . . . . . . . . . . . . . . . . . . . . . 1715

Fla. Bus. Corp. Act § 607.07401 . . . . . . . . . . . 1564, 1658-60

Fla. Bus. Corp. Act § 607.0831 . . . . . . . . . . . . . . . . . 239

Ga. Bus. Corp. Code § 14-2-601 & Comments . . . . . . . . 1102

Ga. Bus. Corp. Code § 14-2-624 & Comments . . . . . . . . 1102

Ga. Bus. Corp. Code § 14-2-742 . . . . . . . . . . . . 1564, 1658

Ga. Bus. Corp. Code § 14-2-744 . . . . . . . . . . . . . . 1659-60

Ga. Bus. Corp. Code § 14-2-830 . . . . . . . . . . . . . . . . . 808

Ga. Bus. Corp. Code § 14-2-853 . . . . . . . . . . . . . . . . 1902

Ga. Bus. Corp. Code § 14-2-854 . . . . . . . . . . . . . . . . 1934

Ga. Bus. Corp. Code § 14-2-1111 . . . . . . . . . . . . . . . 1188

Ga. Bus. Corp. Code § 14-2-1133 . . . . . . . . . . . . . . . 1188

Haw. Bus. Corp. Act § 415-35 . . . . . . . . . . . . . . . . . 2157

Ill. Bus. Corp. Act § 5/7.80 . . . . . . . . . . . . . . . . . . 1598

Ill. Bus. Corp. Act § 6.05 . . . . . . . . . . . . . . . . . . . 1102

Ill. Bus. Corp. Act § 8.75 . . . . . . . . . . . . . . . . . . . 1861

Ind. Bus. Corp. Law § 23-1-32-4 . . . . . . . . . . . . . . 1697-98

Ind. Bus. Corp. Law § 23-1-35-1
. . . . . . . . . . . . . . . . . . . . 239, 688, 730, 816, 1108, 1124

Ind. Bus. Corp. Law § 23-1-37-11 . . . . . . . . . . . . . . . 1935

Ky. Bus. Corp. Act § 271B.8-300 . . . . . . . . . . . . . . . 239

La. Bus. Corp. Law § 12:83 . . . . . . . . . . . 1861, 1978, 2157

La. Bus. Corp. Law § 12:92 . . . . . . . . . . . . . . . . . . 814

Md. Gen. Corp. Law § 2-418 . . . . . . . . . . . . . . 1861, 2157

Mass. Bus. Corp. Law § 50A . . . . . . . . . . . . . . . . . . 1246

Mass. Bus. Corp. Law § 67 . . . . . . . . . . . . . . . . . . . 1948

Mass. Gen. Laws Ch. 149, § 183 . . . . . . . . . . . . . . . . 1327

Me. Bus. Corp. Act § 507 . . . . . . . . . . . . . . . . . . 850, 851

Me. Bus. Corp. Act § 630 . . . . . . . . . . . . . . . . 1564, 1658

Me. Bus. Corp. Act § 632 . . . . . . . . . . . . . . . . . . . 1661

Me. Bus. Corp. Act § 716 . . . . . . . . . . . . . . . . . . . . 239

Me. Bus. Corp. Act § 719 . . . . . . . . . . . . . . . . . . . 1978

Me. Bus. Corp. Act § 902 . . . . . . . . . . . . . . . . . . 850, 851

Mich. Bus. Corp. Act § 450.1107 . . . . . . . . . . . . 1662, 1829

Mich. Bus. Corp. Act § 450.1491a . . . . . . . . . . . . . . . 1661

Mich. Bus. Corp. Act § 450.1493a . . . . . . . . . . . 1564, 1658

Mich. Bus. Corp. Act § 450.1495 . . . . . . . . . 1661-62, 1830

Mich. Bus. Corp. Act § 450.1505 . . . . . . . . . . . . . . 1662

Minn. Bus. Corp. Act § 302A.241 . . . . . . . . . . . . . . 1698

Minn. Bus. Corp. Act § 302A.243 . . . . . . . . . . . . . . 1699

Minn. Bus. Corp. Act § 302A.255 . . . . . . . . . . . . . . 1321

Minn. Bus. Corp. Act § 302A.521 . . . . 1873, 1892, 1931, 1961

1989 Minn. Laws Ch. 172, § 12 . . . . . . . . . . . . . . . . 1699

Miss. Bus. Corp. Act § 79-4-7.42 . . . . . . . . . . . 1564, 1658

Miss. Bus. Corp. Act § 79-4-7.44 . . . . . . . . . . . . . . 1658

Mo. Gen. & Bus. Corp. Law § 351.245 . . . . . . . . . . . 1273

Mont. Bus. Corp. Act § 35-1-543 . . . . . . . . . . . 1564, 1658

Mont. Bus. Corp. Act § 35-1-545 . . . . . . . . . . . . . . 1658

N.C. Bus. Corp. Act § 55-7-40 . . . . . . . . . . . . . . . . 1742

N.C. Bus. Corp. Act § 55-7-42 . . . . . . . . . . . . 1564, 1658

N.C. Bus. Corp. Act § 55-7-44 . . . . . . . . . . . . . . 1662-63

N.C. Bus. Corp. Act § 55-7-49 . . . . . . . . . . . . . . . . 1828

N.C. Bus. Corp. Act § 55-8-30 . . . . . . . . . . . 689, 730, 816

Former N.C. Bus. Corp. Act § 55-55 . . . . . . . . . . . . . 1742

N.D. Bus. Corp. Act § 10-19.1-48 . . . . . . . . . . . . . . 1698

N.D. Bus. Corp. Act § 10-19.1-91 . . . . . . . . . . . . 1873, 1892

N.H. Bus. Corp. Act § 293-A:7.42 . . . . . . . . . . 1564, 1658

N.H. Bus. Corp. Act § 293-A:7.44 . . . . . . . . . . . . . 1658

N.J. Bus. Corp. Act § 14A:3-5 . . . . . . . . . . . . . . . . 2157

N.J. Bus. Corp. Act § 14A:6-1 . . . . . . . . . . . . . . . . 689

N.J. Bus. Corp. Act § 14A:7-2 . . . . . . . . . . . . . . . . 1139

N.J. Bus. Corp. Act § 14A:7-7 . . . . . . . . . . 1102, 1132, 1140

N.M. Bus. Corp. Act § 53-11-4.1 . . . . . . . . . . . . 1978, 2157

N.Y. Bus. Corp. Law § 202 . . . . . . . . . . . . . . . . . . . 321

N.Y. Bus. Corp. Law § 402 . . . . . . . . . . . . . . . . . 231, 1052

N.Y. Bus. Corp. Law § 501 . . . . . . . . . . . . . . . . . . . 568

N.Y. Bus. Corp. Law § 505 . . . . . . . . . 321, 1102, 1103, 1190

N.Y. Bus. Corp. Law § 513 . . . . . . . . . . . . . . . . . . . 1365

N.Y. Bus. Corp. Law § 620 . . . . . . . . . . . . . . . . . . . 1185

N.Y. Bus. Corp. Law § 626 . . . . 1385, 1408, 1427, 1572, 1687

N.Y. Bus. Corp. Law § 627 . . . . . . . . . . . . . . . . . . . 1404

N.Y. Bus. Corp. Law § 713 . . . . . . . . . . 270, 288, 289, 309

N.Y. Bus. Corp. Law § 717 . . . . . . . . . . . . 2, 123, 596, 813

N.Y. Bus. Corp. Law § 719 . . . . . . . . . . . . . . . . . . . . . 231

N.Y. Bus. Corp. Law § 721 . . . . . . . . . . . 1855, 1856, 1960

N.Y. Bus. Corp. Law § 722 . . . . . . . 1855, 1856, 1872, 1873,
1876, 1877, 1880, 1881, 1882, 1884, 1938-39, 1947, 1952, 1959

Former N.Y. Bus. Corp. Law § 722 . . . . . . . . . . . . . . 1881

N.Y. Bus. Corp. Law § 723 . . . . . . . . . . . 1855, 1856, 1857,
1865, 1873, 1888, 1889, 1891, 1892, 1895, 1902, 1906, 1908, 1952

N.Y. Bus. Corp. Law § 724 . . . . . . 1855, 1856, 1936, 1938-40

Former N.Y. Bus. Corp. Law § 724 . . . . . . . . . . . 1865, 1903

N.Y. Bus. Corp. Law § 725
. . . . . . . . . . . . . . 1855, 1856, 1902, 1906, 1941, 1946, 1979

N.Y. Bus. Corp. Law § 726
. . . . . . . . . . . . . . . . . . 1638, 1855, 1856, 1979, 1981-82

N.Y. Bus. Corp. Law § 803 . . . . . . . . . . . . . . . . . . . 1052

N.Y. Bus. Corp. Law § 903 . . . . . . . . . . . . . . . . . . . . 983

N.Y. Bus. Corp. Law § 912 . . . . . . . . . . . . . . . 1103, 1365

N.Y. Bus. Corp. Law § 1320 . . . . . . . . . . . . . . 1945, 1946

N.Y. Debt. & Cred. Law § 271 . . . . . . . . . . . . . . . . . 619

N.Y. Ins. Law § 4312 . . . . . . . . . . . . . . . . . . . . . . 309

Neb. Bus. Corp. Act § 21-2072 . . . . . . . . . . . . . 1564, 1658

Neb. Bus. Corp. Act § 21-2074 . . . . . . . . . . . . . . . . 1658

Nev. Gen. Corp. Law § 78.138 . . . . . . . . . . . . . . . . . 813

Nev. Gen. Corp. Law § 78.330 . . . . . . . . . . . . . . . . . 1238

Nev. Gen. Corp. Law § 78.752 . . . . . . . . . . . 1978-79, 2157

Ohio Gen. Corp. Law § 1701.13 . . . . . . . . . 1892, 1978, 2157

Ohio Gen. Corp. Law § 1701.59 . . . . . 240, 689, 730, 814, 816

Ohio Gen. Corp. Law § 1701.60 . . . . . . . . . . . . . . . 268-69

Ohio Sec. Law § 1707.043 . . . . . . . . . . . . . . . . . 1366-67

Okla. Gen. Corp. Act § 1013 . . . . . . . . . . . . . . . . . 1198

Okla. Gen. Corp. Act § 1038 . . . . . . . . . . . . . . . 1198-99

Pa. Bus. Corp. Law § 515 . . . . . . . 690-91, 730, 815-16, 1193

Pa. Bus. Corp. Law § 518 . . . . . . . . . . . . . . 1968-69, 1978

Pa. Bus. Corp. Law § 1525 . . . . . . . . . . . . . . . . . . 1102

Pa. Bus. Corp. Law § 1711 . . . . . . . . . . . . . . . . . . . 240

Pa. Bus. Corp. Law § 1715 . . . . 24, 241, 690-91, 815-16, 1193

Pa. Bus. Corp. Law § 1743 . . . . . . . . . . . . . . . . . . 1861

Pa. Bus. Corp. Law § 1746 . . . . . . 1887, 1968-69, 1978, 2157

Pa. Bus. Corp. Law § 1782 . . . . . . . . . . . . . . 1387, 1404

Pa. Bus. Corp. Law § 2513 . . . . . . . . . . . . . . . . . . 1102

Pa. Bus. Corp. Law § 2573 . . . . . . . . . . . . . . . . . . . 1367

Pa. Bus. Corp. Law § 2575 . . . . . . . . . . . . . . . . . . . 1367

Pa. Bus. Corp. Law § 2581 . . . . . . . . . . . . . . . . . . . 1327

Pa. Bus. Corp. Law § 2582 . . . . . . . . . . . . . . . . . . . 1327

Pa. Corp. Law § 511 . . . . . . . . . . . . . . . . . . . . . . . . . 240

Pa. Corp. Law § 515 . . . . . . . . . . . . . . . . . . . . . . . 24, 241

Pa. Corp. Law § 516 . . . . . . . . . . . . . . . . . . . . . . . . . 240

Pa. Corp. Law § 518 . . . . . . . . . . . . . . . . . . . . . . . . . 2157

R.I. Bus. Combination Act § 7-5.2-8 . . . . . . . . . . . . . 1193

R.I. Gen. Laws § 28-7-19.2 . . . . . . . . . . . . . . . . . . . 1327

S.D. Bus. Corp. Act § 47-33-4 . . . . . . . . . . . . . . . . . 1193

Tex. Bus. Corp. Act § 1.02 . . . . . . . . . . . . . . . 71-74, 1663

Tex. Bus. Corp. Act § 2.02-1 . . . . . . . . . 1948, 1978-79, 2157

Tex. Bus. Corp. Act § 5.14 . . . . . . 1564, 1571, 1658, 1663-64

Utah Bus. Corp. Act § 16-10a-840 . . . . . . . . . . . . . . . . 239

Utah Bus. Corp. Act § 16-10a-908 . . . . . . . . . . . . . . . 2157

Va. Stock Corp. Act § 13.1-646 . . . . . . . . . . . . . . . . 1102

Va. Stock Corp. Act § 13.1-672.1 . . . . . . . . . . . 1564, 1658

Va. Stock Corp. Act § 13.1-672.4 . . . . . . . . . . . . . 1664-65

Va. Stock Corp. Act § 13.1-690
. . 2, 124, 137, 234-36, 240, 730, 816, 1106, 1155, 1194, 1324

Va. Stock Corp. Act § 13.1-692.1 . . . . . . . . . . . . . . . . . 234

Va. Stock Corp. Act § 13.1-704 . . . . . . . . . . . . . . . . . 1887

Va. Stock Corp. Act § 13.1-728.9
. . . . . . . . . . . . . . . . . . . . 692, 728, 816, 1155, 1194, 1324

Vt. Bus. Corp. Act § 8.50 . . . . . . . . . . . . . . . . . . . . . 1892

Wis. Bus. Corp. Law § 180.0624 . . . . . . . . . . . . . . . . . 1102

Wis. Bus. Corp. Law § 180.0742 . . . . . . . . . . . . . . 1564, 1568

Wis. Bus. Corp. Law § 180.0744 . . . . . . . . . . . . . . . . . 1658

Wis. Bus. Corp. Law § 180.0828 . . . . . . . . . . . . . . 240, 242

Wis. Bus. Corp. Law § 180.0851 . . . . . . . . . . . . . . . . . 1873

Wis. Bus. Corp. Law § 180.0859 . . . . . . . . . . . . . . . . . 1976

**Model Statutes, Restatements and Recommendations:**

Committee on Corporate Laws, Changes in the Model
Business Corporation Act—Amendments Pertaining to
Indemnification and Advance for Expenses, 49 Bus.
Law. 741 (1994) . . . . . . . . . . . 1857, 1885, 1904, 1937, 1962

Committee on Corporate Laws, Changes in the Model
Business Corporation Act—Amendments Pertaining to
Electronic Filings/Standards of Conduct and Standards

of Liability for Directors, 53 Bus. Law. 157 (1997)
. . . . . . . . . . . . . . . . . . . . . . 27, 100, 102-03, 119

Committee on Corporate Laws, Corporate Director's
Guidebook—1994 Edition, 49 Bus. Law. 1243 (1994)
. . . . . . . . . . . . . . . . . . 1, 118-19, 262-63, 266-67, 296

Committee on Corporate Laws, Guidelines for the
Unaffiliated Director of the Controlled Corporation,
44 Bus. Law. 211 (1988) . . . . . . . . . . . . . . . . . . . . . 471-76

Committee on Corporate Laws, Other Constituency
Statutes: Potential for Confusion, 45 Bus. Law. 2253
(1990) . . . . . . . . . . . . . . . . . . . . . . . . . . . . . . . . . 817

1 Model Business Corporation Act Annotated § 2.02
(3d ed. 1996) . . . . . . . . . . . . . . . . . 234, 1878, 2168, 2174

1 Model Business Corporation Act Annotated § 2.06
(3d ed. 1996) . . . . . . . . . . . . . . . . . . . . . . . . . . . . . 1245

1 Model Business Corporation Act Annotated § 3.02
(3d ed. 1996) . . . . . . . . . . . . . . . . . . . . . . . . . . . . . . 321

1 Model Business Corporation Act Annotated § 6.01
(3d ed. 1996) . . . . . . . . . . . . . . . . . . . . . . . . . . . . . 1052

1 Model Business Corporation Act Annotated § 6.24
Official Comment (3d ed. 1996) . . . . . . . . . . . 318, 321, 324

2 Model Business Corporation Act Annotated § 7.21
(3d ed. 1996) . . . . . . . . . . . . . . . . . . . . . . . . . . . . . 1052

2 Model Business Corporation Act Annotated § 7.40-
7.47 Introductory Comment (3d ed. 1996) . . . . . . . . . . . 1384

2 Model Business Corporation Act Annotated § 7.41
(3d ed. 1996) . . . . . . . . . . . . . . . 1386, 1387, 1397, 1403

2 Model Business Corporation Act Annotated § 7.42
& Official Comment (3d ed. 1996) . . . . 1562, 1563, 1570, 1687

2 Model Business Corporation Act Annotated § 7.43
(3d ed. 1996) . . . . . . . . . . . . . . . . . . . . . . . 1570, 1785

2 Model Business Corporation Act Annotated § 7.44
& Official Comment (3d ed. 1996)
. . . . . . . . . . . . . . . . . 1656-58, 1660, 1676, 1782, 1799

2 Model Business Corporation Act Annotated § 7.45
(3d ed. 1996) . . . . . . . . . . . . . . . . . . . . . . . . . . 1408

2 Model Business Corporation Act Annotated § 7.46
(3d ed. 1996) . . . . . . . . . . . . . . . . . . . . . . . . . . 1406

2 Model Business Corporation Act Annotated § 7.47
(3d ed. 1996) . . . . . . . . . . . . . . . . . . . . . . . . . . 1458

2 Model Business Corporation Act Annotated § 8.11
(3d ed. 1996) . . . . . . . . . . . . . . . . . . . . . . . . . . 309

2 Model Business Corporation Act Annotated § 8.24
(3d ed. 1996) . . . . . . . . . . . . . . . . . . . . . . . . . . 1904

2 Model Business Corporation Act Annotated § 8.30
& Official Comment (3d ed. 1996)
. . . . . . . . . . . . . . . . . . . . 2, 100, 109, 117, 118, 200, 1905

Proposed Model Business Corporation Act § 8.30
Official Comment in Committee on Corporate Laws,
Changes in the Model Business Corporation Act—
Amendments Pertaining to Electronic Filings/Standards

of Conduct and Standards of Liability for Directors,
53 Bus. Law. 157 (1997) . . . . . . . . . . . . . . . . . . . . . 2, 80,
84, 85, 100, 101, 120-23, 126, 127, 133, 140, 199, 201, 203, 216

Proposed Model Business Corporation Act § 8.31 &
Official Comment in Committee on Corporate Laws,
Changes in the Model Business Corporation Act—
Amendments Pertaining to Electronic Filings/Standards
of Conduct and Standards of Liability for Directors,
53 Bus. Law. 157 (1997) . . . . . . . . 4, 6, 7, 25, 27, 42, 47, 75,
80-81, 83, 85, 100, 104, 109-10, 112, 113, 128, 134, 137, 168, 273

2 Model Business Corporation Act Annotated § 8.42
(3d ed. 1996) . . . . . . . . . . . . . . . . . . . . . . . . . . . . . 100

2 Model Business Corporation Act Annotated § 8.50
& Official Comment (3d ed. 1996)
 . . . . . . . . . . 1854, 1855, 1876, 1890, 1908, 1952, 1959, 1969

2 Model Business Corporation Act Annotated § 8.51
& Official Comment (3d ed. 1996) . . .   1854, 1855, 1872, 1876,
1877-78, 1880, 1881, 1884, 1885, 1938, 1947, 1952-53, 1959, 1969

2 Model Business Corporation Act Annotated § 8.52
& Official Comment (3d ed. 1996)
 . . . . . . . . . . . . . 1854, 1855, 1858, 1859, 1865, 1952, 1969

2 Model Business Corporation Act Annotated § 8.53
& Official Comment (3d ed. 1996) . . . . . . . . . . . . . . 1854,
1855, 1894, 1895, 1903, 1904, 1905, 1906, 1907, 1908, 1928, 1969

Former Model Business Corporation Act § 8.53  . . . . . . . 1903

2 Model Business Corporation Act Annotated § 8.54
& Official Comment (3d ed. 1996)
. . . . 1854, 1855, 1882, 1885, 1904, 1935, 1937-39, 1946, 1969

2 Model Business Corporation Act Annotated § 8.55
& Official Comment (3d ed. 1996)
. . . . . . . . . . 1854, 1855, 1888, 1889-90, 1891-92, 1893, 1904

2 Model Business Corporation Act Annotated § 8.56
& Official Comment (3d ed. 1996)
. . . . . . . . 1854, 1855, 1856, 1866, 1876, 1908-09, 1953, 1969

2 Model Business Corporation Act Annotated § 8.57
(3d ed. 1996) . . . . . . . . . . . . . . . . . . . . . . . . . . . 1980-81

2 Model Business Corporation Act Annotated § 8.58
& Official Comment (3d ed. 1996)
. . . . . . 1854, 1855, 1867, 1909, 1911, 1931, 1952, 1962, 1969

Former Model Business Corporation Act § 8.58 . . . 1962, 1969

2 Model Business Corporation Act Annotated § 8.59
& Official Comment (3d ed. 1996)
. . . . . . . . . . . . . . . . . 1854, 1855, 1887, 1961, 1967, 1969

2 Model Business Corporation Act Annotated §§ 8.61-
8.63 & Introductory Comment (3d ed. 1996)
. . . . . . . . . . . . . . . . . . . . . . 266, 270, 289-92, 300-01

3 Model Business Corporation Act Annotated § 11.03
(3d ed. 1996) . . . . . . . . . . . . . . . . . . . . . . . . . . . . 983

4 Model Business Corporation Act Annotated § 16.21
(3d ed. 1996) . . . . . . . . . . . . . . . . . . . . . . . . . . . 1979

1 Principles of Corporate Governance: Analysis and
Recommendations § 1.10 (1994) . . . . . . . . . . . . . . . . . 349

1 Principles of Corporate Governance: Analysis and
Recommendations § 1.23 (1994) . . . . . . . . . . . . . . . . . . 71

1 Principles of Corporate Governance: Analysis and
Recommendations § 1.42 (1994) . . . . . . . . . . . . . . . . . . 97

1 Principles of Corporate Governance: Analysis and
Recommendations § 5.03 Comment (1994) . . . . . . . . . . . 1548

1 Principles of Corporate Governance: Analysis and
Recommendations § 6.02 (1994) . . . . . . . . . . . . 693-94, 817

2 Principles of Corporate Governance: Analysis and
Recommendations § 7.02 & Comment (1994)
. . . . . . . . . . . . . 1387, 1388, 1397, 1398, 1399, 1403, 1416

Principles of Corporate Governance: Analysis and
Recommendations § 7.03 & Comment (Tentative Draft
No. 8 Apr. 15, 1988) . . . . . . . . . . . . . . . . . . . . 1564, 1741

2 Principles of Corporate Governance: Analysis and
Recommendations § 7.03 & Comment (1994)
. . . . . . . . . . . . . 1429, 1476, 1563, 1564, 1571, 1665, 1687

2 Principles of Corporate Governance: Analysis and
Recommendations § 7.04 & Comment (1994)
. . . . . . . . . . . . . . . . . . . . . . 1406, 1668, 1680, 1782

2 Principles of Corporate Governance: Analysis and
Recommendations § 7.05 & Comment (1994) . . . . . 1700, 1782

2 Principles of Corporate Governance: Analysis and
Recommendations § 7.06 (1994) . . . . . . . . . . . . 1782, 1785

2 Principles of Corporate Governance: Analysis and
Recommendations § 7.07 (1994) . . . . . . . . . . . . 1668, 1782

2 Principles of Corporate Governance: Analysis and
Recommendations § 7.08 (1994) . . . . . . . . . . . . 1668, 1782

2 Principles of Corporate Governance: Analysis and
Recommendations § 7.09 (1994) . . . . . . . . . 1669, 1700, 1782

2 Principles of Corporate Governance: Analysis and
Recommendations § 7.10 & Comment (1994)
. . . . . . . . . . . . . . . . . . . . . . . . . 1665, 1669-71, 1782

2 Principles of Corporate Governance: Analysis and
Recommendations § 7.11 (1994) . . . . . . . . . . . . . . . . 1782

2 Principles of Corporate Governance: Analysis and
Recommendations § 7.12 (1994) . . . . . . . . . . . . 1673, 1782

2 Principles of Corporate Governance: Analysis and
Recommendations § 7.13 & Comment (1994)
. . . . . . . . . . . . . . . . . 1671-72, 1782, 1799, 1823-25, 1828

2 Principles of Corporate Governance: Analysis and
Recommendations § 7.14 (1994) . . . . . . . . . . . . . . . 1408

Principles of Corporate Governance and Structure:
Restatement and Recommendations § 7.03 (Tentative
Draft No. 1 Apr. 1, 1982) . . . . . . . . . . . . . . . . . . . 1700

2 Principles of Corporate Governance: Analysis and
Recommendations § 7.18 (1994) . . . . . . . . . . . . . . . . 113

2 Principles of Corporate Governance: Analysis and
Recommendations § 7.19 (1994) . . . . . . . . . . 236-38, 2168-69

2 Principles of Corporate Governance: Analysis and
Recommendations § 7.20 & Comment (1994)
. . . . . . . . . . . . . . . . . . . . . . . 1855, 1857, 1867, 1872,

1876, 1879-80, 1881, 1882, 1886, 1887, 1893-94, 1895, 1906, 1908, 1938, 1940, 1947-48, 1952-53, 1959, 1961, 1979-80, 1982

Principles of Corporate Governance and Structure: Restatement and Recommendations Part IV Introductory Note (Tentative Draft No. 1 Apr. 1, 1982) . . . . . . . . . 132

Principles of Corporate Governance and Structure: Restatement and Recommendations § 4.01 Reporter's Note (Tentative Draft No. 1 Apr. 1, 1982) . . . . . . . . . . . 132

Principles of Corporate Governance: Analysis and Recommendations § 4.01 Reporter's Note (Tentative Draft No. 3 Apr. 13, 1984) . . . . . . . . . . . . . . . . . . 132

Principles of Corporate Governance: Analysis and Recommendations § 4.01 Comment & Reporter's Note (Tentative Draft No. 4 Apr. 12, 1985) . . . . . . . . . . . 132, 174

Principles of Corporate Governance: Analysis and Recommendations § 4.01 Reporter's Note (Tentative Draft No. 11 Apr. 25, 1991) . . . . . . . . . . . . . . . . . . 132

Principles of Corporate Governance: Analysis and Recommendations § 4.01 Reporter's Note (Proposed Final Draft Mar. 31, 1992) . . . . . . . . . . . . . . . . . . 132

1 Principles of Corporate Governance: Analysis and Recommendations § 4.01 (1994) . . . . . . . . 106, 118, 132, 215

1 Principles of Corporate Governance: Analysis and Recommendations § 4.01 Comment & Reporter's Note (1994) . . . . . . . . . . . . . . 13, 100, 106, 113, 132, 199, 243

1 Principles of Corporate Governance: Analysis and Recommendations § 4.02 (1994) . . . . . . . . . . . . . . . . . 201

1 Principles of Corporate Governance: Analysis and
Recommendations § 4.03 (1994) . . . . . . . . . . . . . . . . . . 201

1 Principles of Corporate Governance: Analysis and
Recommendations § 5.02 (1994) . . . . . . . . . . . . . . . . 292-93

1 Principles of Corporate Governance: Analysis and
Recommendations § 5.03 (1994) . . . . . . . . . . . . . . . . 319-20

1 Principles of Corporate Governance: Analysis and
Recommendations § 5.05 (1994) . . . . . . . . . . . . . . . 299, 306

1 Principles of Corporate Governance: Analysis and
Recommendations § 5.05 Comment (1994) . . . . . . . . . . . 307

1 Principles of Corporate Governance: Analysis and
Recommendations § 5.10 (1994) . . . . . . . . . . . . . . 376, 471

Restatement (Second) of Contracts § 193 (1979) . . . . . . . . 994

Restatement (Second) of Trusts § 170 (1957) . . . . . . . . . . 879

Uniform Fraudulent Transfer Act §§ 2(a), (b), 7A
U.L.A. 648 . . . . . . . . . . . . . . . . . . . . . . . . . . . . . 619

**Books:**

18B American Jurisprudence 2d Corporations (1985 &
Supp. 1998) . . . . . . . . . . . . . . . . . . . . . . . . . . . . . 15

41 American Jurisprudence 2d Indemnity (1995 &
Supp. 1998) . . . . . . . . . . . . . . . . . . . . . . . . . 1969-70

12A John A. Appleman, Insurance Law & Practice
(1981 & Supp. 1998) . . . . . . . . . . . . . . . . . . . . . . 2139

Henry Ballantine, Ballantine on Corporations (rev. ed.
1946) . . . . . . . . . . . . . . . . . . . . . . . . . . . . . . 243

1 R. Franklin Balotti & Jesse A. Finkelstein, The
Delaware Law of Corporations and Business Organiza-
tions (3d ed. 1998) . . . . . . . . . . . .   3, 5, 132, 139, 151, 195,
238, 270, 368, 1007, 1053, 1343, 1884, 1967-68, 2155, 2157, 2161

2 R. Franklin Balotti & Jesse A. Finkelstein, The
Delaware Law of Corporations and Business Organ-
izations (3d ed. 1998) . . . . . . . . . . . . . . . . . . . . . . 1907

3 R. Franklin Balotti & Jesse A. Finkelstein, The
Delaware Law of Corporations and Business Organiza-
tions (3d ed. 1998) . . . . . . . . . . . . . . . . . . . . . . . . 151

Joseph W. Bishop, Jr., The Law of Corporate Officers
and Directors: Indemnification and Insurance (1981 &
Supp. 1997) . . . . . . . . . . . . . . . . . . . . . . . . 1852, 1975

Joy M. Bryan, Corporate Anti-Takeover Defenses:
The Poison Pill Device (1998) . . . . . . . . . . . 1085, 1195, 1197

Robert E. Burton & Sandra L. Rich, Ohio Corporation
Law & Practice (1989 & Supp. 1991) . . . . . . . . . . . . . . 689

Lewis Carroll, Alice in Wonderland . . . . . . . . . . . . . . 1109

William L. Cary & Melvin A. Eisenberg, Cases and
Materials on Corporations (7th ed. 1995 & Supp.
1997) . . . . . . . . . . . . . . . . . . . . . . . . . . . . 243, 1413

Robert C. Clark, Corporate Law (1986) . . . . . . . . 1299, 1445

19 Corpus Juris Secundum Corporations (1990 &
Supp. 1997) . . . . . . . . . . . . . . . . . . . . . . . . . . . 311

42 Corpus Juris Secundum Indemnity (1991 & Supp. 1997) . . . . . . . . . . . . . . . . . . . . . . . . . . . . 1970

1 David A. Drexler, Lewis S. Black, Jr. & A. Gilchrist Sparks, III, Delaware Corporation Law and Practice (1998) . . . . . . . . . . . . . . . . . . . . . 1004, 1039

2 David A. Drexler, Lewis S. Black, Jr. & A. Gilchrist Sparks, III, Delaware Corporation Law and Practice (1998) . . . . . . . . . . . . . . . . . . . . . . . 1472

Directors' and Officers' Liability Insurance 1989 (Practising Law Institute 1989) . . . . . . . . . . . . . 2040, 2172

Directors' and Officers' Liability Insurance 1993: Impact of the Bankruptcy Laws (Practising Law Institute 1993) . . . . . . . . . . . . . . . . . . . . . . . . . . 1984

Directors' and Officers' Liability Insurance 1994 (Practising Law Institute 1994) . . . . . . . . . . . . . . . 1984

1 David A. Drexler, Lewis S. Black, Jr. & A. Gilchrist Sparks, III, Delaware Corporation Law and Practice (1998) . . . . . . . . . . . . . . . . . . . . . . . . 560

Melvin A. Eisenberg, The Structure of the Corporation: A Legal Analysis (1976) . . . . . . . . . . . . . . . . . 1765

1 Arthur Fleischer, Jr. & Alexander R. Sussman, Takeover Defense (5th ed. 1995 & Supp. 1997) . . . . . . . . . . . . . . . . . . . . . . . . . . 1339, 1345, 1348

Arthur Fleischer, Jr., Geoffrey C. Hazard, Jr. & Miriam Z. Klipper, Board Games: The Changing Shape of Corporate Power (1988) . . . . . . . . . . . . . . . 151

3A William M. Fletcher, Cyclopedia of the Law of
Private Corporations (1994 & Supp. 1997) . . . . . . . . . 100, 244

5A William M. Fletcher, Cyclopedia of the Law of
Private Corporations (1995 & Supp. 1997) . . . . . . . . . . . 315

13 William M. Fletcher, Cyclopedia of the Law of
Private Corporations (1995 & Supp. 1997) . . . . . . . . . . . 1605

15A William M. Fletcher, Fletcher Cyclopedia of the
Law of Private Corporations (1990 & Supp. 1997) . . . . . . . 597

Ernest L. Folk, The Delaware General Corporation
Law 98 (1st ed. 1972) . . . . . . . . . . . . . . . . . . . . . . 1853

1 Ernest L. Folk, Rodman Ward, Jr. and Edward P.
Welch, Folk on the Delaware Corporation Law (3d ed.
1998) . . . . . . . . . . . . . . . . . . . . . . . . . . . . . 1004, 1859

Charles L. Hansen, A Guide to the American Law
Institute Corporate Governance Project (1995) . . . . . . . . . . 293

Harry G. Henn & John R. Alexander, Laws of Corporations and Other Business Enterprises (3d ed. 1983 &
Supp. 1986) . . . . . . . . . . . . . . . . . . . . . . 100, 302, 1413

1 Martin Lipton & Erica H. Steinberger, Takeovers &
Freezeouts (1997) . . . . . . . . . . . . . . . . . . . . . . . . . 1345

National Legal Center for the Public Interest, The
American Law Institute and Corporate Governance:
An Analysis and Critique (1987) . . . . . . . . . . . . . . . . . 105

National Legal Center for the Public Interest, The
American Law Institute Corporate Governance Project
in Mid-Passage: What Will It Mean to You? (1991) . . . . . . 105

John F. Olson & Josiah O. Hatch III, Director and
Officer Liability: Indemnification and Insurance (1997)
1853, 1854, 1870, 1871, 1872, 1947, 1967, 1976, 1979, 1984,
1988-90, 1997, 2008, 2021, 2025, 2030, 2031, 2033, 2040,
2041, 2044, 2046, 2051, 2074, 2093, 2139-40, 2153-56, 2161-64

Thomas Petzinger, Jr., Oil & Honor: The Texaco-
Pennzoil Wars (1987) . . . . . . . . . . . . . . . . . . . . . . . 1001

2 Lee R. Ross & Thomas F. Segalla, Couch on
Insurance 3d (1997) . . . . . . . . . . . . . . . . . . . . . . . . 2139

7 Lee R. Ross & Thomas F. Segalla, Couch on
Insurance 3d (1997) . . . . . . . . . . . . . . . . . . . . . . . 1985

5 Securities Law Techniques (A.A. Sommer, Jr. ed.
1998)
. . 1004, 2021, 2025, 2031, 2037, 2039, 2040, 2044, 2045, 2074

7 Securities Law Techniques (A.A. Sommer, Jr. ed.
1998) . . . . . . . . . . . . . . . . . . . . . . . . . . . . . . . . . 2093

Securities Litigation 1996 (Practising Law Institute
1996) . . . . . . . . . . . . . . . . . . . . . . 1989, 2093, 2135, 2174

Webster's Ninth New Collegiate Dictionary (1988) . . . . . . . 623

1 Robert II. Winter, Mark H. Stumpf & Gerard L.
Hawkins, Shark Repellents and Golden Parachutes: A
Handbook for the Practitioner (1992) . . . . . 822, 1246, 1247-49

2 Robert H. Winter, Mark H. Stumpf & Gerard L.
Hawkins, Shark Repellents and Golden Parachutes: A
Handbook for the Practitioner (1992)
. . . . . . . . . . . . . . . . . . . . . 1055, 1297, 1298, 1299, 1364

4 Robert H. Winter, Robert D. Rosenbaum, Mark H.
Stumpf & L. Stevenson Parker, State Takeover
Statutes and Poison Pills (1992) . . . . . . . . . . . . . 1093, 1115

7C Charles Alan Wright, Arthur R. Miller & Mary
Kay Kane, Federal Practice and Procedure (1986 &
Supp. 1998) . . . . . . . . . . . . . . . . . . . . . . . . . . . . . 1388

13B Charles Alan Wright, Arthur R. Miller & Edward
H. Cooper, Federal Practice and Procedure (1984 &
Supp. 1998) . . . . . . . . . . . . . . . . . . . . . . . . . . . . . 1417

**Articles, Reports and Book Chapters:**

A Flurry of Greenmail Has Stockholders Cursing,
Bus. Wk., Dec. 8, 1986, at 32 . . . . . . . . . . . . . . . . . 1349

ABA Members Applaud NYSE Draft On Disparate
Shareholder Voting Rights, 24 Sec. Reg. & L. Rep.
(BNA) 1443 (Sept. 4, 1992) . . . . . . . . . . . . . . . . . . 1064

Abelson, Investing It; When Boards Say 'No Deal' To
Holders, N.Y. Times, Oct. 6, 1996, § 3, at 1 . . . . . . . . 1173

Adler, D & O Insurers Are Not Liable for Bank's
Settlement: Jury, Bus. Ins., Jan. 23, 1989, at 2 . . . . . . . . 2116

Allen, Independent Directors in MBO Transactions:
Are They Fact or Fantasy, 45 Bus. Law. 2055 (1990) . . . . . 829

American Bar Association Section of Corporation,
Banking and Business Law, Subcommittee on Executive Compensation, Executive Compensation: A Road
Map for the Corporate Advisor, 40 Bus. Law. 219
(1987) . . . . . . . . . . . . . . . . . . . . . . . . . . . . . . . . . 1297

American Bar Association Section of Litigation's Comments to the American Law Institute Project on "Principles of Corporate Governance and Structure: Restatement and Recommendations Tentative Draft No. 1" (Jan. 28, 1983) . . . . . . . . . . . . . . . . . . . . 105, 237

AMEX Files Proposal with SEC on Disparate Shareholder Voting Rights, 23 Sec. Reg. & L. Rep. (BNA) 908 (June 14, 1991) . . . . . . . . . . . . . . . . . . 1064

Another Run at St. Regis?, Bus. Wk., July 16, 1984, at 38 . . . . . . . . . . . . . . . . . . . . . . . . . . . . . . . 1364

Arkin, Should Kidder Advance Jett's Defense Costs?, Nat'l L.J., Oct. 10, 1994, at A21 . . . . . . . . . . . . . . . 1870

Arsht, Indemnification Under Section 145 of the Delaware General Corporation Law, 3 Del. J. Corp. L. 176 (1978) . . . . . . . . . . . . . . . . . . . . . . . . . . . . . 1981

Arsht, The Business Judgment Rule Revisited, 8 Hofstra L. Rev. 93 (1979) . . . . . . . . . . . . . . . . . . 42, 84-85

Arsht & Hinsey, Codified Standard—Safe Harbor But Chartered Channel: A Response, 35 Bus. Law. ix (1980) . . . . . . . . . . . . . . . . . . . . . . . . . . . . . . . 132

Arsht & Stapleton, Delaware's New General Corporation Law: Substantive Changes, 23 Bus. Law. 75 (1967) . . . . . . . . . . . . . . . . . . . . . . . . . 1883, 1965-67

Bader, Takeover and Personal Profit Exclusions in Directors' and Officers' Liability Insurance, in Directors' and Officers' Liability Insurance 1989 (Practising Law Institute 1989) . . . . . . . . . . . . . . . . . . . . . 2040, 2041

Bailey & Lane, The Impact of Bankruptcy Issues on
D & O Insurance and Indemnification, in Directors'
and Officers' Liability Insurance 1994 (Practising Law
Institute 1994) . . . . . . . . . . . . . . . . . . . . . . . . . . . . . 1984

Bainbridge, Interpreting Nonshareholder Constituency
Statutes, 19 Pepp. L. Rev. 971 (1992) . . . . . . . . . . . . . . 819

Bainbridge, The Short Life and Resurrection of SEC
Rule 19c-4, 69 Wash. U.L.Q. 565 (1991) . . . . . . . 1053, 1056

Balotti & Finkelstein, Further Developments in Delaware Disclosure Law, 11 Insights: The Corporate &
Securities Law Advisor No. 1, Jan. 1997, at 21 . . . . . . 535, 539

Barciela, Heavenly Pay, Miami Herald, June 7, 1993,
at B12 . . . . . . . . . . . . . . . . . . . . . . . . . . . . . . . . . . . 308

Barmash, $757 Million Murdoch Offer to St. Regis;
Concern May Find the Bid Hard to Fight, N.Y.
Times, July 19, 1984, at D1 . . . . . . . . . . . . . . . . . . . . 1364

Barnhart & Hodge, Gloomy News About 'D & O', Chi. Trib.,
Jan. 15, 1986, § 3, at 1 . . . . . . . . . . . . . . . . . . . . . . 2164

Bartlett & Andrews, The Standstill Agreement: Legal
and Business Considerations Underlying a Corporate
Peace Treaty, 62 B.U.L. Rev. 143 (1982) . . . . . . . 1368, 1371

Berton, Group of 27 Medium-Sized Audit Firms
Establishes an Offshore Liability Insurer, Wall St. J.,
Aug. 15, 1986, at 36 . . . . . . . . . . . . . . . . . . . . . . . . 2162

Bishop, New Problems in Indemnifying and Insuring
Directors: Protection Against Liability under the Federal Securities Laws, 1972 Duke L.J. 1153 (1972) . . . . 2064-65

Black, The Value of Institutional Investor Monitoring:
The Empirical Evidence, 39 U.C.L.A. L. Rev. 895
(1992) . . . . . . . . . . . . . . . . . . . . . . . . . . . . . . . 1027

Bleakley, Talking Deals; Buying Back, and Buying
Off, N.Y. Times, Nov. 13, 1986, at D2 . . . . . . . . . . . 1350

Block, Radin & Maimone, Derivative Litigation: Current Law Versus the American Law Institute, 48 Bus.
Law. 1443 (1993) . . . . . . . . . . . . . . . . . . . . . . . . . 1673

Bogen, Are Rights Plans Ever 'Draconian'?, 11
Insights: The Corporate and Securities Law Advisor
No. 1, Jan. 1997, at 13 . . . . . . . . . . . . . . . . . . 1089, 1172

Breeden, Acquisitions and Takeovers: What Lies
Ahead for Shareholder Rights 9-10 (Remarks at
Twelfth Annual Institute on Acquisitions and Take-
overs Apr. 26, 1990) . . . . . . . . . . . . . . . . . . . . . . . . 817

Brenner, BankAmerica Captive Offshore Insurer
Raises Legality and Propriety Questions, Am. Banker,
Apr. 26, 1985, at 1 . . . . . . . . . . . . . . . . . . . . . . . . 2153

Brinkley & Lipin, ITT Plans to Split into Three
Companies: Firm to Take on New Debt, Buy Back
Stock in Move to Thwart Hilton Offer, Wall St. J.,
July 17, 1997, at A3 . . . . . . . . . . . . . . . . . . . . 1033, 1278

Brownstein, Takeovers and the Business Judgment
Rule, 20 Rev. Sec. & Comm. Reg. 177 (1987) . . . . . . . . . 822

Brownstein, Takeovers, Fiduciary Duties, and Rights
Plans: A 1996 Status Report, 11 Insights: The Corporate and Securities Law Advisor 12 (Jan. 1997) . . . . . . . . 1086

Brudney & Chirelstein, A Restatement of Corporate
Freezeouts, 87 Yale L.J. 1354 (1978) .............. 378

Byrne, For a So-So CEO, $95 Million in Cash, Bus.
Wk., Oct. 20, 1997, at 40 ..................... 308

Chazen, The Shareholder Rights By-Law: Giving
Shareholders a Decisive Vote, 5 The Corporate
Governance Advisor No. 1, Jan./Feb. 1997, at 8 ....... 1201

Cherno & Sussman, Tender-Offer Litigation, Litigation, Winter 1984, at 41 ...................... 1345

Chiappinelli, Trans Union Unreconsidered, 15 J.
Corp. L. 27 (1989) .......................... 151

Clafman & Schlefer, Recipe for a Management Autoc-
racy, N.Y. Times, Dec. 14, 1986, § 3 at 2 .......... 1086

Coffee & Schwartz, The Survival of the Derivative
Suit: An Evaluation and a Proposal for Legislative
Reform, 81 Colum. L. Rev. 261 (1981) ............. 1765

Cole, Icahn Ends Offer for Phillips; All Shareholders
to Get More, N.Y. Times, Mar. 5, 1985, at A1 ........ 1364
Comment, Directors and Officers Insurance Proceeds
in Bankruptcy: The Impact on an Estate and its Claimants, 13 Bankr. Dev. J. 235 (1996) ............... 1984

Comment, Law for Sale: A Study of the Delaware
Corporation Law of 1967, 117 U. Pa. L. Rev. 861
(1969) ................................. 1906

Comment & Schwert, Poison or Placebo? Evidence on
the Deterrence and Wealth Effects of Modern Anti-
takeover Measures, 39 J. Fin. Econ. 3 (1995) ......... 1086

Corporations Still Flocking to Delaware, N.Y. Times,
Dec. 27, 1997, at D14 . . . . . . . . . . . . . . . . . . . . . . . . . 3

Court Approves Settlement Between 2 Texas Tycoons,
Wall St. J., Dec. 10, 1997, at B12 . . . . . . . . . . . . . . . . 462

Cox, Searching for the Corporation's Voice in Derivative Litigation: A Critique of Zapata and the ALI
Project, 1982 Duke L.J. 959 (1982) . . . . . . . . . . . . . . 1765

Cox & Munsinger, Bias in the Boardroom Physcho-
logical Foundations & Legal Implications of Corporate
Cohesion, 48 L. & Contemp. Probs. 83 (Summer
1985) . . . . . . . . . . . . . . . . . . . . . . . . . . . . . . . . . . . . . . 1766

Crutcher's Chairman and 3 Directors Quit; Lack of
Insurance Cited, Wall St. J., Feb. 12, 1986, at 21 . . . . . . 2174

D & O Policy Addition Covers Investigation of Claims
Against Officers and Board, Corp. Officers & Directors Liability Litig. Rptr. 21182 (May 14, 1997) . . . . . . . 2000

Darlin, Most of Armada's Directors Resign Over
Insurance, Wall St. J., Feb. 5, 1986, at 40 . . . . . . . . . . . 2174

Davis, Approval by Disinterested Directors, 20 Iowa
J. Corp. L. 215 (1995) . . . . . . . . . . . . . . . . . . . . . . . . 293

Dent, The Power of Directors to Terminate Shareholder Litigation: The Death of the Derivative Suit?,
75 Nw. U. L. Rev. 96 (1980) . . . . . . . . . . . . . . . . . . . 1765

Donker, Plaintiffs Lose $243.8 M Suit, Telegram &
Gazette (Worcester, Mass.), June 7, 1997, at B6 . . . . . . . . 619

Dooley, Not in the Corporation's Best Interests,
A.B.A.J., May 1992, at 45 . . . . . . . . . . . . . . . . . . . . . . 17

Dooley, Two Models of Corporate Governance, 47
Bus. Law. 461 (1992) . . . . . . . . . . . . . . . . . . . . . 17, 105

Dooley & Veasey, The Role of the Board in Derivative Litigation: Delaware Law and the Current ALI
Proposals Compared, 44 Bus. Law. 503 (1989)
. . . . . . . . . . . . . . . . . . . 17-18, 105, 110, 1595, 1673, 1771

Eighth Annual Baron de Hirsch Meyer Lecture Series:
ALI Corporate Governance Project, 37 U. Miami L.
Rev. 169-349 (1983) . . . . . . . . . . . . . . . . . . . . . . . 105

Employee Benefit Plans in Control Contests: An Analysis of Participant 'Pass Through' Arrangements, 17
Pens. Rep. (BNA) No. 30 (July 23, 1990) . . . . . . . . . . . 890

Executive Pay Special Report: Tying Pay to Performance is a Great Idea. But Stock-Option Deals Have
Compensation Out of Control, Bus. Wk., Apr. 21,
1997, at 58 . . . . . . . . . . . . . . . . . . . . . . . . . . . . 308

Feit, Pac-Man Defense Upsets Majority Holder Rule,
Nat'l L.J., May 23, 1988, at 33 . . . . . . . . . . . . . . . . 1340

Finkelstein, Antitakeover Protection Against Two-Tier
and Partial Tender Offers: The Validity of Fair Price,
Mandatory Bid, and Flip-Over Provisions under Delaware Law, 11 Sec. Reg. L.J. 291 (1984) . . . . . . . . . . . 1248

Fischel, Organized Exchanges and the Regulation of
Dual Class Common Stock, 54 U. Chi. L. Rev. 119
(1987) . . . . . . . . . . . . . . . . . . . . . . . . . . . . . . . 1053

Fischel, The Business Judgment Rule and the Trans
Union Case, 40 Bus. Law. 1437 (1985) . . . . . . . . . . . . . 151

Fleming Cos.: Board Decides to Terminate Company's
Poison-Pill Plan, Wall St. J., Mar. 19, 1997, at B4 . . . . . 1197

Fleming Cos: Net Income Declines 11% As Sales
Decrease by 8.1%, Wall St. J., May 1, 1997 (avail-
able only in Dow Jones News/Retrieval Publications
Library) . . . . . . . . . . . . . . . . . . . . . . . . . . . . . . . 1197

Fowler, Scarce Corporate Directors, N.Y. Times, Jan.
7, 1986, at D20 . . . . . . . . . . . . . . . . . . . . . . . . . . 2164

From Simple to Bizarre: Ten Ways to Cope with
D & O Insurance Crisis, Corporate Control Alert,
May 1986, at 1 . . . . . . . . . . . . . . . . . . . . . . . . . . 1872

Galante, Corporate Boardroom Woes Grow, Nat'l
L.J., Aug. 4, 1986, at 1 . . . . . . . . . . . . . . . . 2164, 2167-68

Gelfand, "Pun's Oil Sues Toxico": A Comedy of
Errors in (at Least) Four Acts, 11 Del. J. Corp. L.
345 (1986) . . . . . . . . . . . . . . . . . . . . . . . . . . . . . 1001

Georgeson & Co. Inc., Corporate Governance Pro-
posals and Proxy Contests (1992) . . . . . . . . . . . . . . . 1087

Georgeson & Co. Inc., Mergers & Acquisitions:
Poison Pills and Shareholder Value/1992-96, Nov.
1997 . . . . . . . . . . . . . . . . . . . . . . . . . . . . . . . . . 1086

Georgeson & Co. Inc., Poison Pill Impact Study (Mar.
31, 1988) . . . . . . . . . . . . . . . . . . . . . . . . . . . . . . 1086

Georgeson & Co. Inc., Poison Pill Impact Study II
(Oct. 31, 1988) . . . . . . . . . . . . . . . . . . . . . . . . . . 1086

Georgeson & Co. Inc., Response to ISS Analysis of
Georgeson & Co. Inc. Poison Pill Impact Studies
(Nov. 29, 1988) . . . . . . . . . . . . . . . . . . . . . . . . . 1086

Gilson, Drafting an Effective Greenmail Prohibition,
88 Colum. L. Rev. 329 (1988) . . . . . . . . . . . . . . 1349, 1366

Gilson & Kraakman, Delaware's Intermediate Standard
for Defensive Tactics: Is There Substance to Propor-
tionality Review?, 44 Bus. Law. 247 (1989) . . . . . . . . . . . 673

Goldstein, Revision of the Model Business Corporation
Act, 63 Tex. L. Rev. 1471 (1985) . . . . . . . . . . . . . . . . 101

Goldstein & Hamilton, The Revised Model Business
Corporation Act, 38 Bus. Law. 1019 (1983) . . . . . . . . . 1406

Goldwasser, Introduction to Directors' and Officers'
Liability Insurance 1992, in Directors' and Officers'
Liability Insurance (Practising Law Institute 1992) . . . . . . 2173

Goolsby & Whitson, Virginia's New Corporate Code,
19 Rev. Sec. & Comm. Reg. 147 (1986) . . . . . . . . . . . . 126

Greenmail is Back—Just Ask Skadden Arps's Clients,
Corporate Control Alert, Jan. 1987, at 1 . . . . . . . . . . . 1349

Gross, Stiles & Joseph, Director's Duty in Insolvency
Undergoes Shift, Nat'l L.J., Apr. 15, 1991, at 19 . . . . . . . 597

Groves, Lucky Holders, Wary of Restructuring Plan,
OK Reincorporation, L.A. Times, Dec. 23, 1986, at
IV 1 . . . . . . . . . . . . . . . . . . . . . . . . . . . . . . . . 1252

Hamermesh, Repurchases of Shares—State of State
Law, in 5 Securities Law Techniques (A.A. Sommer,
Jr. ed. 1998) . . . . . . . . . . . . . . . . . . . . . . . . . . . 1004

Hamermesh, Responding to Shareholder Demands in Derivative Litigation, 2 Insights: The Corporate & Securities Law Advisor No. 7, July 1988 . . . . . . . . . . . 1595

Hamermesh, The Shareholder Rights By-Law: Doubts From Delaware, 5 The Corporate Governance Advisor No. 1, Jan./Feb. 1997, at 9 . . . . . . . . . . . . . . . . . . 1201

Hamilton, Reflections of a Reporter, 63 Tex. L. Rev. 1455 (1985) . . . . . . . . . . . . . . . . . . . . . . . . . . . 101

Hanks, Non-Stockholder Constituency Statutes: An Idea Whose Time Should Never Have Come, 3 Insights: The Corporate & Securities Law Advisor No. 12, Dec. 1989, at 20 . . . . . . . . . . . . . . . . . . . . . . 818-19

Hanks, Playing with Fire: Nonshareholder Constituency Statutes in the 1990s, 21 Stetson L. Rev. 97 (1991) . . . . . . . . . . . . . . . . . . . . . . . . . . . . . . . 819

Hansen, Other Constituency Statutes: A Search for Perspective, 46 Bus. Law. 1355 (1991) . . . . . . . . . . . . . 822

Hansen, The ALI Corporate Governance Project: Of the Duty of Due Care and the Business Judgment Rule, a Commentary, 41 Bus. Law. 1237 (1986) . . . . . . . . 126

Hanscn, § 8.30 of the Model Business Corporation Act: The Dead Hand Strikes Again, LXVIII Corporation Bulletin No. 10, May 15, 1997, at 1 . . . . . . . . . . . . 170

Harley, Overview of the Directors' and Officers' Insurance Environment, in Directors' and Officers' Liability Insurance 1989 11 (Practising Law Institute 1989) . . . . . . . . . . . . . . . . . . . . . . . . . . . . . . . 2173

Hays, O'Reilly to Step Down As Heinz Chief; Pay
and Style Were Criticized, N.Y. Times, Dec. 3, 1997,
at D1 . . . . . . . . . . . . . . . . . . . . . . . . . . . . . . . . . 308

Hertzberg, Insurers Beginning to Refuse Coverage on
Directors, Officers in Takeover Cases, Wall St. J.,
Jan. 20, 1986, at 3 . . . . . . . . . . . . . . . . . . . . . . 2041, 2167

Hertzberg, Poison Pill Defense No Longer Is Seen as
a Sure Way to Repel Hostile Suitors, Wall St. J., Oct.
31, 1985, at 20 . . . . . . . . . . . . . . . . . . . . . . . . . . . 1093

Hertzberg & Lubove, Wall Street Winces as Belzbergs
Agree to Sell Stock, Run, Wall St. J., Apr. 2, 1986,
at 2 . . . . . . . . . . . . . . . . . . . . . . . . . . . . . . . . . . 1350

Herzel, Law Should Allow Indemnity for Derivative
Suits, Legal Times, Mar. 31, 1986, at 11 . . . . . . . . . . 2174-75

Herzel & Harris, Uninsured Boards Mount Weak
Defense, Nat'l L.J., Apr. 21, 1986, at 19 . . . . . . . . . . . 2175

Herzel & Katz, Smith v. Van Gorkom: The Business
of Judging Business Judgment, 41 Bus. Law. 1187
(1986) . . . . . . . . . . . . . . . . . . . . . . . . . . . . . . . . . 151

Hicks, Ashland to Buy Out Belzbergs, N.Y. Times,
Apr. 2, 1986, at D1 . . . . . . . . . . . . . . . . . . . . . . . . 1350

Hilder, Big U.S. Firms Form Liability Insurer, Wall
St. J., Dec. 23, 1985, at 6 . . . . . . . . . . . . . . . . . . . . 2162

Hilder, Liability Insurance is Difficult to Find Now
for Directors, Officers, Wall St. J., July 10, 1985, at
1 . . . . . . . . . . . . . . . . . . . . . . . . . . . . . . . 2164-66, 2174

Hinsey, Business Judgment and the American Law Institute's Corporate Governance Project: The Rule, the Doctrine, and the Reality, 52 Geo. Wash. L. Rev. 609 (1984) . . . . . . . . . . . . . . . . . . . . . . . . . . . . . . 6, 110

Hinsey, The New Lloyd's Policy Form for Directors and Officers Liability Insurance—An Analysis, 33 Bus. Law. 1961 (1978) . . . . . . . . . . . . . . . . . . . . . . . 1988

Hinsey & Dreizen, Delaware Court Addresses Business Judgment Rule, Legal Times of Washington, June 8, 1981 . . . . . . . . . . . . . . . . . . . . . . . . . . . . . . . 1721

Hofmann, Professional Perils: D & O Buyers Still Not Out of the Woods, Bus. Ins., Oct. 10, 1988, at 3 . . . . . . . 2173

Huber, Business Judgment Rule Probed, Legal Times, Apr. 23, 1984, at 35 . . . . . . . . . . . . . . . . . . . . . . . . . 632

Institutional Shareholder Services, Analysis of Georgeson & Company Poison Pill Study (Nov. 17, 1988) . . . . . 1086

Ipsen, The Crisis in Directors and Officers Insurance, Institutional Investor, Aug. 1985, at 231 . . . . . . . . . . 2164-65

Irv Jacobs is at It Again—At Avco, Bus. Wk., Nov. 19, 1984, at 50 . . . . . . . . . . . . . . . . . . . . . . . . . . . 1364

Is Delaware Supreme Court's Provocative Footnote a Critique of Hollywood Park?, Corporate Control Alert, Apr. 1991, at 2-3 . . . . . . . . . . . . . . . . . . . . . 1296

Johnson, Classes of Common Stock Achieve Key Goals, Legal Times, Mar. 17, 1986, at 15 . . . . . . . 1053, 1054

Johnston, Corporate Indemnification and Liability
Insurance for Directors and Officers, 33 Bus. Law.
1993 (1978) . . . . . . . . . . . . . . . . . . . . . . . . . . . . 1854, 2021

Johnston, D & O Insurance Crisis: How to Fund
Indemnification Arrangements, 1 Insights: The Corporate & Securities Law Advisor No. 2, Aug. 1987, at
3 . . . . . . . . . . . . . . . . . . . . . . . . . . . . . . . 1976, 2153-55

Johnston, Directors' and Officers' and Related Forms
of Liability Insurance, in 7 Securities Law Techniques
(A.A. Sommer, Jr. ed. 1998) . . . . . . . 1988, 1990, 1997, 2093

Johnston, Executive Pay Increases at a Much Faster
Rate Than Corporate Revenues and Profits, N.Y.
Times, Sept. 2, 1997, at D4 . . . . . . . . . . . . . . . . . . . . . 308

Johnston, Harrah's and Union at Odds Over Poison
Pill Vote Tally, N.Y. Times, Apr. 26, 1997, at 38 . . . . . . 1195

Johnston & Alexander, Fiduciary Outs and Exclusive
Merger Agreements Delaware Law and Practice, 11
Insights: The Corporate and Securities Law Advisor
No. 2, Feb. 1997, at 15 . . . . . . . . . . . . . . . . . . . . . . . . 986

Johnston & Alexander, The Effect of Disinterested
Director Approval of Conflict Transactions under the
ALI Corporate Governance Project—A Practitioner's
Perspective, 48 Bus. Law. 1393 (1993) . . . . . . . . . . . . . 293

Karmel, Federalizing Shareholder Voting Rights,
N.Y.L.J., Dec. 8, 1986, at 33 . . . . . . . . . . . . . . . . . . . 1055

Karmel, Is One Share, One Vote Archaic?, N.Y.L.J.,
Feb. 26, 1985, at 1 . . . . . . . . . . . . . . . . . . . . . . 1055, 1056

Karmel, Shareholder Voting Rights Diminishing under
State Law, N.Y.L.J., June 18, 1987, at 1 . . . . . . . . . . 1055

Karmel, The SEC's Power to Regulate Stockholder
Voting Rights, N.Y.L.J., Aug. 21, 1986, at 1 . . . . . . . . 1055

Kennedy, The Standard of Responsibility for Directors, 52 Geo. Wash. L. Rev. 624 (1984) . . . . . . . . . . . . 237

King, Director Protection under Virginia Law, 20
Rev. Sec. & Comm. Reg. 129 (1987) . . . . . . . . . . . . 125, 137

Klein, The Case for Heightened Scrutiny in Defense of
the Shareholder's Franchise Right, 44 Stan. L. Rev.
129 (1991) . . . . . . . . . . . . . . . . . . . . . . . . . . . . . . 1088

Klink, Chalif, Bishop & Arsht, Liabilities Which Can
Be Covered Under State Statutes and Corporate By-
Laws, 27 Bus. Law. 109 (1972) . . . . . . . . . . . . . . . . . 1981

Korn/Ferry International, 23rd Annual Board of Direc-
tors Study (1996) . . . . . . . . . . . . . . . . . . . . . . . . . . . 144

Kuykendall, A Neglected Policy Option: Indemnifica-
tion of Directors for Amounts Paid to Settle Derivative
Suits—Looking Past "Circularity" to Context and
Reform, 32 San Diego L. Rev. 1063 (1995) . . . . . . . . . . 1885

Labaton, American Brands Set to Buy E-II, N.Y.
Times, Feb. 1, 1988, at D1 . . . . . . . . . . . . . . . . . . . 1340

Lawlor, The Auction Process: Can It Ever Be Over?,
22 Rev. Sec. & Comm. Reg. 227 (Dec. 20, 1995)
. . . . . . . . . . . . . . . . . . . . . . . . . . . . . 987, 1002-03

Lesser & Sugimoto, Emerging Trends in the Use of Shareholder Bylaw Amendments, 5 The Corporate Governance Advisor No. 5, Sept./Oct. 1997, at 15 . . . . . . 1196

Lewin, Director Insurance Drying Up, N.Y. Times, Mar. 7, 1986, at D1 . . . . . . . . . . . . . . . . . . . . . 2164, 2174

Lewis, In Restrained Praise of the Derivative Suit, 12 Litigation No. 1, Fall 1985 . . . . . . . . . . . . . . . . . . . . 1804

Linden, Off With Their Perks, Fortune, Dec. 4, 1995, at 54 . . . . . . . . . . . . . . . . . . . . . . . . . . . . . . . 308

Lipin, Big B's Unusual Poison Pill Sparks Lawsuit by Hostile Suitor Revco, Wall St. J., Oct. 1, 1996, at B4 . . . . . . . . . . . . . . . . . . . . . . . . . . . . . . . . 1190

Lipin, Union Pacific Resources' Pennzoil Bid May Prompt the 'Just Say No' Defense, Wall St. J., June 30, 1997, at A3 . . . . . . . . . . . . . . . . . . 1173, 1246-47

Lipin & Machalaba, CSX Agrees to Acquire Conrail For $8.1 Billion In Cash and Stock, Wall St. J., Oct. 16, 1996, at A3 . . . . . . . . . . . . . . . . . . . . . . . . . 665

Lipin & Machalaba, Norfolk Southern Bids $9.1 Billion for Conrail, Wall St. J., Oct. 24, 1996, at A3 . . . . . . . 665

Lipin & Mathews, CSX Will Have to Boost Conrail Bid to Win Over Holders, Analysts Say, Wall St. J., Nov. 14, 1996, at A5 . . . . . . . . . . . . . . . . . . . . . 665-66

Lipin & Mathews, Norfolk Sweetens Hostile Bid for Conrail Hours After CSX Raises Friendly Offer, Wall St. J., Dec. 20, 1996, at A3 . . . . . . . . . . . . . . . . . . . . 665

Lipton, SEC Wrong on 'Poison Pills', Legal Times, Nov. 17, 1986, at 14 . . . . . . . . . . . . . . . . . . . . . . . . 1087

Lipton & Brownstein, Takeover Responses and Directors' Responsibilities—An Update, 40 Bus. Law. 1403 (1985) . . . . . . . . . . . . . . . . . . . . . . . . . . . . . . . . . . . 1339

Long-Term Changes, Softening Seen in D & O Liability Markets, 2 Liability & Insurance Bulletin (BNA) No. 38, at 6 (Apr. 11, 1988) . . . . . . . . . . . . . . . . . . . 2173

Lublin, Higher Profits Fatten CEO Bonuses, Wall St. J., Apr. 21, 1993, at R1 . . . . . . . . . . . . . . . . . . . . . . . 308

Lubin, 'Poison Pills' Are Giving Shareholders A Big Headache, Union Proposals Assert, Wall St. J., May 23, 1997, at C1 . . . . . . . . . . . . . . . . . . . . . . . . . . . . . 1195

Lucky Stores Get Holders' Approval, N.Y. Times, Dec. 23, 1986, at D4 . . . . . . . . . . . . . . . . . . . . . . . 1252

Lyons, Everybody Pays, Forbes, Aug. 6, 1990, at 46 . . . . 2164

Macey, An Economic Analysis of the Various Rationales for Making Shareholders the Exclusive Beneficiaries of Corporate Fiduciary Duties, 21 Stetson L. Rev. 23 (1991) . . . . . . . . . . . . . . . . . . . . . . . . . . . . . 820

Macey & McChesney, A Theoretical Analysis of Corporate Greenmail, 95 Yale L.J. 13 (1985) . . . . . . . 1349, 1364

Macey & Miller, Trans Union Reconsidered, 98 Yale L.J. 127 (1988) . . . . . . . . . . . . . . . . . . . . . . . . . . . . . 151

Mallen & Evans, Surviving the Directors' and Officers' Liability Crisis: Insurance and the Alternatives,

12 Del. J. Corp. L. 439 (1988)
. . 1988, 1991, 2031, 2041, 2154, 2165-66, 2170-71, 2174, 2175

Manning, Reflections and Practical Tips on Life in the
Boardroom After Van Gorkom, 41 Bus. Law. 1
(1985) . . . . . . . . . . . . . . . . . . . . . . . . . . . . . . . . . . 151

Manning, The Business Judgment Rule and the Director's Duty of Attention: Time for Reality, 39 Bus.
Law. 1477 (1984)  . . . . . . . . . . . . . . . . . . . . 102, 110, 144

Manning, The Business Judgment Rule and the Director's Duty of Attention: Time for Reality, 39 Bus.
Law. 1477 (1984)  . . . . . . . . . . . . . . . . . . . . . . . . . . 1619

Marsh, Pritzkers Foot Directors' Bill for Trans Union
Settlement, Crain's Chi. Bus., Aug. 12, 1985, at 19 . . . . . 2166

Mathews, Conrail Directors Advised To Shun Com-
peting Bidders, Wall St. J., Nov. 19, 1996, at A4  . . . . . . . 665

Matthews, Congress Enters the Fray Over Executive
Stock Options Rule, Wash. Post, Aug. 13, 1993, at
G1 . . . . . . . . . . . . . . . . . . . . . . . . . . . . . . . . . . . . . 308

Milligan, The Return of the Captive, Institutional
Investor, Mar. 1986, at 187  . . . . . . . . . . . . . . . . . 2162-63

Minow, Shareholders, Stakeholders, and Boards of
Directors, 21 Stetson L. Rev. 197 (1991) . . . . . . . . . . . . 819

Monteleone, D & O Allocation: Problems and Solutions, XVIII The Risk Report No. 8, Apr. 1996 at 6,
reprinted in Securities Litigation 1996, 997 (Practising
Law Institute 1996)  . . . . . . . . . . . 1989, 2093, 2135-36, 2174

Monteleone & Conca, Directors and Officers Indemnification and Liability Insurance: An Overview of Legal and Practical Issues, 51 Bus. Law. 573 (1996) . . . . . . . . . . . . . . 1898, 1988-89, 1997, 2000, 2007, 2021, 2025, 2032, 2033, 2044, 2046, 2074, 2093, 2129, 2135-37, 2140

Monteleone & McCarrick, D & O Insurance: Settlement Issues in Securities Litigation Involving Directors and Officers, 10 Insights: The Corporate & Securities Advisor No. 9, Sept. 1996, at 7 . . . . . . . . . . . 1996-97, 2039

Monteleone & McCarrick, Practical Concerns Involving Directors' and Officers' Liability Litigation, 7 Insights: The Corporate & Securities Law Advisor No. 11, Nov. 1993, at 15 . . . . . . . . . . . . . . . . . . 2000, 2007

Moore, Business Grows Bolder in Giving Lucrative Golden Parachutes, Legal Times, Mar. 24, 1986, at 1 . . . . . . . . . . . . . . . . . . . . . . . . . . . . . . 1314, 1321

Moscow, Lesser & Schulman, Michigan's Independent Director, 46 Bus. Law. 57 (1990) . . . . . . . . . . . . . . 1662

Moskin, Trans Union: A Nailed Board, 10 Del. J. Corp. L. 405 (1985) . . . . . . . . . . . . . . . . . . . . . . 151

NASD Proposes Voting Rights Rule for All Major Equity Stock Markets, 19 Sec. Reg. & L. Rep. (BNA) 339 (Mar. 20, 1987) . . . . . . . . . . . . . . . . . . . . . . 1057

Nash, Wall Street Bemoans a New 'Greenmail' Season, N.Y. Times, Dec. 28, 1986, at E4 . . . . . . . . . 1349, 1364

National Association of Corporate Directors, Report of the NACD Blue Ribbon Commission on Director Compensation: Purposes, Principles, and Best Practices (June 1995) . . . . . . . . . . . . . . . . . . . . . . . . . . . 308

Nightline: The U.S.'s Overpaid Executives (ABC television broadcast, Apr. 17, 1992) (available on LEXIS, Nexis library) . . . . . . . . . . . . . . . . . . . . . . . . . . 308

Norton is Rescued From British BTR by the Massachusetts Legislature and Saint-Gobain, Corporate Control Alert, May 1990, at 2 . . . . . . . . . . . . . . . . . . . 1246

Not All That Ends Well Is Good, Corporate Control Alert, Dec. 1997, at 2 . . . . . . . . . . . . . . . . . . . . . . 1246

Note, Defenses in Shareholders Derivative Suits—Who May Raise Them, 66 Harv. L. Rev. 342 (1952) . . . . . . . . 1683

Note, Greenmail: Targeted Stock Repurchases and the Management Entrenchment Hypothesis, 98 Harv. L. Rev. 1045 (1985) . . . . . . . . . . . . . . . . . . . . . . . . . . . 1349

Note, Protecting Corporate Directors and Officers: Insurance and Other Alternatives, 40 Vand. L. Rev. 775 (1987) . . . . . . . . . . . . . . . . . . . . . 2154, 2161-63, 2165

Note, Statutory Responses to Boardroom Fears, 1987 Colum. Bus. L. Rev. 749 (1987) . . . . . . . . . . . . . . . . 2174

Note, The Demand and Standing Requirements in Stockholder Derivative Actions, 44 U. Chi. L. Rev. 168 (1976) . . . . . . . . . . . . . . . . . . . . . . . . . . . . . . 1594

Note, The Evolution of Greenmail: A Lawyer's Dilemma in Corporate Representation, 2 Georgetown J. of Legal Ethics 533 (1988) . . . . . . . . . . . . . . . . . . 1364

Nussbaum, The Greenmailers Learn to Play in the Shadows, Bus. Wk., May 5, 1986, at 105 . . . . . . . . . . 1350

Ocampo & Small, General Counsel's Role in Resolving Derivative Litigation: A Personal Perspective, ACCA Docket, Vol. 13, No. 2, Mar./Apr. 1995 . . . . . . . 1596

Olson, The D & O Insurance Gap: Strategies for Coping, Legal Times, Mar. 3, 1986, at 25 . . . . . . . . . 2158, 2165

Orts, Beyond Shareholders: Interpreting Corporate Constituency Statutes, 61 Geo. Wash. L. Rev. 14 (1992) . . . . . . . . . . . . . . . . . . . . . . . . . . . . . . . . . 822

Oslund, Curbing Excesses: Pressure is on to Match Pay of Chief Executives with Performance, Star Trib. (Minneapolis), Nov. 9, 1992, at 1D . . . . . . . . . . . . . . 308

Parks, Insurer Settles Seattle Bank's Liability Claim, Am. Banker, Apr. 26, 1988, at 2 . . . . . . . . . . . . . . . . 2167

Perkins, Proposed Trans Union Settlement: Directors to Contribute to $23.5 Million Settlement Fund, Directorship, Sept. 1, 1985, at 1 . . . . . . . . . . . . . . . . . 151, 2166

Perkins, The ALI Corporate Governance Project in Midstream, 41 Bus. Law. 1195 (1986) . . . . . . . . . . . . . 105

Phillips Shareholders Settle for New Pill and Bylaw but No Cash, Corporate Control Alert, Aug. 1986, at 1 . . . . . . . . . . . . . . . . . . . . . . . . . . . . . . . . . . . 1134

Poison Pills: Aspirin for Corporate Headaches, Corporate Control Alert, Dec. 1989, at 10 . . . . . . . . . . . . . . 1098

Polance & Graul, Indemnification Trusts: Tax and Accounting Implications, 2 Insights: The Corporate & Securities Law Advisor No. 7, July 1988, at 19 . . . . . . . . 1976

Prickett, An Explanation of Trans Union to Henny-
Penny and Her Friends, 10 Del. J. Corp. L. 451
(1985) . . . . . . . . . . . . . . . . . . . . . . . . . . . . . 151

Quillen, Trans Union, Business Judgment, and Neutral
Principles, 10 Del. J. Corp. L. 465 (1985) . . . . . . . . . . . 151

Rehnquist, The Prominence of the Delaware Court of
Chancery in the State-Federal Joint Venture of Providing Justice, 48 Bus. Law. 351 (1992) . . . . . . . . . . . . . . 3

Robbins & Cohen, Ensuring Mandatory Indemnification of Corporate Officers and Directors, 8 Insights:
The Corporate & Securities Law Advisor No. 10, Oct.
1994, at 14 . . . . . . . . . . . . . . . . . . . . . . . . . 1871, 1872

Romano, What Went Wrong with Directors' and
Officers' Liability Insurance?, 14 Del. J. Corp. L. 1
(1989) . . . . . . . . . . . . . . . . . . . . . . . . . . . . . 2164-65

Rovner, Banks Win Approval to Form Captives for
Insurance, Legal Times, Mar. 3, 1986, at 1 . . . . 2153-54, 2162

Rubenstein, Why Geneneral Mills is Suing its Own
Captive Insurance Company: Chasing the Reinsurance
Pot, 2 U.S. Bus. Litig. No. 7, Feb. 1997, at 1 . . . . . . . . 2154

Ruder, Duty of Loyalty A Law Professor's Status
Report, 40 Bus. Law. 1383 (1985) . . . . . . . . . . . . . 365, 368

Sales, Are Top Executives Paid Too Much, Bus. &
Soc'y Rev. No. 90, Summer 1994, at 6 . . . . . . . . . . . . . 308

Sandler, 'Pale Green Greenmail' is Spreading as Firms
Buy Out Raiders as Part of Broader Purchases, Wall
St. J., Nov. 25, 1986, at 59 . . . . . . . . . . . . . . . . . . . 1350

Schares, Directors Resigning Over Lost Insurance,
S.F. Chron., Sept. 9, 1985, at 23 . . . . . . . . . . . . . . . . 2174

Schatz, Directors Feel the Legal Heat, N.Y. Times,
Dec. 15, 1985, § 3 at 12 . . . . . . . . . . . . . . . . . . . . . 2164

Schauer, Ailing D & O Insurance Market Looks for
Cure, 6 Bus. Law. Update 1 (Mar./Apr. 1986) . . . . . . . . 2154

Schwartz & Wiles, Trans Union: Neither New Law
Nor Bad Law, 10 Del. J. Corp. L. 429 (1985) . . . . . . . . . 151

Seafirst Settles Suit Against Five, N.Y. Times, July 9,
1986, at D4 . . . . . . . . . . . . . . . . . . . . . . . . . . . . 2167

Sebring, Recent Legislative Changes in the Law of
Indemnification of Directors, Officers and Others, 23
Bus. Law. 95 (1967) . . . . . . . . . . . . . . . . . 1883, 1967, 1981

SEC Approves NYSE Proposals to Revise Voting
Rights Rules for Listed Companies, 22 Sec. Reg. & L.
Rep. (BNA) 7 (Jan. 5, 1990) . . . . . . . . . . . . . . . . . . 1063

Siconolfi, GE's Kidder Wins Round in Dispute with
Joseph Jett, Wall St. J., Oct. 7, 1994, at C17 . . . . . . . . . 1869

Sills, D & O Insurance: Special Risk, Special Protection, Directorship, May 1988, at 1 . . . . . . . . . . . . . . . 2173

60 Minutes: Easy Money in Hard Times (CBS television broadcast, Apr. 7, 1996) (available on LEXIS,
Nexis library and at 1996 WL 8064836) . . . . . . . . . . . . 308

Sloan, How Much Is Too Much? Huge Checks Make
Even Good CEOs Look Bad, Newsweek, Mar. 17,
1997, at 40 . . . . . . . . . . . . . . . . . . . . . . . . . . . . . 308

Sloane, Insurer-Management Liability Rift Seen Growing, N.Y. Times, Dec. 19, 1985, at D8 . . . . . . . . . 2045, 2167

Sommer, Other Constituency Statutes: "A New Form of Welfarism?," 11 Bus. Law. Update, Sept./Oct. 1990, at 1 . . . . . . . . . . . . . . . . . . . . . . . . . . . . . . . 819

Statement of The Business Roundtable on the American Law Institute's Proposed "Principles of Corporate Governance and Structure: Restatement and Recommendations" (Feb. 1983) . . . . . . . . . . . . . . . . . . . . 105, 237

Stern, The General Standard of Care Imposed on Directors under the New California General Corporation Law, 23 U.C.L.A. L. Rev. 1269 (1976) . . . . . . . . . . 131

Stern & Lublin, Chrysler Has Bold New Idea—In Parachutes, Wall St. J., July 12, 1995, at B1 . . . . . 1297, 1298

Stone, Employees as Stakeholders Under State Non-shareholder Constituency Statutes, 21 Stetson L. Rev. 45 (1991) . . . . . . . . . . . . . . . . . . . . . . . . . . . . . . 822

Strom, Hire Wire Lending Acts: Bridge Loans, Big Trouble in 80's, Are Back, N.Y. Times, July 21, 1995, at D1 . . . . . . . . . . . . . . . . . . . . . . . . . . . . 901

Study Finds 1980s Corporate Defenses Remain Popular, But 'Hot Growth' Seen in Shareholder Action Constraints, 10 Corporate Counsel Weekly (BNA) No. 40, Oct. 18, 1995, at 8 . . . . . . 823, 1053, 1086, 1249-50, 1364

Study Says Restrictive Measures Bear Relation To Poorer Performance, 23 Sec. Reg. & L. Rep. (BNA) 1342 (Sept. 13, 1991) . . . . . . . . . . . . . . . . . . . . . . . 1086

Subak, A Snapshot of the Law Being Carved in Stone, 42 Bus. Law. 761 (1987) . . . . . . . . . . . . . . . . . . . . . . 238

Symposium, 61 Geo. Wash. L. Rev. 871-1293 (1993) . . . . . 105

Symposium: American Law Institute's Corporate Governance Project, 52 Geo. Wash. L. Rev. 495-912 (1984) . . . . . . . . . . . . . . . . . . . . . . . . . . . . . . . . . . 105

Symposium: The Genesis and Goals of the ALI Corporate Governance Project, 8 Cardozo L. Rev. 661-707 (1987) . . . . . . . . . . . . . . . . . . . . . . . . . . . . . . . . . . 105

Symposium on Corporate Governance: 48 Bus. Law. 1267-1483 (1993) . . . . . . . . . . . . . . . . . . . . . . . . . . . 105

Taravella, Alternative Facilities Easing D & O Market, Bus. Ins., Oct. 20, 1986, at 26 . . . . . . . . . . . . . . 2162

Taravella & Shapiro, Psst . . . Do You Know a D & O Insurer?, Bus. Ins., July 29, 1985, at 1 . . . . . . . . 2164

Tauber & Prendergast, Employee Benefit Plans in Takeovers, 16 Rev. Sec. Reg. 937 (1983) . . . . . . . . . . . 887

Taylor, Project Fantasy: A Behind the Scenes Account of Disney's Desperate Battle Against the Raiders, Manhattan, Inc., Nov. 1984, at 60 . . . . . . . . . . . . . . 1364

Tharp, Goldsmith Wins Fight for Crown Zellerbach Corp., Wall St. J., July 26, 1985, at 3 . . . . . . . . . . . 1092

The Dubious Value of Paying Greenmail, Bus. Wk., Mar. 4, 1985, at 83 . . . . . . . . . . . . . . . . . . . . . . . 1364

The Job Nobody Wants: Outside Directors Find That
the Risks and Hassles Just Aren't Worth It, Bus. Wk.,
Sept. 8, 1986, at 56 . . . . . . . . . . . . . . . . . . . . . . . . . 2164

The Siege of Atlanta, Corporate Control Alert, Apr.
1997, at 2 . . . . . . . . . . . . . . . . . . . . . . . . . . . . . 1246

Tracy, Parachutes-A-Popping, Fortune, Mar. 31,
1986, at 66 . . . . . . . . . . . . . . . . . . . . . . . . . . 1314, 1320

Uchitelle, The Origins of the 'Pac-Man' Defense,
N.Y. Times, Jan. 23, 1988, at 35 . . . . . . . . . . . . . . . 1339

Union Pacific Strikes a Dry Well with Pennzoil,
Corporate Control Alert, Dec. 1997, at 7 . . . . . . . . 1172, 1345

Van Der Weide, Against Fiduciary Duties to Corpo-
rate Stakeholders, 21 Del. J. Corp. L. 27 (1996) . . . . . . 821-22

Van Gorkom, The 'Big Bang' for Director Liability:
The Chairman's Report, Directors & Boards, Fall
1987, at 17 . . . . . . . . . . . . . . . . . . . . . . . . . . . . 151

Varallo & Dreisbach, Amsted Industries: Structuring
the Sale of Corporate Control Outside the Auction
Context, 4 Insights: The Corporate & Securities Law
Advisor, May 1990, at 31 . . . . . . . . . . . . . . . . . . . . . 957

Veasey, Duty of Loyalty: The Criticality of the
Counselor's Role, 45 Bus. Law. 2065 (1990) . . . . . . . 85, 829

Veasey, New Insights Into Judicial Deference to
Directors' Business Decisions: Should We Trust the
Courts?, 39 Bus. Law. 1461 (1984) . . . . . . . . . . . . . . . 101

Veasey, Seeking a Safe Harbor from Judicial Scrutiny
of Directors' Business Decisions—An Analytical

Framework for Litigation Strategy and Counselling Directors, 37 Bus. Law. 1247 (1982) ............. 1721

Veasey, The Defining Tension in Corporate Governance in America, 52 Bus. Law. 393 (1997)
.............. 3, 46, 127, 198, 227-28, 230, 538, 1771

Veasey, The Director and the Dynamic Corporation Law with Special Emphasis on Oversight and Disclosure, 5 The Corporate Governance Advisor No. 4, July/Aug. 1997, at 22 .................... 46, 144-45

Veasey, The New Incarnation of the Business Judgment Rule in Takeover Defenses, 11 Del. J. Corp. L. 503 (1986) ............................... 648

Veasey & Finkelstein, New Delaware Statute Allows Limits on Director Liability and Modernizes Indemnification Protection, 6 Bus. Law. Update 1 (July/Aug. 1986) ...................... 237-38, 1884, 2157

Veasey, Finkelstein & Bigler, Delaware Supports Directors with a Three-Legged Stool of Limited Liability, Indemnification, and Insurance, 42 Bus. Law. 399 (1987) ............................. 1967-68

Veasey & Manning, Codified Standard—Safe Harbor or Uncharted Reef? An Analysis of the Model Act Standard of Care Compared with Delaware Law, 35 Bus. Law. 919 (1980) ..................... 132

Veasey & Seitz, The Business Judgment Rule in the Revised Model Act, the Trans Union Case, and the ALI Project—A Strange Porridge, 63 Tex. L. Rev. 1483 (1985) .................. 84, 102, 117, 132, 139

Verespej, Boardroom Roulette, Ind. Wk., Aug. 10, 1987, at 47 . . . . . . . . . . . . . . . . . . . . . . . . . . 2164

Vermont: Land of Green Mountains and Self-Insurance, Bus. Wk., Aug. 21, 1989, at 77 . . . . . . . . . . . . . . 2154

Victor, D & O Canceled and Unocal Sues, Legal Times, July 29, 1985, at 1 . . . . . . . . . . . . . . . . . . . . 1997

Victor, Rhetoric Is Hot When the Topic Is Takeovers, Legal Times, Dec. 23, 1985, at 2 . . . . . . . . . . . . . . . . . 151

Wachtell, Special Tender Offer Litigation Tactics, 32 Bus. Law. 1433 (1977) . . . . . . . . . . . . . . . . . . . . . . 1345

Waldman, Texaco-Pennzoil Case Makes Firms Careful About Merger Moves, Wall St. J., Apr. 15, 1986, at 1 . . . . . 1001

Wallman, Corporate Constituency Statutes: Placing the Corporation's Interests First, 11 Bus. Law. Update, Nov./Dec. 1990, at 1. . . . . . . . . . . . . . . . . . . . . . . 821

Wallman, The Proper Interpretation of Corporate Constituency Statutes and Formulations of Director Duties, 21 Stetson L. Rev. 163 (1991) . . . . . . . . . . . . . . . . . 821

Wander & Jerue, Indemnification and Securities Litigation, in 7 Securities Law Techniques (A.A. § 121 Sommer, Jr. ed. 1998) . . . . . . . . . . . . . . . . . . . . . 1984

Wander & LeCoque, Boardroom Jitters: Corporate Control Transactions and Today's Business Judgment Rule, 42 Bus. Law. 29 (1986) . . . . . . . . . . . . . . . . . . 1321

Weiss, Doing D & O Insurance Right, 4 Bus. Law Today No. 2, Nov./Dec. 1994, at 50 . . 1989, 2000, 2047, 2093

Weiss, Filling the Gaps in D & O Insurance, 6 Bus.
Law Today No. 3, Jan./Feb. 1997, at 44
. . . . . . . . . . . . . 1989, 1996, 2000, 2031, 2046, 2136, 2172

Williams, Advising Committees of Boards of Directors
Formed to Investigate Stockholder Demands, LXII
Prentice Hall Law & Business Corporation Bulletin
No. 6, Mar. 19, 1991 . . . . . . . . . . . . . . . . . . . . . . . 1595

Work, Are Golden Parachutes Turning Platinum?,
U.S. News & World Rep., Feb. 3, 1986, at 49 . . . . . . . . 1314

Wriston, "Risk", the American Law Institute, and the
Corporate Director, in National Legal Center for the
Public Interest, The American Law Institute and Corporate Governance: An Analysis and Critique 7
(1987) . . . . . . . . . . . . . . . . . . . . . . . . . . . . . . . . . 2175

1984 Wyatt Directors and Officers Liability Survey . 2164, 2166

1985 Wyatt Directors and Officers Liability Survey . . . . . 2164

1994 Wyatt Directors and Officers Liability Survey . . . . . 2171

1996 Watson Wyatt Worldwide D & O Liability Sur-
vey Report (1996) . . . . . . . . . . . . . . . . . . . . . . 2172-73

1997 Watson Wyatt Worldwide D & O Liability Sur-
vey Report (1997) . . . . . . . . . . 1895, 2109-10, 2136, 2172-73

# INDEX*

## A

Abuse of Discretion, as Means of Rendering Business Judgment Rule Inapplicable, 39, 84-90, 110

Acquisitions Creating Antitrust Problems for Potential Acquiror, 1332-33

Acquisition Creating Other Regulatory Problems for Potential Acquiror, 1339

Advance Notice Provisions (see Shark Repellent Charter and Bylaw Provisions)

Advancement of Expenses, in Indemnification and Insurance Contexts

    Indemnification, Compared, 1895

    Indemnification Context (see Mandatory Indemnification and Permissive Indemnification headings)

    Insurance Context, 2092-109

    Notice to Shareholders, 1979

    Policy Rationale, 1894-95, 1911, 1921-22, 2092-93

Aiding and Abetting Director Breaches of Fiduciary Duty, 252-54, 615

All-Holders Rule

    Discriminatory Self-Tender or Exchange Offer Context, 1010-11

    Poison Pill Shareholder Rights Plan Context, 1134

Allocation Between Claims, for Insurance Purposes, 2109, 2136-39

Allocation Between Defendants, for Insurance Purposes

    Burden of Proof, 2132-35

---

* AUTHORS' NOTE: This Index does not list the individual cases, statutes, transactions or individuals referred to in this book. This Index is only intended to refer the reader to the legal subjects addressed in the text.

Case Law, 2113-32

Generally, 2109-10

Good Faith Required, 2127-29

Larger Settlement Approach, 2110-11, 2115-25, 2129-31

New Policy Approaches, 2135-36

Proportional Fault/Relative Exposure Approach, 2111-15, 2125

American Bar Association Committee on Corporate Laws (see Committee on Corporate Laws heading)

American Law Institute (see Principles of Corporate Governance heading)

Anti-Greenmail Provisions, 1249, 1364

Antitrust Issues, as Defensive Strategy

Acquisitions Creating Antitrust Problems for Potential Acquiror, 1332-33

Antitrust Litigation, 1333-38

Competitor Standing to Challenge Acquisitions on Antitrust Grounds, 1337-38

Corporation's Standing to Challenge Acquisition on Antitrust Grounds, 1333-37

Antitrust Litigation (see Antitrust Issues, as Defensive Strategy heading)

Appraisal

Definition, 476-77

Determination of Fair Value, 477-83

Breach of Fiduciary Duty Claim, Compared, 483-88

Court Approval Required to Dismiss or Settle Appraisal Proceeding, 488

Inadvertent Tender of Shares Subject to Appraisal, 488-89

When Appraisal Remedy is Available, 370, 476-77

When Appraisal Remedy is Exclusive Remedy, 489-98

Asset Options, as Defensive Strategy, 918-34

Asset Sales, as Defensive Strategy, 904-08

## B

Back End Shareholder Rights Plan Provisions, 1089, 1121-34

Bank Directors (see Financial Institution Directors heading)

Blasius Voting Rule

    Blasius Rule, 790-92

    Business Judgment Rule Inapplicable, 790

    In Delaware, 790-99

    Outside of Delaware, 805-08

    Simultaneous Tender Offers and Proxy Contests, 799-805

Board Size (see Shark Repellent Charter and Bylaw Provisions)

Board's Response to Demand

    Board Entitled to Adequate Time, 1570-71, 1596-1605

    Board May Act on its Own or Upon Advice of Officer, Board Committee or Law Firm, 1595-96

    Board Options: Litigate in Corporation's Name, Let Shareholder Litigate in Corporation's Name or Refuse Demand, 1593-94

    Business Judgment Rule Standard of Review, 1605-49

    Cases Involving Unlawful Conduct, 1649-55

    Discovery in Connection with Motion to Dismiss, 1673-81

    Model Business Corporation Act, 1655-58, 1676

    Neutrality Not Permitted, 1594-95

    No Required Procedure, 1595

    Principles of Corporate Governance, 1665-73, 1680-81

    Section 220 Action, 1677-80

    State Statutes, 1658-65, 1676

    Termination by Special Litigation Committee Where Demand is Excused, Compared, 1689-90, 1711-12

    Universal Demand Requirement (see separate heading)

    Waiver: Board that Delegates Decision-Making Authority with Respect to a Demand Waives Any Claim that Demand is Required and that Board is Disinterested and Independent, 1586-92, 1596

    Wrongful Refusal, 1605-49

Break-Up Fees, 957-79

Bridge Financing, 901-03

Business Judgment Doctrine, 6

Business Judgment Rule

Abuse of Discretion, as Means of Rendering Rule Inapplicable, 39, 84-90, 110

Advancement, 1899-1901, 1911

Applicability in Context of Motion to Dismiss, 27-28

Attaches Ab Initio, 27

Blasius Voting Rule, 790

Burden of Proof, Generally, 18-19, 25-28, 110-11, 264

Burden of Proof, in Corporate Control Transactions (see Revlon-QVC Rule and Unocal Rule headings)

Business Decision, as Element of, 39, 40-41, 110

Business Judgment Doctrine, 6

Cash-Out Merger Transactions (see separate heading)

Codification, 100-06

Compensation (see separate heading)

Controlling Shareholder Transactions (see separate heading)

Corporate Opportunities (see separate heading)

Corporate Control Transactions, Applicability to (see Revlon-QVC Rule and Unocal Rule headings)

D & O Insurance, Relationship to, 1851

Defensive Strategies, Applicability to (see Corporate Control Transactions and Defensive or Protective Strategies headings)

Definition, 4-5, 18, 20-25

Demand Requirement, Relationship to, 1379, 1473, 1479-82, 1605-13

Derivative Litigation, Relationship to, 1379

Disinterestedness, as Element of (see separate heading)

Due Care, as Element of (see separate heading)

Duty of Care, Relationship to, 110-13

Duty of Disclosure, Relationship to, 508-10

Duty of Loyalty, Relationship to, 264-65

Elements of Business Judgment Rule (see separate heading)

Evolution Historically, 7-8, 9-11

Evolution During Last Two Decades, 8

Fairness Standard Where Business Judgment Rule is Inapplicable (see Fairness Standard heading)

Effect of the Rule, Generally, 5, 32-33, 35-39

Fraud, Business Judgment Rule Inapplicable to, 90-91, 110

Freeze-Out Merger Transactions (see separate heading)

Going Private Merger Transactions (see separate heading)

Good Faith, as Element of, 39, 80-84

Illegality, Business Judgment Rule Inapplicable to, 90-93, 110

Indemnification, Relationship to, 1851

Insurance, Relationship to, 1851

Interested Director Transactions, 264

Model Business Corporation Act, 25, 100-04

Officers, Applicability to, 97-100

Parent-Subsidiary Transactions, 370-76

Permissive Indemnification, 1873, 1887-88, 1890-91

Pleading Requirements, 25-28

Presumption, 4-5, 18-25, 106, 110-11

Principles of Corporate Governance, 100, 105-06

Protection of Decisions, 6-7

Protection of Directors, 6-7

Rationale, 12-18

Shareholder Voting, Relationship to, 508-10, 790-805

Special Committees, in Change of Control Transactions, 824-31

Special Committees, in Controlling Shareholder Transactions, 264, 402-08

Special Litigation Committees (see Termination of Derivative Litigation by Special Litigation Committees heading)

Standard of Review, Not Standard of Conduct, 4

Suits by Corporation, 5

Suits by Regulatory Bodies that have Assumed Control of Corporation, 5

Suits by Shareholders as Individuals, 5

Suits by Shareholders Acting as a Class, 5

Suits by Shareholders Acting Derivatively on Behalf of Corporation, 5, 1379

Termination of Derivative Litigation (see Termination of Derivative Litigation by Special Litigation Committees heading)

Ultra Vires Conduct, Business Judgment Rule Inapplicable to, 90-91, 110

Unlawful Conduct, Business Judgment Rule Inapplicable to, 90-93, 110

Waste, Business Judgment Rule Inapplicable to, 93-94, 110

Business Decision Element of the Business Judgment Rule, 39, 40-41, 110

Bylaw Provisions, as Defensive Strategy (see Shark Repellent Charter and Bylaw Provisions heading)

# C

Candor, Duty of, 500

Captive Insurance Subsidiaries, 2153-62

Cash-Out Merger Transactions

Definition, 377

Fairness Standard (see Controlling Shareholder Transaction heading)

Causation, as Element of Breach of Fiduciary Duty, 112-14, 264

Charter Provisions, as Defensive Strategy (see Shark Repellent Charter and Bylaw Provisions heading)

Chewable Shareholder Rights Plan Provisions, 1089-90

Choice of Law

Demand on Directors, 1455-67

Demand on Shareholders, 1686

Director Duties, Generally, 2

Termination of Derivative Litigation, 1455-67

Claims by Early Bidders Against Later Bidders, 1000-02

Claim Made Requirement in D & O Insurance Policies

Claim Made Policies, 1997

Claim Made Versus Claims First Made Policies, 1999

Claim Made Versus Occurrence Policies, 1997-98

Date of Claim, 2007-08

Definition of Claim, When Defined in Policy, 1999-2000

Definition of Claim, When Not Defined in Policy, 2000-07

Definition of Claim, in Context of Regulatory Actions Involving Financial Institutions, 2003-07

Potential Claim Sometimes Sufficient, 1998

Post-Policy Tail Period, 1998-99

Run-Off Policy, 1999

Coercion (see Wrongful Coercion heading)

Committee on Corporate Laws

Corporate Director's Guidebook, 1, 118-19, 262-63, 266-67, 296

Generally, 100, 101

Guidelines for the Unaffiliated Director of the Controlled Corporation, 471-76

Model Business Corporation Act (see separate heading)

Section of Business Law of the American Bar Association, 100, 101

Compensation

Business Judgment Rule, 311-14, 318, 1301

Generally, 308-09

Golden Parachutes (see separate heading)

Model Business Corporation Act, 318

Reasonableness Standard, 309-11, 1301

Principles of Corporate Governance, 318-20

Retroactive Compensation, 315-16

Severance Compensation, 314

State Statutes, 309

Stock Options (see separate heading)

Tax Deductibility of Compensation Exceeding $1 Million, 320

Tin Parachutes (see separate heading)

Waste, 311-13, 1301

Where Approved by Disinterested Directors or Shareholders, 309-15

Where Not Approved by Disinterested Directors or Shareholders, 315-17

Confidentiality Agreements, 772-77

Consent Solicitations (see Shark Repellent Charter and Bylaw Provisions heading)

Contemporaneous Ownership Requirement, 488, 1385-98

Contests for Corporate Control (see Corporate Control Transactions and Defensive Strategies headings)

Continuing Director Shareholder Rights Plan Provisions, 1184-90

Control

    Definition, 344

    Case Law, 344-48

    Controlling Shareholder Transactions (see separate heading)

    Corporate Control Transactions (see separate heading)

    Principles of Corporate Governance, 348-49

Control Premiums, 363-68

Control Transactions (see Corporate Control Transactions heading)

Controlling Shareholders

    Controlling Shareholder Transactions (see separate heading)

    Fiduciary Duty to Minority Shareholders, Generally, 263-64, 342, 349-62

    Fiduciary Duty to Shareholder-Employee, 362

    Rights as Shareholder, 342, 349-62, 777-83

Controlling Shareholder Transactions

    Appraisal (see separate heading)

    Board Responsibilities in Cases Involving Competing Offers, Including One by a Controlling Shareholder, 777-83

    Business Judgment Rule Inapplicable, 264, 405-08

    Business Purpose Requirement In Some Jurisdictions, 467-71

    Control Premiums, 363-68

    Definition of Control, 344-49

    Duties Under Revlon-QVC Rule, 715-16, 777-83

    Duty of Loyalty, Generally, 342

    Fairness Not Required In Tender Offer by Controlling Shareholder to Minority Shareholders, 360-62

    Fairness Not Required Where Controlling Shareholder Does Not Stand on Both Sides of Transactions, 369-70

Fairness Required Where Controlling Shareholder Stands on Both Sides of Transaction, 368-70, 377-78

Fairness Standard, Applications, 380-467

Fairness Standard, Generally, 28-32, 378-80, 399-400

Fairness Standard, Where Disinterested Director or Special Committee Approval is Obtained, 402-67

Fairness Standard, Where Minority Shareholder Approval is Obtained, 400-02

Guidelines for the Unaffiliated Director of the Controlled Corporation, 471-76

Potential Benefits, 342

Principles of Corporate Governance, 471

Corporate Control Transactions

Blasius Voting Rule (see separate heading)

Business Judgment Rule, Generally, 631-49, 733-36, 790

Defensive Strategies (see Defensive or Protective Strategies heading)

Demand on Directors Requirement in Derivative Litigation, 1513-17

Entrenchment, 635-36

Fairness Standard, Where Business Judgment Rule is Inapplicable, 645, 735

Fairness Standard, Where Revlon-QVC Rule Applies But Is Not Satisfied, 735

Fairness Standard, Where Unocal Rule Applies But Is Not Satisfied, 645

Non-Shareholder Constituencies (see separate heading)

Pre-Planned Strategies, 639-40

Principles of Corporate Governance, 693-94, 817

Protective Strategies (see Defensive or Protective Strategies heading)

Retroactive Strategies, 635

Revlon-QVC Rule (see separate heading)

Outside Directors, Generally, 643, 823-32

Simultaneous Tender Offers and Proxy Contests, 799-805

Special Committees, Generally, 823-32

Standing of Potential Acquiror to Challenge Board Actions, 832-34

State Statutes, 688-93, 730, 812-17, 1099, 1102-03, 1190-94, 1321, 1327-28

Unocal Rule (see separate heading)

Corporate Director's Guidebook, 1, 118-19, 262-63, 266-67, 296

Corporate Opportunities

    Business Judgment Rule, Where Applicable, 300-01

    Corporate Opportunity Doctrine, 293-94

    Definition of Corporate Opportunity, 294-300

    Disclosure as Defense, 301-02, 305-08

    Disinterested Director Approval, 300-01

    Fairness Standard of Review, Where Applicable, 301-05

    Model Business Corporation Act, 300-01

    Principles of Corporate Governance, 305-07

Court-Ordered Advancement

    Enforcement of Charter, Bylaw or Contract Right to Mandatory Advancement, 1992-93

    Enforcement of Statutory Right to Mandatory Advancement, 1992-93

    Expenses Incurred in Connection with Enforcing Charter, Bylaw, Contract or Statutory Right to Mandatory Advancement 1933-38

    Model Business Corporation Act, 1937, 1946

    Principles of Corporate Governance, 1937-38, 1946

    Where Advancement Is Not Otherwise Required, 1940-46

Court-Ordered Indemnification

    Enforcement of Charter, Bylaw or Contract Right to Mandatory Indemnification, 1992-93

    Enforcement of Statutory Right to Mandatory Indemnification, 1992-93

    Expenses Incurred in Connection with Enforcing Charter, Bylaw, Contract or Statutory Right to Mandatory Indemnification, 1933-38

    Model Business Corporation Act, 1937, 1938-39

    Principles of Corporate Governance, 1937-38, 1940

    Where Indemnification Is Not Otherwise Required, 1938-40

Crown Jewel Asset Sales, 904-08

Cumulative Voting Rights, 1249

# D

D & O Insurance (see Insurance)

D & O Insurance Crisis of the Mid-1980s

    Causes, 2165-67

    Generally, 1852, 2163-65

    Responses to (see Responses to D & O Insurance Crisis of the Mid-1980s heading)

Damages or Basis for Injunctive Relief

    Duty of Care Action, 112-17

    Duty of Disclosure Action, 530-39

    Duty of Loyalty Action, 264-65

    Nominal Damages, 117

    Rescission, 33-35, 115-16, 461-62

Dead Hand Shareholder Rights Plan Provisions, 1184-90

Debt Shareholder Rights Plan Provisions, 1089, 1121-34

Defensive or Protective Strategies

    Acquisitions Creating Antitrust Problems, 1332-33

    Antitrust Litigation, 1333-38

    Acquisitions Creating Other Regulatory Problems, 1339

    Asset Options, 918-34

    Asset Sales, 904-08

    Break-Up Fees, 957-79

    Bridge Financing, 901-03

    Confidentiality Agreements, 772-77

    Bylaw Provisions (see Shark Repellent Charter and Bylaw Provisions heading)

    Charter Provisions (see Shark Repellent Charter and Bylaw Provisions heading)

    Confidentiality Agreements, 772-77

    Crown Jewel Asset Sales, 904-08

    Disparate Class Common Stock (see Super-Voting Common Stock)

    Dual Class Common Stock (see Super-Voting Common Stock)

Employee Stock Ownership Plans ("ESOPs") (see separate heading)

ESOPs (see Employee Stock Ownership Plans heading)

Exchange Offers (see separate heading)

Expense Reimbursement Provisions, 957-58, 963-65, 969, 972, 974-75, 978-79

Exploding Warrants, 1144-46

Extraordinary Dividends (see separate heading)

Fair Price Provisions, 1248, 1249

Friendly Third Party Stock Acquisitions, 834-53

Golden Parachutes (see separate heading)

Greenmail (see separate heading)

Just Say No, 1171-83

Leg-Up and Lock-Up Stock Options, 909-17

Litigation, 1343-48

Lock-Up Asset Options, 918-34

Market Test or Check Provisions, 769-70, 935, 945-57

No Shop Provisions, 935-42

Options, 909-34

Pac-Man Defense, 1339-43

Pension Fund Assets, Utilization of (see Employee Stock Ownership Plan heading)

Poison Pill Shareholder Rights Plans (see Shareholder Rights Plan heading)

Poison Put Bonds, 1090

Reincorporation, 1249, 1252-53

Repurchase Transactions (see Exchange Offers, Greenmail and Self-Tender Offers headings)

Restrictive Covenants, 1035-38

Sale of Assets, 904-08

Sale of Stock (see White Squire Transactions heading)

Self-Tender Offers (see separate heading)

Settlement (see separate heading)

Shareholder Meeting Dates (see separate heading)

Shareholder Meeting Record Dates (see Shareholder Meeting Dates heading)

Shareholder Rights Plans (see separate heading)

Shark Repellent Charter and Bylaw Provisions (see separate heading)

Springing Warrants, 1144-46

Standstill Agreements, 1349, 1368-77

Stock Options, 909-17

Stock Sales (see White Squire Transactions heading)

Supermajority Provisions, 1247, 1250, 1285-86, 1287

Super-Voting Common Stock (see separate heading)

Termination Fees, 957-79

Tin Parachutes (see separate heading)

Topping Fees, 979-82

White Knight Transactions and Inducements (see separate heading)

White Squire Transactions (see separate heading)

Window Shop Provisions, 935, 942-45

Delaware, Role in Corporate Law, 3-4

Delegation, 198-99, 214-24

Demand on Directors

Allegations that are Insufficient to Excuse Demand, 1488-502

Aronson Test, 1472-74, 1474-75, 1479-529

Board's Response to Demand (see separate heading)

Business Judgment Rule, Relation to, 1379, 1473, 1479-82, 1605-13

Changes in Board Composition, 1474, 1478, 1572-78

Choice of Law, 1455-67

Corporate Control Transactions, 1513-17

Definition, 1407, 1425-29

Director Protection Statutes, 1500-01, 1533

Director's Fees, 1496

Discovery in Connection with Motion to Dismiss, 1673-81

Dismissal With/Without Prejudice for Failure to Make Demand, 1592-93

Due Care Allegations, 1498, 1521-24

Effect of Procedural Context on Level of Interest Required to Disqualify Directors, 1773-75

Evenly Divided Board, 1477-79

Extreme Cases, 1519-21

Financial Ties to Corporation, 1496-97

Forum-Shopping, 1460

Fraud, 1499

Futility, Generally, 1467-71

Futility Under California Law, 1560-62

Futility Under Delaware Law: Aronson, 1472-75, 1479-529

Futility Under Delaware Law: Rales, 1473-75, 1529-43

Futility Under New York Law, 1543-60

Inconsistent with Federal Policy Exception to Demand Requirement, 1456-57, 1460-67

Insured Versus Insured Exclusion, 1500

Interestedness and Lack of Independence Allegations, 1490-1502, 1504-12

Limited Partnership Context (see Limited Partnership Derivative Litigation heading)

Model Business Corporation Act, 1562-64, 1570-71, 1655-58

Need for Prompt Judicial Relief, 1502-04, 1562

Oversight Cases, 145-46, 1537-43

Participation in Alleged Wrongdoing, 1488-90

Pleading with Particularity Requirement, 1427, 1473-74, 1479-82, 1530, 1543-44, 1560

Principles of Corporate Governance, 1562-64, 1571, 1665-73

Rales Test, 1473, 1474-75, 1529-43

Ratification, 1499

Rationale, 1407, 1440-54

Reasonable Doubt, 1475-77, 1549

Refusal of Demand (see Board's Response to Demand heading)

Required Content of Demand, 1427-40

Section 16(b) Demand Requirement, 1415-16, 1684-86

Standing to Raise Demand as a Defense, 1681-84

State Law Governs Unless Inconsistent with Federal Policy, 1455-67

Statute of Limitations, 1501

Substantive Nature of Requirement, 1426

Sue Themselves, Board Colleagues, Friends or Business Associates Allegations, 1492-93

Termination of Derivative Litigation by Special Litigation Committees Where Demand is Required, Relationship to, 1689-90

Time at which Need for Demand is Determined, 1474-75, 1478, 1572

Two Means of Complying with Demand Requirement: Allege that Demand is Excused or Allege that Demand was Made and Wrongfully Refused, 1454-55

Universal Demand Requirement (see separate heading)

Unlawful Conduct, 1499

Voting Rights Allegations, 1517-19

Waiver: Board that Delegates Decision-Making Authority with Respect to a Demand Waives Any Claim that Demand is Required and that Board is Disinterested and Independent, 1586-92, 1596

Waiver: Shareholder Who Makes a Demand Waives Any Claim that Demand is Excused or that Board is Not Disinterested and Independent, 1578-86

Waste, 1524-29

Wrongful Refusal (see Board's Response to Demand heading)

Demand on Shareholders

Choice of Law, 1686

Criticism of Requirement, 1687

Futility, 1687-89

Model Business Corporation Act, 1687

Principles of Corporate Governance, 1687

Rationale, 1687

Required in Some Jurisdictions, 1407

Derivative Litigation

Action Belongs to Corporation, 1379-84, 1440-54

By Fifty Percent Shareholders, 1383

By Majority Shareholders, 1383-84

Confidentiality, 1826-49

Contemporaneous Ownership Requirement, 1385-98

Corporation is Necessary Party, 1382

Corporation's Agreement to Arbitrate Claims Brought Derivatively, 1383-84

Corporation's Right to Defend, 1382

Damages Paid to Corporation, 1381-82

Definition, 1379-80

Demand on Directors (see separate heading)

Demand on Shareholders (see separate heading)

Direct Actions, Distinguished, 1411-1415

Diversity Jurisdiction, 1416-25

Double Derivative Action, 1415-16, 1533-37

Extraordinary Procedural Device, 1454

Extraordinary Remedy, 1454

Fair and Adequate Representation Requirement, 1398-1403

Garner Doctrine, 1820-26, 1828-49

Historical Origins, 1380

Limited Partnership Context (see Limited Partnership Derivative Litigation heading)

Model Business Corporation Act, 1384, 1386-87, 1397, 1403, 1406, 1408, 1562-64, 1570-71, 1655-58

Potential Abuse, 1384-85

Prerequisites and Special Rules, 1384-1425

Principles of Corporate Governance, 1823-25, 1827-28, 1387-88, 1397-98, 1399, 1403, 1406, 1408, 1416, 1562-64, 1571, 1665-73

Privilege, 1819-26, 1828-49

Public Access to Court Filings, 1826-49

Role of Business Judgment Rule, Generally, 1379

Security for Expenses, 1403-07

Settlement, 1408-11

Special Litigation Committees, Where Demand is Excused (see Termination of Derivative Litigation by Special Litigation Committees heading)

Termination of Derivative Litigation by Special Litigation Committees (see separate heading)

Two-Fold Nature of Action, 1381-82

Triple Derivative Action, 1416

Work Product, 1819-20, 1822-23, 1828-49

Different Interests Among Different Shareholder Groups, 67-70, 559-90

Direct Versus Derivative Action, 1411-15

Director Protection Statutes

Ceiling on Liability, 233-34, 236-38

Delaware Cases, 227-30

Demand on Directors, 1500-01, 1533

Duty of Care Claims, Application to, 229

Duty of Disclosure Claims, Application to, 229-30

Duty of Loyalty Claims, Application to, 227

Elimination of Liability, 226-36, 152, 167

Equitable Relief, 228

Financial Institutions, 247-49

Heightened Standard of Culpability, 238-42

Model Business Corporation Act, 234-36

New York Cases, 231-33

Officers, Application to, 228

Origins, 226, 2168

Principles of Corporate Governance, 236-37

Raincoat Provisions, Also Known as, 226

Discriminatory Exchange or Self-Tender Offers, 1008-11

Disinterestedness

Defensive Strategies, 645

Definition of Interest, 41-44

Demand on Directors Context, 1490-1502, 1504-12

Differing Interests among Shareholder Groups, 67-69

Director's Fees, 61-63, 1496

Disqualifying Interest Must Afflict Majority, 42-43, 56-67, 616-17

Disqualifying Interest Must be Material, 44, 47-53

Disqualifying Interest Must be a Financial Interest or Entrenchment, 44

Effect of Procedural Context on Level of Interest Required to Disqualify Directors, 1773-75

Element of Business Judgment Rule, 39, 41-44, 110

Examples, 53-61, 1504-12

Principles of Corporate Governance, 70-71

Ownership of Stock, 63-67

Termination of Derivative Litigation Context, 1744-73

Texas Statute, 71-74

Disparate Class Common Stock (see Super-Voting Common Stock)

Disproportionate Voting Shareholder Rights Plan Provisions, 1135-44

Dividends

Ordinary Dividends, 1039

Extraordinary Dividends, as Defensive Strategy (see Extraordinary Dividends)

Double Derivative Action, 1415-16, 1533-37

Dual Class Common Stock (see Super-Voting Common Stock)

Dual Directorships, 269-70

Due Care

Duty of Care (see separate heading)

Element of Business Judgment Rule, 39, 74-75, 110

Duty of Care

Applies to Decision-Making Process, Not Result, 126

Board Decision Context, 40-41, 126, 134-40

Board Non-Decision or Oversight Context, 40-41, 126-32, 140-46

Business Judgment Rule, Relationship to, 110-13

Decisions Finding Due Care, 179-98

Decisions Finding Lack of Due Care, 146-79, 612-14

Decisions in Demand on Directors Requirement Context, 1521-24

Causation Required to State Breach of Duty of Care Claim, 112-14

Damages or Need for Injunctive Relief Required to State Breach of Duty of Care Claim, 112-17

Delegation, 214-24

Director Protection Statutes, 133-34, 152, 167, 614-15

Disqualifying Lack of Due Care Must Afflict Majority, 75, 1523-24

Elements of Breach of Duty of Care Claim, 110-13

Factors Considered by Courts, 184-95

Generally, 1, 74, 109

Gross Negligence Standard for Liability, 75-77, 124, 132, 134-37, 140-41, 144

Imposition of Liability for Breach of Duty of Care, 109-10, 132-46

Liability for Bad Judgment, 37-39, 84-90, 132-33

Model Business Corporation Act, 2, 103-04, 109-10, 112, 117-18, 119-23, 127-28

Nominal Damages for Breach, Availability of, 117

Non-Shareholder Constituencies (see separate heading)

Permissive Indemnification and Advancement, 1873, 1887-88, 1890-91, 1899-901

Ratification, 112, 224-25

Reasonably Available Material Information, 75, 77-80

No Pre-Set Formula or Required Procedures, 77-80

Reliance, 198-214

Standard of Care, 2, 117-32

Standard of Culpability, 132-46

Unfairness Required to State Breach of Duty of Care Claim, 112, 150-51, 157-67

Duty of Candor, 500

Duty of Disclosure

Applicability Where Shareholder Action Is Sought, 500-01

Applicability Where Shareholder Action Is Not Sought, 501-05

Approval of Corporate Actions Where Required by Statute, 529-30

Burden of Proof, 528

Definition, 107, 499

Duty of Candor, 500

Going Private, Self-Tender Offer and Exchange Offer Transactions, 526-27

Majority of Shareholders Versus Majority of Disinterested Shareholders, 275-76, 529-30

Materiality Standard, Cases Applying, 516-25

Materiality Standard, Generally, 510-16, 521-25

Not Owed by Corporation, 507-08

Owed by Directors and Controlling Shareholders, 499-500

Ratification Context, 528-29

Remedies: Director Protection Statutes, 535-39

Remedies: Injunctive Relief, 530

Remedies: Money Damages, Need to Prove Economic Harm, 530-35

Role of Business Judgment Rule, 508-10

Soft Information, 505-07

Transactions Where Vote Is Controlled by Controlling Shareholder, 527-28

Duty of Loyalty

Advancement of Expenses in Indemnification Context, 1900-03

Business Judgment Rule, Relationship to, 264-65

By Directors, 264, 265-341

By Controlling Shareholders, 264, 342-498

Cash-Out Merger Transactions (see Controlling Shareholder Transactions heading)

Controlling Shareholder Transactions (see separate heading)

Generally, 1, 107-08, 261-64

Causation Requirement, 264

Compensation (see separate heading)

Control Premiums, 363-68

Corporate Opportunities (see separate heading)

Damages or Need for Injunctive Relief, 264-65

Interested Director Transactions (see separate heading)

Model Business Corporation Act, 2, 104

Parent-Subsidiary Transactions (see Controlling Shareholder Transactions heading)

Unfairness Required to State Claim, 264

# E

Elements of Breach of Fiduciary Duty Claim

Causation, as Element of Breach of Fiduciary Claim, 112-14, 204

Damages or Basis for Injunctive Relief (see separate heading)

Duty of Care, 110-17

Duty of Loyalty, 264-65

Elements of the Business Judgment Rule

Business Decision, 39, 40-41, 110

Disinterestedness and Independence (see separate headings)

Due Care (see separate heading)

Good Faith, 39, 80-83, 110, 118

No Abuse of Discretion, 39, 84-90, 110

Employee Tin Parachutes (see Tin Parachutes heading)

Employee Stock Ownership Plans ("ESOPs")

Cases Invalidating ESOPs, 855-70

Cases Upholding ESOPs Pursuant to the Business Judgment Rule, 870-72

Case Upholding ESOP Pursuant to Fairness Standard, 872-76

Director Liability for Trustee Conduct, 883-86

Disclosure Considerations, 855

Dual Service as Director and ESOP Trustee, 879-82

Duties of Trustee in Context of Tender Offer Opposed by Board, 879-80, 887, 888-901

ERISA Considerations, 878-901

Fiduciary Responsibilities Owed by ESOP Trustees, Generally, 853-55

Non-Defensive Uses, 853

Participant "Pass Through" Tendering and Voting Provisions, 887-901

Section 203, 876-78

Usefulness as Defensive Strategy, Generally, 853-54

Enhanced Scrutiny

Revlon-QVC Rule (see separate heading)

Unocal Rule (see separate heading)

Equal Treatment of Shareholders

All-Holders Rule, 1010-11

Common Shareholders, 559-70

Preferred Shareholders, 570-90

Self-Tender Offers and Exchange Offers, 1008-11

Shareholder Rights Plan Provisions, 1096-1103, 1135-44

ESOPs (see Employee Stock Ownership Plans)

Exchange Offers

Case Law, 1004-38

Equal Treatment of Shareholders, 1008-11

Generally, 1003-04

Restrictive Covenants in Debt Securities, 1035-38

Exclusions in D & O Insurance Policies

Acts Prior to Particular Date, 2037

Acts Prior to Particular Date by Some But Not All Insured Directors, 2037

Antitrust Claims, 2037

Bodily or Physical Injury or Death, 2031

Contest for Control Exclusion, 2040-44

Damage or Destruction to Tangible Property, 2031

Discrimination Claims, 2037

Dishonesty, 2030-33

Emotional Distress, 2031

Employment Practice Claims, 2033

Environmental Damage, 2031

ERISA or Comparable State Statute or Common Law Provision Claims, 2030-31

Insured Versus Insured Exclusion (see separate heading)

Illegal Renumeration, 2030

Libel and Slander Claims, 2033

Litigation Filed Prior to Policy's Effective Date or Other Specified Date, 2033-34

Notice Given under Prior Policy or Prior to Policy's Effective Date or Other Specified Date, 2033, 2034-36

Nuclear Accidents, 2031

Personal Profit Without Legal Entitlement, 2030

Punitive Damages, 1986, 2030

Regulatory Exclusion (see separate heading)

Risks Faced by Particular Insureds, 2037

Securities Law or Comparable Common Law Claims, 2037-39

Short-Swing Profit Liability Under Section 16(b), 2030

Takeover Exclusion, 2040

Treble Damages, 1986-87, 2030

Expense Reimbursement Provisions, 957-58, 963-65, 969, 972, 974-75, 978-79

Exploding Warrants, 1144-46

Extraordinary Dividends

Case Law, 1040-52

Comparison to Ordinary Dividends, 1039

Comparison to Self-Tender and Exchange Offers, 1039-40

Use as Defensive Strategy, Generally, 1003, 1039

# F

Fair and Adequate Representation Requirement in Derivative Litigation, 1398-1403

Fair Price/Fair Dealing (see Fairness Standard heading)

Fair Price Provisions, 1248, 1249

Fairness Standard

Applicable Where Business Judgment Rule Does Not Protect Board Conduct, 28-32

Applicable Where Revlon-QVC Rule Applies But Is Not Satisfied, 735

Applicable Where Unocal Rule Applies But Is Not Satisfied, 645

Burden of Proof, 18-19, 28

Comparison to Business Judgment Rule Standard, 19, 32-39

Compensation, 315-17

Controlling Shareholder Transactions, 264, 377-476

Corporate Control Transactions, 645, 735

Corporate Opportunities, 301-05

Duty of Care Context, 112, 150-51, 151-67

Duty of Loyalty Context, 264, 268-69, 282-88, 328-42, 370-76, 377-476

Effect Upon Damages, 33-34, 115-16

Fair Price/Fair Dealing Requirement, 30-31, 284, 378-80, 399-400

Generally, 28-32

Interested Director Context, 264, 268-69, 282-88, 301-05, 315-17, 328-42

Rationale, 29-30

Parent-Subsidiary Transaction Context, 370-76

Perfection Not Required, 31

Stock Option Context, 328-42

Fiduciary Duties

Aiding and Abetting Breach of, 252-54, 615

Breach of Fiduciary Duty Claim, Elements of, 110-17, 264-65

Contract Limitations, 108, 984-1000

Duty of Candor, 500

Duty of Care (see separate heading)

Duty of Disclosure (see separate heading)

Duty of Loyalty (see separate heading)

Equal Treatment of Shareholders (see separate heading)

Fiduciary Out Provisions, 983-84

Financially Troubled Corporations (see separate heading)

Generally, 1-2, 107-08

Not Owed to Prospective Shareholders, 108-09

Owed to and Not by Corporation, 507-08

To Creditors, Generally, 377, 590-96

To Majority of Shareholders Where Majority Does Not Control Board, 1340-43

To Preferred Shareholders, 570-90

Where Different Shareholder Groups Have Different Interests, 67-70, 559-90

Fiduciary Out Provisions, 983-84

Financial Advisor Liability

Aiding and Abetting Director Breach of Fiduciary Duty, 252-54

Breach of Duty to Corporation, 254-56

Breach of Duty to Shareholders, 256-61

Financial Institution Directors

Compared to Other Directors, 242-47, 595

Federal Statutes, 249-52

Principles of Corporate Governance, 243

State Statutes, 248-49

Financially Troubled Corporations

Cases Applying Business Judgment Rule Principles, 600-19, 627-29, 783-90

Cases Applying Trust Law Principles, 599-600, 627-29

Fiduciary Duties to Creditors, Generally, 590-96

Fiduciary Duties to Creditors Upon Insolvency, 596-619

Fiduciary Duties to Shareholders Upon Insolvency, 596-98

When is a Corporation Insolvent, 619-26

Flip In Shareholder Rights Plan Provisions, 1087-89, 1096-1121

Flip Over Shareholder Rights Plan Provisions, 1087-89, 1091-95

Foreign Entities, Takeover Bids by, 1339

Fraud

Business Judgment Rule Inapplicable, 90-91, 110

Demand on Directors Requirement, 1499

Freeze-Out Merger Transactions

Definition, 377

Fairness Standard (see Controlling Shareholder Transactions heading)

Friendly Third Party Stock Acquisitions, 834-53

Funding Trusts

    Golden Parachute Trusts, 1328-32

    Indemnification Trusts, 1976-79

# G

Going Private Merger Transactions

    Definition, 377

    Fairness Standard (see Controlling Shareholder Transactions heading)

Golden Parachutes

    Barriers to Judicial Review, 1299-1301

    Cases Enjoining or Questioning Golden Parachutes, 1312-19

    Cases Upholding Golden Parachutes, 1304-11

    Compensation, Generally (see Compensation heading)

    De Minimus Effect as Defensive Strategy, 1298-99

    Factors Considered by Courts, 1301-04

    Federal Statutes, 1319-21

    Funding Trusts, 1328-32

    Generally, 1296-98

    Shareholder Resolutions, 1321-22

    Standard of Judicial Review, 1301-04

    State Statutes, 1321, 1327-28

    Tin Parachutes (see separate heading)

Good Faith

    Element of the Business Judgment Rule, 39, 80-81, 110

    Generally, 80-83, 118

Greenmail

    Camoumail, 1350

    Cases Questioning Greenmail Transactions, 1356-63

    Cases Upholding Greenmail Transactions, 1351-56

    Charter Provisions, 1249, 1364

    Coercion, Duress and Hobbs Act Claims, 1356

Federal Statutes, 1367-68

Generally, 1349-50

Pale Green Greenmail, 1350

State Statutes, 1365-67

Gross Negligence Standard for Liability, 75-77, 132, 134-39, 140-41, 144

Guidelines for the Unaffiliated Director of the Controlled Corporation, 471-76

# H

Historical Origins

Business Judgment Rule, 9-11

Fiduciary Duties, 1

# I

Illegality

Business Judgment Rule Inapplicable to, 90-93, 110

Board Refusal of Demand, 1649-55

Demand on Directors, 1499

Termination of Derivative Litigation by Special Litigation Committees, 1649-55

Indemnification

Advancement of Expenses (see Mandatory Advancement and Permissive Advancement headings)

Actions by or in the Right of the Corporation, 1880-87, 1983

Actions by or in the Right of the Corporation, Where There is an Adjudication of Liability, 1881-83, 1918-20, 1924-25, 1983

Amounts Paid to Settle Actions by or in the Right of the Corporation, 1883-87

Judgments in Actions by or in the Right of the Corporation, 1883-87

Authorization of Permissive Indemnification (see Permissive Indemnification heading)

Bankruptcy, 1983-84

Business Judgment Rule, Relationship to, 1851

Charter or Bylaw Provisions, 1867-72

Common Law Origins, 1852

Court-Ordered Advancement (see separate heading)

Court-Ordered Indemnification (see separate heading)

Derivative Actions, 1883-87

Directors, Officers, Employees and Agents, Distinctions Among, 1855-57, 1866-67, 1875, 1889

Expenses Incurred as a Party Other Than a Defendant, 1947-49, 1952

Expenses Incurred as a Witness, 1949-52

Expenses Incurred in Connection with Obtaining Indemnification, 1874-75, 1933-38

Federal Savings Associations, 1855, 1866, 1880, 1886, 1894, 1962

Funding Mechanisms, 1976-79

Gaps in Availability, 1983-84

Generally, 1851

Indemnification Contracts, 1867-72

Independent or Special Counsel, 1888, 1891-92, 1893

Insurance, Relationship to, 1851

Mandatory Indemnification (see separate heading)

Model Business Corporation Act, 1854-59, 1865, 1867, 1872, 1875-78, 1880-85, 1887-89, 1891-95, 1904-09, 1911, 1928, 1931, 1937-39, 1946-47, 1952-53, 1959, 1961-62, 1969, 1979

No Distinction Between Actions by Corporation and Actions in the Right of the Corporation, 1881

Non-Exclusivity Provisions, 1886-87, 1959-69

Notice to Shareholders, 1979-80

Permissive Indemnification (see separate heading)

Principles of Corporate Governance, 1855, 1857-59, 1865-67, 1872, 1876, 1878-82, 1885-87, 1893-95, 1905-06, 1937-38, 1940, 1946, 1947, 1952-53, 1959, 1961, 1979

Policy Considerations and Limitations, 1852-55, 1969-76, 1983

Securities and Exchange Commission View, 1975, 1983

Shareholder Decision to Indemnify,

State Statutes, Generally, 1852, 1855

Types of Conduct Covered, 1952-59

Types of Proceedings Covered, 1946-47

Independence

Codifications, 70-74

Demand on Directors Context, 1504-12

Disqualifying Lack of Independence Must Afflict Majority, 42-43, 56-57

Disqualifying Lack of Independence Must Be Material, 44, 47-53

Element of Business Judgment Rule, 39, 42, 45, 110

Examples, 53-61

General Definition of Independence, 45-47

Presence of Controlling Shareholder, 45-46

Principles of Corporate Governance, 70-71

Structural Bias Theory, 1765-73

Termination of Derivative Litigation by Special Litigation Committee Context, 1744-73

Informed Decision Requirement (see Duty of Care heading)

Insurance

Advancement of Expenses, 1989, 2092-109

Allocation Between Claims, 2109, 2136-39

Allocation Between Defendants (see separate heading)

Ambiguity, 1990

Business Judgment Rule, Relationship to, 1851

Cancellation Provisions, 1996

Captive Insurance Subsidiaries, 2153-62

Claims Made Requirement (see separate heading)

Company Reimbursement Part, 1987-88, 2025

Consent to Settlement by Insureds, 1995-96

Consent to Settlement by Insurer, 1994-95

Contest for Corporate Control Exclusion, 2040-44

Current Market, 2172-75

D & O Crisis of the Mid-1980s (see separate heading)

D & O Insurance Not a Substitute for Other Insurance, 2039-40

Declarations, 1989

Deductibles, 1989

Directors and Officers Reimbursement Part, 1988, 2025

Endorsements, 1989

Entity Policies, 1988, 2136

Excess Policies, 1989, 1994

Exclusions (see separate heading)

Federal Savings Associations, 1982-83

Generally, 1851

Hammer Provisions, 1996

Indemnification, Relationship to, 1851

Insured Versus Insured Exclusion (see separate heading)

Limit on Liability, 1989, 1990, 1991-93

Losses Covered (see separate heading)

Misrepresentations in D & O Insurance Policy Applications (see separate heading)

Model Business Corporation Act, 1980-81

Need for, 1983-84

Notice Requirement (see separate heading)

Notice to Shareholders, 1979

Outside Director Policies,

Per Loss or Per Occurrence Limit on Liability,

Policy Applications, 2139-40

Pooling Arrangements, 2162-63

Premiums, 1989

Principles of Corporate Governance, 1982

Privilege, 1991

Public Policy Considerations and Limitations, 1980-81, 1982, 1983-87

Punitive Damages, 1986, 2030

Regulatory Exclusion (see separate heading)

Releases, 1997

Responses to D & O Crisis of the Mid-1980s (see separate heading)

Retentions, 1989

Securities and Exchange Commission View, 1983, 1987

Self-Insurance, 2153-62

State Statutes, 1978-79, 1980-83, 2156-57

Terms and Conditions Describing Claims Procedures, 1989

Treble Damages, 1986-87, 2030

Two-Part Structure, 1987

Typical D & O Insurance Policy Structure and Terms (see separate heading)

Typically No Obligation to Defend, 1990-91

Work Product Doctrine, 1991

Wrongful Act Requirement (see separate heading)

Insured Versus Insured Exclusion in D & O Insurance Policies,

Also Known as "One Versus One" or "1 vs. 1" Exclusion, 2045-46

Bankruptcy Context, 2049, 2068-74

Cases Construing Exclusion, 2047-54

Demand on Directors, 1500

Employment Practice and Wrongful Discharge Claims, 2046, 2050-53, 2053-54

Origin, 2044-45

Regulatory Context, 2054-68, 2084-92

Typical Language Used Today, 2046

Interestedness (see Disinterestedness heading)

Interestedness Director Transactions

Common Law Principle of Automatic Voidability, 265

Compensation (see separate heading)

Corporate Opportunities (see separate heading)

Disinterested Director Approval, 267-69, 271-74

Disinterested Shareholder Approval, 267-69, 274-82, 528-29

Fairness Standard Where Business Judgment Rule is Inapplicable, 268-69, 282-88

Methods of Restricting Interested Director Influence, 272-73

Model Business Corporation Act, 266, 273, 289-92

Potential Benefits, 266-67

Principles of Corporate Governance, 292-93

Shareholder Approval, 267-69, 274-82, 528-28

Safe Harbor Statutes, 267-69, 271, 274, 288-89

Stock Options (see separate heading)

Transactions Between Corporations Having Common Directors, 269-70

## J

Just Say No Defense, 1171-83

## L

Later, Better Offers

    Cases Holding that Directors Cannot Contract Away Fiduciary Duties, 984-94

    Cases Enforcing Merger Agreements Despite Changed Circumstances, 994-1000

    Claims By Early Bidders Against Later Bidders, 1000-02

    Fiduciary Out Provisions, 983-84

    Policy Considerations Supporting Enforcement of Merger Agreements Despite Changed Circumstances, 985-87

Leg-Up and Lock-Up Stock Options, 909-17

Limited Partnership Derivative Litigation

    Demand Requirement, 1805-06

    Special Litigation Committees, 1808-19

    Waiver: Limited Partner Who Makes a Demand Waives Any Claim that Demand is Excused or that General Partners are Disinterested and Independent, 1586, 1807-08

    Wrongful Refusal of Demand, 1806-08

Litigation, as Defensive Strategy, 1343-48

Lock-Up Asset Options, 918-34

Lolli-Pop Shareholder Rights Plan Provisions, 1121-34

Losses Covered by D & O Insurance Policies

    By Corporation, 2025, 2026-27

    By Directors and Officers, 2025

    Criminal Conduct, 1985, 2027

Definition, 2025

Dividend Paid to Settle Shareholder Suit, 2029-30

Indemnification, Distinguished, 2025

Intentional Wrongdoing, 1985, 2027

Return by Directors and Officers of Money or Property Wrongfully Taken from Corporation, 2027-29

Settlement Naming Corporation Rather Than Directors and Officers as Payer, 2026-27

# M

Mandatory Advancement

Business Judgment Made at Time Mandatory Advancement Provision is Adopted, 1911

Conduct Contrary to Corporation's Interests, 1913-14, 1918-28

Cases Enforcing Mandatory Advancement Provisions, 1909-10, 1913, 1914-28

Cases Not Enforcing Mandatory Advancement Provisions, 1926, 1927-28

Federal Savings Associations, 1931 32

Generally, 1894, 1909

Indemnification, Compared, 1895

Model Business Corporation Act, 1894-95, 1909, 1911, 1928, 1931

Policy Rationale, 1894-95, 1911, 1921-22

Punitive Damages Where Mandatory Advancement Provision Is Not Honored, 1910-11

Summary Determinations, 1911-12

Where There Is A Likelihood that Indemnification Will Not Be Allowed, 1914-15

Where Undertaking is Not Secured and Person Seeking Advancement Lacks the Financial Ability to Repay, 1916-17, 1923

Whether Indemnification Includes Advancement, 1928-32

Mandatory Indemnification

Cases Enforcing Mandatory Indemnification Provisions, 1867-68

Charter or Bylaw Provisions Mandating Indemnification, 1867-72

Conduct Contrary to Corporation's Interests, 1869
Directors, Officers, Employees and Agents, Compared, 1866-67
Federal Savings Associations, 1866
Finality Required, 1866
Indemnification Contracts, 1867-72
Model Business Corporation Act, 1857-59, 1865-67
No Business Judgment to be Made, 1869
On the Merits Versus on the Merits or Otherwise, 1857, 1859-65
Partial Success, 1863-65
Successful Versus Wholly Successful, 1858, 1863-65
Permissive Indemnification, Compared, 1858
Principles of Corporate Governance, 1858, 1859, 1867
State Statutes Mandating Indemnification, 1857-67
Market Test or Check Provisions, 769-70, 935, 945-57
Mergers
Cash-Out Merger Transactions (see separate heading)
Freeze-Out Merger Transactions (see separate heading)
Going Private Merger Transactions (see separate heading)
Mergers of Equals, 632, 637, 908-09, 935, 957, 1090
Protective Strategies, 631-32, 637
Unocal Rule Not Applicable, 648
Mergers of Equals, 632, 637, 908-09, 935, 957
Minimum Voting Rights Rule, 1064-68, 1135
Misrepresentations in D & O Insurance Policy Applications
General Principles, 2140-48
Innocent Director Cases, 2148-53
Waiver, 2148
Model Business Corporation Act
Background, 100-01
Board's Response to Demand, 1655-58, 1676
Business Judgment Rule, 25, 100-04
Compensation, 318

Contemporaneous Ownership Requirement, 1386-87, 1397

Controlling Shareholder Transactions (see Guidelines for the Unaffiliated Director of the Controlled Corporation)

Corporate Opportunities, 300-01

Delegation, 216

Demand on Directors, 1562-64, 1570-71, 1655-58

Demand on Shareholders, 1687

Derivative Litigation, 1384, 1386-87, 1397, 1403, 1406, 1408, 1562-64, 1570-71, 1655-58

Director Protection Statutes, 234-36

Duty of Care, 2, 103-04, 109-10, 112, 117-18, 119-23, 127-28

Duty of Loyalty, 2, 104

Fair and Adequate Representation Requirement in Derivative Litigation, 1403

Indemnification and Advancement, 1854-59, 1865, 1867, 1872, 1875-78, 1880-85, 1887-89, 1891-95, 1904-09, 1911, 1928, 1931, 1937-39, 1946-47, 1952-53, 1959, 1961-62, 1969, 1979

Insurance, 1980-81

Interested Director Transactions, 266, 273, 289-92

Liability for Breach of Duty of Care, 103-04, 109-10, 112

Non-Shareholder Constituencies, 817-18

Oversight, 127-28

Reliance, 199-201

Security for Expenses Requirement, 1406

Settlement of Derivative Litigation, 1408

Termination of Shareholder Derivative Litigation by Special Litigation Committees, 1696, 1781-82, 1798-99

Universal Demand Requirement, 1562-64, 1570-71, 1655-58

Multiple Shareholder Classes

Fiduciary Duties to Multiple Common Shareholder Classes, 559-70

Fiduciary Duties to Preferred Shareholder Classes, 559, 570-90

Super-Voting Common Stock (see separate heading)

# N

No Shop Provisions, 935-42

Non-Exclusivity Indemnification Provisions, 1886-87, 1959-69

Non-Shareholder Constituencies

    Case Law, 808-12

    Charter Provisions, 822-23, 1249

    Model Business Corporation Act, 817-18

    Policy Considerations, 817-22

    Principles of Corporate Governance, 817

    Statutes, 124, 595-96, 812-17

Non-Structural Resistance to Contests for Control

    Acquisitions Creating Antitrust Problems for Potential Acquiror, 1332-33

    Acquisitions Creating Other Regulatory Problems for Potential Acquiror, 1339

    Antitrust Litigation (see Antitrust Issues, as Defensive Strategy)

    Golden Parachutes (see separate heading)

    Litigation, 1343-48

    Pac-Man Defense, 1339-43

    Shareholder Meeting Dates (see separate heading)

    Shark Repellent Charter and Bylaw Provisions (see separate heading)

    Tin Parachutes (see separate heading)

Notice Requirement in D & O Insurance Policies

    Constructive Notice, 2013-15

    Information Provided to Underwriting Department and in Renewal Applications, 2011-13

    Must be Given to Insurer in Manner and Form Required by Policy, 2008-11

    Notices Identifying Potential Claims, 2015-21

Notice to Shareholders Concerning Advancement, Indemnification and Insurance, 1979-80

# O

Options, as Defensive Strategy, 909-34

Outside Directors, Generally

Effect of Approval by, in Corporate Control Transaction Context, 643, 823-31

Reluctance to Serve Due to Unavailability of D & O Insurance, 2173-75

Special Committees, in Controlling Shareholder Transaction Context, 264, 402-67

Special Committees, in Corporate Control Transactions Context, 823-32

Special Committees, in Termination of Derivative Litigation Context (see Termination of Derivative Litigation by Special Litigation Committees heading)

Time Typically Devoted to Corporate Business, 143-44

Oversight

Case Law, 128-31, 140-43, 145-46, 1531, 1537-43, 1550-58, 1560-61

Causation, 114

Decision Making Versus Oversight, 126

Description of Oversight Duties, 126-28

Model Business Corporation Act, 127-28

Principles of Corporate Governance, 131-32

# P

Pac-Man Defense, 1339-43

Parent-Subsidiary Transactions

Cash-Out Merger Transactions (see separate heading)

Controlling Shareholder Transactions (see separate heading)

Parent-Subsidiary Transactions, Generally, 370-76

Principles of Corporate Governance, 376

Wholly-Owned Subsidiaries, 376-77

Permissive Advancement

Action Challenging Advancement is Premature Until Action for which Advancement is Sought is Completed and Board Considers Whether to Seek Repayment of Amounts Advanced, 1897-98

Authorization, 1896, 1902-06

Business Judgment Must Be Made, 1899-1901

Directors, Officers, Employees and Agents, Compared, 1907-09

Duty of Care, 1899-1901

Duty of Loyalty, 1900, 1901-02, 1903

Federal Savings Associations, 1906

Generally, 1894-95

Indemnification, Compared, 1895, 1898

Model Business Corporation Act, 1894, 1895, 1904-09

No Requirement that Standard Required for Permissive Indemnification Be Met, 1898, 1902-03, 1915

Policy Rationale, 1894-95

Present Directors and Officers and Former Directors and Officers, Compared, 1908

Principles of Corporate Governance, 1895, 1905-06

Undertaking Required, 1896, 1903, 1906-07

Permissive Indemnification

Actions by or in the Right of the Corporation, 1880-87, 1983

Actions by or in the Right of the Corporation, Where There is an Adjudication of Liability, 1881-83, 1918-20, 1924-25, 1983

Amounts Paid to Settle Actions by or in the Right of the Corporation, 1883-87

Authorization by Directors, 1888-91, 1893

Authorization by Board Committee, 1888

Authorization by Court, 1893

Authorization by Independent or Special Counsel, 1888, 1891-92, 1893

Authorization by Shareholders, 1888, 1892-93

Derivative Actions, 1880-87

Directors, Officers, Employees and Agents, Compared, 1875, 1889

Expenses Incurred in Connection with Obtaining Indemnification, 1874-75, 1933-38

Federal Savings Associations, 1880, 1886, 1894

Generally, 1872-73

Judgments in Actions by or in the Right of The Corporation, 1883-87

May be made Mandatory by Charter, Bylaw or Contract Provision, 1867, 1873

Model Business Corporation Act, 1872, 1875-78, 1880-85, 1887-89, 1891-93

No Distinction Between Actions by Corporation and Actions in the Right of the Corporation, 1881

Non-Exclusivity Provisions, 1886-87, 1959-69

Principles of Corporate Governance, 1872, 1876, 1878-82, 1885-86, 1887, 1893-94

Third Party Actions, 1876-80

Two Questions: Is Indemnification Permissible and Should It Be Granted, 1887-88, 1893-94

Poison Pill Shareholder Rights Plans (see Shareholder Rights Plans heading)

Poison Put Bonds, 1090

Pooling Insurance Arrangements, 2162-63

Pre-Litigation Demand (see Demand on Directors heading)

Pre-Planned Defensive Strategies, Generally, 639-40

Presumption of the Business Judgment Rule, 4-5, 18-25, 106, 110-11

Principles of Corporate Governance: Analysis and Recommendations

    American Law Institute, 100, 104-05

    Background, 104-05

    Board's Response to a Demand, 1665-73, 1680-81

    Business Judgment Rule, 100, 105-06

    Ceiling on Liability, 236-37

    Compensation, 318-20

    Contemporaneous Ownership Requirement, 1387-88, 1397-98

    Control, 348-49

    Controlling Shareholder Transactions, 471

Corporate Control Transactions, 693-94, 817

Corporate Opportunities, 305-07

Delegation, 199, 214-15

Demand on Directors, 1562-64, 1571, 1665-73

Demand on Shareholders, 1687

Derivative Litigation, 1823-25, 1827-28, 1387-88, 1397-98, 1399, 1403, 1406, 1408, 1416, 1562-64, 1571, 1665-73

Director Protection Statutes, 236-37

Disinterestedness, 70-71

Double Derivative Action, 1416

Fair and Adequate Representation Requirement in Derivative Litigation, 1403

Financial Institution Directors, 243

Indemnification and Advancement, 1855, 1857-59, 1865-67, 1872, 1876, 1878-82, 1885-87, 1893-95, 1905-06, 1937-38, 1940, 1946-47, 1952-53, 1959, 1961, 1979

Independence, 70-71

Insurance, 1982

Interested Director Transactions, 292-93

Non-Shareholder Constituencies, 817

Oversight, 131-32

Parent-Subsidiary Transactions, 376

Personal Liability for Breach of Duty of Care, 113

Reliance, 131-32, 201

Security for Expenses Requirement, 1406

Settlement of Derivative Litigation, 1408

Termination of Shareholder Derivative Litigation by Special Litigation Committees, 1696, 1711, 1782, 1798-1800

Universal Demand Requirement, 1562-64, 1571, 1665-73

Waste, 97

Wrongful Refusal of Demand, 1665-73, 1680-81

Prospective Shareholders Not Owed Fiduciary Duties, 108-09

Protective Strategies, Generally, 631-32, 637, 771-72, 909, 1090

# R

Ratification (see Shareholder Ratification)

Raincoat Provisions (see Director Protection Statutes)

Reasonably Perceived Threat to Corporate Policy

    Antitrust and Other Regulatory Issues, 680-81

    Coercive Offer, 663-66

    Corporate Culture Threats, 679-80

    Failure to Provide Shareholders with Option to Remain

    Equity Holders, 677-79

    Generally, 641, 662-63

    Insufficient Time or Information, 672-77

    Price Inadequacy, 666-72

    Two-Tier Offer, 663-66

Reasonable Response to Threat to Corporate Policy

    Coercive Response Not Permitted, 683-84

    Draconian Response Not Permitted, 682-84

    Examples, 684-86, 834-1377

    Preclusive Response Not Permitted, 683-84

    Reasonableness Standard, 681-82, 684

Record Dates, 1241-45

Redemption of Shareholder Rights Plans (see Shareholder Rights Plans)

Regulatory Exclusion in D & O Insurance Policies,

    Ambiguity Considerations, 2074-83

    Public Policy Considerations, 2084-92

Regulatory Issues, as Defensive Strategy

    Acquisitions Creating Regulatory Issues for Potential Acquiror, 1339

    Regulatory Litigation, 1339

    Takeover Bids by Foreign Entities, 1339

Reincorporation, 1249, 1252-53

Reliance, 198-214, 614

Removal of Directors Without Cause, 1248, 1269, 1283-84

Repurchase Rights Plans, 1090

Repurchases (see Non-Targeted Share Repurchases and Targeted Share Repurchases)

Responses to D & O Crisis of the Mid-1980s

    Charter, Bylaw and Contract Provisions Maximizing Indemnification Rights, 1867-72, 1909-1932, 2169

    Director Protection Statutes (see separate heading)

    Funding Mechanisms, 1976-79, 2171

    Pooling Insurance Arrangements, 2162-63, 2171

    Self-Insurance, 2153-62, 2171

    Statutes Increasing Availability of Indemnification and Insurance, 1884-87, 1959-61, 1968-69, 1976-79, 2156-57, 2169

Restrictive Covenants, 1035-38

Retroactive Defensive Strategies, 635

Revlon-QVC Rule

    Auction Not Required to Satisfy Revlon-QVC Rule, 730-31, 735-36, 765

    Auction, Where Conducted, Need Not be Fair to Bidders, 735-36

    Board Responsibilities in Cases Involving Competing Offers, Including One by a Controlling Shareholder, 777-83

    Burden of Proof, 733-35

    Business Judgment Rule Applies Where Revlon-QVC Rule Is Satisfied, 735

    Cases Enjoining Board Conduct Under Revlon-QVC Rule, 736-54

    Cases Upholding Board Conduct Under Revlon-QVC Rule, 754-71, 783-90

    Circumstances Where Revlon-QVC Rule Applies, 694-725

    Enhanced Scrutiny, 730, 732, 733-34

    Evaluating Board Conduct Where Revlon-QVC Rule Applies, 730-90

    Evolution of Revlon-QVC Rule, 695-13

    Factors Considered by Courts Evaluating Board Conduct Under Revlon-QVC Rule, 757-60

    Fairness Standard Applies Where Revlon-QVC Test is Not Satisfied, 735

Generally, 152, 694-98, 730-33

"Lip of Insolvency" Context, 783-90

No Single Blueprint, 730-31, 765-67

Revlon-QVC Rule, 694, 730-31, 733-35

States Other Than Delaware Following and Not Following Revlon-QVC Rule, 726-30

Use of Confidentiality Agreements, 772-77

Use of Shareholder Rights Plan (see Shareholder Rights Plans heading)

Use of Inducements (see White Knight Transactions and Inducements heading)

Rule 19c-4 and its Aftermath, 1057-68

## S

Sale of Assets, as Defensive Strategy, 904-08

Sale of Control at a Premium, 363-68

Sale of Stock, as Defensive Strategy (see White Squire Transactions heading)

SEC Minimum Voting Rights Rule, 1064-68, 1135

SEC Rule 19c-4 and its Aftermath, 1057-68

Security for Expenses in Derivative Litigation, 1403-07

Section 220 Actions, 1677-80

Self-Tender Offers

Case Law, 1004-38

Equal Treatment of Shareholders, 1008-11

Generally, 1003-04

Settlement, as Defensive Strategy

Greenmail (see separate heading)

Standstill Agreements, 1349, 1368-77

Settlement of Derivative Litigation, 1408-11

Share Repurchases

Exchange Offers (see separate heading)

Greenmail (see separate heading)

Self-Tender Offers (see separate heading)

Shareholder Derivative Litigation (see Derivative Litigation heading)

Shareholder Meeting Dates

　Annual Meeting, Generally, 1203-04

　Annual Meeting Requirement Cannot be Satisfied by Use of Consents, 1204

　Cases Invalidating Board Decisions Advancing or Delaying Meeting Dates, 1204-17

　Cases Upholding Board Decisions Advancing or Delaying Meeting Dates, 1217-40

　Decisions Refusing to Enjoin Shareholder Meetings, 1240-41

　Record Dates, 1241-45

Shareholder Meeting Record Dates, 1241-45

Shareholder Meetings

　Blasius Voting Rule (see separate heading)

　Bylaws Regulating Board Nominations, Shareholder Resolutions and Voting (see Shark Repellent Charter and Bylaw Provisions heading)

　Bylaws Regulating Calling of Shareholder Meetings by Shareholders (see Shark Repellent Charter and Bylaw Provisions heading)

　Bylaws Regulating Consent Solicitations (see Shark Repellent Charter and Bylaw Provisions heading)

　Shareholder Meeting Dates (see separate heading)

Shareholder Option Poison Pill Provisions, 1089-90

Shareholder Ratification

　Burden of Proof, 528

　Duty of Care Claims, 112, 224-25, 528-29

　Duty of Loyalty Claims, 272-82, 528-29

　Majority of Shareholders Versus Majority of Disinterested Shareholders, 275-76, 529-30

　Waste Claims, 225-26

　Where Corporate Action is Required by Statute, 529-30

Shareholder Resolutions

　Bylaws Regulating, 1249, 1262-63, 1271-74, 1288-89

　Shareholder Rights Plans, 1194-1202

Shareholder Rights Plans (see Poison Pill Shareholder Rights Plan)

Adoption, 1090-1146

All-Holders Rule, 1134

Back End Provisions, 1089, 1121-34

Chewable Provisions, 1089-90

Continuing Director Provisions, 1184-90

Dead Hand Provisions, 1184-90

Debt Provisions, 1089, 1121-34

Decision Whether to Redeem, 1190-91, 1146-1202

Differing Viewpoints Concerning Value of Rights Plans to Shareholders, 1085-87

Discrimination Among Shareholders, 1096-1103, 1135-44

Disproportionate Voting Provisions, 1135-44

Exploding Warrants, 1144-46

Flip In Provisions, 1087-89, 1096-1121

Flip Over Provisions, 1087-89, 1091-95

Generally, 1085-91

How Rights Plans Work, 1087-90

Lolli-Pop Provisions, 1121-34

Poison Put Bonds, 1090

Redemption, 1090-91, 1146-1202

Repurchase Rights Plans, 1090

Restrictions Upon Authority of Future Boards to Redeem, 1184-90

Shareholder Option Provisions, 1089-90

Shareholder Resolutions, 1194-1202

Springing Warrants, 1144-46

State Statutes, 1099, 1102-03, 1190-94

Use During Contests for Control, Generally, 772, 1090-91, 1146-50

Use in Alternative Restructuring Context, 1161-71

Use in Auction Context, 772, 1150-61

Use in "Just Say No" Context, 1171-83

Shareholder Voting

Approval of Corporate Actions Required by Statute, 529-30

Blasius Voting Rule (see separate heading)

Coercion (see Wrongful Coercion heading)

Ratification (see Shareholder Ratification heading)

Shareholder Ratification (see separate heading)

Shark Repellent Charter and Bylaw Provisions

Anti-Greenmail Provisions, 1249, 1364

Advance Notice Provisions, 1247, 1249, 1257-63, 1269-70, 1271-74, 1286-89, 1292-96

Appointment of Board Members to Committees, 1248-49

Board Nominations, 1249, 1257-62, 1269-70, 1271-74, 1286-87, 1292-96

Board Size, 1248, 1253-57, 1287

Board Vacancies, 1248

Bylaw Provisions Must be Consistent with Charter Provisions, 1245

Calling of Shareholder Meetings by Shareholders, 1246, 1249, 1263-69, 1269, 1270-71

Consent Solicitation Regulation, 1246-47, 1249-50, 1274-78

Cumulative Voting Rights, 1249

Fair Price Provisions, 1248, 1249

Generally, 1245

Must A Bylaw be Waived Where Enforcement Would be Inequitable?, 1292-96

Non-Shareholder Constituencies, 822-23, 1249

Provisions Governing Amendment of Shark Repellent Provisions, 1249, 1283-86

Reincorporation, 1249, 1252-53

Removal of Directors Without Cause, 1248, 1269, 1283-84

Share Ownership Ceiling, 1284-85

Shareholder Approval, Effect of, 1250-53

Shareholder Resolutions, 1249, 1262-63, 1271-74, 1288-89

Staggered Board Provisions, 1246, 1249, 1278-83

Statutory Restrictions, 1289-91

Stock Redemption Provisions, 1248

Super Voting Common Stock (see separate heading)

Supermajority Provisions, 1247, 1250, 1285-87

Voting Rights Ceiling, 1249

Simultaneous Tender Offers and Proxy Contexts, 799-805

Special Committees

Change of Control Transactions, 824-31

Controlling Shareholder Transactions, 264, 402-67

Termination of Derivative Litigation Context (see Termination of Derivative Litigation by Special Litigation Committee heading)

Special Litigation Committees, in Termination of Derivative Litigation Context (see Termination of Derivative Litigation by Special Litigation Committee heading)

Springing Warrants, 1144-46

Squeeze-Out Merger Transactions, 377

Definition, 377

Fairness Standard (see Controlling Shareholder Transactions heading)

Standard of Care for Directors (see Duty of Care heading)

Standing of Potential Acquiror to Challenge Board Actions, 832-34

Standstill Agreements, 1349, 1368-77

Staggered Board Provisions, 1246, 1249, 1278-83

Stock Options

As Defensive Strategy, 909-17

As Form of Compensation, 321

General Standard of Review, 321-24

Options Approved by Disinterested Directors, 324-28

Options Approved by Interested Directors, 328-41

State Statutes, 321

Stock Sales, as Defensive Strategy (see White Squire Transactions heading)

Street Sweep, 844-45

Structural Bias,

Supermajority Provisions, 1247, 1250, 1285-86, 1287

Super-Voting Common Stock 277-97

    Also Known as Disparate Class and Dual Class Stock, 1052

    Cases Enjoining Super-Voting Stock Plans, 1079-83

    Cases Upholding Super-Voting Stock Plans, 1068-79

    Claims Involving Previously Adopted Super-Voting Stock Plans, 1083-85

    Fiduciary Duties to Multiple Common Shareholder Classes, 559-70

    Generally, 1052-54, 1249

    SEC Minimum Voting Rights Rule, 1064-68, 1135

    SEC Rule 19c-4 and its Aftermath, 1057-68

    Statutory Authority, 1054-55

    Stock Exchange Regulation, 1055-57, 1063-68

    Use as Defensive Strategy, 1052-53

    Uses Other Than As Defensive Strategy, 1053-54

# T

Targeted Share Repurchases (see Greenmail heading)

Termination Fees, 957-79

Termination of Derivative Litigation by Special Litigation Committees

    Cases Involving Unlawful Conduct, 1649-55

    Choice of Law, 1455-67

    Considerations Involving Counsel, 1775-81

    Delaware (Zapata) Approach, 1711-38, 1815-19

    Delaware (Zapata) Approach, as Modified by Courts Construing the Law of Other States, 1738-44, 1783-95

    Demand, Relationship to, 1689-90

    Discovery on Motion to Terminate, 1783-1800

    Disinterestedness and Independence Required, 1744-65, 1812-15

    Effect of Procedural Context on Level of Interest Required to Disqualify Directors, 1773-75

    Generally, 1407-08, 1689-90

    Inconsistent with Federal Policy Exception to Demand Requirement, 1456-57, 1460-67

Judicial Review: Auerbach Versus Zapata, 1702-44

Model Business Corporation Act, 1696, 1781-82, 1798-99

New York (Auerbach) Approach, 1702-11, 1795-98

Power to Terminate, 1690-702

Practical Considerations, 1800-04

Principles of Corporate Governance, 1696, 1711, 1782, 1798-1800

Refusal of Demand, Compared, 1689-90, 1711-12

State Statutes, 1696-99, 1782-83, 1798-800

Structural Bias Theory, 1765-73

Tin Parachutes

Cases Enjoining or Questioning Tin Parachutes, 1322, 1325-27

Cases Upholding Tin Parachutes, 1322-24

Generally, 1322

State Statutes, 1327-28

Topping Fees, 979-82

Transactions Between Corporations Having Common Directors, 269-70

Transactions Involving Corporate Control

Corporate Control Transactions (see separate heading)

Defensive Strategies (see separate heading)

Triple Derivative Action, 1416

Typical D & O Insurance Policy Structure and Terms

Advancement of Expenses, 1989, 2092-109

Allocation Between Claims, 2109, 2136-39

Allocation Between Defendants (see separate heading)

Cancellation Provisions, 1996

Claim Made Requirement (see separate heading)

Company Reimbursement Part, 1987-88

Consent to Settlement by Insureds, 1995-96

Consent to Settlement by Insurer, 1994-95

Declarations, 1989

Deductibles, 1989

Directors and Officers Reimbursement Part, 1988

Endorsements, 1989

Entity Policies, 1988, 2136

Excess Policies, 1989, 1994

Exclusions (see separate heading)

Hammer Provisions, 1996

Limit of Liability, 1989, 1990, 1991-93

Losses Covered (see separate heading)

Notice Requirement (see separate heading)

Premium, 1989

Retention, 1989

Terms and Conditions Describing Claims Procedures, 1989

Two-Part Structure, 1987

Typically No Obligation to Defend, 1990-91

Wrongful Act Requirement (see separate heading)

# U

Ultra Vires Conduct, Business Judgment Rule, Inapplicable to, 90-91, 110

Universal Demand Requirement

Demand Required in All Cases, 1562, 1656, 1676

Irreparable Injury Exception, 1562

Model Business Corporation Act, 1562-64, 1570-71, 1655-58

No Federal Universal Demand Requirement, 1566-69

Principles of Corporate Governance, 1562-64, 1571, 1665-73

Rationale, 1563-65

Rejected by Delaware and New York, 1571-72

Standard of Review Where Demand is Refused, 1655-73

State Statutes, 1564, 1570-71, 1658-65

Time Within Which Corporation Must Respond, 1570-71

Unlawful Conduct

Business Judgment Rule, Inapplicable to, 90-93, 110

Board Refusal of Demand, 1649-55

Demand on Directors, 1499

Termination of Derivative Litigation by Special Litigation Committees, 1649-55

Unocal Rule

Applicability Limited to Defensive Conduct, 639, 648-62

Burden of Proof, 641-44, 687

Business Judgment Rule Applies Where Unocal Test Is Satisfied, 644

Coercive Offers as Threat, Generally, 663-66

Demand on Directors Context, 1513-14

Enhanced Scrutiny, 638-45, 681-84,

Fairness Standard Applies Where Unocal Rule Not Satisfied, 636, 645

Generally, 638-49

Mergers, Not Applicable to, 648

Motion to Dismiss Considerations, 644-45, 1115-21, 1150, 1513-14

Pre-Planned Defensive Conduct, 639-40

Principles of Corporate Governance, Compared, 693-94

Rationale, 640-41

Reasonably Perceived Threat to Corporate Policy, Generally (see separate heading)

Reasonable Response to Threat to Corporate Policy, Generally (see separate heading)

Revlon-QVC Modification of Unocal Rule, 733-36

Simultaneous Tender Offers and Proxy Contests, 645-46, 799-805

States Other than Delaware Following and Not Following Unocal, 684-93

Unocal Rule, 638-49

# V

Voting (see Shareholder Voting heading)

# W

Waste

Cause of Action, 94-97

Compensation, 311-13, 1301

    Demand on Directors Context, 1524-29

    Not Protected by Business Judgment Rule, 93-94

    Lock-Up Asset Options Context, 931-34

White Knight Transactions and Inducements

    Break-Up Fees, 957-79

    Expense Reimbursement Provisions, 957-58, 963-65, 969, 972, 974-75, 978-79

    Generally, 771-72, 908-09

    Later, Better Offers (see separate heading)

    Leg-Up and Lock-Up Stock Options, 909-17

    Lock-Up Asset Options, 918-34

    Market Test or Check Provisions, 769-70, 935, 945-57

    No Shop Provisions, 935-42

    Termination Fees, 957-79

    Topping Fees, 979-82

    Window Shop Provisions, 935, 942-45

White Squire Transactions

    Bridge Financing, 901-03

    Employee Stock Ownership Plans ("ESOPs") (see separate heading)

    Friendly Third Party Stock Acquisitions, 834-53

    Generally, 834

    Stock Exchange Limitations Upon Stock Issuances, 834

Wholly-Owned Subsidiaries, 376-77

Window Shop Provisions, 935, 942-45

Wrongful Act Requirement in D & O Insurance Policies

    Definition of Wrongful Act, 2021

    Where Director Has Relationships with Corporation Other Than Service as Director or Officer, 2021-25

Wrongful Coercion

    Generally, 539

    Offers to Purchase Shares, 360-62, 547-59

    Voting, 540-47

Wrongful Refusal of Demand (see Board Refusal of Demand heading)